The Ultimate Source
on Intense Entertainment

CREATURE FEATURES
The Science Fiction, Fantasy, and Horror Movie Guide

John Stanley hosted the popular *Creature Features* TV series in the San Francisco Bay area for six years. He also covered the science fiction, fantasy, and horror scene for the *San Francisco Chronicle* for more than thirty years. He has interviewed dozens of superstars and genre stars, and was named "the Leonard Maltin of horror" by *Fangoria*.

And Joe Bob Briggs is "in awe of the man."

CREATURE FEATURES

THE SCIENCE FICTION, FANTASY, AND HORROR MOVIE GUIDE

Updated Edition

JOHN STANLEY

BERKLEY BOULEVARD BOOKS, NEW YORK

CREATURE FEATURES: THE SCIENCE FICTION, FANTASY, AND HORROR
MOVIE GUIDE, UPDATED EDITION

A Berkley Boulevard Book / published by arrangement with
the author

PRINTING HISTORY
Berkley Boulevard trade paperback edition / August 2000

The Penguin Putnam Inc. World Wide Web site address is
http://www.penguinputnam.com

ISBN: 0-425-17517-0

BERKLEY BOULEVARD
Berkley Boulevard Books are published by The Berkley Publishing Group,
a division of Penguin Putnam Inc., 375 Hudson Street,
New York, New York 10014.
BERKLEY BOULEVARD and its logo
are trademarks belonging to Penguin Putnam Inc.

PRINTED IN THE UNITED STATES OF AMERICA

10 9 8 7 6 5 4 3 2 1

THE CAREER THAT DRIPPED BLOOD
PART II: THE CREATURE MUSE STRIKES BACK

Being John Stanley, I totally understand how horrible it is to be John Malkovich. Whoa, I don't mean being John Malkovich in real life, I mean being John Malkovich in the movie *Being John Malkovich*. With that human being John Cusack crawling around inside his brain, taking control of his life, manipulating him, taking advantage of everything that the poor beleagured actor is and will be. In a perverse way, this 1999 motion picture epitomizes my life, the life of a "Creature Features" reviewer.

You see, being *me*, I know all about being *him*. Because I've got this thing crawling around inside my own brain, searing it white-hot, filling it with images of horror and destruction, sending screams and shrieks howling through its echo chambers like the moans of the dying and the dead. I know how Malkovich feels and why his eyes are often filled with such despair and so maniacally wide in his movies.

We have both been to movie hell and back.

I once modestly put it this way to my psychiatrist: "Doctor," I said, "after seeing thousands of horror and sci-fi movies, I'm trapped in a dungeon of doom, captive to eviscerated evils unimaginable, a prisoner of putrescent pandemonium. Buried up to my armpits in a gorepool created by a thousand vampire bites, fanged werewolf attacks, ghoulish gurglings, baying hellhound teeth gnashing, and man-made monsters babbling their insanity. My existence is a malestrom in which float hundreds of chainsawed arms and legs, filled with buckets of blood from a thousand gaping wounds made by axes, butcher knives, swords, skewers, pikes and picks, and even an occasional Swiss-army pocketknife. Even at this very moment, in the subdued confines of your designer office, Dr. Freudenstein, I wallow in a blood-drenched, gore-soaked atmosphere of horrific visual images."

The good doctor wrote me off as a patient long ago, diagnosing my case as "utterly, completely hopeless." An addendum noted: "He is an incurable moviephile, a sick cinemafiend, a terminal sufferer of flickitis. In short, Mr. Stanley is one of those curiously rare individuals who has seen one horror film too many, and for whom there is no escape." Had I not fled from our last session when, in frustration, the doctor took to the couch and forced *me* to take notes, it is very possible he would have recommended a padded room in a nearby asylum, whose name is chiseled into the granite above the Gothic-arched entranceway.

This thing in my brain, which came from beyond the beyond, from a region of eternal darkness unknown to most other mortals, is what I call my "Monster Muse." (Malkovich calls his version of it a "Cusack Cuddly," but that is his business.) There is nothing "musing" about it, I assure you, but the horror is there, in all its infinite, vicarious, visceral variety. It was created by thousands of hours spent seeing the movies for this "Creature Features" series, the sixth edition of which you now hold in your hands.

Thousands of hours spent observing 2,000 maniacs performing their ungoldly work. Watching unhinged serial killers in masks, watching worm-eaten faces returned from the grave, watching alien bug-eyed monsters with slimy tentacles and oozing, slobbering mouths, eager to lay their extraterrestrial appendages on screaming earth femmes with outlandishly voluptuous anatomies—watching all those things that constitute the Cinema of Doom.

The images go on, unstoppable, swirling through my brain like bad sequel movies: demented doctors (strangely resembling the good Dr. Freudenstein in some ways), cackling scientists driven insane by the sight of their own misshapen, test-tube creations, crazed surgeons flailing along hospital corridors, dispatching their patients with scalpels, chainsaw-armed psychopaths buzzing through human flesh with maniacal intensity, not to mention glee.

Such is the price, dear reader, that I have paid to put this sixth book before you. Since 1981, with the publication of the first modest-in-size edition, I have attempted to provide an ever-growing compendium of reviews covering the genres of science fiction, fantasy, and horror. Modesty of size disappeared as the book kept growing, containing 5,614 titles by its fourth edition. This in spite of whatever damage was being done by my not-so-bemusing "Monster Muse."

These reviews are the product of a single critical sensibility (some have described it as "an insensibility"), for rather than hire a staff of writers that would vary my point of view, I have single-handedly written on well over 6,000 movies in order to achieve a level of comprehensiveness you will not find in any other genre movie guide. The price, as I've described, has been horrendous, but it is one I have been willing to pay, and one I will continue to pay for the good of mankind in general and the readership of this book in particular, if not for myself and my fellow sufferer, John Malkovich.

At one time the material that has so frequently come back to haunt me was limited and manageable. However, since the 1970s—when *Star Wars*, *E.T.*, and *Close Encounters of the Third Kind* spearheaded a trend toward quality, and plots once relegated to B movies suddenly became fashionable for blockbusters and super-epics—there has been an avalanche of classy cinefantastique.

In the early 1980s, the showbiz trade journal *Variety* estimated that 40 percent of major theatrical releases contained fantastical themes. By 1999, that market had burgeoned still more. Of the top 20 moneymakers of all time (that's world-wide box office, not domestic), 14 are science-fiction- or fantasy-driven, including *Star Wars—Episode I: The Phantom Menace* ($922 million), *Jurassic Park* ($920 million), *Independence Day* ($811 million), *E.T.* ($704 million), *The Sixth Sense* ($615 million), *Men in Black* ($587 milion), *Armageddon* ($554 million), *Jaws* ($470 million), and *The Matrix* ($456 million).

It stands to reason that if fantasy has box-office clout, then every producer is going to reach for a piece of the rainbow. So it started raining science-fiction and horror movies one afternoon, and the deluge hasn't stopped yet.

Take, for example, the large number of horror and sci-fi remakes. Theory has it that if a film succeeded once, it should succeed again. Unfortunately, many producers lack the most elemental standards of taste and hence cannot understand why a movie succeeds, thinking that all you have to do is throw in plenty of monsters and special effects. This fallacy, and the lack of taste that is its corollary, was never better demonstrated than in the 1999 remake of the 1963 Robert Wise classic *The Haunting*. Similarly, *The House on Haunted Hill* was an attempt to cash in on nostalgic memories of William Castle's modest 1959 shocker, but with ten times the number of ghosts and bloodlettings. The original was still better. Or take Gus Van Sant's '98 remake of Alfred Hitchcock's all-time classic from 1960, *Psycho*. Good intentions prevailed, but the casting was faulty and it was no improvement. Remakes are almost always lousy, if not worse.

As the world marched into the new millennium, genre movies quickstepped into an age of astounding, astonishing visual imagery. Today's movies, even when they are made fast and cheap, are enhanced by improvements in CGI—computer-generated images. The technology for creating realistic and superi-maginative images seems to get better by the moment, and is forever stretching the imagination of the viewer. That it also stretches the minds of the artists seated behind the computer consoles goes without saying.

Sometimes, though, CGI works to the detriment of the movie, and visuals are given more consideration than story and/or character development. Look to *Armageddon* and *End of Days* as examples. On the flip side, CGI can offer the ultimate enhancement to a well-crafted story. In two recent examples, *The Green Mile* and *Bicentennial Man*, visual effects are used sparingly and only as a means of illuminating the story and characters.

Although *Star Wars—Episode I: The Phantom Menace* now ranks as the number-two box-office winner, just after *Titanic*, George Lucas's reactivation of his classic series was a critical disappointment, failing to recapture the sense of wonder that its granddaddy, *Star Wars*, had engendered in us in 1977. The later film played down to its audience when it should have been playing it smart. Its failure is a testament to the importance of merchandising rights and product marketing rather than story. The characters were stiff and uninteresting, with the exception of the imposing Liam Neeson.

Speaking of technology . . . the one piece of equipment that revolutionized the world of buying and selling of movies for home viewing since 1997 was the Digital Versatile Disc (DVD) player, a machine that takes a CD-size disc and offers a picture superior to that of a VCR. The DVD machine instantly eclipsed the laser-disc market. Like the superior laser discs of yesteryear, the DVD also provides auxiliary material such as movie trailers, documentaries, and running commentaries by actors and filmmakers. Although quality was the keynote, that didn't mean each and every DVD transfer was superior to the laser version. Paramount's DVD version of *War of the Worlds*, for example, didn't begin to compare with the laser format. And some companies dropped cheapie DVDs on the market to prove the old adage that you get what you pay for.

While the more expensive DVD made inroads among elitists, and also became a tool that could be added to the home computer, sci-fi and horror material continued to inundate the videocassette market, which goes on providing an outlet for low-budget B movies not good enough for theatrical release. Then there is the constant flow of network-TV movies and cable-channel originals. Out of all this, one gets plenty. Perhaps too much. Indeed, it's enough to make anyone who has to see it all scream.

Since the fifth edition in this series was released under the Berkley imprint in early 1997, the world of genre movies has gone through some startling trends and reenvisionings. *Scream*, with its repeated allusion to other horror movies and self-consciously aware dialogue about their formulae, resulted in a spate of pictures that often seemed to be more about other movies than about themselves. Boiled down to their essence, however, these tongue-in-cheek offerings turned out to be nothing more than retreaded slasher flicks. In addition to two *Scream* sequels, there was *I Know What You Did Last Summer* (and its sequel *I Still Know What You Did Last Summer*) and *Urban Legend*. A science-fiction film with a similar self-consciousness about the genre to which it belongs was *The Faculty*.

In the wake of this trend came the phenomenally successful *The Blair Witch Project*, which shook up the world of moviemaking by proving that a small picture smartly packaged and prepromoted (with imaginative use of an Internet Web site) could become a runaway smash. Suddenly every would-be producer with a videocamera and a dangling microphone was trying to cash in on this "pseudodocumentary" or "mockumentary" craze. So far the imitations have not found their way into distribution, although there is word that a *Blair* sequel, in which a "Blair Witch Web site" plays a major part, is in the works. Art is always imitating life.

Blair Witch also bore witness to a 1999 trend toward movies that instead of trying to be blockbuster "cinematic happenings" opted for a quieter, more subtle approach—what some were calling "underdevelopment." The classic example of this proved to be *The Sixth Sense*, a supernatural tale about a young boy who sees dead people everywhere he looks that is noteworthy for its underplayed acting and limited use of special effects. The movie ended up ranking ninth in the top box-office hits of all time and proving another adage: in art, sometimes less is more.

The Internet is proving to be a rich mine for those seeking information about horror and sci-fi movies. In addition to my "Creature Features" Web site (*www.netwiz.net/creature*), I highly recommend *www.cinescape* (for news and updates on movie and TV projects in production or being planned) and *chud.com* ("chud" stands for "Cinematic Happenings Under Development"), which highlights movies in various stages of production.

When it comes to analyzing movie trends and genre-movie reviews, some of them by yours truly, it's hard to beat Dennis Willis's *www.soundwavestv.com*, a Web site that presents a potpourri of news and information about hundreds of sci-fi and horror films. Willis started out operating a small video store in Pacifica, CA, and is now a well-respected expert in his field.

Another site I enthusiastically recommend, and would be remiss not to mention, is *www.thecolumnists.com*, where veteran newspaper columnists Gerald Nachman, Murry Frymer, and Ron Miller regale readers with personalized, whimsical glimpses into the world of showbiz—and of genre movies. I'm happy to be able to say that I turn up there on a frequent basis.

Movie collectors quickly learned that if you wanted to save a buck, the Internet was the way to do it. Such Web sites as *amazon.com, reel.com, buy.com, dvdempire.com, cduniverse.com,* and *dvdexpress.com* now offer DVDs and videos at prices lower than retail outlets. Even with the price of shipping, movies sold over the Internet beat out the stores. Great when you're shopping for a bargain . . . but what's going to happen to retail outlets if they don't start competing with the Web sites? Some marketing analysts are already predicting that 40 percent of so-called brick-and-mortar retail businesses are going to fold up. It is sad to imagine half the stores in your now-thriving shopping mall with "Going Out of Business" signs in their windows.

This sixth edition attempts to cover all the major releases, and some minor ones, since 1997. Yet one book's offerings never seem enough. My e-mail and snail-mail box are always loaded with requests for previous editions, so here's your chance to fill the holes on your shelf. For those seeking books in the "Creature Features" series, I still have a limited number of the now-rare 1981 first edition for $25. I also have trade paperback copies of the fourth edition for $10 and hardcover deluxe copies for $20. Send check or money order to P.O. Box 687, Pacifica, CA 94044. I'll also autograph to your specifications.

Meanwhile, at the stroke of every midnight, my "Monster Muse" flashes images of those thousands of fantasy movies I've seen, forcing me to reexperience their most horrendous moments. By day, I continue to see as many horror and sci-fi movies as possible. And you thought watching movies was nothing but fun. I assure you, there is only horror in being John Stanley.

VIDEO/LASERDISC SOURCES

AARDVARK VIDEO
612 N. High St.
Columbus, OH 43215.

ACE VIDEO
19749 Dearborn St.
Chatsworth, CA 91311.

ACME VIDEO
10653 Santa Monica Blvd.
Los Angeles, CA 90025-4900.

ADMIT ONE
P.O. Box 66, Station O
Toronto, Ontario M4A 2M8.

ALTERNATIVE VIDEOS
P.O. Box 270797
Dallas, TX 75227.

ATOMIC PICTURES
P.O. Box 15824
N. Hollywood, CA 91615-5824.

AUDUBON FILM LIBRARY
P.O. Box 7883.
New York, NY 10150-7883.

BANDERA ENTERPRISES INC.
P.O. Box 1107
Studio City, CA 91614.

BARR ENTERTAINMENT
P.O. Box 7878
Irwindale, CA 91706-7878.

BEST FILM & VIDEO
108 New South Rd.
Hicksville, NY 11801-5223.

BLACKEST HEART
1291 Hays St., #360
San Leandro, CA 94577.

BLACKHAWK CATALOG
5959 Triumph St.
Commerce, CA 90048-1688.

BLOOD TIMES
P.O. Box 3340, Steinway Sta.
Long Island City, NY 11103-0340.

CAPTAIN BIJOU
P.O. Box 87
Toney, AL 35773.

CELEBRITY
22052 Ventura Blvd.
Woodland Hills, CA 91365-4112.

CINEFEAR
Keith Crocker
40 S. Brush Drive
Valley Stream, NY 11581.

CINEMACABRE
P.O. Box 10005
Baltimore, MD 21285-0005.

CREATURE FEATURE VIDEO
P.O. Box 602
Northford, CT 06472.

DARK DREAMS
6228 Sand Point Way NE
Seattle, WA 98115.

DISCOUNT VIDEO
P.O. Box 7122
Burbank, CA 91510.

DRIVE-IN VIDEO
P.O. Box 3376
Belleview, FL 34421-3376.

**EDDIE BRANDT'S SATURDAY
MATINEE**
6310 Colfax Avenue
N. Hollywood, CA 91606.

ELETE LASER
(201) 989-4433.

EUROPEAN TRASH CINEMA
P.O. Box 5367
Kingwood, TX 77325.

FACETS VIDEO
1517 W. Fullerton
Chicago, IL 60614
(catalog sales/rentals); (800) 331-6197.
For hard-to-find videos.

FESTIVAL FILMS
6115 Chestnut Terr.
Shorewood, MN 55331.

FILMFAX
P.O. Box 1900
Evanston, IL 60204.

FILM THREAT VIDEO
P.O. Box 3170
Los Angeles, CA 90078-3170.

FRIGHT VIDEO
P.O. Box 179
Billerica, MA 01821.

GRAPEVINE VIDEO
P.O. Box 46161
Phoenix, AZ 85063.

**INTERNATIONAL FILM & VIDEO
CENTER**
989 First Ave.
New York, NY 10022.

J2 COMMUNICATIONS
10850 Wilshire Blvd., #1000
Los Angeles, CA 90024.

LE VIDEO
1239 9th Ave.
San Francisco, CA 94122.

LIGHTNING
60 Long Ridge Rd.
P.O. Box 4000
Stamford, CT 06907.

LOONIC
2022 Taraval St., Suite 6427
San Francisco, CA 94116.

MIDNIGHT VIDEO
5010 Church Dr.
Coplay, PA 18037.

MOVIES UNLIMITED
6736 Castor Ave.
Philadelphia, PA 19149;
(800) 523-0823. For hard-to-find videos.

MPI
15825 Rob Roy Dr.
Oak Forest, IL 60452.

NEW HORIZONS (Roger Corman releases)
2951 Flowers Rd. S., #237
Atlanta, GA 30341.

NOBLE R. BROWN'S HEAVENLY VIDEOS
10306 Trent Court
Indianapolis, IN 46229.

REPUBLIC
12636 Beatrice St.
Los Angeles, CA 90066-0930.

REX MILLER
Route 1, Box 457-D
East Prairie, MO 63845.

RHINO
2225 Colorado Ave.
Santa Monica, CA 90404-3555.

ROAN GROUP
P.O. Box 1615
Thomasville, GA 31799.

SINISTER CINEMA
P.O. Box 4369
Medford, OR 97501-0168
(coded as Sinister/C).

SOMETHING WEIRD
P.O. Box 33664
Seattle, WA 98133
(coded as S/Weird).

THREE-D TV CORP.
(3-D Home Videos)
P.O. Box Q
San Rafael, CA 94913-4316;
(415) 479-3516.

TROMA INC.
733 9th Ave.
New York, NY 10019;
(212) 757-4555.

ULTIMATE VIDEO
1723 Lincoln/Leilay
Peekskill, NY 10566.

VALUE VIEO
P.O. Box 22565
Denver, CO 80222.
(800) 873-7042.

VCI
See **VIDEO COMMUNICATIONS INC.**

VHS DISCOUNT
P.O. Box 130
Remington, VA 22734.

VIDEO COMMUNICATIONS INC.
6535 E. Skella Drive
Tulsa, OK 74145.
(Important for public-domain serials.)

VIDEO SEARCH OF MIAMI
P.O. Box 16-1917
Miami, FL 33116.

VIDEO WASTELAND
214 Fair St.
Berea, OH 44017.

ABADON. See *Vampires*.

ABBOTT AND COSTELLO GO TO MARS (1953) ★★★ A misleading title—the comedy duo lands not on the Red Planet but on Venus (inhabited by an Amazonian race of lovely pin-ups) after wandering aboard an experimental rocket ship and blasting off by accident. Provocative Mari Blanchard is the Queen of Venus and Anita Ekberg and Martha Hyer are among her shapely, sensuous servants. One of the duo's more nostalgic comedies. Howard Christie's production was directed by Charles Lamont from a script by John Grant and D. D. Beauchamp. Robert Paige, Jack Kruschen, Jean Willes. Aka *On to Mars* and *Rocket and Roll*. (MCA)

ABBOTT AND COSTELLO MEET DR. JEKYLL AND MR. HYDE (1953) ★★★★ Frolicking satire with Boris Karloff's bitter half running down London's foggy streets. Robert Louis Stevenson must have rolled over in his literary grave as Bud and Lou run wild . . . fans will be less offended by liberties taken with the tale of dual personality. Nice support from identity-confused Craig Stevens and Helen Westcott, decent scripting by that split personality team of John Grant and Leo Loeb, good schizophrenic direction by Charles Lamont, and Karloff is outstanding as Jekyll/Hyde. John Dierkes, Reginald Denny, Eddie Parker. Originally made as *Dr. Jekyll and Mrs. Hyde*. (Video/Laser: MCA)

ABBOTT AND COSTELLO MEET FRANKENSTEIN (1948) ★★★★ Beloved spoof designed for Bud Abbott and Lou Costello, their bid to kid the cinema's most-adored monsters. Bela Lugosi re-creates Dracula, Lon Chaney, Jr., is tormented Larry Talbot (the Wolfman) and Glenn Strange is the hulking Frankenstein Monster. Even Vincent Price's voice gets into the act as The Invisible Man. Madly uninhibited plot concerns Dracula's attempt to transfer Costello's brain into the head of the Monster. It almost fits. Directed by Charles T. Barton with a flair for the silly, written by John Grant, Frederic I. Renaldo and Robert Lees with a sharp sense of parody, and enlivened by damsels Lenore Aulbert and Jane Randolph. Aka *Abbott and Costello Meet the Ghosts, Meet the Ghosts and The Brain of Frankenstein*. (Video/Laser: MCA)

ABBOTT AND COSTELLO MEET THE GHOSTS. See *Abbott and Costello Meet Frankenstein*.

ABBOTT AND COSTELLO MEET THE INVISIBLE MAN (1951) ★★★½ Comedy-duo programmer has amusing moments as Arthur Franz materializes and dematerializes in "Invisible Man"–genre spoofery. A potpourri of prizefighting, gangsters, rigged bouts, and the obligatory scientific formula that renders invisibility. Directed by Charles Lamont with a knockout comedy punch that wallops the punch-drunk script by Frederic I. Renaldo, John Grant and Robert Lees. Adele Jergens, Sheldon Leonard, Nancy Guild, William Frawley. Aka *Meet the Invisible Man*. (Video/Laser: MCA)

ABBOTT AND COSTELLO MEET THE KILLER: BORIS KARLOFF (1949) ★★★ Satire of the murder-mystery, done by the yuckity-yuckity team with its usual turmoil and louting. Central feature is Boris Karloff as a sinister hypnotist, and he makes it all worthwhile. Directed by Charles T. Barton from a spoofy script by Hugh Wedlock, Jr., Howard Snyder and John Grant. Lenore Aubert, Alan Mowbray, Roland Winters. Aka *Meet the Killer*. (MCA; Goodtimes) (Laser: MCA)

ABBOTT AND COSTELLO MEET THE MUMMY (1955) ★★ You'll get gypped in the crypt and you're a dummy for the mummy if youse gurus waste your taste on this abominable slow-man in gauze, who shambles from his Egyptian tomb to chase two dumb desecrators . . . too bad the bandaged creep never caught them and wrung their ridiculous necks. The least of the A & C film spoofs. Marie Windsor, Michael Ansara, Richard Deacon, Dan Seymour, and Eddie Parker (as the mummy) cannot resurrect Howard Christie's production, written by John Grant. Director Charles Lamont slams home the sarcophagus lid for good measure. Aka *Meet the Mummy*. (Video/Laser: MCA)

ABBY (1974) ★★ Black exploitation ripoff of *The Exorcist* with Carol Speed racing to fall victim to demonic possession with the spirit Eshju and killing men in the most abominable ways. William Marshall (*Blacula*) is a bishop fighting evil. Mediocre effort by genre director William Girdler, who concocted the story with Gordon Cornell Layne. Austin Stoker, Terry Carter, Juanita Moore. Music score by Richard O. Ragland. Aka *Possess My Soul*. (Cinefear)

ABDUCTED (1986) ★ A worthless low-budget psychothriller depicting a female jogger (Roberta Weiss) being held captive by a perverted mountain man (Lawrence King Phillips). The crazy guy's father (Dan Haggerty) wants to help the girl return to civilization but he's crazy too and it becomes one strange bunch of psychoses in them thar mountains. There's no reason to watch this except to torture and hold yourself captive for 90 noncaptivating minutes. Written-directed by Boon Collins. (Prism)

ABDUCTED II: THE REUNION (1994) ★★ Only slightly more competent than the original, this sequel has the advantage of scenic Vancouver Island for its setting, but little else. Dan Haggerty is back as Joe Evans, the strange good-bad guy from *Abducted*. He's guiding big-game hunter Jan-Michael Vincent through the wilderness in a helicopter while, on the ground in Harmony Lake National Forest, his long-dead son (Lawrence King) shows up very much alive to terrorize three beautiful women: Raquel Bianca, Debbie Rochon and Donna Jason. The Boon Collins–Lindsay Bourne script fumbles around with a lot of themes (female Rambo, the evils of stalking helpless game, morality issues up the gazoo) but none of it gels. Another easy one to forget from the noncaptivating director Collins. (Prism)

ABERDEEN EXPERIMENT, THE. See *Scared to Death* (1980).

ABOMINABLE COUNT YORGA, THE. See *The Return of Count Yorga.*

ABOMINABLE DOCTOR PHIBES, THE (1971) ★★★★ Vincent Price at his grotesque best, hamming it up as Dr. Anton Phibes, who employs the Seven Curses of the Pharaohs to avenge his wife's death. Each murder becomes more horrendous, and the morbidity and necrophilia of the nervy ending will have your nerve endings crawling. You'll also laugh to death at the campy elements in the James Whiton–William Goldstein script (aka *Dr. Phibes* and *The Curse of Dr. Phibes*) emphasized by British director Robert Fuest. Phibes is a hideous parody of a man with a skinless face, a speaking tube in his neck and a bad case of acne that fails to repulse lovely assistant Vulnavia (Virginia North). Joseph Cotten, Hugh Griffith. The rousing sequel: *Dr. Phibes Rises Again*. (Vestron) (Laser: Image, with *Dr. Phibes Rises Again*)

ABOMINABLE SNOWMAN, THE See *The Abominable Snowman of the Himalayas.*

ABOMINABLE SNOWMAN OF THE HIMALAYAS, THE (1957) ★★★½ Hammer production, written by Nigel Kneale from his BBC play, *The Snow Creature*, is suspensefully directed by Val Guest. Peter Cushing and Forrest Tucker search for the legendary Yeti in the snowy heights of Tibet. The explorers meet terror at the hairy hands of the ancient creatures. An unusual, thought-provoking ending lifts this out of the potboiler category. This has some very chilling moments, especially when a hairy paw reaches under a tent and gropes for human contact. Maureen Connell, Richard Wattis. Aka *The Abominable Snowman.*

ABRAXUS, GUARDIAN OF THE UNIVERSE (1990) ★ Pro wrestler Jesse Ventura portrays a "Finder," a 10,000-year-old policeman who comes to Earth in search of a renegade cop

(Sven-Ole Thorsen, who does a lousy impersonation of Arnold Schwarzenegger). Most of this Canadian film written-directed by Damian Lee has the two grunt guys fighting it out in snow country while each searches for a child who holds the eye to the future of the Universe—or some such tripe. Michael Copeman, Marjorie Bransfield. (Prism) (Laser: Image)

ABSENT-MINDED PROFESSOR, THE (1961) ★★★ Disney fantasy-farce with slapstick for the young and satire for the adults, so popular it led to a sequel, *Son of Flubber*. Fred MacMurray is a bumbling, lovable scientist who discovers Flubber, a compound that gives its users oddball abilities—such as the ability to fly or bound unimpeded across a basketball court. Scenes of a Model T flying across the sky are standouts. Bill Walsh based his fine screenplay on *A Situation of Gravity* by Samuel Taylor. Wonderful cast includes Nancy Olson as the wife, Keenan Wynn as the villain trying to steal the formula, Ed Wynn, Leon Ames, Edward Andrews. Directed by Robert Stevenson. (Disney offers a colorized video version and black-and-white laser)

ABSENT-MINDED PROFESSOR, THE (1988) ★★ Disney update of its 1961 Fred MacMurray hit vehicle is typically inferior TV time-killer starring Harry Anderson as a physics professor who re-creates Flubber, a form of rubber that enables lubbers to fly. Directed by Robert Scheerer. Cory Danziger, Mary Page Keller. Sequel: *Flubber*.

ABSURD. See *Monster Hunter.*

ABYSS, THE (1989) ★★★★ Writer-director James Cameron (*Titanic; The Terminator; Aliens*) stretches beyond the confining genre forms of previous works in this spectacular underwater fantasy adventure that copped an Oscar for Best Visual Effects. It's a series of cliffhangers as a rescue team (led by Ed Harris, Mary Elizabeth Mastrantonio and Michael Biehn) dives to dangerous depths to find out why a U.S. nuclear sub sank. An alien presence deepens the mystery. Emphasis is on disasters, rescues and underwater chases, and the computerized alien pseudopod effect is revolutionary. But Cameron shifts from ultra-realism to a Spielbergesque fairy-tale ending that gravely dampens the film's climax. The high-tech and fantasy don't mix so well. Leo Burmester, Todd Graff, John Bedford Lloyd, J. C. Quinn, Kimberly Scott, Chris Elliott. (Video/Laser: CBS/Fox)

ABYSS: SPECIAL EDITION, THE ★★★★ Re-edited version of James Cameron's underwater epic, this time with the complete ending of the film running 27 minutes longer than the original. (CBS/Fox)

ACCIDENTS (1989) ★★ Slow-moving paranoia thriller, made in England, in which neurophysical researcher Edward Albert discovers his device for peace (Project Scout, a miniature flying saucer that fires death rays) is being developed for military use by technology chief Jon Cypher. When coworkers begin to die in "accidents," Albert sets out to prove a conspiracy. Director Gideon Amir allows Albert to go bananas in this action film with minimal science fiction. Leigh Taylor-Young, Ian Yule, Candice Hillebrand, Tony Caprari. (Trans World)

ADDAMS FAMILY, THE (1991) ★★★ To recreate Charles Addams's macabre cartoon, Paramount assembled a superb cast: Raul Julia as Gomez, Anjelica Huston as Morticia and Christopher Lloyd as Uncle Fester. Sets and costumes provide an additional touch that keeps faith with Addams's graveyard humor. However, first-time director Barry Sonnenfeld has a hard time holding together a lightweight script by Larry Wilson and Caroline Thompson that fails to propel the Addamses into intriguing situations. What minute plot there is concerns a con woman trying to steal the Addams fortune and planting a Fester lookalike in the ghoulish clan. Still to be savored: morbid love dialogues between Gomez and Morticia; Christina Ricci's superb rendering of daughter Wednesday Addams; hilarious sight gags, one-liners and mordant touches; the appearance of Thing, a severed hand that runs all over the landscape; and Carel Struycken's wordless performance as Lurch the butler. Lloyd plays Fester in every scene with eyeballs bulging and his face on the verge of bursting. Dan Hedaya, Elizabeth Wilson, Judith Malina, Dana Ivey. (Video/Laser: Paramount)

ADDAMS FAMILY VALUES (1993) ★★★½ Charles Addams's cartoon creations, first adapted to fit a TV series during the '60s, then recycled into a box-office smash in 1991, returns as a lavish, big-budgeted sequel with Raul Julia and Anjelica Huston as the heads of the horror house. Carel Struycken is back as Lurch and Christopher Lloyd replays Fester. Other family members include Christina Ricci and Jimmy Workman. The Gomezes are blessed with a newborn, which the other kids try to snuff out in a series of macabre, cartoonish sight gags; and Fester falls prey to a femme fatale (Joan Cusack). Directed by Barry Sonnenfeld from a script by Paul Rudnick. (Video: Paramount) (Laser: Paramount/Pioneer)

ADDICTION, THE (1994) ★★★½ Abel Ferrara's movies always possess a metaphysical edge, and this one, eschewing more commercial values, is a personal statement tapping into that sensibility. It is a dark, brooding, not-easy-to-take tale of a philosophy student (Lili Taylor) bitten by a modern-day vampire and turned into a blood junkie, driven to schizophrenic extremes to get her sanguinary fixes. Set against a New York street atmosphere in stark black-and-white photography, *The Addiction* is a metaphor for all of our obsessive ills (smoking, drugs, alcohol, sex) and our attempt to define evil in the modern world. Taylor's milieu is a non-ending (eternal?) series of attacks on her helpless victims and an exposure to mass murder (photos of the Holocaust) that results in a cynical, schizophrenic personality. At times Nicholas St. John's script is unnecessarily dense, and the characters too bleak to identify with, but there is a compulsion Ferrara creates through his artful direction that holds you fascinated to the more repugnant material. A shocking "orgy of blood" sequence is photographed as if it were a sex orgy, and Christopher Walken appears in an electrifying cameo. If you have the right state of mind to deal with a perverse search for truth in a world of inner and outer horrors, this hard-hitting movie will knock you out. Eddie Falco, Annabella Sciorra. (Video: USA Films).

ADVENTURE IN DINOSAUR CITY (1991) ★★★ Copying elements of TV's *Dinosaurs* and the Ninja Turtle movies, this fantasy-adventure depicts three teenagers whisked through their father's time-vortex device to the land of their favorite TV show. In Tar Town and Saur City, walking-talking lizard and dinosaur creatures ("the hippest dudes from the primordial ooze") mingle with anachronistic cave humans. The kids get caught up in intrigue and battle Mr. Big and his cavemen minions. Especially good is a cantina sequence filled with a plethora of creatures. This pleasing albeit dumb concoction was vigorously directed by Brett Thompson from a script by Willie Baronet and Lisa Morton. Omri Katz, Shawn Hoffman, Tiffanie Poston. (Video/Laser: Republic)

ADVENTURE OF GARGANTUAS. See *War of the Gargantuas.*

ADVENTURES IN THE CREEP ZONE. See *Spacehunter: Adventurers in the Forbidden Zone.*

ADVENTURES OF A GNOME NAMED GNORM, THE. See *A Gnome Named Gnorm.*

ADVENTURES OF BARON MUENCHHAUSEN, THE. See *Baron Muenchhausen.*

ADVENTURES OF BARON MUNCHAUSEN, THE (1989) ★★★ Writer-director Terry Gilliam, infected with Monty Python insanity, is in a world of chaotic extremes, where technology malfunctions and the dark side of man reigns. It's an odd framework for an enduring piece of fantasy literature (the Munchausen stories were written in 1785 by R. E. Raspe). The $40 million film, which went through a chaotic production, is a sight to behold as that irascible soldier of fortune, Baron Munchausen, plunders a sultan's treasure trove and starts a war in which Turkish forces assault a European city. He embarks on an odyssey to round up fellow adventures and encounters a Man on the Moon whose head floats on a platter (played with wild abandonment by Robin Williams), has a race with a speeding bullet, rides a cannonball—and pauses occasionally to tell a flashback adventure. The film sports a superb cast: Oliver Reed as Vulcan, king of Mt. Etna; Eric Idle as a member of an acting troupe; Valentina Cortese as the Queen of the Moon; Uma Thurman as the delectable Venus; and John Neville in the title role, a tour de force. Whatever its contradictions, see this warped and flawed masterwork. (Video/Laser: RCA/Columbia)

ADVENTURES OF BATMAN AND ROBIN. See *Batman and Robin*.

ADVENTURES OF BUCKAROO BANZAI: ACROSS THE EIGHTH DIMENSION (1984) ★★★ Esoteric sci-fi/fantasy adventure, too clever for its own good as it heaps plot on plot that drown the viewer. Buckaroo (Peter Weller) is a contemporary Doc Savage, an intrepid leader of a team of action specialists, who crashes his nuclear-powered racer through solid matter, causing a disturbance in the Eighth Dimension and unleasing aliens on Earth. The Oscillation Overthruster is necessary to prevent global destruction, so Buckaroo and his Hong Kong Cavaliers pursue mad scientist Dr. Emilio Lizardo (John Lithgow, in a campy performance) and his ugly aliens. Although Earl Mac Rauch's script is unnecessarily complex, first-time director W. D. Richter does well with the action sequences. Ellen Barkin, Jeff Goldblum, Christopher Lloyd, Rosalind Cash, Robert Ito, Matt Clark, Vincent Schiavelli. (Video/Laser: Vestron)

ADVENTURES OF CAPTAIN MARVEL, THE (1941) ★★★★ Excellent 12-chapter Republic serial, one of the best of the '40s, with one-time cowboy star Tom Tyler donning the cape of the comic-book superhero (the word "Shazam" changes newsboy Billy Batson into this veritable man of steel) to pursue the evil Scorpion, a supervillain designing a matter transference machine for world domination. The action is slam-bang nonstop thank you, with veteran serial directors William Witney and John England in peak form as the Scorpion attempts to steal lenses that, when fitted together, will give him incredible power. Frank Coghlan, Jr., is corny but adorable as Batson. Harry Worth, Louise Currie, William Benedict, Reed Hadley. (Video/Laser: Republic)

ADVENTURES OF DAVID GRAY. See *Vampyr*.

ADVENTURES OF GALGAMETH, THE (1996) ★ This miserable attempt to blend knights-of-yore action with a medieval fantasy creature will surely disappoint the children for whom it was intended. The creature, a legendary warrior god in the form of a small figurine, looks like a naked Ninja Turtle when the tears of a young king (Devin Oatway) bring it to life. Galgameth starts out in miniature form, but grows in size by eating all the metal he can chew. Pretty soon he resembles an out-of-control Godzilla monster as he leads the peasants to help the youngster and a would-be princess (Johna Stewart) reclaim

their power, which was usurped by the evil Elel (Stephen Macht, in a slimy evil portrayal that is the only thing worth watching in this juvenile misfire). Because the Galgameth creature is so poorly executed, it's impossible to take anything seriously in the Michael Angeli screenplay, which was directed wearisomely by Sean McNamara on Romanian locations. Tim Winters, Tom Dugan, Richard Horvitz, Ken Thorley. (Vidmark/Trimark)

ADVENTURES OF HERCULES II. Video version of *Hercules II* (MGM/UA).

ADVENTURES OF SHERLOCK HOLMES, THE: THE HOUND OF THE BASKERVILLES (1989) ★★★★ A superb adaptation of the Sir Arthur Conan Doyle short story for the superb British TV series starring Jeremy Brett as the Baker Street sleuth and Edward Hardwicke as Dr. Watson. (MPI)

ADVENTURES OF TAURA. See *Starslammer*.

ADVENTURES OF THE STARKILLER. Original working title for *Star Wars*.

AELITA (1924) ★★★★ The avant-garde movement in the Soviet Union during the post-Revolution decade was responsible for this bold, breathtaking adventure set in Russia and on Mars. Its imagery of a futuristic Martian society was a forerunner for the design of American sci-fi (*Flash Gordon* and *Buck Rogers*). Its director was Yakov Protazanov, one of Russia's most successful filmmakers. Designers from the Moscow stage contributed the unique Martian look (heavy on glass and plastics). Based loosely on a story by Alexei Tolstoy, this depicts the love affair between an Earth engineer and the sovereign queen of Mars. Also involved are Gor, "the guardian of planetary energy," the Council of Elders, the dictator Tuskub, and a cast of thousands of Martian laborers. Aka *Aelita: Queen of Mars* and *Revolt of the Robots*. (King on Video; Kino; Sinister/C) (Laser: Image)

AEROBICIDE. See *Killer Workout*.

AFRAID OF THE DARK (1992) ★★★ Offbeat study in abnormal child psychology with such a remarkably low-key performance by young Ben Keyworth that it makes your skin crawl. It's full of startling surprises as Keyworth goes blind and his reveries and nightmares are played out as suspense-terror sequences. Many may find it baffling without being enlightening, but it is full of symbolism and allegory for those willing to search. To say more would be giving away too much. This most unusual thriller—giving new shadings of horror to blindness—was directed by Mark Peploe. James Fox, Fanny Ardant, Paul McGann. (New Line) (Laser: Image)

AFTER DARKNESS (1985) ★★ Before David Cronenberg's *Dead Ringers* there was this misguided psychological horror yarn about twin brothers who undergo childhood traumas. As adults, seemingly sane John Hurt takes disturbed

Julian Sands from an asylum to live with him, but that only makes matters worse as Hurt takes on problems of his sick sibling. Writers-directors Dominique Othenin-Girard and Sergio Guerraz (identified in some U.S. prints as James Foley) create such ambigious characters there's little room for sympathy as they journey from rational to insane. More baffling and irritating than scary or thought provoking, this Swiss-British flick gets lost in its own murkiness. Pamela Salem, Victoria Abril. (Celebrity)

AFTERMATH, THE (1985) ★★★ Well-directed and-edited post-holocaust adventure in which astronaut Steve Barkett (who also wrote and directed) returns from a mission to discover civilization has been ripped apart by nuclear war. The special effects work (with contributions from Jim Danforth) is remarkably good in creating a convincing nuked-out world. Also, Barkett injects considerable emotion into the relationship between the astronaut and an orphan (Christopher Barkett) he adopts from a radioactive-infected museum curator (Forrest J. Ackerman in a cameo). While evil gang leader Cutter (Sid Haig) ravages the countryside, slaughtering survivors, the astronaut builds up his own following, eventually facing Cutter and his gang in a bloody shootout. John Morgan's evocative music score is reminiscent of Bernard Herrmann. A bravura piece of filmmaking. Lynne Margulies, Alfie Martin. (Prism; Starmaker)

AFTER MIDNIGHT (1989) ★★★ Effective horror anthology produced-written-directed by Ken and Jim Wheat. Marc Helgenberger portrays a high school instructor who teaches the "psychology of fear." His students gather to swap three terror yarns, with the framework device providing a fourth climax. #1: Two travelers seek refuge in a lonely mansion after their car breaks down. #2: Four girls are pursued by a madman and his three killer dogs. #3: An answering service operator is trapped with a slasher. #4: The class is subjected to supernatural walking-dead horrors. Fans should enjoy this Wheat crop. Judie Aronson, Marc McClure, Ed Monaghan, Alan Rosenberg, Tracy Wells. (MGM; CBS/Fox)

AFTER PILKINGTON (1986) ★★★ Eccentric albeit original British TV-movie, rich with subtleties of characterization and dialogue. University professor Bob Peck meets old flame Miranda Richardson and is trapped by her neurotic needs and his penchant for lying. He realizes she's a murderess who did in an anthropologist—his body is still in the woods behind the house with scissors protruding from his neck. Simon Gray's offbeat mystery has slight slasher overtones. Watch for clues in Christopher Morahan's direction. Giving a bloody fine performance is Barry Foster as Richardson's unsuspecting but far from dumb husband. (CBS/Fox)

AFTERSHOCK (1989) ★★ Uneven post-Armageddon adventure, its strongest assets well-staged, prolonged martial arts fights, interesting personalities and actual ruins of old factories. A futuristic society is controlled by a "Central Government" (represented by Richard Lynch and John Saxon) that is slaughtering Christopher Mitchum's rebel forces. A compelling twist is that an alien entity (Elizabeth Kaitan) is involved in the war. Jay Roberts, Jr., makes for an uninteresting hero, and one wishes his pal (Chuck Jeffreys, an Eddie Murphy type) had been beefed up. Russ Tamblyn's happy-go-lucky bartender proves a bright light in the drab terrain. Michael Berryman is thrown into the soup too. Chris Derose plays an "apprehender" (read "gunfighter") whose change of heart makes for a few compelling moments. Directed by Frank Harris. (Prism)

AFTER THE FALL OF NEW YORK (1983) ★★ Italian-French imitation of *Mad Max* is a glimpse at a post-holocaust world where splinter factions wage war. A cynical lone wolf is coerced by rebel forces (the Pan-American Federation) to penetrate the ruins of Manhattan where the evil Euraks hold sway, to rescue the only fertile woman on Earth so she can be rocketed to Alpha Centauri. Parsifal's comrades are a cyborg with a hook hand and a gray-haired warrior who downs foes with steel balls on a wire. The rubble of the Bronx and rat-infested sewers provide effective settings. The acting is unsophisticated and Martin Dolman's direction conventional, but the film gallops along. Michael Sopkin, Valentine Moonier, Roman Geer, George Purdom, George Eastman (as Big Ape, who looks like a Caribbean pirate.) (Vestron; Live)

AGAINST ALL ODDS. Video version of *Kiss and Kill* (Republic).

AKAZA, THE GOD OF VENGEANCE. See *Crash!*

AKIRA (1988) ★★★ Animated Japanese feature (based on a comic-book series) set in the 21st century, when Tokyo is ruled by a military government that has brought on urban blight and a disillusioned youth. With imaginative camera angles, director Katsuhiro Otomo brings an unusual sense of cartoon excitement to this convoluted though fascinating morality tale. Two members of a bike gang uncover a secret experiment to develop telekinetic humans to be used in warfare. It's a richly textured tale, demanding full attention. (Streamline) (Laser: Criterion)

ALCHEMIST, THE (1983) ★★ In 1871, Delgado the Alchemist has the hots for raven-haired Lucinda Dooling and forces her lover (Robert Ginty), a Virginia glass maker, to fight for her honor. When she dies the warlock turns Ginty into a tormented man who eats deer. Flash to 1955, when a woman who looks like Dooling happens to drive by Ginty's cabin and is ESPed into his lair in the company of a benevolent hitchhiker. Everyone fights for soul possession as demons jump through a portal of Hell, a grandmother is impaled on a spike and a man is torn in half by the time-continuum threshold. Whew! Directed by Charles Band (as James Amante), written by Alan J. Adler. Viola Kate Stimpson, John Standerford. (Lightning; Vestron; Live)

ALICE, SWEET ALICE (1978) ★★★ Grueling suspense with well-developed characters and psychiatric background, also known as *Communion* and *Holy Terror*. A knife-wielding murderer wearing a doll's mask provides the film's engrossing puzzle. The Catholic Church is the dominating motif, with its omnipresent statues of Christ, madonnas and saints, and its themes of pain and suffering, guilt and innocence. Unknowns (Paula Sheppard, Linda Miller, Mildred Clinton) are supported by Lillian Roth and Brooke Shields. Directed by Alfred Sole, who cowrote with Rosemary Ritvo. (Goodtimes; Spotlite; Video Treasures)

ALIEN (1979) ★★★★★ Just when you thought it was safe to go back into space, along came this ingenious mixture of Gothic horror and sci-fi, a monster movie that lambasts you with shock after shock even after the evil creature is exposed in all its hideous fascination. Credit goes to Swiss designer H. R. Giger for creating the extraterrestrial, ever-changing in its stages of evolution into something larger and deadlier. This revolutionary film unfolds aboard the space freighter *Nostromo*, ordered to set down on an unexplored planet in response to a distress signal. Soon the organic life form is on board, tracking crew members John Hurt, Tom Skerritt, Ian Holm, Yaphet Kotto, Harry Dean Stanton, Veronica Cartwright and Sigourney Weaver. Director Ridley Scott loves cat-and-mouse games, alternating false scares with genuine jolts, all of it deliciously punctuated by the chilling score of Jerry Goldsmith. Dan O'Bannon's screenplay (first called *Starbeast*) not only touches our sense of wonder but reminds us of our fear of the dark and everything unknown or ugly. A splendid paradox giving us those things we dread most, but love to scream at in the dark. Winning an Oscar for Best Visual Effects, it was followed by *Aliens* (another classic) and the lesser *Alien³*. (Video/Laser: CBS/Fox)

ALIEN 2. See *Aliens*.

ALIEN³ (1992) ★★★ If ever there was a set designer's movie, devoted totally to moody, nihilistic ambience, it is this third effort in the popular series. Under the direction of David Fincher, who won this assignment through innovative rock videos, *Alien³* carries over the pictorial qualities and atmosphere of the first two films. Ripley (Sigourney Weaver) crash-lands in a shuttlecraft on a far-off prison planet, Fiorina 161. The only survivor, Ripley learns the ship

has brought an alien with it, and one by one the religious fanatics in the dilapidated penal colony are torn asunder. Since the previous films were more interested in hair-raising suspense and pyrotechnics than characters, it is not surprising *Alien³* lacks any interesting humans other than Ripley, a sympathetic doctor (Charles Dance, who disappears too fast from the story) and a convict (Charles S. Dutton). One of the neat twists to the David Giler–Walter Hill–Larry Ferguson script (Vincent Ward is credited with story): the planet is so rundown, it has no weaponry with which to fight the alien. Unfortunately, the film's climax seems lifted from *Terminator 2* and some maudlin business involving Ripley doesn't work at all. But these quibblings aside, *Alien³* is gripping horror and sci-fi. Brian Glover, Lance Henriksen. (Video/Laser: CBS/Fox)

ALIENATOR (1989) ★ This Fred Olen Ray sci-fi special is derivative of *The Terminator*, but with a female warrior (Teagan Clive) armed with a laser gun who comes to Earth to capture an escapee (Ross Hagen) from a top-security prison in space operated by warden Jan-Michael Vincent. On Earth, game warden John Phillip Law joins with some young travelers and Korean War vet Leo G. Gordon to protect the rebel and fight off the zap-gun-packing lady. She's quite an unusual image in sexy costume, packing that death-ray rod, but she's the only pleasant surprise in this otherwise predictable, clichéd actioner with little brain power to propel the script by Paul Garson. Robert Clarke, Robert Quarry, Richard Wiley, Dyana Ortelli, Jesse Dabson, Dawn Wildsmith. (Prism) (Laser: Image)

ALIENATORS. Japanese laser title for *Shocking Dark*.

ALIEN CONTAMINATION (1980) ★★ When a freighter is found with its crew turned into grisly gruel and a cargo of pulsating egg-shapes, you know you're dealing with body-snatched filmmakers contaminated by *Alien*. When the egg sacs burst open, they spread smoky goo and kill. A conspiracy for world conquest is controlled by a one-eyed Martian glob with a big mouth who hypnotizes humans. The effects in this Italian import are as inferior as the dubbing and the monster will have you laughing, not gagging. Writer-director Luigi Cozzi, who created this as *Contamination: Alien on Earth*, provides an inept charm that makes this fun, especially the inane dialogue. Ian McCulloch, Louise Monroe, Martin Mase. (Cannon; Regal; Paragon; in a heavily edited version from European Creative Films as *Contamination* and from Lettuce Entertain You as *Toxic Spawn*)

ALIEN DEAD, THE (1980) ★★ E.T.s ride to Earth on a meteorite, crash-landing and turning a boatful of kids into raving zombies and other nonsocial creatures. Joining forces to fight them are newsman Ray Roberts and game warden Mike Bonavia. An undistinguished work (also known as *It Fell from the Sky* and *Swamp of the Blood Leeches*) from prolific Fred Olen Ray, who cowrote with Martin Alan Nicholas. Buster Crabbe, in his final role, plays Sheriff Kowalski. (Academy; Genesis; Paragon)

ALIEN FACTOR, THE (1979) ★★ Baltimore filmmaker Don Dohler (writer-producer-director) focuses on a spaceship that crash-lands on Earth. Three aliens emerge to terrorize folks around Perry Hill: The Leemoid, a reptilian being that sucks the life force from humans; the Inferbyce, a clawed gooey-looking creature; and the Zagatile, a tall, furry being. Don Leifert, Tom Griffin, John Cosentino, Larry Schlechter. (Media; United; VCI)

ALIEN FROM L.A. (1987) ★½ The "Alien" is Wanda, a nerdy woman who leaves Malibu to search for her archeologist father, missing in the underground city of Atlantis. This traditional worm-turns fairy tale is a pleasant, oft funny series of misadventures with Kathy Ireland meeting sappy/zappy characters, and endearing her own character with squeaky voice and child-like innocence. In this funky variation on "Alice in Wonderland" that avoids violence, writer-director Albert Pyun (*Sword and the Sorcerer, Cyborg*) proves he's a developing talent. Thom Mathews, Don Michael Paul, Linda Kerridge, Richard Haines. (Media) (Laser: Image)

ALIEN INTRUDER (1992) ★★ Unusual mixture of hardware sci-fi and virtual reality (in the *Westworld* vein) when a seductress E.T. named Ariel (Tracy Scoggins) seduces spacemen to murder for her. Commander Billy Dee Williams brings a ragtag band of ruffians to a floating space station to investigate, where they become involved with "realities" parodying *Casablanca*, Westerns and motorcycle movies. The mediocre effects waylay the film's good intentions, spearheaded by writer Nick Stone and director Ricardo Jacques Gale. Maxwell Caulfield, Gary Roberts, Jeff Conaway, Richard Cody. (PM Entertainment) (Laser: Image)

ALIEN LEGACY, THE (1999) ★★★½ This 67-minute documentary does an excellent job of tracing the history of *Alien*, the 1979 trend-setting science-fiction/horror classic, from the moment screenwriter Dan O'Bannon got the idea from seeing how a wasp paralyzes a spider and lays its eggs in the spider's nest, then waits for its wasp larvae to prey on other spiders. How O'Bannon and cowriter Ronald Shusett got the script together is followed by interviews with H. R. Giger, illustrator Ronn Cobb, costume designer John Mollo, art director Leslie Dilley, director Ridley Scott, effects wizards Brian Johnson and Nick Alider, and many others involved in the making of the film at Shepperton Studios in England. There's also behind-the-scenes footage of cast and crew at work on the original and a few outtakes, too. There's no razzle-dazzle to *The Alien Legacy*, just a straightforward, honest approach. By allowing the sound bites to run their natural course, the film provides insight and depth into how modern movies are made, and does justice to the hard work and inspirational thought that went into the making of *Alien*. (Video/DVD: Fox)

ALIEN MASSACRE. Video version of *Return from the Past* (Academy).

ALIEN MASSACRE. Video version of *The Wizard of Mars* (Regal).

ALIEN NATION (1988) ★★★ Unusual sci-fi thriller, borrowing touches from the buddy-buddy crime flicks to spin its refreshing concept. In the immediate future a shipload of humanoid aliens, labeled "Newcomers," crash-land on Earth and are assimilated into working-class society, evoking a racist reaction among Earthlings. When a gang of aliens begins a wave of crime, cop James Caan volunteers to team with an alien officer to track the killers. What they uncover, while learning about each other's culture, makes for interesting twists while the drug plot unfolds. Writer Rockne S. O'Bannon gives unusual traits to his aliens (they get drunk on milk, and have peculiar body odors) and makes them believable. Caan walks a fine line between tough-guy hardness and his soft spot for his alien buddy. Mandy Patinkin is memorable as Sykes the alien cop. Produced by Gale Anne Hurd and Richard Kobritz, and directed by Graham Baker, this action fantasy became the basis for a syndicated TV series. Terence Stamp, Kevin Major Howard, Leslie Bevins. (Video/Laser: CBS/Fox)

ALIEN NATION: DARK HORIZON (1994) ★★★ This 90-minute TV-movie reprise of the popular TV series deals one more time, and effectively so, with the "Slags" (or "Newcomers"), a race of alien humanoids assimilating itself into American culture, though not without facing racism. In this adventure, an "Overseer" (Scott Patterson) from the planet Tencton is sent to investigate the disappearance of the slaveship Gruza, and discovers that a virus has infected the wife (Michele Scarabelli) and daughter (Laureen Woodland) of Newcomer cop Eric Pierpoint. This virus is about to be unleashed on all Newcomers by the racist Purity '99 movement. Various subplots deal with the series' regulars. The Diane Frolov–Andrew Schneider script was directed by Kenneth Johnson. Terri Treas, Jeff Marcus, Nina Foch, Sean Six. (Video/Laser: Fox)

ALIEN NATION: MILLENNIUM (1996) ★★½ Average TV-movie based on the *Alien Nation* movie and TV series, in which a device called "The Portal" is used by unscrupulous Newcomers to create an illusionary Paradise where everyone is promised peace and contentment.

But it turns out to be your all-too-real scam to sucker money out of the gullible. The cast of regulars from the TV series acts out a mixture of domestic complications and police procedures to round up the con artists. Written-directed by Kenneth Johnson, *Millennium* is unusual only in that it's set a few days before the turn of the century and depicts the eventual coming of A.D. 2000. Gary Graham, Eric Pierpont, Michele Scarabelle, Terri Treas, Laureen Woodland, Sean Six, Jeff Marcus, Kerrie Keane, David Faustino. (Video/Laser: Fox)

ALIEN P.I. See *Alien Private Eye*.

ALIEN PREDATOR(S) (1985) ★ Three bumble-butt youths in a rec vehicle (Dennis Christopher, Martin Hewitt, Lynn-Holly Johnson), traveling through Spain, stop in a town where citizens are controlled by living microbes brought from the Moon by a Skylab satellite. Written-directed by Deran Sarafian, from Noah Bloch's script *Massacre at R.V. Park*, this inferior sci-fier includes a subplot involving Professor Tracer (Luis Predes) and his attempts to find an antidote at a NASA lab. The heroes play the weak material for laughs, but nothing helps this tedious derivative of *Alien*. Also known as *The Falling*. (Trans World; Video Treasures)

ALIEN PREY (1983) ★ Lousy British cheapie, a feeble excuse for torrid, X-rated lesbian scenes between insufferable bitches living in a country estate. Along comes a humanoid alien that eats chickens, foxes and birds, doesn't know how to swim, and turns into a vampire when he's making love. Shoddy exploitation, with terrible makeup and clichéd effects. Directed tastelessly by Norman J. Warren from an equally tasteless script by Max Cuff. Barry Stokes, Glory Anann, Sally Faulkner. Aka *Prey*. (Comet; Cinema Group)

ALIEN PRIVATE EYE (1990) ★ Inferior direct-to-video nonsense about a humanoid (Nikki Fastinetti) named Lemro from the Styx (planet Styx, that is) who uses martial arts to battle enemies while she's on Earth searching for a drug sent to our planet on a black disk. Cliff Aduddell, John Alexander, Robert Axelrod. Written-produced-directed by Vik Rubenfeld. (Raedon)

ALIEN RESURRECTION (1997) ★★★★ If you're going to make an *Alien* sequel, then go all out and make it gross and icky. And carry its concepts into new waters—literally, in the case of an underwater swimming sequence that is one of the scariest and most exciting in this fourth entry in the series. Bring back Sigourney Weaver as Ripley but this time make her stronger and stranger now that she's been implanted with an alien seed. Also, give her a psychic link to the aliens so she knows what they're thinking as well as doing. Hire Jean-Pierre Jeunet to direct, for this French filmmaker is expert at creating a surrealistic world with special focus on its minutiae. Bring in Ron Perlman to play a low-life scumbag space soldier, and counterbalance that by casting Winona Ryder as the one sympathetic character in the whole caboodle. Joss Whedon's script starts out aboard the space station Auriga 200 years after *Alien ³*, with Ripley being cloned into new form (but looking like her old self) from her DNA. Maverick general Dan Hedaya of the United Systems military and mad doctor Brad Dourif are experimenting on alien creatures, but it will come as no surprise when the hideous creatures escape confinement, though it's done in a most graphically clever way. Now everyone on board is potential alien foodstuff. How Perlman and his band of low-life mercenaries (including Michael Wincott, Kim Flowers, and Dominique Pinon as a wheelchair-bound dwarf) make their way to the escape craft, overcoming attacking aliens along the way, swimming through a submerged kitchen, and finding a laboratory of disgustingly mutated life-forms, makes up the bulk of this fanciful and frequently thrilling space adventure. Okay, so the characters aren't much, and relationships are almost nonexistent. What did you expect in an *Alien* movie—intellectuality? Raymond Cruz, Gary Dourdan, Leland Orser. (Video/DVD/Laser: Fox)

ALIENS (1986) ★★★★½ Riveting Oscar-winning action-suspense movie, a supreme sequel to Ridley Scott's *Alien*. Writer-director James Cameron, fresh from *The Terminator*, concocts a thunderyarn reeking with tension and fear, and structured so tightly it moves at lightning pace, so masterful is Cameron at building cliff-hangers within cliff-hangers. Sigourney Weaver returns as the resourceful, hard-driven Ripley, who is rescued 57 years after *Alien* ended and faces a bleak future. Haunted by nightmares of the face-hugger and the belly-busting E.T., she returns to LV-426 to locate colonists who have disappeared. Accompanied back to the windswept planet by commandos equipped with futuristic weapons, she again faces the most hideous creatures of all time. Cameron's focus is the battle between the cynical, well-trained commando team and devious creatures in the dingy corridors and labs of the compound. The humans are only lightly delineated, but some of them come off good, including Michael Biehn, Bill Paxton, Lance Henriksen, Carrie Henn and Jenette Goldsten. Thrills build on thrills until Ripley takes on Mother Alien and her brood in a sequence that qualifies Weaver as the female Rambo of the '80s. Like *Alien*, this exploits our worst fears and carries them to an extreme. All-time classic, brilliantly conceived. (Video/Laser: CBS/Fox)

ALIENS, DRAGONS, MONSTERS & ME (1991) ★★½ Straightforward TV documentary recapping the career of special effects master Ray Harryhausen, narrated by Gary Owens and featuring on-camera interviews with Harryhausen by Eric Boardman. Highlights clips from Harryhausen's earliest animation attempts, including his first experiment with stop-motion (*Cave Bear*), his prehistoric monsters in the unfinished, rarely seen *Evolution*, and his wonderful *Mother Goose* short subjects. Other highlights: clips from *Mighty Joe Young* through *Clash of the Titans*, an interesting interview with producer Charles H. Schneer (who worked with Harryhausen for 30 years plus) and comments by Ray Bradbury, who sums it up well when he says: "Ray is at the center of his films. And we go to see his animals and we go to see him. We don't care what the plot is like as long as it moves.... He stands alone as an artist, a technician and a dreamer." (Cerebus) (Laser: Lumivision)

ALIEN SEED (1989) ★★ Earth woman becomes pregnant via alien presence on Earth as part of an E.T. scheme to create a new "Messiah" to rule the world. Her sister calls on dedicated newsman Erik Estrada to solve the mystery. Okay direct-to-video fare. Heidi Paine, Steven Blade. Written-directed by Bob James and Douglas K. Grimm. (Action International)

ALIEN SPACE AVENGER (1988) ★★ This parody of alien-invasion movies, aka *Space Avenger*, vacillates between tongue-in-cheek physical comedy/campy dialogue and overdone graphic violence, in which humans are blasted into eternity for no particular reason. In 1939, an alien ship carrying escaped prisoners crash-lands and four ugly snake-like monsters take over two men and two women. The story leaps to today as the foursome ventures to New York to tangle with the artist of the "Space Avenger" comic book. The effects consist of showing how the humanoids regenerate new body parts after being blasted to bits. The inability of writer-director-coproducer Richard W. Haines to find a style and stick with it eventually alienates the viewer. A movie in search of fun without finding it. Robert Prichard, Gina Mastrogiacomo, Charity Staley. "Kirk Fairbanks Fogg" is credited as "Space Avenger," but no space avenger appears. (Action International)

ALIEN'S RETURN, THE. See *The Return* (1980).

ALIEN TERROR. Video version of Boris Karloff's *Incredible Invasion* (Sony; MPI).

ALIEN II. See *Alien Contamination*.

ALIEN WARNING. See *Without Warning*.

ALIEN WARRIOR (1985) ★ On a beam of light, a man from another dimension (Brett Clark) arrives on Earth to fight "Great Evil." Clark walks around like he's in a trance, rescues Pamela Saunders from rape, fights drug dealers, and converts minority types at Saunders's reading center. A feeble-minded excuse for voyeuristic sex and bloody shoot-outs with Clark behaving like a superhero as he crashes through walls and

heals his wounds with an inner power. If there's a moral, it's lost in the mindless violence. Ed Hunt directed. Reggie DeMorton, Nelson D. Anderson. Originally released as *King of the Streets*. (Vestron; Live)

ALIEN WITHIN, THE (1994) ★★★ Take a little of *The Abyss*, a touch of *The Thing*, a dab of *Alien* and a smidgen of *Trancers* and you've got this derivative Roger Corman–produced TV-movie set in the year 2020 in an underwater experimental MobilCon lab, where an Alien-like monster gets loose and starts taking over human bodies. Despite its morass of clichés, Alex Simon's script will hold your interest as he spins cat-and-alien games with scientist Roddy McDowall, station captain Alex Hyde-White and lady doctor Melanie Shatner. Director Scott Levy fails to inject much suspense into all this familiar material, but at least he keeps it swimming. Don Stroud, Richard Biggs, Rodger Halston, Emile Levisetti, Sha-Ri Pendleton. (New Horizons)

ALIEN WOMEN (1969) ★ Outer-space cuties, Angvians, battle drab undercover ops in this British production (aka *Zeta One*) from Tony Tenser, which is best described as soft-core porn. Writer-director Michael Cort adapted his story from a comic strip with help from Christopher Neame. Robin Hawdon, James Robertson Justice, Dawn Addams, Charles Hawtrey, Anna Gael. (Front Row Entertainment; Prism; from Sinister/C as *The Love Factor*)

ALIEN ZONE (1975) ★★½ This anthology of David O'Malley's macabre tales is told by ghoulish mortician Ivor Francis to John Ericson, an adulterer fleeing an irate husband. Production values are mediocre but the stories are compelling: A child-hating woman is terrorized by youngsters; a killer photographs women he is about to strangle; two rival detectives try to outwit each other; and a Scrooge-minded man is subjected to mental and physical torture. Ericson's fate provides the fifth tale. Made in Oklahoma, *Alien Zone* is a diverting novelty directed by Sharron Miller. Judith Novgrod, Burr DeBenning, Charles Aidman, Bernard Fox. (From JLT Films as *House of the Dead* and Monarch as *Zone of the Dead*)

ALIVE BY NIGHT. See *The Alien Within*.

ALLAN QUATERMAIN AND THE LOST CITY OF GOLD (1986) ★★½ Richard Chamberlain returns as H. R. Haggard's adventurer (sans British accent) trekking through dangerous Africa in search of his missing brother in an inferior sequel to *King Solomon's Mines* (1986). Quatermain treks with sexy Sharon Stone, native warrior James Earl Jones and cowardly Indian shaman Robert Donner to a shimmering-white metropolis ruled by evil Henry Silva (in an awful fright wig) and Cassandra Peterson (she of Elvira infamy, in a push-up bra). Only the first half has the charm and humor of its predecessor.

Fantasy elements involve snake monsters and Indiana Jones–type ripoffs. Directed by Gary Nelson from a script by Gene Quintano and Lee Reynolds. (MGM/UA)

ALL DOGS GO TO HEAVEN 2 (1996) ★★★ This lacks the hard edge of the original as well as Burt Reynolds's voice for Charlie B. Barkin (this time it's Charlie Sheen), a dog always redeeming himself in the eyes of celestial supervisors. But as a pleasant diversion, with some excellently animated sequences, this first effort from a new MGM cartoon division is a worthy effort. Charlie and his pal Itch (voice by Dom DeLuise) are sent from Heaven to San Francisco to retrieve the lost Gabriel's Horn. The adventures include villainous Carface (Ernest Borgnine); Sasha, a beautiful female (voice by Sheena Easton); and a devil dog named Red (George Hearn). Mainly for children, this sequel is okay stuff. Directed by Paul Sabella and Larry Leker, from a script by Arne Olsen, Kelly Ward and Mark Young. (MGM)

ALLEGRO NON TROPPO (1977) ★★★★ Italian animator Bruno Bozzetto pays homage to Disney's *Fantasia* with six vignettes illustrated to classical music. A scroungy cat is the hero of Sibelius's "Valse Triste"; a Coke bottle figures prominently in Ravel's "Bolero," a tour de force depicting the evolution of life; and a honeybee housewife wreaks revenge on picnickers in Vivaldi's "Concerto in C." The story of Adam and Eve is recounted to Stravinsky's "Firebird"; a white-bearded satyr can no longer please the nymphs to Debussy's "Prelude to the Afternoon of a Faun" and a fable is the core of Dvorak's "Slavic Dance No. 7." This world-famous feature sports live-action wraparound about an orchestra recording music for the cartoons and its silly maestro Maurizio Nichetti, who cowrote the script with Bozzetto and Guido Manuli. (Video: RCA/Columbia) (Laser: Image)

ALLIGATOR (1981) ★★★ Tongue-in-cheek spoof by writer John Sayles (*The Howling*) sets the skin-tone for this takeoff on giant-monster-on-a-rampage movies. A 35-foot-long gator is loose in the sewers and cop Robert Forster is in pursuit—when the monster isn't in pursuit of Forster, jaws slobbering for policeman meat. The creature swims to a theme not unlike John Williams's *Jaws* and carries away entire bodies (look out, gator hunter Henry Silva, you don't stand a chance). Director Lewis Teague (*The Lady in Red, Cujo*) takes none of it seriously and spices the sewer walls with such graffiti as "Harry Lime lives!" If you hate the sight of amphibious entities, you might take along Gator Aid. Dean Jagger, Sue Lyon, Angel Tompkins. (Lightning; Live)

ALLIGATOR II: THE MUTATION (1990) ★★½ Unconnected sequel to the 1981 *Alligator*, in which an oversized gator monster living in the sewers of L.A. decides to have a coming out party—by munching on fishermen and bums. Cop Joseph Bologna rallies forces with the help of police captain Brock Peters and a colorful gator hunter named "Hawk," played with a southern accent by Richard Lynch. Written by Curt Allen, and directed by Jon Hess, this is a phony-baloney monster movie with crummy effects and unconvincing gore attacks. Steve Railsback plays an equally unconvincing villain running an amusement park next to the lake—gosh, does this mean the patrons will also be eaten? Dee Wallace Stone is wasted as Bologna's wife/scientist, and there's a dumb affair between cop Woody Brown and mayor's daughter Holly Gagnier. (Video/Laser: New Line)

ALLIGATOR PEOPLE, THE (1959) ★★★½ Orville Hampton's screenplay is swamped with clichés, but still an entertaining B effort. George Macready is a hypo-happy scientist experimenting with a serum to restore accident victims to normal but which results in scaly skin and glutinous gills. You see, he's been extracting hormones from gators. Richard Crane (TV's *Rocky Jones*) is one of the doc's guinea pigs who's just wed Beverly Garland. When he runs away, she rushes to his Everglades plantation to become a dame in peril. The film is notable for Lon Chaney, Jr., as a modern Captain Hook, and he has a bog-day with his over-the-top role. There's also a great scene of rain-soaked Garland stumbling through a gator-infested swamp. Bruce Bennett lends authority as a psychiatrist. Directed by Roy Del Ruth with a slimy feeling for a swampland horror tale.

ALLIGATORS. See *The Great Alligator*.

ALL OF ME (1984) ★★ Disappointing Steve Martin supernatural "comedy"—a waste of the wild and crazy guy, and of Lily Tomlin. He plays an attorney (moonlighting as a jazz magician) sent to draw up the will of a dying millionairess. Lily is the insufferable moneybags who croaks only to have her soul transferred to Martin's body. Now half of him is him, half of him is her. The Phil Alden Robinson script (based on an Ed Davis novel) is vacuous, giving director Carl Reiner little to work with. A waste of Madolyn Smith, Richard Libertini, Dana Elcar and Victoria Tennant. (Video/Laser: HBO)

ALL THAT MONEY CAN BUY. See *The Devil and Daniel Webster*.

ALMOST DEAD (1995) ★★★ Offbeat TV-movie, based on William Valtos's novel *Resurrection*, in which lithe psychologist Shannen Doherty is haunted by the specter of her dead mother in a small California town, where the only person who believes her story is cop Costas Mandylor. Paranormal events, including spontaneous combustion, ghostly visitations and weird electrical outages plague the slender, leggy, vulnerable Doherty as she tries to unravel the occult mystery. Plenty of atmosphere, an intriguing adaptation by Miguel Tejada-Flores and good direction by coproducer Ruben Preuss make *Almost Dead* very watchable, even if some of its climactic nonsupernatural explanations are disappointing. John Diehl, William R. Moses, Steve Inwood, Eric Christmas, Roy Brocksmith, William Allen Young. (Monarch)

ALMOST HUMAN. See *Shock Waves*.

ALONE IN THE DARK (1982) ★★½ Three wacko cases (Jack Palance, Martin Landau, Erland Van Lidth) escape the asylum of doctor Donald Pleasence, as fruitcake as his patients. The homicidal threesome surrounds the house of a psychiatrist and terrorizes his family. The headshrinker finally resorts to violence to save his loved ones. The bloodbath is gratuitous, and there are moments when writer-director Jack Sholder doesn't explain events. The most depraved scene has Palance under a woman's bed, thrusting upward with a knife through the mattress, the point of the blade emerging between her thighs. A real mixed bag of genres from producer Robert Shaye, who went on to greater success with New Line Pictures. Dwight Schultz, Deborah Hedwall, Lee Taylor-Allan. (RCA/Columbia) (Laser: New Line)

ALPHA INCIDENT, THE (1978) ★ A living microorganism from Mars, brought to Earth on a space probe, terrorizes a motley bunch at a railroad office. The folks bicker and talk and bicker while back at the lab scientists seek an antidote. There's nonsense about not being able to sleep (it's then the microbe destroys the body) so the characters stay awake by playing poker and having sex. Ralph Meeker is wasted as a dimwitted depot manager, and his death scene provides the only effect—his head turning into a puddle of goo. Produced-directed by Bill Rebane and written by Ingrid Neumayer, this low-budgeter (made in Wisconsin as *Gift from a Red Planet*) was no incident. Stafford Morgan, John Alderman, John Goff, Carol Irene Newel. (Media)

ALPHAVILLE (1965) ★★★ Director Jean-Luc Godard also wrote this film set in the near future in which private eye Lemmy Caution (Eddie Constantine) is assigned to rescue a doctor from a city controlled by a computerized brain, Alpha 60, and its creator, Dr. Von Braun (Howard Vernon). Film noir, science vs. intellect, and romance and mythology, vacillating between art film and detective actioner. Anna Karina, Akim Tamiroff, Christa Lang. Aka *Tarzan vs. IBM* and *Alphaville, a Strange Adventure of Lemmy Caution*. (Vintage; S/Weird; Filmfax) (Laser: Criterion)

ALPHAVILLE, A STRANGE ADVENTURE OF LEMMY CAUTION. See *Alphaville*.

ALTAR OF BLOOD. See *Scream of the Demon Lover*.

ALTERED STATES (1980) ★★★ Sci-fi metamorphosis picture given distinguished treatment by Warner Bros. and ballyhooed for its prestigious director (Ken Russell) and screenwriter (Paddy Chayefsky). But in reality it's the same old mad-scientist story, redressed with special-effects razzle-dazzle by Dick Smith and others. Genetics investigator William Hurt climbs into a deepwater think tank and regresses to a primeval state, turning into a hairy ape. There's a real freak-out sequence at the end. Blair Brown, Bob Balaban, Charles Haid, Drew Barrymore. (Video/Laser: Warner Bros.)

ALWAYS (1989) ★★★ Steven Spielberg is a wonderful director but sometimes he over-inflates his films with emotion and turns his characters into schmaltzy goofballs, defeating good intentions. *Always* is an intimate romance, but Spielberg (working with a Jerry Belson script) gives it such epic proportions that the story's flimsiness is apparent. And yet, it's such a good-natured movie, full of charming characters and enhanced by a rousing John Williams score, you can't help but like it. In this loose update of *A Guy Named Joe*, Richard Dreyfuss is an airman fighting fires in Montana, making dangerous runs over burning forests. Holly Hunter is his lover and John Goodman his best buddy. After Dreyfuss dies in a heroic attempt to save Goodman, he finds himself in a netherland where angel Audrey Hepburn tells him he has to perform one last good deed. Yeah, a lot of *Always* is corny, but . . . Brad Johnson, Roberts Blossom, Keith David. (Video/Laser: MCA)

AMANDA AND THE ALIEN (1995) ★★½ This bemused TV-movie adaptation of Robert Silverberg's short story is notable for the performance of Nicole (*Baywatch*) Eggert as a bored, antiestablishment young woman who befriends an alien creature that has taken possession of a human body so she can teach the thing how to behave properly on Earth. The humor in Jon Kroll's adaptation runs from the sublime to the sexual but it's only Eggert who makes any of it very interesting. The creatures are jellyfish-like things of minimal visual interest which pass from being to being, giving cop Michael Dorn and government guy Stacy Keach opportunities to become possessed. As director, Kroll adds little to stir the fire up. You get to see one flying saucer, but so what. Watching *Baywatch* might be more fun. Michael Bendetti, John Diehl, Alex Meneses, David Millbern. (Republic)

AMAZING CAPTAIN NEMO, THE (1978) ★½ Absurd Irwin Allen TV-movie in which two naval officers find the submarine Nautilus abandoned on the ocean floor, with Captain Nemo (Jose Ferrer) preserved in a cryogenic chamber. Nemo leaps out and, forgetting he's just slept for 100 years, pursues a sub commanded by evil Burgess Meredith, who threatens to destroy Washington with a missile. A series of chases featuring force fields, radiation-contaminated waters, laser zap guns, underwater swimming, etc. Robert (*Psycho*) Bloch and Mann Rubin wrote this to Allen's Neanderthal specifications. Lynda Day George, Mel Ferrer, Horst Buchholz, Warren Stevens. Directed perfunctorily by Alex March.

AMAZING COLOSSAL MAN, THE (1957) ★★ Co-writers Bert I. Gordon (producer-director) and Mark Hanna explore the mental anguish undergone by Army colonel Glenn Langan, who's growing ten feet a day after exposure to a plutonium explosion. For one thing, his sex life goes all to hell, to the disappointment of Cathy Downs. Instead of staying on this compelling track, Gordon opts for a rampage of destruction and shoddy effects as the colonel stomps across Vegas to face military forces at Hoover Dam. Good score by Albert Glasser. Camp classic of minimal importance. William Hudson, Larry Thor, Russ Bender, Judd Holdren. The sequel was *War of the Colossal Beast*. (Columbia TriStar; Rhino)

AMAZING EXPLOITS OF THE CLUTCHING HAND. Although this is how the title card reads on the 1936 serial, advertising and other source material reveals only *The Clutching Hand*. See that entry.

AMAZING MR. BLUNDEN, THE (1972) ★★★ Old gentleman (Lionel Jeffries) from the past turns up in the present via the Wheel of Time, and manipulates two children to alter a tragic incident of 100 years ago. Hence, a supernatural tale with paradoxes of time travel and touches of the fairy tale blended with the traditional Victorian ghost story. Based on Antonia Barber's *The Ghosts*, this is an entertaining, clever British film written-directed by Jeffries. Laurence Naismith, Lynne Frederick, Garry Miller, Diana Dors. (Media)

AMAZING MR. H. See *They Saved Hitler's Brain*.

AMAZING MR. X, THE (1948) ★★★ Undeservedly forgotten miniclassic originally released by Eagle Lion as *The Spiritualist* and directed by Bernard Vorhaus. Memorable for its ghostly ambience and atmospheric photography of John Alton, this has dated qualities that now give it a nostalgic patina. Lynn Bari stars as a wistful, lonely woman living in a luxurious cliffside mansion who hears ghostly whisperings of her dead husband (Donald Curtis). On the beach she meets an exotic spiritualist (Turhan Bey, with a raven perched on his shoulder) who puts her in communication with the dead, over the objections of bland boyfriend Richard Carlson, naive sister Cathy O'Donnell and cop Harry Mendoza. This documents the techniques of the phony-baloney medium: floating ectoplasm, ghostly music, spirit cabinets, etc. (Sinister/C; Rex Miller; Filmfax) (Laser: Lumivision)

AMAZING STORIES (1985–87) ★★★½ Steven Spielberg's NBC anthology, which today plays

better than when it premiered, was reedited into TV-movies (subtitles Books 1 through 5) shown exclusively on TV and commercial videotapes (called movies) designed for rental and sell-through. These fantasies range from poignant to comedic to tragic to dark horror, featuring topnotch casts, good scripting and directing, and the ever-present hand of the amazing Spielberg. (MCA)

AMAZING TRANSPARENT MAN, THE (1960) ★½ The plot by Jack Lewis is transparent, the dialogue is vaporous, the acting is invisible and the direction imperceptible in this pellucid piece of nothingness. Douglas Kennedy as a bank robber, Marguerite Chapman as the obligatory skirt and James Griffith as the insidious inventor (planning to create an invisible army of zombies) have every reason to blush unseen as they play shoot-'em-up games before the whole thing vanishes into thin air. You'll see through director Edgar G. Ulmer. (J & J; Sinister/C; S/Weird; Filmfax)

AMAZONS (1984) ★★½ Lost race of Amazon women, depicted in the style of a *Wonder Woman* comic book, is brought into the modern world as busty, crusty conspirators out to pull off a political plot. The paranoia scheme has doctor Madeleine Stowe accused of malpractice, and, in investigating the mystery with cop Jack Scalia, uncovering a drug that turns men mad with fear, a bow-and-arrow charm bracelet and several crossbows. Director Paul Michael Glaser brings more style and mood to this half-baked, confusing tale than it deserves. Tamara Dobson, Jennifer Warren, Stella Stevens, William Schallert. (Western World)

AMAZONS (1986) ★ Lousy acting pulls this Roger Corman sword-and-sorcery adventure to the depths of viewers' despair. It's amateur night in Shanar, land of the Emerald Queen, where huge-breasted, buttocks-busting babes, their bosoms heaving with battle might, square off against "omnipotent" Lord Kalungo, who intends to acquire the Sword of Azendotti and the magical Spirit Stone. Penelope Reed and Danitza Kingsley are gallant wenches who expose their female charms for cinematic art, warring against Kalungo and his one-eyed associate who resembles a Mohawk Indian. As heavy-handed as fingers holding a cannonball, this is dead weight, charmless and produced on the cheap, no doubt in some foreign land where Corman gets discount rates. Directed by Alex Sessa. Joseph Whipp and Jacques Arndt are among the males who are but dirt bumps in the shadows of mighty women. (MGM/UA)

AMAZON WOMEN. Video version of *Gold of the Amazon Women* (America's Best).

AMBULANCE, THE (1990) ★★★½ Fascinating study in paranoia from writer-director Larry Cohen, one of the best independent filmmakers from anywhere. This urban cautionary tale depicts a strange ambulance that picks up diabetic people and whisks them away to the secrert quarters of mad doctor Eric Braeden. Cohen paints eccentric portraits and introduces unexpected plot twists as comic-book artist Eric Roberts searches for Janine Turner with gum-chewing cop James Earl Jones, lady policeman Megan Gallagher and crusty newspaper reporter Red Buttons. Marvel Comics editor Stan Lee appears in a cameo. (Video/Laser: RCA/Columbia)

AMERICAN CYBORG: STEEL WARRIOR (1993) ★★★ Well-made futuristic actioner set in a ruined society (a wartorn city in the Holy Land?) where roving soldier of fortune Joe Lara helps Nicole Hansen take the only living fetus on Earth to safety, battling murderous cyborg John Ryan in a series of exciting combat and hand-to-hand encounters set in actual ruins. Directed by Boaz Davidson from a script by Brent Friedman, Bill Crounse and Don Pequignot. (Video/Laser: Cannon)

AMERICAN GOTHIC (1987) ★★★ Effective horror thriller generates shudders in probing the thin line between sanity and insanity. Sarah Torgov, recovering from a breakdown after the death of her baby, goes on a vacation with two couples and is stranded on an island off Seattle. They find Rod Steiger and Yvonne De Carlo, demented parents of three murderous adults with the minds of children. The film is less concerned with how the vacationers are disposed of than with Torgov's descent into madness. How she resolves this tale is what the film is ultimately about. Director John Hough spares no punches. Michael J. Pollard, Fiona Hutchison, Mark Lindsay Chapman. (Vidmark; from Virgin as *Hide and Shriek*) (Laser: Image)

AMERICAN NIGHTMARE (1981) ★★ Canadian slasher flick in which a cut-and-ask-questions-later madman is on a rampage in Toronto, destroying prostitutes and other wanderers. Meanwhile, pianist Lawrence S. Day searches for his prostitute sister and cop Michael Ironside seeks the razor murderer. Directed by Don McBrearty from a script by John Sheppard. Lora Staley, Neil Dainard. (Interglobal; Media; from Prism as *Combat Shock*)

AMERICAN ORPHEUS (1992) ★★ Modernized version of Jean Cocteau's *Orpheus* from Rick Schmidt (he wrote, produced, directed and edited) in which love extends from beyond the grave between a mother and her young daughter. Jody Esther, Karen Rodriguez.

AMERICAN SCREAM, THE (1988) ★★½ Vacationing family in the Sierra Mountains is terrorized by local freakos and weird dudes, but the Benzingers turn the tables on their tormentors in this horror-comedy written-directed by Mitchell Linden. Kevin Kaye, Jennifer Darling, Kimberlee Kramer. (21st Genesis)

AMERICAN TIGER (1989) ★★½ If there is any one thing to remember about this Italian-produced action movie (shot on location in Miami) with supernatural overtones, it is the scene of evil preacher Donald Pleasence oinking and snorting like a hungry pig during a religious rally, and then turning into a hog monster from the pits of Hell. Otherwise, there's the usual movie mixture of martial arts, car chases and a little magic in the form of a Chinese witch (she lives with a cobra and a cat) who gives rickshaw puller Mitch Gaylord (born in the Year of the Tiger) a legendary Chinese talisman that zaps him with the superstrengths he needs to defeat the preacher and his sadistic henchman-killer. A psychic link exists between the witch and Gaylord, who also has topless dancer Victoria Prouty to help him solve the mystery. Sergio Martino contributed to the story. Martin Dolman directed. (Academy) (Laser: Image)

AMERICAN WAY, THE. See *Riders of the Storm*.

AMERICAN WEREWOLF IN LONDON, AN (1981) ★★★★ This film, with *The Howling*, established new trends in monster movie effects. Rick Baker demonstrates a brilliance in transforming David Naughton into a hairy creature—not with old-fashioned time-lapse techniques but by showing Naughton's body stretching, twisting, expanding and agonizingly popping into its new lycanthropic shape. It's enthralling to watch the transformation—and you know movies can never be the same again. John Landis's scripting and directing are homages to old-fashioned werewolf movies, but he contributes his own tongue-in-cheek comedy through innovative dialogue when a dead friend, Griffin Dunne, keeps returning, in various stages of decomposition, to warn Naughton he will suffer transmutation. Jenny Agutter provides love interest. (Video/Laser: MCA)

AMERICAN WEREWOLF IN PARIS, AN (1997) ★★ This is a thoroughly botched attempt to recapture the magic of John Landis's 1981 classic, *An American Werewolf in London*, which broke new territory with its special effects and its comedic attitudes toward horrific cinema. Instead of a hip, flip script, director Anthony Waller's writing (with the alleged help of Tom Stern and Tim Burns) breaks a lot of wind but little else when American tourist nerds Tom Everett Scott, Vince Vieluf, and Phil Buckman sneak atop the Eiffel Tower one night for a little bungee jumping but end up saving the life of would-be suicide Julie Delpy, who just happens to be endowed with superhuman strength—and the ability to turn into a werewolf when the moon is just right, or when she receives an injection of yellow serum. She's the daughter that David Naughton and Jenny Agutter spawned in Landis's original. While that's interesting, it remains the only real link to the original. Drastically missing is the depth of character that Landis brought to his characters. Instead, Waller strives emptily for a mixture of dark, stark comedy and shock effects through computer-generated werewolves. The results are strained to the limit. No way can this film make any sense when all Waller wants to do is throw every horror trick in the book at you. The loup is really loopy, and really lousy, in this one. The film's one impactful moment is the Parisian location photography behind the opening credits, gargoyles and all. Totally wasted in supporting parts are Julie Bowen as a sexy tourist who likes to get laid in a cemetery (but gets laid to rest instead) and French actors Thierry Lhermitte and Tom Novembre. (Video/ DVD/Laser: Hollywood Pictures)

AMERICA 3000 (1986) ★ A hundred years after the Great Nuke, a band of Amazon women is led by Vena of Frisco, known as the "Tiara," or Queen. This silly example of post-holocaust movie-making is so absurd that it almost becomes entertaining as the warrior dames (the "fraus") engage in political intrigue with other female tribes and hold sway over the "Machos" (male slaves) in a place called Camp Reagan. Writer-director David Engelbach created his own oddball lingo for this picture—thus "negi" is used for "no," "woggo" means crazy, etc. There are times you can't even tell what people are saying, it gets so "woggo." Two young wanderers join a band of guys (Men's Lib?) to stage an uprising in this satirical, never-take-it-seriously action-comedy flicker. "Negi" way, Jose. Chuck Wagner, Laurene Landon, William Wallace, Sue Glosa, Victoria Barrett, Camilla Sparv. (MGM/UA)

AMITYVILLE: A NEW GENERATION (1993) ★★½ This spinoff of *Amityville II: The Possession*, which depicted a teenager killing his family with a rifle, picks up with the son of that teenager, living in a rundown building in L.A., inheriting a haunted mirror from his derelict father. Spirits from behind the glass cause grisly supernatural murders in the building owned by David Naughton as the troubled young man fights internal demons from his family's past. This exploitation thriller places emphasis on psychological aspects and has rewarding moments. It also has a strange twist in the presence of Terry O'Quinn as a special "psychopathology" cop on the case. But much of it is familiar *Omen*-style gore effects with not much done with the mirror, a weakness John Murlowski might have rectified in his directing. Oh well, one must patiently accept the bad with the good in the script by producers Christopher Defaria and Antonio Toro. Ross Patridge, Julia Nickson-Soul, Lala Sloatman, Richard Roundtree. (Video/Laser: Republic)

AMITYVILLE CURSE, THE (1990) ★★ This U.S.-Canadian film appears to be based on a book by Hans Holzer and not Jay Anson's *The Amityville Horror* and is therefore outside the scope of the ongoing *Amityville Horror* series, although its subject matter is similar. It was directed by Tom Berry and stars Kim Coates, Dawna Wightman, Helen Hughes, David Stein and Anthony Dean Rubes. (Vidmark) (Laser: Vidmark/Image)

AMITYVILLE HORROR, THE (1979) ★★★ Jay Anson's best-selling haunted house chiller was allegedly true, documenting the supernatural experiences of a family on Long Island. This version, with James Brolin and Margot Kidder as husband and wife taking over the haunted residence, deviates frequently from the so-called true events, adding to the confusion as to what is fact and/or fiction. There are harrowing moments as the couple experiences ghostly phenomena and a chilling religious subplot unfolds with Catholic priest Rod Steiger, but neither director Stuart Rosenberg nor screenwriter Sandor Stern come close to capturing the terror of Anson's narrative. Good score by Lalo Schifrin and a supporting cast (Murray Hamilton, Don Stroud, Val Avery, John Larch) keep the film on a professional course. (Warner Bros; Goodtimes) (Laser: Vestron)

AMITYVILLE HORROR: THE EVIL ESCAPES—PART IV. See *Amityville 4: The Evil Escapes*.

AMITYVILLE II: THE POSSESSION (1982) ★★ This U.S.-Mexican production begins before *The Amityville Horror*, depicting allegedly true events about a family that lived in the "spirited" house in 1974 and was subjected to supernatural horrors and demonic possessions. (These events were documented in Hans Holzer's book, *Murder in Amityville*.) One night the young son is thoroughly possessed by an evil demon and kills his family in cold blood. Shown in all its bloody details, this crime becomes a tasteless exploitation device. Then the film slides into sheer idiocy as priest James Olson tries to exorcise the youth after helping him to escape jail. The finale—set in the Amityville house—has nothing to do with demonology but everything to do with effects and makeup. The performances by Olson, Burt Young, Rutanya Alda, Moses Gunn and Andrew Prine are on a level of hysteria. A sickening movie, directed by Damiano Damiani and written by Tommy Lee Wallace. (Video/Laser: Nelson)

AMITYVILLE III: THE DEMON. Video version of *Amityville 3-D* (Vestron).

AMITYVILLE 3-D (1983) ★★½ Third entry in the series about an alleged haunted house on Long Island, first popularized in a "true" book by Jay Anson and kept alive by Hollywood exploitation. Unlike its predecessors, this is based on no facts whatsoever, being loosely connected vignettes. Magazine writer Tony Russell buys the accursed estate, laughing contemptuously at the legends, but finds himself sucked into a supernatural netherland. So much for respectable realtors. The effects are decent (a corpse comes to life; a fire-breathing monster emerges from the well in the cellar; and the house goes berserk in the final reel) but the film's power is limited by the weak William Wales screenplay and limpid direction of veteran Richard Fleischer. Tess Harper, Robert Joy, Candy Clark, John Beal. (In 2-D video from Orion and Vestron.) (Laser: Vestron)

AMITYVILLE 4: THE EVIL ESCAPES (1989) ★★½ This plays more like an episode of the *Friday the 13th* series than a sequel to the Amityville series, and it's strictly TV-movie caliber. Based on a book by John G. Jones, director Sandor Stern's telescript focuses on a lamp (set on the base of a gnarly tree stump with personified features) that becomes the new home for the supernatural Amityville evil. This "transmigration" finds the lamp being taken to California, where Jane Wyatt's household is terrorized by all the horror clichés from the earlier Amityville entries. Patty Duke looks totally lost as she joins with priest Fredric Lehne to fight the wicked lamp. Lou Hancock, Brandy Gold, Geri Betzler, Aron Eisenberg, Norman Lloyd. The video version was retitled *The Amityville Horror: The Evil Escapes—Part IV*. (Video: Starmaker) (Laser: Vidmark)

AMITYVILLE '92: IT'S ABOUT TIME (1992) ★★½ By now the phenomena introduced in *The Amityville Horror* have been overused within the genre—but it's refreshing when filmmakers can parade out clichés and still make them work. This time the connection to the 1979 adaptation of Jay Anson's book about a case of haunting on Long Island is a 15th-century clock once owned by a French necromancer who ate the flesh of boys. Architect Stephen Macht brings the clock to his tract home in the San Gabriel valley, where "pure evil" goes into action, slowing down or stopping time to make bad things happen. Macht is bitten by a crazed dog, his daughter becomes a sexual seductress, his son is accused of painting swastikas on a neighbor's door, and his ex-wife and her boyfriend are caught up in inexplicable events. Only the neighborhood supernatural expert, Nita Talbot, knows the truth. You get black, runny goo before the final showdown in Burlwood Estates. Tony Randel effectively directed the script by producers Christopher Defaria and S. Antonio Toro. Shawn Weatherly, Megan Ward, Damon Martin, Jonathan Penner, Dick Miller. (Video/Laser: Republic)

AMOK. See *Schizo* (1976).

AMONG THE LIVING DEAD. See *A Virgin Among the Living Dead*.

AMSTERDAMNED (1987) ★★★½ Dutch filmmaker Dick Maas takes elements of the slasher/underwater/chase genres and does wonders with them in this superior horror tale about a mysterious scuba diver who uses the canals of Amsterdam to conceal his presence until he's ready to strike. In addition to the many suspense and graphic-death sequences, writer-director Maas (best known for *The Lift*) also throws in an exciting underwater sequence à la *Jaws* and stages a fabulous motorboat chase through city streets that is technically flawless and full of dangerous stunts. Amsterdam cop Huub Stapel and girlfriend Monique van de Ven are the principals caught up in the "diver of death" plot, which is full of witticisms and twists. (Vestron) (Laser: Image)

ANACONDA (1997) ★★★½ A really scary snake movie that should please the horror crowd for which it quickly uncoils, even if it does have its lapses and flaws. Who cares when you've got a giant giant giant 40-foot-long serpent of the Amazon that seems to have a personal grudge against snake expert Jon Voight, and who cares if Voight overacts terribly. He knows he's making a genre movie, so he goes right over the top in portraying a man of evil that sometimes behaves as evil as the killer snake. Director Luis Llosa brings a constant tension to the silly proceedings as a documentary film crew (headed by Jennifer Lopez, and including Ice Cube, Eric Stoltz, and Jonathan Hyde) heads up the Amazon to seek a lost tribe. After rescuing a stranded Voight, the boat crew is soon into the thick of it with the colossal snake, a creature created largely through computer animation. And some of the scenes, in which the snake swallows and/or regurgitates entire bodies, are pips. One might wish that screenwriters Hans Bauer, Jim Cash, and Jack Epps, Jr., had put a little more character into their people so we could care about them more, but hey. It's a killer-snake movie, remember? This delivers the goods and has plenty of recoil. Fangs for the memories, you snakes in the grass. Owen Wilson, Kari Wuhrer, Vincent Castellanos. (Video/DVD/Laser: Columbia TriStar)

AND COMES THE DAWN . . . BUT COLORED RED. See *Web of the Spider*.

AND FRANKENSTEIN CREATED WOMAN. See *Frankenstein Created Woman*.

AND NOW THE SCREAMING STARTS (1973) ★★½ Gratuitous Gothic grue from Amacus (produced by Max J. Rosenberg and Milton Subotsky) is set in the House of Fengriffin where a severed hand crawls in the drafty corridors. It's a legendary curse the tormented characters must endure. Directed by Roy Ward Baker. Peter Cushing, Herbert Lom, Stephanie Beacham, Patrick Magee, Guy Rolfe. Aka *Fengriffen* and *I Have No Mouth but I Must Scream*. (Media; Prism; Nostalgia Merchant)

ANDROID (1982) ★★★ Better-than-average sci-fi adventure, exploring man's relationships with robots. Klaus Kinski, bordering on the psychosis of Dr. Frankenstein, lives on a far-flung space station with Max 404, an android assistant

(Don Opper, who cowrote with James Reigle). The doctor creates a beautiful blond android to keep Max company. Conflict erupts when three escaped convicts hide on the station. Directed by Aaron Lipstadt, onetime assistant to Roger Corman. Brie Howard, Nobert Weisser. (Media) (Laser: Image)

ANDROID AFFAIR, THE (1995) ★★ Mediocre, predictable TV-movie in which beautiful robotics expert Harley Jane Kozak helps to create Android #905 under the tutelage of evil doctor Ossie Davis and helper Saul Rubinek (wearing a wild flow of hair). As the android, Griffin Dunne struggles with the script by director Richard Kletter (based on Isaac Asimov's short story "Teach 109") but it's slow, tedious going. In short, poor programming and bad short circuiting. Peter Outerbridge, Natalie Radford. (Video/Laser: MCA)

ANDROMEDA STRAIN, THE (1971) ★★★★½ Robert Wise's adaptation of Michael Crichton's best-seller, scripted by Nelson Gidding, is a sci-fi thriller brilliantly designed, well-acted and -plotted in the style of an exciting detective story. A deadly bacterium brought to Earth by a U.S. satellite destroys a desert community (except for an old man and newborn baby). The survivors are isolated in an underground research center where Arthur Hill, Kate Reid, James Olson and Paula Kelly unravel the bacterium mystery. Although the climax is contrived, the film is brilliant in all departments. (Video/Laser: MCA)

AND SOON THE DARKNESS (1970) ★★½ British terror thriller in which two women bicycle across Europe while a slasher waits in the bushes. Directed by Robert Fuest, who gave us *The Abominable Dr. Phibes*. Screenplay by Terry Nation and Brian Clemens. Pamela Franklin, Michele Dotrice, John Nettleton. (HBO)

ANDY AND THE AIRWAVE RANGERS. See *Andy Colby's Incredible Video Adventure*.

ANDY COLBY'S INCREDIBLE VIDEO ADVENTURE (1988) ★ Below-average Roger Corman TV-movie in which Randy Josselyn, while watching a video, is sucked into the tube by Lord Chroma (Chuck Kovacic), the ruler of a world within the TV set. The Jed Horovitz–Deborah Brock script is an excuse for Corman to reuse footage from *Space Raiders*. Bo Svenson plays . . . Kor the Conqueror? Directed by Deborah Brock. Aka *Andy and the Airwave Rangers*. (RCA/Columbia)

AND YOU THOUGHT YOUR PARENTS WERE WEIRD (1991) ★½ This weak-kneed comedic imitation of *Short Circuit* is a failure, and its attempts to be sentimental are cloying. Joshua Miller and Edan Gross are brother inventors who create an R2D2-looking robot endowed with the spirit of their deceased father, who helps them outwit dimwitted thief John Quade and his inventor son (Eric Walker) from stealing

the robot. Writer-director Tony Cookson makes this an irritating bore. The voice of Alan Thicke serves as the robot-father. Sam Behrens, Susan Gibney. (Vidmark)

ANDY WARHOL'S DRACULA (1974) ★★ A most singular vampire movie (also called *Blood for Dracula, Young Dracula* and *Andy Warhol's Young Dracula*) which has dated badly and now is more laughable than horrific. Its European accents ("virgin" emerges "where-gin") and foppish performances by the androgynous-looking Udo Kier and Arno Juerging give it an unintentional comedic edge it didn't have in the '70s. The dialogue is uproariously campy ("the blood of this whore is killing me!") and Joe Dallesandro's American accent creates howls when he takes his axe and goes after the vampire. The plot has Kier as a Romanian count looking for a virgin in the family of Vittorio DeSica, but his daughters keep coming up ravished by Dallesandro, leaving Kier to drink tainted blood. You really need patience and a love for Warhol's memory to sit through this. Written-directed by Paul Morrissey. (Video Gems)

ANDY WARHOL'S FRANKENSTEIN (1974) ★★ Bloodletting, excessive violence, necrophilia, gore murders. A sickening exercise in black humor . . . You'll need a strong stomach, and an even stronger sense of curiosity, to endure this low point in cinema, also known as *Andy Warhol's Young Frankenstein, Flesh for Frankenstein* and *The Frankenstein Experiment* and sometimes referred to as *Warhol's Frankenstein*. Paul Morrissey directed (and cowrote the awful screenplay with Tonino Guerra), Carlo Rambaldi handled the gore effects. Joe Dallesandro, Monique Van Vooren, Carla Mancini. Originally conceived as *Up Frankenstein* and *The Devil and Dr. Frankenstein*. (Video Gems; in 3-D format from 3-D TV Corp.)

ANDY WARHOL'S YOUNG DRACULA. See *Andy Warhol's Dracula*.

ANGELA (1996) ★½ This is the kind of emptyheaded, pretentious claptrap art theaters love to play under the guise of "socially significant." Superficial and as messed up in plotting as the lives of the disturbed people it depicts, *Angela* is about a troubled 10-year-old girl (Miranda Ruth Rhyne) who sees strange figures (the Virgin Mary, beckoning to her; a cherubic angel, saying that he loves her) as she refuses to relate to her sluttish mother (beautiful Anna Thompson) and vacillating father (John Ventimiglia), and romps about meaninglessly with her younger sister (Charlotte Blythe). Written-directed by Rebecca Miller, the daughter of playwright Arthur Miller, this is rampant with meaningless religious symbols and has all the depth of a drained duck pond.

ANGEL HEART (1987) ★★★★ One strange private-eye story in the film noir tradition, seguing into a startling supernatural thriller. Director Alan Parker has a bleak vision of this dark tale, giving it ambience, atmosphere and intriguing symbolism. In 1955, private eye Harry Angel (Mickey Rourke) is hired by Mr. Cyphere (Robert De Niro) to find singer Johnny Fortune, missing since 1943. The trail leads Angel to New Orleans and voodoo rites, and it's littered with corpses as Angel gets closer to the occult solution. Clever viewers will spot the surprise ending in advance, but it's still a staggering viewing experience with its nihilistic views. Lisa Bonet (of the *Cosby* TV show) engages in a heavy R-rated sex scene. Charlotte Rampling. (IVE) (Laser: Image)

ANGEL OF DEATH (1986) ★★ Dr. Mengele, the butcher of Auschwitz who conducted "medical experiments," is found alive in Brazil by Nazi-hunters Fernando Rey and Christopher Mitchum. Mengele is conducting new experiments in genetics with a monkey monster. Directed by Andrea Bianchi and Jesus Franco. Howard Vernon, Jack Taylor, Robert Foster, Susan Andrews. (New World)

ANGEL OF H.E.A.T.—THE PROTECTORS: BOOK #1 (1982) ★★ There's a green door and Marilyn Chambers goes behind it but doesn't find an orgy of excitement—it's mad scientist Dan Jesse with a sound-frequency device that shatters metal, and a gang of horny androids. This nutty professor, plotting to steal microchips programmed with high-security data, is too daffy to be an interesting villain and the film fails as soft-core exploitation, having too little sex and nudity. Marilyn may be well-suited (or un-suited?) for X-rated fare, but as sexy spy Angel Harmony (leader of Harmony's Elite Assault Team), her shapely body does little for forward thrust. Even Mary Woronov's lesbian role adds nothing. The best thing in this film, produced-directed by Myrl A. Schreibman (*Clonus Horror*), is Lake Tahoe scenery. If you can't stand H.E.A.T., get out of the kitsch. Originally made as *The Protectors: Book #1*. (Video/Laser: Vestron)

ANGEL OF PASSION (1991) ★ Adulteress wakes up in Limbo Heaven with Dr. Guardian, who assigns her to atone for her sexual wrongdoings by returning to Earth and casting a spell that will give pleasures to others. A flimsy excuse for soft-core sex scenes and stripteases, performed lustfully if not artistically. Written-directed by Jason Holt as amateurishly as the acting. Lisa Petrund, Douglas McHail, Lynn Chase, Tim Sullivan, Tuscany.

ANGEL ON MY SHOULDER (1946) ★★★½ Deliciously wonderful supernatural comedy with Claude Rains as a devious Devil who arranges for deceased gangster Paul Muni to return to Earth to pose as a well-respected judge. The H. Segall–Roland Kibbee script is witty and Archie Mayo directs with a fine blend of melodrama

and tongue-in-cheek. Anne Baxter, Onslow Stevens, Jonathan Hale, Fritz Leiber. (Sinister/C; Nostalgia) (Laser: Road)

ANGEL ON MY SHOULDER (1980) ★★★½ Well-done TV-movie remake of the '46 fantasy-comedy has the advantage of a looser moral code that doesn't straitjacket the writers. With gusto and insight, Peter Strauss portrays a wisecracking crook who's sent to the chair. Next stop: Hell, where he weaves a deal with the Devil to return to Earth and take over the body of a D.A. and set him up for a political fall. It's delightful to watch Strauss undergo subtle changes and pull a double-cross on old Satan (underplayed by Richard Kiley) and make passes at Barbara Hershey. Directed by John Berry. Janis Paige, Scott Colomby, Murray Matheson. (Sultan)

ANGELS (1992) ★★★ Influences of Dennis Potter and Charles Dickens hang over this British TV-movie in which guardian angels Tom Bell, Cathy Tyson and Eric Mallett become guides for three tormented souls, one of whom has torn the "cosmic fabric" by not dying at his appointed time. How the spirits, operating out of a heavenly way station (distinguished by a bleached-out black-and-white look) come to terms with these confused humans makes for comedy and pathos. Directed by Philip Saville. Warren Clarke is especially good as a sadistic entertainer. Louise Lombard, James Purefoy.

ANGER OF THE GOLEM. See *It!*

ANGRY RED PLANET, THE (1960) ★★½ Low-budget space thriller strains to be different but the effects crew only gets H for hernias. Astronauts Gerald Mohr, Les Tremayne, Jack Kruschen and Nora Hayden land on an expressionistic Martian landscape. They encounter a giant spider-bat and globular entities, but none of these goofy E.T.s is convincing. The script by director Ib Melchoir and Sidney Pink evokes unintended chuckles. This was called "Cinemagic"—referring to a tinting, that of orange cellophane. Stanley Cortez's cinematography is superior to the material. First made as *Invasion of Mars* and *Journey to Planet Four*. (HBO) (Laser: Image, with *Journey to the Seventh Planet*)

ANGUISH (1987) ★★★ This might have been a masterpiece of psychoterror had Spanish director Bigas Luna opted for a less disgusting story (he cowrote with Michael Berlin) and gone for classy suspense and shocks. That criticism aside, *Anguish* is still a humdinger. For 20 unsavory minutes we watch crazyman Michael Lerner, a hospital orderly, slice up innocent victims and remove their eyeballs. He also endures hypnotic trances induced by daffy mother Zelda Rubinstein (Tangina in the *Poltergeist* series). Suddenly we realize we're watching a movie called *The Mommy*, playing at a theater in Culver City where a serial killer with a mother fixation is on the verge of a murderous rampage. An odd parallel develops when, in *The Mommy*, Lerner enters a Barcelona theater where Willis O'Brien's *The Lost World* is playing. Now we have two movies of almost identical story lines (and don't forget you, watching *Anguish*.) This overcomes poor taste with clever construction. Talia Paul, Angel Jove, Isabel Garcia Lorca. (Video/Laser: Fox)

ANIMAL FARM (1954) ★★★★ Louis de Rochemont's adaptation of George Orwell's cautionary fable about how false governments rise up to enslave their people is still as effective as when it was made. Orwell couched his message as a parable about Manor Farm, run by drunken Farmer Jones. When they are badly mistreated, the animals revolt and take over under Napoleon the boar hog. The parallels to communism are obvious as Napoleon turns into a Stalin, fattening his own stomach at the expense of others. Providing an interesting irony is the fact the animals are Disneyesque—but there's nothing cute about their suffering. Under the direction of producers John Halas and Joy Batchelor, this is a powerful film, showing how animation can be an effectively powerful propaganda tool. (Vestron; Media; Video Yesteryear; Amvest)

ANNA TO THE INFINITE POWER (1982) ★★★ Unusually sensitive film, based on a book by Mildred Ames, depicts telekinetic teenager Martha Bryne and her involvement with spies, who misuse her in a scientific experiment. An intriguing, oblique narrative produced-directed by Robert Wiemer. Dina Merrill, Mark Patton, Jack Gilford, Donna Mitchell. (RCA/Columbia)

ANOTHER FLIP FOR DOMINICK (1982) ★★★ Intriguing sequel to the intriguing *The Flipside of Dominick Hide* (see that title). In this British TV-movie, Peter Firth portrays a time-traveling agent for a governmental agency in the 21st century, which tampers with the past to make the future better. Assignment chief Patrick Magee sends Hide into the past after a missing agent, but Hide gets mixed up with a woman whose son he sired. How Hide solves his new mystery and untangles family complications provide a poignant, offbeat fantasy. Directed by Alan Gibson, who cowrote with Jeremy Paul. Pippa Guard, Caroline Langrishe, Michael Gough.

ANSWER, THE. See *The Hands of Orlac* (1960).

ANTHROPOPHAGUS/ANTHROPOPHAGUS BEAST, THE. See *The Grim Reaper*.

ANTHROPOPHAGUS II. See *Monster Hunter*.

ANTICHRIST, THE (1976). See *The Omen*.

ANTICHRIST, THE (1974). See *The Tempter*.

ANTS (1977) ★★ This TV-movie was originally shown as *It Happened at Lakewood Manor*, but Lakewood is minor as far as horror is concerned. Penned by Guerdon Trueblood, this nature-gone-berserk thriller is preposterous: Swarms of irate ants attack a resort, imprisoning dull and unimaginative individuals inside. Ants' antisocial behavior is blamed on pesticides and man's carelessness toward nature, but hasn't that already been overworked by frogs? The suspense is ersatz, the menace of these Hymenoptera uninvolving . . . you wouldn't hesitate to go on a picnic. In fact, do—it beats this dreary stuff. Directed by Robert Scheerer. The best screamer in the cast is Suzanne Somers. Robert Foxworth, Lynda Day George, Myrna Loy, Bernie Casey, Steve Franken. Aka *Panic at Lakewood Manor*. (Great if you're planning to take your VCR on a picnic) (USA; Live)

A*P*E (1976) ★★ U.S.-Korean 3-D production in which a 36-foot-high relative of K*I*N*G K*O*N*G is discovered on a Pacific island, captured, lost and then stalked by pursuers to Korea, where the hairy one wreaks revenge. Not very O*R*I*G*I*N*A*L, is it? Directed and coproduced by P*a*u*l L*e*d*e*r. Rod Arrants, Joanne De Verona, Alex Nicol. Aka *The New King Kong* and *Super Kong*. (New World; in 3-D from 3-D TV Corp. as *Hideous Mutant*)

APE, THE (1940) ★ Moronic Monogram mess, a waste of Boris Karloff even though the Englishman gallantly attempts to bring the Curt Siodmak–Richard Carroll material up from the primeval muck. Karloff portrays a misunderstood doctor developing a spinal fluid to cure paralysis. His heart is in the right place but his twisted methods (running around in an ape costume to extract fluid from humans) are purely macabre. Directed by William Nigh. Maris Wrixon, Henry Hall, George Cleveland. Aka *Gorilla*. (Kartes; Sinister/C; Filmfax; Video Yesteryear)

APE MAN, THE (1943) ★ This inexpensive Monogram monstrosity depicts Bela Lugosi mutating into a hairy beast—it shouldn't happen to a gorilla. Wallace Beery, Henry Hall, Louise Currie and Emil Van Horn (as the ape) are wasted under William Beaudine's inept direction. Sam Katzman–produced cheapie, written by Barney Sarecky from Karl Brown's story "They Creep in the Dark." Aka *Lock Your Doors*. (Cable; Video Yesteryear; Kartes; Filmfax; Nostalgia)

A.P.E.X. (1993) ★★★½ Intriguing, well-produced high-tech sci-fi actioner (produced by Talaat Captan) blending computer special effects with rough-and-tumble combat-adventure footage, plus an interesting time-travel paradox twist. The script by director Phillip J. Roth and Ronald Schmidt has time experimenter Richard Keats traveling from the year 2073 back to the Mojave Desert in 1973, setting into motion a parallel universe in which back in 2073 killer robots have attacked mankind, leaving the world in one sorry state. How Keats joins with a band of hardened commandos to fight the robots, restore time to normalcy and get back the woman who was his wife in a former time-zone makes for one rousing combat movie, with explosions all over the funky terrain. The only problem is, if those robots have such great firepower technology, how come they always miss the heroes with their superzap ray-gun explosions? Oh well, *A.P.E.X.* was designed to sate your visceral needs and for achieving that, it reaches an apex. Mitchell Cox, Lisa Ann Russell, Marcus Aurelius, Adam Lawson, David Jean Thomas. (Video/Laser: Republic)

APOLOGY (1986) ★★★½ Taut TV psychothriller in which a killer of homosexuals stalks Manhattan artist Lesley Ann Warren who has an "apology" answering service for those who want to get sins off their chests. Hitchcockian in structure, this unfolds with cop Peter Weller following the clues. George Loros, Ray Weeks, Harvey Fierstein. Directed by Robert Bierman, scripted by Mark Medoff. Music by Maurice Jarre. (HBO)

APPLE, THE (1980) ★★ Borrowing from *Privilege*, this is a futuristic parable about a rock 'n' roll star manipulated by fascistic forces. At its core is an intriguing idea, set in 1994 at the Worldvision Song Contest. Buggallow (all satanic symbolism) seduces a young singer into perversion, while he seeks solace with hippies left over from the '60s. Good intentions are destroyed by the piousness of producer-director-writer Menahem Golan, who spews out an ending in which a man in a white suit comes to Earth in a '60s automobile and takes good souls to Heaven. Grace Kennedy, Catherine Mary Stewart, George Gilmour, Allan Love. *The Apple* shouldn't be picked. (Cannon; Paragon)

APPLEGATES, THE (1989) ★ An absurd cautionary tale (originally written by director Michael Lehman and Redbeard Simmons as *Meet the Applegates,* the film's release title), about a family of jumbo-jet beetles living in a South American rain forest who mutate into human beings and move to Median, Ohio. Still with us? The "Applegates" assimilate into society, making enough dumb mistakes to pad out this excuse for a comedy. Has to be seen to be believed, but do you want to waste the time? Ed Begley, Jr., Stockard Channing, Bobby Jacoby, Cami Cooper, Dabney Coleman (in drag yet). (Media) (Laser)

APPOINTMENT, THE (1981) ★★½ Intriguing though problematic British film about Edward Woodward having a communications problem with daughter Samantha Weyson. Is she creating nightmares for Woodward, or taxing him with adolescent witchcraft power? In his nightmares, Woodward's car is attacked by dogs and it runs off a cliff. Slowly we see the dream (the appointment, or rendezvous with fate) come true. Writer-director Lindsey C. Vickers lets monot-

onous scenes run too long (filled with Trevor Jones' music of doom), but the film pays off with a hair-raising accident sequence. Shot in England. Jane Merron, John Judd. (Sony)

APPRENTICE TO MURDER (1987) ★★½ A fire-and-brimstone preacherman (Donald Sutherland) called a "Powwow Doctor," believing Satan walks in various guises, trains young Chad Lowe in detecting evil, and commits a murder with the boy's help in the name of fighting Satan. For this they are sentenced to prison. This offbeat film, based on a true-life murder case, was directed by R. L. Thomas. Mia Sala, Rutanya Alda, Knut Husebo. (New World/Starmaker; Hollywood Home Entertainment) (Laser: Image)

APRIL FOOL'S DAY (1985). See *Slaughter High.*

APRIL FOOL'S DAY (1986) ★★½ Frank Mancuso, Jr., producer of the *Friday the 13th* series, attempts a variation on the slasher flick by placing prank-oriented teenagers in a deserted island mansion where they meet violent demises. Because of a pending surprise twist, the murders cannot be graphically depicted, with director Fred Walton preferring to treat his story as a poor man's *Ten Little Indians*. Genre fans will find this tedious going, with a payoff that may not please everyone/anyone. Jay Baker, Pat Barlow, Deborah Foreman, Lloyd Berry. (Video/Laser: Paramount)

AQUARIUS. Video version of *Stage Fright.*

ARABIAN KNIGHT (1995) ★★★ Call this full-length cartoon feature a poor animator's version of Disney's *Aladdin*. For while it offers up some dazzling, stylistic animation and occasional bursts of storytelling bravura, it is handicapped by a bland hero (a cobbler living in Bagdad in the days before Ali Baba or Sinbad) and logic gaps in narrative. If anything makes this piece of work by animator Richard Williams shine, it is Vincent Price's voice work as Zigzag, the evil vizier, and Jonathan Winters's as the amusing Thief. And there are several amusing songs, one sung by a band of hapless, dumb desert brigands. The plot involves several evil forces trying to get the three golden balls of Bagdad, which contain magical powers. The cartoon film went through a depressing series of production problems and was never fully realized by Williams, who cowrote the script with Margaret French. Other voices: Jennifer Beals (as Princess Yum Yum), Matthew Broderick (as Tack, that colorless hero), Eric Bogosian (as Phido) and Toni Collette (the Good Witch). A gallant attempt, marred by bad business mishaps more than anything else. (Video/Laser: Miramax)

ARACHNOPHOBIA (1990) ★★★½ Tongue-in-cheek scare flick about the fear of spiders (see title) and how a lethal prehistoric crawler escapes from a Venezuelan jungle to hide out in the barn of Jeff Daniels and Harley Jane Kozak, urbanites newly moved to a California town. Director Frank Marshall (long-time associate of Steven Spielberg) parades out every "scare thrill" imaginable. The Don Jakoby–Wesley Strick script allows Daniels's phobia to build to a crescendo in a climax that pits him against a nest of killer spiders. The kind of flick that puts "fun" back into moviegoing. John Goodman stands out as an obese bug exterminator. Julian Sands, Stuart Pankin, Brian McNamara, Henry Jones, Mark L. Taylor, James Handy. (Video/Laser: Hollywood Pictures/Touchstone)

ARCADE (1993) ★★½ A Charles Band fantasy in the vein of *TRON*, depicting how "virtual reality" becomes exactly that when Vertigo Tronics introduces a new video game, Arcade, in Dante's Inferno, a video arcade run by sinister John DeLancie. When the souls of their friends are trapped inside the seven-level game, Megan Ward (a teenager troubled by the recent suicide of her mother) and boyfriend Peter Billingsley work their way to the final level, facing death within an assortment of landscapes loaded with computerized effects ("digital imagery"). David S. Goyer's script emphasizes Ward's problems and so you care about her during the life-and-death ordeal inside Arcade. Directed by Albert Pyun. Sharon Farrell (as Ward's mom), Seth Green, Humberto Ortiz, Jonathan Fuller. (Video: Paramount) (Laser: Full Moon)

ARENA (1990) ★★★½ All the boxing clichés are recycled through this refreshingly different sci-fi fight movie produced by Charles Band and Irwin Yablans. On a "work world" spaceship that resembles a wrench, floating through the Quasar Nebula, Paul Satterfield (who looks like a young Christopher Reeve) is forced to box aliens (including a centipede creature) to pay off his debts and is trained by a 4-handed manager and sexy good girl Claudia Christian. (Four-armed is forearmed, I guess.) The Danny Bilson-Paul DeMeo script is a throwback to *Champion* and *Rocky*, with champ pugilist Steve Armstrong manipulated by a corrupt promoter and lured into training by exotic Shari Shattuck. Director Peter Manoogian brings a vitality to this unusual floating world. Hamilton Camp, Armin Shimerman, Jack Carter. Score by Richard Band. (Video/Laser: Columbia TriStar)

ARIZONA RIPPER. Alternate TV title for *Bridge Across Time.*

ARMAGEDDON (1998) ★★★ If ever there was a movie designed to be in your face for 150 minutes, here is a whipped-cream-and-meringue combination certain to make a loud SPLAT. There isn't a single dull moment as it tries to manipulate you into believing that Bruce Willis is the only man on Earth (name: Harry S. Stamper) who can save the planet from complete destruction. It's full of rousing action sequences overloaded with terrific special effects, there

isn't a single subtle performance in it, and you will have your emotions whipped up like whipped cream. Although you could call it an "end of the world" saga, it's really just a spin-off from *The Magnificent Seven*. Take a handful of experts (in this case a team of roughnecks who specialize in deep-core oil drilling), give them an iconoclastic, emotion-racked boss (that would be Willis) with plenty of larceny in his soul, and you've got a mission like no other: save mankind from Armageddon! This Jerry Bruckheimer–Gale Anne Hurd–Michael Bay production is really something, with overjuiced direction by Michael Bay, a rambunctious script by Jonathan Hensleigh and J. J. Abrams, and rousing performances by Billy Bob Thornton, Ben Affleck, and Steve Buscemi. What Willis and crew have to pull off is the destruction of an asteroid on a collision course with Earth. Just rocket to the asteroid, drill down into its unstable surface, and set off a nuclear device that will blow the accelerating rock into tiny pebbles. They also have to get away in time so the blast doesn't get them, too. The sentimentality is really bad at times (Willis's daughter, played by Liv Tyler, provides a lot of that), but you get so sucked into this movie early on that you don't care. You will be overwhelmed by the outer-space effects and the incredible cliffhangers that are piled one on top of the other. This is one that should be studied for the art of crafting crowd-pleasing genre movies that hold nothing back. (Video/DVD: Buena Vista)

ARMAGEDDON 1975. See *Escape from Planet Earth.*

ARMY OF DARKNESS (1993) ★★★ This is actually *Evil Dead 3*, but Universal was afraid the title would debauch society and concealed its true origins. *Army of Darkness* still made money all over the world. This time that warm-hearted, marshmallowy director Sam Raimi (writing with brother Ivan) has concocted a marvelous horror parody in which smart alec Bruce Campbell (also coproducer) travels back in time with his trusty chain saw to encounter terrors of the Dark Age as he (Ash) is assaulted by Deadites, an army of skeletal monsters on horseback; demons; and time-space distortions. Again, it's stylish filmmaking, refusing to take itself seriously but still building to effective shocks. In short, it's "groovy." Danny Elfman's "March of the Dead" theme figures prominently, and Bridget Fonda has a cameo. (Video/Laser: MCA)

ARNOLD (1973) ★★½ Contemporary Grand Guignol spoof in which curvaceous Stella Stevens marries a corpse, but a necrophilous nut she's not—she wants to inherit a wad of delicious money. The corpse, Arnold, hails from a family of kooks, nuts, perverts, misfits and other everyday people who are murdered in comedic-horrible ways. This whacky horror comedy, directed by Georg Fenady, has macabre humor and graphic bloodletting. Elsa Lanchester, Roddy McDowall, Farley Granger, Victor Buono, Patric Knowles. (Lightning; Live)

ARRIVAL, THE (1990) ★★★½ Offbeat mixture of a vague sci-fi plot with a sympathetic portrait of a serial killer and his attempt to find true love. There's an unusual element of sensitivity in director David Schmoeller's handling of the Daniel Ljoka script, which opens in the town of Mayfair on the night a beam of light smashes into a field near grandfather Robert Sampson. An unseen alien presence enters his body and reverses his aging process, so that within months he's a handsome man in his 20s, played by Joseph Culp. However, the alien presence needs estrogen to survive and turns into a killer of women. John Saxon plays the thoughtful agent who tracks the murderer. A shortage of exposition about the alien is puzzling, but the film achieves a level of emotional power. Gore is at a minimum. Robin Frates, Geoff Hansen, Danny Fendley, Joseph Culp, Michael J. Pollard (in a cameo). (Prism) (Laser: Image)

ARRIVAL, THE (1996) ★★★½ Credit writer-director David Twohy (*Grand Tour: Disaster in Time*) with being more literate than most science-fiction filmmakers. This is a conspiracy/paranoia thriller in the vein of *Invasion of the Body Snatchers* and it spends half its running time building up plot and character as SETI radio astronomer Charles Sheen, after receiving a signal from space, discovers it's being covered up by boss Ron Silver. The trail of clues leads to Mexico, where Sheen meets fellow astronomer Lindsay Crouse and learns a race of aliens is secretly heating up our atmosphere for an ultimate invasion. No one, of course, believes him except maybe girlfriend Teri Polo, and they're on their own as the special effects and monster makeup kick in and *The Arrival* turns into a rousing sci-fi adventure. Sheen suffers from overacting at times, but his intensity finally carries the film to an exciting climax. Richard Schiff, Leon Rippy. (Video: Orion; Artisan Entertainment/DVD: Artisan)

ARRIVAL II (1998) ★★ This sequel to the 1996 Charlie Sheen conspiratorial alien-invasion thriller trots out all the tried-and-blue clichés as it picks up with computer expert Jack Addison (Patrick Muldoon), the brother of Sheen, finding out his brother is dead. Did the aliens do him in? Muldoon and *New York Sentinel* investigative reporter Jane Sibbert (Bridget Riordan by name) receive papers from the dead Sheen that the aliens are still trying to block our ozone in order to raise the temperature and make the planet inhabitable for hordes of aliens to come. After a tediously slow beginning, the movie kicks into gear as they escape a trap set for them by the evil E.T.s and spend the rest of the footage on the run from femme-fatale alien Catherine Blythe and her mean-looking henchmen. These dastards send a mechanical killer spider after Michael Sarrazin, who plays a scientist named (of all things) Dr. Zarkoff, and try to retrieve a pyramid-shaped device that allows Muldoon and Sibbert to enter alien-created realities, where, with the help of Muldoon's computer expertise, they seek ways to stop the alien takeover. The climax occurs in a Canadian nuclear-power station after the usual car chases and narrow escapes and attempts by the aliens to make the heroes look like villains to the rest of society. It's all cut-and-dried stuff for an obvious direct-to-video project. Schlockmeister Kevin S. Tenney (*Witchboard, Night of the Demons*) makes sure all the stereotypes are firmly in place as he faithfully follows Mark David Perry's hackneyed screenplay. Mike Scherer, Larry Day. (Video/DVD: Artisan Entertainment)

ARSENIC AND OLD LACE (1944) ★★★★ Actually filmed in 1942, but not released until the play's Broadway run had concluded, this adaptation of the rollicking, whacky comedy by Joseph Kesselring is a superb example of black comedy at its best, before that term got bandied about in later years. It's about two sweet, elderly sisters who give poison to male callers (they feel sorry for them, you see) and bury their bodies in the cellar. Director Frank Capra creates a zany world for the bizarre and crazed characters who parade through the sisters' home, including two prison escapees played by Raymond Massey and Peter Lorre. The Massey role was written for Boris Karloff, but his stage commitment curtailed him from appearing in the film. A masterpiece of farce, scripted for the movies by Julius J. Epstein and Philip G. Epstein. Cary Grant, Priscilla Lane, Josephine Hull, Jean Adair, Jack Carson, James Gleason. (MGM) (Laser: Criterion/MGM)

ARTHUR C. CLARKE'S MYSTERIOUS WORLD (1985) ★★★ Original title for a syndicated TV series of intriguing documentaries dealing with assorted real-life mysteries and featuring the famous science-fiction author and satellite inventor introducing the episodes from his home in Sri Lanka, and popping in and out to make comments. The great mysteries of our universe include flying saucers, abductions, reincarnation, precognition, fairies, phantoms, stigmata, magic, superstition, etc. These shows are on video from Pacific Arts as *Arthur C. Clarke's Mysterious World* (in six one-hour tapes) and *Arthur C. Clarke's World of Strange Powers* (in twelve 30-minute tapes) and were produced by Adam Hart-Davis and Simon Wolfare and directed by Charles Flynn.

ART OF DYING, THE (1990) ★★ Producers Joseph Merhi and Richard Pepin have gone on to make excellent action pictures, but this early collaboration is a misfire in its failed attempt to portray the sleazy underbelly of Hollywood pornography. Gary Werntz plays a complete fruit-cake who re-creates scenes from famous movies (*Psycho, The Deer Hunter, Joan of Arc*), murdering the participants while filming them. Cop Wings Hauser tracks the death-porno gang with a vengeance, resorting to vigilantism. Photographed by Pepin and written by Merhi, *Dying* was also directed by Hauser and co-stars Michael J. Pollard as an offbeat detective, Kathleen Kinmont as Hauser's kinky girlfriend and Sarah Douglas as another cop on the case. (PM Entertainment)

ASPHYX, THE (1972) ★★★½ An ambience of morbidity hangs over this British supernatural terrorizer, creating a queasiness about death singularly fascinating in the hands of director Peter Newbrook. Scientist Robert Stephens discovers that within each person is a soul (or spirit) called for at the moment of death by a being from another dimension called the Asphyx. Using a special beam-control device, Stephens captures an Asphyx coming to claim his own soul; hence, this develops into a thoughtful, atmospheric tale of immortality. The themes are thoroughly intriguing, and there's a shock ending. Effectively photographed by Freddie Young. Robert Powell, Alex Scott, Fiona Walker, Jane Lapotaire. (Interglobal; VCI; Magnetic; from Media as *Spirit of the Dead*)

ASSASSIN (1986) ★★ TV-movie clone of *The Terminator,* of no particular distinction. Humanoid robot Richard Young is designed to be the perfect killer, but something goes ker-spung and he/it goes on a killing spree. Retired agent Robert Conrad is coerced into tracking him with scientist Karen Austin, who designed him. Young, whose face alternates between deadpan and maniacal glee, plays the role as if he were cast in a slasher movie. Robert Webber is the CIA chief. Written-directed by Sandor Stern. (Academy)

ASSAULT (1970) ★★ School for women is under attack from a sex fiend in this pre-slasher-trend British psychoterror flick. Lesley-Anne Down and Suzy Kendall are among the beauties. Frank Finlay, Freddie Jones, James Laurenson, Tony Beckley. Aka *Tower of Terror, The Creepers* and *In the Devil's Garden.* Directed by Sidney Hayers. (Embassy; Sultan)

ASSAULT ON PRECINCT 13 (1976) ★★★½ Writer-director John Carpenter pays tribute to *Night of the Living Dead* by depicting a youth gang, a mindless army of kill fanatics, attacking an isolated police station without regard for life or limb. The hoodlums show no more emotion than George Romero's walking corpses. The defenders are led by a black policeman and a hard-boiled office employee, who behave in the macho manner of Howard Hawks's characters. A cult favorite among Carpenter aficianados. Darwin Joston, Austin Stoker, Laurie Zimmer, Martin West, Tony Burton. Carpenter also wrote the music score. (Media) (Video: Image)

ASSIGNMENT ISTANBUL. See *The Castle of Fu Manchu.*

ASSIGNMENT TERROR (1970) ★½ Humanoid aliens from a freezing, dying planet exploit our superstitions as part of an invasion plot in this Spanish horror job, the fourth in the series to star Paul Naschy as werewolf Waldemar Daninsky. The ridiculous idea, set forth by writer Jacinto Molina (actor Naschy) and further muddled by producer-director Tulio Demichelli, is to revive the Frankenstein Monster, the Mummy and other monsters to terrorize humans. Hey, these freaked-out E.T.s have seen too many Universal monster movies! Poorly dubbed for the U.S. market—Michael Rennie's real voice wasn't even used. Rennie, assistant Karin Dor and the Werewolf and Frankenstein (the latter two played by Naschy) are all that can prevent our destruction. Zounds! Aka *The Man Who Came from Ummo.* Craig Hill, Patty Sheppard. The next film in this series was *Fury of the Wolfman.* (From UAV as *Dracula vs. Frankenstein*)

ASTRAL FACTOR, THE. See *Invisible Strangler.*

ASTRONAUT'S WIFE, THE (1999) ★★½ This is a cold, impersonal movie about people who keep their emotions bottled up inside, and live in antiseptic steel-gray apartments, and never respond warmly to each other. And out of all that angst and chill comes a strong sense of atmosphere for stylish director Rand Ravich. But it's difficult to get close to his movie and it's impossible to like any of the characters in his original screenplay. Charlize Theron, who played a similar role in *The Devil's Advocate,* is the titular wife who lives in a very troubled world. Johnny Depp is her husband, a spaceman for NASA who underwent an inexplicable two-minute experience while walking in space. His partner (Nick Cassavetes) underwent the same experience only he dies soon after from a heart ailment. Only we suspect it's not a heart ailment. And his wife commits suicide by taking her radio into the hot tub. Only we suspect it's not a suicide. Then there's some rough, hot sex and Depp is no longer Depp the astronaut. Who is he? Better yet: what is he? Now the iceberg that is Theron is pregnant with not one child but two, and living in New York, where her husband has moved to work for an industrial firm building a new fighter plane. This modernized *Rosemary's Baby* (substitute unexplained alien being for Satan) builds tension and suspense, but it never offers much of an explanation, or what the mysterious E.T. force is. In the end,

The Astronaut's Wife is all style but not much substance, with enigmatic subplots that seem to enhance the cold overview of the movie, but which do not add to the characters or main story line. There's finally a dramatic showdown between husband and wife, but it too is ambiguous and leaves many questions unanswered. Joe Morton appears as a paranoid-driven NASA official, Samantha Eggar makes a brief appearance as an OB-GYN, and Tom Noonan is Depp's new boss. (Vido/DVD: New Line)

ASTRO-ZOMBIES (1969) ★ Grade Z abomination is so incompetently handled, it's a must-see. Mad scientist Dr. De Marco (John Carradine) murders for body organs so he can assemble a new being. Wendell Corey is the G-man hot on the trail of the human leftovers. Notable for being one of Tura Satuna's few films besides *Faster Pussycat! Kill! Kill!* Director Ted V. Mikels (*The Corpse Grinders*) co-wrote with coproducer/actor Wayne Rogers. Rafael Campos, Wally Moon, Joan Patrick, Tura Satama. (VCI; from Wizard as *Space Zombies* and Cult as *Space Vampires*)

ASYLUM (1972) ★★★★ Ripping good Amicus anthology film (known on TV as *House of Crazies*) cleverly scripted by Robert Bloch and adroitly directed by Roy Ward Baker. Four terror tales from the Bloch canon ("Frozen Fear," "The Weird Tailor," "Lucy Comes to Stay" and "Mannikins of Horror") are told through patients in an insane asylum. There's even a fifth story (a payoff for the framework) with a jolt ending. Superior fare. Britt Ekland, Herbert Lom, Peter Cushing, Patrick Magee, Barry Morse, Barbara Parkins, Robert Powell. (Prism; Starmaker; Media) (Laser: Image)

ASYLUM EROTICA. Video version of *Slaughter Hotel* (Nostalgic Merchant; Meteor; Amvest).

ASYLUM OF HORROR. See *The Living Dead* (1931).

ASYLUM OF THE INSANE. See *The Flesh and Blood Show*.

AT GOOD OLD SIWASH. See *The Remarkable Andrew*.

ATLANTIS, CITY BENEATH THE DESERT. See *Journey Beneath the Desert*.

ATLANTIS, THE LOST CONTINENT (1961) ★★★ Elaborate George Pal spectacle vacillates between Greek tragedy-melodrama and sword-and-sandal action with special effects by Jim Danforth. Daniel Mainwaring's screenplay (from a play by Sir Gerald Hargreaves) focuses on Greek fisherman Anthony Hall rescuing Atlantis princess Joyce Taylor and finding his way into her underwater kingdom, where intrigue is afoot to take over the world with an Atlantean death ray. Producer-director Pal makes it visually appealing. John Dall, William Smith, Edward Platt, Frank de Kova. (Video/Laser: MGM/UA)

ATLAS AGAINST THE CYCLOPS (1961) ★★ Italian import showcasing that one-eyed monstrosity of mythical infamy—and the muscles of Mitchell Gordon. A sexy babe, Capys (daughter of Circe), shafts Penelope the Queen and forces Atlas to attack the Cyclops. Not a legendary movie, but it has its share of grunts and groans. Directed by Antonio Leonviola. Chelo Alonso, Aldo Padinotti, Vira Silenti. Aka *Maciste in the Land of the Cyclops, Maciste vs. The Cyclops* and *Monster from the Unknown World.* (From S/Weird as *Atlas in the Land of the Cyclops*)

ATLAS IN THE LAND OF THE CYCLOPS. Video version of *Atlas Against the Cyclops* (Sinister/C; Video Yesteryear).

AT MIDNIGHT I'LL TAKE YOUR SOUL (1963) ★★★ This is the first in the Coffin Joe horror films from Brazilian filmmaker Jose Mojica Marins. For starters, the titular gravedigger searches for the sexy woman who will provide him with an heir. Others in this series: *This Night I Will Possess Your Corpse, Strange World of Coffin Joe, Hallucinations of a Deranged Mind* and *The Bloody Exorcism of Coffin Joe.* (S/Weird)

ATOM AGE VAMPIRE (1960) ★★★ Italo-French horror film, of interest to fans of cinematographer Mario Bava, who later became a major horror director. Here his work is moody in a film-noir vein. The film is better than average with a good cast headed by Alberto Lupo as an obsessive doctor whose Derma 28 formula restructures human cells and restores the beautiful face of blond stripper Susanne Loret after she's badly burned. This works not only as a throwback to the 1950s but develops Lupo's flawed doctor, turned into the mad beast Sadak, who makes nocturnal excursions to murder women for hormones. Director Anton Giulio Majano (alias: Richard McNamara) emphasizes the doctor's perverted love and study of A-bomb victims. Sergio Fantoni, Roberto Berta. (Loonic; Sinister/C; S/Weird; Filmfax; V/Yesteryear; Nostalgia)

ATOMIC BRAIN, THE (1964) ★ Aka *Monstrosity,* a fitting description for this mad-scientist melodrama in which the doc transplants brains from cranium to cranium. Low I.Q.s result for everyone. Directed brainlessly by Joseph Mascelli. Erika Peters, Judy Bamber. (Sinister/C; S/Weird; Filmfax; Nostalgia)

ATOMIC MONSTER. See *Man-Made Monster.*

ATOMIC MONSTER. Early title for *It Came from Outer Space.*

ATOMIC ROCKETSHIP. Reedited first half of the 1936 *Flash Gordon* serial.

ATOMIC SUBMARINE, THE (1959) ★★ UFO hidden in the ocean depths disrupts routine aboard Arthur Franz's submarine. Before long a one-eyed E.T. invader is creating havoc for the crew. This has so many recognizable B-movie faces, it's worth seeing: Dick Foran, Brett Halsey, Tom Conway, Bob Steele, Sid Melton, Joi Lansing, Jack Mulhall. Directed by serial king Spencer Bennet, written by Orville Hampton, produced by Alex Gordon. (Monterey; Sinister/C)

ATOM MAN VS. SUPERMAN (1950) ★★★ Sequel to Sam Katzman's 1948 *Superman* stars a more affected Kirk Alyn as the Man of Steel, but it holds up as an entertaining depiction of Superman vs. archvillain Lex Luthor, well portrayed by Lyle Talbot. Luthor doubles as Atom Man, a weird dude in a helmet who talks with a metallic voice and intends to take over the world using fantastic gimmicks: a coin that makes a man appear or disappear, a disintegrator ray, and a device that sends enemies into the Empty Doom, a void of lost souls. Directed by King of the Cliffhangers, Spencer Bennet, this is enhanced by Noel Neill as Lois Lane and Tommy Bond as Jimmy Olson. The rich, booming voice of Knox Manning opens and closes each chapter. Call it silly, call it naive, but it's irresistible. (Warner Bros.)

ATOR. This is a sword-and-sorcery hero in the style of Conan the Barbarian who was played by Miles O'Keeffe in a number of action films in the early 1980s, shot in Europe and released under various titles, sometimes confusingly. For the first in the series see *Ator the Fighting Eagle*.

ATOR THE BLADE MASTER (1984) ★★ Inconsequential sequel to *Ator* with Miles O'Keeffe still in a blond wig and wielding a sword with less than astounding agility. Sagacious inventor Akronos has harnessed atomic energy ("Geometric Nucleus") so he sends daughter Lisa Foster to fetch Ator to fight villainous Zovv (Charles Borromin). Meanwhile, Ator, the daughter and karate-swordsman Thong (Chen Wong) protect a tribe against cutthroat warriors who worship a serpent god. The only good scene: cuties being fed to the snake, and Ator battling the colossal asp. Marred by stilted acting and less than artistic directing-writing by David Hills (aka Aristide Massaccesi). (From Media as *The Blade Master*)

ATOR THE FIGHTING EAGLE (1983) ★★ Dumbest sword-and-sorcery picture imaginable with Miles O'Keeffe as a sword wielder in loincloth and blond wig. When O'Keeffe's virgin bride is abducted on her wedding day by the Spider King, Ator is in hot-blooded pursuit, abetted by an outlaw (Sabrina Siani) in laughable adventures in the Cave of the Ancient Ones, the Cavern of Blind Warriors, the Land of the Walking Dead, the Room of the Shadow Warrior, the Temple of the Spider, etc. Written-directed by David Hills (aka Aristide Massaccesi). Sequels: *Ator the Blade Master, Iron Warrior* and *Quest for the Mighty Sword*. (HBO)

ATOR THE INVINCIBLE. See *Ator the Blade Master*.

ATOR III. See *Iron Warrior*.

ATOR III: THE HOBGOBLIN. Mistitled series entry. It's actually the fourth, on tape from Columbia, with Aristide Massaccesi credited as writer-director. The U.S. version (Al Bradley credited as director) is *Quest for the Mighty Sword*. See that entry.

ATTACK OF THE AZTEC MUMMY. See *The Aztec Mummy*.

ATTACK OF THE BEAST CREATURES (1985) ★★ The "Beast Creatures" aren't the beastliest beasts you've ever seen, but you might get a few laughs out of this amateurish tale, made in Connecticut, in which shipwreck survivors meet zombies as miniature people. The Puppetmaster is at work! Robert Nolfi, Robert Lengyel, Julia Rust. Directed by Michael Stanley. Aka *Hell Island*. (Western World)

ATTACK OF THE BLIND DEAD. See *Return of the Blind Dead*.

ATTACK OF THE BLOOD LEECHES. See *Attack of the Giant Leeches*.

ATTACK OF THE CRAB MONSTERS (1957) ★★½ Roger Corman exploitationer (he produced-directed), cheap in depicting stranded travelers on a Pacific island inhabited by giant nuclear-poisoned crustaceans. Strictly in the shrimp league, yet by being shoddy and laughable, Corman creates an entertaining framework with Charles Griffith's script. A charming naïveté is at work as monsters gobble up characters (some scenes are gruesome) and then send out victims' thought patterns to lure the living into a trap. Richard Garland, Pamela Duncan, Russell Johnson, Leslie Bradley, Mel Welles.

ATTACK OF THE 50-FOOT WOMAN (1958) ★★ Women's Lib should embrace this cheapie as a determined dame rises above the men in her life; men will be intrigued by the largest breasts in the world towering above them. This has earned cult status as an incompetent example of '50s sci-fi but should be viewed from a modern perspective as a metaphor for woman's revenge. Direction (Nathan Juran) and scripting (Mark Hanna) are on a poverty-row level when an alien crash-lands in the desert and detours voluptuous Allison Hayes, causing her metabolism to accelerate. The well-endowed Ms. Hayes, her bosom heaving with passion, takes it out on the men in her life, including a jerkola husband. Still, she isn't head and shoulders above the rest of the cast: William Hudson, Yvette Vickers, Roy Gordon, Ken Terrell. (Key) (Laser: CBS/Fox, with *The House on Haunted Hill*)

ATTACK OF THE 50-FOOT WOMAN (1993) ★★ This TV-movie remake of the 1958 sci-fier, produced by Debra Hill, presents Daryl Hannah as quite a hunka woman who's exposed to a ray from a flying saucer and grows to towering proportions. Because she's been so abused by lousy husband Daniel Baldwin and uncaring father William Windom, she goes on a short-lived rampage for revenge. Some of it is fun, but a lot of script possibilities are missed in Joseph Dougherty's rewrite, and the effects seem only half-hearted. You wonder why they didn't improve more on an old B movie. Directed by Christopher Guest. (Video/Laser: HBO)

ATTACK OF THE GIANT HORNY GORILLA. See *A*P*E.

ATTACK OF THE GIANT LEECHES (1959) ★ Leo Gordon's plot is as crudely shaped as the mutated beasts in a swamp, stealing bodies and storing them as food for their leech-erous appetite in an underwater cavern. This unconvincing swamp water is the pathetic producing efforts of Gene and Roger Corman. The aquarian bloodsuckers, caused by falling debris from rockets from nearby Cape Canaveral, are human forms with canvases pulled around their bodies and sucker pods stuck on their faces. The only time the film comes alive is when a sluttish woman (Yvette Vickers) shows off her shapely legs and seduces a good-looking guy while her fat cuckolded husband runs around the marsh firing his shotgun. Such absurdities abound, including inept underwater shots. The direction by Bernard L. Kowalski is limboesque. Ken Clark, Bruno Ve Sota, Jan Shepperd. Aka *The Giant Leeches, Demons of the Swamp* and *Attack of the Blood Leeches.* (Sinister /C; S/Weird; Filmfax; Nostalgia)

ATTACK OF THE KILLER TOMATOES (1979) ★★ Rampaging red-colored monsters of a circular shape attack mankind in San Diego in an international spoof of horror movies. It's much talked about by those who haven't seen it, but those who have are less impressed, for its humor tends to wither on the vine. (Even so, three sequels have resulted.) Writer-director John DeBello scores more misses than "splats" with his shotgun approach, but some of the giant killer tomatoes, rolling to the attack, are funny— for a while. A curiosity garden piece with its threadbare plot finally getting squished. Love that fruit! David Miller, Sharon Taylor, Eric Christmas. Sequels: *Return of the Killer Tomatoes, The Killer Tomatoes Strike Back* and *Killer Tomatoes Eat France.* (Media; Disney)

ATTACK OF THE LIVER EATERS. See *Spider Baby.*

ATTACK OF THE MARCHING MONSTERS. See *Destroy All Monsters.*

ATTACK OF THE MAYAN MUMMY (1963) ★ Sequences from Mexico's *Aztec Mummy* film series were reedited by U.S. producer Jerry Warren and incorporated with new footage with American actors Richard Webb, Nina Knight and John Burton. A very boring film resulted. (Sinister/C; Loonic; Nostalgia; S/Weird; Filmfax).

ATTACK OF THE MONSTERS. See *Gamera vs. Guiron.*

ATTACK OF THE MUSHROOM PEOPLE (1963) ★★½ Pull up a toadstool and see tourists on a luxury yacht washed onto a fog-shrouded Pacific isle. They decide a fungus is among us when face-to-face with monstrous walking incredible edibles. Akiro Kubo and Yoshio Tsuchiya head the Japanese cast. That *Godzilla* team, director Inoshiro Honda and effects artist Eiji Tsuburaya, pick the mushrooms. Aka *Matango—Fungus of Terror* and *Curse of the Mushroom People.* (S/Weird)

ATTACK OF THE PHANTOMS. See *Kiss Meets the Phantom of the Park.*

ATTACK OF THE PUPPET PEOPLE (1957) ★★ Producer-director-writer Bert I. Gordon pulls the wires but his marionette melodrama dances short of *The Incredible Shrinking Man.* John Hoyt gives a sympathetic performance as a lonely, deranged puppetmaster named Franz who runs a toy shop, Dolls Inc. No matter how crazy he seems, you still like the guy, he's so sweet with kids who love the tiny cat he keeps in a matchbox. Franz designs a machine that miniaturizes John Agar and June Kenny so they are "wee the people," but he only belittles himself in the process. Gordon did his own effects, but their cheapness leaves you dangling. Nice "strings," though, by composer Albert Glasser. Scott Peters, Susan Gordon, Michael Mark. Aka *Six Inches Tall.* (From Sinister/C as *The Fantastic Puppet People*)

ATTACK OF THE ROBOTS (1967) ★★★ This French-Spanish production stars Eddie Constantine as an Interpol agent on the trail of an insidious madman (Fernando Rey) and his evil female companion (François Brion) who are controlling everyone with Type O blood via an army of zombie monsters. Strictly a computerized programmer with automated acting. Directed by Jesus Franco from a script by Jean-Claude Carriere. Aka *Cards Face Up* and *Cards on the Table.* (Sinister/C; S/Weird; Video Yesteryear)

ATTACK OF THE 60-FOOT CENTERFOLD (1995) ★ This awful, unimaginative rip-off of *Attack of the 50-Foot Woman* is a major waste of time. Producer-director Fred Olen Ray is barely trying with Steve Armogida's script as sex kitten J. J. North (a knockout blonde with giant breasts but eeny-weeny acting ability) grows into a giant cover girl after swallowing a doctor's rejuvenation formula that causes cell-growth acceleration. Everything about this Roger Corman effort is halfhearted, even when sexy Raelyn Saalman and Tammy Parks take off their bras to show that they have breasts as big as North's. Guest cameos by Michelle Bauer, Russ Tamblyn, Tommy Kirk, Ross Hagen and George Stover merely point to the emptiness of the project. Simply put, *Attack* is unwatchable. Tim Abell, Ted Monte, Jay Richardson, Stanley Livingston, John LaZar. (New Horizons)

AT THE EARTH'S CORE (1976) ★★★ Second in a stylish series of Edgar Rice Burroughs adaptations produced in England (coming after *The Land That Time Forgot*) with Doug McClure as an adventurer trapped in isolated settings inhabited by monsters. In this adventure, he is isolated in the kingdom of Pellucidar, an underworld inhabited by loathsome Sagoths. The Wing People are dominated by the Sagoths, giving cause for McClure and explorer Peter Cushing to lead an uprising. Effects consist of mock-up monster models. Kevin Connor directed John Dark's screenplay. Cy Grant, Caroline Munro, Keith Barron. The series continued with *The People That Time Forgot* and *Warlords of Atlantis*. (Warner Bros.)

ATTIC, THE (1980) ★★★ In-depth psychodrama with Gothic touches (sinister house, electric storms, a corpse in a closet) and a horrific climax in which repressed Wichita librarian Carrie Snodgrass is trapped in her ultimate nightmare. This is a clinical portrait of a sexually deprived spinster forced to care for her sadistic father (Ray Milland). She imagines his death or humiliation, revealing her own psychotic tendencies. Writer-director George Edwards is sensitive to the plight of the lamentable librarian. More intriguing for its insights into the aberrant mind than for visual shocks. Ruth Cox, Rosemary Murphy. (Unicorn; Monterey; CBS/Fox)

AUDREY ROSE (1977) ★★★½ Compelling study of reincarnation, superbly directed by Robert Wise but deteriorating when the issue of life after death is introduced as courtroom melodrama. Anthony Hopkins (as an Englishman who believes his dead daughter has been reincarnated) is most intense and believable. The other characters wallow in self-pity and unreasoning hysteria. The film states an unusually positive case for believing in reincarnation. Scripted by Frank DeFelitta from his own novel. Marsha Mason, John Beck, Susan Swift, John Hillerman, Norman Lloyd. (MGM/UA)

AUSTIN POWERS: INTERNATIONAL MAN OF MYSTERY (1997) ★★★½ Yes, this slapstick spoof of the James Bond films and the mod trend of the sixties gets pretty dumb, yet that dumbness adds to the fun of this box-office hit, a credit to star Mike Myers, who also wrote the screenplay. Myers portrays an idiotic British agent with buckteeth who is inexplicably irresistible to women. He also plays the film's idiotic villain, Dr. Evil, patterned after, and made up to look like, Donald Pleasence's Blofeld. After Powers and Dr. Evil are revived from cryogenics chambers (where they have slumbered since 1967), Dr. Evil resumes his reign of terror against Earth with the intention of holding it

ransom for $100 million or he will bore into its center and set off a nuclear device. (The fact that the blast would destroy him, too, never seems to bother him.) Beautiful Elizabeth Hurley's presence is an enormous asset as she portrays the virginal agent assigned to help Powers track Dr. Evil; Michael York has fun as the assignment boss known as Chief Exposition, and Robert Wagner plays the one-eyed No. 2 (although one wishes his part had been expanded). Director Jay Roach sprinkles in *Mad* magazine-style visuals, including a few sex gags that are really funny, even if they are juvenile and in utterly terrible taste. And he populates the sets with babes and broads dressed in the styles of the sixties, so it's easy on the eyes. A femme fatale named Alotta Fagina (Fabiana Udenio) is thrown into the soup and the music soundtrack is a mixture of pop songs from the era and pastiches of John Barry's Bond motifs. Myers, atoning for the awful *So I Married an Axe Murderer,* struck just the right chord in concocting the superspy nonsense and the film was a box-office smash, followed by an equally smash sequel. Mimi Rogers, Seth Green (as Dr. Evil's son), Paul Dillon, Charles Napier, Mindy Sterling. (Video/DVD: New World)

AUSTIN POWERS: THE SPY WHO SHAGGED ME (1999) ★★★ Michael Myers's phenomenally successful 1997 spoof of the sixties mod scene and James Bond movies showed off an irreverent, wild sense of visual comedy and lampooning of a randy, raunchy kind. However, this follow-up flick of tastelessness ("I'm ready to shag you, baby") has too thin an idea. Rather than explore fresh territory, the script by Myers and Michael McCullers returns to the tried-and-tired as once again Myers's chauvinistic, sex-obsessed British spy tracks the supervillain Dr. Evil (also played by Myers and made up to resemble Donald Pleasence as Blofeld) and the same kind of visual and verbal sex jokes are trotted out. Director Jay Roach goes for brightly lit mod-ish scenes, just as in the first Powers film, and doesn't seem to be concerned with helping us make much sense out of the chaotic story line. There also comes a point when slapstick takes over totally, and any attempt to make the film exciting or fresh is lost to a kind of timidity. Michael Myers, timid? Only creatively speaking, of course. The film opens dubiously with a series of scenes of a naked Myers romping through downtown London, everyone oblivious to his nudity. Strategic placing of props to suggest sex acts were used in the original, and here it's carried to its extreme, hinting that this retread is going to offer little that's new. That proves to be true. The story opens with Elizabeth Hurley returning as secret agent Vanessa Kensington, but her part is brief as the "real she" has been replaced by a "fem-bot" killer that is blown to bits on Myers's honeymoon night. She is soon replaced by Felicity Shagwell (the drop-dead-beautiful Heather Graham), who is great to look at in short-shorts and halter tops. When the jokes fall flat, her roundedness prevails. Myers also portrays Fat Bastard, a Scottish villain who weighs "a metric ton" and has chicken fat rubbed all over his body. This character is gross and unnecessary and isn't funny for a moment, especially when he goes to bed with Graham. Michael York is back as Basil Exposition, the assignment chief, who sends Myers back to 1967 so he can retrieve his "mojo" (substitute "sexual energy" and you've got the idea). Also back is Robert Wagner wearing an eye patch as No. 2, Evil's right-hand man, but he vanishes almost immediately to be replaced by a younger version of himself played by Rob Lowe, who then proceeds to do an impression of an older Robert Wagner. Wagner should have stayed, as he knows how to play against Myers's absurdities better than Lowe does. There's a lot of time traveling back and forth, but little is done with this element; there aren't even any good special effects to jazz up the wearisome fish-out-of-water concept. Seth Green is amusing as Dr. Evil's misunderstood, whining son ("You never kill Powers when you have the chance, Dad") but less successful is Mini Me, a miniature clone version of Dr. Evil played by Verne Troyer, who does mean-spirited, unfunny things. One fun element is composer George S. Clinton's pastiches of the old John Barry themes for the Bond films and the clever way they are worked into the soundtrack. Enjoyable are surprise cameos by Burt Bacharach, Elvis Costello, Willie Nelson, Tim Robbins (as our president), Jerry Springer (hosting a TV show with Dr. Evil as surprise guest), Woody Harrelson, and Fred Willard. Myers needs to take a serious look at the vacuum into which his concept has been sucked. It's time for something new. How about this, Michael: "Wayne's World Gets Shagged"? (Video/DVD: New World)

AUNTIE LEE'S MEAT PIES (1992) ★★ Five gorgeous dames run a meat pie business that tastes so good. They should. The delicacies contain the flesh of now-deceased men. Yummy yummy. Directed by Joseph F. Robertson. Karen Black, Noriyuki "Pat" Morita, Pat Paulsen, Huntz Hall, Michael Berryman. (Video/Laser: Columbia TriStar)

AURORA ENCOUNTER, THE (1985) ★★ Cantankerous Jack Elam playing checkers with a bald-headed midget from space (Mickey Hays) and snorting Dr. Neptune's Elixir is as enthralling as this family-oriented morality tale gets. The time is the 19th century, in the town of Aurora, which is visited by a "flying craft" and the benevolent little E.T. A female newspaperwoman tries to expose the story, visits governor Spanky McFarland and argues with town sheriff Peter Brown, while three little girls go into a cave where they find a magical crystal. This saccharine, gentle story, with filmmaker Charles B. Pierce appearing as a preacherman, was produced at the Big D Ranch near Dallas by producer-director Jim McCullough and son Jim Jr., who wrote and coproduced. Carol Bagdasarian, Dottie West. (New World)

AUSTRIA 1700. See *Mark of the Devil.*

AUTOMATIC (1994) ★★★ Another *Die Hard Meets the Cyborg Man* action movie (similar to the *Shadowchaser* flicks), in which leggy heroine Daphne Ashbrook is trapped in the RobGen Corp. building with The Automatic (Olivier Gruner), a benevolent but warriorlike android designed "to serve and protect." The Corporation (headed by smooth-talking John Glover) wants to cover up an accidental death by having the android and woman destroyed, and it calls in a pair of well-armed bounty hunters to finish the job. But The Automatic proves a worthy opponent in a series of cliffhanging action pieces, some of which are quite exciting. But with too little plot in the Patrick Highsmith–Susan Lambert script, director John Murlowski doesn't have enough to work with, and the movie goes nowhere from midpoint on. If all you want is action plus pseudofuturistic sci-fi, this one is automatically yours. Penny Johnson, Jeff Kober, Marjean Holden, Dennis Lipscomb, Annibelle Gurwitch. (Video/Laser: Republic)

AUTOPSY (1974) ★★ An Italian morgue is an eerie place with Ennio Morricone's music swelling on the soundtrack—but don't expect much in the way of visual thrills. This is about as scary as walking through your local horror wax museum blindfolded. Mimsy Farmer portrays a young woman working in the morgue, and she's so silly, she deserves every touch of terror thrown at her by writer-director Armando Crispino. Barry Primus, Angela Goodwin. Also known as *Tarot.* (Mogul; Prism; MPI)

AVENGERS, THE (1998) ★★½ Who can explain how a movie based on one of the most popular TV series of all time—the British superspy spoof starring Patrick Macnee as John Steed and Diana Rigg as Emma Peel—could have gone so wrong? Was it the casting of Ralph Fiennes as Steed? Uma Thurman as Peel? Sean Connery as a totally charmless villain? Even though screenwriter Don MacPherson uses the classic lines and situations, and even makes it seem like an episode of *The Avengers,* the chemistry is horribly lacking between Fiennes and Thurman, and Connery has no redeeming value as a mad scientist who unleashes horrible weather over London to blackmail the world into "buying" good weather from him. The special effects are all in place, with some of the storm sequences and destruction of London looking spectacular, but without much of a story to tie them together, the movie jumps around without logical threads. That includes a sequence in which mechanical-bee creatures are sent after the Avengers, resulting in the film's one wild-and-woolly action sequence. In the beginning was a good concept, but in the end was a muddled mess in the hands of director Jeremiah Chechik. Tim Broadbent is rather amusing as "Mother," the head of the ministry, whom the Avengers work for, and Fiona Shaw has moments as his female counterpart named "Father," but the film remains without charm and ultimately lacks the satire on which the TV series thrived. An adaptation of *Secret Agent,* anybody? Eddie Izzard, Eileen Atkins, John Wood. (Video/DVD: Warner Bros.)

AVENGING BRAIN, THE. See *The Monster and the Girl.*

AVENGING CONSCIENCE, THE (1914) A silent-screen high point in the career of writer-director D. W. Griffith as he explores works by Edgar Allan Poe: "The Tell-Tale Heart" and "Annabel Lee." Henry B. Walthall, Donald Crisp, Dorothy Gish, Blanche Sweet. Aka *Thou Shalt Not Kill.* (Grapevine; Video Yesteryear; LSVideo)

AVENGING SPIRIT. Video version of *Dominique Is Dead* (Impulse; Simitar).

AWAKENING, THE (1980) ★★ Adaptation of Bram Stoker's *Jewel of Seven Stars* (by Allan Scott, Chris Bryant and Clive Exton) becomes scrambled mumbo jumbo not even an Egyptologist could decipher. Archeologist Charlton Heston uncovers a long-lost tomb of a wicked princess, whose spirit is transmitted into Heston's newborn daughter. Stephanie Zimbalist becomes the possessed girl, but she never conveys a captured spirit. The Egyptian tomb set is magnificent and Jack Cardiff's desert photography is stunning. But in trying to imitate the gore of *The Omen,* director Mike Newell merely looks like a copycat. Susannah York, Jill Townsend. (Warner Bros.)

AWAKENING OF CANDRA, THE (1981) ★★★ This TV-movie, reportedly based on a true 1975 incident, will be of interest to horror fans for the effective way it deals with the brainwashing of a young newlywed (Blanche Baker) at the hands of a psychotic drifter (Cliff De Young) who murders her groom and pet dog and leads her away on a rope into the wilds, there to humiliate her sexually and work on her mind until she's putty in his hands. Tom Lazarus's psychological script gets into Ms. Baker's head and allows you to feel her psychic pain. As directed by Paul Wendkos, Baker is supported by an outstanding cast: De Young is an all-too-realistic killer, Richard Jaeckel is the cop who believes in her and helps to break her mental blocks, and Parley Baer is the cantankerous sheriff. (Video Gems)

AWFUL DR. ORLOFF, THE (1961) ★★★ Howard Vernon portrays a sadistic doctor who fondles beautiful victims before plunging his scalpel into their wriggling, screaming bodies in his sanguinary experiments to graft their skin onto the face of his horribly disfigured daughter. This Spanish shocker, written-directed by Jess Franco from a book by David Kuhne and aka *Cries in the Night, Screams in the Night* and *The Demon Doctor,* spawned the sequels *Dr. Orloff's Monster, The Diabolical Dr. Z, Orloff Against the Invisible Man* and *Orgies of Dr. Orloff.* Perla Cristal, Diana Lorys. (With subtitles from Video Search; S/Weird; Tapeworm)

AXE! (1974) ★ Originally *California Axe Massacre* and then *Lisa, Lisa,* this was rereleased in 1983 to cash in on the slasher-movie craze. It's as low budget as they come, about a gang of cheap, sadistic hoods terrorizing a southern belle and her crippled grandfather. The young woman turns on her assailants and gives 'em what fer, yes indeedie. Written-directed by Frederick R. Friedel, who plays a criminal. Jack Canon, Leslie Lee. Dull-edged. (Astrovideo; from Best Film & Video with *Scream in the Streets*)

AXE FOR THE HONEYMOON. See *A Hatchet for the Honeymoon.*

AXE MURDERS, THE. See *Axe!*

AYESHA, DAUGHTER OF SHE. See *The Vengeance of She.*

AYESHA, THE RETURN OF SHE. See *The Vengeance of She.*

AZTEC MUMMY, THE (1957) ★ Mexican "classic" that started the "Aztec Mummy" series. If ever a film demanded total imbecility and moronic attention spans, here it is, amigos (also known as *Attack of the Mayan Mummy* and *The Mummy Strikes*). Rafael Portillo directed this depiction of the mummy Popoca and the vengeance it wreaks. Ramon Gay, Rosita Arenas. Sequels were *The Robot vs. the Aztec Mummy, Curse of the Aztec Mummy* and *The Wrestling Women vs. Aztec Mummy.* (In 1963, schlock producer Jerry Warren recut the film for the U.S. market as *Attack of the Mayan Mummy,* adding scenes with Richard Webb, Nina Knight, John Burton and Bruno Ve Sota. They didn't help.)

AZTEC MUMMY DOUBLE FEATURE. Video packaging of *The Robot vs. the Aztec Mummy* and *The Curse of the Aztec Mummy.*

AZTEC MUMMY VS. THE HUMAN ROBOT (1957). Variant title for *The Robot vs. the Aztec Mummy.*

BABY, THE (1972) ★★★ A 21-year-old Mongoloid idiot—still wearing diapers and called "Baby" by mother Ruth Roman—is befriended by social worker Anjanette Comer. When it appears Roman and her two sisters are homicidal, Anjanette kidnaps the "infant"—but for reasons that will startle you. Ted Post's direction is first-rate. Not pablum . . . grotesque. Marianna Hill, Suzanne Zenor, David Manzy. (Western World; King of Video)

BABY BLOOD. See *The Evil Within.*

BABY DOLL MURDERS, THE (1992) ★★½ Cliched psychokiller thriller in which a knife-wielding strangler in a black jumpsuit murders big-breasted woman always naked at the time of attack. The masked murderer leaves a doll by the corpses as a calling card. Obsessed cop Jeff Kober thinks he knows who the killer is but boss John Saxon and you the viewer know better as writer-director Paul Leder trods on familiar slasher-whodunit territory. Other than watching the buxom women in stages of undress, this offers too little too late. Melanie Smith, Bobby DiCicco, Tom Hodges. (Republic)

BABY KILLER. See *It's Alive.*

BABYLON 5 (1993) ★★★ TV-pilot in the vein of *Deep Space Nine*, depicting life aboard a five-mile-long-space station that serves as a neutral zone for governments hailing from different solar systems. Someone is trying to destroy Babylon 5 and it's up to Commander Jeffrey Sinclair (Michael O'Hare) to find out who—or what. Imaginative amalgam of space hardware, space-age costumes, exotic alien life-forms, model work and computer-generated graphics, so well produced that this led to a syndicated series. Jerry Doyle, Tamlyn Tomita. Created by J. Michael Straczynski. (Warner Bros.)

BABY: SECRET OF THE LOST LEGEND (1985) ★★★½ Entertaining Disney adventure-fantasy set in Africa where paleontologist Sean Young and sports writer-husband William Katt find a mother and father brontosaurus (known to natives as "mokele-mobembe") hovering over a newly hatched "baby." Anthropologist Patrick McGoohan and African mercenaries tranquilize the mother, kill the father and pursue the infant, who is befriended by Young and Katt. The creatures are believable, and a warmth is generated for the "brontes," giving this fantasy an unusual versimilitude. Directed on the Ivory Coast by Bill L. Norton. (Video/Laser: Touchstone)

BABYSITTER, THE (1980) ★★★ The theme of the stranger (an embodiment of evil) entering a household to seduce its members has been explored in *The Servant* and *Something for Everyone*, but in this TV-movie the seductress (Stephanie Zimbalist, in a fine performance) is a murderess, and might be a spawn of a devil force, for she talks to an unseen entity. Zimbalist disrupts the household of William Shatner (a Seattle doctor) and alcoholic wife Patty Duke Astin on a Canadian island. The range of the

woman's influence moves from the sublime to the dastardly under Peter Medak's direction. John Houseman is good as the neighbor who suspects foul play and Shatner has good scenes as he falls under Zimbalist's sexual spell. Kenneth Tigar, Virginia Kiser. (Cannon) (Laser: HBO)

BABYSITTER MURDERS. Original title of *Halloween.*

BACK TO THE FUTURE (1985) ★★★★ Delicious Steven Spielberg production, a time-travel comedy with Michael J. Fox as a teenager involved with zany scientist-inventor Christopher Lloyd, who has a sports car with a "Flux Capacitor" capable of time jumping. Circumstances whisk Fox back to his hometown in 1955 to make sure his father and mother fall in love to ensure his own birth. Characters are charming, dialogue crisp and witty. Director Robert Zemeckis (who collaborated on the script with producer Bob Gale) builds to an exciting climax as Fox, with the help of a younger Lloyd, races against "time" to get back to the future, which is our present. This deals wonderfully with the paradoxes of time travel. The filmmakers rely on the cleverness of story and character, using effects sparingly. Crispin Glover, Claudia Wells, Marc McClure, Lea Thompson. (Video/Laser: MCA)

BACK TO THE FUTURE II (1989) ★★★½ Bob Gale's clever sequel script picks up where *Back to the Future* left off, with Michael J. Fox being whisked ahead into time with professor Christopher Lloyd aboard his time-traveling Delorean. They're tampering with time to prevent Fox's future family from going wrong. However, they affect the past and time-hop back to 1955, where scenes from the original picture are repeated, but from a different perspective. And therein is the fun. With director Robert Zemeckis at the wheel, it's energetic, imaginative and sometimes slapstickish—a fascinating, funny blend. The unresolved ending was a teaser for the third *Back to the Future*. Lea Thompson, Thomas F. Wilson, Harry Waters Jr. (Video/Laser: MCA)

BACK TO THE FUTURE III (1990) ★★★½ This sequel to the sequel is every bit as funny and intriguing as preceding installments in the misadventures of time travelers Michael J. Fox and Christopher Lloyd who, this time, land in 1885 in Hill Valley. The clichés of the Wild West are brought to life by director Robert Zemeckis, and there's the unusual fillip of a romance between Lloyd and schoolteacher Mary Steenburgen. Especially wonderful is the cliffhanging sequence in which the characters attempt to return to the future aboard a speeding train. You won't be killing time watching—you will improve your disposition and increase your smile. Thomas F. Wilson, Lea Thompson, Elisabeth Shue, Matt Clark, Pat Buttram, Harry Carey. (Video/Laser: MCA)

BACKWOODS (1987) ★ Subhuman being (Jack O'Hara) and his Neanderthal-like father (Dick Kreusser) terrorize folks in the forest by biting them in the neck. Aka *Geek*, this is about as lowbrow as movies get. Directed by Dean Crow. Christina Noonan, Brad Armacost. (Cinema Group; New Star)

BACKWOODS MASSACRE. Video title for John Russo's *Midnight*. (Midnight)

BAD BLOOD (1989) ★ Psychological horror thriller from director Chuck Vincent is a showcase for pornie actress Georgina Spelvin, who plays a wealthy painter who gets caught up in a murder-poison-confused identity thriller. Troy Donahue, Gregory Patrick, Ruth Raymond, Linda Blair. Aka *A Woman's Obsession*. (Academy)

BAD CHANNELS (1992) ★★★½ One of producer Charles Band's more creative sci-fi comedies, fashioned by director Ted Nicolaou to make fun of rock and roll music, Alien-like monsters, CNN-styled networks and gooey effects. Paul Hipp plays hip, nasty radio disk jockey "Dangerous" Dan O'Dare, 666 on the radio band. His studio is besieged by a tall E.T. with a giant buglike head and a cutesy-pie robot who cover everything with a green fungus and miniaturize beautiful girls, zapping them into tiny bottles. For listeners they produce a hallucination of a rock 'n' roll band (Blue Oyster Cult, who wrote the musical soundtrack). The satire is thick as cable network news-types gather outside, as the Pahoota townspeople disappear mysteriously and as O'Dare finds a way out of his fungus-covered dilemma. None of it is adequately explained, but then nobody watches Full Moon productions for logic . . . do they? Martha Quinn, Aaron Lustig, Ian Patrick Williams. (Paramount) (Laser: Full Moon)

BAD DREAMS (1988) ★★★ Gratuitously gory shocker is a rehash of familiar horror material, focusing on a survivor of the Unity Fields cult massacre, in which guru leader Richard Lynch set fire to the members. Thirteen years later Jennifer Rubin awakens to find herself in a "borderline personality" therapy group under Bruce Abbott, and hallucinates that Lynch is back, luring her and friends into *Omen*-style murder situations. Chopped up bodies, impalings, a car/body squash and suicide leaps from buildings are among the bloody deaths which baffle Abbott and cop Sy Richardson. The script by Steven E. de Souza and director Andrew Fleming makes interesting comment about modern drugs for mental patients. Produced by Gale Anne Hurd. Dean Cameron, Harris Yulin, Susan Barnes. (Video/Laser: CBS/Fox)

BAD GIRLS FROM MARS (1990) ★ Serial killer is knocking off the leading ladies of the flick *Bad Girls from Mars*. Fred Olen Ray directed, coproduced and wrote as Sherman Scott. The good thing here is the undulating body of Edy Williams, who fondles her ample bazooms and has a lesbian bit with Brinke Stevens. Jay Richardson, Gary Graver, Oliver Darrow, Grant Austin Waldman (the latter also produced). (Vidmark)

BAD SEED, THE (1956) ★★★½ Maxwell Anderson's Broadway play, based on a William March novel, sprouts into a fascinating film under the green thumb of producer-director Mervyn LeRoy. Nancy Kelly believes her mother was a murderess and that she has genetically transferred homicidal traits to her own 8-year-old daughter (Patty McCormack). Sure enough, the sweet thing turns into a horrid, deceiving little killer, at heart a conniving monster. Eileen Heckart, William Hopper, Paul Fix and Jesse White add to the believability of the premise, as does Henry Jones as a dim-witted handyman bright enough to recognize Rhoda Penmark's deceit. Screen adapter John Lee Mahin was forced to tack on an undesirable deus ex machina ending demanded by Hollywood's morality code, but otherwise it's a fascinating watch. (Video/Laser: Warner Bros.)

BAD TASTE (1988) ★★★ A government group, the Alien Investigation and Defense Service, whose job is to keep Earth safe from invasion, discovers a small town is being taken over and moves in for the kill. A bloody battle ensues that should please splatter and action fans, so graphic are the disembowelments and other acts of mayhem in this New Zealand–produced gorefest. Peter Jackson, Terry Potter, Mike Minett, Craig Smith. Written-produced-directed by Peter Jackson. (Magnum) (Laser)

BALLAD OF HILLBILLY JOHN. See *Legend of Hillbilly John*.

BALLAD OF VIRGIL CANE. See *Shadow of Chikara*.

BAMBI MEETS GODZILLA (1969) ★★★★ One of the great short-short cartoon pieces of all time (all of 30 seconds), satirizing our penchant for adorable characters and bestial movie monsters. Produced by Marvin Newland. Contained in many anthologies, including *Bambi Meets Godzilla and Other Weird Cartoons*. (Rhino)

BAMBOO SAUCER, THE (1967) ★★ After test pilot John Ericson claims he was buzzed by a UFO, he is assigned to parachute into China with Dan Duryea's combat team to locate an alien saucer. The squad works with a Russian team and behind-enemy-lines clichés abound as the men bicker over ideologies, Ericson falls for Russian scientist Lois Nettleton, etc. Finally there's a poorly staged shootout with Chinese regulars and Ericson and Nettleton fly the saucer at the speed of light toward Mars. Minor message movie from director-writer Frank Telford. Bernard Fox, Vincent Beck. Aka *Collision Course*. (Republic)

BANANA MONSTER. Video version of *Schlock* (Western World).

BANKER, THE (1989) ★★ This slasher flick didn't draw much interest and was deposited directly on video. It's a no-account account of a serial killer (Duncan Regehr) who lays away prostitutes, mutilating and spindling them as he undergoes a South American ritual, splashing paint on his face like a fanatical native. He also uses a crossbow to stalk victims. Hot on his trail is cop Robert Forster. We suggest an immediate withdrawal. Shanna Reed, Jeff Conaway, Richard Roundtree. Directed by William Webb. (Video/Laser: MCEG)

BARAN. See *Varan the Unbelievable*.

BARBARELLA: QUEEN OF THE GALAXY (1968) ★★★½ Imaginative adaptation of the French cartoon strip by Jean-Claude Forest with Jane Fonda as the wide-eyed innocent space traveler of A.D. 40,000 with bulging bosom and an incompetency for sex as she encounters close extraterrestrial adventures of the bizarre kind. Roger Vadim directed with an eye for psychedelic detail and treats matters neither seriously nor inanely, allowing the viewer to indulge in the fun. The set design is wonderfully, incredibly weird; Barbarella is attacked by man-eating Barbie dolls, trapped in the Chamber of Dreams and blows the fuse of the Pleasure Machine. Silly, absurd, funny, outrageous, utterly visual . . . the ridiculousness won't stop. John Phillip Law, Milo O'Shea, David Hemmings and Ugo Tognazzi are among the oddly garbed grotesqueries. (Video/Laser: Paramount)

BARBARIANS, THE (1987) ★★½ Musclemen brothers Peter and David Paul (billed as the Barbarian Brothers) star in this ridiculous Cannon spoof of the sword-and-sorcery canon. The brothers start out as kids with a tribe called Ragniks, whose queen Canary possesses a magical ruby. Richard Lynch (as villainous Kadar) wants the stone for evil purposes and imprisons the group. The boys grow into strongarm louts Kutchet and Gor, who proclaim their prowess with Tarzan-style battle cries and escape to lead a revolt against Lynch and his sorcerers, and partake in battles with warriors, swamp skeleton monsters and a dragon. You might call this *Butch Cassidy and Sundance Meet Conan*. Filmed in Italy under director Ruggero Deodato, the film's cast plays it for laughs, using anachronisms. Michael Berrymore is especially campy as the Dirtmaster. Eva La Rue, Virginia Bryant. First made as *The Barbarians and Co.* (Media) (Laser: Image)

BARBARIC BEAST OF BOGGY CREEK, THE, PART II. Alternate title for *Boggy Creek II*.

BARB WIRE (1995) ★★★ As comic-book adaptations go, this version of Dark Horse's futuristic adventure about an erotic-looking dame who plays neither side in the Second Civil War in A.D. 2017 is pretty good, having more than enough plot and sympathetic writing for secondary characters. (Credit screenwriters Chuck Pfarrer and Ilene Chaiken for the subtleties.) Underneath its sci-fi gimmicks and funky Steele City milieu (the only neutral place in a war between the Congressional Directorate [i.e., Nazis] and The Rebels), Barb Wire is paying homage to *Casablanca*. Pamela Anderson Lee is a standout—in more ways than one—as the sexually provocative owner of a night club where everyone comes (just like Rick's). She's a wet-dream fantasy, but look out! She has no loyalties and acts as a bounty hunter for monetary gain, using her sexy wiles and physical agility to conquer the meanest of bad guys. Tough, cynical and asexual (she never allows anyone to get into her pants and only gives a kiss or two to an old flame), Barb Wire could have used some softening and undergone more character transition to make her a bit more approachable, but what the hey—it's a comic-book tale, right? There's plenty of double crosses, stunt action, explosions, overturning vehicles and a terrific fight atop a tall crane as director David Hogan goes for the jugular. Udo Kier is good as Barb's club manager and Clint Howard gives his sleazy-creep performance some nice touches. Temuera Morrison, Victoria Rowell, Jack Noseworthy, Xander Berkeley, Steve Railsback. (Video/Laser: PolyGram)

BARE-BREASTED COUNTESS, THE. See *Erotikill*.

BARN OF THE NAKED DEAD. Video version of *Terror Circus*. (Showcase Productions Inc.)

BARON BLOOD (1972) ★★★ Mario Bava directed this Gothic tale about the spirit of Baron Otto von Kleist haunting the halls of the family castle and wreaking vengeance with torture devices. Taut chase sequences, grisly gore effects and eerie photography give Bava's clichéd script vitality, as do Joseph Cotten (as the Baron) and heavy-breathing Elke Sommer, who does wonders for the low-cut blouse/ miniskirt industry. Aka *Chamber of Tortures, The Blood Baron, The Thirst of Baron Blood*. Antonio Cantafora, Massimo Girotti, Alan Collins. (From HBO as *Torture Chamber of Baron Blood*) (Laser: Image, with *Circus of Horrors*)

BARON MUENCHHAUSEN (1943) ★★★ During World War II, Hitler ordered his UFA film division to produce a nonpropaganda entertainment for his Third Reich. This spectacular, richly textured film, first released as *The Adventures of Baron Muenchhausen*, was the result, but released into a society so devastated by war that few saw it. This subtitled version is a film historian's delight with its period costumes, elegant sets, excellent color, and fine cast. It features many of the fantasy-adventures that Terry Gilliam re-created in *The Adventures of Baron Munchausen*. Watch for the funny sequences in Catherine the Great's court and in the Sultan's harem. The effects were unusually good for their time, but more important to the film's sense of fairy-tale charm. Directed by Josef von Baky. Hans Albers is wonderful as the Baron, Brigitte Horney is exactly that as the sensuous Catherine of Russia, and Wilhelm Bendow is the Man on the Moon. Aka *The Extraordinary Adventures of Baron Muenchhausen*. (Video City)

BARON OF TERROR. See *The Brainiac*.

BARON'S AFRICAN WAR, THE (1943) Whittled-down TV version of the Republic serial *Manhunt in the African Jungle*, made as *Secret Service in Darkest Africa*.

BARRACUDA (THE LUCIFER PROJECT) (1978) ★★ Fish poisoned by mankind's pollution take a human to lunch in the waters off Florida. Munch munch with plenty of crunch. This tale of ecological revenge involves Dr. Jason Evers and his experiments in low blood sugar that could affect the entire town. Wayne David Crawford, the blandest hero ever cast in a horror movie, sets out to solve the mystery. Harry Kerwin directed and cowrote with Crawford. Comedy relief consists of an obese deputy sheriff. Bert Freed, Roberta Leighton, William Kerwin, Cliff Emmich. (VidAmerica)

BARTON FINK (1992) ★★★½ A metaphor for the expression "writer's hell"—that region of the mind where wordsmiths suffer when they face creative constipation. New York playwright John Turturro is hired in 1941 by a Hollywood studio to write a wrestling movie. The Earl Hotel, where the motto is "a day or a lifetime," becomes Turturro's hell, his neighbor in the next room (John Goodman) a form of the Devil. There are portions of this Coen brothers film (they cowrote; Ethan produced and Joel directed) that explore other aspects of the writer's difficulties in creating, one of the studio's writ-

ers (John Mahoney) being based on William Faulkner. Michael Lerner's performance as the studio boss is an undisguised satire of Louis B. Mayer, one-time king of MGM, and it's a gem. An exercise in style that blends realistic and surreal elements, and which is fascinating in the enigma it presents. (Video/Laser: CBS/Fox)

BASIC INSTINCT (1993) ★★★½ One helluva slasher-with-sex thriller with enough kinky stuff going down (!) to satisfy your own basic instincts. Michael Douglas is a brutal, disturbed homicide cop who falls for a murder suspect (Sharon Stone, playing a bisexual, hardbitten novelist who loves to tease men with her cool sexuality) only to get caught up in the whirlpool of a series of ice-pick murders. Joe Eszterhas's screenplay gets too convoluted and contrived, but Paul Verhoeven directs it with such energetic force, the film can't fail to hold your attention (not to mention the interrogation scene wherein Ms. Stone uncrosses her legs). Jerry Goldsmith wrote the score. George Dzundza, Jeanne Tripplehorn, Denis Arndt. (Video/Laser: Live)

BASKET CASE (1981) ★★★½ Cinema of the Grotesque lives! The wicker basket Kevin Van Hentenryck carries into Times Square contains something that snarls and chomps on burgers. It's director Frank Henenlotter's homage to monster macabre, full of spattering blood à la Herschell G. Lewis (to whom the film is dedicated) and visually unsettling: "it" is a blob with monstrous head and gnarly arms, a Siamese twin mutant, avenging itself on the flaky doctors who separated him from brother Kevin at birth, and on low-life city trash. Henenlotter uses Times Square's derelicts, whores, drug addicts and quacks for an outrageous acting effect. (Media) (Laser: Image)

BASKET CASE 2 (1991) ★★★ Because an R rating was desired, writer-director Frank Henenlotter (a "filmmaking subversive") played down this sequel to his 1981 black-comedy shocker. This is the continuing saga of Kevin and Belial—the former a normal-looking guy, the latter a grotesque parody of a man concealed in a basket when he isn't out murdering. In this love story (!), Belial ends up in an attic of monsters and falls in love with a huge operatic mouth called Lorenzo, while his brother Kevin has an affair with a normal woman. The ending is comically dark. Kevin Van Hentenryck, Annie Ross, Ted Sorel. (Shapiro Glickenhaus) (Laser: Image)

BASKET CASE 3: THE PROGENY (1991) ★★★ Writer-director Frank Henenlotter scores high marks for his imaginative, over-the-top filmmaking bravura, though some may find his grotesque themes more than they can bear. Henenlotter continues to explore the world of freak-monsters (where normal-looking people are the real monsters) for new nuances, so each sequel plunges into new horror territory. Picking up where Part 2 left off, Belial's bride gives birth to "12 baby Belials" when a menagerie of monsters under Annie Ross's care goes to the countryside to escape the "horrors" of the city. The gory effects are more comedic than real, and a sense of twisted satire works on one's sensibilities rather than shock or outrage. These films remain anomalies of the video marketplace—amusing, outrageous, but stylish, with an insightful sense of irony and comedy. Kevin Van Hentenryck, Gil Roper. (Video/Laser: MCA)

BAT, THE (1959) ★★ "Old dark house" horror-drama (from the creaky Mary Roberts Rinehart-Avery Hopwood play), originally made in 1915, 1926 and in 1930 as *The Bat Whispers*. Vincent Price is involved in events surrounding a caped figure flitting about a weird mansion, The Oaks, inhabited by "batty" dames. Agnes Moorehead, John Sutton and Gavin Good keep the old-fashioned concepts moving under Crane Wilbur's direction. (Sinister/C; S/Weird; Filmfax)

BATES MOTEL (1987) ★ Disappointing TV pilot spinning off from Robert Bloch's novel *Psycho* and Hitchcock's film adaptation. Bud Cort portrays a lovable nerd locked up in an asylum who befriends Norman Bates and inherits his run-down motel when the psychopathic killer dies. Cort remodels and opens for business with street-smart waif Lori Petty and carpenter Moses Gunn. He is mysteriously bothered by a strange figure (Mrs. Bates?). The motel's first customer, a woman about to commit suicide, has a fling with the supernatural. Cort is too silly and the thrills too weak. Written-produced-directed by Richard Rothstein. Kerrie Keane. (MCA)

BATMAN (1943) ★★★ Columbia's 15-chapter serial is one of the studio's best cliffhangers and holds up well despite its anti-Japanese sentiments and J. Carrol Naish's performance as Dr. Daka, an enemy agent with a brain-zapping device that turns men into zombies. Naish is out to steal a radium supply, and also steals the show with his campy performance. Lewis Wilson (Batman) and Douglas Croft (Robin) prove worthy crimefighters. Directed by Lambert Hillyer. William Austin, Shirley Patterson, Charles Middleton. (Goodtimes)

BATMAN (1966) ★★★ Spinning off from the hit TV series with Adam West and Burt Ward, this feature seems better today than when it was released. Batman and Robin fight four archcriminals (the Catwoman, the Joker, the Penguin and the Riddler) who plan to use a Dehydration Machine to convert us to dust. Screenwriter Lorenzo Semple, Jr., unfolds this superhero tale in the zany tradition of TV and there's not much more to say about it. Director Leslie H. Martinson treats it like just another quickie TV epi-

sode. Lee Meriwether, Cesar Romero, Burgess Meredith and Frank Gorshin are the villains. Stafford Repp, Neil Hamilton. (Video/Laser: Fox)

BATMAN (1989) ★★★★ Director Tim Burton carries the comic-book concept into a dark realm, creating a vision of Gotham City and its crimefighters in a gothic style. Because the Sam Hamm–Warren Skaaren script gives a psychological cause for Batman's Robin-less crusade against crime, Burton spins a tale with all the ironic comedy, tragedy and doom of a Shakespearean saga. The surrealistic imagery by designer Anton Furst provides an unrelenting sense of fear for the lost society in which Bruce Wayne–Batman must tread. As Batman, Michael Keaton brings a brooding angst to the character that is refreshing. Jack Nicholson shines as the Joker, driven by an inner demon that never loosens its maniacal grip. Sinister and brooding, as is Danny Elfman's doom-laden score. Visually it's stunning—to the point its underdeveloped screenplay suffers. But so much is going on, the portrayals so larger than life, and the hardware so fabulous, it's a gripping experience. Kim Basinger plays Vicki Vale to good effect. Robert Wuhl, Pat Hingle, Billy Dee Williams, Michael Gough, Jack Palance. The sequels: *Batman Returns, Batman Forever* and *Batman and Robin*. (Video/Laser: Warner Bros.)

BATMAN AND ROBIN (1949) ★★½ Sam Katzman's 15-chapter Columbia serial (originally shot as *The New Adventures of Batman and Robin*) stars Robert Lowery as Batman and John Duncan as Robin as they battle the insidious Wizard, a hooded madman who has stolen a valuable invention that could lead to mankind's destruction. Spencer Bennet directed this slugfest of cliffhanging fun. Jane Adams, Lyle Talbot, Ralph Graves, Don Harvey, House Peters Jr. (Goodtimes)

BATMAN AND ROBIN (1997) ★★★ Of all the feature-length *Batman* movies, this offers the least development of Bruce Wayne and the psychological reasons he is a dedicated crimefighter. At least Michael Keaton and Val Kilmer were given some personality as Gotham City's savior against the archvillains of the world. However, as a very expensive comic-book movie with dazzling special effects and Joel Schumacher at the directorial helm, *Batman and Robin* is a fun if empty-headed excuse to kill two hours. If the action is outrageously incomprehensible and defies all laws of physics, the production design is stunning. George Clooney, in a rubber suit that emphasizes nipples and well-rounded butt, takes up the fight (along with Chris O'Donnell's Robin the Boy Wonder and Alicia Silverstone's Batgirl) against two colorful archvillains, but ironically they are the personalities who emerge strongest in Akiva Golds-

man's script: Arnold Schwarzenegger as Mr. Freeze and Uma Thurman as the femme fatale Poison Ivy (fatale is right—her lips are caked with a lethal substance that kills on kissing contact). Arnie, his face painted silver gray to suggest the subtemperature of his body, goes over the top in a metallic silver suit, cracking with "The Iceman Cometh!" and "Chill out!" before he freezes his adversaries into icicles with a freeze rifle. (He's a former good scientist who fell into a tank of freezing water that altered his blood and iced his brain into evil, and he must now live in chilly temperatures.) Thurman starts out as a mousy botanist who is infected with plant substances that bring out her man-killing sexuality; as Poison Ivy, she flits about making sexual references and blowing a red "love dust" into the faces of those she wishes to beguile. (As if oomph-girl Uma couldn't do it without the "love dust.") Her strong-arm assistant is a grunting wrestler type named Bane (Jeep Swenson). While earlier movies in this series kept the action to some standard of believability, and Batman was always depicted as a gallant crimefighter without superpowers, Schumacher and Goldsman throw that all away to depict Batman and Robin "surfing" from incredible heights down to earth on aircraft doors. And Batman forever in this movie is firing off bat-pulley ropes on his utility belt that crunch through thick walls, wrap around some support, and enable him to swing wherever he wants, in any direction. It totally defies explanation. Some action sequences are poorly staged, such as a chase that resembles a hockey game, with pucks being used to push around a diamond. Or a motorcycle chase at a high altitude that couldn't possibly exist in any given metropolis. O'Donnell's Robin is an impetuous spoiled brat, always arguing with Batman, and Silverstone's Batgirl is utterly unbelievable, doing stunts that would have taken her months of training to perfect. Michael Gough is back as Alfred the Butler, and he faces a life-threatening crisis of his own, one of the few gentler moments this comic-book movie offers. Poor Clooney. He could have used some emergency screenwriters to save his rubber-covered butt. Ultimately it is Schwarzenegger's Freeze (who playfully pines over the fact that his true love is cryogenically kept alive in a tank of water) and Thurman's Poison Ivy that keep the franchise going. *Batman and Robin* is the kind of movie you must set your brain on zero to watch if you are to enjoy it. (Video/DVD: Warner Bros.)
BATMAN FOREVER (1995) ★★★½ Following Tim Burton's *Batman* and *Batman Returns*, this third in the Warner Bros. Dark Knight series could be the ultimate comic-book action movie. It's bursting with visual excitement, excellent camera work and direction (the latter by Joel Schumacher), and a gallery of larger-than-life characters that maintain an intriguing grip. What is most compelling is the ability of the script (by Lee and Janet Scott Batchler and Akiva Goldsman) to present an abundance of high-tech action and still slide effectively into the psychological dark side of Batman/Bruce Wayne and why he is a compulsive crimefighter. Replacing Michael Keaton, who gave up the role because he thought the villains had too much screen time, is Val Kilmer, who takes over cape and cowl effortlessly to carry on in the Batman tradition with the finest arsenal of weapons and craft ever assembled to stave off such evil forces as Two-Face (played with wild abandon and psyche-confusion by Tommy Lee Jones) and the Riddler (a mad inventor gone even madder in the hands of Jim Carrey, whom Schumacher does nothing to hold back from duplicating the wildness of his role in *The Mask*). An interesting new rub is the introduction of Robin/Dick Grayson to the series, with Chris O'Donnell giving the role youthful zing, and adding to the psychological traumas of the story. Michael Gough returns to play Alfred the Butler and Pat Hingle is back as Commissioner Gordon. Drew Barrymore and Debi Mazar add sexy spice as Two-Face's babes. It does go overboard at times, and logic is often cast away for spectacular action, but *Batman Forever* forever entertains you. (Video/Laser: Warner Bros.)
BATMANIA (1989) ★★★ Documentary history of Bob Kane's *Batman* comic strip and the movies and other media events that have evolved out of the character. (Video Treasures)
BATMAN: MASK OF THE PHANTASM (1993) ★★★½ Animated feature in the "Dark Knight" vein as a troubled Batman/Bruce Wayne fights the Joker and falls in love with a woman whose father is mixed up with crooks. Moody, loaded with angst and action. Directed by Bruce Timm and Eric Radomski, story by Alan Burnett. Voices by Kevin Conroy, Hart Bochner, Abe Vigoda. Aka *Batman: The Animated Movie*. (Video/Laser: Warner Bros.)
BATMAN RETURNS (1992) ★★★½ Triumphant sequel to the 1989 smash, with Tim Burton displaying a flashy directorial style in one groovy comic-book adaptation. Michael Keaton is back as the angst-riddled crimefighter who faces formidable adversaries: the Penguin, played to the max by Danny DeVito, and Catwoman, one supersexy villainess as scratched out by Michelle Pfeiffer. These psychotic whackos team with city tycoon Max Shreck (wig-covered Christopher Walken) to bring about Batman's downfall in bizarre battles. There are holes in the Daniel Waters script, but this is where powerful, overwhelming visuals are

everything. Michael Murphy, Pat Hingle, Vincent Schiavelli, Michael Gough. The sequel: *Batman Forever.* (Video/Laser: Warner Bros.)

BATMAN: THE ANIMATED MOVIE. See *Batman: Mask of the Phantasm.*

BATMEN OF AFRICA. Chopped-up TV-feature version of *Darkest Africa.*

BAT PEOPLE, THE (1973) ★ Low-budget vampire-drama (originally entitled *It's Alive* and *It Lives by Night*) in which John Beck and Marianna MacAndrew suffer from vampire bat bites and undergo transformation. A grisly climax is the only payoff to producer Lou Shaw's screenplay, set in a desert community. Sluggishly directed by Jerry Jameson. Stewart Moss, Michael Pataki, Arthur Space, Paul Carr. (HBO)

BATS (1999) ★★ If kinetic energy and a fast-paced script were all that counted, *Bats* would ring plenty of bells in everyone's belfry. But since it lacks any original characters, and some of its cutting is so jumpy as to make the close-up action blurry and confusing, and its story is riddled with genre-movie clichés, the film hasn't got much bite, even if it is ultimately a pain in the neck. It certainly holds your interest with its swift story movement, but you realize afterward that you've seen it all before, and it's really as empty as a bat cave in the dead of night. Everything in this movie blows up, whether it should or not, indicating that director Louis Morneau (who did a much better job on *Retroactive,* if not on *Carnosaur 2*) and screenwriter John Logan could care less about motive or realism. If it looks exciting on the screen, hell, go ahead and do it. Don't slow the plot down with logic or reason. Clichés, clichés. Take the characters, for example. Lou Diamond Phillips plays a dedicated sheriff who is fearlessly heroic and keeps telling everyone to hurry before it's too late, Dina Meyer is a pretty blond bat expert who isn't afraid to crawl in and out of bat abodes and who keeps talking about the annihilation of mankind if they don't act quickly, Leon is a wisecracking comedy-relief character who almost borders on the old stereotypical role that blacks were forced to play 50 years ago, and Bob Gunton is a traditional mad scientist who looks sinister even when he shouldn't. Gunton's Dr. McCabe has created a superintelligent, highly aggressive "flying fox" bat by infecting lab specimens with a virus. Of course, the prototypes escaped and created thousands more, and that bat bunch is now attacking Gallup, Texas, killing folks right on the main street of town and in its bars and stores. The killer bats come swooping down on you or they sneak up, signaling their attacks with a chilling chittering sound. And are they intelligent. They're smart enough to prevent the dumb humans from finding their cave, which is beneath an old abandoned mine just outside of town. The climax has Phillips and Meyer, without an ounce of concern for their own safety, plunging into a bat cave with only minutes to spare since a wing of fighter planes is approaching to drop bombs on the site. (The usual disagreement between levelheaded scientists and military forces who believe in massive destruction is a subplot.) Down in the subterranean depths, the intrepid adventurers find themselves wading through a river of bat guano. They are literally up to their ears in this bubbly, offensively smelling stuff when you suddenly realize that you, too, because you chose to watch *Bats,* are up to your own ears in pretty much the same substance. (Video/DVD: Warner Bros.)

BATTERIES NOT INCLUDED (1987) ★★★½ This Steven Spielberg production is a soft-hearted, warm fantasy parable with cutesy-pie hardware. The setting is a building in the Bronx where a café is run by Hume Cronyn and Jessica Tandy. Evil forces are at work to remove them, but miniature alien saucers (their crews are never shown; the ships take on human personification) act as fairies for the good folks in the building. The UFO effects are wonderful, and director Matthew Robbins gives the film a blend of fantasy and harsh realism without making it depressing. Frank McRae, Elizabeth Pena. *E.T.*-type music score by James Horner. (Video/Laser: MCA)

BATTLE BEYOND THE STARS (1968). See *The Green Slime.*

BATTLE BEYOND THE STARS (1980) ★★★½ Roger Corman's version of *Star Wars* is also a space-opera remake of *The Seven Samurai,* with Richard Thomas flying through the universe seeking mercenaries to help his planet Akirian combat warlord John Saxon, who's blowing up everyone with his Stellar Converter. John Sayles's script has a redeeming tongue-in-cheek quality often subservient to the space effects. George Peppard is an amusing cowboy who loves to drink; Robert Vaughn revives his *The Magnificent Seven* role as a "gunfighter" haunted by his past; and Sybil Danning is a buxom space jockey whose breasts threaten to pop out of her bra and through the screen. The film's spirit of fun (under Jimmy T. Murakami's direction) should send you into orbit. (Vestron) (Laser: Image)

BATTLE FOR THE PLANET OF THE APES (1974) ★★ Fifth and final entry in Arthur Jacobs's *Planet of the Apes* series, and the least effective. This was relegated to the B category, as witness the decreased production values and a less incisive script by John William Corrington and Joyce Hooper Corrington. Upstart apes plot to promote a culture that treats men and apes equally, but insurrectionist gorillas thwart this movement with the help of mutant humans. Roddy McDowall is back as Caesar and Claude Akins is the leader of the growlin' dissidents. Director J. Lee Thompson throws it all away in favor of action, but even shoot-'em-up mayhem can't keep everyone from looking like monkeys. Lew Ayres, Paul Williams, John Huston, France Nuyen, Paul Stevens, Pat Cardi, John Landis. Originally written as *Colonization of the Planet of the Apes*. (Playhouse)

BATTLE OF THE ASTROS. See *Godzilla vs. Monster Zero*.

BATTLE OF THE GIANTS. See *One Million B.C.*

BATTLESTAR GALACTICA (1979) ★★★ A 125-minute space adventure reedited from the three-hour pilot that opened the TV series. It's intergalactic war between the Cylons, robots programmed to destroy mankind, and a ragtag fleet of starships returning to Earth after colonies are attacked and nearly destroyed by the Cylons. John Dykstra, contributor to the *Star Wars* effects, has ingenious spacecraft, aerial dogfights, massive explosions, alien landscapes. Glen A. Larson's script is derivative of *Star Wars* with Richard Hatch and Dirk Benedict emulating Luke Skywalker and Han Solo as warriors racing to their battlecruisers. Richard A. Colla began directing but was replaced by uncredited Alan J. Levi. Lorne Greene, Jane Seymour, Ray Milland, Lew Ayres, Wilfrid Hyde-White. (MCA; Goodtimes) (Laser: MCA)

BATTLETRUCK. See *Warlords of the 21st Century*. (Laser: Image)

BAXTER (1988) ★★★½ A bull terrier narrates this strange French depiction of canine angst as a psyched-out pooch from Paris searches for the perfect master, but brings to humans only unhappiness and death. This is not a "killer dog" movie, but a sincere attempt to get inside a dog's head and find out why man's best friend isn't always so. Based on *Hell Hound*, a novel by Jacques Audiard, it was written-directed by Jerome Boivin, who feels this is a "shaggy-dog story in which the dog is more human than the humans." Lise Delamare, Jean Mercure. (Fox Lorber; New Video Group) (Laser: Lumivision)

BAY COVEN. See *Eye of the Demon*.

BAY OF BLOOD, A (1972) ★★ Italian scarer (aka *Twitch of the Death Nerve, Bloodbath Bay of Blood, Carnage* and *The Ecology of a Crime*) about sadistic murderers fighting over the estate of Countess Federica and featuring 13 gore murders, each carried out in a diabolically bloody way. Graphically revolting, stained with blood from beginning to end. Mario Bava wrote, directed and photographed this bloodbath that features such "cutting-edge" technology as cleavers, spears and other flesh-penetrating weapons. Claudine Auger, Claudio Volonte, Luigi Pistilli. (Gorgon; MPI)

BEACH BABES FROM BEYOND (1993) ★ Three humanoid aliens built like brick chickenhouses are vacationing from their planet Zerko when they crash land their "T-Bird Ship" on Beta 35 (Earth). The place just happens to be a beach and so the E.T. chicks, dressed in Frederick's of Hollywood outfits, go looking for fun in the sun with some buffy, surf-happy dudes and an older guy named Uncle Bud (Joe Estevez). So what we have here is a titty movie (an estimated 14,000 breasts were bared) with some R-rated love-making sequences, and three billion comely wenches in the skimpiest of bikinis, dancing to rock 'n' roll music on Zuma Beach. Some day film historians will look back upon this hunka innocuousness and call it the *Beach Blanket* movie of the '90s. Or something. You'll call it a dud what with all of its corny special effects, dumb teenage humor and inane plot involving a bikini contest and a superduper suntan lotion. For some reason, parts of this were shot in Mexico. Vaya con Dios. Directed with a *Bill & Ted* mentality by Ellen Cabot (aka David DeCoteau). (The writer demanded his name not be included in the credits.) Sarah Bellomo, Tamara Landry, Nicole Posey, Jacqueline Stallone, Burt Ward, Linnea Quigley, Joey Travolta, Don Swayze. (Paramount) (Laser: Torchlight Entertainment)

BEACH GIRLS AND THE MONSTER, THE (1965) ★ Jon Hall directed and stars in this primitive piece of putrescence (originally released as *Monster from the Surf*) about a nutty oceanographer who spends half his time watching bikini girls and the other half creating a creature that preys on the cuties. So what else is new, professor? Sue Casey, Walker Edmiston, Dale Davis, Read Morgan. Aka *Invisible Terror* and *Surf Terror*. (Sinister/C; S/Weird; Filmfax).

BEAKS THE MOVIE (1986) ★ Aka *Birds of Prey*, this is a steal of Hitchcock's *The Birds* with nothing new—just inferior thrills when the bird population, rebelling against pollution, hunts and pecks humans to death. Some of the attack sequences are well done but writer-director-producer Rene Cardona, Jr., lines his cage at every opportunity, relying on clichés. Rather than rent this strictly-for-the-birds video, pick up *The Birds* again. *Beaks*, which reeks, was filmed in Madrid. Christopher Atkins, Michelle Johnson, Salvador Pineda. (IVE)

BEANSTALK (1994) ★★ A lame Charles Band production in the style of the *Prehysteric!* series, a wobbly attempt to make fun of the Jack and the Beanstalk legend, with mediocre David Allen effects. J. D. Daniels, living in the town of Rockville, throws some seeds out his window and a giant tree grows—atop which he and an obnoxious climbing companion find a family of giants ruled over by Richard Moll in lousy facial makeup. The gag here is that Moll and family are just ordinary suburbanites, with a fear of "the tiny people" reportedly living below the clouds. The script by writer-director Michael Paul Davis is belabored with "fe-fi-fo" jokes and a plot involving a greedy land developer trying to claim Daniels's home. It only comes to life when Margot Kidder is on screen as a nerdy, bumbling scientist who studies "cryptozoology," the study of creatures "that may or may not exist." Otherwise, this isn't worth the effort it takes to throw a handful of beans out your window. Amy Stock-Payton, Patrick Renna, David Naughton, Cindy Lou Sorenson, Stuart Pankin. (Paramount) (Laser: Moonbeam)

BEAST, THE. One of the early proposed titles for *King Kong*.

BEAST, THE. Video version of *Equinox*. (Wizard)

BEAST FROM HAUNTED CAVE (1960) ★★½ Director Monte Hellman dovetails a gangster and monster story (by Charles Griffith) into an unusual melange in this Gene Corman production. Crooks are holed up in a ski resort when a creature in a nearby cave begins a reign of terror. Made in Deadwood, S. Dakota. Sheila Carol, Michael Forest, Wally Campo. Produced by Gene Corman as *Creature from the Cave*. (S/ Weird; Filmfax; Discount)

BEAST FROM SPACE. See *20 Million Miles to Earth.*

BEAST FROM 20,000 FATHOMS (1953) ★★★½ Colossal-monster-on-a-rampage thriller, enhanced by the effects of Ray Harryhausen, working solo after an apprenticeship with *King Kong* mover Willis O'Brien. Although his stop-motion was to undergo refinement, this remains a trend-setting miniclassic, tense and ferocious. The titular entity is a dinosaur freed from its ten-million-year hibernation by an atomic blast at the North Pole. The creature ravages New York City, swallowing one traffic cop whole and attacking a roller coaster. Directed by Eugene Lourie and co-written by Fred Freiberger (*Star Trek*'s producer in its final season) and Lou Morheim (of *The Outer Limits*). Inspired by Ray Bradbury's "The Foghorn." Paul Christian, Paula Raymond, Cecil Kellaway, Kenneth Tobey, Donald Woods, Lee Van Cleef, King Donovan. (Video/Laser: Warner Bros)

BEAST KILLS IN COLD BLOOD, THE. See *Slaughter Hotel.*

BEASTMASTER, THE (1982) ★★★½ Sword-and-sorcery adventure from producer-director Don Coscarelli: Bronzed hero Dar (Marc Singer), searching for barbarians who slaughtered his village, telecommunicates with anmals and birds and uses an eagle, a panther and two ferrets to carry out his bidding. Some effects are nice, but the plot suffers from bad dialogue. Tanya Roberts is merely decorative as a slave girl who bares her breasts briefly in a pool sequence, and Rip Torn is horribly unrestrained as the villain Maax. John Amos shines as Seth, Dar's fighting companion, even though it is a silly role. There's much to be enjoyed: Bird Men, Zombie Monsters, and a night battle. This popular film was followed by two sequels. (Video/Laser: MGM/UA)

BEASTMASTER 2: THROUGH THE PORTAL OF TIME (1990) ★★★ Suitable sequel to the 1982 adventure, with Marc Singer back as Dar, the benevolent barbarian who travels through the land of Arok in the company of his animal friends in his new battles against the evil ruler Arklon (Wings Hauser). Sarah Douglas, as a wicked sorceress, learns the secret to a time portal that takes them all to modern-day L.A. where Arklon seeks the Neutron Detonator for world dominance. The comic-book action is plentiful, Douglas makes for a fetching, humorous villainess and Singer is a likable presence, no matter how hokey the R. J. Robinson–Jim Wynorski–Ken Hauser–Doug Miles script gets in adapting a novel by Andre Norton. Director Sylvio Tabet holds the nonsense together. And there's an above-average score by Robert Folk. Kari Wuhrer, Charles Young, James Avery, Robert Z'Dar, Michael Berryman. (Video/Laser: Republic)

BEASTMASTER III: THE EYE OF BRAXUS (1995) ★★½ This is a middling entry in the popular series starring Marc Singer as the blond, bronzed warrior Dar, who travels with his now-familiar cadre of beasts. It suffers badly from cheap interior sets, mediocre fight choreography and poor performances, notably by David Warner as evil Lord Agon and Olaf Pooley as Agon's wizard, Maldor. As always, Singer is believable and likable as the determined, driven Beastmaster; Sandra Hess is worthy as a sharp-tongued warrioress, and Lesley-Anne Down is a lot of fun as a tease of a witch who has the hots for Dar's sidekick Seth (Tony Todd, playing his role with a bemused attitude). In this fantasy adventure, Agon's Crimson Warriors kidnap King Tal (Dar's brother) and torture him on the Shroud of Agony while Dar rushes to save him and the magical green ruby called the Eye of Braxus. Scripted by producer David Wise with some tongue-in-cheek dialogue (but not nearly enough) and directed by Gabrielle Beaumont, this Sylvio Tabet production is sadly beneath the potential this series offers. Singer deserves better. (Video/Laser: MCA)

BEAST MUST DIE, THE (1973) ★★½ Assorted types are invited to the mansion of millionaire Calvin Lockhart, who knows one of them is a werewolf. He has electronic lycanthropic-detecting equipment in and around the estate to trap the four-legged attacker. This modern touch is okay but it still boils down to old Wolf Man clichés with a dog dressed to look like a werewolf. Directed by Paul Annett; from a Michael Winder script based on James Blish's novelette "There Shall Be No Darkness." Peter Cushing, Charles Gray, Anton Diffring. (Starmaker; from Impulse as *Black Werewolf*) (Laser: Image)

BEAST OF BLOOD (1970) ★ Filipino sequel to *Mad Doctor of Blood Island*, in which insidious Dr. Lorca (Eddie Garcia) keeps a decapitated creature alive. Writer-producer-director Eddie Romero needed to inject more life into this listless horror film, as abominable as the dead forces it depicts. John Ashley, Celeste Yarnall. Aka *Blood Devils, Horrors of Blood Island, Return to the Horrors of Blood Island.*

BEAST OF HOLLOW MOUNTAIN (1956) ★★ Willis O'Brien, the major contributor to stop-motion animation with *King Kong*, utilized Regiscope to animate a cattle-hungry Tyrannosaurus Rex in this U.S.-Mexican production made in Mexico by Edward and William Nassour, under the title *Valley of the Mists*. It's your basic Western but with monster touches, starring Guy Madison as a rancher being forced out by a land baron. Matters pick up with the arrival of Patricia Medina wearing low-cut blouses . . . and finally comes the long-awaited attack by the Rex with the pecs from his mountain lair, but the beast isn't on screen long enough. Directorial chores were shared by Edward Nassour and Ismael Rodriguez. Scripted by Robert Hill from an idea by O'Brien. Eduardo Noriega, Carlos Rivas. (Laser: MGM/UA)

BEAST OF THE DEAD. See *Beast of Blood.*

BEAST OF YUCCA FLATS, THE (1961) ★ Tor Johnson, a brutish actor often seen sneaking up on Bela Lugosi in grade-Z horror jobs directed by Ed Wood, has his sole leading role as a Soviet scientist pursued into the desert by Russian agents and accidentally exposed to radiation when an A-bomb is exploded. This blast turns Johnson—for reasons never explained by writer-director Coleman Francis—into a maniacal killer. Johnson doesn't have a single line of dialogue as he stumbles around cacti and rocks. A primer in how not to expose film inside a camera, *Beast* is one of the poorest excuses for a movie that exists, consisting of little dialogue and a narration track that sometimes defies explanation. The photography is simply awful, and Francis deserves to go to the bottom of the Ed Wood class. In fact, he makes Ed Wood look *great*. Douglas Mellor, Barbara Francis, Bing Stafford. (Sinister/C; S/Weird; Filmfax; Cinemacabre)

BEASTS. Video version of *The Twilight People.* (Direct)

BEASTS. Video version of *Claws* (1985). (ANE)

BEAST WITH FIVE FINGERS (1947) ★★★½ No need to give Warner Bros. the finger: the studio did an adept job palming off W. F. Harvey's short story to screenwriter Curt Siodmak,

who turned it into a superior piece of psychological horror. The severed hand of a maddened pianist scuttles repulsively to and fro . . . or is Peter Lorre imagining an old friend has returned from the grave to strangle him? Lorre goes mad as only Lorre can, nailing the ghastly quintet of digits to a board and flinging it into a fire. Give a big hand to director Robert Florey and a round of applause with sweaty palms to Robert Alda, Andrea King, Victor Francen and J. Carroll Naish. And kudos to Max Steiner for his enriched score. (MGM/UA)

BEAST WITHIN, THE (1982) ★★★ *The Omen* producer Harvey Bernhard fashioned a horror-monster entertainment with good transformation effects by Thomas Burman. Ronny Cox's wife is raped by an unseen spirit; a son is born possessed by an evil being who takes on new shape before launching a homicidal rampage. One of the film's virtues is the bravura acting by Paul Clemens, who conveys the teenager's demonic pain without makeup in early scenes. There is a dark, moody atmosphere to Philippe Mora's direction. Made in the small town of Raymond, Miss. Edward Levy's novel was loosely adapted by Tom Holland. Bibi Besch, Don Gordon, R. G. Armstrong, L. Q. Jones. (MGM/UA)

BEAST WITH TWO HEADS. See *The Thing with Two Heads.*

BEAUTIFUL SCREAMERS. See *Silent Madness.*

BEAUTY AND THE BEAST (1946) ★★★★★ Writer-director Jean Cocteau's adaptation of the classic fairy tale is a poetic, dreamlike fantasy that still delights new generations. Costuming, sets, music—it is a synthesis of the cinema arts. A surrealistic autumn air hangs over a decaying mansion where Belle (Josette Day) encounters candelabra held by human hands thrust from wall sconces, wooden faces that come to life, walls that whisper to her and the Beast (Jean Marais), a prince trapped in a werewolf's body until he finds a woman to love him. Marais's creature, although fanged and hirsute, is a poet-intellectual who expresses the pain of the human heart. French director René Clement acted as technical adviser to Cocteau. Marais portrays three roles: the Beast, Belle's handsome but uninspired village suitor, and the Prince Charming waiting to be restored. Marcel André, Mila Parely, Michel Auclair. Music score by Georges Auric. (Embassy; Nelson) (Laser: Nelson; Voyager; Criterion)

BEAUTY AND THE BEAST (1961) ★★ This United Artists release lacks the poetry of the 1946 Cocteau version, and is a commercialized vehicle retold in the pedantic terms of the swashbuckler of the '50s. It was directed flatly by Edward L. Cahn from a rather hackneyed, prosaic script by George Bruce and Orville Hampton in which duke Mark Damon is cursed to turn into a werewolf at night. The makeup by

Jack Pierce is identical to that in *The Wolf Man* with effects consisting of time-lapse photography. Michael Pate is the villain trying to take over the duke's throne and Joyce Taylor is the sympathetic beauty. There's little chemistry between her and Damon, leaving the period costumes and castle settings the only things of interest. Eduard Franz, Merry Anders, Dayton Lummis, Walter Burke.

BEAUTY AND THE BEAST (1987) ★★★½ "Once Upon a Time in New York," the two-hour pilot for the cult TV series, introduces Vincent, a warm, sensitive man living in a subterranean society beneath New York City. His only problem is, he's half monster, resembling a hairy (but still visually attractive) werewolf. He rescues a beautiful D.A.'s assistant and takes her into his world, where they fall in love. It's a fascinating relationship that was to fuel this unusual TV series for several seasons. Ron Perlman and Linda Hamilton make a great team. Other tapes/lasers in this series: "Siege" and "No Way Out"; "Masques" and "The Beast Within"; "Nor Iron Bars a Cage" and "Song of Orpheus"; "Though Lovers Be Lost"; "Above, Below and Beyond." (Video/Laser: Republic)

BEAUTY AND THE BEAST (1991) ★★★★ One of the best Walt Disney cartoons and a winner of the Academy Award for Best Picture. An effervescent adaptation of Madame De Beaumont's eternal fairy tale about an enchanted beast and his love affair with a beautiful young woman during the late 18th century. It is in a musical tradition, with several production numbers—superb renderings thanks to lyrics by Alan Menken and music by Howard Ashman. The main characters have charm and depth, and the supporting "cast" is made up of household items (candlestick, clock, tea kettle and tea cup, etc.) that are unforgettably funny. Linda Woolverton's script, the direction by Gary Trousdale and Kirk Wise and the voices of Robby Benson (the beast), Paige O'Hara (Belle the beauty), Angela Lansbury, David Ogden Stiers and many others contribute to the excellence of this tale, Disney's 30th feature cartoon. (Video/Laser: Disney)

BEDEVIL (1993) ★★½ Trilogy of horror tales from Australian writer-director Tracey Moffatt. In "Mr. Chuck," with Diana Davidson and Jack Charles, the spirit of a U.S. soldier haunts a suburban home; "Choo Choo Choo Choo," with Moffatt and Banula (David) Marika, concerns the spirit of a blind girl; "Lovin' the Spin I'm In," with Lex Marinos and Dina Panozzo, has lovers as ghosts.

BEDLAM (1946) ★★★ Last of the horror films produced by Val Lewton for RKO. Mark Robson directed his screenplay (inspired by Hogarth's painting "Bedlam," and first known as *Chamber of Horrors*), which depicts horrific conditions in the St. Mary of Bethlehem Asylum of London in 1761. Anna Lee is incarcerated for meddling in the affairs of the cruel asylum-keeper, Master Sims, devilishly played by Boris Karloff. The costuming and mood of the period are expertly evoked and the cast is superb: Ian Wolfe, Jason Robards, Sr., Robert Clarke, Ellen Corby, Billy House. (Nostalgia Merchant; Media; Fox Hill) (Laser: Image; Turner)

BEE GIRL, THE. See *The Wasp Woman*.

BEES, THE (1978) ★★ If you've seen one swarm, you've seen them all. Yet another "B" thriller movie (written-produced-directed by triple-stinger Alfredo Zacharias) about South American killer bees attacking our hemisphere, with John Saxon, Angel Tompkins and John Carradine out to destroy the little sneaks. Expect to break out in hives. (Warner Bros.)

BEETLEJUICE (1988) ★★★★ A bizarre, outrageous comedy you will love. In a mood of no-holds-barred, exploratory storytelling, writers Michael McDowell and Warren Skaaren concoct an afterlife where recently deceased Alec Baldwin and Geena Davis are trapped in their home unless they step outside, in which case they find themselves in this crazy way station where souls wait for reclassification. The thrust of the story has the couple trying to scare a new family in their house—weirdos nuttier than the ghosts. In desperation the ghosts turn to the titular whacko who exorcises humans. As played by Michael Keaton, Betelgeuse is an absolute trouble-making rascal. Director Tim Burton allows uninhibitedness to rule and the characters' bizarre non sequitur antics are utterly insane. The goofiest supernatural comedy ever made. Jeffrey Jones, Catherine O'Hara, Glenn Shadix, Winona Ryder, Sylvia Sidney, Dick Cavett, Annie McEnroe, Robert Goulet. (Video/Laser: Warner Bros.)

BEFORE I DIE. See *Targets*.

BEFORE I HANG (1940) ★★★ Effective programmer designed for Boris Karloff. As Dr. John Garth, he seeks a serum to fight off aging, even after being sent to prison for a mercy killing. Some fanciful pseudoscience enhances all the double-talk about medicine for the good of mankind, but it finally boils down to Karloff turning into a human monster à la Dr. Frankenstein. Directed by Nick Grinde, scripted by Robert D. Andrews and Karl Brown. Evelyn Keyes, Bruce Bennett, Edward Van Sloan, Don Beddoe, Robert Fiske. (RCA/Columbia)

BEFORE THE FACT. See *A Bay of Blood*.

BEGINNING OF THE END (1957) ★ Atomic radiation affects the genes of nature, and hopping out of the grass hoppin' mad are the biggest grasshoppers you'll ever see. But the buggy behemoths move as haltingly as the dialogue, so you know you must be watching a Bert I. Gordon epic. You are! Hence, you're watching one of the weakest of the Giant Bug movies of the

1950s. Peter Graves is unconvincing as a scientist who devises a supersonic sound-wave device to stop the juggernauts. The Fred Freiberger–Lester Gorn script does not have legs. Peggie Castle, Morris Ankrum, Thomas Henry, Richard Benedict. (Video Treasures)

BEHEMOTH/BEHEMOTH, THE SEA MONSTER. See *Giant Behemoth*.

BEHIND THE DOOR. See *The Man with Nine Lives*.

BEHIND THE MASK (1946) ★★ Although based on the Shadow character from the pulp magazines, this features none of the supernatural or metaphysical attributes of Lamont Cranston to cloud men's minds so they cannot see him. All Kane Richmond does as the playboy about town is cast a sinister shadow while wearing a cape, mask and fedora and threaten his adversaries. Most of George Callahan's script wastes its time making fun of Margo Lane (Barbara Reed) as she's always getting in the way of the investigation of a murdered newspaper columnist. Directed by Phil Karlson, the film is fun to watch but has little action and no fantasy whatsoever. Robert Shayne, George Chandler, Dorothea Kent. (Grapevine)

BEING, THE (1982) ★ Blatant ripoff of *Alien*: the titular monster has slavering jowls, gnashing teeth and an ornery disposition. The spawning ground for this one-eyed monstrosity is nuclear waste at a plant outside Pottsville, Idaho. Pornie film king William Osco turned legit to produce this schlocker, which under the direction of wife Jackie Kong (she penned the script) and Robert Downey (uncredited), is boring clichés. Osco costars as Rexx Coltrane, portraying a gallant hero who rescues Marianne Gordon from ludicrous cliffhangers. Martin Landau, Dorothy Malone, Ruth Buzzi and Jose Ferrer are townspeople who become fodder for the beast. Aka *Freak* and *Easter Sunday*. (HBO)

BEING JOHN MALKOVICH (1999) ★★★★ *Alice in Wonderland* plunged you downward into a Carrollesque world; this movie carries you sideways through a vertical tunnel into a Malkovichian world. Malkovichian as in John Malkovich, the movie actor. Or call it a Kaufmanesque world, as in Charles Kaufman, the screenwriter who dreamt up this bizarre, hard-to-define movie. It all begins, in a gloriously refreshing and original way, when down-and-out puppeteer John Cusack, who stages slightly pornographic shows on sleazy street corners in Manhattan, discovers he can enter the mind of the movie actor, and eventually ends up controlling Malkovich and taking over his body for personal gain and celebrityhood. Along the way his wife (Cameron Diaz, looking dowdy and frowzy) also gets into Malkovich's mind while he's making love to one of Cusack's office workers (Catherine Keener), for whom Diaz has

the hots. Everything is kinky and twisted in this delightfully perverse stretch of the imagination, which emerges as one of Hollywood's oddest and freshest mainstream movies since Terry Gilliam's *Brazil*. Malkovich as himself is brilliant, never really allowing us to see into what he's really like, as if he wanted to remain as mysterious as the forces that created this movie. In one fascinating sequence, he enters a world of hundreds of living, breathing John Malkoviches, and the sight almost drives him to the brink of madness. Orson Bean contributes as Cusack's utterly eccentric boss, Mary Kay Place is a stuttering secretary, and Charlie Sheen and Sean Penn appear as themselves, satirizing their own movie personalities. There are constant O. Henry–style surprises and plot manipulations— some of which work fine. Other outrageous U-turns only confuse and muddle up the already hard-to-follow storyline, but somehow this oddball movie still moves with the speed of a strong laxative moving toward the intestines. What ultimately emerges from director Spike Jonze's stylish presentation is a topsy-turvy universe where nobody is quite what he or she seems. Just in case none of this is what Kaufman had in mind, maybe *Being John Malkovich* is about invisible forces pulling our strings, and how we witlessly dance to the music of some God up there on high. This movie is an American original, and its unique nature places it in a genre all its own. Call it "film malkovich-noir." (Video/DVD: Columbia TriStar)

BELA LUGOSI COLLECTION, THE. Lumivision laser disc set of *The Devil Bat* and *Scared to Death*.

BELA LUGOSI MEETS A BROOKLYN GORILLA (1952) ★★★ So awful it's enjoyable watching Bela Lugosi portray a mad doctor with a serum that turns men into gorillas. Tim Ryan's script focuses on stranded USO entertainers Duke Mitchell and Sammy Petrillo, Dean Martin–Jerry Lewis imitators who parody their counterparts well. Muriel Landers is a native girl pursuing Duke, while Sammy is chased by an overweight gal through jungle sets. Directed by William Beaudine, a specialist at schlock. Associate producer was Herman Cohen. Aka *The Boys from Brooklyn*, *Lugosi Meets a Brooklyn Gorilla* and *The Monster Meets the Gorilla*. (Sinister/C; S/Weird; Filmfax; Admit One)

BELA LUGOSI SCRAPBOOK (197?) ★★★ This documentary of the horror-film actor includes his classic screen roles as well as flubbed outtakes and other novelty footage. (Discount; Rex Miller)

BELIEVERS, THE (1987) ★★★ Gripping tale of black magic and voodoo set in Manhattan, where police psychiatrist Martin Sheen is recovering from his wife's death while investigating gruesome cult murders. Sheen is caught up in a conspiracy that also involves hard-boiled cop Robert Loggia. Director John Schlesinger maintains an intense sense of foreboding. A subtexture deals with our powers of belief in the supernormal, so this is a thinking man's horror film with ample gore and violence. Helen Shaver, Lee Richardson, Elizabeth Wilson. (Video/Laser: HBO)

BELLS. TV title for *Murder by Phone.*

BELOVED (1998) ★★★½ This adaptation of Toni Morrison's unusual ghost novel—directed by Jonathan Demme, with script by Akoua Bush, Richard LaGravenese, and Adam Brooks— seems to achieve the impossible: it spins one very strange supernatural yarn, yet it remains a sometimes ultrarealistic slice-of-life portrait of a black mother and her daughter. They live on the outskirts of Cincinnati in 1873, on "124 Bluestone Road." Oprah Winfrey (also coproducer) stars as Sethe, the mother who carries a dark secret about her family from the days right after the Civil War. To set the stage for the supernatural elements, the film opens with an 1865 prologue in which a furious poltergeist is at work within a house, hurtling a dog across the kitchen after plucking out one of its eyeballs and breaking one of its legs. Then comes a character study of day-to-day life for Sethe, her daughter Denver (Kimberley Elise), a former slave Sethe knew years before named Paul D (Danny Glover), and a strange young woman (Thandie Newton) who wanders out of nowhere one day surrounded by supernormal clues that hint she is not earthly. At first this newcomer appears to be mentally ill, but when she announces that her name is "Beloved" (the name of one of Sethe's dead children), it becomes clear that she is a ghostly manifestation, and a key to that horrible incident from Sethe's past. However, in no way is *Beloved* a genre ghost story. Beloved doesn't pop in and out like a spectral visitor. She's solid flesh and blood and she lives in the house, interacting with the others. Presumably she is a baby spirit transferred into an older body, for she struggles to learn the simplest tasks and talks like a retarded child. Newton's performance is nothing short of remarkable, given the demands of this role. How do you play a nontraditional ghost? Demme does not make this an easy movie to watch. Many segments are unsettling and past and present are intermingled to show that Sethe never escapes the memories that haunt her. Costuming, sets, and an intense attention to period detail re-creates life in and around Cincinnati at a time when the black population was adjusting to a new way of life. *Beloved* definitely has a heightened sense of time and place. Winfrey, Glover, and Elise are all excellent. (Video/DVD: Buena Vista)

BE MY VALENTINE, OR ELSE. See *Hospital Massacre.*

BEN (1972) ★★ Sequel to *Willard* is cheapjack exploitation, poorly scripted by Gilbert Ralston and routinely directed by Phil Karlson. Demented Lee Harcourt Montgomery finds the survivors of the first movie (a pack of well-trained rats) and hides them in the city's sewers. Joseph Campanella is in charge of stopping the rogue rodents. Arthur O'Connell, Rosemary Murphy, Meredith Baxter, Kenneth Tobey. (Prism) (Laser: Image)

BENEATH THE PLANET OF THE APES (1970) ★★★ First sequel to *Planet of the Apes*, less than its predecessor but still an exciting actioner. Astronaut James Franciscus, in search of the first lost expedition, is swept up in a time warp and lands on Earth to find it devastated by atomic war. In an underground city (remnants of New York), he stumbles across humans with ESP powers. On the surface, meanwhile, apes, gorillas and orangutans form an attack party. The direction by Ted Post is taut, the screenplay by Paul Dehn is lean and literate, and John Chambers' makeup is in the tradition of the original film. Beneath the masks: Kim Hunter, Maurice Evans, Jeff Corey, Thomas Gomez and James Gregory. Among the humans: Linda Harrison (as Nova, speechless native girl), Victor Buono, Tod Andrews, Paul Richards and Charlton Heston, returning as the lost-in-time astronaut Taylor. Early proposed titles: *Planet of the Apes Revisited* and *Planet of the Men.* (Video/Laser: CBS/Fox)

BERMUDA DEPTHS, THE (1978) ★★★ Aboveaverage TV-movie with a small touch of *Jaws* and a big touch of *Moby Dick* in depicting an expedition searching for a giant sea turtle. Burl Ives is the Ahab biologist obsessed with the capture of the turtle and Connie Sellecca portrays Jennie Haniver, a mysterious brunette believed to be the spirit of a woman who once made a pact with the turtle and is still aqua-maiding 300 years later. Effects are surprisingly good. Written by William Overgard, directed by Tom Kotani, produced by the animation team of Saul Bass and Arthur Rankin, Jr., Leigh McCloskey, Carl Weathers, Julie Woodson, Ruth Attaway. Aka *It Came up from the Depths.*

BERNARD AND THE GENIE (1991) ★★★ This BBC-TV fantasy, written by Richard Curtis and directed by Paul Weiland, is a whimsical entertainment made fun by Lenny Henry's performance as a lively, hip genie who's been corked away for 2,000 years when nerdish art dealer Alan Cummings uncorks him. With each of his wishes granted, Bernard Bottle (Cummings) wreaks revenge on the boss who just fired him and his cheating girlfriend. Light, frothy and frivolous, it's Henry's film all the way as he plays "Joe Sephis." (CBS/Fox)

BERSERK (1968) ★★½ Joan Crawford is the dearest owner of a big top plagued by mysterious deaths: one performer is impaled on bayonets, another has a spike driven into his head, yet another is sawed in half. Despite its Grand Guignol trappings, it's a glorified whodunit, ably directed by Jim O'Connolly from a script by producer Herman Cohen and Aben Kandel. Ty Hardin, Diana Dors, Michael Gough, Judy Geeson. Aka *Circus of Blood* and *Circus of Terror*. (Video/Laser: Columbia TriStar)

BERSERKER (1987) ★★ Students tramping through the woods hear about an old legend in which "berserkers," Viking warriors, were once cursed by the Nordic gods. Who should turn up but one of those resurrected warriors, who tears apart flesh with his bare hands. Written-directed by Jef Richard. Joseph Alan Johnson, Valerie Sheldon, Gregg Dawson. (Starmaker; Prism)

BEVERLY HILLS BODYSNATCHERS (1989) ★★½ Unpleasant mortuary humor—embalming jokes and the lot—is the main motivation behind this comedy that is an undertaker's equivalent to the *Bill & Ted* misadventures. Two nerds (Rodney Eastman and Warren Selko) are forced by their underworld "Uncle Vito" (Art Metrano) to take jobs as mortician's assistant's assistants. They end up stealing bodies for boss Vic Tayback and mad doctor Frank Gorshin, who does an imitation of Boris Karloff as he invents a formula that brings life to the dead. Gorshin is the only funny actor in this misfire of a black comedy. Director Jon Mostow knows nothing about comedy or the timing it requires, and the jokes fall flat when Gorshin is offscreen. Seth Jaffee, Brooke Bundy, Keone Young. (Shapiro Glickenhaus; South Gate) (Laser: Image)

BEVERLY HILLS VAMP (1989) ★★ Another effort from prolific genre filmmaker Fred Olen Ray. This one mixes Hollywood satire (Britt Ekland is a vampire running a brothel in the hills of Beverly) and bloodsucking thrills as Eddie Deezen becomes an enthusiastic vampire hunter with a cross fashioned on his shorts and the words: "Eat crucifix bitch!" Tim Conway, Jr., Jay Richardson, Michelle Bauer, Debra Lamb, Robert Quarry. (Vidmark)

BEWARE MY BRETHREN. See *The Fiend.*

BEWARE OF THE BLOB/BEWARE! THE BLOB. See *Son of Blob.*

BEWARE OF THE BRETHREN. See *The Fiend.*

BEYOND ATLANTIS (1975) ★★★ Good fantasy-adventure (originally made as *Sea Creatures*) with excellent underwater photography. Add to that shapely Leigh Christian and this comes up a winner. Adventurers John Ashley and Patrick Wayne track Atlantean pearls to a native-inhabited island. Eddie Romero's direction is okay and Charles Johnson's script features a neat twist of fate. George Nader looks a bit silly as a native chief, but what counts is the two-fisted action. Eddie Garcia, Vic Diaz. (United)

BEYOND DARKNESS (1992) ★★ The spirits of witches burned at the stake centuries earlier plague a family that has just moved into a New England house. Directed by Clyde Anderson. Gene Le Brock, David Brandon, Barbara Bingham. (Imperial) (Laser: Image)

BEYOND DREAM'S DOOR (1988) ★★★ Effective low-budgeter, made at Ohio State, tells the surrealistic tale of Nick Baldasare, whose nightmares unleash a monster. Clever editing keeps the inferior effects to a minimum and powerful camera angles suggest more than is there. Above-average for a video production. Written-directed by Jay Woelfel (who also wrote the score). Rich Kesler, Susan Pinsky, Norm Singer, Daniel White. (VidAmerica)

BEYOND EVIL (1980) ★★½ When Lynda Day George takes possession of a house on a Pacific island, she's possessed by the spirit of the previous owner, who needs her for sacrificial ceremonies to the Devil. Director Herb Freed cowrote with Paul Ross. John Saxon, Michael Dante, David Opatoshu. (Media)

BEYOND OBSESSION. See *Beyond the Door.*

BEYOND THE BERMUDA TRIANGLE (1976) ★★★ TV-movie exploits the hysteria surrounding the Devil's Triangle theory in a low-key, subtle fashion with a tasteful telescript by Charles McDaniel and the sensitive direction of William A. Graham. Fred MacMurray, after losing his fiancée off the coast of Florida, begins an obsessive search in strange waters. There's a melancholy gentleness about his remorse that MacMurray pulls off without sentimentality. Sam Groom, Donna Mills, Suzanne Reed, Dana Plato. (Magnum)

BEYOND THE BRIDGE. See *Olivia.*

BEYOND THE DOOR (1975) ★★½ Italian imitation of *The Exorcist*, set in San Francisco, in which Juliet Mills has a baby in her tummy tum-tum capable of opening/closing doors, knocking crockery off shelves and turning mama into a bitch witch who spits up greenish vomit. How this bratty beastie got into her womb only the Devil would know, if you get our drift. Nice photography of Sausalito and the Golden Gate Bridge, but also long, dull stretches of Richard Johnson walking around (he's supposed to be a go-between for the Devil) and the cliché playroom scenes where the toys come to life. Writer-director Oliver Hellman (aka Ovidio G. Assonitis) fails to breathe life into this ripoff. Aka *Beyond Obsession* and *Who?* (Media; RCA/Columbia) (Laser: RCA/Columbia)

BEYOND THE DOOR II (1977) ★★ Sequel to *Beyond the Door* with Daria Nicolodi in the Juliet Mills role—a mother still suffering the terrors of a son possessed by the spirit of her deceased husband, a son who plays terror games and uses wicked psychokinetic powers. The kid even tries to get sexual. Mom gets hysterical, boy goes bonkers, audience dozes off. Director Mario Bava allows the door to close on his own screenplay without much of a slam. David Colin, Jr., is the mean little kid, Ivan Rassimov the dense new husband. Lamberto Bava contributed to the script. Aka *Shock (Transfer Suspense Hypnos)*, *Shock* and *Suspense*. (Media)

BEYOND THE DOOR III (1991) ★★ This has nothing to do with *Beyond the Door*—better it should be called *Runaway Train of Horror*. L.A. students ("junior ambassadors") are sent to Belgrade, Serbia, only to fall prey to a Balkan devil cult that wants a virgin (Mary Kohnert) to mate with Lucifer. The group is trapped on a train out of control and the students die horrible deaths one by one. The best parts of Ovidio G. Assonitis's production are the sequences dealing with attempts to stop the train, and not the blood-and-gore scenes. Bo Svenson is wasted in the role of a Yugoslav professor. William Geiger, Renee Rancourt, Jeremy Sanchez, Alex Vitale. Directed by Jeff Kwitny. (Video/Laser: Columbia TriStar)

BEYOND THE FLAME BARRIER. See *The Flame Barrier*.

BEYOND THE FOG. Retitling of *Horror on Snape Island*. See *Tower of Evil*.

BEYOND THE GATE. See *Human Experiments*.

BEYOND THE LIVING (1977) ★★ Muddled supernatural thriller in which a cult leader dies in a hospital just as his spirit possesses the curvy body of a nurse. She knocks off the characters with cleavers, knives and other sharp/blunt instruments. Meanwhile, there's an absurd subplot in which a black football star–patient turns up with a voodoo amulet to ward off evil. Poorly directed by Al Adamson. Released as *Nurse Sherri*. Jill Jacobson, Marilyn Joi, Mary Kay Pass, Geoffrey Land. (From World's Worst Videos as *Hospital of Terror*, from Marathon as *Terror Hospital*, from Lettuce Entertain You as *Hands of Death* and from Iver as *Killer's Curse*)

BEYOND THE LIVING DEAD (1974) ★★ Spanish fright flick stars Paul Naschy as a nasty nut resurrecting corpses and programming them to knock off folks standing in the way of scientific progress. Beyond the comprehension of most living viewers. Directed by John Davidson (Naschy). (Unicorn; from Western World as *The Hanging Woman* and from Wizard as *Return of the Zombies*)

BEYOND THE RISING MOON (1988). See *Star Quest: Beyond the Rising Moon*.

BEYOND THE STARS (1963). See *Unearthly Stranger*.

BEYOND THE STARS (1989) ★★★ Heartfelt, moving story of an Apollo astronaut (Martin Sheen) who discovers a secret on the moon and is exposed to radiation, and the effect these have upon him when he becomes a recluse in Cedar Bay, Oregon. It's told from the viewpoint of a teenager (Christian Slater) undergoing problems with his divorced parents, who builds a friendship with Sheen and a love affair with Olivia D'Abo. Writer-director David Saperstein sometimes gets too preachy (especially with F. Murray Abraham as a man who studies whale communications) but he spins a compassionate story. Sheen, Slater and Robert Foxworth (as the boy's estranged father) are wonderful, as is Sharon Stone as Foxworth's girlfriend. (Video/Laser: IVE)

BEYOND THE TIME BARRIER (1960) ★ Robert Clarke takes off in an experimental supersonic rocket and, after passing into a time warp, lands in 2024 to find a subterranean world that has survived a cosmic nuclear plague. It's a dreary civilization, making our present-day world, even with its faults, seem Utopian in comparison. Although directed by cult favorite Edgar G. Ulmer, it is marred by terribly amateurish acting, chintzy production values, and an awful script by Arthur G. Pierce (aka *The War of 1995*). Darlene Tompkins, John van Dreelen, Arianne Arden, Vladimir Sokoloff. (Sinister/C; S/Weird; Nostalgia)

BE YOUR AGE. See *Monkey Business*.

BICENTENNIAL MAN (1999) ★★★★ If only the great science-fiction writer Isaac Asimov were alive to see and enjoy the splendid job screenwriter Nicholas Kazan, director Chris Columbus, and star Robin Williams have done in adapting his robotics novel *The Positronic Man*, which was written with Robert Silverberg in 1976 to mark the American Bicentennial. Focusing on character and keeping futuristic settings, robot creatures, and other science-fictional trappings to a minimum, *Bicentennial Man* is the 200-year-long saga of a robot's journey to understand humanity and ultimately become human. In the process, it becomes a heartfelt study of man himself, with the message that all the things we take for granted day to day are fully appreciated, ironically, by a mechanical creation. Kazan's script deals with all the major issues of being human—freedom vs. slavery, relationships, sexuality, nobility, mortality—and the passages that life takes all of us through. For Columbus, this movie demonstrates a maturity and restraint he has never exhibited before as a director, and might well be his own rite of passage to becoming a better filmmaker. Even if Kazan's script sometimes seems schmaltzy or overly sentimental, there are so many brilliant bits of dialogue (the robot's description of sex: "You get to go to heaven but you come back alive!") and warm, fleshed-out characters that one can forgive him for being so compassionate and for grabbing for your heartstrings. Williams has an unusual role in that during the first half of the two-hour film he is inside a robot's body designed by special-effects veteran Steve Johnson: "NDR-14 Domestic"—a mechanical unit created for domestic home service. While the structure of the face does resemble Williams's, with soft eyes and an expression that suggests naïveté, he is only heard but never seen as he matures under the tutelage of his owner, Sir (played by a very restrained Sam Neill), Sir's wife (Wendy Crewson), and the daughter Little Miss (Hallie Kate Eisenberg as a child, Embeth Davidtz as an adult). The soft-spoken Sir comes to realize that "Andrew" (the name he christens the robot) is an assembly-line anomaly with individual traits and a sense of curiosity that make him unique. Once NDR-14 learns all he can from Sir and family, he asks for and receives his freedom, a concept he has read about and senses he needs to be more complete. With a large fortune Sir allowed him to amass through his woodworking and clock-making abilities, Andrew begins a nomadic life alone, wandering through a technically advancing world in search of other robots like himself, but finding that there are no other surviving anomalies because of newer robot technologies. (The changes over the 200-year span are shown via shots of San Francisco and Washington, D.C., with computer-graphic enhancements, so that familiar landmarks are mingled with major skyline alterations and such sci-fi visuals as sky cars.) It isn't until he finds eccentric robotics-android scientist Rupert Burns (Oliver Pratt) that life begins to turn for Andrew. With artificial flesh covering his metallic exterior, the full-bodied Robin Williams now enters the picture, ready to assimilate himself into the world of humans by returning to the descendants of Sir's family. Andrew renews his friendship with Little Miss, who now is quite older, and is attracted to her granddaughter Portia (also played by Davidtz). With the added enhancement of a central nervous system he has designed with Rupert's help, Andrew is ready for his first romantic interlude and sexual experience. As decades pass, Andrew and his love face the reality that he is immortal while she is not, and soon they will be separated by death. How Andrew finally resolves this, in taking his last step to being a complete human being, gives *Bicentennial Man* a teary but uplifting ending. Throughout this positive story, Columbus takes from Kazan's script a sense that man, despite all his problems and his destructive nature, is headed into a prosperous future. An exciting, decent world waits for generations yet unborn. (Video/DVD: Touchstone)

BIG (1988) ★★★★ Warm fantasy-comedy in which a 13-year-old is given the body of an adult by a fortune-teller machine at an amusement park. Before you can say G.I. Joe, the boy turns into Tom Hanks and is made vice-president of a toy company under boss Robert Loggia—for who understands toys better than a kid? When Elizabeth Perkins falls in love with him, and Hanks responds as a youth, this becomes a delightful comedy under Penny Marshall's poignant direction. Charm and good humor grace the Gary Rose–Anne Spielberg script. John Heard, Jared Rushton. (Video/Laser: CBS/Fox)

BIG CAIMANO RIVER, THE. See *The Great Alligator.*

BIG DUEL IN THE NORTH SEA. See *Godzilla vs. the Sea Monster.*

BIG FOOT (1971). See *Yeti: The Giant of the 20th Century.*

BIGFOOT (1987) ★★½ Innocuous, pleasant children's fluff, depicting how two hiking kids in the Walla Walla mountains are saved by a pair of loving Sasquatch creatures while adults scurry around looking for them and a Bigfoot pursuer closes in for the kill with a tranquilizer-dart rifle. The creature faces are good, but it's still a couple of guys in hairy suits and there's nothing in the way of excitement or effects. The presence of Colleen Dewhurst however, gives this triviality a lift. James Sloyan, Gracie Harrison, Joseph Maher, Adam Carol, Bernie White. Written by John Groves and directed by Danny Huston (John Huston's son), this plays like a TV-movie.

BIGGEST BATTLE ON EARTH, THE/BIGGEST FIGHT ON EARTH, THE. See *Ghidrah, the Three-Headed Monster.*

BIGGLES: ADVENTURES IN TIME (1986) ★★★ Offbeat time-travel adventure depicting how frozen-food executive Alex Hyde-White travels through time and space whenever his life is in jeopardy to World War I, where he meets Sopwith Camel ace Neil Dickson, who is trying to destroy a supersonic device the Germans use to knock down Allied airships. Hyde-White pops in and out of the time-stream at the oddest moments. It's rousing good fun enhanced by Peter Cushing as an officer giving exposition. Directed by John Hough. (New World/Starmaker)

BIG HURT, THE (1987) A reporter investigates mind-expanding experiments being conducted secretly at the Waldon Club, where torture is the order of the night. Directed by Barry Peak. Nick Waters, David Bradshaw, Lian Lunson, Simon Chilvers. (Laser: Image)

BIG MAN ON CAMPUS (1989) ★★★½ A gallant attempt to satirize *The Hunchback of Notre Dame* in modern guise (made as *The Hunchback of UCLA*) but a failure for not coming to terms with the sociological satire inherent in screenwriter Allan Katz's premise—that a "wild man" can be educated and brought into the folds of society despite man's fear to the contrary. Katz also portrays the primitive dude living in the campus bell tower who becomes the student body's strangest body when he's assimilated into the educational system by professor Tom Skerritt and tutor Gerrit Graham. Only during the second half does this misguided project seem to move toward its truth, but not even prestigious director Jeremy Paul Kagan can overcome deficiencies of narrative. Melora Hardin, Corey Parker, Cindy Williams, Jessica Harper. (Vestron) (Laser: Image)

BIG MEAT EATER (1982) ★★ This comedy-parody of movie genres (written-directed by Chris Windsor) blends so many together into a "kitchen sink" approach that the drain gets clogged. It's a musical with lampoonish production numbers, it's an alien-invader story with toy robots inside a flying saucer, it's a comedy set in a butchershop where a crazed black named Abdullah destroys meat with his cleaver and cuts up the town Dalmatian into delicacies. There's also a Russian family involved and a mayor who is killed and restored to life by aliens. If any of it makes any sense, write us an explanation. George Dawson, Big Miller, Andrew Gillies. (Media)

BIG SPACE MONSTER GUILALA. See *X—The Unknown.*

BIG TROUBLE IN LITTLE CHINA (1986) ★★★ Ghosts, kung fu, a monster, a subterranean Chinese city and a touch of mysticism . . . ingredients for a lively fantasy-adventure, but director John Carpenter is only partially successful. The main problem is, nothing about this martial arts ghost story ever ignites the viewer. The best thing is Kurt Russell as a wisecracking truck-driver who thinks he's John Wayne; he's swept into a mystery in which a 2,000-year-old demon must marry the heroine in order to turn back into a man. Action, comedy and light-show effects are part of the brew, but it still emerges lightweight. Dennis Dun, Kim Cattrall. (Video/Laser: CBS/Fox)

BIKINI GENIE. See *Wildest Dreams.*

BIKINI ISLAND (1991) ★½ Girls in skimpy bathing suits are the main reasons to watch this ogler's fantasy in which the chicks turn up on an island for a photo spread, and then are killed one by one. Produced-directed by Anthony (*Invisible Maniac*) Markes. Holly Floria, Alicia Anne, Jackson Robinson, Shannon Stiles, Sherry Jackson. (Video/Laser: Prism)

BILL AND TED'S BOGUS JOURNEY (1991) ★★½ Sequel to *Bill and Ted's Excellent Adventure* is inferior horseplay; the material is no longer fresh but retread stuff, stupidly plotted. Writers Chris Matheson and Ed Solomon are back with cyborg versions of Bill and Ted that time-travel from the future to kill our heroes. They do, and the dudes (Keanu Reeves and Alex Winter) go to Hell, where they play Battleship and Clue with the Grim Reaper (William Sadler) in order to return to Earth alive to stop a plot engineered by futuristic dictator De Nomolos

(Joss Ackland). This means we also get to visit a bleached-white Heaven and its Pearly Gates. The bodacious vocabulary of the lovable if dumb guys from San Dimas, CA, is still in evidence, and George Carlin appears briefly as Rufus with his time-traveling phone booth. The best part is the closing titles, in which Bill and Ted appear on magazine covers. Now that's "Excellent." Directed by Peter Hewitt. (Orion) (Laser: Image)

BILL AND TED'S EXCELLENT ADVENTURE (1989) ★★★ A box office success among teens because of the appeal of Keanu Reeves and Alex Winter as Ted Logan and Bill S. Preston—two "cool dudes" who hope to launch a rock band, the Wyld Stallyns, but first they must pass their history course. To accomplish this, they travel through time with Rufus (George Carlin) in a telephone booth, picking up Napoleon, Billy the Kid, Socrates, Genghis Khan, Abraham Lincoln, Mozart and Sigmund Freud and bringing them to the present for a high school show. The Chris Matheson–Ed Solomon screenplay is very clever or totally dumb, or perhaps both. In spite of its imbecilities, it does have a way of grabbing you. The crazy vocabulary of the boys, and their reactions to the people and customs of assorted time zones, contribute to the appeal, if not the intellectualism. Director Stephen Herek keeps this thing moving, ignoring the huge holes in logic. Terry Camilleri, Dan Shor, Tony Steedman, Rod Loomis. (Video/Laser: Nelson/Orion)

BILLY THE KID VS. DRACULA (1965) ★ When he was alive, John Carradine considered this his worst film. Watch and find out why. Directed by William "Crank-'em-Out-Fast" Beaudine and written by Karl Hittleman, the film abounds in absurdities and vampire lore miscalculations, such as having Carradine/Dracula creeping around in daylight. By all means, don't see it if you can miss it. Bing Russell, Roy Barcroft, Harry Carey Jr., Olive Carey, Roy Barcroft. (Embassy; S/Weird; Nostalgia; Video Yesteryear)

BIOHAZARD (1984) ★ Awful monster movie, poorly executed by writer-producer-director Fred Olen Ray, who during the closing credits resorts to amusing outtakes, writing off the picture as a joke. An *Alien* ripoff with psychic Angelique Pettyjohn not only making contact with an alien ship and teleporting it to Earth but showing off her enormous breasts. When the alien escapes its container, it's on a rampage of gory death. Christopher Ray plays the cheesy monster. Aldo Ray, William Fair, Frank McDonald. (Cinema Group; Continental; MNTEX)

BIONIC EVER AFTER? (1994) ★★ Further adventures of the Six Million Dollar Man (Lee Majors) and the Bionic Woman (Lindsay Wagner) when they decide to get married—but before they can enjoy biobliss, each undergoes breakdown from a "computer virus" introduced into their systems by a scheming OSI agent. They become involved with a terrorist gang holding the U.S. Embassy in the Bahamas hostage, and threatening to blow up the area with an atomic-warhead SCUD missile. An average TV-movie, almost listlessly directed by Steven Stafford from a telescript lacking conviction by executive producer Michael Sloan and Norman Morrill. Richard Anderson, back as Oscar the assignment chief, served as coexecutive producer. Anne Lockhart makes for a lovely villain. Martin E. Brooks, Alan Sader, Geordie Johnson.

BIONIC SHOWDOWN (1989) ★★½ TV-movie based on TV's *The Six Million Dollar Man* and *The Bionic Woman*, with Lee Majors and Lindsay Wagner re-creating their roles. An enemy bionic man has infiltrated OSI and a new bionic woman helps Steve, Jamie and Oscar fight the enemy at the World Unity Games. Typical TV action stuff moves under director Alan J. Levi. Majors and Richard Anderson served as coproducers. Bill Conti wrote the music. Sandra Bullock, Jeff Yagher, Martin E. Brooks, Lee Majors II, Robert Lansing.

BIRDS, THE (1963) ★★★★★ Alfred Hitchcock's masterpiece of suspense, scripted by Evan Hunter from the Daphne du Maurier story. For reasons never explained, only pontificated on, winged creatures turn against mankind and attack without warning. Rod Taylor and Tippi Hedren are trapped in a farmhouse and the attacks are spine tingling. (Hedren claims Hitch set hungry birds against her to capture ultimate realism.) The ending is ambiguous, as was the short story, but Hitchcock's masterful direction makes it work. Bernard Herrmann provided the eerie bird "sounds" and Lawrence A. Hampton pulled off the complicated effects, combining real and fake birds in stunning fashion. An all-time favorite worth reseeing. Jessica Tandy, Suzanne Pleshette, Veronica Cartwright, Charles McGraw, Doodles Weaver. (Video/Laser: MCA)

BIRDS II: LAND'S END, THE (1994) ★★ Colorless sequel to Hitchcock's '63 classic set on an island off the coast of Florida, where unhappily married Brad Johnson and Chelsea Field bring their two kids and lovable dog for a holiday, only to become pecking targets for sea gulls and crows as the winged creatures lead a new revolt against mankind, presumably because of polluted ocean waters. The problems of the couple, which consume most of the film's 90 minutes, seem at odds with the horrific elements, as if writers Ken and Jim Wheat and Robert Eisele needed padding. Padding for a sequel to Hitchcock's great '63 special-effects extravaganza? Daphne du Maurier's short story was ill served with this TV-movie that recycles Tippi Hedren from the original—but even she

is wasted in a nothing role. *Birds II* just never flies. James Naughton, Jan Rubes. If you're wondering who director Alan Smithee is—that's an alias for Rick Rosenthal. (MCA)

BIRDS OF PREY. See *Beaks the Movie.*

BLACK AUTUMN. See *Psychomania* (1963).

BLACK CASTLE, THE (1952) ★★★ Call this an "old dark castle" thriller. Swashbuckler Richard Greene visits baron Stephen McNally in his medieval digs to seek a missing friend. Lurking at the arras as castle retainers, and giving this a touch of the sinister, are Boris Karloff and Lon Chaney, Jr. Now-classic Gothic suspense programmer with additional villainy from Michael Pate and John Hoyt. Directed by Nathan Juran from a Jerry Sackheim script. (MCA)

BLACK CAT (1990) ★★ Luigi Cozzi wrote-directed this movie about a cast making a horror film in a haunted house. Brett Halsey, Caroline Munro. (Columbia)

BLACK CAT, THE (1934) ★★★ One of the strangest of Universal's horror films thanks to surreal direction by Edgar G. Ulmer and the abstract script by Peter Ruric, who threw away Poe's tale for more bizarre proceedings. Boris Karloff, leader of a cult of devil worshipers, lives in a strange house constructed over a fort, where he is keeping the corpse of Bela Lugosi's wife. Karloff and Lugosi are antagonists to the death, symbolized by a game of chess. Eerie images (credit photographer John Mescall), sadomasochism and torture, bizarre gimmicks, unexplained characters. It's enigmatic, but chillingly so. Aka *House of Doom* and rereleased as *The Vanishing Body.* (Media; on MCA cassette and laser with *The Raven*)

BLACK CAT, THE (1980) ★★ Just how scary is a black pussy? This Italian supernatural thriller directed by Lucio Fulci answers that question. Not a helluva lot. And how scary are close ups of Patrick Magee's eyeballs? Not a helluva lot. Magee is a village nut recording tapes with voices from the dead whose evil is transported into a black cat . . . or is the evil of the cat overtaking him? Scotland Yard cop David Warbeck investigates murders linked to Magee and his cat and nosy photographer Mimsy Farmer thinks the pussy is pulling off the homicides. Murders include a body falling on a pitchfork, a woman burned alive, claws across hands and other feline felonies. Please, no catty remarks. (Rhino; Media)

BLACK CAULDRON, THE (1985) ★★★ Long-awaited (five years in the making!) and expensive ($25 million) animated feature from Disney, based on Lloyd Alexander's *The Chronicles of Prydain.* The evil Horned King seeks the Black Cauldron, that Spectral Stewpot with the power to conquer the world. Standing in his way is Taran, a naive hero who proves his nettle with a magic sword, a beautiful scullery maid, a roving minstrel, a fuzzy cute animal creature that mutters, and an oracle-divining pig. An odd blend of styles (some cartoonish, some grittily realistic) and characters (some old-fashioned Disney, others like extras from *Conan*) results in a stunningly visual piece that still seems trivial. Directed by Ted Berman and Richard Rich. John Huston narrates the introduction; voices: John Hurt as the Horned King, Grant Bardsley as Taran and Susan Sheridan as Eilonwy. (Disney)

BLACK CHRISTMAS (1963). See *Black Sabbath*.

BLACK CHRISTMAS (1974) ★★★ This predates the slasher cycle and establishes tone and ambience for which the subgenre was to become known, so producer-director Robert Clark deserves credit for establishing precedent in this Canadian film, aka *Stranger in the House* and *Silent Night, Evil Night*. A fiendish killer remains hidden in the attic of a sorority house while police run weary looking for missing persons who are dead in the garret. The killer's identity is never known (writer Roy Moore sets it up so it doesn't matter) but knowledge of the killer's whereabouts contributes to the tension. Olivia Hussey, Margot Kidder, Keir Dullea, John Saxon, Art Hindle. (Warner Bros.)

BLACK COUNTESS, THE. See *Erotikill*.

BLACK DEMONS (1991) ★ Brazilian voodoo terror stalks Keith Van Hoven, Joe Balogh and Sonia Curtis during a Rio vacation in this Italian horror thriller directed by Umberto Lenzi.

BLACK DEVIL DOLL FROM HELL (1985) ★ Vidjunk in which a woman is trounced on by a ventriloquist's dummy, a monster programmed by its creator to murder. Directed by Chester T. Turner. Shirley T. Jones, Rickey Roach. (Hollywood Home Theater)

BLACK DRAGON OF MANZANAR. Reedited TV version of the Republic serial *G-Men vs. Black Dragon*.

BLACK DRAGONS (1942) ★★ Monogram programmer with Bela Lugosi wasted as a plastic surgeon operating on Japanese spies so they can infiltrate America. It's the "yellow horde" menace, a polemic mangled by writer Harvey Gates and squashed to death by director William Nigh. Has the dubious distinction of Lugosi in two roles. Clayton Moore, Joan Barclay. (Sinister/C; Filmfax; Nostalgia)

BLACK ELIMINATOR. Video version of *Death Dimension*. (Unicorn)

BLACKENSTEIN (1973) ★ Unsavory take-off on *Blacula*, in which mad doctor John Hart turns a Vietnam basket case into a monster. *Blackenstein* only blackens the names of producer-writer Frank Saletri and director William Levey. Andrea King, Liz Renay. Aka *Return of Blackenstein* and *Black Frankenstein*. (Media)

BLACK EVIL. Video version of *Blood Couple*. (Lettuce Entertain You)

BLACK FRANKENSTEIN. See *Blackenstein*.

BLACK FRIDAY (1940) ★★★ Boris Karloff portrays a sympathetic scientist who transplants the brain of a criminal into an injured colleague, with the patient taking on gangster characteristics. Bela Lugosi appears in a small role as a hoodlum. The Curt Siodmak–Eric Taylor script bears resemblance to Siodmak's own *Donovan's Brain*. Not a distinguished Universal horror film of the period, but of interest for its cast. Arthur Lubin directed. Stanley Ridges, Anne Nagel, Anne Gwynne, Paul Fix, James Craig. (MCA)

BLACK HARVEST OF COUNTESS DRACULA, THE. See *The Werewolf vs. the Vampire Women*.

BLACKHAWK (FEARLESS CHAMPION OF JUSTICE) (1952) ★★ Kirk (Superman) Alyn portrays the noble leader of an international band of flyers fighting foreign agents led by sultry Carol Forman, who is out to steal an Electronic Combustion Ray. This 15-chapter Sam Katzman serial for Columbia has the flyers driving around in black-painted 1950 Fords most of the time, with only an occasional airplane in sight. This action serial is based on the comic book drawn by Reed Crandall, but it's seriously missing the sense of aviation adventures that set Blackhawk apart. Directed by Spencer Bennet. (Heavenly)

BLACK HOLE, THE (1979) ★★½ The Black Hole of Space is an astronomical theory that when a star dies it becomes a compressed mass, where laws of physics cease to exist. This Disney effort, an answer to *Star Wars*, is a compressed mess. Many effects artists (including Peter Ellenshaw) were brought in to assist, but the Jeb Rosebrook–Gerry Day screenplay belies their efforts with cardboard characters and feeble premises. A survey ship, dangerously close to a Black Hole, is approached by another ship from which robots (cutesy-pie creatures) zap the expensive sets with their blasters. Even the trip through the Black Hole, intended as an abstraction, is a misfire for director Gary Nelson. Anthony Perkins, Robert Forster, Joseph Bottoms, Yvette Mimieux, Ernest Borgnine, Maximilian Schell. Robot voice by Slim Pickens. (Video/Laser: Disney)

BLACK LAGOON. Original title of *Creature from the Black Lagoon*.

BLACK MAGIC (1991) ★★★ There's a Preston Sturges zaniness to this whacky comedy set in Istanbul, S.C., where Judge Reinhold shows up to find out how his brother was killed. Seems his sibling has returned from the dead to torment Reinhold to find his killer. The madcap search leads to a would-be witch (Rachel Ward, in a sensuous, ambiguous role), a town crazy (Brion James) and other oddball characters. A most unusual supernatural comedy, so more power to writer-director Daniel Taplitz. Anthony LaPaglia, Richard Whitting, Wendy Markena. (Video/Laser: MCA)

BLACK MAGIC MANSION. TV title of *Cthulhu Mansion*.

BLACK MAGIC RITES—REINCARNATIONS. See *The Reincarnation of Isabel*.

BLACK MAGIC WOMAN (1990) ★★★ Exotic and sexy Apollonia Kotero provides an eyeful when she falls for gallery curator Mark Hamill, over objections of girlfriend Amanda Wyss. Black magic rituals (dead rooster hanging above his bed, poisonous snake under his pillow, severed human fingers) soon have Hamill voodooized. When a dead servant winds up as "cold cuts" in a refrigerator, you can figure the hexer means business. The twist ending to Gerry Daly's screenplay is neat if predictable. A smooth whodunit directed by Deryn Warren. Victor Rivers, Larry Hankin. (Video/Laser: Vidmark)

BLACKOUT (1985) ★★★ Intriguing psychothriller with Richard Widmark as a policeman obsessed by a quadruple family murder—presumably committed by the missing husband. What gives this a wrenching twist is that Keith Carradine, an accident victim, could be the father suffering from amnesia. Does he now have a split personality, reverting to homicidal tendencies at times? Is he terrorizing his bride Kathleen Quinlan? Or is a former lover plotting to drive her bonkers? Intriguing questions to hold your interest. Michael Beck, Gerald Hiken. Directed by Douglas Hickox. (Fox Hills)

BLACKOUT (1988) ★★ Has Gail O'Grady's father come back from the dead to haunt her attic? And what are those strange dreams she's having about her childhood? Since the screenwriter is producer Joseph Stefano, you know you're in *Psycho* territory. Directed by Doug Adams. Carol Lynley, Michael Keys Hall. (Magnum)

BLACKOUT: THE MOMENT OF TERROR. Video version of *Blood Couple*. (Fantasy)

BLACK RAINBOW (1989) ★★★ Solid work by writer-director Mike Hodges about an evangelist (Rosanna Arquette) with prescient abilities who inadvertently gets involved in a murder plot to cover up a chemical plant scandal. The real story, though, involves Arquette's relationship with alcoholic father Jason Robards and reporter Tom Hulce. Arquette is an actress of unusual caliber and her fans will be delighted when she goes nude in a sizzly love scene with Hulce. The film's theme is summarized when a traveling preacherman remarks, "We steal when we touch tomorrow. It's God's." Mark Joy, Ron Rosenthal, John Bennes, Linda Pierce. (Media; Fox; Video Treasures) (Laser: Image)

BLACK RAVEN, THE (1943) ★½ Minor horror overtones of the "old, dark house" school permeate this ordinary whodunit of the '40s in which horror figure of the period George Zucco, as the owner of the Black Raven Inn, plays host to stranded travelers, who die one by one at the hands of a shadowy, hooded figure. It's woefully written (by Fred Myton) and directed (by Sam Newfield). Glenn Strange, strangely enough, is the comedy relief, and Charles Middleton plays a dumb sheriff to no particular avail. (Sinister/C; Rex Miller)

BLACK ROOM, THE (1935) ★★★ Identical twins (Boris Karloff & Boris Karloff) are caught up in macabre events that lead to the fulfillment of an ancient curse. Assorted bodies are thrown on spikes or skewered in a torture chamber. Karloff, portraying a sympathetic and a hateful character in the same film, shows his mettle under the direction of Roy William Neill. Script by Henry Myers. Thurston Hall, Edward Van Sloan, Katherine DeMille, Marian Marsh. Aka *The Black Room Mystery*. (RCA/Columbia; Goodtimes) (Laser: RCA/Columbia; Image)

BLACK ROOM, THE (1981) ★★ Ghoulish brother-and-sister team lures unsuspecting victims into the family mansion, photographs them having sex through two-way mirrors in the titular bedroom, and murders them so the brother can have a transfusion to stave off a blood disease. My, what a fun-loving movie. Directed by Elly Kenner and Norman Thaddeus Vane (he wrote the script). Stephen Knight, Cassandra Gaviola, Jim Stathis, Linnea Quigley. (Vestron)

BLACK ROOM MYSTERY, THE. See *The Black Room* (1935).

BLACK ROSES (1988) ★★★½ Above average video horror flicker that vacillates between thoughtful, almost literate portions of characterization and dialogue, and the cheap thrills of the slasher genre. The town of Mill Basin is in an uproar over satanic rock 'n' roll group Black Roses, led by singer Damian. Bluenose Julie Adams predicts disaster—and her forecast comes true when Damian (a demon in human form) hypnotizes the town's youngsters to commit murders. English professor John Martin tries to stop the terror. Ken Swofford, Sal Viviano, Frank Dietz. Directed by John Fasano. (Imperial) (Laser: Image)

BLACK SABBATH (1963) ★★★★ One of the best Italian horror pictures directed by Mario Bava, and the film that best reflects his attitude toward psychothrillers. He once said that a man alone in a room, confronting his own fears, intrigued him most, and *Black Sabbath* is three studies in abject fear, each introduced by an amusingly morbid Boris Karloff. In "A Drop of Water," based on a Chekhov story, nurse Jacqueline Soussard removes a ring from a dead body and is stalked by the corpse. This is absolutely chilling, for Bava uses color for psychological effect. "The Telephone" concerns strange calls to a beautiful woman from a man believed to be dead. Although the least effective yarn, it has ironic twists and brilliant use of color. This stars Michele Mercier and Lydia Alfonsi. Tolstoy's "The Wurdalak" stars Karloff as a vampire who can only kill those he loves. This is reeking with the kind of gothic atmosphere that Bava was best at achieving. Mark Damon, Suzy Anderson. The music is by Les Baxter. Aka *Black Christmas*, *The Three Faces of Fear* and *The Three Faces of Terror*. (HBO; Sinister/ C) (Laser: Image, with *Black Sunday*)

BLACK SCORPION (1995) ★★★ A pure comic-book superhero movie, with frustrated cop Joan Severance turning vigilante while wearing a sexy black costume that puts her somewhere between Batman and Catwoman. Her nemesis is a Darth Vader-type villain called The Breathtaker, who plots to poison the atmosphere with a gang called the Red Dragons, crooks who all suffer from asthma. This campy crap is rather fun to watch as Black Scorpion bounces around on bolts of lightning, jiggling her wonderful breasts and driving a car that molecularly changes its structure. And there's some sexy scenes with her cop partner Bruce Abbott. A gas and a half for voyeurs. Darryl M. Bell, Casey Semaszno. (New Horizons)

BLACK SCORPION, THE (1957) ★★½ Willis O'Brien's effects are the only commendable feature in this multi-legged monsterama in which a Mexican volcano spews up king-size mutant spiders. Richard Denning and Mara Corday race through south-of-the-border locations in search of a way of stopping the attack. Edward Ludwig directed this Warner Bros. flick written by David Duncan and Robert Blees. Unless you like scuttling bugs, you'd better scuttle elsewhere. (Fright)

BLACK SLEEP, THE (1956) ★½ Film lacks acting character but has plenty of character actors: Lon Chaney, John Carradine, Akim Tamiroff, Bela Lugosi, Tor Johnson—what a menagerie! Mad doctor Basil Rathbone performs perverted surgery to create a "gallery of creeps." Low-brow script by Reginald Le Borg (who also directed) and John Higgins. Barely watchable despite zoo-like cast. Aka *Dr. Cadman's Secret*. (Channel 13)

BLACK SUNDAY (1960) ★★★★ Milestone Italian film marked cinematographer Mario Bava's directing debut and made a horror star of Barbara Steele. Bava pumps so much Gothic atmosphere into this adaptation of Gogol's *The Vij* that it's a masterpiece continually coming back to haunt the viewer. It opens with a horrific sequence in which a spiked mask is placed over Steele's face (she's a witch being burned at the stake) and a curse is placed on her family. Two centuries later Steele's corpse rises to stalk her modern counterpart (also played by Steele). Helping her bring terror to the family is her evil brother, his face a countenance of twisted hate. Arturo Dominici's performance in this role is remarkable. John Richardson, Ivo Garrani, Andrea Cecchi. Music by Les Baxter. Aka *The Demon's Mask*, *The Hour When Dracula Comes*, *Mask of the Demon*, *Revenge of the Vampire* and *House of Fright*. (Filmfax; Movies Unlimited; S/Weird; Sinister/C carries a British version; in heavily edited form as *The Mask of Satan*) (Laser: MCA, with *Black Sabbath*)

BLACK VAMPIRE (1973) ★ Heavily altered video version of *Ganja and Hess*, which is also in video as *Blood Couple*. This version is of poor quality, featuring some credits as pseudonyms. The box carries another set of fictional names that don't match the credits at all. Puzzling. (Simitar; Video Gems)

BLACK WEREWOLF. Video version of *The Beast Must Die*. (Media; Prism; Impulse)

BLACK WIDOW, THE (1947) ★★★ Republic's 13-chapter serial is one of the studio's more campy, gassy post–World War II offerings, featuring a teleportation machine that allows evil Asian ruler King Hitomu (scowling Theodore Gottlieb) to travel from continent to continent. (The writers, apparently, were trying to revive the Yellow Horde peril.) His equally evil daughter, Sombra the Spider Woman (Carol Forman in sexy, spiderish outfits), can assume other identities by applying lookalike face masks. She and bad dad (with the insidious help of henchman Anthony Warde and demented scientist I. Stanford Jolley) are out to swipe Ramsay Ames's atomic rocket and other superweapons— but standing in their way is mystery writer-turned-investigator Steve Colt (Bruce Edwards) and *Clarion* reporter Virginia Lindley, the latter a bubbly creature you come to adore. There's campy dialogue between them as they track Sombra. Directed by Spencer G. Bennet and Fred C. Brannon, masters of the hang-by-your-thumbs crowd. The feature-length TV-movie version is *Sombra the Spider Woman*. (Video/ Laser: Republic)

BLACULA (1972) ★★★ Racist twist on the old vampire cliché: A black African Prince (William Marshall) is resurrected in Transylvania and shipped to L.A. As if the city isn't cursed enough, Prince Mamuwalde inflicts his own pain via punctures in the neck. Blacula falls for a reincarnated princess and pursues low-life types and cops through ghetto streets. It's such bloody good fun, it's a crying shame when the sun comes up. William Crain directed. Vonetta McGee, Denise Nicholas, Thalmus Rasulala, Elisha Cook, Jr., Charles Macauly (as Dracula). Sequel: *Scream, Blacula, Scream*. (HBO)

BLACULA II/BLACULA IS BEAUTIFUL/BLACULA LIVES AGAIN. See *Scream, Blacula, Scream*.

BLADE (1998) ★★½ An extravagant special-effects movie that is all spectacle without substance, a soulless movie without the beat of a heart. Based on the Marv Wolfman–Gene Colan comic book, David S. Goyer's screenplay focuses on a half-vampire, half-human super-antihero who stalks a major American city, slaughtering gangs of vampires that belong to a widespread cult planning to take over the world under the leadership of mad would-be vampire god Deacon Frost (Stephen Dorff). Portraying Blade as if he were a sadistic madman who gets his jollies from killing is Wesley Snipes, who brings not a whim of humor or humanity to his dark, stark, grim-jawed characterization. That makes Blade—with all his submachine guns, shotguns, knives, and samurai sword—as undesirable as the blood-drinking vampires he's taking out. Only N'Bushe Wright, as a forensics doctor taken under Blade's wing after almost becoming a vampire herself, brings any sense of warmth to this ruddy, bloody gorefest. She's aided a bit by Kris Kristofferson as Blade's right-hand man, Abraham Whistler, who is wise in the ways of destroying vampires (they're allergic to silver, garlic, sunlight, and ultraviolet rays) and who prepares the serum Blade needs to keep himself from turning into a bloodsucker. (Seems that Blade was born to a half-vampire mother, inheriting the cult's superpowers.) But even Kristofferson gets killed far too soon for the film's own good. Snipes is really lost in this bloody mess, struggling to bring anguish to an already cold-blooded character but having too little to work with within the threadbare plot. Okay, so the sequences showing Blade destroying vampires (who dissolve away to skeletons and then disintegrating pieces in startling computer-animated sequences) are eye grabbing. But where's any people or story substance in this anything-goes-with-plot movie? The wild-and-crazy climax, when Dorff gathers his sanguinary companions (including Traci Lords and Donal Logue) into a subterranean temple and awaits a transformation into an unkillable leader, is visually fascinating but makes no sense. The only thing that keeps this fiasco going is the kinetic direction of Stephen Norrington. A lot of glitzy, fast editing and good action choreography help, but one wishes desperately for story and character to be more than they are. Can't we have just a little hope with the garlic injections? Hell, even Blade's mom turns out to be evil and becomes a target for his vengeance. Ugh. (Video/Laser: New Line)

BLADE IN THE BODY. See *The Murder Clinic.*

BLADE IN THE DARK, A (1983) ★★ Italian psychothriller, directed by Lamberto Bava, in which a movie composer isolates himself in a villa to write a horror score while a killer armed with a razor and/or knife stalks victims. Clues the composer uncovers suggest each woman in the cast is a suspect, but clever viewers (like you) will figure out the killer's identity aided by pseudopsychiatric flashbacks. A fair time-killer, cutting slowly into your credulity veins. Andrea

Occhipinti, Anny Papa, Fabiola Toledo. Aka *House of the Dark Stairway.* (Lightning; Vestron; Live)

BLADE MASTER, THE. Video version of *Ator the Blade Master.* (Media)

BLADE OF THE RIPPER (1984) ★★½ Surprise twists heaped atop each other during the climax of this German chiller make up for mediocre production values and lousy U.S. dubbing/scanning. The "Razor Killer" is slashing the throats of Vienna's rich women. An intended victim is the neglected wife (Edwige Fenech) of the first secretary of the American Embassy. She receives flowers from a former lover, strikes up an affair with mysterious George Hilton and is blackmailed by a stranger. Which one—if any—is the murderer? Nothing is what it seems in this Euro-erotic psychothriller loaded with nudity and bloody slashings. Also called *Next.* (Saturn; the Regal video carries no writing/directing credits)

BLADE RUNNER (1982) ★★★★ A visual stunner, directed by Ridley Scott with the same eye for atmosphere that made *Alien* a hit. Graphic designers have created an L.A. of 1999 brilliant in its acid-rain wretchedness. The Hampton Fancher–David Peoples script, based loosely on Philip K. Dick's *Do Androids Dream of Electric Sheep?*, is such a downer the film operates without a soul. Harrison Ford is washed-out private eye Deckard, assigned to destroy rebellious replicants (humanoid robots). Deckard is worldweary, his voice-over monotonic narration, in the Mike Hammer style, contributing a nihilistic touch. Rutger Hauer is the head replicant, suggesting character complexities with the mere twist of a smile. The final confrontation in the Bradbury Building is an atmospheric, action-packed knockout. All style and no humanity; yet, recommended for compelling visuals and Scott's directorial eye, as well as Douglas Trumbull's effects. (Reissued theatrically in 1991 without the narration and with a different ending, it was described as "the director's original cut." However, this was untrue, according to Scott, who claimed it was a test work print. So in 1992 another version was released as the "director's cut," or what Scott wanted. Got that straight?) Sean Young, Joanna Cassidy, Daryl Hannah, Edward James Olmos, Hy Pyke, Joseph Turkel, Brion James. (Embassy; Nelson; RCA/Columbia) (Laser: Nelson; Criterion; Voyager; Warner Bros.)

BLADES (1988) ★ An absurd premise (lawnmower comes back from the junkpile, unmanned, to get even for being replaced by Japanese equipment) is played straight by screenwriter William R. Pace, who sold his bill of goods to director Thomas R. Rondinella. The mind boggles, watching this traumatic Troma production, how Pace's script exactly follows the events of *Jaws*, the mulcher replacing the killer shark. An unexciting hero and heroine (Robert North, Victoria Scott) slow the Pace-ing down as they join with greens keeper Jeremy Whelan at the Tall Grass Country Club to track the killer machine. Everyone's behavior is as inexplicable as where the machine gets its gas and oil. (Media) (Laser: Image)

BLAIR WITCH PROJECT, THE (1999) ★★★ A handful of inexperienced filmmakers throws a century of technical improvements in filmmaking to the winds and returns to a crude level of production with a story about the most elemental instinct in man—survival motivated by abject fear. *Blair Witch* is largely told with a handheld camera in pseudo-documentary style, with a prologue that tells us that three filmmakers, while making a documentary in a region of Maryland alleged to be haunted by an evil witch, disappeared during a field trip and were never seen again. Their videotapes, found a year later, are now being presented to us in an edited form that tells of their demise. As one of the characters remarks during the expedition into doom: "It's not quite reality . . . it's fictional reality. You're pretending everything is not quite the way it is." Which is exactly what *Blair Witch* is all about. In the beginning, the catalyst for the project (Heather Donahue) and her team—soundman Joshua Leonard and cameraman Michael Williams—are shown in a small town taking black-and-white footage of citizens relating what they know about the Blair Witch, a supernatural urban legend dating back to the days of the Salem witch trials. It is further suggested that a rash of child murders in 1940 in and around the Black Hills Forest was committed by a hermit driven to violence by the old witch. Through crude color footage, the threesome is shown setting out in a spirit of fun, though they only infrequently enter the frame, most of the footage being of surrounding countryside. Their conversations seem very real and no doubt were largely improvised. Heather is revealed to be a hard-edged, sharp-tongued woman who can hold her own with men, using their swear words and drinking Scotch in an attempt to bond. Of the three, she is always the dominant force, with Joshua or Michael displaying little initiative. However, Heather inexplicably begins to lose her way, then misplaces her map, then finds out one of the guys threw the map away—an act suggesting he has been mentally tampered with by unseen demonic powers. A fight erupts with name-calling and accusations. Civilization has been stripped away to reveal the beasts of the jungle, though they are frightened beasts. Something sinister continues to affect the characters and they begin behaving erratically and walk aimlessly in circles, even though they are guided by Heather's compass.

When they find strange piles of rocks and weird stick formations, and hear voices crying out in the night, they really fall apart. Joshua disappears, leaving Heather and Michael to sweat it out alone on the last night. Finally, in the film's best sequence, Heather finds a bloody object inside a piece of Joshua's shirt and undergoes a complete breakdown, making a "confession" on camera. She apologizes to her parents for getting lost and takes responsibility for the impending doom she senses. "We've ended up," she whispers, tears rolling down her cheeks, "hungry, cold, and HUNTED. I'm scared to close my eyes, or open them." The screenwriters-directors, Eduardo Sanchez and Daniel Myrick, understand the power of the unseen, that less can be more in a horror movie. They also rely on "the theater of the mind," what made old-time radio work so well, allowing imagination to supply all the gory details and ugly characters that seem to be lurking just out of camera frame (and which they no doubt could not afford to create.) Some of the scariest segments take place with only a black frame (Heather's camera rolling unattended at night) filling the screen and voices expressing total dread of what's out there. Be sure to see the companion piece, *Curse of the Blair Witch,* which is a full-length "documentary" about events surrounding the disappearances and the history of the Blair Witch. Another film made in a similar vein is *The Last Broadcast,* which no doubt inspired Sanchez and Myrick. However, they have succeeded in taking the concept into a more profitable arena. The Web site that helped to build up the film's reputation, even before it was released, is www.blairwitch.com. (Video/DVD Artisan)

BLANKMAN (1994) ★★★ Succeeding where Robert Townsend's *The Meteor Man* failed, *Blankman* is an amusing black man's fantasy about becoming a superhero to improve the quality of life. Damon Wayans, who cowrote with J. F. Lawton, plays a nerdish Rube Goldberg–styled inventor whose creations include a bulletproof fabric out of which he fashions a ridiculous costume in which to fight crime. With the help of his brother David Alan Grier (who works for the TV tabloid show *Hard Edition*) and his amusing, half-crazed inventions, Wayans battles gangsters in a semi-inept fashion, winning the heart of newswoman Robin Givens (in a sweet part) and beating evil underworld kingpin Jon Polito and his henchmen. Director Mike Binder employs parodies of the TV *Batman* series along the way, and makes this a pleasant diversion. Christopher Lawford, Lynn Thigpen, Nicky Corello, Jason Alexander. (Video/Laser: Columbia TriStar)

BLAST OFF (1967) ★★★ Jules Verne–style adventure/fantasy set in Victorian days with Burl

Ives, Troy Donahue, Gert Frobe (remember *Goldfinger?*), Hermione Gingold and Lionel Jeffries as high-flying aviators with a penchant for slapstick. It's a zany plot about sending a ship to Venus. Jolly silly fun. Aka *Jules Verne's Rocket to the Moon, Journey That Shook the World, P. T. Barnum's Rocket to the Moon, Rocket to the Moon,* and *Those Fantastic Flying Fools.* Directed by Don Sharp from a script by Dave Freeman. (HBO)

BLIND DATE (1983) ★★★½ Above-average psychothriller unfolds in the style of a Dario Argento jolter. The fascinating premise is that Joseph Bottoms is blinded while fleeing a killer, and agrees to have Dr. Steiger (Keir Dullea) implant a device in his brain that feeds computer-like images to his mind, allowing him to "see." Using the device, he sets out to find the killer in Athens, where this was photographed. The women are sexy (the killer has a penchant for TV models) so it's easy on the eyes. Unfortunately, Kirstie Alley's role is never heavily integrated and one wishes she were around more. James Daughton, Lana Clarkson, Gerald Kelly. Written-produced-directed by Nico Mastorakis, who no doubt digs those Argento thrillers. (Lightning; Vestron)

BLIND DEAD, THE (1972) ★★★ Spanish horror flick has eerie atmosphere and decent gorefects in recounting the legend of a 13th century cult, the Templarios, sadistic knights who murdered thousands of women in blood sacrifices. Written-directed by Amando De Ossorio, this was the first of four films in a series: *Return of the Evil Dead* (or *Return of the Blind Dead*), *Horror of the Zombies* (or *The Ghost Galleon*), *Night of the Seagulls* (or *Night of the Death Cult*). Cesar Burner, Lone Fleming, Maria Sylva, Joseph Thelman, Helen Harp, Rufing Ingels. Aka *Night of the Blind Dead.* (Paragon; from Midnight Video in a superior version as *Tombs of the Blind Dead*)

BLIND FEAR (1989) ★★ Blinded Shelley Hack is trapped in a mountain lodge with killers and must use her wits to save herself. Is this *Wait Until Dark* all over again, or what? Canadian feature directed by Tom Berry. Jack Langedijk, Kim Coates. (Academy) (Laser: Image)

BLIND FURY (1989) ★★★ Rutger Hauer, blinded during the Vietnam War, is trained in martial arts by native rescuers. When he returns stateside to see an old buddy, he gets caught up in a fight with the mob in Reno, using his fighting prowess to help his dead friend's son. Hauer has a psychic sense when he battles, similar to the metaphysical powers of Japan's blind swordsman, Zatoichi. Directed by Philip Noyce. Brandon Call, Terry O'Quinn, Lisa Blount, Nobel Willingham, Meg Foster, Nick Cassavetes. (Video/Laser: RCA/Columbia)

BLIND JUSTICE (1994) ★★★ Inspired by but not attributed to the Jonah Hex comic-book character, this HBO TV-movie is a dark, macabre western with strange religious symbolism that draws a parallel to the Jesus Christ legend. Armand Assante is effective as a near-blind Civil War survivor named Canaan who travels the West with a newborn baby (shades of the Babycart series from Japan), has keen senses, and is haunted by nightmares of his wartime experiences. Director Richard Spence captures a sureal feeling for the Arizona landscape and the Daniel Knauf telescript, while drawing on many elements, is nevertheless full of excellent dialogue and unexpected characters and situations. Elisabeth Shue, Robert Davi, Adam Baldwin. (HBO)

BLIND MAN'S BLUFF (1991) ★★ Foolish, unconvincing TV-movie that is a hodgepodge of pseudopsychiatry, split personality behavior, serial murders performed with a hammer, and a little touch of *Wait Until Dark* tossed in. Robert Urich portrays a blind novelist stalked by a murderer and gets involved with stolen coins, suspicious cops, his best friend, his psychiatrist and a former flame. Whew! Lisa Eilbacher, Patricia Clarkson, Ron Perlman. Directed by James Quinn.

BLIND MAN'S BUFF. Video version of *Cauldron of Blood.* (Vidcrest)

BLIND VISION (1991) ★★½ This Canadian TV-movie is reminiscent of 1980's *Fade to Black* in its depiction of a sexually repressed, social misfit (Lenny Von Dohler), a pathetic mailroom worker who falls for the beautiful girl (Deborah Shelton) in his office but can only watch her through his telescope from afar, too frightened to attempt a real relationship—until a mysterious stranger (Robert Vaughn, identified as Mr. X) turns up to hassle her and Von Dohler comes to her rescue. There isn't much in the way of visual thrills, but Von Dohler delivers a convincing performance. Ned Beatty as a cop and Louise Fletcher as a landlady contribute nice character bits. Written by director Shuki Levy and Winston Richard. (World of Video) (Laser: Image)

BLIND WITNESS (1989) ★★ TV-movie terror tale of a woman trapped in her home environment with killers (a genre established by *Wait Until Dark*). Victoria Principal, whose husband has been murdered, is terrorized in the aftermath of his death. Produced-directed by Richard Colla. Paul LeMat, Stephen Macht, Matt Clark.

BLINK (1993) ★★★ After an eye operation that restores her sight, Madeleine Stowe experiences "ocular flashback"—images out of their proper sequence in time. Since her visions involve a serial killer, she's quickly embroiled with cop Aidan Quinn. This offbeat thriller with mild supernatural overtones is stylishly directed by Michael Apted. Laurie Metcalf, James Remar. (Video/Laser: New Line)

BLOB, THE (1958) ★★★ Gelatin-like lumpy-glumpy substance comes to Earth aboard a meteor and grows each time it sucks up a human being, which is often, as Theodore Simonson and Kate Phillips don't want any blobs growing under their script. Steve McQueen and town juveniles set out to warn folks, but nobody listens . . . until the icky-sicky invades a movie theater and then it's too late to stop the ever-growing glunky junky. Tongue-in-cheek fun if you can roll with the World's Biggest Jello Ball. Director Irvin S. Yeaworth Jr. deserves credit for turning this into a cult favorite known for being icky sicky. Aneta Corseaut, Olin Howlin, Earl Rowe. Rejected titles included *The Glob, The Glob That Girdled the Globe, The Meteorite Monster, The Molten Meteorite* and *The Night of the Creeping Dead.* (Video Gems; Video Warehouse) (Laser: Voyager/Criterion, with trailers and an interview with Steve McQueen)

BLOB, THE (1988) ★★★½ This remake of the classic 1958 Steve McQueen vehicle is a monster movie with a capital M—a wonderful send-up of the original, ashine with gross but fun special effects. Director Chuck Russell (who co-authored with Frank Darabont) knows what elements of the scare genre make us leap from our seats or pull our feet up from the floor when the film re-creates the famous movie theater scene when the ploppy gloppy pours through the projection portal. Once again the glob Blob is a mindless force but this time was created during a human-genetics experiment in space. We see it ingesting people, changing its shape, and behaving as a scary monster should, at one moment literally sucking a human victim down a tiny drain. Kevin Dillon and Shawnee Smith flee the creature in the sewer system and fight it out (aided by the townspeople) in a battle royal. Hoyt Yeatman spearheaded the effects team and Lyle Conway designed the Blob. Donovan Leitch, Candy Clark, Del Close. (RCA/Columbia) (Laser: Image)

BLONDE HEAVEN (1994) ½ This wobbly tale about a fledgling beauty who arrives in Hollywood and wants to become "eternal" by becoming a movie star, and then falls into the clutches of a female vampire coven, is merely a feeble-minded excuse for a lot of sex play between men and women and women and women, and comes as close to pornography as you can get without an X marking their spots. Three alleged writers (Kenneth J. Hall, Mack Millenko and Matthew Jason Walsh) can't even come up with a single good idea, so director Ellen Cabot (aka David DeCoteau) just goes for the sex. Not a viewer's heaven, that's for sure. Julie Strain,

Raelyn Saalman, Michelle Bauer, Joe Estevez, Alton Butler, Jason Clow. (Paramount/Torchlight)

BLOOD AND BLACK LACE (1964) ★★★ Italian-French horror thriller focuses on a fiendish killer and the step-by-step enactment of crimes against beautiful models in a fashion salon run by Eva Bartok. In a compelling script by Marvello Fondato, Mario Bava and Giuseppe Barilla, the killer wears a stocking that makes the face an empty blank and there is a merciless choice on director Bava's part to show gore murders in drawn-out, excruciating sequences. One woman has her face shoved against a hot grill, for example. One-time cinematographer Bava uses primary colors to psychological effect, creating the paradox of a beautiful-looking movie about death. Aka *Fashion House of Death* and *Six Women for the Murderer.* Cameron Mitchell, Thomas Reiner, Harriet White. (Media) (Laser: Polygram)

BLOOD AND DONUTS (1995) ★★★ This off-the-wall Canadian production is less a vampire thriller than an exercise in how to write dialogue for eccentric, angst-ridden misfits and monsters. Gordon Currie portrays a shy, repressed vampire (aroused after sleeping since man set foot on the moon in 1969) who wanders through the night in a run-down part of the city meeting an abused cabdriver (Justin Louis), a lonely gal (Helene Clarkson) who serves donuts and coffee in an all-night café, two small-time hoods working for crime boss David Cronenberg (the filmmaker), and a onetime lover of Currie's who is now trying to kill him. But, as Currie remarks, "You can't kill someone who's not alive." This exercise in mood and low-life characters was written with a sardonic sense of humor by Andrew Rai Berzins and directed stylishly, if not too flamboyantly, by Holly Dale. There's some gore that might offend some, but genre fans should take it in the unusual spirit in which this film was conceived. Louis does an especially good job with his cabbie role. Fiona Reid, Frank Moore, Hadley Kay. (Live)

BLOOD AND ROSES (1961) ★★★ Director Roger Vadim's version of J. Sheridan Le Fanu's *Carmilla* (he cowrote with several collaborators) was brutalized by U.S. censors years ago who removed 13 minutes of lesbian activity. What's left of this tale tells of a woman with a family history of vampirism who is obsessed by an ancestor's spirit and an overpowering craving for blood of both sexes. Mel Ferrer, Elsa Martinelli, Annette Vadim. Aka *To Die with Pleasure.* (Paramount/Gateway, with much lesbianism and violence restored)

BLOOD BARON, THE. See *Baron Blood.*

BLOOD BATH (1966) ★★ Schizophrenic beatnik painter in the L.A. suburb of Venice murders women, lowering their still-warm bodies into a boiling vat. He thinks he's the reincarnation of a vampire. This exploitation flick will be of interest to fans of William Campbell, who costars with Marissa Mathes, Lori Saunders, Sandra Knight and Jonathan Haze. Written-directed by Jack Hill and reportedly finished by Stephanie Rothman after Hill was fired by producer Roger Corman. Also contains reedited footage from a Yugoslavian film. (From Sinister/C and 21st Genesis as *Track of the Vampire*)

BLOODBATH. See *A Bay of Blood.*

BLOODBATH AT THE HOUSE OF DEATH (1984) ★★½ In one bloody night, 18 died in Headstone Manor: four skewered, two killed by lightning, six frozen in a locker, two axed, one hanged, one blown up and two sliced open. Now investigators and psychics are in the house to check out why it's radiating radioactivity. This parodies specific horror films and was intended by writer-director Ray Cameron as a vehicle for British comedian Kenny Everett, who plays Dr. Lucas Mandeville. Vincent Price stars as the Sinister Man, a cult leader. For the farcically minded. Pamela Stephenson, Gareth Hunt, Don Warrington, Joe Fortune, John Stephen Hill. (Media)

BLOODBATH BAY OF BLOOD. See *Bay of Blood.*

BLOODBATH IN PSYCHO TOWN (1989) ★ While a movie is being shot in a small town, a sinister hooded figure begins to knock off the crew members one by bloody one. Written-directed by Alessandro DeGaetano. Helen Benton, Terry Brown, Claudia Peyton. (Video)

BLOOD BEACH (1980) ★★ Bathers are sucked into sandy Santa Monica beach by an unseen subterranean creature, baffling cops John Saxon and Burt Young. Writer-director Jerry Bloom builds a modicum of suspense, but the sandsucker is an uninspired blob creature, its origins unexplained. Marianna Hill, David Huffman, Otis Young, Stefan Gierasch. (Media)

BLOOD BEAST FROM HELL. See *Blood Beast Terror.*

BLOOD BEAST FROM OUTER SPACE. See *Night Caller from Outer Space.*

BLOOD BEAST TERROR (1967) ★★★ Although Peter Cushing considers this his worst, it doesn't seem that bad on rereview. Backed by Hammer production qualities and a strong cast, Cushing portrays a 19th century police inspector who goes undercover to discover that mad doctor Robert Flemyng has turned beautiful Wanda Ventham into a death's-head moth. Cushing's daughter (Vanessa Howard) is threatened as she also goes undercover. Vernon Sewell does a good job of directing Peter Bryan's script. Russell Napier, David Griffin. Also known as *Blood Beast from Hell* and *The Vampire Beast Craves Blood.* (Monterey)

BLOODBEAT (1982) ★★★ Writer-director

Fabrice-Ange Zaphiratos deserves a nod for making a gore film in which he blends psychic and slasher genres. A samurai warrior with a glowing aura terrorizes a rural family gathered for Christmas, in which mother and sister have mental powers. Gore is minimal as Zaphiratos goes for weirdness through music (some classical), enigmatic characters and a sexual link between the sister and the spectral samurai. Helen Benton, Terry Brown, Claudia Peyton, James Fitzgibbons. (Trans World)

BLOOD BRIDES. See *A Hatchet for the Honeymoon.*

BLOOD BUTCHERS. See *Toxic Zombies.*

BLOOD CASTLE (1970). Alternate video version of *Scream of the Demon Lover* (Lightning).

BLOOD CASTLE. Video version of *The Legend of Blood Castle.*

BLOOD CASTLE (1972). See *The Blood-Sp(l)attered Bride.*

BLOOD CITY. See *Welcome to Blood City.*

BLOOD COUPLE (1973) ★½ Released as *Ganja and Hess*, and known as *Double Possession* and *Vampires of Harlem*, this heavily cut version is the vampiric tale of a black doctor's assistant inflicted with a desire for blood after stabbed with a knife from a long-extinct black Nigerian civilization called Myrthia. This deals with black traditions in a well-intended but mind-dulling fashion, its pacing slow and its moments of action infrequent. Director-writer Bill Gunn appears in the cast with Duane Jones, Marlene Clarke, composer Sam Waymon and Leonard Jackson. Good black music accompanies the tale, but nothing saves this from its own stuffiness. (Video Gems; from Simitar and Impulse as *Black Vampire*, from Lettuce Entertain You as *Black Evil*, from Fantasy as *Blackout: The Moment of Terror*)

BLOOD CREATURE. Video version of *Terror Is a Man.*

BLOOD CULT (1985) ★½ At a Midwest college, coed murders lead to the discovery of a witches' coven that dates back to the Salem trials. A sheriff and girlfriend close in on the hags and crones. Made in and around Tulsa, Oklahoma, by Linda Lewis (producer) and Christopher Lewis (director), this was one of the first video movies, but it's undistinguished. Julie Andelman, Charles Ellis. (United)

BLOOD CULT OF SHANGRI-LA. See *The Thirsty Dead.*

BLOOD DEMON. See *The Castle of the Walking Dead.*

BLOOD DEVILS. See *Beast of Blood.*

BLOOD DINER (1987) ★ Tasteless sleazeball low-budgeter redeemed by its satirical humor directed at the artificialities of horror films. Director Jackie Kong makes fun of the genre as two nerds running a greasy spoon dig up their long-dead uncle, remove his brain and construct a new body from severed virgins' limbs and torsos. Purpose: to summon the great Goddess Sheetar. Mighty Kong allows every crummy joke and sick gag imaginable and spares none of the gore, although it's poorly done (on purpose, one hopes). If ever there was an armpit movie, this is it. Rick Burks, Carl Crew. (Vestron)

BLOOD DOCTOR. See *Mad Doctor of Blood Island.*

BLOOD DRINKERS, THE. See *Return from the Past.*

BLOOD EVIL. Video version of *Demons of the Mind* (Academy).

BLOOD FEAST (1964) ★★★ Exploitation gore flick, directed-photographed-scored by Herschell Gordon Lewis, who also did special effects. Lewis is legendary as the Grossest Filmmaker of All, and this is exemplary of his "work." We're talking gore gore here. Women are dissected, organ by organ, as a madman restores life into an Egyptian goddess. A sickening spectacle as Lewis preys on vicarious needs of lowbrows. The squeamish are advised not to watch, although intellectuals and other thinkers might get off on the sociopathic implications. Coproduced by another master of exploitation, David F. Friedman, and scripted by A. Louise Downe. Connie Mason, Thomas Wood. Aka *Feast of Flesh.* (Comet; Rhino; VCI; S/Weird) (Laser: Hollywood Home Theater)

BLOOD FEAST (1974). Video version of *Night of a Thousand Cats.* (Academy)

BLOOD FIEND, THE. See *Theatre of Death.*

BLOOD FOR BLOOD. Variant video version of *Vengeance Is Mine.* (Lettuce Entertain You)

BLOOD FOR DRACULA. Japanese laser title for *Andy Warhol's Dracula.*

BLOOD FREAK (1985) ★★ A vampire's myths are punctured when he learns the blood of drug addicts taint so good. Steve Hawkes, Heather Hughes, Dana Cullivan. Directed by Hawkes and Brad Grinter. (Video Treasures; Simitar offers an edited version; Regal's is said to be unedited)

BLOOD FRENZY. Either a video of *Bloody Frenzy* or a misspelling in some listings.

BLOOD FROM THE MUMMY'S TOMB (1972) ★★ Seth Holt's final directorial assignment—he died during production and was replaced by Michael Carreras. Acting and cinematography in this Hammer production are topnotch but Christopher Wicking's script, about a buxom young woman who resembles a long-dead Egyptian princess, is turgid stuff. Based on Bram Stoker's *The Jewel of Seven Stars.* Andrew Keir, Valerie Leon, George Coulouris. Remade as *The Awakening.*

BLOOD GAMES (1989) ★★★ This manipulative, exploitative burst of violence is another revenge metaphor for the war between men and women. Babe and the Ballgirls, an all-women's baseball team, outplay some rednecks, so insulting their macho pride that they go after the sexy gals with intent to do bodily harm, especially since they've killed their boss's sadistic son (in self-defense is beside the point). How the women unite into formidable fighters against male aggressors (using baseball bats, rifles and sex) is an intriguing if repulsive procedure in the hands of director Tanya Rosenberg, working from a script by four men. Artistic photography and a cast of fair-complected women raise this blood-and-gore thriller to greater heights than the material deserves. Gregory Cummings, Laura Albert, Shelley Abblett, Ernest Wall. (Video/Laser: RCA/Columbia)

BLOOD HARVEST (1986) ★½ Tiny Tim tiptoes through the bloody tulips in this low-budget, lowbrow imitation of the slasher genre in which he portrays Marvelous Mervo, a crazed hayseed in the whiteface and costume of a circus clown. But is he the demented dork who's kidnapping local folks, hanging them up like so many pigs to the slaughter and slitting their throats? This regional horror film was made in Wisconsin by writer-director Bill Rebane. Itonia Salochek sheds her clothes for lightcore sex scenes. Dean West, Frank Benson. (UAV)

BLOOD HOOK (1987) ★ One of the stranger variations on *Friday the 13th,* set at a lake in Muskie, Wisconsin, where fishermen gather for a contest. A killer uses a giant hook to "catch" his prey and then yank them apart. The murderer also shoves a hook through their mouths after they're dead and ties them together like a string of fish, this cheap movie's most ghastly effect. Other effects are amateurish (blame that on director James Mallon). The kind of movie you can fast-forward through because the majority of it is idle chatter among boring characters. Mark Jacobs, Patrick Danz, Sara Hauser, Christopher Whiting. (Prism; Paramount)

BLOOD HUNGER. Video version of *Vampyres—Daughters of Darkness* (Lettuce Entertain You).

BLOOD HUNT. Video version of *The Thirsty Dead* (Simitar).

BLOOD ISLAND (1966) ★★ Unfaithful version of a novelette by H. P. Lovecraft and August Derleth. That was a good horror story—this is just a horror. After so many horrendous murders, performed by something locked up in a weird house, it is utterly impossible to swallow the explanation offered about what is hiding in the shuttered room. This "monster" would have a difficult time kicking sand into the face of a 90-pound weakling, let alone throttling half the cast. A waste of Gig Young, Carol Lynley, Oliver Reed, Flora Robson and Bernard Kay. Directed by David Greene. Originally made as *The Shuttered Room.* (Ace)

BLOOD IS MY HERITAGE. See *Blood of Dracula.*

BLOOD LAKE (1987) ★ Teenagers are the commonplace fodder for the sharp-edged weapons of a crazed slasher-killer who stalks the unwitting (and witless) prey around the perimeter of a body of water isolated in the desolate wilderness of the countryside.

BLOOD LEGACY (1971) ★ Incompetent psychothriller in which four heirs to a country estate spend the night in the homestead to qualify for the family fortune. Each is murdered in horrible fashion; even the head of sheriff Rodolfo Acosta ends up on a turkey platter in the fridge. Jeff Morrow, John Carradine, John Russell and Faith Domergue are all squandered by producer-director Carl Monson. A pox on the horror house of writer Eric Norden. (Video Gems)

BLOOD LINK (1983) ★★★ Clinically detailed portrait of a perverted psychokiller murdering women in Hamburg and Berlin. It's also the study of Siamese twins: Michael Moriarity plays the killer and a doctor experimenting in brain control. Intriguing twists and good production make this Italian thriller above average. However, the sexual violence is a turn-off, creating a fascinating story unpleasant to watch. Penelope Milford, Geraldine Fitzgerald, Cameron Mitchell, Virginia McKenna. Music by Ennio Morricone. Directed by Albert de Martino. (Embassy; Video Treasures)

BLOODLUST (1961) ★½ Variation on "The Most Dangerous Game": Crazed hunter Dr. Balleau (Wilton Graff) chases humans with a bow-and-arrow rig, displaying the remains as trophies in glass containers. Written-produced-directed with a minimum of lustiness by Ralph Brooke and starring unknowns except for Robert Reed, who became a TV star in "The Brady Bunch." Lilyan Chauvin, June Kenny, Joan Lora. (Sinister/C; S/Weird; Filmfax)

BLOODLUST (1976) ★★ Swiss horror film about a man obsessed with stealing parts of corpses from mortuaries and putting the pieces in bottles. Directed by Marijan Vajda from a Nangoni Supasi script. Werner Pochath, Ellen Umlauf, Birgit Zamula. Aka *Mosquito*.

BLOODLUST (1981). Video of *Dr. Jekyll and Miss Osbourne* (Citadel; King of Video).

BLOODLUST (1992) ★ Australian-produced vampire shocker in which three femme fatale bloodsuckers rove Melbourne searching for sex-seeking men. Gore, softcore sex and mediocre everything. Written-directed by Richard Wolstencroft and Jon Hewitt. Jane Stuart Wallace, Kelly Chapman, Robert James O'Neill.

BLOODLUST: SUBSPECIES III (1993) ★★★ Third and final bloodspatter in Charles Band's *Subspecies* series—is this the end for vampire Radu (Anders Hoe) and Mummy dearest (Pamela Gordon)? Picking up right where *Bloodstone: Subspecies II* left off, Melanie Shatner is back looking for sister Denice Duff, imprisoned

in Radu's Transylvanian castle. Gooey, gory and blood-smeared with some great death scenes enhanced by good effects. Certain to please bloodsucking fans. Written-directed by Ted Nicolaou. (Paramount)

BLOOD MANIA (1970) ★ Wicked, wanton sexpot speeds up her father's demise so she can help her depraved boyfriend pay off a blackmail debt. These unsavory characters finally get chopped into little pieces, but this merciful act comes too late to benefit the viewer. Directed by Robert Vincent O'Neil. Peter Carpenter, co-producer with Chris Marconi, stars. (Academy; VCI)

BLOOD MASSACRE (1987) ★½ Not released on video until 1991, this Don Dohler production (he produced and directed) depicts outlaws on the run who stop at a farmhouse, not knowing a cannibalistic family lives there. Such sweet people, the Parkers—they intend to take the gangsters to lunch. If you get the drift. George Stover, Robin London, James Di Angelo.

BLOOD MONSTER. See *Vampire Men of the Lost Planet*.

BLOOD MONSTER (1972). Production title for Ray Dennis Steckler's *The Chooper*.

BLOOD MOON. Video version of *The Werewolf vs. the Vampire Woman* (AIR).

BLOODMOON (1989) ★★★ The first half of this Australian psychothriller is deadly dull. Teenagers in Cooper's Bay, which happens to have St. Elizabeth School for Girls and the Winchester School for Boys in close proximity, are being murdered by a killer with a barbed-wire garrote as they have sex, so there's nudity and love-making to keep you awake. The second half builds to a suspenseful climax, aided by Brian May's music. Leon Lissek is memorable as an impotent biology teacher–serial killer protected by wife Christine Amor. In Australia the film featured a "Fright Break" (an idea stolen from William Castle's *Homicidal*). Directed by Alec Mills. Ian Williams, Helen Thomson, Suzie MacKenzie. (Live) (Laser: Image)

BLOOD OF DRACULA (1957) ★½ Would you believe a vampire movie with songs? Would you believe hypnosis turning Sandra Harrison into a bloodsucker? Would you believe an all-girls' school where the headmistress has evil powers? Would you believe . . . naw, you wouldn't believe. Director Herbert L. Strock and screenwriter Ralph Thornton have justifiably remained obscure but producer Herman Cohen went on to *I Was a Teenage Frankenstein*, *Konga*, etc. Louise Lewis, Gail Ganley. Aka *Blood Is My Heritage* and *Blood of the Demon*. (RCA/Columbia)

BLOOD OF DRACULA'S CASTLE (1967) ★ Dreadfully produced flop (Rex Carlton's script is also known as *Dracula's Castle*) which drains weak laughs from the formula by updating it to modern California, but results are anemic, even with cinematographer Laszlo Kovacs assisting and with John Carradine (as a faithful butler to the Dracula clan) and Lon Chaney, Jr. A gross misuse of the Count's non-good name by producer-director Al Adamson, assisted in directing by Jean Hewitt. Alex D'Arcy and Paula Raymond are Mr. and Mrs. Dracula, chaining up beautiful chicks in the cellar. Robert Dix, Ray Young, Vicki Volante. (Interglobal; United; Grand Entertainment; VCI)

BLOOD OF DR. JEKYLL, THE (1981) ★★½ Polish filmmaker Walerian Borowczyk's interpretation of Stevenson's classic is fraught with erotic imagery and bloodletting. Udo Kier, Marina Pierro, Patrick Magee, Howard Vernon. Aka *Dr. Jekyll and Miss Osbourne.* (From Citadel as *Bloodlust*)

BLOOD OF FRANKENSTEIN. See *Dracula vs. Frankenstein.*

BLOOD OF FU MANCHU. See *Kiss and Kill.*

BLOOD OF GHASTLY HORROR (1970) Video version of *The Man with the Synthetic Brain.* (VidAmerica; Movies Unlimited).

BLOOD OF HEROES, THE (1989) ★★★½ Surprisingly good existential glimpse into a futuristic world—a welcome change in the post-Armageddon genre. In a desert landscape, battered bands of warriors rove, training for battle games ("The League") staged for the upper crust. Rutger Hauer teams with feisty Joan Chen and other scarred "heroes" to take on the best the League offers in bone-crunching gladiatorial contests. The games become a metaphor for man's fight to achieve and survive, and the script by director David Peoples builds to a satisfying climax despite barren production values. It's Hauer and Chen who make it work intellectually and viscerally. Max Fairchild also shines as Hauer's adversary, giving his brutish character dimension. Made in Australia as *Salute of the Jugger.* Vincent Donofrio, Anna Katarina, Delroy Lindo. (HBO) (Laser: Image)

BLOOD OF THE DEMON. See *Blood of Dracula.*

BLOOD OF THE UNDEAD. See *Schizo* (1976).

BLOOD OF THE VAMPIRE, THE (1958) ★★★½ Inspired by the sanguinary efforts of Hammer, screenwriter Jimmy Sangster offers up sinister Callistrastus (Donald Wolfit, of grand theatrics) who conducts blood experiments in an asylum. A superior British chiller, reeking with period atmosphere and doom. Full of the blood and gore Hammer made so fashionable, enhanced by Barbara (*Cat Woman*) Shelley as a heroine undergoing blood transfusions and Victor Maddern as the Igor-style aide-de-campy to the mad doc. Directed by Henry Cass. Milton Reid, John Le Mesurier. (Magnet; MPI; Gorgon)

BLOOD OF THE WEREWOLF. See *I Was a Teenage Werewolf.*

BLOOD ON HIS LIPS. See *The Hideous Sun Demon.*

BLOOD ON SATAN'S CLAW, THE (1971) ★★★ Gruesome British supernatural chiller (tensely directed by Piers Haggard from Robert Wynne-Simmons' script) concerns the Devil afoot in 17th-century England, turning the kiddies in surrounding farmlands into cauldron-stirring witches and warlocks. Exorcism is employed by a noble Englishman (Patrick Wymark) sworn to destroy the cult. Period atmosphere and costuming are excellent. Aka *The Devil's Touch, Satan's Skin* and *Satan's Claw.* Linda Hayden, Barry Andrews, Tamara Ustinov. (Paragon; Cannon)

BLOOD ORGY. See *The Gore Gore Girls.*

BLOOD ORGY OF THE SHE-DEVILS (1973) ★ Quadruple threat Ted V. Mikels (writer/director/producer/editor) offers little blood during sacrificial rites, a few hardly dressed she-devils (their choreography would roll Busby Berkeley over in his grave) and no orgy at all. It's black magic mumbo jumbo as a queen of the witches, living in a California mansion (in Orange County, maybe?), practices the blackest of arts on the lowest of budgets. Lots of dialogue about psychometry, regression, white magic, etc., but it builds to a big letdown. Lila Zaborin, Leslie McRae, Tom Pace. (Western World; from Lettuce Entertain You as *Female Plasma Suckers*)

BLOOD RAGE (1983) ★ This *Halloween* imitation has but a single twist: A slasher killer recently escaped from an asylum has a lookalike twin, and no one can tell them apart. So, pals, which one is the real killer? And that's all this independent film (made in Jacksonville, FL) has to offer. Ed French's makeup and gore effects are nothing special and the murders are all telegraphed. Directed flatly by John M. Grissmer. Louise Lasser, Mark Soper, Marianne Kanter, Julie Gordon. Aka *Nightmare at Shadow Woods.* (Prism)

BLOODRAGE (1979) ★ Pointless bloodbath as a mental case stalks the sleazy districts of New York City, attacking anyone he can get his homicidal hands on. Directed by Joseph Bigwood. Lawrence Tierney, Ian Scott, James Johnston. (Marquis; from Best Film & Video as *Never Pick Up a Stranger*)

BLOOD RELATIONS (1988) ★★★ Respectable Canadian-produced chiller set in a mansion where surgeon Jan Rubles is grieving over his wife's death when his son (Kevin Hicks) and girlfriend (Lydie Dernier) visit. What they don't know: Rubles has stored his wife's brain in a fresh cranium. Ray Walston plays an old man in the house who is dying. Frankenstein horror mixed with who'll-get-the-inheritance plot. Directed by Graeme Campbell. (Video/Laser: Nelson)

BLOOD RITES. See *The Ghastly Ones.*

BLOOD ROSE (1969) ★★ Plastic surgeon Howard Vernon steals the faces of beautiful women and grafts them onto the fire-scarred countenances of his once-gorgeous wife in this sexually alive French horror film written-directed by Claude Mulot. Frederic Lansac, Elizabeth Teissier, Philippe Lemaire, Michele Perello, A. Duperey. Aka *The Burnt Rose*, *The Flayed Rose* and *Ravaged*. (Video)

BLOOD RUBY. See *Ruby*.

BLOOD SABBATH (1972) ★★ Wandering guitarist Tony Geary falls for Yala the water nymph (Susan Damante) and is willing to sacrifice his soul to Aloyta, Queen of the Witches (Dyanne Thorne), for Yala's love. Good ideas in William Bairn's script are weakened, however, by gratuitous nudity (granted us by sexy members of Aloyta's coven) and mediocre gore effects. Its shoddy visuals designed by Hugo Grimaldi are in contrast to a languid love mood. (JLT Films)

BLOOD SALVAGE (1989) ★★★½ In the dark-comedy jugular vein of the *Texas Chainsaw* series, this macabre tale depicts rednecks running a wrecking yard who rig highway accidents and take surviving victims to a barn of horrors, where the family's daffy patriarch (Danny Nelson) slices-dices the bodies. The choicest parts he sells to black marketeer Ray Walston. "Mad Jake" and demented sons close in on traveler John Saxon and family. Crippled daughter Lori Birdsong is subjected to a litany of indignities and horrors. It's a battle of moribund humor as Birdsong outfoxes the brothers, Saxon escapes the barn–dissection center and an alligator slithers around. Done to the tune of "Bringing in the Sheep." Director Tucker Johnston cowrote the subversive script with producer Ken C. Sanders. Christian Hesler, Ralph Pruit Vaughn. (Magnum; Turner; from Malo as *Mad Jake*) (Laser: Image)

BLOOD SCREAMS (1988) ★ Monastery in a Mexican village is haunted by the ghost of a high priest who once ordered a slaughter for the local coven. Trouble begins when traveling magician Russ Tamblyn comes to town. Stacey Shaffer, Ron Sands, James Garrett. Written-directed by Glenn Gebhard. (Warner Bros.)

BLOOD SEEKERS. See *Blood Thirst*.

BLOOD SEEKERS, THE. See *Dracula vs. Frankenstein*.

BLOOD SHACK. Director's cut of *The Chooper* (Mascot).

BLOOD SHED. Video version of *Crazed* (Regal).

BLOOD SISTERS (1973). See *Sisters*.

BLOOD SISTERS (1986) ★ New sorority pledges are taken to an old house where they spend the night. Unknown to all, someone connected with murders 13 years before is stalking the premises, murdering the gals in graphic fashion. The women also hallucinate images of ghosts and eerie phenomena wandering the creepy joint.

Written-directed by Roberta Findlay. Amy Brentano, Shannon McMahon. (Sony; RCA/Columbia)

BLOOD SONG (1982) ★★★ Something to sing about: An unusually tense psychothriller with Frankie Avalon forsaking his clean image to portray a mental patient who escapes from an asylum and stalks a young woman (Donna Wilkes) after axing her father (Richard Jaeckel) to death. Good scary thriller. Directed by Alan J. Levi and Robert Angus. Antoinette Bower, Dane Clark. (Abacus; Coast to Coast; from HQV as *Dream Slayer*)

BLOOD-SP(L)ATTERED BRIDE, THE (1969) ★★ Spanish variation on Le Fanu's "Carmilla," as newlyweds Simon Andreau and Maribel Martin, after a slow wedding night, finally get down and dirty with depravity and perversion. This sets the mood for a shrouded woman (Alexandra Bastedo), a reincarnation of long-dead Carmilla who enjoys blood from a human wrist and making lesbian passes at Maribel. The first hour moves slowly under Vincente Aranda's writing-direction. When murders occur, it's too late. Dean Selmier, Monserrat Julio. Aka *Blood Castle*. (Gorgon; MPI; heavily edited from Vestron as *Til Death Do Us Part*)

BLOODSPELL (1988) ★★ This video feature has plot twists that make it semi-endurable. Anthony Jenkins is possessed by his father's spirit, a form of monster who intends to live inside his son's body and draw off energy. The invaded youth, staying at St. Boniface, a center for disturbed youngsters, turns telekenetic powers to evil means, creating force fields that cause accidents and death for companions. Effects are okay, acting passable. Aaron Teich, Alexandra Kennedy, John Reno. Directed by Deryn Warren. (Forum; MCEG)

BLOOD SPLASH. Video version of *Nightmare* (1981) (Platinum).

BLOODSTALKERS (1976) ★★★ A thinking buff's gore flick, structured by writer-director Robert W. Morgan as a metaphor for man's indifference to his fellow man, and man's isolationism from responsibility. Also known as *The Night Daniel Died*, it starts as a psychological study of two men and two women vacationing in the Florida Everglades. Themes of cowardice and redemption arise when hairy creatures (called "Bloodstalkers" by rural yokels) close in and one of the men (Jerry Albert) seeks help from a community that treats him as an outsider. In a spinoff from *Straw Dogs*, Albert turns into the very character that has spawned his predicament. If this sounds profound, rest assured the film has graphic violence: two are dispatched with an axe, a scythe pinions two more to a wall, and one is hung up to bleed to death. Morgan (who also plays a redneck killer) meshes it into an intriguing tale, and even gets artsy at a gospel church where the action is pantomimed and the soundtrack taken over by black singers. Kenny Miller, Celea-Anne Cole, Toni Crabtree. (Vidmark)

BLOODSTONE: SUBSPECIES II (1993) ★★★½ This sequel to *Subspecies* benefits from Transylvanian/Romanian locations, but Charles Band's vampire thriller is full of disgusting blood drinking, flesh ripping and other distasteful depictions that rob the tale of potential charm. Anders Hove is back as Radu, that Nosferatu-like vampire with the clawy hands, and Denice Duff is the innocent in a filmy nightgown fleeing his clutches, taking with her the mythical relic (the Bloodstone) said to contain the blood of saints. Pamela Gordon steals the show as Radu's "Mummy," a Crypt Keeper type of ghoulish crone who cackles her way into your heart. Meanwhile, Melanie Shatner shows up as Duff's sister and Kevin Blair is an ineffectual State Department jerkola. If you like 'em gross, by all means. Written-directed by Ted Nicolaou. Next: *Bloodlust: Subspecies III.* (Paramount)

BLOOD SUCKERS. Title for *Dr. Terror's Gallery of Horrors*, which was reretitled *Return from the Past.* See that entry.

BLOODSUCKERS (1966). See *Man-Eater of Hydra.*

BLOODSUCKERS (1970) ★★ Vampirism is treated as sexual perversion in this British adaption (by Julian More) of Simon Raven's novel, *Doctors Wear Scarlet.* Released in England as *Incense for the Damned*, it stars Peter Cushing and Patrick Macnee and is enhanced by Cypriot location shooting. A woman searches for her lost fiancé amidst a cult of Satan lovers. Directed by Robert Hartford-Davis as Michael Burrowes. Edward Woodward, Patrick Mower, Imogen Hassal. (Media; Sinister/C; VCL)

BLOODSUCKERS FROM OUTER SPACE (1984) ★ Attempt to parody the sci-fi genre, shot around Hamilton, Texas, is an example of a misfire in the hands of amateurs. An invisible life force "from beyond our atmosphere"—its presence signaled by a strong wind—takes over one's bloodstream, bleeds out all the blood through orifices, then reanimates the body. Effects and acting are substandard and attempts by writer-director Glen Coburn to poke fun at warmongering army officers, mad doctors and narrow-minded Southerners are strained. Thom Meyers, Laura Elis. Pat Paulsen cameos as the U.S. president. (Lorimar; Warner Bros.)

BLOODSUCKING FREAKS. Video version of *The Incredible Torture Show* (Vestron).

BLOODSUCKING NAZI ZOMBIES. Video version of *Oasis of the Zombies* (Trans World).

BLOODSUCKING PHARAOHS IN PITTSBURGH (1989) ★½ In the vein of the *Police Academy* series, stuffed with vomiting, dildo jokes and other gaggery in poor taste, this regionally produced attempt at comedy-horror is as exciting as visiting Pittsburgh. A mysterious figure, pulling a power unit to which electrical tools are plugged in, kills women and takes their bodies to perfect a formula for eternal life. Two dumb cops follow the trail of Jackie Cairo to the Egyptian part of town (full of camels and snake charmers). One funny slasher gag has the killer jamming a parking meter into a victim's stomach as the "Time Expired" flag pops up. Makeup by Tom Savini; script by Dean Tschetter; directed by Alan Smithee (pseudonym). *Bloodsucking Pharaohs* is the pitts. Jake Dengel, Joe Sharkey, Susann Fletcher, Shawn Elliott. (Paramount)

BLOOD THIRST (1965) ★ Another "Blood-Runner" from the Philippines, depicting bloodthirsty sun cultists. Watch this too long and you'll see spots in front of your eyes. Directed by Newt(on) Arnold. Robert Winston, Yvonne Nielson, Judy Dennis, Vic Diaz, Eddie Infante. Aka *The Horror from Beyond* and *Blood Seekers.* (Sinister/C)

BLOOD THIRST (1979). Retitled video version of *Salem's Lot* (On Line Cinema).

BLOODTHIRSTY BUTCHERS (1970) ★ Terrible rehash of *Demon Barber of Fleet Street*, the Sweeney Todd sanguinary saga. Grotesque oddity that panders to the lowest common denominator, dripping with intestines and blood. A batty barber (Berwick Kaller) and a psychotic pastry preparer meld their perversions into one to mutilate victims and sell the leftovers as bargain basement pies. It's the work of infamous cameraman-writer-director Andy Milligan. John Borske, John Miranda. (Midnight/Select-A-Tape)

BLOOD TIDE (1981) ★½ Aka *The Red Tide*, this is a ripoff of *Jaws* in which archeologist James Earl Jones disturbs a sea monster from its "ancient sleep." Island natives Jose Ferrer and Lila Kedrova know legends about the slimy, gnashing Kraken requiring a virginal sacrifice but aren't telling Jones, Mary Louise Weller, Lydia Cornell and Deborah Shelton. Poor Lydia gets eaten while swimming without a bra. Director Richard Jeffries (who wrote with coproducer Nico Mastorakis) never shows the briny beast, just slobbering jaws in flash cuts. It's ebb tide for *Blood Tide.* (Continental; Cinema Group; Planet)

BLOOD TIES (1991) ★★ Failed TV-pilot created by scripters Esther and Richard Shapiro—a blend of vampire horror with the "Dallas"-type series. *Blood Ties* still offers interesting variations on the theme. Belgian actor Patrick Bauchau is the corrupt patriarch of a vampire family working its way up in the business world in Long Beach, CA, and is a kind of "globfather" image to bloodlusting relatives. A nephew (Harley Venton) who works as a newsman tries to escape his heritage by romancing D. A. Kim Johnston-Ulrich, but sex brings out the beast in him and this creates conflicts. And there are times when suave Bauchau turns into a snarling beast—a compelling metaphor for the ruthless businessman. Well produced and directed by Jim McBride. (New Horizons) (Laser: Image)

BLOOD TRACKS (1986) ★★ Rock group in the Rockies (ha ha) shooting a Rock(ies) Video (ha ha) is attacked by crazies living beneath an old factory. Gore and sex aplenty. Directed by Mike Jackson. Jeff Harding, Michael Fitzpatrick, Naomi Kaneda. (Vista)

BLOOD VOYAGE (1977) ★★ Pleasure sailboat bound for Hawaii is the claustrophobic world in which a psycho killer armed with meat cleaver and knives knocks off passengers. These include a troubled Vietnam vet, a buxom bleached blond scheming to murder her stepfather, a drug addict and a lecherous cook. The horror effects are minimal and director Frank Mitchell brings little style or tension to the thriller, which ends with a twist that seems unnecessarily immoral. The only recognizable actor is John Hart, who once played the Lone Ranger. Here he's white haired with matching beard. Jonathan Lippe, Laurie Rose, Mara Modair. (Cinematex; Monterey's version is cut)

BLOOD WEDDING. See *He Knows You're Alone*.

BLOOD WILL HAVE BLOOD. See *Demons of the Mind*.

BLOODY BIRD. See *Stagefright*.

BLOODY BIRTHDAY, THE (1980) ★★ *The Bad Seed* played as a slasher film: Two boys and a girl (all born during a solar eclipse) are instilled with homicidal tendencies on their tenth birthday. Emotionlessly, they beat a man over the head with a shovel, strangle his girlfriend with a rope, kill dad (the sheriff of peaceful Meadowvale) with a bat, shoot a schoolteacher (Susan Strasberg) and ogle a naked girl through a peephole. Is this sick or what? Director Ed Hunt proves you can have your cake and slice people too, but it can't hold a candle to other slasher movies. It'll just frost you. Jose Ferrer, Ellen Geer, Melinda Cordell. Aka *Creepers*. (Prism; Starmaker)

BLOODY CEREMONY. See *The Legend of Blood Castle*.

BLOODY EXORCISM OF COFFIN JOE, THE (1972) ★ In this entry in the Brazilian Coffin Joe series, filmmaker Jose Mojica Marins appears as himself, analyzing what makes Coffin Joe tick . . . tick . . . tick. Gradually his documentary turns into fiction when members of his family become possessed by evil spirits. Others in this series: *At Midnight I'll Take Your Soul, This Night I Will Possess Your Corpse* and *Hallucinations of a Deranged Mind*. (S/Weird)

BLOODY FIANCEE. See *The Blood-Sp(l)attered Bride*.

BLOODY FRENZY (1987) ★ Psychiatrist takes his confused clients into the desert for tranquil analyses, but the group is beset by a psycho killer. Directed by Hal Freeman. Wendy MacDonald, Lisa Loring. (Vestron; Hollywood Family Entertainment)

BLOODY GIRL. Video version of *Fangs of the Living Dead*.

BLOODY MOON (1981) ★ Two killers on a rampage during the Festival of the Moon terrorize Olivia Pascal in this Italian gorefest directed by Jesus Franco and written by Rayo Casablanca. Watch with delight as a woman is burned to death in a wheelchair. Christopher Brugger, Nadja Gerganoff. (CIC; Trans World)

BLOODY NEW YEAR (1987) ★ A boatload of British teenagers occupies an old hotel on an island haunted by attendees of a 1960 New Year's Eve's party, who somehow have gotten mixed up in a time-space continuum warp-bend. At least that's what screenwriter Frazer Pearce says. Directed by Norman J. Warren. Aka *Time Warp Terror*. Suzy Aitchison, Nikki Brooks, Colin Heywood. (Academy)

BLOODY PIT OF HORROR (1965) ★½ Italian mishmash of torture scenes should delight sadists, masochists and other flagellators. Mickey Hargitay, one-time hubby of movie queen Jayne Mansfield, cracks a mean whip as the Crimson Executioner in a castle equipped with the latest torture devices. Visiting the high stone are beautiful models to pose for book covers, but instead they pose their last for Mickey. Massimo Pupillo (as Max Hunter) directed this form of viewing torture from the torturous (to read) script by Roberto Natale and Romano Migliorini. Allegedly based on the memoirs of the Marquis de Sade; his spirit should return and sue for defamation, if not residuals. Walter Brandi, Louise Barrett, Ralph Zucker. Aka *The Castle of Artena, The Red Hangman, The Crimson Executioner, Some Virgins for the Hangman, Virgins for the Hangman, The Scarlet Executioner, The Scarlet Hangman* and *A Tale of Torture*. Whew! (Sinister/C; S/Weird; Filmfax)

BLOODY POM-POMS. See *Cheerleader Camp*.

BLOODY SCREAM OF DRACULA. See *Dracula—Prince of Darkness*.

BLOODY SECT, THE (1982) ★ The sperm of the Devil is deposited in an artificial insemination bank and used to impregnate three women. Will one of them give birth to a little Devil? Spanish film directed by Steve McCoy from a John Wood script. Mery Kerr, Carlos Martos, Josephine Varney, John Zanni.

BLOODY VAMPIRE, THE (1960) ★★ Footage from a Mexican serial reedited by American producer A. K. Gordon Murray. It's Count Cagliostro, good aristocracy, against Count Frankenhausen, evil aristocracy. Directed-written by Miguel (Michael) Morayta. Carlos Agosti, Begona Palacios, Raul Farrell. Sequel to *Invasion of the Vampires*. Aka *Count Frankenhausen*. (Sinister/C; S/Weird; Filmfax)

BLOODY WEDNESDAY (1985) ★★★ Offbeat study of a man (Raymond Elmendorf) who slowly sinks into madness to become a mass murderer. Based on the 1984 incident at a San Diego hamburger shop where diners were killed by a rampaging gunman, this was written and coproduced by veteran screenwriter Philip Yordan. The incidents are an odd mix of reality and hallucination. Harry is staying in a deserted hotel and he meets an old bellboy who tells him of a past that begins to recur. Another oddity is the presence of hoodlums, who pursue Harry and become involved in sparking his final act of insanity. Directed by coproducer Mark G. Gilhuis. Pamela Baker, Navarre Perry. (Prism)

BLUEBEARD (1972) ★★ Ladykiller Richard Burton can't make love to ladies so he kills them as they surrender sexually. And what lovely victims: Raquel Welch (as a nun), Nathalie Delon, Karin Schubert, Marilu Tolo, Virna Lisi, Sybil Danning. Each curdling murder is recounted by Bluebeard to his bride/next-victim-to-be Joey Heatherton, who psychoanalyzes the Count one dark night. Director Edward Dmytryk provides titillation, soft-core nudity, lesbianism, sadism. But scenes are played so flatly, one doesn't know if to laugh or scream. So just cry. (USA; IVE)

BLUE BOY, THE (1994) ★★★½ This *Masterpiece Theater* presentation is a chilling horror tale with a gothic British twist. Emma Thompson and Adrian Dunbar are a married couple undergoing marital nonbliss when Dunbar's former lover (Eleanor Bron) turns up just when Thompson learns she's pregnant. Set in a dark, brooding area of the Scottish Highlands, *Blue Boy* is chilling in its use of the supernatural (the title refers to a youth drowned in a nearby lake many years before) and realistic in its depiction of man-woman conflict. Thompson and Dunbar capture the couple's anguish and Bron is a real bitch as the other woman. Written-directed by Paul Murton.

BLUE DESERT (1991) ★★★ Courteney Cox, a New York City comic-book artist whose specialty is a femme strip called "The Iron Medusa," is a victim of recurring rapist attacks so she leaves Big Town to live modestly in a small desert community where she meets a demented motorcyclist (Craig Sheffer) and a friendly sheriff (D. B. Sweeney). One of them is out to mislead and murder her, but you won't know for sure which one it is, as director Bradley Battersby (who cowrote the script with Arthur Collis) keeps you guessing with one cat-and-mouse Hitchcockian game after the other, making each suspect seem guilty-innocent, guilty-innocent an equal number of times. Cox gives quite a cred-

ible performance as a repressed, lonely woman, and Sheffer is especially effective at capturing the confused state of the drifter. Joel Goldsmith's music helps this minor effort that strives mightily to be different. Philip Baker Hall, Pete Schrum, Sandy Ward. (Academy/Laser: Image)

BLUE FLAME (1993) ★½ If anyone out there can make sense out of this alleged sci-fi mind-games adventure, written-directed by Cassian Elwes, please fax in the details. Until then, here's what seems to be happening: Brian Wimmer is an investigator for ACTCON, a government unit dealing with alien contact in A.D. 2018. His daughter is kidnapped by humanoid E.T.s Wind (sexy Kerri Green) and Fire (Jad Mager) who, two years later, begin a series of inner-mind deceptions, designed to lead Wimmer to his missing daughter, that take place in "another dimension." Is this Wimmer's mind? Some alternate reality created by aliens? A Virtual Reality vidgame? Who knows? It's computerized crap. Anyway, Wimmer, a violent, hate-filled cop, is seduced and shot several times, always emerging in one piece to undergo the next ridiculous encounter in which characters talk in riddle-me-this dialogue and philosophical balderdash. This is so unbelievably incomprehensive, one wonders what exec producer David Niven, Jr., saw in the muddled material. Fax us, Dave. Melissa Behr, Ian Buchanan, Joel Brooks, Cecilia Peck, Charley Hayward. (Video/Laser: Columbia TriStar)

BLUE HOLOCAUST. See *Buried Alive* (1979).

BLUE MAN, THE. See *Eternal Evil*.

BLUE MONKEY (1987) ★★★½ Monster thriller set in a county hospital where a man cut by a thorn on a flower plant spits up a caterpillar-like form, which turns into an insect. When the leggy creature is sprayed with NAC-5, a life-force accelerator, it turns into a giant monster spawning new larvae. After the thing go cop Steve Railsback, doctor Gwynyth Walsh and entomologist Don Lake. While this Sandy Howard production is an *Alien* rip-off, it builds suspense and has believable characters, thanks to George Goldsmith's script, which brings in a laser experiment and a quarantine. Director William Fruet rolls his camera through a labyrinth of corridors and photographs the final battle, in a laser lab, breathlessly. Above average for a video movie. John Vernon portrays the head of the hospital. Susan Anspach, Robin Duke, Joe Flaherty, Judith Glass. (RCA/Columbia; from Winson as *Insect*)

BLUE SUNSHINE (1977) ★½ LSD derivative causes students to lose their hair and sanity. Writer-director Jeff Lieberman (he who gave us *Squirm*) weaves a detective story (Zalman King searches for the source of "blue sunshine") and a political cover-up plot. But it doesn't cover up what amounts to a bad trip. You'll feel blue and need sunshine. Deborah Winters, Robert Walden, Mark Goddard, Ann Cooper. (Vestron)

BLUE THUNDER (1983) ★★★★ State-of-the-art helicopter (with infrared and eavesdropping devices, not to mention knockout firepower) traverses the skies over L.A., eventually engaging in combat with another superchopper. It's a rousing high-tech actioner with pilots Roy Scheider and Daniel Stern picking up on a military conspiracy and shooting it out in super-exciting fashion with bad guy Malcolm McDowell amidst skyscrapers. Great movie action, technically superior. Directed by John Badham, scripted by Dan O'Bannon and Don Jakoby. Warren Oates, Joe Santos, Candy Clark. (Video/Laser: Columbia TriStar)

BLUE TIGER (1994) ★★★ An ancient Japanese legend hangs over this mystical tale of revenge: The Blue Tiger is always in search of the Red Tiger, and fate will bring them together. After her son is killed in a pharmacy shootout between rival gangs fighting over the tour-bus trade, Virginia Madsen gets a Blue Tiger tattoo from Harry Dean Stanton and transforms herself into a femme fatale who infiltrates the Yakuza, the Japanese Underworld, to nail those who killed her son—on both sides. A psychic relationship develops between Madsen (who is excellent in this role) and assassin Toru Nakamura as Joel Soisson's script depicts a number of violent shootouts in the John Woo tradition. Director Noberto Barba captures a sense of mysticism with his shots of L.A.'s Little Tokyo, and *Blue Tiger* comes off as very odd and compellingly hypnotic. Dean Hall, Ryo Ishibashi, Sal Lopez, Yuji Okumoto. (Columbia)

BLUE YONDER, THE See *Time Flyer*.

BLUNT. See *The Fourth Man.*

BOARDING HOUSE (1982) ★ Pretty girls move into a haunted house, oblivious to warnings about its bloody past. Sure enough, a woman's spirit haunts the premises, and blood flows hot only after it's run cold. Directed by John Wintergate. Alexandra Day, Joel Riordan. (Paragon; from Classical as *Housegeist*)

BOARDING SCHOOL, THE (1969) ★★★ Polished Spanish horror film set in a 19th-century boarding school for young women. A touch of class is provided by Lilli Palmer as the headmistress. The film excellently captures the oppressive sexual needs of the girls with erotic artsy intercutting, heavy lesbian overtones and one intense hazing scene. Suddenly the girls are attacked by a knife killer. It's the style of director Narciso Ibañez Serrador that makes this enjoyable. Scripted by Luis Verna Penafiel. Cristina Galbo, Mary Maude, John Moulder Brown. Aka *The House That Screamed.* (Vestron)

BODIES BEAR TRACES OF CARNAL VIOLENCE, THE. See *Torso.*

BODY BAGS. See *John Carpenter Presents "Body Bags."*

BODY BENEATH, THE (1970) ★ Writer-director-photographer Andy Milligan offers you a painful, tedious (to watch) experience in which reverend Gavin Reed and wife Susan Heard take over Carfax Abbey. Aha, they're from a long-descending line of vampires that inbreeding is destroying. Now the Rev needs to rev up with a blood transfusion. Meanwhile, innocent descendant Jackie Skarvellis shows up (the in-house coven wants her child to shore up the family tree) to be terrorized by an Igor-style assistant. One maid gets her eyes punctured with stakes, a man is nailed to the door of Old Souls' Church and other bloodletting abounds, and all one can do is pray it will end quickly—the film, we mean. Aka *Vampire's Thirst.* Berwick Kaler, Richard Ross, Emma Jones. (Western World)

BODY COUNT (1988) ★ Slasher thriller starring Bernie White as a nutty guy who escapes from a mental institution and kills all those he meets. Marilyn Hassett, Dick Sargent, Steven Ford, Greg Mullavey. Aka *The Eleventh Commandment.* Produced-written-directed by Paul Leder. (Forum; MCEG)

BODY DOUBLE (1984) ★★★½ Brian De Palma's most outrageous work—he takes narrative liberties and defies credulity to spin this strange story about a horror film actor (Craig Wasson) fascinated by a woman he spies on through a telescope. Soon Wasson is into a mystery that includes a terrifying electric drill murder and a sleazy glimpse into the L.A. underground of pornographic moviemaking. De Palma is a master at suspense in the Hitchcock tradition, and uses bits from his own films, even satirizing *Dressed to Kill* in the closing credits. Gregg Henry, Melanie Griffith (as Holly, pornie queen), Deborah Shelton (as erotic, alluring Mrs. Revelle), Guy Boyd (as the cop). (Video/Laser: Columbia TriStar)

BODY MELT (1993) ★★ Gruesome gore stuff, from Australia, in which mad doc Ian Smith discovers a vitamin pill that causes its takers to hallucinate and undergo self-destruction, such as exploding when it's least appropriate. Plenty of graphic carnage earmark this film from writer-director Philip Brophy. Gerard Kennedy, Andrew Daddo, Vince Gil. (Video/Laser: Prism)

BODY PARTS (1991) ★★★½ It took Hollywood 25 years to make this, but it was worth the wait, for it's a macabre horror tale establishing good characters and suspense before delivering a ghoulish climax. It was inspired by *Choice Cuts*, the award-winning 1965 novel by French writers Pierre Boileau and Thomas Narcejac, whose earlier fictions became the films *Diabolique* and *Vertigo.* Prison psychiatrist Jeff Fahey loses his arm in an auto accident and sinister Dr. Webb (Lindsay Duncan) grafts on the arm of an executed killer. When the arm starts to control itself with acts of cruelty, Fahey discovers three others also have parts of the killer's body and are suffering similar symptoms. What follows makes for one helluva thriller. The adaption is by Norman Snider and Eric Red, who also directed with a sure hand (his own, of course). Give an arm and leg to see this one. Brad Dourif, Peter Murnik. (Video/Laser: Paramount)

BODY PUZZLE (1993) ★★ This Italian psychothriller appears to be a direct ripoff of *Body Parts* (no script credit is given in the dubbed U.S. version) and stars Italians whose names have been Americanized (i.e., Tom Aaron and Frank Quinn), with the exception of Ms. Joanna Pacula, who portrays a woman caught up in a cat-and-mouse game of murder when a killer sends her body parts removed from his victims. This crazy guy, who kills whenever he hears "Night on Bald Mountain" playing on the soundtrack, is of minimal interest as a villain, and the background as to why he's committing the hideous knife murders is all muddled. Directed by Larry Louis. (Tribono)

BODY SHOP (1971) ★ Goremeister Herschell Gordon Lewis would have applauded this pastiche of his bloodworks—a direct steal of *The Bride of Frankenstein* in which mad doctor Don Brandon (billed in the credits as ("America's No. 1 Magician") slices up bodies of sexy women with the help of snarling hunchback assistant Gregory, who smokes cigars during the breaks and is told at one point, "You may as well clean up the mess." Without any story, or even an ending (it just suddenly stops), *Body Shop* is distinguished only by the fact that William B. Girdler, who went on to a brief career as a horror director, wrote the music and contributed to the effects. Written-produced-directed by J. G. Patterson. Jenny Driggers. (Paragon; from United as *Dr. Gore*)

BODY SNATCHER, THE (1945) ★★★½ Val Lewton, specialist in low-budget films suggesting the unseen, produced this literate adaptation of Stevenson's macabre tale in which body snatcher Boris Karloff inherits the trade of Burke and Hare, creating his own corpses when the cemetery runs dry. Directed by Mark Robson from a Philip MacDonald–Carlos Keith script (Keith is a Lewton nom de plume). Henry Daniell, Bela Lugosi, Edith Atwater, Robert Clarke, Rita Corday. (RKO) (Laser: Image; Turner)

BODY SNATCHERS (1993) ★★★½ "They get you when you sleep," says one who knows of the conspiracy. If that sounds familiar, then be prepared for the fact that there's nothing new in this third adaptation of Jack Finney's classic sci-fi novel, except that this time we get to see how the seed pods from space steal one's soul and shape a lookalike humanoid form inside the or-

ganic pod itself. This is more a sequel than an adaptation, being set in and around a military installation where toxic waste is stored. The pods, as one might expect, are taking over the surrounding communities one by one, and it's up to Gabrielle Anwar and Terry Kinney to escape the clutches of the human monsters and destroy them and warn the rest of mankind—if anyone is left to listen, that is. The paranoia that earmarked the first two versions called *Invasion of the Body Snatchers* (Don Siegel's in 1956; Philip Kaufman's in 1978) is here with all the subtext about alienation, indifference and what happens when we lose the power and humanity of our emotions. It's just disappointing that the excellent filmmakers involved (Abel Ferrara directed; Stuart Gordon, Dennis Paoli and Nicholas St. John wrote the new script) didn't come up with some fresh twists. But hey, fans, you gotta see it. R. Lee Ermey, Billy Wirth, Christine Elise, Meg Tilly, Forest Whitaker. (Video/Laser: Warner Bros.)

BODY STEALERS, THE. See *Invasion of the Body Stealers.*

BOG (1978) ★½ There's this Bog Lake, see, where a fisherman is dynamiting fish, only he shakes up the slumbering Incredible Slime Creature. The rubber-suited hulker kills while baffled sheriff Aldo Ray seeks answers from pathologist Gloria De Haven and doc Marshall Thompson. (He should know, he conquered *The Fiend Without a Face*.) They stare into microscopes and speculate about the creature's blood and breeding habits, since it appears he thrives on type A and loves to smooch with females—human. Finally we see the Bog Monster. Wow! Glug glggglggg . . . Directed by bogged-down Don Keeslar. Leo Gordon turns up as a bayou monster expert from the city. A witch named Adrianna has a psychic link with the monster, and in an odd bit of casting, De Haven plays her too. Thoroughly glgg glgg glgglggg. (Prism)

BOGEY MAN, THE. See *Boogeyman.*

BOGGY CREEK II (1985) ★★ When word leaks out old "Boggy" is on the rampage again, terrifying folks in the South, an anthropologist leads an expedition into the bayou with computerized equipment. Meanwhile, a hermit captures Big Foot's offspring, holding him captive. This is producer-director Charles B. Pierce's soggy sequel to *The Legend of Boggy Creek.* Retitled *The Barbaric Beast of Boggy Creek Part II.* Cindy Butler, Serene Hedin. (Video/Laser: Media)

BONE COLLECTOR, THE (1999) ★★★★ The literary tradition of Sir Arthur Conan Doyle, in which rational detective Sherlock Holmes engages in a battle of wits with his archnemesis Dr. Moriarty, is given a refreshing new context in this taut suspense thriller with overtones of the horror genre. Written by Jeremy Iacone, the film is based on the novel by Jeffrey Deaver, who cleverly disguised the Doyle antecedents by setting his duel of wits in a contemporary albeit sinisterly dark, dank Manhattan. Moriarty has been replaced by a fiendish serial killer who purposely leaves physical clues at the eerie murder scenes. Not obvious clues, but ones that need interpretation in connection with other clues. This brain game is designed to challenge a modern Holmes: NYPD forensic investigator Lincoln Rhyme (love that name!), who is bedridden following an accident that left his body half-crushed. As a man who constantly undergoes attacks to his nervous system and who could become a vegetable if any one attack is too severe, Rhyme is brilliantly played by Denzel Washington, who gives the character charm, humor, a sense of impending doom, and a never-ending drive to solve the crimes from his apartment, which has been equipped with computers and other forensic tools to help in the race against time. (The killer is always setting a deadline and hoping that Rhyme will arrive too late to save the endangered victim.) While *The Bone Collector* might seem overly contrived during its first hour, discerning viewers will spot some of the giveaway clues that hint that the story is not quite what it seems—that there is something far more diabolical at work, that the contrivance is less the screenwriter's than the serial killer's. The supporting cast, working with exceptional Australian director Phillip Noyce, etches memorable characters, especially Angelina Jolie (daughter of actor Jon Voight) as a beat policewoman who first finds the clues at a homicide location that bring Rhyme into the investigation. He sees the makings of a brilliant inspector in her and sends her to the next suspected murder location, where she must face the darkness alone in a tunnel system beneath Manhattan streets. Although Jolie deals with all the clichéd lone-woman-in-peril situations (the script goes out of its way to find rational explanations for sending her into frightening places alone, without the usual police backup), she carries off the part with a mixture of professionalism and terror. Michael Rooker plays the detective in charge of the case who doesn't buy Lincoln Rhyme's techniques and hence is as much a hindrance to a solution as the killer; Queen Latifah is sassy as Rhyme's constant bedside nurse; Luis Guzman is lively as a technician at Rhyme's bedside. Noyce's directorial style captures a twilit New York City with spectacular helicopter shots and murky scenes in train tunnels, sewers, deserted piers, etc. One cannot help but think of *Seven* and *The Silence of the Lambs*, serving as inspiration. Leland Orser, Ed O'Neill, Mike McGlone, John Benjamin Hickey. (Video/DVD: MCA Universal)

BONEYARD, THE (1990) ★★ Psychic Deborah Rose, aided by a detective getting long in the tooth, tracks a cult killer and the trail leads to zombie critters. Written-directed by James Cummins. Ed Nelson, Norman Fell, Phyllis Diller, Denise Young. (Prism) (Laser: Image)

BOOBY HATCH (1985) Superscientist with supererotic scientific equipment sets out to test sexual responses in this sci-fi comedy of the flesh written-directed by John Russo and Rudy Ricci. Sharon Joy Miller, Ruby Ricci, Doug Sortino. (Super)

BOOBY TRAP. See *Wired to Kill.*

BOOGEYMAN (1980) ★★½ Supernatural exploitationer kicks off as a psychostudy of an adolescent knife murderer who grows into a troubled mute. Story line veers to a haunted mirror, pieces of which cause grisly murders à la *The Omen.* Then it segues into a poor man's *Exorcist* as all hell breaks loose with a Catholic priest, flying knives, glowing windows, etc. Finally, disjointed elements refuse to jell and the film babbles to an incoherent closing. Directed by Ulli Lommel, an arty West German filmmaker who went "commercial." Suzanne Love, John Carradine, Nicholas Love. (Wizard; Magnum; Hollywood Home Entertainment) (Laser: Image)

BOOGEYMAN II (1982) ★ This picks up where *Boogeyman* left off with Suzanne Love (also credited with writing the script with producer Ulli Lommel) recapping the plot, which permits director Bruce Starr to use footage from the original and save a buck. But this is twice as awful as its predecessor as a spirit with a piece of mirror embedded in his palm terrorizes half of Hollywood's aspiring young performers. Its only statement is about the filmmaking culture of Hollywood as aspirants (Shannah Hall, Ashley Dubay) gather poolside to discuss vagaries of producers. Otherwise, Ulli still seems hung up on impalings and things shoved into victims' mouths. Barely watchable, said the Elgin salesman without his clothes on. Also known as *Revenge of the Boogeyman.* Shoto von Douglas, Bob Rosenfarb. (VCII)

BOOGIE MAN WILL GET YOU, THE (1942) ★★★ Did you hear the one about the traveling salesman who stopped off at the old Colonial Inn and ended up in a state of suspended animation? He (Boris Karloff) was only a mad scientist but he sure knew how to make his thunder bolt. Bless Karloff's patriotic heart—he wants to transform ordinary men into superheroes for the war effort. Director Lew Landers and writer Edwin Blum play this for light farce, as do Peter Lorre, Maxie Rosenbloom, Jeff Donnell, Don Beddoe and Larry Parks.

BOOK OF THE DEAD. Original title of *The Evil Dead.*

BORDELLO OF BLOOD. See *Tales from the Crypt Presents Bordello of Blood.*

B.O.R.N. (1989) ★ Title is an acronym for Body Organ Replacement Network, a secret organization run by mad sawbones William Smith, who kidnaps women for their organs and sells them for black market transplants. Amanda Blake, in one of her last roles, helps in the search for Ross Hagen's missing daughter. P. J. Soles, Russ Tamblyn, Clint and Rance Howard. Hagen doubled as director and cowriter with Howell. (Prism)

BORN OF FIRE (1984) ★★ Eastern mysticism and religion are the keynotes of this limited-interest tale about a flutist (Peter Firth) and his search for the Master Musician (Oh-Tee), a supernormal being planning to blow up the world. How Firth and girlfriend Suzan Crowley (an ethereal astronomer named Anoukin) will "learn to control forces of the earth" is one of many vaguenesses of this esoteric movie. A djinn runs around (it takes form as snake, scorpion, beast of prey, man or woman) and figures pop in and out to give the film a hallucinatory quality. But watching a deformed man (the Silent One, played by a deformed man, Rabil Shaban) scuttle and seeing Crowley give birth to an insect monster are unpleasant. Far East theologians will dig it the most. Directed by Jamil Dehlavi. (Vidmark) (Laser: Image)

BORROWER, THE (1989) ★★★½ John McNaughton, director of *Henry: Portrait of a Serial Killer*, combines his penchant for chilling horror with a sci-fi theme to spin this bizarre tale about a buglike creature from another planet that is sentenced to exile on Earth, the worst place in the Universe. The alien has been given a human body but keeps losing his head, so he rips off the head of another human and sticks it atop his bloody torso, absorbing that person's personality. (???) So the alien goes from being Tom Towles to Antonio Fargas to . . . meanwhile, hardboiled cop Rae Dawn Chong and her more sensitive partner Don Gordon are on the thing's trail. *The Borrower* is occasionally fun, frequently perverse and gallops toward a double twist-ending. Neil Giumtoli, Pam Gordon. (Video/Laser: Cannon)

BORROWERS, THE (1993) ★ British adaptation of Mary Norton's fantasy novels about a family of people only six inches high living under the floorboards of a normal family is tediously executed, capturing little of the story's effects possibilities. Adapted by Richard Carpenter, directed by John Henderson. Ian Holm, Penelope Wilton, Rebecca Callard. (Turner)

BORROWERS, THE (1997) ★★★ Although stealing from the beleaguered, inept criminals in *Home Alive* and all its subsequent imitators, this is nevertheless a delightfully fun adaptation of the stories by Mary Norton about a family of mini-people (à la *The Incredible Shrinking Man*) living in the basement of a British home and how they defend themselves against Ocious P. Potter, a ruthless property-hungry villain played with relish (and mustard) by John Goodman. Goodman intends to take over and remodel the house, causing no end of troubles for the Clock family—mom and dad (Jim Broadbent and Celia Imrie) and the two kids (Flora Newbigin and Tom Felton). In a world where what we take for granted can be the stuff of traumas and catastrophes, the Clocks fight for survival against not only Potter but his exterminator man (Mark Williams, in a role that's very funny). There's a swirl of special effects and oversized props and a wild and crazy plot, but you are never in doubt that the Clocks will clock in okay. The fun here is watching Goodman and Williams get their comeuppances and seeing the little people extract themselves from cliffhanger situations. Director Peter Hewitt milks all the comedy from the Gavin Scott–John Kamps screenplay, including the sequence where Arriety Clock (Newbigin) is trapped inside a milk bottle as it moves along the assembly line in a milk-bottling plant. (Video: Polygram/DVD: USA Films)

BOUNTY HUNTER 2002 (1992) ★½ Another cheaply produced *Mad Max* wannabe, although it does have the advantage of a sense of humor as reflected through Phil Nordell (as the bounty hunter), who roves the desert in search of a virgin, which in A.D. 2002 brings big bucks. Nordell portrays a traditional antihero, in this case an alcoholic working for a Japanese consortium that wants the virgin. She's played by Francine Lapensee, and she's one tough fighter (and an unconvincing virgin). Jeff Conaway, who plays a crazed religious fanatic, and Vernon Wells, who is Nordell's rival, were associate producers on this crudely made actioner that was directed by Sam Auster. (Action International) (Laser: Image)

BOURBON STREET SHADOWS. See *Invisible Avenger.*

BOWERY AT MIDNIGHT (1942) ★★ Lowbrow Monogram potboiler (aka *Burial at Midnight*) runs out of steam even with Bela Lugosi as the star. In a dual role (as Professor Brenner and as Karl Wagner), Lugosi deposits the victims of his murderous sprees in his basement. What wretched behavior—and what a creaky old Sam Katzman movie. Directed by Wallace Fox from a script by Gerald Schnitzer. John Archer, Tom Neal, Wanda McKay, Dave O'Brien. (Sinister/C; Filmfax; Nostalgia; from Admit One with *Dick Tracy vs. Cueball*)

BOWERY BOYS MEET THE MONSTERS, THE (1954) ★★½ Late-in-life attempt by Leo Gorcey, Huntz Hall and the gang to recapture their goofy encounters with supernatural/sci-fi creatures. In this menagerie of mirthy monsters, the guys fall prey to mad doc John Dehner, whose mansion contains a clumsy robot, Gorgog; sweet old lady Ellen Corby who nourishes a man-eating plant; a formula that turns men into hairy beings; a femme fatale in the tradition of Morticia (Laura Mason); a Lurch-like butler, "Gruesome" Grisham; and a gorilla with an IQ higher than Gorcey and Hall combined. Written by Elwood Ullman and Edward Bernds, who also directed.

BOXING HELENA (1993) ★★★ Jennifer Chambers Lynch, daughter of filmmaker David Lynch, made an auspicious debut as writer-director with this psychological horror tale—an uncompromising study into aberrant human behavior and sexual obsession. Doctor Julian Sands has a thing for the town slut (Sherilyn Fenn, who plays her beautiful, self-indulgent bitch to perfection) and turns her into a captive after an accident leaves her without arms and legs. This macabre joke becomes grounds for a study of sexual behavior as Lynch examines each character's possessive nature. There's no blood or gore; it's the exploration of things hidden in the darkness of man's subconscious that makes this a memorable study. Kurtwood Smith, Bill Paxton. (Orion) (Laser: Image)

BOY AND HIS DOG, A (1975) ★★★½ Harlan Ellison's prize-winning novella about life after nuclear holocaust, faithfully adapted by producer-director L. Q. Jones and assistant producer Alvy Moore. In 2024, young Vic (Don Johnson) roves the devastated surface searching for food and encountering mutant bands. His canine companion, Blood, is capable of ESP and has a radarlike mind. Love among the ruins with beautiful Susanne Benton leads Vic to Down Under, a subterranean society where the males are sterile and Vic is needed to inseminate the gals. Less successful once Up Above is left behind, but still an engrossing sci-fi experiment. Jason Robards, Charles McGraw, Alvy Moore. (Media; Front Row Entertainment; Critics' Choice) (Laser: Image)

BOY AND THE PIRATES, THE (1960) ★★ Bert I. Gordon, king of schlock Z's, slants this innocuous fare for the juvenile set. A youth, propelled through time by a genie, has adventures aboard a pirate ship commanded by Blackbeard. For adults, this picture is equivalent to walking the plank. Filmed in something producer-director Gordon calls Perceptovision. A little "percepto" wouldn't have hurt Gordon. One nice element is Albert Glasser's rousing musical score. Charles Herbert, Susan Gordon, Murvyn Vye.

BOY GOD (1986) ★ Lackluster Filipino production for juveniles, but with such poor effects today's young will sneer at it with adults. Nino Muhlach portrays a youngster blessed with Immortality and superhero powers, who goes on a quest to free his parents from a purgatory in which they are doing penance. He meets bearded guy Vulcan (resembling Old Shazam from Captain Marvel) and fights vampire and lizard men (i.e., actors in ill-fitting animal skins) in poorly choreographed battles. Dreary stuff, dreadfully dubbed. Directed by J. Erastheo Navda. Jimi Melendrez, Isabel Rivas. (Video City)

BOYS FROM BRAZIL, THE (1978) ★★★½ From the best-seller by Ira Levin, who delivered *Rosemary's Baby* and married us to *The Stepford Wives*. The clever plot deals with a Nazi DNA cloning scheme by master German war criminal Dr. Mengele, played unevenly by Gregory Peck. Hot on Mengele's trail, trying to solve a mystery surrounding 94 Hitler clones, is Jewish avenger Lieberman, played with dogged weariness by Laurence Olivier. Franklin J. Schaffner directed. Lilli Palmer, James Mason, Uta Hagen, Michael Gough, John Dehner, Denholm Elliott. (Video/Laser: Fox)

BOYS FROM BROOKLYN, THE. Video version of *Bela Lugosi Meets a Brooklyn Gorilla.*

BOY WHO COULD FLY, THE (1986) ★★★½ The resourcefulness of the human spirit, and the power of positive thought, are the themes of this moving drama written-directed by Nick Castle, best known for *The Last Starfighter.* A mute lad, who has withdrawn into himself and dreams of flying, is befriended by a new family next door undergoing its share of trauma. The small-town ambience, Castle's ability to parody movie form, a collection of benevolent characters, and a lilting musical score enhance this fantasy. Lucy Deakins, Jay Underwood, Bonnie Bedelia, Fred Savage, Colleen Dewhurst, Fred Gwynne. (Warner Bros.) (Laser: HBO)

BOY WHO CRIED WEREWOLF, THE (1973) ★★½ Director Nathan Juran and actor Kerwin Mathews teamed for this lycanthropic tale, but the winning combination that made *The Seventh Voyage of Sinbad* a hit is nowhere in evidence. Mathews is bitten by a werewolf and turns into same, threatening the life of his son. Bob Homel's script is a rehash of wolf man clichés. Elaine Devry, Robert J. Wilke, Jack Lucas, Paul Baxley.

BOY WITH GREEN HAIR, THE (1948) ★★★ Joseph Losey, who was later blacklisted, directed this anti-war allegory about orphan Dean Stockwell, who wakes up one morning to find he has green hair. He is ostracized by his small community except for a band of war orphans (spirits of the dead) who tell him how to put his uniqueness to good use. Gentle, thoughtful, underrated film. Robert Ryan, Pat O'Brien, Barbara Hale, Dwayne Hickman, Russ Tamblyn, Regis Toomey, Walter Catlett. (Nostalgia Merchant) (Laser: Image)

BRAIN, THE (1962) ★★★ Variation on Curt Siodmak's *Donovan's Brain*: Well-meaning doctor Peter Van Eyck keeps alive the brain of a sadistic millionaire who gradually compels the doctor to carry out his evil bidding. This German/British coproduction makes the old material work effectively. Directed by Freddie Francis from a script by Robert Stewart and Philip Mackie. Anne Heywood, Cecil Parker, Bernard Lee, Miles Malleson. Aka *Vengeance, A Dead Man Seeks His Murderer* and *Over My Dead Body*. (Media; Monterey; Nostalgia; Sinister/C; S/Weird; Filmfax)

BRAIN, THE (1971) ★ Sleazy, amateurish mad doctor clunker with Kent Taylor transplanting the brain of a Middle East ruler into the body of Gor, a brute with a putty face who took lessons at the Tor Johnson Acting School. Poor are the performances and wretched are the camera work and music score. Even the sound stinks. There's a dwarf (the doc's assistant), a blond femme (Vicki Volante) and a doltish hero (Grant Williams). Meanwhile, Reed Hadley's voice keeps coming out of Gor's mouth until the brain is switched to Hadley's body. Difficult stuff to endure. Filipino production, directed by Al Adamson and (un)written by Joe Van Rodgers and Kane W. Lynn. Also called *Brain of Blood* and *The Creature's Revenge*. (Star Classics; New Horizon)

BRAIN, THE (1988) ★★½ David Gale, whose "severed" head was an unforgettable element in *Re-Animator*, returns as another crazed doctor, a TV show host using airwaves to brainwash viewers. In his lab is a giant brain that keeps gnashing its teeth and waving its spinal cord tail. This oversized cranium hypnotizes everyone. A paranoia plot is activated when Tom Breznahan and Cyndy Preston are involved with Blake's Psychological Research Institute. While this comments on misuse of TV, and our fear of authority, Barry Pearson's script relies too much on *Alien* clichés. Director Edward Hunt is laden with dreary Canadian locations. Watch for Gale's head in a homage to *Re-Animator*. (IVE) (Laser: Image)

BRAIN DAMAGE (1988) ★★★ Writer-director Frank Henenlotter, mastermind behind *Basket Case*, offers another cult favorite with funky sets and bizarre characters. The monster is Aylmer ("all inspiring famous one"), a thick wormlike thing with teeth and hooks. The hooks he sinks into Rick Herbst's neck, giving his brain a jolt of psychedelic goodies, "color, music and euphoria." Aylmer enjoys boring into your brain and eating it up. For those who think deep, there's a penis fixation to the phallic-looking Aylmer, with sexual references as Aylmer shoots "juice" to the youth. And there's a prostitute who remarks "you've got a monster in there" before undoing Herbst's zipper and coming face to face with Aylmer. The theme comments on our drug culture and dependence on "monsters" such as cocaine and heroin. Gordon MacDonald, Theo Barnes, Lucille Saint-Peters.

One subway scene pays homage to *Basket Case* with Kevin Van Hentenryck in a cameo. (Paramount)

BRAIN DAMAGE. See *The Brain* (1971).

BRAIN DEAD (1989) ★★ Director Adam Simon found an unproduced 1963 Richard Beaumont script and updated it. Result: An instant video movie. In a lab of jars filled with brains, neurologist Bill Pullman studies the aberrations of the mind, in particular a mad mathematician played by Bud Cort. There are dreams within dreams within nightmares within fantasies as this convoluted, twisted pretzel of a movie unfolds in the craziest way. Bill Paxton, Nicholas Pryor, Patricia Charbonneau, George Kennedy. (MGM/UA)

BRAINDEAD. Theatrical title of *Dead Alive*.

BRAIN EATERS, THE (1958) ★★ This exemplifies the atomic-era paranoia genre, with director Bruno Ve Sota creating a bleak world through tilted camera angles and black-and-white photography. Although he stages the action sequences stiltedly, a semi-documentary effect emerges. From inner earth comes small crawling parasites that bore into victims' necks, taking over their brains. The community of Riverdale faces the onslaught with Ed Nelson (who produced the film) heading the scientific investigators. Leonard Nimoy (billed as "Nemoy") plays an old man in a robe but the script by Gordon Urquhart (based on Robert Heinlein's *The Puppet Masters*) muddles up what he's doing there. Alan Frost, Jack Hill. Aka *The Keepers, The Brain Snatchers* and *Keepers of the Earth*. (Columbia TriStar; Nostalgia; Cinemacabre)

BRAIN FROM PLANET AROUS, THE (1956) ★★ Delightfully campy sci-fi schlocker with John Agar as a nuclear scientist whose head is invaded by Gor, a floating brain that looks like a huge golf ball with half moons for eyeballs. Gor plans to take over Earth but Val, a good-brain "golf ball" from Arous, hides in a dog's head and waits to strike at Gor's "fissure of Orlando," which when injured will render Gor useless. Does one dare call Ray Buffum's script brainless? This "hot blast of gamma" will send you into convulsions of laughter or bore you to tears with the incompetence of Nathan Hertz's direction (he's better known as Nathan Juran). Joyce Meadows plays Agar's long-suffering wife. Makeup by Jack Pierce. (Cinemacabre; Interglobal; Rhino; S/Weird; Filmfax) (Laser: Image)

BRAINIAC, THE (1961) ★ He munched on brains, this wretched-smelling abomination who, 300 years ago, was a respectable baron, until he was burned at the stake by the Spanish Inquisition. He returns to Earth aboard a meteor (?!) in the shape of a hairy monster with long snout, pincerlike hands and droopy forked tongue (?!), thirsting for vengeance. Watch out as that tongue slurps up your intellect. It came from Mexico, but it refused to die, and it comes back to haunt us on *The Late Show*. An Abel Salazar production (he also appears in the cast) directed with complete ineptitude by Chano Urueta and written with equal failings by Adolpho Portillo. German Robles, Rene Cardona. A U.S. version was prepared by K. Murray Gordon. (Hollywood Home Theater; Filmfax; Sinister/C; Dark Dreams; S/Weird)

BRAIN MACHINE, THE (1972). Alternate video version of *Grey Matter* (Paragon).

BRAIN OF BLOOD. Alternate video version of *The Brain* (1971) (Magnum; Regal).

BRAIN OF FRANKENSTEIN, THE. See *Abbott and Costello Meet Frankenstein*.

BRAINSCAN (1994) ★★★ Unusually dark and intense horror film about a young computer user (Edward Furlong), recently scarred in a car accident and living alone, who becomes trapped in the nightmarish world of a new computer game (Brainscan), where he commits a murder and is pursued by a strange cop (Frank Langella). Out of the computer pops The Trickster (T. Ryder Smith), a vile character that represents Furlong's uglier side. This has more depth of character than most horror films thanks to director John Flynn. Amy Hargreaves, Jamie Marsh. (Video/Laser: Columbia TriStar)

BRAINSNATCHER, THE. See *The Man Who Lived Again*.

BRAIN SNATCHERS, THE. See *The Brain Eaters*.

BRAINSTORM (1983) ★★★½ Offbeat sci-fi thriller distinguished by the visuals of director Douglas Trumbull, whose effects excelled in Kubrick's *2001: A Space Odyssey*. Scientists Christopher Walken and Louise Fletcher develop a sensory gadget that records thoughts and emotions onto tape and plays them back via a headpiece, so the receiver undergoes an identical experience. The research sequences are fascinating, with implications that the device allows one to pass to a higher plane of being through a recording of the death experience. Benevolent research director Cliff Robertson gives in to clandestine military forces (who want the device for war), and Walken fights to keep the system out of the wrong hands. The climax is an abstract neoreligious death sequence, but what Trumbull intended is as nebulous as the heavens in which it is set. *Brainstorm*, as written by Robert Stitzel and Philip Frank Messina, tries to reach a metaphysical level, but gets locked out of the Pearly Gates. Joe Dorsey, Alan Fudge, Jordan Christopher. Natalie Wood drowned during filming. (Video/Laser: MGM/UA)

BRAINSUCKER, THE (1988) ★ A murderer posing as a psychiatrist named Dr. Suck uses a corkscrew to knock off his victims in this horror corker from writer-director Herb Robins (*The Worm Eaters*). Shot in Santa Fe, New Mexico. Jonathan Middleman. (Raedon)

BRAIN THAT WOULDN'T DIE, THE (1959) ★★ Transplanted plot about transplanted brains is lifted from brainless horror flicks that should have died. Jason Evers is your run-of-the-slab scientist keeping his fiancée's head alive after her decapitation in a car crash. Now his only problem is to find a female body that turns him on. Once the head is attached, he can proceed with wedding plans. Yucky stuff, as lowbrow as Z movies get, with an awful scene where a monster in a closet yanks a man's arm from its socket. Joseph Green wrote-directed this cheapie, which has developed a cult following among weirdos. Virginia Leith, Adele Lamont. Aka *The Head That Wouldn't Die*. (Warner; Rhino; Filmfax; S/Weird; Sinister/C has an unedited version)

BRAIN TWISTERS (1991). A conspiracy is afoot within a software company to carry out mind-control experiments on its buyers through computer games. Written-directed by Jerry Sangiuliano. Terry Londeree, Farrah Forke, Joe Lombardo.

BRAINWAVES (1982) ★★★½ German writer-producer-director Ulli Lommel helmed this fascinating thriller: Accident victim Suzanne Love, suffering brain damage, is fed (via computer) the thought impulses from a brain donated to a lab run by strange Dr. Clavius (Tony Curtis). While the impulses are designed to return her to normal, she has memories of a murdered woman. How Love and Keir Dullea track down the murderer and deal with the psychological terrors make for an unusual plot. Curtis has an odd role as hoarse-voiced Clavius. Vera Miles, Percy Rodrigues, Paul Willson. (Embassy; Sultan)

BRAM STOKER'S DRACULA (1992) ★★★★ Francis Ford Coppola cleverly concocted an entertainment designed for the art crowd, his own cult followers and aficionados of traditional vampire movies. This opulent, imaginative version of Stoker's classic novel unabashedly plunges into self-indulgence on occasion, yet producer-director Coppola maintains a sure experimental hand. Coproduced by Michael Apted and Robert O'Connor, it was written by James V. Hart and closely follows Stoker's novel, evolving its own visual style and moods. Gary Oldman is superb in the title role, appearing in various guises and special makeups as he matures from Vlad the Impaler in a surrealistic sequence (a high point of many high points) to a centuries-old Dracula to a chilling gargoyle-like version. It's a perverse love story as Oldman's Dracula pursues Winona Ryder's Mina; their "romance" soars to new heights of screen erotica in this movie for the senses. Anthony Hopkins is an eccentric Van Helsing, Keanu Reeves is Jonathan Harker, Richard E. Grant is Dr. Jack Seward, Tom Waits is Renfield. (Video: Columbia TriStar) (Laser: Voyager)

BRAVESTARR (1988) ★★ American cowboy and supernatural sidekick Tex Hex are asssigned to rescue the planet of New Texas from a robot-monster invasion in this animated feature directed by Tom Tataranowicz. Voices: Charles Adler, Susan Blu, Pat Fraley. (Celebrity)

BRAZIL (1986) ★★★½ Prepare for two hours of the bizarre in this high-tech, high-energy surrealistic fantasy set in a futuristic quasidictatorship, where everything is askew in a Monty Python way, thanks to writer-director Terry Gilliam. Jonathan Pryce, as a worker in the Ministry of Information, plots against a bumbling "Big Brother" government in hilarious ways and fantasizes himself as a warrior always rescuing a blonde from a giant samurai. Imaginative and free-wheeling, sometimes to the detriment of story and character: It's difficult to relate to people who act so unpredictably. The sets and model work are fabulous, but one wishes Gilliam had restrained his indulgencies to tell a more impactful narrative. Don't miss it, however. Robert De Niro assists as a furnace repairman acting as a terrorist-commando against the regime. Ian Richardson, Kim Greist, Bob Hoskins, Michael Palin. (Video/Laser: MCA)

BREAKDOWN. See *Freeway Maniac*.

BREAKFAST OF ALIENS (1989) ★★ Milquetoast Vic Dunlop swallows a miniature alien and is taken over by the E.T. force within him. It's enough to put a lump in your throat. Written by Dunlop (a stand-up comedian) and coproducer/director David Lee Miller. Indy Shriner, John Hazelwood, Steve Franken. (Hemdale)

BREAKING POINT (1993) ★★ Another derivative serial-killer thriller, this one about "The Surgeon," a homicidal, knife-wielding maniac and part-time male stripper (Jeff Griggs) who plays cat-and-mouse with ex-cop Gary Busey by threatening to murder his wife (Kim Cattrall). Filmed in Vancouver under the direction of Paul Ziller, *Breaking Point* has all the stereotypes and clichés of the genre (blame screenwriters Michael Berlin and Eric Estrin for that) and only the presence of Darlanne Fluegel to liven up things, for she's a feisty, beautiful cop out to avenge the death of her sister.

BREEDERS (1986) ★ Uneven attempt to blend visual sci-fi with softcore sex, the latter cheapening an idea better played without titillation. Manhattan virgins are impregnated by an otherworld beast to the puzzlement of doctor Teresa Farley and cop Lance Lewman. They discover the breeding grounds beneath the hospital, where babes drench themselves in a tub of alien sperm. Effects are good but director-writer Tim Kincaid goes wrong in casting the virgins against type. There isn't a single one that could

pass the test—these women have been around! Ed French, a doctor under the alien's spell, designed the effects. (Wizard; Vestron)

BRICK BRADFORD (1947) ★★ Fifteen-chapter Columbia serial based on the adventure comic strip by William Ritt and Clarence Gray, starring Kane Richmond as an adventurer who travels to the moon through a "crystal door" in an effort to stop madman Charles Quigley from using the Interceptor Ray, a new guided missile that could destroy Earth. Directed by Spencer Gordon Bennet, produced by schlockmeister Sam Katzman. Rick Vallin, Linda Johnson, John Merton, Pierre Watkin. (Heavenly Video)

BRIDE, THE (1985) ★★★½ Excellent variation on Shelley's *Frankenstein*, beginning where *The Bride of Frankenstein* left off and reminiscent of Hammer's gothic thrillers. After a rousing opening as lightning bolts bring a woman to life in the Baron's lab, this follows the Baron (played sensitively by Sting) teaching worldly ways to the bride-to-be; and the Monster (Clancy Brown, wearing little makeup and emphasizing the emotional rather than physical) joining a dwarf circus performer (David Rappaport) on the road to Budapest to learn he must "follow your heart." A fresh visualization of the parable aspects of Shelley's book, handsomely directed by Franc Roddam. Jennifer Beals, as the Bride, develops into an independent woman. Anthony Higgins, Geraldine Page. (Fox) (Laser: RCA/Columbia)

BRIDE AND THE BEAST, THE (1960) ★ "Nightmare from the jungle! A human bride, enslaved victim of gargantuan HORROR!" But that's the ad; the movie is never as exciting. Hunter Lance Fuller decides an African safari is what wife Charlotte Austin needs—until she's stolen away by an ape. Produced-directed by Adrian Weiss; scripted by Edward D. Wood Jr., who gave us *Plan 9 from Outer Space*. Aka *Queen of the Gorillas*. Johnny Roth, Stevel Calvert. (Weiss Global; Admit One)

BRIDE OF BOOGEDY (1987) ★★★ Part of a series of TV programs produced by Walt Disney about Mr. Boogedy, a New England ghost with a magical cloak, this TV-movie is a fun-filled supernatural comedy for children in which the mean-spirited spirit plagues gag-toy designer Richard Masur and his family when they move into Boogedy's old mansion in Lucifer Falls. The Halloweenish special effects and scary tomfoolery will please the kids, and there's the added bonus of Karen Kondazian playing a crystal ball-gazing fortune teller and Vincent Schiavelli as creepy graveyard keeper Lazarus. Mimi Kennedy, Tammy Lauren, David Faustino, Joshua Rudoy.

BRIDE OF FENGRIFFEN. See *And Now the Screaming Starts*.

BRIDE OF FRANKENSTEIN, THE (1935) ★★★★★ James Whale's sequel to *Frankenstein* is a masterpiece of macabre humor and Gothic horror thanks to an intelligent script by William Hurlbut and John Balderston. Colin Clive is again at work in the lab as the ambitious, misguided doctor resurrecting the dead and seeking to create a "mate" for the Monster. A delightful subplot involves the miniaturization of beings by the glint-eyed Dr. Pretorious (Ernest Thesiger), and there's the meeting between the Monster and the blind beggar, spoofed so well in *Young Frankenstein*. Boris Karloff recreates his shambling entity of evil and pathos, while Elsa Lanchester doubles as the bride and Mary Wollstonecraft Shelley. Valerie Hobson, Dwight Frye, John Carradine, Una O'Connor, Billy Barty. Music by Franz Waxman. Early proposed titles: *The Return of Frankenstein* and *Frankenstein Lives Again!* (Video/Laser: MCA)

BRIDE OF CHUCKY (1998) ★★½ The only thing that makes this fourth entry in the *Child's Play* horror series watchable is screenwriter Don Mancini's visual and verbal gags as he attempts to inject new satirical life into the dead-doll franchise. Chucky, the doll possessed by the soul of the Lakeside Strangler, is rescued from an "Evidence Repository" by sexy blond Jennifer Tilly, who once loved the serial killer when he was still in human form. Resurrecting Chucky with the help of the usual incantation and a pentagram, the femme fatale encourages the doll to kill her lover Damien (Alexis Arquette) just for laughs. But then Tilly becomes too bitchy for her own good and gets electrocuted in her bubble bath—by Chucky, of course. Chucky (voice by Brad Dourif) does the usual incantation and Tilly's soul pops into a bridal doll named Tiffany. The pair of lover dolls' domestic quibbles is where the fun comes in for the next hour, with Mancini's minimal plot taking second position. "That's the work of a true homicidal genius," comments Tiffany (voice by Tilly) on Chucky's bloody handiwork, then adds: "I wouldn't marry you if you had the body of GI Joe." Then they're seen reading *Voodoo for Dummies,* because Chucky needs a magical amulet that was buried with the Lakeside Strangler. So off the poisonous playthings go in a van with runaway teens Katherine Heigl and Nick Stabile, after the treacherous toys have killed Heigl's mean old father (John Ritter) by driving nails into his forehead. *Bride of Chucky* really goes freaky when everyone reaches the Hackensack grave site where Chucky seeks the amulet, the only device that will enable him to transfer his soul to a human. Director Ronny Yu (*Warriors of Virtue*) tries to be as irreverent and shocking as possible, and stages a graphic final battle between the two dolls, who after a few days of married life would rather kill each other

than members of the human cast. This outrageous movie ends on a revolting note that would allow a fifth film to follow, no doubt called *The Son of Chucky and Tiffany*. How the loving couple pull it off can only be explained with blueprints of their plumbing systems. Details to follow from producer David Kirschner, who also designed Chucky and Tiffany. The "Double-Devil-Doll-Package" should be in the stores any day now. (Video/DVD: Universal)

BRIDE OF RE-ANIMATOR (1989) ★★★½ Although not as impactful as Stuart Gordon's trend-setting *Re-Animator*, this sequel is worth seeing for its surreal, nightmarish climax. Dr. Herbert West (Jeffrey Combs), the creation of H. P. Lovecraft, is back with his green serum that gives life to dead tissue. It's eight months later at Miskatonic Medical School and Dr. West joins Dr. Cain (Bruce Abbott) to graft the head of Cain's dead lover onto various body parts: the feet of a ballet dancer, the legs of a prostitute, the womb of a virgin, the hand of a sculptress, another hand of a murderess, and the arms of a lawyer. Meanwhile, the head of Dr. Hill (David Gale) returns to life, zombie creatures break loose and a cop with a severed hand runs rampant. It's one helluva horror scene when these components merge. Brian Yuzna directed the Woody Keith–Rick Fry script. Grand effects work by David Allen, the K.N.B. EFX Group and Screaming Mad George. Claude Earl Jones, Fabiana Udenio (as the thankless, jeopardized love interest), Kathleen Kinmont (as the Bride), Mel Stewart. (Live) (Laser: Image)

BRIDE OF THE ATOM. See *Bride of the Monster*.

BRIDE OF THE MONSTER (1955) ★★ Edward D. Wood Jr. "classic," originally *Bride of the Atom* and *The Monster of the Marshes*, revealing a Bela Lugosi ravaged by drugs and alcohol. The plot (Alex Gordon helped Wood with the concept) has Lugosi creating a race of atomic supermen, without a lot of luck, and feeding victims to a swamp monster that looks like half of an octopus. Tor Johnson, the obligatory brainless brute, makes a grab for Lugosi in one of the most pathetic fights ever photographed. And dig those amateurs, Tony McCoy and Loretta King. You have to see it to believe it. (Video Yesteryear; Sinister/C; Filmfax) (Laser: Lumivision)

BRIDES OF BLOOD/BRIDES OF BLOOD ISLAND/ BRIDES OF DEATH. See *Brides of the Beast*.

BRIDES OF DRACULA (1960) ★★★ After *Horror of Dracula*, Christopher Lee refused to play the caped count for a few years, so David Peel assumed the role. Peter Cushing returns as Dr. Van Helsing, the "exorcist" of Transylvania. This excellent Hammer film features silver chains, holy water and a strangely formed "cross" which repels the handsome Peel. Terence Fisher directed using heavy Freudian symbolism. Anthony Hinds produced; Jimmy Sangster cowrote with Peter Bryan and Edward Percy. Martita Hunt, Yvonne Monlaur, Freda Jackson. (Video/Laser: MCA)

BRIDES OF DR. JEKYLL. See *Dr. Orloff's Monster.*

BRIDES OF FU MANCHU, THE (1966) ★★½ In this sequel to *The Face of Fu Manchu*, the insidious, inscrutable Asian mastermind (Christopher Lee) has another incredible scheme—to kidnap sexy daughters of government officials and throw the world into political chaos. Out to thwart the scheme is Nayland Smith (Douglas Wilmer) of the Yard. Lee also has a new Death Ray. Directed by Don Sharp, who coscripted with Harry Alan Towers (as Peter Welbeck). Preceded by *The Face of Fu Manchu* and followed by *The Vengeance of Fu Manchu, Kiss and Kill* and *The Castle of Fu Manchu*. Howard Marion-Crawford, Burt Kwouk, Tsai Chin, Marie Versini, Rupert Davies. (Warner Bros.)

BRIDES OF THE BEAST (1968) ★★ First in the "Blood Island" Filipino series produced by Eddie Romero, aka *Brides of Blood, Brides of Death, Orgy of Blood, Terror on Blood Island* and *Brides of Blood Island*. Mad doctor Kent Taylor uses radiation to turn the living into monsters that love to munch on normal folk. Romero was so overcome as director, he hired Gerardo de Leon to help him direct the traffic. John Ashley is the hero, Beverly Hills and Eva Darren the screaming heroines. (Regal)

BRIDES WORE BLOOD, THE (1972) ★ Lackluster vampire flop in which not even the fangs look genuine. Produced in Florida by director Robert R. Favorite, this spins the Legend of the De Lorca Family Curse. In order to make the curse work, old man De Lorca lures four beauties to his mansion. Pedantic and productionless, *Brides* unfolds at a plodding pace, never arousing interest, no matter how much gibberish from Madame Van Kirst, psychic medium, or "conjurations" by De Lorca. Dolores Heiser, Chuck Faulkner, Jan Sherman. (Regal; New Horizon; from Magnum as *Blood Bride*)

BRIDGE ACROSS TIME (1985) ★★★ The London Bridge—transported to Lake Havasu, Arizona, and reconstructed there stone by stone—is the showpiece for this TV-movie in which Jack the Ripper reappears to murder women in his inimitable style. William F. Nolan's teleplay, though an inspired idea, is predictable and follows the standard cat-and-mouse games of stalked victims, baffled police, town politicians wanting to cover up lest tourism decline, etc. E. W. Swackhamer directs with a constant eye on the bridge. It's not bad, just ordinary. David Hasselhoff, Randolph Mantooth, Clu Gulager, Lindsay Bloom, Rose Marie, Adrienne Barbeau. Aka *Arizona Ripper*. (On video from Fries as *Terror at London Bridge*)

BRIGHTON STRANGLER, THE (1944) ★★ Actor John Loder is so obsessed with his role as a strangler in a British stage hit that a concussion during the London Blitz deludes him into thinking he's the murderer he's playing. He takes the train to Brighton to carry out a murder, but the girl he meets, June Duprez, tries to help him sort out his confusion . . . right up to the twist ending. Similar to the 1947 Academy Award winner *A Double Life*, but not as classy. Max Nosseck directed and cowrote with Arnold Phillips. Ian Wolfe, Miles Mander, Rose Hobart, Gilbert Emery. (On a "double bill" from RKO with *Before Dawn*)

BRIMSTONE AND TREACLE (1982) ★★★ Dennis Potter wrote this unusual British study of good vs. evil depicting a stranger (Sting, in one powerful and weirdo role) entering a family's home only to introduce it to supernatural troubles. Metaphysical symbolism and related special effects abound. Directed by Richard Loncraine. Denholm Elliott, Joan Plowright, Suzanne Hamilton. (MGM)

BRITANNIA HOSPITAL (1983) ★★★½ Bizarre British film wavering between satire and outrageous black comedy, well directed by Lindsay Anderson from an imaginative script by David Sherwin. While it makes sport of English institutions, David Sherwin's script has a universality. The setting is a London hospital undergoing turmoil on the day Her Royal Highness visits. A subplot involves a mad doctor who pieces together a Frankenstein Monster from assorted body organs and limbs. When the Creature is brought to life and bites the hand of the doctor that fed it life, this is gruesome and requires strong stomachs. There's also a giant brain called Genesis controlling the administrators. The most irreverent scene has police clubbing rioters while H.R.H. listens to "God Save the Queen." Leonard Rossiter, Malcolm McDowell, Mark Hamill, Alan Bates. (HBO)

BRONX EXECUTIONER (1989) ★ Cyborg killers on a rampage (aren't those mean old cyborg killers always?) in the futuristic Manhattan you loved so much in *Escape from New York*. Woody Strode, Margie Newton, Chuck Valenti. Directed by Bob Collins. (Cannon)

BRONX WARRIORS. See *1990: Bronx Warriors*.

BROOD, THE (1979) ★★½ Disturbing tale from Canada's "king of horror," David Cronenberg, depicting a therapy called psychoplasmics in which the patient changes cell structure through internal anger. Doctor Oliver Reed experiments with Samantha Eggar, who produces a womblike sac on her tummy and gives birth to a brood of deformed, monstrous dwarves who enjoy hammering innocent people to death. In one sickening sequence, Samantha breaks open the membrane of her sac, removes a malshaped human form and licks away the blood. An intriguing idea, but blatantly offensive. Art Hindle, Cindy Hinds, Susan Hogan, Henry Beckerman, Nuala Fitxgerald. (Embassy) (Laser: Image)

BROTHER FROM ANOTHER PLANET, THE (1984) ★★★ A thoughtful, esoteric sci-fier, so satiric in its overview of humans that it becomes precious. Joe Morton portrays a black humanoid alien with three-toed feet and an ability to touch anything broken and make it work. The Brother, stranded on Earth, never speaks during his adventures in Harlem, object lessons in human behavior. Trailing the alien are two interstellar cops. Writer-director John Sayles (one of the aliens) plays them for laughs. A low-budget experimental film, gritty yet charming, with Morton's mimed performance a tour de force. Darryl Edwards, Steve James. (Key)

BROTHER FROM OUTER SPACE (1985) ★ Oh, brother. Send messages via Western Union, not via crummy sci-fi movies. That's an axiom that director Roy Garrett (who cowrote this with John L. Martin) might consider. Maudlin and mawkish to the extreme, this foreign-produced *E.T./Close Encounters* ripoff is allegedly based on a "true" account, but not for a moment does it smack of the truth. Martin Balsam is a Catholic priest who helps a blind woman and her friend to shield a little E.T. twerk in a silver spacesuit from the Army after the creature lands in a small capsule, which has been dropped by a huge gleaming mothership. Man's inhumanity to his fellow man (and extraterrestrials) is the blatant theme of this nonentertaining, mind-deadening nothing movie, which appears to have been filmed in and around San Luis Obispo, CA. Agostina Belli, Silvia Tortosa Davis, William Beger, Geoffrey Reyli.

BROTHER FUTURE (1991) ★★★ Rapper Phill Lelas of modern Detroit is transported through time to Charleston, 1822, awaking to find himself in the midst of a slave revolt. This dramatized history lesson, with no scientific explanation of how Lelas travels through time, shapes into a serious drama with only mild comedic touches when Lelas introduces modern rap lingo to fellow slaves. Based on a true incident (the slave revolt), *Brother Future* is mildly interesting with good performances by Lelas, Carl Lumbly, Moses Gunn and Frank Converse. Written-directed by Roy Campanella II. (Public Media)

BROTHERHOOD OF SATAN, THE (1971) ★★★ Produced by Alvy Moore and L. Q. Jones, and directed by Bernard McEveety, this low-budget supernatural thriller is well photographed and acted by Strother Martin (as the leader of a Satanic cult), with Moore and Jones also in the cast. A coven in a Southwestern town needs children to feed the Devil during sacrificial offerings. William Welch's script has many chilling moments as well as one eerie dream sequence. Charles Bateman, Anna Capri. (RCA/Columbia; Goodtimes) (Laser: Image)

BRUCE GENTRY—DAREDEVIL OF THE SKIES (1949) ★★★ A remote-controlled flying disc of explosive powers is the deadly weapon of the Recorder, an enemy agent who learns it isn't easy to be a dastard when daredevil pilot Bruce Gentry is around. Gentry, created for the comics by Ray Bailey, is played by Tom Neal with gusto in this 15-chapter Columbia serial that features a number of well choreographed fist-fights. Directed by Spencer Gordon Bennet and Thomas Carr; produced by Sam Katzman. Judy Clark, Ralph Hodges, Forrest Taylor. (Heavenly Video)

BRUTE MAN, THE (1946) ★★ Rondo Hatton was a limited talent who enjoyed brief fame as a film ugly. He needed no makeup, for he suffered from a pituitary gland disease. Hatton's popularity was due to his portrayal of the Creeper, a character introduced in *The Pearl of Death*. That character's origin is recounted in this shoddy thriller. A football hero is disfigured in a lab explosion and, in a beauty-and-beast variation, falls in love with a blind pianist between strangulations. These murders are depicted with Hatton's grotesque shadow on a wall as he moves his gnarly hands toward human throats. Call it pathos/bathos terror. Universal considered it repulsive (though it is only dull today) and sold it to PRC, a grade-Z studio. Hatton died the same year *The Brute Man* was released. Directed by Jean Yarbrough. Tom Neal, Jane Adams, Jan Wiley. (Sony; Republic; Admit One) (Laser: Sony)

BRUTES AND SAVAGES. See *Eaten Alive* (1976).

BUBBLE, THE (1966) ★★½ Arch Oboler produced-directed this sci-fi mystery about a community surrounded by a force-field where humans are under alien scrutiny. Some 3-D effects are startling (such as a tray of beer floating out to the audience), others fail miserably. What's really unforgivable: Oboler's script is one-dimensional. Rereleased as *Fantastic Invasion of Planet Earth*. Michael Cole, Deborah Walley, Johnny Desmond, Virginia Gregg, Vic Perrin. (In 3-D from 3-D TV Corp. as *The Zoo*)

BUCKAROO BANZAI. See *The Adventures of Buckaroo Banzai.*

BUCKET OF BLOOD (1959) ★★★½ This classic American-International release (produced-directed by Roger Corman as an exercise in dark humor) depicts the Beat Generation, when pretentious poets wore berets and sat in coffeehouses reciting their works. Dick Miller plays Walter Paisley, a browbeaten busboy at the Yellow Door Coffeehouse who kills a cat and turns it into a sculpture, "Dead Cat." Admired for his "talent," Walter turns to murdering people (a nosy cop, a nude model) and "sculpting" them too for his one-man show. Charles B. Griffith's hip, flip script is full of amusement, such as when a newsboy croaks, "Read all about the man cut in half! Police can find only part of the body!" Paisley was resurrected in Corman's 1985 *Chopping Mall* and enjoyed a 1995 TV revival in a remake. Barboura Morris, Anthony Carbone, Ed Nelson, Bert Convy. (Rhino; Sinister/C; S/Weird; Filmfax)

BUCKET OF BLOOD (1995) ★★★½ A worthy remake of Roger Corman's 1959 satire on the beatnik world, with an updated script that retains all the good satire from the original. Anthony Michael Hall re-creates the role of busboy Walter Paisley, who turns into a murderer who covers his "subjects" in plaster of paris and offers them to the Jabberjaw crowd as "objects of art." Since the fans are all intellectual phonies, Walter fits right into their pretentious scheme of things. Credit the success of this delightfully droll TV-movie to director Michael James McDonald, who cowrote with Brendan Broderick. Thanks, Rog, for not screwing up a good thing. Justine Bateman, Sam Lloyd, Alan Sues, Patrick Bristow, Darcy DeMoss, Paul Bartel. (New Horizons)

BUCK ROGERS (1939) ★★★ In the style of *Flash Gordon* serials also starring Buster Crabbe, this 12-episode Universal cliffhanger, which was directed by Ford Beebe and Saul Goodkind, depicts Buck and Buddy Wade (Jackie Moran) crashlanding their dirigible on a mountaintop and put into suspended animation by a "nirvano" gas. They awaken 500 years later to find the world taken over by Killer Kane (Anthony Warde). Buck battles Kane with Dr. Huer (C. Montague Shaw), Wilma (Constance Moore) and a race of Saturnians. Not as well produced or written as the *Flash Gordon* shows, but still great fun as writers Norman Hall and Ray Trampe conceived it. Feature versions are *Planet of Outlaws* (1953) and *Buck Rogers: Destination Saturn* (1965). (Complete in 12 chapters from UAV and Foothill; in feature form from CBS/Fox as *Buck Rogers Conquers the Universe*)

BUCK ROGERS CLIFFHANGER SERIALS VOLS. I & II. The 1939 full-length serial in a two-box video set. (United)

BUCK ROGERS CONQUERS THE UNIVERSE. Video version of *Buck Rogers*. (CBS/Fox)

BUCK ROGERS IN THE 25TH CENTURY (1979) ★★★ Theatrical version of the TV-pilot produced by Leslie Stevens and Glen A. Larson. A pastiche of *Star Wars* with awesome mothership, comedy-relief robots and cardboard heroes and heroines. Sexual double entendres give it a false sense of being "adult," but it's cornball space opera with Gil Gerard as Buck, Erin Gray as space jockey Wilma Deering, Henry Silva as Killer Kane and Pamela Hensley as the sexually

arousing Princess Ardala Darco. The voice of Twiki the robot is Mel Blanc's. So is the voice of Dr. Theopolis, a miniaturized computer in the shape of a neon disc worn about Twiki's neck. Daniel Haller directed the Larson-Stevens script. Tim O'Connor, Julie Newmar. (Video/Laser: MCA).

BUFFY THE VAMPIRE SLAYER (1992) ★★★ This is not a great vampire comedy but it's fun to watch attractive Kristy Swanson use somersaulting abilities as a cheerleader to battle vampires sucking blood out of the L.A. population. The Valley Girl's chief antagonists are cult leader Rutger Hauer and daffy aide Paul Reubens, but they're too campy to be menacing, so you have to settle for the laughs. Buffy is the descendant of a vampire stalker from the Dark Ages and it's her heritage to carry on the anti-bloodsucker war. Her mentor is Donald Sutherland, a joy to watch as he trains her in fangbusting, and Kristy learns martial arts. Directed by Fran Rubel Kuzui. Luke Perry, Michele Abrams, Candy Clark. (Video/Laser: Fox)

BUG BUSTER (1998) ★ This epitomizes the bad B movie cranked out by inexperienced filmmakers, for it never makes up its mind if it's a dumb-and-dumber comedy or a killer-bug movie with gory thrills. So much does Malick Khoury's script vacillate, not even director Lorenzo Doumani knows what to do with the scenes. On the one hand, he allows Randy Quaid to play ridiculous bug exterminator "General George" (imitating George C. Scott imitating General George S. Patton), and then shows a young woman having nightmares as killer cockroaches and ugly bugs crawl all over her body, including up her leg toward . . . Brenda Epperson Doumani is a serious-minded scientist who provides the background exposition, while Downtown Julie Brown plays an absurd TV reporter named Katie Cunning. Then director Doumani allows bad racist comedy with George Takei as a Japanese bug expert, and then he has James Doohan play it straight as a small-town sheriff, as if he's in the world's most serious movie. Other uninteresting characters are played by Katherine Heigl, Meredith Salenger, Ty O'Neal, David Lipper, and Anne Lockhart. The setting is a rural district where insects have mutated through fish in a nearby lake. When a DDT-type insecticide is sprayed via crop duster, the bugs mutate to worse proportions and begin eating everyone alive. The only special-effects monster is a giant spider in a cave, and that's played for laughs. As one critic of this movie wrote, "Scotty, beam this movie outta here!" (Video/DVD: DMG Entertainment)

BUMP IN THE NIGHT. See *The Final Terror*.

BURBS, THE (1989) ★★★ When weird Addams Family types move into his neighborhood, Tom Hanks and his buddies go dingy, suspecting the newcomers of murder, mayhem and things even worse. Although this is a dumb comedy, aiming for the lowest common denominator, there are sections that look like they were lifted out of horror movies. For that reason, its pseudosupernatural elements might appeal to buffs. Directed by Joe Dante. Carrie Fisher, Rick Ducommun, Corey Feldman, Brother Theodore, Bruce Dern. (Video/Laser: MCA)

BURIAL AT MIDNIGHT. See *Bowery at Midnight*.

BURIAL GROUND (1979) ★ Unengaging Italian zombie-gore flick in which a number of guests at a country mansion gather at the request of "The Professor," a nitwit using arcane Etruscan practices to raise the dead in a nearby cemetery. Corpses with white faces, their skin crawling with maggots, attack and tear apart the humans, munching on their flesh. This George Romero rip-off tripe (script by Piero Regnoli) is more revolting than terrifying, and a scene of a woman (beauteous Maria Angela Giordan) having her nipple bitten off by her adolescent son is almost more than even a dedicated zombie fan will want to bear. Director Andrea Bianchi contributes nothing new to the zombie pantheon with the cliché beheadings, intestine munching, etc. Karin Well, Peter Bark, Gian Luigi Chirizzi, Simone Mattioli, Roberto Caporali. Aka *Zombie Horror* and *Zombie 3*. (Vestron; Live)

BURIED ALIVE (1979) ★ Italian gore thriller from director Aristide Massaccesi (Americanized as Joe D'Amato) about a deranged taxidermist who does strange things with corpses following a fouled-up childhood—such as injecting them with a preservation serum. Aka *Blue Holocaust*. Kieran Canter, Ann Cardini. (Thrillervideo)

BURIED ALIVE (1990) ★★ South African horror flicker features John Carradine in reportedly his last role and is bolstered marquee-wise by Robert Vaughn and Donald Pleasence. The setting is Ravenscroft Asylum where horror is enhanced by the themes of Edgar Allan Poe. Harry Alan Towers production directed by Gerard Kikoine (pornie filmmaker). Karen Witter, Nia Long, Ginger Lynn Allen. (RCA/Columbia)

BURNDOWN (1989) ★★ Corpses clicking with high radiation counts are found outside a coastal Florida town, where sheriff Peter Firth fights a local-government coverup and reporter Cathy Moriarty uses sexual wiles on the lawman to investigate the gory murders. A nuclear power plant nearby makes it obvious where the killer is coming from. Stuart Collins's novel was adapted for this mediocre whodunit with apocalyptic overtones by Anthony Barwick and producer Colin Stewart. James Allen's direction gives the low-budget film a nihilistic touch. Hal Orlandini, Hugh Rouse. (MCEG/Virgin) (Laser: Image)

BURNING, THE (1982) ★★ At Camp Blackfoot, stupid teenagers pull a prank on Cropsy the caretaker, who is horribly burned. When he's released from the hospital, Cropsy returns armed with giant shears and eager to wreak vengeance. Another sleazy scuzz-bag slasher-sickness flick with gory murders. Features the massacre of several stupid kids simultaneously, adding to its close-your-eyes-before-the-knife-descends gruesomeness. Producer Harvey Weinstein, a stickler for realism, claims the Cropsy tale is true; or maybe he just saw *Friday the 13th*. Directed by Tony Maylam; written by Weinstein and Peter Lawrence. Makeup by Tom Savini. Brian Matthews, Leah Ayles, Larry Joshua. (Thorn EMI)

BURNT OFFERINGS (1976) ★★½ Modern Gothic with excellent effects, and fine performances by Oliver Reed, Karen Black and Bette Davis (*not* playing a crazy old bat). But alas, it goes awry because of an ambiguous script by producer-director Dan Curtis and William F. Nolan (based on the novel by Robert Marasco). The theme of the "house possessed by evil" never comes off due to a lack of expository material. Instead, it's a mishmash. Even a twist ending cannot save it. Nice try turns to ashes. Burgess Meredith, Eileen Heckart, Dub Taylor. (MGM/UA)

BURNT ROSE, THE. See *Blood Rose*.

BURN, WITCH, BURN (1962) ★★★ Based on a Fritz Leiber novel, *Conjure Wife*, this better-than-average British supernatural thriller (aka *Night of the Eagle*) stars Peter Wyngarde as a professor lecturing against witchcraft and Janet Blair as his wife, armed with charms to ward off evil. Some wild things happen and you'll be unnerved, even if you can see wires propelling a killer bird when it pops off the face of the campus tower. Directed by Sidney Hayers, written by George Baxt, Charles Beaumont and Richard Matheson.

BURN, WITCH, BURN! (1970). See *Mark of the Devil*.

BUTCHER, THE (1971) ★ This is one chopped up mess of a movie, amateurishly axed to death by director Paulmichel Mielehe, who also massacred the script. What makes it perversely intriguing to watch (if you can stand it) is the presence of Vic Tayback (destined to run Mel's Diner on TV) as Smedke, a demented butcher shop owner who sells human meat, and Robert Waldon (destined to be a reporter working for Lou Grant) as his halfwit assistant chopper, who goes berserk in a cloud of flying feathers as he chases chickens through the shop and hacks off their heads. Then there's Talia Shire as a parenthood social worker who's hanging around town for no obvious reason. The setting is a small California town where mute girl Maxie (R. G. Baumann) gets wise to the scheme and her father (Morgan Upton) goes in search of her after Walden kidnaps her in a really sleazy sequence. Some of the footage is light-struck, so poorly was this shot and edited. Its original title appears to be *Maxie*. David Peoples codirected. Ford Clay, Richard Hilliard, Charles Dorsell. (Entertainment International Ltd.; from Star Classic as *Murderers' Keep*)

BUTCHER, THE (1981). Video version of *Psycho from Texas* (Bronx).

BUTCHER, BAKER, NIGHTMARE MAKER. See *Night Warning*.

BUTCHER BOY, THE (1998) ★★½ Scottish filmmaker Neil Jordan (*The Crying Game*), in this offbeat movie, strikes at the heart of what makes the Irish tick—and explode. It's a chilling psychological study of a youth (Eannon Owens) growing up in a rural town and the forces of life that eventually lead him to sadism and murder. Owens's is a tour de force performance as he captures the boy's sensitivity and cruelty. All told, by the way, with Jordan's usual dark comedy and raw irony. He makes beautiful things ugly and ugly things beautiful. Based on a novel by Patrick McCabe, who cowrote the script with Jordan, *The Butcher Boy* has moments of pure fantasy, such as when Owens imagines monsters from Hollywood sci-fi movies, atomic explosions, and the appearance of a guardian angel (singer Sinead O'Connor). The film also has its moments of blood and gore when the youth turns on his lifelong village nemesis (Fiona Shaw) and slaughters her like a pig, hiding her butchered corpse under rotting cabbages. Owens's Francie Brady is a character you won't soon forget as we see how his alcoholic, trumpet-blowing father (Stephen Rea, who also plays Francie as a grown man) and insane mother get his life off on the wrong foot, and how his anger is soon displaced onto others as a psychotic, alienated person rolls off into an unhappy sunset. (Video: Warner Bros.)

BUTCHER'S WIFE, THE (1991) ★★★½ Warm, wonderful study of the needs and absurdities of romance as filtered through a sweet, naive but clairvoyant farm girl who marries a New York City butcher on impulse and resettles in Manhattan. Her ability to foresee the romantic futures of her husband's customers leads to unforeseen complications for her (Demi Moore), the butcher (George Dzundza), the neighborhood psychiatrist (Jeff Daniels) and a mousy woman turned bar-lounge singer (Mary Steenburgen in a tour-de-force role). An unusual commentary on romance, told in a lightly comedic vein by screenwriters Ezra Litwak and Marjorie Schwartz, and tastefully directed by Terry Hughes. Frances McDormand, Margaret Colin, Max Perlich, Miriam Margoyles. (Video/Laser: Paramount)

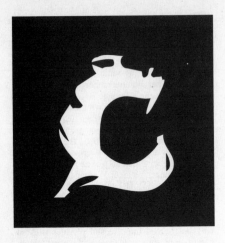

CABINET OF CALIGARI, THE (1962) ★ Robert Bloch scripted this updated version of the silent German classic *The Cabinet of Dr. Caligari*, but claims producer-director Roger Kay butchered his script. This is loaded with Freudian symbolism and dream sequences, and despite Bloch's reaction is still an interesting experiment, for nothing is what it seems as distraught Glynis Johns, after her car breaks down, stays in a strange house in the country presided over by sinister Dan O'Herlihy. J. Pat O'Malley, Estelle Winwood, Lawrence Dobkin.

CABINET OF DR. CALIGARI (1919) ★★★★ Silent German classic in Expressionism, an attempt to explore psychological horror. It's a nightmare told by an asylum inmate, depicting a carnival hypnotist, his somnambulistic zombie, murders, etc. Contemporary audiences may find this cumbersome with outmoded acting but it remains a hallmark in experimentation. Robert Wiene directed the script by Fritz Lang and Carl Meyer. Werner Krauss, Conrad Veidt, Lil Dagover. (Kino; Sinister/C; Republic; Moore) (Laser: Republic)

CAFE FLESH (1982) ★★½ Set in an improbable future, after the world has been nuked and turned into a rubble heap, and many survivors have lost all desire for sex and are called Sex Negatives. Still, they go to Cafe Flesh to watch Sex Positives perform X-rated sexual dances. Written-directed by Rinse Dream. Andrew Nichols, Paul McGibbony, Pia Snow, Marie Sharp.

CAGE. Video version of *Mafu Cage* (Magnum).

CAGLIOSTRO. See *The Mummy* (1932).

CALIFORNIA AXE MASSACRE. Video version of *Axe!* (Malibu).

CALIFORNIA AXE MURDERS. See *Axe!*

CALLING, THE. See *Murder by Phone.*

CAMERON'S CLOSET (1989) ★★★ Intense thriller about a youngster (Scott Curtis) with telekinetic powers who brings an ancient Mayan demon out of hibernation to live in his closet. Although Gary Brandner (adapting his own novel) is unable to avoid convoluted plot devices, the film intriguingly pulls cop Cotter Smith and psychiatrist Mel Harris into the supernatural shenanigans. Armand Mastroianni's direction is hampered by dull lighting, but otherwise this little movie gallops along, aided by Tab Hunter as Cameron's father. Chuck McCann, Leigh McCloskey, Kim Lankford. (Sony) (Laser: Image)

CAMPSITE MASSACRE. See *The Final Terror.*

CANADIAN MOUNTIES VS. ATOMIC INVADERS (1953) ★★★ Of the serials produced by Republic after 1950, this is possibly one of the best. Key to the success of these 12 chapters of action in the northwest territory is Bill Henry (as Mountie Don Roberts), who provides a ring of authenticity that was often lacking in Republic's leading men. Then there is the well-rounded bosom of Susan Morrow, although director Franklin Adreon does not give it the attention it deserves. While portions were obviously filmed on the back lot, there is good stock footage of snow country: ice floes, a herd of stampeding reindeer, huskies and wolves running wild, and excellent action choreography as Roberts (doubled by stunt genius Tom Steele) leaps off cliffs into moving vehicles. Written by Ronald Davidson, *Canadian Mounties* involves a foreign agent named Marlof (Arthur Space disguised as a rummy trapper named Smoky Joe) plotting to establish atomic missile launching platforms to blow up American cities. This is all thwarted by one Mountie, carrying a six-shooter. Amazing! But what fun to watch the craftsmanship that went into these bygone serials. Harry Lauter turns up in the last chapter, perhaps as a kind of screen test so he could star the next year in his own serial, *Trader Tom of the South Seas.* The TV-movie version is *Missile Base at Taniak.* (Video/Laser: Republic)

CANDLE FOR THE DEVIL, A. See *It Happened at Nightmare Inn.*

CANDYMAN (1992) ★★★★½ As a supernatural-horror thriller this is a superb adaptation of Clive Barker's story "The Forbidden." Writer-director Bernard Rose skillfully crafts a blood-and-guts tale that has a fascinating subtext about urban legends and how they affect our culture. Virginia Madsen portrays a brave woman studying the legend of "Candyman," a boogeyman-figure within a black ghetto. Her nosing around highrise slums leads to a confrontation with an evil spirit (equipped with a hook hand) and nightmarish events refreshing to the horror genre. Barker acted as executive producer, which may account for the superiority of this gore flick. Tony Todd is electrifying as the slave returned to life as a serial killer. Vanessa Williams is good as Madsen's assistant. Evocative Philip Glass score with pseudoreligious undercurrents. (Video/Laser: Columbia TriStar)

CANDYMAN 2: FAREWELL TO THE FLESH (1995) ★★★½ Another example of Clive Barker functioning well as a producer in telling an unpleasant, extremely horrific and gory tale with pseudoreligious overtones. An excellent musical track by Philip Glass enhances the return of Tony Todd as the urban legend known as Candyman. This time the setting is New Orleans, background to the original story of artist Daniel Robitaille, who was murdered by whites but has returned as an evil spirit to murder with his hook hand. The focus is on an Old New Orleans family as its members die horribly at the hand of Candyman and deep, dark secrets are revealed. Bill Condon's direction is a superior example of atmospheric and moody filmmaking that doesn't waste one opportunity to chill you or make you jump from your chair with a series of false scares, intermingled with real ones. Some of the performances are cameo gems, and everyone contributes to the film's overall impact. Kelly Rowan, Timothy Carhart, Veronica Cartwright, William O'Leary, Fay Hauser, Matt Clark. (Video/Laser: Polygram)

CANNIBAL. Variant video version of *The Last Survivor* (AIR).

CANNIBAL APOCALYPSE. Uncut video version of *Invasion of the Flesh Hunters* (Midnight Video).

CANNIBAL CAMPOUT (1988) ★½ Beautiful women are tasty morsels for a gang of flesh-eating freakos. Directed by Jon McBride and Tom Fisher. Carrie Lindell, Richard Marcus. (Donna Michelle)

CANNIBAL FEROX. See *Make Them Die Slowly*.

CANNIBAL GIRLS (1972) ★★ In a Canadian town, three dead women with a penchant for human flesh haunt a restaurant where Eugene Levy and Andrea Martin spend the night. Avant-garde supernatural thriller of interest because it was the first work of producer-director Ivan Reitman. Original theatrical prints contained a buzzer sound to warn viewers of pending violence. Written by coproducer Robert Sandler. Ronald Ulrich, Bonnie Neilson. (No buzzer on CIC's version)

CANNIBAL HOOKERS (1987) ★ Amateurish video movie written-produced-directed by one-time fertilizer salesman Donald Farmer in which two chicks pose as prostitutes and are turned into zombies with a taste for human flesh. Gary J. Levinson, Eric Caidin, Sheila Best. (Camp)

CANNIBAL MASSACRE. See *Invasion of the Flesh Hunters*.

CANNIBAL ORGY. See *Spider Baby*.

CANNIBALS ARE IN THE STREETS. See *Invasion of the Flesh Hunters*.

CANNIBAL VIRUS. See *Night of the Zombies* (1983).

CANNIBAL WOMEN IN THE AVOCADO JUNGLE OF DEATH (1988) ★★½ This sendup of *Apocalypse Now*, safari adventures and sex comedies is talkative and full of tongue-twisting rhetoric on a satirical level. The blend is not the rollicking parody its title suggests. Shannon Tweed portrays Margo Hunt, a feminist on safari with bumbling hunter Brett Stimely and sexy Karen Mistal (that gal from *Return of the Killer Tomatoes*) to find "Kurtz," another feminist (Adrienne Barbeau in loincloth) leading a tribe of Piranha Women in the wilderness of California where they eat men after sex. This hodgepodge is by writer-director J. D. Athens (pseudonym for J. F. Lawton). Barry Primus, Bill Maher. (Video/Laser: Paramount)

CANTERVILLE GHOST, THE (1944) ★★★★ Whimsical, hilarious version of the Oscar Wilde story, directed by Jules Dassin from an Edwin Blum script. A cowardly ghost (Charles Laughton, in one fine role) is doomed to walk the family castle until a descendant performs a heroic deed. Updated to incorporate the Nazi threat. Robert Young, Margaret O'Brien, Peter Lawford and Rags Ragland. (MGM/UA)

CANTERVILLE GHOST, THE (1986) ★★★ TV version of Wilde's comedy, set in modern England when Andrea Marcovicci and Ted Wass inherit a castle in Worcester, where this was filmed. Stalking its halls, with supernatural ball and chain, is Sir John Gielgud as the irascible, blustering specter; he alone makes this worthwhile. Good effects enhance this old tale in which the ghost must force earthlings to perform an heroic act. Directed by Paul Bogart. (RCA/Columbia)

CANTERVILLE GHOST, THE (1995) ★★★★ Patrick Stewart brings a classic touch to his portrayal of Oscar Wilde's famous ghost, Simon of Canterville, in this superbly written TV-movie adaptation made in England and coproduced by Stewart. Eschewing the more comedic elements of Wilde's supernatural morality tale, Stewart emphasizes the pathos and tragedy of Simon, who has been condemned to a living death for 400 years, and is finally befriended by a sympathetic teenage daughter when an American family rents the hall. Neve Campbell is also excellent as the young woman with the courage to enter the Realm of Darkness with the ghost to help free him of his curse. There's an alienated daughter subplot (her father thinks she's faking all the ghostly manifestations) and a minor love affair with a neighboring duke. Credit Robert Benedetti for the script and Sid Macartney for the fine direction. Leslie Phillips, Daniel Betts, Donald Sinden, Cherie Lunghi. (Hallmark)

CAPE CANAVERAL MONSTERS, THE (1960) ★½ Writer-director Phil Tucker, who established new incompetency levels in *Robot Monster*, dips to even greater lows. Two bathers are attacked by beams of light (what a great effect!), die in a car crash and return possessed by alien energy fields. Nadja and Hauron (aliens) foul up rocket launchings by pointing a bazooka-shaped zap gun and firing. They address their E.T. boss on an "interplanetary receiver"—a TV set in which a pancake floats. Katherine Victor and Jason Johnson convey no menace as the turgid invaders, who grow uglier as more putty is heaped on their faces. At control center, a Jewish scientist operates phony-looking equipment while Scott Peters and Linda Connell stumble around the aliens' cave. Mercifully short (69 minutes) but still not short enough!

CAPTAIN AMERICA (1944) ★★★ This 15-chapter Republic serial, based loosely on the Marvel comic-book character, is an exciting action cliffhanger with Dick Purcell as a D.A. who takes to the Captain America costume to fight the evil Scarab, who uses a poison called "The Purple Death" to kill his enemies and steal such new devices as a "dynamic vibrator" called the Thunder Bolt that knocks down a skyscraper, a Re-Animation Machine that brings a criminal back to life, and other weapons of the "Death Ray" school. The fistfights are great, the action is nonstop, Lorna Gray is fine as the obligatory heroine, Lionel Atwill shines as a perverted sophisticate, and the direction by John English and Elmer Clifton has unusually good camera angles for the period. Aka *The Return of Captain America*. (The Video Treasures transfer is mediocre; for some strange reason, Republic has not released this on tape.)

CAPTAIN AMERICA (1989) ★★★ Unlike previous versions based on the comic-book hero of World War II, who was revived in the '60s by Marvel, this captures the flavor of the original by pitting Captain America (Matt Salinger) against his grand Nazi nemesis, The Red Skull (Scott Paulin). It's grand, uninhibited comic-book action as the warriors clash in 1943. Through circumstances that could only happen in a four-color magazine, Steve Rogers/Captain America (product of a top-secret experiment) is left in suspended animation in the Arctic while the Red Skull plots the assassinations of the Kennedys and Martin Luther King. Revived from the ice, the red-white-and-blue superhero, armed with a boomerang-like shield, takes on the Skull and his sexy assassins led by his daughter after they've kidnapped the U.S. President (Ronny Cox). Director Albert Pyun ignores logic and goes for pacing to make this a satisfying adaptation. Ned Beatty, Darren McGavin, Michael Nouri, Melinda Dillon, Bill Mumy. (Video/Laser: Columbia/TriStar)

CAPTAIN KRONOS—VAMPIRE HUNTER (1972) ★★★½ Exciting Hammer actioner, also known as *Vampire Castle* and *Kronos*. Horst Janson is the dedicated Kronos, who embarks on Quixotic hunts for bloodsuckers with hunchback Professor Grost (John Cater). Writer-director Brian Clemens creates a blend of satire and swashbuckling action with overtones of an old-fashioned serial. Exotic Caroline Munro is Kronos's helper. Shane Briant, Ian Hendry. (Paramount) (Laser: Japanese)

CAPTAIN MEPHISTO AND THE TRANSFORMATION MACHINE (1945). Feature version of Republic's serial *Manhunt of Mystery Island*.

CAPTAIN NUKE AND THE BOMBER BOYS (1995) ★★ Bungled comedy from producer Roger Corman attempts to ridicule authority figures (Martin Sheen as an egocentric FBI agent; Rod Steiger as a befuddled, Dixie-style U.S. President) while three high school nerds blackmail America for improved youth rights by threatening to set off a home-made nuclear bomb they found accidentally. These kids are really dumb and obnoxious, and not funny for a moment. Also threatening the government (because he also accidentally found the bomb) is bumbling petty crook Joe Mantegna (in a role far beneath his capabilities, but hey, an actor has to eat). Slapstick gags and schtick routines (such as Sheen going off the deep end over his own greatness) all fall flat as a dud bomb under the direction of Charles Gale, whose inane script set this abortion into (slow) motion. Joanna Pacula, Ryan Thomas Johnson, Michael Bower, Joshua Schaefer, Kate Mulgrew, Joe Piscopo. (New Horizons)

CAPTAIN SINBAD (1963) ★★★ Made in Germany by Frank and Henry King (of *Gorgo* fame), this colorful fantasy written by Samuel B. West and Harry Relis stars Guy Williams as the sailor of the Arabian Nights adventures who pursues his fiancée, a damsel trapped in the clutches of wicked Pedro Armendariz (in his final screen role). Sinbad is tortured, battles a giant hand (winning thumbs down) and seeks to cut out the evil caliph's heart. All ages will enjoy the costumes, sets and Byron Haskin's stylish direction. (MGM/UA)

CAPTAIN VIDEO (1951) ★★½ A 15-chapter Columbia serial spinning off from a once-popular TV show, *Captain Video and His Video Rangers*, one of TV's first sci-fi series. Of all the cliffhangers that Sam Katzman produced for Columbia, this is the wildest and perhaps the most fun to watch. The writers pulled out all the stops in creating sci-fi gadgets: jetmobile, inertia stungun, sonic air cushion, floating space platform, cloak of invisibility, etc. Directed by Spencer Gordon Bennet and Wallace A. Grissell, it's nonstop nonsensical action as Captain Video (Judd Holdren) and Video Ranger (Larry Stewart) battle Vultura (Gene Roth), the evil ruler of the planet Atoma. Most of it, however, takes place on Earth (in the foothills of L.A.) with Captain Video mainly fighting Dr. Tobor

(George Eldredge), an inventor who uses his own gadgets to help Vultura conquer the world. Needless to say, Vultura and Tobor don't succeed. This also sports some of the silliest sound effects ever used in a serial. Don't miss it. (Noble R. Brown's; Heavenly)

CAPTAIN YANKEE. See *Jungle Raiders*.

CAPTIVE PLANET: A NIGHTMARE OF LIVING HELL. See *Star Odyssey*.

CAPTIVE WILD WOMAN (1943) ★★½ Acquanetta walks zombielike as a mysterious native woman transformed into a member of the monkey family by a mad doctor—but everyone associated with this Universal quickie, including John Carradine as Dr. Sigmund Walters and Milburn Stone and Evelyn Ankers as the sympathetic heroes who are members of a circus, is engaged in monkey business. Surprisingly, this tasteless B effort sparked sequels: *Jungle Woman* and *Jungle Captive*, equally as cheap, Jack. Edward Dmytryk directed. Lloyd Corrigan, Paul Fix, Grant Withers. (MCA)

CAPTURE OF BIGFOOT, THE (1979) ★ An insufferable kid, two bad-guy hunters, a forest ranger and his girlfriend, a dumb, disbelieving sheriff, an old trapper named Jake, and a wise Indian are the inept characters running around Cloud Lake in winter, pursuing two extras from Central Casting in furry white suits and monster faces. Hell, them abominations look more like Yetis. Oh well, it's the Legend of Aurak unleashed on us hapless movie-watchers by writer-producer-director Bill Rebane. The cast stumbles through snowdrifts without ever getting the drift. Stafford Morgan, Richard Kennedy, Katherine Hopkins, Otis Young, John Goff. (Active)

CARNAGE (1972). See *A Bay of Blood*.

CARNAGE (1983) ★½ A poor man's *Amityville Horror* from producer-writer-director-cameraman Andy Milligan, depicting newlyweds Deeann Veeder and Chris Georges committing suicide in their new two-story mansion. Three years later a new couple (Leslie Den Dooven and Michael Chiodo) takes over the house and, at first, undergo harmless poltergeist activity. Then the vengeful spirits of the bride and groom get murderous, using psychic energy to throw hatchets and other sharp-edged weapons. While Milligan has a grasp on the psychology of hauntings, his gore murders and effects are unconvincingly executed, and his editing lacks the pacing required to build to a suspenseful crescendo. He doesn't have a ghost of a chance. John Garritt, Chris Baker, Rosemary Egan. (Media; Video Treasures)

CARNIVAL OF SOULS (1962) ★★★½ Obscure cult favorite was revived in 1989, with missing footage restored by producer-director Harvey (Herk) Harvey. It's funky and crude but compelling, for its story avoids clichés—in fact,

George Romero credits it with inspiring *Night of the Living Dead*. Candace Hilligloss wanders in limbo between life and death, with death symbols tugging at her. The mood generated by Harvey and cowriter John Clifford and the oddball characters overwhelm the amateurishness to give this a unique touch. The film was created around a deserted pavilion near Salt Lake City, which became a central location for this low-low budgeter made in and around Lawrence, Kansas, and Salt Lake. It lacks graphic shocks but its psychological content is superior. (Goodtimes; S/Weird; Filmfax) (Laser: VidAmerica; Image)

CARNOSAUR (1993) ★★★ Although an apparent attempt to cash in on the *Jurassic Park* hoopla, this Roger Corman low-budgeter is a good monster-gore movie, well written-directed by Adam Simon. Genetics scientist Diane Ladd, as mad as a hatter, crosses chicken eggs with DNA from dinosaurs (gosh, does this sound familiar or what?) and gets a modest-sized *T. rex* creature monster juggernaut that shreds plenty of human flesh. Raphael Sbarge, Jennifer Runyon, Harrison Page. (New Horizons) (Laser: Image)

CARNOSAUR II (1994) ★★★½ Excellent Roger Corman production, a worthy sequel and one helluva exciting adventure set in Yucca Mountain, a secret government installation where dinosaurs have been created through DNA. After the garrison is wiped out except for young Rick Dean, a special squad led by Don Stroud and John Savage arrives with argumentative government guy Cliff De Young only to become trapped in the tunnel systems. The effects get effectively gory when the ferocious beasts tear an arm off one of the women, and bite the head off an EVAC soldier. It's finally up to the youth to stop the rampaging creatures. A lot of good suspense is brought out of Michael Palmer's fast-paced, no-nonsense script by director Louis Morneau. This is one you wanna see. Arabella Holzbog, Miguel A. Nunez, Jr., Neith Hunter. (New Horizons) (Laser: Image)

CARNOSAUR 3: PRIMAL SPECIES (1996) ★★½ Imagine *Jurassic Park Lizard Monsters in the Lost World of Aliens Meets the Deep Blue Sea of Exploding Ships* and you have your standard Roger Corman pastiche of currently popular genre movies, albeit with substandard pyrotechnics and inferior special effects. In this third (and hopefully final) glimpse at a government project to clone dinosaurs, a terrorist team hijacks a convoy of trucks, thinking they are stealing a uranium shipment. However, the terrorists become a fine-flavored meal for two raptors and one T-Rex being transported to a lab where scientist Janet Gunn intends to extract elements that could cure many human diseases. But it's up to a commando team led by Scott Valentine (doing an impression of Sylvester Stallone in *First Blood*) to try to take the creatures alive for the sake of research. Whether running through a warehouse or skulking through the corridors of a cargo ship, the commandos are just cannon fodder for the monsters and the monsters aren't even state-of-the-art. Gore-and-action buffs might still forgive director Jonathan Winfrey for keeping the plot moving right on out to sea aboard a freighter and they might console screenwriter Scott Sandin for the campy dialogue and ludicrous characters. In one scene, a guy soldier arm-wrestles a girl soldier, forgetting there are man-eating monsters not far away waiting to eat lunch. These Corman movies certainly have a way of boggling one's mind. Rick Dean, Rodger Halston, Anthony Peck, Terri J. Vaughn, Billy Burnette, Morgan Englund. (New Horizons)

CARRIE (1976) ★★★★½ Producer-director Brian De Palma's treatment of Stephen King's first novel, a lurid tale of modern Gothic horror, has two sequences that'll make you leap from your seat. It's a psychological study of mousy teenager Sissy Spacek who uses telekinetic power to wreak vengeance after a macabre joke is played on her at the high school prom. Tension between Spacek and mother Piper Laurie, a religious fanatic, is riveting and her "Crucifixion" scene is unforgettable. A powerful horror film of the '70s. John Travolta, Nancy Allen, Amy Irving, William Katt. (MGM/UA; Paramount) (Laser: Voyager; Criterion)

CARRIER, THE (1988) ★½ When an isolated community is struck by an epidemic (an allegory of AIDS?), the infected turn into gooey piles of custard. Produced in Michigan on a shoestring budget, this was written-directed by Nathan J. White and stars Gregory Fortescue, Steve Dixon, Paul Urbanski, N. Paul Silverman. (Magnum)

CARRION. See *The Jar.*

CARRY ON SCREAMING! (1966) ★★ This spoof in the "Carry On" series pokes spirited fun at Universal's horror monsters: a mad doctor who regenerates corpses, his Vampira-like assistant Valaria (exotic Fenella Fielding), a wolfman named Ozbod, and a stuffy butler. Two inept Scotland Yard cops, Bung and Slowbottom, bungle through an investigation to find out why six women disappeared from Hocombe Woods. Turns out our crazed physician has a way of turning them into solid statues with a special dip. Jolly good fun directed by Gerald Thomas. Harry H. Corbett, Kenneth Williams, Charles Hawtrey, Jim Dale, Joan Sims. Aka *Carry On, Vampire* and *Screaming.* (Movies Unlimited)

CARS THAT EAT PEOPLE, THE (1974) ★★ Peter Weir began his directing-writing career in Australia with this bizarre though poorly produced,

grainy parable horror tale. Half chilling, half satirical, it's set in the Australian desert town of Paris, where the demented community survives by rigging auto accidents and then living off the profitable aftermath—including transplant organs. John Meillon plays an unimaginative, manipulatable young man who survives an "accident" to undergo psychological mind games played on him by a freaky psychiatrist (Kevin Miles). It's a study in empty-headed comformity and human indifference. This faltering though interesting film only hints at the talent Weir (who also cowrote the script) would demonstrate in much better films to come (*Road Warrior*, maybe?). There's a kind of mild *Road Warrior* touch in a spiked-covered car used by the crazed "Parisians," but it's really a cynical comment on man's willingness to destroy his fellow beings for profit. Terry Camilleri, Rick Scully, Max Gillies. Aka *Cars That Ate Paris.* (RCA/Columbia; Double A; New Line offers an uncut version that is the only good way to see this film)

CASE OF JONATHAN DREW, THE. See *The Lodger* (1926).

CASE OF THE MISSING BRIDES. See *The Corpse Vanishes.*

CASPER (1995) ★★★★ Like *Jurassic Park*, this shows off aspects of computerized animation when it is creatively blended with live action, and like *Jurassic Park*, this is an Amblin Entertainment production with Steven Spielberg contributing as producer if not director. Who would have thought the old Harvey comic-book character, Joseph Oriolo's Casper the Friendly Ghost, would work in a feature-length format? Well, pal, that old spectral splash of surrealplasm works well indeed, for he/it/that sheeted cutesy pie entity is at the center of a rollickingly funny spoof of the supernatural as conceived by writers Sherri Stoner and Deanna Oliver, and executed with uncanny precision by director Brad Silberling. Trapped in the 19th-century mansion where he died as a youth, Casper is an animated cartoon figure superimposed with Bill Pullman (as Dr. Harvey, a psychiatrist out to help spooks finish their business on Earth so they can cross to the other side), his daughter Christina Ricci and a couple of baddies played by Cathy Moriarty and Eric Idle. A threesome of other ghostly cartoon characters (Stretch, Stinkie and Fatso) almost steal this show with their slapstick antics and parodies. Yes, it gets morally hokey at times, and unnecessarily raucous with an uninhibited number of subplots, but the magic of the animation, and the hopeful potentials it bodes for the future of film, carries the day. A definite step upward in the imaginative use of technology. (Video/Laser: MCA)

CASSANDRA (1987) ★★½ A psycho killer writes "Who Killed Cock Robin?" on the mirrors of his victims in this muddled Australian psychological profile of a prescient child and her parents. As Cassandra, Tessa Humphries relives her mother's death-by-shotgun and has psychic flashes of new murders as they happen, including the slasher-death of her father's girlfriend. Deep family secrets are at the root of the script by director Colin Eggleston, Chris Fitchett and John Ruane. Shane Briant, Kit Taylor, Lee James. (Virgin Vision) (Laser: Image)

CAST A DEADLY SPELL (1991) ★★★½ Offbeat, catchy TV-movie combines the private-eye genre with cosmic horror of H. P. Lovecraft. Set in a parallel universe in 1948, where everyone can perform magic tricks, L.A. private eye H. Phillip Lovecraft (Fred Ward) is after "The Necronomicon," which holds the key to unleashing evil Elder Gods from their dimensional prisons to earthly environs. Rich recluse David Warner wants the book to control the world; so does night club gangster Raymond O'Connor, while sexy torch singer Julianne Moore just wants Lovecraft. Director Martin Campbell keeps it moving with gremlins, zombies and beasts as part of the black magic. Producer Gale Anne Hurd includes atmospheric matte paintings that enhance this low-budget effort. You'll enjoy this kooky world in which the cop is named Bradbury. Clancy Brown, Alexandra Powers, Charles Hallahan. The loose sequel is *Witch Hunt*. (Video/Laser: HBO)

CASTLE FREAK (1995) ★½ Mark this as one of the last of the Full Moon films from producer Charles Band. The company went out with a fizzle, not a bang! *Castle Freak* is a genuine thud bomb from director Richard Gordon, who rejoins with his *Re-Animator* stars Jeffrey Combs and Barbara Crampton to spin another perversely horrific tale. But this time the attempt to shock falls flat, with a nude, demented cannibal monster hidden away in an old Italian castle. (It appears the thing is wearing a "skin suit," genitals and all showing, but it's laughable, not frightening.) To the castle comes Combs, wife Crampton and blind daughter Jessica Dollarhide. He's there to claim his inheritance, which happens to be the castle. But Combs is haunted by the memory of having accidentally caused the death of his son, and Crampton hates him for being weak and sexually impotent. Combs finally gets drunk and brings a prostitute to the castle one dark night (the sex scene is rather graphic, fans) and that's when the chained-up "thing in a cell" breaks loose and starts chewing on the cast members. A few by-the-numbers murders and plenty of blood and gore are what you get until Combs and the crazed creature fight it out to the death in the dingy castle. Gordon dreamed up the half-baked idea and Dennis Paoli scripted it. Music by Richard Band. Jonathan Fuller, Massimo Sarchielli, Elisabeth Kaza, Luca Zingaretti, Helen Stirling, Raffaella Offidani. (Video/DVD: Koch Full Moon)

CASTLE OF ARTENA, THE. See *Bloody Pit of Horror*.

CASTLE OF BLOOD (1962) ★★★ Above-average Italian horror flick in which George Riviere spends a night in a haunted castle after accepting a bet from Edgar Allan Poe. Naturally, he proceeds to lose his mind as he bears witness to ghostly spirits. Among them is Barbara Steele, who provides a great lift. Directed by Anthony M. Dawson, who remade the story as *Web of the Spider*. Ah, but that's another night of horror. Aka *Castle of Terror, The Long Night of Terror, Tombs of Horror, Coffin of Terror, Dimensions in Death* and *Danse Macabre*. Margaret Robsahn, Sylvia Sorente, Henry Kruger. (Sinister/C; Filmfax)

CASTLE OF BLOODY LUST. See *Castle of the Creeping Flesh*.

CASTLE OF DEATH. Video version of *The Devil's Nightmare* (Premiere).

CASTLE OF DOOM. See *Vampyr*.

CASTLE OF FU MANCHU, THE (1968) ★★½ Final entry in the British series with Christopher Lee as the insidious Asian with another nefarious scheme to throw the world into chaos. Helping old Fu in this new grue is his dastardly daughter, death rays and torture devices in the Sax Rohmer tradition. Directed by Jesus Franco. Aka *Fu Manchu's Castle, Assignment Istanbul* and *The Torture Chamber of Fu Manchu*. Preceded in the series by *The Face of Fu Manchu, The Brides of Fu Manchu, Vengeance of Fu Manchu* and *Kiss and Kill*. Richard Greene, Maria Perschy. (American Videotape; Moore)

CASTLE OF LUST. See *Castle of the Creeping Flesh*.

CASTLE OF TERROR (1963). See *The Terror*.

CASTLE OF TERROR (1964). Video version of the Barbara Steele horrifier *Castle of Blood* (S/Weird).

CASTLE OF THE CREEPING FLESH (1968) ★ Mad doctor Howard Vernon tries to bring his murdered daughter back to life by killing for body organs. Aka *Castle of Bloody Lust*. Directed by Percy G. Parker (Adrian Hoven). Elvira Berndorff, Claudia Butenuth, Janine Reynaud. (Magnum; Videodrome)

CASTLE OF THE LIVING DEAD (1964) ★★½ Troupe of entertainers stops at Christopher Lee's castle, where bizarre murders commence. Ample lurking through secret passageways before the show biz gang (dwarf and all) discovers Count Drago (Lee) is preserving the dead. You'll get a kick out of Donald Sutherland as a comedy relief policeman (he also appears as an old witch). Directed by Herbert Wise (real name: Luciano Ricci), scripted by Warren Kiefer. Gaia Germani, Philippe Leroy. Aka *Crypt of Horror*. (Sinister/C; S/Weird; Filmfax)

CASTLE OF THE WALKING DEAD, THE (1969) ★★★ German-produced excursion into 19th-century horror with haunted woods (body parts embedded in branches and trunks) and spooky castle of torture chambers, trapdoors, snake pit and mad-doctor laboratory. Lex Barker and Karin Dor portray aristocracy invited to Andimi Castle, home of the dreaded Count Regula. They watch helplessly as the Count is brought to life as Christopher Lee, who plays the madman without charm. Seems he has the blood of 12 virgins, but needs Dor's to complete his formula for eternal life. Manfred Kohler's script borrows Poe's *The Pit and the Pendulum* for one sequence. The acting, sets and direction by Harald Reinl make this watchable despite its datedness. Aka *Blood Demon*, *Pendulum*, *The Snake Pit*, *The Snake Pit and the Pendulum*, (Interglobal; from Magnum as *The Torture Chamber of Dr. Sadism* and *The Snake Pit*.)

CASTLE OF UNHOLY DESIRES. See *Castle of the Creeping Flesh*.

CAT. See *Night Creature*.

CATACLYSM. Variant video version of *The Nightmare Never Ends* and *Night Train to Terror* (Academy; Fox)

CATACOMBS (1988). Original video title of a Charles Band film rereleased as *Curse IV* (Transworld).

CAT CREATURE, THE (1973) ★★ Robert Bloch supernatural teleplay with in-jokes about movie cats, but it's pallid stuff. Gale Sondergaard, one-time Spider Woman, is a cat goddess claiming victims to possess a golden amulet. Kent Smith, of *Curse of the Cat People*, has a cameo. Curtis Harrington needed nine lives to direct David Hedison, Stuart Whitman, Keye Luke, John Carradine; Peter Lorre, Jr., turns up in one scene with a knife in his back. Has the bite of a kitten instead of a jungle marauder.

CAT GIRL (1957) ★★ Barbara Shelley, in her first British film, inherits a family curse that promises "the craving for warm new flesh and blood." Cuckolded by her devious husband, Barbara unleashes a phantom cheetah on him and girlfriend—a transference that in turn unleashes the curse and sets in motion vengeful murders. Alfred Shaughnessy directed Lou Rusoff's script. Robert Ayres, Kay Callard, Paddy Webster. Aka *The Cat-Woman*. (Paramount; Columbia)

CATHARSIS. See *Terror in the Crypt*.

CATHY'S CURSE (1976) ★ French-Canadian horror flick borrowing from *Carrie* in dealing with an 8-year-old girl possessed by the demonic spirit of her aunt, who was killed in a fiery auto crash. Housekeeper plunges from an upper window to her death, family dog is destroyed, other "web of horror" clichés ensue.

Special effects are undistinguished, Eddie Matalan's direction is tedious, and Randi Allen as Cathy seems more insufferable than evil. Curses on everyone involved. Alan Scarfe, Beverly Murray, Roy Wiltham. (Planet; Continental)

CAT O' NINE TAILS (1971) ★★★ Karl Malden, who portrays a blind man specializing in solving crossword puzzles, considers this one of his best low-budget features, a tribute to the talents of writer-director Dario Argento. This blends mystery and psychoterror in telling of a murderer whose blood is tainted with homicidal tendencies. James Franciscus is a reporter on the killer's trail. Catherine Spaak, Cinzia de Carolis. Music by Ennio Morricone. (Simitar; Bingo) (Laser: Japanese)

CAT PEOPLE, THE (1942) ★★★★ Classic supernatural shocker from RKO producer Val Lewton, who stressed unseen horror in his low-budget assignments. Simone Simon is a fragile European bride fearful she is turning into a panther whenever her sexual desires are aroused. We never witness the transformation, only shadowy figures on windswept streets and the hint of something prowling just out of camera range. A genuinely eerie atmosphere created by director Jacques Tourneur, with Dewitt Bodeen's script remarkably literate. Kent Smith, Tom Conway, Jane Randolph, Jack Holt. (Nostalgia Merchant; Media; King of Video; RKO) (Laser: Voyager; Image; Turner)

CAT PEOPLE (1982) ★★½ Paul Schrader directed this barely-a-remake of the '42 version, emphasizing the sexual side of humans turning into animals. It's kinky: Malcolm McDowall mutates into a panther whenever sex is on his mind, and so should his relative Nastassia Kinski, only she's a virgin and hasn't developed the impulses. Schrader deals with this depravity in vivid visuals. Yet the exposition is so uncertain, he suggests more than he ultimately shows, an ironic twisting of Lewton's technique. Even the effects by Tom Burman (human arm popping out of leopard's stomach; arm being ripped out of its socket; man-to-animal transmutation) are brief, as if Schrader was afraid to include shocks lest he not be taken seriously. In his vain attempt to remain "honorable" and still be trendily "box office" he creates a film that isn't enough to satisfy hardcore horror/gore buffs, and that is too obscure to please a mass audience. The Alan Ormsby script borrows sequences from the '42 version, but is not an improvement. John Heard, Annette O'Toole, Ruby Dee, Ed Begley, Jr. (Video: MCA) (Laser: Voyager/Criterion)

CAT'S EYE (1985) ★★★ Anthology film combining screenwriter Stephen King and director Lewis Teague, who first dealt with King material in *Cujo*. A well-made film (superbly photographed by Jack Cardiff) of three tales linked by a superintelligent tail—a tabby who intervenes in affairs of men for non-evil purposes. The opener is black comedy in which habitual smoker James Woods seeks help from Quitters Inc. and finds that Alan King employs a harsh cure. The middle narrative concerns underworld kingpin Kenneth McMillan forcing his wife's lover (Robert Hays) to walk a high building ledge on a bet. Nice O. Henry twist here. Final story is the strongest: Our tabby follows a gnomelike minimonster (created by Carlo Rambaldi) into a rural home to defend Drew Barrymore from ferocious attacks. The menacer is a gremlin dressed as a court jester and the battle in the toy-ridden bedroom is a classic. One of the better King movies. Candy Clark, Jared Naughton. (Video/Laser: Fox)

CAT WITH THE JADED EYES, THE. See *Watch Me When I Kill*.

CAT-WOMAN, THE. See *Cat Girl*.

CAT WOMEN OF THE MOON (1953) ★ Dreadful 3-D programmer, so unconvincing and stodgy it isn't even so-bad-it's-good. It's just so-bad-it's-unbearable. See it if you must but don't believe that baloney about it rivaling *Plan 9 from Outer Space* for sheer ineptitude. Some schlock has it, some doesn't. This don't. Sonny Tufts, Victor Jory, Douglas Fowley and Marie Windsor are on a loony lunar expedition but you'll howl at the Sears spacesuits and Woolworth zap guns. The "cat women" are ballet dancers in tights. Cat-o'-nine tails for producer Al Zimbalist (*Robot Monster*), director Arthur Hilton and scripter Roy Hamilton. Remade in 1960 as *Missile to the Moon*, and aka *Rocket to the Moon*. (Nostalgia Merchant; Sinister/C; Filmfax; from Rhino in 3-D)

CAULDRON OF BLOOD (1971) ★½ Spanish-American grue (produced in 1967 in Madrid, but not released until after Boris Karloff's death) in which Karloff portrays a blind artist (mis)used by murderous wife Viveca Lindfors to dispose of corpses in a most unusual fashion. Karloff is in a wheelchair most of the time because he was ill. This is one cauldron that fails to boil under the stirring of director-writer Edward Mann (Santos Alcocer). Jean-Pierre Aumont doesn't bubble the pot, either. Aka *Blind Man's Buff*, *The Corpse Collectors*, *Death Comes from the Dark* and *The Shrinking Corpse*. (Republic; Vidcrest)

CAVE DWELLERS, THE. See *One Million B.C.*

CAVE GIRL ISLAND (1994) ★½ This loose sequel to *Beach Babes from Beyond* has the three galaxy-traveling bimbos Luna (Stephanie Hudson), Xena (Sarah Bellomo) and Sola (Tina Holliman) dropping their ship onto a primitive planet and then dropping their bras and panties to indulge in some simulated sex with handsome cavemen. Lenny Rose portrays a guy in a cave with a virtual reality control board who calls out a dinosaur and has an idiot for an assistant.

Nothing in Mark Michelini's script makes any sense—it's all a feeble excuse for a frequently graphic sex romp, again directed by David DeCoteau under the name Ellen Cabot. Rodrigo Botero, Stefan Galio, Kenny Johnson, Guy Payne. (Paramount) (Laser: Torchlight Entertainment)

CAVE MAN. See *One Million B.C.*

CELIA—CHILD OF TERROR (1989) ★★★ Although released in theaters as *Celia*, Trylon Video added *Child of Terror* to make it look like a horror film à la *The Bad Seed*. Exploitation aside, it's a psychological profile of an Australian girl (Rebecca Smart) growing up in a rural area during the 1950s and encountering corruption, indifference, sadism and other "normal" aspects of mankind. Except for brief moments involving imaginary Aussie creatures called Hobyahs, and unexpected acts of violence during its climax, horror fans will feel misled. Directed-written by Australian film maker Ann Turner, who was appalled by the lurid packaging. Nicholas Eadie, Victoria Longley. (Trylon)

CELLAR, THE (1989) ★★½ A Comanche legend tells of the evil spirit Queg-Why, the "bastard of the raven." The four-legged, ugly creature feasts on human flesh, lives beneath a desert ranchhouse and pops up just for meals. A kid new to the territory (Patrick Kilpatrick) sees it but nobody believes him—including father Chris Miller, whose domestic life is on the verge of collapse. This rendering of a story by Dr. David Henry Keller, adapted by John Woodward, boils down to the familiar confrontation between man and beast. And director Kevin S. Tenney fails to build suspense by showing too much of the creature too soon. Suzanne Savoy, Michael Wren, Lou Perry. Only old-time actor Ford Rainey, as an old desert rat, brings character to the film. (South Gate; Hemdale)

CELLAR DWELLER (1988) ★★★ This monster thriller, filmed by Charlie Band in Rome, is distinguished by comic-book horror art cleverly intercut with live action to create a nice fantasy effect. John Carl Buechler, a special effects man who turned director with *Troll*, again shows he has an appreciation for the genre as director. Artist Debrah Mullowney arrives at lonely Throckmorton Institute for the Arts as a specialist in horror imagery, her inspiration the work of a famous comic-book artist who died there 30 years before. By reading "The Curse of the Ancient Dead," she resurrects a monster, and by drawing comic pages highlighting the killer-beast she kills off her real-life enemies: Unlikable headmistress Yvonne De Carlo, old rival Cheryl-Ann Wilson, and snoopy private eye Vincent Edwards. Comic-book fans will dig the artwork, a homage to E.C. comic books. Jeffrey Combs, Brian Robbins, Pamela Bellwood. (New World) (Laser: Image)

CEMETERY GIRLS. See *Dracula's Great Love*.

CEMETERY HIGH (1989) ★ Incredibly unwatchable comedy send-up on splatter movies follows four dumb "teenage slasher sluts" running around campus murdering sexually aggressive, rude jocks. The guys get blown away in a variety of ways (except the way they would like to) while the dames make wise cracks. This incomprehensibly bad movie was directed by Gorman Bechard. It features "The Gore Gong" (to warn you things are turning bloody) and "The Hooter Honk" (to warn you sexual material is coming). Two more reasons not to waste your time. Debi Thibeault, Karen Nielsen, Lisa Schmidt. (Unicorn; Hollywood Home Entertainment)

CEMETERY MAN (1993) ★★½ Graveyard humor prevails during the first half of this French-Italian coproduction starring Rupert Everett as a cemetery caretaker named Frencesco Dellamorte. The soil in this particular cemetery brings the dead back to life and the "returners" have to be shot in the head to be stopped. As satire on horror movies, this material unfolds grotesquely but is very funny in its own dark way, and director Michele Soavi is in control. Everett plays it deadpan with his drooling Igor-like assistant Nagy (Francois Hadji-Lazaro) providing a touch of parody as a mental deficient. But then writer Gianini Romoli gets too metaphysical and turns Everett into an inept serial killer, and Soavi loses control. The movie goes all over the place, making comments about life and death, about pain and sex, about love that can never be. And finally *Cemetery Man* buries itself under an avalanche of skewered thinking and instead of entertaining you, only disturbs and confuses.

CEMETERY TRAMPS. See *Dracula's Great Love*.

CERTAIN MR. SCRATCH, A. See *The Devil and Daniel Webster*.

CHAIR, THE (1986) ★★½ Quirky characterizations and a non-genre approach to this story about an old prison haunted by a warden electrocuted two decades earlier should have turned *The Chair* into a comfortable offering. But it doesn't set easy (not enough shock value, maybe?). The action centers around High Street Correctional Facility when psychologist James Coco and warden Paul Benedict (once a guard at High Street) reopen the old prison to look after "eight fragile psychies." Helping out is naive, neophyte psychologist Trini Alvarado, unaware Benedict is going off the deep end. Electricity becomes an evil force, leading to deaths, amputations, etc. Director Waldemar Korzeniowsky's tone vacillates between horror and comedy. Gary McCleery, Stephen Geoffreys, Ron Taylor. (Imperial) (Laser: Image)

CHAMBER OF FEAR. Video version of Boris Karloff's *The Fear Chamber* (Unicorn).

CHAMBER OF HORRORS (1940) ★★★ Entertaining Edgar Wallace story (based on *Secret of the Door With Seven Locks*) set in a weird mansion where Dr. Manetta (Leslie Banks, a great of the 1930s) houses torture instruments. Lilli Palmer is a lovely heroine who falls into his trap, and Gina Malo is refreshing comedy relief as a vacationing American. "I love frolicking in a morgue," remarks Ms. Palmer when trapped with boyfriend Richard Bird. There's nothing supernatural about it but it's charming in its antiquated fashion. Written-directed by Norman Lee. Remade as *The Door with Seven Locks* in 1962. (United; Sinister/C; Filmfax; Nostalgia)

CHAMBER OF HORRORS (1946). See *Bedlam*.

CHAMBER OF TORTURES. See *Baron Blood*.

CHANCES ARE (1989) ★★★ This has such appealing characters it transcends its dumb premise—that of a dead husband returning from Heaven in a new body to fall in love with his former wife and to have (but reject) the opportunity to have sex with his own daughter. It also overcomes our suspension of belief in its casting of characters who never seem to age during a 23-year period. Credit screenwriters Perry and Randy Howze and director Emile Ardolino for taking the chance. Cybill Shepherd, never looking lovelier, plays the widow pursued these 23 intervening years by Ryan O'Neal, but remaining in love with her deceased husband. Mary Stuart Masterson is beautiful as the daughter and adds a strong romantic rival for the attentions of Robert Downey, Jr., as the returning spouse. Maurice Jarre's music fleshes out this love tale, as does the camera work of William Fraker. Chances are, you're going to be richly entertained by *Chances Are*. (Video/Laser: RCA/Columbia)

CHANDU ON THE MAGIC ISLAND (1934) ★★ Last eight chapters of the serial *Return of Chandu*, with Bela Lugosi as Frank Chandler, also known as Chandu. He's a drab magician (once a popular radio hero) fighting the Black Magic Cult of Ubasti on Lemuria. The first seven reels were also reedited as *Return of Chandu*. Directed by Ray Taylor. (Video Yesteryear has a feature version; Sinister/C has the full-length serial)

CHANDU'S RETURN. See *The Return of Chandu*.

CHANDU THE MAGICIAN (1932) ★★ Feature version of the radio serial, with Edmund Lowe as a magician who materializes and dematerializes at will. Bela Lugosi, who would later play Frank Chandler in a Chandu serial (*Return of Chandu*), portrays Roxor, a mad priest who intends to conquer the world by stealing a Ray Disintegrator. Directed by William Cameron Menzies and Michael Varnel. Photographed by James Wong Howe. (Rex Miller)

CHANGELING, THE (1980) ★★★★ Superior

haunted house tale heavy with creepy atmosphere, structured by writers William Gray and Diana Maddox. Composer George C. Scott, recovering from the deaths of his wife and child, discovers the mansion is haunted by a murdered child. Director Peter Medak keeps this tense story unfolding on several levels—as a pure ghost story, as a psychological study of Scott's recovery from tragedy, as a morality tale of good vs. evil. The ending is far out but enhances this unusually excellent supernatural tale. Trish Van Devere, Barry Morse, Melvyn Douglas, Jean Marsh, John Colicos. (Video/Laser: Vestron)

CHARLEY AND THE ANGEL (1973) ★★ Poor producer's version of *It's a Wonderful Life*, set in a rural town during the Depression, in which shopkeeper Fred MacMurray, taking his family for granted, is warned by angel Harry Morgan he had better mend his ways. MacMurray, too nice a guy to seem even remotely negligent, sees the light but has troubles with bootleggers. Lightweight Disney comedy with little conviction, although the cast is pleasant and reflects a different age of Disney filmmaking. Cloris Leachman is the confused but faithful wife and Kurt Russell has a small role. Roswell Rogers based his script on Will Stanton's novel *Golden Evenings of Summer* and Vincent McEveety directed. Vincent Van Patten, Kathleen Cody, Barbara Nichols, George O'Hanlon, Ed Begley, Jr. (Disney)

CHARLIE'S GHOST STORY. See *Charlie's Ghost: The Secret of Coronado*.

CHARLIE'S GHOST: THE SECRET OF CORONADO (1994) ★ This bland, endlessly boring adaptation of a Mark Twain story stars Trenton Knight as a misunderstood kid and Anthony Edwards (who also directed) as his archeologist father who never has time for his son—so the ghost of Spanish explorer Francisco Vásquez de Coronado (in the form of always-laughing Cheech Marin) pops up to make quips and give advice. Despite a good supporting cast (Charles Rocket, J. T. Walsh, Linda Fiorentino, Daphne Zuniga), there isn't an ounce of energy in the script by Clint Hutchison and Lance W. Dreeesen or in the direction by Edwards. Aka *Charlie's Ghost Story*.

CHEERLEADER CAMP (1988) ★ This was made so teenagers could watch nubile, bouncing young girls in short skirts and tight sweaters rehearsing at Camp Hurrah. Poor Betsy Russell keeps having strange dreams and darned if a killer doesn't start knocking off the babes one by one. Could it be Leif Garrett, who wants to love Betsy but she won't let him? Or could it be sleazy handyman Buck Flowers? Anyhow, one girl gets clippers through the back of her head and out her mouth. She's left speechless.

John Quinn produced-directed this cheerless *Friday the 13th* clone, aka *Bloody Pom-Poms*. Lucinda Dickey, Lorie Griffin, Teri Weigel. (Prism; Paramount)

CHEERLEADER CAMP II (1990) ★ If you saw *Cheerleader Camp I* there isn't much point in seeing *Cheerleader Camp II* unless you enjoy eyeballing retread psychomurder cheapie bombs—and torturing yourself. (Prism)

CHERRY 2000 (1986) ★★★ Intriguing action/sci-fi adventure set in 2017 when female robots are love-making machines. When his Cherry 2000 model shorts out while making love in an overflow of soap suds, a dumb male (David Andrews) decides to find a replacement in the Zone—an area of Nevada where outlaw bands and crazy characters rove. His guide is Melanie Griffith (a character named E. Johnson), who leads him into bizarre situations—some of them cliffhangers. Old-timers Ben Johnson and Harry Carey Jr. add professionalism to the raucous proceedings. Director Steve de Jarnatt does all he can to beef up the Michael Almereyda script. Tim Thomerson, Brion James. (Video/Laser: Orion)

CHILD, THE (1977) ★½ Ripoff of *The Exorcist*, in which a murderous moppet calls upon ghoulish graveyard demons to carry out her revenge against despicable characters. Directed by Robert Voskanian from a Ralph Lucas script. Rosalie Cole, Laura Barnett. Also known as *Zombie Child*. (Best; from FHE and Paragon as *Kill and Go Hide*)

CHILD OF DARKNESS, CHILD OF LIGHT (1991) ★★★ The Angel of Death is back in this fascinating *Omen*-style TV-movie based on *Virgin*, a novel by James Patterson. Brian Taggert's teleplay compellingly depicts the efforts of priest Anthony John Denison (a "church cop") to investigate the virgin pregnancies of two 15-year-olds (Kristen Dattilo and Sydney Penny). One of the babies will be the Antichrist—but which one? Meanwhile, the world is plagued by disease and pestilence. Denison is aided by nun Sela Ward, who soon falls prey to the Devil's manipulation of her repressed sexual desires. Director Marina Sargenti moves it at a brisk pace and doesn't telegraph a climactic twist that'll hit hard. Brad Davis, Paxton Whitehead. (Paramount)

CHILD OF SATAN. Video version of *To the Devil a Daughter* (Olympus).

CHILD OF THE NIGHT. See *What the Peeper Saw*.

CHILDREN, THE (1963). Proposed title for *Children of the Damned*.

CHILDREN, THE (1980) ★★★ Kind-of-fun variation on *The Night of the Living Dead* in which leakage from a nuclear plant causes a cloud of radiation that turns a busload of children into hollow-eyed zombies. You're in for juvenile jars, kiddie killings and moppet mayhem because the merest touch from a child's atomic-charged fingers causes adults to smoke and turn into rotting flesh. The disgusting idea that adults must go out with machetes and cut off the kids' hands gives this a perverse twist. Producer Max Kalmanowicz directs it like a monster flick of the '50s. Also known as *The Children of Ravensback*. Martin Shakar, Gil Rogers, Gale Garnett. (Vestron; Rhino)

CHILDREN OF BLOOD. Video version of *Cauldron of Blood* (Republic).

CHILDREN OF THE CORN (1984) ★★ Lousy adaptation of a story from Stephen King's collection *Night Shift* and a prime example of filmmakers (director Fritz Kiersch, screenwriter George Goldsmith) taking a master's work and turning it into schlock. Peter Horton and Linda Hamilton are travelers detoured into a rural community in Nebraska lorded over by a cult of youngsters slaughtering adults as a sacrifice to a corn god. The corncob icon shows up in the climax but is so poorly photographed, one never knows what "it" is. R. G. Armstrong, John Franklin. (Embassy; Starmaker) (Laser: Image)

CHILDREN OF THE CORN [2]: THE FINAL SACRIFICE (1992) ★★★ Corn stalks Hollywood again when Stephen King's revengeful cornfield god, He Who Walks Behind the Rows, returns to Gatlin, NE, to manipulate the town's young ones to carry out his/her/its evil bidding, a form of vengeance for man's toxic poisoning of the corn industry. Ned Romero as Dr. Frank Red Bear, an Indian professor, steals the show. Director David F. Price fails to pick up the pacing and this horror film drags except for a few homicidal set pieces: a man bleeds to death in church during a hellfire sermon; a house falls on an old woman; a doctor is punctured to death by hypos; an invalid in a wheelchair crashes through a plate glass window, disturbing a bingo game. Terence Knox, Paul Scherrer, Ryan Bollman, Christie Clark. (Paramount)

CHILDREN OF THE CORN 3: URBAN HARVEST (1995) ★★★ Horror fans, lend me your ears—of corn, that is—for this is a major terrorizer with plenty of kernels (generally speaking). Almost every horror and monster cliché imaginable is brought into play by screenwriter Dode B. Levenson, and with makeup by Screaming Mad George adding to the visual fun you can't go wrong with this nonstop genre pleaser, designed to fill your vicarious needs for blood, gore and death. Daniel Cerny plays Eli, head of the killer-kiddie cult of the cornstalks, who with Ron Melendez turns up to live on a peaceful farm. But not peaceful for long, as Eli conjures up demonic evil and kills almost everyone in town (not to mention the cast in due course) to appease He Who Walks Behind the Rows. This

time He turns out to be a huge ugly creature with long tentacles and a tendency to swallow victims whole (you get to see one of those eaten beings cut out of its body). It's all horrific style with little logic. Director James D. R. Hickox (related to producer Anthony Hickox, no doubt) sure knows how to keep his camera on the goriest events. Ah shucks, twern't nothin'. Michael Ensign, Jon Clair, Mari Morrow, Duke Stroud, Rance Howard. (Video/Laser: Buena Vista)

CHILDREN OF THE CORN [4]: THE GATHERING (1996) ★★★ Another gorefest for genre aficionados that carries on the tradition of young children being the homicidal monsters controlled by outside evil forces in the cornfields of America. Set in Grand Island, Nebraska, *The Gathering* depicts how the young but dead spirits of evil Caleb and Zeke invade the bodies of numerous innocent children, turning them into scythe-swinging murderers. That means doctor William Windom gets cut in half (sawed off at the waist by the sawed-off runts), Karen Black is dragged to a horrible farm-implement death, and Samaria Graham dies by hypodermic needle crucifixion—well, you get the idea. The Stephen Berger–Greg Spence script is pure horror-movie stuff, and therefore fun if a bit predictable. Spence, who also directed, loves to fling blood on walls and show flash-cut monster faces. Naomi Watts and Brent Jennings play the adults who finally get wise and turn killers themselves, but for a good cause: to wipe out those evil kids. Samaria Graham, Jamie Renee Smith, Brandon Kleyla. (Video/Laser: Buena Vista)

CHILDREN OF THE CORN V: FIELDS OF TERROR (1998) ★★ If you're going to make a body-count shocker, then make it fun to count the bodies. First we have a farmer who gets levitated, struck by bolts of lightning, and charred to a crisp. Not an ounce of fun, even when the body falls from the sky and scrunches against the earth. Now, that could have been fun. Then we have a woman in a cornfield scythed to death. Bloody, but so solemnly presented, it's not fun. It might have been a barrel of laughs. Then her boyfriend is scythed through the stomach and beheaded. A repetitive bore, and where's the fun in that? The script by director Ethan Wiley gets especially boring when four boring young people (make that two guys and two chicks) turn up stranded in the Midwest corncob town where He Who Walks Behind the Rows walks and his young disciples make sacrifices to a silo that contains a pit leading to hell. A lot of nothing happens, then local crazy David Carradine and redneck sheriff Fred Williamson get killed—Carradine's head and torso are split open like a cleavered orange, and Williamson is engulfed by flames. Not a bit of fun, and why did these two worthy actors bother with a picture of this caliber? And nothing new in terms of murder weapons. The same old knives, chain-saws, and farmer's tools with sharp points. Didn't the first four *Children of the Corn* movies do some of that? *Fields of Terror* ends with one of the chicks throwing some stuff into the pit that ticks off He Who Walks Behind the Rows and causes him/it to explode and blow up the silo. You don't even get to see a monster. It's hard to say just what the hell Wiley intended with all this pointless stuff. It sure isn't fun for you, the viewer, and it couldn't have been any fun for the participants: Stacy Galina, Alexis Arquette, Adam Wylie, Greg Vaughan, Eva Mendez, Ahmet Zappa, Olivia Burnette, Angela Jones. (Video/Laser: Dimension)

CHILDREN OF THE CORN 666: ISAAC'S RETURN 1999) ★ The only reason to keep doing sequels to Stephen King's short story about a cult of devil worshipers in a midwestern county called Gatlin is to keep up the body count for gore fans, so here goes: one man electrocuted (no blood or gore, just sizzling sparks and screaming), one suicide by falling on a scythe with the blade sticking up in the air (close-up of blade penetrating male body), a woman split in half by a sword (close-up of head dividing down the middle), a steel pole through a human torso (close-up of area of entry with blood spattered on all sides), and a couple of others I can't remember now, having gone out to get some lunch. Thanks goes to Tim Sulka and John Franklin (screenwriters) for maintaining a lively lineup of homicides and to director Kari Skogland for not failing to demand graphic close-ups. Oh, the story. Almost forgot. Angst-ridden Nancy Ramsey (playing a gal named Hannah) is psychically drawn back to Gatlin in her beat-up convertible and learns, when she hits town, she is the Chosen One. That means the devil's son Gabriel (Paul Popowich) is going to lay her before midnight and spawn the next evil leader of the devil pact that worships He Who Walks Behind the Rows. Ramsey's mom (Nancy Allen) tries to save her daughter from this fate, worse than death, and so does world-weary doctor Stacy Keach, on leave from narrating a TV show about disastrous true-life events. But it doesn't work. Popowich squirts a water hose all over Ramsey's nude body and that turns her on. She really gets horny and then they make the baby that you know is gonna give everyone a helluva time. Franklin, in addition to writing every other word of the script, returns to the series as Isaac, a short little guy who's always conjuring up demons in a cornfield. Isaac is first shown in a coma in a hospital room, accounting for his absence from the last couple of pictures. Awakened from his slumber, little Franklin hurries out into the nearest cornfield and tears into everyone with a vengeance, spouting all the prophecies that keep coming true in these mov-ies, because that's the way they were written in the script. But even Isaac gets some surprises from Gabriel, who really blows his horn before bloodbath No. 6 is over. No. 7 is all set up now for the birth of the new devil child, so you can be sure of a continuing body count. That's a relief. (Video/DVD: Dimension)

CHILDREN OF THE DAMNED (1963) ★★★ Sequel to *Village of the Damned* (aka *Horror!*) is superior thanks to a literate script by John Briley that touches on aggressive behavior. A group of highly intelligent children, created by an alien race which impregnated Earth mothers from deep space, is brought to London, where the government intends to destroy them. The kids are wise to the conspiracy and wrest control. Thoughtfully directed by Anton M. Leader; based on ideas from John Wyndham's *The Midwich Cuckoos*. Alan Badel, Ian Hendry, Clive Powell, Bessie Love, Frank Summerscales. Early titles: *The Children* and *The Children Return*. (MGM/UA) (Laser: MGM, with *Village of the Damned*)

CHILDREN OF THE NIGHT (1971). Video version of *Daughters of Darkness* (Ariel).

CHILDREN OF THE NIGHT (1991) ★★ Produced by the *Fangoria* magazine empire, this monster-gorefest should satisfy undemanding horror fans, but it offers nothing fresh or unusual to the vampire genre. The children in Allburg USA ("a quiet town") are imprisoned in suspended animation to provide blood for the number one adult vampire (David Sawyer). A few of the images are memorable—such as teenage girls swimming in a water-filled crypt, and a truck careening with a giant stake thrust ahead of it—but it's all derivative, and its attempts at black humor are out of place. Tony Randel directed in Michigan. Karen Black, Peter DeLuise, Ami Dolenz. (Columbia TriStar)

CHILDREN RETURN, THE. Proposed title for *Children of the Damned*.

CHILDREN SHOULDN'T PLAY WITH DEAD THINGS (1972) ★ A hammy traveling troupe journeys to an island to stage a satanic play, pretending to raise the dead. But corpses in the graveyard aren't pretending—they're out for blood! This vacillates between stupidity and cheap thrills in the hands of producer-director Bob Clark, who coscripted it as *Zreaks* with Alan Ormsby, doubling as the troupe's director. Intelligent viewers shouldn't waste time with dumb movies. Anya Ormsby (Alan's wife), Bruce Solomon. (Gorgon; MPI; from True World as *Revenge of the Living Dead*) (Laser: Japanese)

CHILD'S PLAY (1988) ★★★ Considering how preposterous the precise is, this horror tale works thanks to director Tom Holland's suspension of our disbelief. A strangler is tracked down by cop Chris Sarandon and killed, but not before he transfers his soul into a department store doll. The doll finds its way into the hands of a youngster and sets out to kill for revenge, including Sarandon. The boy's mother, Catherine Hicks, has a thankless role, exclaiming such lines as "My God, the doll's alive!" But it is her bravura and acting abilities that also help to save the picture. There are moments when the doll, designed by producer David Kirschner, captures a note of terror despite its small size. Alex Vincent, Brad Dourif, Dinah Manoff. (Video/Laser: MGM)

CHILD'S PLAY 2 (1990) ★★★ Chucky, the doll's body inhabited by the spirit of the Lakeside Strangler, is back for more cat-and-mouse games in producer David Kirschner's follow-up to his box office smash. There are few surprises in Don Mancini's script—just more of the same terror tactics. After Chucky is brought back to life by a toy corporation's research department, he turns into a demonic killer, seeking out the youth of the first film to claim his body as a new hiding place. The best sequence comes at the toy manufacturing center's assembly line with a chase involving Chucky. Directed by John Lafia. Alex Vincent, Jenny Agutter, Gerrit Graham, Peter Haskell. (Video/Laser: MCA)

CHILD'S PLAY 3: LOOK WHO'S STALKING (1991) ★★ A despicable horror film, crassly made to cash in on the overworked "Chucky the Killer Doll" concept. Chucky goes on his third (and one hopes final) rampage at a military school for boys after his evil spirit is brought back to life when the Chucky-toy assembly line is reactivated. Don Mancini's screenplay is devoid of originality—once again it's a set-up for chuckling Chucky to trap victims and close in for the kill. The climax, set in a horror-amusement ride in a carnival, is gratuitous. Directed by Jack Bender, who deserved a better feature debut after helming TV's *The Dreamer of Oz*. Justin Whalin, Perrey Reeves. (Video/Laser: MCA)

CHILLER (1985) ★★★ Producer Richard Kobritz (*Salem's Lot, Christine*) adds to his good credits with this TV horror movie. Writer-producer J. D. Feigleson's story centers on a malfunction in a Cryonics "mausoleum" that allows doctors to restore life to long-dead Michael Beck—but Beck returns to life without a soul, subjecting everyone to physical and mental tortures. Director Wes Craven sustains suspense and tension. Paul Sorvino is the family minister, Beatrice Straight is the devoted mother. Makeup work by Stan Winston.

CHILLERS (1989) ★ Direct-to-video anthology horror tales told by passengers in a lonely depot waiting for a bus that never seems to come. Five narratives in all, all spun without much luster, on a nothing budget by writer-producer-director

Daniel Boyd. Jesse Emer, Marjorie Fitzsimmons. Jim Wolff. (Raedon; Simitar; Prism)

CHILLING, THE (1989) ★★ Lab assistant Linda Blair, mad doctor Troy Donahue and security guard Dan Haggerty are Kansas City residents facing cryogenic corpses returned to life on Halloween by bolts of electricity. Written-produced-directed by Jack A. Sunseri and Deland Nuse. Ron Vincent costars. Aka *Gamma 693*. (Coyote; Hemdale; Satellite)

CHIMERA (1990) ★★★ In the vein of the Quatermass films, this British TV-movie depicts science out of control and the efforts of society to clean up the mess. Originally made as *Monkey Boy* in four one-hour installments, but edited to two hours for U.S. TV, this opens at the Jenner Clinic, where an experiment is underway to create a chimera, a creature with the DNA of man and monkey. A slaughter of the doctors leads to an investigation headed by the powerful and strange Hennessey (Kenneth Cranhaw), essayed in the style of Dr. Quatermass. Stephen Gallagher fashioned the telescript from his novel, and it was directed by Lawrence Gordon Clark. Christine Kavanagh, John Lynch. (Prism) (Laser: Image)

CHINCHERO. TV title for *The Last Movie*.

CHOKE CANYON (1984) ★★★ Rousing adventure with a minor sci-fi theme: physicist Stephen Collins sets up a computer in a Utah canyon to capture soundwaves (from Halley's Comet) to be turned into "safe energy." But the Pilgrim Corp. is dumping toxic waste and a battle-to-the-death erupts. Although the aerial scenes between a bi-winged plane and helicopter are exciting, an irony is at work: If Collins wants energy for peaceful reasons, why is he willing to destroy property and lives? That aside, director Chuck Bail gets lively performances from Janet Julian as the corp. daughter who turns against her father, Lance Henriksen as a slimy henchman, Bo Svenson as a sympathetic hitman (Capt. Oliver Parkside) and Victoria Racimo as Collins' loyal lab assistant. (Media)

C.H.O.M.P.S. (1980) ★★ Juvenile comedy produced by Joe Barbera, king of Saturday cartoons. The title stands for Canine Home Protection System, a shaggy dog robot built with X-ray vision, superstrength, in-house sound effects and the ability to detect crime. Industrialist Jim Backus plots to steal the "dog" from inventor Wesley Eure. The cast plays for cute: Conrad Bain, Valerie Bertinelli, Chuck McCann, Red Buttons, Hermione Baddeley, Robert Q. Lewis. At best, a lightweight diversion, something to catch between buses. Don Chaffey directs with an eye on the nearest fire hydrant. (Orion)

CHOOPER, THE (1971) ★ "The Chooper Man," a legendary Indian spirit haunting a farmhouse, turns out to be a silly-looking man in black who runs around with a long sword, killing snoopers.

This crude effort by cult director Ray Dennis Steckler is substandard, with sound as unintelligible as the story line. Even Steckler's followers will find this excruciatingly painful as the frequent killings are padded out with useless rodeo footage and scenes of pensive Carolyn Brandt walking around as she narrates the threadbare plot. Aka *Blood Monster* (original title) and *Blood Shack*. Jason Wayne, Laurel Spring, John Bats, Peanuts the Pony. (Mascot; from Premiere as *Curse of the Evil Spirit*)

CHOPPER CHICKS IN ZOMBIETOWN (1990) ★★ Troma drama doesn't live up to its promising title as it plumbs lower depths of the "walking dead" genre. Call it "Dykes on Bikes" when motorcycle mamas ride into the desert town of Zariah (pop. 128) where the dead are resurrected to work in a mine, and shambling corpses eat flesh of the living. The klutz sluts with the struts have guts and fight against the flesh-munching undead, knocking off their heads with bats, setting them afire, etc. The chopper-boppers then ride off into the sunset. It's a dreary, uninspired effort to blend parody with gore. Written-directed by Dan Hoskins and Vicki Frederick. Jamie Rose, Catherine Carlen, Lycia Naff, Kristina Loggia. (Video/Laser: RCA/Columbia)

CHOPPING MALL (1986) ★★★ A combination of *Westworld, Aliens* and any movie about malfunctioning robots, this Julie Corman production is loaded with in-jokes and Roger Corman memorabilia. Mary Woronov and Paul Bartel appear as Mr. and Mrs. Bland from *Eating Raoul*, there's a store called "Roger's Little Shop of Pets," and Dick Miller is janitor Walter Paisley (a character he created in *Bucket of Blood*). Otherwise it's your basic robots-run-amok in the Park Plaza 2000 Shopping Center, where teenagers are spending the night. Director Jim Wynorski cheapens the effect with unnecessary nudity and clichés as the "killbots" (the original title) mindlessly murder, concluding each homicide with "Have a nice day." The kids are well armed (from "Peckinpah's Sporting Goods") but bullets bounce off the robots as our heroes dodge killer zap rays, and they must resort to more exotic weaponry. Karrie Emerson, Kelli Maroney, Barbara Crampton. (Lightning)

CHOSEN, THE (1977) ★★ Italian-British production, originally *Holocaust 2000*, is a rehash of the THE OMEN, with Kirk Douglas as an industrialist who specializes in nuclear power plants and suspects he is fulfilling biblical prophecies and setting the world on a disaster course. You see, Simon Ward, his son, is the Son of Satan, or the Antichrist. A fine international cast struggles with a muddled screenplay: Anthony Quayle, Virginia McKenna, Alexander Knox. Directed by Alberto De Martino. (Vestron; Fox)

CHRISTINE (1983) ★★★ Stylish, well-lubricated adaptation (by Bill Phillips) of Stephen King's novel about a 1958 Plymouth Fury possessed by evil powers. Director John Carpenter shifts into high gear as the car knocks off its "rivals." The car, you see, is "Fury-ously" jealous. For this is a love story about a boy and his car. Call it auto-eroticism. There's a great scene of the auto in flames, speeding through the night. The movie works because of our love affairs with cars, an extension of our sexual energies. Gee, are we getting deep. But don't worry about subtext—focus on that Plymouth as it becomes a frightening "character." Keith Gordon, John Stockwell, Alexandra Paul, Harry Dean Stanton. (Video/Laser: RCA/Columbia)

CHRISTMAS EVIL. Video version of *Terror in Toyland* (Saturn).

CHRONICLES OF NARNIA, THE (1989) ★★★ A BBC-TV miniseries consisting of three live-action C. S. Lewis fantasy adaptations: *The Lion, the Witch and the Wardrobe; The Silver Chair* and *Prince Caspian and the Voyage of the Dawn Treader*. Originally aired as part of the *Wonderworks* series. Directed by Alex Kirby. Barbara Kellerman, Jeffrey Perry, Richard Dempsey, Jonathan Scott, Sophie Cook, Tom Baker. (Public Media; Facets Multimedia)

C.H.U.D. (1984) ★★★ Contamination Hazard Urban Disposal is dumping toxic wastes into N.Y. sewers. Also out there are Cannibalistic Humanoid Underground Dwellers, a clan infected by radioactivity. Parnell Hall has shaped an intelligent script focusing on cop Christopher Curry trying to solve his wife's disappearance, and uncovering a conspiracy between government and Manhattan authorities. *C.H.U.D.* has more class than other films about creatures in slimy sewers. Director Douglas Cheek (as in Tongue In) photographed underground New York with atmospheric know-how, and Tim Boxell's monster designs are effective (creatures have drippy fangs, white glowing bulbs for eyes, stretchable necks). What gives it versimilitude are its Soho locations, grubby street people and T-shirts stained with perspiration. The film sports the tag: "Filmed in and under New York City." John Heard, Laurie Mattos, Justin Hall. (Media) (Laser: Image)

C.H.U.D. II: BUD THE CHUD (1989) ★★ A sequel in name only, this failure indulges in tongue-in-cheek comedy, none of which works in the hands of director David Irving. The screenplay by Ed Naha, writing as "M. Kane Jeeves," a one-time pseudonym for W. C. Fields, is a compendium of stolen ideas and completely fizzles in detailing how a cannibal-zombie, the result of a military project, turns the town of Winterhaven into ghoulish killers. Robert Vaughn has fun as the demented officer in charge of the aborted project and is surrounded by Larry Linville, Bianca Jagger, Norman Fell,

June Lockhart, Clive Revill—even the director's mother, Priscilla Pointer, joins in the idiotic activities. There's no way to describe adequately how awful this crud *C.H.U.D.* is. Brian Robbins, Bill Calvert, Tricia Leigh Fisher. (Video: Vestron) (Laser: Image)

CHURCH, THE (1988) ★★ Italy's gore master, Dario Argento, concocted this horror tale with director Michele Soavi. Curiously, it fails to engage the viewer despite powerful images of a Budapest church—it's a case of bland characters. Seems Teutonic Knights once buried bodies and an encoded parchment beneath the church. When a librarian-cataloguer deciphers it, and slides open a long-locked hatch leading to a pit below, he unleashes demons that possess his body and that of a woman working in the church. In fact, everyone gets possessed and all hell breaks loose when tourists are locked inside the cathedral. There are unpleasant overtones of child molestation and the usual fright-monsters and spooky imagery, not to mention the oppressive atmosphere of the church. Hugh Quarshie, Tomas Arana, Feodor Chaliapin. (South Gate)

CINEMAGIC (1985) ★★ Compilation of horror/sci-fi vignettes: "Nightfright"; "Illegal Alien"; "Dr. Dobermind"; "The Thing in the Basement." Also released as *Frightshow*. (MPI)

CIRCLE OF IRON (1979) ★★½ Martial arts film, produced by Sandy Howard in Israel as *The Silent Flute*, is an odd mix of kung fu/Zen philosophy, based on a Bruce Lee–James Coburn idea expanded by Stirling Silliphant and Stanley Mann. Blind sage David Carradine holds the key to all knowledge in a mythical kingdom ("a land that never was and always is") where warrior Jeff Cooper is on the Odyssey of Knowledge, passing ordeals which test strength and cunning. Each adversary is Carradine in makeup—as the Monkey Man, the Rhythm Man and Death. When Cooper reaches Christopher Lee, he learns the meaning of life: Beware Pretentious Movies Bearing Messages. Roddy McDowall plays the White Robe and Eli Wallach is a man in a tub of oil. Dialogue runs to lines like "Tie two birds together; they have four wings yet cannot fly" and "The fool is the twin of the wise." Potential fools have been forewarned. Directed by Richard Moore. (Embassy)

CIRCUITRY MAN (1990) ★★★ Stylish, amusing sci-fi hardware actioner set in a near future when society, the environment completely poisoned, has moved underground. This has a rogues' gallery of oddball characters: Plughead (Vernon Wells), a criminal kingpin with sensory inputs in his head (a "biosynthetic"); female kingpin Juice (Lu Leonard); adventurer Leech (Dennis Christopher) and lesbian-tough broad Yoyo (Barbara Alyn Woods). The titular character (Jim Metzler) is a humanoid synthetic man

who joins bodyguard Lori (Dana Wheeler-Nicholson) to take microchips across country to New York. Two sequences stand out: when Circuitry Man and Plughead meet in Plughead's mind, and when Circuitry Man creates a romantic environment for his affair with Lori. Directed by Steven Lovy, who scripted with Robert Lovy. (Video/Laser: RCA/Columbia)

CIRCUITRY MAN II: PLUGHEAD REWIRED (1994) ★★★ Despite a confusing, chaotic script by producers Steven and Robert Lovy, this sequel is certain to please *Circuitry Man* cultists and sci-fi fans with its funky technology and assortment of amusing characters who all play over the top. Directed by both Lovy brothers, this has FBI agent Deborah Shelton (one of the better built agents of that agency) taking the pleasant-mannered "bio-synthetic" Circuitry Man (Jim Metzler) to the headquarters of his archenemy Plughead (Vernon Wells, who screams his role rather than acts it) in some underground location, where Plughead intends to "rape" Metzler's mind with a probe designed to give him the DNA secret to world domination. Again, the surface world is poisoned and one needs an "oxy" mask to survive. Paul Willson and Andy Goldberg portray two rocket pilots who never really fit into the plot, but you have Dennis Christopher and Nicholas Worth on a trek of their own to Plughead's plug-in place, portraying a kind of Laurel and Hardy of the desert. Traci Lords appears as a miniskirted bioengineer to spice up proceedings. (Video/Laser: Columbia TriStar)

CIRCUS OF BLOOD. See *Berserk*.

CIRCUS OF FEAR. Video version of *Psycho Circus*, featuring new footage and a new introduction with John Carradine. For full details, see *Psycho Circus* (Saturn; Sinister/C; Nostalgia).

CIRCUS OF HORRORS (1959) ★★★ Engrossing British shocker about a plastic surgeon (Anton Diffring) who leaves his patients hideously deformed. Meanwhile, Diffring runs his three-ring circus like a madman, causing grisly gore murders under the Big Top. Wonderfully graphic deaths in all three rings. Sick but engaging. Directed by Sidney Mayers from an engaging script by George Baxt. Yvonne Monlaur, Erika Remberg, Yvonne Romain, Donald Pleasence. Aka *Phantom of the Circus*. (HBO) (Laser: Image, with *Baron Blood*)

CIRCUS OF TERROR. See *Berserk*.

CITY LIMITS (1985) ★ Fifteen years "from now" a plague decimates mankind, and for no reason discernible, society ends up as gangs of survivors, bikers called the DAs and the Clippers, who maintain an uneasy truce and hold jousting contests. One gang is influenced by evil Robby Benson (who never moves from behind his desk) and does the forbidden—uses weapons to gain control. From the team that made *Android*, this is a pointless excuse for biking stunts, though it avoids being a *Mad Max* imitation. Directed by Aaron Lipstadt, scripted by Don Opper. Darrell Larson, Kim Cattrall, Rae Dawn Chong, James Earl Jones. (Vestron; HHE) (Laser: Image)

CITY OF ANGELS (1998) ★★★ Here's a new kind of "men in black" for you: lonely angels clad in heavy, black overcoats who hover above Los Angeles, serving as guardians to us hapless humans. But because these beings have never been "human," they know nothing about the five senses and thus are emotionless. Sometimes their presence helps us, and naturally they take away dead souls to the Great White Light. If these wingless sentinels, who can read the thoughts of people and who can be seen only when they choose, sound vaguely familiar, that's because this Hollywood movie is an adaptation of Wim Wenders's 1987 West German film *Wings of Desire*. In this heavily romanticized version drafted by Dana Stevens, doctor Meg Ryan (in the original, the love interest was a circus aerialist) awakens the unfulfilled needs of angel Nicolas Cage (in the original, this role was filled by Bruno Ganz). To experience love, and following the example set by "renegade angel" Dennis Franz, Cage (or Seth, as he has been named) decides to give up his guardianlike duties to turn human. Once he bleeds and feels pain, Cage knows he's made the transition and begins an idyllic affair with Ryan. As soft as the skins of oranges, Cage and Ryan both give gentle, underplayed performances under Brad Silberling's direction. *City of Angels* leaves many questions unanswered, feels inconsistent and incomplete in spinning its fanciful love story, and deals with the harsh realities of being human only for a brief moment when Cage is beaten up by a roving L.A. gang. But the film does have a heart, and never gets too maudlin, so who's to complain? On the other hand, how come there are no lady angels watching over us? What kind of chauvinistic universe is God running up there? Andre Braugher, as the only other angel personified in the script, provides a nice foil for Cage's philosophical conversations. Colm Feore, Robin Bartlett, Joanna Merlin. (Video/DVD: Warner Bros.)

CITY OF BLOOD (1987) ★★ Prehistoric tribal witch doctor materializes in Johannesburg, killing prostitutes. A medical examiner (Joe Stewardson) pursues the supernatural specter. Written-directed by Darrell Roodt. Ian Yule, Dudu Meltize, Susan Coetzer. (New World)

CITY OF LOST CHILDREN, THE (1995) ★★★★½ Those who love surrealistic movies will be entranced by this French follow-up to *Delicatessen* from the directing team of Jean-

Pierre Jeunet and Marc Caro. Again they join screenwriter Gilles Adrien to create a bizarre world of abnormal characters, dark humor and an oddball technology, where attention is often focused on the most microscopic details. Crazed doctor Daniel Emilfork keeps a thinking brain in a solution (voice by Jean-Louis Trintignant) and a team of clone researchers in an ocean laboratory, and kidnaps children from a nearby coastal city for purposes of dream experiments. Sideshow strongman Ron Perlman (a lovable brute called "One") searches for his kidnapped brother with the help of a sensitive youngster (Judith Vittet) and undergoes numerous (mis)adventures that often boggle the mind. There's an Underwater Man living in a cavern who collects harbor junk, a venomous flea that jumps onto humans and turns them crazy, two sisters who are hooked together to one body and train kids to steal, and a sect of blindmen who see through an electronic third "eye." And a collection of Rube Goldberg–inspired devices reinforce the Jeunet-Caro attitude of a berserk universe, in which this is decidedly set. It sure isn't the real world. Fascinating stuff, beautifully shot. Dominique Pinon, Jean-Claude Dreyfus. (Video/Laser: Sony)

CITY OF LOST MEN. Truncated version of Mascot's 12-chapter serial *The Lost City* (1935).

CITY OF THE DEAD. See *Horror Hotel*.

CITY OF THE LIVING DEAD. Video version of *The Gates of Hell* (Pacesetter).

CITY OF THE WALKING DEAD (1980) ★★★ If you savor zombie monsters slaughtering with guns and knives and if you relish bodies torn asunder and the blood sucked from their throats, you'll rollick in the bloodthirsty joy of this Italian-Spanish goreburst, a loose sequel to Lucio Fulco's *Zombie*. This is the retitled U.S. version of *Nightmare City*, aka *Invasion by the Atomic Zombies*. These vampiric creatures have been subjected to atomic radiation and their cells given "abnormal strength." Director Umberto Lenzi brings nihilism to this doomsday thriller, suggesting through military leaders Mel Ferrer and Francisco Rabal that mankind is doomed. Newsman Hugo Stiglitz and wife Laura Trotter flee across country, barely escaping perilous encounters with bloodsuckers. The violence is ultragraphic: a woman's breast is cut open and an eye gouged out, etc. Maria Rosaria Omaggio, Sonia Viviani. (Cinema Group; Continental; New Star)

CLAIRVOYANT, THE (1982) ★★★ Refreshingly offbeat slasher flick, with believable characters caught up in a maelstrom of mayhem. "The Handcuff Murders" are sweeping Manhattan when TV talk-show host Perry King begins a vendetta against the killer, helping psychic artist Elizabeth Kemp, who draws impressions of the murders. She is caught between the manipulative host and sincere cops as the web tightens. Armand Mastroianni directs with restraint. Norman Parker, Kenneth McMillan. (Magnum; from CBS/Fox as *The Killing Hour*)

CLASH OF THE TITANS (1981) ★★★★ The last work of stop-motion pioneer Ray Harryhausen and producer Charles Schneer (who teamed on many fantasy successes), and hence the end of an era. Harryhausen's techniques seem outmoded (coming in the wake of the effects revolution) and one senses *Titans* spelling doom for hand-crafted stop motion and heralding the coming of computer-animation technology. This paean to Greek mythology has all that Grecian royalty atop Mt. Olympus in the personages of Laurence Olivier, Claire Bloom, Maggie Smith and Ursula Andress. The hero (Harry Hamlin) and heroine (Judi Bowker) are—Zeus bedamned!—purely squaresville. When Harryhausen unleashes the horned brute Calibos (Lord of the Marsh), the Medusa, the Kraken (a monster of the deep), the two-headed Dioskilos wolf dog and other beasties, the film finally comes alive. Script by Beverly Cross; direction by Desmond Davis. Burgess Meredith is a standout as chronicler Ammon. (Video/Laser: MGM)

CLASS OF 1999 (1990) ★★★ There's a vitality and spirit to this action film, the handiwork of director Mark L. Lester, who keeps it moving even when the C. Courtney Joyner script crumbles. It's a freaky blend of *The Terminator*, every post-holocaust movie ever made, *Mad Max* craziness, *Robocop* and *Class of 1984*, to which this could be a loose sequel. By 1999 gangs have taken over our high schools, forcing educators to drastic measures—in this case Stacy Keach brings to Seattle's Kennedy High three androids programmed to teach without sparing the rod. When the robots go out of control, good guy Bradley Gregg unites rival gangs. The pyrotechnics, battle effects and android work are powerful, and Pam Grier, Patrick Kilpatrick and John P. Ryan as the berserk humanoids give the film a tongue-in-cheek tone that matches the campy lines in Joyner's script (based on an idea by Lester). (Vestron)

CLASS OF 1999 II: THE SUBSTITUTE (1993) ★★½ This sequel to Mark Lester's 1990 box-office hit is a lesser piece of filmmaking that is uncomfortably violent. That discomfort comes from a mixed sense of morality as high school students of a vicious kind are murdered by their teacher because they are rebellious. That teacher appears to be a "battle droid, A-77 series," a leftover from the cyborgs that were all allegedly destroyed in the previous film. The bloodletting is extreme as the "droid" engages in numerous unpleasant murders, including some with a combat knife. A bloodbath is featured as the film's climax, and there's a "surprise" ending that makes little sense. A poorly structured project (blame it on the neanderthalic script by Mark Sevi) that director Spiro Razatos photographs with a penchant for bloody violence. Sasha Mitchell, Nick Cassavetes, Caitlin Dulany, Jack Knight, Gregory West, Rick Hill. (Video/Laser: Vidmark)

CLASS OF NUKE 'EM HIGH (1986) ★ Loose sequel to *Toxic Avenger*, set in the same town: Tromaville, the "nuclear waste capital of the world." Again there's a spillage (from the Tromaville Nuclear Facility) into the drinking water at the local high school that causes teens to go berserk, regurgitating *Alien*-like monsters and behaving in a farcical style. It took two directors (Lloyd Kaufman, as Samuel Weil, and Richard W. Haines) but it's still out of control—a wild parody of catastrophe movies. Hell, nuke the movie. Janelle Brady, Gilbert Brenton. (Media)

CLASS OF NUKE 'EM HIGH PART II: SUBHUMANOID MELTDOWN (1990) ★ You need the mentality of MTV-watching to endure this out-of-control Troma bombardment of gross images and depraved behavior. We return to Tromaville, where students were exposed to radiation and turned into creatures. Things are no better as campus newspaper reporter Brick Bronsky (looking more like a blond jock than a writer) discovers that crazed Professor Holt (Lisa Gaye) has created monsters (stop-motion style) and is keeping "subhumanoids" in the Tromaville Institute of Technology. "Bizarre" is the only word that describes costumes, characters and behavior as everyone runs amok as if attending an orgy of sex and rock 'n' roll. It climaxes (no pun intended) with a tiny squirrel mutating into a giant Godzillalike monster and stomping hell out of everything. Director Eric Louzil fails the coherency test. Leesa Rowland, Michael Kurtz, Scott Resnick. (Media; Fox) (Laser: Image)

CLASS OF NUKE 'EM HIGH 3: THE GOOD, THE BAD, AND THE SUBHUMANOID (1995) ★ Picking up only moments after Part II left off, this outrageous Troma trauma from producers Lloyd Kaufman and Michael Herz, in their tradition of chaotic madness, resumes the adventures of jock journalist Brick Bronsky when he mates with a subhumanoid (Lisa Star, with the most incredible hairdo in history) and becomes father to twins. With Eric Louzil directing again, these twins (who instantly grow up to become Brick Bronsky clones) can turn inert objects radioactive, so the evil Dr. Slag (John Tallman) has all his crazily dressed minions out to capture the brothers. All the loony stuff that the name Troma stands for is paraded out nonstop, and you'll get a kick out of all the gags in the closing credits. If you've seen the previous two films, you'll know what to expect. If you haven't, you won't be watching this one either. Lisa Gaye, Albert Bear, Phil Trivo. (Troma)

CLASS REUNION MASSACRE. Video version of *The Redeemer* (Continental; VCI).

CLAW MONSTERS, THE. Feature version of Republic's serial *Panther Girl of the Kongo*.

CLAWS (1977) ★★ An old Indian legend purports that Kush Ta Ka is a demon grizzly that attacks Alaskan farm folks, so forest ranger Jason Evers puts on his Smoky the Bear hat and joins others in the pursuit of the evil spirit creature. Leon Ames, Anthony Caruso, Glenn Sipes, Myron Healey. Directed by Richard Bansbach and R. E. Pierson. Aka *Devil Bear*. (UAV; Video Gems)

CLAWS (1985) ★ A farm lad is attacked by "feline mutants." Jason Roberts, Brian O'Shaughnessy, Sandra Prinsloo. (Western World; from ANE as *Beasts*)

CLEO/LEO (1989) ★★ Male chauvinist pig Scott Baker is turned into a woman (Jane Hamilton/Veronica Hart) and learns the true meaning of understanding between the sexes. Silly comedy produced-written-directed by Chuck Vincent. Alan Naggar, Ginger Lynn Allen (one-time porn actress). (New World; Media)

CLIMAX, THE (1944) ★★★ Boris Karloff portrays Dr. Hohner, a Svengali impresario casting a hypnotic spell over opera singer Susanna Foster, whom he believes is the reincarnated soul of his dead wife. *Phantom of the Opera* sets (circa 1943) were reused in this Universal thriller, which has a tense atmosphere despite a too-chatty script by Curt Siodmak and Lynn Starling (based on a play by Edward Locke). George Waggner directed. Turhan Bey, Gale Sondergaard, June Vincent, Scotty Beckett. (Video/Laser: MCA)

CLOCKWORK ORANGE, A (1971) ★★★★ Writer-producer-director Stanley Kubrick's masterpiece on brainwashing and the price we pay for conformity, based on Anthony Burgess's novel. The setting is the not-too-distant future of England when "droogs" (ruffians and malcontents) rove the countryside, pillaging and raping. When one of these youths (Malcolm McDowell) is arrested for murder, he is processed through a rehab center until he reaches a pacifistic state. The Kubrick touch dominates this unusual tale. Patrick Magee, Michael Bates, Adrienne Corri, David Prowse (Darth Vader). (Video/Laser: Warner Bros.)

CLONES, THE (1974) ★★ Low-budget sci-fier about asexual reproduction is a dull B thriller. The Government duplicates four scientists 52 times and places them in meteorological stations to control the weather. A real scientist discovers the plot and escapes—the rest is standard chase material across rooftops and down boulevards.

Lamar Card and Paul Hunt co-directed Steve Fisher's script. Gregory Sierra, Michael Greene, Otis Young, Alex Nichol, Bruce Bennett. Aka *Dead Man Running, The Cloning of Dr. Appleby, The Cloning* and *The Mindsweepers*. (Lightning; Live)

CLONING, THE. See *The Clones*.

CLONING OF DR. APPLEBY, THE. See *The Clones*.

CLONING OF JOANNA MAY, THE (1991) ★★★½ Excellent writing, deep characterizations and insightful acting raise this three-hour British TV-movie to intriguing heights. It depicts the love-hate relationship between powerful nuclear industrialist Brian Cox (superb as Carl May) and former wife Patricia Hodge (superb in the title role). That relationship is tinged with murder, lust, infidelity and a "DNA implantation" that leads this emotionally involving story into speculative science. The three cloned daughters (Emma Hardy, Helen Adie, Laura Eddy) become a symbolic threesome that leads to Carl May's own downfall—one of many singular twists under Philip Saville's taut direction. Billie Whitelaw, Jean Boht.

CLONUS HORROR, THE (1979) ★★★ Terse low-budgeter depicting a "breeding farm" where a race is created through cloning. One subject breaks free to warn of this diabolical conspiracy, so you're in for chase excitement as writer-director Robert Fiveson maintains a brisk pace. Dick Sargent, Paulette Breen, Peter Graves, Keenan Wynn, Timothy Donnelly. (Lightning; from Catalina as *Parts—The Clonus Horror*.)

CLOSE ENCOUNTERS OF THE THIRD KIND (1977) ★★★★★ Steven Spielberg's awesome masterpiece in special effects sci-fi . . . depicting man's first contact with aliens in a spiritually uplifting style. Spielberg draws on documented lore of UFOs and, with the cinematic trickery of Douglas Trumbull, creates staggering effects. The "Mother Ship" is a mindblower and the smaller saucers flit behind glaring lights, looking solid one moment, multi-dimensional and transparent the next. Less effective is Spielberg's script about power lineman Richard Dreyfuss, who is subjected to the saucer phenomena. But the meager plot is overshadowed by the beauty of the saucers, the integrity of the effects, and the neoreligious mood. French director François Truffaut portrays a UFO investigator heading an international team that travels the world in pursuit of the saucer mystery. What a positive way to prepare us for our next step in space exploration. Another great score by John Williams. Teri Garr, Melinda Dillon, Bob Balaban, Cary Guffey, Carl Weathers, Bill Thurman, Hal Barwood. (Columbia Tristar) (Laser: Voyager; Criterion; Columbia Tristar, with "production essay")

CLOSE ENCOUNTERS OF THE THIRD KIND: SPECIAL EDITION (1980) ★★★★ After the theatrical release of *Close Encounters of the Third Kind*, Steven Spielberg restored excised footage and took out some of the original, hoping to reach a new state of perfection. The end result seems no better or worse than the original, with story line unchanged. Either gives you satisfying results. (Video/Laser: RCA/Columbia)

CLOWNHOUSE (1987) ★★ Teenagers trapped in a mansion with escaped maniacs dressed as circus clowns is such a hackneyed premise you hope these obnoxious kids get killed fast. Alas, screenwriter-director Victor Salva is not so kind. The main kid (Nathan Forrest Winters) behaves so contrary to someone his age that the film defies all plausibility and fails to generate more than a modicum of thrills, and then only clichéd ones. Brian McHugh, Sam Rockwell. (Salva went on to make the impressive *Powder*.) (Video/Laser: RCA/Columbia)

CLOWN MURDERS, THE (1975) ★ Halloween evening finds those in costumes getting less of a treat than they expected in this cut-'em-up-alive thriller. John Candy, Susan Keller, Al Waxman, Lawrence Dane. Directed by Martyn Burke. (Trans World)

CLUB, THE (1993) ★★½ Following a high school prom dance, several graduates are trapped in an ancient mansion which once housed a Suicide Club, and an evil force is unleashed on them. This is a rather infuriating Canadian horror thriller that is more noisy than scary, and which offers a few morphing special effects but precious little else to thrill one. [A] castlelike setting and atmosphere are good, but dull characters make you want to quit *The Club*. Written by Robert C. Cooper, directed by Brenton Spencer. Jel Wyner, Andrea Roth, Rino Romano, Zack Ward, Kelli Taylor. (Video/Laser: Imperial)

CLUB DEAD. Video version of *Terror at Red Wolf Inn* (Electric).

CLUB DEAD (1989) ★★ The winner of a travel contest finds herself staying at a secluded resort where the guests disappear under mysterious circumstances. Hmm. Directed by Bud Townsend. Arthur Space, John Neilson, Mary Jackson, Linda Gillin.

CLUB EXTINCTION (1989) ★★★★ Compelling, complex thriller with sci-fi overtones, inspired by Fritz Lang's silent classics about Dr. Mabuse. (And hence, also known as *Dr. M.*) In this updated version from director Claude Chabrol, Alan Bates portrays the insidious mastermind Dr. Marsfeldt, who designs a method of broadcasting subliminal messages on Berlin TV that makes thousands commit suicide, often taking others with them in spectacular accidents. This German/Italian/French coproduction becomes a metaphor for the Berlin Wall and the trapped feelings of Berliners. Outstanding is Jan Niklas as policeman Klaus Hartman, who tracks the mystery of the "suicide virus" through Jennifer Beals, a model whose face appears on citywide "videoboards." This fantasy deals with ideas and is recommended for thinking viewers. Hans Zischler, William Berger, Andrew McCarthy, Wolfgang Preiss. (Video/Laser: Prism)

CLUTCHING HAND, THE (1936) ★★½ This creaky, dated serial, told in "15 Thunderbolt Chapters!," is nevertheless watchable for its campy corniness as Dr. Gironda (Robert Frazier), a professor with a formula for synthesizing gold, is kidnapped by an evil force who calls himself The Clutching Hand ("hee hee hee hee") and stalks about in a slouch hat, casting his gnarly shadow on walls and cackling with an insane madness that can only be described as hilarious. Detective Craig Kennedy (Jack Mulhall) proves indefatigable in a series of fistfights and chases. At least the identity of the titular villain (who overacts horribly in the final chapter) will come as a surprise. Marion Shilling portrays the heroine and famous stuntman Yakima Canutt portrays Henchman #8, William Farnum and Reed Howes contribute. Jon Hall appears as a subplot villain, Hobart, under the billing of Charles Locher. Directed, with some well-staged fisticuffs for the period, by Albert Herman. (Captain Bijou; Sinister/C; Nostalgia; Video Dimensions; VCI)

COBRA WOMAN (1944) ★★★ Colorful fantasy (written by Richard Brooks and Gene Lewis) of the most entertaining kind, no matter how hokey it gets. A South Seas island is ruled by a hooded cobra, who can be placated only by beautiful princess Maria Montez, who in one campy sequence does a dance coordinated to a snake's movements. Maria's a great looker but a terrible actress . . . but who cares when we can groove on her voluptuous figure, sacrifices to the volcano, sequined fabrics, and jungle boy Sabu. This Universal hooey bears no resemblance to H. R. Haggard's story. Directed with a flash for trash by Robert Siodmak. Lon Chaney, Jr., Lois Collier. (Grapevine)

COCOON (1985) ★★★★ Richard Zanuck–David Brown's production, about aging seniors and how they face dying, is only slightly sugarcoated by its fantasy premise. Aliens from another galaxy wearing human skin (Brian Dennehy, Tahnee Welch, Tyrone Power, Jr.) retrieve pods from the ocean floor off Florida. These contain life-forms in need of nourishment. Senior citizens (Don Ameche, Wilford Brimley, Hume Cronyn) swim with the pods, emerging with renewed sexual drive and proof hearts can be young and gray. Tom Benedek's script (from a David Saperstein novel) sincerely deals with the problems of the men; with wives Jessica Tandy, Gwen Verdon and Maureen Stapleton; with Jack Gilford's negativism; with greediness destroying a good thing. Ron Howard directs without becoming sentimental, and never succumbs to effects unless needed. Steve Guttenberg, Linda Harrison, Clint Howard, Rance Howard. (Video/Laser: Fox)

COCOON: THE RETURN (1988) ★★½ This sequel to the 1985 hit was a flop, failing to recapture the magic. The lovable characters are back, but the directorial touch of Daniel Petrie cannot compare to Ron Howard's. Perhaps the story is too sentimental to work, although the feel of the film is similar to the original. Whatever the reason for failure, it is a subtle one. Anyway, the characters who left for the planet of Antarea return to St. Petersburg, FL, for a holiday, only to be faced with new crises. The Jack Gilford character is harder to take in this new context, one of the film's failings. Don Ameche, Wilford Brimley, Hume Cronyn, Steve Guttenberg, Maureen Stapleton, Jessica Tandy, Gwen Verdon, Elaine Stritch, Courteney Cox. Produced by Richard D. Zanuck/David Brown. (Video/Laser: Fox)

CODE NAME: TRIXIE. See *The Crazies*.

COFFIN OF TERROR. See *Castle of Blood*.

COLD-BLOODED BEAST. See *Slaughter Hotel*.

COLD HEAVEN (1992) ★★★ A study of guilt and infidelity told with a walking dead man and religious miracle—hence, a strange movie with a unique ambience. Credit goes to director Nicolas Roeg, working with a script by producer Allan Scott based on a novel by Brian Moore. Theresa Russell is at the heart of this allegory—her infidelity causes dead husband Mark Harmon to return to life and brings about a visitation of the Virgin Mary. Outré as only Roeg can make them. James Russo, Talia Shire, Will Patton. (Video/Laser: Hemdale)

COLD ROOM, THE (1984) ★★★ Amanda Pays portrays a spoiled coed who travels to East Berlin to patch up a shaky relationship with father George Segal. She undergoes hallucinations which create two time streams: Her own deterioration set in the present, and her transformation into a girl in Nazi Germany caught up in love and betrayal. The time streams flow together for a nice climax. Intriguing premise, helmed by writer-director James Dearden in Berlin. Renee Soutendijk, Warren Clarke, Anthony Higgins. (Media)

COLD SWEAT (1993) ★★½ Routine erotic thriller that qualifies for this book only because hit man Ben Cross is haunted by the ghost of one of his victims (Maria Del Mar). This fascinating premise could have been a movie in itself but it's only a subplot of little consequence, and all that's left is a series of double crosses within double crosses as sizzly Shannon Tweed and lover boy Adam Baldwin plot to do in her hubby (Dave Thomas), etc., etc. Written

by Richard Beattie, directed by Gail Harvey. (Paramount)

COLLISION COURSE. See *The Bamboo Saucer*.

COLONIZATION OF THE PLANET OF THE APES. See *Battle for the Planet of the Apes*.

COLONY, THE (1995) ★★★ Remember that strange community in which Rock Hudson found himself after starting a new identity in *Seconds*? This TV-movie has a similar twist of suspicion, paranoia and the horror of conformity when security-system designer John Ritter opts to move into a crime-free suburban tract called The Colony, where everyone is forced to live by strident rules under the thumb of designer Hal Linden and surveillance cop Marshall Teague. There's also a fascist aspect at work in the schools, where the children are taught class snobbery. This metaphor about the dangers of modern living when certain conservative attitudes prevail was conceived by writer-director Rob Hedden, who keeps it taut and fast-moving as Ritter slowly awakens to the truth of the manipulations. The implications of the right wing one day taking us over are chilling, as are the performances by Linden, Teague and June Lockhart (as a sweet school principal). Todd Jeffries, Alexandra Picatto, Cody Dorkin, Frank Hauner.

COLOR ME BLOOD RED (1966) ★★ Blood-dripping obscenity from writer-director Herschell G. Lewis, gore specialist, and exploitationer producer David F. Friedman. A deranged artist retains blood of female victims to splash on his impressionistic canvases. Color it morbid. ... Joseph, Candi Conder, Scott H. Hall. ...met; Rhino; Video Dimensions; S/Weird; ... BFPI as *Model Massacre*)

... OR OF NIGHT (1994) ★★★ Diehard Bruce ...is fans will be disappointed in this bizarre ...hothriller in which Willis portrays a sensi... psychiatrist solving the murder of his best-...nd headshrinker (Scott Bakula), committed b... ne of five neurotic, whacked-out patients in a therapy group. There are several excellent gore-murder sequences and some hot and heavy love-making sessions between Willis and Jane March (including a bout of underwater grappling in a swimming pool), but the script by Matthew Chapman and Billy Ray is full of glaring inconsistencies and sports a climax more ludicrous than thrilling. If the film excels at all, it is in the offbeat direction of Richard Rush, who has an incredible eye for detail and makes clever use of locations and props. Willis's Dr. Capa is as nutty as the group neurotics (who include Lance Henriksen, Brad Dourif, Lesley Ann Warren and Kevin J. O'Connor) and has an is-he-crazy-or-not? scene stolen right out of Hitchcock's *Spellbound*. Willis is too limited an actor to carry the load of absurdities, and the image of his high-tech action movies are indelibly superimposed over his screen persona. Some things do die hard. (Video/DVD: Hollywood Pictures)

COLOSSUS 1980. See *Colossus: The Forbin Project*.

COLOSSUS OF NEW YORK (1958) ★★★ Excellent low-budget sci-fi thriller, intelligently directed by Eugene Lourie and written by Thelma Schnee. When genius Ross Martin is struck down by a truck, his father (Otto Kruger) removes his brain and forces his second son (John Baragrey, who looks and sounds like MacDonald Carey) to create a robot to house the mind. It's a mixture of *Donovan's Brain*, Gort the Robot, Svengali the Hypnotist and *Demon Seed* as the brain is stricken by insanity and the robot goes on a murderous spree at the UN, killing with an X-ray beam through its visor. Ed Wolff plays the ten-foot metal man, Mala Powers is the beautiful wife and Robert Hutton is the colorless love interest.

COLOSSUS: THE FORBIN PROJECT (1968) ★★★★ Tense, exciting sci-fi about a supercomputer designed to maintain peace in the world but which takes control of missile systems, forcing all people to bow to its demagogic whims. Fine effects by Albert Whitlock, sharp direction by Joseph Sargent and a well-honed script by James Bridges (from the D. F. Jones novel). Eric Braeden, Susan Clark, William Schallert. Aka *The Day the World Changed Hands* and *Colossus 1980*. (MCA)

COMA (1978) ★★★ Robin Cook's best-seller, faithfully adapted by director Michael Crichton. Nurse Genevieve Bujold discovers patients are dying mysteriously under comatose conditions and with Michael Douglas reveals a shocking plot. Good thriller, ample suspense. Richard Widmark, Elizabeth Ashley, Rip Torn, Lois Chiles. (Video/Laser: MGM/UA)

COMBAT SHOCK. Video version of *American Nightmare* (Prism).

COMEBACK, THE (1977) ★★ Singer Jack Jones is writing new material in an eerie estate when he is haunted by his wife's ghost. Her murderer comes to the mansion, where a confrontation is played out with buckets of blood. Produced-directed by Peter Walker, scripted by Murray Smith and Michael Sloan. Richard Johnson, David Doyle. Aka *The Day the Screaming Stopped*. (Warner Bros.; Lorimar)

COMEDY OF TERRORS, THE (1963) ★★★★ Sidesplitting parody: Undertakers Vincent Price and Peter Lorre plot to finish off landlord Basil Rathbone but bumble to their own demises. Boris Karloff is in a hysterical role as an old geezer, with Joe E. Brown and buxom Joyce Jameson adding to the macabre merriment. Director Jacques Tourneur (*Curse of the Demon*) makes sport of horror clichés with a cast that made the clichés famous. Classic "black com-

edy" script by Richard Matheson, first written as *The Graveside Story*. (HBO; Movies Unlimited) (Laser: Image, with *The Oblong Box*)

COMIC BOOK CONFIDENTIAL (1988) ★★★★ Intriguing documentary on the comic books with emphasis on the 1954 congressional hearings that led the industry to impose a censorship code on itself. Filmmaker Ron Mann focuses on the E.C. comics of the period and interviews Al Feldstein, William M. Gaines and Harvey Kurtzman for memories of those turbulent times. Several horror comics of the period are dealt with—but the film also covers comics up to modern time, with Stan Lee explaining why superheroes became popular in the 1960s and underground artists (Robert Crumb, Gilbert Shelton, Bill Griffith, Art Spiegelman) commenting on how they brought about changes in the '60s. Highlighted is Will Eisner, whose "Spirit" comic is documented as a major artistic force. Any self-respecting comic book fan will not want to miss this informative, amusing film. (Pacific Arts) (Laser: Voyager)

COMIC BOOK KIDS, THE (1981) ★★ Strictly kiddie fare photographed on a soundstage, before a live audience of kids, and taken from a TV series. Joseph Campanella keeps appearing as the frustrated boss of a comic-book company harassed by artist Marvin (Mike Darnell), who draws the Fanto the Comic Book Wizard. Two obnoxious kids (Robyn Finn and Jim Engelhardt) wear "transporter belts" to project themselves into Fanto's world. Appearing in guest spots in the two half-hour episodes here ("The Worried Wizard" and "The Princess and the Goblin") are Anjelica Huston and Billy Barty. Directed by Gene Weed. (Cinemaker)

COMING SOON (1984) ★★★ Compilation of footage from Universal's horror and sci-fi movies, as well as trailers and behind-the-scenes footage, such as Steven Spielberg making *E.T.* Written by Mick Garris and producer John Landis, who also directed. Narrated by Jamie Lee Curtis. (MCA)

COMMANDO CODY. Feature-length video version (85 minutes) of the Republic serial *Radar Men from the Moon* (Worldwide).

COMMANDO CODY, SKY MARSHAL OF THE UNIVERSE. This is a compilation of episodes from a TV version of the serial *Radar Men from the Moon*, with Judd Holdren in the title role that George Wallace played in the 12-chapter cliffhanger. Directed by Fred C. Brannon, Harry Keller and Franklin Adreon. Aline Towne, William Schallert, Lyle Talbot.

COMMUNION. (1978). See *Alice, Sweet Alice*.

COMMUNION (1989) ★★★ Whitley Strieber's 1986 best-seller, in which he claimed to have been subjected to medical testing by alien life-forms, became an independent feature coproduced and written by Strieber and directed by

Philippe Mora. Hence, it is Strieber's point of view—a disturbing fact if you are less than convinced the well-read horror novelist lived through these weird events. However, in all fairness, the film is a compelling study of the abduction phenomenon, and submerges itself into the metaphysical side of the mystery. The creatures—androgynous saucer-eyed humanoids and dark blue, rotund reptilians—are presented as benevolent beings and the film ends on an uplifting note. Christopher Walken as Strieber limns an eccentric, ironic character as he undergoes his sinister encounters. Lindsay Crouse, Joel Carlson, Francis Sternhagen, Andrea Katsulas. (MCEG Virgin) (Laser: Image)

COMPANION, THE (1976). See *Die, Sister, Die!*

COMPANION, THE (1994) ★★★ Ray Bradbury's "Marionettes Inc." seems to be the inspiration behind this TV-movie written by Ian Seeberg and directed by Gary Fledler. It's set in a vague, futuristic time and place, when we have improved electronics but everything else looks the same. Romantic novelist Gillian Tanner (Kathryn Harrold) buys a human android (Bruce Greenwood) from Personal Electronics (the G-45 series) to take with her to the lake, where she's writing a new book. She keeps reprogramming the "guy" (from greater sexuality to "random data," which makes him fully human) until the android becomes possessive and homicidal. The believability of it all hinges on Greenwood, who does a formidable job of conveying the growing levels of intelligence as he is reprogrammed. Brion James gives a nice cameo as a sculptor who lives nearby. Talia Balsam, Joely Fisher, James Karen, Bryan Cranston, Tracey Walter. (Video/Laser: MCA)

COMPANY OF WOLVES, THE (1985) ★★★★ Beautiful British film mixing man-into-animal effects with ominous symbolism and literary metaphor to retell "Little Red Riding Hood" as a werewolf horror story. Director Neil Jordan (who went on to direct *Interview with the Vampire*) makes this audacious idea work because the fictional never-never land is a foreboding forest, and the theme depicted in graphic horror terms. (One sequence shows a man skinning his own head while wolf parts pop out of his body; another has a wolf's tongue darting out of a human mouth.) Sarah Patterson dreams she and her family are in a village in a past century, threatened by killer wolves or men with "the beast within them." Angela Lansbury is gnarly and wise as the grandmother who tells "once upon a time" werewolf tales. Several wolf-narratives within wolf-narratives build to the confrontation between Patterson (Ms. Riding Hood) and Huntsman-turned-fang-monster (Micha Bergese). This works as an exercise in art design, mood and allegory. The photography is exquisite, capturing an autumnal tone that adds

to the sinister qualities of the medieval times. David Warner. (Video/Laser: Vestron)

COMPUTER GHOSTS (1987) ★ Silly Australian TV-movie depicting the efforts of a bogus security company, Crooksnatchers, to create phony computer-generated hauntings in order to buy up abandoned property cheaply at auction. This innocuous comedy, directed by Marcus Cole, is nearly worthless as an entertainment, especially when the supernatural themes are intermingled with a "Heavenly" subplot in which an old man (who could be the son of God) sends a pair to Earth to circumvent the devious minds behind Crooksnatchers. The comedy is labored beyond belief. Nicholas Ryan, Peter Whitford.

COMPUTER KILLERS. See *Horror Hospital.*

COMPUTER WORE TENNIS SHOES, THE (1970) ★★★ Electronic memory bank of a computer is injected into Kurt Russell's brain in this Disney comedy written by Joseph L. McEveety. Cesar Romero is the bumbling bad guy trying to steal the new discovery. Directed by Robert Butler. Joe Flynn, William Schallert. The sequel was *Now You See Him, Now You Don't.* Remade for TV in 1995. (Disney)

COMPUTER WORE TENNIS SHOES, THE (1995) ★★ In this remake of the 1970 Disney comedy, a Scott Immergut TV production, Kirk Cameron portrays the college student whose brain is filled with data after he's shocked in a laboratory computer accident. Directed by Peyton Reed and written by Joseph L. McEveety and Ryan Rowe, based on the film originally written by McEveety. Anne Marie Tremko, Dean Jones, Andrew Woodworth, Mathew McCurley.

CONAN THE BARBARIAN (1982) ★★★★ Robert E. Howard's sword-and-sorcery hero with bulging biceps, who prays to the god Crom, reached the screen as Arnold Schwarzenegger, one-time muscle champ. Despite a "barbaric" Austrian accent, it was good casting. John Milius's direction and script (with cowriter Oliver Stone) give the first half-hour an episodic sense, then indulge the clichés of the quest. The main thrust is Conan's search for his parents' murderer: Thulsa Doom, a snake cultist etched in acid by James Earl Jones. Of interest is Conan's romance with a female warrior, Sandahl Bergman. Mako and Gerry Lopez are of minor interest as Conan's chronicler and sidekick. Ron Cobb's visual designs are imaginative. Sequel: *Conan the Destroyer.* William Smith, Franco Columbo, Max Von Sydow. (Video/Laser: MCA)

CONAN THE DESTROYER (1984) ★★★ Strong follow-up to (but no substitute for) *Conan the Barbarian*, directed by Richard Fleischer and scripted by Stanley Mann. Arnold Schwarzenegger is back as the sword-wielding warrior, assigned to escort a teenage princess to a castle where awaits a precious stone with magical powers. His band includes two-faced Wilt Chamberlain, a beanpole of a warrior (Grace Jones) and witty chronicler Mako. The villain is a warlock, Dagoth (created by Carlo Rambaldi), who indulges his fighting whims in a room of mirrors. Tracey Walter, Sarah Douglas, Jeff Corey. (Video/Laser: MCA)

CONDORMAN (1981) ★★ Cartoonist Michael Crawford experiences the adventures he created for his hero, Condorman, by donning his Condorman costume to fight for the CIA, surrounded by beautiful operatives (Barbara Carrera for one) and gadgets that enable him to fly, drive supercars, etc. Disney spoof of James Bond is watered down kids' stuff. Directed by Charles Jarrott; written by Marc Stirdivant from Robert Sheckley's book *The Game of X*. Oliver Reed, Dana Elcar, James Hampton. (Disney)

CONEHEADS (1993) ★★★ A movie spinoff from the *Saturday Night Live* sketches, from producer Lorne Michaels, depicts a family of pinheaded aliens accepted as normal by people on Earth. Dan Aykroyd and Jane Curtin (from the original cast) are back to have a silly time as they portray "illegal aliens" pursued by INS agents. The sci-fi elements are stylish and the direction by Steve Barron appropriately fast-moving to keep one from noticing any lack of logic. Michelle Burke, Michael McKean, Jason Alexander. (Video/Laser: Paramount)

CONGO (1995) ★★★ Rousing, well-produced version of Michael Crichton's adventure novel, directed by Frank Marshall with a sense for what's good in an old-fashioned trek-through-jungle movie and adapted with an ear for unusual dialogue by John Patrick Shanley. *Congo* is a mixture of many African themes (safari made up of assorted soldiers-of-fortune and adventurers, each with a personal agenda; communication between man and gorilla; King Solomon's lost city and diamond mine; a colony of gray killer gorillas) which are all expertly blended. The climax is a grand payoff as the nearby restless volcano finally erupts, the ground cracks open to swallow anything that doesn't hang on for dear life, and heroine (and one-time CIA operative) Laura Linney, "great white hunter" Ernie Hudson, diamond seeker Tim Curry, gorilla trainer Dylan Walsh and a benevolent gorilla named Amy run for their lives. Bruce Campbell, Grant Heslov, Joe Don Baker. (Video/Laser: Paramount)

CONNECTICUT YANKEE IN KING ARTHUR'S COURT, A (1949) ★★★ Musical-comedy based on Mark Twain's fantasy about a man who travels in time to King Arthur's court. It's a handsome showcase for Bing Crosby and his crooning, colorfully directed by Tay Garnett. Neat time-travel paradoxes as Crosby croons and clowns. Victor Young's score is memorable and the cast well chosen: Rhonda Fleming, William Bendix, Sir Cedric Hardwicke, Henry Wilcoxon, Alan Napier, Virginia Field. (Video/Laser: MCA)

CONNECTICUT YANKEE IN KING ARTHUR'S COURT, A (1989) ★★★ An amusing satirical TV-movie that deviates from Mark Twain's fantasy. Instead of a man traveling through time to the days of yore, a young girl (Keshia Knight Pulliam, star of "The Cosby Show") faces the lance of Sir Lancelot and becomes involved in the king's court, imposing women's lib attitudes and taking advantage of Dark Age superstitions to appear magical. There's a fairy-tale quality and a spirit of fun that director Mel Damski maintains throughout the adventurous tomfoolery. Jean Marsh, Rene Auberjonois, Emma Samms, Whip Hubley, Michael Gross. (Family Home Entertainment)

CONQUEROR WORM, THE (1968) ★★★ The final film of director Michael Reeves, a cult filmmaker who died at 25 from a drug overdose, is a stylish horror thriller about witchhunter Vincent Price burning women at the stake when Cromwell was deposing the King of England. Based on a Poe poem, it was written by Reeves and Tom Baker. Ian Ogilvy, Hillary Dwyer, Patrick Wymark, Rupert Davies. Aka *The Witchfinder General*. (HBO) (Laser: Image)

CONQUEST (1984) ★★ Italian-Spanish-Mexican job from Italian director Lucio Fulci, a specialist in graphic horror. It's sword and sorcery in a setting where muscular warriors do battle with she-devil Ocron (Sabrina Siani) and hairy beasts. Script (by Gino Capone) and direction are poor, although Claudio Simonetti's rock score is exciting, if inappropriate to Neanderthal locations. Jorge Rivero. (Media)

CONQUEST OF SPACE (1954) ★★ Chester Bonestell's paintings of alien landscapes (from a book written by Willy Ley) are the highlight of this science-minded adventure about a flight to Mars and the psychological problems of the crew. Directed by Byron Haskin, from James O'Hanlon's script, George Pal's film is an attempt to reflect space travel in a realistic fashion, but that realism is in contrast to the unconvincing characters. Walter Brooke, Eric Fleming, Phil Foster, Ross Martin, William Hopper, William Redfield. Aka *Mars Project*. (Paramount)

CONQUEST OF THE PLANET OF THE APES (1972) ★★★★ One of the best in the Planet of the Apes series, depicting a futuristic Earth when apes are trained as slaves. Ceasar the chimpanzee (Roddy McDowall), who has powers of speech and reasoning, forms the slaves into gorilla guerrillas and stages a revolt. Fine direction by J. Lee Thompson, an excellent script by Paul Dehn and intriguing morality lessons make this compelling. Don Murray, Ricardo Montalban, Hari Rhodes, Natalie Trundy, John Randolph. (Video/Laser: CBS/Fox)

CONSPIRACY OF TERROR. See *House of Secrets* (1993).

CONTACT (1996) ★★★★★ This adaptation of Carl Sagan's novel depicts man's first discovery of an alien-generated radio signal from deep space and the adventures of young scientist-astronomer Ellie Arroway, who will utimately become the first woman to travel through time and space to another galaxy/dimension/center of the universe (the choice is ultimately yours). *Contact* is certainly one of the most mature films to deal with these hard-core science-fiction themes and it does so in a heartfelt and honest way as we watch how mankind handles (and frequently mishandles) such a monumental event. At its core is an excellent and moving performance by Jodie Foster as Ellie. Fragile and intelligent, and burdened by a scientist's disbelief in God as a supreme being, Ellie finds that the spirit of purity she has for her job with SETI, searching for extraterrestrial life in the universe by listening for radio signals, is more than trampled on by government bureaucracy, militant suspicions and paranoia, and a strong pro-God movement that interprets the radio signals as a message from God Himself. Ellie must also handle her personal affairs with lover Matthew McConaughey (his views differ from hers, but their romance constantly rebinds them), a rival scientist (Tom Skerritt), a government cynic (James Woods), a White House administrator (Angela Bassett), and an eccentric millionaire (John Hurt) whose place in all of this may not be what it first seems. David Morse gives a moving performance as Ellie's father (who turns up in the darnedest places) and Ken Ralston's special effects of Ellie being jettisoned through the universe are a fascinating blend of science and fantasy. The script adaptation by James V. Hart and Michael Goldenberg provides one excellent scene after another and reveals a key plot twist at just the right moment. Director Robert Zemeckis brilliantly brings all the complex themes together in a style that is nonintrusive yet still captures the scope and the emotional depth of the story. And although the film runs long (2 ½ hours), it never seems long. In fact, the characters emerge so vividly you want the story to continue. The film is dedicated to Sagan, who is credited as coproducer but who died before its release. William Fichtner, Rob Lowe, Jake Busey. (Video/DVD: Warner Bros.)

CONTACT UFO: ALIEN ABDUCTIONS (1991) ★★½ Pseudodocumentary report on alleged abduction cases, including a couple that have startling documentation. (Video/Laser: MPI)

CONTAGION (1988) ★★ Real estate man John Doyle is lured to a dilapidated mansion and forced by ghosts to commit crimes of sex and passion for reasons never made clear by director Karl Zwicky. Nicola Bartlet, Roy Barrett, Nathy Gaffney. (Sony) (Laser: Image)

CONTAMINATION. Heavily edited version of *Alien Contamination* (European Creative).

CONTAMINATION: ALIEN ON EARTH. Original title for *Alien Contamination*.

COOL WORLD (1992) ★★½ This wasted opportunity to follow in the paw tracks of Roger Rabbit is a mixture of live action and animation that is so far off the mark one wonders what producer Frank Mancuso, Jr., and director Ralph Bakshi had in mind when they concocted this schizophrenic glimpse into a cartoonist's mind. There's wonderful animation but the Michael Grais–Mark Victor script is disconnected from cohesive storytelling. Gabriel Byrne plays the wacko cartoonist who travels between Las Vegas and "Cool World," a netherland in his own mind (?) where his cartoons live as "doodles"—drawn characters set against real backgrounds. Sexy Yankee "doodle" dancer-singer Holli Would (patterned after counterpart Kim Basinger) wants to "get real" so she can stay in our world, but why she keeps going from flesh to animation and back again, and why Brad Pitt is a "Cool World" private eye are never made clear. One memorable highlight is a "Superduperman" parody image that deserves more screen time. Michele Abrams, Deidre O'Connell, Carrie Hamilton. (Video/Laser: Paramount)

COOPERSTOWN (1992) ★★★ Alan Arkin plays an eccentric in this light-hearted character study. He's an aging baseball coach who never had the pitching career that he dreamed of, and who is haunted by the spirit of his dead catcher friend (Graham Greene). For years Arkin has harbored a grudge against his one-time playing companion, and this details how he revisits people and places from his past to find a new inner peace. It's a pleasant mixture well directed by Charles Haid, who also appears in the cast. Ed Begley, Jr., Josh Charles, Paul Dooley, Hope Lange. (Turner)

COPPERHEAD (1984) ★ Video release, made in Missouri, focusing on a crazy swamp family fleeing with a rare necklace. The father is a crazy guy who enjoys blowing away poisonous snakes, but those slimy critters get their revenge. Written-directed by Leland Payton. Jack Renner, Gretta Ratliff. (VCI)

COPYCAT (1995) ★★★★ There are many serial killer/slasher movies out there, and while this is just as contrived as most, demanding that you set your credulity button on zero, it rises to the top because of the extra care screenwriters Ann Biderman and David Madsen took in shaping the characters. Holly Hunter portrays one of the cops on the case (M. J. Monahan) with a deliciously different take on female homicide investigators, using her quirky attitude and charm to get what she wants from the San Francisco Police Department as she investigates a series of grisly murders. And Sigourney Weaver, as serial-killer expert Dr. Helen Hudson, brings believability to the story with her mental breakdown, panic attacks and agoraphobic condition. And there is, for this genre, a genuinely surprise twist ending that is chilling in its implications. The story deals with how Hunter and Weaver work together to expose a murderer who is copying the horrendous crimes of real-life killers. Laszlo Kovacs's photography for director Jon Amiel gives him all he needs to make this look and feel like a horror picture. Dermot Mulroney, John Rothman, Will Patton, Harry Connick, Jr. (Video/Laser: Warner Bros.)

CORMORANT, THE (1993) ★★★ A chilling if sometimes enigmatic tale of possession, and an allegory of what happens to man when he loses control to nature à la *The Birds*, this British TV-movie is based on a novel by Stephen Gregory and is set on the bleak Welsh coast. Ralph Fiennes and Helen Schlesinger inherit a strange seabird and have to live in a house on the lonely frontier taking care of it. The sinister bird with a long bill begins to take over—first by killing the family cat, then by taking over Fiennes. It's a dark, moody psychological study of human deterioration adapted by Peter Ransley and directed by Peter Markham, who captures the loneliness and coldness of Wales. Thomas Williams, Buddug Morgan.

CORPSE COLLECTORS, THE. See *Cauldron of Blood*.

CORPSE GRINDERS, THE (1971) ★ Bad, bad exploitationer, as stomach-churning as its title subtly suggests. At a cat-food factory, house tabbies, fed human flesh turned into hamburger patties, become snarling beasts, attacking innocent cat-lovers. The canning was done by producer-director Ted V. Mikels, who (mis)conceived *The Astro Zombies*. Arch Hall and Joseph Cranston wrote the tin labels. Tasteless. Sean Kenney, Monika Kelly. (Western World)

CORPSE-MAKERS, THE. See *Twice-Told Tales*.

CORPSE VANISHES, THE (1942) ★½ Vapid potboiler with Bela Lugosi as an unhinged botanist restoring youth to his aging wife by stealing brides' blood. Barrel-bottom production with hammy performances by Lugosi, Luana Walters (wife), Minerva Urecal (crazy old lady), Frank Moran (crazy son) and Angelo Rossitto (cackling dwarf) send this up in a disappearing wisp. Directed by Wallace (*Vanishing*) Fox, produced by Sam (*Thin Air*) Katzman and written by Harvey (*Evaporation*) Gates. Aka *Case of the Missing Brides*. (Kartes; Sinister/C; Filmfax; Nostalgia; Admit One carries this on a dual cassette with *Dick Tracy, Detective*)

COSMIC MAN, THE (1959) ★½ Direct steal of *The Day the Earth Stood Still* with humanoid alien John Carradine crash-landing on Earth (make that Bronston Canyon in L.A.) in a ship that resembles a golf ball and seeking scientist Bruce Bennett, who has been brought in by the military to find out if the golf ball is dangerous. Carradine is actually a good alien, attempting to help us feeble-minded Earthlings reconcile our political differences so we can live in peace with the Universe. Herman Greene's direction varies from absolutely corny to halfway decent, and Arthur Pierce's script has some okay dialogue and character relationships but gets hopelessly corny with a crippled kid and a long-suffering mother. Lyn Osborne, Paul Langton. (Rhino; S/Weird; Sinister/C)

COSMIC MONSTERS (1959) ★★ Scientist Forrest Tucker blows a hole in the ionosphere with his new invention, allowing rays from space to turn bugs into jumbo Insidious Insects and Behemoth Bugs in Breilly Woods. Adapted from Rene Ray's BBC serial *Strange World of Planet X* by Paul Ryder and directed by Robert Gunn, this is the sort of quickie that gives '50s sci-fi a crummy name. The monster effects are unconvincing, no matter how much scientific gibberish Tucker exchanges with a humanoid visitor from space, who speaks with a British accent yet. Yikes! Gaby Andre, Martin Benson. Aka *The Crawling Horror*. (Media; Rhino; VCI; S/Weird; Filmfax; Sinister/C)

COSMONAUTS ON VENUS. See *Planeta Burg*.

COSMOS KILLER. See *Miami Horror*.

COUNT DRACULA (1970) ★★ Spanish-British adaptation of Bram Stoker's *Dracula*, produced by cowriter Harry Alan Towers and directed by Jesus Franco. However, a gap remains between honorable intentions and execution and the film still falls short of its goals, with sloppy camera work and bad zooms. Christopher Lee believes this to be among his best work but it's certainly not the best *Dracula*. Herbert Lom is Van Helsing and Klaus Kinski is Renfield. Fred Williams, Soledad Miranda. Aka *Bram Stoker's Count Dracula*, *Dracula '71* and *The Nights of Dracula*. (Republic)

COUNT DRACULA AND HIS VAMPIRE BRIDE (1973) ★★ Lacking in Hammer's usual Gothic flavor and detail, Christopher Lee is surrounded by a cheap devil cult and speaks—a blasphemy that destroys the mystique Lee established in earlier films. Lorimar Van Helsing is again essayed by gaunt, indefatigable Peter Cushing, an extra staying power. The final showdown is contrived and half-hearted, as if director Alan Gibson and scripter Don Houghton hoped this would be the series' death knell. It was. Lee never again donned the Dracula cape. Joanna Lumley, Michael Coles, William Franklyn, Freddie Jones. Aka *The Satanic Rites of Dracula* and *Dracula Is Dead . . . and Well and Living in London.* (From ABC Liberty as *The Satanic Rites of Dracula*)

COUNT DRACULA'S GREATEST LOVE. Video of *Dracula's Great Love* (S/Weird; Filmfax).

COUNTERATTACK OF THE MONSTERS. See *Godzilla Raids Again.*

COUNTESS DRACULA (1970) ★★ Based on Valentine Penrose's historical study *The Bloody Countess*, this Hammer slammer written by Jeremy Paul tells the "true" story of Countess Elizabeth Bathory who, in the 16th century, slaughtered virgins in her dungeons and bathed in their blood. Meanwhile, cop Nigel Green investigates the corpses littering the countryside. Not for the squeamish. Directed by Peter Sasdy. Lesley-Anne Down, Maurice Denham.

COUNTESS DRACULA (1972) See *The Legend of Blood Castle.*

COUNT YORGA—VAMPIRE (1970) ★★ Producer Michael Macready and writer-director Bob Killjan teamed to make this low-budget horror film, successful enough to be followed by a sequel, *The Return of Count Yorga.* In an eerie castle outside L.A., Transylvania count Robert Quarry sets up headquarters invaded by stake-wielding teenagers. Goofy today, trendy when released. Roger Perry, Michael Murphy, Donna Anders, Judith Lang. Narrated by George Macready, Michael's dad. *Aka Loves of Count Iorga.* (HBO) (Laser: Image, with *Cry of the Banshee*)

COURTYARD, THE (1995) ★★½ A head-/arm-/legless torso, a severed head in a plastic bag and a corpse that drops in unexpectedly are among the horror visuals in this otherwise tame TV-movie murder-mystery whodunit that is most memorable for its quirky, nervous lead character (Andrew McCarthy as an architect) who is known by the killer and can't quite get connected to the cop on the case (played stylishly by Cheech Marin). McCarthy's troubles begin when he takes a spacious apartment at Shangri-La. He should have known he was in trouble when the owner turns out to be mysterious, creepy Vincent Schiavelli. Written by Wendy Hiller and Christopher Hawthorne; directed by Fred Walton. Madchen Amick, Bonnie Bartlett, David Proval, Jonathan Penner. (Republic)

COVEN. Video of *The Demon Lover* (BFPI).

CRADLE WILL FALL, THE (1983) ★★ James Farentino's eyeballs roll madly as a doctor seeking the formula for a "Fountain of Youth" serum—the better to inject into his patient, Lauren Hutton, a hardworking D.A. TV-movie based on a novel by Mary Higgins Clark and directed by John Llewelyn Moxey. Ben Murphy co-stars. (Lorimar; Warner Bros.)

CRAFT, THE (1996) ★★★ One of the better supernatural thrillers to deal with witchcraft and the nature of witches, a poor man's *The Witches of Eastwick.* Director Andrew Fleming (who co-wrote the intelligent script with Peter Filardi) makes the most of special effects but also emphasizes the relationships between four high school girls (dysfunctional or plagued by assorted problems) who discover they possess witchcraft powers. This is told from the point of view of sympathetic Robin Tunney, and enhanced by fine acting by Neve Campbell, Fairuza Balk and Rachel True as the others. Gradually the young women discover the dire consequences of their ungodly actions, and one of them is totally corrupted by evil after making her pact with the dark forces. There's a great snake sequence that rivals the one in *Raiders of the Lost Ark* and there's imaginative camera work to capture the frenzied, mad and impassioned world in which these 4 witches live. (Video/Laser: Columbia)

CRASH! (1977) ★ A total wreck that merely rusts in the sun. An antique auto possesses powers to kill, sending Sue Lyon scurrying for a traffic cop. Jose Ferrer, John Carradine, Leslie Parrish and John Ericson pop their clutches. *Crash!* is a mangled mess with director Charles Band at the wheel and writer Marc Marais in the crankshaft. Aka *Akaza, the God of Vengeance* and *Death Ride.*

CRASH AND BURN (1990) ★★★ Offbeat Full Moon Production, directed by Charles Band from a J. S. Cardone script, set in July 2030, when the ozone layer is depleted and Earth is bombarded with ultraviolet light and men wear "cool suits" outside. The setting becomes a TV station–power center where several characters are stranded, and a killer "synthoid" (a government humanoid-robot) is on a rampage to protect the UNICOM government. Paul Ganus, a UNICOM agent, learns the truth but turns against the company to protect the innocent people the robot stalks. There's nothing supergreat about this video movie but there are unusual effects and the cast is competent. Ralph Waite, Megan Ward, Bill Moseley, Eva Larue, Jack McGee, Katherine Armstrong, John Davis Chandler. (Video/Laser: Paramount)

CRAVING, THE (1980) ★ Ninth entry in Paul Naschy's werewolf series from Spain, with the hairy guy meeting up with Hungary's reigning blood queen, Liz Bathory. In the Carpathians, an evil chick digs up Liz and brings her to life by dripping blood over her face. Yech! It's the old silver-dagger-in-the-heart-on-the-night-of-the-full-moon. Spanish gore; ya want more? Directed by Naschy as "Jack" Jacinto Molina. Aka *Return of the Wolf Man.* (Media; Vestron)

CRAWLERS, THE (1990) ★★ Nuclear waste from a rural power plant is sucked up by the roots of trees, turning the roots into snakelike monster-tentacles that attack human beings. Mary Sellers and Jason Saucier organize the town to fight off the attackers. Poorly done effects and lousy acting earmark this Canadian sci-fi thriller with ecological overtones. Bubba Reeves, Chelsi Stahr, Vince O'Neil. Directed by Martin Newlin. (Columbia Tristar)

CRAWLING EYE, THE (1958) ★★ Old-fashioned alien invader-monster movie with the hoary clichés and bad effects of the '50s. On the plus side is crisp black-and-white photography and a sense of doom when a cloud formation hovers around Mt. Trollenberg in the Alps, something in its interior killing mountain climbers. UN investigator Forrest Tucker is drawn into the mystery by sisters (Janet Munro and Jennifer Jayne) who have a mind-reading stage act. The "Eye Monster" is a tentacled blob that's pretty corny when the showdown arrives. Jimmy Sangster based his tense, stereotyped script on a BBC teleplay by Peter Key, *The Trollenberg Terror.* Great to curl up and watch, even if you have to laugh occasionally. Directed by Quentin Lawrence. Warren Mitchell, Laurence Payne. Aka *The Flying Eye, The Trollenberg Terror, Creature from Another World* and *The Creeping Eye.* (Fox Hills; Media; Sinister/C; Dark Dreams; Filmfax) (Laser: Image)

CRAWLING HAND, THE (1963) ★★½ Delightfully sleazy B in which the X-20 lunar rocket returns with a madman aboard, his molecules stricken with Cosmic Rayitis. After his ship is blown up by scientists Kent Taylor and Peter Breck, Rod Lauren finds his severed arm and takes it home. The hand comes alive, clutching human throats and hypnotizing victims. What makes this watchable are Allison Hayes as lab assistant, Tris Coffin as cop, Richard Arlen as lunar project boss and Alan Hale as sheriff. The digited "hand-me-down" beast is finally trapped in a city dump. Tension mounts. Moral: Never fight the hand that bleeds you. Written-directed by Herbert L. Strock. Aka *Don't Cry Wolf, The Creeping Hand* and *Tomorrow You Die.* (Video Gems; Rhino; Nostalgia) (Laser: Image)

CRAWLING MONSTER, THE. See *The Creeping Terror.*

CRAWLING TERROR, THE. See *The Cosmic Monsters.*

CRAWLSPACE (1986) ★ Pointless psychokiller movie exploiting human madness without insight into the madman's character. Klaus Kinski, son of a Nazi war criminal, has inherited his father's desire to murder. "Killing is my opiate, my fix," mumbles Kinski, during one of his soul-searching sessions, which are frequent in this Empire film produced in Rome. An ex-doctor from Buenos Aires, who was responsible for 60 deaths, KK rents flats to young women, then spies on them from the ventilator shaft (crawlspace) or kills their sex partners after watching them coupling. In his lab of horrors, KK keeps a woman in a cage and body pieces in bottles. Blood and gore are minimal. Directed by David Schmoeller. Talia Balsam, Barbara Whinnery. (Lightning; Vestron)

CRAZE (1973) ★ Antique collector Jack Palance sacrifices humans to an African idol, going bonkers in eyeball-rolling fashion and bringing his wonderful maniacal menace to this dreadful dreck. A Herman Cohen film made in England, directed by Freddie Francis. Cowritten by Cohen and Aben Kandel, who adapted Henry Seymour's *The Infernal Idol.* Diana Dors, Julie Ege. (Saturn; from VCR as *The Demon Master*)

CRAZED (1982) ★★ Quirky psychological portrait of an impotent man (Laszlo Papas) living in a boardinghouse with a cranky, chatty old woman (Belle Mitchell) unfolds in an offhanded way and is loaded with eccentric characters, such as a skid-row hotel owner and a writing instructor. Beverly Ross portrays the lonely woman/diabetic with whom the social misfit falls in love. Circumstances finally force him to commit murders. Writer-director Richard Cassidy, who has a penchant for the bizarre, maintains a sense of sympathy for this demented character. (Trans World; from Regal as *Blood Shed* and Genesis as *Slipping into Darkness*)

CRAZIES, THE (1975) ★★★ Director George Romero attempts to duplicate his *Night of the Living Dead* by depicting the population of Evans City, PA, going stark raving bananas after exposure to a deadly virus unleashed by the military into the town's drinking water. Grim civil-war sequences ensue as the debilitating virus brings on madness, then death, while the militia tries to restore order. A frightening commentary on martial law. Fast-paced editing breathes an exciting tempo into this low-budget film, Romero's personal favorite. Originally made as *Code Name: Trixie*; aka *The Mad People.* Lane Carroll, Harold Wayne Jones. (Vista) (Laser: Japanese)

CRAZY MUSIC. Rerelease title of *The Five Thousand Fingers of Dr. T.*

CREATED TO KILL. Video of *Embryo* (Ace).

CREATION OF THE HUMANOIDS (1962) ★★½ Although plagued by cheapness, and static scenes under the direction of Wesley E. Barry, this is an earnest attempt to tell a postatomic-war cautionary tale, depicting life thousands of years after the Apocalypse when mankind has robots to tend to his needs. Robotic science leads to humanoid robots, but a guerrilla war breaks out when these are programmed to feel emotion and the militant Order of Flesh and Blood stamps out the new models. Reportedly Andy Warhol's favorite movie, *Creation* has a strange atmosphere due to the stylized (if inexpensive) sets, a prejudicial theme reflected through humanoid robots ("clickers") treated as inferiors, the color cinematography by Hal Mohr, the makeup by Jack Pierce (of *Frankenstein* fame) and occasional brilliant bits of dialogue by Jay Simms. Head android is Dudley Manlove of *Plan 9 from Outer Space* fame. Don Megowan, Frances McCann. Aka *Revolt of the Humanoids*. (Raedon; Monterey; Sinister/C)

CREATOR (1985) ★★★½ Heartfelt story about a crusty but lovable scientist (Peter O'Toole) who tries to re-create his long-dead wife in his lab by fertilizing an embryo with her cells. So wonderful is O'Toole as Harry Dr. Wolper, and so witty and philosophical is Jeremy Leven's script (adapted from his novel), this is a joy to behold. It's a love story—of O'Toole's undying feelings for his wife, of his platonic relationship with a sexually free nymph named Mellie (Mariel Hemingway). It's also about love between O'Toole's lab assistant (Vincent Spano) and a technician (Virginia Madsen). Accolades to director Ivan Passer for a sensitive film that says so much about the joy and pain of life. David Ogden Stiers, John Dehner, Jeff Corey. (Video/ Laser: HBO)

CREATURE (1984) ★★½ Obvious steal of *Alien*, at best an ambitious failure. What detracts is a spirited attempt to duplicate the *Alien* look but without striving for originality. An archeological expedition travels to Titan, a moon of Jupiter, to discover a derelict ship inhabited by a hideous beast that munches avidly on victims or attaches control devices to victims. Numerous gory touches and resurrected corpses, but director William Malone does not create tension or suspense. The cast is slightly above the teen-age acting level, taking its sense of hysteria from Klaus Kinski, who turns up as a Mad German. Aka *The Titan Find*. Stan Ivar, Wendy Schaal, Lyman Ward. (Media; Magnum) (Laser: Media)

CREATURE FROM ANOTHER WORLD. See *The Crawling Eye*.

CREATURE FROM BLACK LAKE (1976) ★½ Two anthropologists search for a long-armed relative of Big Foot, seen loping around in a sinister lake. Dub Taylor and Jack Elam as good ole swamp boys give the film character, and the Louisiana bayou photography is okay, but the younger characters and their search are hampered by tomfoolery. The film (aka *Demon of the Lake*) ends with a harrowing chase, but it comes too late. Directed by Joy Houck, Jr., from a Jim McCullough, Jr., script. Dennis Fimple, Catherine McClenny (Morgan Fairchild's sister). (Lightning; Vestron)

CREATURE FROM BLOOD ISLAND. See *Terror Is a Man*.

CREATURE FROM GALAXY 27, THE. See *Night of the Blood Beast*.

CREATURE FROM THE BLACK LAGOON (1954) ★★★★★ A truly classic monster movie, one of Universal's best ever, originally written as *Black Lagoon* and shot in 3-D. The excellent underwater photography lifts the somewhat mundane Harry Essex–Arthur Ross story line

out of the doldrums as scientists travel to South America in search of a "gillman." Ben Chapman and Riccou Browning share credit for playing the Monster, one of Hollywood's best rubbersuit jobs. Richard Denning and Richard Carlson head the expedition, fighting over lovely Julia Adams. In one sequence she goes swimming alone and the monster swims with her, creating an eerie "beauty and the beast" aquatic ballet. Jack Arnold directed in inspired fashion, contributing ambience and action. Equally fine are Whit Bissell, Nestor Piava (as the superstitious captain) and Antonio Moreno. The H. J. Slater/ Henry Mancini musical score is suitably horrendous—and memorable. With the sequels *Revenge of the Creature* and *The Creature Walks Among Us*, this is one series that swam all the way to the bank. (MCA; Goodtimes; Hollywood Movie Greats) (Laser: MCA)

CREATURE FROM THE CAVE. See *Beast from Haunted Cave*.

CREATURE FROM THE HAUNTED SEA (1960) ★★ Roger Corman produced/directed film (shot in Puerto Rico) blends horror and satire in a spoof of the Warner Bros. gangster films of the '30s. Charles Griffith's script has gangster Anthony Carbone helping members of Batista's government flee Cuba with a gold cache. Carbone plans to kill them and blame it on a sea monster. Remade as *Up from the Depths*. Betsy Jones Moreland, Edward Wain, Robert Bean. (Sinister/C; Viking; Video Home Library; S/ Weird; Filmfax; Nostalgia)

CREATURE OF DESTRUCTION (1967) ★ Incompetent schlock, plain utterly awful. Les Tremayne portrays a stage hypnotist who puts beautiful Pat Delaney into a trance, turning her into a sea monster that rises from the surf to murder, kill and slaughter, but not necessarily in that order. Described as a remake of *She Creature*, this is the botched work of producer-director Larry Buchanan. Aron Kincaid, Neil Fletcher. (S/Weird)

CREATURES, THE. Re-release title of *From Beyond the Grave*.

CREATURES FROM BEYOND THE GRAVE. See *From Beyond the Grave*.

CREATURES OF THE PREHISTORIC PLANET. See *Vampire Men of the Lost Planet*.

CREATURES OF THE RED PLANET. Alternate title for *Vampire Men of the Lost Planet*.

CREATURE'S REVENGE. See *The Brain* (1971).

CREATURES THE WORLD FORGOT (1971) ★★★ A Hammer prehistoric fantasy-adventure, but producer-writer Michael Carreras dropped stop-motion dinosaurs and focused on a different creature—the kind that arouse men in a special way. The creature he picked was Julie Ege. There's nothing prehistoric, though, about Julie's figure, which bulges out of her animal skins. Carreras's monosyllabic screenplay shows how Julie, daughter of a tribal chief, is given to the chief of a rival clan. Don Chaffey directed this entertainment, which has not a serious bone in its cinematic body. Brian O'Shaughnessy, Tony Bonner, Robert John. (RCA/Columbia)

CREATURE WALKS AMONG US, THE (1956) ★★★½ Third and final release in Universal's *Black Lagoon* series is still better than most B efforts. Scientists Jeff Morrow and Rex Reason capture the Gillman and mutate its lungs so it can live on land. But the murderous passions of man and some hints of sex send the Creature into a primeval rage. Arthur Ross's script builds sympathy for the Creature and deals with unusual philosophical issues. Directed with an ambience of moral decay by John Sherwood. Ricou Browning repeats his underwork role as the Creature, Don Megowan takes over on dry land. Leigh Snowden, Gregg Palmer. (Video/Laser: MCA)

CREATURE WASN'T NICE, THE. See *Spaceship*.

CREATURE WITH THE ATOM BRAIN (1955) ★★ They were mindless humanoid robots, their brains wired with vengeful circuitry and programmed to kill, kill, kill. These monstrosities mutilate, bash, crash and make hash of human targets. Standing tall in this sea of mangled bodies is Richard Denning, who short-circuits the mad doc responsible for the destruction. Delightfully inept Sam Katzman production, totally watchable. Thank writer Curt Siodmak and director Edward L. Cahn for the yocks. Angela Stevens, Harry Lauter, Tris Coffin.

CREEPER, THE (1981). See *Rituals*.

CREEPER, THE (1984). Video version of *The Dark Side of Midnight* (AVR).

CREEPERS (1980). See *The Bloody Birthday*.

CREEPERS (1984) ★★★ Italian director Dario Argento returns to his *Suspiria* themes to spin this shivery yarn about Jennifer Connelly at a girls' school in "Swiss Transylvania" who finds crawling maggots and/or worms while insect researcher Donald Pleasence seeks a hooded killer who murders with a knife on a pole. This has that surreal quality that made Argento a cult favorite; his camera follows Jennifer as she chases a fallen telephone down a tunnel and as she plunges into a pit of gooey slime. Despite its murders and "perils of Pauline," though, *Creepers* (written by Argento and Franco Ferrini) never sustains the drive of *Deep Red*. Daria Nicolodi, Dalila Di Lazzaro. Aka *Phenomena*. (Media)

CREEPERS, THE (1968). See *Island of Terror*.

CREEPERS, THE (1970). Video version of *Assault* (Genesis; Saturn).

CREEPING EYE, THE. See *The Crawling Eye*.

CREEPING FLESH, THE (1973) ★★½ British chiller with Peter Cushing as a scientist exploring New Guinea who discovers a skeleton that,

when injected with a serum mixed with his blood, comes to life and causes havoc. Cushing injects daughter Lorna Heilbron with serum and she too develops antisocial tendencies. Christopher Lee lends strong presence as an asylum curator. Don't try to make sense of it, just enjoy. Directed by Freddie Francis, written by Peter Spencely and Jonathan Rumbold. Lorna Heilbron, George Benson, Michael Ripper. (Media; RCA/Columbia) (Laser: Image)

CREEPING HAND, THE. See *The Crawling Hand*.

CREEPING TERROR, THE (1964) ★ Reputedly "the worst film of all time," although *Plan 9 from Outer Space* deserves equal rank. Made at Lake Tahoe, NV, it depicts an elongated alien resembling a clumsy shag rug that devours people through a gaping maw, overturns cars and takes forever to shamble ten feet. Surely an example of superior ineptitude, so kudos to director Art(less) Nelson and (un)writer Arthur Ross. There's no dialogue, just narration—reportedly, the soundtracks were lost in the lake. Maybe the creature gobbled them up. Vic Savage, Shannon O'Neill. Aka *The Crawling Monster* and *Dangerous Charter*. (United; VCI; Rhino)

CREEPING UNKNOWN, THE (1956) ★★★ Hammer's version of Nigel Kneale's TV play *The Quatermass Experiment*, the first in the Quatermass trilogy that includes *Enemy from Space* and *Five Million Years to Earth*. Brian Donlevy portrays a driven scientist who tracks down the only surviving member of a rocket crew infected by an alien spore that turns into a putrescent blob and engulfs the Tower of London. It's up to Quatermass (naturally!) to stop it. Directed by Val Guest, who cowrote the adaptation with Richard Landau. Margia Dean, Jack Warner, Richard Wordsworth, Lionel Jeffries. Aka *Shock*. (Discount; from Sinister/C as *The Quatermass Experiment*) (Laser: MGM/UA)

CREEPOZOIDS (1987) ★½ Substandard *Alien* ripoff set in 1998 in a post-holocaust world where five deserters from the U.S. Army take refuge from acid rainstorms in an isolated lab. It's a "containment center" for a Government experiment that's created a Hideous Monster (once human, now mutated by "internal genetic synthesis") and a Giant Killer Rat. The effects are really bad, the rat and the monster obviously puppets pushed around by hand. Especially bad is a fight between a deserter and a newborn baby monster that looks identical to the one in *It's Alive*. Directed by David DeCoteau. Linnea Quigley, Ken Abraham, Michael Aranda, Richard Hawkins. (Urban Classics) (Laser: Shadow Entertainment)

CREEPS. See *The Bloody Birthday*.

CREEPSHOW (1982) ★★★½ George Romero, a lover of horror comics, directs 5 tales plus a wraparound from Stephen King's script, a homage to the E.C. comics of the '50s, a blending of Gothic horror and black humor. "Father's Day" is a graveyard tale of a walking corpse wreaking revenge; King appears in "The Lonesome Death of Jordy Verrill," portraying a bumpkin who sees a meteor crash near his farmhouse and spread green fungus ("meteorcrap") over everything; "The Crate" is the grisliest, showing how a creature caged up for a century is freed to feed on humans; the weakest entry, "Something to Tide You Over," is another walking-corpse story and thus redundant; the creepiest entry, "They're Creeping Up on You," is a man-vs.-nature allegory about an eccentric millionaire (E. G. Marshall) vs. cockroaches. Tom Savini's effects are outstanding. Hal Holbrook, Adrienne Barbeau, Fritz Weaver, Leslie Nielsen, Viveca Lindfors. (Video/Laser: Warner Bros.)

CREEPSHOW II (1987) ★★ Inferior sequel to the 1982 collaboration between writer Stephen King and director George Romero, copying the format of an old E.C. comic book with a character named The Creep (Tom Savini, the makeup artist) introducing three stories by King. (This time Romero produced, with Michael Gornick directing.) "Old Chief Wood'nhead" is a revenge yarn in which a general store wooden Indian in the dying town of Dead River comes alive after store owners George Kennedy and Dorothy Lamour are shot by killers. "The Raft" is a touch better, depicting 4 teenagers trapped on a lake where an oil-slick monster waits to take each of them to a gooey death. Only with "The Hitchhiker" does the film come to life, with Lois Chiles as an adulteress who runs over a pedestrian only to be pursued by his spirit. The tales are interspersed with Saturday morning–style animated sequences. (New World) (Laser: Image)

CRIES IN THE NIGHT (1961). See *The Awful Dr. Orloff*.

CRIES IN THE NIGHT (1981). See *Funeral Home*.

CRIMES IN THE WAX MUSUEM. See *Nightmare in Wax*.

CRIMES OF DR. MABUSE, THE. Video version of *The Testament of Dr. Mabuse* (Sinister/C; Filmfax).

CRIMES OF PASSION (1984) ★★½ Primarily the study of a prostitute and her sexual games and roles in life, but included here because of Anthony Perkins's role as a defrocked, perverted man of the cloth who hangs around skid row and gets his jollies by wielding a knife. Director Ken Russell opts for an ending that steals from *Psycho* and plays as an obscene joke. Kathleen Turner portrays the whore-by-night, working-woman-by-day. As freakish as it sounds. Annie Potts, Bruce Davison. (Video/Laser: New World)

CRIME ZONE (1988) ★★ Offbeat post-Armageddon society story that avoids *Mad Max* clichés and has the feel of an allegory. In a futuristic society, Soleil, a militant police force (bossed by David Carradine) controls a population of social classes and has "sex" checks to make sure you're not breaking any procreation rules. Peter Nelson and Sherilyn Fenn are "subgrades," lowlife types trying to escape the bleakness of their world. They pull off a heist to earn that escape, but are caught up in doublecrosses and betrayals. There are moments of the Orwellian world of 1984, and there's even a touch of Bonnie and Clyde in the Daryl Haney screenplay. There's a funkiness about the characters and settings that is grating, but a sense of tragic character holds one's interest thanks to producer-director Luis Llosa. Roger Corman and Carradine produced. (MGM/UA)

CRIMINAL ACT (1989) ★½ Any criminal act involved is on the part of the filmmakers who cranked out this video movie. Catherine Bach and Charlene Dallas portray news investigators tracking down giant humanoid rats in the city's sewer system. Vic Tayback plays the exterminator. Directed by Mark Byers, scripted by producer Daniel Yost. Nicholas Guest, John Saxon. (Prism)

CRIMINALS OF THE GALAXY. See *Wild, Wild Planet*.

CRIMSON CULT, THE (1970) ★★ Produced as *The Curse of the Crimson Altar*, and aka *Witch House, The Reincarnation* and *Spirit of the Dead*, this is one of Boris Karloff's last films. He portrays a hero, Professor Marshe, an expert in witchcraft. In the English village of Greymarsh, the descendant of a witch burned at the stake forms a cult and is preparing new sacrifices. Said to be based on Lovecraft's "Dreams in the Witch House." Directed by Vernon Sewell. Christopher Lee, Michael Gough, Barbara Steele, Mark Eden. (Movies Unlimited) (On laser from HBO/Image as *Curse of the Crimson Altar* with *The Haunted Palace*)

CRIMSON EXECUTIONER. See *Bloody Pit of Horror*.

CRIMSON GHOST, THE (1946) ★★★½ Cliffhanger fans! Here's all 12 chapters of a rousing Republic serial featuring a crude dude who wears a skeleton's mace face, strobe robe and scowl cowl. His henchmen are out to steal the Cyclotrode, a cool tool capable of short-circuiting electrical currents. Charles Quigley, as criminologist Duncan Richards, fights the kook spook with the yelp help of Linda Stirling ("Queen of the Serials"). Plenty of action and action and action from matinee kings William Witney and Fred C. ("Cannon") Brannon. Clayton Moore, "The Lone Ranger," is the Crimson Ghost's chief henchman. Stanley Price, Rex Lease. There's a feature-length TV colorized version, and a condensed TV version, *Cyclo-trode X*. Run with the fun. (Republic; Video Connection)

CRIMSON THE COLOR OF BLOOD (1973) ★ This turgid, unwatchable Spanish fiasco plays more like a gangster shoot-'em-up than a horror picture despite its theme of brain transplants. A criminal (Paul Nash, aka Paul Naschy) is given a brain transplant and turns into a homicidal killer-within-a-killer. The only horrifying scene involves a train decapitating a head from a corpse, and the head rolling down an embankment. And that's about it for horror buffs. Sorry, gang, this is one you don't need. Directed by Jean Fortuny. Sylvia Solar, Oliver Matthews, Evelyn Scott, Richard Palmer. (Wizard; Lightning)

CRITICAL LIST. See *Terminal Choice*.

CRITTERS (1986) ★★★ Entertaining sci-fi/horror comedy. Criminal aliens (Krites, small fur balls with teeth) escape a space prison and fly to Earth, pursued by two bounty hunters with shape-changing powers. Director Stephen Herek goes for laughs and thrills, and while the latter are least effective, the film maintains a constant charm by not taking itself seriously and by having fun with the Jekyll-Hyde bounty hunters. Above average and popular enough to warrant many sequels. Dee Wallace Stone, M. Emmet Walsh, Billy Green Bush, Scott Grimes, Don Opper. (Video/Laser: Columbia/Tristar)

CRITTERS 2: THE MAIN COURSE (1988) ★★★ This sequel is equal to the original in maintaining a balance between thrills and comedy as those outer-space porcupine balls, the Krites, return to Grover's Bend. Again, all hell breaks loose, and this time the bounty hunters from space—Ug, No-Face and Charlie—aren't as effective in stopping them. It's left up to adolescent Brad Brown (Scott Grimes), Harv the ex-sheriff and the townspeople to stop the slimeballs. The Chiodo Brothers have again done a commendable job in keeping the creatures rolling along (literally) and in presenting an image of these teethy beasts that vacillates between menace and parody. Good directorial job by Mick Garris, who cowrote with D. T. Twohy. Don Opper, Tom Hodges, Sam Anderson, Liane Curtis. (Video/Laser: RCA/Columbia)

CRITTERS 3: YOU ARE WHAT THEY EAT (1991) ★★½ "I gotta go where the cosmic winds blow me," remarks bounty hunter Charlie (Don Opper) when he turns up to help families trapped in an L.A. apartment building under siege from those furry, rolling fuzzballs with teeth that came from space in *Critters* and its sequel. Although inferior to the first two entries, this works okay as a video feature and establishes continuity for a long-running series featuring Opper as the alien-blasting good guy/nerd. Written by David J. Schow and directed by Kristine Peterson. Aimee Brooks, John Calvin, Katherine Cortez, Leonardo DiCaprio. (Video/Laser: New Line)

CRITTERS 4 (1992) ★★★ This commences where the third film left off, with bounty hunter Charlie McFadden (Don Opper) going into space with the only surviving Krite in an effort to prevent the species from dying out. Cut to the Saturn Quadrant A.D. 2045 aboard a space research station where the crew of the spaceship RSS *Tesla* is soon engaged in battle with Krites. Opper, awakening from suspended animation, tries to warn the crew of the dangers from the critters. The most amusing aspect of this oddball mixture of comedic horror and sci-fi is Brad Dourif's battle of wits with the central computer, Angela—a metaphor for our ability to create a technology we cannot control. The Joseph Lyle–David J. Schow script is clever in its development of character and director Rupert Harvey (coproducer with Barry Opper) injects satiric elements. Paul Whitthorne, Angela Bassett, Anders Hove, Eric DaRe. (New Line) (Laser: Image; New Line)

CROCODILE (1986) ★½ *Jaws*-style plot about an atomic-poisoned crocodile that grows to enormous size (its tail can destroy whole grass villages) and a boatload of adventurers who pursue the creature. Filmed in Thailand, and purely a croc. Directed by Sompote Sands (an alias for Herman Cohn?). Nat Puvania, Kirk Warren, Tiny Tim. (HBO)

CRONOS: IMMORTAL CURSE (1992) ★★★ This is one weird, macabre Mexican movie that puts most American equivalents to shame. It'll have your skin crawling and your flesh creeping as it spins a strange narrative about "The Cronos Device," a small golden box invented by a 16th-century alchemist who claimed it was the key to eternal life. The box falls into the hands of antiques dealer Federico Luppi and soon the device's claws and needle puncturers are automatically emerging to poison Luppi's blood and turn him into a living zombie with vampiric traits. In pursuit of the box comes Ron Perlman as the nephew of a dying rich man. (Perlman's performance is remarkably peculiar.) This film's dark comedy and sense of style (credit director Guillermo Del Toro) will intrigue you. With English subtitles when needed. Claudio Brook, Margarita Isabel. (Video/Laser: Vidmark)

CROSSROADS (1986) ★★★ Americana Negro folk tale, nostalgic in its music and languid in its mood. It's the old one about a man selling his soul to the Devil for fame and fortune, only Old Scratch is short-changing Blind Dog, a harmonica blues artist who's fallen on hard times despite having sacrificed his soul years before. A youth nicknamed Lightnin' Boy helps the geezer by confronting the Devil's minion in a musical playoff, aided only by Blind Dog's

Louisiana voodoo charm. The characters are warm and poignant, the music right on, and director Walter Hill and writer John Fusco capture the grass-roots essence of soul and gospel country. Ralph Macchio, Joe Seneca, Jami Gertz, Joe Morton, Harry Carey, Jr. Music by Ry Cooder. (Video/Laser: RCA/Columbia)

CROSSWORLDS (1996) ★★ The most exciting thing about this direct-to-video sci-fi fantasy? The short miniskirt that rebel fighter Andrea Roth wears for the film's 86 minutes. Whenever she leaps, rolls, jumps, curtsies, bows, karate-kicks, or falls, one's eye cannot help but dart directly to her lithe, slender legs ending in boot-encased toesies. The next most exciting thing? The low-cut blouse she wears for those 86 minutes. When she bends or leans forward, or makes some martial-arts movement to disable an insolent male attacker, her small but cozy breasts are partially revealed. Clearly the most important artist working on this film behind the scenes was the costume designer. That's the exciting stuff. Now let's get to the plot conceived by Krishna Rao (who also directed) and Raman Rao: Josh Charles (*Hairspray, Threesome*) is this nonheroic type ("Just leave me alone, will-ya?") who meets Roth at a party; but instantly she disappears. Bam, she returns that night while he's asleep in his bedroom, and this begins an odyssey through several different dimensions that are ruled over by "warlords." Warlord Ferris, the biggest wheel of all (played by Stuart Wilson in a business suit—God, what happened to the budget?), has the powers of a wizard more than a warlord. He can fire bolts of lightning out of his fingers and make ropes bind themselves around heroes. He wants the Scepter of Dyracchra as well as a crystal (which nonheroic Charles wears around his neck on a chain) because when put together, this cuts holes in reality and tears holes in dimensions. So Roth and Charles team up with wisecracking warrior type Rutger Hauer (yeah, he's wearing one of those robes from his wardrobe) to fight Ferris and little short sycophant Perry Anzilotti. In and out of dimensions they go—mostly desert. One looks normal, another has a reddish cast, and everyone is out of phase, as if the sprocket holes of the film had not lined up properly inside the camera. There's one action scene in snow country. The rules for how the Scepter of Dyracchra works? The Raos keep that part of it a secret. So anything goes. And everything does. (Video/DVD: Trimark)

CROW, THE (1994) ★★★ This is the film that claimed the life of its star, Brandon Lee (son of Bruce Lee), who was accidentally shot on the set in early '93. It's a dark, surreal version of James O'Barr's comic-book series about Eric Draven, a rock musician who is murdered and returns from the dead to wreak revenge against the sleazy criminals who did in him and his fiancée. The title refers to a supernatural bird that leads Draven through his bloody, vengeful experiences. The plot is nothing special but the film is notable for its atmosphere (a decaying city with wet, glistening streets), kinetic editing, dynamic action pieces and the unique directorial style of Alex Proyas. Not a work of art but certainly an example of bravado filmmaking. Script by David Schow and John Shirley. Ernie Hudson, Michael Wincott. (Miramax) (Laser: Miramax/Image)

CROW: CITY OF ANGELS, THE (1996) ★★½ This is a disappointing follow-up to the 1994 supernatural hit that starred the late Brandon Lee (he was accidentally shot and killed during production) and was based on James O'Barr's surrealistic horror comic books. Vincent Perez is totally inadequate as the new embodiment of Lee's character of Ashe, a murdered man who returns from the beyond to wreak terrible vengeance. Directed by rock-video maker Tim Pope, this sequel is a hodgepodge of nonclarity, and lacks all the robust, violent action of the original. It is less a story than a jumble of scenes that costar Richard Brooks and Iggy Pop as villains and Mia Kirschner as a tattoo artist who befriends Ashe through a psychic bond. The script by David S. Goyer seems to miss all the qualities that made the first effort work so well. (Video/DVD: Miramax)

CROWFOOT (1995) ★★ Obviously the pilot for a series idea from "Magnum P.I." producer Donald P. Bellisario, this TV-movie has the advantage of scenic Hawaiian locations as a young private eye of American Indian heritage (played by newcomer Jim Davidson) meets the ghost of a murder victim (Kate Hodge) and sets out to find her killer with the aid of an intriguing Chinese detective (played by Tsai Chin with a touch of the Dragon Lady thrown in). As Davidson is also psychic, and has visions when he touches corpses and other clue-lending props, *Crowfoot* is an intriguing idea helped along by a good cast: Mike Genovese, Bruce Locke, Erin Gray and Michael Watson.

CRY DEMON. See *The Evil.*

CRYING CHILD, THE (1996) ★★½ Unexceptional, by-the-numbers supernatural thriller, with modest spectral special effects, set on an isolated island where Mariel Hemingway (who has just lost her baby at birth) begins hearing a paranormal crying in the family estate she has inherited. Friend Finola Hughes is the only one who believes her story, but gradually they learn that an evil spirit haunts the house and convince disbelieving males George Delhoyo and Kin Shriner. Based on the Barbara Michaels novel; scripted by Rob Gilmer; produced-directed by Robert Lewis.

CRY OF THE BANSHEE (1970) ★★ Ugly witch

Oona calls up a spirit from the beyond—a servant of Satan to claim a psychotic witch-hunter. Villain Vincent Price chews the scenery in this British chiller directed by producer Gordon Hessler from a script by Tim Kelly and Christopher Wicking. Stylish fun, with surprise ending. Sally Geeson, Quinn O'Hara, Hugh Griffith. Good music score by Les Baxter. (HBO) (Laser: Image, with *Count Yorga—Vampire*)

CRY OF THE WEREWOLF (1944) ★★½ Nina Foch portrays Celeste La Tour, Queen of the Trioga Gypsies, who inherits the lycanthropic curse from her mother (her transformation takes place offscreen, unfortunately for you werewolf lovers). This mild Columbia horror thriller, set in New Orleans, was directed by Henry Levin from a script by Griffin Jay and Charles O'Neal. Fritz Leiber, Barton MacLane, John Abbott. Aka *Daughter of the Werewolf*. (Movies Unlimited)

CRYPT AND THE NIGHTMARE, THE. See *Terror in the Crypt*.

CRYPT OF HORROR (1963). See *Terror in the Crypt*.

CRYPT OF HORROR (1964). See *Castle of the Living Dead*.

CRYPT OF THE BLIND DEAD. See *The Blind Dead*.

CRYPT OF THE LIVING DEAD (1972) ★★ A turkey made in Turkey with new U.S. footage directed by Ray Danton. Archeologists Andrew Prine and Mark Damon warn superstitious natives on an island that a long-dead bloodsucker is about to awaken and drink their life fluid. The first hour is spent with the Wild Man, a one-eyed henchman, murdering all interferers; the last half-hour details how Prine rescues Patty Sheppard from killer Teresa Gimpera. Originally called *Hannah—Queen of Vampires*, by someone who doesn't know the difference between vampires and witches. The gore was edited for TV but the tedium is intact as Julio Salvador wrote-directed it. Aka *Young Hannah, Queen of the Vampires* and *Vampire Women*. (Direct; United; VCII)

CRYPT OF THE VAMPIRE, THE. See *Terror in the Crypt*.

CRYSTALSTONE (1987) ★★ Legend has it that the magical Crystalstone is the key to happiness on earth, and two children seek it while being pursued by an evil guardian. Directed by Antonio Pelaez. Kamlesh Gupta, Frank Grimes, Laura Jane Goodwin. (MCEG)

CTHULHU MANSION (1990) ★★½ "Inspired" by H. P. Lovecraft, this horror film produced in Spain depicts a mansion in which a satanic force is unleashed by hoodlums who hold magician Chandu (Frank Finlay) and daughter (Marcia Layton) hostages. Chandu once tampered with the supernatural (using a book of Cthulhu incantations) and caused his wife Leonor (a homage to Poe?) to burn to death. There are a few good touches amidst the chaos: amphibianlike claw hands that emerge from a fridge, demon makeup, and a woman's body being engulfed by tendrils of ivy. Nondiscriminating fans will find it diverting. Written and directed by J. P. Simon. Brad Fisher, Melanie Shatner, Paul Birchard, Kaethe Cherney. The TV version is *Black Magic Mansion*. (Republic)

CUBE (1997) ★★½ This abstract Canadian "thinking man's" horror picture will not be everyone's cup of grue, especially since it only offers abstract answers to many of its intriguing puzzles. A handful of individuals, who prove to be more symbolic than human, wake up inside a huge labyrinth of interlocking square rooms, lined with different-colored glass. The idea is to work their way out of the maze by going room to room, but only into compartments that do not contain hideous death traps. (One such snare slices up a hapless human into many pieces via invisible-to-the-eye laser rays). The notion offered by director Vincenzo Natali and cowriters Andre Bijelic and Graeme Manson is that this is an abandoned government project that never really had a purpose except to allow bureaucrats to spend money and justify their meaningless existences. What is intriguing is the way the few survivors finally figure out how to escape. But don't count on *Cube* offering a happy ending. This nihilistic comment on man's plight must have a nihilistic resolution, to make its point. Right? Ahem. Well, as a riddle trapped inside a puzzle wrapped in an enigma, it's an interesting poser, but as a movie, it leaves a lot to be answered. Nicole DeBoder, Nicky Guadagni, David Hewlett, Andrew Miller, Julian Richings, Wayne Robson, Maurice Dean Wint. (Video/DVD: Vidmark/Trimark)

CUJO (1983) ★★★½ Dogged adaptation of Stephen King's best-seller (by Don Carlos Dunaway and Lauren Currier) about a rabid St. Bernard that traps Dee Wallace and son Danny Pintauro in a Ford Pinto and holds them at bay, attacking maniacally. Director Lewis Teague displays expertise as a suspense-genre craftsman as the siege becomes a harrowing ordeal. The St. Bernard portraying Cujo (Spanish for "unconquerable force") is deserving of a lifetime supply of Alpo for meeting script demands for a rabies-maddened critter that slobbers, drools and goes for the throat on the theory man is dog's best din-din. Daniel Huh-Kelly, Ed Lauter, Christopher Stone, Mills Watson. (Video/Laser: Warner Bros.)

CULT OF THE COBRA (1955) ★★½ Faith Domergue metamorphoses into a cobra and attacks GIs who infiltrate a snake cult in the Far East in 1945. No attempt is made by director Francis D. Lyon to capture a '40s ambience and Domergue lends nothing to her role (she might have tried to look sinuous instead of sensuous) as Marshall Thompson, Richard Long and David Janssen fall under her spell. No cult movie, this. (MCA)

CULT OF THE DEAD. Video version of *The Snake People* (MPI).

CURDLED (1995) ★★★ A deeply dark sense of humor, aided greatly by the presence of Quentin Tarantino as executive producer, earmarks this most unusual and eccentric serial-killer tale, which is more a satire than a thriller under the care of writers John Maas (also a producer) and Reb Braddock, who also directed. A childlike young woman (Angela Jones, who is excellent) is obsessed with serial killers in general and Miami's "Blueblood Killer" in particular, a handsome sadist who lures beautiful upper-crust women into his lair of horrors, stabs them repeatedly with a knife, and then decapitates them. William Baldwin brings a weird twist to this role as he tortures the beauties in a most unpleasant manner. Meanwhile, Jones applies for a job with the Post-Forensic Cleaning Service (PFCS), which under the guidance of Barry Corbin cleans up murder scenes after the cops are finished. How Jones and Baldwin finally come face-to-face at one of the bloody murder scenes, and dance a macabre "ballad of death" with Jones clutching a butcher knife, will intrigue and fascinate you. Keep an eye on Jones's facial expressions. They're delicious. And you will love the final surprise ending. It may not curdle your blood, but it will certainly tickle it. Bruce Ramsay, Mel Gorham, Daisy Fuentes, Lois Chiles. (Touchstone)

CURIOUS DR. HUMPP, THE (1970) ★ Freaky sex exploitation flicker about mad doctor Aldo Barbero, who collects exotic dancers so he can extract their libidos in an effort to find the secret of eternal youth. Much of this consists of the crazed doc watching dancing babes or couples engaged in the mating ritual. Directed by Emilio Vieyra. (S/Weird; Tapeworm)

CURSE, THE (1987) ★★★ Get beyond the stomach-churning graphics of this Ovidio G. Assonitis film, made as *The Farm*, and you'll find food for thought. When a meteor crashes in Tellico Plains, TN, it contaminates the water of farmer Claude Akins, mutating vegetables and fruits and turning livestock and people into monsters. Fundamentalism gets a swift kick in the seat when Akins becomes a religious fanatic who closes his eyes to the poisoned environment, and there is a cynical attitude toward land developers destroying nature for condos. The tale has a touch of innocence from the view of young Wil Wheaton, an outsider in a family of repressed personalities. Director David Keith maintains an eerie sense of doom and ends on an apocalyptic note. Malcolm Danare, Cooper Huckable, John Schneider, Ann Wheaton, Steve

Carlisle. (Video Treasures; HBO) (Laser: Image)

CURSE II: THE BITE (1989) ★★★ The best of the "Venom-Fanged Killer Snake" movies. Although this has no relationship to *The Curse* (1987), it's a superbly slithery tale that will give snake-lovers and -haters mongoose bumps. Jill Schoelen and boyfriend J. Eddie Peck are crossing the Arizona desert, which has been lambasted by radioactive fallout that gives snakes a venom that replaces the DNA structure in human flesh. Peck's hand turns into a serpent's head, and scaly critters are dropping out of his mouth faster than quarters from a Vegas slot machine. There's a great scene where their car runs over serpents stretched across the desert highway. The whole film has a creepy quality and was directed with style by Fred Goodwin. Jamie Farr is good as a salesman and Bo Svenson is also good as a redneck sheriff. Frankly, we were bitten by this movie. (Trans World)

CURSE III: BLOOD SACRIFICE (1990) ★★½ It's reassuring to hear Christopher Lee (as a doctor in East Africa circa 1950) remark, "I've seen things that can't be explained by modern science." The reassuring presence of Lee, however, is the only asset of this British-produced voodoo movie, unrelated to *The Curse* or *Curse II*. A plantation owner's pregnant wife (Jenilee Harrison) interrupts a witch doctor's sacrifical rite and is singled out to be sacrified to a scaly beast conjured up by voodoo. Chris Walas's monster is another rubber-suited entity (although he carries a machete—an interesting touch). Directed by Sean Barton. Aka *Panga*. (Video/Laser: RCA/Columbia)

CURSE IV: THE ULTIMATE SACRIFICE (1988) ★★ Originally made as *Catacombs* by Charles Band, this was initially released on video by Worldvision, then retitled for the *Curse* home-video series. As with most films Band produced in Italy, this is well photographed and acted. It is also well directed by David Schmoeller. Set in the church at St. Pietro, Italy, a demon (imprisoned in the church's catacombs) is unleashed when a new Father Superior takes over. The drama is limited to a few encounters with the demon and the death of a few characters; effects are also limited. Timothy Van Patten, Laura Schaefer, Jeremy West, Feodor Chaliapin. (Video/Laser: Columbia TriStar)

CURSED (1990) ★ When a gargoyle falls off a church during a thunderstorm, pieces are taken to a lab by a scientist and his female assistant; the debris is possessed by evil and acts against the doctor's genetic experiments. Directed by Mychel Arsenault. Ron Lea, Catherine Colvey, Tom Rack.

CURSED MOUNTAIN MYSTERY, THE (1993) ★ Sher Mountain provides sheer horror in this thriller involving a rare gem with magical powers that falls into the wrong hands. European boxing champ Joe Bugner, making his film debut, portrays the "Protector" of the rock and knocks off bad guys one by one. Directed by Vince Martin, written by Denis Whitburn. (Columbia TriStar)

CURSE OF COUNT YORGA. See *The Return of Count Yorga.*

CURSE OF DARK SHADOWS. See *Night of Dark Shadows.*

CURSE OF DEMON MOUNTAIN. Video version of *Shadow of Chikara* (United American).

CURSE OF DR. PHIBES, THE. See *The Abominable Dr. Phibes.*

CURSE OF FRANKENSTEIN (1957) ★★★½ Opener in the Hammer *Frankenstein* series, originally called *Birth of Frankenstein*, with Peter Cushing as the inspired albeit demented doctor who yearns to resurrect the dead and Christopher Lee as the Monster, in new makeup. Outstanding horror picture (an international hit) with a Gothic flavor and set design that established standards for scores of Hammer films. Written by Jimmy Sangster, directed by Terence Fisher. Hazel Court, Robert Urquhart, Valerie Gaunt, Noel Hood. (Warner Bros.)

CURSE OF KING TUT'S TOMB (1980) ★★★½ Legendary incidents behind the curses surrounding the boy king's burial chamber, and the deaths of those who desecrated the treasure trove, are exploited at a hysterical pitch in this TV-movie directed by Philip Leacock, narrated by Paul Scofield and starring Raymond Burr (in a turban), Eva Marie Saint, Harry Andrews, Wendy Hiller and Tom Baker. How much is true? You'll have to reread history to separate fact from the fiction of Herb Meadow's script. Perhaps *Behind the Mask of Tutankhamen*, the Barry Wynne book on which this pyramid of sensationalism is based. (RCA/Columbia; Goodtimes)

CURSE OF THE AZTEC MUMMY (1957) ★ Crummy mummy confronts bumbling dummy (a weary dreary superhero dubbed the Angel) when his flipped crypt is desecrated by cinematic defilers. Another unforgivable Mexican production (shambling in the wake of *The Aztec Mummy*) imported by K. Gordon Murray, from the forgettable *Aztec Mummy* series with Roman Gay. Dr. Krupp squares off against the heroic gauzeman, Popoca. Others in the series: *The Robot vs. the Aztec Mummy* and *Wrestling Women vs. the Aztec Mummy*. Directed by Rafael Portello. (Sinister/C; S/Weird; Filmfax; as *Aztec Mummy Double Bill*)

CURSE OF THE BLACK WIDOW (1977) ★★★ Producer-director Dan Curtis repeats the formula of his *Night Stalker* with a Giant Killer Spider. There's the investigator hot on the legs of the creature, a research expert who spots the spidery clues, and innocent, sexy victims. The

plot (by Robert Blees and Earl W. Wallace) scampers along, supported by Anthony Franciosa, Donna Mills, Patty Duke Astin, June Lockhart, June Allyson, Jeff Corey, Sid Caesar and Vic Morrow as the cop. Originally shown as *Love Trap*. (Continental)

CURSE OF THE BLAIR WITCH (1999) ★★★ Whatever you may personally think about *The Blair Witch Project*—and the reaction to its unusual approach to filmmaking has been mixed—this "documentary" stands alone as a remarkable pastiche of "reality" TV series. It was cleverly designed as a promotional piece for the movie, but instead of going "behind the scenes" to show us "the making of . . ." the producers chose to make it seem as if the three filmmakers who disappeared in Black Hills Forest of Maryland really *had* vanished. Using all the documentary techniques commonplace on today's cable networks, the film reminds one of the "News on the March" opening of *Citizen Kane*, which offers "newsreel" footage to present the life of its *fictional* protagonist. In *Curse*, interviews with eyewitnesses and experts, footage from an old TV-show, black-and-white motion-picture footage that looks like it was lifted out of a Hollywood feature about Salem witches, readings of old records, and historical photographs are all brilliantly blended with narrator Peg O'Keef intoning the tragedy and mystery of it all. Heather Donahue, Michael Williams, and Joshua Leonard—they are three students from Montgomery College, Maryland, who vanished in October 1994 while making a student film about the legendary "Blair Witch." Relatives express the sadness of their loss and a film professor (Michael DeCoto) describes the background to the project, and how Heather and Joshua were really ill suited for each other (subtle hint of personality clashes that are revealed in the feature movie). From there we flashback to 1785, when an old woman/accused witch, Ellie Kedward, was banished into the woods and left to die. But suddenly the following year her accusers mysteriously began to vanish, and the citizens ultimately abandoned the settlement of Blair. A story grew over the next two centuries about how the ghostly spirit of Ellie returned every 50 years to wreak new vengeance in and around what was renamed Burkittsville. Horrible things happened to whoever was hanging around Black Hills Forest or Coffin Rock (an entire search party was found disemboweled there in 1886) or the infamous Tappy East Creek, where a child was drowned under mysterious circumstances and strange wooden sticks were found. Let's not forget the infamous serial killer of 1940, who claimed to be possessed by the spirit of Ellie Kedward and did unspeakable things to young children before being brought to justice. This "factual" information is passed on to us via Bill Barnes (crusty historian of Burkittsville); footage lifted from a 1971 "documentary" series called *Mystic Occurrences* featuring a modern "witch"; Burkittsville sheriff Ronald Cravens; witchcraft expert Clarence Moorehead; and hard-boiled investigator Buck Buchanan. Then, in 1994, the finding of a backpack and a few cans of 16mm film belonging to the missing threesome. A few choice scenes from this "missing" film are, of course, scenes from the finished print of *The Blair Witch Project*. Kudos to producers Robin Cowie, Gregg Hale, and Mike Monello (assuming they even exist) and to writers Ben Rock, Eduardo Sanchez, and Daniel Myrick. The latter two do exist, for they are the creators and directors of *The Blair Witch Project*. This will go down in history as a classic put-on alongside Orson Welles's radio play *The War of the Worlds* and the segment of *Citizen Kane* alluded to above. (Artisan Home Entertainment)

CURSE OF THE BLUE LIGHTS (1988) ★★ Uninspired, derivative video "tale of terror" set in the hick town of Dudley, where stupid teenagers discover a band of ghouls and the statue of a monster that once walked the land. The campy creature makeup and dialogue are strictly from hunger, and the acting pathetic. Don't blame Mame, blame the lame (brained, that is). That would be writer-producer-director John Henry Johnson. Also guilty are Brent Ritter as the leader of the Ghouls, Loath (some actor), Bettina Julius (as The Witch), Patrick Keller and Becky Golladay. (Magnum)

CURSE OF THE CANNIBAL CONFEDERATES. Variant title for *The Curse of the Screaming Dead.*

CURSE OF THE CAT PEOPLE, THE (1944) ★★★½ This sequel to *The Cat People* has Kent Smith and Simone Simon re-creating their characters, but has nothing to do with cats. Producer Val Lewton was cashing in on the success of his previous low-budget winner, agreeing to the title but refusing to compromise the story. Scripter DeWitt Bodeen came up with a poetically moody tale about a girl's fantasies which produce a fairy godmother (Simone) to protect her from a mysterious stranger in the woods. An eldritch fairy tale, so different it will surprise you. Codirected by Robert Wise and Gunther V. Fritsch. Ann Carter, Elizabeth Russell, Jane Rudolph. (RKO; Turner has a colorized version) (Laser: Image; Turner)

CURSE OF THE CRIMSON ALTAR. Laser title for *The Crimson Cult* (HBO/Image).

CURSE OF THE CRIMSON CULT. See *The Crimson Cult.*

CURSE OF THE CRYSTAL EYE (1993) ★★ A lethargic, poorly directed adventure in the Indiana Jones style, but without any style, and offering a lifeless performance by Jameson Parker as a soldier of fortune who tracks down Ali

Baba's treasure in a desert cavern. The best thing about this Roger Corman release, written by Mike Angel, are the sets in which Parker and girlfriend Cynthia Rhodes venture with an expedition of explorers, overcoming death traps and natural obstacles to find the cache of pearls, jewels and crystals. The action sequences are wretchedly directed by Joe Tornatore, and, believe it or not, "Open Sesame" actually opens the cave. Curses! Mike Lane, Andrew Jacobs, David Sherwood. (New Horizons)

CURSE OF THE CYLONS. See *Battlestar Galactica.*

CURSE OF THE DEAD. See *Kill, Baby, Kill.*

CURSE OF THE DEMON (1957) ★★★½ Based on "Casting the Runes," a classic short story by M. R. James, a British historian noted for quiet, antiquarian tales of supernatural horror. This British chiller, which has won cult status, was directed by Jacques Tourneur, a disciple of Val Lewton. Psychic investigator Dana Andrews comes to England to probe a devil cult, only to find the supernatural. The Charles Bennett–Hal F. Chester script is full of suspense and highlights a classic climax. Peggy Cummins, Niall MacGinnis, Maurice Denham, Athene Seyler, Liam Redmond, Percy Herbert. Aka *Night of the Demon* and *Haunted*. (Goodtimes; Mike Lebell's) (Laser: Image)

CURSE OF THE DEVIL (1973) ★ A hodgepodge of confusing details plagues this Spanish horror thriller (sequel to *Mark of the Wolfman*), seventh in the series with Paul Naschy (Jacinto Molina) as the nobleman Valadimir Daninsky of Transylvania, who is always turning into a hairy wolfman. First a witch being burned at the stake curses her inquisitors. Then Nashy shoots a running dog, the corpse of which turns into a man. Then a sexy gal drops by the manor and gives him a bite that transforms him into a monster when the moon is full. Only when the tormented Valadimir meets his true love, the seductive Faye Falcon, does the film evoke compassion amidst its bloody murder sequences. The women are knockouts and Nashy/Molina comes off sympathetically. Directed by Charles Aured. Aka *The Return of Walpurgis* and *The Black Harvest of Countess Dracula*. (United American; Sinister/C; Dark Dreams; S/Weird; Filmfax)

CURSE OF THE EVIL SPIRIT. Alternate video version of *The Chooper* (Premiere).

CURSE OF THE FACELESS MAN (1958) ★★½ Screenwriter Jerome Bixby concocted a variation on the mummy movie, the evil being a stone man, Quintillis Orilius, turned to rock during the destruction of Pompeii in A.D. 79. Painter Elaine Edwards is a reincarnation of a woman the creature loved and now, 2000 years later, he's risen from an archaeology "dig" to fulfill his affair. Described as "the son of Etruscan gods," Quintilius is a shambling creature anyone could escape if they just left the room. Archaeologists Richard Anderson and Adele Mara try to save the day, but it's a compendium of monster-menacing-woman clichés, with old-fashioned voice-over narration. Charles Gemmorah is the monster. Luis Van Rooten, Gar Moore. Directed by Edward L. Cahn.

CURSE OF THE FLY (1965) ★★ Third and least effective entry in *The Fly* series. The DeLambres, experimenting with a teleportation machine that still has bugs in it (ha), are suffering from genetic mutations and frequently family members turn into hideous creatures. Director Don Sharp's pacing is slow, the action in Harry Spalding's script too long in coming. Half-hearted attempt features Brian Donlevy as a DeLambres, but not even that old pro, who did so much to bring Professor Quatermass to life, can overcome the inadequacies. George Baker, Carole Gray, Michael Graham, Burt Kwouk.

CURSE OF THE GOLEM, THE. See *It!*

CURSE OF THE KARNSTEINS See *Terror in the Crypt.*

CURSE OF THE LIVING CORPSE (1964) ★★★ Roy Scheider is caught in the jaws of death in this exercise in Grand Guignol in which torso murders appear to be the handiwork of a dearly departed spirit (a millionaire who was buried alive). Writer-producer-director Del Tenney makes this a lively, stylish gore flick. Candace Hilligoss, Helen Waren, Margo Hartman. (Prism)

CURSE OF THE LIVING DEAD (1967) Alternate video version of *Kill, Baby, Kill* (Electric).

CURSE OF THE LIVING DEAD (1979) Alternate title for *Nightstalker.*

CURSE OF THE MUSHROOM PEOPLE. See *Attack of the Mushroom People.*

CURSE OF THE PHARAOH. See *The Pharaoh's Curse.*

CURSE OF THE SCREAMING DEAD, THE (1982) ★ Sleazy deer hunters arouse Civil War–killed corpses in a churchyard, setting into motion a walking-rebel gorefest of the give-'em-what-fer-you-all kind. Produced-directed by Tony Malanowski, who also made the Civil War horror film *Night of Horror.* Script by Lon Huber. Aka *Curse of the Confederate Cannibals.* Steve Sandkuhler, Christopher Gummer, Rebecca Bach. (Mogul)

CURSE OF THE STONE HAND (1959) ★ U.S. producer Jerry Warren purchased two films, directed new footage with John Carradine, and released a new monstrosity to an unsuspecting public as a fresh feature. The Mexican footage (directed by Carl Schleipper) revolves around a story about an Incredible Creeping Crawling Hand (you've seen it before, only done better),

the Chilean footage is about a suicide club. Accursed viewing. Ernest Walch; Sheila Bon; Katherine Victor. (Loonic; Nostalgia)

CURSE OF THE SWAMP CREATURE (1966) ★ In the steaming depths of the deadly Everglades a maniacal doctor is crazily at work creating a half-human reptile monster. You'd think the Alligator People would have knocked him off by now. John Agar looks as though he's still searching for the brain from planet Arous. Produced-directed by bogged-down Larry Buchanan, king of swamp schlock, and written by Tony Huston. Francine York, Bill Thurman, Shirley McLine. (S/Weird; Vidmark; Movies Unlimited; Video Dimensions)

CURSE OF THE VAMPIRE (1960) ★ One stormy night five showgirls seek refuge in a spooky castle. The gals reveal a penchant for Baby Doll nighties and stiletto heels while Count Gabor Kernassy (Walter Brandi) lurks about, mixing chemicals in his lab and amazed how one babe resembles an old relative. Gosh, it sounds like "Carmilla." Fang marks in a woman's throat are the height of effects in this dreary Italian job, written-directed by Piero Regnoli. Not even the strip-tease sequence is exciting. This picture, dated even when it was produced, just rolls over and dies. Lyla Rocco, Mario Giovannini. Aka *The Playgirls and the Vampire, Desires of the Vampire, Daughters of the Vampire, The Last Prey of the Vampire* and *The Vampire's Last Victim.* Whew!

CURSE OF THE WEREWOLF, THE (1961) ★★★ A shapely wench is thrown into a cell with an incarcerated werewolf and raped, later giving birth to a baby that grows into hairy manhood in this version of Guy Endore's *The Werewolf of Paris,* transported to Spain in the 1730s. Hammer's production values are high and Oliver Reed is an excellent tormented monster. Sexual frustrations caused by Catherine Feller finally bring out the beast in Reed and he attacks. Directed by Terence Fisher from a script by John Elder (Anthony Hinds). Yvonne Romain, Clifford Evans, Anthony Dawson, Michael Ripper. (Video/Laser: MCA)

CURTAIN CALL (1998) ★★½ This Starz TV-movie original attempts to blend supernatural tomfoolery with a romance about an idealistic New York publisher (James Spader) with middling results. Each ingredient might have worked without the other, but telewriter Todd Alcott's attempt to combine the two is a series of big letdowns. The supernatural stuff comes in the form of two ghosts, played by Michael Caine and Maggie Smith in period costumes, who turn up as permanent guests when Spader buys their old, dilapidated home in Manhattan. Director Peter Yates pulls excellent performances out of his all-star cast (Polly Walker as

Spader's confused lover, Buck Henry as a publisher whose company has just merged with Spader's, and Francis Sternhagen as a harassed secretary) but the *Topper* style of humor doesn't evoke many laughs, and the romance kind of just fizzles along, instead of sizzling along. Producer Andrew Karsch provided the story idea. Sam Shepard, Marcia Gay Harden. (DVD: Image)

CURTAINS (1982) ★★ Irritating Canadian slasher film, written by Robert Guza, Jr., paints characters in muddy fashion. Actress Samantha Eggar commits herself to an asylum to experience madness so her next film will be more believable. Hubby-producer John Vernon leaves her in the nuthouse and gathers six beauties in his isolated mansion, subjecting them to degrading sexual games. That's when the slasher, wearing an old hag's mask, strikes, and that's when it's curtains for *Curtains*. There's nothing clever or suspenseful about the murders, and the climax is neither riveting nor surprising. The direction by Jonathan Stryker (real name: Richard Ciupka) rambles. Linda Thorson, Annie Ditchburn. (Vestron)

CURVE, THE (1997) ★★½ Call it a myth or an urban legend, but there's this belief in some collegiate quarters that if your campus roommate commits suicide, the dean will give you an automatic 4.0 grade average for the semester. How writer-director Dan Rosen uses this unusual bit of university malarkey makes for more of a psychological study of twisted, abnormal students than a blood-and-guts horror film, but then sometimes an exploration of the dark side of the psyche makes for a more compelling kind of "horror" experience than the obvious clichéd stuff. There's nothing great about this movie, which was retitled *Dead Man's Curve* for TV. It was shot on the cheap in and around Baltimore, MD, has almost zero production values, and there's nothing very flashy about Rosen as a moviemaker. But the acting is unusually good and the surprise twists keep coming, so nobody is quite what they seem. Heading the cast is Matthew Lillard as the chief student of deception and deceit, with Michael Vartan as a confederate you can sympathize with. Randall Batinkoff is the campus jerk you want to hate and Keri Russell and Tamara Craig Thomas are the women caught up in their schemes. Unusually rough cops are played by Anthony Griffith and Bo Dietl; Dana Delany has a subdued role as the campus psychiatrist. Recommended if you're looking for something offbeat. (Video: Two Left Shoes/DVD: Vidmark/Trimark)

CUTTING CLASS (1989) ★★½ Here's how the characters get knocked off by a slasher in a high school: A math teacher gets a fire ax through the brain, an art teacher is baked alive in his kiln, a gym instructor is pinioned with a U.S. flagpole, a vice principal is strangled with her face against a Xerox machine, and a teenager has his throat mundanely cut open with a knife. It's the usual body count amidst the usual inane teenagers who enjoy playing grab-ass and smooching while everyone around them is dying. This perversion of teenage sex and blood-spilling is the work of director Rospo Pallenberg, who gets an F. Donovan Leitch, Jill Schoelen, Brad Pitt, Nancy Fish and Mark Barnet are assisted by Roddy McDowall (as a lecherous principal) and Martin Mull in a comedy cameo. (Video/Laser: Republic)

CYBER BANDITS (1994) ★★★ You take this tubular device, point it at your enemy, say "Go to Hell" or "Go to the bottom of the ocean" and your enemy is sent into a kind of permanent state of virtual reality, doomed to spend the rest of his/her life undergoing the horrific idea suggested. That's the weird superweapon that everyone is after in this oddball actioner starring Martin Kemp as a sailing navigator who has the weapon's formula tattooed on his back at the suggestion of adventuress Alexandra Paul. Both are fleeing from bloodthirsty killers dispatched by Robert Hays, a sadistic millionaire who has financed Henry Gibson (playing a crazed, almost silly German doctor) to make the device. The James Robinson–Winston Beard script defies description, but Erik Fleming directs it like nothing is out of the ordinary about these bizarre characters and crazy situations. What a strange movie. Adam Ant, Grace Jones, James Hong. (Video/Laser: Columbia TriStar)

CYBER CHIC. TV title for the wretched *Robo-C.H.I.C.*

CYBERNATOR (1991) ★ Science-fiction actioner depicting cyborg assassin squads going freelance. Directed by Robert Rundle. William Smith, Lonnie Schuyler, Christina Peralta, James Williams.

CYBER NINJA (1994) ★ Japanese comic-book fantasy adventure mixing modern science-fiction devices with old-fashioned samurai warriorism. Hanbel Kawai, Hiroki Ida. (Fox Lorber)

CYBERTRACKER (1994) ★★★½ While maybe the world doesn't need another cyborg-killer movie made for direct release to video, at least this Joseph Merhi–Richard Pepin production is a competent sci-fi actioner, with no pretentions of being anything else. Don "The Dragon" Wilson (also a coproducer) stars as a security bodyguard for an evil corporation. He's set up to take a fall for murder, and is aided in his fight against an unstoppable machine monster (Jim Maniaci, playing the usual mindless assassin with amazing firepower) by the UHR (Union of Human Rights), a freedom movement resisting the idea of androids as policemen licensed to kill. Without an ounce of subtlety, this slam-bammer was directed by Pepin from a script by Jacobsen Hart. Richard Norton, Stacie Foster, Abby Dalton, Steve Burton, John Aprea. (PM Entertainment) (Laser: Image)

CYBERTRACKER 2 (1995) ★★★½ Another rousing sci-fi actioner from producers Joseph Merhi and Richard Pepin, almost nonstop in its delivery of cyborg shootouts, complex vehicular chases and exploding buildings and on-fire bad guys. As Eric Phillips, the same Secret Service agent he played in the first *Cybertracker*, Don ("The Dragon") Wilson is once again on the run after high-level cyborg technology conspirators create cyberassassins that resemble his wife (Stacie Foster) and him. While unit #9 (Jim Maniaci) was a bad cyborg in the original, here he's a good guy machine cop who supports Wilson. The script by Richard Preston, Jr., is jam-packed with suspense and action, and Pepin directs it with panache and elan. Tony Burton, Anthony DeLongis, Stephen Rowe, Steve Burton. (PM Entertainment) (Laser: Image)

CYBERZONE (1995) ★★½ Tongue-in-cheek humor livens up an otherwise routine android melodrama set in 2077, when Phoenix is now a seaport and New Angeles is an underwater city promising no crime. "Droid gunner" Jack Ford (Marc Singer) is hired to look for four missing (and very sexy) "pleasure droids" and is joined in the search by beautiful Rochelle Swanson. The action, under the direction of Fred Olen Ray, is rather ordinary, but he spices it up with some sleazy striptease dances, and colorful character cameos with Ross Hagen (as a one-eyed bartender) and Robert Quarry as a smuggler who lives like Emperor Ming. There's little in the line of special effects, and William C. Martell's script could have used more comedy to make it all bearable. It's still passable—barely. Kin Shriner, Robin Clarke, Cal Bartlett, Brinke Stevens. (New Horizons)

CYBORG (1973). See *The Six Million Dollar Man.*

CYBORG (1989) ★★★ Granted, this has empty-headed characters and gratuitous violence, but director Albert Pyun makes these things with panache and style. *Cyborg*, scripted by Kitty Chalmers, is memorable for its dynamic editing and stunt coordination. That aside, this is your basic *Mad Max* retread with Jean-Claude Van Damme as a muscle guy trapped in a post-holocaust world where the Flesh Pirates are after a cyborg programmed with the new cure to a plague. Van Damme, playing Gibson (haha!) Rickenbacker, has prolonged battles with troops of the blackest pirate of all, Fender Tremolo (Vincent Klyn), and finally with Tremolo himself. Dayle Haddon plays Pearl Prophet, the pivotal cyborg. TV title:

Masters of the Universe II: The Cyborg. (Cannon) (Laser: Warner Bros.)

CYBORG 2 (1993) ★★ The insidious Pinwheel Robotics Inc. designs a humanoid cyborg to destroy a rival Japanese corporation in this action-packed, violent glimpse into a chaotic future. Production values are high as writer-director Michael Schroeder has cyborg Angelina Jolie and heroic guy Elias Koteas fighting bounty hunter Billy Drago (playing one of his crazies) and stormtroopers sent out by evil president Allen Garfield. Jack Palance plays an oddball named Mercy. (Video/Laser: Vidmark)

CYBORG 3: THE RECYCLER (1995) ★★★ This sci-fi action film has a more thoughtful script than most of its ilk, and brings an element of depth to its protagonists and chief villain. That villain is one-eyed Anton Llewelyn, a "recycler" (or bounty hunter) who preys on benevolent cyborgs in a futuristic *Mad Max*–type world. Richard Lynch's portrayal of Anton is the best thing in the Barry Victor/Troy Bolotnick script. Not that Zach Galligan (as a sympathetic human scientist) and Khrystyne Haje (as a cyborg unit with a "cybernetic womb and cyrogenic sperm bank") aren't also given some development. It's just that Lynch runs with his role and wallows in its evilness, making it a delicious viewing experience. With some okay effects by John Carl Buechler thrown in, *Cyborg 3* has a balanced mixture of action and plot and captures the bleakness of a burned-out world as innocent cyborgs face bloodthirsty humans in a final confrontation over possession of a womb-baby created by Haje. Directed by Michael Schroeder.

CYBORG COP (1993) ★★★ Derivative but diverting actioner with sci-fi overtones, depicting the efforts of maverick DEA agent David Bradley to find his brother, taken captive during a drug raid on the Caribbean HQ of nutty scientist John Rhys-Davies and turned into a cyborg killing machine. Rhys-Davies's Kessel is a larger-than-life villain with homosexual suggestions, but the real concern of writer Greg Latter is formula action between cyborgs and mortal men, plus a little rolling in the hay between Bradley and Alonna Shaw, who plays an international reporter without conviction. Bradley is a one-dimensional actor who only shines during fight scenes, when he brings intensity to his combat. But basically it's slam-bam, thank you, viewer. Directed by Sam Firstenberg. Todd Jensen, Rufus Swart. (Video/Laser: Vidmark)

CYBORG COP II (1994) ★½ Will Tom Clancy sue the producers of this comic-book movie because they named their hero Jack Ryan? That's just one stolen idea in this ripoff of a dozen other cyborg movies in which half-man, half-machine creatures run amok, killing the very mankind that created them. This time they're called the "Cyborg Quad Team" and come equipped with "pulsating laser generator," "gatling gun" and "Olympic Torch flamethrower." One of these hulkers is Jesse Starkraven (Morgan Hunter), a cold-blooded killer who was sent to prison by DEA agent David Bradley (from *Cyborg Cop*) and whom the government has turned into a hideous machine monster. So much for government funding. Jon Stevens's script is totally lacking in any logic and director Sam Firstenberg just keeps killing people and sending Bradley flying through the air each time a laser zap is fired. As Ryan, Bradley is an unpleasant, arrogant hero, as despicable and chauvinistic as the bad guys he pursues. Action movies should at least try to bring a smile to your lips—this brings only a snarl. Jill Pierce, Dale Cutts, Victor Mellaney. (Video/Laser: Vidmark)

CYBORG: THE SIX MILLION DOLLAR MAN. See *The Six Million Dollar Man.*

CYCLE PSYCHO (1972) ★ Serial killer Joseph Turkel (what's he doing in this stinker?) kills the wife of businessman Tom Drake for money, then blackmails Drake into getting him young girls he can carve up with his knives. Drake hires the Savage Disciples motorcycle gang to carry off the abduction of two innocents just arrived in wicked L.A. This movie is as depraved as its sleazy characters and not even the motorcycle shots are good. Noncredit goes to writer-producer-director John Lawrence. Aka *Savage Abduction* and *Numbered Days*. Stephen Oliver, Sean David Kenney, Amy Thomson, Stafford Repp. (Academy)

CYCLONE (1987) ★★ This exploitation shoot-'em-up stars the shapely torso of Heather Thomas, who comes into possession of a supercycle that the government and other forces are fighting over. It's one blazing firefight and vehicle chase after another with no plot twists to brag about or motivated characters. Another whizbang from captain/director Fred Olen Ray. Jeffrey Combs, Ashley Ferrare, Dar Robinson, Martine Beswick, Martin Landau, Huntz Hall. (Video/Laser: RCA/Columbia)

CYCLOPS, THE (1956) ★½ Horror fans prefer to watch this Bert I. Gordon production (he wrote-produced-directed) with one eye shut; general audiences prefer both eyes shut. You have a choice as Gloria Talbott leads an expedition into Mexico in search of her missing lover boy, a crashed aviator grown into a 50-foot monstrosity who moans and groans most of the time. Lon Chaney, Jr., hams it up as a berserk uranium hunter always undermining the expedition and James Craig and Tom Drake are along to watch modern lizards in macrophotography scenes and other incompetent special effects. (IVE; Mike Lebell's)

CYCLOTRODE X. Reedited feature version of the Republic serial *The Crimson Ghost.* One version is colorized. (Video Connection; Mike Lebell's)

DADDY'S DEADLY DARLING (1972) ★½ This unappetizing psychothriller focuses on disgusting elements: Toni Lawrence, a demented young woman knife-kills her father when he tries to rape her; she escapes an asylum to meet pig farmer Marc Lawrence, who feeds victims to his hogs and finds in Toni a kindred murderous spirit. Jesse Vent portrays the good ole boy sheriff and Katherine Ross (but not that Katherine Ross) believes pigs are possessed by reincarnated people's souls. Lawrence produced-directed this slop, which he wrote as F. A. Foss. Need we add Lawrence makes a boor of himself as he hogs the screen? Aka *The Killer, Lynn Hart, The Strange Love Exorcist, The Strange Exorcism of Lynn Hart*. (Paragon; from Simitar and Home Video as *Pigs*; from HVQ as *Horror Farm*)

DADDY'S GONE A-HUNTING (1969) ★★★ Good psychomystery in which jilted lover Scott Hylands terrorizes ex-girlfriend Carol White, with many visual touches à la Hitchcock by producer-director Mark Robson. The "McGuffin" is a kidnapped baby carried through San Francisco in a poodle basket. Mild horror touches are combined with the suspense and shocks. Paul Burke, Rachel Ames, Mala Powers. (Warner Bros.)

DAGORA, THE SPACE MONSTER (1963) ★ Out of the depths of the Pacific it undulates, a quivering mass of octopod mutation jelly jiggling across land to turn cities into seaweed-stained rubble. The monstrosity absorbs diamonds, so why isn't it after Mae West? Japanese monster sci-fier written-directed by Inoshiro Honda. Hiroshi Koizumi, Yoko Fujiyama. Aka *Space Monster Dagora*. (Video Yesteryear; S/Weird)

DALEKS—INVASION EARTH 2150 A.D. (1966) ★★ Sequel to *Dr. Who and the Daleks*, featuring that lovable curmudgeon doctor (Peter Cushing) who moves through the dimensions in his time machine. In this adventure written by producer Milton Subotsky, Dr. Who (a character created on the BBC by Terry Nation) squares off against the Daleks (mutated beings in R2D2-like movable units) who have conquered our planet. Directed by Gordon Flemying. Bernard Cribbins, Ray Brooks, Andrew Keir, Jill Curzon. Aka *Invasion Earth 2150 A.D.* (HBO/Cannon)

DAMIEN—OMEN II (1978) ★★★ Murderous moppet of *The Omen*, the Antichrist as predicted in the Book of Revelation, is now 13 and using supernatural powers to the max. Grisly death scenes again—including a humdinger in an elevator. Although Harvey Bernhard's production never achieves the horror of its predecessor, cast and direction still make this a must-see. Directed by Don Taylor from a Michael Hodges–Stanley Mann script. William Holden, Lee Grant, Jonathan Scott Taylor, Robert Foxworth, Lew Ayres, Elizabeth Shepherd, Sylvia Sidney. (Video/Laser: CBS/Fox)

DAMNATION ALLEY (1977) ★★ Roger Zelazny's post-Holocaust novel, turned into a hackneyed version of *Stagecoach* by scripters Alan Sharp and Lukas Heller. Civilization has been wiped out by atomic missiles and the terrain is littered with giant scorpions and armor-plated cockroaches. In place of the 'coach is the Land Master, a futuristic tank piloted by Air Force officer George Peppard, underling Jan-Michael Vincent and other dull characters. There's nice effects work when the Earth returns to its proper axis, but other effects are downright awful. Jack Smight directed. Paul Winfield, Murray Hamilton, Dominique Sanda. (Key)

DANCE MACABRE (1991) ★★ Robert (Freddy Krueger) Englund leads a group of dancers training in Russia, but his personality takes a pirouette for the worse and splits into evil and good halves. One of those halves is a serial killer. Directed by Greydon Clark. Michelle Zeitlin, Marianna Moen. (Video/Laser: RCA/Columbia)

DANCE, MEPHISTO. See *The Oblong Box.*

DANCE OF DEATH. Video version of Karloff's *House of Evil* (MPI; Sony).

DANCE OF THE DAMNED (1989) ★★ Call this *Last Tango in Shadowland*. It's a sexual encounter between handsome vampire Cyril O'Reilly and brooding stripper Starr Andreeff, who spend a night discussing the meaning of life, the ennui of an eternal vampire in search of blood, and the importance of sun on the body. There's little here but mood, and there's tons of mood. From the team that made the *Stripped to Kill* flicks: Andy and Katt Shea Ruben, he producing, she directing, together writing. Deborah Ann Nassar, Maria Ford, Athena Worthy. Remade by producer Roger Corman as *To Sleep with a Vampire*. (Virgin Vision) (Laser: Image)

DANCE OF THE DWARFS. See *Jungle Heat.*

DANCE OF THE VAMPIRES. See *The Fearless Vampire Killers.*

DANGEROUS CHARTER. See *The Creeping Terror*.

DANGEROUS GAME (1990) ★★ A computer expert and pals penetrate the security system of a department store, only to be stalked by a killer. Miles Buchanan, Sandy Lillingston, Kathryn Walker, John Polson. Directed by Stephen Hopkins. (Academy)

DANGERS OF THE CANADIAN MOUNTED (1947/48) ★★ Considering that action specialist Yakima Canutt codirected (with Fred Brannon) this 12-chapter Republic serial, *Dangers* is a disappointment, being one of the studio's more stilted, slow-moving and clumsy-footed attempts at a cliffhanger, despite the fact much of it was filmed in rugged redwoods country. Jim Bannon is incredibly bland as mountie Chris Royal, who is faced with stopping Mort Fowler (Anthony Warde, excellent in this kind of badguy role) from stealing the legendary treasure of Genghis Khan, which is hidden in an old ship. Fowler and his cronies trick professor I. Stanford Jolley into studying hieroglyphics to figure out the hiding place while Royal goes through dull cliffhangers. There's one good sequence involving an ancient statue in a cave, but that's about it. Virginia Belmont helps Bannon in his northwestern adventures but it's very tired, compared to other Republic serials of the period. One can only assume Canutt was denied an adequate budget and just gave up. Dorothy Granger (as Skagway Kate), Tom Steele, Bill Van Sickel, Phil Warren. The TV-feature version is *R.C.M.P. and the Treasure of Genghis Khan*. (Video/Laser: Republic)

DANIEL AND THE DEVIL. See *The Devil and Daniel Webster*.

DANSE MACABRE. See *Castle of Blood*.

DAREDEVILS OF THE RED CIRCLE (1939) ★★★ One of Republic's better serials, primarily because of on-location action pieces directed by cliffhanger kings William Witney and John English. Master criminal #39013 (Charles Middleton) disguises himself as a millionaire and uses deadly Delta Killer Rays against three ex-circus daredevils. Nonstop, rugged action, the kind men (and kids) like. Charles Quigley, Herman Brix (Bruce Bennett), David Sharpe, Carole Landis, Miles Mander, C. Montague Shaw. (Republic; Video Connection)

DARIO ARGENTO'S INFERNO. See *Inferno*.

DARIO ARGENTO'S TRAUMA (1993) ★★★ Italy's master of horror and suspense helms this psychothriller (aka *Trauma*) about a killer called the Headhunter, who cuts off human anatomy from the neck up with a power-tool device whenever it's raining. This has that warped sense of storytelling that makes Argento an unusual filmmaker, with characters who behave bizarrely, as if they all belonged in a rest home for psychos. Among the oddball characters (not even counting the decapitator) are Frederic Forrest as the crazed Dr. Judd (weird, weird, weird) and Brad Dourif as a freaked-out guy in the Brad Dourif style. Cowritten by Argento with T. E. D. Klein, this features location footage of the worst parts of Minneapolis. Christopher Rydell, Asia Argento, Laura Johnson, James Russo, Hope Alexander-Willis, Piper Laurie. Special makeup by Tom Savini. (World of Video, in rated and unrated versions)

DARIO ARGENTO'S WORLD OF HORROR (1986) ★★ Vid-documentary on Italian writer-producer-director Dario Argento, best known for *Deep Red: The Hatchet Murders* and *Suspiria*. Features segments from *Creepers, The Bird With the Crystal Plumage, Demons*, etc. Directed by Michele Soavi. (Vidmark) (Laser: Image)

DARK, THE (1979) ★ Hare-brained mixture of sci-fi/horror when an unfrightening 7-foot alien in a fright mask (with glowing red eyeballs) tears off victims' heads and disintegrates them with a laser. Cathy Lee Crosby, William Devane, Keenan Wynn, Richard Jaeckel, Casey Kasem and Biff Elliott run around Hollywood looking bewildered, no thanks to director John "Bud" Cardos and scripter Stanford Whitmore. It's the old Frankenstein Monster resurrected in alien form and killing without motive. (Media; from Simitar as *The Mutilator*)

DARK, THE (1993) ★★½ Eerie photography in a tunnel beneath a cemetery enhances this Canadian horror thriller in which a maverick ex-FBI agent (Brion James) pursues a genetic monster that feeds on dead bodies. One twist in Robert C. Cooper's script is that the toothy, hairy creature is semi-benevolent when a drifter (Stephen McHattie) and greasy-spoon waitress (Cynthia Belliveau) join in the search. However, Cooper's narrative is muddled—a deficiency that Craig Pryce's direction cannot overcome. Jaimz Woolvett, Dennis O'Connor, Neve Campbell. (Imperial) (Laser: Image)

DARK AGE (1988) ★★ Remember *Jaws*? Remember *Alligator*? Remember *Crocodile*? Well, now remember (or would you rather forget?) Australia's *Dark Age*, the tale of the legendary 25-foot-long Numunwari, a demon salt-water croc/gator/jawsbreaker feared and revered by the Arnhem Land Aborgines. Three men—a ranger and two natives, one of them with an ESP connection to ole Numunwari—set out to find the creature after he's enjoyed human hors d'oeuvres. Sound familiar, or what? The difference here is that they want to keep the croc alive—it's the last of its species. Written by Sonia Borg (from a Grahame Webb novel) and directed by Arch Nicholson. John Jarratt, Nikki Coghill, Max Phipps, Burnam Burnam. (Video/Laser: Charter)

DARK ANGEL. See *I Come in Peace*.

DARK ANGEL: THE ASCENT (1994) ★★★ One of the strangest offerings, and one of the last, from Charles Band's Full Moon Entertainment company. The first 15 minutes are set in Hell and play like a scene from Dante's *Inferno*, where tormented souls are being eternally beaten to death while flames rage around them. (These scenes were shot in a 17th-century Romanian castle.) The young daughter of the headmaster rebels like a teenager against her Hellish way of life and she runs away from home—surfacing on Earth with her dog Hellraiser, there to carry out bloody acts of retribution against criminals as if she were an "avenging angel." What makes Matthew Bright's script compelling and confusing at the same time is the film's reluctance to distinguish between good and evil, as Heaven and Hell seem to be interactive, God controlling everything that happens. Director Linda Hassani brings a lot of artsy-fartsy stuff to this oddball horror flick and there is the added location atmosphere of Romania. The cast is good (especially Angela Featherstone as Monica Teresa Maria Valeria Iscarius of Hell; Nicholas Worth as her demon father with minihorns; and Michael C. Mahon as a cop). This is one that'll have you scratching your head, wondering what the Hell it's all about. Exactly! Daniel Markel, Charlotte Stewart, Michael Genovese, Milton James. (Paramount) (Laser: Full Moon)

DARK AUGUST (1976) ★ Slow-moving, predictable tale of the supernatural (first made as *The Hant*) in which an old man curses the driver of the Jeep that accidentally ran down his daughter. The cursed guy (J. J. Barry) seeks help from a mystic named Adrianna Puttnam (Kim Hunter), but his efforts to follow her advice are thwarted by ironic intervention. This low-budget quickie never builds momentum. Scripted by Martin Goldman (who also directed) and the female lead, Carole Shelyne. (Lightning; Vestron)

DARK BACKWARD, THE (1991) ★★ This intriguing attempt to make a morbid comedy within a surreal setting fails because of frequent lapses of taste and an ugly attitude toward people. A little restraint by writer-director Adam Rifkin could have guided this into a more acceptable area. Judd Nelson plays the ultimate nobody—a shy, repressed nerd who grows a third arm out his back when he turns stand-up comedian. His friend (Bill Paxton) is an obnoxious, disgusting character who fornicates with three fat women, licks a woman's corpse in a garbage pit and cackles hysterically. Wait until you see Wayne Newton as talent manager John Chrome, or Rob Lowe as a talent scout, or Lara Flynn Boyle as a sexually repressed hash slinger. Ugh. (Video/Laser: RCA/Columbia)

DARK CITY (1997) ★★★½ This intriguing fable of apocalyptic proportions blends science fiction, fantasy, and horror into a stunningly original tale that borders on being an allegory about creation. A sinister alien race of thin-bodied humanoids in dark overcoats and slouch hats is tampering with people's minds (they have no individual thoughts, only collective memories) in a strange metropolis that seems an amalgamation of different periods. Stumbling through this vast mystery is an amnesiac (Rufus Sewell), a weird doctor (Kiefer Sutherland), a beautiful woman (Jennifer Connelly), and a sardonic cop (William Hurt). Is Sewell a serial killer, or is he being manipulated by the aliens with a talent for "quning," the ability to change reality? *Dark City* unfolds as a fascinating mystery-thriller scripted by director Alex (*The Crow*) Proyas, who collaborated with Lem Dobbs and David S. Goyer and coproduced with Andrew Mason. The computerized effects are brilliant in this experiment in style and metaphysical atmosphere. The convoluted story requires full attention, but those who love literate sci-fi will groove on its visual and mind-boggling delights. (Video/DVD:New Line)

DARK CRYSTAL, THE (1982) ★★★ Muppet mastermind Jim Henson and *Star Wars* producer Gary Kurtz collaborated on this fantasy on a faraway planet ruled by Skekses, a race of lizard creatures. It's a kingdom where characters are hand puppets or people in costumes and face masks. David Odell's script, from an idea by Henson, has two Gelflings setting out to find a crystal piece that, when restored to the mystical Dark Crystal, will remove blight from the land. The Skekses and the Mystics, a race of ponderous thinkers, are brilliantly designed, but the Gelflings are lifeless puppets. Brian Froud's fantasy world is well realized, but anyone expecting this to be a cutesy romp will be disappointed. Codirected by Henson and Frank Oz. (Video/Laser: HBO)

DARK DEALER, THE (1995) ★★½ Although cheaply shot and ragged around a lot of its edges, this independent, Texas-made anthology of horror tales will find favor with monster buffs, and those who enjoy discovering a promising new talent, in this case director Tom Alexander. His scripting is also ragged around the edges, but there are moments of visual style worth waiting for. The wraparound portion of *Dark Dealer* deals with three characters playing blackjack with Death, which doesn't work. The best of the tales is "Cellar Space," with two punk killers invading the rundown room of a weirdo named Nicodemus (Gordon Fox), only to undergo grim demises as ole Nic keeps turning into different horrendous creatures. "Blues in the Night," about an entertainment lawyer (Kevin Walker) who steals the songs of a dead man (Vincent Gaskins) only to be haunted by his ghost, takes a close second, with a third tale about an evil sphere of light that attacks some characters breaking into a pharmaceutical lab lagging way behind. Uneven, but give it a try if you dig tyros giving their all. (Stardance Entertainment)

DARK DREAMS. Video title for *Erotic Dreams.*

DARKEST AFRICA (1936) ★★★ Republic's first serial ever, with wild-animal trainer Clyde Beatty trekking with jungle boy Baru (a chubby lad well-versed in subduing wild animals with a whip) and Bonga the ape in search of the lost city of Joba. They're also looking for Baru's sister—a missing beauty named Dagna, the unwilling Goddess of Joba—but thwarting them are winged warriors (called Bat Men) and two crooks after a fortune in diamonds. Did we forget to mention the volcano and earthquake? Directed breathlessly by B. Reeves Eason (an action specialist) and Joseph Kane, although the acting is pretty corny. Lucien Prival, Manuel King, Edmund Cobb, Elaine Shepard. Various working titles: *The Hidden City* and *King of the Jungleland.* TV-feature version: *Batmen of Africa.* (Video/Laser: Republic)

DARK EYES. See *Demon Rage.*

DARK EYES OF LONDON. See *The Human Monster.*

DARK EYES OF LONDON, THE. See *The Dead Eyes of London.*

DARK FORCES. Video version of *Harlequin* (Media).

DARK HALF, THE (1991) ★★★ Stephen King's popular novel is given a bang-up job by writer-director George Romero, and Timothy Hutton does a bang-up job as best-selling writer Thad Beaumont, and as his alter ego, a serial killer. Eventually "the dark half" works his way toward Beaumont's New England home. Only during an apocalyptic ending, involving swarms of sparrows, does the tale turn ridiculous and overwrought. But during its suspenseful buildup, with Romero utilizing the conventions of the slasher genre, the film is compelling. Amy Madigan is Beaumont's wife, Michael Rooker is the sheriff, and Julie Harris is Beaumont's colleague. (Orion) (Laser: Image)

DARKMAN (1990) ★★★★ Sam (*The Evil Dead*) Raimi distinguishes himself again as a director of style, whose visual virtuosity is striking. *Darkman* is reminiscent of the old serials and pulps of the '40s but with a modern black-comedy twist when Dr. Peyton Westlake (Liam Neeson) discovers a formula for synthetic skin, but then is mutilated by gangsters. Barely surviving, and gruesomely disfigured, Dr. Westlake moves from light into darkness to wreak his revenge on enemies by wearing masks that allow him to assume other identities. This watershed movie has the gothic spirit of *Batman*, the split personality of *Dr. Jekyll and Mr. Hyde*, the deformities of *The Phantom of the Opera* and the doomed romantic relationship of *The Fly.* Fr-

ances McDormand, Jenny Agutter, Larry Drake (as nemesis Robert G. Durant), Nelson Mashita. (Video/Laser: MCA)

DARKMAN II: THE RETURN OF DURANT (1994) ★★★ A direct-to-video sequel to *Darkman,* this Sam Raimi–Robert Tapert production has all the style and destructive special-effects of the original as Larry Drake's evil villain, Robert G. Durant, is resurrected from his death in *Darkman* and given a new life as a gangleader plotting to take over the city's rackets with the help of a new laser rifle. But Dr. Peyton Westlake (back as Arnold Vosloo) is still creating his synthetic face masks, which enable him to fight Durant in a series of explosive action sequences. All the important elements of the original seem to be here in Steven McKay's script, and cameraman/director Bradford May shows he has the same dynamic, stylish eye as Raimi, so it's an effective reprise. Next in the series: *Darkman III: Die, Darkman, Die!* Kim Delaney, Renee O'Connor, Lawrence Dane. (Video/Laser: MCA)

DARKMAN III: DIE DARKMAN DIE (1995) ★★★ Another fine direct-to-video follow-up to the hit *Darkman,* with producers Sam Raimi and Robert Tapert maintaining the quality and integrity of this surprisingly good series by allowing cameraman-director Bradford May to stay at the helm. Arnold Vosloo is back as Peyton Westlake (described as "an Urban Bigfoot") who is still trying to perfect a lasting synthetic skin formula. His new nemesis is drug kingpin Jeff Fahey, who maintains respectability with a wife (Roxann Biggs-Dawson), daughter and mansion. How the slimy Fahey and the sexy Darlene Fluegel trick Westlake/Darkman with a new "microsurgery" sets into motion a series of deceptions involving Westlake's face masks. The Michael Colleary/Mike Werb script emphasizes character as well as explosive action and sci-fi gimmicks, allowing Westlake to carry on his angst and for Fahey to develop a despicable villain you love to watch go bonkers. (MCA)

DARK NIGHT OF THE SCARECROW (1981) ★★★ Unusually gory, violent TV-movie, startlingly refreshing. Bubba, a halfwit accused of murder, is shot by angry farmers, who pump 22 bullets into his quivering body before learning he is innocent. The town acquits the men but Bubba returns as a scarecrow, killing farmers with their own equipment. One gets dropped into a thrashing machine, another is suffocated in a grain silo. The J. D. Feigelson teleplay is filled with surprises, ending on a shocker director Frank De Felitta never tips beforehand. Charles Durning, Larry Drake, Lane Smith, Jocelyn Brando. (Fox/Key; Front Row Entertainment)

DARK OF THE NIGHT (1984) ★ New Zealand imitation of *Christine* (aka *Mr. Wrong*) recycles the theme of the haunted automobile but in a slow-moving, eccentric way that makes this low-budget effort of minimal interest. A Jaguar Mark IV becomes the property of Heather Bolton, who soon discovers its former owner was a young woman (Perry Percy) who was murdered. Strange things happen when a stranger (David Letch) turns up. Written by coproducer/director Gaylene Preston from a story by Elizabeth Jane Howard. (Live; Lightning)

DARK POWER (1987) ★★½ Lash LaRue, one-time western hero who specialized in cracking a whip in a black outfit, made a modest comeback in this tale about evil Indian spirits that haunt a home in North Carolina, only to feel the sharp sting of Lash's whip. For sadists only. Directed by Phil Smoot. (Midwest; Magnum)

DARK REFLECTION (1993) ★★★ Good suspense thriller with sci-fi genetics overtones as computer expert C. Thomas Howell comes to realize he is the result of a cloning experiment and his lookalike brother (also Howell) plans to replace him. That old ploy, which-one-is-which?, is cleverly used by director Jack Sholder. Lisa Zane, Miko Hughes, Ethan Phillips. (Fox)

DARK RIDE (1977) ★ Fictionalized case history of serial killer Ted Bundy, spun as a mixture of police procedure (with cop James Luisi doggedly on the killer's trail) and gore murder thriller, although the gore is minimal and lacks impact. The only thing this low-budgeter offers is John Karlen as the murderer. Set in San Francisco but filmed mostly in L.A. Directed by Jeremy Hoenack. Susan Sullivan, Martin Speer. (Media)

DARKROOM (1990) ★½ Something never gets developed in the think-tank as director Terrence O'Hara overexposes the plot. The image: a slasher on the loose, motivated by incest. Negative results. Sara Lee Wade, Jeffrey Allen Arbaugh, Aarin Teich, Jill Pierce. (Quest Entertainment; VCL)

DARK SANITY. Video version of Aldo Ray's *Straight Jacket* (Marquis; Genesis; Prism).

DARK SECRET OF HARVEST HOME, THE (1978) ★★ Tom Tryon's excellent novel was made into a TV-movie by producer Jack Laird, depicting life in a New England village, Cornwall Coombe, where cultlike activities suggest human sacrifice and satanism. Faithful to Tryon's concepts, including the unsettling ending. Bette Davis stars as Widow Fortune, a dowager with powers of witchcraft. Directed by Leo Penn. Joanna Miles, David Ackroyd, Rosanna Arquette, Earl Keyes. (MCA)

DARK SHADOWS (1991) ★★★ This two-part TV-movie revived Dan Curtis's daytime supernatural serial of the 1960s—and served as the pilot for a short-lived series that brought a new sense of horror and darkness to the sanguinary history of a family of vampires. Jonathan Frid is not here as Barnabas Collins (that part passed to Ben Cross) and that may disappoint fans—but those same fans should be happy about this well-produced, atmospheric and oppressive fang-fantasy. Barbara Blackburn, Jim Fyfe, Joanna Going, Roy Thinnes, Barbara Steele, Jean Simmons. Curtis directed. (MPI)

DARK SHADOWS. (1966–1971) MPI has issued at least 28 cassettes containing episodes from the daytime serial.

DARK SHADOWS. See *House of Dark Shadows* and *Night of Dark Shadows* for description of feature versions.

DARK SIDE OF MIDNIGHT, THE (1984) ★ Trauma-inducing film from the Troma folks about the Creeper, a slasher-smasher-basher knocking off people in Fort Smith, Arkansas. Watching the second hand of your clock ticking toward midnight might be more exciting. James Moore, Wes Olsen. Written-produced-directed by Olsen. (Prism; from AVR as *The Creeper*)

DARK SIDE OF THE MOON, THE (1989) ★★★½ Taut, well-produced, no-nonsense sci-fi mystery set in 2022 aboard Spacecore 1, a ship on a mission to repair (or "refab") nuclear-armed satellites rotating Earth. When the ship malfunctions it drifts into "Cypress B-40" (code name: dark side of the moon). There, the crew encounters a derelict shuttlecraft that leads to a mystery involving the Bermuda Triangle, walking corpses, and the Devil. The Carey W. Hayes–Chad Hayes script presents the scientific puzzles in an intriguing fashion. Director D. J. Webster keeps it tense. Joseph Turkel, Will Bledsoe, Alan Blumenfeld, Robert Sampson, John Diehl, Wendy MacDonald. (Vidmark) (Laser: Image)

DARK STAR (1975) ★★★½ Sci-fi with the shining: A starship roves the Universe, armed with thermonuclear bombs to explode unstable suns. The John Carpenter–Dan O'Bannon script captures the claustrophobia of space travel and the mental deterioration of ennui-softened crewmen. A malfunctioning computer results in one of the strangest villains in any space movie. The only flaw is a form of alien life, obviously an inflated beachball with clawed feet. Carpenter produced-directed with the original title *Dark Star: A Science Fiction Adventure*. O'Bannon stars with Brian Narelle. (Video Dimensions; VCI) (Laser: Image)

DARK TOWER (1987) ★★ Sandy Howard production shot in Barcelona, Spain. The first half-hour of this tale of a haunted highrise has a few twists and only minor chills as accidents and murders occur in the building. But then it completely crumbles. Architect Jenny Agutter, who designed the building, is haunted by her dead husband. Michael Moriarty, striving to bring characterization to a woefully written cop role, probes the case with quirky psychics Theodore Bikel and Kevin McCarthy. All these actors—including Carol Lynley in a thankless part as Agutter's secretary—deserve better. This turned out so poor, director Freddie Francis used the pseudonym Ken Barnett. (Forum; MCEG Virgin) (Laser: Image)

DARK UNIVERSE (1992) ★ While aboard the spacecraft *Nautilus*, an astronaut turns into an *Alien*-like monster that looks like it was borrowed from *Deep Space*, another film produced by the ubiquitous Fred Olen Ray. This evil entity lands in Florida (where this incredibly inept cheapie was shot) and proceeds to kill everyone in the cast by sticking its pointed tongue through the belly and sucking out all of one's life source. Call it "Spawn of the Yawn," it's so boring. Directed by Steve Latshaw (destined to do the equally dismal *Jack-O* for Ray); written by Patrick Moran. Grant Austin Waldman coproduced with Ray and Jim Wynorski. Blake Pickett, Cherie Scott, Bently Tittle, John Maynard. (Prism) (Laser: Image)

DARK WIND, THE (1991) ★★★½ Mild Indian mysticism and witchcraft overtones are woven throughout this excellent mystery thriller starring Lou Diamond Phillips as Navajo reservation cop Jim Chee, who is caught up in a mystery involving a cache of drugs, crooked Federal agents and an assortment of colorful Navajo and Hopi characters. The New Mexico landscapes are beautifully and eerily captured through the unusual direction of documentary filmmaker Errol Morris. Coproduced by Robert Redford. Gary Farmer, Fred Ward (as Joe Leaphorn), John Karlen. The Neal Jimenez–Eric Bergin script was adapted from a Tony Hillerman novel. (Video/Laser: New Line)

D.A.R.Y.L. (1985) ★★ Boring juvenile fantasy about young robot D.A.R.Y.L. (Data Analyzing Robot Youth Lifeform), labeled a "test tube experiment in artificial intelligence," who escapes from the lab and seeks refuge with Mary Beth Hurt and Michael McKean. He learns the meaning of "human" as he demonstrates his powers and learning abilities. The baddies come looking for him and he becomes an object lesson. Uninspired; dully photographed. Directed by Simon Wincer. Colleen Camp, Kathryn Walker. (Video/Laser: Paramount)

DATE WITH AN ANGEL (1987) ★★★ There are warm moments in this fantasy morality tale written-directed by Tom McLoughlin—and there's a tenderness too. Emmanuelle Beart is wonderful as an angel found floating in a swimming pool by Michael E. Knight, who's about to marry Phoebe Cates. Beart is so beautiful you believe she's an angel as Knight finds himself caught up in misunderstandings with his fiancée, her parents and his teen-age pals. The story takes on social issues when Cates's father (Da-

vid Dukes), president of a cosmetics firm, exploits the angel. Fluffy entertainment, but harp-and-halo above most of its ilk. Phil Brock, Albert Macklin. (Video/Laser: HBO)

DAUGHTER OF A WEREWOLF. See *Legend of the Wolfwoman.*

DAUGHTER OF DR. JEKYLL (1957) ★½ Wonderfully ridiculous premise for a cheesy B flick: Gloria Talbott thinks she's tainted by the split personality of her infamous father, and stalks hapless victims at night. The monster myths really go awry in producer-writer Jack Pollexfen's script when a werewolf gets a stake through the heart. Directed by Edgar G. Ulmer. John Agar, Arthur Shields, John Dierkes, Martha Wentworth. (Fox/Key)

DAUGHTER OF FRANKENSTEIN. See *Lady Frankenstein.*

DAUGHTER OF HORROR (1953) ★★★½ A powerful, shocking film noir in black and white, from the imagination of writer-producer-director John Parker, who displays great understanding of psychology and mood filmmaking. Originally released as *Dementia*, this is the nightmare of a woman (Adrienne Barrett) whose mental deterioration blurs the line separating reality from fantasy. She drifts through a nocturnal world populated by a fat man, a sadistic policeman and other lowlifes. Parker's strengths lie in his depiction of the woman's illness through her whorish mother and cruel father. Ed McMahon narrates the lurid prose for this avant-garde masterpiece. Great music by George Antheil, enhanced by Marni Nixon's vocals. (S/Weird; Thunderbird; Sinister/C)

DAUGHTER OF THE WEREWOLF. See *Cry of the Werewolf.*

DAUGHTERS OF DARKNESS (1971) ★★★ Belgium's Harry Kumel wrote-directed this contemporary vampire tale which projects Elisabeth Bathory, 16th-century Hungarian countess who bathed in the blood of virgins, into a luxury hotel on the coast of Belgium. As Bathory, Delphine Seyrig gushes with sophistication, glamour and lesbian innuendo which turns blatant when she seduces a newlywed and her husband. While there is blood and gore, Kumel explores the dark side of human sexuality in fascinating fashion, using erotica and symbolism. Achieves an aura of decadence strangely compelling. Aka *Erzebeth, The Promise of Red Lips, The Redness of the Lips* and *The Red Lips.* Daniele Ouimet, John Karlen. (Cinema Group; from AIR as *Children of the Night*)

DAUGHTERS OF DARKNESS/DAUGHTERS OF DRACULA. See *Vampyres—Daughters of Darkness.*

DAUGHTERS OF THE VAMPIRE. See *Curse of the Vampire.*

DAWN OF THE DEAD (1979) ★★★ George A. Romero's sequel to *Night of the Living Dead.*

The unrestricted movie code now allows writer-director Romero to be more graphic, and while overshock lessens the impact, he still has a primitive power that sets him apart from (if not always above) his contemporaries. This succeeds as a stomach-churning glimpse at man's prowess to destroy himself with up-to-date weaponry, and as a spoof on *Living Dead* itself. For sometimes the walking zombies are treated menacingly, other times as jokes. The plot involves a small band trapped in a shopping mall. *Day of the Dead* was the third and final chapter in this sanguinary saga. David Emge, Ken Foree, Scott H. Reininger. Aka *Zombies* and *Dawn of the Living Dead*. (HBO; Republic) (Laser: HBO)

DAWN OF THE LIVING DEAD. See *Dawn of the Dead*.

DAWN OF THE MUMMY (1981) ★★ Hashish smokers in a Cairo square are as exciting as it gets in this tale of a bandaged-enwrapped hunk of Egyptian royalty circa 3000 B.C. who rises from his desecrated crypt to create an army of flesh-eating monsters. Heads are ripped off with wild abandon and one unfortunate Egyptian is skewered on a hook. Egyptian pyramid locations are a plus, but the only plus. The script by producer-director Frank Agrama, Darda Price and Ronald Dobrin depicts magazine models posing for cheesecake shots in the crypt of royal king Zevraman. Definitely a lowbrow shambling-dead flick. The sun sets quickly on *Dawn of the Mummy*. Brenda King, Barry Sattels. (HBO)

DAY AFTER, THE (1983) ★★★½ TV-movie written by Edward Hume and directed by Nicholas Meyer for $8 million depicting nuclear war in and around Lawrence, Kansas. It begins as an average day for several citizens . . . then news of pending attack creates panic. Finally, the Apocalypse comes with twin explosions in which Kansas City is destroyed, women and children vaporized and thousands radiated in the aftermath. The day after is more terrifying as countless bodies are heaped on pyres, people die of radiation poisoning, etc. As grim as anything made for TV. Jason Robards, Georgann Johnson, Kyle Aletter, Bibi Besch, Steve Guttenberg, JoBeth Williams, John Lithgow. (Video/Laser: Embassy)

DAY BEFORE HALLOWEEN (1983) ★★ Australian paranoia thriller depicts a woman chased by a lecherous photographer, a half-crazed boyfriend, a notorious lesbian and a sculptor who puts a severed pig's head in her bed. All of them want to exploit and drive this innocent (Chantal Contouri) bonkers. Simon Wincer directed this strange novelty. Aka *Snap-Shot*. Music by Brian May. (Catalina)

DAYBREAK (1993) ★★ Bleak glimpse into a "near future" when a sexual disease affects society to the point many are being quarantined under mysterious circumstances and an underground resistance movement has risen up. Writer-director Stephen Tolkin brings a social conscience to this TV-movie but it's too downbeat and unapproachable to pass as entertainment. Cuba Gooding, Jr., Moira Kelly, Omar Epps, Alice Drummond. (Video/Laser: HBO)

DAY IT CAME TO EARTH (1977) ★ Radioactive meteorite falls to Earth, unleashing E.T. forces of evil into the corpse of a criminal who comes to life and goes on a rampage. Directed by Harry Z. Thomason, written by Paul Fisk. Roger Manning, Wink Roberts, George Gobel. (Paragon)

DAY NEW YORK WAS INVADED, THE. See *The Mouse That Roared*.

DAY OF JUDGMENT, A (1981) ★★½ This could be the world's only religious slasher flick, a lesson in following the Ten Commandments—or else. It's couched as a parable and the climax has all the excitement of a Sunday sermon. Anyway, a man in black, carrying a scythe and symbolizing Retribution, rides into a Southern town in the '20s and stalks less-than-genteel types: a banker foreclosing on a farmer, a half-crazed widow who poisons a harmless goat, an adulterer and adulteress, a son who schemes to send his mom and dad to an asylum. The gore is largely offscreen. From North Carolina producer Earl Owensby. Directed by C. D. H. Reynolds. William T. Hicks, Harris Bloodworth. (HBO)

DAY OF THE ANIMALS (1977) ★★½ Earth's ozone layer is damaged by aerosol and turns animals into killers. A little of *Jaws*, a little of *The Birds*. Beware of anything on four legs as an expedition is attacked, each member dying a horrible death. Christopher George heads the snivelers and arguers: Leslie Nielsen, Lynda Day George, Richard Jaeckel, Paul Mantee, Ruth Roman, Michael Ansara. Directed by William Girdler. (Media; from Action Inc. as *Something Is out There*)

DAY OF THE DEAD (1985) ★★★ Third and final installment in the *Night of the Living Dead* series from writer-director George A. Romero. The world is now made up of walking zombies with only a few "normals" left. Survivors hide in an underground center where Dr. Logan (Richard Liberty) experiments on the dead. Loco Logan comes into conflict with a military unit which wants to curtail the sickening experiments. (This modern Frankenstein has the dedication of a quack at Dachau.) This conflict seems unnecessary when 9,000 zombies are trying to break in. Romero, who once had fun with zombies, here takes himself seriously, relying on effects for horror scenes that revolt rather than entertain. There's the expected chomping on body parts and unstringing of intestines, and thanks to Tom Savini we see a human body ripped apart. A clumsy, unresolved conclusion to the trilogy. Lori Cardille, Terry Alexander, Howard Sherman. (Media; Video Treasures) (Laser: Image)

DAY OF THE MANIAC. Video version of *Demons of the Dead* (Super; from Vogue as *They're Coming to Get You*).

DAY OF THE TRIFFIDS (1963) ★★½ John Wyndham's novel was mangled by screenwriter Philip Yordan in this British version, at one point deteriorating into man-battling-rampaging-monsters. Still, some of Wyndham's unusual end-of-mankind story remains intact, showing how most of the world's population is blinded by a meteor shower. Spared their vision, Howard Keel and Nicole Maurey flee to safety, surrounded by armies of Triffids: spores from the meteors which grow into unpruned plantlike beings which yank up their roots and stalk mortals, their pods delivering a lethal sting. Directed by Steve Sekely and Freddie Francis. Janette Scott, Mervyn Johns, Kieron Moore. Aka *Revolt of the Triffids* and *Invasion of the Triffids*. (Media) (Laser: Fox; Image)

DAY OF THE WOMAN. See *I Spit on Your Grave*.

DAY THE EARTH CAUGHT FIRE, THE (1961) ★★★½ Doff your fire helmet to British screenwriters Val Guest and Wolf Mankowitz for giving us an intelligent sci-fi thriller. Two governments set off atomic explosions that result in a shift of the Earth's axis and an eccentric, unstable path for our planet. Mankind heads inexorably toward its doom. Edward Judd is a drunken newspaperman, Leo McKern a crusading science editor, Janet Munro the love interest. Guest also directed. Michael Goodliffe, Bernard Braden. Aka *The Day the Sky Caught Fire*. (HBO; Republic)

DAY THE EARTH STOOD STILL, THE (1951) ★★★★★ One of the finest sci-fi movies of the '50s, thanks to director Robert Wise's concern for atmosphere and characterization. Harry Bates's short story "Farewell to the Master" was altered by writer Edmund North but the essence is kept. Michael Rennie is Klaatu, an alien who lands his flying saucer in Washington, D.C., to warn us we must settle our geopolitical differences, or else. Wounded by soldiers, he is hospitalized, but goes undercover to locate a brilliant scientist (Sam Jaffe) in order to gather the intelligentsia to hear his plea. To prove he means business, Klaatu stops all machinery on Earth for one hour. The score by Bernard Herrmann is a classic and even theologians have studied the peculiar Christ symbolism North inserted into the script. Patricia Neal is the love interest who befriends the alien and seeks out a seven-foot robot, Gort, to utter "Klaatu barada nikto," to keep Gort from destroying the world. Gort was Lock Martin, a 7'7" doorman. Hugh Marlowe, Billy Gray, Harry Lauter, Drew Pearson. (Video/Laser: Fox)

DAY THE SCREAMING STOPPED, THE. See *The Comeback*.

DAY THE WORLD CHANGED HANDS, THE. See *Colossus: The Forbin Project*.

DAY THE WORLD ENDED, THE (1955) ★★★ Producer Alex Gordon/director Roger Corman horror/sci-fi flick, as ludicrous as it is entertaining as conceived as scripter Lou Rusoff. Paul Birch has designed a modernistic house free from radioactive contamination in which he and daughter Lori Nelson take refuge on the day of Armageddon. However, a stripteaser, gigolo, gold prospector, gangster and moll turn up for shelter. While they bicker, a hideous mutant (a reminder of atomic horrors in the world beyond) pokes around with the hope of carrying away Lori in her high heels. Richard Denning, Paul Dubov, Adele Jergens, Jonathan Haze. Mike Connors is billed as Touch Connors.

DAY TIME ENDED, THE (1978) ★★ Filmed as *Vortex* and aka *Timewarp*, this Charles Band effort stars Jim Davis as head of a family in a desert solar home as the effects of a supernova reach Earth. A green pyramid appears and tiny creatures dance in stop-motion animation. The house is in a time warp (dig those fighting dinosaurs, gang). Effects by Jim Danforth and David Allen are nice, and the cast is watchable (Christopher Mitchum, Dorothy Malone, Scott Kolden, Marcy Lafferty), but the story is slight and pseudo-Spielbergish. Directed by John "Bud" Cardos from a script by producer Wayne Schmidt, Larry Carroll and David Schmoeller. (Media) (Laser)

D DAY ON MARS. Edited version of the Republic serial *The Purple Monster Strikes*.

DEAD AGAIN (1991) ★★★ This Kenneth Branagh-directed murder-mystery thriller with supernatural/reincarnation overtones is a compelling bit of bravura filmmaking and acting. Amnesia victim Emma Thompson has nightmares about a 1948 Hollywood murder (shown in black-and-white flashbacks) as private eye Branagh helps her to unravel her past aided by hypnotist Derek Jacobi. Unfortunately, Frank goes off the deep end with too many co-incidences and the film plunges into self-parody, its excesses overwhelming the cast. Still, many portions are superb, with Andy Garcia contributing as a jaded prize-winning journalist. Robin Williams, in an uncredited cameo, plays a disbarred psychiatrist. Sydney Pollack produced. (Video/Laser: Paramount)

DEAD ALIVE (1992) ★★★ Outrageous gore-splatter comedy blending the morbid parody of Frank (*Basket Case*) Henenlotter and the macabre styles of Sam Raimi and George Romero. Made in New Zealand, it depicts what happens when simian raticus ("the rat monkey of Sumatra") is brought from Skull Island in 1957 and placed in a zoo. The creature's bite (rendered in stop-motion animation) instantly turns a woman into a monster that ferociously kills. The mom's nerdy son and girlfriend try to contain the corpses in mom's mansion but the living dead keep increasing. The only way to control them? Stick a hypodermic up their nostrils. This features chopped-off limbs and heads by the score, a lawnmower that churns bodies into puree gore, hypos into noses and eyes, exploding bodies, a mutant baby running rampant and a karate-trained minister. This blatant attempt to offend and still bring a smile to your lips is the work of director Peter Jackson. A must for genre fans, but general audiences will find this too subversive. (Video/Laser: Vidmark, also in an unedited version)

DEAD AND BURIED (1981) ★★★ Offbeat Dan O'Bannon–Ronald Shusett horror tale, set in coastside Potter's Bluff, where townspeople slaughter strangers by setting them afire or poking them with knives, pitchforks and other handy tools. And snapping photos all the while, for the scrapbooks. It's up to sheriff James Farentino to solve the puzzle. By keeping us in the dark about the why (if not the who), the film under Gary A. Sherman's direction builds to a suspenseful climax. The odd mixture includes witchcraft, voodooism, zombieism. Melody Anderson is Farentino's schoolteacher wife and Jack Albertson is the town coroner. Effects by Stan Winston. (Vestron)

DEAD CALM (1989) ★★★½ This Australian adaptation of Charles Williams's novel was reshaped by screenwriter Terry Hayes into a slasher-horror shocker set aboard a yacht manned by Sam Neill and Nicole Kidman, who are on a sailing holiday. The lone survivor (Billy Zane) of a ship massacre comes aboard and the terror begins. It's a fascinating concept to have victims isolated on the ocean with a killer, and director Philip Noyce captures a sense of claustrophobic horror. (Video/Laser: Warner Bros.)

DEAD CERTAIN (1990) ★★★½ This is one weird serial-killer movie that predates *Silence of the Lambs*, so don't call it a rip-off. If anything, it's unique in its dark approach to the genre and for its unrelenting, uncompromised portrait of burned-up alcoholic cop Francesco Quinn, who is obsessed with capturing a murderer. At first it appears that the killer is Brad Dourif (who gives one of his inimitable oddball performances), but as the body count builds, Quinn realizes that maybe he isn't. Writer-director Anders Palm does a bangup job with this character-driven duel of wits between Quinn,

Dourif and a man who appears to be the real killer. Or is he? It's grim, moody and murky, and if you like them that way, you will certainly dig *Dead Certain*. Karen Russell, Joel Kaiser, Jonathan Grinner, Angelo Celeste. (Hemdale)

DEAD END CITY (1989) ★★ Evil forces in U.S. Government implement a new "urban renewal" policy by forcing gangs to wipe themselves out, making it safe for law-biding citizens. As the gangs shoot it out, factory owner Greg Cummins refuses to vacate and defends his property. Dennis Cole, Christine Lund, Robert Z'dar. Written-produced-directed by Peter Yuval. (Action International)

DEAD-END DRIVE IN (1986) ★★ In the 1990s, after civilization collapses and anarchy sets in, teenagers are trapped in a drive-in movie lot in a '56 Chevy. It's a compound for teenagers, and our young hero sets out to escape. What results in this Australian political fantasy are car crashes, blazing submachine-guns and cliffhanging chases. Directed by Brian Trenchard-Smith. (New World)

DEAD EYES OF LONDON, THE (1961) ★★ West German remake of the 1940 horror flick *The Human Monster*, aka *Dark Eyes of London*, based on Edgar Wallace's *The Testament of Gordon Stuart*. Heavily insured old men are dying too frequently and the clues lead Scotland Yard's Joachim Fuchsberger to a ring of blind murderers led by a reverend. Directed by Alfred Vohrer in Hamburg, from a script by Trygve Larsen. Klaus Kinski, Karin Baal, Anna Savo. (S/Weird; Sinister/C; Filmfax)

DEAD GIRLS (1990) ★★ Women, hearing the song "You've Got to Kill Yourself" with such lyrics as "Life is a total bummer—death ends all," decide to commit suicide. One survives and goes to a hideway to recover with friends—and the friends are murdered by a masked killer, who uses weapons described in songs she wrote. Directed by Dennis Devine. (Raedon)

DEAD HEAT (1988) ★★★ Pushing outrageously into the zone of *Reanimator* and other wall-busting films, this is many things (the press book calls it a "gleeful mixture of action, adventure, fantasy, horror, mystery, romance and flat-out comedy"). It's best as a comedy of zombie and buddy-cop movies as mad Arthur P. Loudermilk (Vincent Price) rejuvenates dead humans with a machine of electric bolts and sends out zombies to hold up jewelry stores. L.A. cops Treat Williams and Joe Piscopo, a Butch Cassidy–Sundance Kid comedy duo, trail the monsters with coroner Lindsay Frost. The picture, directed by Mark Goldblatt, takes a bizarre turn when Williams becomes a zombie and goes after the bad guys. The best sequence occurs in a restaurant when the carcasses of dead animals (pig, chicken, duck, etc.) attack the cops. Darren McGavin, Keye Luke, Toru Tanaka, Robert Picardo. (New World) (Laser: Image)

DEAD KIDS. See *Strange Behavior.*

DEADLOCK (1991) ★★★ Rutger Hauer brings a light touch to his role as a jewel thief who is doublecrossed and sent to Camp Holliday, a futuristic prison in which convicts wear collars set to explode. When Hauer and Mimi Rogers escape, the film becomes a poor man's *Defiant Ones*, with the mismatched pair forced to stick close or risk being blown up. Hot on their tails is Hauer's former flame, Asian killer Joan Chen. Although there are not enough futuristic gimmicks to create an intriguing society of tomorrow, Broderick Miller's script has enough action and amusements to make this a pleasing entertainment, and it's well directed by Lewis Teague. James Remar, Stephen Tobolowsky. (HBO; Video Treasures; Fox) (Laser)

DEADLOCK 2 (1995) ★★★ An action-packed TV-movie follow-up to *Deadlock*, this presents more adventures with people who have deadly, explosive collars around their necks in a prison of the future. This time the falsely accused prisoners are Esai Morales and Nia Peeples, who escape Playland (an amusement park used as a prison) but have to stick close together or their collars will explode. The cliffhangers are delicious and involve a train, moving vans and parachutes. The telescript by Broderick Miller, Chris Cosby and Mel Friedman is intricately challenging, involving crooked businessman Stephen McHattie, a crooked politician, computer scams and embezzlement. A pleasing entertainment directed by Graeme Campbell. Jon Cuthbert, Sarah Strange, Douglas Arthurs. (Hallmark) (Video: Image)

DEADLY AND THE BEAUTIFUL, THE (1973) ★★½ If you can endure the schlock and crude crap of this Filipino hunkahorror (originally shot in Manila as *Wonder Women*), you will discover some campy stuff that's insanely fun, what with Ross Hagen (also producer) playing his Bond spoof for laughs, and Nancy Kwan playing Dr. Su, an insane scientist who practices "Brainsex" and surrounds herself with machine gunpacking, scantily clad babes. She runs a racket in which her gang kidnaps athletes so she can use their bodies for organ transplants for aging or dying millionaires. Suzy Wong may have been on the skids, but she was having a few laughs. Directed semi-incompetently by Robert Vincent O'Neil, who cowrote with Lou Whitehill. Dig leggy Maria De Aragon as she runs through downtown Manila in high heels and leads Hagen on a wildly crazy bus chase full of slapstick comedy bits. Roberta Collins, Sig Haig, Vic Diaz. Aka *Women of Transplant Island.* (Media)

DEADLY BLESSING (1981) ★★ Botched Wes Craven effort, an imitation of many genre films, has little logic as a family of Hittites, a religious sect, terrorizes women living in a farmhouse. One memorable scene has a rattlesnake crawling into a hot tub with a naked woman. We defy you to keep your eyes open during this sequence. The rest is raunchy sex and violence. Maren Jensen, Susan Buckner, Jeff East, Lisa Hartman, Lois Nettleton (in a going-bonkers role), Ernest Borgnine. (Embassy)

DEADLY DANCER (1990) ★★ Your standard movie psycho killer is on a new rampage, killing dancers/strippers in Los Angeles' Club Metro. Adolfo Quinones, Smith Wordes, Walter W. Cox, Steve Johnson. Directed by David A. Prior. (Action International) (Laser: Image)

DEADLY DREAMS (1988) ★★ Mitchell Anderson is haunted by dreams of when his parents were murdered by a man in an animal mask. Has the killer returned from the dead to kill Anderson? Directed by Kristine Peterson. Juliette Cummins, Xander Berkeley, Thom Babbes. (Virgin Vision) (Laser: Image)

DEADLY EYES (1982) ★★ Mutant rodents grow to giant size in the London subway, devouring babies and other innocents. The rabid rats finally meet their match when science teacher Sam Groom buys giant mousetraps. Meanwhile, Scatman Crothers goes to an eerie doom while inspecting a sewer. Creatures average the size of dachshunds—in fact, those are dachshunds under the rat skins. An insult to James Herbert's novel, being a typical horror film (directed by Robert Clouse, written by coproducer Charles Eglee) in which most characters are gnawed on before the final fade. The low budget shows in Ron Wisman's effects and there's a distracting (but sizzling) love affair between Groom and Lisa Langlois. Cec Linder, Lesleh Donaldson. Aka *Night Eyes* and *The Rats.* (Warner Bros.)

DEADLY FRIEND (1986) ★★ Writer Bruce Joel Rubin (adapting Diana Henstell's *Friend*) wants to tell a bittersweet love story between a Polytech student (who studies human brains and designs robots) and his next-door girlfriend (a victim of fatherly abuse). Director Wes Craven wants to retell *A Nightmare on Elm Street*, loading up on nightmares, tacked-on shock scenes and effects for their own sake (i.e., the basketball bit). Sympathy for the girl, after she's killed and restored to life (via a robot circuitry in her damaged brain), is nil once she begins killing those who wronged her. Matthew Laborteaux, Anne Twomey. (Video/Laser: Warner Bros.)

DEADLY GAME (1991) ★★★ Several individuals are summoned to an island and set loose as prey for a killer named Osiris. They flee for their lives and avoid death traps à la "The Most Dangerous Game." Each character's guilt is revealed in a flashback (the settings are Vietnam, Cambodia, the Mardi Gras, etc.) and a profile of Osiris builds. Director/coproducer Thomas J. Wright keeps it moving. Among the fleers are Roddy McDowall, Marc Singer, Mitchell Ryan, Jenny Seagrave, Soon-Tech Oh, Frederic Lehne, John Pleshette. (Paramount)

DEADLY GAMES (1982) ★★½ Esoteric slasher film (first produced as *Who Fell Asleep?*) dealing with the relationship between killer and victim. A black-mask killer is murdering women, but writer-director Scott Mansfield narrows the possibilities to demented policeman Sam Groom or melancholoy theater manager Steve Railsback. The murders are not gory, suggesting Mansfield prefers dealing with drama rather than cliché knife murders. His subtleties cause the film to go in and out of focus, and there are counterpoint idyllic moments when a would-be victim (Denise Galin) enjoys fun and games with the two suspects, unaware one of them is the slasher. Jo Ann Harris, June Lockhart, Colleen Camp, Alexandra Morgan, Dick Butkus, Gale Sayers. (Monterey)

DEADLY INTRUDER (1985) ★ Unimpressive psycho-killer flick: A slasher villain escaped from a nuthouse is loose in a community, where cop Stuart Whitman is always a few clues behind an arrest. Most of the violence is kept off screen by director John McCauley. Writer/coproducer Tony Crupi turns up as Drifter. Molly Cheek, Chris Holder. (HBO)

DEADLY INVASION: THE KILLER BEE NIGHTMARE (1995) ★★★ Suspenseful TV-movie of the people-trapped-in-a-house-surrounded-by-monsters genre, the "monsters" being a swarm of venomous African bees. In recent years many predictions have been made that one day the strain (which took root in South America many years ago) will invade the U.S., and this deals with that theory. Set in the central California town of Blossom Meadow, *Deadly Invasion* depicts the ordeal that Robert Hays and his family undergo when nearby hives are disturbed and the killers close in to put the sting on humans. The effects work is good and the tension plentiful during the siege segments. Dennis Christopher plays an expert on bees who briefly provides exposition in the telescript by Paul Hudson, Steven Rea and William Bast. Director Rockne S. O'Bannon pulls it all together into an ominous package that leaves you dangling with uncertainties about the dangers of the African bee: There is no known way to stop their migration should they ever head north. Nancy Stafford, Ryan Phillippe, Gina Philips, Gregory Gordon, Michael A. Nickles. (Video/Laser: Fox)

DEADLY LOVE (1995) ★★★½ Rob Gilmer adapted Sherry Gottlieb's novel *Love Bite* into a superior TV-movie script, which in turn was directed by Jorge Montesi with unusual sensitivity, especially in the sensual bedroom scenes between Susan Dey (playing a photographer who is a vampire) and Stephen McHattie as the cop investigating the murders she has committed. The issues of morality and good vs. evil are set aside to explore these two unusual characters, so don't expect the usual climaxes or denouements. Dey and McHattie are both excellent and succeed in transcending vampire clichés to make this a fascinating exploration of the darker side of man's soul. Also excellent are Eric Peterson as the beautiful Dey's protector and Julie Khaner as McHattie's outspoken cop partner. This is one vampire love story with real bite. Robert S. Woods, Jean Leclerc.

DEADLY MANTIS, THE (1957) ★★★ Sci-fi effects thriller (aka *The Giant Mantis* and *The Incredible Preying Mantis*) in which a giant mantis is released from an iceberg by an earthquake and begins a wave of destruction, knocking over Washington Monument and hiding in Holland Tunnel. This will appeal to those who enjoy '50s rampaging monsters. Craig Stevens is the officer out to stop the creature, William Hopper the scientist looking for a killing device and Alix Talton the love interest. Directed by Nathan Juran; effects by Clifford Stine. (Video/Laser: MCA)

DEADLY OUTBREAK (1995) ★★★ When U.S. government turncoat Ron Silver takes over a lab in Israel to steal a virus that could destroy mankind were it unleashed, it's up to security guard Jeff Speakman to rescue scientist Rochelle Swanson, kill all the bad guys in shootouts and karate fights, and save the world in general—wisecracking all the while. This variation of *Under Siege* and *Die Hard* has by now become standard movie action stuff, and while the fights are well-staged, it's all very derivative and by-the-numbers predictable. Directed by Rick Avery from a script by Harel Goldstein and Charles Morris Jr. (Live)

DEADLY PREY (1987) ★ Yet another variation on *The Most Dangerous Game* as a gang of soldiers of fortune hunt human victims for sport. Cameron Mitchell, Troy Donahue, Ted Prior, Fritz Matthews. Written-directed by David A. Prior. (AIP)

DEADLY RAY FROM MARS. Video version of *Flash Gordon Conquers the Universe* (Questar).

DEADLY REACTOR (1989) ★ Although this is set in a post-holocaust world, it has the trappings of the old-fashioned Hollywood western as a mean old motorcycle gang terrorizes folks. The "sheriff" is also the film's writer and director, David Heavener. He goes after Hog (Darwyn Swalve) and his sadists. Stuart Whitman, Allyson Davis. (Action International)

DEADLY SPAWN, THE. See *Return of the Alien's Deadly Spawn*.

DEADLY STING, THE. See *The Alien Within*.

DEADLY WEAPON (1988) ★★★½ Unusually sensitive Charles Band production with an underlying, subtle theme about teenage suicide. Rodney Eastman gives a moving performance as a troubled youth in rural King Bee, Arizona, who finds a pistol that fires anti-gravity X-ray beams—zap rays to you. From a dysfunctional family (runaway mother, drunken father, nasty sister), Eastman uses the weapon for self-defense but this only gets him into trouble during a siege. Surrounded by military forces out to retrieve the lethal weapon, the youth tries to find a peaceful way out. Director Michael Miner's script has an element of tragedy. Kim Walker, Gary Frank, Michael Horse, Barney Martin, Ed Nelson. (Trans World)

DEADLY WEB (1996) ★★½ Routine TV-movie variation on the woman-in-peril theme with beautiful, leggy Gigi Rice (usually in miniskirts) pursued by a serial killer called CyberGod, a "killer computer whiz" who uses WorldNet to harass and terrorize his victims by altering records and assorted cat-and-mouse computer tricks. Alan Ormsby's teleplay is filled with the usual contrivances and red herrings of this genre. Directed by Jorge Montesi, *Deadly Web* isn't likely to entangle you very much, but it's a competent time killer. Ed Marinaro, John Wesley Shipp, Robin Quivers, Andrew Lawrence, Ted McGinley, Raphael Sbarge. (Fried)

DEAD MAN RUNNING. See *The Clones*.

DEAD MAN SEEKS HIS MURDERER, A. See *The Brain* (1962).

DEAD MAN WALKING (1987) ★★ Unpleasant sci-fi cautionary tale set in a depressing future when a plague has wiped out most of mankind and a corporation called Unitus rules. Those dying of the plague are Zero Men, and clubs have been designed for them to play out games of suicide. Such a Zero Man is Luger (Wings Hauser), hired by corporation man Jeffrey Combs to find his boss's daughter, kidnapped by escaped criminal Decker (Brion James). They enter the Plague Zone, and murder, mayhem and car crashes result. Drearily unappealing, set against drab Southern California and styled without pace, sympathetic characters or purpose. It features such revolting images as men playing suicide with a chainsaw and pistols, and a man set on fire in a nightclub act. Produced-directed by Gregory Brown. (Republic)

DEAD MATE (1989) David Gregory plays a multiple wife-murderer who uses electricity to bring their corpses back to life. He whisks waitress Elizabeth Mannino away into his trap of death. Plenty of gore as she tries to escape. Written-directed by Straw (Boss) Weisman. Lawrence Bockins, Adam Wahl, Judith Mayes. (Prism)

DEAD MEN DON'T DIE (1990) ★ When TV newsman Elliott Gould is killed when pursuing a drug story, cleaning woman Mabel King uses voodoo to bring him back to life. Gould goes after his killers posing as a live man and trying not to look like a dead one. Melissa Anderson, Mark Moses, Philip Bruns, Mabel King. Written-directed by Malcolm Marmorstein. (Academy)

DEAD NEXT DOOR, THE (1989) ★ When a virus creates corpses that walk, a special "Zombie Squad" is dispatched to blow the dead-alive creatures to bloody bits. Peter Terry, Scott Spiegel. (Tempe; Movies Unlimited)

DEAD OF NIGHT (1945) ★★★★★ Superlative British ghost story anthology—possibly the most influential horror film of the '40s. In a drawing room several characters recount frightening incidents. Basil Dearden directed the first story (by E. F. Benson) in which a race driver receives a supernatural warning. The second, directed by Alberto Cavalcanti, is the brooding tale (also adapted from Benson) of the ghost of a little boy murdered by his sister in a tower room. "The Haunted Mirror," directed by Robert Hamer, is a gripper in which an ornate looking-glass reflects a Victorian bedroom and almost compels its owner to commit murder. H. G. Wells's "The Inexperienced Ghost," set on a golf course and directed by Charles Crichton, is of a comedic nature and the weakest tale. "The Ventriloquist" (directed by Cavalcanti) is the most frightening, with entertainer and dummy shifting personalities. The final tale involves the storytellers and brings the film full circle with a climactic surprise. The eerie score is by Georges Auric. Michael Redgrave, Googie Withers, Mervyn Jones, Miles Malleson, Sally Ann Howes. (HBO; Republic; Rex Miller) (Laser: Image)

DEAD OF NIGHT (1972). See *Deathdream*.

DEAD OF NIGHT (1976) ★★★ During the '70s Universal resurrected the anthology format with two pilots directed by Dan Curtis. The first was *Trilogy of Terror*; this, the second, features three tales written by Richard Matheson. "Second Chance" is a *Twilight Zone* clone with Ed Begley, Jr., as a man traveling through time in his 1926 Jordan Playboy. "No Such Thing as a Vampire" stars Patrick MacNee, Anjanette Comer, Elisha Cooke Jr. and Horst Buchholz in a revenge yarn with pseudohorror overtones. "Bobby" is the best one, about a grieving mother (Joan Hackett) who asks for her drowned son back and gets more than she bargained for when Lee H. Montgomery knocks on her door. (Thrillervideo, hosted by Elvira; HBO; MPI)

DEAD OF NIGHT (1987). Original theatrical/TV title for a horror movie now on video as *Mirror of Death*.

DEAD OF NIGHT (1997) ★½ Don't confuse this

Playboy-produced direct-to-video vampire movie with the 1945 British ghost story anthology. That was a classic—this is not. Kathleen Kinmont stars as an L.A. nurse who turns out to be the reincarnation of a woman who died in London in 1889. Her then-husband (Robert Knepper) gave up his soul to a vampire cult so he could spend the rest of eternity tracking down the body into which she would be reborn. (At least Kinmont has a good enough body to make his years of waiting worthwhile.) If that premise isn't ridiculous enough, screenwriter Karen Kelly keeps piling it on by having Knepper as part of a bloodsucker gang that lures young women and men into its pad and then hypnotizes them and takes control of their souls. This gives director Kristoffer Tabori an excuse for ample soft-porn footage as the vampires have sex (in twosomes and threesomes) with their victims before drinking their blood and turning them into slaves. Larry Poindexter, Alex Rocco and Paul Winfield play cops who get involved with Kinmont when she comes around to complain about the prostitutes hanging around her neighborhood (that seems to have something to do with London 1889, but it's vague). Coproduced by actor Andrew Stevens, *Dead of Night* was first made as *Dark Hunger*. And from hunger it strictly is. John Enos, Diana Frank, Scott Kraft, Sherry Hursey.

DEAD ON: RELENTLESS II. See *Relentless II: Dead On.*

DEAD ON SIGHT (1994) ★★½ Another retread serial-killer thriller featuring a woman in peril (Jennifer Beals) who has precognitive dreams about "The Clock Killer," a "recreational killer" working out of Kingston, Virginia. Daniel Baldwin, whose wife was murdered, teams with pal Kurtwood Smith and Beals to pin the rap on a local café owner (William H. Macy). The whodunit script by Lewis Green is totally predictable and there's not a single new idea to advance the genre. Directed by Ruben Preuss. (MCEG)

DEAD PIT (1989) ★★ Take your average *Snake Pit* environment, mix in *Night of the Living Dead* zombies and this is what you get from director Brett Leonard, working with a script he cowrote with producer Gimel Everett. Cheryl Lawson, playing a mentally disturbed woman haunted by traumatic childhood incidents, ends up in the State Institute for the Mentally Ill, underrgoing psychohypnosis under Dr. Jeremy Slate. She's haunted by the specter of a mad "surgeon" with eyes that glow red who once performed horrible lobotomies. An earthquake breaks open a pit of corpses and they rove the hospital, murdering fresh victims. It's familiar territory that should sate gore buffs. Danny Gochnauer. (Imperial)

DEAD RINGERS (1988) ★★★ This study of twin brothers (based on *Twins* by Bari Wood and Jack Geasland) is loaded with psychological twists, and pushes this Canadian-produced film into the arena of psychiatric horror. It is so morbidly presented by writer-director David Cronenberg that one is prevented from sympathizing with the characters. It's disturbing to watch two brilliant gynecologists, who have spent their lives together building careers and are now so locked together in spirit they are destroying themselves. Again, Cronenberg turns to the theme of our bodies being invaded by foreigners—the twin doctors are always inserting gynecological tools into their patients, and designing their own instruments judged "radical" by the medical industry. Jeremy Irons is brilliant in the dual roles but even he cannot generate enough sympathy to cancel out the unsettling feelings. The same is true of Genevieve Bujold, who turns on the doctors when they discover she has a freakish uterus. An unnerving experience. Heide Von Palleske, Barbara Gordon, Stephen Lack. (Media) (Laser: Image)

DEAD SLEEP (1991) ★ Nurse Linda Blair, working in the experimental ward of a Brisbane, Australia, hospital, discovers that patients subjected to deep sleep testing are dying. This imitation of *Coma* was directed by Alec Mills. Tony Bonner, Andrew Booth. (Vestron)

DEAD SPACE (1990) ★ Remember Roger Corman's 1981 ripoff of *Alien*, called *Forbidden World*? Well, he ripped that off too and cranked out this cheap remake. With footage borrowed from previous Corman sci-fiers, *Dead Space* has a red face when space jockey Marc Singer and his half-functioning robot Chim-Pan arrive on Phabon, where a genetic experiment with the Delta 5 virus results in a "metamorphic mutant." The creature races around the space station murdering folks, while "freelance contributor" Singer can never hit it with his laser zap gun, he's such a lousy shot. Onions to director Fred Gallo. Laura Tate, Bryan Cranston, Judith Chapman, Lori Lively. (Video/Laser: RCA/Columbia)

DEAD THAT WALK, THE. See *Zombies of Mora Tau.*

DEADTIME STORIES (1986) ★★ "Nobody lives happily ever after," promise the producers of this anthology film, made in Greenwich, CT, as *Freaky Time Tales*. It's a trilogy of tongue-in-cheek horrors told by daddy to a sleepless junior. "Peter and the Witches" is a medieval grim fairy tale in which a fisherman's son helps two cackling crones prepare a human sacrifice. "Little Red Runninghood" is a modern variation on the fairy tale but it's predictable, including the verbal punchline. "Goldilox and the Three Bears" is the weakest of the threesome, played tongue-in-cheek by director Jeffrey Delman.

Scott Valentine, Melissa Leo, Cathryn De Prume, Phyllis Craig. (Cinema Group; Continental) (Laser: Image)

DEAD WEEKEND (1995) ★★½ One strange parable about man's destructive nature spun as science fiction. Set in "the near future," society is so close to anarchy that a fascist police called True World Forces (TWF) has the power to evacuate L.A. in order to (a) wipe out street gangs and (b) apprehend an alien from another planet. That alien is an exotically sexy woman with Quadra Synapse Syndrome (QSS), the ability to change from one racial identity to another. A horny soldier named Weed (Stephen Baldwin) falls for "Amelia," who is played at various times by Bai Ling, Afifi Alaouie, Blair Valk, Jennifer McDonald and Barbara Alyn Woods (all of whom make steamy, hot love with Baldwin). A surreal, Kafka-esque quality hangs over this TV-movie written by Joel Rose and directed with multicamera setups by Amos Poe. Its message of brotherly love gets in the way of the action and despite its thematic virtues, this heavyhandedness ultimately weighs it down and saps its effectiveness. David Rasche, Perry Lang, Alexis Arquette, Nicholas Worth, Tom Kenny. (Paramount)

DEAD WOMEN IN LINGERIE (1990) ★ Despite its clever title, this has to be one of the lousiest serial-killer movies ever made. A complete misfire, *Dead Women* is slow moving, has no gore effects, and no suspenseful buildup to the finding of the killer of 3 Mexican-American models working in a lingerie sweat shop for ulcer-riddled Jerry Orbach in April 1987. It isn't even sexy. As an L.A. private eye working on the case, John Romo is kind of cute (a Jim Belushi type) and Maura Tierney might have made for an interesting lady-in-danger if the script (by Romo and director Erica Fox) had any danger in it. Which it doesn't. Everything about this movie is so so wrong. June Lockhart, Lyle Waggoner, Dennis Christopher. (Monarch)

DEAD ZONE, THE (1983) ★★★★ Loyal adaptation of Stephen King's best-seller, a riveting portrait of Johnny Smith, who wakes up from a five-year coma to discover he can predict the future. How he copes with this "gift" is enthralling, with director David Cronenberg avoiding clichés. Christopher Walken's performance is tops, Brooke Adams is excellent as Johnny's girl (their affair is bittersweet) and Martin Sheen chillingly plays politician Greg Stillson, whom Johnny intends to assassinate when he foresees Stillson's psychotic condition leading America into war. The film poses difficult, controversial issues but doesn't offer simple solutions. Cronenberg's restraint (except for one death sequence involving the Castle Rock Killer) makes for a thoughtful ESP melodrama, insightfully

structured by screenwriter Jeffrey Boam. Tom Skerritt is the sheriff, Herbert Lom is Dr. Weizak, Anthony Zerbe is the influential Roger Stuart, Colleen Dewhurst the mother. (Video/Laser: Paramount)

DEAN KOONTZ'S PHANTOMS (1997) ★★★½ The first half hour of this adaptation of the popular novel (adapted by Koontz himself) plays like a good old-fashioned horror movie, when Rose McGowan and Joanna Going arrive in the mountain town of Snowfield, only to find many of its residents with their heads and hands chopped off or corpses drained of blood. But then it veers off into the wild-and-woolly land of scientific mumbo jumbo, replete with weird tentacles and assorted uglies that suck into human flesh and take over people's souls, turning them into killing tools for the mother monster. The only man who understands all this, Peter O'Toole's Timothy Flyte (a discredited scientist reduced to writing articles for a weird-mysteries news sheet), arrives in Snowfield to assume that the "Ancient Enemy" they face is a globular entity at the center of the earth that sends out "phantoms" (or feelers) to absorb human intelligence in order to take over the planet from mortal beings. Plenty of ugly black tentacles run rampant as a handful of survivors figures out a way to destroy the subterranean blob while men in radiation suits get demolished by the "it." Koontz's plot becomes ridiculous at times, but horror buffs should enjoy all the variations-on-a-monster and the half-crazed performance of O'Toole, who definitely runs away with the concept. Director Joe Chappelle must have had his hands full, indeed. Watch for Bo Hopkins as a freaked-out FBI agent. Liev Schreiber, Ben Affleck, Nicky Katt, Clifton Powell, Rachel Shane. (Video/DVD/Laser: Dimension)

DEAN R. KOONTZ'S THE SERVANTS OF TWILIGHT. See *The Servants of Twilight*.

DEAN R. KOONTZ'S WHISPERS. See *Whispers*.

DEAR DEPARTED (1987) ★ Whacked-out Australian comedy, so unrestrained in creating a zany universe in which the real world and the afterworld intermingle, it reaches remarkable heights of incomprehensibility. Sexy Pamela Stephenson kills actor-husband Garry McDonald and others to be haunted by their "wronged spirits." There are monster faces, electrical charges of light that encircle bodies and a kind of Halloween nonsense about the hauntings. The characters are so unapproachable that only the most tolerant viewer will endure to the ironic ending. Dear, depart early from *Dear Departed*. Su Cruickshank, Marian Dworakowski.

DEATH AND THE GREEN SLIME. See *The Green Slime*.

DEATH AT LOVE HOUSE (1975) ★★ Pseudosupernatural TV-movie—poppycock about a writer and wife (Robert Wagner, Kate Jackson) who move into the mansion of a once-famous movie star to write a script of her life. (The location is the old Harold Lloyd estate.) Wagner's father once had an affair with fiery Lorna Love, and Wagner becomes obsessed by the spirit of the depraved actress. Jim Barnett's teleplay is pure baloney, with a mysterious woman in white flitting around the mansion. If only director E. W. Swackhamer hadn't played it so straight. Sylvia Sidney, Marianna Hill (Lorna Love), Joan Blondell, Dorothy Lamour, John Carradine, Bill Macy. (Prism)

DEATH BECOMES HER (1992) ★★★★ This dark comedy is a blend of satire, sex, special-effects jokes and commentary on man's greed, with touches that spoof Hitchcock movies. Revenge is the motif when aging Broadway actress Madeline Ashton (Meryl Streep, never looking lovelier) steals plastic surgeon Ernest Menville (Bruce Willis) from fiancée Helen Sharp (Goldie Hawn). After Hawn turns into a superfat blob grieving the loss, she vows come-uppance, and plots to steal Willis back and arrange Streep's "accidental" death. Enter Isabella Rossellini in an exotic, erotic role as a half-naked seductress who sells the elixir of eternal youth to Streep. Ken Ralston's effects and Dick Smith's makeup come into play, with characters bodily damaged in hilarious ways. The morality of this is brought into crystal focus in a marvelously zany ending. The script by Martin Donovan–David Koepp is ingenious and producer-director Robert Zemeckis photographs it on magnificent sets, creating a rich Beverly Hills lifestyle contrasted by the unpleasant characters. Ian Ogilvy, Adam Storke, Nancy Fish, Alaina Reed Hall, and movie director Sydney Pollack in a cameo. (Video-Laser: MCA)

DEATH BED. See *Terminal Choice.*

DEATH BITE. See *Spasms.*

DEATH CAR ON THE FREEWAY (1979) ★★ The Fiddler—a maniac driver in a van, who loves to play bluegrass music as he attacks—roves L.A. freeways, seeking helpless woman whom he kills in fiery crashes. "Fiery crashes" are the key to this TV-movie, designed by director Hal Needham, onetime Hollywood stunt man, and writer William Wood as an effects vehicle. Some crashes are great, but the story is banal as TV reporter Shelley Hack tracks the killer. There's a weak relationship with TV exec George Hamilton to pad out the script. Peter Graves is an ineffectual cop. Harriet Nelson, Dinah Shore, Abe Vigoda, Frank Gorshin, Barbara Rush.

DEATH COLLECTOR (1988) ★ Dumb, immature blending of sci-fi and westerns when Daniel Chapman, in a future time period, goes after the guys who killed his brother. Philip Nutman,

Ruth Collins. Produced-directed by Tom Gniazdowski. (Raedon; Video Treasures)

DEATH COMES FROM THE DARK. See *Cauldron of Blood.*

DEATH CORPS. See *Shock Waves.*

DEATH CURSE OF TARTU (1966) ★ From the writer-director of *Stanley* comes this nonthriller about an Indian witch doctor who stirs in his crypt while natives beat on drums. But William Grefe does little to bolster his supernatural theme by picking teenagers who dance rock 'n' roll in the Everglades and swim in shark-infested waters. You want to see them get killed quickly, so insufferable is their behavior. Grefe uses a snake as a killing device but the cottonmouth is made of rubber, so not even the creepy-crawlie aspects are challenging. But the color photography is . . . colorful. Fred Pinero, Babbette Sherrill, Bill Marcus. (Active)

DEATHDAY. See *Madhouse.*

DEATH DIMENSION (1978) ★ Killer bomb could freeze our planet—and ruin TV viewing. Or damage brain cells from underfed story. Dimensionless feature, death to watch, directed by Al Adamson. Jim Kelly, George Lazenby, Harold Sakata. (Budget; from Unicorn as *Black Eliminator,* from Movietime as *The Freeze Bomb* and Academy as *Kill Factor*)

DEATH DORM. See *The Dorm That Dripped Blood.*

DEATHDREAM (1972) ★★ Aka *The Night Walk, Dead of Night, The Night Andy Came Home* and *The Veteran,* this is from director-producer Bob Clark (*Porky's*) and screenwriter Alan Ormsby, who borrowed from "The Monkey's Paw." Richard Backus portrays a dead Vietnam soldier whose spirit is brought home by his grief-stricken mother, but now he's a vampire killer. Well-staged chases and a macabre climax. John Marley, Anya Ormsby. (MPI)

DEATH DREAMS (1991) ★★★½ Offbeat TV-movie based on the William Katz novel and adapted by Robert Glass in which a mother accuses her husband of drowning her child. Marg Heldenberger's evidence against stepdaddy Christopher Reeve is based on ESP dreams in which the child returns from the dead to give her clues. Robert Glass does an excellent job of adapting the offbeat narrative into a supernatural thriller (and director Martin Donovan gives it chilling moments) that retains verisimilitude when it turns into a courtroom conflict. Fionnula Flanagan is good as an occultist who befriends Heldenberger. (New Line) (Laser: Image)

DEATHHEAD VIRGIN, THE (1973) ★ The last virgin princess of a legendary Moro tribe of the Philippines guards a treasure in a galleon sunk in 1850. Her spirit is aroused when a treasure hunter finds an ancient medallion. The unconvincing monster is a sexy gal wearing a skull-face mask. Philippine locations help this poverty-stricken production, poorly written by Ward Gaynor (an alias for cast members Larry Ward and Jock Gaynor, who portray underwater adventurers) and indifferently directed by Norman Foster. Diane McBain provides plot turns but one wishes she had more scenes in a bikini—she's the only visual excitement. (Academy)

DEATH HOUSE (1988) ★★ John Saxon directed and stars in this prison horror thriller as a federal agent with a bad streak who is utilizing a new drug to create unbeatable warriors. Dennis Cole, Tane McClure, Anthony Franciosa, Michael Pataki. (Action International)

DEATH IN FULL VIEW. See *Deathwatch.*

DEATH IS CHILD'S PLAY. See *Island of the Damned.*

DEATH ISLAND. See *Man-Eater of Hydra.*

DEATH KISS (1932) ★★ This is listed purely for completist elitists who must see every Bela Lugosi movie ever made, no matter what. In this Hollywood whodunit, as old-fashioned as Klieg lights and catwalks, our *Dracula* star portrays the manager of Tiffany Studios, where a murder is committed on the set of a thriller. Turgid and predictable, with Lugosi behaving strangely. Maybe he's scowling at John Wray, Mona Maris, Adrienne Ames, Edward Van Sloan and David Manners for overacting under Edwin L. Marin's dreary direction. (Prism; Kartes; Sinister/C; Thunderbird)

DEATH LIST. See *Terminal Choice.*

DEATH MACHINE (1995) ★★ High-tech sci-fi thriller in which a defense systems designer unleashes "the ultimate fighting unit." Directed by Stephen Norrington. Brad Dourif, Ely Pouget, William Hootkins, John Sharian. (Video/Laser: Vidmark)

DEATH MAGIC (1992) ★★ Five magicians gather to raise the dead and then wish they hadn't when a mass murderer from the year 1875 returns to wreak revenge. Anne Caffrey, Keith DeGreen, Jack Dunlap, Danielle Frons. Written-directed by Paul E. Clinco. (Video)

DEATH OF THE INCREDIBLE HULK, THE (1990) ★★ In this final installment of the TV-movie series, based on the Marvel Comics character, director Bill Bixby (who plays scientist David Banner) evokes a tragic feeling for the misunderstood scientist who turns into a green entity when angered. The Hulk portions, as usual, feature Lou Ferrigno on a rampage, but thanks to Bixby's sensibilities it's a better-than-average entry. Banner becomes involved with spies leaking secrets from a top-secret security lab, and falls for Elizabeth Gracen before facing his final "demise." Philip Sterling, Barbara Tarbuck, Ann Katerina, John Novak. (Rhino)

DEATH PENALTY. See *The Satan Killer.*

DEATH RACE 2000 (1975) ★★★★ Roger Corman cult favorite, directed by Paul Bartel. It's a real with-it script by Robert Thom and Charles B. Griffith (from an Ib Melchior idea) set in the future during a transcontinental race. Since America is a fascist land, anything goes, and that includes running over pedestrians, bombing opponents and taking whatever steps are necessary to win. David Carradine is a maniacal driver (nicknamed "Frankenstein" because he is so brutally scarred). Sylvester Stallone scores big as Machine Gun Joe Viterbo. Other standouts: Simone Griffith, Mary Woronov, Roberta Collins, Joyce Jameson. (Warner Bros.)

DEATH RAY MIRROR OF DR. MABUSE/DEATH RAYS OF DR. MABUSE. See *Secret of Dr. Mabuse.*

DEATH RAY 2000 (1979) ★★½ Average Quinn Martin TV-movie with Cliff Gould's script imitating the James Bond superspy films, first telecast as a pilot for the series *A Man Called Sloane* and aka *T. R. Sloane.* Robert Logan portrays a smooth-talking government man out to recover the hijacked Dehydrator, a device that sucks the moisture out of your body, leaving you a shriveled up raisin (or prune). Villain Clive Revill pets spiders and snakes and sics strong-man Ji-Tu Cumbuka on his enemies. Ji-Tu has a stainless steel hand embedded with claws and knives, so there's nice fights staged by director Lee H. Katzin. And Ann Turkel as Logan's love is a pleasing presence. But this is so clichéd and predictable only the most diehard Bond-imitation fans will be compelled to watch. Dan O'Herlihy (as Logan's assignment chief), Maggie Cooper, Paul Mantee. (Worldvision; Movies Unlimited)

DEATH RIDE. See *Crash!*

DEATH RING (1993) ★★ Mediocre, slow-paced actioner based loosely on *The Most Dangerous Game,* with crazed Billy Drago playing a "game master" who kidnaps survivalist Mike Norris to his isolated island where sadists and murderers pay for the pleasure of pursuing him for the kill. A sound idea by screenwriter George T. LeBrun is given only half-hearted treatment by director R. J. Kizer. Chad McQueen shines as Norris' pal to the rescue, with Drago taking second-place honors for his portrayal of a sociopath. Don Swayze, Elizabeth Fong Sung, Isabel Glasser. (Video/Laser: New Line)

DEATHROW DINER (1988) ★★ A movie studio mogul, sent to prison for a crime he didn't commit, is executed, brought back to life and goes on a rampage of revenge. Jay Richardson, Michelle Bauer, John Content.

DEATHROW GAMESHOW (1987) ★★ In an alternate universe, where the U.S. government allows death row inmates to gamble their lives on a TV game show, emcee Chuck Toedan (John McCafferty) leads a hard life—pursued by criminals, threatened by kooks and nuts, and the target of feminist Gloria Sternvirgin (Robin Blythe). This parody of how TV sets trends and enforces revised values on our morality, written-directed by Mark Pirro, is amusing, but forces the issue with vulgarities and tasteless gags. Mark Lasky, Darwyn Carson. (Media) (Laser: Image)

DEATH SCREAMS (1982) ★★ "The last scream you hear . . . is your own!" Psychohorror flick depicting the machete murders of college beauties, with plenty of nudity. Directed by David Nelson. Susan Kiger, Jody Kay, Martin Tucker. (Video Gems)

DEATHSHEAD VAMPIRE, THE. See *The Blood Beast Terror.*

DEATH SHIP (1980) ★★★ A freighter deserted on the high seas, haunted by the misery and sadism of the Nazis who once had a torture chamber aboard, is boarded by Richard Crenna, George Kennedy and other survivors of a sea disaster, who learn of its horrors too late. There's the torture gallery, decomposing bodies, parts that move supernaturally, and Kennedy, who thinks he's a murderous captain. Directed by Alvin Rakoff, scripted by John Robins. Sally Ann Howes, Kate Reid, Nick Mancuso. (Embassy)

DEATH SPA (WITCH BITCH) (1987) ★★ Starbody Health Spa is run by a computer that fouls up, turning a shapely customer into a human lobster. Subsequent foul-ups include flying shower tiles, broken diving board, a hand chopped off in a Quasar, and broken pipes that emit scalding water on nubile bodies. It's not so much the computer as the guy who runs it, whose sister was burned alive. It appears her spirit is invading his body, turning him into a murderous transvestite. This supernatural flick is one strenuous workout with its *Omen*-style deaths. What can you say when a dead fish comes alive and bites a man to death except "Cod damn it!" Director Michael Fischa emphasizes other red herrings that won't scare anyone. William Bumiller, Brenda Bakke, Merritt Butrick. (MPI)

DEATHSPORT (1978) ★★½ A thousand years from now the good guys are Ranger Guides who use swords to make their point. The bad guys are Statesmen (we aren't kidding about this) who ride cycles called "death machines." So they go battle, with crashes and exciting stuff like that. Meanwhile, David Carradine and Claudia Jennings are gladiators in a sporting arena who escape into the desert. Carradine does his kung fu bit against Richard Lynch while Jennings looks fetching in glamorous rags. Unintentional comedy from writer-director Henry Suso (real name: Nicholas Niciphor), codirector Allan Arkush and Donald Stewart. (Warner Bros.)

DEATHSTALKER (1983) ★★½ Sword-and-sorcery fantasy (produced by Roger Corman) with a Conan-style hero who kills mercilessly, grabs pretty girls and never lets scruples stand in his way. "I steal and kill to stay alive—not for the luxury of glory," he remarks, but deep inside Deathstalker is a good guy pursuing the Amulet of Light, Chalice of Magic and Sword of Justice. There are soft-core sex scenes (wow, you see the bare boobs of Barbi Benton, former Hugh Hefner roommate) and abundant violence in Howard Cohen's script that director John Watson does not spare. Richard (Rick) Hill is a hero-hunk in a phony blond wig, and Barbi makes for a beauteous damsel. Richard Brooker snarls as the villain Oghris, but what do you expect in a witchcraft/action flick—subtlety? Lana Clarkson, Bernard Erhard. (Video/Laser: Vestron)

DEATHSTALKER II: DUEL OF THE TITANS (1987) ★★★ Entertaining satire on sword-and-sorcery flicks, capturing a comedic element that makes the hokey production values and acting bearable. Director Jim Wynorski treats Neil Ruttenberg's script with just the right touch. Everyone speaks in a modern idiom, with timely in-jokes sustaining the quest plot. Stealing the show are John Terlesky as the devil-may-care adventurer and Monique Gabrielle, who plays a princess posing as a fortune teller. She also plays a clone femme fatale, showing a sexier, seductive side—say, this gal has talent. John La Zar is the villain-magician Jarek. Tony Naples is attractive and hammy as Sultana, and Maria Scocas leads a gang of Amazons with a twinkle in her eye. Filmed for producer Roger Corman in Argentina. (Vestron) (Laser: Image)

DEATHSTALKER III: THE WARRIORS FROM HELL (1988) ★★ This lacks the roguish charm of Rick Hill in the first film and the tongue-in-cheek anachronisms of the second, but it does have a lot of swordplay as John Allen Nelson (third and least Deathstalker) seeks a diamond crystal and finds the secret treasure city of Erendor. This tired quest formula limps along (blame it on Howard R. Cohen's script) with bursts of energy from Carla Herd (playing twin sisters—one a sweet thing, the other a princess who falls into evil ways), Claudia Inchaurregui (as a sexy warrior proficient with bow and arrow), Terri Treas (as evil Queen Camisarde) and Thom Christopher (as daffy necromancer Troxartas, who creates zombie soldiers). Another Roger Corman epic, made in Mexico under director/coproducer Alfonso Corona. Aaron Hernan, Roger Cudney. (Vestron) (Laser: Image)

DEATHSTALKER IV: MATCH OF TITANS (1990) ★★ That wisecracking barbarian is back, longer in the tooth but still living by that old axiom, "It's a man's instinct to hunt, to fight and to ravish women." However, the joy has dissipated since his satirical romp through the second film, and writer-director Howard R. Cohen treats this new adventure indifferently, as though he were vacationing in Bulgaria, where this was produced. Deathstalker (Rick Hill), searching for his missing magical sword, attends a tournament of champions in a castle ruled by empress Kana and her army of zombie stone men. Involved is a deposed princess, Kana's henchman and a strongman virgin. Huh? (New Horizons) (Laser: Image)

DEATH TRAIN, THE (1978) ★★ Slow-chugging Australian TV-movie of eccentric characters and supernatural ambiguities. After a man is apparently run over in his backyard by a train, his ankle bone protruding through his neck, an insurance investigator uncovers a land-development plot. Whether a "phantom train" exists or not remains a head-scratching mystery as Hugh Keays Bryne probes for the answer. This film becomes extremely strange when Bryne flees through the night in his underwear, pursued by a killer bulldozer. And just when you think the enigma has been explained, the occult rears its ugly head. Directed by Igor Auzins. (Paragon)

DEATH TRAP. See *Eaten Alive.*

DEATH VALLEY (1981) ★★ Director Dick Richards is saddled with a sleazy slasher script (by coproducer Richard Rothstein) and his efforts to make it significant are wasted as soon as the graphic violence begins. Then the poor writing and dumb characterizations completely befuddle him. The plot has young Peter Billingsley witness to murder and pursued by mad-dog killers in Death Valley. Paul LeMat, Catherine Hicks, Edward Herrmann, A. W. Brimley. (MCA)

DEATH WARMED UP (1984) ★★★½ Grotesquely unpleasant New Zealand film, unrestrained in gore as surgeon Gary Day experiments in brain surgeries that turn men into kill-happy zombies. Four people come to Day's island headquarters, Trans Cranial Applications. One of them (Michael Hurst, his hair bleached snowy blond) has a strange link to the doctor as the quartet is subjected to zombie horrors and a chase through red-lit tunnels. An ax in the stomach, exposed intestines, a man impaled on a spike and a gun that fires light beams into the zombies (the only way to kill them) are among the "gorities" by director David Blyth and cowriter Michael Heath. Grim stuff; wishy-washies beware. (Vestron)

DEATHWATCH (1980) ★★½ Set in a bleak futuristic society (Glasgow, Scotland) in which an evil TV network holds sway over depressed people, this German-French tale is more didactic than visual. Coproducer-director Bertrand Tavernier brings tragedy and pain to its characters, giving heart to their desolation. Based on David Compton's novel *The Continuous Katherine Mortenhor* (or *The Unsleeping Eye*), it depicts Harvey Keitel as a man who can transmit pictures with a video camera device in his head and Romy Schneider as a dying woman. The network under Harry Dean Stanton (playing a likable villain) wants to show Romy withering away and Keitel is treacherous in befriending her. But when they fall in love, the film detours into character exploration. Max Von Sydow is a philosopher who guides the characters toward a final destiny. Aka *Death in Full View.* (Video/Laser: Embassy)

DEATH WHEELERS, THE. See *Psychomania* (1973).

DECEIT (1993) ★★ Humanoid aliens from another planet, who specialize in destroying "polluted" worlds, decide Earth needs to be cleaned up and come to Earth to check out the babes first. Scott Paulin, Norbert Weisser, Samantha Phillips. Written by Kitty Chalmers and directed by Albert Pyun. (RCA/Columbia)

DECEIVERS, THE (1988) ★★★ This fanciful retelling of how the British occupational forces of India discovered a gang of murderers—Thugs worshiping the goddess of destruction, Kali—is structured by Michael Hirst (adapting John Masters's novel) as a thriller with overtones of eastern mysticism. British officer Pierce Brosnan goes undercover as a Thug to discover that the spirit of Kali is more real than he thought. This Ismail Merchant production, directed by Nicholas Meyer, captures the perverseness of what Brosnan is undergoing, and Brosnan fascinates as the civilized man exposed to barbarism. Shashi Kapoor, Saeed Jaffrey, Helene Michell, Keith Michell. (Video/Laser: Warner Bros.)

DEEP BLUE SEA, THE (1999) ★★★½ Director Renny Harlin blends the clichés of the *Jaws* genre with those of the disaster-at-sea adventure story, where a handful of characters are trapped underwater and must work their way to the surface. Also thrown into the maelstrom are some superb special effects of massive destruction and a sci-fi touch in which a new species of extra-large mako shark (45 feet long) has superintelligence—enough to engage in a war of wits with human beings. However, to his credit and to the credit of the slick screenplay by Duncan Kennedy, Donna Powers, and Wayne Powers, *The Deep Blue Sea* creates a few original waves of its own and is an absolute crowd pleaser, never allowing the absurdities of the premise to linger long and focusing instead on a constant series of goose-bumpy cat-and-mouse games of terror. Just when you thought you'd seen it all before, and wanted to take a swim in the deep blue sea, Harlin churns the clichéd waters, creating an assortment of visual surprises and shocks. The setting is Aquatica, a multilevel deep-sea laboratory where corporate boss Samuel L. Jackson arrives to learn that the giant-shark project has resulted in a new brain substance that appears to cure Alzheimer's disease. Saffron Burrows is the cold, calculating scientist who feels the project must succeed at all costs (her coolness in the face of overwhelming danger is one of the unusual elements she brings to the project, and she looks great when she strips to panties and bra to lure one of the sharks into a trap). Thomas Jane is the standard hero, a "shark wrangler," and LL Cool J is a religious-leaning cook, Preacher, whose closest friends are a wine bottle and a green parrot. Lesser characters include Jacqueline McKenzie, Michael Rapaport, Stellan Skarsgard, and Aida Turturro. Although characterization is never a strong point in this type of adventure, as most of them get eaten before they have a chance to develop, it is to Cool J's credit that he comes off unusually well. When he's trapped in his half-submerged kitchen with one of the three killer sharks, he crawls into an oven to escape being eaten, only to realize it's set at 500 degrees. How he eludes his toothy adversary is definitely a high point of *The Deep Blue Sea*. There are the expected graphic eating sequences with a lot of wide-open jaws and rows of terrifying teeth—yet they are still startling in the way Harlin works them out. Especially a scene involving Jackson. But to tell more would be spoiling it. (Video/DVD: Warner Bros.)

DEEP IMPACT (1998) ★★★★ Rarely does a special-effects movie designed on a grand scale reach the pathos of this most unusual DreamWorks production. Here's a movie with a heart, even when it seems we are all doomed. Producers David Brown and Richard D. Zanuck obviously wanted those ethical values firmly in place. And they have achieved a balance between sheer spectacle and the smaller individual stories of family ties and romantic love. A comet is streaking toward Earth and most of mankind is doomed, and this is the story of how man prepares for the grand-scale disaster and also tries to avert it by sending a team of astronauts into space led by Robert Duvall. Their mission is to land on the surface of the comet and implant nuclear devices that will blow it to bits, thereby averting the collision with our planet. Of course, it isn't quite that easy, as screenwriters Michael Tolkin and Bruce Joel Rubin turn the sequence into a memorable setpiece of suspense and special effects. Most of the story centers around the burdened U.S. president (played with quiet dignity by Morgan Freeman), a TV newswoman (Téa Leoni), close to mother Vanessa Redgrave but at odds with father Maximilian Schell, and two young lovers—amateur astronaut Elijah Wood (who helped in the discovery of the comet) and girlfriend Leelee Sobieski. The astronauts' story is also presented in detail by director Mimi Leder, and she does a good job of imparting a sense of

reality to monumental events. There is also a sense of doom hanging heavy over the events, and yet the climax (an effective tidal wave that destroys Manhattan and other famous landmarks) leaves one feeling uplifted, since it involves sacrifice by a few to save millions (more about that we don't want to divulge without giving it all away). This is definitely a worthwhile, well-intended film, enhanced by Hans Zimmer's score, a film that shows a respect on the part of its producers for its audience, and for a return to the basic values that seem to keep vanishing from our society. *Armageddon* tells this same story but without the heart. James Cromwell, Ron Eldard, Jon Favreau, Laura Innes, Richard Schiff, Blair Underwood. (Video/DVD/Laser: Paramount)

DEEP RED (1994) ★ A woman who has been exposed to an alien, and whose blood has been altered as a result, becomes the test subject for an evil doctor. Directed by Craig R. Baxley from a D. Brent Mote Script. Michael Biehn, Joanna Pacula, John de Lancie. (MCA)

DEEP RED: THE HATCHET MURDERS (1976) ★★★★ Mini-masterpiece of psychoshock from Italian director-writer Dario Argento, with David Hemmings as a pianist who witnesses the knife murder of a psychiatrist in Rome. Ingenious killing after ingenious killing follows, with the murderer playing cat-and-mouse games with victims. Among the highlights: a woman being scalded to death in her bathroom, a man being dragged to pieces by a truck. Then Hemmings himself becomes the target for the killer. Also known as *Dripping Deep Red* and *The Sabre Tooth Tiger*. Daria Nicolodi. (HBO)

DEEP RISING (1998) ★★★ This is pure science fiction and horror with no pretensions, designed from the ground up to be a scary B movie with A production values. So what's not to enjoy even if it is hokey and contrived? Stephen Sommers wrote-directed with a continuous homage to *Alien* and a thousand other scary flicks and peppers it with hard-boiled characters. The movie jet-rockets forward at all times in telling the slam-bang action tale of seafaring adventurer Treat Williams (giving a tongue-in-cheek performance that helps to keep the film in balance) as he rides his boat-for-hire into dangerous waters. Dangerous because the men who've hired him are mercenaries on a mission involving a ship hijacking and nuclear warheads. When Treat and his buddy mechanic Kevin J. O'Connor arrive at the world's greatest luxury liner, the *Argonautica*, they discover a deserted ship and what could be the world's largest sea monster (created by Rob Bottin). It's quite a mega-squid with dozens of endless tentacles that reach anywhere into the ship, little mouths on their tips opening up to swallow human beings whole. Famke Janssen adds a lot as a small-time thief who joins Treat and the mercenaries as they try to escape from the ship without becoming hors d'oeuvres. Yes, the action gets pretty impossible at times, but the visceral shocks keep coming and you're guaranteed to be jumping out of your seat a few times. Anthony Heald, Wes Studi, Derrick O'Connor, Jason Flemying. (Video/DVD: Buena Vista)

DEEP SPACE (1987) ★★★ Low-budget director Fred Olen Ray rises above his previous programmers, for this sci-fi/horror meringue is well handled and the screenplay (by Ray and T. L. Lankford) has good characters and dialogue. The U.S. Government has created an unstoppable *Alien*-like monster but the space lab containing the ugly thing crashlands in an L.A. junkyard and begins killing. Cops Charles Napier and Ron Glass are hot on its trail, browbeaten by Bo Svenson. Napier and Ann Turkel (unconvincing as a cop) track the giant bastard to Arkham Alley for a battle to the death with a chainsaw, an axe, assorted firearms and bare hands. Part of the fun is watching character actors Anthony Eisley, Peter Palmer, James Booth and Julie Newmar. (TransWorld)

DEEPSTAR SIX (1989) ★★★ Above-average blending of the best elements of disaster films with touches of *Alien*. Sean Cunningham's direction captures tension in an underwater lab besieged by a behemoth fish-monster. Rather than rely on tried-and-grue clichés, the Geof Miller-Lewis Abernathy script emphasizes human endurance under duress, relegating the flesh-eating amphibian to second position. One weakness are the so-so underwater effects, but the cast and realism of the lab make up for it. Nancy Everhard, Greg Evigan, Miguel Ferrer. (Video/Laser: Live)

DEF BY TEMPTATION (1990) ★★★ Troma's answer to Spike Lee is James Bond III (not a gag pseudonym), who wrote-produced-directed this all-black portrait of a female vampire who preys on men in New York bars; it's also the story of a divinity student lured into her seductive traps. An unusual intelligence is at work here, and the low-low-budget film is loaded with angst, mood and colorful dialogue. The horror aspects (barful of zombies; the vampire turning into a demon) are the least effective parts of this allegorical study of today's black society. Kadeem Hardison, Samuel L. Jackson, Minnie Gentry, John Canada Terrell. (Shapiro Glickenhaus) (Laser: Image)

DEF-CON 4 (1985) ★★½ Astronauts orbiting Earth in a satellite watch as the U.S. and Russia are obliterated in nuclear holocaust. When the spacecraft crashes, survivor Maury Chaykin is caught in a war between cannibals, ordinary people and a sadistic militant band. Odd mixture of *A Boy and His Dog* and *Mad Max* as the gangs shoot it out. All the while, unknown to the parties, a missile is counting down to detonation. The space scenes are good high-tech stuff under Paul Donovan's direction but the land warfare footage is commonplace. Kate Lynch, John Walsch. (New World/Starmaker) (Laser: Image)

DEFENDING YOUR LIFE (1991) ★★★ Albert Brooks's films are always oddball mixtures of social comedy and quirky relationships but in this outing he steps into the Twilight Zone to make points about the human condition. After Brooks is killed in a collision with a bus he winds up in a pleasant purgatory, where he must defend his recent existence to determine what new incarnation he will affect. His defense attorney (Rip Torn) locks horns with the prosecution (Lee Grant) as his past life is examined. The gags are amusing as Brooks evaluates his life, falling in love with another defendant (Meryl Streep). Very strange but poignant. (Warner Bros.) (Laser: Pioneer)

DEJA VU (1985) ★★ Unconvincing reincarnation story (based on the novel *Always* by Trevor Meldal Johnsen) finds novelist Nigel Terry regressing to the 1930s when he was a choreographer in love with ballerina Brook Ashley. Who does Ashley turn out to be but the previous soul of Terry's wife, Jaclyn Smith. The regression scenes evolve around tarot reader Shelley Winters, as unbelievable as the rest of this British film with Claire Bloom as the dancer's domineering mother. Director Anthony Richmond wasn't on his toes—he slouched when he should have pirouetted. (Video/Laser: MGM/UA)

DELICATESSEN (1991) ★★★½ A crazy post-holocaust movie and winner of several awards for directors Jean-Pierre Jeunet and Marc Caro. This French film defies description as it depicts events in a rundown building in a ruined city. The inhabitants are bizarre individuals driven to the edge of insanity by whatever has happened to the rest of the world (that part is never explained). The owner of the hotel-deli is a cannibal who keeps meat in the shop by cutting up his tenants; a woman keeps attempting suicide without success; a man lives in a basement of frogs; and there's a commando team that travels through sewers, acting as a police force. The camera plunges into dark holes and travels through pipes and conduits to create a macabre mood. The horrific elements of the script by comic-book writer Gilles Adrien, Jeunet and Caro are tinged with a satirical quality, and the action exaggerated. One weird movie, bon ami. Marie-Laure Dougnac, Jean Claude Dreyfus, Karin Viard. (Video/Laser: Paramount)

DELIRIA. See *Stagefright*.

DELIRIUM (1978) ★★½ Fair blending of two mystery plots. One is about a psycho killer who slaughters shapely women (one is impaled on a spear, another is pitchforked in the neck, another is drowned), the other is about respectable St. Louis businessmen on "The Council," a secret vigilante band that kills murderers and makes their deaths look like suicides. Two homicide cops with the help of a woman close in on the two elements. Directed by Peter Maris. Turk Gekovsky, Debi Chaney, Terry Tenbroek, Barron Winchester. (Paragon; Caravan; from Viz as *Psycho Puppet*)

DELUSION (1981) ★★ Psychological thriller of the *Psycho* school, underplayed by director Alan Beattie, who emphasizes the subtleties of Jack Viertel's script. Patricia Pearcy is a nurse who arrives at Joseph Cotten's home to care for him, discovering a crazy youth locked up in the cellar. The characters die one by one . . . but it won't take a genius to figure out the "surprise" ending. David Hayward, John Dukakis. Aka *The House Where Death Lives*. (Sultan) (Laser: HBO)

DEMENTED (1980) ★★ Sallee Elyse is no Catherine Deneuve but she tries to pull off a portrayal of a demented woman in the style of Roman Polanski's *Repulsion*. It's strictly a poor man's version in this thriller directed by Alex Rebar. After being gang-raped in a horse stall, Elyse returns halfway around the bend to her husband-surgeon Bruce Gilchrist, who's two-timing her for a nymphomaniac. When Elyse flips, she corners pranksters in clown masks and eliminates them with cleaver, shotgun, piano wire, etc. The horrific aspects are minimal and, despite pretensions at characterization, it's a dud. Deborah Alter, Kathryn Clayton. (Media)

DEMENTIA. See *Daughter of Horror*.

DEMENTIA 13 (1963) ★★★ Francis Ford Coppola's first directorial-writing job was this Roger Corman cheapie shot in and around an Ireland castle. Luana Anders arrives to claim her family inheritance (after helping her weak-hearted husband take a dive into a lake). She unlocks ghastly secrets in the family closet, unleashing an axe murderer. The death-gore scenes are moderately exciting but it's easy to spot the killer. William Campbell, Patrick Magee, Barbara Dowling, Bart Patton. Aka *The Haunted and the Hunted*. (World Video Picture; Cable; Hollywood Home Theater; K-Tel; Filmfax; S/Weird; Nostalgia; Sinister/C; LSVideo)

DEMOLITION MAN (1993) ★★★½ Refreshing futuristic action-comedy blockbuster that includes a tongue-in-cheek look at tomorrow. That world (A.D. 2032) is one in which violence has been eliminated and police are benevolent beings incapable of stopping a master criminal (Wesley Snipes, wearing a white wig and playing it for laughs) who has escaped from a cryogenic prison. Thawed out from his deep-freeze container because he's the only man who can stop the evil Simon Phoenix is another criminal, framed ex-cop John Spartan, wonderfully played by Sylvester Stallone. The film's action pieces, when it isn't satirizing social mores, are fabulously directed by Marco Brambilla. Sandra Bullock is a standout as a lady cop who works with Spartan and introduces him to a form of "virtual reality" sex. Nigel Hawthorne, Benjamin Bratt. (Video/Laser: Warner Bros.)

DEMON. See *God Told Me To*.

DEMON, THE (1981) ★★ A slasher, dispatched by the Devil, wears a mask and uses clawed hands and strangulating plastic bags on victims. Psychic cop Cameron Mitchell tracks the monster. The film comes alive when a blonde is trapped with the Demon and runs naked through a house. Directed-written by Percival Rubens. Jennifer Holmes, Craig Gardner. Aka *The Unholy*. (VidAmerica; HBO)

DEMON DOCTOR, THE. See *The Awful Dr. Orlof*.

DEMONIC TOYS (1991) ★★★ Imaginative night of horror and gory violence in a toy warehouse begins when cop Tracy Scoggins, pursuing illegal-arms dealers, is trapped with an evil spirit ("The Demon Kid") who brings to life playthings that attack and kill. Among them: Baby Oopsy-Daisy ("I can even shit my pants"), a clown jack-in-the-box, a robot that shoots laser fire, and a flesh-eating bear that grows into a giant. Trapped with Scoggins: fat security cop Pete Schrum, "Chunky Chicken" delivery man Bentley Mitchum (Robert's grandson), derelict Ellen Dunning and sadistic killer Michael Russo. This Charles Band production is earmarked by rambunctious, lively direction by Peter Manoogian. Toys by John Buechler. (Paramount) (Laser: Full Moon)

DEMON IN MY VIEW, A (1991) ★★½ No one portrayed madness better than Anthony Perkins, and in this German production shot in Hamburg and London he is "The Kenbourne Killer," a serial murderer who strangles streetwalkers. Plagued by hallucinations, this guy is so warped and wretched that he makes love to a mannequin and writes poison pen letters. Writer-director Petra Haffter, from a Ruth Rendell novel, structures an unusual portrait of a lonely, sick man, and in one of his last roles Perkins restrains his performance. The romantic subplot involving Uwe Bohm and Sophie Ward seems out in left field until it brings an ironic film-noir touch to the action. Stratford Johns, Brian Bovel, Terence Hardiman, James Aubrey. (Video/Laser: Vidmark)

DEMON KEEPER (1993) ★★½ After a bare-breasted beauty is burned at the stake, unleashing flashes of lethal energy-light that kill her inquisitors, we flash to modern day as psychic investigator Edward Albert conducts a druid "Prohibition Sabbath" to raise the sleeping spirit of Amadeus the Horned Demon (Mike Lane in a devil suit). Once Amadeus is unleashed in a mansion cut off from the rest of the world by an intense thunderstorm, the séance attendees are murdered one by one, the demon preying on their weaknesses. This is an uninspired Roger Corman thriller, made in South Africa to save a buck, that dredges up every Demon cliché imaginable (with plenty of bare breasts to spice the tasteless broth). Not a single spark of originality is to be found in Mikel Angel's script. Produced-directed by Joe Tornatore. Dirk Benedict, Andre Jacobs, Adrienne Pearce, David Sherwood. (New Horizons) (Laser: Image)

DEMON LOVER (1976) ★★½ Despite stupid gore killings and a dumb teen mentality, this is grisly stuff that sticks in the memory (and the craw) thanks to writers-directors Donald G. Jackson and Jerry Younkins. Enough idiotic kids to fill a cemetery get involved with a witchmaster who conjures a horned demon from Hell. Especially memorable is the kid who gets an arrow through his groin and grovels on the floor. Luridly compelling if thoroughly tasteless. This stars Gunnar (Leatherface) Hansen. (Unicorn; from Regal as *Devil Master* and from Premiere as *Master of Evil*)

DEMON MASTER (1973). Video of *Craze* (VCR).

DEMON MASTER (1976). A more complete video version of *Demon Lover* (Regal).

DEMON OF THE LAKE. Video version of *Creature from Black Lake*.

DEMONOID—MESSENGER OF DEATH (1982) ★★ A 300-year-old hand (severed from a desecrator of a Mexican devil cult) is crawling in modern times when Roy Cameron Jenson discovers the tomb with wife Samantha Eggar. It's one severed hand after the other and mumbo jumbo about possession as the "hand" life force passes from person to person. It's a meandering story line writer-director Alfred Zacharias and coauthor David Lee Fein are handing us. Stuart Whitman is a boxing Inglewood priest. Aka *Macabra*. (Media)

DEMON PLANET, THE. See *Planet of the Vampires.*

DEMON POSSESSED (1989) ★★½ Unusually restrained supernatural tale about six snowmobile explorers trapped on Black Friar Lake. They seek refuge in abandoned Camp St. Dominic, where satanic activities once were held. A hooded shadow is brought out of limbo when the explorers find a ouija board called "The Devil's Eye." Finally, the gore murders: one body chopped up by a freezer locker fan; one punctured through the head with a falling icicle; another hanged; another impaled on barbed wire; yet another crushed under a snow plow. It's told as a memory flashback and the narration captures a quality the rest of the film lacks. Produced-directed by Christopher Webster in Wisconsin. Dawn Laurrie, Aaron Kjenaas, Connie Snyder, David Fields. (Action International) (Laser: Image)

DEMON RAGE (1982) ★ Huge-breasted Lana Wood (sister of Natalie) is some eyeful in this weak-kneed supernatural thriller (aka *Fury of the Succubus* and *Satan's Mistress*) in which a "lonely spirit" from beyond (Kabir Bedi) rapes Ms. Wood as frequently as writer-director James Polakof can reload his cameras. Tedious, predictable and taking forever to build to its nonarousing climax. John Carradine is wasted in a thankless cameo as a priest. Britt Ekland (as a psychic) and Ms. Wood appear in semistages of undress, but this needs more than tantalizing flesh. Tom Hallick. (HarmonyVision)

DEMONS (1985) ★★★½ Dario Argento production, shot in Berlin, and directed by Lamberto Bava (son of Mario Bava), who brings surrealism to this shocker set in the Metropol theater. The audience is watching a film about Nostradamus when a viewer turns into a demon and it's a zombiethon with hideous makeup, foaming green bile, claws, fangs. Really weird things happen (our hero rides through the auditorium on his motorbike, killing zombies with a sword; a helicopter crashes through the roof; two lovers are strangled while they kiss) and it turns out the whole world is infected with demon-mania. (New World) (Laser: Image)

DEMONS 2: THE NIGHTMARE RETURNS (1986) ★★★ Worthy follow-up to *Demons*, strictly for gore lovers as it depicts an army of humans, infected by a strange blood malady, terrorizing sections of Rome. Director Lamberto Bava, with producer Dario Argento, creates a surrealistic world in which a young woman watching a horror movie is attacked by a demon through a TV set. This mingling of reality and media is a fascinating subtext touching on our penchant for violent movies. Anyway, the demon creates an army (contagion is spread through the fingernails) rampaging through the highrise apartment building. There's a memorable battle to the death between a pregnant woman and a newly born demon baby. David Knight, Coralina Cataldi Tassoni, Bobby Rhodes. (Imperial) (Laser: Japanese)

DEMON SEED, THE (1977) ★★★ Sci-fi thriller combines dazzling computer effects with a literate story (written by Robert Jaffe and Roger O. Hirson, from a Dean R. Koontz novel) dealing with man's rape of Earth and machine's rape of man, in this case lovely Julie Christie. The ultimate computer decides it is greater than its creator and malfunctions to conceive a child that will embody its own genius. Among the effects: a machine having a sexual climax. Donald Cammell directed. Computer voice: Robert Vaughn. Fritz Weaver (as the creator of Proteus IV), Gerrit Graham, Berry Kroeger. (Video/Laser: MGM/UA)

DEMON'S MASK, THE. See *Black Sunday.*

DEMONS OF LUDLOW, THE (1983) ★ Low-budget supernatural tale with woefully inadequate effects, made in Wisconsin by producer-director Bill Rebane. The New England town of Ludlow faces horror when a long-dead puritan-warlock returns as a haunted piano (?!). Among the out-of-tune weirdo stuff is a phantom noose from another dimension, a demon hand that pops up from the floorboards, haunted toy dolls and sword-wielding duelists. Paul Von Hausen, Stephanie Cushna, Carol Perry, James R. Robinson. (Trans World)

DEMONS OF PARADISE (1987) ★ Filmed in and around Kihono, on the island of Hawaii, this grade-B monster movie is predictable from stereotyped beginning to hackneyed ending. Nothing can save this movie relying on stolen *Jaws* subplots and *Black Lagoon* replays. Akua, an ancient fish-demon feared by the natives, is disturbed by fishermen using dynamite and begins to kill natives and tourists. The creature, of the unconvincing rubber-suit school, is impervious to bullets and explosions and has the strength to down a helicopter. Directed by Cirio H. Santiago. Kathryn Witt, William Steis, Laura Banks. (Warner Bros.)

DEMONS OF THE DEAD (1975) ★★★ Effective Italian psychothriller, made in England, is best when the camera is swirling and spinning to capture the fright of a woman recovering from a car accident that caused her to lose her unborn baby. Made in "Chill-O-Rama," *Demons* follows her into a coven of witchcraft practitioners. If you love pseudopsychology, you'll dig this mess. Directed by Sergio Martino. George Hilton, Edwige Fereck, Ivan Rassimor. (From Super as *Day of the Maniac* and from Vogue as *They're Coming to Get You*)

DEMONS OF THE MIND (1972) ★★★ Hammer shocker deals with satanic possession resulting from incestuous sex and is "intense." Shane Briant and Gillian Hills are children kept imprisoned by their father. Patrick Magee is the family physician who learns the dark secrets. The visual horror only comes at the end. Directed by Peter Sykes from a Christopher Wicker script. Paul Jones, Michael Hordern, Yvonne Mitchell. Aka *Blood Will Have Blood* and *Nightmare of Terror*. (HBO; Republic; from Academy as *Blood Evil*)

DEMONS OF THE SWAMP. See *Attack of the Giant Leeches*.

DEMONSTONE (1989) ★★½ R. Lee Ermey and Jan-Michael Vincent as fun-loving, shit-kicking Marine Corps buddies out to solve grisly murders in Manila are the best things in this action-horror thriller that uses Filipino political unrest as a subplot. The supernatural amulet of the title involves a 400-year-old curse; Ermey and Vincent have to find out what has unleashed a ferocious supernatural power, but the film's structure is that of an action film with careening automobiles and blazing submachine-guns. The Demonstone gets second billing, with limited effects. Director Andrew Prowse is to be commended for making his shoot-outs believable. Pat Skipper, Peter Brown. Aka *Heartstone*. (Fries) (Laser: Image)

DEMON TOWER. See *Demon Lover*.

DEMONWARP (1987) ★ Dumb movie filled with young people behaving stupidly, and abounding with monsters and masks, gore and goo. In Demonwood, a Bigfoot creature attacks George Kennedy and daughter. Then the teenagers turn up and the hunt is on for the beast. Turns out an alien craft landed in the vicinity and an E.T. beasty is responsible. The story by John Buechler—who designed the monster—was turned into a worthless script by Jim Bertges and Bruce Akiyama and directed empty-headedly by Emmett Alston. David Michael O'Neill, Billy Jacoby, Pamela Gilbert. (Vidmark)

DEMON WIND (1989) ★★★ Monster and gore fans will enjoy this variation on *Night of the Living Dead* with demonic overtones, a production by Paul Hunt, Michael Bennett and Peter Collins. The setting is a farmhouse (sound familiar?) in which young people amass to fight off legions of walking dead, a cloven-footed, horned demon and gooey-faced freaks. Writer-director Charles Philip Moore fills it with dream sequences and other tricks-within-tricks that undercut the horror, but he still manages a fast pace, horrendous makeup and a few surprises. Eric Larson, Francine Lapensee, Bobby Johnston, Lynn Clark. (Paramount) (Laser: Prism/Image)

DEMON WITHIN, THE. Video version of *The Mind Snatchers* (Ace).

DENTIST, THE (1996) ★ This is really a down-in-the-mouth horror film, and certainly displays a certain tongue-in-molar quality. Undergoing a root-canal operation without any painkillers, however, might possibly be more entertaining. The script by Dennis Paoli, Stuart Gordon, and Charles Finch—appealing to our lowest-common-denominator fear of those who wield drills and inject novocaine—depicts bloody oral surgery, unnecessary tooth drilling, extractions with pliers, root explorations, gum sticking, dental-floss stretching, and other standard dental-horror practices. Dr. Alan Finestone, who loves opera music and is a stickler for cleanliness in a "dirty" world, is breaking down as this mouthful of a movie begins. He suspects his beautiful wife, Linda Hoffman, of having an affair with the pool cleaner, he shoots to death a neighbor's dog, and he begins mouthing off to his patients down at the office. When he finally flips out, he rapes a beauty queen, murders his IRS agent (the unkindest yank of all), kills a couple of dental assistants, and chases a young girl wearing braces through the dental building. Corbin Bernsen, who went on to play Finestone with much more comedic madness in *The Dentist 2*, denigrates tooth doctors (not to mention tooth fairies) everywhere when he finally cuts out the tongue of his lovely wife, all in the name of personal hygiene. Better you should avoid this Brian Yuzna–directed mess and make an appointment to see the sequel. Incidentally, this did not get an "open wide" distribution when it was first released. The producer does make the claim that if you see this movie, you will very definitely brush after every meal in the days that lie ahead. Molly Hagan, Ken Foree, Virginya Keehne, Patty Toy, Jan Hoag, Earl Boen. (Video/DVD: Vidmark-Trimark)

DENTIST 2: BRACE YOURSELF, THE (1998) ★½ That "Psycho Dentist," the not-so-fine Dr. Finestone, who enjoys an occasional "kill drill" to spice up his life, escapes his straitjacket environment (where he settled in at the end of the highly inferior *The Dentist*) and starts a new life in the small midwest town of Paradise. His motto: "The Yank Is Coming" or "I've Got Pull in This Town." It doesn't take him long to kill off (how about "extract"?) the only dental practitioner in the community to take over his business. But then, tooth is stranger than fiction. As Finestone, Corbin Bernsen is totally whacked out and does a delightful job as a one-hundred-percent fruitcake. He cuts himself constantly on the arm as a kind of self-punishment for murdering innocent people, hallucinates about people with horribly deformed teeth, and fantasizes about how his first wife (Linda Hoffman) cheated on him and he cut out her tongue. Just watching Corbie going bonkers is more fun than watching your favorite root-canal specialist getting ready to examine your family roots. With the repeated request "Open wide!", Bernsen/Finestone makes root-canal work seem like a pleasure in comparison to his own sadistic pastime of probing decayed teeth with a sharp pick and drilling into painful places from which pops out pus and other gooey substances. *The Dentist 2* is definitely on the droll side . . . oops, we mean drill side, under the pulsating direction of Brian Yuzna, but Richard Dana Smith's script still lacks the biting wit of, say, *Dr. Giggles* or *The Surgeon* or even *The Nurse*. Jillian McWhirter is the small-town beauty who doesn't get wise to Bernsen until it's too late, and Clint Howard turns up as a comedy-relief character with a . . . yeah, you guessed it, a throbbing, pounding, unbearably painful, God-awful toothache. The ending is totally bizarre, by the way, as if everything suddenly goes surreal. But then, I've seen the interior of some dentists' offices that were really surreal, too. Susane Wright, Jim Antonio, Lee Dawson, Ralph P. Martin. (Video/DVD: Vidmark-Trimark)

DEPTHS OF THE UNKNOWN. See *The Time Travelers*.

DERANGED. Video version of *Idaho Transfer* (Satellite).

DESERT WARRIOR (1985) ★½ Rip-off of *Mad Max* with anti-hero Trace (Gary Watkins) battling the villainous Scourge who has kidnaped his sister. Trace's pals are a fast gun (Laura Banks) and a kid with ESP (Linda Grovenor). Made in the Philippines by director-producer Cirio H. Santiago. (Prism)

DESERT WARRIOR (1988) ★ In a post-holocaust world of roving bands, mighty warriors fight over one of the few women still capable of bearing children. Lou Ferrigno, Shari Shattuck, Kenneth Peer, Anthony East. Directed by Jim Goldman. (Prism)

DESIRES OF THE VAMPIRE. See *Curse of the Vampire*.

DESTINATION INNER SPACE (1966) ★★ Laughable low-budget "junkie" (subtitled *Terror of the Deep*) with an alien that looks like a rejected version of the Black Lagoon creature. An underwater lab commanded by Scott Brady is invaded by a monster from a spaceship that splashed down nearby. Scripter Arthur C. Pierce duplicates the tricks of *The Thing* but director Francis D. Lyon is no Howard Hawks. Sheree North, Gary Merrill, Roy Barcroft, Mike Road.

DESTINATION MOON (1950) ★★★ George Pal production depicting man's first flight to the moon—19 years before it happened. The pseudodocumentary style emphasizes difficulties of space walks, weightlessness and other scientific curiosities. Authentic for its day, it now seems tame. Chesley Bonestell's lunar drawings are excellent. Irving Pichel directed. Good score by Leith Stevens. Robert Heinlein cowrote the script. Warner Anderson, John Archer, Erin O'Brien-Moore, Tom Powers. (Nostalgia Merchant; S/Weird) (Laser: Image)

DESTINATION SATURN. Reedited video version from Cable Films of Universal's 12-chapter *Buck Rogers* serial. See *Buck Rogers*.

DESTINY TO ORDER (1989) ★★ Frustrated writer (Stephen Ouimette), through an electrical jolt to his computer, is suddenly in touch with his characters and takes on different guises to save them from bikers led by Michael Ironside. Canadian film written-directed by Jim Purdy. Alberta Watson, Victoria Snow. (Off Hollywood)

DESTROY ALL MONSTERS (1969) ★★ Inoshiro Honda, who brought us Godzilla, unites Japan's hulkers (Godzilla, Godzilla, Jr., Ebirah, Wenda, Rodan, Anzilla, Gorasorus, Barugan, Mothra, Varan) in a destruction marathon. When Earth is attacked by spacemen called Kilaaks, they unleash the monsters from Ogaswara Island, sending each to destroy a city. Effects by Eiji Tsuburaya, including a battle atop Mount Fuji.

Akira Kubo, Jun Tazaki. Aka *Operation Monsterland, Attack of the Marching Monsters* and *The March of the Monsters*. (Fright) (Laser: Japanese)

DESTROY ALL PLANETS (1968) ★★ Japanese monster mauling as "hero monster" Gamera the Flying Turtle (making his fourth appearance, by contractual arrangements with producer Hidemasa Nagata) falls under the control of aliens. But two small children set the thick-shelled creature free and he attacks Viras the Incredible Sea Squid. Eastern enthrallment directed by Noriaki Yuasa. Also known as *Gamera vs. Outer Space Monster Viras*. (S/Weird; Sinister/C; from Celebrity as *Gamera vs. Viras*) (Laser: Japanese)

DESTROYER (1988) ★★ The corpse of electrocuted convict Ivan Moser (played by a hulk, Lyle Alzado) stalks an abandoned prison, murdering members of a film crew making "Death House Dolls." Moser is subjected to assorted deaths along with his victims. The screenplay by producers Peter Garrity and Rex Hauck makes little sense, and director Robert Kirk is stuck trying to make something out of nothing. An oddity is the presence of Anthony Perkins as a film director. Deborah Foreman, Clayton Rohner. (Virgin Vision) (Laser: Image)

DEVIL AND DANIEL WEBSTER, THE (1941) ★★★★ Stephen Vincent Benét's classic story, produced-directed by William Dieterle, is an American folk tale depicting how Senator Webster, an orator-statesman in the rotund shape of Edward Arnold, defends farmer James Craig when Old Scratch, grandiosely etched in brimstone by thunderous Walter Huston, comes to claim his soul. The jury is made up of Benedict Arnold, Captain Kidd and Blackbeard. Robert Wise was editor, Bernard Herrmann wrote the score, Benét collaborated with Dan Totheroh on the script. Aka *Here Is a Man, A Certain Mr. Scratch* and *All That Money Can Buy*. H. B. Warner, Jeff Corey, Simone Simon, Anne Shirley, Jane Darwell, William Alland. (Embassy; RCA/Columbia; Home Vision) (Laser: Criterion; Voyager; Nelson)

DEVIL AND DR. FRANKENSTEIN, THE. See *Andy Warhol's Frankenstein*.

DEVIL BAT, THE (1941) ★ A depressing reminder of Bela Lugosi's plummeting career in the '40s, this PRC release (written by John T. Neville) stars him as a mad scientist who trains a killer bat to carry out his evil bidding. Lugosi guides the night flapper to the target by giving victims a special perfume. Directed by Jean Yarbrough. Suzanne Kaaren, Dave O'Brien, Guy Usher, Hal Price. Aka *Killer Bats*. A loose sequel was *Devil Bat's Daughter*. (Prism; Sinister/C; Filmfax; Nostalgia) (Laser: Lumivision, with *Scared to Death*)

DEVIL BAT'S DAUGHTER (1946) ★★ Rosemary LaPlanche (one-time beauty queen) believes she is possessed by the spirit of her father, who presumably turned into a bat when he died. This sequel to *The Devil Bat* is borderline horror with whodunit overtones. It wasn't the butler, but you won't have much trouble figuring out who is guilty, due to no subtleties from producer-director Frank Wisbar or writer Griffin Jay. Eddie Kane, John James, Monica Mars. (RCA; Sony)

DEVIL BEAR. See *Claws*.

DEVIL CAT. See *Night Creature*.

DEVIL COMMANDS, THE (1940) ★★★ Boris Karloff gives another riveting performance as a driven, obsessed man of science determined to unlock nature's secrets: Dr. Julian Blair, who discovers a way of recording human brain waves in his mansion isolated on Barsham Harbor. After the accidental death of his wife, he finds a method of communicating with the dead through an odd head contraption and joins with phony spiritualist Anne Revere (her cold, evil demeanor makes for a chilling performance) in macabre experiments that require corpses from a nearby cemetery. Based on William Sloane's superb novel *The Edge of Running Water*, the Robert D. Andrews/Milton Gunzburg script is highlighted by an eerie narration read by Karloff's daughter and laboratory scenes depicting corpses in odd body and head rigs. Effectively directed by Edward Dmytryk. Aka *When the Devil Commands* and *The Devil Said No*.

DEVIL DOG: THE HOUND OF HELL (1978) ★ Uninspired TV-movie, directed by Curtis Harrington from a script by Stephen and Elinor Karpf. The Mangy Mutt from Beyond terrorizes suburbanites Richard Crenna and Yvette Mimieux. The yip is a gyp. Kim Richards, Victor Jory, Ike Eisenmann, R. G. Armstrong, Martine Beswick. (Vestron; Lightning)

DEVIL DOLL (1963) ★★★ Compelling British shocker blending touches of Svengali with the ventriloquist tale from *Dead of Night*. Bryant Halliday is the Great Vorelli, a stage magician-hypnotist with a dummy that walks and talks. Vorelli, a dabbler in the mysteries of India, is no dummy—he knows secrets of soul transference. Lindsay Shonteff directed the Lance Z. Hargreaves and George Barclay script with a starkness matched by Gerald Gibbs's photography. William Sylvester, Yvonne Romain. (Gorgon; MPI)

DEVIL DOLL, THE (1936) ★★★ This well-produced MGM revenge-fantasy, one of the last films directed by Tod (*Dracula*) Browning, is superior for its era, with enthralling miniaturized effects. It was adapted from Abraham Merritt's *Burn Witch Burn!* and Browning's own *The Witch of Timbuctoo* by Garrett Fort, Guy Endore and Erich von Stroheim. Lionel Barrymore goes drag to pose as a sweet old lady who sells life-like dolls in Paris. What his/her purchasers don't realize is that the dolls are real—a doctor has devised a formula for shrinking people and now Barrymore, escaped from Devil's Island after being sent there for a crime he didn't commit, uses these creatures to carry out his revenge. Henry B. Walthall, Maureen O'Sullivan. (MGM/UA)

DEVILFISH (1984) A richly textured storyline by Lewis Coates (Luigi Cozzi), Don Lewis and Martin Dolman enhances this Italian production directed by Lamberto Bava (identified in the credits as John Old, Jr.). It's Bava's variation on *Jaws* when a seemingly prehistoric shark, 40-feet-long with tentacles and huge teeth, shows up off the Florida coast to eat the local swimming population. Turns out, however, that a nearby underwater-study institute has been conducting secret experiments under the name Sea Killer and the thing is only eight months old, so the plot is busy busy busy with murders, double crosses and hidden agendas that will have you guessing. Unfortunately, the special effects are only passable, and the creature not all that convincing. But Bava holds your interest and makes something out of the hodgepodge. Aka *Monster Shark* and *Red Ocean*. William Berger, Michael Sopkiw, Mortimer Monnier, John Garko, Iris Peynado, Dagmar Lassander. (Vidmark)

DEVIL GIRL FROM MARS (1954) ★½ Patricia Laffan, in a fetching outfit all the rage on the canals this season, and her robot Chani invade Earth with an eye on the men—she has breeding in mind. Directed by David MacDonald and written by John C. Maher and James Eastwood, this has no subtleties in depicting how a big-breasted woman would conquer mankind. Hazel Court, Hugh McDermott, Adrienne Corri. (Nostalgia Merchant; Rhino; MPI; Sinister/C; S/Weird)

DEVIL GOT ANGRY, THE. See *Majin, Monster of Terror*.

DEVIL IS A WOMAN, THE. See *The Velvet Vampire*.

DEVILISH DR. MABUSE, THE. See *The Secret of Dr. Mabuse*.

DEVIL MASTER. Another video version of *Demon Lover*. This, from Regal, is said to be more complete than the Unicorn tape.

DEVIL RIDES OUT, THE. See *The Devil's Bride*.

DEVIL SAID NO, THE. See *The Devil Commands*.

DEVIL'S ADVOCATE, THE (1997) ★★★½ Anyone who thinks we live in a morally decaying world, where decadence seems to manifest itself in many deceptive forms and the bad guys too often win, will find plenty to identify with in this cool, cautionary tale of the supernatural. At a time when the world seems to be going to hell all too quickly, *The Devil's Advocate* has something to say about our collapsing society, and just might be the most elaborate antilawyer joke ever told. And it does so with a sense of sardonic humor and perverse pleasure. Two unusual performances emerge: Keanu Reeves as self-centered defense attorney Kevin Lomax, who defends all the wrong people but has never lost a case yet, and Al Pacino as John Milton, the dynamic and deceptively charming head of a power-packed Manhattan law firm known as Milton, Chadwick & Waters. When Reeves is lured away from Florida to join the firm, his mother (Julie Ivey) cites Revelation 18 to warn him of the dangers of New York City: "Fallen, fallen is Babylon the great; it has become a dwelling place for Demons . . . I send you out as sheep amidst the wolves." Lomax should have listened to Mom. When he and happy-go-lucky wife Charlize (*The Astronaut's Wife*) Theron arrive at the firm, Paradise seems to be offered by Pacino's gregarious Milton as they walk on the building's unusual rooftop, where a pool of water appears to cascade over the edge. Manhattan is spread out below and is all Lomax's for the taking—but look out, pal, you could plunge off the edge if you're not careful. In defending an accused killer (Craig T. Nelson), Lomax settles into his old self-assured indulgent self, neglecting his wife and succumbing to some (if not all) of the temptations his new milieu offers. At first he's totally blind to the reality that he's gone to work for the devil; but then his conscience kicks in to provide the morality fight that leads him into confrontation with his mentor Milton. Theron, a lot quicker to realize the evil that surrounds her in their Fifth Avenue apartment, sinks deeper and deeper into depression and madness, and sees that some of the "friends" from the firm often lapse into looking like demons (Rick Baker designed the makeup). A fellow attorney (Jeffrey Jones) tries to warn Lomax, but he's slower than we are to glom onto the truth: Milton's firm is the 20th century's center of pure evil. Lomax finally has his face-to-face with Milton, in which all the moral ideas of Andrew Neiderman's novel are strikingly articulated by screenwriters Jonathan Lemkin and Tony Gilroy. This is one of director Taylor Hackford's best works, for he helms the film with a sense of restraint and taste, holding back the devil's lambasting blasphemy until the climactic moments in Milton's lavish office when a bas-relief (seemingly of religious figures) suddenly wriggles to life and becomes a sex orgy. The film has a twist ending that doesn't quite work, but it does suggest that evil can never be defeated, that it will always rise up again and laugh in your face. Connie Nielsen, Tamara Tunie, Debra Monk, Ruben Santiago-Hudson. (Video/DVD: Warner Bros.)

DEVIL'S BRIDE, THE (1968) ★★★½ Hammer's superb version of Dennis Wheatley's *The*

Devil Rides Out. While weaknesses in Richard Matheson's script cannot be denied, Terence Fisher's direction is remarkably fluid, the juxtaposition of scenes excellent and the flavor of Britain in the '20s well preserved. Christopher Lee fights to destroy Charles Gray's devil cult. The "Death on Horseback" sequence is a shocker, and suspense mounts as Lee and force seek protection in a pentagram under assault from supernatural forces.

DEVIL'S BROOD, THE. See *House of Frankenstein.*

DEVIL'S DAUGHTER, THE (1991) ★★ The Devil sends out his bad guys to make life miserable on Earth for us humans. With Herbert Lom and Kelly Curtis. Directed by Michele Soavi. Produced and cowritten by Dario Argento. Aka *The Sect.* (Video/Laser: Republic)

DEVIL'S EYE. See *Eyeball.*

DEVIL'S GIFT, THE (1984) ★½ Monkey doll with sinister eyes (it's inhabited by a demon) carries out evil deeds by hypnotizing a housewife. Filmed in the Santa Rosa–Petaluma area, this low-budgeter is incredibly chintzy, lacking in production except for a weird opening that is partially animated. The drabness of the people and locales, plus the fact the script by Hayden O'Hara, Jose Vergelin and producer-director Kenneth J. Berton was lifted from Stephen King's "The Monkey," make this an excruciating experience. *The Devil's Gift* is no gift to you. Bob Mendlesohn, Vicki Saputo. (Vestron)

DEVIL'S LONGEST NIGHT, THE. See *Devil's Nightmare.*

DEVIL'S NIGHTMARE (1971) ★★ Campy dialogue and silly premise provide laughs in this Italian-Belgian flop chiller about a Nazi general whose family has a pact with the Devil. Each generation's eldest daughter is born an evil witch lusting to kill. Flash to present day as seven travelers seek refuge one stormy night in Castle von Rhoneberg. These idiots (bubbleheaded sexy blondes, a glutton, and so on) meet grisly deaths: quicksand, guillotine, Iron Maiden, impalement on spikes, etc. The priest in the group stands to fight a religious battle. Erika Blanc, Jean Servais. Directed/cowritten by Jean Brismee. Also known as *The Devil's Longest Night.* (Monterey; New Horizon; from Premiere as *Nightmare of Terror,* from Regal as *The Devil Walks at Midnight* and from Applause as *Succubus*)

DEVIL'S RAIN (1975) ★★½ Ernest Borgnine is Jonathan Corbis, a goat demon heading a coven somewhere in the Southwest. Innocent passersby stumble across the secret and must be silenced. Trashy film, barely salvaged in the final minutes when the Evil Ones are drenched in a satanic rainstorm, turning into oozing, melting puddles of multi-colored wax. Not even director

Robert Fuest (*The Abominable Dr. Phibes*) comes in out of the rain. William Shatner, Ida Lupino, Eddie Albert, Tom Skerritt, John Travolta, Keenan Wynn. (United; VCI) (Laser: Image)

DEVIL'S TOUCH, THE. See *The Blood on Satan's Claw.*

DEVIL'S UNDEAD, THE (1975) ★★★ Christopher Lee produced (and stars in) this decent adaptation of John Blackburn's *Children of the Night,* in which a school of youngsters are injected with serum that contains memory genes of an adult murderess that turns them into frolicking psycho cases. However, Brian Hayles's adaptation treats this dark tale more as a mystery than a horror film as retired detective Lee, with the help of biochemist Peter Cushing and newshound Georgia Brown, pursue a mother (Diana Dors) suspected of murder. Only during the climactic scene (reminiscent of *The Wicker Man*) does director Peter Sasdy have a chance to deal effectively with horrific images and their implications. Coproduced by Anthony Nelson Keys. Keith Barron, Fulton Mackay, Gwyneth Strong. Aka *The Resurrection Syndicate.* (Monterey; from Trend Video Concepts as *Nothing but the Night*)

DEVIL'S WEDDING NIGHT, THE (1975) ★★★ Dracula's Nibelungen ring, which lures virgins to a sacrificial party, is the pivotal device in this Italian film (*The Full Moon of the Virgins*), which offers ample nudity. Another variation on the Countess Bathory legend, in which Sara Bay (as the Countess) caresses her skin with virgins' blood. Mixture of blood, sex and lesbianism, directed by Paul Solvay (Luigi Batzella). Mark Damon has a dual role as twin brothers. Francesca Romana Davila, Stan Papps. Aka *Countess Dracula.* (Wizard; VCI; Midnight)

DEVIL TIMES FIVE (1974) ★ During the snowy season around Lake Arrowhead, lodge owner Papa Doc (Gene Evans) is caught up in a supernatural mystery involving five strangers led by a child who could be possessed by the Devil. Low-budget schlock-bottom job is dully paced by writer John Durren (who doubles as an actor) and director Sean MacGregor. Sorrell Booke, Taylor Lacher, Joan McCall. Also called *People Toys* and *The Horrible House on the Hill.* (Video Treasures; Media; Sinister/C)

DEVIL WALKS AT MIDNIGHT. Video version of *Devil's Nightmare* (Regal; Saturn).

DEVIL WITHIN HER, THE (1976) ★ British rip-off of *The Exorcist,* as messy as Nicholas Carlesi's diapers, who by the tender age of 30 days has pushed his nanny into the Thames and dunked a dead mouse in a teacup. Joan Collins, who birthed this cradled creature after being hexed by a sinister dwarf, wonders why so much mayhem from a toddler. Doctor Donald Pleasence has suspicions. Lack of motivation and obscure demonic background turn this (also known as *I Don't Want to Be Born, The Monster, The Baby* and *Sharon's Baby*) into a cinematic nightmare for director Peter Sasdy and writer Stanley Price. Ralph Bates, Caroline Munro. (Axon)

DEVONSVILLE TERROR, THE (1983) ★½ German filmmaker Ulli Lommel directed this slow-moving witchcraft/sorcery tale. It begins centuries ago with a Salem witch burning and jumps to modern day, when descendants of the witch stalkers are plagued by a curse. Suzanna Love, one of three women new in town, would appear to be a witch, but it takes forever for townspeople to catch on. Meanwhile, worms infect doctor Donald Pleasence. The script by Lommel, Love (his wife) and George T. Lindsey never comes to life. Robert Walker, Paul Willson, Angelica Rebane. (Embassy; Sultan)

DIABOLICAL DR. MABUSE, THE. See *The Thousand Eyes of Dr. Mabuse.*

DIABOLICAL DR. VOODOO. See *The Incredibly Strange Creatures Who Stopped Living and Became Mixed-Up Zombies.*

DIABOLICAL DR. Z, THE (1966) ★★★ Murky atmosphere enhances, rather than detracts from, this Spanish-French sequel to *The Awful Dr. Orlof* with Howard Vernon back as the mad doc. His daughter (Mabel Karr) takes lab center to gain control of a woman dancer nicknamed Miss Death (Estella Blain) for revenge by using a long needle that plunges into victims. Directed by Jesse Franco. Mabel Karr, Antonio J. Escribano, Guy Mairesse. Aka *Miss Muerte, Miss Death* and *Miss Death and Dr. Z in the Grip of the Maniac*. (Sinister/C; S/Weird; Filmfax)

DIABOLIQUE (1996) ★★★ It's puzzling why filmmakers take an old classic and remake it, abandoning many of the original concepts for their own twists, as if to say they can do better. This lack of understanding why the original worked so well, and the ability to turn a silk purse into a sow's ear, is mightily reflected in this feature-film redo of the 1955 French thriller from director Henri-Georges Clouzot. Still following the original novel by Pierre Boileau and Thomas Narcejec, Don Roos's screen rewrite is all over the place with inconsistent, muddled characters, love affairs difficult to track, and a restructuring of the policeman character that's nothing short of lame. Sharon Stone is as cold as ice as the scheming mistress of Chazz Palminteri and the lesbian lover of Palminteri's mousy wife Isabelle Adjani. How they carry out Palminteri's graphic death (first by drugging him and then holding him underwater in a bathtub) is still one of the best murder pieces of all time, but after that the story really falls to pieces as Kathy Baker shows up as a nosy out-of-work cop (the original role inspired the creation of

Columbo) and all the red herrings appear to make it look as though Palminteri is back from the dead seeking revenge. Jeremiah Chechik's direction is darkly sinister, capturing the bizarreness of the characters' behavior, but the script ultimately doesn't work. Especially grating and bad are the multiple "twists" at the climax as the film finally abandons its inspiration and goes all out for new, and very poor, shocks. The TV-movie versions of the original include *Reflections of Murder* and *House of Secrets.* (Video/ Laser: Warner Bros.)

DIAL: HELP (1989) ★★★ Spinning, tonish Italian supernatural thriller epitomizes the frustration of long-distance dialing when Charlotte Lewis taps into a psychic energy field containing the spirit of a dead operator. Suddenly her friends are dying and psychic doctor William Berger investigates. Directed by Ruggero Deodato, who cowrote the taut script. (Prism)

DIAMOND MOUNTAIN. Video version of *Shadow of Chikara* (Mintex).

DIAMONDS ARE FOREVER (1971) ★★★½ Seventh entry in the 007 series stars Sean Connery in his last fling in the role prior to quitting in 1972. In this adaptation of Ian Fleming's novel, 007 searches for Blofeld, who is firing his diamond laser at missile bases. The settings range from the lunar landscape to Las Vegas to the Nevada desert. There's a car chase down the main street of Vegas, a race with a moonmobile, lady karate attacks and two gay villains. Jimmy Dean portrays a Howard Hughes–type recluse, Jill St. John is the beautiful Tiffany Case (oh does she love diamonds), Lana Wood appears as sexy Plenty O'Toole, and Charles Gray is the dastardly cat lover, Blofeld. Directed by Guy Hamilton in flashy fashion and written tongue-in-cheek by Richard Maibaum and Tom Mankiewicz. (CBS/Fox) (Laser: MGM/UA)

DIAPHANOIDS, BRINGERS OF DEATH. See *War of the Planets* (1965).

DIARY OF A MADMAN (1963) ★★½ Tormented performance by Vincent Price enhances the threadbare script by producer Robert E. Kent, based on Guy de Maupassant's "The Horla." Price is a 19th-century Parisian magistrate, haunted by an invisible entity that forces him to slash beautiful Nancy Kovack to pieces. A quasi-religious ending is in keeping with the morality of the times. The "invisible man" tricks are unimpressive and the weight falls on Price's shoulders. Directed by Reginald LeBorg. Chris Warfield, Ian Wolfe, Stephen Roberts. (Facets Multimedia; MGM)

DIARY OF THE DEAD (1976) ★★½ Macabre overtones enhance this oddly structured Hitchcockian thriller starring Hector Elizondo as a pure heel, an out-of-work crossword solver with a shrew of a mother-in-law (Geraldine Fitzgerald). How he sets out to knock her off for her $80,000 inheritance leads to a labyrinth of deadly twists and turns under Arvin Brown's subtle direction. Salome Jens is Elizondo's browbeaten wife. (Vista)

DICK TRACY (1937) ★★★½ The first of four action-packed, dynamite Republic serials based on Chester Gould's comic-strip character has angular-faced Ralph Byrd portraying the jaw-jutting detective to corny perfection. In this adventure the Chicago plainclothesman is turned into a glorified G-Man as he goes up against the Spider (George Morgan), a club-footed fiend (aka the Lame One) who works in harmony with Moloch (John Piccori), an eyeball-rolling mad hunchbacked scientist who turns Tracy's brother (Carleton Young) into a villain through brain surgery. Among the highlights of this wonderfully fast-paced serial is a Flying Wing aircraft, used in an attempt to destroy the newly opened San Francisco Bay Bridge with a vibration device, and assorted hair-raising cliffhangers involving boats, planes, etc. The 15 chapters were directed by Ray Taylor and Alan James. Kay Hughes, Smiley Burnette (as comic relief Mike McGurk), Lee Van Atta (as the kid Junior). (Burbank; United; Sinister/C; Video Yesteryear; VCI; Goodtimes offers a two-cassette packaging) (Laser: Image)

DICK TRACY MEETS GRUESOME (1947) ★★½ Comic-book movie (aka *Dick Tracy's Amazing Adventure* and *Dick Tracy Meets Karloff*) based on Chester Gould's cop (Ralph Byrd) stars Boris Karloff as a heavy who robs banks with a paralyzing nerve gas. He borrowed it from the Green Hornet, maybe? Directed perfunctorily by John Rawlins from an Eric Taylor–Robertson White script. Anne Gwynne is Tracy's wife, Tess Trueheart. Howard Ashley, June Clayworth, Robert Clarke, Lex Barker. (Video Yesteryear; Sinister/C; Nostalgia; Rhino; United American; Silver Screen) (Laser: Image)

DICK TRACY MEETS KARLOFF. See *Dick Tracy Meets Gruesome.*

DICK TRACY'S AMAZING ADVENTURE. See *Dick Tracy Meets Gruesome.*

DICK TRACY'S G-MEN (1939) ★★★ In this, the third in Republic's *Dick Tracy* serials, Ralph Byrd goes against scientist Zarnoff, who uses a drug to bring himself back from the dead after his prison execution. It's nonstop action under directors William Witney and John English. Irving Pichel, Ted Pearson, Walter Miller. And dig that Phylis Isley—she became Jennifer Jones! (VCI) (Laser: Image)

DICK TRACY VS. CRIME INC. (1941) ★★★ William Whitney and John English directed this 15-chapter Republic serial (the studio's fourth and last) in which Chester Gould's comic-strip cop tangles with the Ghost, a dastard capable of making himself invisible as he terrorizes the city. Action-packed. Ralph Byrd reprises his role as Tracy, assisted by Frank Morgan. Aka *Dick Tracy vs. the Phantom Empire.* (United; VCI) (Laser: Image)

DICK TRACY VS. THE PHANTOM EMPIRE. See *Dick Tracy vs. Crime Inc.*

DIE, DIE! MY DARLING! (1966) ★★★ Grand Guignol horror (aka *Fanatic*) with Stefanie Powers trapped in a house of crazies governed by religious zealot Tallulah Bankhead, who goes bonkers in eye-rolling, scenery-chomping fashion. The graphic murders are of such an abhorrent nature, the film has a singular gripping fascination. Donald Sutherland is Tallulah's nutty handyman, and he's impressive. Directed by Silvio Narizzano, scripted by Richard Matheson from Anne Blaisdell's *Nightmare.* Maurice Kaufman. (RCA/Columbia)

DIE LAUGHING (1980) ★★★½ A formula for altering atomic waste into plutonium bomb components is the McGuffin in this spy spoof with Robby Benson as a cabbie who falls into possession of a cute monkey holding the key to the secret. Accused of murder, Benson rushes all over San Francisco with dumb villain Bud Cort in pursuit. A spirit of fun is at work. Directed by Jeff Werner from a script by Benson and Scott Parker. Charles Durning, Elsa Lanchester. (Warner Bros.)

DIE, MONSTER, DIE! (1965) ★★½ Loose-as-a-noose adaptation of H. P. Lovecraft's "The Colour Out of Space," produced in England as a vehicle for Boris Karloff and aka *Monster of Terror* and *House at the End of the World.* The setting is H. P.'s infamous Arkham County where a desolate tract of land has been stricken by a diseased power from space that turns everyone into monsters. Director Daniel Haller provides isolated moments of fear and mystery, but the majority of Jerry Sohl's script is muddled. Nick Adams is the American who comes to a weird mansion looking for his bride-to-be (Suzan Farmer). Freda Jackson is a woman who keeps her hideous appearance hidden beneath a veil, and Patrick Magee is a doctor. (HBO) (Laser: Image, with *Lust for a Vampire*)

DIE, SISTER, DIE (1976) ★ Weak, talkative psychothriller in which Jack Ging hires nurse Antoinette Bower to kill shrewish sister Edith Atwater. Kent Smith and Robert Emhardt add strength to the cast but Tony Sawyer's lukewarm script and Randall Hood's limp direction do nothing to make this rise above the level of a competent TV movie. First released as *The Companion.* (Gorgon; MPI)

DIGITAL MAN (1994) ★★½ As far as its computerized graphics, flying spacecraft and superweaponry are concerned, this special-effects sci-fi actioner should please high-tech freakos and explosion lovers. But there's something dumb about how all this futuristic technology is used, and how frequently it misses, given all of its radar controls. Which means you get a lot of destruction and mayhem, but not much logic, when the "perfect soldier," a cyborg aka Digital Man (Matthias Hues), goes on a mission to take out some terrorists and ends up with the launch codes for 250 missile silos. When Digital Man goes renegade, an assault team (half-human, half-cyborg) also goes into action. From then on it's mindless mayhem, effects by Todd Masters. Directed by Phillip Roth, who cowrote the all-over-the-map script with Ronald Schmidt. Ken Olandt, Kristen Dalton, Paul Gleason, Ed Lauter, Don Swayze. (Video/Laser: Republic)

DIMENSIONS IN DEATH. See *Castle of Blood.*

DINOSAUR ISLAND (1994) ★★½ This is one hilariously campy comedy-adventure with a strong attraction for girlwatchers and other lovers of natural things who enjoy watching bountiful women in animal skin bras and panties, jiggling to their hearts' content (if you get our drift). Joining forces to produce and direct this wild male fantasy are Jim Wynorski and Fred Olen Ray, who spare all the subtleties to bring us such wonderful wenches as Michelle Bauer, Toni Naples and Antonia Dorian in all their fleshy glory. The excuse for a plot (by unwriters Bob Sheridan and Christopher Wodden) has a team of professional soldiers stranded on an island where dinosaurs and other monsters (under the care of special effects wizard John Carl Buechler) run wild. The bouncy, bounding broads strip to throw water all over each other (bumping breasts on occasion) and behave as any self-respecting chauvinist pig would demand. The whole thing is a superfunny send-up, but definitely insulting to women. Ross Hagen, Richard Gabai, Steve Barkett, Peter Spellos, Tom Shell. (New Horizons) (Laser: Image)

DINOSAUR: SECRET OF THE LOST LEGEND. See *Baby: Secret of the Lost Legend.*

DINOSAURUS (1960) ★★½ The funniest sci-fi movie ever made—unintentionally, that is. This bizarre variation on the Three Stooges—a prehistoric caveman, a tyrannosaurus and a friendly brontosaurus—will have you in stitches as they run wild on a tropical island after being blasted out of their hibernational digs. One hilarous scene has the caveman (Gregg Martell) fleeing in terror from a woman in pincurlers. The Jean Yeaworth–Dan Weisburd script is side-splitting from beginning to end . . . kids will love it. Paul Lukather, Ward Ramsey, Kristina Hanson. Directed by Irvin S. Yeaworth, Jr., of *Blob* fame. (New World/Starmaker; Sinister/C; S/Weird; Filmfax)

DISASTER IN TIME. See *Grand Tour: Disaster in Time.*

DISCIPLE OF DEATH (1972) ★ Insanely inept, ludicrously laughable British mishmash with Mike Raven as a priest who seeks out virgins,

whom he sacrifices to Satan. Raven is so hammy, and the cast so underdirected by co-producer/coscreenwriter Tom Parkinson, this is hopeless gore-junk. The setting is 18th-century England and there are "Dracula's Brides" and a cackling dwarf. Marguerite Hardiman, Ronnie Lacey, Virginia Wetherell. (Unicorn)

DISCIPLE OF DRACULA. See *Dracula—Prince of Darkness.*

DISCIPLES OF DEATH. See *Enter the Devil.*

DISTORTIONS (1986) ★★½ Slow-paced psychothriller in which it appears Olivia Hussey is having hallucinations following the death of her husband at the hands of a homosexual killer. Insanity, you see, runs in her family. A charred face pops up to haunt her, but discerning viewers will see through the red herrings in John Goff's screenplay. It's saved from total tedium by Steve Railsback as the understanding boyfriend, Piper Laurie as the scheming aunt, June Chadwick as a friend of Olivia's, Rita Gam as a grocery store lady, and Edward Albert as the handsome husband. Director Armand Mastroianni never overcomes the limitations. (Academy)

DISTURBANCE, THE (1989) ★★ Disturbing portrait of a crazy guy (Timothy Greeson) with a mother complex who has a demon inside his body and kills women. Directed by MTV's Cliff Guest and written by Laura Radford. Lisa Geoffrion, Ken Ceresne. (VidAmerica)

DISTURBED (1990) ★★½ Goofball study of psychiatrist (Malcolm McDowell) who goes crazy within the walls of Bergen Field Clinic. Seems that Dr. Russell rapes his pretty patients and forces them to commit suicide. It's goofball because McDowell plays as if he were in a screwball comedy while everyone else maintains straight faces. Director Charles Winkler, who cowrote the wacky script with Emerson Bixby, achieves a dark macabre overtone. The proceedings, including hallucinations and comedy acting by McDowell and Geoffrey Lewis, leads to a twist ending. McDowell's campy performance is joined to Winkler's askew camera angles to suggest madness. Priscilla Pointer is a gas as a devoted nurse and Irwin Keyes and Clint Howard go bonkers as inmates. Pamela Gidley is a victim. (Live) (Laser: Image)

DISTURBING BEHAVIOR (1998) ★★★ Somewhere between *The Stepford Wives* and *Invasion of the Body Snatchers* walks this cautionary tale of what happens when science wants to control us or change us so we conform fully to a standard. James Marsden plays a newcomer to Cradle Bay High School, located on Crescent Island off the coast of Vancouver. He wants to fit in, but unless you're part of the campus's elite Blue Ribbon bunch, you remain an outsider at this oddball school. Strange how those Blue Ribbon members have eyes that suddenly glow red, and they turn angry and get violent, and have superhuman strength to knock down and bloody up their adversaries. Equally unusual is how the parents accept this behavior, all because the Blue Ribbon gang is clean-cut, well dressed, and drawing straight A's. How blind adults are when it comes to images. Nick Stahl is a paranoid pal of Marsden's who's wise to something wrong and tries to warn him, but suddenly Stahl has been turned into one of the automaton nice boys with blue coat and haircut. When Marsden and girlfriend Katie Holmes (another outsider) find out that the organizer of the Blue Ribbon gang (Bruce Greenwood) is a doctor of dubious character practicing neuropharmacology (mind-control science) in a nearby mental institution, they drop in to investigate and discover experiments are going on that change the personalities of the students. From here on, Scott Rosenberg's screenplay gets disturbingly bizarre, with all the hospital's patients behaving like extras in *The Snake Pit,* cop Steve Railsback going maverick, and the local handiman (William Sadler) turning out not to be retarded at all, but wise to the conspiracy and there to help our heroes. Director David Nutter, who made a couple of *Tracers* movies for Charlie Band before directing episodes of *The X-Files,* is really not in control of this overblown material, which is totally lacking in subtlety; conspiracies should be conducted in a low-key, underplayed manner. There is one viscerally exciting scene when Marsden is strapped into the mad doctor's chair and is about to be zombified, and you scream at him to escape. If other parts of the movie had been as well done, *Disturbing Behavior* might have earned a Blue Ribbon of its own. (Video/DVD: MGM)

D.O.A. See *The Monster and the Girl.*

DOC SAVAGE—MAN OF BRONZE (1975) ★★½ George Pal's campy treatment of a pulp magazine superhero (created by Kenneth Robeson) is one of his last—and least—efforts in a distinguished career as a producer of fantasy movies with trend-setting effects. Ron Ely (TV's Tarzan) has eyes that literally sparkle as he embarks on a mission to South America to find the killers of his father. His Fabulous Five, associates skilled in sciences and martial arts, are far from the characters conceived in the stories, making this seem unfaithful to the source novels. Michael Anderson directed, Pal and Joe Morheim adapted. Paul Gleason, Paul Wexler, Pamela Hensley, Carlos Rivas. (Warner Bros.)

DOCTOR AND THE DEVILS, THE (1985) ★★★ Dylan Thomas's script, resurrecting the Burke and Hare case of old Edinburgh, was first written in 1945, but considered too Grand Guignol for a movie until producer Mel Brooks and director Freddie Francis turned it into a morality drama. Timothy Dalton is the self-righteous anatomical instructor Dr. Rock (based on Dr. Knox) who buys corpses from body snatchers Jonathan Pryce and Stephen Rea. Pryce's portrait of a totally evil man is chilling and the period detail fascinating; in fact, it's so real, capturing the poverty of Edinburgh, that it becomes uncomfortable viewing. Twiggy, Julian Sands. (Key)

DOCTOR BLOODBATH. Video version of *Horror Hotel* (Bingo).

DOCTOR BLOOD'S COFFIN (1961) ★★★ Sidney J. Furie cut his directorial teeth (fangs?) on this well-photographed British horror thriller enhanced by rugged coastal Cornwall settings where old tin mines were once active. Peter Blood, son of a doctor (Ian Hunter) who dabbles in the arcane, uses a curare poisoning that paralyzes his victims while he pitilessly experiments on them in a secret cavern. Kieron Moore makes a compelling mad doctor, torn between science and evil, and has the appearance of a decent chap to mislead others. But at heart he's your basic crazed Dr. Frankenstein, raving in the end. Fetching is his nurse, buxom Hazel Court, who screams so beautifully and scrambles across the rocks poised on her high heels. Nicolas Roeg served as camera operator for this intriguing film. Kenneth J. Warren, Andy Alston, Fred Johnson, Paul Stockman. (Alpha; Sinister/C; Dark Dreams; S/Weird; Filmfax)

DOCTOR OF DOOM (1960) ★ First in Mexico's "Wrestling Women" series (aka *Wrestling Women vs. the Aztec Mummy*) in which brain transplants by a mad doctor leave several empty craniums, one of which was the producer's. Heroic Golden Rubi and Gloria Venus take on gorilla Gomar and her pain-brain companion, Vendetta, in this attempt to liven up the Aztec Mummy by surrounding him/it/whatever with shapely femmes. Written with grunts and groans by Alfred Salazar, directed by Rene Cardona. Armando Silvestre, Lorena Velasquez. (Sinister/C; Hollywood Home; Timeless; Filmfax; from Rhino as *Rock 'n' Roll Wrestling Women vs. the Aztec Mummy*)

DOCTORS WEAR SCARLET. See *Bloodsuckers* (1970).

DOCTOR WHO (1996) ★★★ This British-U.S. TV-movie is just wild and crazy enough to satisfy fans of the ongoing BBC science fiction series about a "time lord" who travels through time and space in a phonebooth. In this special effects–laden adventure, written by Matthew Jacobs, an evil entity called "The Master" (who takes over the body of paramedic Eric Roberts) winds up on Earth in 1999 and uses the Eye of Tardes to try and suck the Earth through a vortex (or something like that). Who (Paul McGann) and doctor Daphne Ashbrook, with the help of pleasant young hoodlum Yee Jee Tso, set out to prevent the apocalypse. Director Geoffrey Sax gives it plenty of razzle-dazzle. Sylvester McCoy, John Wovak.

DOCTOR X (1932) ★★★ This early Warner Bros. horror Technicolor whodunit is set in the Gothic house of Blackstone Shoals, where "The Full Moon Killer" is one of several eccentric doctors Lionel Atwill has gathered to reenact the crimes, which consist of a scalpel insertion at the base of the neck and cannibalism. Atwill's performance is intriguing, but other characters are stereotyped, such as Fay Wray as the daughter always screaming at the sight of her mysterious father, and Lee Tracy's wisecracking reporter, disruptive to the somber mood established by director Michael Curtiz. Despite predictabilities, *Dr. X* retains a nostalgic charm and morbid fascination. Preston Foster, Mae Busch. (Video/Laser: MGM/UA)

DOGMA (1999) ★★½ This is a difficult movie for serious-minded Catholics who don't feel their religion should be the brunt of outrageous iconologist humor, and it's going to be a difficult movie for non-Catholics who might miss some of the finer points about the religion. It's also going to be a difficult movie for moviegoers who couldn't care less about Catholics, irreverence and bad taste, and just want to have a movie that keeps them entertained. For writer-director Kevin Smith allows his characters to talk on screen incessantly. They are often satirizing aspects of modern religion and probing the strengths and weaknesses of Catholicism, but the conversations become too convoluted. Instead of being the benevolent souls depicted on TV's *Touched by an Angel,* Smith's beings from heaven talk and act as if they were modern teenagers, using foul language, brandishing weapons, speaking street slang, and even resorting to physical violence. The plot is a dense thicket of ideas and characters: Outcast angels Loki (Matt Damon) and Bartelby (Ben Affleck), who are killing all the sinners they meet, want to get back into Heaven and have found a loophole circumventing God's will. However, once back to the celestial cloud, the two angels will cause God's downfall and that will result in the end of existence for all things. So the Voice of the Lord (Alan Rickman, playing a world-weary angel beautifully) appeals for help from an earthling (Linda Fiorentino, who turns out to be "the great-great-great-great-great-great grandniece of Jesus Christ"), the 13th Apostle (Chris Rock), The Muse (Salma Hayek, who also plays a stripper), and two oddball angels (Jason Mewes and Kevin Smith). Together they fight off some demons from Hell and meet an ugly creature that comes out of a toilet and is called "The Shit Monster." (This is one time when Smith goes totally wrong.) It's difficult to describe the odyssey that finally takes them to New Jersey for an apocalyptic showdown at the doors of a Catholic church that has just introduced (with the help of priest George Carlin) a new statue of Jesus called "Buddy Christ" and a less depressing version of the crucifix. Suffice to say, the story becomes such a mishmash of inexplicable events and characters that the satire finally collapses under its own weight. (Video/DVD: Lion's Gate)

DOGS (1976) ★ Man's Best Friend does an about-tail and doglegs to the left to chase after (or retrieve, in the case of bird dogs) human flesh as though it were upgraded Kal-Kan. This film's bite is worse than its bark as the murderous mutts, cursed curs and psychopurebreds take over management of all pounds and kennels. What a time they have with fire hydrants, with the SPCA out of business. David McCallum leads the human pack, with Linda Gray nipping at his heels. No puppy love in this family. Directed by Burt Brinckerhoff on point, who hounded the cast for better performances, and written by O'Brian Tomalin, who loves to be scratched behind his ears. Therein lies the tail of this tale.

DOGS OF HELL (1982) ★ Regional filmmaker Earl Owensby shot this in Georgia in 3-D as *Rottweiler.* An Army experiment involving surgical implants in animals turns Rottweilers into killers, a "loss of human affection response." The dogs escape and invade the Lake Lure resort, where campers, farmers and passerby die horribly in the jaws of the killer pack. Tom McIntyre's script takes forever to get yipping and director Worth Keeter dogs it. Producer Owensby also plays the sheriff but he's without bite. Robert Bloodworth, Bill Gribble, Kathy Hasty, Ed Lilliard, Jerry Rushing. (Media)

DOIN' TIME ON PLANET EARTH (1988) ★★½ Oddball comedy about misfit Nicholas Strouse in Sunnydale, AZ, who is told by his computer that he is an alien and it's time to go home. He's visited by other oddballs (Adam West and Candice Azzara) who claim they too are aliens, and they want Ryan to turn his father's revolving restaurant atop a Holiday Inn into a flying saucer for the flight home. Screenwriter Darren Star never makes it explicit if this is real or in Ryan's imagination, but one thing is sure: Andrea Thompson plays a sexy lounge singer who helps Ryan "explode" the DNA knowledge in his system. Directed by Charles Matthau (son of Walter), this has cute moments, but ultimately is forgettable. Hugh Gillin, Gloria Henry, Hugh O'Brian, Martha Scott, Roddy McDowall, Maureen Stapleton. (Warner Bros.)

DOLLMAN (1990) ★½ One of the lesser efforts of video producer Charles Band, beneath his usual production standards. The effects never believably integrate a 13-inch-high humanoid policeman with the full-scale humans. This wee guy hails from the planet Arturos and crashlands on Earth while in pursuit of a villain in the form of a floating head (and we don't mean a portable toilet). Tim Thomerson essays the psychotic, triggerhappy cop Brick Bardos in a flat fashion and director Albert Pyun fails to trick up shots convincingly. Screenwriter Chris Roghair deals with the characters on a shallow level, especially a young mother and her son trapped in the ghetto of New York. This only snorts to life when Pyun uses documentary techniques to capture street life in the Bronx, where the film was shot. Jackie Earle Haley, Kamala Lopez. The sequel: *Dollman vs. the Demonic Toys*. (Paramount) (Laser: Pioneer)

DOLLMAN VS. THE DEMONIC TOYS (1993) ★ Charles Band crossover vidflick teaming space cop Brick Bardo (13 inches in height) from *Dollman* with the shrunken nurse Ginger ("Doll Chick") from *Bad Channels* to fight the ugly entities introduced in *Demonic Toys*. Back as cop Judith Grey (from *Demonic Toys*) is Tracy Scoggins, who hires Bardo (Tim Thomerson, star of the *Trancers* series) and Ginger (sexy and appealing Melissa Behr) to do battle against the evil playthings, including Baby Upsy Daisy and a new one, Zombie Man. Despite all the tricks, producer-director Band can't make the miniaturization theme believable and Craig Hamann's script, in spite of all the talent at work, falls flat. Phil Brock, Phil Fondacardo, William C. Carpenter. Soundtrack by Quiet Riot. (Paramount) (Laser: Full Moon)

DOLLS (1986) ★★½ Ed Naha's predictable script has stranded travelers trapped in the mansion of a couple that specializes in making dolls—more to the point, of turning humans into miniaturized entities they control for evil purposes. Guy Rolfe and Hilary Mason are good in these benevolent-malevolent roles. Carrie Lorraine is a lovable child who discovers the couple's secret and tries to warn the adults. There's enough gore to please the splatter freaks, and one or two nice scenes as the dolls, en masse, close in for the kill. But there's nothing in this film that hasn't been done before, and one wonders what extraordinary director Stuart Gordon saw in it. Ian Patrick Williams, Carolyn Purdy-Gordon. (Vestron)

DOLLY DEAREST (1991) ★★★ You thought Chucky was yucky. Here's a ripoff that humiliates the screen's goriest killer doll with a female counterpart that can be just as homicidal. The body of a toy is filled with the spirit of Sanzia the Devil Child, a Mexican spawn of Satan. When a tomb is desecrated, the spirit escapes to a toyshop where the Dolly Dearest models are infected with evil—so you got skirt-wearing Chuckies running round trying to kill archeologist Rip Torn, toymaker Sam Bottoms, wife Denise Crosby and their two kids (Chris Demetral, Candy Hutson). Writer-director Maria Lease should pay residuals to the Chucky creators. Lupe Ontirveros, Will Gotay, Alma Martinez. (Video/Laser: Vidmark)

DOMINION (1995) ★★★ In yet another variation on *The Most Dangerous Game*, six hunters venture into the wilderness on a hunting trip only to face the wrath of a madman, driven to slaughtering innocent game stalkers after his young son was accidentally shot to death in the forest. In this direct-to-video feature, there's little depth to Brion James's homicidal tendencies (he's portrayed as a typically mindless slasher killer) as he drives his bayonet into bodies and shoots hunters at random. The frail script (by director Michael Kehoe and actor/coproducer Woody Brown) is strengthened by the presence of Brad Johnson as a vacationing cop who demonstrates heroic prowess under fire and Tim Thomerson as his buddy, a wisecracking bartender who does John Wayne impressions. Some of the sequences consist of suspenseful cross-cutting, and there's a good piece of action on a suspension bridge, but this is standard stuff, showing little ingenuity, with an unresolved ending suggesting there might be a sequel. Steve Gianelli, Richard Riehle, Geoffrey Blake. (Turner)

DOMINIQUE. See *Dominique Is Dead*.

DOMINIQUE IS DEAD (1978) ★★★ Millionaire Cliff Robertson is grieving over the death of wife Jean Simmons when he sees her spectral image in the hall. The spirit continues to haunt him, and while he should wise up to the possibility of Hitchcockian tricks, he's a real fall guy to the end. This kind of pseudosupernatural thriller has been done to death, but director Michael Anderson injects it with class. Edward and Valerie Abraham adapted Harold Lawlor's *What Beckoning Ghost*. Jenny Agutter, Simon Ward. (Prism; from Impulse and Simitar as *Avenging Spirit*)

DONOR (1991) ★★★½ Macabre, gory TV-movie is a rehash of *Coma* and *X-Ray* in which an aspiring, easily-made-hysterical doctor (Melissa Gilbert-Brinkman) uncovers a hospital conspiracy to exploit indigent patients for their pituitary glands and create a new formula for agelessness. A scalpel killer stalks Melissa, leading to a grisly sequence in a formaldehyde corpse tank. Effective script by Michael Braverman, directed for shock values by Larry Shaw. Jack Scalia is Melissa's love interest, Pernell Roberts is the chief of staff, Marc Lawrence is an aging patient and Gregory Sierra is a baffled cop.

DONOR, THE (1994) ★★★ A nightmarish air of conspiracy and paranoia so surrounds movie stuntman Billy Castle (Jeff Wincott), the central character in this Canadian-produced medical mystery thriller, that *The Donor* gives plenty in terms of suspense, duplicity and surprising twists of plot as conceived by scriptwriters Neal and Tippi Dobrofsky. Wincott is seduced one night and wakes up the next morning to discover one of his kidneys is gone—taken by a gang of organ transplanters. The psychological traumas he undergoes, his therapies, his suspicions—all contribute to this offbeat, thoughtful study in character and terror directed by Damian Lee. Michelle Johnson, Gordon Thomson, Richard Zeppieri, Joseph Scorsiani. (Imperial)

DONOR UNKNOWN (1995) ★★★ Good thriller with mild horrific overtones is enhanced by Peter Onorati's excellent performance as a tough insurance investigator who undergoes a heart attack and awakens with a transplanted heart. Curious about the donor, Onorati discovers he's at the center of a transplant racket involving crooked doctor Sam Robards and sadistic ex-cop Clancy Brown. The psychological implications and nightmarish world in which Onorati finds himself are ably captured by director John Harrison, who based his script on William H. Mooney's novel *Corazon*. Alice Krige is also fine as Onorati's wife. Leo Garcia, Christina Solis. (Video/Laser: MCA)

DONOVAN'S BRAIN (1953) ★★★½ Curt Siodmak's classic novel (first produced in 1943 as *The Lady and the Monster*) was remade by producer Tom Gries into a superior version thanks to the literate writing and direction by Felix Feist. Well-meaning scientist Lew Ayres keeps a tyrannical tycoon's brain alive in a solution, but the brain gains mental control, forcing Ayres to commit acts against his will. Chillingly effective. Nancy Davis (now better known as Nancy Reagan), Steve Brodie, Gene Evans, Tom Powers. (MGM/UA) (Laser: Image)

DON'T ANSWER THE PHONE (1981) ★½ Aka *The Hollywood Strangler*, this was (un)inspired by the L.A. Hillside Strangler case. A disturbed Vietnam vet (Nicholas Worth) rushes around Hollywood, choking women with a stocking. The violence is gratuitous and has no redeeming values, nor does the Michael Castle script shed insight into psychopathic killers. The couch is empty for writer-producer-director Robert Hammer. James Westmoreland, Pamela Bryant. (Media)

DON'T CRY WOLF. See *The Crawling Hand*.

DON'T GO IN THE HOUSE (1980) ★½ Sicko movie mess about a psycho (Dan Gramaldi) whose mother burned him as a kid, so now he sets naked women on fire with his flame-thrower and watches them burn, all because he hates his now-deceased mother—and all women remind him of her. He keeps the charred corpses in his private charnel house. Written-directed by Joseph Ellison; produced by Ellen Hammill, who cowrote this insultive diatribe against women with Ellison and Joseph Masefield. Don't go in the theater. (Media)

DON'T GO IN THE WOODS (1980) ★ Knife-killer low-budget exploitationer from producer-director Jim Bryan and word-chopper Garth Eliasson. Buck Carradine, Mary Gail Artz and James P. Hayden can't see the forest through the trees. (Media; Vestron)

DON'T LOOK IN THE ATTIC (1981) ★★ A film about a haunted house that contains the spirits of cows. Say, are they trying to milk the supernatural theme? One hopes the producers had plenty of pull. Directed by Carl Ausino. Jean-Pierre Aumont. (Mogul)

DON'T LOOK IN THE BASEMENT (1973) ★★★ An aura of madness clings to this low-budget, a credit to producer-director S. F. Brownrigg and writer Tim Pope. In an insane asylum, nurse Rosie Holotik takes over after the previous director was axed to death. Gradually the inmates seize the asylum and the film sinks into a snake pit of insanity. Full of thrills and shocks. Ann McAdams, William McGee, Gene Ross. (VCI; Gorgon; MPI; VidAmerica)

DON'T LOOK NOW (1973) ★★★½ Daphne du Maurier's story becomes an engrossing psychological horror film directed by Nicolas Roeg, featuring erotic love scenes between Donald Sutherland and Julie Christie. Sutherland, a restorer of European churches, foresees his daughter's drowning. His power of prescience increases—and so does the inexplicable mystery. Ambiguous and enigmatic, but its psychic themes are fascinating. Hilary Mason, Clelia Matania. (Video/Laser: Paramount)

DON'T OPEN THE DOOR (1979) ★★ The maker of *Don't Look in the Basement*, S. F. Brownrigg, is back with another woman (Susan Bracken) faced with madness when she returns to Texas to ponder who stabbed mother to death. A sense of sexual depravity makes this unpleasantly compelling when Ms. Bracken realizes a transvestite killer is in her house. Psycho wackos galore. Gene Ross, Annabelle Weenick. (Video Gems)

DON'T OPEN THE DOOR. See *The Orphan*.

DON'T OPEN TILL CHRISTMAS (1984) ★★★ He's making a kill list and checking it twice in Britain's answer to *Silent Night, Deadly Night*, with a psycho killer knocking off English Santas. The murders are graphic: a spear through the mouth, a cleaver across the face, two strangulations, a terrifying castration and knife plunges into stomachs. The suspense is well handled by director Edmund Purdom, especially a stalking sequence in the London Dungeon. Purdom also plays a Scotland Yard cop on the case. Caroline Munro appears in a skin-tight dress. Written by Derek Ford. Belinda Mayne. (Vestron)

DON'T WALK IN THE PARK. See *Kill, Baby, Kill*.

DOOM ASYLUM (1988) ★★ Long-dead Michael Rogan springs to life like a trampoline acrobat to kill in this comedy slasher flick, shot in New Jersey by Richard (*Deathmask*) Friedman. Gore aplenty plus clips from Tod Slaughter pics. Patty Mullen, Ruth Collins. (Academy)

DOOM OF DRACULA. Early title of *House of Frankenstein*.

DOOMSDAY. See *Escape from Planet Earth*.

DOOMSDAY MACHINE, THE. See *Escape from Planet Earth*.

DOOMWATCH (1972) ★★½ Chemicals dumped into waters surrounding a British island create human mutations when fish netted from the waters are eaten. Directed by Peter Sasdy; written by Clive Exton from a British TV special. Some hideously good monster makeup. Ian Bannen, Judy Geeson, George Sanders, Percy Herbert, Simon Oates, George Woodbridge. (Monterey; Embassy)

DOORMAN, THE. See *Too Scared to Scream*.

DOPPELGANGER (1969). See *Journey to the Far Side of the Sun*.

DOPPELGANGER: THE EVIL WITHIN (1992) ★★★½ A better-than-average genre horror film—thanks to writer-director Avi Nesher for creating two interesting L.A. culture characters, the sexy performance of Drew Barrymore and a couple of gooey but effective monsters. The characters are movie writer Patrick Highsmith (George Newbern), a likable nerd who klutzes his way to victory over evil, and his cowriter, a sharp-tongued, amusing young woman played by Leslie Hope. The pouty, exotic Barrymore—always in high heels and minidresses when she isn't stripping to make love to Newbern—undergoes a split personality, or a supernatural evil half is walking around outside her body. Nesher's ability to create ambiguity enhances the film's suspense. At the climax, in a bit of monster-shop tour de force, Barrymore splits into two alien-looking entities, fights a battle with evil, then merges back together. George Maharis and Sally Kellerman are wasted in bit roles. Dennis Christopher, Stanley De Santis, Peter Dobson, Dan Shor. (CBS/Fox's videobox bears the above title, but the print itself reads only *Doppelganger*.) (Laser: CBS/Fox)

DORM THAT DRIPPED BLOOD, THE (1981) ★ Formula stuff from writers-producers-directors Jeffrey Obrow and Stephen Carpenter, a killer-on-the-loose, dumb-trapped-teenagers story set in Dayton Hall, which is closed for renovation. That gives the characters lonely rooms to wander in while the slasher-basher stalks them. The kids are given little to do but scream and die. Downbeat ending. Laurie Lapinski, Stephen Sachs, Daphne Zuniga. Aka *Death Dorm* and *Pranks*. (Media)

DOUBLE, DOUBLE, TOIL AND TROUBLE (1993) ★★★ This light-hearted Halloween TV-movie proves to be a worthy showcase for Cloris Leachman, who portrays twin sisters—one is an evil witch who uses a green moonstone to work her diabolical stuff, the other is a benevolent lady trapped in a mirror by magic. Leachman plots against young twin sisters Mary-Kate and Ashley Olsen when they join forces with a black vagrant, a gnome and a frightened grave digger to steal the moonstone and free the imprisoned sister. A delightful touch prevails throughout this pleasant family diversion written and directed by Jeff Franklin. Meshach Taylor, Phil Fondacaro, Eric McCormach. (Warner Bros.)

DOUBLE DRAGON (1995) ★★★ Call this one *Bill & Ted Meet Fu Manchu*. It's a Kitchen Sink comedy-adventure with something for everyone: martial arts fighting; skinhead gangs; car chases; ample explosions; computerized animation and effects; motorboat stunts; and walking zombies. There's nothing to be taken seriously in the Michael Davis–Peter Gould script in which evil Robert Patrick wants to take control of New Angeles A.D. 2007 with the use of a mythical medallion. But he has only half the medallion—two nerds, the Lee Brothers, have the other half and so they fight for 90 minutes. Director James Yukich bolsters this nothing premise with an army of stuntmen performing vigorous athletics. It's mirthy, mindless mayhem with George Hamilton putting in a campy cameo as a TV broadcaster. Patrick has a lot of fun and so does the rest of the cast: Julia Nickson, Alyssa Milano, Mark Dacascos, Scott Wolf, and Michael Berrymore (in a too-brief cameo). Especially good is Kristina Malandro Wagner as Lash, a sadistic brunette who swings a wicked whip. (Video/Laser: MCA/DVD: GoodTimes)

DOUBLE EXPOSURE (1981) ★★ A slasher film (aka *The Photographer*) about an ice-pick murderer stalking L.A. prostitutes . . . focus shifts to a girlie mag photographer (Michael Callan) who fears he is the killer. He suffers from dreams in which he slaughters his models (in one case by sticking her head into a bag containing a rattlesnake). Is he dreaming or did he commit these heinous crimes? Not even psychiatrist Seymour Cassel knows for certain. Callan's relationship with his one-armed, one-legged brother (James Stacy) is a mixture of repressed affection, macho backslapping and sibling rivalry. Pamela Hensley and Robert Tessier are cops working with chief Cleavon Little but their contributions are minor as writer-director William Byron Hillman keeps focus on Callan and girlfriend Joanna Pettet. A peculiar non sequitur to the genre. (Vestron)

DOUBLE GARDEN, THE (1970) ★★ Mad doctor James Craig uses thunder and lightning to turn carnivorous plants into man-eating bloodsuckers. (From Regal as *The Revenge of Dr. X*)

DOUBLE JEOPARDY. See *Olivia*.

DOUBLE POSSESSION. See *Ganja and Hess*.

DRACULA (1931) ★★★★ Bela Lugosi's performance is the saving grace of this Universal milestone movie, establishing the vampire formula for all time. Tod Browning's direction is strangely static, and the Garrett Ford–Dudley Murphy adaptation (from the Hamilton Deane–John Balderston play, in turn from Bram Stoker's novel) is as stuffy as the drawing room in which too much of the action is set. Only the early Transylvania sequences, when Renfield (Dwight Frye) coaches across the eerie moor and arrives at the Gothic Dracula castle, convey the atmosphere the rest of the film screams for. It is the affected stage-style acting of Lugosi, the malignant evil he suggests, and the hypnotic spell he holds over females that keeps one rapt. The supporting cast becomes mired in the stilted style of the period. Edward Van Sloan portrays the Van Helsing character, Helen Chandler one of Dracula's victims. Makeup by Jack Pierce (who also did Karloff's Frankenstein Monster), cinematography by Karl Freund. (Video/Laser: MCA)

DRACULA (1931) ★★★★ A Spanish-language version of Tod Browning's *Dracula* with a different cast but on the same sets and with the same costumes, lighting and production values. George Melford directed, and some feel he did as good a job, if not better, as Browning. Carlos Villarias plays Dracula. Lupita Tovar, Eduardo Arozamena, Pablo Alvarez Rubio. (MCA)

DRACULA (1958). See *Horror of Dracula*.

DRACULA (1973) ★★★½ Richard Matheson scripted this Dan Curtis TV-film which met mixed reaction: Many critics felt it was slow-paced and dull, others were encouraged to see Jack Palance attempt a sympathetic, tormented portrait of the King of Vampires. This refreshing shift of pace is worth the serious buff's attention. Nigel Davenport appears as Van Helsing. Simon Ward, Fiona Lewis. Directed by Curtis. (MPI; IVE) (Laser: MPI)

DRACULA (1974). See *Andy Warhol's Dracula*.

DRACULA (1979) ★★★★ Stylish, atmospheric remake of the hoary old Hamilton Deane–John Balderston play (based on Bram Stoker's historic novel). Frank Langella, fresh from the Broadway version, is a sensual, sexy vampire radiating an uncommon amount of lust as he seduces Van Helsing's daughter. That foe of vampires is essayed with passionate histronics by Sir Laurence Olivier. Walter Mirisch's production reeks with period decor and costumes, with enough bloodletting and "undead" chills to satisfy specialty crowds as well as general audiences. Well directed by John Badham, with some startling shots of Dracula crawling along the side of a building. Donald Pleasence, Kate Nelligan, Trevor Eve. Score by John Williams. (Video/Laser: MCA)

DRACULA: A CINEMATIC SCRAPBOOK (1990) ★★½ Subtitled "A Treasury of Trailers Starring the Thirsty Transylvanian," this is a one-hour, fun-to-watch compilation of minimal narration and previews of coming attractions beginning with the original Bela Lugosi *Dracula* and winding up with the Hammer series starring Christopher Lee. Highlights include the *London After Midnight* trailer, some *Spooks Run Wild* footage, an occasional Lugosi tidbit ("I gave all of me! I was more real than any vampire!") and color footage from *Scared to Death*. Written-directed by Ted Newsom. (Rhino)

DRACULA A.D. 1972 (1972) ★★★ With its throbbing rock 'n' roll soundtrack, and its lack of Gothic trappings and atmosphere with Dracula and Van Helsing in contemporary England, Hammer broke too much tradition for its own good, perhaps, yet this entry in the series holds up pretty good. In this one, Drac is resurrected by a gang of modish partiers and avenges himself against a descendant of Professor Van Helsing. Peter Cushing, after an 11-year absence from the series, is back as the updated Van Helsing, tracking the vampire to an old church after his beautiful granddaughter (the wonderfully busty Stephanie Beacham, and she really lets it all hang out) has been lured into Drac's domain. Christopher Lee is still imposing as the bloodsucker with the bloodshot eyes and his battles with Cushing are well staged, although some of the demises are based on now-predictable clichés, and some effects have dated. Directed by Alan Gibson, written by Don Houghton. Caroline Munro, Marsha Hunt, Philip Miller, Michael Kitchen, Christopher Neame. Original titles: *Dracula Today, Dracula '72, Dracula Chelsea '72, Dracula Chases the Mini Girls*. The next in this Hammer series: *The Satanic Rites of Dracula*. (Warner Bros.)

DRACULA AGAINST FRANKENSTEIN. See *Dracula vs. Dr. Frankenstein*.

DRACULA & SON (1976) ★★ Mixture of horror, comedy and political polemic: The Communists ruling Transylvania feel vampires are bad for the party's image, so Dracula and son are exiled to England, where the film community welcomes them as stars. But talk about typecasting: the boys are hired to play cinema vampires. Directed and cowritten by Eduardo Molinaro. Christopher Lee, Bernard Menez, Raymond Bussieres, Anna Gael. (Goodtimes; Columbia TriStar)

DRACULA AND THE SEVEN GOLDEN VAMPIRES. See *The Legend of the Seven Golden Vampires*.

DRACULA CHASES THE MINI GIRLS. See *Dracula A.D. 1972*.

DRACULA CHELSEA '72. See *Dracula A.D. 1972*.

DRACULA: DEAD AND LOVING IT (1995) ★★★½ Mel Brooks in harness, eschewing toilet-room jokes and raunchy sexual references? Excuse the irreverence, but maybe Mel is just getting old. Whatever Mel's excuse, this parody of Bram Stoker's famous vampire novel, and the countless movie adaptations since the Bela Lugosi version in the early '30s, is an experiment in Brooksian restraint, coming off as a family comedy with most of the jokes tasteful (if you'll excuse the expression). While it's missing the madcap fun of *Young Frankenstein*, it is something of a joy to behold Leslie Nielsen doing his takeoff on the infamous Count in the company of Peter McNicol as an amusing Renfield, producer-director Brooks as Van Helsing (who has the funniest lines in the picture) and beautiful Amy Yasbeck and Lysette Anthony as the lovely ladies whose throats are pursued by old Drac. Strangely enough, Brooks is very faithful to the original novel (the script is by Brooks, Rudy De Luca and Steve Haberman) and, if the funny asides had been removed, almost plays as a straightforward horror film. Two sequences stand out as having the Brooks touch—Steven Weber (as Jonathan Harker) staking one of Dracula's brides and getting drenched with blood, and Renfield eating insects while Dr. Seward (Harvey Korman) has breakfast on the lawn. Cameo appearances by Clive Revill, Mark Blankfield, Anne Bancroft (as a gypsy woman), Avery Schreiber and Cherie Franklin. (Video/Laser: Columbia)

DRACULA HAS RISEN FROM THE GRAVE (1968) ★★½ Heavy (handed) use of religious symbolism earmarks this third film in Hammer's series to star Christopher Lee as the infamous count. In John Elder's (actually John Samson and Anthony Hinds) script he is reduced to a one-dimensional vampire suggesting tons of evil but unsupported by a strong plot. Two priests climb to Castle Dracula to resurrect the antihero and control his bloodletting for purposes of revenge. A giant crucifix figures ludicrously in the blood-gushing climax. Many scenes were shot through a red filter to cast a sanguinary motif, but this technique, a poor choice by director Freddie Francis, calls attention to itself whenever the camera pans. The beauteous Veronica Carlson is an eyeful in her flimsy nightgowns. Rupert Davies, Barbara Ewing, Michael Ripper. Good music by James Bernard. Next in this Hammer series: *Taste the Blood of Dracula*. (Video: Warner Bros.) (Japanese laser: Warner Bros.)

DRACULA IN THE CASTLE OF BLOOD. See *Web of the Spider*.

DRACULA IS DEAD . . . AND WELL AND LIVING IN LONDON. See *Count Dracula and His Vampire Bride*.

DRACULA—PRINCE OF DARKNESS (1965) ★★★ After *Horror of Dracula*, Christopher Lee refused to reappear as the Count for several years. This Anthony Nelson Keys–produced film, however, lured him back into the fold of the cape, so it is often referred to as the sequel to *Horror* even though another Hammer feature, *The Brides of Dracula*, was produced in 1960. Two English couples traveling through Transylvania spend the night at you-know-who's castle, where the bloodsucker is restored to life in a bizarre ceremony, a perversion on religious resurrection. Then old Drac goes after Barbara Shelley and Suzan Farmer to make them new "brides." One of the best films in the series, directed by Terence Fisher from a script by John Samson and Anthony Hinds writing as John Elder. Aka *Disciple of Dracula, Dracula 3, Revenge of Dracula* and *The Bloody Scream of Dracula*.

DRACULA, PRISONER OF FRANKENSTEIN. See *Dracula vs. Dr. Frankenstein*.

DRACULA RISING (1992) ★★★½ Unusually ethereal, metaphysical vampire tale from producer Roger Corman, with Stacey Travis as a painter hired to restore old paintings in a European monastery where she is introduced to the ways of bloodsucking by vampire Vlad (handsome Christopher Atkins). With good location work under director Fred Gallo, and a literate script by Rodman Flender and Daniella Purcell, this comes off as one of Corman's better efforts. Doug Wert, Tara McCann. (New Horizons) (Laser: Image)

DRACULA'S CASTLE. TV title for *Blood of Dracula's Castle*.

DRACULA'S DAUGHTER (1936) ★★½ Vintage Universal production picks up where *Dracula* left off—with Professor Van Helsing (again played by Edward Van Sloan) under arrest for murdering the Transylvanian Count (after all, he did drive a stake through the chap's cold, cold heart). Female offspring Gloria Holden goes on a new spree of murder. Let the name of Countess Marya Zaleska drip with blood! The film is okay as a time-killer but has none of the legendary proponents of its predecessor. Directed by Lambert Hillyer, scripted by Garrett Fort. Otto Kruger, Marguerite Churchill, Irving Pichel, Hedda Hopper, E. E. Clive. (Video/Laser: MCA)

DRACULA'S DESIRE. See *My Son, the Vampire*.

DRACULA'S DOG (1978) ★ Nonclassic goes to the dogs with a howling-funny plot in which a Romanian tomb under Soviet guard is disturbed and a vampire slave (Reggie Nalder) escapes his coffin. Since the last descendant of Dracula now lives a normal life in L.A., the gnarly-faced entity, accompanied by the vampiric hound Zoltan, travels to America. The untainted Dracula (Michael Pataki) has taken his family on a vacation, so most of this cheap Albert Band–directed film takes place at a lake with the toady siccing devil dogs (the Baskerville variety, with blazing demonic eyes) on hapless humans. One harrowing sequence has Soviet policeman Mel Ferrer and Pataki trapped in a tiny 1-room shack; another that anticipates *Cujo* has Pataki trapped in his car. Jan Shutan, Libbie Chase. (United; from Thorn EMI and VCI as *Zoltan—Hound of Dracula*)

DRACULA '71. See *Count Dracula.*

DRACULA '72. See *Dracula A.D. 1972.*

DRACULA'S GREAT LOVE (1973) ★★★ Reedited version of a Spanish film imitating the Hammer style, the eighth and final entry in the Waldemar Daninsky werewolf series starring Paul Naschy. Previously you were subjected to *Frankenstein's Bloody Terror, Nights of the Werewolf, The Werewolf vs. the Vampire Women, Assignment Terror, Fury of the Wolfman, Dr. Jekyll and the Werewolf* and *The Hunchback of the Morgue.* What more could you ask to see? So get with it, for this has good set designs and costumes, but . . . acting and story line are as anemic as the victims of the old Count, 4 lovely señoritas hanging out in an abandoned sanitorium. Dubbing is listless, blood effects are heavily edited and plot sorely in need of a hero. Drac seeks a virgin so he can restore his "evil superiority" and allow his long-dead daughter to rise from her crypt. Paul Naschy is the fanged creature with a more gentle side than most vampires. The swelling bosoms belong to Rossana Yanni, Ingrid Garbo and Mista Miller. Aka *The Great Love of Count Dracula, Count Dracula's Greatest Love, Cemetery Girls, Cemetery Tramps* and *Dracula's Virgin Lovers.* Written-directed by Javier Aguirre. After this eighth in a series, Naschy buried Daninsky once and for all and went on to make unconnected supernatural thrillers. (MPI; Gorgon; Sinister/C)

DRACULA'S LAST RITES (1980) ★★ Alucard is now in the cover-up business: He's the mortician in a town where folks don't catch on when you murder them by sucking their blood. Spell his name backwards (as they did in *Son of Dracula*) and you discover the nature of the walking dead around him. Aka *Last Rites*, something this film needed from the start. Written-directed by Dominic Paris. Patricia Lee Hammond, Gerald Fielding. (Paragon; Warner Bros.; Cannon)

DRACULA'S VIRGIN LOVERS. Video version of *Dracula's Great Love.*

DRACULA'S WIDOW (1988) ★½ That *Emmanuelle* gal, Sylvia Kristel, as a vampire named Vanessa, "the true wife of Dracula"? Just because Sylvia did a lot of sucking in some of her previous films was no reason to typecast the poor girl in this, a cheapie, creepy, sleepy little nothing movie. Her coffin is delivered to the Hollywood House of Wax where she begins a reign of terror, mesmerizing museum curator Lenny Von Dohlen, wiping out a devil cult and chasing after a descendant of Van Helsing (his grandson is now an L.A. antiques collector).

The numerous murders are done without style or imagination, and Sylvia is really a terrible vampire, performing without charm or menace, and not even providing anything sexy to the part. Stephen Traxler, who gave us *Slithis*, was one of the producers. Written by Kathryn Ann Thomas and Christopher Coppola; Coppola also directed this undistinguished, ho-hum affair. Josef Summer, Marc Coppola, Rachel Jones. (HBO)

DRACULA, THE GREAT UNDEAD (1985) ★★ Recycled TV documentary hosted by Vincent Price, detailing the myths surrounding blood-sucking vampires. Strictly historical stuff with a few clips of Bela Lugosi. (Active; Videotakes; Facets Multimedia)

DRACULA: THE LOVE STORY. See *To Die For.*

DRACULA 3. See *Dracula—Prince of Darkness.*

DRACULA TODAY. See *Dracula A.D. 1972.*

DRACULA VS. DR. FRANKENSTEIN (1972) ★★ Spanish-French concoction blending werewolves, vampires and beasties of the night. Written-directed by the indomitable Jesus Franco. Dennis Price plays the bad doctor badly, Howard Vernon plays the vampire vampily. Aka *Dracula, Prisoner of Frankenstein.* (From VCI as *The Screaming Dead*; with subtitles as *Erotic Rites of Frankenstein*)

DRACULA VS. FRANKENSTEIN (1970). Video version of *Assignment Terror* (United American).

DRACULA VS. FRANKENSTEIN (1971) ★ Depressingly bad pastiche of Universal horror pictures of the '40s has a campy nostalgia, brought about by a cast that has gone to that great graveyard in the sky. Lon Chaney, Jr., and J. Carrol Naish were in their declining, almost decrepit, years. The makeup is dreadful, the lighting amateurish and the music track horrendous, and yet one pines for these gallant scare-stalwarts of the screen. The ludicrous plot (by schlockers W. Pugsley and Samuel M. Sherman) is a hodgepodge of creatures and motiveless actions. Al Adamson directed in his shamelessly bad way. Forrest J. Ackerman has a bit role as a victim. Aka *Blood of Frankenstein, They're Coming to Get You, The Blood Seekers, Satan's Bloody Freaks* and *Teenage Dracula.* Anthony Eisley, Regina Carol, Jim, Davis, Zandor Vorkov, Russ Tamblyn. (VidAmerica; Sony; Super; from Duravision as *Revenge of Dracula*)

DRAGONFIGHT (1990) ★★★½ Fascinating metaphor for the immoral behavior of corporations during the '80s, couched in metaphysical images and presented as a morality play within an action frame. In a futuristic society, corporations earn millions by staging gladiatorial contests. But fighter Falchion (Paul Coufos) rebels against the system, refusing to do battle in the Arizona desert with a bellowing warrior (Robert Z'Dar) named Lockaber. So Lockaber goes on a rampage, killing tourists while fleeing Falchion is befriended by ranger Charles Napier and desert rat George "Buck" Flower and his daughter. A mystical quality prevades over the desert footage. A sexy high priestess, who has power to rejuvenate Lockaber, gives the film another unusual push. Budd Lewis's script is never predictable and reveals a sense for sensitive characters. Director Warren Stevens balances these elements. Alexa Hamilton, Michael Paré, Joe Cortese, James Hong. (Warner Bros.)

DRAGONHEART (1996) ★★★★½ A thoroughly satisfying mythical adventure/special effects movie that brings computer animation a step higher in perfection, and a fairy-tale spectacle that will please adults and children. Although Dennis Quaid plays a dragonslayer named Bowen in 10th-century England, and he's very colorful as the cynical, wisecracking swordsman, the real star of *Dragonheart* is Draco the Dragon, with the voice (and sometimes the mannerisms) of Sean Connery as it/he achieves things on the screen no previous dragon dared try. (Draco was created by Phil Tippett and carried out by Lucas's IL&M company.) The dragon is the last of its kind and has a heart, a sense of humor and the soul of a philosopher, and joins in with Quaid to carry out assorted deceptions. This is such a delightful mixture of action, comedy and SPX razzle-dazzle, it is like seeing your first Robin Hood adventure movie all over again, but with new treats added. Director Rob Cohen captures the magic of Charles Edward Pogue's literate script (though still giving the story a gritty edge that captures the cruelty and hardships of the time) and allows the cast to rollick in some of the script's witticisms and anachronisms. Among the supporting players are David Thewlis as the evil young king who has half the dragon's soul, Pete Postlethwaite as a delightful roving chronicler of Quaid's exploits (more of this character would have been appreciated), Julie Christie as the king's sympathetic mother, and Dina Meyer as Quaid's modest love interest. This is a milestone movie any self-respecting fantasy lover should not miss. (Video/Laser: MCA)

DRAGONSLAYER (1981) ★★★★ Outstanding fantasy-adventure capturing a sense of action, mystery, menace and magic, thanks to the doting care doled out by Matthew Robbins (director) and Hal Barwood (who coscripted with Robbins). Effects master Dennis Muren pioneered new animation techniques in bringing to life a fire-breather named Vertithrax that flies and breathes fire. The tone is set by Ralph Richardson as the delightful sorcerer Ulrich, while Peter MacNichol as young hero Galen and Caitlin Clark as his maiden are suitably naive and venturesome. Baby dragons provide some of the best moments. Albert Salmi, Peter Eyre, John Hallam. Score by Alex North. (Video/Laser: Paramount)

DRAGONS OF KRULL. See *Krull*.

DRAGONWORLD (1994) ★★★½ An unusually sensitive and well-conceived Charles and Albert Band production for their Moonbeam Productions, well scripted by director Ted Nicolaou and Glazener Naha, and intelligently acted by all concerned, thanks to Nicolaou's superb handling of all the difficult ingredients of this heartfelt special effects–laden fantasy-adventure. When Courtland Mead, 8, goes to Scotland to live with his grandfather (Andrew Keir, in a wonderful role as a castle-owning Scotsman), he finds a baby dragon for his companion. Years later, he's grown into Sam MacKenzie, who now owes enough back taxes on the castle that he allows an unscrupulous promoter (John Woodvine) to put the dragon on display at an amusement park. How MacKenzie gets his dragon back, with the help of documentary TV producer John Calvin and beautiful blond Lila Kaye, makes up the rest of this enjoyable effort that highlights excellent dragon effects by Mark Rappaport and stop-motion master David Allen. Richard Band's music is a perfect accompaniment with its Scottish overtones. (Video/Laser: Paramount)

DR. ALLEN. Video version of *I Was a Teenage Sex Mutant* (Video/Laser: Paramount).

DR. BLACK AND MR. HYDE (1975) ★★½ Black exploitationer written by Larry Le Bron with Bernie Casey (as Dr. Henry Pride) experimenting with the regeneration of dying cells in liver patients and finding a formula that turns him into an albino-white killer. He has a childhood phobia about prostitutes and kills the streetwalkers in Watts. This puzzles policeman Ji-Tu Cumbuka, who looks almost as tall and lean as the Watts Towers. A genre film needs an aura of entertaining fantasy, but director William (*Blacula*) Crain captures the drabness and squalor of Watts, inflicting depression rather than terror. Aka *The Watts Monster*. Rosalind Cash, Stu Gilliam, Marie O'Henry. (VCI)

DR. BUTCHER M.D. (MEDICAL DEVIATE) (1979) ★★ Originally *Queen of the Cannibals*, this spaghetti-scarer belongs to the "cannibal school" with its torture and mutilation. It's a mad-doctor-on-a-lonely-Pacific-island tale in which Donald O'Brian creates zombies while Alexandra delli Colli and Ian McCullough investigate. Flesh-munching and organ-ripping keep this lively in the hands of writer-director Frank Martin. Aka *Zombie Holocaust* and *Island of the Last Zombies*. (Paragon; Thrillervideo) (Laser: Japanese)

DR. CADMAN'S SECRET. See *The Black Sleep*.

DR. CALIGARI (1989) ★ The titular, tit-plated

doc is granddaughter of the silent-screen Caligari, and she's so insane, running the Caligari Insane Asylum, that she's using folks for hormone experimentation. A stylish, campy film directed by Stephen (*Café Flesh*) Sayadian. Madeleine Renal, Laura Albert, Fox Harris. (Starmaker) (Laser: Image)

DR. CYCLOPS (1940) ★★★ Ernest B. Schoedsack, cocreator of *King Kong*, returned to the genre to direct this tale of a mad scientist (Dr. Thorkel, played by Albert Dekker) who miniaturizes people to doll size. Unfortunately, the rear projection and matte shots are unimaginatively executed and the characters are stereotypes, including Dekker's unbalanced doc. Still, Tom Kilpatrick's script has period charm, and this is one of the first features to use Technicolor for menacing effect. Janice Logan, Thomas Coley, Victor Killian, Frank Yaconelli. (Video/Laser: MCA)

DR. DEATH: SEEKER OF SOULS (1973) ★ Need a soul for that dead body lying around the house? Just pick up the phone and call Dr. Death ("This is Dr. Death. I'm not in right now, but if you'll leave your name after the beep . . ."). All he has to do is make a house call, pop open the vial around his neck and instruct the wispy vapor that drifts out to enter the cadaver. John Considine is the physician; co-souls belong to Barry Coe, Florence Marley, Cheryl Miller, Jo Morrow and TV horror host Seymour. Directed-produced by Eddie Saeta from a script by Sal Ponti. (Prism)

DREAM A LITTLE DREAM (1989) ★★★ An intelligence and conviction is behind this fantasy-comedy, and an emotional ring in the dialogue sets it apart from other personality-transference movies, but the fantasy premise is so intellectualized this eventually loses its impetus. It's difficult to explain why the minds of aging Jason Robards and teenager Corey Feldman are merged, but how each faces life afterward provides the gist for this morality fable, with emphasis on Feldman's romance with lovely Meredith Salenger. Director Marc Rocco, who produced and cowrote the script with Daniel Jay Franklin and coproducer D. E. Eisenberg, hired his dad, Alex Rocco, to play Feldman's dad. Piper Laurie, Harry Dean Stanton, Corey Haim, Susan Blakely. (Vestron) (Laser: Image)

DREAM A LITTLE DREAM 2 (1993) ★★½ A pair of magic glasses are sought by underworld figures (a sexy dame in miniskirts; a fat slob; a hit man) while teenager Corey Feldman (playing the same dumb kid he played in *Dream a Little Dream*, and acting as coproducer) runs around on fire escapes and down corridors escaping various death traps. This has none of the class of its predecessor, with a lightweight (featherweight?) script by David Weissman and Susan

Forman. It's perfunctorily directed by James Lenno. Robyn Lively, Stacie Randall, Michael Nicolosi, Bobby Costanzo, Corey Haim. (Columbia TriStar)

DREAM A LITTLE EVIL (1992) ★ Another disgusting, dumb teenage horror comedy, the kind that gives intellectualism and rocket science a bad name. Two geeky brothers in a huge L.A. mansion feud with each other while one spends all his time in his bedroom making love to his shapely girlfriend and the other invents a headpiece-device that grants him his disgusting, dumb wishes. His biggest wish turns into a witch who vomits all over the guys and turns uglier and uglier with each reel. Finally, she turns into a grotesque monster, gooey and drippy. Lyle Waggoner (out of work?) appears briefly as Death (Lyle who?). Writer-producer-director Royce Mathew is more than a triple threat. He's a tripe threat. He's a menace to society, upchucking material like this. It's enough to make you go chunky style. Richard Sebastian, Ducan Rouleau, Michelle Gaudreau, Katy Smith.

DREAMANIAC (1986) ★ Sleaz-iac quickie-sickie (made for video) about a heavy metal composer who heavily composes up a succubus to suck a bust or two at a sorority hash-brownies party. Amateurish production marked by buckets of unconvincing blood, tons of sex and nudity and tons of sex and nudity. The bare-skinned monotony and bad acting just won't quit. You will become a blithering screamaniac. Directed by David DeCoteau. Thomas Bern, Kim McKamy. (Wizard)

DREAM DEMON (1988) ★★ Virgin Jemma Redgrave, presumably because she's fearful of sexually consummating her pending marriage, has terrifying nightmares, only the demons in them converge with the real world and gruesome, gory murders result. This British flicker has plenty of monsters and hideous makeup for shock lovers. Directed by Harley Cokliss. (Warner Bros.)

DREAMER OF OZ, THE (1990) ★★★★ Warm TV-movie chronicling the life of L. Frank Baum, who wrote *The Wonderful Wizard of Oz* and 13 other books about Dorothy in the magic land of the Emerald City. Richard Matheson's teleplay (from an idea by exec producer David Kirschner) shows the ups and downs of Baum's career and how he became a best-seller in his twilight years, writing fables that fascinated children and adults. This features excellent fantasy sequences with makeup by Craig Reardon and effects by Sam Nicholson. As Baum, John Ritter captures the boy trapped in a man's body, Annette O'Toole is good as his faithful wife and Rue McClanahan is amusing as Baum's mother-in-law. An enchanting, fascinating biodrama.

Directed by Jack Bender. Charles Haid, David Schramm.

DREAM KILLER, THE. See *The Night Walker*.

DREAM LOVER (1986) ★★★ After Kristy McNichol undergoes a traumatic rape experience, in which she kills her assailant with a knife, she is so plagued by nightmares she seeks the help of dream researcher Ben Masters but only gets in deeper when her dreams become reality. Elements of this psycho-mystery are fascinating, but McNichol portrays the troubled woman with such coldness, one can never feel empathy for her. Directed by Alan J. Pakula. Paul Shenar, Justin Deas. (MGM/UA)

DREAM LOVER (1993) ★★★½ If you appreciate psychological horror stories that probe the complexities of the human mind, you will appreciate the subtleties and plot twists of this most unusual tale of madness, in which it's hard to tell where sanity leaves off and schizophrenia cuts in. Handsome James Spader plays a reserved, somewhat repressed architect who falls for Madchen Amick, a quiet, mysterious beauty whose secret past begins to come out after they are married and have two children. Writer-director Nicholas Kazan introduces a number of clever surprises and symbolic dreams as Spader (whose sanity we have begun to doubt) sinks into paranoid delusions—or is it a trick by Amick to have him institutionalized? Therein lies the rub—and the fascination. As Spader falls apart, you are not quite sure who is sane or insane, and Kazan finally takes Spader to the extreme limits. This movie demands a lot of attention, but it pays off if you are willing to give. Bess Armstrong, Frederic Lehne, Larry Miller, Kathleen York.

DREAM NO EVIL (1970) ★ Half-baked ripoff of Robert Bloch's *Psycho*, and a hapless career moment for Edmond O'Brien, who portrays a farmer who rises from the autopsy table to kill undertaker Marc Lawrence by ripping open his back with a surgical knife. He also uses a scythe to dispense with an obese sheriff. O'Brien talks hellfire and brimstone with his nymphomaniac daughter (sexy Brooke Mills). Its pseudo-Freudian overtones are explained by harebrained psychiatrist Arthur Franz. As for writer-director John Hayes, don't dream of seeing his "evil." Aka *Now I Lay Me Down to Die*. (Active; Star Classics)

DREAMSCAPE (1984) ★★★½ Tightly honed script by David Loughery, Chuck Russell and director Joseph Ruben makes for an exciting excursion into the subconscious mind (the dreamscape) as telepathic subjects undergo dream testing. Psychic Dennis Quaid is hired by research scientists Max Von Sydow and Kate Capshaw to link with sleeping subjects and experience their nightmares. Christopher Plummer is a sinister government man who wants the dreamlink for assassination purposes, Eddie Albert is a U.S. President troubled by nuclear nightmares. Although Peter Kuran's effects are limited, they capture the spirit of bad dreams, especially in the form of a Snake Creature. Makeup specialist Craig Reardon contributes cadaverous faces. Fine music track by Maurice Jarre. (Video/Laser: HBO)

DREAM SLAYER. Video of *Blood Song* (HQV).

DRESSED FOR DEATH (1972) ★★★ Obscure Hammer psychothriller, originally released as *Straight on Till Morning*, is designed for ambience and characterization as it unfolds leisurely. It is fascinating because of imaginative crosscutting and its sympathy for a man who records the voices of his murder victims. Director Peter Collinson and screenwriter Michael Peacock try to be arty and it works—thanks to the editing tempo and the moods of Rita Tushingham (as a mousy, shy thing) and the killer, Shane Briant, a confused psychotic who befriends Rita, then draws her into his spider's lair. Produced by Michael Carreras, this is also known as *Till Dawn Do We Part*. Tom Bell, Annie Ross. (Academy)

DRESSED TO KILL (1980) ★★★★ Lulu of a horror film from writer-director Brian De Palma—a macabre black joke as he follows sex-starved housewife Angie Dickinson to her death at the hands of a knife murderess in an unforgettable elevator sequence. More jolting surprises are in score when the murdered woman's son and a prostitute (Nancy Allen) join forces to track the killer. De Palma's direction is brilliant, the film opening and closing with erotic shower sequences. They don't make shockers better than this. Michael Caine, Keith Gordon. (Warner Bros.; Goodtimes) (Laser: Orion/Image)

DR. FRANKENSTEIN'S CASTLE OF FREAKS (1973) ★ Boring Italian menagerie horror film that wastes Rossano Brazzi, Michael Dunn and Edmund Purdom. Same old hoary clichés as the evil doc creates freako anomalies with his Electric Accumulator. And dig the results: Goliath the Giant, Kreegin the Hunchback and Ook the Neanderthal Man. Directed by Robert H. Oliver. Only watchable things: busty lovelies who reveal their enormous breasts. Aka *Monsters of Frankenstein* and *Terror Castle*. (Magnum; Sinister/C)

DR. GIGGLES (1992) ★★★½ True-grue horror fans will find this a delightfully evil formula of slasher-movie gags brilliantly woven by director Manny Coto, who co-wrote the satirical script with Graeme Whifler. Larry Drake is hysterically macabre as a doctor who uses every instrument in his black bag to slaughter townspeople responsible for hanging his father. So what if dad was stealing the hearts of his patients—literally. Now dear Dr. Evan Rendell, his warped offspring, is stealing them and the body count is climbing! What makes this blood-bath so delightful are the tasteless doctor puns that punctuate (pardon that word) each murder. This is one of the funniest put-ons within the horror-film canon. Drake is over the top as the doctor who makes house calls—without being asked! If you want a second opinion, go ahead, but we urge you to see this. Now, open wide . . . Holly Marie Combs, Cliff De Young, Glenn Quinn. (Video/Laser: MCA)

DR. GOLDFOOT AND THE BIKINI MACHINE (1966) ★ Comedy-mystery starring Vincent Price as the titular madman who plans world domination with lady robots, capable of seducing the average male. A hodgepodge of ideas and performers, directed by Norman Taurog and written by Elwood Ullman and Robert Kaufman. Followed by *Dr. Goldfoot and the Girl Bombs*. Dwayne Hickman, Frankie Avalon, Fred Clark, Deborah Walley, Susan Hart, Annette Funicello. (AIP; Orion)

DR. GOLDFOOT AND THE GIRL BOMBS (1966) ★ Vincent Price, that creator of robotic pulchritude, is back from *Dr. Goldfoot and the Bikini Machine* with a hot plot to start a war between major powers with his mass-produced androids—literal sexbombs set to explode while making love to military leaders. "Bomb" is the word for this indulgence in idiocy directed by Mario Bava. Louis Heyward and Robert Kaufman helped with the script. Fabian, Franco Franchi, Laura Antonelli. Aka *Dr. Goldfoot and the Love Bomb, Dr. Goldfoot and the S Bomb, The Spy Came from the Semi-Cold* and *Spies Come from Halfcold*. (Orion)

DR. GOLDFOOT AND THE LOVE BOMB. See *Dr. Goldfoot and the Girl Bombs*.

DR. GOLDFOOT AND THE S BOMB. See *Dr. Goldfoot and the Girl Bombs*.

DR. GORE. Video version of *Body Shop* (United; VCI).

DR. GOUDRON'S SYSTEM. See *Dr. Tarr's Torture Dungeon*.

DR. HACKENSTEIN (1987) ★★ Quaint send-up of *Frankenstein*, directed with style by Richard Clark, who wrote the spoofy script. Hackenstein is a misguided scientist with no moral judgment, but he's still an amusing figure as he murders for assorted body parts to put his wife back together. Phyllis Diller appears as a complaining town socialite; Anne and Logan Ramsey are body snatchers in a black-comedy vein. The gore never is offensive as this pleasant comedy unfolds. David Muir, Stacey Travis, Catherine Davis Cox. (Forum; MCEG)

DR. HECKYL AND MR. HYPE (1980) ★ Incredibly unfunny-unsavory spoof of Stevenson's classic tale of schizophrenic personality, botched by writer-director Charles B. Griffith. Oliver Reed is awful as a podiatrist whose normal countenance is ugly, and who turns normal when his monstrous side surfaces. Switching the faces of good and evil might sound clever but it's presented as non sequiturs with stupid characters: the fragile, sexy young girl who thinks ugly Dr. Hekyll is beautiful; a crazed guy with a feather fetish, Dr. Who; detective Lt. Mac Druck (or "Il Topol"); dumb uniformed cop Sgt. Flea Collar (Jackie Coogan); and Flynn the trash-bin man (Dick Miller). The only decent feature about this flop is Richard Band's music and the only funny line is: "There's a vile, green, garbage-eating monster on the loose." Well, sort of funny. Corinne Calvet. (Paragon)

DRILLER KILLER, THE (1979) ★ This poor man's *Taxi Driver* depicts a disturbed, very depressed painter named Reno (Abel Ferrara billed as Jimmy Laine) exposed to mentally ill derelicts and crime on New York streets. He's finally driven off the deep end by a rock 'n' roll band constantly practicing in a nearby flat. He takes out his power drill and murders street people in depressingly graphic penetration attacks. And then when a gallery owner hates his latest painting of a buffalo, Ferrara really freaks out. This dark, perverse movie is difficult to watch. It was the first effort of director Ferrara and screenwriter Nicholas St. John, who went on to become a respected filmmaking team. You could say this film is full of bit parts. Call it a big "bore." Carolyn Marz, Harry Schultz, Baybi Day. (Wizard; Magnum)

DRIPPING DEEP RED. See *Deep Red*.

DRIVE-IN MADNESS (1989) Anthology of horror trailers intermixed with interviews with genre filmmakers (George Romero, John Russo, Tom Savini) who describe the making of *Night of the Living Dead*. And Sam Sherman talks about *Satan's Sadists*. Sexy heroines Linnea Quigley and Bobbie Bresee also appear. Written-produced-directed by Tim Ferrante. (Imagine)

DRIVE IN MASSACRE (1976) ★ Producer-director Stuart Segall's tribute to the "passion pit" consists of two overweight cops looking for a killer who terrorizes moviegoers with a long sword, severing their heads from their bodies and piercing two bodies with a single thrust while they make out in a car. The Buck Flower–John Goff script is slow going, failing to achieve style. We can't even recommend that you see this at a drive-in. Adam Lawrence, Jake Barnes. (Magnum) (Laser: Image)

DRIVING FORCE (1989) ★ In a post-nuked world, bad guys called the Black Knights terrorize Sam J. Jones and other holocaust survivors. Cheapjack job directed by A. J. Prowse. Catherine Bach, Don Swayze. (Academy)

DRIVING ME CRAZY (1990) ★½ The Edsel of "fantasy car" movies—a shiftless mess that will drain your mental battery. German inventor Thomas Gottschalk (who speaks with a British accent) invents a car that runs on "tubular vegetables" and exceeds 200 mph. When this naive jerk arrives in L.A., mogul Dom DeLuise steals the car and forces Gottschalk, his pal Billy Dee Williams and his girl Michelle Johnson to chase after him. But first the film runs out of gas and pistons a lot of comedians (Milton Berle, Morton Downey, Jr., etc) through its hollow cylinders before breaking down. The jokes are flat—ach, it's a lemon. Steve Kanaly, James Tolkan, George Kennedy, Richard Moll. Directed without gas by Jon Turteltaub. (Video)

DR. JEKYLL AND MISS OSBOURNE. See *The Blood of Dr. Jekyll*.

DR. JEKYLL AND MR. HYDE (1920) ★★★ Silent-screen classic (and the first version of Stevenson's novel) with John Barrymore as the well-intended doctor who tampers with science to create a monster within himself. A tour de force for Barrymore, who underwent the transformations without the aid of trick photography or makeup. Directed by John S. Robertson. Nita Naldi, Brandon Hurst. (Kino; Viking; Republic; Sinister/C; Moore; Critic's Choice) (Laser: Republic)

DR. JEKYLL AND MR. HYDE (1932) ★★★★ Rouben Mamoulian's direction and the acting of Fredric March and Miriam Hopkins have held up well over the years, making this an endurable film version of Stevenson's oft-abused narrative. The Samuel Hoffenstein-Percy Heath script is unusually adult. As the split personality, March underwent on-camera transfigurations achieved with special lenses and unique makeup by Wally Westmore. Hopkins as the prostitute is extremely seductive and her smoldering sensuality is wonderful to behold. March won an Oscar for his performance, but it is the whole that is greater than any part. Rose Hobart, Holmes Herbert, Edgar Norton. (Video/Laser: MGM/Turner)

DR. JEKYLL AND MR. HYDE (1941) ★★★½ MGM's version of the Stevenson horror classic, with Spencer Tracy in the dual role as the doctor whose evil side surfaces while taking a drug that by today's standards would be "hallucinogenic." While its production standards are high, and its cast includes Ingrid Bergman, Donald Crisp, Lana Turner and Ian Hunter, it lacks the impact of the 1932 version. Still, it's worth seeing. Victor Fleming directed the John Lee Mahin script. Barton MacLane, C. Aubrey Smith, Sara Allgood. (Video/Laser: MGM/UA)

DR. JEKYLL AND MR. HYDE (1973) ★★★ A musical of the Stevenson classic? With Kirk Douglas as the schizophrenic doctor? From a major TV network? What's the world of horror coming to? But what a cast! Susan George, Stanley Holloway, Michael Redgrave, Donald Pleasence. David Winters directed. (Sony) (Laser: Image)

DR. JEKYLL AND MRS. HYDE. Original title for *Abbott and Costello Meet Dr. Jekyll and Mr. Hyde*.

DR. JEKYLL AND MS. HYDE (1995) ★★ A failed comedic attempt to spoof Robert Louis Stevenson's beloved fantasy classic in modern terms using DNA experimentation. Tim Daly plays Dr. Jacks, a perfume inventor who inherits Dr. Jekyll's old notebooks, and who comes up with an injection that turns him into beautiful Sean Young, who uses her wily sexuality to seduce the boss so she can get credit for inventing a new perfume for Polly Bergen's perfume company. There's an interesting battle-of-the-sexes theme that underlies the script by director David Price, and Kevin Yagher's transformation special effects are nifty, but much of the humor (especially the seduction jokes) falls flat and the film strays afield of its own ingenuities, as out of control as a mad scientist's experiments. Lysette Anthony, Harvey Fierstein. (HBO/Savoy)

DR. JEKYLL AND SISTER HYDE (1972) ★★★ Bizarre variation on the Jekyll-Hyde theme: Instead of a good man metamorphosing into a bad man, a good man metamorphoses into a bad woman. This turnabout is considered fair play in Brian Clemens's script. Ralph Bates is the doctor, Martine Beswick his counterpart. Directed by Roy Ward Baker. (HBO; Republic)

DR. JEKYLL AND THE WEREWOLF. Video of *Dr. Jekyll and the Wolfman* (Sinister/C).

DR. JEKYLL AND THE WOLFMAN (1971) ★★ The sixth in the Spanish-produced series to star Paul Naschy as the werewolf Waldemar Daninsky, a follow-up to *Frankenstein's Bloody Terror, Nights of the Werewolf, The Werewolf vs. the Vampire Women, Assignment Terror* and *Fury of the Wolfman*. Directed by Leon Klimovsky, scripted by Jacinto Molina (none other than Naschy), the story has Waldemar, poor soul, being turned from a werewolf into a Hyde-like beast. Monsterism just doesn't go away in the Daninsky clan, man. The next film in this remarkably ongoing series: *The Hunchback of the Morgue*. (From Sinister/C as *Dr. Jekyll and the Werewolf*, from S/Weird as *Dr. Jekyll vs. the Wolfman*, from Filmfax as *Dr. Jekyll vs. the Werewolf*)

DR. JEKYLL'S DUNGEON OF DARKNESS. See *Dr. Jekyll's Dungeon of Death*.

DR. JEKYLL'S DUNGEON OF DEATH (1979) ★ Great-grandson of Dr. Jekyll–Mr. Hyde has a serum that transforms criminals into martial-arts battlers. Unwieldy mixture of genres from San Francisco producer-director James Wood. Writer James Mathers stars as Jekyll, and Wood did his own lighting, music and sound. Threadbare, stretched as thin as Wood himself. John Kearney, Tom Nicholson. Also known as *Dr. Jekyll's Dungeon of Darkness*. (Wizard; Magnum; Genesis)

DR. JEKYLL'S MISTRESS. See *Dr. Orloff's Monster.*

DR. JERKYLL AND MR. HYDE. See *The Nutty Professor.*

DR. M. See *Club Extinction.*

DR. MABUSE, THE GAMBLER (1922) ★★★ Fritz Lang's earliest depiction of Norbert Jacques' supervillain, a mathematical genius who turns his creativity to evil with murderers, rapists, thieves and counterfeiters engaged in bringing about social upheaval. The architectural madman (Rudolph Klein-Rogge) assumes disguises (banker, psychiatrist, gambler, drunken sailor) to flood the economy with fake money. In 1933 Lang produced a sound version, *The Testament of Dr. Mabuse*, followed in the '60s with a series of German productions, the first of which (*The Thousand Eyes of Dr. Mabuse*) he directed. Followed by *The Return of Dr. Mabuse, Dr. Mabuse vs. Scotland Yard* and *The Secret of Dr. Mabuse.* (Embassy; Sinister/C; Nostalgia; Moore)

DR. MABUSE'S RAYS OF DEATH. See *The Secret of Dr. Mabuse.*

DR. MABUSE VS. SCOTLAND YARD (1964) ★★ German madman, out to conquer the world, just might pull it off this time. No matter that Mabuse is dead. He returns to life and takes possession of an invention that turns citizens into killers and conquerers. This German production, directed by Paul May from a script by Ladislas Fodor, was part of a series that gave rebirth to Norbert Jacques's archvillain, first popularized by Fritz Lang in the '20s. Peter Van Eyck, Klaus Kinski. Aka *The Scarlet Jungle, Scotland Yard vs. Dr. Mabuse, Scotland Yard in Pursuit of Dr. Mabuse* and *Scotland Yard Hunts Dr. Mabuse.* (Video Yesteryear; Sinister/C; S/Weird; Filmfax)

DR. MANIAC. See *The Man Who Lived Again.*

DR. MORDRID: MASTER OF THE UNKNOWN (1992) ★★½ Subdued, sometimes sublime fantasy codirected by producer Charles Band and his father Albert, depicting a wizard (Jeffrey Combs) who stands guard over the gateway "between our world and darkness" in his Manhattan apartment. His only companion is the raven Edgar Allan. Brian Thompson is Dr. Mordrid's nemesis, Kabal, but the battles they fight are tame (a few lightning bolts, a few magical tricks) and the payoff a bit disappointing. Emphasis is more on criminologist Yvette Nipar, who lives in Dr. Mordrid's building and helps him on the earthly plane. The high point of C. Courtney Joyner's script is Dave Allen's stop-motion animation of two dinosaur skeletons battling in a museum. Jay Acovone, Ritch Brinkley, Keith Coulouris. Features a moody score by Richard Band. (Paramount)

DR. NO (1963) ★★★★½ Granddaddy of the superspy films—first in the James Bond (Agent 007) series. The suave, cold-blooded British spy was created in popular novels by ex–British intelligence agent Ian Fleming, and these early films produced by Harry Saltzman and Albert R. Broccoli have slick, tongue-in-cheek action with glittering gadgets, superweapons and abundant female pulchritude. In his screen debut, 007 battles SPECTRE, a gang of terrorists headed by Dr. No, a master criminal operating an underwater city off Jamaica. Sean Connery is slick with the femmes fatales, yet ruthless with his Baretta, shooting a man in cold blood, or coolly watching enemies die in fiery traps. Terence Young's stylish direction set the standard. Ursula Andress is provocative as Honey, bikini-clad adventuress; Joseph Wiseman is slimy-great as the evil Dr. No; Jack Lord is contact agent Felix Leiter. Bernard Lee and Lois Maxwell bow as assignment chief M and his secretary, Miss Moneypenny. (CBS/Fox) (Laser: MGM/UA)

DROP DEAD FRED (1990) ★★★ Phoebe Cates's imaginary childhood playmate Drop Dead Fred comes back to haunt her during adulthood in the form of Rik Mayall. Red-headed, wild-bouffant Fred (only Phoebe can see him) is a crazy *Beetlejuice*-style character who behaves like a Warner Bros. cartoon character, smoke drifting out of his ears and his eyeballs bulging while helping Phoebe handle her problems, which include a philandering husband and a bossy mom. The zany antics wear thin and it's the cast (Marsha Mason, Tim Matheson, Carrie Fisher) that keeps the premise afloat. Ate de Jong (a pseudonym?) directed. (Live) (Laser: Live; Pioneer)

DR. ORLOFF'S MONSTER (1964) ★½ An evil scientist creates a stalking hulk of abominable mankind, putrescent of flesh, hideous of countenance. Spanish/Austrian sequel to *The Awful Mr. Orlof* (notice how one "f" got lost in translation, along with coherence) was written-directed by Jesse Franco. Aka *The Secret of Dr. Orloff, The Brides of Dr. Jekyll, Dr. Jekyll's Mistress* and *The Mistresses of Dr. Jekyll.* Agnes Spaak, Hugh White, Jose Rubio. (Sinister/C; S/Weird; Filmfax)

DR. PHIBES. See *The Abominable Dr. Phibes.*

DR. PHIBES RISES AGAIN (1972) ★★★ Sequel to *The Abominable Dr. Phibes* with Vincent Price (under the direction of Robert Fuest, who cowrote the imaginative script with Robert Blees) again on a rampage, seeking an eternal elixir in Egypt to restore his long-dead wife to life. Robert Quarry (Count Yorga) isn't the best hero material but he works overtime to outwit the devious Phibes. More macabre murders, each attempting to top the last in grisliness. Valli Kemp plays Vulnavia. Hugh Griffith, Terry-Thomas, Beryl Reid, Fiona Lewis, Peter Cushing. (Vestron) (Laser: Image)

DR. SATAN'S ROBOT. TV-movie version of *The Mysterious Dr. Satan* (Video Connection).

DR. SEUSS' 5000 FINGERS OF DR. T. Video version of *The 5,000 Fingers of Dr. T.*

DR. TARR'S PIT OF HORRORS. Video version of *Dr. Tarr's Torture Dungeon* (Electra).

DR. TARR'S TORTURE DUNGEON (1972) ★ This unusual adaptation of Edgar Allan Poe's "The System of Dr. Tarr and Professor Feather," directed in Mexico by Juan Lopez Moctezuma, who coscripted with Carlos Illescas, is an amusing study in madness more than it is a horror exploitationer. This is the one about the inmates taking over the asylum when a psychologist gentleman is sent to check up on a certain doctor's techniques for curing madness. Pretty soon he, his woman and his strongarm servant are subjected to an amusing series of adventures in which their tormentors are totally bonkers. The film is also mildly interesting for its large-scale sets and cast of insane extras. Aka *Dr. Tarr's Pit of Horrors, House of Madness, The Mansion of Madness, The System of Dr. Tarr and Professor Feather* and *Dr. Goudron's System.* Claudio Brook, Arthur Hansel, Ellen Sherman, David Silva. (Magnum)

DR. TERROR'S GALLERY OF HORRORS. Video version of *Return from the Past* (Ingram).

DR. TERROR'S HOUSE OF HORRORS (1965) ★★★ Amicus anthology with Peter Cushing as an uncanny tarot-card reader who confronts five passengers aboard a speeding train and "reads" their futures. Hence, five tales: Art critic Christopher Lee is pursued by a beast with five fingers; Roy Castle is haunted by a voodoo curse; Neil McCallum wishes he hadn't when he wrestles with a werewolf; Alan Freeman is attacked by a peculiar vine plant; and Donald Sutherland sharpens his stake for a vampiric kill. The framework aboard the train provides one final, fatal twist. Directed by Freddie Francis, scripted by Milton Subotsky. Max Adrian, Peter Madden, Katy Wild, Michael Gough, Jennifer Jayne. (Republic)

DRUMS OF FU MANCHU (1940) ★★★½ For its time, this was an unusually well written Republic cliffhanger, based on Sax Rohmer's infamous Asian mastermind. Played here by Henry Brandon in a way that makes him far more interesting than his adversary Sir Dennis Nayland Smith (William Royle) or crusading newspaper guy Allan Parker (Robert Kellard), Fu Manchu gets to use creative death traps and killer devices in his quest for Genghis Khan's scepter, which he intends to use to conquer the world. Especially creepy are Fu's henchmen: mindless, obedient servants called "Dacoits," who have undergone frontal lobotomies. This serial constantly shifts gears and scenery and moves to a satisfying climax, in which Fu Manchu survives and vows to fight another day. Directed by William Witney and John English. (Heavenly Videos; Second Chance)

DR. WHO AND THE DALEKS (1965) ★★★ *Dr. Who* remains a popular British sci-fi TV series in America; this feature version is aimed at the same youthful, fantasy-oriented audience. As the kindly inventor, Peter Cushing journeys forward in time to a planet where the good Thals fight off the evil Daleks, strange beings who wear metallic coverings to keep out lethal radiation. Directed by Gordon Flemying, scripted by producers Milton Subotsky and Max J. Rosenberg. Jennie Linden, Roy Castle, Robert Tovey, Geoffrey Toone. (Thorn EMI; Goodtimes)

DUEL (1971) ★★★★½ Although this appears to be a non-fantasy suspense TV-movie about a motorist (Dennis Weaver) pursued by an insane trucker, director Steven Spielberg never allows the homicidal driver to be seen and the semi takes on an evil personification, sliding into the realm of *The Twilight Zone.* Weaver's building sense of terror and the cat-and-mouse tactics of the trucker build to a nerve-wracking climax of action and menace. Richard Matheson's script (from his short story) functions on several levels, but viewed just as a shocker, it's a pip. First made for TV, this was released abroad in a longer version, now available to TV. (MCA)

DUEL OF THE GARGANTUAS. See *War of the Gargantuas.*

DUEL OF THE SPACE MONSTERS. See *Frankenstein Meets the Space Monster.*

DUNE (1984) ★★½ Long-awaited version of Frank Herbert's classic novel is a complicated, disappointing Dino De Laurentiis film. David Lynch seems incapable of bringing cohesiveness to his script or direction. The story desperately needs humor and levity to contrast the bleakness of Lynch's unrelenting sobriety. Plot: Everyone needs the planet Dune for a spice from its sands that enables a race of mutants to provide astral space travel to migrating alien cultures. Protecting the spices are worm creatures with mystical links to mankind. *Dune* is the story of a Messiah who leads the people of Dune out of bondage. The Messiah is Kyle MacLachlan; Kenneth McMillan is the hated Baron Harkonnen, whose corpulent body floats in astral projection; Jose Ferrer is Emperor Shaddam IV; Linda Hunt is Shadout Mapes (a wasted role); Silvana Mangano is Rev. Mother Ramallo; Sting is Feyd Rautha; Max von Sydow is Dr. Kynes. And on and on, just like this 140-minute movie. *Dune* is all grit, no substance. This was recut in a longer version and rereleased to TV. (Video/Laser: MCA)

DUNE WARRIORS (1992) ★½ This imitation of *Road Warrior* is also a remake of *The Magnificent Seven* without the magnificence. Set in New California in A.D. 2040, Roger Corman's production pits roving Samurai warrior David Carradine against bad guy Luke Askew, who pillages the countryside with bandits. Jillian McWhirter commissions Carradine and good-hearted mercenaries to defend her village. The fighting, while well staged, is overloaded with mock heroics and doesn't make up for the poor writing by T. C. McKelvey. Produced-directed in the Philippines by an old hand at this *Mad Max* nonsense, Cirio H. Santiago. Rick Hill, Blake Boyd, Val Garay. (Video/Laser: RCA/Columbia)

DUNGEONMASTER, THE (1985) ★★½ Purveyors of sword-and-sorcery computer games will find this tedious going—as much fun as watching an Apple or Atari crashing. Charles Band's production overinvests in effects without a plot to support its gross-outs. Hence, hero and heroine are swept from adventure to adventure with a disregard for logic, undergoing seven encounters to reach . . . what? It's a ripoff of role-playing without the psychological undercurrents of role-playing. The script by Allen Actor provides ill-defined roles for swashbuckling Jeffrey Byron, tied-to-the-stake heroine Leslie Wing and scenery-chewing Richard Moll as Mestema, a minion of the Devil. Seven directors are credited with the stew: Rosemarie Turko handled "Ice Gallery"; John Buechler was responsible for "Demon of the Dead"; David Allen helmed "Grand Canyon Giant"; Stephen Ford carved a name for himself with "Slasher"; Peter Manoogian caved in to do "The Cave Beast"; Ted Nicolaou megaphoned "Desert Pursuit"; and Band provided the wraparound stuff. Buechler also designed the makeup. Aka *Ragewar*. (Lightning) (Laser: Vestron)

DUNGEONS AND DRAGONS (1981). Video of *Rona Jaffe's Mazes and Monsters* (Showtime).

DUNGEONS AND DRAGONS (1983). See *Krull*.

DUNGEONS OF KRULL. See *Krull*.

DUNWICH HORROR, THE (1969) ★★ Producers have major difficulties adapting the cosmic horror tales of H. P. Lovecraft, as evidenced by this fiasco with Dean Stockwell and Sandra Dee (voted the girl least likely to succeed in a horror film role) as students at Miskatonic University. Someone has lifted the infamous Necronomicon volume from the campus library and is using its incantations to summon "The Old Ones" (ancient, banished gods of pure evil) from another dimension during orgiastic, satanic rites. Sounds

like pure Lovecraft, but this remains far from the Arkham territory H. P. so vividly explored in his literate, blood-chilling tales. Directed by Daniel Haller. Les Baxter's music is the best thing in this James H. Nicholson–Samuel Z. Arkoff production written by Curtis Lee Hanson, Henry Rosenbaum and Ronald Silkosky. Ed Begley, Sam Jaffe, Lloyd Bochner. (Embassy)

DUPLICATES (1992) ★★★ Well-produced TV-movie depicting how Gregory Harrison and wife Kim Greist, while searching for their missing son and her missing brother, stumble across a government-sponsored brainwashing program conducted by doctors Kevin McCarthy and Cicely Tyson. Honorable intentions (to replace the criminal mind with a clean one) are being subverted to create secret assassins, and Harrison and Greist become victims of mind-controlling experiments. Director Sandor Stern, who cowrote the script with Andrew Neiderman, provides clever twists to familiar material. Lane Smith, William Lucking, Scott Hoxby. (Paramount)

DUST DEVIL (1992) ★★½ Pretentious and heavyhanded as it is, this is an unusual film told by an unseen narrator as a South African folk tale about a supernatural spirit, a "wind from nowhere," that wanders the earth as a "black magician, a shape shifter, gaining power through the ritual of murder." That evil entity in human form is Robert Burke, who commits his ritualistic murders with a knife and takes a finger from each victim. His newest "intended" is an unhappy wife (Chelsea Field) fleeing a bad marriage with her upset husband in pursuit. Zakes Mokae makes for an unusual black detective on the trail of the Dust Devil. Weird African symbolism, music and sound effects are used by writer-director Richard (*Hardware*) Stanley, who stresses mood and ambience more than plot. Shot in Namibia. John Matshikiza, Rufus Swart, William Hootkins, Marianne Sagebrecht. (Paramount)

DYING TO REMEMBER (1993) ★★ Fashion designer Melissa Gilbert is plagued by nightmares from her previous life—or so her psychiatrist tells her—in this modest reincarnation thriller set in San Francisco. You'll be smarter than Gilbert in solving the 1963 murder case she finds herself tracking with the help of two cops and a real-estate developer. Directed by Arthur Allan Seidelman. Scott Plank, Jay Robinson, Ted Shackelford. (Paramount)

EARTHBOUND (1981) ★★ Disabled alien spacecraft lands near Gold Rush, where dumb sheriff John Schuck and even dumber deputy Stuart Pankin can't control the crowd when word gets out E.T.s have invaded Earth. It's actually a benevolent humanoid family (led by parents Christopher Connelly and Meredith MacRae) seeking the help of grandfather Burl Ives and his grandson Todd Porter. Hot on their trail is Joseph Campanella as a government guy plotting betrayal of the aliens. Directed witlessly by James L. Conway from a Michael Fisher script.

EARTH DEFENSE FORCE. See *The Mysterians*.

EARTH GIRLS ARE EASY (1990) ★★★½ A goofy pop-bop sci-fi comedy-parody with the odd look of a Day-Glo Buck Rogers comic strip. Three dumb space jockeys (Jeff Goldblum, Jim Carrey, Damon Wayans) from another planet crashland into the swimming pool of Valley Girl Geena Davis and go on a spree to experience the L.A. life-style, love and sex. This oddball comedy features dance numbers well staged by director Julien Temple and satiric slaps at social mores. Although an eccentric burlesque, it's a fetching concoction, refreshing and funny in a dumb way. Charles Rocket and Michael McKean costar. (Video/Laser: Vestron)

EARTHRIGHT. See *The Return*.

EARTH 2 (1994) ★★★ This two-hour pilot for a sci-fi TV series, set in the year 2192, vacillates between a lost-wilderness family situation, of minimal impact, and a metaphysical subplot enhanced by good special effects. A colony ship from Earth crashlands on Planet 6889 in a distant galaxy and must not only confront an unknown race of aliens but trek to a rendezvous point to help others. The aliens are mysteriously good (lean, frightening creatures that can pass through solid objects and burrow through the ground like moles) and only relate to humans on a strange dream level. The big cast includes Debrah Farentino, Antonio Sabata, Jr., Rebecca Gayheart, Jessica Steen, Clancy Brown, Joel Zimmerman and Sullivan Walker. Written by Billy Ray, Michael Duggan, Carol Flint and Mark Levin. Directed by Scott Winant.

EARTH VS. THE FLYING SAUCERS (1956) ★★★ Although Ray Harryhausen's stop-motion effects are blatant swipes from George Pal's *War of the Worlds*, and this Columbia release directed by Fred F. Sears is hampered by a low budget, it's of historic importance for helping to keep '50s science fiction in the forefront, and for advancing special effects. The George Worthington Yates–Raymond T. Marcus script has Earth satellites being knocked out of the sky, followed by alien saucers staging a full-scale invasion against tourist attractions in Washington, D.C. On the downside is Hugh Marlowe, miscast as a scientist-hero who forever slows down the already-lumbering plot to romance Joan Taylor. And just when the film needs original music, producer Sam Katzman throws themes swiped from other pictures. Still, it's a must-see. Harry Lauter, Morris Ankrum, Grandon Rhodes, Donald Curtis. Aka *Invasion of the Flying Saucers*. (Columbia TriStar; Goodtimes) (Laser: Columbia TriStar w/Harryhausen interview; Image)

EARTH VS. THE GIANT SPIDER. See *Earth vs. the Spider*.

EARTH VS. THE SPIDER (1958) ★½ Producer-director Bert I. Gordon, who works harder than any other producer-director to save a buck, gets entangled in a web of ineptitude in presenting a giant mutant spider living in a cave outside of a town crawling with unbearable two-legged teenagers. As visualized by screenwriters George W. Yates and Laszlo Gorog, the eight-legged monstrosity turns out to be eight times duller than most giant movie spiders. Ed Kemmer, of *Space Patrol*, stars as the adult to the rescue. June Kenney, Gene Roth. Aka *The Spider* and *Earth vs. the Giant Spider*. (RCA/Columbia)

EASTER SUNDAY. See *The Being*.

EAT AND RUN (1986) ★½ Dumb comedy-satire on sci-fi and legal-system movies, with the jokes falling as flat as tasteless food under Christopher Hunt's direction. Heavyset R. L. Ryan, portraying an alien dubbed Murray Creature, starts eating up Manhattan's Italian section when he develops a taste for human salami. Cop Ron Silver (deserving of better material) captures Ryan but is thwarted when a liberal judge (Sharon Schlarth), who happens to be his bedmate, is too lenient. Any attempt at satire is lost. Belch! (Starmaker)

EATEN ALIVE (1976) ★ After *The Texas Chainsaw Massacre*, Tobe Hooper directed this sickening misfire (the ultimate underbelly of sleaze movies) with an utterly bananas Neville Brand running a dilapidated hotel (The Starlight) in the Louisiana swamp. Next door is a pit containing a hungry alligator who eats animals—and individuals. An unwatchable film (unless you're a hopeless sadist), especially when the beast is going to eat a little puppy. Mel Ferrer, Stuart Whitman, Carolyn Jones, Marilyn Burns. Aka *Death Trap, Horror Hotel Massacre, Starlight Slaughter* and *Brutes and Savages*. (Prism)

EATEN ALIVE (1980) ★½ From the warmhearted sentimentalists who gave you *Make Them Die Slowly* comes this molar-moving cannibalistic tale of human flesh frying on the barbie. Italian director Umberto Lenzi provides a story involving a jungle cult that parallels the Jim Jones tragedy of 1978 and a woman seeking her lost sister in the jungles of New Guinea. Rather than satisfy your appetite it will undoubtedly grumble your stomach juices. Aka *Eaten Alive by the Cannibals*. Ivan Rassimov, Mel Ferrer. (LD Video; from Continental as *Emerald Jungle*)

EATING RAOUL (1982) ★★★ Writer-director Paul Bartel concocted (with cowriter Richard Blackburn) this outré black comedy about Paul and Mary Bland (Bartel and Mary Woronov), an average L.A. couple who lure creeps into their home pretending to be swingers, when what they really want to do is kill the deviates for their money. Demurely, Mary seduces them and Paul bangs them—over the head with a skillet, with no visible damage to their moral sensitivities. A hilarious movie, great satire on the L.A. culture. Robert Beltran, Ed Begley, Jr., Buck Henry, Garry Goodrow, Charles Griffith. (CBS/Fox)

EBIRAH, HORROR OF THE DEEP/EBIRAH, TERROR OF THE DEEP. See *Godzilla vs. the Sea Monster*.

ECHOES (1983) ★★★ Moody supernatural chiller directed by Arthur Allan Seidelman in New York City, capturing a Manhattan ambience that enhances this weird psychological tale by Richard J. Anthony of an artist (Richard Alfieri) haunted by dreams in which he is a once-famous Spanish painter befouled by love, passion and murder. Psychic Gale Sondergaard believes he is plagued by a "twin spirit" from another dimension, while mother Ruth Roman tells him about a miscarriage she had that might be responsible for an "unborn brother." Nathalie Nell, Mercedes McCambridge, Michael Kellin. (VidAmerica)

ECHO OF TERROR. See *Man with the Synthetic Brain*.

ECOLOGY OF A CRIME, THE. See *A Bay of Blood*.

ED AND HIS DEAD MOTHER (1993) ★★★½ A bemusing, clever satire on the morality of small-town America, as told through hardware store owner Steve Buscemi, who is having a hard time adjusting to his mother's death. (Uncle Ned Beatty feels otherwise, having been haunted by her when she was alive.) Along comes Happy People Corporation's cryogenics pitchman (John Glover, white-haired and clad in

a white suit) to resurrect her—for a fee of course. Back in action, dear old mom (Miriam Margolyes, the essence of apple pie Americana) has this strange need to eat bugs, and human flesh when she starts up her chainsaw. Dark humor written by Chuck Hughes and directed with wacky twists by Jonathan Wacks. Sam Jenkins, Rance Howard. (Video/Laser: Fox)

EDGAR ALLAN POE'S BURIED ALIVE. See *Buried Alive* (1990).

EDGAR ALLAN POE'S ONE MINUTE BEFORE DEATH. See *The Oval Portrait*.

EDGAR ALLAN POE'S THE OBLONG BOX. See *The Oblong Box*.

EDGE OF HELL, THE (1989) ★ The incompetence is complete and the ineptitude is exquisite in this amateurish horror flick that throws monsters and special effects at the audience. In an inexplicable turn of events the film segues from a slasher yarn, in which hard-rock musicians gather in a country estate to rehearse their act, into a religious parable in which Triton the Archangel squares off against Satan in the form of a beast. At no time do director John Fasano and writer Jon-Mikl Thor (who doubles as Triton) give any indication they are making a rollicking comedy. Jillian Peri, Frank Dietz. (Academy)

EDGE OF SANITY (1989) ★★★ A must-see film for the overwrought performance of Anthony Perkins, who brings to Dr. Henry Jekyll (aka Jack Hyde) the madness that earmarks his deliveries in *Psycho* and *Crimes of Passion*. Perkins is indeed on the "edge of sanity" in this foreign-produced R-rated thriller. And if Perkins also teeters on the edge of campiness, it still doesn't detract from this offbeat remake of the Stevenson classic, which throws in Jack the Ripper. Director Gerard Kikoine, known for pornie flicks, crosses into mainstream with a plethora of perversion and Victorian Era sex. Unfortunately, Kikoine's garish excesses (and depiction of sexy clothing styles too modern to belong here) eventually sicken and repel, with only Perkins's performance to bring one back to the fold. The perversity, mixed with many slashed throats, makes this for the strong of heart. Made in Hungary. Glynis Barber, Sarah Maur-Thorp, David Lodge. (Virgin Vision) (Laser: Image)

EDGE OF THE AXE (1989) ★ Crazed madman carrying a long-handled wood-chopping, stump-smashing woodcutter's sharply-honed tool terrorizes hapless citizens of a rural community. Directed by Joseph Braunstein. Barton Faulks, Marie Lane, Page Moseley. (MCEG; Forum)

EDICT. See *Z.P.G.*

EDWARD SCISSORHANDS (1990) ★★★★ Masterpiece from director Tim Burton is a contemporary fairy tale with black-comedy overtones, commenting on good and evil within the human spirit. Burton's surrealistic style matches Caroline Thompson's script (from an idea by

Burton) about a young man with pruning shears for hands who lives in a strange castle perched above a tract community. It's a unique world of Burton's own making, seemingly normal but definitely off-kilter. And he captures a warm, magical feeling for his characters that makes the film very approachable. An Avon lady (warmheartedly portrayed by Dianne Wiest) takes the misfit youth (Johnny Depp) home to care for him, never questioning his oddities—nor does Wiest's husband, Alan Arkin, who essays another eccentric character. Depp is an intriguing image dressed in black, with white face, who pantomimes his part with minimum dialogue, and whose steel-bladed hands (designed by Stan Winston) become a fascinating prop. Winona Ryder, the film's love interest, was never more beautiful. Anthony Michael Hall, Kathy Baker. (Video/Laser: CBS/Fox)

ED WOOD (1994) ★★★★ Any self-respecting horror fan should not miss this fascinating, esoteric portrait of the man now proclaimed the worst filmmaker of all time. You should know Ed Wood by now: the U.S. Marine who fought the battle of Tarawa wearing women's underwear, who returned to civilian life to write pornographic novels wearing angora sweaters and to make the movies *Bride of the Atom* and *Plan 9 from Outer Space* with an unparalleled incompetence. Directed by Tim Burton, *Ed Wood* is a charming, oft-amusing piece of Hollywood history, although its explanation of why Wood (played with innocence and likability by Johnny Depp) was so lousy as a filmmaker only scratches the surface. What stands memorably at the heart of this labor of love is Martin Landau's Oscarwinning performance as Bela Lugosi, a has-been by the early '50s who was befriended by Wood to star in *Glen or Glenda?* and the epics mentioned above. Landau captures the essence of Lugosi with a stunning perfection, as well as the pain of his drug addiction and his need to act again, even when his performances verge on the hammy. The supporting cast adds to the flavor of low-budget moviemaking in the Hollywood '50s (the period of Wood's life the film confines itself to): Sarah Jessica Parker and Patricia Arquette as the women in Wood's life; Jeffrey Jones as Criswell "the prophet"; Bill Murray as Bunny Breckinridge (his performance is a highpoint of this fanciful biography); George "The Animal" Steel as Tor Johnson; and Lisa Marie as Vampira. One of the most important "Creature Features" movies ever attempted. A pat on the back to writers Scott Alexander and Larry Karaszewski, who based their script on Rudolph Grey's oral history *Nightmare of Ecstasy: The Life and Art of Edward D. Wood, Jr.* G. D. Spradlin, Vincent D'Onofrio, Mike Starr. (Video/Laser: Touchstone)

ED WOOD: LOOK BACK IN ANGORA (1994) ★★★ One-hour documentary about the extraordinarily incompetent filmmaker profiled in *Ed Wood*, told with tongue-in-cheek perceptions by writer/producer/director Ted Newsom. Interviews with producer Steve Apostolof, actor Conrad Brooks, leading lady Dolores Fuller, ex-Marine Joe Robertson and Mrs. Kathy Wood show a sweet, misunderstood and ultimately sad side to Wood. But it's Newsom's witty writing that carries the day: "He triumphs over all obstacles, including his own singular lack of ability. . . . His stream-of-consciousness dialogue was like a ransom note pasted together from words randomly cut out of a Korean electronics manual." Narrator Gary Owens camps it up more than necessary with that booming voice of his. (Rhino)

ED WOOD STORY: THE PLAN 9 COMPANION, THE (1992) ★★★ Even if you're only mildly curious about the man proclaimed the worst filmmaker of all time, and who was lovingly profiled in Tim Burton's biodrama *Ed Wood*, this documentary will fascinate you with its insights into not only the oddball man who was Ed Wood, Jr., but Hollywood moviemaking and its esoteric characters. The main thrust of writerdirector Mark Patrick Carducci is on Wood's "master opus" *Plan 9 from Outer Space* and what has made it so "endearing" despite its utter incompetency. Interviews with Vampira, Conrad Brooks, Paul Marco, makeup man Harry Thomas and numerous others sheds wonderful light on an arena of Hollywood appreciated but seldom explored. Adding their comments are those who were influenced (or not influenced) by Wood: Sam Raimi, Eric Caidin, Bill Warren, Joe Dante, Tony Randel and Harry Medved. At 111 minutes, this is pure joy to watch and is a must-see for any horror/sci-fi fan intrigued with the creative process. Lee Harris helped Carducci in writing the script. (MPI; from Atomic Video as *Flying Saucers over Hollywood: The Plan 9 Companion*)

EEGAH! (1962) ★ Arrrrgggghhhhh!! What an incredibly astonishing fantasy (miswritten by Bob Wehling) for brainless teenagers! The dumbest caveman in film history chases a pretty girl through the desert. Arrrrggghhhh!!! Director Nicholas Merriwether's camera work has to be seen to be disbelieved. Unknown cast reaches unsurpassed heights of ineptitude. Did we say unknown? The caveman is Richard Kiel, destined to become Jaws in the James Bond series. Arch Hall, Jr., Marilyn Manning, Ray Steckler. Aaarrrgghhh!!! (Rhino; Sinister/C; Cinema) (Laser: Image)

EERIE MIDNIGHT HORROR SHOW, THE (1978) ★ Released as *Tormented*, and aka *The Obsessed* and *The Sexorcist*, this is an Italian imitation of *The Exorcist*, depicting a young woman's terror when she is possessed by a spirit embodied in a statue. Undistinguished and contrived, featuring R-rated soft porn and sadism. Directed by Mario Gariazzo. Stella Carnacina. (Continental; Planet; from HQV as *Enter the Devil*)

EGGS FROM 70 MILLION B.C. See *Josh Kirby . . . Time Warrior!*

EIGHTEEN AGAIN! (1988) ★★★ Pleasant fantasy-comedy in the switched-bodies tradition, with 81-year-old George Burns trading personalities with 18-year-old grandson Charles Schlatter, who swaggers through the role, cigar in hand, capturing the witty, sagacious manner of the old-timer. It's moderate, oft-underplayed humor and director Paul Flaherty plays up the characters' charm and appeal. Jennifer Runyon as the girlfriend, Red Buttons as an old family friend and Tony Roberts as the misunderstood son of cantankerous Burns provide morality subplots. Only Anita Morris, as a supersexy sexpot, seems a little out of place, as if the filmmakers felt they had to comment on Burns's legendary "sex prowess." (New World) (Laser: Image)

EIGHTH WONDER, THE/EIGHTH WONDER OF THE WORLD, THE. See *King Kong* (1933).

ELECTRIC DREAMS (1984) ★★★ This "fairy tale for computers" is a lighthearted look at our computerized fetishes: a love story between Lenny Von Dohlen (nerdish architect) and Virginia Madsen (happy cello player) and a love story between Von Dohlen and Edgar, an entity created within his home computer. Rusty Lemorande's script is gentle and whimsical, often told in computerized images, with Giorgio Moroder's score capturing an electronical "passion." Director Steve Barron (he helmed the first Ninja Turtles movie) tells a pleasant story with pleasant images. Filmed in San Francisco. Maxwell Caulfield, Bud Cort. (Video/Laser: MGM/UA)

ELECTRIC MAN, THE. See *Man-Made Monster*.

ELECTRONIC LABYRINTH. Alternate title of the short experimental student film that George Lucas produced as *THX 1138-4EB*.

ELEPHANT MAN, THE (1980) ★★★ John Hurt is John Merrick, a real-life freak of the last century who suffered terrible physical and mental discomforts from his malformities until befriended by a doctor (Anthony Hopkins) who nursed his anguish. Merrick was a learned man, which makes his internal grief all the more touching. A tearjerker in many ways, but memorable for Hurt's makeup as the grotesque-looking Merrick, his pain-racked performance, and Freddie Francis's black-and-white photography, which captures the drabness of industrial England. Anne Bancroft, John Gielgud. Directed by David Lynch, produced by Mel Brooks and written by Lynch with Christopher Devore and Eric Bergren, from the nonfiction books *The Elephant Man and Other Reminis-*

cences by Sir Frederick Treves and *The Elephant Man: A Study in Human Dignity* by Ashley Montagu. (Video/Laser: Paramount)

ELEVENTH COMMANDMENT, THE. See *Body Count.*

ELIMINATORS (1986) ★★½ Lively adventure-satire from producer Charles Band depicting a "mandroid" and how he/it seeks the help of a lady scientist, soldier-of-fortune and martial arts champ to do battle with a mad scientist and his army. Filmed in Spain under Peter Manoogian's direction, the film has Patrick Reynolds as a half-man, half-machine character but he's uninteresting compared to the female lead (Denise Crosby), the adventurer (Andrew Prine) and the ninja (Conan Lee). Indiana Jones isn't sweating over this film, but it certainly has its moments of action and humor. John Carl Buechler did his usual good effects job. (Fox/Playhouse)

ELVES (1990) ★★½ Neo-Nazis hiding in Colorado Springs plan to breed an elf with a virgin to create a new Master Race. Along comes Dan Haggerty as a department store Santa Claus to thwart the plot. Directed by Jeff Mandel. Julie Austin, Deanna Lund. (Action International)

ELVIRA, MISTRESS OF THE DARK (1988) ★★ Cassandra Peterson was always sexually sizzling as L.A.'s horror-movie hostess, her enormous bosom falling out of her slinky black slit-dress as she cracked wise about some awful cinematic wonder. In the starring role of a film, Peterson still looks sexually sizzling and is a total gas. Best moments are at film's end when Elvira performs a fabulous tassle-twirling act in Las Vegas, her gigantic boobs overfilling the screen (or boob tube). The Mystery Hostess leaves her L.A. show for Massachusetts when her great aunt dies and bequeaths her a dark old house. It's a Puritan center where old fogies are up-tight about Elvira, and all young people love her (or wish they could, in the case of guys). Fantasy elements: a monster that Elvira has to shove down a sink, a shape-changing poodle, and a wicked uncle (W. W. Morgan Sheppard) who turns into a warlock. The workable script is by Peterson (her husband, Mark Pierson, helped but he is uncredited), Sam Egan and John Paragon. Directed by James Signorelli. Edie McClurg, Pat Crawford Brown, William Duell. (New World) (Laser: Image)

EMBRACE OF THE VAMPIRE (1994) ★★½ A whole lotta perversity is going on in this R-rated erotic vampire thriller, and one-time TV child actress Alyssa Milano (*Who's the Boss?*) shows she can be the boss as a naughty femme fatale, engaging in some hot-and-heavy lesbian and orgy sequences with multiple partners at which she bares her ripe breasts for kissing and petting. Milano portrays a sweet young college fresh(wo)man who loses her innocence to an evil bloodsucker who comes to her in dreamlike sex fantasies. This is basically your soft-core vampire movie and the fact a woman (Anne Goursaud) is at the directing helm gives the film a sensual eroticism often missing from "erotic thrillers." But its perverse nature makes this an unpleasant film to watch when vampire Martin Kemp licks blood off a door and Alyssa sticks her finger into the crotch of lesbo lady Charlotte Lewis. The meandering, almost formless script by Halle Eaton, Nicole Coady and Rick Bitzelberger (originally conceived as *The Nosferatu Diaries*) has too many unnecessary characters and undeveloped subplots, and Jennifer Tilly is wasted in a cameo. Harrison Pruett, Jordan Ladd, Rachel True. (Video/Laser: New Line)

EMBRYO (1976) ★★ B-movie material by Anita Doohan and Jack W. Thomas about a scientist (Rock Hudson) experimenting with a human fetus, elevated by moody photography (Fred Koenekamp's) and direction (Ralph Nelson's). In only a few days the fetus evolves into a woman (Barbara Carrera), tutored by Hudson in mathematics and sex—emphasis on the latter. But she turns into a homicidal maniac looking for a new formula to prevent her accelerated aging. Diane Ladd, Roddy McDowall, Dr. Joyce Brothers. (USA; IVE; Starmaker; from Ace as *Created to Kill*)

EMERALD JUNGLE, THE. Video version of *Eaten Alive* (1980) (Continental).

EMPIRE OF ASH II (1985) ★ The setting is "New Idaho" in a post-holocaustic time as horseback guys fight motorcycle guys. Horsebacker Thom Schioler teams up with Melanie Kilgour to search for her missing sister. Produced-directed by Lloyd Simandl and Michael Mazo. See *Empire of Ash III* for more (less!) (From AIP as *Maniac Warriors*)

EMPIRE OF ASH III (1985) ★ This clone of *Mad Max*, set in the post-Armageddon world of 2050, is not simply below average—it's beneath contempt. Has there ever been one of these after-the-nuclear-bombs-fall movies as bad as this? Probably, but we'd rather not search for it. We lasted 60 minutes through this atrocity to set a world record—and we're not bragging. And what's a good actor like William Smith doing as the evil leader who now rules Earth? Digging ditches would have been better, Bill. The blame for this series of incoherent submachine-gun battles, vehicles racing through a jungle and liberal doses of lesbianism and sadomasochism can be placed on producer Lloyd A. Simandl, the indescribable script of Chris Maruna and the direction by Simandl and Michael Mazo. Melanie Kilgour and Ken Farmer are among those whose careers turned to ash immediately after this was released. (From AIP as *Last of the Warriors*)

EMPIRE OF THE ANTS (1977) ★★ Subtitled *How the Pest Was Won*, this is superschlock from producer-director Bert I. Gordon. Dull characters (Joan Collins, Robert Lansing, Albert Salmi, John David Carson, Robert Pine, Jacqueline Scott) are trapped in a seaside resort with mutant ants, grown to enormous size from radiation. Gordon's special effects are slipshod and the plot (from an H. G. Wells short story) is ludicrous. The giant picnic crashers have taken over a nearby town and hypnotized the residents and . . . see what we mean by superschlock? (Embassy; Sultan)

EMPIRE OF THE DARK (1991) ★★★ Steve Barkett (*The Aftermath*) is an all-around filmmaker: writer, director, editor, actor. This work excels with its pacing, kinetic editing and Bernard Herrmann–like score by John Morgan. This fantasy-adventure has a satanic cult that exists in an alternate dimension; a 50-foot demon from Hell (stop-motion style); serial killings; a private eye–bounty hunter searching for a killer; and ninja-type battles. While Barkett's film suffers from clichés and clumsy acting, this video flick is worth enduring. Barkett stars as the private eye. Christopher Barkett (Steve's son), Richard Harrison, Terry Hendrickson, Dan Speaker. (Nautilus)

EMPIRE STRIKES BACK, THE (1980) ★★★★ Sequel to *Star Wars* didn't disappoint fans who returned time and again to cheer Luke Skywalker, Princess Leia, C3PO, R2D2, etc. Darth Vader, still the Scourge of the Universe, sends Imperial forces against rebels on the ice planet Hoth, where battles with Emperial Walkers are the major highlight of the film, but only the beginning of new adventures. Luke searches for Yoda, a mentor who furthers his knowledge of the Force; Han Solo and Chewbacca the Wookiee escape the Imperial fleet in an exciting Asteroid Belt sequence; Lando Calrissian, rogue adventurer, is introduced; and Luke faces Vader in a light-saber showdown that is a splendid piece of choreographed action. Producer George Lucas turned direction over to Irvin Kershner, and the script (by Leigh Brackett and Lawrence Kasdan) has greater philosophical interest. Lucas's third in this series (*Return of the Jedi*) rounded out the unresolved elements of this script but this proved to be the most mature. Hence, it seems to have greater depth, though the emphasis remains on action. Mark Hamill, Carrie Fisher, Peter Mayhew, Harrison Ford, David Prowse (as Vader with voice by James Earl Jones), Anthony Daniels (as the golden robot), Billy Dee Williams (as Lando), Alec Guinness (as a spectral image). (Video/Laser: Fox)

ENCINO MAN (1992) ★ Dumb teenage comedy becomes so silly that one gives up in abject frustration and rolls with the slap-happy punches. Sean Astin (in a role beneath his talents) finds a Cro-Magnon man in suspended animation and proceeds, with the help of buddy Pauly Shore, to dress him up and pose him at their high school as an exchange student. Brendan Fraser (as Encino Man) is too good to be wasted in such ridiculous fare. Directed by Les Mayfield. Megan Ward, Robin Tunney, Michael DeLuise, Mariette Hartley. (Disney)

ENCOUNTER AT RAVEN'S GATE (1988) ★ Gory sci-fi monster actioner in which punk musicians tangle with alien creatures. Eddie Cleary, Steven Vidler. Directed by Rolf de Heer. (Hemdale) (Laser: Image)

ENDANGERED SPECIES (1982) ★★★½ Enthralling, offbeat suspenser dealing with mutilated cattle. This explores the mystery with research and taste, offering a solution that involves a secret military organization conducting tests as part of a clandestine germ-warfare program. Around this semi-plausible premise director-writer Alan Rudolph and cowriter John Binder fashion a melodramatic mystery in which burned-out New York cop Robert Urich settles in a Wyoming community, only to become caught up in the enigma. JoBeth Williams, Paul Dooley, Hoyt Axton, Harry Carey, Jr. (MGM/UA)

ENDGAME (1983) ★★½ In the post-holocaust world of 2025 A.D., warriors square off in a bloodsport called "Endgame" while stormtroopers in Nazi helmets gun for them. The best Endgame player, Shannon (Al Cliver), talks his roughest opponents (burly brute, martial art oriental, etc.) into helping him escort mind-reading Mutants to safety, promising them a fortune in gold. Endless battles as the band encounters sadists, killers and blind priests. Italian *Mad Max* imitation directed by Steven Benson. Laura Gemser, George Eastman. (Media)

ENDLESS DESCENT (1989) ★★ In the vein of *The Abyss* and *Leviathan*: Sub inventor Jack Scalia dives in *Siren II* with by-the-book Captain R. Lee Ermey to find out why *Siren I* vanished in the depths. Turns out a DNA cloning experiment created monsters with tentacles, and human-shaped monstrosities, in an underwater cavern. This tries for the thrills of *Aliens* but misses by leagues. Ray Wise, Deborah Adair, John Toles Bey. Originally produced as *The Rift*. (Live) (Laser: Image)

END OF DAYS (1999) ★★½ Casting difficulties throw a pall over this overblown mixture of big-scale action sequences and a supernatural plot in which the devil attempts to destroy mankind: Gabriel Byrne as "The Man" from hell, and Arnold Schwarzenegger as an alcoholic security guard who finds the strength to take on evil single-handedly to save the world. Byrne comes off as a wisecracking grade-B-movie demon seemingly patterned on Christopher Walken's Gabriel the Archangel in the inferior *Prophecy* series. And Schwarzenegger has the impossible task of forcing us to put aside memories of the lighthearted action hero he used to play (*Total Recall, True Lies*, etc.) so we might accept him

as a new kind of action hero—one who still robustly performs the stunts and heroic deeds but who is a tragic figure searching to restore his lost faith and ultimately sacrifice himself for the good of mankind. Clearly, his Jericho Cane is a terrible case of miscasting and that only adds to the ludicrousness of this horror adventure. If the devil can blow up buildings, bring dead people back to life, and cause all kinds of mayhem in Manhattan, why is he so incompetent when it comes to finding just one woman? Wouldn't he have the supernormal resources to pluck her up and do with her what he wants, and to hell with everything else? It is this kind of illogic that often plagues supernatural movies, but it would have been so easy for director-writer Peter Hyams to plug up such a hole. By not establishing "the rules" for the movie to follow, it becomes a plotting mess and a narrative nightmare. The dumb premise has a baby of the devil being born in 1979 and anointed with rattlesnake venom, while the pope tells his followers in the Vatican City to protect the girl child, even though he knows that in 20 years (according to the Book of Revelation) she will become the mother of a devil child herself. That child will grow into the Antichrist and destroy mankind. The catch is, the devil has to fornicate with her one hour before midnight of the millennium, December 31, 1999. Schwarzenegger portrays a mentally depressed security cop as the movie begins, on the verge of committing suicide because he's unable to get over the murder of his wife and child. He's interrupted by partner Kevin Pollak (in a wasted role), who picks him up for an assignment to protect "a businessman." The businessman is Byrne, the body the devil has taken over upon arrival in Manhattan. The devil is first presented as a shimmering space warp (à la *Predator*) that comes up through the sewers of Manhattan and immediately blows up a restaurant after stealing Byrne's body. A religious fanatic tries to kill Byrne and Arnie chases him while dangling from a helicopter rope. Turns out a squad of Vatican commandos is trying to finish off the young woman. (Good guys trying to kill the good girl is the only original idea in this movie.) Robin Tunney is pretty good as the bewildered young woman who has nightmares about "The Man" and eventually she goes on the run with Arnie, as nobody can be trusted, what with the way the devil resurrects dead cop C. C. H. Pounder to do his evil bidding. One person they trust is a priest played intensely by Rod Steiger, but his strong character doesn't have enough scenes. To his credit, Hyams provides a rousing subway action sequence and a surprisingly good hand-to-hand struggle between Schwarzenegger and Tunney's housekeeper (Miriam Margolyes). However, it's ultimately so silly and contrived that no matter how hard Hyams struggles to make the action pieces exciting and grimly dark in atmosphere, *End of Days* never builds any suspense or momentum. Yes, the devil finally manifests into a huge dragonlike monster with wings, but like the rest of the supernatural stuff, it's schlocky. Derrick O'Connor, Udo Kier, Victor Varnado Michael O'Hagan, Mark Margolis. (Video/DVD: Universal)

END OF THE WORLD (1977) ★½ Poverty level sci-fier from producer Charles Band and director John Hayes, whose plodding work (also reflected in his pitiful editing) is tedious. Christopher Lee portrays Zandi, who possesses the body of a priest and plots to blow up Earth because (get this, readers) mankind is contaminating the Universe. Frank Ray Perilli's script ends on a whimper! Dean Jagger, Lew Ayres, MacDonald Carey, Sue Lyon. (Media)

END OF THE WORLD, THE. See *Panic in Year Zero*.

ENEMY FROM SPACE (1957) ★★★ Second in Hammer's series about determined scientist Bernard Quatermass, again played by Brian Donlevy, who established the role in *The Creeping Unknown*. A superior effort, from Nigel Kneale's screenplay (based on his TV serial) to Gerald Gibbs' stark photography to Val Guest's direction. Quatermass discovers a malevolent alien race in control of an isolated industrial station at Wynerton Flats. Vera Day, Bryan Forbes, Michael Ripper. (From Corinth under this title and as *Quatermass II: Enemy from Space*)

ENEMY MINE (1985) ★★★ A promising theme kicks off this big-budgeted adventure: An Earthman (Dennis Quaid) and a lizard creature called a Drac (Louis Gossett, Jr., in heavy makeup and scaly costume) laser each other out of the heavens during a space war and crashland on a barren planet where they must learn tolerance over mutual hatred. The arm's-length relationship shapes into friendship; a twist of fate leads to an exciting rescue situation. The landscapes are realistically harsh and the action sequences superbly designed, with the story making its human points while remaining solid entertainment. Directed by Wolfgang Peterson. (Video/Laser: CBS/Fox)

ENTER THE DEVIL. Video version of *The Eerie Midnight Horror Show* (HQV).

ENTITY, THE (1983) ★★★½ Above-average supernatural thriller, allegedly based on a true case that occurred in L.A. and adapted by Frank de Felitta from his own book. A widowed mother (Barbara Hershey) is attacked by an invisible demon and raped. On a literate level this deals with believers vs. nonbelievers and science vs. ESP. Focus is on characters, dialogue and tension as director Sidney J. Furie maintains a fearful atmosphere and refuses to show the "entity" in detail. Excellent makeup by Stan Winston and James Kagel. Ron Silver, David Labiosa, Alex Rocco. (CBS/Fox)

ENTITY FORCE. See *One Dark Night*.

EQUALIZER 2000 (1987) ★½ Ripoff of the *Mad Max* genre, produced by Roger Corman in the Philippines, where wall-to-wall action unfolds in furious, ludicrous fashion under Cirio H. Santiago's direction. A narrator tells us it's "one hundred years after the Nuclear Winter," and we're in an "arid desert" where the Ownership (i.e. bad guys) has control and a rebel wing is trying to restore order. A loner hero named Slade (Richard Norton, never cracking a smile in a black leather outfit) and a sexy gal (Corinne Wahl, ex–*Penthouse* pin-up) join forces to fight Mordon, a villain who is after Slade's fantastic weapon, which seems to have more firepower than all the Rambo movies together. It ain't dull as armies of men in black leather scamper over old mining digs, blazing away with machine-guns. William Steis, Robert Patrick, Frederick Bailey, Rex Cutter. (MGM/UA)

EQUINOX (1971) ★★½ Four teen-age hikers find an ancient witchcraft tome that unleashes supernatural entities, including a horned creature with pterodactyl wings and pitchfork tail. Well-intended effort by writer-director Jack Woods has early David Allen–Jim Danforth effects. Prize-winning sci-fi writer Fritz Leiber turns up as a geologist. The film took four years to complete, so the characters age before your very eyes. Producer Dennis Muren became an award-winning effects artist. Frank Bonner, Edward Connell, Barbara Hewitt. (From Wizard and VCI under this title and from Lightning as *The Beast*)

EQUINOX (1993) ★★★½ One of writer-director Alan Rudolph's strangest films, and one of his most satisfying. Set in the near future in a strange city, *Equinox* is a moody, atmospheric, slow-paced twisted fairy tale about twin brothers (both played by Matthew Modine) of opposite personalities. One is an introverted garage worker afraid of his own shadow, the other is a nasty gangster. How they finally meet is what makes this quirky, life-is-just-fate movie so intriguing. Rudolph has a way of creating oddball characters that slowly grow on you, and the lost, sometimes downcast people in *Equinox* become fascinating if not always lovable. Lara Flynn Boyle, Marisa Tomei, Tate Donovan, Lori Singer, M. Emmet Walsh, Fred Ward. (Video/Laser: Columbia TriStar)

ERASERHEAD (1978) ★★★★ Surrealistic nightmare from avant-garde filmmaker David Lynch (writer-director-producer–special effects), who suffers from an obsession with prenatal dreams. The camera plunges into black holes, squishy worm-things float like spermatozoa and a hideous mutant baby squawls its anger. "Midnight" cult film has stunning moments, with unsettling visuals and low-life characters. Jack Nance, Charlotte Stewart, Jeanne Bates, Laurel Near. (Video/Laser: RCA/Columbia)

ERIK THE VIKING (1989) ★★½ Monty Python–styled parody of adventure movies, written-directed by Python alumnus Terry Jones. Tim Robbins stars as a sword-wielding member of a plundering-blundering gang of warriors pillaging during the Age of Ragnarok. Erik decides he's tired of raping and murdering and searches for the Halls of Valhalla. The comedy-adventures are plentiful (see the Dragon of the North Sea, look out for Halfdan the Black, behold the Pit of Hell, keep an eye out for the Edge of the World, and scale the Rainbow Bridge at your own risk). Robbins is supported by John Cleese as the villain, Mickey Rooney as the grandfather, Eartha Kitt as Freya the Witch, Tim McInnerny as Sven the Berserk and Freddie Jones as Harald the Missionary. Never has pillaging been so much fun. (Video/Laser: Orion)

EROTIC ADVENTURES OF SIEGFRIED. See *Long, Swift Sword of Siegfried.*

EROTIC DREAMS (1988) ★ Soft-core sex-fantasy comedy in which Robert Miles, a practitioner of black magic, might lose his soul to the Devil if he doesn't control his sexual desires. Strictly for flesh purveyors. Directed by Robert F. Pope. Nathan Lanes, Stephanie Goldwin. (Celebrity; also in video as *Dark Dreams*)

EROTIC RITES OF FRANKENSTEIN. Video version of *Dracula vs. Dr. Frankenstein* (Nightmare; from Video Search with English subtitles).

EROTIKILL (1975) ★ Aka *The Black Countess* and *The Bare-Breasted Countess,* this is a rock-bottom French-Belgium vampire atrocity, poorly acted, incompetently photographed, feebly dubbed. Linda Romay bares her considerable assets as Irina, a bloodsucker who terrorizes love-hungry men. Devoid of story, suspense and everything else filmmakers put into movies. Directed by Jesus Franco under the alias of J. P. Johnson. Jack Taylor, Alice Arno, Monica Swin. This is heavily edited footage from *Sicarius—The Midnight Party* (or *Jacula* or *The Last Thrill*), a very X-rated effort that has been deballed into various eunuchs. (Lightning; from Luna and Media in more erotic form as *The Loves of Irina*)

ERZEBETH. See *Daughters of Darkness* (1970).

ESCAPE FROM GALAXY 3 (1986) ★ Chintzy and unconvincing Italian space opera in the *Star Wars* vein, which never hits the jugular. This is the kind of anemic space opera where giant spacecraft float past the camera, villains wear cowls and scowls, and heroes call for the "Uranium Vapor Rocket," "Megaray Shield" and "Astral Scanner." When Oraclon, King of the Night, invades the peaceful planet of Exilan, a handsome young rocket pilot and Queen Bellestar escape to the planet Earth, where they discover the meaning of sex and love in exchange for their immortality. (If they were so indifferent to sex, how come Bellstar always dresses so provocatively?) Then it's back to deep space to confront the villain in a ridiculous denouement. Silly sound effects for zap ray guns finally undermine this effort which features mild nudity and love-making sequences. Directed by Ben Norman (an alias, no doubt) from an anemic script by John Thomas. Cheryl Buchanan, James Milton, Don Powell, Auran Cristea, Margaret Rose. (Prism)

ESCAPE FROM L.A. (1996) ★★★½ This long-delayed follow-up to John Carpenter's 1982 hit, *Escape from New York,* is a half-crazed, goofy remake with essentially the same plot but with hardened warrior Snake Plissken (Kurt Russell's imitation of Clint Eastwood, aided by an eyepatch and a clipped vocabulary) infiltrating the island of Los Angeles, which is surrounded by water following a major earthquake in the next century. As a new penal colony for America's criminals and misfits under a dictatorial president (Cliff Robertson), the City of Angels has become a place of demons—a burned-out hellhole of social disorder (is this a metaphor or what?) and Disneyland is a watering hole for gang boss George Corraface and girlfriend Utopia (A. J. Langer). She's the president's runaway daughter who has stolen a doom's-day device that could stop all things mechanical on the entire planet if Corraface has his way. In a race against time, Plissken has only hours to retrieve the device, and he uses the help of Map to the Stars Eddie (Steve Buscemi), sympathetic street dame Valeria Golino and a gang led by transsexual Pam Grier. The script by director Carpenter, producer Debra Hill and Russell (also an exec producer) is at times muddled and not all the gimmicks work so well the second time around, especially Russell's forced, hoarse-voiced performance. But so much of *Escape from L.A.* is a gas, what with the surfing down Hollywood Boulevard and other satiric touches, that you should be willing to forgive Carpenter his trespasses. Sort of. Stacy Keach is effective as the president's closest aide-de-camp. Bruce Campbell, Paul Bartel, Robert Carradine and Peter Fonda have cameo bits. (Video/Laser: Paramount)

ESCAPE FROM NEW YORK (1981) ★★★ One of John Carpenter's best, moving at a roadrunner's pace as escapist fantasy. The writer-director (with cowriter Nick Castle) populates this imaginative narrative with hard-boiled characters. The plot is an outrageous joke (Manhattan, by 1997, is a maximum-security prison) and gallops headlong with stark atmosphere. Kurt Russell, an eyepatch over one eye, does his Clint Eastwood impression as Snake Plissken, a rebel assigned by security chief Lee Van Cleef to penetrate NYC to bring out the U.S. President (Donald Pleasence), whose Air Force 1 jet has crash-landed. Adrienne Barbeau, Harry Dean Stanton, Isaac Hayes, Season Hubley, Ernest Borgnine. (Embassy; Nelson; RCA/Columbia; A New Line's version has a 20-minute interview with Carpenter) (Laser: Nelson; New Line/Image, with new footage, interviews and original trailer)

ESCAPE FROM PLANET EARTH (1967) ★ Sci-fi space film lacking in everything except Stanley Cortez's cinematography. A rocket piloted by Henry Wilcoxon and Grant Williams is halfway to Venus when nuclear war destroys Earth. What to do next? Scriptwriter Stuart James Byrne settles on bickering among the passengers (Ruta Lee, Bobby Van, Mala Powers, Mike Farrell, James Craig, Denny Miller) and a meeting with a superintelligence deep in space that will provide the answer for mankind's new beginnings. Aka *Armageddon 1975*, *The Doomsday Machine*, and *Doomsday*, this film doesn't end— it just stops. Directed by Lee Sholem and Harry Hope. (Academy)

ESCAPE FROM SAFEHAVEN (1989) ★ Nuked-out New York City: in the holocaustic ruins a gang called the Colts is attacked by an evil gang led by Roy MacArthur. It's one hairy battle in this derivative *Mad Max* clonehouse. Directed by Brian Thomas Jones and James McCalmont. Rick Gianasi, Mollie O'Mara. (Sony)

ESCAPE FROM THE BRONX (1984) ★ Sequel to *1990: The Bronx Warriors*, in which the Bronx is a danger zone of roving gangs and *Road Warrior*-type freakos. Trash, the bash-boss, leads his men against Henry Silva, assigned by the Corporation to wipe out everyone in the Bronx. There's plenty of action—but that's all there is in this Italian release directed by Enzo G. Castellari. Mark Gregory, Valeria D'Obici, Timothy Brent. (Media)

ESCAPE FROM THE PLANET OF THE APES (1971) ★★ Third entry in the *Planet of the Apes* series is a talky effort, with screenwriter Paul Dehn overindulging in comedic comparisons between man and monkey. A trio of chimps travels back in time in a space capsule to present day. But because the talking creatures pose a threat, the government forms a conspiracy. This film's outcome led to *Conquest of the Planet of the Apes*. Dehn and director Don Taylor score best in generating empathy for the beleaguered chimps, are less successful with satiric jabs. Roddy McDowall, Kim Hunter, Sal Mineo, Eric Braeden (as the villain), Ricardo Montalban, Jason Evers, Albert Salmi, Natalie Trundy. (Video/Laser: Fox)

ESCAPEMENT. Video version of *Electronic Monster* (Sinister/C; Filmfax).

ESCAPE OF MEGAGODZILLA, THE. See *Terror of Mechagodzilla*.

ESCAPES (1986) ★★ Five stories in the tradition of *The Twilight Zone*, but not as satisfying. Host Vincent Price has little to do but look sinister as he spins miniyarns: "A Little Fishy" is a swipe of a famous E.C. tale about a fisherman who picks up a sandwich on the beach; "Coffee Break" is the strange-town-visited-by-an-outsider story in which a van driver gets his comeuppance; "Who's There" is a flop of a story about a jogger who meets forest elves; "Jonah's Dream" features an old woman meeting a flying saucer; and "Think Twice" is about the thin line separating fantasy from reality. Directed by David Steensland. (Starmaker; Prism)

ESCAPE 2000 (1983) ★★★ Unusual Australian futuristic adventure, set in an Orwellian society. A concentration camp for "deviates" is run by sadistic guards under a perverted commandant. Three sexual sickos drop in for sport in the style of *The Most Dangerous Game*. Five prisoners are set free and the commadant and his sporting pals follow with high-powered rifles, explosive arrows and other flesh-rending weaponry. The bloody action is almost nonstop. Much gore was cut for the U.S. Produced by David Hemmings, directed by Brian Trenchard-Smith. Music by Brain May. Olivia Hussey, Steve Railsback, Michael Craig, Carmen Duncan. Released to theaters as *Turkey Shoot*. (Embassy; Starmaker)

ESPY (1986) ★★ Japanese sci-fi actioner in which a spy with ESP powers, in the company of a German Shepherd named Cheetah, goes after a gang that uses psychokinetic powers to carry out evil. Script by Ei Ogawa. Directed by Jun Fukuda. (Paramount)

E.T. AND ME. Early working title for *E.T.—The Extra-Terrestrial*.

ETERNAL, THE (1998) ★★★ This is one odd psychological horror story with a Gaelic flavor about a 2,000-year-old Druid witch that possesses the body and mind of an alcoholic woman visiting her grandmother in a seacliff mansion shrouded in gloom and doom on the Dublin coast. It's the kind of stylized movie you will either dig for its different qualities or dismiss as incomprehensible, as nothing is really adequately explained. Writer-director Michael Almereyda (who made the equally strange vampire tale *Nadja*) has a peculiar style that avoids the clichés of the genre, and he stresses atmosphere and style as he attempts to get into the mind of the woman played by Alison Elliott. She keeps having hallucinations and nightmares, so she and husband Jared Harris (who drinks too much, but has better control) and son (Karl Geary) arrive at the mansion where Uncle Bill (Christopher Walken, in one of his curiously sinister roles) is taking care of granny, who apparently is a witch herself, and where the corpse of the Druid witch is kept in the cellar. Many plot details are purposely left unclear (I am giving Almereyda the benefit of the doubt here), so one has to do some imaginative guessing. If you don't care for subtlety, skip this one. Jason Miller, Paul Ferriter, Rachel O'Rourke, and Jeffrey Goldschrafe contribute nice character bits, and the location photography enhances the eeriness of a most unusual supernatural adventure. Aka *Trance* (Video/DVD: Vidmark-Trimark)

ETERNAL EVIL (1985) ★★ Made in Montreal as *The Blue Man*, this unusual astral-projection horror tale stars Winston Rekert as a filmmaker undergoing a series of dreams in which he commits out-of-body murders. He seeks the help of psychiatrist Karen Black. Meanwhile, Montreal cop John Novak carries on his own investigation. Directed by George Mihalka with a fluid camera, but it's quite bewildering. Andrew Bednarsky, Patty Talbot, Lois Maxwell. (Lightning) (Laser: Image)

ETERNAL FIST. See *Fist of Steel.*

ETERNITY (1989) ★★½ At two hours, five minutes, this reincarnation feature runs on eternally—but it's still a sincere movie that marked Jon Voight's return to the screen after a five-year hiatus. Voight portrays a TV news investigator who has dreams about a former life, during a medieval age, when he and Armand Assante were rivals for maiden Eileen Davidson. Now Assante is a ruthless TV station mogul and Davidson an actress whom Assante tries to wrest from Voight. An unlikely TV trial-for-libel on Assante's network gives Voight opportunity to deliver a plea for the brotherhood of man. Voight helped shape the preachy script with director Steven Paul and Paul's wife, Dorothy Koster Paul. Wilford Brimley, Kaye Ballard, Eugene Roche. (Academy) (Laser: Image)

E.T.—THE EXTRA-TERRESTRIAL (1982) ★★★★★ To think: the great box office smash is a simplistic but heartfelt parable in which boy meets alien, boy loves alien, boy loses alien. Steven Spielberg's masterpiece was fashioned from a script by Melissa Mathison, who borrowed such Spielbergian themes as suburban settings; ordinary kids and adults coping with realities; an awesome attitude toward lights in the sky and alien life. Comedy touches keep E.T. from becoming too sentimental, and even when the story turns serious, and men are shown as menaces, one feels for E.T.'s plight in wanting to overcome prejudice on Earth to return home. Carlo Rambaldi created E.T., and although the cutie at times seems clumsy and too cute, the cuteness wins you over. Great score by John Williams; fine flying sequences by Dennis Muren. Dee Wallace, Peter Coyote (the man with keys), Robert MacNaughton, Drew Barrymore, Henry Thomas, Milt Kogan. Early working titles: *E.T. and Me* and *Night Skies.* (Video/Laser: MCA)

EUREKA (1983) ★★ Surrealistic portrait of the world's richest man, overburdened with the esoterica and eccentricities of cameraman-director Nicolas Roeg to the point of excruciation. Gene Hackman does a good job of etching Jack McCall, a man made unhappy by his good fortune, but the narrative is incoherent, full of symbolic asides (such as a voodoo orgy) and erotic extravagances. Others lost in this muddle: Theresa Russell, Rutger Hauer, Ed Lauter, Joe Pesci. (MGM/UA)

EVE OF DESTRUCTION (1991) ★★★½ Good combination of high-tech sci-fi and action in which humanoid robot Eve VIII goes haywire during a holdup in San Francisco and is locked in "battlefield mode." The robot's creator, who programmed Eve VIII with her own memories, personality and image, joins antiterrorist specialist Gregory Hines to stop the monster. There's a balance of suspense and action in the script by director Duncan Gibbins and Yale Udoff, with an apocalyptic element that adds a race against time. Hines is effective as the agent and Sweden's Renee Soutendijk shows a wide range in portraying Eve VIII and her creator. Michael Greene, Kurt Fuller, John M. Jackson, Kevin McCarthy. (RCA/Columbia; Orion, Sultan) (Laser: Nelson/New Line)

EVENT HORIZON (1997) ★★★½ This is a superb and exciting deep-space action-mystery thriller set in 2047, with outstanding special effects, a pace that never falters, an intriguing premise, and visually shocking graphics—all the stuff a sci-fi fan expects but rarely gets. *Lewis & Clark*, a search-and-rescue spaceship, is assigned to take inventor Sam Neill to Neptune, where the research vessel *Event Horizon* has been found after being lost for seven years. Neill has designed man's first "dimensional gateway," enabling a spacecraft to jump from one point in the universe to another, but when he arrives at the massive ship (which obviously has warped into space) with a rescue team made up of commander Larry Fishburne, medical officer Kathleen Quinlan, and other crew members Joely Richardson, Richard T. Jones, Jack Noseworthy, Jason Isaacs, Sean Pertwee, and Peter Marinker, they find the crew slaughtered. Before long, Philip Eisner's script has the space jockeys exposed to their worst fears and all hell breaks loose. The effects are dazzling and come nonstop as Fishburne tries to keep the team together and figure a way out of the blood-and-gore horrors that wipe out the team one by one. Director Paul Anderson, who filmed in a London studio, never allows a dull moment to creep into this creepy, scary sci-fi blast, which even suggests that the possessed spaceship might have been to hell and back. (Video/DVD/Laser: Paramount)

EVE, THE WILD WOMAN. See *King of Kong Island.*

EVICTORS, THE (1979) ★★ Writer-producer-director Charles B. Pierce purports this is a true story of a "haunted" farmhouse but his execution lacks conviction or the pseudodocumentary air that earmarked his *Legend of Bigfoot*. Surprises are telegraphed and cat-and-mouse suspense is tepid. Michael Parks and Jessica Harper are victims of scheming realtor Vic Morrow. Toss out *The Evictors*. (Vestron) (Laser: Japanese)

EVIL, THE (1978) ★★½ Along come Joanna Pettet and Richard Crenna to convert a mansion into a rehab center, unaware of the house's bloody history. First thing they know, people and animals are going crazy at the height of electric storms, the house trembles as though it were '06 again and there's a corpse in the dumbwaiter. There's also the lurking presences of Andrew Prine and Victor Buono, the latter as a demon from Hell. "This house is trying to kill us all," remarks Crenna once he catches on to Donald Thompson's plot gimmick. The rent would kill anyone. Directed by Gus Trikonis. Aka *Cry Demon*. (Embassy)

EVIL ALTAR (1989) ★★ The best thing about this video-movie is villain William Smith, who portrays evil on a level few other actors can attain. As a minion of the Devil, Smith is collecting souls for Hell in the community of Red Rock with the help of cop Robert Z'Dar. Directed by Jim Winburn. Pepper Martin, Theresa Cooney, Tal Armstrong. (South Gate; Hemdale)

EVIL BELOW (1889) ★★ Mixture of underwater action and ersatz supernatural thrills when Wayne Crawford and June Chadwick search for a treasure that went down off the coast of Africa in the 17th Century. Art Payne's script was directed by Jean-Claude Dubois. (Raedon)

EVIL CLUTCH (1988) ★★ Excessively gory Italian film executed without artistic finesse or an understanding of what makes the genre bleed best. In short, this was made to sicken you without artistic merit. A vacationing couple comes to a village haunted by a malignant supernatural force (no further explanation given). The couple is set upon by ghouls, demons and the walking dead, depicted as ugly, depraved creatures. For your money you get a man's penis ripped off by a woman's vagina (in the shape of a clawlike hand), arms, hands and heads yanked (or chopped) off, blood spurting through severed arteries, zombie monsters and people screaming, cackling and going crazy without subtlety. A chaotic film with lengthy countryside shots that pad the storyless plot. Written-directed by Andreas Marfori. Coralina C. Tassoni, Diego Ribon. (Rhino offers the uncut version) (Laser: Image)

EVIL DEAD, THE (1983) ★★★ Powerful cult favorite appreciated for excessive gore effects and sledgehammer techniques from a triumvi-rate of producers (line executive Robert Tapert, writer-director Sam M. Raimi and actor Bruce Campbell). Made in Tennessee and Michigan, the film (original title: *Book of the Dead*) concerns young adults finding a Book of the Dead from the Sumerian period in a wilderness cabin. Recited incantations open portals to another dimension and hideous demons wreak havoc. And havoc it is, as bodies are hacked to pieces—the only way to stop the evil entities. A crude effort full of visual shocks, reflecting gore talents to come. Duck those flying body parts and look out for the spattering blood. Sarah York, Betsy Baker, Ellen Sandweiss, Hal Delrich. (HBO) (Laser: Image)

EVIL DEAD 2: DEAD BY DAWN (1987) ★★★★ This is so stylishly, hysterically overdone that it stands out as a first-class comedy gore flick. "There's something out there" (a line from the film, believe it or not) exemplifies the tongue-in-cheek approach of director-writer Sam Raimi, who works with cowriter Scott Spiegel in keeping close to the original film's story. Once again the Book of the Dead allows invisible demons to rove the forest, animating inanimate objects and possessing animate ones. Raimi is out to startle you with the most blatant visuals. A man chainsawing off his own hand, a woman gulping an eyeball, tree roots and tendrils strangling humans, and demons cackling their evil are among the perverted delights. There's a wonderful parody of the Rambo trailer in which hero Campbell arms himself, concluding with his approval: "Groovy." The overacting finds acceptability within the gushing blood (sometimes green, sometimes red), the flesh-destroying effects and wide-angle-lens shots that are, well, "groovy." Denise Bixler, Kassie Wesley, Dan Hicks, Theodore Raimi. (Video/Laser: Vestron)

EVIL DEAD 3. See *Army of Darkness*.

EVIL EYE. See *Manhattan Baby*.

EVIL EYE, THE (1962) ★★½ Historically this is the first of the Italian "giallo" films, in which more attention is paid to the stalkings and the murders than to the investigations, and the killer is presented as a disguised fiend who shows no bounds in depravity. Directed by Mario Bava in Rome, it depicts a tourist (Leticia Roman) who is witness to a terrible street murder and is caught up in bloody slayings. Years later, Dario Argento took the genre to new heights of horror with *The Bird with the Crystal Plumage* and *Deep Red*. John Saxon, Valentina Cortese. (Sinister/C)

EVIL IN THE SWAMP (1989) ★ Children living in a swamp are stalked by photographer James Keach. John Savage, Robby Benson, Samantha Eggar. Aka *All the Kind Strangers*. (Chiron Industries; MNX)

EVIL JUDGMENT (1985) ★★ Is a psychopathic judge responsible for a series of vicious murders? Pamela Collyer plays an investigator checking out that very question. Directed by Claude Castravelli. Jack Langedyk, Nanette Workman. (Video Treasures; Media)

EVIL LAUGH (1988) ★★ A rundown, empty orphanage serves as the setting for this psycho-killer screamer in which a killer is knocking off volunteer medical workers. Directed by Dominick Brasscia, who scripted with coproducer Steven Baio. Baio is also in the cast with Kim McKamy, Tony Griffin, Jody Gibson. (Celebrity)

EVIL OF FRANKENSTEIN, THE (1964) ★★ Hammer's third entry in its Frankenstein series, produced by Anthony Hinds, is one of its least efforts, providing only laboratory-worn results. Director Freddie Francis and writer John Elder (Hinds) needed a good solid bolt of electricity in the as . . . pirations. Peter Cushing is back as the Baron with a yen for resurrecting the dead, and Kiwi Kingston, as the Monster, lumbers in caves and laboratories under Francis's own lumbering direction. The monster, preserved in a glacier, doesn't get moving until late in the proceedings. A new prologue was added for U.S. TV with William Phipps. Peter Woodthorpe, Duncan Lamont, Katy Wild. (Video/Laser: MCA)

EVIL PASSAGE. See *The Power* (1984).

EVILS OF THE NIGHT (1983) ★★ Neville Brand and Aldo Ray portray pawns of outer space invaders who terrorize teenagers. John Carradine, Tina Louise, Julie Newmar. Produced-directed by Mardi Rustam. (Lightning; Live)

EVIL SPAWN (1987) ★ Originally released by Camp Video, this horror vehicle for sexy Bobbie Bresee was reedited, with new material added by Fred Olen Ray. The result was *The Alien Within*. See that entry.

EVILSPEAK (1982) ★★ Dressed-up revamping of the-worm-that-turns tale. Clint Howard (Ron's brother) is a klutzy cadet at a military academy, picked on by juvenile peers. Uncovering a volume on satanic rituals, Clint conjures up Estabar the Demon, who chops off the heads of virgins. Howard uses a computer to call up the devil in a dungeon beneath the school's chapel. This is not a particularly good film and becomes slightly disgusting when a puppy is slaughtered by Howard's tormentors. What makes the film work, though, is Howard's ability to engender sympathy. R. G. Armstrong is wasted as a drunken night watchman. Eric Weston's direction is adequate. Some critics speak evil of *Evilspeak*. Don Stark, Claude Earl Jones, Haywood Nelson. (CBS/Fox)

EVIL SPIRITS (1990) ★★ Take a gloomy mansion, populate it with eccentrics, give it a landlady who murders boarders and you have a "black humor" shocker with an above-average cast. Directed by Gary Graver, whose lighting

and gothic imagery give this low-budget effort class, *Evil Spirits* focuses on Karen Black, a "lovely" landlady as wacky as a gold-plated ax. Among her roomers: Martine Beswick as a spaced-out dancer; Michael Berryman as a Peeping Tom; Bert Remsen and Virginia Mayo as Beverly Hills folk; Mikel Angel (the screenwriter) as a sot; and Debra Lamb as a psychic. Oh, don't forget the wheelchair-bound husband with whom Black communicates psychically, and the guy chained in the cellar who gnaws on human hands. Along comes Social Security inspector Arte Johnson. That still doesn't stop batty Black from burying new bodies in her yard, the smell of which bothers nosy neighbor Yvette Vickers. Robert Quarry is a doctor and Anthony Eisley is a cop. (Prism) (Laser: Image)

EVIL TOONS (1990) ★★ This is one sorry excuse for a horror movie, wasting the talents of David Carradine as a 16th-century warlock who returns from the dead to the house where he hung himself, a book under his arm that has a talking cover. Inside the book is an animated (read: cartoon) monster in the Tex Avery style that pops out and inhabits the bodies of its slaughtered victims. Among those victims are several shapely house cleaners in short shorts who frequently expose their large breasts for no good reason. Fred Olen Ray coproduced and directed the nothing script by Sherman Scott, casting such lovelies as Monique Gabrielle, Suzanne Ager, Stacey Nix and Michelle Bauer as the fleshpots. Dick Miller is thrown into the potpourri to make fun of himself and horror movies, but his presence only points out the barrenness of this misguided project. Arte Johnson, Madison Stone, Don Dowe. (Prism) (Laser: Image)

EVIL TOWN (1987) ★★ A stranger in town discovers zombies created by a traditional mad scientist. A mishmash of a movie composed of footage from three projects and strung together with the help of Elmer's Glue, rubber bands and paper clips. Directed by Edward Collins, Larry Spiegel and Peter S. Traynor. Dean Jagger, James Keach, Michele Marsh, Robert Walker, Jr. (Transworld; Starmaker)

EVIL WITHIN, THE (1989) ★★★ This French horror film, borrowing cinematic touches of the macabre from Frank Henenlotter, David Cronenberg and Larry Cohen, is definitely not for the squeamish. Voluptuous Emmanuelle Escourrou, a beauty working in a circus animal act, becomes the host for a snakelike creature that bursts out of the insides of a panther and crawls up into her vagina. It communicates telepathically with her, insisting it needs human blood to grow, so lovely Emmanuelle knives males to death. This unusually graphic movie wallows in blood, as does Escourrou as her search for edible gore becomes desperate. The birth sequence (monster by Benoit Lestang) is unsettling and there is a distastefulness about it all as random passersby are slaughtered. Director Alain Robak (who cowrote with Serge Clikier) opts for ambiguity about the whys of it all (an opening prologue hints this evil thing was created at the dawn of time) and it ends on an inconclusive note. Leave it to the French to blend neo-reality with pure horror. Your flesh will crawl and your skin will creep. First made as *Baby Blood*. Jean-François Gallotte. (A-Pix)

EWOK ADVENTURE, THE (1984) ★★★½ Endor's moon, as any *Return of the Jedi* viewer knows, harbors intelligent creatures known as Ewoks, who speak an unintelligible language in groans and sighs and are adept with crude weapons. In this TV-movie from George Lucas, a starcruiser carrying a family of four crashlands. The parents are kidnapped by a snorting giant called the Gorax and two kids (Aubree Miller and Eric Walker) are befriended by the little furry ones and trek to find the Gorax. They encounter a vicious Tree Snake, hulking beasts, a lake that entraps those who fall into it and a firefly named Izirna. Bob Carrau's script is juvenile entertainment, but refreshing. Produced by Tom Smith and directed by John Korty in and around Marin County. Special effects by Dennis Muren, Michael Pangrazio, Phil Tippett and Jon Berg. Released in Europe as *Caravan of Courage: An Ewok Adventure*. Fionnula Flanagan, Guy Boyd. (Video/Laser: MGM/UA)

EWOK: THE BATTLE FOR ENDOR (1985) ★★★½ Sequel to *The Ewok Adventure*, less a children's story and more an action adventure in the *Star Wars* tradition. Aubree Miller is back as the lost Earthling, Cindel, who sees her parents killed in an attack by the evil alien Kerak and his seven-foot henchmen (lizardmen called Marauders). She escapes with Wicket the Ewok to begin adventures that lead her to a derelict named Noa (Wilford Brimley) and a cute little creature, Teek, who zips around the Endor landscape like a flash. Action is nonstop when Cindel and Wicket are kidnapped by the evil witch Charal and taken to Karek's castle. Climactic battle is a steal from *Return of the Jedi*, but still a rousing time. Again, Tom Smith (the genius behind Industrial Light and Magic) is producer and again the story idea is George Lucas's. Jim and Ken Wheat cowrote and codirected. The effects are plentiful, featuring a killer dragon in a cave, stop-motion beasts of burden, a flying spaceship, and other delights for which Lucas is famous. Warwick Davis is good as Wicket, but it's Teek who almost steals this show. (Video/ Laser: MGM/UA)

EXCALIBUR (1981) ★★★ John Boorman's interpretation of the King Arthur legend etches a brutal vision of the Middle Ages, intermingling myth and magic with gritty day-to-day hard-

ships. Arthur (Nigel Terry) pulls the mystical Excalibur sword from a rock and with Merlin the Magician (Nicol Williamson) forges a kingdom symbolized by the gallant Knights of the Round Table. But there is also betrayal from his Queen Guinevere (Cherie Lunghi) and the royal knight Sir Lancelot (Nicholas Clay), and the ordeal of the Quest for the Holy Grail. Themes of success, failure and redemption run throughout this strange, lengthy period saga. (Video/Laser: Warner Bros.)

eXistenZ (1999) ★★★ David Cronenberg has always had an obsession for things that look like sexual parts but really aren't, and acts that resemble sexual encounters but really aren't. Gooey openings, drippy appendages, mounds with tips on them, organic squishy things— these objects are always popping up in the Cronenberg worlds. This time the offbeat Canadian filmmaker enters the world of virtual reality, following in the wake of *The Matrix, The Game*, and *The Thirteenth Floor*. In all of these films, one is never certain where reality ends and "the game" begins. Unlike the other films, *eXistenZ* does not feature spectacular special effects. Instead, visual-effects artist Jim Isaac creates a normal-looking world wherein only a few props look weird. That is the Cronenberg touch. Well, to get to the plot: *eXistenZ* is a brand-new fantasy role-playing game invented by a brilliant woman named Allegra Geller (Jennifer Jason Leigh) who is introducing her brainchild to test subjects. Immediately you know Cronenberg is at work when you see the "cable" that connects from the control board to a "bioport" at the base of the player's spine. It looks like an umbilical cord. And the control board looks like an organic cutout of some of those sexual organs referred to above. You squeeze it and fondle it and rub your hands over the bumps and it makes squishy noises and writhes around weirdly. Suddenly an assassin (apparently from a band of terrorist rebels trying to prevent people from playing these games, since it destroys one's concept of reality) shoots Jason Leigh with an organic pistol made out of the carcass of a two-headed toad. This unusual weapon shoots not bullets but human teeth. Since teeth don't necessarily kill you instantly, Leigh jumps up and escapes with a public-relations guy (Jude Law) who works for Antenna (the company that put up the $5 million to create the eXistenZ game). On the run, dodging more assassins and rebels, they look for a "country gas station" and darned if they don't find one (identified as "Country Gas Station" on the side of the building) where a hard-looking guy named Gas (Willem Dafoe) inserts a "bioport" into Law so that he and Leigh can play the game. Now we go into the eXistenZ game, where deception and trickery are commonplace, and Law begins to lose his ability to tell reality from fantasy. There are more oddball characters who come and go, secret passwords are given, characters jump in and out of the story, and there is an introduction to a laboratory where the game control boards are shown to be made from amphibious creatures and synthetic DNA. There's one of Cronenberg's revolting scenes (he loves to throw these into his films) where Law eats some awful-looking amphibian creatures in a Chinese restaurant, only to discover the picked bones form a pistol—with human teeth yet. It will come as no surprise to anybody tuned into this genre of movie that a "twist ending" is in store. But Cronenberg is too late—others already beat him to the punch, and did it better. You can see it coming for a mile. The excellent cast includes Ian Holm, Don McKellar, Callum Keith Rennie, Sarah Polley, and Robert A. Silverman. (Video/DVD: Dimension)

EXORCIST, THE (1973) ★★★★★ Thinking man's horror picture juxtaposing graphic shock with allegorical levels of religion vs. evil, with William Peter Blatty adapting his best-seller for director William Friedkin. Everyone was shocked by the nauseous horrors suffered by young Linda Blair as she is possessed by an evil spirit: green vomit, ghastly makeup, foul-mouthed blasphemy, glassy sulfurous green eyes, a head that makes a 360-degree turn, etc. In the process, viewers overlooked many of the story's subtleties, which are of greater interest. How, for example, does the mother of priest Jason Miller fit in? How did the amulet come to be found by cop Lee J. Cobb? Concern yourself with these details, and less with bilious visuals, and you will find it richly rewarding. Excellently photographed by Owen Roizman and Billy Williams. Max von Sydow, Ellen Burstyn, Jack MacGowran, Kitty Winn. Mercedes McCambridge provided the ugly voice of the Demon that blurts from Blair's mouth. (Warner Bros.; RCA/Columbia) (Laser: Warner Bros.)

EXORCIST II: THE HERETIC (1977) ★ An absolute fiasco directed by John Boorman—audiences laughed this hunkajunk off the screen, and it deserved debasing, emerging an unintentional parody. Richard Burton, as a priest assigned to investigate the death of Father Karras (from *The Exorcist*) overplays to absurdity. And Louise Fletcher, as a psychiatrist probing the mind of Regan (Linda Blair), is amateurish. The William Goodhart plot involves James Earl Jones as African chief Kokumo and more mumbo jumbo than most witch doctors hear in a lifetime. The only good things about this failure are the cinematography by William Fraker, the set design, and the Ennio Morricone score. Max von Sydow returns in flashbacks. Ned Beatty, Kitty Winn, Paul Henreid. (Warner Bros.)

EXORCIST III: LEGION (1990) ★★★ William Peter Blatty, who wrote the novel on which *The Exorcist* was based, wrote-directed this third film in the series (based on Blatty's *Legion*), which stars George C. Scott as Lt. Kinderman (Lee J. Cobb in the original). New murders lead Kinderman to conclude that the spirit of a serial killer nicknamed Gemini has possessed the body of incarcerated criminal Brad Dourif, who promises to escape to murder again. Blatty goes for unusual scare tactics. Ed Flanders is a priest, Nicol Williamson is the new exorcist, and Patrick Ewing (the Knicks basketball player) is a guardian angel (!?). (Video/Laser: CBS/Fox)

EXPEDITION MOON. See *Rocketship X-M.*

EXPLORERS (1985) ★★★ The gentler side to director Joe Dante, who focuses on three teenagers: One is a dreamer, another is a junior scientist while the third is a youth alienated from his family. They make contact with space creatures, discover how to build a rocket and fly to meet the E.T.s. That meeting is the funny side to *Close Encounters* as the bug-eyed creatures are TV lovers, who recite lines from cartoons and movies. A charming science fantasy, written by Eric Luke, with cute aliens by Rob Bottin. Ethan Hawke, River Phoenix, Jason Presson, Mary Kay Place. (Video/Laser: Paramount)

EXTERMINATORS OF THE YEAR 3000 (1984) ★★ Italian-Spanish ripoff of *Road Warrior* set in a post-holocaust world where men fight for water after the ozone belt is destroyed. Our Mad Max lookalike drives a beat-up wreck equipped with weapons and radar called "The Exterminator," and battles a funky fleet of wheels commanded by Crazy Bull, a grotesque guerrilla who calls his men "Mother Grabbers." Directed by Jules Harrison. Alicia Moro, Alan Collins, Eduardo Fajardo, Luca Valentini. (HBO)

EXTRAORDINARY ADVENTURES OF BARON MUENCHHAUSEN. See *Baron Muenchhausen.*

EXTRATERRESTRIAL NASTY. See *Night Fright.*

EYE, THE. See *Eyeball.*

EYEBALL (1974) ★ Here's one to turn on gore lovers: murderer kills, then pops out his victim's eyeballs. Nearsighted Italian-Spanish release is about as exciting as watching an eye chart in an optician's office. Director-writer Umberto Lenzi is in need of a Seeing Eye dog, and this is a dog. John Richardson, Martine Brochard. Aka *The Eye* and *The Devil's Eye.* (Prism)

EYE CREATURES, THE (1965) ★½ E.T. invaders resembling huge upright marshmallows with black gaping holes for mouths invade a rural community while stupid Army personnel surrounds their flying saucer. Action centers on kids making out on lovers' lane and how they outsmart the hulking entities. This crude TV quickie is an inferior remake of *Invasion of the Saucermen*, produced-directed ineptly by Larry Buchanan. Its only interesting feature is a severed alien hand that does an impression of the

Beast with Five Fingers. John Ashley, Cynthia Hull, Chet Davis, Warren Hammack. (Sinister/C; S/Weird; Filmfax; Nostalgia)

EYE OF THE DEMON (1987) ★★½ Despite swipes from *Rosemary's Baby* and *The Omen*, this TV-movie has intriguing moments when yuppies Pamela Sue Martin and Tim Matheson escape the rat race to live on an island off the East Coast haunted by a witchcraft past. It appears Matheson is part of a cult staging a conspiracy trip on Martin, who keeps seeing things that later aren't there. You've seen it before, but there are scary moments and the climax pays off. Directed by Carl Schenkel. Barbara Billingsley, Jeff Conaway, Inga Swenson, Woody Harrelson. Originally shown on TV as *Bay Coven*. (Video/Laser: Vidmark)

EYE OF THE EVIL DEAD. See *Manhattan Baby*.

EYE OF THE SERPENT (1992) ★★½ A half-baked sword-and-sorcery adventure-fantasy with not enough fantasy and too much steamy sex. Roving sword warrior Tom Schultz gets caught up in a war between two evil sisters, fighting for possession of two legendary swords (said to contain gems that will open the gates to Paradise) and the beautiful, innocent daughter of one of those sisters. The script by Stewart Chapin–Mark Seldis–Tracy Young spends a lot of time depicting one evil queen sitting around her castle, urging a scholar to translate an old rune, and plenty of time with those lovemaking sequences. Director Ricardo Jacques Gale needed better fight coordinators. The action sequences are lousy. Diana Frank, Lenore Andriel, Lisa Toothman, Chuch Mavich. (Video: Academy/DVD; Laser: Image)

EYE OF THE STORM (1992) ★★★ Offbeat psychothriller with surprise twists: Two brothers, after surviving the murder of their parents, turn into maladjusted adults running a roadside café-hotel, stopping place for drunken millionaire Dennis Hopper and wife Lara Flynn Boyle. Craig Sheffer and Bradley Gregg bring interesting nuances to the whacked-out brothers, one of whom . . . well, we don't want to give it away. Atmospheric direction by Yuri Zeltser. (Video/Laser: New Line)

EYES. See *Mansion of the Doomed*.

EYES BEHIND THE STARS (1972) ★½ Photographer and model are taking photos when the cameraman senses an alien presence. Eventually he has an encounter too close for comfort. Cheap UFO pseudothriller showing how the government suppresses flying saucer reports. Written-directed by Roy Garrett (real name: Mario Gariazzo). Martin Balsam, Nathalie Delon, Robert Hoffmann. (United; National)

EYES OF A STRANGER (1980) ★★½ The Miami Strangler is terrorizing women with obscene calls, then strangling and sexually abusing them.

Some charmer. Lauren Tewes is a TV newswoman who goes after him when she suspects he's a resident of her apartment building. Jennifer Jason Leigh portrays a vulnerable blind girl. The Mark Jackson–Eric L. Bloom script is sleazy, demeaning to women, unnecessarily brutal and simple-minded. Tom Savini's graphic makeup grotesqueries seem subdued. Director Ken Wiederhorn adds no directorial tricks. John DiSanti, Peter DuPre. (Warner Bros.)

EYES OF DR. CHANEY. See *Mansion of the Doomed*.

EYES OF EVIL. See *The Thousand Eyes of Dr. Mabuse*.

EYES OF FIRE (1984) ★★ This artistic, melancholy period supernatural tale is only partly successful. Its photography, capturing a dank, dark forest with strong beams of light and clouds of mist etching its characters, is strong and sensual. But the story by director Avery Crounse is ponderous and a hodgepodge of imagery. The time is 1750 when the townspeople of Dalton's Ferry attempt to hang their adulterous preacher. The man of the cloth is saved by a witch girl and flees to set up a new stockade in a valley inhabited by mud people and a demon. Symbolism and allegory make it literate but nothing about the characters or "monsters" creates suspense. Aka *Cry Blue Sky*. Dennis Lipscomb, Guy Boyd. (Video/Laser: Vestron.)

EYES OF HELL. See *The Mask* (1961).

EYES OF LAURA MARS (1978) ★★ Chic photographer Faye Dunaway, a specialist in blending sex and sadism in her morbid layouts, is inexplicably linked to a psycho killer, but this link is never explored, and the film becomes a simple-minded one-murder-after-the-other plot until the maniac closes in on Dunaway. John Carpenter's original concept was revised by David Zelag Goodman. Directed by Irvin Kershner. Tommy Lee Jones costars as the investigating cop. Intriguing premise ultimately suffers from producer Jon Peters's blindness to story quality. Brad Dourif, Rene Auberjonois, Raul Julia. (RCA/Columbia; Goodtimes) (Laser: Columbia)

EYES OF THE AMARYLLIS, THE (1982) ★★★ Gentle, restrained ghost story about a young girl (Natalie Babbitt) who comes to Nantucket Island in 1880 to live with her grandmother—a strange woman who keeps an even stranger vigil for the return of a lover who drowned at sea. This is more a coming-of-age tale than a supernatural thriller, as writers Frederick O'Harra and Stratton Rawson emphasize character and atmosphere. Director Frederick King Keller plays the same game. Ruth Ford, Jonathan Bolt, Guy Boyd. (Vestron; Live)

EYES WITHOUT A FACE. Video version of *The Horror Chamber of Dr. Faustus* (Interama; Filmfax) (Laser: Image).

FABULOUS BARON MUNCHAUSEN, THE (1961) ★★★ From the Czechs who made *The Fabulous World of Jules Verne*, here is another ingenious blending of live action with animation, based on Gustav Doré engravings. A first-man-on-the-moon story told by writer-director Karel Zeman with panache. (Live; Vestron; Tapeworm; also in video from American Video and on laser from Image as *The Original Fabulous Adventures of Baron Munchausen (Baron Prasil)*

FABULOUS JOURNEY TO THE CENTER OF THE EARTH. See *Where Time Began.*

FACELESS (1988) ★★½ Dr. Flamono (Helmut Berger) attempts to restore a woman's beautiful countenance after her face has been disfigured by acid. Also being held in the batty doc's lab is Caroline Munro, whose father (Telly Savalas) sends private dick Christopher Mitchum to find her. Howard Vernon and Anton Diffring also appear in this horror entry from Italian director Jesus Franco. The French version (from Import Horror) is uncut.

FACELESS MONSTER, THE. See *Nightmare Castle.*

FACELESS VAMPIRE KILLERS. See *The Fearless Vampire Killers.*

FACE OF ANOTHER, THE (1966) ★★ Producer-director Hiroshi Teshigahara, who helmed *Woman in the Dunes*, offers another haunting tale with allegorical overtones: A man horribly disfigured in an accident turns into an outcast and is driven to a psychiatrist-plastic surgeon who produces a lifelike mask of a stranger's face. Nakadai assumes the stranger's personality. Aka *I Have a Stranger's Face.* (Sony, with English subtitles)

FACE OF EVIL, THE (1973). See *A Name for Evil.*

FACE/OFF (1997) ★★★½ John Woo directs action movies like no one else, and when his talent for blazing shoot-outs and fiery crashes is combined with a script that has unusual personality twists, the result is a rousing experience. Sometimes this movie is purely visceral, other times it's purely psychological. A most unusual blend. Adding to the success of this over-the-top action film, from an original screenplay by Mike Werb and Michael Colleary, are intriguing science-fiction touches and two excellent performances—Nicolas Cage as sadistic sociopath Castor Troy, who kills for the joy of it, and John Travolta as Sean Archer, a dedicated FBI agent driven to avenge Troy's murder of his son. Now, wait a minute. Those are the characters Travolta and Cage play in the beginning half hour. After that, with Troy captured and in a coma, Archer agrees to exchange faces with his old adversary in order to trick Troy's brother Pollock (Alexandro Nivola) into revealing the hiding place of a bomb that could wipe out Los Angeles. Archer undergoes an incredible operation that not only gives him Troy's face, but he gets a computer chip in his laryx so he

sounds like Troy. But then, as you might expect, while Archer is in a maximum-security prison carrying out the subterfuge, Troy wakes up in the hospital facility, forcing the doctor to graft Archer's face on him and killing all those who knew of the switch. That leaves Archer, now looking like Troy, stuck in prison and Troy, now looking like Archer, taking over the FBI spot and making love to Archer's long-suffering wife (Joan Allen). Each actor must now "impersonate" the other, and you frequently have to remind yourself that good guy is bad guy, and bad guy is good guy. Identity lines are further blurred by the fact that Archer (now Troy) kills numerous prison guards and SWAT team members to save himself. In other words, the good guy is killing good guys, while the bad guy is helping the good guys. Also, each character has to adapt to new environments and gets involved in the other's life, assuming some of the other's traits. It's an amazing bit of writing and acting. Meanwhile, the action is nonstop with large-scale shoot-outs, confrontations, bodies crashing through glass walls and rooftops, and a spectacular motorboat chase. A good supporting cast includes Gina Gershon (as the real Troy's wife), Harve Presnell as Archer's FBI chief, C. C. H. Pounder as a fellow agent, and Dominique Swain as Archer's troubled daughter. Face it: this is one to savor. (Video/DVD: Paramount)

FACE OF FEAR. See *Peeping Tom.*

FACE OF FEAR, THE (1990) ★★★ This TV-movie, based on a Dean R. Koontz novel, was adapted by Koontz and Alan J. Glueckman. It's a contrived slasher thriller in which a serial killer, The Butcher, traps magazine editor Lee Horsley and girlfriend Pam Dawber in an office building one night and pursues them floor by floor. Although Horsley has a fear of heights, he and Dawber, with a convenient mountain-climber's rig, escape by descending the side of the building. There's some tense moments but the silliness of the situation, and the unbelievable characters established by director Farhad Mann, defeat an all-too obvious contrivance.

FACE OF FU MANCHU, THE (1965) ★★ Hammer's resurrection of the Sax Rohmer villain, with Christopher Lee as the insidious Asian planning to destroy the world with a poison invented by a German he holds prisoner. Nigel Green is Sir Nayland Smith of Scotland Yard. Don Sharp directed Harry Alan Towers's production, which Towers wrote. Tsai Chin is Fu's daughter, Karin Dor a hapless captive, Walter Rilla the scientist. Original title: *The Mask of Fu Manchu.* This film proved to be so successful that a series resulted: *The Brides of Fu Manchu, Vengeance of Fu Manchu, Kiss and Kill* and *The Castle of Fu Manchu.* (Warner Bros.)

FACE OF MARBLE (1946) ★★ While creaky in terms of its antiquated techniques, this Monogram thriller from the Frankenstein school has such an unusual plot that it's entertaining and offbeat. John Carradine, in one of his sympathetic roles, and Robert Shayne portray doctors in a cliffside mansion conducting electrical experiments in restoring life to the dead. Brutus, the family Great Dane, becomes a test experiment, but the dog turns into a phantom that passes through solid walls and drinks the blood of its prey. Not much of this is explained but there's an attraction in watching the female leads, Maris Wrixon and Claudia Drake, run around the castle in nightgowns that emphasis their heaving bosoms. Willie Best is a servant, Thomas E. Jackson is a cop. Scripted by Michel Jacoby, directed by William Beaudine. (Fang)

FACES OF FEAR. See *Olivia.*

FACULTY, THE (1998) ★★★ In *Scream* screenwriter Kevin Williamson made fun of slasher flicks by having his characters discuss the do's and don'ts of the formula. Borrowing from *Invaders from Mars, Invasion of the Body Snatchers,* and other alien-invasion thrillers, he has similar fun with the sci-fi formula, though to a lesser degree. His story (proposed by Bruce Kimmel and David Wechtler) deals with teenage characters at Herrington High, somewhere in Ohio. Stokely (Clea Duvall) reads Robert Heinlein's sci-fi novels and Jack Finney's pod-takeover conspiracy book and knows all about alien invasions, extraterrestrial parasites, etc. Casey (Elijah Wood) has seen all the flicks from *Aliens* to *The Puppet Masters.* After some strange incidents on campus, they decide that filmmakers like Spielberg and Lucas have been feeding us all those E.T. movies so that when the aliens do strike, nobody will believe it. Mom and Dad and all the cops in America will chalk it up to "delusions" from seeing too many killer-cyborg movies. And they discover that an amphibious "mother monster" has sent her miniaturized parasitical fish creatures into the school to take over the faculty. After that, the students will be converted into host bodies controlled by the mother-monster intelligence. From there the host bodies will take over all of society. It's the body snatchers without the pods. Without Williamson's use of the lore of genre movies, *The Faculty* would be just another special-effects horror/sci-fi thriller depicting paranoid people trying to convince authorities but failing and finally taking their own steps to destroy the transgressors. Director-editor Richard Rodriquez does a good job of building up the handful of characters who will try to save the world, but it's standard stuff, showing off none of the bravura he displayed in *From Dusk to Dawn.* The final showdown occurs in the locker room of the gymnasium as the mother-monster (a big-tentacled ugly thing straight out of the school of bug-eyed monsters) traps the surviving characters. This includes the campus drug dealer (John Hartnett), a cheerleader (Jordana Brewster), a fallen quarterback (Shawn Hatosy), the newcomer (Laura Harris). Among the faculty bodies occupied by the alien parasites are football coach Robert Patrick, principal Bebe Neuwirth, teacher Piper Laurie, science-lab instructor Jon Stewart and nurse Salma Hayek. (Video/DVD: Dimension)

FADE TO BLACK (1980) ★★★ Compelling study of lonely Dennis Christopher who fantasizes images from movies and assumes guises of such monsters as the Mummy, Dracula, etc. Finally, reality and fantasy are indistinguishable and Christopher turns on his abusers. These killings are cleverly conceived—in fact, the film feels original (credit writer-director Vernon Zimmerman). Linda Kerridge is a wonderful Marilyn Monroe lookalike, Tim Thomerson is a cop. Clips from *The Creature from the Black Lagoon.* (Media)

FADE TO BLACK (1993) ★★ Marginal psychothriller, a kind of poor man's *Rear Window,* with barely any suspense and graphic murder. Psychologist Timothy Busfield witnesses a killing in a neighboring apartment but can't convince police so he sets out to prove he recorded the crime on videotape. Unfortunately, Douglas Barr's telescript strains credulity time after time as Busfield and other characters behave in outrageous ways. What finally emerges from the material are messy unbelievable events, with one or two mild surprises that briefly bring the film back on track. But director John McPherson, for all his hard work, can only fade away at the end. Cloris Leachman has a cameo as Busfield's alcoholic neighbor, and Heather Locklear has sexy scenes dressing and undressing, but the rest of the cast (Michael Beck and David Byron) fade with McPherson. (Video/Laser: Paramount)

FAHRENHEIT 451 (1966) ★★★ The title refers

to the temperature at which paper catches fire—
à propos to a plot set in the future when books
have been outlawed and special "firemen" seek
out and destroy any volumes still in existence.
Oskar Werner is such a fireman who discovers
the delights of reading and rebels against the
regime. Based on the novel by Ray Bradbury,
and directed by François Truffaut, this has met
with mixed emotions—some feel it captures the
poetry of Bradbury, others feel the premise is
too absurd. I think it's a literate contribution to
the genre. Julie Christie appears in a dual role.
Truffaut coscripted with Jean-Louis Richard.
Nicolas Roeg photographed it, Bernard Herrmann wrote the wonderful music. Anton Diffring,
Cyril Cusack, Anna Palk. (Video/Laser: MCA)

FAIL-SAFE (1964) ★★★★ Sidney Lumet's
version of the Eugene Burdick–Harvey Wheeler
best-seller (scripted by Walter Bernstein) approaches impending nuclear war as a politico-
horror thriller, a portrait of inexorable doom.
Stark black-and-white photography by Gerald
Herschfeld and electrifying acting by Henry
Fonda, Dan O'Herlihy and Walter Matthau
make this superior apocalypse science fiction
which comments on our militancy and inability
to control technology. A U.S. bomber accidentally unleashes a nuclear device on Moscow. To
keep peace, the President (Fonda) faces sending
one of our own planes to bomb New York City.
Dark and gripping. Larry Hagman, Dom De-
Luise, Fritz Weaver. (RCA/Columbia; Goodtimes) (Laser: Columbia)

FAIR GAME (1988) ★★½ This Italian film
(made as *Mamba*) has a fascinating premise: a
woman (Trudie Styler) is trapped in her apartment with a deadly black mamba while her husband uses a TV-monitoring system to interfere
with her efforts to avoid the fatal bite. Unfortunately, the direction by Mario Orfini is mediocre
and the snake's point-of-view shots ineffectual
and clichéd. What should have been the ultimate
in horror loses its bite (excuse us). Gregg Henry
is superb as the crazed husband. The music is by
Giorgio Moroder, who also served as associate
producer on this threadbare film. Fangs, but no
fangs. (Video/Laser: Vidmark)

FAIRYTALE: A TRUE STORY (1997) ★★★★
This is a challenging, fanciful mixture of fact and
fantasy that combines into one very unusual
movie, seemingly designed to rekindle within us
that sense of wonder we had as children, and may
have lost becoming adults. While it is based on a
true incident in the annals of so-called "supernatural photography" (a case known as "The Cottingley Fairies"), the film clearly deviates from the
truth of that incident to spin a fanciful metaphor
and pose some intriguing questions: What is illusion? What is reality? Should we believe what
we think our eyes are seeing? Is it better to be a
hard-headed realist, or someone who dreams and

has faith in magic, and believes in things that
cannot be real? The true incident occurred in England in 1917 when two adolescent girls claimed
they had taken pictures of fairies near their home
in Cottingley Glen. The photographs found their
way to Sir Arthur Conan Doyle, who believed
they were genuine. (They were not—the girls
had used paper cutouts from a children's book,
Princess Mary's Gift Book, and years later admitted to the playful hoax.) Doyle, who had just
lost his son in the European war and who believed in life after death, turned the girls into ce-
lebrities. End of facts, for Ernie Contreras's
screenplay (based on an idea by Contreras, Tom
McLoughlin and Albert Ash) leaves history behind to spin pure fantasy, in which there is a clan
of fairies living in the children's garden. Doyle
(wonderfully played by Peter O'Toole) becomes
involved in the investigation of the two girls
(Florence Hoath and Elizabeth Earl) with help
from escape artist/illusionist Harry Houdini
(Harvey Keitel), who is touring England at the
time. They are exceptional opposites, for Houdini is a disbeliever in the photos, and a debunker
of phony spiritualism rackets. The magician offers the suggestion that we often create a reality
that is really just an illusion, but there are always
those who will believe in the illusion. "Never try
to fool children," he says. "They expect nothing,
and therefore see everything." While the portrayal of Houdini may not be totally faithful to
his real-life beliefs, the story nevertheless has a
gentle, whimsical quality that is purely sublime.
This odd mixture of the real and the made-up, as
directed by British director Charles Sturridge,
climaxes with a sweet and charming sequence of
fairies flying into the home of the children as they
sleep soundly in their beds. The supporting cast,
including Paul McGann and Phoebe Nicholls, is
excellent. (Video/DVD: Paramount)

FALCON'S GOLD. See *Robbers of the Sacred
Mountain.*

FALL BREAK. (1983) See *The Mutilator.*

FALLEN (1998) ★★★ Nicholas Kazan's
screenplay tenaciously follows in the tracks of
heroic big-city cop Denzel Washington (he feels
that "cops are the chosen people") as he (1)
watches a serial killer he captured put to death
in a prison gas chamber and (2) follows up on
a series of new murders that point back to the
now-deceased convict. What he gradually
learns, from a set of puzzling visual clues that
keep popping up mysteriously, is that an evil
spirit known as Azazel (described as "a fallen
angel") has left the killer's body and is now
passing from person to person by a mere touch
as it plays a cat-and-mouse game with Washington, his brother and young son. Unfortunately, Kazan convolutes his story with a lot of
extraneous detail that's hard to swallow. There
are two brilliant sequences directed by Gregory

Hoblit depicting the spirit passing from body to body, each individual changing personality when touched, and then passing it along. There's a consistently rainy-city atmosphere that gives this work a film-noir sensitivity totally lacking in any sentiment or romance. Oddly, *Fallen* has almost no special effects (except for some weirdly lit Azazel point-of-view shots) and no attempt is made to depict Azazel in a supernatural or pseudoreligious style. The downbeat ending is right out of O. Henry, which makes it more suitable for the thinking crowd than the action crowd. Don Sutherland and John Goodman provide strong support as Washington's fellow cops. (Video/Laser: Warner Bros.)

FALLING, THE. See *Alien Predator(s).*

FALLING FIRE (1997) ★★½ Given the cheap nature of Showtime's "Roger Corman Presents," or given the cheap nature of Roger Corman himself, this sci-fi adventure inspired by *Deep Impact* and *Armageddon* features some decent special effects as a spacewheel known as The Spirit of '49 guides a wayward asteroid toward Earth by changing its pathway with nuclear explosions. The plan is to put the rock into orbit around Earth and provide enough jobs to boost a faltering world-wide economy sometime in the not-too-distant future. While copilot Michael Pare argues with the captain, his wife (a secret service agent played by Heidi von Palleske) is taken prisoner by demented cult leader Lopez (Christian Vidosa) who believes Earth should be destroyed because man is an evil being. To achieve this, the fruitcake guru has placed a spy on the ship who will sabotage the works and set the asteroid on a collision course with Earth. Which in the handful of crew members is the saboteur? Although suffering from the usual Corman-didn't-give-us-much-to-make-this-one, *Falling Fire* at least has an interesting story (credit the script to director Daniel Dor, coproducer G. Philip Jackson and Peter I. Horton) that plays out with some surprise twists. MacKenzie Gray, Zehra Leverman, Jacklyn Francis, Michaela Matthieu, Cedric Turner. (New Horizons)

FALL OF THE HOUSE OF USHER, THE. Video version of Roger Corman's *The House of Usher The* (Warner Bros.; Goodtimes) (Laser: Image, coupled with *The Pit and the Pendulum*).

FALSE FACE. See *Scalpel.*

FAN, THE (1981) ★★ Weak slasher film failing to believably portray disturbed Michael Biehn and his reign of terror directed against an aging but attractive Broadway actress (Lauren Bacall). James Garner is wasted as Lauren's husband, although Maureen Stapleton is good as the actress's personal secretary caught up in the knife horrors. Directed by Edward Bianchi. From a novel by Bob Randall. Aka *Trance.* (Video/Laser: Paramount)

FANATIC (1965). See *Die, Die! My Darling!*

FANATIC (1982). See *The Last Horror Film.*

FANGORIA'S WEEKEND OF HORRORS (1986) Footage of a horror convention features interviews with makeup artist Rick Baker, directors Tobe Hooper and Wes Craven and actor Robert Englund. (Media)

FANGS (1978) ★ Killer reptiles and serpents put the bite on the enemies of a snake lover. Proved to be poisonous at the box office. Directed by Vittorio Schiraldi. Les Tremayne, Janet Wood, Bebe Kelly. (United America; Video Gems; Moore)

FANGS OF THE LIVING DEAD (1968) ★½ "The coldness of the grave is in my blood," remarks a buxom, frilly-gowned vampire woman in this Italian rehash of *Dracula.* The star is Anita Ekberg, who plays (hold your breath) a virgin. Inheriting a castle, she arrives to discover a suspicious baron and a harem of busty, lusty bloodsuckers. The color, production and ladies are nice on the eyes but this is an exercise in tedium. Anyway, fangs for the mammaries, Anita. Written-directed by Amando De Ossorio. Also known as *Malenka the Vampire, The Niece of the Vampire, The Vampire's Niece* and *Bloody Girl.* Julian Urgarte, Diana Lorys. (Sinister/C; S/Weird; Filmfax)

FANTASIA (1941) ★★★★ Amalgam of cartoon art set to classical music (by Leopold Stokowski and the Philadelphia Orchestra) was a revolutionary experiment by Disney, animated by artists visually interpreting the music. Each sequence explores an element of the fantastic—from a Bach of abstract designs to a "Nutcracker Suite" of magical sprites and dancing mushrooms; from Mickey Mouse in "The Sorcerer's Apprentice" to Stravinsky's "The Rite of Spring," a pageant of life's evolution depicting primeval ooze, dinosaurs and global holocaust. Centaurettes, cupids and winged horses frolic in Beethoven's "Pastoral Symphony," followed by Ponchielli's "Dance of the Hours" featuring pirouetting hippopotami. Moussorgsky's "Night on Bald Mountain" is of macabre design. (Disney) (Laser: Disney; Image)

FANTASIST, THE (1986) ★★★ A strange literate psycho-killer movie thanks to the direction and writing by Robin Hardy, better known for *The Wicker Man.* Adapting Patrick McGinley's novel *Goosefoot,* Hardy etches the portrait of Dublin teacher Moira Harris, whose sexually repression is caused by her Protestant upbringing in a dysfunctional family. Eccentric American Timothy Bottoms could be "The Phone Call Killer," who calls women with non-obscene erotic poetry that appeals to their repressions, then attacks them with a knife. Policeman Christopher Cazenove is as odd as the rest of the gallery of eccentric personalities in this metaphorical statement about the Irish character. Harris's final confrontation with the killer is psychological and arousing, featuring a bizarre love-making sequence. (Republic)

FANTASTIC INVASION OF PLANET EARTH. See *The Bubble.*

FANTASTIC PLANET (1973) ★★★★ Imagine a world in which humanoids are only inches high and treated like frivolous pets or domestics. Such a world is Ygam, where the masters are the 40-foot-tall Draags, and we earth beings are Oms. Winner of the Grand Prix at Cannes, this French animated film is the work of artist Roland Topor and director Rene Laloux. The parable aspects are fascinating, for they tap into the roots of human existence. Also impressive are the organic drawing styles and oddball flora and fauna of the planet. The plot involves occasional exterminations of the Oms and the outlaw band's attempt to escape to Fantastic Planet, a satellite world where Draags go to meditate. A fascinating sci-fi fable. Voices for the U.S. version: Marvin Miller, Barry Bostwick, Jane Waldo. Aka *The Savage Planet.* (Video Yesteryear; United America; Sinister/C; Filmfax; from Vidcrest as *Planet of Incredible Creatures*)

FANTASTIC PUPPET PEOPLE, THE. Video version of *Attack of the Puppet People* (Sinister/C).

FANTASTIC VOYAGE (1966) ★★★½ Submarine and crew are miniaturized to microscopic size and injected into the bloodstream of a scientist who has been shot by foreign agents and will die unless the crew can voyage through his body to his brain and destroy a bloodclot with a laser beam. Imaginatively executed, with tremendous effects for their time. In this bizarre inner world of the body, the simplest things become obstacles: an artery is a whirlpool, blood corpuscles are deadly attackers, etc. Richard Fleischer directed the Harry Kleiner script, adapted by David Duncan. Stephen Boyd, Arthur Kennedy, Raquel Welch, Donald Pleasence, Arthur O'Connell, Edmond O'Brien. Early titles: *Microscopia* and *Strange Journey.* (RCA/Columbia) (Laser: CBS/Fox)

FANTASTIC WORLD OF D. C. COLLINS (1984) ★★ Imaginative child Gary Coleman is caught up in spy shenanigans with Soviet agents over possession of a videotape that holds the key to the prevention of nuclear war. As he undergoes the chase, Coleman daydreams he's Clint Eastwood, James Bond, Indiana Jones and Luke Skywalker in parody flashbacks. Routine TV-movie, strictly for kids. Bernie Casey, Shelly Smith, Michael Ansara, George Gobel, Marilyn McCoo. Directed by Leslie Martinson. (New World/Starmaker)

FANTASY FILM WORLD OF GEORGE PAL, THE (1986) Fascinating documentary on one of Hollywood's most beloved producers of fantasy and sci-fi, whose *Destination Moon, When Worlds Collide* and *War of the Worlds* established new trends. Tony Curtis, Ray Bradbury and Ray Harryhausen discuss Pal's warm character and contributions to cinema. Footage from many of Pal's productions. Written-directed by Arnold Leibovit. (Starmaker) (Laser: Image)

FAR AWAY, SO CLOSE! (1993) Wim Wenders's sequel to *Wings of Desire,* picking up where that film left off with angel Cassiel (Otto Sander) atop the Angel of Victory tower in Berlin. Joining him is Nastassia Kinski as the angel Raphaela. Horst Buchholz, Heinz Ruhmann, Bruno Ganz, Willem Dafoe. Guest cameos by Peter Falk and Lou Reed. (Columbia TriStar)

FAREWELL TO THE PLANET OF THE APES (1974) ★ Turgid, unexciting reedited episodes of the TV series *Planet of the Apes,* which lasted on the CBS-TV network only four months. Roddy McDowall (the only carryover from the movie series) stars as Galen the chimpanzee, who is always helping two time-traveling Earthlings who have become trapped on an Earth ruled by simians. In the first episode, Galen poses as a slavemaster when the astronauts (Ron Harper and James Naughton) pose as spear fishermen and swim to avoid sharks. In the second of these less-than-inspired adventures, Galen and the astronauts are involved with a man creating a flying machine, a device considered dangerous by the orangs and monkey leaders. Unworthy follow-up to the excellent film series. Directed by Don McDougall and J. M. Lucas. Roscoe Lee Browne, Joanna Barnes, Frank Aletter. A number of these shows were rereleased to TV under the generic title *New Planet of the Apes.*

FAR FROM HOME (1989) ★★ Lightweight killer-on-the-loose terror tale with unusual desert photography. Magazine writer Matt Frewer and teenager daughter Drew Barrymore are stranded in a rundown Nevada burg, where a series of murders dogs them. Predictable and only occasionally exciting, with Susan Tyrrell shining as a shrew of a mother who runs a trailer park. Based on a script by Tommy Lee Wallace and directed by Meiert Avis. Richard Masur, Karen Austin, Jennifer Tilly, Dick Miller. (Video/Laser: Vestron)

FARM, THE. See *The Curse.*

FASHION HOUSE OF DEATH. See *Blood and Black Lace.*

FATAL CHARM (1991) ★★ Set in Ukiah, CA, this psycho-killer flick went through enough production ills that the director used the pseudonym Alan Smithee. Nicolas Niciphor's script deals with teenager Amanda Peterson falling for a serial killer and writing to him in prison after he's found guilty of heinous crimes. Why? Because he's handsome and has "fatal charm." Ha! The film attempts to set up the viewer for a surprise twist, but that surprise is telegraphed. This cynicism is distasteful and *Fatal Charm* is a hollow cliché. The cast is wasted, especially Christopher Atkins as the accused killer. Mary Frann, James Remar, Andrew Robinson, Peggy Lipton,

Lar Park Lincoln, Robert Walker, Jr., (MCEG; Academy) (Laser: Academy)

FATAL GAMES (1983) ★ An awful slasher flick in the hands of total incompetents. The setting is the Falcon Academy of Athletics, where teenagers preparing for the 1984 Olympics don't realize they are guinea pigs for a doctor with a new superstrength formula not unlike steroids. They are also cannon fodder for a mad killer armed with a javelin, who spikes his victims while they work out. The most ridiculous scene has the javelin jerkola lurking underwater while a beautiful swimmer passes above him—an obvious homage to the Black Lagoon Creature. The incoherent script was speared to death by Rafael Bunuel and director Michael Elliott. Sally Kirkland, Lynn Banashek, Sean Masterson, Michael O'Leary, Teal Roberts. Produced as *The Killing Touch*. (Media)

FATAL IMAGES (1982) ★★½ Is a still camera demonically possessed by the serial killer who previously owned it? Each time its new owner clicks the shutter on a beautiful model, she is doomed. David Williams, Kay Schaver, Lane Coyle. Directed by Dennis Devine. (Active)

FATAL PULSE (1988) ★½ Uninspired dash of slash that imitates so many predecessors that it doesn't have an original thought in its doltish script. A killer wearing black gloves closes in on sorority chicks who always happen to be naked or semi-undressed. The dumbest of the murders has the killer using the edge of a record to slit a student's throat. Producer-director Anthony J. Christopher brings nothing special to the material, although Martin Mayo's synthetic score works when it's jazzy. Joe Phelan (Martin Sheen's brother), Michelle McCormick, Ken Roberts, chCindra Hodgson join porn actor Herschel Savage, billed as Harvey Cowen. (Celebrity)

FATAL SKY. TV title for *Project Alien*.

FATHERLAND (1994) ★★½ This is a "What if" story, or a "parallel universe" tale. The "what if" is "What if Hitler had won World War II?" In 1964, at a time when Hitler is about to make a cold war peace with President Joseph Kennedy, newswoman Miranda Richardson is caught in political intrigue and murder with sympathetic SS officer Rutger Hauer. A dark secret of Nazi Germany is being hidden and only they can expose it. As carried over to film from Robert Harris's novel by telewriters Stanley Weiser and Ron Hutchinson, *Fatherland* is far more intriguing in idea than execution. Director Christopher Menaul never quite makes it convincing—a vital factor in a "What if" story. Chalk up this TV-movie, made in England, as average. Peter Vaughan, Mabel Kitchen, John Woodric, John Shrapnel, Jean Marsh. (Goodtimes)

FBI VS. DR. MABUSE, THE. See *The Return of Dr. Mabuse*.

FEAR (1977). See *Night Creature*.

FEAR (1988) ★★ A brutal film about a Vietnam vet who freaks out and goes on a killing spree, this is also an attempt by director Robert A. Ferretti to capture the chaotic, schizophrenic mind of a victim of war. It may repel you, but its nightmarish interpretations of the berserk killer's mind make this unusual. The plotline follows four escapees (including Frank Stallone) who go on a murder spree, terrorizing vacationers Cliff De Young and Kay Lenz. (Virgin Vision) (Laser: Image)

FEAR (1990) ★★★ Psychic Ally Sheedy helps police track serial killers, writing best-sellers with her manager Lauren Hutton. The twist to director Rockne S. O'Bannon's script is that a serial killer known as "The Shadow Man" is just as much a psychic as Sheedy, and he uses his power to terrify her because her fear turns him on. "I give great fear," Sheedy cries. This is notches above the usual dame-in-peril fare, enhanced by a Henry Mancini score and John Agar (as another serial killer), Stan Shaw (cop), Keone Young (another cop) and Dina Merrill (publisher's wife). Produced by Richard Kobritz. (Vestron)

FEAR, THE/FEAR IN THE CITY OF THE LIVING DEAD. See *The Gates of Hell*.

FEAR CHAMBER, THE (1974) ★ One of four Mexican-produced cheapies made by Boris Karloff in 1968 shortly before his death, but not released for years. Karloff fans will not be impressed—the Master has only a few scenes as a benevolent scientist who keeps a living rock in his laboratory, unaware underlings are feeding it women to control its appetite. Written by Jack Hill, who codirected with Juan Ibanez. Yerye Beirut, Julissa, Carlos East. Aka *Torture Zone*. (Filmfax; from Sinister/C as *Chamber of Fear* and from MPI as *The Torture Chamber*)

FEAR IN THE CITY OF THE LIVING DEAD. See *The Gates of Hell*.

FEAR IN THE NIGHT (1947) ★★ Cornell Woolrich's "Nightmare" is the basis for this low budgeter with DeForest Kelly as a musician who wakes up thinking he committed a murder. He turns to a policeman relative (Paul Kelly) for help but evidence mounts that he did it. Written-directed by Maxwell Shane, who remade this in '56 as *Nightmare*. Ann Doran, Kay Scott, Jeff York, Robert Emmett Keane. (Sinister/C; Filmfax; HBO)

FEAR IN THE NIGHT (1973) ★★ Hammer psychothriller with Judy Geeson as a bride being terrorized at a deserted school for boys. Everyone thinks she's recovering from a breakdown and is still nuts, but we know better, right fans? Trick ending by writers Jimmy Sangster and Michael Syson is telegraphed, so this shocker has few surprises. Sangster also produced and directed. Joan Collins, Ralph Bates, Peter Cushing. (HBO; Republic; from Magnum as *Dynasty of Fear*)

FEARLESS VAMPIRE KILLERS, THE, OR PARDON ME, BUT YOUR TEETH ARE IN MY NECK (1967) ★★★ Roman Polanski's lampoon of the vampire genre is an uneven olio, a mixture of cleverness and inanity that still deserves a look. There's plenty of idiotic clowning as professor Jack MacGowran and his assistant (Polanski) invade the castle of Count Von Krolock (Ferdy Mayne). Because these characters are dunderheads, the foils (and fools) of parody, they are of little interest no matter how much fun is made of wooden stakes and other vampire-hunting accoutrements. Sharon Tate is a girl in a bathtub, and her scene is the funniest. Aka *Dance of the Vampires*. Alfie Bass, Fiona Lewis, Ian Quarrier, Ron Lacey. (Video/Laser: MGM/UA)

FEAR NO EVIL (1981) ★★★ Director Frank LaLoggia helms this above-average, below-expensive supernatural tale featuring some zippy effects. The plot is implausible (three archangels descend to Earth to take on human guises to combat Lucifer and his zombies), and there's too much emphasis on a plot involving teenagers, but overall execution and artistry are good. Made as *Mark of the Beast*. Elizabeth Hoffmann, Dick Burt, R. J. Silverthorn. (Embassy; Columbia)

FEAST FOR THE DEVIL (1987) ★★ A woman searching for her missing sister ends up in the evil clutches of a crazed doctor, who hypnotizes beautiful women trapped in his sinister castle. Krista Nell, Thomas Moore, Teresa Gimpera. Directed by John Lacy. (Mogul)

FEAST OF FLESH. See *Blood Feast*.

FEDERAL AGENTS VS. UNDERWORLD INC. (1949) ★★ Republic's 12-chapter serial spotlights an evil network of criminals that has stolen a famous artifact, the Golden Hands, which an ancient legend says is cursed. A nonstop battle erupts between the evil Nila (Carol Forman) and her henchmen against square-jawed federal agent Dave Worth (Kirk Alyn, who that same year played Superman). Alyn battles hired guns and seeks to stop Nila from using an Asian drug that controls men's minds. Fred Brannon directed with all the cliffhangers in place. Rosemary La Planche, Roy Barcroft, James Dale, Bruce Edwards, Tris Coffin. The edited TV-movie version is *Golden Hands of Kurigal*. (Republic)

FEMALE BUTCHER. See *The Legend of Blood Castle*.

FEMALE FIEND. See *Theatre of Death*.

FEMALE PLASMA SUCKERS. Video of *Blood Orgy of the She-Devils* (Lettuce Entertain You).

FEMALE SPACE INVADERS. See *Starcrash*.

FENGRIFFEN. See *And Now the Screaming Starts*.

FERTILIZING THE BLASPHEMIZING BOMBSHELL (1990) ★ Made as *Mark of the Beast* (Rhino Video), this TV version has an inappropriate title (it's a serious movie, not a comedy) suppos-

edly describing what happens when a woman looking for her missing sister in the desert region of the Devil's Playground stumbles across a satanic cult. If the title was supposed to set this movie apart, it only sets it apart into the scrap heap of hunkajunk movies one should avoid. The heroine, intended as a human sacrifice, runs around the dunes in panties and blouse until sheriff Bo Hopkins comes to her rescue. It's blasphemy this was even produced. Sheila Caan, Denise King, Rick Hill.

FIELD OF DREAMS (1989) ★★★★ An extraordinary fantasy that is a metaphor, an allegory, a parable. It is an American fairy tale standing for desires and unfulfilled dreams, the search for inner contentment, and the fight against the Establishment to be special. Kevin Costner is a farmer who hears a voice telling him to build a baseball field in his pasture. Costner does—and soon the field is filled with ballplayers long dead, and Costner is sent on an odyssey in search of the truth. Based on *Shoeless Joe*, a novel by W. P. Kinsella (whom Costner plays), this involves a dropout advocate of the 1960s (James Earl Jones) and a doctor (Burt Lancaster) before Costner returns to the field for an encounter with his dead father. Writer-director Phil Alden Robinson pulls these elements together in a fascinating way. Amy Madigan, Ray Liotta. (Video/Laser: MCA)

FIEND (1980) ★ Regional horror thriller from writer-producer-editor-gofer Don (*The Alien Factor*) Dohler and cofilmmaker Don Leifert about a supernatural firefly that takes over music teacher Tom Leifert and eats its way into corpses, bringing them to life. Richard Nelson, Elaine White, George Stover. (Monterey; Prism).

FIEND, THE (1971) ★★★ Taut British thriller in which beautiful women are murdered by a Londoner practicing soul possession, in a style that would warm the cold heart of Jack the Ripper. Produced-directed by Robert Hartford-Davis from a script by Brian Comport. Patrick Magee, Ann Todd, Suzanna Leigh, Percy Herbert. Aka *Beware My Brethren* and *Beware of the Brethren*. (Monterey)

FIENDISH PLOT OF DR. FU MANCHU (1980) ★★ Peter Sellers's last film (made under the title *Fu Manchu*) is not his best as he portrays Sax Rohmer's insidious Asian in search of an eternal youth serum, with fantasy contraptions randomly thrown in. Sellers plays Fu Manchu at 168, a younger Fu after drinking the youth elixir, an antiques dealer, and detective Nayland Smith. Smith's stuffiness and British demeanor are the funniest touches in this mess directed by Piers Haggard. David Tomlinson, Helen Mirren, Steve Franken, Burt Kwouk. (Video/Laser: Warner Bros.)

FIEND WITHOUT A FACE (1958) ★★★ A favorite "alien invader" thriller (written by Herbert J. Leder from Amelia Reynolds Long's "The Thought Monster") with grotesque brainspine creatures which attach to heads and suck away human brains . . . positively unsettling, unforgettable movie monsters. Locale is a Canadian Air Force base where rocket experiments have caused human thoughts to be turned into the attacking brain creatures. This Richard Gordon production is recommended for its macabre overtones. Directed by Arthur Crabtree. Marshall Thompson, Kim Parker, Terence Kilburn. (Video/Laser: Republic)

FIEND WITH THE ATOMIC BRAIN. See *The Man with the Synthetic Brain.*

FIEND WITH THE ELECTRONIC BRAIN See *The Man with the Synthetic Brain.*

FIFTH ELEMENT, THE (1997) ★★★ This $70 million French sci-fi extravaganza from stylish director Luc Besson has some wonderful moments in depicting the whacky world of A.D. 2259, especially when ex-government agent now-cabbie Korben Dallas (Bruce Willis) is involved in the blazing action and flamboyant special effects. But there's such a wild mixture of styles and so many failed attempts at satiric humor that ultimately the Kitchen Sink approach defeats Besson's purposes to tell a rousing, tongue-in-cheek fantasy. The script (by Besson, from his own original ideas, and plot-flesher Robert Mark Kamen) incorporates a fireball planet on a collision course with Earth, a race of evil, ugly-looking mercenary aliens equipped with huge blasting rifles, a villain (Gary Oldman) after the devices that could save Earth, a humanoid woman (Milla Jovovich) who has the knowledge and energy to save mankind, a diva from another planet (Maiwenn Le Besco), a high priest (Ian Holm) who "sort of" knows how to save the world, a radio disc jockey dressed as a drag queen (Chris Tucker), a floating pleasure ship in a farflung galaxy, and a president (Tommy Lister Jr.) manipulating all of the above for sundry reasons, with Brion James as his powerful minion. L.A. is a city of flying craft (a la *Judge Dredd* and *Blade Runner*) and there's an amusing sequence with Willis at the controls of his futuristic taxi cab. The race against time works effectively for a while, but gets a bit overstretched for a climax that is more predictably wearisome than thrilling. A tightening of the freestyle script, an elimination of the humor that doesn't work, and a rethinking of the Tucker craziness would have helped this movie to find consistency. Luke Perry, Lee Evans, John Neville. (Video/DVD: Columbia TriStar)

FIGHTING DEVIL DOGS (1938) ★★★ Twelve-chapter Republic serial, directed by that unbeatable triumvirate of action directors: William Witney, John English and Robert Beche. Marine Corps lieutenants Lee Powell and Herman Brix (soon to be Bruce Bennett) square off against the Lightning, a caped hooligan who destroys things with bolts of electricity. The artificial thunderbolt machine (a clap trap?) becomes their target and the action is nonstoppable. The TV-feature version is *Torpedo of Doom.* (Republic; Video Connection)

FILMGORE (1983) Compilation of blood-and-gore scenes from horror movies: *The Texas Chainsaw Massacre, Driller Killer, Snuff, 2,000 Maniacs, Blood Feast,* etc., etc. Produced by Charles Band, directed by Ken Dixon, with music by Richard Band. Hosted by Elvira. (Wizard; Force)

FILM HOUSE FEVER (1986) A compilation of film clips from cult and genre movies. Included are scenes from *Blood Feast.* Hosts include Jamie Lee Curtis, Harvey Korman, Lon Chaney, Jr., and James Keach. (Veston; Live)

FINAL APPROACH (1991) ★★ Psychological sci-fi technological thriller in which amnesiac fighter pilot James B. Sikking undergoes interrogation by psychiatrist Hector Elizondo to find out the truth behind a cover-up in the military ranks involving a new bomber. Directed by Eric Steven Stahl. Madolyn Smith, Kevin McCarthy, Cameo Kneuer, Wayne Duvall. (Video/Laser: Vidmark)

FINAL CONFLICT, THE (1981) ★★★ Third and final film in *The Omen* series, as godless as its predecessors. Damien Thorn (Sam Neill), the Antichrist, has become Ambassador to the Court of St. James's to be near the birth site (near London) of the Son of God, whose Second Coming is prophesized in the Book of Revelation. The gory murders are numerous (though not as imaginative as in *The Omen* and *Damien: Omen II*) as the Son of Satan defends himself against priest-assassins armed with the Seven Sacred Daggers of Meggido. The "final conflict" between the Antichrist and the Son of God is poorly developed by scriptwriter Andrew Birkin, but producer Harvey Bernhard's film still has a compelling "sickness" and a good pseudoreligious score by Jerry Goldsmith. And it's nicely directed by Graham Baker. Rossano Brazzi, Don Gordon, Lisa Harrow, Mason Adams, Barnaby Holm. (Video/Laser: Fox)

FINAL COUNTDOWN, THE (1980) ★★★ Filmed aboard the USS *Nimitz,* this is an excellent semidocumentary approach to showing the U.S. Navy and Air Force in action. The plot—in which the carrier is caught in a time warp and sent back to Pearl Harbor in 1941 on the eve of the Japanese attack—sounds ingenious, but assorted screenwriters never came to grips with the promising twists. Kirk Douglas, Martin Sheen, Katharine Ross, James Farentino, Ron O'Neal, Charles Durning work with limited material; the jet fighters come off looking better. Directed by Don Taylor. (Video/Laser: Vestron)

FINAL EQUINOX (1995) ★★½ This is your basic action-thriller with only a modicum of sci-fi technology—namely a device called The Regenerator (which apparently was stolen from an alien race with long, bony fingers and which apparently restores the surfaces of dying planets. Two factions of mean-looking guys—one a gang of terrorists led by Martin Kove, the other a band of black-coat-wearing CIA renegades sanctioned to be as dirty as the baddies—fight over possession of the Hitchcockian McGuffan by blowing each other apart with shotguns and automatic weapons. Meanwhile, special agent Joe Lara has martial problems with wife, Tina May Simpson, and gang member David Warner plots to steal the thing himself. Writer-director Serge Rodnunsky strives to be different but it's still an action movie, though perhaps not as mindless as most, with Lara playing both ends against the middle in the style of a Kurosawa-style swordsman. Vincent Klyn, Robin Joi Bronw, Rowdy Jackson. (Monarch)

FINAL EXAM (1981) ★½ Tame slasher made in South Carolina, a clone of *Halloween*. Writer-director Jimmy Huston saves the goriest scenes for last as a fiendish murderer slaughters dumb college students. Most of the time *Final Exam* deals with pranks, hazings and crude jokes, and engages in idle chatter designed as character "development." Huston's writing is so weak, the killer's identity is never given, his motives never made clear. Cecile Bagdadi, Joel S. Rice. (Embassy; Columbia)

FINAL EXECUTIONER, THE (1983) ★½ Lame-brained *Mad Max* imitation, set in a post-holocaust world where "Hunters" kill off contaminated people. In search of the woman he loves, William Mang is trained in combat by ex-cop Woody Strode, then invades the stronghold of the hunters, killing them off one by one. The murders on both sides are so violent, one can never feel sympathy for Mang and this becomes nothing but a bloodbath. Directed with neanderthal elan by Romolo Guerrieri. Marina Costa, Harrison Muller. Aka *The Last Warrior*. (MGM/UA)

FINAL JUDGMENT (1992) ★★★ A gross mixture of serial-killer clichés, sexy striptease dances and Catholic guilt/innocence produces an unusual psychothriller carried by its very neurotic, hysterical exploitation of reverent themes. Brad Dourif plays an ex-hoodlum turned pistol-packing priest ("the fastest gun in the pulpit") who tries to help low-life types, and who behaves in an unorthodox manner when he finds his daughter (a beautiful stripper) strangled. Like a Dirty Harry with a white collar, Dourif sets out to find the killer in the underbelly of L.A., a sick dude (David Ledingham) with religious fetishes who paints each victim before the big murder. The script by Kirk Honeycutt and director Louis Morneau is so over the top it's actually a gas, and

the picture moves with energetic frenzy. The cast includes Orson Bean, Bert Williams, Isaac Hayes, Simone Allen and Karen Black (the latter in a bit part as the killer's naive mom). (New Horizons) (Laser: Image)

FINAL MISSION (1992) ★★½ Jet fighter pilots testing a new "virtual reality" training system begin to die off so hot-shotter Billy Wirth noses into the truth: an Air Force conspiracy to use men as guinea pigs for a new post-hypnotic zombie-making computer system. Meanwhile, he makes love to beautiful Elizabeth Gracen. Okay thriller cowritten and directed by Lee Redmond. Steve Railsback, Corbin Bernsen, Richard Bradford. (Vidmark)

FINAL NOTICE (1989) ★★½ Lightweight slasher/private-eye thriller that drags out every cliché imaginable. Gil Gerard portrays less-than-thrilling PI Harry Stoner who's in search of the Library Slasher, a knife-plunging maniac who cuts up female forms in art books, and real female forms, too. John Gay's telescript (based on a Jonathan Valin novel) is predictable, with Melody Anderson turning up as a librarian with glasses who takes them off to become . . . wow, a raving beauty. You'll spot the killer in advance of the climax. Directed by Steven Hilliard Stern. Jackie Burroughs, Kevin Hicks, Louise Fletcher, David Ogden Stiers. (Paramount) (Laser: Pioneer)

FINAL SANCTION (1989) ★★ After war breaks out between the U.S. and Russia, the factions decide to settle the dispute by putting two men into an arena in a fight to the death. Ted Prior is the American, Robert Z'Dar is the Commie. Written-directed by David A. Prior. (Action International; Hollywood Home Entertainment)

FINAL TERROR, THE (1983) ★½ Samuel Arkoff's film (made as *Campsite Massacre*) stars Rachel Ward and Daryl Hannah before they found big-time success. A busload of fire rangers and girlfriends travels into the gloomy woods near Crescent City, CA, to be stalked by a toothless hag who eats raw dogmeat and keeps severed hands in her Mason jars. A sunless forest and always-dreary sky provides a chilly mood but body count is low, making this of minimum interest to splatter seekers. Director Andrew Davis went on to make topnotch action movies. John Friedrich, Adrian Zmed, Mark Metcalf and Lewis Smith are the louts messing up our beautiful forests. Aka *Bump in the Night* and *The Forest Primeval*. (Video/Laser: Vestron)

FIRE AND ICE (1982) ★★★★ Excellently animated sword-and-sorcery fantasy-adventure set in a world where evil ice king Nekron uses glacial spears to destroy his enemy, namely the kingdom of Firekeep. His mother Juliana orders the kidnapping of Firekeep's princess, a sexy number who is rescued by a young hero during a series of exciting adventures. What makes this outstanding is the superb art by Frank Frazetta, who worked under writer-producer-director Ralph Bakshi. The film was rotoscoped to give it a life-like quality. Comic-book fans will groove on it. Voices by Leo Gordon, Susan Tyrrell, Randy Norton, Sean Hannon, Cynthia Leake. (Video/Laser: RCA/Columbia)

FIREFIGHT (1987) ★★ Gangs of convicts rove a post-holocaust world in an attempt to gain power. James Pfeiffer, Janice Carraher, Jack Turner. Directed by Scott Pfeiffer. (TransWorld; Star Classics)

FIREFOX (1982) ★★½ One of Clint Eastwood's lesser pictures: dark, melancholy, clumsy, when it should be zappy and fast-paced. As director, Eastwood doesn't seem to be comfortable with a spy thriller. *Firefox* depicts has-been pilot Mitchell Gant (Eastwood) being sent to Russia to steal a jet fighter equipped with weapons controlled by human thought. Little is made of this premise—the plot unfolds like a grade-B spy movie. John Dykstra provides nice flying sequences, but they don't make up for deficiencies in the Alex Lasker–Wendell Wellman script, adapted from Craig Thomas's novel. (Video/Laser: Warner Bros.)

FIRE IN THE SKY (1993) ★★★½ A controversial UFO abduction case, the singular affair of Travis Walton, is dramatized in this Paramount release written by Tracy Torme (*Intruders*) and directed by Robert Lieberman. In 1975 Arizona lumberjack Walton allegedly observed a saucer with six other woodsmen. Walton ran toward the UFO, was zapped by a bolt of blue and thrown ten feet, according to eyewitnesses. Thinking Travis dead, the axmen fled. Walton turned up five days later, claiming to have been kidnapped and examined by aliens. How true the Walton incident is has been debated. That aside, *Fire in the Sky* is a heightened experience of sight and sounds. The saucer interior sequence is gruesome, with Walton awakening in a womblike, organic environment. These scenes resemble a nightmare with life and death symbols and is a gross exaggeration of what Walton says he experienced, but as film it's chillingly awesome. James Garner is a disbelieving sheriff. D. B. Sweeney, Robert Patrick, Craig Sheffer, Henry Thomas, Bradley Gregg. (Video/Laser: Paramount)

FIRE MAIDENS FROM OUTER SPACE (1956) ★½ British sci-fi with a ridiculous plot concocted by writer-director Cy Roth: Space explorers (ineptly led by Anthony Dexter) discover women carrying out sacrifices to the black gods on a moon near Jupiter. By all means, catch it if you want to have a thousand laughs at the expense of Susan Shaw, Paul Carpenter and Harry Fowler. And dig the females dancing to Borodin's music! First made as *The Thirteenth Moon of Jupiter*. (Cinemacabre)

FIRE MONSTER. See *Godzilla Raids Again*.

FIRE NEXT TIME, THE (1993) ★★ Craig T. Nelson and wife Bonnie Bedelia make an odyssey to Canada when the U.S. is hit hard by an ecological disaster in the year 2017. TV-movie directed by Tom McLoughlin from a James Henerson script. Jurgen Prochnow, Richard Farnsworth, Charles Haid. (Cabin Fever)

FIREPOWER (1993) ★★½ A futuristic martial-arts actioner, with a whodunit element behind it, set in a city of tomorrow where scores of bad guys called Hell Riders dwell in the Hell Zone, into which police do not venture. When a female cop is shot during a raid on the local precinct, wisecracking law enforcers Chad McQueen and Gary Daniels do venture into the Hell Zone, there to undergo a series of action-packed chases and brawny battles. There isn't much originality in Michael January's script (if we may be august and march out an opinion) but Richard Pepin has directed it with a penchant for the funky and the grungy as he depicts the awfulness of urban living, disguising his metaphor as a routine action picture with few other pretenses. Huh? Joseph Ruskin, George Murdock. (PM Entertainment) (Laser: Image)

FIRESTARTER (1984) ★★ Stephen King ranks this among the worst of his adaptations, and he struck the match right on the head. It's an effects movie, at the expense of a cohesive narrative, adapted by Stanley Mann and directed by Mark L. Lester. Flying fireballs and other inflammatory bolts of energy are hurled by Drew Barrymore, a kid who can turn her anger into flaming revenge. In short, she lights up your life. Government agents and foreign powers are after Barrymore to harness her ESP abilities. George C. Scott fulfills a very odd role. Filmed in North Carolina; the Mike Wood–Jeff Jarvis effects are the best things in this never-catches-fire picture. David Keith, Martin Sheen, Heather Locklear, Art Carney, Louise Fletcher, Moses Gunn. (Video/Laser: MCA)

FIRST MAN INTO SPACE, THE (1958) ★★½ Cosmic rays turn Earth's first astronaut—an obsessed man who takes his spacecraft higher than ordered—into a hideous, encrusted monster who craves human blood. Writers John Cooper and Lance Z. Hargreaves engender sympathy for the malformed being instead of making him a killer monster. A commendable effort from producer Richard Gordon, director Robert Day and screenwriters John C. Cooper and Lance Z. Hargreaves. Wyatt Ordung (an alias of Roger Corman?) is credited as idea man. Marshall Thompson is the scientist attempting to communicate with the gnarly man. Carl Jaffe, Marla Landi, Bill Nagy. Aka *Satellite of Blood*. (Filmfax; Rhino; Media; S/Weird; Discount; Monterey)

FIRST MEN IN THE MOON (1964) ★★★★ Marvelous adaptation of H. G. Wells's novel about a Victorian spaceship blasting off from

Earth and flying to the lunar surface; the expedition's adventures are riveting. Ray Harryhausen (also associate producer) provides excellent stop-motion effects, notably the insect moonmen. His lavish alien civilization and its creatures are a satisfying example of what a ton of imagination on a nominal budget can achieve. Edward Judd, Martha Hyer, Lionel Jeffries, Peter Finch. Written by Nigel Kneale and Jan Read; directed by Nathan Juran. Charles H. Schneer produced. (RCA/Columbia) (Laser: Pioneer)

FIRST OF JANUARY, THE. See *Z.P.G.*

FIRST POWER, THE (1990) ★★½ Lou Diamond Phillips portrays L.A. cop Russ Logan, who specializes in capturing serial killers. Sadistic killer Patrick Channing (Jeff Kober) is electrocuted and his spirit returns from the hereafter to terrorize Logan—a plot similar to *Shocker* and *The Horror Show* and hence not as fresh as writer-director Robert Resnikoff might have thought. Logan teams with psychic Tracy Griffith and has religious help from nun Elizabeth Arlen . . . all these derivative ingredients are blended with ample fights, usually high above the ground. Resnikoff shows promise but needs to get out of the cliché bin. Mykel T. Williamson, Dennis Lipscomb, Carmen Argenziano. (Video/Laser: Nelson)

FISH MEN, THE. See *Screamers* (1978).

FIST OF STEEL (1991) ★½ This post-holocaust actioner, set in a desert where roving bands of men fight for ownership of water, is just an excuse for Dale "Apollo" Cook (world kickboxing middleweight champion) and Don Nakaya Nielsen (U.S. kickboxing heavyweight champion) to square off in an endless series of duels. What little plot there is has Cook helping Cynthia Khan find revenge against the roving renegades that destroyed her village, led by Mainframe (Nielsen). Directed by Irvin Johnson. Gregg Douglass, James Gaines. Originally made as *Eternal Fist*. (Video/Laser: Action International)

FIST OF THE NORTH STAR (1995) ★★★½ A worthy adaptation of the graphic fantasy novels by Buronsont and Tetsuo Hara, thanks to the stylish direction of Tony Randel, who cowrote the script with Peter Atkins. Randel conveys a sense of tragic destiny for the vengeful martial-arts warrior Kenchido (Gary Daniels), who is doomed to rove a post-holocaust landscape ruled over by the Southern Cross. His father (Malcolm McDowell in a brief guru-type role) having been ruler of the North Star, Kenchido has psychic and magical powers of destruction and must eventually curb his warlike tendencies to beat the evil men of the Southern Cross and claim his rightful heritage. The martial arts battles are well choreographed, the villains are grotesque and plentiful (Clint Howard gives one of his unchecked portrayals of sadism), and the violence and mayhem are considerable, although

to his credit Randel gives the bloodletting a stylish touch. Costas Mandylor, Chris Penn, Isako Washio, Melvin Van Peebles, Downtown Julie Brown, Tracey Walter. (DVD: Fox Lorber)

FIVE GRAVES FOR A MEDIUM. See *Terror Creatures from the Grave*.

FIVE MILLION YEARS TO EARTH (1968) ★★★★ Third in the Quatermass series (see *The Creeping Unknown* and *Enemy from Space*) is perhaps Nigel Kneale's best—it is the most outré, replete with religious and mythical overtones. An alien spaceship is uncovered during excavations in London, and corpses of giant grasshoppers are found onboard. Mankind is related to these E.T.s through experiments carried out centuries before. Then it really gets weird as ESP and energy force fields come into play. Andrew Keir assumes the Quatermass role. Directed by Roy Ward Baker, written by Kneale. Aka *The Mind Benders* and *Quatermass and the Pit* (the latter is the title for the original BBC-TV production of 1958). Barbara Shelley, James Donald, Duncan Lamont.

FIVE SINISTER STORIES. See *The Living Dead* (1931).

FIVE THOUSAND FINGERS OF DR. T, THE (1953) ★★★ Producer Stanley Kramer's offbeat fantasy (Aka *Crazy Music*) reflects the ultimate nightmare for children forced to learn music against their will. One such child (Tommy Rettig) dreams he is imprisoned with 500 others in the prison of Dr. Terwilliker (Hans Conried), a crazed piano instructor owning the world's largest piano. The Dr. Seuss fantasy attempts to recapture a *Wizard of Oz* flavor but the choreography is so odd and listless, the film remains consistently offkey. Retuning was in order, maybe? Directed by Roy Rowland, scripted by Dr. Seuss and Alan Scott. Peter Lind Hayes, Mary Healy. (Xenon; from RCA/Columbia as *Dr. Seuss' 5,000 Fingers of Dr. T.*) (Laser: Columbia TriStar)

FLAME BARRIER, THE (1957) ★½ Purely a flameout, this undistinguished grade-B potted-plant thriller with few thrills and plenty of potted plants has intrepid explorer Arthur Franz and bickering, alcoholic brother Robert Brown leading naive Kathleen Crowley (in skirt and high heels yet) into the Yucatan Peninsula in search of her missing husband, who just happened to be nosing around where an experimental rocket, the X-117, crashed by accident. In a cave, they discover a glowing ball of glop that gives off an energy field. Is it an extraterrestrial substance or just a ball of glowing glop? Who knows? You won't care. The most exciting scene in this nonexciting movie is a fer-de-lance that rises up to bite Ms. Crowley on her acetates. You'll be rooting for the snake and hissing just as much. Directed by Paul Landres from a Pat Fielder–George W. Yates script. Aka *Beyond the Flame Barrier* and *It Fell from the Flame Barrier*.

FLASH, THE (1990) ★★★ Well-produced TV-movie depicting the comic-book superhero who moves faster than light and is but a blur in the eyeball of mankind. This pilot for the CBS series has delightful effects of the speeding Flash, and also captures the angst of his alter ego, Barry Allen, a forensic specialist for the LAPD. Written by Danny Bilson and Paul De Meo (also producers) and directed by Rob Iscove. John Wesley Shipp is effective in both roles. Amanda Pays, Alex Desert, Paula Marshall, Tim Thomerson, Priscilla Pointer. (Video/Laser: Warner Bros.)

FLASH 2: REVENGE OF THE TRICKSTER, THE (1991) ★★ The Flash's greatest nemeses, Trickster and Prank, are on the prowl, hoping they can think faster than the fastest-moving superhero in the world. John Wesley Shipp, Amanda Pays, Mark Hamill, Richard Belzer. (Warner Bros.)

FLASH GORDON (1936) ★★★ First of three Universal serials to star Buster Crabbe as the space hero created for the comics by Alex Raymond. (The other two: *Flash Gordon's Trip to Mars* and *Flash Gordon Conquers the Universe.*) In one of the best action cliffhangers ever, Flash, girlfriend Dale Arden and scientist Dr. Zarkov try to prevent the planet Mongo (ruled by Ming the Merciless) from conquering Earth. On Mongo, it's all-out action as Flash and followers meet Ming's sexy daughter Aura, the Lion Men, the dragon-lizard monster Gocko, and an underwater race led by King Kala. Jean Rogers is Arden, Charles Middleton the evil emperor, Priscilla Lawson the busty Aura and Frank Shannon the dedicated Zarkov. Stylishly directed by Frederick Stephani. The 12-chapter serial has been released in abbreviated versions as *Spaceship to the Unknown, Space Soldiers* and *Atomic Rocketship.* (From NPS in its original form; Video Yesteryear and Prism as *Flash Gordon: Rocketship*) (Laser: Image)

FLASH GORDON (1980) ★★★ Dino De Laurentiis's paean to Alex Raymond's comic-strip space hero features a Lorenzo Semple, Jr., script that walks a fine balance between action and satire. The costumes and sets are fabulous and the cast finely picked: Sam Jones as Flash is perhaps too naive but his enthusiasm makes him acceptable; Max von Sydow makes movie history as one of the great villains, Ming the Merciless; Melody Anderson is a liberated Dale Arden, and Topol a daffy, dedicated Dr. Zarkov. Brian Blessed thunders his way through the stylish action as Vultan the Hawkman. The great sky battles are faithful to Raymond's designs. Only the rock score by Queen seems out of place. A real fantasy funhouse directed by Mike Hodges. (Video/Laser: MCA)

FLASH GORDON CONQUERS THE UNIVERSE (1940) ★★★ The third serial in Universal's *Flash Gordon* series (the comic-strip character created by Alex Raymond) finds Earth subjected to Ming the Merciless's latest ploy to conquer Earth: the Plague of the Purple Death, a "death dust" that Ming's minions radiate into our atmosphere. Flash, Dale Arden, Dr. Zarkov and Prince Barin, ruler of Arboria, take on Ming with renewed strength, their adventures rocketing them to Frigia, a frozen wasteland. This marked the series' end and is the least of the trilogy, but it's still great fun. Directed by Ford Beebe and Ray Taylor. Carol Hughes, Charles Middleton, Frank Shannon, Beatrice Roberts, Anne Gwynne. Reedited as *Purple Death from Outer Space, Space Soldiers Conquer the Universe* and *Perils From the Planet Mongo.* (From Video Yesteryear, Sinister/C; United and Filmfax in 12 chapters)

FLASH GORDON: MARS ATTACKS THE WORLD. Feature video of *Flash Gordon's Trip to Mars* (VCI; Cable).

FLASH GORDON: ROCKETSHIP. Feature video of *Flash Gordon* starring Buster Crabbe (Video Yesteryear; Prism, Cable).

FLASH GORDON: SERIAL ONE: SPACE SOLDIERS. A 2-cassette repackaging of the initial *Flash Gordon* serial starring Buster Crabbe (NPS Home Video).

FLASH GORDON: SERIAL TWO: FLASH GORDON'S TRIP TO MARS. A 2-cassette repackaging of the second *Flash Gordon* serial starring Buster Crabbe (NPS Home Video).

FLASH GORDON: SPACESHIP TO THE UNKNOWN. Feature version of the original *Flash Gordon* serial (Questar).

FLASH GORDON'S TRIP TO MARS (1938) ★★★ The second Buster Crabbe Flash Gordon serial by Universal, based on Alex Raymond's famed comic strip, finds Flash, Dale Arden and Dr. Zarkov flying to Mars to stop Ming the Merciless from stealing the nitrogen from Earth's atmosphere. Adventures involve the Clay People, Azura the Queen of Magic, the White Sapphire, the Tree People, Prince Barin, Tarnak and Happy. Rousing action directed by Ford Beebe and Robert F. Hill. Jean Rogers, Frank Shannon, Charles Middleton, Beatrice Roberts. Reedited as *Deadly Ray from Mars, Space Soldiers' Trip to Mars* and *Mars Attacks the World.* (NPS Video; also on video as *Flash Gordon: Mars Attacks the World*)

FLASH GORDON: THE DEADLY RAY FROM MARS. Feature video version of *Flash Gordon Conquers the Universe* (Questar; Nostalgia; Sinister/C).

FLASH GORDON: THE PERIL FROM PLANET MONGO. Feature video of *Flash Gordon Conquers the Universe* (Questar).

FLASH GORDON: THE PURPLE DEATH FROM OUTER SPACE. Feature video of *Flash Gordon Conquers the Universe* (Questar).

FLASH GORDON VOL. I–III (1953) Episodes from the TV series of 1953–54 (produced in

Germany) in which Steve Holland starred in 39 episodes as Flash, Irene Champlin was Dale Arden and Joe Nash was Dr. Zharkov. Among the extraterrestrial enemies fought in these cheaply shot episodes were the Mad Witch of Neptune, the Great God Em of Odin and the Evil Queen of Cygnil. (Discount)

FLATLINERS (1990) ★★★½ Eschewing genre-film stereotypes, this unusual film probes the frontier of death—specifically the near-death experience. A group of medical college students experiments by "killing" one of its kind and bringing the individual back from complete death at the last possible moment. The suspense is sometimes unbearable. But each student who survives the self-imposed ordeal is haunted by his or her past. Director Joel Schumacher injects a surreal style into Peter Filardi's screenplay in trying to visualize the realm of death (in the same way that Douglas Trumbull explored it in *Brainstorm*). Kiefer Sutherland, Julia Roberts, Kevin Bacon, William Baldwin, Oliver Platt. Recommended. (Video/Laser: RCA/Columbia)

FLAYED ROSE, THE. See *Blood Rose.*

FLESH AND BLOOD SHOW, THE (1973) ★★ British actors audition for a Grand Guignol show as part of a film, but it turns out the auditioner in a sinister hood is setting them up for the kill—literally. A sputtering "splatter" movie, originally shot in 3-D by director Peter Walker. Jenny Hanley, Robert Askwith, Tristan Rogers, Luan Peters. Aka *Asylum of the Insane.* (Wizard; Monterey)

FLESH AND FANTASY (1943) ★★★★ A dreamlike quality pervades over this trilogy directed by Julian Duvivier and dealing with that primitive level of the imagination giving birth to fear and superstition. In the framework for the weird tales, Robert Benchley is disturbed by a bad dream and a friend reads from an old book to allay his dread. Betty Field and Robert Cummings star in a story about a homely seamstress whose love for a man causes a miracle; Charles Boyer is a tightrope walker haunted by images of circus aerialist Barbara Stanwyck. The best tale is Oscar Wilde's "Lord Arthur Savile's Crime," with Edward G. Robinson as an American solicitor in London who meets fortune teller Thomas Mitchell with dire predictions. A fourth story, "Destiny," was cut from the script, expanded and released as the feature film *Destiny.* Aka *Six Destinies* and *Obsessions.*

FLESH CREATURES. See *Vampire Men of the Lost Planet.*

FLESH CREATURES OF THE RED PLANET. See *Vampire Men of the Lost Planet.*

FLESH EATER. See *Revenge of the Living Zombies.*

FLESH EATERS, THE (1964) ★½ Assorted squabblers are stranded on a secluded island where an idiotic scientist has created amoeba

monsters which devour people with considerable glee and gnashing. Some effects aren't bad, but overall quality is poor and the visuals are sickening. Directed by coproducer Jack Curtis from a script by fellow producer Arnold Drake. Martin Kosleck is the insane inventor, Rita Morley, Ray Tudor and Byron Sanders the victims. (Monterey; Sinister/C)

FLESH EATING MOTHERS (1988) ★★★ The gore crowd should get a few laughs out of this send-up depicting lovable mothers being turned into cannibals when they contract a virus after having sex with a promiscuous husband about town. Besides the AIDS metaphor, James Aviles Martin offers a nice directorial style. Its numerous arm-and leg-chewing sequences (Carl Sorenson's effects are grossly amusing), its funny bit in which an alley cat is stretched into two pieces, and its pun lines add up to a good time. Robert Lee Oliver, Valorie Hubbard. (Academy has two tape versions, one unrated)

FLESH FOR FRANKENSTEIN. Japanese laser title for *Andy Warhol's Frankenstein.*

FLESH GORDON (1974) ★★★ Rollicking sex parody of *Flash Gordon* serials was heavily pornographic when produced by William Osco in 1972, but later was cleaned up for theatrical release. It's a lively romp with Flesh, a half-naked Dale Ardor and Dr. Flexi Jerkoff penetrating the kingdom of Emperor Wang's world of Porno. The props and creatures are visualized sex jokes or phallic imagery. Overshadowing the sophomoric humor, amateurish acting and raunchy sex and gropings are imaginative effects of E.T. monsters in the Ray Harryhausen vein, achieved by Dave Allen and Jim Danforth. Mike Light wrote-directed what remains an anomaly. Makeup by fandom world figure Bjo Trimble. Jason Williams, Suzanne Fields, William Hunt, John Hoyt, Lance Larsen, Candy Samples. (Media; Video Dimensions; Front Row Entertainment) (Laser: Image)

FLIGHT OF BLACK ANGEL (1990) ★★★★ Uncompromising, hard-edged, disturbing TV-movie, well written by Henry Dominick, about a "loose cannon"—a U.S. fighter pilot turned renegade who shoots down his own planes after he's stolen an atomic warhead. He intends to blow up Vegas, and you know this religious nut will do it. It's up to Peter Strauss to stop him. William O'Leary is all too real as the warped pilot. Taut direction by Jonathan Mostow. James O'Sullivan, K. Callan. (Video/Laser: Vidmark)

FLIGHT OF THE NAVIGATOR (1986) ★★★ Charming juvenile sci-fi adventure from Disney, in which David Freeman, 12, returns one day after he's been missing for eight years, having not aged a day. A government investigation reveals that he went into space at the speed of light for four hours. Freeman escapes testing headquarters to find he was befriended by an alien collecting specimens for an intergalactic zoo. The benevolent alien is only a voice controlling an E.T. ship, and an amusing relationship develops. Meanwhile, NASA official Howard Hesseman is trying to find Freeman. Takes a while to get going, then it soars. Directed by Randal Kleiser. Veronica Cartwright, Cliff De Young, Sarah Jessica Parker. (Video/Laser: Disney)

FLIGHT TO A FAR PLANET. See *Queen of Blood.*

FLIGHT TO MARS (1951) ★ Cheap Monogram space opera, cranked out by Arthur Strawn, in which Martians turn out to be humanoids from the Screen Actors Guild, women's costumes are miniskirts (at least that part of the film came true) and the plot is pure pulp nonsense. A rocket crew from Earth (including Cameron Mitchell and Arthur Franz) finds an underground city of dying Martians ruled by Ikron the Heinous. Because the society needs a gas called Corium to survive, PG&E intrigue is rampant. Morris Ankrum, Marguerite Chapman, John Litel, Robert Barrat and Virginia Huston are among those misdirected by Lesley Selander. (Nostalgia Merchant; Media) (Laser: Image)

FLIPSIDE OF DOMINICK HIDE, THE (1980) ★★★ Intriguing British TV-movie dealing with time paradoxes and set in a society 150 years from now. Time travel is a government business (watched over by Patrick Macnee) in which timehoppers return to the past to correct history so things will turn out better in the present. Peter Firth keeps returning to 1980 in a flying saucer contraption and begins a romance that, unbeknownst to him, will have an effect on the future. Written intelligently by Jeremy Paul and director Alan Gibson. Pippa Guard, Caroline Langrishe. The sequel was *Another Flip for Dominick.*

FLOWERS IN THE ATTIC (1987) ★★★ Faithful in some ways to V. C. Andrews's best-selling book, and faithless in others, this version is the compelling work of screenwriter-director Jeffrey Bloom, an allegory about how we imprison ourselves in pursuit of life's riches, and often turn evil for material needs. The film introduces a happy family but with a sense it's really dysfunctional. When the father dies, mother Victoria Tennant takes her four children to Foxworth Hall, there to be restored into her father's will. But because Victoria has married her own uncle, the kids are deemed the "Devil's spawn" and locked into a room with adjoining attic by their grandmother, played evilly by Louise Fletcher in a role that rivals her Nurse Ratched for hissability. The four prisoners create their own world of love and hate. The four youths (Kristy Swanson, Jeb Stuart Adams, Ben Granger, Lindsay Parker) excellently convey the reactions of teens and adolescents to the plight, and Tennant goes bonkers in believable style. (New World) (Laser: Image)

FLUBBER (1997) ★★½ What might have been an insufferable comedy with a lot of special effects to bolster its sluggish storyline is instead made watchable by the presence of Robin Williams. He plays Professor Phillip Brainard, a descendant of Professor Ned Brainard, the nerd played by Fred MacMurray in the 1961 Disney comedy *The Absent-Minded Professor.* It's a very nice performance by Williams, who brings a sense of sympathy to a man who can't even remember to show up for his own wedding three times in a row. He makes this unbelievable cliché of a character seem almost possible, and even generates a feeling of vulnerability for an otherwise comedic cliché. The title refers to a magical substance Brainard accidentally discovers one day in his laboratory and names "Flubber," a combination of "flying rubber." This is a globular gunk of green stuff that keeps changing shape and makes cute gurgling noises, as if it were a newborn baby. When the translucent gunk falls to the floor, it instantly richochets through the air at supersonic speed, smashing and crashing anything it hits and rebounding again and again like a rifle bullet. In defying the laws of gravity, Flubber enables a car to fly through the sky, an image taken directly out of the MacMurray version. So is a basketball-game sequence where the players bound all over the gymnasium court thanks to the magical properties of the malleable flubber. The new script by John Hughes (the original author, Bill Walsh, is given credit for writing this one, too) is formula stuff, combining elements of *Home Alone* by having two shady characters (Clancy and Brown and Ted Levine) always trying to steal the professor's secret formula and getting bonked and banged on the head repeatedly for their efforts or flying through the air to unbelievable heights (and back down again to a very hard earth). Behind the plot to get the Flubber formula is millionaire Raymond Barry after his son, Wil Wheaton, has been flunked in chemistry class by Brainard. Then there's the wife-to-be, Marcia Gay Harden, who is president of Brainard's university, which is on the verge of bankruptcy. This is all manipulated and resolved by the numbers and barely holds one's attention. What does keep you watching are the nice special effects, the chemistry between Williams and Harden, and an overall sharp performance by Williams. Although Les Mayfield seems to be a firm follower of the John Hughes style of directing, he should get some credit for pulling that performance out of Williams. (Video/DVD: Walt Disney)

FLUKE (1995) ★★★ Surprisingly good adaptation of James Herbert's novel about a man (Matthew Modine) who dies in a car accident and returns as a puppy of mixed breed (actually a talented Golden Retriever named Comet). The script by director Carlo Carlei and James Carrington is a story for children that also has enough serious themes to make it accessible to adults as that aforementioned pup grows into a mature canine that keeps having flashbacks to its humankind days. After adventures in the city with a wise older dog named Rumbo (voice by Samuel L. Jackson), including a well-staged escape of animals from an experimental lab, Fluke tracks down his former wife (Nancy Travis) and son (Max Pomerane), and sets out to solve the mystery of that strange car chase and crash that opens the picture and involves Modine's business rival Eric Stoltz. Carlei has a razzle-dazzle visual style that almost allows this to be labeled an art film. There's sentiment and sweet stuff sprinkled throughout this episodic dog adventure that features an inspired music score by Carlo Siliotto. Nice cameos are provided by Ron Perlman (as a meanie), Jon Polito (as a wrecking yard owner) and Bill Cobbs (as a hash slinger who befriends dogs). (Video/Laser: MGM/UA)

FLY, THE (1958) ★★★½ If you can overlook inconsistencies in this version of George Langelaan's story (scripted by James Clavell), you will enjoy this unsettling sci-fi/horror classic about research scientist David (Al) Hedison, who discovers the secret of teleportation. During an experiment, a housefly buzzes into the transfer chamber. The result is two incredibly mixed-up beings: a tiny fly with human head, a human with the fly's head. Think about it and it doesn't bear scrutiny. Even so, it's well directed by Kurt Neumann and enhanced by the histrionics of Vincent Price (as a member of the cursed Delambre family) and Herbert Marshall (as investigating cop). The sequels were *Return of the Fly* and *Curse of the Fly*, and there were two remakes in the '80s. Patricia Owens portrays the long-suffering wife. (CBS/Fox) (Laser: CBS/Fox, doubled with *Return of the Fly*)

FLY, THE (1986) ★★★ Scientific update of the 1958 classic, utilizing gene-splitting and computers to explain how the molecules of a human and a housefly are intermixed. Director David Cronenberg (who cowrote with Charles Edward Pogue) is again fascinated with deformity and the "beasts from within" theme as scientist Jeff Goldblum devises "telepods" to teleport matter. Chris Walas's Oscar-winning human/fly effects are a knockout, but the story defies credulity when girlfriend Geena Davis still loves this ugly man in metamorphosis. Sympathy is shown the monster once it emerges, but some may find it hard to get past the gore, especially when the fly-creature vomits on a man's hand and foot with an icky goo that dissolves them. John Getz plays a magazine editor involved with the fly-by-night. (Fox) (Laser: CBS/Fox)

FLY II, THE (1989) ★★ Chris Walas, an Oscar winner for creating the horrific effects in the 1986 *The Fly*, was further rewarded with his

first directorial assignment, and he does a good job in re-creating the disgusting but effective Fly creature. However, the script by Mick Garris, Jim and Ken Wheat and Frank Darabont recycles the sentimental love story from the original without success, but does succeed with its thrills, effects and gooey gore. This tale of son-like-father begins with the birth of the Fly's son, who grows at an accelerated rate. Soon he's Eric Stoltz, a guinea pig in a rich industrialist's research center, where teleporter pods are again in action. As the Son of the Fly undergoes genetic change, the film races to an exciting, scary conclusion. The last half-hour is every horror fan's delight as the hideous monster goes on a murdering spree, but still retaining human traits. Daphne Zuniga gets lost as the love interest, Lee Richardson is good as the industrialist Bartok. John Getz, Frank Turner, Ann Marie Lee. (Video/Laser: Fox)

FLYING DISC MAN FROM MARS (1950) ★★½ Twelve-chapter Republic serial is nonstop action in the cliffhanger vein. Walter Reed stars as Kent Fowler, a pilot who does battle with the evil Martian Mota (Gregory Gay). The Thermal Disintegrator and other wild gadgets provide the fantasy elements. By 1951 Republic was giving its serials short shrift/thrift so compared to previous studio efforts this might seem a touch shoddy in the writing and effects. But director Fred C. Brannon gives it that Saturday-matinee feeling that former kids will love reexperiencing. (The whittled-down TV version is called *Missile Monsters*.) If you love nostalgia, you couldn't find a better example. Lois Collier, James Craven, Harry Lauter, Tom Steele. Republic's *Radar Men From the Moon* is similar in plot. (Republic)

FLYING EYE, THE. See *The Crawling Eye*.

FLYING SAUCER, THE (1950) ★½ A travelogue/espionage thriller more than a sci-fi adventure with Mikel Conrad as an unlikely Secret Service agent posing as a sportsman/playboy dispatched to Alaska to track the mystery surrounding a UFO. Filmed in and around Juneau under Conrad's direction, this minor independent feature sports long stretches of beautiful aerial photography, but there's little drama, a dollop of romance (with lovely Pat Garrison) and no effects to mention. The ubiquitous Conrad also cowrote the script with Howard Irving Young. Hanz von Teuffen, Lester Sharpe, Denver Pyle, Roy Engel. (United; Rhino; Wade Williams)

FLYING SAUCERS OVER HOLLYWOOD: THE PLAN 9 COMPANION. Variant video version of *The Ed Wood Story: The Plan 9 Companion* (Atomic).

FLYING SERPENT, THE (1946) ★½ PRC flick of the so-bad-it's-hilarious-school (thanks to Sherman Scott's uproarious script), with George Zucco outstandingly atrocious as a mad doctor who cages Quetzalcoatl (the Killer Bird God) and sends the winged killer out to murder after he has placed a feather from the bird on the intended victim. Acting and music are equally laughable; wires propelling the creature are discernible even to the most nondiscerning eyeball. Loose remake of *The Devil Bat*; Quetzalcoatl was updated in 1982 for *Q*. Directed by Sam Newfield. Ralph Lewis, Hope Kramer. (Video/DVD: Image)

FOG. Original title of *A Study in Terror*.

FOG, THE (1980) ★★★ Memorable exercise in supernatural horror as a sinister fog engulfs a coastal California town; within the swirling mist are maggot-decaying pirates armed with pikes, hooks and other flesh-ripping weapons, seeking revenge for wrongs committed last century. Director John Carpenter (who cowrote with producer Debra Hill) plays against our innermost fear of the dark, delivering shock after shock as the fog draws closer. Adrienne Barbeau, Jamie Lee Curtis, Janet Leigh, Hal Holbrook, John Houseman. (Video/Laser: Columbia)

FOLKS AT RED WOLF INN, THE. Original theatrical title for *Terror at Red Wolf Inn*.

FOLLOW ME IF YOU DARE. Original title of *Mysterious Two*.

FOLLOW ME QUIETLY (1949) ★★★ More '40s film noir than a horror flick, this offbeat thriller depicts cop William Lundigan pursuing a strangler known as the Judge. When the cops set up a mannequin in their office, the killer takes the figure's place to keep abreast of what the police are up to. Tight little shocker, well directed by Richard Fleischer. Dorothy Patrick, Jeff Corey, Nestor Paiva. (Turner; Rex Miller)

FOOD OF THE GODS, THE (1976) ★ Bert I. Gordon wrote-produced-directed this horrible horror movie based on an H. G. Wells story. At least a portion of it—the title—is based on Wells. It's low-grade schlock as Marjoe Gortner goes hunting with pals to encounter giant wasps, extra-large chickens and overgrown rats. If only Marjoe, Ralph Meeker, Ida Lupino and Pamela Franklin had 5,000 pounds of American cheese, they might stand a chance. On second thought, Swiss would be better—it would match the thousands of holes in the plot. Jon Cypher, Belinda Balaski. (Orion; Vestron)

FOOD OF THE GODS II (1989) ★★ Only loosely joined to its 1976 inspiration, this Canadian production (also known as *Gnaws*) is a misfire, trying to follow in the pawtracks of such fare as *Willard, Ben* and other rat-infested flicks but ending up a mouse. The effects (consisting mainly of giant rat heads) are ludicrous rather than frightening, and there is more comedic result than horror. Paul Coufos is a lab scientist experimenting with 192 Mathianol, a growth hormone that results in the king-sized rodents. Directed by Damian Lee. Lisa Schrage, Karen

Hines, Colin Fox, Frank Moore. (Video/Laser: IVE)

FOOL KILLER, THE (1965) ★★★ Here's an offbeat Western noir with overtones of *Psycho*, brimming with brooding characters and stark photography. Anthony Perkins makes the Wild West wilder as an ax murderer (during the Civil War yet!). Great stuff from director Servando Gonzalez. Don't be a fool and miss this one. Edward Albert, Dana Elcar, Henry Hull, Salome Jens, Arnold Moss. Aka *Violent Journey*. (Republic)

FORBIDDEN PLANET (1956) ★★★★★ Classic film science fiction, set in A.D. 2200 on the planet Altair II, where an Earth ship lands to contact Professor Morbius (Walter Pidgeon) and his beautiful daughter Alta (Anne Francis). Suddenly the ship (*C-57-D*) is attacked by an invisible entity, whose beastlike outline is only visible when it touches the vessel's force-field shield. Nicholas Nayfack's MGM production has overtones of a whodunit thriller (what is this bizarre alien killer and where does it come from?) and has outstanding technology—from Robby the Robot to the subterranean city of the long-dead Krell race to Morbius's futuristic home to the spacecraft and land cruisers. Spacemen Leslie Nielsen, Earl Holliman and Warren Stevens remain second bananas to the witty Robby. Odd electronics score by Louis and Bebe Barron. Directed by Fred McLeod Wilcox from a Cyril Hume script said to be inspired by Shakespeare's *The Tempest*. (Video/Laser: MGM/UA; Voyager)

FORBIDDEN SUN (1989) ★★ The most distinguishing feature about this British release, originally called *Bulldance*, is that the script is by Robin Hardy, director of *The Wicker Man*. Olympic hopefuls, coached by Lauren Hutton, are on the isle of Crete when one of the women is attacked and violently raped. The others set out for revenge. Cliff De Young, Renee Estevez. Directed by Zelda Barron. (Video/Laser: Academy)

FORBIDDEN WORLD (1982) ★½ This loose Roger Corman–produced sequel to *Galaxy of Terror* is an *Alien* ripoff depicting space ranger Mike Colby (Jesse Vint) at a research station on a far-flung world. An experiment in genetic engineering has spawned a mutation that's turning humans into piles of gooey leftovers. However, gore can't take the place of suspense. The attitude of director Allan Holzman is so condescending to his characters that the film lapses into laughableness. The women, for example, quickly strip and leap into bed with Colby, or rush stupidly through the corridors, trying to communicate with "it" or fleeing from its gnashing, slobbering jaws. Dawn Dunlap, Linden Chiles, June Chadwick. Aka *Mutant*. (Nelson; Embassy; Sultan) (Laser: Image)

FORBIN PROJECT, THE. See *Colossus: The Forbin Project*.

FORCE, THE (1994) ★★★ An offbeat TV-movie mixture of corrupt-cops intrigue and the supernatural when the spirit of a murdered plainclothesman (Gary Hudson) passes into patrolman Jason Gedrick, who is then motivated to solve the homicide. As he probes deeper into the crime, having the knowledge of the dead man possessing him, Gedrick uncovers crooked cops involved in a prostitution racket. The Pierre David production, written by Steve Kallaugher, Mitch Marcus and Randall Frakes, is average but director Mark Rosman gets good performances out of his cast (including Cyndi Pass, Gerald Anthony, Dennis Lipcomb and Lyman Ward) and makes atmospheric use of the deserted L.A. county jailhouse. (Republic)

FORCE BEYOND, THE. See *The Evil*.

FOREST, THE (1983) ★½ Poorly executed low-budget indie, in which a wife killer turned cannibal (Michael Brody) terrorizes four dull campers. Writer Evan Jones provides plot twists, such as having two children wandering the woods turning out to be ghosts, but it's all predictable, with drawn-out flashbacks and a lack of effects to complement the gore killings. Producer-director Don M. Jones fails to evoke believable performances from Dean Russell, Elaine Warner, John Batis and Ann Wilkinson. Aha, a critic can see the sleaze through *The Forest*, after all. (Prism; Starmaker)

FOREST PRIMEVAL. See *The Final Terror*.

FOREVER: A GHOST OF A LOVE STORY (1992) ★★★ Unusual supernatural comedy-drama blended with soft-core sex as rock-music-video director Keith Coogan rents the one-time home of murdered Hollywood director William Desmond Taylor and is haunted by Mabel Normand and other real-life movie stars of the '20s. Sally Kirkland, as a movieland agent, spends most of her time seducing Coogan and disbelieving his story. This is an oddball offering that generates only mild interest despite its probing of a real unsolved murder case. Sean Young, Diane Ladd, Terence Knox, Renee Taylor, Steve Railsback. Directed by Thomas Palmer, Jr.; written by Palmer and Jackelyn Giroux. (Crystal Vision)

FOREVER EVIL (1987) ★ Video original made in Houston and Coldspring, Texas, involving a demon baby with red-glowing eyes, an Elder God (Yog Cothar, a name stolen from H. P. Lovecraft) imprisoned on a quasar, and a humanoid monster whose identity is kept a secret. Cheaply shot, with amateur talent, this only comes to life with the appearance of a zombie-like creature that cannot be killed, and the efforts of hero and heroine to do the monster in. Oh, there's also some crap about a mythical dagger. If you're a masochist, go ahead and rent it. Roger Evans directed. Charles Trotter, Howard Jacobson, Red Mitchell. (United; VCI)

FOREVER YOUNG (1992) ★★★½ Entertaining family picture that recaptures many of the storytelling values of the '40s, a definite feather in the cap of its producer and star, Mel Gibson. He portrays a test pilot in 1939 whose fiancée is paralyzed in an accident. So stressed out, he puts himself into a deep-freeze experiment under scientist George Wendt, hoping to be reawakened when she comes out of her coma decades later. When he is revived, the disoriented Gibson begins a series of heart-tugging adventures with Jamie Lee Curtis and her two adolescents. Sure, it's corny and manipulative, but it has so many wonderful and sweet moments, you can't help but like Gibson's sympathetic performance. Credit director Steve Miner for also capturing an adolescent romance. Forever successful! Elijah Wood, Isabel Glasser, Joe Morton, Nicholas Surovy. (Warner Bros.)

FORGOTTEN ONE, THE (1989) ★ Slow-moving ghost story with few scares, produced in Denver, in which Terry O'Quinn (*The Stepfather*) takes over an old house haunted by the spirit of a woman who committed suicide there in 1891. Even though O'Quinn would rather be in love with neighbor Kristy McNichol, he's gradually seduced by the beautiful spectral brunette in a series of unexciting incidents with unimaginative effects. Lethargically written-directed by Phillip Badger. Elisabeth Brooks, Blair Parker. (Academy) (Laser: Image)

FOR LOVE OR MURDER. Video version of *Kemek* (Neon).

FORMULA, THE (1980) ★★½ Steve Shagan's best-seller was a compelling detective-mystery and this film version emphasizes the cynical theme as cop George C. Scott uncovers a formula that can produce gas from synthetic products, first used by Hitler in World War II. There is a conspiracy by a major oil company to suppress the formula. Marlon Brando exemplifies the conspiratorial side as a cynical, greedy oil magnate. John Avildsen directed Shagan's script. Marthe Keller, John Gielgud, G. D. Spradlin. (CBS/Fox; MGM) (Laser: Japanese)

FORTRESS (1992) ★★★ Well-produced, intense sci-fi thriller set in a maximum-security prison of the future, run by a private corporation called Mentel. Prisoner behavior is controlled by an explosive ("intestinate") placed in the stomach of each convict; a "mind wipe chamber" where one's memories are erased; and "enhancers," prison officials who have been turned into creatures that live on amino acids. Although the basic form is that of the prison action picture, this has so many intriguing ideas that one is swept along with its effectively brutal torture sequences and the climactic escape attempt. Christopher Lambert and Loryn Locklin play husband and wife who have been imprisoned for breaking the breeding laws—Loryn is pregnant with child. Kurtwood Smith is slimy as the head "enhancer"—his evilness steals the picture. Directed with the gore and violence one expects from Stuart Gordon, who re-animated himself into a first-class director with this superb fantasy-action flick. Jeffrey Combs, Lincoln Kilpatrick, Tom Towles. (Video/Laser: Live)

FORTY YEARS OF SCIENCE FICTION TELEVISION (1990) ★ The only reason to collect this superficial study of TV sci-fi from 1959–90 is its inclusion of the *Star Trek* bloopers. Otherwise, it's clips with cursory commentary from a droning voice. Scenes lifted from early stuff (*Tom Corbett, Space Cadet*) through *Science Fiction Theater* through *Batman, The Prisoner, Kolchak*, etc. Also called *A History of Sci-Fi Television*. (Simitar)

FOR YOUR EYES ONLY (1981) ★★★½ The 12th James Bond adventure, more restrained than many, though it still features exciting chases, futuristic gadgets and vehicles designed to keep Agent 007 one step ahead of the villains. Director John Glen emphasizes character and suspense, allowing 007 (Roger Moore) to appear more human than Superman. The British agent is after the tracking system of a sunken nuclear submarine stolen by a ruthless mercenary. The Derek Meddings–John Evans effects are outstanding, Alan Hume's cinematography is topnotch and Bill Conti's music is whistleable. The acting by Topol, Lynn-Holly Johnson and Carole Bouquet is just strong enough to hold attention until the next action sequence. A mountain-scaling feat is one of the film's more suspenseful bits. (Video/Laser: CBS/Fox)

FOUR SKULLS OF JONATHAN DRAKE, THE (1959) ★ Familiar beware-the-family-curse plot is at work in this cheapie from producer Robert E. Kent. Despite its abundance of shrunken heads, the appearance of a Jivaro native with his mouth sewed shut and threads dangling from his chin is as horrific as it gets as Orville Hampton's threadbare story, about a family whose male members are always beheaded at 60, unfolds. Henry Daniell is appropriately menacing as Jonathan Drake, who keeps all the skulls in his private collection. Turns out Drake is a 2,000-year-old walking zombie. Zounds four times. Inexpensive sets, lethargic direction by Edward L. Cahn and a long sharp stiletto that bends like a piece of rubber are in store for you, the cursed viewer. Valerie French and Eduardo Franz bring a grain of versimilitude to the proceedings.

FOURTH MAN, THE (1984) ★★★ Paul Verhoeven, director of *Total Recall*, spins a weird allegorical tale about a homosexual writer who suffers hallucinations and undergoes horror when he meets a Black Widow whose husbands have all died mysteriously. A multilayered Dutch film (with subtitles), this may offend some with its sexual and violent content, but art-film lovers should find it fascinating. Jeroen Krabbe, Renee Soutendijk, Jon De Vries. Aka *Blunt*. (Media; Xenon) (Laser: Image)

FRANCIS THE TALKING MULE (1950) ★★★ A talking mule with Chill Wills's voice? Yep, it's time for that fun-loving Universal-International comedy with Donald O'Connor as a World War II dogface who gets thrown into a psycho ward when he tries to explain about the articulate ass that saved his life in a Japanese ambush. Written by David Stern from his novel and directed by Arthur Lubin, with ZaSu Pitts, Eduard Franz, Mikel Conrad, Patricia Medina and Ray Collins providing platoon support. This rollicking comedy was the "pilot" for a long-braying, money-making series, after which Lubin created the TV series about the talking horse, *Mr. Ed*. Others in this series, also on video, are *Francis Covers the Big Town, Francis Goes to the Races, Francis Goes to West Point, Francis in the Haunted House, Francis in the Navy* and *Francis Joins the WACs*. (Video/Laser: MCA)

FRANK. See *The Being*.

FRANKENHOOKER (1989) ★★★ Black-comedy parody of *Frankenstein* in the *Re-Animator* vein from writer-director Frank Henenlotter, coming after *Basket Case* and *Brain Damage*. It's madcap lampoonery of the darkest kind as mad doctor James Lorinz salvages body parts of his sister after she's mulched up in a mowing machine. After hilarious adventures in Times Square with hookers, he puts her together again. A cult "midnight" movie, designed for those who enjoy gory horror and aren't easily offended. There's nudity and softcore sex. Patty Mullen, Charlotte Helmkamp, Lia Chang, Louise Lasser. (Shapiro Glickenhaus) (Laser: Image)

FRANKENSTEIN (1931) ★★★★★ Grand-daddy of the Walking Monster films, so cleverly directed by James Whale it takes on greater classicality with each viewing. Boris Karloff, as Frankenstein's Monster in the makeup of Jack Pierce, projects a paradoxical mixture of pathos and horror. Whale's vision was years ahead of its time, influencing a superb adaptation of Mary Shelley's novel (by Garrett Ford, Robert Florey, Richard Shayer, John L. Balderston, Francis E. Faragoh) and crisp, Gothic-inspired camerawork by Arthur Edeson. Whale went on to make *Bride of Frankenstein*, which many feel is superior to the original . . . but unquestionably this established a cinema trend. Whale's superb cast includes Colin Clive as Dr. Frankenstein ("It's alive! Alive!"), Mae Clarke, John Boles, Edward Van Sloan, Dwight Frye. A new video version contains the controversial scenes cut from the original of the Monster drowning a little girl in the village pond. (Video/Laser: MCA)

FRANKENSTEIN (1969). See *Assignment Terror*.

FRANKENSTEIN (1973). See *Andy Warhol's Frankenstein*.

FRANKENSTEIN (1973) ★★ Originally shown on ABC-TV in two parts, this is a long, tedious Dan Curtis production (exceeding two hours) in which Robert Foxworth plays an unlikable, intense Dr. Frankenstein and Bo Svenson is his monstrous creation—an articulate, intellectual shambler who spends too much time talking. The low-budget, lumbering production never escapes the sound-stage look, and director Glenn Jordan zooms his camera too much. Strasberg provides love interest. Heidi Vaughn, Robert Gentry, Philip Bourneuf. (Thrillervideo)

FRANKENSTEIN (1984) ★★ U.S.-British TV video blending Hammer's Gothic influences with Mary Shelley into an entertaining brew. Robert Powell portrays Dr. Victor Frankenstein with an element of depraved madness, while Carrie Fisher is his innocent sister who is always lifting her period bustle to walk room to room. John Gielgud appears as the blind man in the forest. Terence Alexander is the young assistant and Susan Woolridge his love interest. David Warner brings little pathos to the Monster and his makeup is hideous without being stunning or original. James Ormerod's direction has that anonymous clarity that plagues all taped dramas. Ripley Castle in England is the setting. (Lightning; Live)

FRANKENSTEIN (1993) ★★★★ Shot in England and Poland for cable TV by British writer-producer-director David Wickes, this adaptation of Shelley's novel stars Randy Quaid as the Monster, Patrick Bergin as Dr. Frankenstein and John Mills as the blind man in the forest. It's a richly ornate version with the obsessed doctor creating his monster with a force-field device that provides the film with its goriest sequence. Quaid is effective as the Monster, and Wickes is faithful to some parts of the book if not to others. Quite similar in style to Branagh's 1994 version, *Mary Shelley's Frankenstein*. Lambert Wilson, Fiona Gillies. (Turner)

FRANKENSTEIN (1994). See *Mary Shelley's Frankenstein*.

FRANKENSTEIN: A CINEMATIC SCRAPBOOK (1990) ★★ A "treasury of movie trailers" of all the Frankenstein movies in Universal's and Hammer's horror series, with a sprinkling of oddball and independent movies such as *Frankenstein 1970* and *Frankenstein's Daughter*. The narration by producer-director Ted Newsom offers an occasional tidbit, such as Boris Karloff appearing in monster makeup at a 1941 baseball game. (Rhino)

FRANKENSTEIN AND THE GIANT LIZARD. See *Frankenstein Conquers the World*.

FRANKENSTEIN AND THE MONSTER FROM HELL (1973) ★★ Final entry in Hammer's *Frankenstein* series, at its best with laboratory black humor. Shane Briant, a young disciple of Baron Frankenstein, is sent to Carlsbad Asylum for the Insane for his heinous acts, but once there is befriended by Frankenstein (the utterly delightful, and mad, Peter Cushing). Assisted by mute Madeleine Smith, the team takes a genius violinist's brain and places it in David Prowse's cranium, resulting in new mayhem. The script by John Elder (aka producer Anthony Hinds) is clichéd and half-hearted; Terence Fisher's direction is weary; it's but a ghostly shadow of earlier films in this historic series. Bernard Lee, Charles Lloyd-Pack. (Paramount/Gateway) (Laser: Japanese)

FRANKENSTEIN BROTHERS, THE. Unproduced sequel to *War of the Gargantuas*.

FRANKENSTEIN (BY ANDY WARHOL) See *Andy Warhol's Frankenstein*.

FRANKENSTEIN CONQUERS THE WORLD (1966) ★ Made as *Frankenstein vs. the Giant Devil Fish* ... but in a cutting room the Devil Fish was spliced out. Destructive mayhem, however, was not cut; so rampage-mayhem-chaos fans can rejoice. The battle royal is between Baragon, a rampaging dinosaur, and a human who is 30 feet high after swallowing a heart created by Dr. Frankenstein for the Nazis. Nick Adams headlines the cast to give the film international appeal. *Godzilla* director Inoshiro Honda helms the action, with effects by his pal Eiji Tsuburaya. Tadao Takashima.

FRANKENSTEIN CREATED WOMAN (1967) ★★★ A Hammer horror film for transsexuals. Peter Cushing, as Baron Frankenstein, has mastered the black science of capturing the spirit of a corpse. A male wraith is transplanted into the body of a beauty with heaving bosom (Susan Denberg), who goes around stabbing folks with a knife, her bosom still heaving. Production values are outstanding and the cast ably manipulated by director Terence Fisher, a specialist at motivating heaving bosoms. Screenplay by John (Heaving) Elder, produced by Anthony Nelson-Keys. Thorley Walters, Robert Morris. Originally made as *And Frankenstein Created Woman*. Aka *Frankenstein Made Woman*.

FRANKENSTEIN 80 (1972) ★½ Italian rehash of the Frankenstein legend is a blood-splattered flicker with effects by Carlo Rambaldi and direction by Mario Mancini. Gordon Mitchell portrays a mad doctor who creates "Mosaico," a hulking evil that escapes the lab to wreak revenge on sexy women. Marisa Travers, John Richardson. (Gorgon; MPI)

FRANKENSTEIN '88. See *The Vindicator*.

FRANKENSTEIN EXPERIMENT, THE. See *Andy Warhol's Frankenstein*.

FRANKENSTEIN GENERAL HOSPITAL (1988) ★★★ Improv-comic genius Mark Blankfield (*Jekyll and Hyde ... Together Again*) stars in this spoof as Dr. Robert Frankenheimer who, with the help of assistant Iggy (Leslie Jordan), puts together a new body from body leftovers. The scenes in his subterranean lab are in black and white because it has been "drained of color"—one of the few gags in this film that works. Another cute bit is set in Tushman's Terminated Teenager Mortuary. Most of the flat humor evolves out of smutty scatology tomfoolery, body parts jokes, nerdy nurse nutties, sexually depraved puns and pratfalls. Irwin Keyes, as the Monster, is cute and never menacing. Kathy Shower and Katie Caple show off their ample bosoms—it does liven up the tedium. Direction by Deborah Roberts is as flat as the jokes. Jonathan Farwell, Hamilton Mitchell, Ben Stein. (Video/Laser: New Star)

FRANKENSTEIN ISLAND (1981) ★½ So bad it has to be seen to be appreciated: Balloonist-cum-scientist Robert Clarke and three pals plus Melvin the dog land on an island where alien women in leopard-skin bikinis dance to tomtoms, pirate Steve Brodie wears an eyepatch and cackles like a madman, schooner captain Cameron Mitchell recites poetry locked in a cage, and the floating head of John Carradine (Dr. Frankenstein) screams "Power! Power! Power!" You also get mad Dr. Van Helsing and his peroxide-blond wife, Sheila, and a Frankenstein Monster in a tub of water, surrounded by zombie guards in dark glasses. What does it all mean? Producer-director Jerry Warren never does say. Andrew Duggan, Robert Christopher, Patrick O'Neil, Katherine Victor. Aka *Frankenstein's Island*. (Monterey)

FRANKENSTEIN JUNIOR. See *Young Frankenstein*.

FRANKENSTEIN LIVES AGAIN! Early title for *The Bride of Frankenstein*.

FRANKENSTEIN MADE WOMAN. See *Frankenstein Created Woman*.

FRANKENSTEIN MEETS THE SPACEMEN. See *Frankenstein Meets the Space Monster*.

FRANKENSTEIN MEETS THE SPACE MONSTER (1965) ★ And you'll meet with boredom from this poverty-stricken heap about an "astrorobot" with half a face (and less of a brain) fighting Princess Marcuzan and her alien-invader hordes. This has nothing to do with the Frankenstein Monster, but who cares? Produced in Puerto Rico as *Mars Invades* (or *Attacks*) *Puerto Rico*; directed by Robert Gaffney. James Karen, Nancy Marshall. Aka *Duel of the Space Monsters* and *Frankenstein Meets the Spacemen*. (Prism)

FRANKENSTEIN MEETS THE WOLF MAN (1943) ★★★★ Fanged, drooling battle between the Frankenstein Monster and Lawrence Talbot, the misunderstood lycanthrope, was declared the "Clash of the Century" by Universal. The rematch of these box-office monsters, written by Curt Siodmak and directed by Roy William Neill, is fun movie-watching. Lon Chaney, Jr., is back as Talbot and Bela Lugosi proves he's no Boris Karloff as he shambles ineptly as the Monster. Boy, what a cast of horror favorites: Patric Knowles as Dr. Mannering, who resurrects the Monster; Lionel Atwill as the village mayor; Maria Ouspenskaya as the gypsy woman who intones the classic "wolfbane curse." Dwight Frye, Dennis Hoey, Ilona Massey. (Video/Laser: MCA)

FRANKENSTEIN MUST BE DESTROYED (1970) ★★★ In this, fifth in Hammer's *Frankenstein* series, Peter Cushing cuts apart cadavers to create a hulking entity of evil. The Bert Batt script succeeds in being nauseating, as in a Grand Guignol sequence where a busted water pipe forces a buried victim up through the mud. Buffs will enjoy this hokum from producer Anthony Nelson-Keys and director Terence Fisher; others may find it unstomachable or tedious as Cushing dons a fright mask to attack victims, cuts open skulls to extract human brains, and forces assistant Simon Ward to claim the body of Veronica Carlson, quite beautous in her diaphanous nightgowns. Freddie Jones plays the Monster. (Warner Bros.)

FRANKENSTEIN 1960/FRANKENSTEIN 1975. See *Frankenstein 1970*.

FRANKENSTEIN 1970 (1958) ★★½ Instead of harnessing electricity to resurrect man-mad monsters, Baron Victor von Frankenstein (Boris Karloff) uses atomic energy. Oh well, even horror films have to swing with the modern age. Anyway, the unhinged Baron (victim of Nazi torture) allows a movie crew (feisty Don "Red" Barry is its director) onto his castle grounds, horrified to discover the tinseltown troupe is making a fright flick. How horrible! But the Baron knows cast and crew will supply the bodies he needs for his nuclear reactor. The surprise ending is quite predictable. Directed by Howard Koch, scripted by George W. Yates and Richard Landau. Tom Duggan, Jana Lund, Mike Lane, Charlotte Austin. Discarded earlier titles: *Frankenstein 1960* and *Frankenstein 1975*.

FRANKENSTEIN'S BLOODY TERROR (1971) ★★★ Spanish import, redesigned for U.S. consumption, has nothing to do with Frankenstein or his Monster—it's about a clan called Wolfstein and depicts a man becoming a werewolf, and then watching helplessly (while chained to a wall) while two vampires seduce his girl. Despite poor dubbing, this has good color photography and nice nocturnal scenes of the vampire playfully leading a young woman into the night. Directed by Enrique L. Equiluz. Paul Naschy portrays the werewolf in this, the first of eight wolfman dim-witted dilemmas. Aka *Hell's Creatures*, *The Mark of the Wolfman*, *The Werewolf's Mark*, *The Vampire of Dr. Dracula* and *The Wolfman of Count Dracula*. Whew.

FRANKENSTEIN'S CASTLE OF FREAKS. Video version of *Dr. Frankenstein's Castle of Freaks*.

(S/Weird; Filmfax; AstroVision; from Best Film & Video with *The Mad Butcher*)

FRANKENSTEIN'S DAUGHTER (1958) ★½ Wretched Z flick, so compellingly awful it's required viewing for schlock fans. Exemplary of '50s genre, with amateurish actors, condescending script (by H. E. Barrie) and uninspired direction by Richard Cunha. The grandson of Dr. Frankenstein perfects the drug Degeneral, which degenerates Sandra Knight into a hideous, fanged she-creature comparable to what you see on Halloween night at the front door, asking for a treat. Meanwhile, some teenagers try to solve the mystery while a cop dumbly investigates. Wonderfully incompetent. John Ashley, Harold Lloyd, Jr., Voltaire Perkins, George Barrows (the Monster). Aka *She Monster of the Night*. (Media; Rhino; Nostalgia; VCI)

FRANKENSTEIN'S GREAT-AUNT TILLIE (1985) ★ Mexican production, shot in English with a U.S.-British cast—figure that one out. Writer-director Myron J. Gold goes for laughs when the Transylvanian town of Mugglefugger lays claim to the Frankenstein Castle because of unpaid taxes. Along come Victor, Jr. (Donald Pleasence), buxom June Wilkerson and 109-year-old Great-Aunt Tillie (Yvonne Furneaux) to search for the family fortune hidden in the castle. Nothing aloof about this spoof. Zsa Zsa Gabor, Rod Colbin, Garnett Smith. (Video City)

FRANKENSTEIN SINGS . . . THE MOVIE (1994) ★★ Based on the musical play "I'm Sorry, the Bridge Is Out, You'll Have to Spend the Night" by Sheldon Allman and Bobby Pickett, this adaptation written and directed by Joel Cohen and Alec Sokolow is a complete misfire in its attempt to recapture the campy magic of *The Rocky Horror Picture Show*, of which it is an obvious parody. The car of two nerdy kids (Ian Bohen and Candace Cameron) breaks down on a lonely road (wwhhaatt???) and they seek shelter in a spooky gothic castle inhabited by a menagerie of supernatural beings who clown around, sing and dance. Hence, a musical comedy. Bobby Pickett portrays the crazy Dr. Frankenstein ("of the Hyannis Port Frankensteins") but the only time he's good is when he sings "Monster Mash." There's Dracula (Anthony Crivello), Drac's bride (Sarah Douglas, looking very fetching and worthy of better material), the Frankenstein Monster (Deron McBee) and Jimmie Walker. What's wrong here is that it's not nearly wild and crazy enough, and the choreography and original songs lack energy. It's just drab on the slab. Adam Shankman, Mink Stole, John Kassir. (Turner/Prism)

FRANKENSTEIN'S ISLAND. See *Frankenstein Island*.

FRANKENSTEIN: THE COLLEGE YEARS (1991) ★★½ Good natured, if frequently dumb, TV-movie making slapstick out of the Frankenstein

Monster legend. When college scientist Lippzigger dies he leaves his formulae to young student William Ragsdale and pal Christopher Daniel Barnes. Together they resurrect a benevolent creature (Vincent Hammond) who is integrated into campus life as a student and football quarterback. Most of the characters behave stupidly or nerdish, and the humor is of the a-belch-is-funny school. A few of the parody gags will evoke chuckles, but the tee-hees are few. Directed by Tom Shadyac. Larry Miller, Andrea Elson.

FRANKENSTEIN 3-D. See *Andy Warhol's Frankenstein*.

FRANKENSTEIN UNBOUND (1990) ★★★ Roger Corman's first directorial effort in 20 years is a well-made film if not a great one. But who ever expected greatness from the master of the B horror movie? This adaptation of a popular Brian W. Aldiss novel by screenwriter F. X. Feeney (with rewrite help from Roger baby) follows Dr. Buchanan (John Hurt) in the year 2031 when he's hurled backward through time to 1817 just as Dr. Frankenstein (Raul Julia) is creating a mate for his first monster, which is on a murderous rampage. Filmed in Italy, this has many fascinating elements. Bridget Fonda, Nick Brimble, Catherine Rabett. Aka *Roger Corman's Frankenstein Unbound*. (Video/Laser: CBS/Fox)

FRANKENSTEIN VS. THE GIANT DEVIL FISH. See *Frankenstein Conquers the World*.

FRANKENWEENIE (1984) ★★★ This 30-minute short subject produced by Disney was the showcase piece that launched Tim Burton into the Hollywood big time. As idea man and director, he burst out of animation obscurity with this satirical variation on *Frankenstein*, in which Daniel Stern's pet dog Sparky is run over by a car and buried in a graveyard that resembles something out of *The Nightmare Before Christmas*. Inspired by lab teacher Paul Bartel's use of electricity to get a postmortem reaction out of a dead frog, Stern sparks Sparky back to life, causing no end of trouble for mom (Shelley Duvall) and dad (Barret Oliver). The surreal imagery and inspired direction are all Burton's, and it's all too short. This idea (scripted by Lenny Ripps) could easily have carried over into a full-length film, with its upbeat direction and excellent cast. Joseph Maher, Roe Braverman. (Buena Vista)

FREAKED (1994) ★½ At the heart of this tasteless, failed excuse for a satire on movie horror (originally shot as *Freekz*) is cowriter/star Alex Winter, who portrays a goofy chemical salesman for an unscrupulous corporation. Winter is sent to South America to track down Zygrot 24, a wonder fertilizer invented by Elijah C. Skuggs (Randy Quaid), a Frankenstein-type doctor running a sideshow of freaks with the help of Mr. Toad, an Igor type. What Quaid does is turn everyone into freaks, and it doesn't take him long to turn Winter and others into monstrosities via bizarre injections. A number of minor stars humble themselves in cameos (Morgan Fairchild, Bobcat Goldthwait, Brooke Shields, Mr. T, etc.) but it's all terrible stuff, ranging from rancid vomit and toilet humor to hideous but pointless monster makeup by Screaming Mad George. The script (director Tom Stern and Tim Burns helped in its misconception) is a hodgepodge of incoherence, Stern's direction is uncontrolled and without focus, and the whole thing just squizzles around like a pile of . . . Zygrot 24, whatever the hell that is. We didn't care. You won't either. Michael Stoyanov, William Sadler, Megan Ward, Alex Zuckerman, Ray Baker, Patti Tippo. (Video/Laser: Fox)

FREAK FROM SUCKWEASEL MOUNTAIN, THE. See *Geek Maggot Bingo*.

FREAKMAKER, THE (1974) ★★½ This British nightmare thriller, like Tod Browning's *Freaks*, features real-life sideshow freaks. Donald Pleasence portrays a biologist who sees the world dying and decides crossbreeding man and plants is the answer to survival. His experiments create hideous mutants and a man-eating plant to dispose of any cadavers left lying around. Directed by Jack Cardiff, this was Michael Dunn's last film before his untimely death. Tom Baker is Pleasence's assistant and Jill Haworth and Julie Ege provide shapely bodies and screaming mouths. Brad Harris, Scott Anthony. Aka *Mutations* and *The Mutation*. (Vidcrest)

FREAKS (1932) ★★★★ Tod (*Dracula*) Browning produced-directed this disturbing portrait of carnival life, also known as *Barnum, Forbidden Love, Nature's Mistress* and *The Monster Show*. A stickler for realism, Browning hired real circus freaks to act out a macabre tale about the circus world. Two normal-sized performers try to swindle an inheritance from a well-to-do midget by poisoning him on his wedding night. The sympathetically portrayed freaks turn against the pair, providing a shock ending that disgusted '30s viewers. A Classic of the Grotesque based on Tod Robbins's "Spurs." Among the misshapen: a living torso, pinheads, a "living skeleton" and Siamese twins. Wallace Ford, Roscoe Ates, Olga Baclanova, Edward Brophy. (Video/Laser: MGM/UA)

FREAKY FAIRY TALES. See *Deadtime Stories*.

FREDDY'S DEAD: THE FINAL NIGHTMARE (1991) ★★½ Sixth entry in the *Nightmare on Elm Street* series is as much a fizzle as the previous three, offering nothing new for Freddy Krueger to do but make tepid wisecracks and threaten teenagers with his knife-hand. In this final adventure, Freddy (Robert Englund) terrorizes more troubled teens: Lisa Zane, Ricky Dean Logan, Lezlie Deane, Shon Greenblatt. And there's flashbacks showing how Freddy killed his wife and went after his own child—tasteless material

for what is basically an entertainment. The last 10 minutes were filmed in 3-D but it's cheesy stereovision, the images similar to those in a Disneyland horror ride. If Freddy's really dead, good! Directed by Rachel Talalay. (Video/Laser: New Line)

FREEJACK (1992) ★★★ Robert Sheckley's *Immortality Inc.* was the basis for this sci-fi/adventure, directed with big-budget flair by Geoff Murphy, in which racing car driver Emilio Estevez is yanked forward into time by Mick Jagger, to serve the evil purposes of corporate bigwig Anthony Hopkins. Most of this is action and vehicle chases, never rising above the ordinary as Estevez escapes the cliffhangers. However, when the film enters Hopkins's mind and duplicates his mental landscape, it comes to life in a unique way. Computerized images, however, are still not enough to make up for the clumsily constructed Ron Shusett–Steve Pressfield–Dan Gilroy script. Rene Russo, Jonathan Banks, David Johansen, Grand Bush. (Video/Laser: Warner Bros.)

FREEKZ. Original title of *Freaked*.

FREEWAY (1988) ★★★ A haunting ambience hangs over this study of an excommunicated priest turned religious nutcake who cruises the L.A. freeway system, killing randomly with his .44 revolver. Besides giving it mood, director Francis Delia etches the unhappy, obsessed characters of Darlanne Fluegel, whose husband was a victim of the freeway killer, and nihilistic ex-cop James Russo. Other disturbing albeit fascinating characters: Richard Belzer as a radio talk host whom the murderer calls during his attacks, Michael Callan as a harassed but caring cop, Clint Howard as a sex-crazed mechanic, and Billy Drago as Heller, the killer who uses quotations from the Bible. (Nelson; Starmaker) (Laser: New World)

FREEWAY MANIAC (1989) ★★½ Paul Winters directed this exercise in murderous behavior that depicts a madman taking refuge on the set of a sci-fi movie and killing again and again. The script was fashioned by Gahan Wilson, the (in)famous macabre cartoonist. Loren Winters, James Courtney, Shepard Sanders. A "thank-you" credit salutes Robert Bloch and Stan Lee, for reasons not explained. Also known as *Breakdown*. (Media)

FREEZE BOMB. Video version of *Death Dimension*. (Movietime)

FRENCHMAN'S FARM (1987) ★★ Tracey Tainish witnesses a murder that police tell her was committed in 1944. She and law student David Reyne try to unravel the supernatural mystery. Directed-written by Ron Way. Norman Kaye, John Meillon. (Magnum)

FRENZY (1972) ★★★ Alfred Hitchcock's good suspense shocker, depicting in unusually graphic style (with some nudity) the strangulations committed by London's infamous Necktie Murderer. There's a classic scene in the back of a potato truck and other clever directorial touches to this unsettling psychological tale of sex and murder, which Hitch jokingly and perversely links to food. Jon Finch, Anna Massey, Barbara Leigh-Hunt, Barry Foster. (Video/Laser: MCA)

FRIDAY THE THIRTEENTH (1980) ★★★ A lucky day for producer-writer-director Sean Cunningham: This trend-setting slasher movie was a runaway smash, followed by an endless series of sequels, all in a similar vein. A blood-drenched psycho killer named Jason is knocking off his victims (for revengeful purposes) at Camp Crystal Lake. This is a curiosity piece, mainly to see the different ways the victims are done in—there are no 2 deaths alike. Some of the modi operandi are clever, others ludicrous. Tom Savini made his reputation for gore effects on this film. Adrienne King, Betsy Palmer, Harry Crosby, Mark Nelson. (Video/Laser: Paramount)

FRIDAY THE THIRTEENTH PART 2 (1981) ★★★ A vast crowd-pleaser under Steve Miner's direction, delivering numerous graphic murders, with impalings being the favorite of scripter Ron Kurz. The mutilations are ghastly as that beloved unstoppable killer, Jason Voorhees, returns to Camp Crystal (aka "Camp Blood") to knock off ill-mannered teenagers just asking for swift dispatching via a poker through the eye, a machete through the jugular, a spear through two bodies at once. Oh, there's also a pitchfork, a chainsaw, and decapitating mechanisms. The cast is negligible (except as cannon fodder) and technical credits adequate if not stunning. Adrienne King, John Furey, Amy Steel, Warrington Gillette, Betsy Palmer. (Video/Laser: Paramount)

FRIDAY THE THIRTEENTH PART 3 (1982) ★★ The main titles leap out at you in 3-D and it's a whopper of an effect. And then the movie begins. There isn't a whopper to follow it as the body count builds at Crystal Lake, where more dumb teenagers are on an outing, laughing at that old legend about Jason the Killer. Well, before you can say "Son of the Chainsaw Massacre Meat Cleaver Driller Killer Strikes Again," Jason is back in his funny mask to knock off juvenile jerks one by bloody one. And do those kids deserve what they get! Directed by Steve Miner. Dana Kimmell, Richard Brooker, Catherine Parks. (Video/Laser: Paramount)

FRIDAY THE THIRTEENTH PART 4: THE FINAL CHAPTER (1984) ★★ A tepid entry in the series, depicting the slaughterous adventures of Jason Voorhees (an unkillable supernatural wraith) in and around Crystal Lake. Writers Barney Cohen and Frank Mancuso couldn't dream up new ways for bodies to be slashed, skewered or impaled, so Paramount kept the bloodletting and gore effects by Tom Savini to flash cuts. Six teens rent a summer cottage and face death by butcher-knife beheading, hacksaw hacking, corkscrew twisting, stomach knife-punctures, etc. The characters are witless, the dialogue inane and Joseph Zito's direction feeble. Despite the title, the denouement set up an obvious sequel in which Jason returned. Kimberley Beck, Peter Barton, Corey Feldman, Alan Hayes. (Video/Laser: Paramount)

FRIDAY THE THIRTEENTH PART 5: A NEW BEGINNING (1985) ★★½ Fifth in the popular slasher series, a tired formula affair with nothing new about Jason Voorhees, the inhuman killer who delights in wearing a hockey mask. So, this collapses like a balloon with a butcher knife shoved into it. This time the isolated rural setting is a rehab center for the mentally deranged, where ill-defined characters are knocked off by road-flare-shoved-into-mouth, commonplace beheadings and impalings, an axe in the brain, garden shears in the eyeballs, a spike in the brain, ad nauseam. Danny Steinmann directed, but telegraphs every punch. The cast (Melanie Kinnaman, John Shepherd, Shavar Ross, Marco St. John) behaves like refugees from a school for the teenaged deranged. An unnecessary and mean exercise in gratuitous violence. (Video/Laser: Paramount)

FRIDAY THE THIRTEENTH PART 6: JASON LIVES (1986) ★★★ Not quite the same old gore murder crap centered around the masked madman, Jason Voorhees. Writer-director Tom McLoughlin has seen fit to inject touches of humor into his script, suggesting none of us should take this too seriously. Not that anyone would. By now Jason is a menaceless parody of himself as he stalks his youthful victims in rural settings. One of the gags is that Crystal Lake has been renamed Forest Green County and the cemetery is called Eternal Peace. Here's the body count: machete thrust for two, impaling on a spear, broken bottle into throat, bare fist through a stomach, 360-degree head twist, and assorted stabbings and decapitations. Duck the splatter from the head on a platter. Thom Mathews, Jennifer Cooke, David Kagen. (Video/Laser: Paramount)

FRIDAY THE THIRTEENTH PART 7: THE NEW BLOOD (1988) ★★ A weak entry in the Paramount series starring Jason Voorhees, the world's greatest hockey mask salesman, as he is resurrected from the cliffhanger in Part VI. There's nothing new under the electrical storm as Voorhees again stalks the grounds of Camp Crystal, this time faced with the telekinetic powers of a young woman (Lar Park Lincoln) who sets everything on fire everytime she gets pissed off. Director John Carl Buechler hasn't the slightest idea what to do with this retreaded tired tire, as he telegraphs each murder. The thin storyline has Ms. Lar undergoing psychiatric testing by cruel headshrinker Terry Kiser and arguing with her mother (Susan Blu) while the usual dumb teenagers provide cannon fodder for Jason's pointed instruments. Jennifer Banko, John Orrin, Kevin Blair, Susan Jennifer Sullivan. (Video/Laser: Paramount)

FRIDAY THE THIRTEENTH PART 8: JASON TAKES MANHATTAN (1989) ★★ The title suggests a parody of the Jason Voorhees series, but not so. The hockey-masked killer is back with a vengeance, using spearguns, knives, and other "penetrating" weaponry to kill off young people. But there are twists: Part of the film is set aboard a ship, getting the series away from Crystal Lake and that damn barn. And there are good scenes of Jason in the Big Apple—Times Square, the subway, the rat-infested alleys, the waterfront, etc. Writer-director Rob Hedden should have set the entire picture there. It would have been a real gas. There's also a decent subtext in which the ghost of young Jason comes back to haunt Jensen Daggett. At least they seemed to be trying with this one, even though the endless murders are, by now, all tired retreads. Scott Reeves, Peter Mark Richman, Barbara Bingham. (Video/Laser: Paramount)

FRIDAY THE THIRTEENTH PART 9. See *Jason Goes to Hell: The Final Friday.*

FRIDAY THE 13TH . . . THE ORPHAN. See *The Orphan.*

FRIGHT (1971) ★★½ Peter Collinson directed this British shocker (written by Tudor Gates as *Night Legs*) with babysitter Susan George trapped in a spooky house with an escapee from an insane asylum. An interesting undercurrent of sexual energy develops as killer Ian Bannen develops fixations. Honor Blackman portrays Bannen's wife. John Gregson, George Cole, Dennis Waterman. (Movies Unlimited; Republic)

FRIGHT, THE. See *The Visiting Hours.*

FRIGHTENERS, THE (1996) ★★★★ New Zealand director Peter Jackson followed up his *Bad Taste, Dead Alive* and *Heavenly Creatures* success with this Hollywood-produced macabre comedy that is a masterful blend of supernatural special effects, screwball humor, and edge-of-your-seat thrills. Michael J. Fox portrays a whacked out psychic investigator aided by three spectral ghosts (John Astin, Jim Fyfe and Chi McBride) as he hunts a Grim Reaper image representing Death. In this crazed world, Fox is the only one who can see images of the supernatural and struggles to protect Trini Alvarado from the scythe-armed figure, which is somehow associated with an executed serial killer (Jake Busey) returned to life, and his repressed girlfriend (Dee Wallace Stone). Jackson directs at a frenetic pace, throwing jolt after jolt into the uneven but intriguing stew, which he wrote with Fran Walsh. Jeffrey Combs is a standout as a loony FBI investigator, and R. Lee Ermey does a

ghostly parody of his drill-instructor persona. Peter Dobson, Troy Evans. (Video/DVD/Laser: Universal)

FRIGHTENING SECRET OF DR. HICHCOCK, THE. See *The Horrible Dr. Hichcock.*

FRIGHT HOUSE (1989) ★★ Two tales of blood-curdling (you hope!) terror: "Fright House" depicts witches prepping for a meeting with the Devil; "Abandon" is about a teacher who never ages and must explain to her pupils. Al Lewis, Duane Jones—the latter in his final role. Produced-directed by Len Anthony. (Studio Entertainment; Shooting Star)

FRIGHTMARE (1974) ★★ Disgusting but effective British chiller about a mother (Sheila Keith) who craves (and carves) human flesh and a husband (Rupert Davies) who covers up for her. There's a hot poker murder, a pitchfork homicide and an ax murder or two in David McGillivray's script, and producer-director Peter Walker has the decency to look the other way when the gore splatters. Well, some of the time, anyway. Deborah Fairfax, Paul Greenwood. Also known as *Once upon a Frightmare*. (From Prism as *Frightmare II*)

FRIGHTMARE (1981) ★★½ "I've never died before, but I want to do it right," proclaims vampire film actor Conrad Radzoff, "The Prince of Ham." And after pushing his director to his death for exhibiting boorish temperamental symptoms, Radzoff dies from acute overacting. Where do washed-up horror players go after death? Right back to the living: He's conjured up from the dead by a medium. So Radzoff (Ferdinand Mayne) continues to chew scenery—and bodies—by terrorizing the dumb teenagers who stole his corpse from a mausoleum. It's a campy send-up by writer-director Norman Thaddeus Dane, who first conceived of this as *The Horror Star*. Luca Bercovici, Nita Talbot, Jennifer Starrett. (Vestron)

FRIGHTMARE II. Video of 1974's *Frightmare* (Prism).

FRIGHT NIGHT. TV title of *Night Fright.*

FRIGHT NIGHT (1985) ★★★½ Writer-director Tom Holland (author of *Psycho II*) uses the "boy cried werewolf" plot but with ingenious twists. William Ragsdale is convinced a vampire lives next door—but mom, his girlfriend and best friend aren't. Roddy McDowall is marvelous as a late-night "Creature Features" host to whom Ragsdale turns for help. Eventually the girl (Amanda Bearse), a school chum (Stephen Geoffreys) and McDowall enter the vampire's abode, and a "night of terrors" begins, with Richard Edlund providing effects in all their fury. Chris Sarandon has great fun as the vampire, knowing when to be subtle and when to ham it up. He has a handsome assistant (Jonathan Stark) and a homosexual relationship is suggested but never elaborated on. And dig that sequence in a disco when the vampire mesmerizes Bearse. A box-office hit that was followed by *Fright Night Part 2*. (Video/Laser: RCA/Columbia)

FRIGHT NIGHT PART 2 (1988) ★★★ This is one sequel that borrows the elements of success from the original. Back from Tom Holland's 1985 hit are Charley Brewster (William Ragsdale) and "Fright Night" TV host Peter Vincent (Roddy McDowall) to stalk new vampires. Director Tommy Lee Wallace and writers Tim Metcalfe and Miguel Tejada-Flores understand what made the first film work—the Brewster-Vincent relationship, the erotic aspects of vampirism, a clever use of effects. Outstanding in the erotic department is Julie Carmen as Regine, a vampire related to the one killed off in the original. With effectively sensual choreographed dances, she proves to be a worthy foe. Traci Lin, Russell Clark, Brian Thompson, Jonathan Grieg. (IVE) (Laser: Image)

FRIGHT SHOW. Video of *Cinemagic* (MPI).

FRISSONS. See *They Came from Within*.

FROG, THE. See *Psychomania* (1973).

FROG DREAMING. See *The Quest*.

FROGS (1972) ★★ Frightened by the image of frogs, toads and related amphibians leaping to the attack, croaking a melody of death? Then you'll quiver in your wading boots as nature rampages against man (presumably because of our polluting habits). Personifying man's evil side (along with DDT and insecticides) is land-owner Ray Milland, who feels the attack just isn't cricket and then orders frogleg soup. The attacking frogs, leaping to the music of Les Baxter, the typewriter strokes of Robert Hutchison and Robert Blees and the directorial commands of George McCowan, also have control over snakes and other swamp crawlies as the crowd closes in on Milland's private island, inhabited by quibblers Sam Elliott, Joan Van Ark, Adam Roarke, Judy Pace and William Smith. (Warner Bros.; Vestron)

FROGS! (1994) ★★ If watching frogs (or facsimiles from the special-effects department) hopping around in a reedy swamp is your idea of a good time, then don't miss this *rivet*-ing drama of metamorphosis, designed primarily as a children's tale for the TV "Wonderworks" series and directed by David Grossman. Poor Scott Grimes turns into a frog after he meets nerdish nightclub singer Gus Prince (Paul Williams). Despite the dumbness of the Mark Herder–David Arata teleplay, *Frogs!* still has a sweet quality to its romance (Grimes falls for Amy Lynne) and captures the innocence of young love. The fantasy highpoint is a guest appearance by Judith Ivey as Passionatta, a parody of a fairy-tale princess that's a real gas. Elliott Gould and Shelley Duvall are Grimes's disbelieving parents. Robin Tunney, Paul Dooley. (PM Entertainment; Home Vision Cinema) (Laser: Image)

FROGTOWN II (1990) ★★ This is not quite as amusing or as clever as *Hell Comes to Frogtown*, but it has campy moments as the Texas Rocket Rangers (inspired by Republic's trilogy of serials that began with *King of the Rocket Men*) fight against the evil Star Frogmeister, who is planning to "turn the world green" by injecting all humans with a frog serum. Rocket Ranger Sam Hell, with the help of his computer F.U.Z.Z.Y., goes up against Commander Toty on the "Frogtown Mutant Reservation." The film works best when its oddball characters (a nerdy scientist played by Brion James; a frog hand-puppet; a sexy mutant nurse who only gets turned on by humans) chew up the scenery. Writer-director Donald G. Jackson pays homage at the same time he spoofs movie cliffhanger conventions. Robert Z'Dar, Denise Duff, Charles Napier, Don Stroud, Lou Ferrigno. (York)

FROM A WHISPER TO A SCREAM. See *The Offspring*.

FROM BEYOND (1986) ★★★ Director Stuart (*Re-Animator*) Gordon has such a distinct style (frenetic pacing, bizarre characters, no-holds-barred horror) that he overcomes the shortcomings of this unrestrained horror thriller from producer Charles Band. Crazy Doc Pretorious (name sound familiar?) has invented the Resonator, which taps into another dimension, allowing a grotesquely awful monster into our world, at the cost of everyone's sanity. Despite all the gooey effects and horrific visuals, the film works because of the overwrought performance of Barbara Crampton as Dr. Roberta Bloch, a psychiatrist who loses all control (sexually and otherwise) to become a kinky anti-heroine (and her bared breasts get pawed by the monster, too). Jeffrey Combs is Crawford Tillinghast. (Characters have genre names provided by scripter Dennis Paoli, who based this loosely on a story by H. P. Lovecraft.) (Vestron) (Laser: Image)

FROM BEYOND THE GRAVE (1973) ★★★ Amicus anthology film featuring four stories by R. Chetwynd-Hayes, linked by an antique shop setting where owner Peter Cushing foresees the doom of customers trying to cheat him. As adapted by Robin Clarke and Raymond Christodoulou, the stories are "The Gate Crasher," "An Act of Kindness," "The Elemental" and "The Door." Director Kevin Connor presents them with a flourish of atmosphere and production value; recommended. David Warner, Margaret Leighton, Donald Pleasence, Ian Bannen, Diana Dors, Lesley-Anne Down, Nyree Dawn Porter. Aka *The Undead, Tales from Beyond the Grave, Tales from the Beyond* and *The Creatures*. (Warner Bros.)

FROM DUSK TILL DAWN (1995) ★★★★ One of the most outrageously violent vampire movies ever made, and one of the best U.S. gorefest movies in a long while thanks to an audacious, raucous script by Quentin Tarantino, who isn't afraid to explore old territory by treading into it with innovative, mind-stomping ideas. Tarantino also portrays one of two cold-blooded brother-killers on a rampage through Texas. The other is George Clooney, and together they make a frightening, sadistic pair as they gun down their victims with a despicable glee. But they're also very funny because this blend of genres never takes itself seriously, and you aren't supposed to take it seriously either. At first you will think this is one of those Tarantino crime movies done up by director-editor Robert Rodriguez with stylish tongue-in-cheek gusto. But at midpoint, the brothers arrive at their rendezvous point in Mexico to divvy up stolen loot with Cheech Marin (who plays three roles—border guard, Titty Twister pitchman, and the brothers' contact), taking ex-preacherman Harvey Keitel and his kids (Juliette Lewis and Ernest Liu) along as hostages. At the Titty Twister, the most bizarre topless club you'll ever see, it turns into a goofy battle between humans and vampires, the latter reflecting all the cinematic state-of-the-art special effects and computerized animation tricks. Helping out is Fred Williamson, who, with several other familiar faces, makes a guest appearance. The film's profanities of sex and violence may stun the more squeamish, but genre buffs will really get off on Tarantino's twisting of old, familiar clichés. Selma Hayek, Marc Lawrence, John Saxon. (Dimension)

FROM DUSK TILL DAWN 2: TEXAS BLOOD MONEY (1998) ★★★ Although it comes nowhere near the satirical outrageousness of its money making predecessor, this sequel about the vampire game that hangs out at the Titty Twister "sleaze" bar somewhere in Mexico should satisfy undemanding gore-and-violence genre fans. Producer Quentin Tarantino (for the "Los Hooligans" production company) is back with another stylish director, Scott Spiegel, who wrote the script with actor Duane Whitaker. From the outset, Spiegel's design is to make everything extravagantly over-the-top with uncommonly lengthy stretches of film that are pure cinematic action and gore-letting. Unfortunately, there is only one sequence set at the Titty Twister, so there is little that connects this to the original film. (After all, it was the Titty Twister that gave the first film its sweet charm.) So here's the minimal plot: gang leader Luther Hex (Whitaker) escapes from prison and orders his partner-in-crime Robert Patrick to round up three other crooks (Texas cowboy-type Muse Watson, crazy Mexican Raymond Cruz, and nice guy Brett Harrelson) to form an "Unmagnificent Five" to rob a bank down in Bravo, Mexico. They stay at the El Coyote Motel after

driving there in a convertible with the license plate BYT. MEE. But Luther, coming alone in his Jeep, is hit by a flying vampire bat on a desert highway and turns into a nocturnal bloodsucker when he's bitten by the bartender from the Titty Twister. But hell, even a vampire needs cash to keep on the lam, so he still carries out the heist, one by one turning members of the gang into fellow bat monsters. The last third of the film is a nonstop standoff with Mexican police troops surrounding the bank and trapping the robbers inside. Patrick escapes and tries to convince cop Bo Hopkins (a sworn adversary of Luther) to use anti-Dracula techniques and forget about routine service-revolver bullets or ineffectual semiautomatic fire. He doesn't listen, so there's a tremendous bloodbath as the Mexican force is annihilated. Rockets blow up squad cars, bodies fly beautifully through the air, blood flows and spurts and often covers the camera lens. As if those delightful visuals were not enough, Spiegel spices up his directorial style with several clever insert shots and unusual special-effects close-ups that enhance the satirical nature of the lowbrow material. Somewhere in all this mess are Bruce Campbell, Danny Trejo and curvy Tiffani-Amber Thiessen. (Video/DVD: Dimension)

FROM DUSK TO DAWN 3: THE HANGMAN'S DAUGHTER (2000) ★★★ Cult followers of the first blood-drenched vampire saga set at the Titty Twister should enjoy the uninhibited number of impalings, beheadings, disembowelings, severings, fang-sinkings and other methods of bodily destruction in this "origin" tale of how the bloodsucking gang came to hang out in the Mexican desert and how vampire Princess Santanico Pandemonium came to be. The year is 1915 in the midst of Pancho Villa's Revolution, with famous American fiction writer Ambrose Bierce (Michael Parks) arriving to join in the fight. A cynical alcoholic, jaded beyond hope, Bierce becomes the passive observer of what starts out as a raunchy, bullet-riddled "spaghetti western." Sadistic outlaw Johnny Madrid (Marco Leonardi) escapes the rope of hangman Temuera Morrison and takes the sadistic ropemaster's daughter (lovely Ara Celi) with him in a prolonged chase that ultimately ends up at the tavern/bordello. Although a "Band Apart/Los Hooligans" production with Quentin Tarantino acting as coproducer and Robert Rodriguez also hanging around as coproducer and costory idea guy, in no way does this have the inventive cleverness of the original—just its outrageous, politically incorrect violence. Nudity, sexual orgies, and the cutting off of at least one sex organ are among the graphic delights. In fact, the screenplay by Alvaro Rodriguez (who got help from Rodriguez) is a chaotic, messy affair with hardly any sympathetic characters to root for, offering up scene after scene of unrelenting death and destruction. Even the Madrid character, the closest thing to a hero this movie has, despicably allows a woman to hang while he rides away, preoccupied by his own problems. Lennie Loftin is a Bible-toting newlywed hot to get into wife, Rebecca Gayheart's underpinnings, Danny Trejo returns as Razorblade Charlie, and Sonia Braga, Jordana Spiro, Orlando Jones and Kevin Smith play assorted outlaws and vampires. Director P. J. Pesce is no Rodriguez, but he does have a pretty good sense of location (the desert shots were done with a reddish cast, in keeping with all the sanguinary themes of the series), and he knows how to direct action sequences. (Video/DVD: Dimension)

FROM HELL IT CAME (1957) ★½ A tree trunk named Tabanga branches out when possessed by the radioactive spirit of a dead native. But what a sap! Leaving its shady past behind, the trunk stalks the jungles of a Pacific island, murdering anyone passing through. The performance of the tree (Paul Blaisdell, who was soon after put out to pasture) is equaled only by the wooden acting of Tod Andrews and Tina Carver (but she does have shapely limbs). The *Roots* of horror. The seeds for this were sown by writer Richard Bernstein and planted by producer Jack Milner and director Dan Miller.

FROM RUSSIA WITH LOVE (1964) ★★★★ Second in the James Bond series produced by Harry Saltzman and Albert R. Broccoli, and still a superior spy thriller. The bone of contention is a Soviet decoding machine, the Lektor, which S.P.E.C.T.R.E. is trying to steal from Russia's cryptographic headquarters in Istanbul. Bond is employed by M (Bernard Lee) to steal the device aided by agent Kerim Bey (Pedro Armendariz). And soon our heroic British spy is embroiled with beautiful women (Daniela Bianchi is ravishing) and enemy agents Red Grant (Robert Shaw) and Rosa Klebb (Lotte Lenya). Director Terence Young keeps the pace brisk and the visuals dazzling, capturing every nuance of Richard Maibaum's adaptation of Ian Fleming's novel. The action includes chases in motorboats and helicopters, a fiery belly dance contest climaxed by a gunbattle, and a fight aboard a speeding train. Martine Beswick, Aliza Gur, Lois Maxwell. (CBS/Fox) (Laser: MGM/UA)

FROM STAR WARS TO JEDI: THE MAKING OF A SAGA (1983) ★★★ Behind-the-scenes documentary footage of how George Lucas produced the *Star Wars* trilogy, with emphasis on special effects. Directed by Lucas, with on-camera appearances by David Prowse (the man under Darth Vader's headpiece), Harrison Ford, Carrie Fisher, Billy Dee Williams and Alec Guinness. (Fox; Films Inc.)

FROM THE DEAD OF NIGHT (1989) ★★★ Despite its use of horror genre clichés and frequent red herrings, and despite its heroine behaving stupidly at times, this four-hour TV-movie sweeps one along. Based on Gary Brandner's novel *Walkers* it's the mystery of fashion designer Joanna Darby (Lindsay Wagner), who undergoes a harrowing life-after-death experience, only to discover she is pursued by six dead spirits who have one month to get her—so watch for six supernatural attackers. Wagner is bolstered by two boyfriends: Robin Thomas as a jerkola who never believes any of it, and Bruce Boxleitner, a tarot card reader who buys it all. It's director Paul Wendkos who keeps the dubious plot going when William Bleich's script doesn't. Diahann Carroll, Robert Prosky, Merritt Butrick, Joanne Linville. (Action International)

FROM THE EARTH TO THE MOON (1958) ★★ The best features in this adaptation of Jules Verne's scientific adventure are Victorian settings and costumes. Inventor Joseph Cotten uses a new explosive to launch a missile to the moon. He and Debra Paget end up in each other's arms, facing the hazards of space flight. Literate, well produced but not very exciting. Directed by Byron Haskin, scripted by Robert Blees and James Leicester. George Sanders, Don Dubbins, Patric Knowles, Morris Ankrum. (United; VCI) (Laser: Image)

FROSTBITER: WRATH OF THE WENDIGO (1991) ★½ This Troma pick-up is one of those homemade potpourris where a little of everything gets thrown into the kettle. Made on location in Tecumseh, MI, it's the campy retelling of an ancient legend about a snow beast which is kept in check by "The Guardian," a monstrous looking guy who lives in a log cabin surrounded by human skulls. When "The Guardian" (Mike Missler) gets blown away by some dumb hunters on Manitou island, Frostbiter goes wild, taking such forms as "Evil Mom," "Miss October" and "The Witch." Finally it becomes a Harryhausen-esque skeletal thing with a moose's antlers that jerks around in stop-motion style, killing all the hunters and turning them into *Night of the Living Dead* zombie extras. Writer-producer-director Tom Chaney, knowing he has little money to make it believable, plays it for laughs. The best thing you can say about this amateurish outing (with an endless track of rock music) is that it's stupid enough to be a little bit enjoyable as a monster comes out of a chili pot, a skeleton strangles a man, and a man's head is bitten off. Ron Asheton, Lori Baker, Patrick Butler, Devlin Burton. (Troma)

FROZEN ALIVE (1964) ★★ More experimentation in the art of preserving dead bodies with freezing techniques, tinged with sci-fi overtones. The Evelyn Frazer script deals mostly with the legal ramifications when scientist Mark Stevens is arrested for killing his wife, when her body is really in suspended animation. Directed by Bernard Knowles. Delphi Lawrence, Marianna Koch, Walter Rilla. (Movies Unlimited)

FROZEN DEAD, THE (1966) ★★★ Don't give it a cold shoulder—it's a chilling (ha ha!) tale depicting a loyal Nazi (Dana Andrews, speaking with an accent that borders on parody) who devises a method to keep German soldiers alive in suspended animation. But something is wrong with their brains and the doctor has a cellarful of mindless Nazis. The doc drills a hole in a brain, severs the head of a strangled woman and keeps it alive, and creates a wall of severed arms that he can tingle back to life with electricity. Mad, you say? Yes, isn't writer-producer-director Herbert J. Leder wonderful. Anna Palk portrays the doctor's niece who enters into telepathic rapport with the detached head, and Philip Gilbert (a specialist in severed heads from America) provides bland love interest. Kathleen Breck, Karel Stepanek, Philip Gilbert. Produced in England.

FROZEN GHOST (1945) ★★½ Entry in Universal's minor *Inner Sanctum* series, B mysteries introduced by a head floating in a crystal ball—or was it a goldfish bowl? Lon Chaney, Jr., plays another misunderstood character: Gregor the Great, a hypnotist who fears he committed murder. Chaney is stiff in the thankless role, and gets no help from director Harold Young. The script was chiseled from an iceburg by Barnard Schubert and Luci Ward. Evelyn Ankers, Milburn Stone, Elena Verdugo, Douglas Dumbrille, Martin Kosleck.

FROZEN SCREAM (1980) ★ Incompetently made time-waster about crazy doctors creating zombie creatures who cackle and look bug-eyed. It's so muddled, there's voice-over narration to explain the plot involving a dumb cop and his terrorized girlfriend, but even that only adds to the confusion. The acting is pathetic, the direction by Frank Roach totally inadequate. The Michael Soney–Celeste Hammond plot is about prefrontal cranial circuitry lobotomies. It's enough to freeze anyone's mind. Renee Harmon, Lynne Kocol. (VEC; from Continental with *Executioner II*)

FROZEN TERROR (1980) ★ First feature from Lamberto Bava is a wild beginning for the son of Mario Bava, famed horror director. Bernice Stegers stars as a wacky broad who keeps the severed head of her husband in her bed—a head endowed with supernatural powers. This killer has attributes of both Jack Frost and Jack the Ripper! Double your horror pleasure. Originally produced as *Macabro*. Veronica Zinny, Robert Posse, Stanko Molnar. (Lightning; Vestron; from CIC as *Macabre*)

FULL CIRCLE. Variant video version of *The Haunting of Julia* (Media).

FULL ECLIPSE (1993) ★★★ Fascinating variation on the werewolf theme when heroic urban cop Mario Van Peebles is asked to join a secret group of police who take a serum that gives them superpowers and brings out the animal instincts in them. The kinetic, stylish direction of Anthony Hickox gives the Richard Christian Matheson–Michael Reaves script an added boost, especially when Hickox resorts to violence in the John Woo style. Above average TV-movie. Patsy Kensit, Jason Beghe, Paula Marshall. (Video/Laser: HBO)

FU MANCHU. Original title of *Fiendish Plot of Dr. Fu Manchu.*

FU MANCHU AND THE KEYS OF DEATH. See *Kiss and Kill.*

FU MANCHU AND THE KISS OF DEATH. See *Kiss and Kill.*

FU MANCHU'S CASTLE. See *The Castle of Fu Manchu.*

FU MANCHU'S KISS OF DEATH. See *Kiss and Kill.*

FUNERAL HOME (1981) ★★ Busty Lesleh Donaldson helps grandmother Kay Hawtry run a tourist home, formerly a funeral parlor until her grandfather, Mr. Chalmers (rhymes with "embalmers"), disappeared. In the cellar, late at night, strange voices can be heard. Is Grandma keeping a dark secret? This Canadian film is half-hearted exploitation, not quite a gore movie and not quite a character study. Barry Morse has a minor role as a husband looking for his missing wife. William Fruet's direction is workaday, and Ida Nelson's script is too derivative of *Psycho* to stand on its own. Good track by Jerry Fielding. Aka *Cries in the Night.* (Paragon)

FUNHOUSE, THE (1981) ★★★ That *Texas Chainsaw Massacre* lovable, Tobe Hooper, restrains himself for the first half hour of this chiller to establish four teenagers who spend the night in a spooky carnival. But then director Tobe pulls out the stops! A sexually repressed midway helper (mine Wayne Doba) wears a fright mask to hide the fact that underneath is an even worse countenance—something to give the Frankenstein Monster nightmares. Script by Larry Block. Sylvia Miles, Kevin Conway, William Finley, Cooper Huckabee, Elizabeth Berridge, Miles Chapin. Effects by Craig Reardon and Rick Baker. (Video/Laser: MCA)

FURTHER ADVENTURES OF TENNESSEE BUCK, THE (1988) ★★ Unusual lesbian overtones earmark this satire of the Indiana Jones series made in Sri Lanka, directed by and starring David Keith as the adventurer who leads a jungle expedition with inadequate husband Brant van Hoffman and sexy wife Kathy Shower, who looks great in same with clothing off. A rubdown of Kathy's inspiring body is the high point of this sexually activated actioner. (Media) (Laser: Image)

FURTHER TALES FROM THE CRYPT. See *The Vault of Horror.*

FURY, THE (1978) ★★½ Insufficient exposition weakens this Brian De Palma horror-adventure about a young man (Andrew Stevens) with psychic powers who becomes a pawn between spy factions. Superspy Kirk Douglas (Stevens's father) tries to rescue him from the villainous John Cassavetes. Emphasis of the John Farris script is on suspense and pursuit, with smashed-up cars, special effects and makeup (Rick Baker). Carrie Snodgrass, Amy Irving, Charles Durning. Music by John Williams. (Video/Laser: CBS/Fox)

FURY OF THE SUCCUBUS. See *Demon Rage.*

FURY OF THE WOLFMAN (1971) ★★ Paul Naschy tries to get it off his chest—the sign of the Pentagram, we mean. If he doesn't, he'll turn into a hairy killer when the moon is full, just as he did in four previous films in this Spanish series: *Frankenstein's Bloody Terror, Nights of the Werewolf, The Werewolf vs. the Vampire Women* and *Assignment Terror.* Directed by Jose Maria Zabalza, *Fury* will only make horror fans furious when Waldemar Daninsky goes to the Tibetan mountains and gets bitten, just like that dude in *Werewolf of London.* Naschy (Jacinto Molina) also scripted. Perla Cristal, Veronica Lujan, Mark Stevens. The next entry in this series: *Dr. Jekyll and the Wolfman.* (Unicorn; Charter; Sinister/C; Loonic; Filmfax; S/ Weird; Alpha)

FURY WITHIN, THE (1999) ★★ Given that *Poltergeist* exhausted the special-effects possibilities of extrasensory perception and ghostly manifestations, does the world need another exploitation flick made on a shoestring budget? Especially if it's a cheapjack USA Network original movie? Probably not, but there's the never-ending craving for genre flicks, no matter how lousy. What we have here is a variation on the Id from *Forbidden Planet*—a force of evil created from the vivid imagination of one of the film's characters. Which one? I'll never tell, but you don't have to be a rocket scientist to figure it out. Ally Sheedy plays a mother with a misunderstood adolescent (Vincent Berry) who seems to be conjuring up a hulking, snarling entity of evil of the "demon from hell" variety, created by a "limpic brain" and its "source of primitive drives such as hunger, sex, fear, and rage." Then there are rocks falling from the sky and a dog turned rabid and a whole lot of set shaking and teeth rattling going on when ESP investigator Steve Bastoni sticks his nose into these strange things. He wishes he hadn't when the demon comes after him, too. The William Bast–Paul Huson script tries to be a whodunit as well as a horror story, and even throws in some domestic problems when Sheedy's wandering hubby (Costas Mandylor) has an affair with Jodie Dry (provocative in miniskirts and skintight sweaters). Under Noel Nosseck's direction, *The Fury Within* finally fizzles out to an unhappy ending. As for the beautiful Dry, she ends up being pursued by the demon and falls into a huge fan. Now all they have back at the crime scene is a lot of Dry rot. (Paramount)

FUTURE COP (1976) ★★½ One-joke concept teaming cop Ernest Borgnine with a robot cop (Michael Shannon) who is poorly programmed and always klutzing it up. Poorly programmed is right. This TV-movie directed by Jud Taylor became a series that brought back Borgnine, Shannon and John Amos, then it was the inspiration for another TV-movie, *Cops and Robin*, with the same cast. And the concept was recycled for the 1980 feature *Superfuzz*, again with Borgnine. (Paramount)

FUTURE COP (1985). See *Trancers.*

FUTURE FORCE (1989) ★★½ This claptrap actioner features such a laid-back performance by David Carradine that it's almost worth enduring—almost. Carradine is John Tucker, top gun of Civilian Operated Police Systems, an organization of bounty hunters that has replaced the police, so ineffectual has law enforcement become in fighting lawlessness. Carradine, acting like John Wayne, blasts the heavies (led by crooked "cop" William Zipp) and his own men to protect a TV reporter with good-looking legs (Anna Rapagna) who knows too much about Zipp's organization. Carradine even has a metal armpiece that fires laser bolts. Credit writer-director David A. Prior, who went on to make a sequel, *Future Zone.* Can nothing stop this man? Robert Tessier, Patrick Culliton. (Action International)

FUTURE HUNTERS (1988) ★★ Filipino director Cirio H. Santiago usually turns out *Mad Max* imitations, but here he indulges in *Indiana Jones*–type fantasy adventures energetic and swiftly paced. In a long prologue in 2025, in a post-holocaust setting, hero Richard Norton finds the head of the magical spear that pierced Jesus Christ's body on the Cross. To prevent the doom of mankind, Norton must find the spear's missing head. He travels to his past, our present (1986), and turns over his mission to an anthropology student (vivacious Linda Carol) and her boyfriend (Robert Patrick). They embark on a series of adventures involving neo-Nazis (Ed Crick and Bob Schott), Amazon warriors, a Mongolian horde and a benevolent race of dwarves in the Philippine jungle. Patently ridiculous, yet entertaining. (Vestron) (Laser: Image)

FUTURE KICK (1991) ★★½ Lively if frequently clichéd Roger Corman production set in a society ruled by corporations with "cyberons" to enforce peace. However, since these android lawmen have morals, they must be destroyed by the men who created them. The soul surviving robot warrior (played woodenly by kickboxing champ Don "The Dragon" Wilson) helps Meg Foster find the psychotic assassin who murdered her husband with a double-bladed device in a smog-ruined world reminiscent of *Blade Runner*. Writer-director Damian Klaus pads his movie with footage lifted from at least ten other Corman actioners. Christopher Penn, Eb Lottimer, Al Ruscio, Jeff Pomerantz. (New Horizons) (Laser: Image)

FUTURE KILL (1985) ★ Look at Splatter: He's the leader of a punk gang, an android-man whose hand is a claw device that rips flesh at the wriggling of a finger. Big Splatter and his Little Splatters are cruising the city, following social collapse, looking for members of a fraternity who witnessed Splatter commit a murder. A sickening movie (originally *Splatter*) with nothing to counterbalance its violence and nihilistic viewpoints. As Ronald W. Moore has written-directed it in Austin, Texas, this has zero entertainment values. Edwin Neal, Marilyn Burns. (Video/Laser: Vestron)

FUTURE SHOCK (1993) ★½ A failed attempt of recut footage from three movies tied together by having the main character of each visit psychiatrist Martin Kove, who sends them into a trance or listens to their woeful tales. "Jenny Porter" is about a paranoiac woman (Vivian Schilling) trapped in her home by mad dogs. Directed by Eric Parkinson and costarring Brion James. "The Roommate" stars Scott Thompson as a nerdy morgue attendant plagued by a roommate from hell (Bill Paxton). Directed by Francis G. Oley Sassone. "Mr. Petrified Forest" is a surreal, terribly confused tale of Sam Clay going through a death experience, or so it seems. Directed by Matt Reeves. The only horrific sequence opens the film: mad scientists experiment with virtual reality on a dumbbell. What does it all mean? Who knows. (Video/Laser: Hemdale)

FUTURESPORT (1998) ★★★ At $9 million, this is considered to be one of the most expensive TV movies ever made. (Or was it intended to be a feature film that was deemed unreleasable?) Whatever, *Futuresport* came to TV once and then went into the little cardboard box. It's set in the year 2025 in a New Orleans arena where a new international game dominates the sporting world: Futuresport. This is an oddball combination of basketball (get an electrified ball through a small hole), Roller Derby (guys and gals on skates), skateboards that can be levitated, and long metal poles with which one can block the advances of an opponent. The players dress in outfits reminiscent of *Judge Dredd;* if a player holds the ball for more than five seconds he/she gets electrical shocks through the body.

Since there is an abundance of characters and situations, Robert Hewitt Wolfe's screenplay needs explanation. The world has divided into two political halves—the North American Alliance (all the good guys) and "The Comm" (Russians, Chinese, like that). In Hawaii, there is a band of terrorist rebels called the HILO (Hawaiian Liberation Organization), which both factions are hoping to control. The world comes to the brink of war over Hawaii, so the greatest Futuresport star, a cocksure athlete named Tremain "Pharoah" Ramzey (played by Dean Cain), suggests that a team from each side battle it out in the Futuresport arena, winner getting Hawaii. Wesley Snipes, who is executive producer of this strange mixture of genres, also plays the creator of Futuresport—Obike Fixx. Fixx is a cool dude who might or might not be on the side of the good guys. Cain, who goes from being in love with himself to a fair man with the other players, enjoys a love interest with TV reporter Vanessa L. Williams and becomes a target for the HILO, resulting in a few action sequences requiring firepower and martial-arts expertise. The final showdown game provides the climactic action, although by then any child can figure out the outcome. A few R-rated scenes have been added since the TV run to spice this up for the action-video market. Although *Futuresport* drags in spots, it has so many subplots that ultimately its far-flung ideas and energy carry you to the end. (Video/DVD: Columbia TriStar)

FUTUREWORLD (1976) ★★★ This sequel to *Westworld* (about a bizarre fantasy paradise that malfunctioned and killed vacationers) picks up when the malfunctions are corrected and Westworld functions alongside Futureworld, where your sci-fi dreams come true. However, crusading reporters Peter Fonda and Blythe Danner suspect a cabal of power-mad villains is using the facilities to take over the world. The Mayo Simon–George Schenk script makes for an exciting thriller with wonderful sets (including the real Houston Space Center) and ample intrigue. Yul Brynner reappears as the Gunfighter in Black. Directed by Richard T. Heffron. Arthur Hill, Allen Ludden, John Ryan, Stuart Margolin, Robert Cornthwaite. (Warner Bros.; Goodtimes; Vestron) (Laser: Image)

FUTURE ZONE (1990) ★★ Sequel to *Future Force*, with David Carradine re-creating his role as maverick lawman of the future John Tucker, who draws his weapon according to his own code. In a plot by David A. Prior (who also directed), a cowboy (Ted Prior) rides in from the future to alter the destiny of the gunfighter. Gail Jenson, Patrick Culliton, Ron Taft, Renee Cline. (Action International) (Laser: Image)

GALACTICA III: CONQUEST OF THE EARTH.
Video of *Conquest of the Earth* (MCA).

GALACTIC GIGOLO (1987) ★½ Gorman Bechard directed this science-fiction satire about a vegetable from outer space that sprouts up on earth and takes root in society only to discover it has a taste for Earthling women, or "tomatoes." How does a vegetable entertain women? It needs plenty of lettuce, that's for sure. Carmine Capobianco, Debi Thibealt, Ruth Collins.

GALAXINA (1980) ★★ Through the 31st century soars a starship piloted by Captain Butt (Avery Schreiber) and his misfits, creatures and robots. Their mission: retrieve the Blue Star, a powerful crystal, from robot villain Ordric. This comedy-parody, written-directed by William Sachs, is not a rollicking lampoon but does have isolated laughs. Title character is a sexy robot (Dorothy Stratten, a *Playboy* centerfold who was murdered shortly after production). Nice try, but no extraterrestrial cigar. Stephen Macht, James D. Hinton. (Video/Laser: MCA)

GALAXIS (1995) ★★★ An entertaining if somewhat mindless sci-fi actioner with enough explosive special effects and computerized graphics to make it easy on the eyes. It opens as a *Star Wars* clone on the planet Centaria, where fighting factions blaze away at each other. The losing side can only save its planet from conquest by sending Brigitte Nielsen to Earth to retrieve a powerful crystal, but following her is bad guy Kyla (Richard Moll), a Darth Vader with superzap. On Earth, the common man with the crystal, John H. Brennan, is caught up in the quest and undergoes amazing adventures. Nonstop action with stereotyped characters (sadistic gang leader, black cop, female cop, etc.) is the best you can expect from writer Nick Davis. In her powerbra armor plating, with her blond hair cut short, Nielsen is an imposing though dimensionless heroine who throws men around right and left—the film's one social comment (about male chauvinistic behavior?). This was directed by William Mesa, a special effects artist. Roger Aaron Brown, Fred Asparagus, Craig Fairbrass, Michael Paul Chan, Sam Raimi (in a guest cameo). (Turner)

GALAXY CRIMINALS. See *Wild, Wild Planet*.

GALAXY INVADER (1985) ★½ Alien is hunted by Earthlings after it crash lands its rocket on the surface of Terra. Low budgeter directed by Don Dohler. Richard Ruxton, Faye Tilles, Don Liefert, George Stover. (VCI; United; National Entertainment)

GALAXY OF TERROR (1981) ★★★ Well-produced B job from Roger Corman, a horror/sci-fi tale about a crew on a desolate planet. Each member meets a horrible death—opportunities for blood, gore and multitentacled monsters. The best attack scene is when a sluglike monster "rapes" a beautiful astronaut after stripping away her spacesuit. This moves so fast under Bruce Clark's direction, there's no time to

contemplate illogical behavior. Graphic design is satisfying but the ending is needlessly metaphysical. Ray Walston, Erin Moran, Edward Albert. Aka *Quest, Planet of Horrors* and *Mindwarp: An Infinity of Horrors*. A loose sequel was entitled *Forbidden World*. (Video/Laser: Nelson)

GALAXY QUEST (1999) ★★★½ This spoof of TV space-adventure shows is a funny glimpse into pop culture that makes sport of sci-fi fandom, stardom, and the clichés of *Star Trek* and other series of its kind. It takes a handful of down-and-out Hollywood actors, who 18 years earlier starred in a hit series entitled *Galaxy Quest,* and throws them headlong into a "real" situation with aliens called Thermians in the deep space of the Klatu Nebula. The make-believe space heroes must now become their TV counterparts, relying on plots of past episodes to get out of cliffhanger situations and even seeking help from fans back on Earth who know more about the shows than they do. With Tim Allen as their Kirk-ish captain and Alan Rickman as an alien humanoid à la Mr. Spock, the actors have a ball in this lighthearted send-up featuring an assortment of goofball characters you eventually grow to like, no matter how silly some of them are in the beginning. To the credit of screenwriters Robert Gordon and David Howard, this is not a cynical or condescending put-down of the shows or their fervent fans. Director Dean Parisot even lets the film have a feel-good ending, and thus it ends up a heartfelt homage to the memory of Gene Roddenberry and those starship crews that have been traveling our TV and theatrical-release spaceways since 1966. Adding to the fun is Sigourney Weaver's sexpot actress, whose ditzy Lieutenant Tawny Madison shows off ample cleavage before the space ride is over. Among the film's best special-effects shots (brought to fruition by George Lucas's Industrial Light & Magic) are those of the humans being "beamed up" to a space station (although not in the way they used to do it on *Star Trek*), and one dazzling sequence in which Tim Allen is exposed to the wonders of the universe for the very first time. Stan Winston also contributed to the effects, which include an imaginative creature formed by boulders and a race of little cutesy-pie aliens—cutesy, that is, until they bare their sharpened teeth and swoop to the attack. How Allen and his crew help the Thermians defeat a race of lizard monsters is more fanciful fantasy than science fiction, but hey. There's a lot of visual fun and media satire to be found in *Galaxy Quest*. The amusing supporting cast features Tony Shalhoub, Daryl Mitchell, Sam Rockwell, and Enrico Colantoni. (Video/DVD: DreamWorks)

GALLERY OF HORRORS. Video version of *Return from the Past* (Academy).

GAME OF SURVIVAL (1989) ★½ Zane, a warrior from another planet, battles six warriors from various parts of the Universe. Directed by Armand Gazarian. Nikki Hill, Roosevelt Miller Jr., Cindy Coatman. (Raedon)

GAMERA, THE INVINCIBLE (1966) ★★ Wow! Look at that! A hot-breathed, jet-propelled, bi-winged prehistoric monster! And a turtle to boot! Get a load of Japanese monster movie-making at its zappiest! This is the first in a series starring Gamera as a wannabe Godzilla—actually he/she/it is a flying turtle always sticking its neck out to save mankind from a fate worse than watching Japanese monster marathons. In this origin tale directed by Noriaki Yuasa, Gamera is cantankerous and intends to stomp on Tokyo. The U.S. version contains footage with Brian Donlevy, Albert Dekker and Diane Findlay. Originally this tale about a turtle beast was called *Gammera*, but an M got lost in the translation, maybe? Gammera obscura? Eiji Funakoshi, Harumi Kiritachi. (Filmfax; Sinister/C: Just for Kids; Sinister/C; Celebrity's *Gamera the Invincible* is without the U.S. footage.) (Laser: Image, with *Gamera Vs. Guiron*)

GAMERA VS. BARUGON. Video of *War of the Monsters* (Celebrity) (Laser: Japanese).

GAMERA VS. GAOS (1967) ★★ Japanese monster movie with plenty of snap—its main protagonist being that giant turtle Gamera (he/she/it debuted in *Gamera the Invincible*), who comes out of his shell when Gaos, a winged monstrosity that fires laser bolts through its mouth, attacks Earth without pity. Kazufumi Fujii's effects include earthquakes and spewing lava, in case the titans bore you with routine destruction. Actually the effects are good . . . but you must appreciate these Asian slam-bang affairs to reach the bitter end. Directed by Noriyaki Yuasa. Aka *Return of the Giant Monsters*.

(Celebrity; Just for Kids) (Laser: Image, with *Gamera Vs. Zigra*).

GAMERA VS. GIGER (1970) ★★ Aka *Monsters Invade Expo '70* and *Gamera Vs. Monster X*, this Japanese monster marathon stars that giant flying turtle at Expo '70, where ferocious, noisy battles occur between Gamera and Jiger, a bitchy female who spits spears (!) through her jagged mouth. Crash bam thud. Directed with subtlety by Noriaki Yuasa. (Celebrity)

GAMERA VS. GUIRON (1969) ★★ This has "Made in Japan" stamped all over it. From what other part of the world would you find a film with Gamera the giant turtle battling Guiron to rescue Earthlings from brain-eating space beauties from planet Tera? Aka *Attack of the Monsters*. Directed by Noriaki Yuasa. Nobuhiro Kashima, Chris Murphy. (Celebrity, Just for Kids) (Laser: Image, with *Gamera*).

GAMERA VS. MONSTER X. See *Gamera Vs. Giger*.

GAMERA VS. OUTER SPACE MONSTER VIRUS. See *Destroy All Planets*.

GAMERA VS. THE DEEP SEA MONSTER ZIGRA. See *Gamera Vs. Zigra*.

GAMERA VS. VIRAS. Video version of *Destroy All Planets* (Celebrity).

GAMERA VS. ZIGRA (1971) ★★ Aliens called Zigrans plot to conquer Earth, but first have to kill the heroic turtle Gamera. Call it the old shell game. Kids bring Gamera to life and it engages in a rousing battle with a monster-battleship. Incomprehensible for adults; matinee fodder for the toddler. Directed by Noriyaki Yuasa. Aka *Gamera Vs. the Deep Sea Monster Zigra*. (Celebrity) (Laser: Image, doubled with *Gamera Vs. Gaos*)

GAMES (1967) ★★★ Director Curtis Harrington's thriller with Hitchcockian overtones: James Caan and Katharine Ross conceive diabolical mind-playing "games" . . . but Simone Signoret turns sport into nightmare. Resolution of the supernatural elements may disappoint buffs but suspense fans will enjoy Gene Kearney's twist ending, if they haven't seen through the gossamer fabrications. Don Stroud, Kent Smith, Estelle Winwood, Ian Wolfe. (GoodTimes)

GAMMA 693. See *Night of the Zombies* (1983).

GANDAHAR. Rene Laloux's original French-language version of what was retitled *Light Years*.

GANG BUSTERS (1942) ★★ The diabolical Professor Mortis (Ralph Morgan) uses a secret formula to bring dead criminals back to life and then forces them to join his "League of Murdered Men" to carry out acts of sabotage against the city government. Despite a promising premise, this is a dreary, lackluster cliffhanger that never uses Kent Taylor and Irene Hervey (as hero and heroine) to best advantage. They really cut the budget on this one, and it shows badly. Directed by Ray Taylor and Noel Smith. (VCI)

GANJA AND HESS (1973) This vampire film directed by Bill Gunn was recut after its release and retitled *Blood Couple*, but was so altered it qualifies as a totally different film. See *Blood Couple* for details about various video versions and retitlings.

GANJASAURUS REX (1987) ★ Parody/satire/lampoon of Japanese monster movies in which a 400-feet-high dinosaur terrorizes California marijuana growers, looking for a bed of grass to rest his tail in. Paul Bassis, David Fresh, Rosie Jones. Directed by Ursi Reynolds. (Rhino)

GARBAGE PAIL KIDS MOVIE, THE (1987) ★★ Writer-director Rod Amateau has turned out a mean-spirited satire based on the offensive creatures in the Topps Chewing Gum card set. It's a mixed bag of foul frolicking, in which violence and grotesque humor are blended with the ugly characters from space who land on Earth in a garbage can and live in Anthony Newley's magic shop. The songs are forgettable as the characters (Valerie Vomit, Ali Gator, Greaser Greg and Messy Tessie, among others) romp with Mackenzie Astin and Katie Barberi in an absurd plot that involves senseless gang violence and the Home for the Ugly guarded by Leo Gordon. John Buechler did the monster creations. A misfire that belongs in the bucket. It pales beside garbage. (Atlantic; Kartes) (Laser: Paramount)

GARGANTUA (1998) ★ This TV movie, which first ran on the Fox Network as a U.S.-Australian coproduction, is an inferior throwback to the giant-monster movies of the fifties. Not to the good ones, to the lousy ones with unconvincing monsters of gargantuan proportions. Take any Godzilla title of your choice, throw in a Gorgo theme in which mama is looking for little lost baby, and add some cutesy boy-loves-creature E. T. stuff and you have the inconsequential *Gargantua*. Aussie helmsman Bradford May (who did much better work in *Darkman II* and *Darkman III*) allows parts of Australia to stand in for a tropical South Pacific island (Malau) where scientist Adam Baldwin and son Bobby Holsea find a nine-foot-long creature that is a mutation, caused by chemicals secretly dumped into a nearby bay. Not only do we have a salamander-toad-lizard creature swimming around (the filmmakers never can make up their minds and blend in elements of several species), but there's also an angry, Godzilla-sized mother out there beyond the waves, searching for her little baby. That little baby is a cuddly lizard creature with moony eyes that becomes pals with the kid when Holsea feeds him breakfast cereal. Nothing like

Cheerios or Cap'n Crunch to beef up a growing lizard baby. There's the usual plot about the military wanting to destroy the creatures (allowing for some explosions and crushed-bodies scenes). Meanwhile, Julie Carmen (the weak love interest) and the guys try to save the misunderstood creatures. There's also a wishy-washy subplot about some bad guys trying to get the creatures for personal profit that falls flat. *Gargantua* sinks faster than a metal-suit undersea diver who's oxygen line has just been severed by the beak of a swordfish. Credit scripter Ronald Parker for that one. (Fox)

GARGON TERROR, THE. See *Teenagers From Outer Space.*

GARGOYLES THE MOVIE: THE HEROES AWAKEN (1994) ★★★ Excellently produced Japanese feature-length cartoon adventure, featuring the voices of Jonathan Frakes, Keith David, Marina Sirtis, Ed Asner and Salli Richardson to give it added U.S. appeal. What provides Michael Reaves' script with an edge is the humanity he brings to Goliath, the leader of a band of gargoyles guarding a Scottish castle in 994 A.D. That castle, along with Goliath and his pals Brooklyn, Broadway, Lexington and Bronx, is brought to New York City in modern times and the grotesque but benevolent creatures become "defenders of the night." Betrayal, unrequited love and other adult themes give added depth to what is basically an animated adventure with ample action sequences. Directed by Kazuo Terada, Saburo Hashimoto and Takamitsu Kawamura, *Gargoyles the Movie* should find favor with children and adults. (Video/Laser: Buena Vista)

GATE, THE (1987) ★★★ This is purely an effects movie without much logic, a box-office hit without a soul. Stephen Dorff is a kid troubled by a hole in his backyard after a tree is hit by lightning and removed. The hole is a passageway for killer imps to come from another dimension and terrorize Dorff and fellow dorks. It ends up five kids trapped in a house where energy manifests itself in various forms until the Big Monster à la Spielberg arrives. How Dorff defeats the beast is dorfy dumb. Directed by Tibor Takacs. Louis Tripp, Christa Denton, Kelly Rowan, Ingrid Venninger. (Video/Laser: Vestron)

GATE II (1989) ★★ Except for good monster effects ranging from a man in a scaly suit to stop-motion animation, this sequel to the 1987 hit offers little with its juvenile storyline and dull characters. Nerdy Louis Tripp makes contact with the Trinity of Demons and has fantasy-horror adventures with girlfriend Pamela Segall and pals Simon Reynolds and James Villemaire. One never senses peril for the oddball foursome, for this is harmless fun from director Tibor Takacs. It sat for three years before a release in '92. Neil Munro, James Kidnie. (RCA/Columbia) (Video/Laser: Vision P.D.G./Sony)

GATES OF HELL, THE (1981) ★★½ In Dunwich, USA, stomping grounds of H. P. Lovecraft, a priest hangs himself in a graveyard, opening portals to Hades. Christopher George has three days to close that door or every corpse on Earth will never rest again. (Won't George Romero like that!) Director Lucio Fulci (*Zombie*), who cowrote this with Dardano Sacchetti as *Twilight of the Dead*, is more interested in showing a woman vomit her guts out, a drill penetrate a man's head and a brain squashed out of a woman's head. Very pointless (except for the drills) and revolting. Strong stomachs required. Katherine MacColl, Venantino Venantini. Aka *The Fear* and *Fear in the city of the Living Dead*. (Paragon; New Vision; Embassy offers a subtitled version; from Iver as *City of the Living Dead*)

GATTACA (1997) ★★★½ This is a smart, compelling glimpse into the future of cloning and DNA science in which a society in the "not-too-distant future" has the capability to test a baby's blood and determine immediately how healthy it will be, how long it will live and other vital statistics. If those statistics are good, the baby will grow up to be a member of a genetic elite group. If they are bad, the baby will be relegated to the category of "de-gene-rate" or "In-Valid" and have no opportunities in life. Vincent (Ethan Hawke) has been born defective, so the best job he can get is that of a janitor (working under Ernest Borgnine), even though he dreams of becoming an astronaut. To achieve this in a sterile, green-shaded world that denies him everything, he trades identities with an elite cripple named Jerome Morrow (Jude Law) by substituting blood and urine samples. Within the government complex where the space project is being developed, Vincent/Jerome gets away with the impersonation and wins the heart of fellow worker Uma Thurman—until one of the directors is murdered. Investigators Alan Arkin and Loren Dean (his background provides a surprise twist to the story) suspect the killer works at the Gattaca Complex and the game of cat-and-mouse suspense is on. Will Vincent/Jerome be uncovered? (Even a fallen hair from an eyebrow could give away his true identity.) But the murder is only a subplot in the script by writer-director Andrew Niccol, a New Zealand filmmaker who brings a subtle touch to this futuristic adventure. Niccol gets good performances from his cast with insightful dialogue and never compromises his theme for the sake of box office. He remains true to a melancholy mood that prevails throughout *Gattaca*, which in the final analysis is a parable for the human condition—of striving to be more than we are, of achieving beyond our social limitations, of having the inner strength to overcome physical handicaps and reach, as Vincent/Jerome does, "for the stars." (Video/DVD: Columbia TriStar)

GEEK. See *Backwoods*.

GEEK MAGGOT BINGO (1983) ★★ Amateur 16mm monster-horror parody for midnight audiences (aka *The Freak From Suckweasel Mountain*), written-produced-directed-edited by the only and one Nick Zedd. Dr. Frankenberry (Robert Andrews) is trying to do a Frankenstein number by piecing together assorted body parts when his daughter is nabbed by vampire queen Scumbalina (Donna Death). Sleazy effects and crude camera work and lighting abound as the crazed doc hires the Formaldehyde Man (Tyler Smith) to rescue her. Narrated by Zacherley, one-time horror host. Enough Zedd? (Penetration Films; Monday/Wednesday/Friday; Movies Unlimited)

GEMINI TWINS, THE. See *Twins of Evil*.

GENE AUTRY AND THE PHANTOM EMPIRE. See *The Phantom Empire*.

GENGHIS COHN (1993) ★★★ Off-the-wall British TV-movie starring Anthony Sher in a tour de force performance as a Jewish night-club ventriloquist (his dummy: Adolf Hitler) who is persecuted by the Nazis until he's murdered by SS officer Robert Lindsay at Dachau in 1945. In 1958, Lindsay has become the chief of police in a small Bavarian town where the ghost of Sher comes back in the form of a concentration camp inmate to haunt Lindsay and drive him to madness in the midst of a police hunt for a serial killer in his small village. As grim as it sounds, this oddity is played as a dark comedy, with cleverly constructed monologues for Sher, and is enhanced with the sexy presence of Diana Rigg as the village countess. Matthew Marsh, Paul Brocke. (A&E Entertainment)

GET SMART, AGAIN! (1989) ★★½ This TV-movie retread of the TV spoof of the 1960s returns with Don Adams as Agent 86 and Barbara Feldon as Agent 99. Other agents (Hymie the Robot, Larabee, etc.) are also back, and they lend their humor to Leonard B. Stern's script, which brings the bumbling agents out of retirement to track down a weather-controlling machine in the hands of KAOS. Meanwhile, Agent 99 has written her CONTROL memoirs and that subplot dovetails with Dr. Hottentot's stolen climate formula. The "Would you believe . . . ?" and "And loving it!" gags are repeated and still evoke a chuckle. Directed by Gary Nelson. Bernie Kopell, Dick Grautier, Robert Karvelas, Harold Gould, Kenneth Mars. (Worldvision)

GETTING EVEN (1986) ★★★ A high-tech slam-bam action film with horror/fantasy overtones, first made as *Hostage—Dallas*. Industrialist soldier-of-fortune Taggar (Edward Albert) steals a Russian nerve gas from a secret base in Afghanistan (code name Project Viper) so it can be analyzed . . . meanwhile, evil rancher Joe Don Baker plots to steal it. The gas "ravages the flesh" and "devours people" as it "feeds on the atmosphere." (Well, that's what they say!) There are disturbing scenes of victims being turned into jelly and puddies of goo and action bits with helicopters, submachine-guns, hand grenades and other modern devices. Director Dwight H. Tittle sure keeps it lively. Audrey Sanders, Billy Streater. (Vestron)

GETTING LUCKY (1989) ★ No luck for you, the viewer. An unbearable teen comedy appealing to prurient interests as nerdy Steven Cooke finds an Irish "genie" in a bottle (nicknamed "Lepre") who will grant the stupid hero three wishes to win a girlfriend and marry her. As conceived by writer-director Michael Paul Girard, it's unwatchable. Leslie Z. McCraw, Rick McDowell, Jean Stewart. (Raedon, Hollywood Home Entertainment)

GET WELL SOON. See *Visiting Hours.*

GHASTLY ONES, THE (1969) ★ This period gore thriller was cowritten-produced-directed by Andy Milligan, with a madman running around a mansion chopping folks into little pieces and eating animals alive. The really ghastly one is Milligan, who remade this as *Legacy of Horror* in 1978—it was just as terrible bad ugh. Veronica Radbur, Maggie Rogers. Aka *Blood Rites.* (Video Home Library)

GHASTLY ORGIES OF COUNT DRACULA. See *The Reincarnation of Isabel.*

GHIDORA, THE THREE-HEADED MONSTER. See *Ghidrah, the Three-Headed Monster.*

GHIDRAH, THE THREE-HEADED MONSTER (1965) ★★ Another of director Inoshiro Honda's exercises in global destruction and monstrous mayhem when Ghidrah, the fire-breathing ET dragon, battles Godzilla (in his first role as a good creature), Rodan and Mothra atop Mt. Fuji. Made when Eiji Tsuburaya's effects were still well produced. Eiji Okada, Yosuke Natsuki. Aka *Ghidora, the Three-Headed Monster, The Biggest Fight on Earth, The Biggest Battle on Earth, The Greatest Fight on Earth* and *Monster of Monsters—Ghidrah.* (Goodtimes; Interglobal; Prism; Hollywood Home Theater; Video Connection; VCII; S/ Weird; Video Treasures)

GHOST, THE (1963) ★★ Scotland, 1919. Peter Baldwin and Barbara Steele have an affair that drives husband Leonard Elliott to twisted jealousy. Elliott dies but returns from Deathland (using his housekeeper as a medium) to wreak revenge on the ill-tempered lovers. Elliott plays the titular character from *The Horrible Dr. Hichcock,* so this is a loose sequel. Directed by Riccardo Freda. Aka *The Spectre.* (United; Sinister/C; Filmfax; Liberty; S/Weird)

GHOST (1990) ★★★★ Take an old cliché (man is terrorized by a ghost) and switch it around (ghost is terrified by man) and you have an original premise and a delightful supernatural comedy-drama that works as a morality lesson. Bruce Joel Rubin's script is a beautiful cinematic device that Jerry Zucker directs with taste. Patrick Swayze portrays a murdered New York businessman still existing on the earthly plane, invisible except for his voice, which is heard only by phony spiritualist Whoopi Goldberg. The film deals with how Swayze learns to become a ghost (with the help of eternal subway dweller Vincent Schiavelli), communicate with live-in mate Demi Moore and find his killer. The picture won an Oscar and so did Goldberg. Tony Goldwyn, Rick Aviles, Gail Boggs. (Video/Laser: Paramount)

GHOST AND MRS. MUIR, THE (1947) ★★★★ In this atmospheric supernatural comedy with a whimsical, witty touch, thanks to the masterful adaptation of R.A. Dick's novel by Philip Dunne, widow Gene Tierney lives in a seacoast mansion and collaborates on a best-seller with the salty spirit of sea captain Rex Harrison. Excellent period flavor, superbly directed by Joseph L. Mankiewicz. George Sanders, Natalie Wood, Vanessa Brown. This inspired a '60s sitcom. (Video/Laser: CBS/Fox)

GHOST BREAKERS (1940) ★★★★ Hilarious comedy directed by George Marshall and written by Walt DeLeon (from a comedy play by Paul Dickey and Charles W. Goddard), proving Bob Hope was a master at screen spoofery. A haunted house in Cuba is owned by Paulette Goddard and frequented by ghosts and zombies. The first version of this popular play was a silent film in 1922; Dean Martin and Jerry Lewis did the same story in 1952 as *Scared Stiff,* though with lesser results. Richard Carlson, Anthony Quinn, Paul Lukas, Paul Fix, Willie Best, Pedro de Cordoba. (Video/Laser: MCA)

GHOSTBUSTERS (1984) ★★★★ Inspired, ingenious supernatural comedy of refreshing images from writers Dan Aykroyd and Harold Ramis and producer-director Ivan Reitman. Bill Murray (Dr. Peter Venkman), Aykroyd (Dr. Raymond Stantz) and Harold Ramis (Dr. Egon Spengler) are Manhattan spirit smashers who transfix spirits with laser guns and imprison evil protoglops in a ghost gaol. An official feels they're polluting the environment, and allows the wraiths and spectral creatures to escape. Now the city is threatened with a "ghost wave." Richard Edlund's effects are brilliant. Murray is the aloof ghostbuster who would rather bed beautiful clients, and his asides are hysterical. Aykroyd is the buffoon and Ramis the straight-faced, textbook expert spouting jargon about multidimensional ectoplasmic invasions. Sigourney Weaver discovers an ancient God in her refrigerator. (RCA/Columbia) (Laser: Voyager)

GHOSTBUSTERS II (1989) ★★★ Once again the premise of men working as demon exterminators with the attitude of firemen is wonderful, with the added twist that evil supernatural slime gains strength through millions of unhappy New Yorkers. But this attempt is strained and often silly without the underpinings of satire. The gang is back (Bill Murray, Dan Aykroyd, Harold Ramis, Ernie Hudson) and so is Sigourney Weaver, whose baby is the target of a sacrifice. The script is by Ramis and Aykroyd, with Ivan Reitman back as director. Despite faults, there's still enjoyment to be derived from this sequel. Rick Moranis, Peter MacNicol, David Margolies. (Video/Laser: RCA/Columbia)

GHOST CHASE (1989) ★★★ Pleasant, innocuous supernatural-comedy set in Hollywood and depicting how a grandfather clock gives off the spirit of an old familiar retainer. The spirit, inhabiting the "body" of a cute alien (in the style of *E.T.*) being readied for a feature film, sets out with two filmmakers to track down an old house, which will provide the solution to a family scandal. The Roland Emmerich–Thomas Kubsch screenplay, as slight as it is, is given a nice directorial touch by Roland Emmerich. Jason Lively, Tim McDaniel, Leonard Lansky, Jill Whitlow, Toby Kaye. (MCEG) (Laser: Image)

GHOST DAD (1990) ★★ "Can I take you to show-and-tell?" a child asks her father, when he turns up at home as a ghost. And that's about as funny as this vehicle for Bill Cosby gets. Most of the high points are special effects as Cosby falls through floors and ceilings, flies through the air, poses as "The Invisible Man," passes through the center of a bus and transports himself through a telephone wire to confront his caller. And the sequence leading up to his "death" is a masterful series of near-disasters and stunts. Sidney Poitier brings a sense of vitality to his direction. Music by Henry Mancini. Kimberley Russell, Denise Nicholas, Barry Corbin. (Video/Laser: MCA)

GHOST FEVER (1986) ★ Stupefyingly dumb comedy spoofing the "old dark house" genre with stupid cops Sherman Hemsley and Luis Avalos (playing Buford and Benny) assigned to evict tenants from Magnolia House, haunted by a black man (Hemsley in heavy makeup as a black assigned to "keeping spooks in line"), a Southerner (Myron Healey with a Robert E. Lee accent) and an invisible rebel (Pepper Martin) who finally appears as a vampire with a torture chamber, operating room and walking zombies. *Groins of the Darker Species*, a book Hemsley reads in a library sequence, is the only funny joke. Smokin' Joe Frazier plays a goofy boxer and Deborah Benson and Jennifer Rhodes are Southern belles. Directed in Mexico by Lee Madden, who uses the alias Alan Smithee. (Charter) (Laser: Nelson)

GHOST GALLEON, THE. See *Horror of the Zombies*.

GHOSTHOUSE (1988) ★★ Undistinguished "possessed house" shock-crock in which the spirit of a juvenile girl and her life-size clown-doll haunt a rundown joint near Boston. Hanging around the environs is a crazy handyman with ax and pitchfork—and along comes human fodder. Lara Wendell screams so much, you wish the killer would get her. Insomniacs will find this a sure cure. Greg Scott, Mary Sellers and Kristen Fougerousse are unknowns whom director Humphrey Humbert directs. Foundationless script by Cinthia McGavin. (Imperial) (Laser: Image)

GHOST IN THE MACHINE (1993) ★★★ Imaginative, well-executed computerized special effects distinguish this horror thriller in which the soul of "The Address Book Killer" is captured inside a computer complex during an electric storm. The evil spirit begins to ply its murderous trade through the city's computer network, using pages from the lost address book of Karen Allen. She, her son and a computer expert drive hard to trap the floppy disc killer and RAM it to the byte-sized bastard in a series of clever maneuvers designed to make him a permanent terminal case. The William Davies–William Osborne script is a lively paced tale and will make an impression on your memory. Directed by Rachel Talalay as a window of opportunity for her career. Chris Mulkey, Ted Marcoux, Will Horneff, Jessica Walter. (Video/Laser: Fox)

GHOST IN THE SHELL (1995) ★★★ A superbly rendered Japanese animation sci-fi adventure set in a futuristic city; as "film noir" it is very atmospheric and has effective action sequences as it follows the affairs of a beautiful cyborg warrior cop tracking a criminal called the Puppet Master. Based on the comic book series by Masamuna Shirow, *Ghost* offers compelling ideas about how the new life of computers is taking on an intelligence parallel to our own, and might eventually overtake us, and hence is a warning about technology gone awry. Sometimes the plot gets too convoluted for its own good, but if you dig Japanese animation you will find this work from Mamoru Oshii to be challenging, and you will groove on the music by U2 and Brian Eno. (Manga)

GHOST MOM (1993) ★★ In this Halloween TV-movie, an obnoxious, possessive mother (Jean Stapleton) returns from the dead to help her surgeon son (Geraint Wyn Davies) find the Stone of Ise (a Japanese artifact with magical powers) and avoid an Asian gang. Stapleton is so grating it's hard to care for her or her son, and it's a long time before one's sympathy kicks in. Directed by Dave Thomas. Denis Akiyama, Shae D'Lyn, Jayne Eastwood, Zachary Bennett.

GHOST OF FLETCHER RIDGE (1988) ★ Supernatural elements don't come into play until the conclusion of this tale about city boy Campbell Scott falling for hillbilly girl Virginia Lantry and getting caught in a shotgun feud between two families. Of minimal interest to genre fans; mainly a backwoods morality piece. Directed by Michael Borden. Bernie White, Len Lesser, Sean McGuick, John Durbin. (Simitar)

GHOST OF FRANKENSTEIN, THE (1942) ★★★ Fourth film in Universal's Frankenstein series, directed by Erle C. Kenton and written by W. Scott Darling, has Bela Lugosi returning as the revengeful Ygor (from *Son of Frankenstein*) and Lon Chaney Jr. lurching uncontrollably as the Monster. W. Scott Darling's script involves Lionel Atwill putting Ygor's brain into the monster. A must see. Sir Cedric Hardwicke, Ralph Bellamy, Evelyn Ankers, Dwight Frye. (Video/Laser: MCA)

GHOST OF SLUMBER MOUNTAIN, THE (1919) ★★★ Willis O'Brien, pioneer in stop-motion animation (*King Kong*), provided effects for this short depicting dinosaurs and other prehistoric beasts. The story opens with Uncle Jack telling children about Mad Dick, an old hermit with a telescope to see the creatures. Among the highlights: a battle between a giant bird and snake, a fight to the death between triceratops, and Jack being chased by a dinosaur. Of importance to O'Brien aficionados. Written-produced-directed by Herbert M. Dawley. (LSVideo)

GHOSTRIDERS (1987) ★ Cheap regional supernatural thriller (produced around Dallas) that doesn't have a single spectral effect worth mentioning. An outlaw gang returns from 1886 to terrorize researchers. Not one scene is scary, an attempt to emulate *Night of the Living Dead* is misguided, and a dire lack of pacing, editing and story blasts this worthless crap out of the saddle. It's lynching time for director Alan Stewart. Bill Shaw, Jim Peters, Cari Powell. (Prism; Starmaker)

GHOSTS CAN'T DO IT (1989) ★★ John and Bo Derek have made oddball films before (*Tarzan, Bolero*) but none quite as oddball as this. Bo, still possessing that spectacular body, is distraught after the suicide death of husband Anthony Quinn. In heaven, Quinn is confronted by fledgling angel Julie Newmar (whose body is as gorgeous as Bo's) who sends him back to Earth to be with Bo. They can talk but sex is a no-no so Quinn (depicted as a floating head) plots to kill handsome Leo Damian and take over his body. Meanwhile, Bo dances in the rain (the water pressing her dress' thin material against her braless breasts), Bo strips to the buff on a beach, Bo takes a shower and Bo goes for a naked swim. Hubby John's camera lingers lovingly on her lumpy lovelies. Don Murray portrays Bo's traveling companion, Donald Trump appears at a negotiating table, and attorney Gerry Spence

presides over Quinn's mountaintop funeral. Huh? (Video/Laser: RCA/Columbia)

GHOST SHIP, THE (1943) ★★★ A frightening psychology voyage (produced by Val Lewton, directed by Mark Robson and written by Donald H. Clarke) set on a sailing ship commanded by homicidal captain Richard Dix, who hides behind a veneer of respectability. Third officer Russell Wade suspects the truth, but can't prove it, even to an inquiry board. One unforgettable sequence has Lawrence Tierney being crushed by an anchor cable in a cargo hold; another has Wade trapped in his quarters and under siege. Edith Barrett, Skelton Knaggs, Ben Bard. (Laser: Turner)

GHOST SHIP (1953) ★★★ Trim, skimming British supernatural tale, set aboard the Cyclops, a luxury yacht haunted by apparitions ever since it was found adrift with no one aboard. Hazel Court and Dermot Walsh purchase the craft, then learn of its ugly history. Finally, a medium discovers there are corpses of two tormented souls buried below deck, and a murderous captain on the loose. Writer-director Vernon Sewell has tacked on a whodunit ending to give it that is-the-supernatural-real-or-not? A tenseness pervades that will have you clutching your preserver. Hugh Burden, John Robinson. (VCI; Filmfax; Nostalgia; S/Weird; United)

GHOST STORIES. See *Kwaidan.*

GHOST STORIES: GRAVEYARD THRILLER (1986) ★ Actors stand in a graveyard and relate tales of terror. That's it. No reenactments, no special effects, no production of any kind. Directed by Lynn Silver. (Vestron)

GHOST STORY (1974). Video version of *Madhouse Mansion* (Comet; Cinema Group).

GHOST STORY (1981) ★★½ Peter Straub's convoluted best-seller (possessing the chilling qualities of M. R. James) was clumsily transferred to the screen; screenwriter Lawrence D. Cohen oversimplifies Straub's narrative, limiting the variety of ghosts, among other deficits. One horrible face after another (from the "walking dead" school of graphic countenances) is all you get. However, the premise is intriguing: The Chowder Society, a group of old men, gathers to swap ghost stories. Its members—Douglas Fairbanks Jr., John Houseman, Fred Astaire, Melvyn Douglas—share a dark secret from their youth. How a wronged wraith (a drowned woman) avenges herself across the veil of death makes for the supernatural thrills—but oh, Straub's novel was so much more. Directed by John Irvin. Craig Wasson, Alice Krige, Patricia Neal, Ken Olin. (Video/Laser: MCA)

GHOST TOWN (1988) ★★ Offbeat Charles Band production is set in a desert ghost town outside Tucson, where modern-day deputy sheriff Franc Luz tracks a missing woman—only to be thrown into the past where he confronts a gunslinging demon (Jimmie F. Skaggs) and the other townspeople of the 19th century. Director Richard Governor is stuck with a slender storyline by Duke Sandefur to go with cinematographer Mac Ahberg's groovy imagery blending the old West with the supernatural. Catherine Hickland, Bruce Glover. (New World) (Laser: Image)

GHOST WARRIOR (1985) ★★ An Iceman cometh: A 400-year-old samurai warrior, a kind of "Frozen Shogun" in a cavern in Motosuka, Japan, is revived at a cryogenics hospital in L.A. where Dr. Jane Julian introduces him to modern life. But this warrior out of time and place must wield his sword against evil in this offbeat Charles Band fantasy-actioner produced as *Swordkill*. Hiroshi Fujioka is good as Yoshita as he tangles with modern gangs and is etched in stark relief against skyscrapers, cars, TV sets and pursuing helicopters. Directed by Larry Carroll. John Calvin, Charles Lampkin. (Vestron)

GHOST WRITER (1990) ★★½ Lightweight, innocuous comedy with Audrey Landers as a writer who settles in a haunted Malibu beachhouse, where thirty years before sexy actress Billie Blaine committed suicide by drowning in the surf. Actually, she was poisoned . . . and now she's rematerialized to ask the writer's help to find the murderer. The most compelling aspect of this TV-movie is Judy Landers, a poor man's Marilyn Monroe. There are the usual invisible (wo)man shticks in director Kenneth J. Hall's script. Jeff Conaway is Audrey's boyfriend, David Doyle a tabloid editor and Anthony Franciosa the heavy. Joey Travolta, John Matuszak, the Barbarian Brothers, Dick Miller, Kenneth Tobey. (Prism)

GHOUL, THE (1933) ★★★ British chiller of the "walking dead" school . . . Boris Karloff is a professor of Egyptology in possession of the Eternal Light, a priceless jewel of mysterious properties. Vowing to rise from the dead should anyone tamper with the stone, Karloff dies . . . and lives up to his promise when his servant (Ernest Thesiger) steals the Eternal Light. Now it's going to be Eternal Night for that dude. Directed by T. Hayes Hunter from a script by Rupert Downing. Anthony Bushell, Cedric Hardwicke, Ralph Richardson, Kathleen Harrison. (Sinister/C; Nostalgia; Filmfax)

GHOUL, THE (1975) ★★ British Gothic horror thriller (aka *The Thing in the Attic*) is set in the 1920s and based on *The Reptile*: Wild flappers hold a car race across foggy moors. When one car breaks down, its beautiful driver seeks refuge in Peter Cushing's mansion, unaware he is a defrocked minister whose son is infected with a love for Kali. Now he is a ghoul, feeding on fresh flesh. John Hurt, in an ugly role, plays the crazed groundskeeper who rapes the beauties before the son munches at lunches. A lumber-

ing, disgusting, pointless movie with nihilistic overtones in John Elder's (Anthony Hind's) script. Veronica Carlson, Don Henderson, Alexandra Bastedo. Directed by Freddie Francis. (Media; Electric; VCL; Active)

GHOULIES (1985) ★★ Charles Band's turgid imitation of *Gremlins*, unimaginatively plotted by producer Jeffery Levy and director Luca Bercovici, and only coming to life in a few effects sequences. The setting is a creepy old house in Hollywood where Peter Liapis and wife Lisa Pelikan come under Black Magic. Mischievous monsters pop in and out to provide the only moments of vitality and humor. Michael Des Barres, Jack Nance, Peter Risch and Tamara de Treaux are among the midgets in makeup. (Vestron) (Laser: Japanese)

GHOULIES II (1988) ★★ Innocuous morality tale is a weak sequel to the popular *Ghoulies*, so it has nowhere to go but down. There's something quaint about its beginnings: Four of the creatures escape to a carnival, where they become part of an attraction, murdering patrons and hiding bodies in the props. A subplot has a money-minded owner threatening to close the show down. This Charles Band production, made in Rome, was directed by Albert Band and sports the hand puppets of John Buechler. Damon Martin, Royal Dano, Phil Fondacaro, Anthony Dawson. (Vestron) (Laser: Image)

GHOULIES III. See *Ghoulies Go To College.*

GHOULIES GO TO COLLEGE (1990) ★★ He who possesses a copy of the comic book *Ghoulish Tales* possesses the key to controlling those mischievous little gremlin imitations from another dimension, who always pop up out of a toilet. The setting for this third entry in the *Ghoulies* series is Glazier College, appropriate to the soporific teenage pranks, sex jokes and other lowbrow content. Humanities teacher Kevin McCarthy brings the impish ones back while college factions vie for the "Prank Wee" crown. The stiff, not-always convincing ghoulies were designed by John Carl Buechler, who also directed what amounts to a series of *Porky*-like sequences ranging from burping jokes to panty raids in reverse (the women strip the men) to firing squirt guns of "goofy glue." Evan Mackenzie, Eva La Rue. (Vestron)

GHOULIES IV (1993) ★★ One thing you have to say for director Jim Wynorski: He casts some of Hollywood's most beautiful women in his low-budget films, encasing them in miniskirts and sexy outfits. Barbara Alyn Woods plays a gorgeous blonde homicide detective; Stacie Randall is Alexandra, a femme fatale in a black outfit that exposes most of her breasts, and Raquel Krelle is a cop's knockout girlfriend in bra and panties. Other than that, there isn't much to say about this third sequel in a so-so series. Pete Liapis plays a sleepy L.A. cop caught up in a search for a magical ruby sought by Faust, his dark half from Hell, conjured up within pentagrams by exotic Alexandra. Bobby DiCicco plays a nerdy cop who's controlled by Faust. The only two ghoulies (Tony Cox as "Ghoulie Dark" and Arturo Gil as "Ghoulie Lite") are almost afterthoughts, contributing little to a plot that really doesn't need them. You could say Mark Sevi's script is all backwards. Producer Gary Schmoeller is capable of better stuff than this messy, oft-demeaning movie. (Vestron)

GIANT BEHEMOTH, THE (1959) ★★ Stop-motion animator Willis O'Brien provides only mediocre effects for this British creature-on-the-rampage production. The brontosaurus hulker ravages downtown London with its radioactive eyes, burning flesh from bodies. Scientist Gene Evans should have seen *The Beast From 20,000 Fathoms* for monster-destroying pointers. Eugene Lourie, who co-directed with Douglas Hickox, wrote the screenplay. Aka *Behemoth* and *Behemoth the Sea Monster*. Andre Morell, Leigh Madison, Jack MacGowran, John Turner, Henry Vidon. (Warner Bros.)

GIANT CLAW, THE (1957) ★ Inane, incredulous, incompetent—one of the truly laughable sci-fi turkeys of the '50s and a classic low-water mark for schlockmeister producer Sam Katzman, who had it written by Samuel Newman and Paul Gangelin as *Mark of the Claw*. The titular talon is attached to a giant bird from space, which resembles a stuffed Thanksgiving turkey and is obviously pulled by wires. The size of a battleship, the ET winged warlord is surrounded by an antimatter force field which makes it impervious to atomic bombs. Jeff Morrow and Mara Corday devise a "mu-meson projector" to down the combed conquerer, cheered on by "birdwatchers" Morris Ankrum, Edgar Barrier and Robert Shayne. The asinine avian avenger, with long neck, bulging eyeballs and a plucked look, will have you rolling in the aisles. Directed by Fred F. Sears, who winged it. (Movies Unlimited)

GIANT GILA MONSTER, THE (1959) ★ Produced by actor Ken Curtis, this low-budget quickie is an uninteresting potpourri of hot rods and teenagers facing a mystery in the New Mexican desert. "What do you suppose is out there?" and "I think I saw something moving" exemplify the dialogue by director Ray Kellogg and Jay Sims. The monster is a harmless lizard enlarged by a macro lens. Kellogg went on to direct John Wayne's *The Green Berets*, Curtis became Festus on *Gunsmoke*. The gila monster's contract was not renewed. Don Sullivan, Lisa Simone, Shug Fisher, Yolanda Salas. (Sinister/C; Rhino; S/Weird; Filmfax) (Laser: Image)

GIANT LEECHES, THE See *Attack of the Giant Leeches.*

GIANT MANTIS, THE. See *The Deadly Mantis.*

GIANT YMIR, THE. See *20 Million Miles to Earth.*

GIFT FROM A RED PLANET. See *The Alpha Incident.*

GIGANTIS, THE FIRE MONSTER. See *Godzilla Raids Again.*

GILALA. See *X From Outer Space.*

GILL WOMEN, THE. See *Voyage to the Planet of Prehistoric Women.*

GILL WOMEN OF VENUS. See *Voyage to the Planet of Prehistoric Women.*

GIRLFRIEND FROM HELL (1989) ★★★ A supernatural/sci-fi spoof so dumb that it's fun to watch thanks to good performances by an appealing cast. Dana Ashbrook portrays Chaser, a character from Purgatory jetting through the universe as a beam of light who ends up on Earth in human form pursuing the Devil in the shapely form of Liane Curtis, who proceeds to "suck the souls" out of male attendees at a birthday party, while their girlfriends stand around trying to figure out what to do about the unearthly femme fatale. The heroine becomes Lezlie Deane, who knocks the crap out of Ashbrook and Curtis. Maybe there's too much made of bashing, with the guys mostly taking it on their chins, but within the context of a silly comedy, how can you get too serious about social issues? Written-directed by Daniel M. Peterson. James Daughton, Anthony Barrilo, Brad Zutaut, James Karen, Alba Francesca. (IVE) (Laser: Image)

GIRL FROM MARS, THE (1991) ★★★ Engaging and thought-provoking TV-movie depicts teenager Sarah Sawatsky, who has telekinetic powers and claims to be from Mars. This latter point remains ambiguous to the end, one of the charms of this Canadian–New Zealand production. Sawatsky's father (Edward Albert) is a politician struggling with conservation issues that also touch a scientist (Eddie Albert) who befriends the girl. Something very gentle and touching is at work here under Neill Fearnley's direction. Gary Day, Christianna Hirt. (New Line)

GIRL FROM TOMORROW, THE (1990) ★★★ Entertaining children's TV-movie in which teenager Katherine Cullen, resident of the year 3000 A.D., becomes a pawn in a time-travel experiment gone awry that sends her to 1992 with James Findlay, a fugitive from the year 2500. How Cullen convinces earthlings of her true origins and overcomes the evil intentions of Findlay (with the help of a laser beam called the "transfuser") comprises this Australian production directed by Kathy Mueller. Melissa Marshall, Andrew Clarke, Helen O'Connor, John Howard.

GIRL IN A SWING, THE (1989) ★★ Meg Tilly marries a rich Englishman (Rupert Frazier) but they can't find happiness when she is plagued by ghostly visitations from her past . . . or does she have some strange psychic power? Directed by Gordon Hessler, from the novel by Richard Adams. Elspet Gray, Lynsey Baxter, Jean Boht. (HBO) (Laser: Image)

GIRL IN ROOM 2A, THE (1975) ★★ Poor Italian gore flick about a cult of sadists led by a killer in red mask and gloves, who sticks spears into beautiful women after abducting them. Newly paroled Daniela Giordano appears to be next when she takes residence in a strange house. While she hallucinates, we see a man's hand burned on a fireplace grate, bodies probed with pokers and knifes, a blood spot that appears on the floor, and dull characters searching for missing persons. The dubbing is atrocious, the gore without redeeming social values and the performances, under director-producer William L. Rose, are lousy, including Raf Vallone's. (Prism)

GIRLS NITE OUT (1983) ★★½ A slasher dressed in a giant bear suit, equipped with razor-sharp talons, runs around Dewitt University on Scavenger Night, knocking off the prettiest of young coeds. This imitation of *Friday the 13th* (originally shot as *The Scaremaker*) is strengthened only by the presence of Hal Holbrook as a campus security chief trying to get a handle on the killer's MO. Otherwise, it's all quite familiar. Directed by Robert Deubel. Richard Barclay, Julie Montgomery, James Carroll, David Holbrook. (HBO)

GIRLS' SCHOOL SCREAMERS (1984) ★½ At the Trinity School for Girls, exemplary students are singled out to spend a few days at the Wildwood Estate (allegedly haunted) to take inventory of valuable antiques. A feeble excuse for giggling teenagers to become victims of a slasher-killer who uses knife, pitchfork and meat hooks. Written-directed by John P. Finegan Jr. Mollie O'Mara, Sharon Christopher, Mari Butler. (Lightning)

GIRL WITH THE HUNGRY EYES, THE (1993) ★★½ An artistic avant-garde piece of work inspired by Fritz Leiber's short story of the same title, this vampire tale is not your average blood-drinking saga. Although Christina Fulton wears fangs most of the time, there is little else that will look familiar to genre fans. Instead, writer-director Jon Jacobs goes for style, erotica and a lot of unexplained stuff that he hopes will pass for art. Some passes as gas, unfortunately. But let's give him an A for artsy (as in artsy fartsy) in the telling of this sanguinary saga about a "deco model" who commits suicide in a Miami hotel, The Tides, in 1937. Jump to modern day as her hanging sequence is run in reverse and she returns to life as a ditsy, flitzy dame who runs wild with a fashion photographer (Isaac Turner) in the seedy environs of Miami, occasionally deserting him to kill gangsters and other forms of lowlife for her blood supply. A lot of sound and crafty camera angles don't make for much of a story, but Fulton's oddball behavior as a kooky vampire adds up to one batty performance, rolling eyeballs and all. If you dig pretension, here's your shovel, baby. Leon Herbert, Bret Carr. Executive produced by David Niven Jr. and Cassian Elwes. (Video/Laser: Columbia Tristar)

GLADIATOR COP: SWORDSMAN II (1994) ★ Lorenzos Lamas is back as L.A. cop Andrew Garrett who has psychic visions whenever he touches a blood-drenched corpse that's been slaughtered with the sword of Alexander the Great. This time the sword is stolen from its museum niche by evil curator Frank Anderson, who uses the weapon in illegal bouts-to-the-death between modern gladiators wielding swords, battle axes, and other weapons from antiquity. Anderson portrays one despicable villain in a movie that is totally despicable and devoid of any sense of humanity. Lamas wanders through the scenes with an indifference that is only broken whenever he is jolted by touching the dead bodies. Then he cries out with pain and rolls around on the floor. Maybe this is neo-method acting. James Wong shows up as a possible reincarnation of the treacherous general who once led a revolt against Alexander the Great—the script by director Nick Rotundo and cowriters Paco Alvarex and Nicolas Stiliadis never makes it that clear. This lousy B-movie is just an excuse for a lot of arena sequences in which brawny men bash each other half to death before one or the other delivers the coup de grace, usually a sword thrust through the torso or a slice across the throat or a discompassionate twist to the neck that snaps it with a loud C-R-U-N-C-H on the soundtrack. Ugly and unchallenging to the intellect, this tasteless movie epitomizes the worthless direct-to-video movie made solely to pander to visceral tastes and mindless viewers who want only action and blood, though not necessarily in that order. There's good action movies and unwatchable ones, and this is definitely unwatchable. (Video: Monarch)

GLEN AND RANDA (1971) ★★★ Avant-garde Apocalyptic-vision film set 40 years after the Bomb. The title characters are members of a tribe that lives in ignorance of mankind's past. But Glen (Adam?) is curious about Metropolis (the city he read about in old *Wonder Woman* comics) and he and a pregnant Randa (Eve?) trek through the wilderness of Idaho. Images linger afterward of a tree growing through a rusting car, gas pumps in a weed patch, Randa eating grass like a horse, the pair eating bugs from old boards, and Glen brutally beating salmon trapped in a stream. Director Jim McBride goes for esoteric effect—this could be viewed as hippies seeking the answers to life's riddles. McBride wrote the script with Lorenzo Mans and Rudolph Wurlitzer. Steven Curry, Shelley Plimpton, Garry Goodrow. (United; IME) (Laser: VCI)

GLEN OR GLENDA? (1953) ★★★ A sympathetic study of transvestism from transvestite writer-director Edward D. Wood Jr., who went on to become the diabolical designer of *Plan 9 From Outer Space* and *Bride of the Monster*. (The story behind this film is fictionally recounted in Tim Burton's *Ed Wood*.) It opens with non sequitur shots of Bela Lugosi reading from a tome, but nothing he says has anything to do with the rest of the film. Cop Lyle Talbot visits doctor Timothy Farrell to discuss two sexually confused men, Glen/Glenda and Alan/Ann. Flashbacks consist of humdrum documentary footage mixed with staged shots absolutely hysterical for their bad acting and writing. Occasionally Wood makes a salient point in building empathy for the transvestites, then he negates it with scenes of two struggling women in bondage-sadism-lesbian footage, or indulges in heavy-handed symbolism. Known at various times as *I Led Two Lives, I Changed My Sex*, and *Transvestite*. Dolores Fuller, Conrad Brooks, Daniel Davis. (Video Yesteryear; Sinister/C; Nostalgia) (Laser: Lumivision)

GLOB, THE/GLOB THAT GIRDLED THE GLOBE, THE. Rejected titles for *The Blob* (1958).

GLUMP. See *Please Don't Eat My Mother!*

G-MEN VS. BLACK DRAGON (1943) ★★★★ Twelve-chapter Republic serial starring Rod Cameron as good old American Secret Service investigator Rex Bennett, a role he played in the sequel *Secret Service in Darkest Africa*. Bennett fights the evil Haruchi and his insidious Black Dragon Society, baddies armed with fantastic devices. (The whittled-down TV version is *Black Dragon of Manzanar*.) It's all sinisterly administered by director William Witney with some of the finest fistfights ever filmed. In short, the action serial at its best. Constance Worth, C. Montague Shaw. (Republic; Nostalgia Merchant) (Laser: Republic)

GNAW. See *Food of the Gods II*.

GNOME NAMED GNORM, A (1993) ★★★½ An amusing and sometimes charming fantasy, aka *The Adventures of a Gnome Named Gnorm*, blending a cops-and-robbers whodunit plot with the bonding of a furry creature from Inner Earth with a blundering cop (Anthony Michael Hall) working on a murder case. What elevates this out of the ho-hum humdrum of videomovies is the presence of a delightful and sympathetic being who digs his way to the surface to recharge a crystal that gives life to his subterranean world and becomes witness to a homicide. Gnorm is just realistic enough to tug at your heart a little and provide some nice comedy touches to the

script by coproducer Pen Densham and John Watson. It was directed by special-effects wizard Stan Winston. Jerry Orbach lends strength as Hall's cop boss and Claudia Christian is good as Hall's girl pal. Eli Danker, Robert Z'Dar, Mark Harelik. (PolyGram)

GOBLIN (1993) ★ In their new home, newlyweds discover that a bloodthirsty creature doesn't want them to have a happy life together. Bobby Westrick, Matt Lewis, Kim Alber, Mike Hellman, Tonia Monahan, Jenny Admire. Directed by Todd Sheets. (Tempe)

GODS AND MONSTERS (1998) ★★★½ Christopher Bram's novel *Father of Frankenstein* served as the foundation for this excellent character study that blends elements of surreal fantasy and classic scenes from the first two Frankenstein movies made at Universal in the early 1930s. For this is a depiction of the final days in the life of Hollywood director James Whale, who became known for his gothic horror films before he suddenly quit making movies at the peak of his cinematic powers in the late 1930s. He retired to a reclusive life at his L.A. estate, where he was found dead, floating in his swimming pool, in 1957. This film is an attempt to capture his deteriorating health and state of mind, and the memories of healthy youth that plagued him in those final weeks. All excellent stuff in the hands of screen adaptor-director Bill Condon, who was rewarded with three excellent performances: from Ian McKellen, who plays the aging homosexual with empathy and understanding; Brendan Fraser, who portrays the gardener who becomes friendly with Whale and poses nude for him, even though he is not homosexual; and from Lynn Redgrave as Whale's housemaid, who feels that her charge's lifestyle has condemned him to hell, even though she loves him dearly and looks after him faithfully. Intermingled with his final days are surreal recreations of scenes from the Frankenstein series and fantasies of Whale's days as an active homosexual. One of the high points of the film draws Whale to a George Cukor cocktail party, where Boris Karloff and Colin Clive show up. This superbly honest and direct film, coproduced by Clive Barker and Stephen P. Jarchow, is a moving and rewarding experience. Lolita Davidovich, David Dukes, Kevin J. O'Connor. (Video/DVD: Universal)

GODSEND, THE (1979) ★½ Mysterious woman leaves her newborn baby girl with English farmers. When the child grows up, she is responsible for several deaths through evil emanations. What sounds like an *Omen* rip-off is a fair British chiller focusing on psychology rather than gore. Produced-directed by Gabrielle Beaumont from a script by Olaf Pooley. Cyd Hayman, Malcolm Stoddard, Angela Pleasence. (Vestron)

GOD TOLD ME TO (1976) ★★★ Writer-producer-director Larry Cohen's revisionistic look at the Jesus Christ legend will never be sanctioned by the Catholic Church but will fascinate sci-fi fans, iconoclasts, atheists and agnostics. Indiscriminate killings are linked to a Jesus figure (Richard Lynch) conceived when a virgin was artifically inseminated in a flying saucer in 1951. Equally bizarre is the cop (Tony Lo Bianco) investigating the case who was similarly conceived and has psychic powers. Then comes confrontation between the "brothers" as they use their energy beams in a death duel. Irreverent film provides religious food for thought—and controversy. An odd, misunderstood project that was banned, boycotted and theatrically distributed minimally as *Demon*. Sandy Dennis, Deborah Raffin, Andy Kaufman, Sylvia Sydney, Harry Bellaver. (Charter) (Laser: Image)

GODZILLA (1998) ★★★ After the box-office success of *Independence Day,* filmmakers Roland Emmerich and Dean Devlin chose to make an updated version of the popular Japanese monster series, which has been fascinating movie audiences all over the world since its intrusion on mankind's well-being in 1954 as *Gojira.* Unfortunately, Emmerich and Devlin chose to appeal almost exclusively to children and teenagers in bringing the giant lizard/prehistoric dinosaur to New York City for a destruction derby of mammoth proportions. The main problem is that Godzilla, the mutated result of French nuclear testing in the Polynesia area of the Pacific, might have been given some personality in the Ray Harryhausen style, but instead is depicted as a mindless, towering, hulking entity of destruction as it stomps through downtown Manhattan. Nor do Emmerich and Devlin (in addition to coproducing, Emmerich directed, and cowrote the script with Devlin) give any intelligence to the military forces trying to stop the onslaught. They fire rockets and blast away with machine guns that destroy and blow up the Chrysler Building and other edifices of the Big Apple as if it didn't matter. (Maybe it's a way of cutting down on the city's population.) This downgrading is really unforgivable, and so is the playing up to the popularity of special effects at the expense of logic and good storytelling. As for the human race, it comes in a narrow second behind Godzilla for believable acting. How dumb do movie characters have to be just so we know it's an entertainment? Matthew Broderick as a Greekborn biologist for the Nuclear Regulatory Commission provides most of the limited exposition (Godzilla, he explains, is a hybrid caused by atomic fallout and is "the dawn of a new species") and isn't very believable; even worse is cutie-pie Maria Pitillo, who just happens to be an old girlfriend of Broderick's. She plays her role as a would-be TV reporter as if she were in a Woody Allen comedy. Jean Reno, as a member of the French Secret Police who's got a guilty conscience about the mess, seems totally out of place. Instead of French, how about a Japanese scientist or secret agent? After all, isn't that where it all started, at Toho Studios? Well, okay, despite all these negatives, there are a few exciting sequences. One scene that doesn't lay an egg is set at Madison Square Garden, where Godzilla has laid hundreds of eggs that hatch open to reveal an army of baby Godzillas. Although it looks like outtakes of the raptors from *Jurassic Park,* this is exciting, fun footage. How Broderick and the others escape and still get the creatures destroyed accounts for some good cliffhangers; then there's a spectacular climax on the Brooklyn Bridge with a taxi full of our characters firmly lodged in the giant lizard's mouth; and there's a good submarine attack on Godzilla in New York Harbor. Still, one constantly wishes there could have been more class to this expensive production. Others in the cast include Hank Azaria as a TV cameraman (he is wasted except for one scene where he narrowly misses getting stepped on by Godzilla), Kevin Dunn as a military bigwig, Michael Lerner as a fatuous mayor, Vicki Lewis as another field scientist, and Harry Shearer as a supercilious reporter. Godzilla was designed by Patrick Tatopoulos (the same name that is jokingly given to Broderick's character) with "visual effects" by Volker Engel. (Video/DVD: Columbia TriStar)

GODZILLA FIGHTS THE GIANT MOTHRA. See *Godzilla Vs. Mothra.*

GODZILLA–KING OF THE MONSTERS (1954) ★★★ Japanese classic directed by Inoshiro Honda (who co-wrote with Takeo Murata), with effects by Eiji Tsuburaya. It was imported to the U.S. with new footage shot by director Terry Morse of Raymond Burr as newspaperman Steve Martin. In this trend-setting monsterthon (the first in a long-running series), Godzilla, a 400-foot-high *Tyrannosaurus rex,* is aroused from hibernation by an A-bomb and rampages through Tokyo. Serious critics have interpreted Honda's inspiration to present a fire-breathing, radioactive monster as an allegory of the nuclear age. Meanwhile, kids filled the theaters of the world to cheer the dueling titan. Akira Takarada, Momoko Kochi. Aka *Gojira.* (Video/Laser: Paramount)

GODZILLA: 1985 (1984) ★★★ After a ten-year hibernation, Japan's reigning King of Monsters returns mean and snarling as he blows his radioactive breath on downtown Tokyo while giving it his famous two-step stomp. Like the origin movie, this features Raymond Burr as a newspaperman in footage shot for the U.S. Nothing new in this revival—the effects are what you would expect, and there are obligatory scientists and military leaders declaring the dangers of Godzilla's wrath. What's different is a sympathy toward the monster, as if the juggernaut was just looking for a little love. Forget that the large lizard just crushed 3,000 Asians. Directed by Koji Hashimoto and R. J. Kizer. Shin Takuma, Ken Tanaka. (New World) (Laser: Image)

GODZILLA ON MONSTER ISLAND (1972) ★★ The leapin' lizard (with monster pal Angorus) battles three-headed Ghidrah and Gigan (an obnoxious bird creature with a buzzsaw in its chest cavity) near an amusement park featuring a Godzilla tower. All this is instigated by cockroach aliens invading Earth. Buildup to the battle is repetitive and tedious. Directed by Jun Fukuda. Hiroshi Ichikawa, Yuriko Hishimi. (Sinister/C; Filmfax; from Starmaker as *Godzilla Vs. Gigan*)

GODZILLA RAIDS AGAIN (1955) ★★★ Sequel to *Godzilla, King of the Monsters* features the towering infernal as Gigantis. The destructor of Tokyo is trailed to an island where he/she/it battles Angorus, a spiked creature with wings. After some soothing mayhem, Gigantis-Godzilla stomps toward Tokyo to make it a tail of one city. Directed by Motoyoshi Oda, with effects by Eiji Tsuburaya. The 1959 U.S. version was directed by Hugo Grimaldi. Aka *Gigantis the Fire Monster, The Volcano Monster, The Return of Godzilla, Godzilla's Counterattack* and *Counterattack of the Monster*. (Paramount; Video Treasure)

GODZILLA'S COUNTERATTACK. Another title for *Gigantis the Fire Monster*.

GODZILLA'S REVENGE (1969) ★★½ By now the Godzilla series was shamelessly borrowing footage from earlier films to keep Eiji Tsuburaya's special effects costs down. The setting is Monster Island, where Godzilla and son Minya fight Baragon and other monster stereotypes without compelling personalities. Bad dubbing, although the grunts are more articulate than usual. Directed by Inoshiro Honda. Kenji Sahara. Aka *Terror of Godzilla*. (Simitar) (Laser: Paramount)

GODZILLA VS. BIOLLANTE (1989) ★★½ A colossal mutated plant is the latest enemy of the Giant Lizard from Tokyo in this sci-fi monster marathon directed by Kazuki Omori. Kunihio Mitamura, Yoshiko Tanaka. (Video/Laser: HBO)

GODZILLA VS. GIGAN. Video of *Godzilla on Monster Island* (Starmaker; IME) (Laser: Image, with *Godzilla Vs. Mechagodzilla*).

GODZILLA VS. HEDORA. Japanese laser version of *Godzilla Vs. the Smog Monster*.

GODZILLA VS. MECHAGODZILLA. Video of *Godzilla Vs. the Cosmic Monster* (Starmaker) (Laser: Image, with *Godzilla Vs. Gigan*).

GODZILLA VS. MEGALON (1973) ★★½

Clumsy-footed entry in the Godzilla series. The 400-foot-tall green lizard is aided by a jet-packed robot in fighting off Megalon (a giant cockroach with Zap Killer Beam), Baragon the stomper, and a race of underground Earthlings, the Seatopians. Written-directed by Jun Fukuda. Katsuhiko Sasaki, Hiroyuki Kawase. (Goodtimes; Nostalgia; United American; S/Weird)

GODZILLA VS. MONSTER ZERO (1966) ★½ And Zero is what this monster flick scores on the Entertainment Scale. *Godzilla* director Inoshiro Honda and effects buddy Eiji Tsuburaya are up to usual tricks with Monster Zero, a hulking entity of evil resembling three-headed Ghidrah. Also involved are Godzilla and Rodan, lured from Earth by Planet X fiends so they won't interfere with a force invading Earth. It's incomprehensible but lean back and enjoy the explosive effects, atrocious dubbing and Nick Adams playing an astronaut (not the same character he played in *Frankenstein Conquers the World*). Aka *Invasion of the Astro Monsters, Battle of the Astros, Invasion of Planet X* and *Monster Zero*. Akira Kubo, Akira Takarada. (Paramount; Simitar)

GODZILLA VS. MOTHRA (1964) ★★★ The giant saurian wars with the giant moth Mothra, which lays an egg—literally speaking, of course. From the egg hatch two caterpillar progeny which weave a shroud of silk around hapless Godzilla, leaving him "stranded." A subplot about miniaturized people makes for a good laugh. Directed by Inoshiro Honda; effects by Eiji Tsuburaya. Akira Takarada, Yurito Hoshi. Aka *Godzilla Vs. the Giant Moth, Godzilla Vs. the Thing, Godzilla Fights the Giant Moth; Mothra Vs. Godzilla* and *Mothra Vs. Godzilla*. (Paramount; Fusion)

GODZILLA VS. THE BIONIC MONSTER. Video version of *Godzilla Vs. the Cosmic Monster* (Sinister/C; Filmfax).

GODZILLA VS. THE COSMIC MONSTER (1974) ★★½ This sequel to *Terror of Mechagodzilla* is Japanese sci-fi sukiyaki with the King of Monsters battling a cyborg Godzilla controlled by aliens bent on conquest. A huge rodent creature said to embody Asian spirits comes to the real Godzilla's aid when the languid lizard squares off against antagonistic Angorus. Written-directed by Jun Fukuda. (United American; Video Yesteryear; from Sinister/C as *Godzilla Vs. the Bionic Monster* and New World as *Godzilla Vs. Mechagodzilla*)

GODZILLA VS. THE GIANT MOTH. See *Godzilla Vs. Mothra*.

GODZILLA VS. THE SEA MONSTER (1966) ★★ Aka *Ebirah—Terror of the Deep* and *Big Duel in the North Sea*, this exercise in cardboard mayhem stars the saucy saurian, the King of Monsters, as a crusty critter suffering a case of crabs when he's attacked by colossal crustaceans and does battle with the Red Bamboo bad-guy gang. Jun Fukuda directed, Eiji Tsuburaya did the still-classy effects. Akira Takarada, Toru Watanabe. (Interglobal; Discount; Hollywood Home Theater; Video Treasures)

GODZILLA VS. THE SMOG MONSTER (1972) ★★★ A Japanese industrial city has an ecology woe: its miasmic bay of waste and rotting animal life breeds Hedorah, which shoots laser beams from its eyepods and flies at will. It intakes nourishment by sitting atop smokestacks and ingesting waste, which is expelled as human-killing smog. To the rescue comes the flat-footed Godzilla to indulge in a duel-of-the-titans. Written-directed by Yoshimitsu Banno. Akira Yamauchi, Toshie Kimura. Aka *Godzilla Vs. Hedora.* (Orion; Simitar) (Laser: Image, with *Monster From a Prehistoric Planet*; on Japanese laser as *Godzilla Vs. Hedora*)

GODZILLA VS. THE THING. See *Godzilla Vs. Mothra.*

GOIN' UP. See *The Lift.*

GOJIRA. See *Godzilla—King of the Monsters.*

GOLDEN CHILD, THE (1986) ★★½ When Eddie Murphy is on camera, making delightful wise-guy cracks, *Golden Child* is all that glitters. But when coproducer Dennis Feldman's script resorts to action and monster-movie clichés, he's fool's gold, barely rising above a TV-movie. Director Michael Ritchie glitzes up the weaknesses but when fantasy can make anything happen, there's no sense of fun—just hodgepodge. This blends martial arts impossibilities, a demon from hell (Sardo Numspa, played by Charles Dance) and a quest for a magical sword. Murphy portrays the Chosen One, decreed by an ancient Asian scroll to rescue the kidnapped Golden Child in the City of Angels. Charlotte Lewis, Victor Wong. (Video/Laser: Paramount)

GOLDENEYE (1995) ★★★★ This, the 17th entry in the long-surviving James Bond series, is a dynamic, dynamite action-adventure, brought to life by modern technology and special-effects artistry and by the performance of a new (and the fifth actor to play the role) Bond: Pierce Brosnan, who was almost selected over Timothy Dalton in the late '80s, and who this time proves he's the right chap for the assignment. Bond is back in a bang-up, pre-credits action sequence set in Russia, where he leaps off the lip of a dam for one damn plunge to bust into a chemical factory with the help of a fellow agent (Sean Bean). This is a rousing bit of blazing action that includes a remarkable (though preposterous) aerial stunt involving a parachute and an airplane. Then the Jeffrey Caine-Bruce Feirstein script gets down to serious/satirical business as Bond tracks Soviet renegades who steal two missiles from a Siberian base (after wiping it out

to the last man but forgetting the last lady, Izabella Scorupco) and plot to destroy London, if not the entire world. The nonstop action is delicious, Brosnan's sexual encounters and exchanges are given a modern twist (especially with a brutal Soviet ladykiller played by Famke Janssen), and there's a terrific sequence with Bond at the controls of a Soviet tank in downtown St. Petersburg (and manning the tank against an oncoming train). And so on and so on. Director Martin Campbell blends all this action with just enough character stuff and spy double crosses to remind us that somewhere in a Bond adventure you have to have a little plot, no matter how ridiculous it seems. Daniel Kleinman's main credits pay homage to the late Maurice Binder, who did the early Bond films. A winner all the way with Joe Don Baker (as a CIA operative), Judi Dench (as a new uptight female M), Samantha Bond (as a more youthful Moneypenny), Desmond Llewelyn (still playing Q and still coming up with nifty new weapon devices), Robbie Coltraine, Gottfried John. (Video/Laser: MGM/UA)

GOLDEN HANDS OF KURIGAL (1949). TV-feature version of *Federal Agents Vs. Underworld Inc.*

GOLDEN VOYAGE OF SINBAD, THE (1974) ★★★★ Ray Harryhausen's effects excitingly capture the Arabian Nights in this excellent fantasy adventure. Marvel at the duel with the six-armed Kali; a battle between a centaur and a griffin; a ship's masthead painfully coming to life and attacking; and a devious homunculus. For these visual treats alone this Charles Schneer production is worth repeated viewings, as well as for the score by Miklós Rózsa. Brian Clemens' script (originally entitled *Sinbad's Golden Voyage*) is weak on character development, and John Phillip Law portrays the familiar sword-swinging hero with indifference, but it is Harryhausen who keeps it alive. Another outstanding feature is Tom Baker as the Black Prince, whose villainy is convincing. Also appealing is the semi-draped Caroline Munro, whom fans will want to ogle. A miniclassic. Martin Shaw, Douglas Wilmer. Directed by Gordon Hessler. (RCA/Columbia) (Laser: RCA/Columbia; Pioneer)

GOLDEN YEARS. See *Stephen King's Golden Years.*

GOLDFINGER (1964) ★★★★★ Best of the James Bond 007 glossy thrillers for tongue-in-cheek thrills, comedy, gimmicks and gadgets, thanks to scripters Richard Maibaum and Paul Dehn. Director Guy Hamilton provides style and pacing and there has never been a better supervillain than Gert Frobe as gold-hungry Auric Goldfinger. Sean Connery is in top form and so is Shirley Eaton as the bikini girl. The plot concerns the robbery of Fort Knox, a nuclear bomb (to which Bond is handcuffed) and a unique Asian villain, Oddjob (Harold Sakata). Also a flying team of shapely femmes led by Pussy Galore (Honor Blackman). (MGM/UA) (Laser: MGM/UA; Criterion)

GOLD OF THE AMAZON WOMEN (1979) ★★½ The fabled Cities of El Dorado are sought by explorer Bo Svenson in this absurd TV-movie. Svenson, after a bow-and-arrow fight in downtown Manhattan, finds a tribe of Amazons in form-fitting Playtex zebra skins. Their leader is buxom Anita Ekberg, who looks uncomfortable in her Maidenform leopard spots. Donald Pleasence is after the treasure too. Fortunately, director Mark L. Lester emphasizes the camp elements. Richard Romanus, Robert Minor, Bond Gideon. (Embassy; Sultan; from America's Best as *Amazon Women*; from Euro Scan as *Quest for the Seven Cities*)

GOLIATH AND THE ISLAND OF VAMPIRES. See *Goliath and the Vampires.*

GOLIATH AND THE VAMPIRES (1964) ★ Onetime Tarzan Gordon Scott portrays a muddled muscleman who flexes his biceps (but seldom his brain) to destroy zombie slaves and bloodsuckers. Maciste (his name isn't Goliath or Hercules) misses by a mile. Aka as *The Vampires, Goliath and the Island of Vampires*, and *Maciste Vs. the Vampire*. Directed by Giacomo Gentilomo. Gianna Maria Canale.

GOMAR THE HUMAN GORILLA. See *Night of the Bloody Apes.*

GOOD NIGHT GOD BLESS (1987) ★★ A psycho-killer priest described as "from Hell" is on a murderous rampage. And God bless you too. Emma Sutton, Frank Rozelaar Green. Directed by John Eyres. (Magnum)

GOOD SON, THE (1993) ★★ *The Good Son* is one bad movie—an obvious ripoff of *The Bad Seed* but done without a shred of psychological reasoning behind why cute little Macauley Culkin is such a homicidal maniac at his tender age, given that mom and dad are so loving and his home life has such rustic charm. Elijah Wood portrays Culkin's cousin, whose mother has just died and who comes to live with Culkin and family during a cold winter. Cold is right— before you can stretch your bubblegum or crack a Marvel comic, Culkin shoots a nasty dog with a crossbow device, causes a major highway pileup of cars, and sends his sister (Quinn Culkin, Macauley's real-life sibling) under a thin sheet of ice during a skating party. Sheet! Ian McEwan's script just plain defies explanation, with Wood going paranoid in all the wrong places when he should be keeping a cool head. Director (and coproducer) Joseph Ruben photographs it well, and there's a great cliffhanging finale (in a literal sense) with remarkable camera angles, but there's little else in this vapid kiddie litter. Wendy Crewson, David Moses, Daniel

Hugh Kelly, Jacqueline Brookes. (Video/Laser: Fox)

GOOD, THE BAD, AND THE SUBHUMANOID. See *Class of Nuke 'Em High 3: The Good, the Bad, and the Subhumanoid.*

GOONIES (1985) ★★½ Overdone children's fantasy produced by Steven Spielberg, directed by Richard Donner and written by Chris Columbus. A group of kids is propelled into an exotic adventure in underground Oregon caverns in search of pirates' treasure. It has the madcap tempo of a roller coaster ride, but there is never a real sense of jeopardy even though the caves have death traps and the featherweight story is treated as an epic when modesty was needed. *Goonies* is skilled filmmaking, and certainly has youthful vitality provided by Sean Astin, Josh Brolin, Jeff Cohen and Corey Feldman. (Video/ Laser: Warner Bros.)

GOR (1987) ★★★ John Norman's sword-and-sorcery novels make for a wild fantasy adventure with armies of swordsmen, harem women in scanty costumes and larger-than-life characters. Urbano Barberini portrays American college professor Cabot who travels to another dimension ("The Counter Earth") via a magical ring. The nerdy Cabot is quickly turned into a warrior when he helps a subservient band fight evil King Sarm (Oliver Reed). Director Fritz Kiersch fills the tavern and harem scenes with ample naked flesh and there's battle after battle as Cabot infiltrates the barbarian's fortress. Rebecca Ferratti in a sexy costume, Paul L. Smith as an obese ruffian and Jack Palance as a villain for a sequel add to the color. (Warner Bros.)

GOR II. See *Outlaw of Gor.*

GORATH (1962) ★★½ *Godzilla* director Inoshiro Honda, with effects pal Eiji Tsuburaya and sci-fi happy scribe Takeshi Kimura, weaves more sublime outer-space thrills with giant monsters. A planet on a collision course with Earth forces scientists to move our planet from its orbit by firing rockets into the stratosphere. Ryo Ikebe, Akihiko Hirata. (Discount; Video Gems; Prism)

GORE GORE GIRLS, THE (1972) ★★ The last of the exploitation films produced-directed by Herschell Gordon Lewis, who also cranked out the music score. Aka *Blood Orgy*, this has amusing moments (some of them intended) as it parodies the movie whodunit, and forecasts slasher flicks to come. Private eye Abraham Gentry is investigating the deaths of strippers Suzy Creampuff and Candy Cane—go-go broads sliced up by a masked killer. You see a hot iron dropped on a face, a knife stuck into an eyeball and bare buttocks flailed in an act of "tenderization." Thrown in are an anti-stripper protest movement, a Vietnam vet who chops up vegetables and fruits, a girl Friday for Mr. Gentry and comedian Henny Youngman as a club owner. There's an element of fun at work here. Frank Kress, Hedda Lubin. (Midnight; Movies Unlimited)

GORE-MET ZOMBIE CHEF FROM HELL (1987) ★★ A spoof of gore flicks, in which a blood-sucker opens a seafood cafe and knocks off customers to sate his evil appetite. Directed by Don Swan. Theo Depuay, Kelley Kuricki, C. W. Casey, Alan Marx. (Camp)

GORGON, THE (1964) ★★½ Greek legend claims three sisters (Stheno, Euryale and Medusa) can turn bone to stone should you chance to glance the flakes of snakes writhing atop their dead heads. From that theme, producer Anthony Nelson-Keys and writer John Gilling have fashioned a Hammer vehicle with Christopher Lee as an investigator who realizes that brain surgeon Peter Cushing is harboring beauty Barbara Shelley for reasons slitheringly sinister. Directed by Terence Fisher. Richard Pasco, Michael Goodliffe, Jack Watson. (RCA/Columbia; Goodtimes) (Laser: Image)

GORILLA. See *The Ape* (1940).

GORY CREATURES, THE. See *Terror is a Man*.

GOTHAM (1988) ★★★ Call it a Manhattan ghost story. Down-at-the-heels private eye Eddie Martel Mallard (Tommy Lee Jones) has hit the skids when a guy hires him to make his wife stop bothering him. It sounds like a routine 'tec job, until Mallard learns the wife (Virginia Madsen) drowned ten years ago. A moody, offbeat tale of the supernatural as Mallard falls in love with the woman. Writer-director Lloyd Fonvielle blends a ghost story with the P. I. genre. Jones is excellent as the tormented Mallard, and Madsen is sexy as the ghost. Denise Stephenson, Kevin Jarre, Frederic Forrest. (Video/Laser: Cannon; Warner Bros.)

GOTHIC (1987) ★★½ On the night of June 16, 1816, poet Lord Byron played host at his Villa Diodati to writer Percy Shelley, his future bride Mary Wollstonecraft, her half-sister Claire Clairmont and Percy's physician, Dr. Polidori. Yes, but what is this movie about? Since the director is Ken Russell, it's an exercise in Russellian grotesqueries with incoherent plotline. It was on this famous night Mary Shelley conceived the idea for *Frankenstein*. These haunted characters take drugs, have an orgy, rush through drafty corridors and behave as if in a Shakespearean nightmare. Color it depraved, call it freako as Russell explores homosexuality, masochism and decadence. Leeches, maggots, demons, monsters. Gabriel Byrne (Byron), Julian Sands (Percy Shelley), Natasha Richardson (Mary), Myriam Cyr (Claire), Timothy Spall (Dr. Polidori). (Vestron) (Laser: Image)

GRADUATION, THE. See *The Prowler*.

GRADUATION DAY (1981) ★★★ Above-average slasher film with clever camera work, good point-of-view shots and pacing. After a young woman dies from a blood-clot attack, the members of the campus track team are murdered one by one in bloody ways. Herbert Freed wrote-produced-directed. Christopher George, Michael Pataki, E. J. Peaker, Linnea Quigley, Vanna White. (RCA/Columbia)

GRAND TOUR: DISASTER IN TIME (1992) ★★★★ David N. Twohy wrote-directed this excellent adaptation of the sci-fi story "Vintage Season" by Henry Kuttner and C. L. Moore. In this superior time-travel yarn, Jeff Daniels is a hotel owner who encounters travelers from the future who venture to past time zones to watch spectacular disasters—and a disaster is on its way to Daniels' town, and he must tamper with time to avert tragedy. This is the way science fiction should be told on the screen—with taste, interesting characters and respect for the source material. Emilia Crow (as a sexy lady from tomorrow), Ariana Richards (as the "tour guide"), Jim Haymie, David Wells, Nicholas Guest, Robert Colbert. (Academy) (Laser: Image)

GRANNY, THE (1995) ★★★ As a macabre gorefest comedy designed to please fans of the genre, *The Granny* satisfies. Writer-director Luca Bercovici (who also appears in a cameo as Namon Ami, a guru-type who possesses the Holy Grail) knows what pleases fans of these things, and he has crammed his outrageous movie with an exorcism scene, plenty of living-corpses made up by Christopher Nelson, exploding bodies, and crypt quips from Stella Stevens, who stars as the titular grandmother. Granny is finished off by her greedy, foul relatives but returns from the dead because she has drunk the elixir from the Holy Grail. Bercovici's yarn is all messed up in terms of logic, but gore buffs seldom demand that. So what the hey, it serves its purpose. Besides Stevens' Krueger-like performance, Shannon Whirry shines as the only sympathetic member of the family, who fights the rest when they transform into ghouls and bloodsuckers. Brant von Hoffman, Sandy Gelberg, Ryan Bollman, Heather Elizabeth Parkhurst, Pat Sturges. (Warner Bros.)

GRASP OF THE LORELEI. See *When the Screaming Stops*.

GRAVE, THE (1995) ★★★ Though not a horror film in the traditional sense, this is a fascinating "sleeper" that deals with man's insatiable greed and his willingness to do evil to satisfy his avarice, and it emerges a creepy, macabre tale. While it is cast as a modern fable, gothic images from *The Body Snatchers* and *The Premature Burial* will flash through your mind when the film gets into grave-robbing and tomb-desecrating. Josh Charles and Craig Sheffer are inmates in a maximum security prison in North Carolina, who learn that a fortune was buried in a millionaire's tomb. They bust out to find the treasure, but events only lead them to other nasty lowlifes with their own devious plans to find and bust into the burial-hiding place. How all these despicable, untrustworthy characters (including Anthony Michael Hall and Donal Logue) intermesh and destroy each other leads to a couple of O'Henry–style surprise twists. The script by Jonas and Josh Pate is rich with dark comedy and Jonas Pate's direction captures a genuine sense of the Deep "redneck" South as the vicious good ol' boys (and one gal, Gabrielle Anwar) try to outfox each other. Keith David, John Diehl, Giovanni Ribisi. (Republic)

GRAVE DESIRES. See *Brides of the Beast*.

GRAVE OF THE VAMPIRE (1972) ★★½ Michael Pataki portrays a vampire who rapes a pretty coed near a mauseoleum. The offspring, brought up on mother's blood, is William Smith, who spends years seeking the rapist—only to confront dear dead dad, and realize heritage is everything in life, after all. Directed by John Patrick Hayes, who based the script he cowrote with David Chase from Hayes' novel *The Still Life*. Lyn Peters, Jay Adler, Inga Neilsen. Aka *Seed of Terror*. (Unicorn)

GRAVE ROBBERS FROM OUTER SPACE. See *Plan 9 From Outer Space*. Or don't see *Plan 9 From Outer Space*. See if we care.

GRAVE SECRETS (1989) ★★★ Offbeat ghost story in the *Poltergeist* tradition in which Paul LeMat, a college professor obsessed with contacting the dead, is asked by Renee Soutendijk to investigate her haunted bed-and-breakfast inn. Spectral manifestations, moving objects (i.e., a flying ax), ghostly sounds and eerie winds are the phenomena that plague LeMat and transmedium David Warner. A headless man and the unlocking of dark family secrets become the thrust. Sincere effort by director Donald P. Borchers to weave an original supernatural tale. Olivia Barash, Lee Ving, John Crawford. (Shapiro Glickenhaus) (Laser: Image)

GRAVE SECRETS: THE LEGACY OF HILLTOP DRIVE (1992) ★★★ This TV-movie, based on an alleged true incident recounted in the book *The Black Hope Horror*, could be the real-life counterpart to *Poltergeist*. Patty Duke and David Selby move into a rural tract home and undergo hauntings and ghostly manifestations. An intelligently told tale dealing with the legal ramifications of hauntings. Effectively chilling in the hands of director John Patterson. David Soul, Blake Clark, Kelly Rowan, Jonelle Allen. (Worldvision)

GRAVESIDE STORY, THE. Original title for *The Comedy of Terrors*.

GRAVEYARD, THE (1974) ★★★½ Superior psychological British thriller: Lana Turner is a vindictive mother subjecting her bastard son to persecution to get even for the way men in her life mistreated her. The boy turns crazy and drowns the family cats in bowls of milk, burying their bodies in a minigraveyard concealed in a labyrinth. As an adult (Ralph Bates), he still bears the brunt of mother's evil when she kills his child and arranges for his wife to find him in the arms of another woman. But Bates has his revenge. Stark, taut film with first-rate performances by Turner (looking well-preserved), Bates, Trevor Howard as the secret father, Olga Georges-Picot as the seductress and Suzan Farmer as the wronged wife. Directed by Don Chaffey. Aka *Persecution* and *Terror of Sheba*. (Interglobal; VCL; Electric)

GRAVEYARD OF HORROR (1971) ★★ Cemetery, hidden cave, grave robber, hairy corpse that comes to life, innocent victims—all blended by Spanish writer-director Miguel Madrid (also known as Michael Skaife) into substandard horror genre material. They'll dig you . . . you won't dig them. Aka *Necrophagus*. William Curran, Catharine Ellison, Frank Brana. (Super; from All American as *Necromaniac*)

GRAVEYARD SHIFT (1987) ★★½ Canadian quickie about a taxi driver who also happens to be a vampire, and his adventures with a TV director seeking a sexual experience. Boy, does she get it! The experience we mean. Written-directed by Gerard Ciccoritti. Silvio Oliviero, Helen Papas, Cliff Stoker (any relation to Bram, Cliff?). A loose sequel was *The Understudy: Graveyard Shift II*. (Virgin Vision) (Laser: Image)

GRAVEYARD SHIFT (1990) ★★ Disappointing adaptation of a Stephen King story, which translates here as a series of hoary clichés. The setting is a cotton mill next to a cemetery—and living in the subterranean depths is a tentacled blob that eats anything it can. The characters are so dark and unappealing that sympathy for their eventual plight, when trapped in the monster's breeding grounds beneath the rat-infested mill, is virtually nil. Adaptor John Esposito's script never escapes the B-movie category, rendering director Ralph S. Singleton as helpless as the cast. David Andrews, Kelly Wolf, Stephen Macht, Brad Dourif. Aka *Stephen King's Graveyard Shift*. (Video/Laser: Paramount)

GRAVEYARD SHIFT II. See *The Understudy: Graveyard Shift II*.

GREAT ALASKAN MYSTERY, THE (1944) ★★★ At a time when Universal was making slow-moving, often boring serials, this 13-chapter cliffhanger has abundant action (in the style of a Republic serial, yet) and a lot of good stock footage of Alaska in the early episodes as Milburn Stone (the son of a mine owner) ventures to the North Country to help scientist Ralph Morgan keep his Peratron out of the hands of Nazi spy Martin Kosleck and a gang of masked outlaws. That Peratron, your standard Death Ray of the '40s, is the single fantasy element and it's put to good use in blowing up aircraft, burning up trees and obliterating a few human souls. Directed by Ray Taylor and Lewis D. Collins, *The Great Alaskan Mystery* is not great: there's not much mystery and Alaska is mainly rear projection, but it's fun most of the time, especially with Edgar Kennedy providing an unusual amount of comedy relief as Stone's bumbling pal and Fuzzy Knight having a few good scenes. As usual, Anthony Warde's henchman bad guy is a highpoint of the serial's villainy. Marjorie Weaver hangs around as the obligatory skirt. This one is definitely worth seeing. Samuel S. Hinds, Joseph Grehan, Harry Cording. First produced as *The Great Northern Mystery*. (VCI)

GREAT ALLIGATOR, THE (1981) ★★½ Tropical island tourists Barbara Bach and Mel Ferrer could be dinner for an angry tribal god, Kuma, who assumes the form of an overgrown, scaly creature that would one day make about 5,000 pairs of walking pumps. This Italian film, directed by Sergio Martino, was made as *Big Alligator River*. Aka *The Big Caimano River* and *Alligators*. Richard Johnson, Claudio Cassinelli, Romano Puppo. (Gorgon; MPI)

GREAT AMERICAN MASSACRE, THE. See *Bloody Wednesday*.

GREATEST FIGHT ON EARTH, THE. See *Ghidrah, the Three-Headed Monster*.

GREATEST GIFT, THE. Original title of *It's a Wonderful Life*.

GREAT LOVE OF COUNT DRACULA, THE. See *Dracula's Great Love*.

GREAT MONSTER YONGARY. See *Yongary, Monster From the Deep*.

GREAT NORTHERN MYSTERY, THE. See *The Great Alaskan Mystery*.

GREEN ARCHER, THE (1940) ★★★ Victor Jory is a standout in any serial, and in this 15-chapter Columbia cliffhanger he's private eye Spike Holland, helping to solve the mystery surrounding Garr Castle, where the spectral image of a masked archer flits about, firing warning arrows and disappearing into secret passageways. Also a standout is James Craven, the head of a gang out to claim the castle for himself, who gets so frustrated by his incompetent underlings that he makes choice remarks on several occasions. Director James W. Horne is a master at making such nonsense palatable (witness *The Spider's Web* and *The Shadow*). If not a great serial, certainly a fun one. Iris Meredith, Robert Fiske, Dorothy Fay, Jack Ingram. (Video Yesteryear; Nostalgia, Video Connection).

GREEN MAN, THE (1990) ★★★½ Intriguing ghost tale in the British tradition, based on a novel by Kingsley Amis. It's a psychological portrait of alcoholic Albert Finney, proprietor of the Green Man, a country inn haunted by the spirit of a 17th-century occult practitioner who comes to symbolize the self-destruction within Finney. This British TV-movie also glimpses into the dark side of Finney's sexuality. Effective hair-raiser directed by Elijah Moshinsky. Linda Marlowe, Sarah Berger, Nicky Henson, Michael Hordern. (A & E; Tamarelle's) (Laser: Lumivision)

GREEN MILE, THE (1999) ★★★★ Strip away from Stephen King's stories all the vampires, werewolves, demons, alien entities, and supernaturally endowed beings and you always find strong human characters, people who grow and change and learn from their experiences. Failure to stress these human elements is often why King films or TV movies seem less than the books or stories on which they are based. *The Green Mile* is perhaps one of the best of the King movie adaptations, being a glimpse into prison life during the Depression years that becomes a full-blown story of people under stress. It is always this humanity that is at the core of the film, and that drives its plot and characters. Written and directed by Frank Darabont, who also made the King prison film *The Shawshank Redemption*, this three-hour (but never too long) adaptation is set on death row of a Louisiana state prison in 1935, where head guard Tom Hanks maintains control over several doomed inmates with the help of fellow guards David Morse, Barry Pepper, and Jeffrey DeMunn. Into their grim but regulated world, in which the floor leading to the electric chair is painted green, comes tall black actor Michael Clarke Duncan as condemned-to-die John Coffey (note the initials J. C.). On death row for rape and murder, Coffey is an uneducated gentle giant with strange healing powers, whose guilt or innocence eventually comes into question (though this is not what the movie is about). After grasping a person to "absorb" his or her "illness," Coffey is racked by pain, then releases a swarm of insects as a way of clearing his system. It's a startling effect created by Lucas's Industrial Light & Magic. But emphasis in *The Green Mile* is not on the special effects or the miraculous or the supernormal; it is more on how this miraculous, godlike healing power affects the lives of Hanks (whose urinary problems are cured) and his staff of guards, including the newcomer to the cellblock (Doug Hutchison), a cowardly, sadistic bastard, and the sympathetic warden (James Cromwell). Even Hanks's personal life with wife Bonnie Hunt is touched. Hanks, who unerringly continues to accept roles that allow him to soar and grow as an actor, makes his guard a gentle, understanding man, but he also displays a brutal side that reminds us that prison life creates viciousness in even the best. The long running time, rather than being detrimental, gives Darabont opportunity to flesh out these compelling characters and thus the performances are strong, including that of Patricia Clarkson as the warden's dying wife. The first clue that Coffey has "miraculous" powers comes in the form of a mouse nicknamed Mr. Jingles, who begins performing tricks and isn't afraid of people. This unusual development, while sounding corny, is so well handled that sympathy is engendered for the small creature as well as the prisoner (Michael Jeter) who befriends it. Other prisoners who enhance the story are "Wild Bill" (a nutcase played over-the-top by Sam Rockwell) and a quiet American Indian (Graham Greene). Each reflects a different way of accepting death. The film depicts three executions in an electric chair dubbed "Old Sparky." One of these executions, which goes awry, is a chilling statement about capital punishment, but it also provides a catalyst for character changes; another execution provides a wrenching, heartfelt sequence that is the film's most powerful moment. Yes, there is the expected symbolism and religious imagery. This analogy reaches crystal clarity in one stunning shot as Coffey sits watching *Top Hat* with Fred Astaire singing "I'm in heaven" and the projection light behind him forming a halolike effect around his head. It is with this scene that Darabont hits his stride. (Video/DVD: Warner Bros.)

GREEN SLIME, THE (1969) ★★½ U.S.-Japanese sci-fi serving set on Gamma III, a space station where astronauts Robert Horton and Richard Jaeckel confront protoplasmic aliens of a hue between yellow and blue on the color spectrum. Producers Ivan Reiner and Walter Manley were not green with envy about the inadequate effects work, and fans have remained an indifferent hue due to technical deficiencies. The monsters are one-eyed entitites with tentacles they want to wrap around curvy Lucianna Paluzzi. Directed by Kinji Fukasaku. Aka *Death and the Green Slime* and *Battle Beyond the Stars*. (MGM/UA)

GREEN WOMAN, THE. See *Queen of Blood*.

GREMLINS (1984) ★★★★ Steven Spielberg's production is the brainchild of screenwriter Chris Columbus, director Joe Dante and producer Mike Finnell, who have concocted a morality fable blending dark macabre humor with serious horror and the air of a fairy tale. Chris Walas designed and articulated the gremlins. Madcap inventor Hoyt Axton brings home a cuddly, wide-eyed creature he calls "Gizmo." Although Gizmo is benevolent, he passes through an odd reproductive stage leading to the birth of impish, malevolent critters who create havoc. The gremlins are repulsive and amusing. Polly Holliday, Harry Carey Jr., Dick Miller, Edward Andrews, Scott Brady, Kenneth Tobey and Belinda Balaski bring an added touch of fun. (Video/Laser: Warner Bros.)

GREMLINS 2: THE NEW BATCH (1990) ★★★ A sequel worth seeing—a worthy successor to the 1984 hit—that breaks down the fourth wall to let us laugh at filmmaking itself. Director Joe Dante and writer Charlie Haas have pulled out the stops to make this zanier and crazier than the original. There are new wrinkles when the Gremlins take over a high-tech office building in Manhattan: one talks, one turns into a giant spider monster, another into a bat flyer. Rick Baker's gremlins are incredibly realistic (Gizmo less so) and the gags they pull are nothing but fun. It's *Mad* magazine, *Hellzapoppin'* and William Castle rolled into a satisfying monster comedy. Zach Galligan and Phoebe Cates are back as young lovers challenged by the rampaging gremlins; John Glover is hysterically funny as the rich building designer, Clamp; Christopher Lee is marvelous as a genetics scientist (would you believe "designer genes"?). (Video/Laser: Warner Bros.)

GREY MATTER (1973) ★★ Metaphysical ideas are lost to poor production and mediocre acting in this scientific thriller originally made as *The Brain Machine*. A government conspiracy allows for an experiment involving a Brain Machine in the National Environmental Control Center, but questions of immortality and truth lead to human disintegration. Directed and co-written by Joy N. Houck Jr. James Best (as a reverend), Barbara Burgess, Gil Peterson, Gerald McRaney. (Bancorp; Premiere; from Academy as *Mind Warp*)

GREYSTOKE: THE LEGEND OF TARZAN, LORD OF THE APES (1984) ★★★★ Fresh approach to the cinematic rendering of Edgar Rice Burroughs' jungle hero, with director Hugh Hudson and writers P. H. Vazak (a pseudonyn for Robert Towne) and Michael Austin showing the nitty gritty of growing up as the son of a pack of apes. The film is fascinating as little Tarzan passes through various ages until he emerges a disciplined jungle man. It's when he's domesticated and taken back to Victorian England that the film becomes a strange love story more difficult to relate to. Tarzan fans may resent the heavy realism, while Burroughs purists will have to respect this attempt to recapture the spirit of the Tarzan novels. Christopher Lambert is fine as John Clayton–Tarzan and Sir Ralph Richardson is superb as the Sixth Earl of Greystoke. Ian Holm, James Fox, Andie MacDowell, Cheryl Campbell, Nigel Davenport, Ian Charleson. (Video/Laser: Warner Bros.)

GRIM (1995) ★ A by-the-numbers monster cheapie, distinguished solely by the natural wonders of Clearwell Caves in Glouchester, England, where a Neanderthal gorilla monster (for want of a better term, since no explanation is given about the origins of the titular monstrosity) passes through rock walls and growls a lot.

He/she/it has been conjured up by a group of Ouija-board players, and now it's free to pull people through a time-space continuum that writer-director-editor Paul Matthews never bothers to explain either. Why let a coherent, interesting plot get in the way of a genre blood-and-guts beastie flick? There are no characters, just stupid cave explorers getting killed one by one as Peter Tregloan, in the gorilla suit and headpiece designed by Niell R. Gorton, runs wild and keeps some humans captive, apparently for future meals. The hapless cast must deal with the hopeless noncharacters: Emmanuel Xuereb, Tres Hanley, John Chancer, Kadamba, Michael Fitzpatrick. Plenty of ugliness and bloodletting, though without redeeming social values. (Video; Una-Pix/DVD: Image)

GRIM PRAIRIE TALES (1990) ★★★ Offbeat anthology horror flick with two strangers sitting around a desert campfire spinning western terror tales. In this low-budget feature (the first for writer-producer-director Wayne Coe), the storytellers (Brad Dourif as a sensitive intellectual; James Earl Jones as a grubby, snarling bounty hunter) build to such interesting dimensions that their wraparound material overpowers the vignettes, structured like old E.C. comic stories with twist endings: (1) A cowhand dares to cross an Indian burial ground; (2) a man encounters a strange prairie woman who proceeds to seduce him; (3) a young girl learns the truth about her bigoted frontier father; and (4) a rich rancher has hired guns shoot it out to find the fastest. There's a low-key element that makes the stories sublime. Will Hare, Marc McClure, Michelle Joyner, William Atherton, Lisa Eichhorn. (Academy; Facets Multimedia) (Laser: Image)

GRIM REAPER, THE (1981) ★★½ Italian platter of splatter for nongourmets with Tisa Farrow leading a pack of American tourists to a Greek island where a murderous cannibal is eager to become part of the have-a-tourist-for-lunch bunch. Also known as *Anthropophagus, The Anthropophagus Beast* and *Man Eater*, this slowly gnaws away at you as the corpses pile up and as knife after knife is shoved into human flesh. The victims die horribly, by throat-biting, hair-pulling and other unrelenting, sickening means. A flood of blood with bash and splash. The sequel was *Absurd* (or *Anthropophagus II*). Directed by Joe D'Amato (Aristide Massaccesi). George Eastman, Bob Larson, Vanessa Steiger. (Fries Entertainment; Monterey)

GRINDHOUSE HORRORS (1992) Movie trailers of obscure horror and exploitation fare from the 1960s through the '80s. Titles include *Cult of the Damned, Deep Red, Journey Into the Beyond* and *The Virgin Witch*. Most is high-class trash. (Ecco; Killgore)

GRIP OF THE STRANGLER. See *The Haunted Strangler*.

GRIZZLY (1976) ★★ This imitates *Jaws* in every detail, but on dry ground. A 15-foot-tall superbear terrorizes Georgia State Park, devouring backpackers and hunters until forest ranger Christopher George and Richard Jaeckel track it down using neomodern weapons. William Girdler directed. Andrew Prine, Lynda Day George, Joan McCall, Joe Dorsey. Aka *Killer Grizzly*. (Media) (Laser: Japanese)

GROTESQUE (1987) ★★½ Linda Blair and Donna Wilkes show up at Linda's place for a weekend outing to become targets for Robert Z'Dar (*Maniac Cop*) and his gang of bikers. Tab Hunter plays a plastic surgeon. Plenty of lousy filmmaking to please those who like a good bad movie. Directed grotesquely by Joseph Tornatore. Brad Wilson, Guy Stockwell. (Media) (Laser: Image)

GROVE, THE. See *A Name for Evil*.

GRUESOME TWOSOME, THE (1967) ★ The inane tone for this gorebore from producer-director-cameraman Herschell Gordon Lewis is set by wigged mannequin heads holding a conversation that leads into the story of an old lady (Elizabeth Davis) who runs "The Little Wig Shop." She turns her beautiful customers over to her slobbering son (Chris Martel), who works on them with an electric carving knife, scalping them and pulling out their intestines. Snoopy teenager Gretchen Wells, a "female James Bond," tracks the missing nubile co-eds. What makes this bearable is its parody. (Midnight; VCI; Rhino)

GUARDIAN, THE (1990) ★★½ A major disappointment from director William Friedkin—at best a grade-B supernatural thriller. The Steven Volk/Dan Greenburg/Friedkin script (based on the novel *The Nanny* by Greenburg) is a bloody fable about a tree in a forest that lives on the blood of newborn babies—babies provided by a sexy wood nymph in the shape of Jenny Seagrave. The characters are so poorly developed, one can never quite get into their emotional states. Dwier Brown, Carey Lowell, Brad Hall, Miguel Ferrer. (Video/Laser: MCA)

GUILTY AS CHARGED (1991) ★★★★ This dark-humor morality tale, beautifully photographed in a surreal way and enhanced by a Steve Bartek score, is really wired to charge you up for laughs (and "shocks"). Rod Steiger plays a wonderfully demented avenger who kidnaps dastardly criminals and electrocutes them in his own prison with the help of God-fearing Aloyshus (Isaac Hayes) and Deek (the wonderfully underrated Irwin Keyes). The electric chair murders are powerfully stunning. The tongue-in-cheek satire on politics, power and the justice system by writer Charles Gale is right on, giving *Guilty as Charged* high-voltage delivery. Besides Steiger's religious kook you have power-hungry Lauren Hutton (wife of a politician), sassy housemaid Zelda Rubinstein and Heather Graham as an innocent young thing working as a parole officer surrounded by some of the craziest criminals you've ever seen. Directed by Sam Irvin, this is a sleeper. Lyman Ward, Michael Beach, Mitch Pileggi. (Video/Laser: RCA/Columbia)

GULLIVER'S TRAVELS (1977) ★★½ Anglo-Belgian blend of animation and live action with Richard Harris as the shipwrecked adventurer who gets mixed up with little people and giants. Not an auspicious credit for Peter Hunt, whose direction is static. The Don Black script makes only token effort to deal with Jonathan Swift's political satire; mainly for children. Catherine Schell, Norman Shelley. (United; Lucerne Media; HHE)

GULLIVER'S TRAVELS (1995) ★★★★ This two-part TV-movie is the definitive adaptation of Jonathan Swift's 1726 classic satirical fantasy, and presents Ted Danson in the best role of his career as Lemuel Gulliver, who for eight years wanders on an odyssey through unbelievable adventures in five different lands. Simon Moore's teleplay, far outweighing previous film versions, blends Gulliver's present (presumed mad as he spins his tales to his wife Mary Steenburgen, he is placed in an insane asylum by evil doctor James Fox) and chunks of adventures past, moving in and out of both time zones with imaginative transitions. Gulliver's incredible destinations include Lilliput, the land of little people; Brobdingnag, the kingdom of giants; a flying city; a city in Luggnagg where royalty drinks water that makes them eternal; the land of talking horses (Houyhnhnms) and primitive natives (Yahoos). Finally, Gulliver faces an insane-asylum board to determine his fate. Excellent supporting performances from Steenburgen, Geraldine Chaplin, Sir John Gielgud, Peter O'Toole, Robert Hardy, Omar Shariff and Graham Crowden enhance this British production which is rampant with special effects and a variety of moods and comedy styles under Charles Sturridge's direction. (Video/Laser: Hallmark)

GUY NAMED JOE, A (1943) ★★★★ Big-budgeted MGM fantasy scripted by Dalton Trumbo and directed by Victor Fleming, with touches of World War II propaganda and some excellent special-effects combat footage unusually effective for its time. Spencer Tracy, a flying hero who dives his flaming fighter into a Japanese warship, returns to his base as a wise-cracking spirit (with his spirit guide to Barry Nelson) to hang around the recruits and pass along his elan by whispering in their ears. But the going gets tough for Tracy when his old flying buddy Ward Bond falls for his former girl Irene Dunne, and fledgling pilots Don Defore and Van Johnson have to earn their wings. This is an inspired production, the characters being memorable and the dialogue first rate. Remade in 1990 by Steven Spielberg as *Always*. Lionel Barrymore, James Gleason, Esther Williams. (MGM).

GUYVER, THE (1991) ★★★½ A wild and crazy monster-action entertainment mixing martial arts, genetics sci-fi and creatures usually found in Japanese movies. David Gale, portraying an unrestrained crazy scientist, sends his minions (including Michael Berryman) after the Guyver, a device that turns man into the ultimate warrior, *Ultraman*-style. Gale's minions are a motley collection of ugly but funny beasties battling Mark Hamill, the underdog who fights back as the Guyver. Producer/director Brian Yuzna put together this amusing actioner, which features spectacular fistfights among the monsters. The energetic script is by Jon Purdy; Screaming Mad George and Steve Wang teamed to create the monster effects. Jeffrey Combs and Linnea Quigley in cameos, Vivan Wu, Jack Armstrong, Jimmie Walker, Peter Spellos. (Video/Laser: New Line)

GUYVER 2: DARK HERO (1994) ★★★ Special effects man Steve Wang is back as producer-director of this rousing two-hour sequel to one of the wildest, woolliest monster-action flicks of the '90s. It's another wild romp as that good-guy creature (played this time by David Hayter) goes after the Xoinoid monsters working for the evil Kronos Corp. A cave has been discovered housing an alien spaceship so Hayter turns up in the dig to expose a doublecross being carried out against archeologist Kathy Christopherson. The battles royal between the Guyver and assorted Japanese-like monsters are frequent and lengthy, the acrobatics and special effects are fun, Hayter conveys the anguish and angst of having to kill his foes, and the film should satisfy those who enjoy unsophisticated monster bashing. The script by Nathan Long has just enough depth to keep you interested during lulls in the fighting. Bruno Gianotta, Christopher Michael, Stuart Weiss. "Creative effects" by Wang and Moto Hata. (Video/Laser: New Line)

GWANGI. See *The Valley of Gwangi*.

HACK-O-LANTERN (1987) ★½ A hysterical, stylized movie villain, Hy Pyke, plays a grandfather in control of a satanic band who kills to protect its secrecy on All Hallows' Eve. Years later, Pyke must pick his successor in the cult. Direct-to-video chiller-diller-thriller of minimum importance directed by Jag Mundhra. Gregory Scott Cummins. (from Legacy as *Halloween Night*)

HALL OF THE MOUNTAIN KING. Video version of *Night of the Howling Beast* (Majestic).

HALLOWEEN (1978) ★★★★ This low-budget money-maker, which launched director John Carpenter's career and five sequels, is a paean to October 31—a series of jolts designed to shock, rock and knock as it depicts a psychopathic madman who escapes from an asylum and terrorizes babysitters and their boyfriends in a small Midwestern town. The killer is unkillable, allowing for a surprise ending. Director Carpenter, who scripted with producer Debra Hill, knows his scare tactics, never letting the viewer relax. The graphic, stylish murders helped establish the slasher trend. Donald Pleasence portrays the psychiatrist; Jamie Lee Curtis is the screaming target who experiences the ultimate in blood-curdling horror. Nancy Loomis, Nick Castle (the killer), Charles Cyphers, P. J. Soles. Original title: *The Babysitter Murders*. (Media) (Laser: Image, Criterion)

HALLOWEEN II (1981) ★★½ This picks up on the same night as the original, as Jamie Lee Curtis is hospitalized with psychiatrist Donald Pleasence close at hand. The Bogeyman Slasher, as you suspected, is alive and well—well-angered, that is, shambling zombielike to get poor Jamie in the hospital. Unfortunately, it's a weak premise (co-authored by producers Carpenter and Debra Hill), with the hospital so poorly lit, one wonders how the nurses can find patients. A hypodermic needle thrust into an eyeball, slashed throats and a head dipped into scalding water are among the jolly sights. You almost wish the killer would hurry up and knock off Curtis. Directed by Rick Rosenthal and Carpenter. Charles Cyphers, Jeffrey Kramer, Lance Guest. (Video/Laser: MCA)

HALLOWEEN III: SEASON OF THE WITCH (1982) ★★ See a man's eyes squeezed out of their sockets. See a man set himself on fire. See a head twisted off its torso. See a boy's face explode in a shower of beetles, roaches and rattlesnakes. Had enough? If not, catch this John Carpenter/Debra Hill-produced flick, with all the imagery of a Halloween nightmare. But don't be misled by the title. This has nothing to do with the first two *Halloween* flicks. Dan O'Herlihy is a designer of children's fright masks (creations of Don Post) with a fiendish plot: In each mask is a device that will explode while children are watching a TV commercial. It's up to Tom Atkins and Stacey Nelkin to thwart the diabolical plan. Director-writer Tommy Lee Wallace creates a few scary sequences, but an element of fun is missing. (Video/Laser: MCA)

HALLOWEEN 4: THE RETURN OF MICHAEL MYERS (1988) ★★ Disappointing sequel to *Halloween* and *Halloween II*, with the Boogeyman Slasher committing more mayhem. Sorely needed is writer-director John Carpenter, for he understood what made the slasher-killer theme work; stand-in director Dwight H. Little does not. It's more an imitation of the *Friday the 13th* series, so Michael Myers is a substitute Jason Voorhees. Myers is being transferred to a new mental hospital and escapes. He plans to knock off blood relatives in Haddenfield, so a handful of characters lock themselves in a dark, eerie house, becoming perfect targets. Not a single murder is believable or shocking, and Donald Pleasence (as the headshrinker) reaches new heights of hysteria. Ellie Cornell, Danielle Harris. (Video/Laser: CBS/Fox)

HALLOWEEN 5: THE REVENGE OF MICHAEL MYERS (1989) ★★★½ Surprisingly good of its kind, capturing an intensity through the overwrought performance of young Danielle Harris as Jamie, niece of the infamous Boogeyman Slasher, who's physically linked to her uncle and knows when he's going to kill. Another overwrought performance is given by Donald Pleasence as Dr. Loomis, who is now quite mad and a delight to watch as he goes bonkers. These key performances aside, No. 5 is an endless series of clichés, although to his credit director Dominique Othenin-Girard keeps his camera fluid, and the editing makes it more thrilling than it really is. The victims fall prey to Myers in the usual dumb ways, with costumed teenagers retiring into dark places to carry out pranks and sex games. Wendy Kaplan, Ellie Cornell, Donald L. Shanks. (Video/Laser: CBS/Fox)

HALLOWEEN [6]: THE CURSE OF MICHAEL MYERS (1995) ★★ So shoddily and sloppily written by Daniel Farrands, and so darkly photographed by Billy Dickson as to make it almost impossible to see anything, this is one sorry excuse for a horror movie, and an insult to John Carpenter's 1978 original. The familiar psycho killer (George P. Wilber as "The Shape") returns to the Illinois' rural Haddonfield to slaughter anyone, and it's one gory death after another although it's difficult to make out what some of the murder weapons are in the underexposed footage. Apparently some farm implements figure into it. But who cares? The only reason to see this pathetic effort is for the final screen performance of Donald Pleasence (as Dr. Loomis), who died shortly after the film was finished. Director Joe Chappelle and everyone else connected with this diminishing series should take a hint: It's time for a treat instead of a trick. Mitch Ryan, Marianne Hagan, Paul Rudd, Leo Geter. (Video/Laser: Dimension)

HALLOWEEN: H2O TWENTY YEARS LATER (1998) ★★ One can imagine that Jamie Lee Curtis resisted doing these kind of films even if they had brought her fame as a "scream queen" and beyond. So what lured her back for this seventh entry in the series? An obscene sum of money, perhaps? She certainly portrays an obscene character. The lovable Laurie Strode of John Carpenter's original has been replaced by a shrewish woman who escaped her identity to hide from the nightmares of the past by becoming boarding-school headmaster Keri Tate. Keri/Laurie curses all the time, drinks too much, and is half-crazed with images of unstoppable killer Michael Myers (her brother, if you will recall your genetics) coming back to get her once and for all. It is impossible to care about her. Nobody else in the story is likable either; everyone seems to be driven exclusively by greed, sex, or other dumb motives. Michael Myers, in fact, seems to be the only decent person around—if only he would stop knifing to death everyone he meets. In Curtis's favor is the moment when she decides not to take it any longer and, picking up a fire ax, starts tracking Myers in the deserted school, ready to murder him. It's a Sigourney Weaver takeoff that ultimately has a startling payoff. But believe me, the payoff to Curtis is bigger than any payoff the film hands you. Also in the cast of this undistinguished movie are Adam Arkin as Keri/Laurie's lover, Janet Leigh as an administration assistant, Josh Hartnett as Keri/Laurie's son, Chris Durand as the alabaster-faced Myers, and LL Cool J as a comedy-relief security guard. Steve Miner really took a step backward to direct the Robert Zappia–Matt Greenberg screenplay. (Video/DVD/Laser: Dimension)

HALLOWEEN NIGHT. Video version of *Hack-O-Lantern* (Legacy).

HALLOWEEN NIGHT (1990) ★ Small town is attacked by evil on that grand night for goblins, ghosties and things that go thump in the night. Hy Pyke, Katrina Garner. Directed by Emilio P. Miraglio. (Atlantic)

HALLOWEEN PARTY. See *Night of the Demons*.

HALLOWEEN TREE, THE (1993) ★★★★ A very special Hanna-Barbera TV-movie adaptation, in animated form, of Ray Bradbury's wonderful children's novel. Bradbury adapted the book and narrates some of the more beautifully poetic passages in the telling of four children on Halloween evening who embark on a 4,000-year-history of All Hallows' Eve under the "tutelage" of the weird Mr. Moundshroud (voice by Leonard Nimoy). The children want to save the life of a sick friend and after seeing how religions were once persecuted in Europe and Mexico's "Day of the Dead," they make a gallant sacrifice. The traditional Halloween images are well blended with many themes and morality lessons, all filtered through the sensitivities of grand Mr. Bradbury. One topnotch effort from producer David Kirschner. Produced-directed by Mario Piluso. (Video/Laser: Turner)

HALLUCINATIONS OF A DERANGED MIND (1970) ★★ Another entry in Brazilian filmmaker Jose Mojica Marins' series about gravedigger Coffin Joe. In this disturbing tale, a young man finds his dreams invaded by Coffin Joe. Others in this series: *At Midnight I'll Take Your Soul*, *This Night I Will Possess Your Corpse*, *Strange World of Coffin Joe* and *The Bloody Exorcism of Coffin Joe*. (S/Weird)

HAND, THE (1981) ★★★ Thinking man's *Beast With Five Fingers*, in which cartoonist Michael Caine, after losing his right hand in a freakish car accident, sinks into madness, with the severed hand knocking off anyone who has wronged him. Or is Caine committing the murders and hallucinating? Writer-director Oliver Stone has done a thoughtful job of adapting Marc Brandel's *The Lizard's Tail*, exploring Caine's insanity with the use of black-and-white film, distorted camera angles, etc. Makeup and effects by Stan Winston, Tom Burman and Carlo Rambaldi. Music by James Horner. Andrea Marcovicci, Viveca Lindfors, Annie McEnroe. (Video/Laser: Warner Bros.)

HANDMAID'S TALE, THE (1990) ★★★ Interesting adaptation of Margaret Atwood's allegorical novel about the kingdom of Gilead, where women undergo a tyrannical training program at the hands of Aunt Lydia (Victoria Tennant) to become nunlike childbearers. Natasha Richardson becomes a symbol of rebellion after she undergoes the horrors of being forced to have sex with a commander (Robert Duvall, who brings many nuances to his basic-villain role) while wife Faye Dunaway assists. However, director Volker Schlondorff demonstrates taste in these kinky sequences. Harold Pinter adapted the book. Aidan Quinn, Elizabeth McGovern, Blanche Baker, Traci Lind, David Dukes. (HBO) (Laser: Image)

HANDS OF A STRANGER (1962) ★★ Interesting variation on Maurice Renard's *The Hands of Orlac* in which a doctor must sever the damaged hands of a concert pianist and graft on the hands of "a stranger." While in previous versions the hands belonged to a killer, in this version we never do find out who they belonged to. Writer-director Newton Arnold creates good characters and dialogue but there are times when he goes off the Freudian end. Paul Lukather delivers an intense performance as the pianist driven by his own madness rather than anyone else's and the murders are treated as "accidents." As powerful as this film-noirish effort is, the best version is still *Mad Love*. Joan Harvey, Ted Otis, Irish McCalla, Larry Haddon, Sally Kellerman, Barry Gordon. Aka *The Answer*. (Worldvision; Sinister/C; S/Weird; Filmfax)

HANDS OF A STRANGER. See *The Hands of Orlac*.

HANDS OF DEATH. Video version of *Beyond the Living* (Lettuce Entertain You).

HANDS OF ORLAC, THE (1935). See *Mad Love*.

HANDS OF ORLAC, THE (1960) ★★★ Second film version of Maurice Renard's classic tale of physician (Donald Wolfit) who grafts the hands of a murderer onto the wrists of a pianist (Mel Ferrer). Christopher Lee costars as a stage magician. French-British film was directed by Edmond T. Greville. Donald Pleasence, Danny Carrel, David Peel, Felix Aylmer, Basil Sydney. Aka *Hands of a Stranger*. (Sinister/C; Filmfax; S/Weird)

HANDS OF STEEL (1986) ★ Cyborg assassin (Daniel Greene) can't carry out his new assignment when his human side prevails, so he goes on the run. Italian copy of *The Terminator* directed by Martin Dolman. John Saxon, Janet Agren, George Eastman. (Vestron; Lightning)

HANDS OF THE RIPPER (1971) ★★★ Offbeat Hammer thriller directed by Peter Sasdy with Angharad Rees as the daughter of jolly Jack the Ripper. The L. W. Davidson script emphasizes psychological effects as Rees is obsessed with memories of gory murders and possessed by the spirit of not-so-dear old dad. Now she must carry out his unholy cravings and carvings. Eric Porter portrays the headshrinker helping her. Ripping good. Jane Merrow, Keith Bell, Derek Godfrey. (VidAmerica)

HANGAR 18 (1980) ★★★ Intriguing variation of a legendary story in UFO annals (the 1947 Roswell incident, about which see *Roswell*) in which a flying saucer and a NASA missile collide in space and the bodies of aliens are retrieved from a desert crash site, then taken to a top-security military base. Where the film falters is in its cheap effects. Directed by James L. Conway from a Steven Thornley script. Robert Vaughn, Darren McGavin, Gary Collins, Philip Abbott, William Schallert, H. M. Wynant. The TV version, with a different ending, is *Invasion Force*. (Worldvision) (Laser: Image)

HANGING WOMAN, THE. Video of *Beyond the Living Dead* (Western World; VCI; Unicorn).

HANNAH—QUEEN OF THE VAMPIRES. See *Crypt of the Living Dead*.

HANT, THE. See *Dark August*.

HAPPINESS CAGE, THE. See *The Mind Snatchers*.

HAPPY BIRTHDAY TO ME (1981) ★★★ Above-average slasher flick, featuring a top star (Glenn Ford), a name director (J. Lee Thompson) and a major studio (Paramount). While this qualifies as an imitation of *Halloween*, it has ingenious twists and turns of its own. The plot revolves around teenagers who are murdered one by one, and it seems obvious who the killer is . . . or does it? Pseudopsychiatric motivations and mental-breakdown nonsense give the film a compelling perversity and sense of madness. Don't be put off by the shish-kebab skewering . . . it's only the tip of the . . . fork? Melissa Sue Anderson, Sharon Acker, Lawrence Dane. (Video/Laser: RCA/Columbia)

HAPPY HELL NIGHT (1991) ★★ Slasher crasher built around a "Hell Night," derivative of several serial-killer movies you will instantly recognize. Two students, as part of a hazing, are ordered to photograph a madman in an asylum, unaware he is a supernatural entity who, 25 years before, slaughtered fraternity members of Phi Delta Sigma at Winfield College. Those students who aren't massacred by the evil one's ice ax perform a ritual to send the demon back to Hell, under the guidance of Darren McGavin, who unleashed the creature way back when. Despite its potential for mayhem, *Happy Hell Night* is peculiarly unexciting, for director Brian Owens completely fails to generate suspense or menace. In fact, the ugly-faced killer makes an occasional wisecrack in the Freddy Krueger vein, unbecoming his evil character. Made in Canada and Yugoslavia. Nick Gregory, Laura Carney, Ted Clark, Charles Cragin.

HARDROCK ZOMBIES (1984) ★ Is this the film that led to the downfall of Cannon Pictures? If not, it should have. Everyone connected with this abortion must have been firmly zoned out on LSD or other mind-destroying drugs. It has zombies, dwarf-sized monsters, Adolf Hitler, ax-wielding madmen and a severed walking hand, among other "things." A rock band called Holy Moses (E. J. Curcio, Geno Andrews, Sam Mann and Mick Manz) stops at the mansion of a beautiful blond who murders people with the help of her oddball family of monsters. In the nearby town, total idiots hold a town meeting to ban rock 'n' roll concerts. Finally, after being slaughtered, the dead rock 'n' rollers rise from their beat-meat peat graves to engage in a little bunk junk funk punk. The metal's heavy, man, heavy, when the great-filled dead is pushing open the mausoleum door. Produced-directed by Krishna Shah, who cowrote the alleged script with David Ball. Unbelievable, in the extreme. Lisa Toothman, Jennifer Coe, Ted Wells. (Vestron; Cannon)

HARD TIMES FOR DRACULA/HARD TIME FOR VAMPIRES. See *Uncle Was a Vampire.*

HARD TO DIE (1994) ★ This loose sequel to *Sorority House Massacre 2* is a sequel only in that mentally deficient handyman Orville Ketchum is back, this time to pose a seeming threat to five beautiful babes who run around in sexy underwear in the "Acme Lingerie" office in a highrise building—when they aren't taking showers for no other reason than to show off large breasts. Forrest J. Ackerman plays an archeologist who knows something about a "soul box," out of which springs an evil spirit that takes possession of one of the babes; she runs wild with a submachine gun, murdering the others in slasher, one-by-one fashion. Bouncing flesh is the main dramatic ingredient with Robyn Harris, Lindsay Taylor, Debra Dare, Melissa Moore and Bridget Carvey. Actor Jurgen Baum was also cameraman on this shoot. Directed by (who else?) producer Jim Wynorski from a script (?) by Mark McGee and James B. Rogers. (New Horizons) (Laser: Image)

HARDWARE (1990) ★★★ A messy post-holocaust world is the setting for this punk-funk flick in which an elaborate cyborg killing machine, dubbed Mark 13, goes on a rampage, allowing the effects boys to destroy property and life. Human characters include scavengers who cross the blighted, rubbled landscape and their women. Written-directed by Richard Stanley, who brings an unusually good feel for doom to otherwise familiar material to fans of the *Mad Max* genre. Dylan McDermott, Stacey Travis, John Lynch, William Hootkins. Iggy Pop appears as Angry Bob. (HBO) (Laser: Image)

HARDWARE WARS & OTHER FILM FARCES (1977) ★★★ The title piece is a laugh-a-second, 13-minute parody of *Star Wars*, a cult favorite from the wacky mind of Berkeley filmmaker Ernie Fosselius. This bright, inspired send-up of Lucas' characters and concepts has ordinary home appliances replacing the spaceships and weaponry. The "Other Film Farces" include *Bambi Meets Godzilla*, *Porklips Now* and *Closet Cases of the Nerd Kind*. (Warner Bros.; Pyramid)

HARLEQUIN (1980) ★★ Puzzling Australian film with Robert Powell as a supernatural clown with powers of healing who saves a politician's dying son (shades of Rasputin?). The politician (David Hemmings) is a puppet of unscrupulous industrialist Broderick Crawford and must decide between righteousness, as dictated by the Harlequin, or corruption. The moral battle is compelling, Powell's performance is sympathetic and Simon Wincer's direction is tense. Aka *The Minister's Magician.* (From Media as *Dark Forces*)

HARRISON BERGERON (1995) ★★★ An excellent TV-movie adaptation (shot in Ontario) of the Kurt Vonnegut short story set in the year 2053, when mediocrity and conformity are the rules of the day. It is also a satire on television and how the media controls our lives. A benevolent form of dictatorship keeps emotions in check by having everyone wear headbands that puts a limit on how much one can use his/her intelligence. And everyone drives cars from the 1950s—a period considered complacent and happy. Sean Astin gives a powerful, passionate performance as a superintelligent young man who comes to question the limits imposed on society, and who fights back in a special way. Arthur Crimm did the remarkably compelling script; Bruce Pittman directed it with compassion and understanding. Christopher Plummer (as the fatherly authority figurehead) heads an excellent supporting cast that includes Buck Henry, Howie Mandell, Miranda de Pencier, Andrea Martin and Eugene Levy. Sean's dad, John Astin, appears in a cameo as a sports broadcaster. Don't miss this one. (Republic)

HARRY AND THE HENDERSONS (1987) ★★★★ Excellent comedy in the vein of *E.T.*, in which a middle-class Seattle family takes in a Bigfoot creature and learns to love him despite his clumsy, destructive ways and strong body odor. Rick Baker's hairy Harry is the real star of this Spielberg/Amblin production, which constantly tugs at the heartstrings and isn't afraid to wallow in a little sentiment. The result is above-average entertainment with John Lithgow and Melinda Dillon heading the lovable Spielbergite family. David Suchet is an intense but still sympathetic villain (a hunter in pursuit of Bigfoot) and Don Ameche brings charm as an anthropologist. Oscar winner for makeup, and another feature in the directing cap of William Dear. (Video/Laser: MCA)

HARVEY (1950) ★★★★ This superb whimsical fantasy won a Pulitzer Prize for playwright Mary C. Chase and an Oscar for supporting actress Josephine Hull as a wonderfully daffy old aunt. More than just the story of oddball Elwood P. Dowd (James Stewart) who insists his constant companion is a six-foot-high invisible rabbit . . . it is a commentary on our society and the thin line dividing sanity from insanity. This screen version, adapted by Chase and Oscar

Brodney, also makes poignant comments about our lack of communication. But enough heavy-handed analysis! This is a wonderful satiric comedy involving classic misunderstandings, character mix-ups and other old devices cleverly revitalized. It will stir your funny veins and touch your sensitive bones. Directed with a deft touch by Henry Koster. Cecil Kellaway, Jesse White, Wallace Ford, Charles Drake, Peggy Dow, Nana Bryant. (Video/Laser: MCA)

HATCHET FOR THE HONEYMOON (1971) ★★★ One of Mario Bava's best directorial jobs is to be savored in this Spanish-Italian coproduction. This assumes the point of view of a handsome designer (Stephen Forsyth), but beneath the charm is a psychotic killer who loves to hack up shapely models in wedding gowns. It is disconcerting to see someone mild-mannered turn into a fiend. Forsyth, a character patterned loosely on the Bluebeard legend, is haunted by visions of a childhood trauma that accounts for his antisocial behavior with the hatchet. His wife (Laura Betti) wonders: Whatever happened to nuptial happiness? And just when Forsyth thinks he's a masterful hacker, Betti's recently departed spirit returns in the form of a ghost to give him the abject willies. Bava demonstrates an understanding of how color adds effect to horror themes. A major contribution to European horror cinema. Also known as *Blood Brides, An Axe for the Honeymoon, The Red Sign of Madness* and *The Red Mark of Madness.* (Charter; VCII; Media; Timeless)

HATCHET MURDERS, THE. Video title for Dario Argento's *Deep Red* (HomeVision).

HAUNTED (1957). See *Curse of the Demon.*

HAUNTED AND THE HUNTED, THE. See *Dementia 13.*

HAUNTED HARBOR (1944) ★★★ Monster fans will delight in seeing a sea monster rearing its ugly head out of the Republic Studios tank in this rousing 15-chapter serial (aka *Pirate's Harbor*) directed by Spencer G. Bennet and Wallace Grissell. Kane Richmond is the crusading seaman out to clear his name of murder as he tangles with a murderous gang that preys on local superstition to keep away the gringos. You know the rest. Just focus on the great fistfights and cliffhangers. Kay Aldridge, Roy Barcroft, Forrest Taylor, Kenne Duncan, Tom Steele, Robert Wilke, Marshall Reed. (Republic)

HAUNTED PALACE, THE (1963) ★★★ Good horror film (aka *The Haunted Village*) produced-directed by Roger Corman, based on a poem by Poe and H. P. Lovecraft's novella, "The Case of Charles Dexter Ward." But any similarities are purely by accident. Charles Beaumont's script describes a warlock (Vincent Price) who possesses a descendant to wreak revenge against those who burned him at the stake. The most

interesting device, besides creepy characters with fright faces, is a Thing in a well, a banished "Elder God," the one real Lovecraftian touch. Lon Chaney Jr., Debra Paget, Elisha Cook Jr., Leo Gordon. (HBO) (Laser: Image, with *Curse of the Crimson Altar*)

HAUNTED PLANET, THE. See *Planet of the Vampires.*

HAUNTED SCHOOL, THE (1986) ★★ Lightweight pseudosupernatural Australian TV-movie more gentle than frightening, its ghosts and goblins explained away as natural phenomena. Carol Drinkwater portrays a British school marm who arrives in a backward community where uneducated adults resist her efforts to start a school in the ruins of an old inn that burned up mysteriously and where spirits are said to rove. Helen Cresswell's telescript (from an idea by Drinkwater) is a morality lesson that should appeal to children. Directed by Frank Arnold. James Laurie, Michael Becher, Emil Minty, Grant Navin.

HAUNTED STRANGLER, THE (1957) ★★★ "The Haymarket Strangler" was executed 20 years ago for garroting and slashing five women and now, in 1880 London, obsessed mystery writer/criminologist Boris Karloff is afraid the wrong man was accused. Soul possession sets in when Karloff picks up a scalpel at Scotland Yard's Black Museum and duplicates the heinous murders, his face a twisted, gnarly frightmess. Interesting variation on the Jekyll-Hyde theme; produced in Britain by Richard Gordon, directed by Robert Day with nice can-can scenes; written by Jan Read and John C. Cooper. Aka *Grip of the Stranger* and *Stranglehold.* Anthony Dawson, Elizabeth Allan, Jean Kent. (Media; MPI; Gorgon) (Laser: Image)

HAUNTED SUMMER (1988) ★★ This covers the same ground as Ken Russell's *Gothic*, but without the hysterical melodrama or startling images or sexual perversity. Once again it's the summer of 1815 and those literary greats-to-be Lord Byron (Philip Anglim), Mary Wollstonecraft Godwin (Alice Krige), Percy Shelley (Eric Stoltz) and Dr. Polidori (Alex Winter) have gathered for games of sex, drugs and philosophical interchanges. The monumental crux is that Mary will become Mary Shelley and write *Frankenstein.* But the potential for horror is limited to a couple of drug-crazed sequences—hardly enough to warrant listening to Lewis John Carlino's turgid dialogue or enduring director Ivan Passer's melancholic pacing. Based on the novel by Anne Edwards, the film is well-intended but it plods along, more mysterious than enlightening. Laura Dern. (Video/Laser: Media)

HAUNTED: THE FERRYMAN (1986) ★★ Horror novelist and his wife, resting in the country, realize one of his books is coming true when they are haunted by a drowned ferryman. British TV-movie directed by John Irvin. Adapted by Julian Bond from a Kingsley Amis story. Jeremy Brett, Natasha Parry, Leslie Dunlop. (Prism)

HAUNTED VILLAGE, THE. See *The Haunted Palace*.

HAUNTED WORLD, THE. See *Planet of the Vampires*.

HAUNTING, THE (1963) ★★★★★ Robert Wise's production is one helluva scary supernatural thriller, among the best ever made. Credit Wise's incredibly precise direction and Nelson Gidding's adaptation of Shirley Jackson's *The Haunting of Hill House*. It's truly scary because the horrors remain unseen and play heavier on the imagination. Richard Johnson, a psychic ghost chaser, picks "sensitives" to help him investigate an old mansion steeped in psychic phenomena. (Much of this is based on true cases.) Psychological problems of spinstress Julie Harris are related to the ghostly events. Guaranteed to chill you, and recognized as a classic. Claire Bloom, Russ Tamblyn, Lois Maxwell. (Video/Laser: MGM/UA)

HAUNTING, THE (1999) ★★ Isn't it ironic that this second film version of a classic Shirley Jackson ghost novel should forget the very things that made the book, and the 1963 adaptation directed by Robert Wise, so superior. Both Jackson and Wise understood that less is more when it comes to the horrible images one can dredge up from the darkest depths of the imagination. And yet, as if they never read the book or saw the first movie, screenwriter David Self and director Jan De Bont proceed to turn *The Haunting* into a ridiculous haunted-house extravaganza, believing that the bigger everything is, the scarier it will be. They should have taken a lesson from Wise, who chose to let the atmosphere of his eerie mansion become a personality that wrapped itself around and squeezed the characters trapped within it. However, our filmmakers of the nineties have become fixated on elaborate computer-generated special effects that keep getting bigger and bolder, until they finally erupt in a howlingly funny climax that is more suited to a movie called *Casper the Ghost—New Manifestations Part II* than *The Haunting*. In this updated version, Richard Johnson's parapsychologist is replaced by Liam Neeson, who is studying fear instead of the paranormal. The members of his experimental team are similar: Lili Taylor plays Nell (originated by Julie Harris), whose haunted past is used by the house to become her haunted present, and whose memories of her dying mother are activated by the ghostly essence of the house; Catherine Zeta-Jones is the subtle lesbian Theo (originated by Claire Bloom) and Owen Wilson plays the young guy (originated by Russ Tam-

blyn). In small supporting roles are Bruce Dern and Marian Seldes as the superstition-driven caretakers. At times, Self's script seems more parody than serious movie. What is visually stimulating is the house itself. The exteriors are those of Harlaxton Manor in Nottinghamshire, England, and the bone-chilling design of the interiors is the creative work of Eugenio Zanetti. The mansion does finally take on a personality of its own, even if the film does not. In the end, this is a hollow movie, epitomized by a line of dialogue uttered by Theo when she first enters the house: "It's like Charles Foster Kane meets the Munsters." Emphasis on the Munsters. (Video/DVD: Dreamworks)

HAUNTING FEAR (1990) ★★ Inspired by Poe's *The Premature Burial*, this Fred Olen Ray production would have been better titled *The Immature Burial*, so silly is Ray's attempt at an erotic thriller with *Psycho* underpinnings. Brinke Stevens is suffering from nightmares and hallucinations, unaware her husband (Jay Richardson) is having an affair with sexpot secretary Delia Sheppard. Brinke's only really good nightmare features Michael Berryman as a ghoulish morgue attendant. Most of Sherman Scott's slow-moving script focuses on the lovers as they plot to bury Brinke alive—a phobia caused by her father's death. Ray spices up the cast with Jan-Michael Vincent as a strongarm man posing as a cop, Karen Black as a hypnotist-psychiatrist, Robert Clarke as the family doctor and Robert Quarry as a hoodlum, but the story falls to pieces when Brinke goes on a cackling rampage in her nightgown. (Rhino) (Laser: Image)

HAUNTING OF BARNEY PALMER, THE (1992) ★★ Margaret Mahy's *The Haunting* formed the basis for this episode from TV's *Wonderworks* series, with Ned Beatty portraying a man haunted by the ghost of his great uncle. Alexis Banas, Eleanor Gibson. (Public Media; Facets Multimedia)

HAUNTING OF HAMILTON HIGH. Theatrical title for *Hello, Mary Lou: Prom Night II*.

HAUNTING OF HARRINGTON HOUSE (1982) ★★ Dominique Dunne portrays a young inhabitant of an alleged haunted house whose camera picks up images of ghosts. Oddball characters (fortune teller, magician, suspicious maid, 95-year-old sisters, etc.) spring to life under Murray Golden's direction. Roscoe Lee Browne, Edie Adams, Phil Leeds, Vitto Scotti. (Video Gems)

HAUNTING OF JULIA, THE (1976) ★★ Moody, slow-moving British-Canadian horror film (produced in London as *Full Circle*), based on *Julia*, a lesser-known Peter Straub novel. Mia Farrow, who has just lost her daughter, moves into a strange house haunted by a perverted young girl.

Mia becomes obsessed with investigating the child's past. This is lyrical and full of ambience, under the subtle direction of Richard Loncraine. Tom Conti, Keir Dullea, Jill Bennett, Cathleen Nesbitt. (Media; Magnum)

HAUNTING OF LISA, THE (1995) ★★★ Predictable albeit well produced whodunit TV-movie with psychic overtones in which Cheryl Ladd, who had psychic powers as a girl, discovers that her 9-year-old daughter (Aemilia Robinson) also has the power when the daughter sees visions of a 30-year-old murder. The main drama of Don Henry's script is Ladd's reluctance to allow Robinson to become involved in police chief Duncan Regehr's investigation, complicated by the fact she's about to marry him. It's red herrings and everyone-is-a-suspect when it becomes apparent the killer is a main character. Don McBrearty directs all these contrivances with professional touches. Don Allison, Kate Lynch, Tony Rosato, Wayne Northrop.

HAUNTING OF MORELLA, THE (1989) ★★½ Within the canon of films directed by Jim Wynorski, this ranks as one of his better ones—as if producer Roger Corman said, "Now you be a good boy, Jim, and cut back on all that silly sex and violence you usually give." Corman appears to be recapturing the essence of his earlier Edgar Allan Poe adaptations as R. J. Robertson's script pays homage to EAP even if the tale does get a bit twisted with its modest amount of sex and bloody violence. David McCallum lends authority to his role as a blind man whose witch-wife was burned at the stake. Her spirit returns in the body of her grown daughter, and a reign of terror begins with sacrifical bloodletting, blasts of lightning from the Heavens and a wanton demon woman causing the death of others. Christopher Halsted, Lana Clarkson, Jonathan Farwell. (New Horizons) (Laser: Image)

HAUNTING OF SARAH HARDY, THE (1989) ★★★ TV-movie recycles the shopworn premise of the woman being driven crazy by a ghost—or is a plot afoot to drive her bonkers so someone can inherit the family fortune? Sela Ward portrays a sweet thing who once watched her mother drown in the surf near their mansion, The Pines. Now she's happily married to Michael Woods, but the spectral image of dear ole mom haunts her. Thomas Baum's adaptation of Jim Flanagan's novel *The Crossing* segues midstream from Sarah's point of view to her husband's, allowing for new surprises. Director Jerry London concludes with a snap ending. Polly Bergen, Morgan Fairchild. (Video/Laser: Paramount)

HAUNTING OF SEACLIFF INN, THE (1994) ★★½ This TV-movie, directed by Walter Klenhard and based on a script he wrote with Tom Walla, is a rather obvious, clichéd haunted-house tale; and yet it has interesting characters (Ally Sheedy and William R. Moses as a troubled couple trying to start over again by opening a bed-and-breakfast place on the Mendocino coastline) and a storyline that deals with domestic problems as well as supernatural ones when the mansion they buy turns out to be possessed by angry spirits. Since you've seen all the haunting devices before (house controls itself, causing a few deaths along the way), it's basically an okay time-killer with Lucinda Weist as a fetching siren who lures Moses into her trap and who occasionally turns into a dangerous wolfhound. Louise Fletcher, Tom McCleister, Maxie Stuart. (Video/Laser: MCA)

HAUNTING PASSION, THE (1983) ★★★ Restrained TV-movie which handles its sexual theme tastefully: Jane Seymour is romanced by an invisible ghost in her coastside home. This deals as much with Seymour's problems with her TV newscaster husband (Gerald McRaney); he's undergoing a midlife crisis and cannot perform sexually, leaving an opening for the surrogate ghost. Hiro Narita's camera captures the rugged Pacific Coast and it comes together under John Korty's direction. Executive producer Douglas Schwartz wrote the telescript. Paul Rossilli, Millie Perkins, Ruth Nelson. (USA; IVE)

HAUNTS (1976) ★½ Only the bad scripting by Anne Marisse and directing by Herb Freed (who cowrote with Marisse) will haunt you . . . A madman wielding scissors attacks pretty girls in a small community, while in a farmhouse outside town May Britt fears that her father, Cameron Mitchell, is responsible for the scissors attacks. Aldo Ray hangs around town as the sheriff. E. J. Andre, William Gray Espy. Original title: *The Veil*. (Media; Twilight)

HAUNTS OF THE VERY RICH (1973) ★★★ TV-movie directed by Paul Wendkos borrows from the *Outward Bound* premise: Passengers aboard an airliner don't know how they got there or where they're going. Eventually they reach a tropical island (à la *Fantasy Island*) where weird things happen. It's apparent Lloyd Bridges, Cloris Leachman and Anne Francis are caught up in a Is-it-Heaven-or-Hell? plot. The allegory is contrived by writer William Wood but compelling. Edward Asner, Tony Bill, Moses Gunn, Donna Mills (Vidmark)

HAWK, THE (1992) ★★★½ One really offbeat, weird British TV-movie dealing with a serial killer called the Hawk, who kills his female victims (often mothers with two children) with a hammer, then pecks their eyes out like he were . . . yeah, a hawk. Housewife Helen Mirren, a neurotic, paranoid mother of two, suspects her husband (George Costigan) is the slasher-murderer, but one isn't sure if she's hallucinating or . . . David Hayman's unusual, frenetic direction gives this story added tension and one never knows where the script by Peter Ransley (based on his novel) is going. For those who like their whodunits out of the standard mold with plenty of red herrings. Rosemary Leach, Melanie Hill, Clive Russell. (Academy) (Laser: Image)

HAWK OF THE WILDERNESS (1938) ★★★ A 12-chapter Republic serial directed by William Witney and John English, and starring Mala and Herman Brix (soon to be Bruce Bennett). An uncharted island is inhabited by a jungle boy and superstitious natives living in dread of a volcano. An expedition arrives to rescue the boy and that sets into motion a series of narrow escapes. Monte Blue, Jill Martin, Noble Johnson, Tom Chatterton, William Royle. The truncated TV-feature version is *Lost Island of Kioga*. (Nostalgia Merchant; Video Connection)

HAWK THE SLAYER (1980) ★★ British sword-and-sorcery actioner, about rival brothers in search of supernatural powers, is structured like a Western, with fights staged as gun battles. It reeks of Oedipus overtones as the evil brother Voltan (Jack Palance) seeks to destroy the good (John Terry, armed with Mindsword, a blade that appears out of thin air when needed). Settings are foggy and mystical, characters gritty and determined, and the effects, though not stupendous, are palatable. Director Terry Marcel tends to take it too seriously: acting is of the grandiose, scenery-chewing school. Roy Kinnear, Patrick Magee, Harry Andrews. (USA; IVE) (Laser)

HEADHUNTER (1989) ★★½ A voodoo curse resurrects an evil spirit named Chitatikumo that flies through the air, destroying natives before it moves on to Miami, where it runs amok, much to the chagrin of cops Kay Lenz and Wayne Crawford. It always rips off its victims' heads, causing Lenz to remark, "Maybe we can find this guy's head around here somewhere. That would be nice, huh?" Sure would be more sanitary. Since the only way it can be destroyed, according to an old medicine man, is to dismember its body parts, scripter Len Spinelli has a chainsaw-massacre climax. Standard gore-fest stuff directed by Francis Schaeffer. Steve Kanaly, June Chadwick, John Fatooh. (Academy) (Laser: Image)

HEADLESS EYES (1971) ★ Despicable junk that has zero entertainment value and disgusts from beginning to end. Down-on-his-luck New York artist Bo Brudin has his eye poked out while robbing a woman's apartment. This turns him into a serial killer with a patch over one eye. He kills women he sees on the street, then hangs their eyeballs from the ceiling or implants them

in his work of "art." An insult to women in particular and mankind in general. Call it blind filmmaking with unsightful writing. Directed by Kent Bateman. (Vestron; Wizard; VCI)

HEADS (1993) ★★½ An oddball Canadian-produced whodunit with horrific overtones set in the small town of Dry Falls, where John Cryer, a maladroit, repressed bumbler-turned-reporter tracks the Town Decapitator, a killer responsible for gory decapitations. If there's any good reason to watch this amalgam of dumb comedy and occasionally serious drama it's for the performance of Ed Asner as newspaper publisher Abner Abbot, a cantankerous, ironically humored "Lou Grant" of the small-town weeklies. He's great to watch; it's just too bad this couldn't have been a more suitable vehicle for his talents. Paul Shapiro does direct it with a sense of style, capturing the expansive wheat regions of Manitou, Canada, to add to the film's peculiar tone, and he gets a good performance out of sexy Jennifer Tilly as Asner's wayward daughter. Script by Jay Stapleton and Adam Brooks. Roddy McDowall has a cameo as the town's rich guy. Shawn Alex Thompson, Wayne Robson, Earl Pastko, Nancy Drake. (Republic)

HEAD THAT WOULDN'T DIE, THE. See *The Brain That Wouldn't Die*.

HEARSE, THE (1980) ★★★ Nicely crafted vehicle of horror (pun intended). Trish Van Devere, recovering from a mental collapse, settles in a town where she is unwelcome because the house she has inherited is allegedly haunted. At night, an antique corpse wagon turns up to terrorize her. The terror builds well under George Bowers' direction. Joseph Cotten, David Gautreaux. (Media)

HEART CONDITION (1990) ★★ Dark comedy from director James O. Parriott in which racist, insubordinate L.A. cop Bob Hoskins dies from a coronary (bad eating habits, angry temper) and is given the heart of a black attorney just killed in a car crash. The ghost of the attorney (Denzel Washington) is visible only to Hoskins as they set out together to find the guys who set up Washington's car "accident." This partnership is tough for the guys to handle because Washington once took away Hoskins' white girlfriend (Chloe Webb). Parriott vacillates between comedy and serious crime and goes for some sentiment, but the drabness of the L.A. milieu and the grim climactic shootout make the film difficult to take to heart. It's also difficult to like Jack Moony (Hoskins' character), the way he barnstorms through this desolate movie. (Video/Laser: RCA/Columbia)

HEART OF MIDNIGHT (1988) ★★★ Interesting more for its psychological portrait of a confused woman with a psychiatric history than for its supernatural elements, which are erratic and never brought into perspective by writer-director Matthew Chapman. Jennifer Jason Leigh is excellent as Carol Rivers, who inherits a night club called the Midnight from her deceased Uncle Fletcher, a sex pervert who ran a house of "sex games" in the upstairs rooms. Leigh lives in this haunted environment in a state of confusion, receiving help from crisis worker Denise Dummont (a strangely exotic woman), a stranger (Peter Coyote) and policeman (Frank Stallone) who doubts Rivers' sanity. There are a few suspenseful moments as Leigh creeps around the eerie night club, but the menacing factors of Uncle Fletcher remain muddled. Gale Mayron, Sam Schact, Brenda Vaccaro, James Rebhorn. (Virgin Vision) (Laser: Image)

HEARTSTONE. See *Demonstone*.

HEARTSTOPPER (1992) ★★ A doctor is hanged for being a vampire and two hundred years later returns from the dead. Directed by John Russo. Kevin Kindlin, John Hall, Moon Zappa, Tom Savini. (Tempe)

HEATSEEKER (1994) ★½ Superlousy kickboxing actioner set in 2019 A.D., when the Sianon Corporation (a specialist in cyborg technology) holds a world championship pitting various cyber-implant warriors against human champ Chance O'Brien. To ensure he fights, the bad guys kidnap his girlfriend, zap her with brain implants and force her to fall in love with O'Brien's cyborg enemy Xao. The fights are boringly photographed—in fact, the whole venture is poorly directed by Albert Pyun, who cowrote the empty script with Christopher Borkgren. *Heartseeker* is cold. Don't seek it out. Keith H. Cooke, Thom Mathews, Norbert Weisser, Tim Thomerson (with a shock of red hair), Tina Cote. (Vidmark)

HEAVEN (1998) ★★½ Although its subject matter is sleazy and unpleasant, this New Zealand film by writer-director Scott Reynolds develops a compelling fascination as it blends its clairvoyant theme with a violent tale of nightworld characters and a fight between divorcés over custody of their son. Reynolds also plays with the time line of his film, holding back chunks of expository material to mislead the viewer, and moving back and forth in time as well. This technique pays off handsomely in the end, allowing Reynolds to pull off a few surprises. But be forewarned: this movie makes you work; if you stay with it, though, the characters will begin to grow on you. Martin Donovan gives an outstanding performance as the divorcé with a gambling addiction that keeps taking him back to the Paradise, a low-life nightclub run by control freak and sadist Richard Schiff. What a club: its strippers/sex dancers are actually male cross-dressers and transves-

tites, chief among them being Heaven (Danny Edwards). There's also a blond hunk of a bouncer (Karl Urban) called "The Sweeper." Heaven has powers that allow her to see into the future, but it's only bits and pieces, and hence her predictions are always shrouded in mystery. Donovan decides to use Heaven's strange powers to win at poker and eventually she even helps him in his custody battle against ex-wife Joanna Going (an utterly stunning brunette), who has been having an affair with therapist Patrick Malahide, who secretly has the hots for Heaven. Yeah, this plot gets a little complicated, but it pays off. Edwards's performance is a moving, convincing one, and after a while you forget it's a man playing this sympathetic "woman." Basing his movie on a novel by Chad Taylor, Reynolds includes one startling suicide scene and fills the climactic confrontations with violent killings and blood-dripping fights in the back alleys of a major city. (Video/DVD: Miramax)

HEAVEN CAN WAIT (1943) ★★★ Worthwhile comedy produced-directed by Ernst Lubitsch, featuring Laird Cregar as the Devil, who must listen to playboy Don Ameche describe his life history before deciding if he should be sent to Hell permanently. A colorful depiction of American life at the turn of the century, fired up by a musical score by Alfred Newman. Scripted by Samson Raphaelson. Gene Tierney, Charles Coburn, Spring Byington, Signe Hasso, Allyn Joslyn. Not to be confused with the 1978 Warren Beatty fantasy-comedy—that was based on *Here Comes Mr. Jordan*. (Video/Laser: CBS/Fox)

HEAVEN CAN WAIT (1978) ★★★ Amusing escapism comedy starring Warren Beatty who cowrote with Elaine May and codirected with Buck Henry. Beatty stars as a football star whose soul is prematurely taken and who demands a replacement body. What he gets is the aging carcass of a millionaire industrialist—and naturally he wants to play quarterback for the L.A. Rams. A remake of the 1941 *Here Comes Mr. Jordan* with Julie Christie, James Mason (as the overseer from above), Jack Warden, Dyan Cannon, Charles Grodin, Vincent Gardenia, Buck Henry. (Video/Laser: Paramount)

HEAVENLY CREATURES (1994) ★★★★ A brilliant piece of filmmaking, writing and acting, conceived with imagination by New Zealand director Peter Jackson and written by Jackson and Frances Walsh with insight and understanding of teenage behavior. Based on a true-life 1954 murder case in New Zealand, this unusual movie depicts two young murderesses-to-be (Kate Winslet as Juliet Marion Hulme and Melanie Lynskey as Pauline Yvonne Parker) in a sympathetic light and interprets the "fourth world" in which they escape together as a kind of Oz land where Borovnian creatures (gray, claylike beings) romp about. These special-effects characters become substitutes within their individual fantasies as the teenagers (Pauline is a dour introvert; Kate is an outgoing, precocious, adorable creature) discover lesbian sex and contemplate eliminating stumbling blocks (such as Pauline's disciplinarian mother) for their greater happiness, unaware of the consequences. The insight into this horrific murder (the teens beat the mother to death with a brick after luring her into Victoria Park) and the use of child-like fantasy images gives this film a sensitivity and visual power that lingers on. Sarah Peirse, Diana Kent, Clive Merison, Simon O'Connor. (Video/Laser: Miramax)

HEAVENLY KID, THE (1985) ★★½ Unusually sappy teenage fable in which dragster Lewis Smith is killed when his car plunges off a cliff and is doomed to ride a subway train for eternity . . . unless, he's told by a heavenly emissary named Rafferty (Richard Mulligan), he redeems himself by returning to Earth and helping nerdish Jason Gedrick make it with the chick of his dreams. That's what writers Cary Medoway (who also directed) and Martin Copeland call a premise. There's nothing heavenly about it. It's just plain dull and maudlin. (HBO)

HEAVY METAL (1981) ★★★ Spinoff from the illustrated fantasy magazine, an imaginative mixture of sci-fi, fantasy, horror and surrealism in different animation styles. The results are uneven but the highs outnumber the lows. The youth market was attracted by the hard-rock music track (Black Sabbath, Cheap Trick, Blue Öyster Cult) and comic fans dug the adaptations of Richard Corben and Bernie Wrightson. One tale is about a cabbie in a half-destroyed, futuristic New York City, another is about a haunted B-17 during World War II. A green ball of "universal evil" threads in and out of the narratives, but otherwise the stories have little connection. A dazzling anthology. Directed by Gerald Potterton. (Columbia)

HEIRESS OF DRACULA, THE. See *The Heritage of Dracula.*

HE KILLS NIGHT AFTER NIGHT. Video version of *Night After Night After Night (He Kills)* (Monterey)

HE KNOWS YOU'RE ALONE (1980) ★★ Psycho-killer flick in which women are terrorized then murdered in a manner most foul. The slaughterer of brides-to-be plays ugly cat-and-mouse games with victims, striking when you least expect the knife to fall. It's terrifying in an excruciating way, and bloodcurdling. Directed by Armand Mastroianni. Don Scardino, Caitlin O'Hearney, Tom Rolfing. Tom Hanks appears in a cameo. Aka *Blood Wedding.* (MGM/UA)

HELLBENT (1989) ★★ Down-and-out bandleader Phil Ward makes a deal with the owner of a bar (the Devil) for success in exchange for his soul. Some deal. Lyn Levand, Cheryl Slean, David Marciano. Written-directed by Richard Casey. (Raedon)

HELLBOUND (1993) ★★★ While it's rare to find Chuck Norris karate-kicking his way through a horror picture, his presence lends sparkle and sex appeal to this otherwise routine supernatural tale about Prosatanos ("The Soul of Darkness, Satan's Emissary"). In the opening, King Richard (David Robb) kicks Prosatanos' ass during a battle in a dungeon in 1186 A.D. Cut to Chicago where cops Norris and Calvin Levels encounter the emissary in the sleazy Blue Ritz Hotel, where a rabbi's heart has just been ripped out. Off they go to Tel Aviv, where director Aaron Norris (Chuck's stuntman brother) has ample opportunity for scenic shots. Chuck discovers there are nine pieces of a scepter that Prosatanos (played by Christopher Neame) is putting together to strengthen his evil power. Ultimately the nosy cops track the Evil One to a dungeon, just when he's about to sacrifice the film's only modest love interest, Sheree J. Wilson. And you have your grand battle of magic and might. There's little in the Brent Friedman–Donald C. Thompson script that's surprising. It's Norris that makes the day. (Cannon)

HELLBOUND: HELLRAISER II (1988) ★★★ Clive Barker's *Hellraiser* was a dark, disturbing horror film, which reached new heights in horrifying imagery. This follow-up is just as unsettling as once again Kirsty (Ashley Laurence) must enter the labyrinth of Hell to confront the Cenobites and solve the Lament Configuration Puzzle Box. The eeriness is unrelenting, somber to its core, and the images are stark and painful. Peter Atkins' script (based on a Barker outline) is concocted from no logic known to man, and the story is chaotic. First-time director Tony Randel still manages to make it an auspicious debut. Clare Higgins, Kenneth Cranham, Imogen Boorman, William Hope. (New World) (Laser: Image)

HELL COMES TO FROGTOWN (1988) ★★½ One wacked-out *Mad Max* imitation, which laughs at itself and has a modicum of directorial style from R. J. Kizer and Donald G. Jackson. Sam Hellman (Roddy Piper) is singled out in a post-Armageddon society as a breeding machine needed to "impregnate fertile women" and assigned to accompany Sandahl Bergman and Cec Verrell in a pink van into mutant territory, where fertile babes have been taken by renegades. The community of Frogtown is a campy one, inhabited by a race of toads and ruled over by Commander Toty (characters destined to croak?). Adding to the whimsical nature of this nonsense is Rory Calhoun as old prospector Looney Tunes; adding to the villainy is William Smith as Count Sodom, a sadist with a vendetta against Hellman. The sequel is *Frogtown II*. (New World) (Laser: Image)

HELL CREATURES. See *Invasion of the Saucermen*.

HELLFIRE (1995) ★★★½ Above-average TV-movie production from Roger Corman (co-produced with Eastern Europeans) in a 19th-century setting in which Baron Jean Oktavia writes "The Devil's Symphony" and murders prostitutes with piano wires. After he's put away (drawn and quartered, actually) his niece (Jennifer Burns), many years later, finds the unfinished manuscript and hires unemployed composer Ben Cross to finish it. Out of the grave comes the spirit of the Baron to possess Cross to murder more prostitutes and to rekindle an old affair with his housekeeper (Beverly Garland). Good scripting by Tara McCann, Beverly Gray and David Hartwell provide director David Tausik with enough action and sex to make this one worthwhile. (New Horizons)

HELLFIRE ON ICE. Video version of *Sweet Sugar* (Hurricane).

HELLGATE (1989) ★★½ Direct-to-video junk designed for visual shocks rather than coherency. A motorcycle gang, The Strangers, rapes the daughter of the man who owns Hellgate, a ghost-town attraction. Years later the father finds a crystal that (1) restores life to the dead and (2) exudes a destructive laser. The dead daughter lures Ron Palillo and pals into a trap for a showdown in Hellgate. None of this hangs together—but director William A. Levey and cast hang together, by the neck until dead. Abigail Wolcott (she of big chest dimensions), Carel Trichardt, Petrea Curran. (Vidmark) (Laser: Image)

HELL HIGH (1989) ★★ A little girl playing in a rural dollhouse accidentally kills an obnoxious biker and his girlfriend . . . 18 years later she's a science teacher on the edge of insanity, tormented by four dumb students. Of course, the tormentors soon become the stalked when the gal flips out and goes on a rampage. This is an excruciating viewing experience, probably more painful than the few deaths that it depicts in usual slasher-movie style. Producer-director Douglas Grossman is to blame. Maureen Mooney, Christopher Stryker. (Prism)

HELLHOLE (1985) ★★½ Women-behind-bars sleazebagger from producer Samuel Z. Arkoff, who breaks tradition with asses-and-jugs-in-the-jug by adding a Frankenstein plot: Doctor Marjoe Gortner tests a brain serum on inmates of Ashland Sanitarium for Women, assisted by psychiatrist Mary Woronov to satisfy her bisexual perversities. (She offers an intense depiction of a lesbian.) But Gortner's "chemical loboto-

mies" create madwomen. Meanwhile, inmate Judy Landers (a dull actress) is stalked by humming killer Ray Sharkey. Edy Williams fans will delight in watching her fondling women in soft porn segments. Director Pierre De Moro gives this trash style. Terry Moore, Robert Darcy. (Video/Laser: RCA/Columbia)

HELL HUNTERS (1988) ★½ Stewart Granger stars in this West German production as a Nazi who invents a spider serum that turns people into fascists. However, war criminal hunters Maud Adams and William Berger thwart the insidious plot. Produced-directed by Ernst R. von Theumer. George Lazenby, Eduardo Conde, Candice Daly. (New Star)

HELLISH FLESH (1970) ★½ Another graphic gore thriller from Brazil's Jose Mojica Marins, the hombre who gave el mondo the Coffin Joe spookers. Marins stars as a mad scientist who loves to dissolve human bodies with his new Super Acid. Ugly stuff. (S/Weird)

HELL ISLAND. See *Attack of the Beast Creatures*.

HELLMASTER (1990) ★★½ "If God created the world in six days, and I can make Hell of it in one night, then God must be dead," cackles John Saxon as the evil biochemist conducting the Nietzsche Experiment in this gory, gooey, God-awful ghastfest. Wearing a three-needle hypo hand, which he shoves into victims, the crazed doc has a serum that turns teenagers and a nun into murderous monsters. In turn, the deformed maniacs attack teachers and students on the campus, killing with a scythe. More unpleasant than entertaining, but if you like to see puncture wounds, you'll get the points. Written-produced-directed by Douglas Schulze. David Enge, Amy Raasch, Edward Stevens. (Action International) (Laser: Image)

HELL NIGHT (1982) ★★★ Clever blending of slasher and haunted house clichés, building to many successful suspense sequences—you even grow to like four teenagers locked in the old Garth Mansion overnight as part of the Alpha Sigma Rho initiation rites. The killers are deformed creatures hiding in tunnels under the house or in secret passageways within. Linda Blair runs screaming through the house, killer in hot pursuit. Well directed by Tom De Simone, scripted by Randolph Feldman. Kevin Brophy, Vincent Van Patten. (Media)

HELLO AGAIN (1987) ★★ Misfire from director Frank Perry that asks: Can a once-mean dead woman come back from the grave and find acceptance from those she mistreated? A good answer is never provided. Shelley Long is Lucy Chadman, a pathetically clumsy, unliked woman who is the wife of a yuppish plastic surgeon. She chokes on a South Korean chicken ball and dies. Her zany sister (Judith Ivey) brings her back to life with astrological mumbo-jumbo. How she's rejected by hubby (Corbin Bernsen), reestablishes a relationship with her kitchen-loving son, and finds romance with Kevin Scanlon form the core of this lethargic movie, which fails to generate any enthusiasm. Just say goodbye and forget it. Sela Ward, Austin Pendleton. (Video/Laser: Touchstone)

HELL OF THE LIVING DEAD. See Vincent Dawn's *Night of the Zombies* (1983).

HELLO MARY LOU: PROM NIGHT II (1987) ★★½ *Prom Night* was your standard slasher flick—this is more a remake of *Carrie* with dabs of *The Exorcist*. In 1957, superslut Mary Lou is accidentally set ablaze as Homecoming Queen. Thirty years later, on the eve of Hamilton High's homecoming dance, sweet Wendy Lyon is possessed by the spirit of Mary Lou, with demonic winds blowing. Principal Bill Nordham (Michael Ironside, who helped to kill Mary Lou in '57) tries to save his son from death as the evening ends in an explosion of special effects—including a body breaking open and a different person popping out. Ron Oliver's script is predictable, as is Bruce Pittman's direction. Justin Louis, Richard Monette. (Video/Laser: Virgin Vision)

HELLRAISER (1987) ★★★½ Stephen King proclaimed British writer Clive Barker "the future of horror," and to prove it Barker wrote-directed his first feature, believing that "good fantastique should be dangerous, leading us into dreams and night, giving us a map of unexplored territory." *Hellraiser* is certainly that: Its "charnel house" subject matter is truly graphic, and Barker is in a bloody rush to show us all the grotesqueries he can. Three demons called Cenobites escape from a small box in which they are trapped to create havoc in a house in England. A corpse is resurrected in the film's best sequence, then lures an old flame into a new love affair. An undercurrent of sexual perversity, coupled with blunt hammer murders, gives Barker's story a disgusting twist. There is a terrific monster guarding the corridor to Hell, and the Cenobites suggest intriguing concepts about pleasure and pain. (New World) (Laser: Image)

HELLRAISER II. See *Hellbound: Hellraiser II.*

HELLRAISER III: HELL ON EARTH (1992) ★★½ Despite the influence of Clive Barker as executive producer, this is a tired retread of those boys from Hell, the Cenobites, as they battle with Terry Farrell for possession of the Lament Configuration Puzzle Box, the gateway to Hell. Peter Atkins' script (from a story concocted with director Tony Randel) has Farrell crossing an eerie battlefield in a limbo between Heaven and Hell; the removal of a prostitute's skin; the slaughter of a night club's decadent rock 'n' rollers; and Farrell's flight down a street as supernatural explosions occur around her. It's loaded with pyrotechnics, electrical zap rays and

a plethora of other effects, and the rules of the game keep changing so you never can figure out what's happening. But the fans for whom this was intended could no doubt care less. Anthony Hickox (*Waxwork*) directed. Doug Bradley, Paula Marshall. (Video/Laser: Paramount)

HELLRAISER IV: BLOODLINE (1996) ★★★ This fourth entry in Clive Barker's never-ending series about Pinhead, the demon from the bowels of Hell, is strictly for dyed-in-the-wool horror fans who like stark and dark, and who revel in movies that are unrelenting in the physical violence and ugly graphics they portray. There isn't a chuckle or a pretty sight in 100 minutes of ongoing bloodletting, torture and skin ripping. Those hooks and chains of Pinhead tear assorted humans to shreds, while he gloats about and promises unimaginable new horrors scheduled to arrive soon from the depths of hellfire and damnation. This *Hellraiser*, produced by Barker, has a science-fictional framework (script is by Barker disciple Peter Atkins) and is set in the year 2029, on the space station Minos. Bruce Ramsay has just unlocked Pinhead (Doug Bradley, looking hideously good) from the puzzle box, and explains in flashbacks how his ancestors in the 17th century designed the puzzle box for a warlock, and set into motion all of Pinhead's evil. Down through the raging ages, the symbol of eternal evil becomes Valentine Vargas, a witch with blazing eyes and murderous designs. Now the entire universe is in danger, and stuff like that. A face being punctured and ripped apart by a claw, and two heads merging together are among the hideousness. The director, unhappy with the final results, assumed the traditional alias of Alan Smithee. Kim Myers, Christine Harnos, Charlton Chatton.

HELL'S BELLS. See *Murder by Phone.*

HELL'S CREATURES. See *Frankenstein's Bloody Terror.*

HENRY: PORTRAIT OF A SERIAL KILLER (1989) ★★★ An unsettling film attacked when released for being of questionable "moral content." That's putting it mildly. However, *Henry* is not an exploitation movie but a sincere attempt by director John McNaughton (who cowrote with Richard Fire) to profile a man who murders random victims. The nihilistic point of view, realistic psychological touches and downer ending add up to one shocking film, which never cops out to the bitter end. Michael Rooker is unforgettable as the serial killer. Also excellent are Tracy Arnold (as a young woman who falls in love with Henry) and Tom Towles as a low-life accomplice to some of Henry's crimes. (Video/Laser: MPI)

HERCULES (1959) ★★½ First in the Italian series about the son of Jupiter (Steve Reeves) using superhuman biceps in his search for the Golden Fleece. Sylva Koscina is lovely to look at, and delightful for Reeves to hold during romantic clenches, but there's little else to recommend in this poorly dubbed sword-and-sandals enterprise. Cinematography by Mario Bava. Written-directed by Pietro Francisci. Gianna Maria Canale, Arturo Dominici. Aka *The Labors of Hercules*. (Embassy; Vid-America; S/Weird; VCI; Embassy; Video Connection) (Laser)

HERCULES (1983) ★½ Stupefying Italian interpretation of Greek mythology, imitating *Clash of the Titans* by having Zeus and lesser Gods on Mt. Olympus overseeing the affairs of mortals. What makes this so unviewable is Lou Ferrigno (TV's Incredible Hulk) . . . the muscleman is a helluva hunk, but when he tries to emote, it makes you realize how great Arnie Schwarzenegger is. Writer-director Lewis Coates sinks beneath camp to become insufferably dull. Sybil Danning (her breasts threatening to pop out of her halter like overripe tomatoes), Brad Harris, Rossana Podesta and William Berger are at the mercy of wretched dialogue. The special effects are amateurish . . . One's mind gibbers insanely. (Video/Laser: MGM/UA)

HERCULES II (THE ADVENTURES OF HERCULES) (1984) ★½ He's back, that invincible Son of Zeus, and the gods can have him. Lou Ferrigno continues to grunt with macho gusto as he searches for the seven thunderbolts of Zeus, stolen by "rebel gods." So Herc the Jerc, on yet another odyssey, finds the warrior Goris, a Chewbacca-like beast; the Mire People in the Forbidden Valley; the Lair of Lakunt in the Land of the Little People; the Amazons of Scythia; and the Oracle of Death. Oh, we almost forgot to mention the Wasteland of Hisperia and Normacrill, the only substance in the entire Universe that can face Antus the Fire Monster. Ferrigno delivers his usual Method Acting. Written-directed by Lewis Coates. William Berger, Milly Carlucci, Sonia Viviani, Carlotta Green, Laura Lenzi, Margi Newton. (MGM)

HERCULES AGAINST THE MOON MEN (1964) ★★ Straight from wars on the lunar surface comes a race of moon mongrels ruled by a sorceress, Queen of the Lunar Loonies. The only man who can stop their moon-iacal deeds is Hercules, bulging to life as Alan Steel (brace yourself!). Written-directed by Giacomo Gentilomo. Jean Pierre Honore. Aka *Hercules Vs. the Moon Men* and *Maciste Vs. the Moon Men*. (Sinister/C; S/Weird; Goodtimes)

HERCULES AND THE PRINCESS OF TROY (1966) ★★½ Gordon Scott rides a mythical white horse impervious to arrows, muscles his way out of assorted death traps set by treacherous Trojan warriors, and stops a sluglike, sluggish sea creature from devouring Diana Hyland, she in a flowing white robe. Paul Stevens makes with the

jokes as Diogenes. Everett Sloane narrates. Produced-directed by Albert Band. Aka *Hercules Vs. the Sea Monster*. (Sinister/C; S/Weird)

HERCULES AND THE QUEEN OF LIDIA. See *Hercules Unchained.*

HERCULES AT THE CENTER OF THE EARTH. See *Hercules in the Haunted World.*

HERCULES GOES BANANAS. Video version of *Hercules the Movie* (Unicorn).

HERCULES IN NEW YORK. Video version of *Hercules the Movie* (MPI).

HERCULES IN THE HAUNTED WORLD (1961) ★★ "Hercules Descending" might be the subtitle for this adventure in Hell, where old Herc (beefcaker Reg Park) searches for the Magic Apple which will allow him to rescue a beauty held in bondage by evil sorcerer Christopher Lee. While the story is tired, and the action unconvincingly choreographed, there is a visual power to the fantasy sequences from director Mario Bava. Memorable images include Hercules crossing a rope above a pit of boiling lava, and an army of corpses charging while he hurls huge stones into their ranks. Aka *Hercules at the Center of the Earth, Hercules Vs. the Vampires, The Vampires Vs. Hercules* and *With Hercules to the Center of the Earth*. Eleonora Ruffo, Giorgio Ardisson, Marisa Belli. (Saturn; Rhino; Sinister/C; S/Weird)

HERCULES: THE LEGENDARY JOURNEYS (1994) ★★★ This was a series of excellent two-hour TV-movies, which were treated more like features than video fodder by producer Sam Raimi and creator Christian Williams, and which led to a more traditional one-hour follow-up series in 1995. These reflect the Raimi touch, as they are amusing, entertaining adventures crammed with special effects, monsters, sexy women, knock-down drag-out fights, anachronistic humor, and a pleasing titular hero in the form of pleasant, seemingly nonheroic Kevin Sorbo. In this version, set in "a time of myth and legend," Herc is half-human, half-God (his father is Zeus, played with tongue-in-cheek gusto by Anthony Quinn) whose wife is Tawny Kitaen. These are the superb series openers that sword-and-sorcery fans should seek out:

HERCULES AND THE CIRCLE OF FIRE: In this odyssey adventure, Hercules must find a cure for his friend's unhealing wound as well as prevent his mother Hera from taking away all fire from Earth (in the form of the Eternal Torch) and leaving it a freezing hell. There are some rousing fights with Hera's minions, a tree that turns into a talking monster, and a nearly frozen Prometheus. Tawny Kitaen, Kevin Atkinson, Stephanie Barrett.

HERCULES IN THE UNDERWORLD: The Earth opens up outside a small village and begins engulfing everyone in a fatal green flame, which forces beauty Marlee Shelton to seek Hercules' help. But Herc must consider his mortality if he is to face the demons of Hell. Directed by Bill L. Norton, this episode is full of beautiful women, three of whom try to seduce Herc in Hades by lashing their snakelike tongues around his body. The Andrew Dettman–Daniel Truly teleplay, which also features a satyrlike character, is playful but also allows Sorbo to do some serious acting as he tries to maintain his love for his wife in the face of seduction and betrayal. Marlee Shelton, Cliff Curtis.

HERCULES IN THE MAZE OF THE MINOTAUR: This final two-hour episode in the miniseries highlights many of the excellent special effects and fight sequences from the previous three shows, with a slight new plot by Andrew Dettmann and Daniel Truly involving Hercules' boredom with home life and his final trek, with a braggart pal (Michael Hurst), to a battle royal for the titular monster. A satisfying compendium directed by John Becker. Tawny Kitaen, Anthony Ray Parker, Anthony Quinn (as Zeus).

HERCULES THE MOVIE (1970) ★½ One of the oddest of the Hercules movies ever made, and Arnold Schwarzenegger's first starring role, although it would take him a decade (and more) to make up for the damage this must have wreaked on his fledgling career. (He was first billed as Arnold Strong, but later prints billed him by his real name.) Aubrey Wisberg's script approaches this comedy with the proper tongue-in-cheek attitude ("That's a fine chariot," Herc says to a forklift driver, "but where are the horses?"). However, Arthur Allan Seidelman's direction is turgid, Schwarzenegger's voice is horrendously dubbed, and the physical and verbal humor is dreary. The premise is that Zeus, ticked off because Hercules is knocking over pillars and throwing papier-mâché boulders, banishes the sinew-swelling strongman to contemporary Earth, there to undergo adventures with Arnold Stang (as comedy relief) and lovely Deborah Loomis. Somewhere in all of this is Taina Elg. James Karen, Ernest Graves. (From MPI as *Hercules in New York* and Unicorn as *Hercules Goes Bananas*) (Laser: Disc Factory)

HERCULES UNCHAINED (1960) ★★★ Mythology-happy sequel to *Hercules*, directed by Pietro Francisci. Steve Reeves returns as the biceps-bulging beefcaker and lovely Sylva Koscina is his wife with her own well-rounded muscles. Hercules loses his memory to a magical water and is a prisoner in the male harem of the Queen of Lydia. Dreadfully dubbed, but Mario Bava's camera work is excellent, and this Italian film is superior to its countless imitators. Primo Carnera does battle with Reeves. Aka *Hercules and the Queen of Lydia*. (VidAmerica; S/Weird; Sultan; Video Connection) (Laser: Nelson)

HERCULES VS. THE HYDRA. TV title for *Loves of Hercules*.

HERCULES VS. THE MOON MEN. See *Hercules Against the Moon Men*.

HERCULES VS. THE SEA MONSTER. See *Hercules and the Princess of Troy*.

HERCULES VS. THE VAMPIRES. See *Hercules in the Haunted World*.

HERE COMES THE BLOB. Original title of *Beware the Blob*.

HERE IS A MAN. See *The Devil and Daniel Webster*.

HERITAGE OF CALIGULA—AN ORGY OF SICK MINDS, THE. Video version of *The Incredible Torture Show* (Magnum).

HERITAGE OF DRACULA, THE (1970) ★★ Jesus Franco–directed vampire flicker repeats *Dracula* clichés in graphic fashion. Susan Korda, Dennis Price, Ewa Stromberg. Aka *Lesbian Vampires; Lesbian Vampires—The Heiress of Dracula; The Heiress of Dracula; The Strange Adventure of Jonathan Harker, The Sign of the Vampire* and *The Vampire Women*.

HERO AND THE TERROR (1988) ★★½ This Chuck Norris vehicle, an urban thriller with horrific overtones, is based on actor Michael Blodgett's sexually explicit novel about mass murderer Simon Moon. Norris is a dedicated L.A. cop (nicknamed Hero) haunted by nightmares of his one-on-one with Moon, during which he was almost drowned. When Moon escapes an insane asylum, Norris musters up the courage to face the mindless killer again. While there are never any doubts of the battle royal to come, Norris registers more emotional response than usual, and there's a heavy emphasis on his romance with Brynn Thayer. Directed by William Tannen. Jack O'Halloran is menacing as Terror. Steve James, Jeffrey Kramer, Ron O'Neal. (Media) (Laser: Image)

HEX (1973). Theatrical title for *The Shrieking*.

HIDDEN, THE (1987) ★★★½ Exciting sci-fi thriller set (à la *The Terminator*) in an urban environment, which adds to the versimilitude of Bob Hunt's far-fetched tale. An alien creature that enters human bodies by way of mouth and controls the mind is loose in L.A. with strange FBI agent Kyle MacLachlan hot on the ET's trail. Humans inhabited by the alien can't be killed easily, so this film is loaded with grim violence and slam-bang action sequences as MacLachlan and homicide cop Michael Nouri pursue the seemingly unstoppable killer. It's told mostly through action, with a minimum of exposition. Director Jack Sholder whisks the cast along, making this a knock-out action picture. Ed O'Ross, Clu Gulager, Claudia Christian. (Video: Media) (Laser: Media; Lumivision w/extra material)

HIDDEN II, THE (1993) ★★ This sequel is inferior to the 1987 sci-fi actioner that inspired it, with Raphael Sbarge taking the place of Kyle MacLachlan as the good-guy alien inside a human body who is on Earth to destroy an evil alien (a buglike monster) that, as a parasite, passes from body to body. The one interesting twist here is that Sbarge is slowly being consumed by a cancer that will inexorably turn him into an evil alien, and this endangers his relationship with Kate Hodge, the daughter of cop Michael Nouri from the first film. Other than that, this is predictable, clichéd action pieces with bodies being blasted full of lead, and the sluglike creature choosing new bodies. Written-directed by Seth Pinsker, *The Hidden II* never reveals itself to be much more than another lousy sequel. Jovin Montanaro, Christopher Murphy, Michael Weldon, Michael A. Nickles. (Video/Laser: New Line)

HIDDEN CITY. Working title for the serial *Darkest Africa*.

HIDDEN OBSESSION (1992) ★★ Insignificant slasher murder mystery that never builds much suspense as it falls back on such clichés as the escaped convict-maniac on the loose, a beautiful woman (Heather Thomas) alone in her country place, a thunderstorm and a strange man at the front door. There's an attempt by screenwriter David Reskin to make it a whodunit, but the identity of the real killer is barely hidden and will hardly become an obsession. John Stewart directed with little flourish, failing to evoke an adequate performance from Thomas (unconvincingly portraying a TV broadcaster) and barely getting one out of Jan-Michael Vincent. A crud dud. (Video/Laser: MCA)

HIDDEN RAGE. See *Perfect Victims.*

HIDDEN ROOM OF 1000 HORRORS. See *The Tell-Tale Heart.*

HIDDEN VALLEY, THE. See *The Land Unknown.*

HIDE AND GO SHRIEK (1987) ★★★ What begins as a clichéd slasher-film setup (eight purposely lock themselves into a furniture warehouse for a night of hide-and-seek games and love-making) develops into an interesting affair despite extreme brutality toward women. The fact the warehouse is full of mannequins allows director Skip Schoolnik to have some unusual fun. If you get through the excruciating first half, you'll find the second half, with large-breasted women stripping, rewarding enough. Donna Baltron, Brittain Frye, Annette Sinclair. (New Star) (Laser: Image)

HIDE AND SHRIEK. Video version of *American Gothic* (Virgin).

HIDEAWAY (1995) ★★★½ A fantastically effective special-effects horror tale, an extremely dark and disturbing adaptation of Dean R. Koontz's novel from director Brett (*Lawnmower Man*) Leonard. The film attempts to depict the death experience of a serial killer (Jeremy Sisto) through a series of dazzling effects that simulate that experience through a macabre time and space, where evil dominates. Meanwhile, Jeff Goldblum, after a harrowing car accident involving him, his wife (Christine Lahti) and daughter (Alicia Silverstone), also undergoes a death experience but is pulled back from the dead by doctor Alfred Molina. Now he and the serial killer (returned to life by the same doctor) are psychically linked, and each undergoes interconnected traumas including a series of bloody knife killings. The film climaxes with a wild confrontation between metaphysical forms of good and evil as Goldblum and Sisto fight to the death. The stark, moody photography is unrelenting as this grim but fascinating tale unfolds. Script by Andrew Kevin Walker and Neil Jimenez. Rae Dawn Chong, Kenneth Welsh, Mara Duronslet. (Video/Laser: Columbia Tri-star)

HIDEOUS SUN DEMON, THE (1959) ★★ Robert Clarke produced, directed and stars in this cheapie, demonstrative of the mutated-monster craze of the '50s. He portrays a physicist exposed to radiation who, under sun rays, transmutates into a scaly, homicidal creature. Clarke conveys the torment this brings to the human soul, but such sympathetic touches are secondary to the murder and mayhem he wreaks. Just plain hideous. Aka *Blood on His Lips, Terror From the Sun* and *The Sun Demon.* Patricia Manning, Del Courtney. (Rhino; Nostalgia Merchant; S/Weird)

HIDER IN THE HOUSE (1989) ★★★ Chilling and disturbing psychological thriller in which escaped killer Gary Busey hides in the home of a wealthy family (Mimi Rogers and Michael McKean), spying on them and becoming obsessed with intervening in their affairs. Directed by Matthew Patrick. Candy Hutson, Christopher Kinder. (Vestron) (Laser: Image)

HIGH DESERT KILL (1989) ★★ Three mountain hunters and an old-timer in the New Mexico highlands are subjected to terror from an unseen alien presence. Old sci-fi hands will quickly see that the humans are being experimented on by Mr. E.T. Bad Creature. Chuck Connors is good as the old man and Marc Singer strikes an interesting chord as a macho hunter, and some of the desert photography is striking, but it's confusing clichés. Directed by Harry Falk. Anthony Geary. (MCA)

HIGH FREQUENCY (1988) ★★ Oddball high-tech Italian-produced thriller, with deeply psychological overtones of suspicion and paranoia, in which Vincent Spano, a satellite station operator in the Alps, witnesses a murder and uncovers a Washington D.C.–based spy ring through strange visual transmissions he receives at his snowbound, isolated post. With the help of a young boy (Oliver Benny) he communicates with via radio, he closes in on the ring. Director Faliero Rosati (who conceived the idea and coauthored the script) is less interested in the mystery than in Spano's reaction to his isolation, the communications problems that arise, and the warm relationship Spano builds with the youth via long-distance. Some questions remain unanswered in this study of human behavior only thinly disguised as a mystery. Anne Canovas, David Brandon, Maurizio Onadoni. (MCG)

HIGHLANDER (1986) ★★★★ Stupendous fantasy-adventure, directed with great imagination by Russell Mulcahy, who employs a fluid camera to tell this cosmic-level story about a race of immortals who duel over the centuries with magical swords to claim "The Prize." This covers four centuries by cross-cutting between past and present to dramatize the growth of a Scotsman (Christopher Lambert) trained by mentor Sean Connery. Their common enemy is Kurgen, a malevolent immortal. The fights are brilliantly staged in this stylish screen fantasy. Watch for the great stairway sword duel. Roxanne Hart, Clancy Brown. (HBO) (Laser: Image)

HIGHLANDER 2: THE QUICKENING (1991) ★★ Australian director Russell Mulcahy is a visual stylist and once again he dazzles with camera movement combined with well-choreographed swordfights as the immortal warriors of the planet Zeist battle each other for the power on Earth. Back are Christopher Lambert as Macleod and Sean Connery as his teacher Ramirez, resurrected from the dead to help fight Katana (Michael Ironside). The botched plot, which never makes clear the rules by which the immortals function, involves the depleted ozone layer in the 21st century, a barrier around Earth that has created perpetual night, a scheme between an Earth corporation and Katana, and a pretty woman (Virginia Madsen) thrown in for a perfunctory romance. (Video/Laser: Columbia Tristar)

HIGHLANDER 3: THE FINAL DIMENSION (1995) ★★ Although this Canadian-French-British production avoids the claptrap junk of the second feature in this fantasy-adventure series, and gets back to *Highlander* basics as established in the opening actioner directed by Russell Mulcahy, it is nevertheless a disappointing effort in dramatizing the moody, melancholy immortal man Connor MacLeod (Christopher Lambert, still a strangely attractive and sometimes mysterious screen presence) as he squares off in duels against a new archenemy named Kane. Mario Van Peebles plays Kane with all the stops off, curling his lip, sneering and popping off a few quips when he isn't chopping heads off to gain more power from other immortals, but it's strictly a one-dimensional character caught in a

mess of a plot as concocted by Paul Ohl. It was directed darkly by British TV director Andy Morahan under the original title of *Highlander 3: The Sorcerer*, but Morahan should have spent more time with the action sequences and less with mood. The sword combat is repetitious and without the energy or fascination that Mulcahy gave it in the opener. Deborah Unger, Mako, Mark Neufeld. (Video/Laser: Columbia)

HIGHLANDER 3: THE SORCERER. See *Highlander 3: The Final Dimension*.

HIGH RISE. See *Someone's Watching Me!*

HIGH SPIRITS (1988) ★★½ Madcap comedy set in a drafty Irish castle which owner Peter O'Toole turns into a "haunted" tourist attraction. Writer-director Neil Jordan (*The Company of Wolves*) keeps the slender idea afloat like so much ghostly ectoplasm by having riotous characters flapping about like the Three Stooges. The players (O'Toole as a balmy Irishman, Steve Guttenberg as an American with a yen for 200-year-old ghost Daryl Hannah, and Beverly D'Angelo as Guttenberg's sexy wife) bolster the spectral elements. It will certainly lift your—ahem—spirits. Jennifer Tilly, Peter Gallagher, Liam Neeson. (Media) (Laser: Image)

HIGHWAY TO HELL (1991) ★★★ Imaginative "black comedy" in which Chad Lowe and Kristy Swanson take a desert shortcut to Vegas. But it's a time-space continuum to Hell, where "Hell Cop" C. J. Graham kidnaps Swanson, and Lowe pursues in his beat-up coupe to Hell City. It's nonstop action-mayhem, puns, jokes about death, and the Devil as Beezle (Patrick Bergin, who brings comedy to the role). Plenty of pizzazz/energetic direction by Ate De Jong. There's such mind-blowing set pieces as a roadside café for the dead, a hall where famous evil men sit and bore each other, the river Styx, and severed hands that serve as "handcuffs." Adam Storke, Pamela Gidley, Robert Farnsworth. (Video: HBO)

HILLS HAVE EYES, THE (1977) ★★★ A man's skull is split open with a crowbar; a caveman mutant rips the head off a canary and drinks its blood; a German shepherd rips open a man's foot and throat; a knife plunges into a twitching torso; a man is tied to a yucca plant, drenched in gasoline and set aflame; a baby is kidnapped and prepared for barbecue. And that's during the prologue . . . yes, it's fun and games from Wes Craven, that modern intellectual who gave us *Last House on the Left*. Craven's screenplay has a Cleveland family searching for a desert mine when it is attacked by degenerate cavemen and -women who carry walkie-talkies and cackle with homicidal glee. This pandering plunge into depravity and death does, however, have a social comment: When innocent people resort to violence, they become no better than their nemeses. John Steadman, Dee Wallace, Susan Lanier, Martin Speer, Robert Houston, James

Whitworth, Michael Berryman. (Magnum; Harmony Vision) (Laser: Image)

HILLS HAVE EYES II, THE (1984) ★★★ Back we go into Wes Craven territory, those hills around Yucca Valley where young folks inevitably meet their deaths at the hands of barbaric cannibals. A busload of eight youthful ones is stranded—among them a survivor of the original film plus a reformed cannibal from that same movie, now a vegetarian. What we get is a rock crushing a cyclist's head, a spear into a human chest cavity, a hatchet into a brain and other grisly deaths ending up in a charnel house of corpses. One of two survivors is blind, so writer-director Craven gets to play *Wait Until Dark* too. James Whitworth and Michael Berryman fare best as the bone-chompers. (HBO; Republic)

HISTORY OF SCI-FI TELEVISION, A. See *Forty Years of Science Fiction Television.*

HITCHER, THE (1986) ★★★ Psycho-killer movie with such ill-defined motives and surreal plotting that the easiest way to watch is to accept it as a nightmare from which one can't wake up. David Howell, driving across Texas, picks up hitchhiker John Ryder (Rutger Hauer) to become the victim of Hauer's conspiracy to make him look guilty of grisly murders. Howell goes through harrowing experiences, with Hauer involving him with police and then protecting him from capture. There's an undercurrent of homosexual masochism in Eric Red's terse script with images of chains and leather, and a weird psychic link between the two men. There's a human finger on a plate of French fries, a woman tied between trucks and shotgun murders. Many find this despicable, others are intrigued by its enigmas. Directed by Robert Harmon. Jennifer Jason Leigh, Henry Darrow. (Video/Laser: HBO)

HOBGOBLINS (1987) ★½ Some little critters escape from a vault to terrorize citizens. Jeffrey Culver, Tom Bartlett. Directed by Rick Sloane. (Trans World)

HOCUS POCUS (1993) ★★½ Witches who keep alive by sucking up the life essence of little children? Doesn't sound like a promising Disney premise, but since it's played as a comedy, with the trio of witches etched by Bette Midler, Sarah Jessica Parker and Kathy Najimy, this comes off as a pleasing grue. Described as "The Three Stooges on Broomsticks," *Hocus Pocus* was directed by Kenny Ortega from a script by co-producer Mick Garris and producer David Kirschner and is set in Salem, MA, where the tricky threesome is conjured up by teenager Omri Katz. (Video/Laser: Disney)

HOLLOWGATE (1988) ★ Producers Richard Pepin and Joseph Merhi would prefer you forget about this early effort; it's about as rank as they get. Four kids on a Halloween spree meet a killer (Addison Randall) at a ranch called Hollowgate. He's a kid gone psycho because his sadistic father beat him up on Halloween, so he terrorizes the foursome and finally feeds one of them to his Golden Retrievers. Golden Retrievers as killer canines? It's just one of many amateurish convulsions this worthless movie goes through before the surviving woman (Katrina Alexy) ends up in a psycho ward. There ain't no justice in brainless horror movies. Richard Dry, J. J. Miller, George Cole. Written-directed by Ray Dizazzo. (City Lights)

HOLLYWOOD CHAINSAW HOOKERS (1987) ★★★ This campy spoof depicts—hold your breath—a cult of chainsaw-sacrifice worshipers with a demented, pot-bellied guru (Gunnar Hansen, Leatherface in *The Texas Chainsaw Massacre*) and sexually-charged prostitutes who murder in blood-spattered orgies. Script is credited to Dr. S. Carver and B. J. Nestles, who are really director Fred Olen Ray and writer T. L. Lankford. This "Savage Cinema" production, loaded with bare breasts and clumsily simulated sex, is shaped as a private eye thriller as shamus Jack Chandler (Jay Richardson) looks for a missing teenager. Don't miss the Virgin Dance of the Double Chainsaws! The closing credits promise a sequel: *Student Chainsaw Nurses*. Michelle Bauer, Linnea Quigley, Dawn Wildsmith. Ray is now deserving of an anthropological study. (Camp) (Laser: Roan Group)

HOLLYWOOD GHOST STORIES (1986) ★★ Pseudodocumentary about Hollywood stars whose ghosts have reportedly haunted Tinseltown, including spectral sightings of George Reeves and Valentino. Sexy German actress Elke Sommer talks about a haunted house she once lived in. Narrated by John Carradine. Directed by James Forsher. (Warner Bros.)

HOLLYWOOD HAUNTING. ★★ Edward Mulhare hosts this excursion into the people who allegedly haunt Hollywood, such as Jean Harlow, Lionel Barrymore, Harry Houdini and other stars. A séance is held to raise the spirit of John Wayne. (Video: MPI)

HOLLYWOOD'S NEW BLOOD (1988) ★★ Ghosts from hell haunt a film crew working in the movie capital. Directed by James Shyman. Bobby Johnson, Francine Lapensee. (Video Treasures)

HOLLYWOOD STRANGLER. Video version of *Don't Answer the Phone* (Active; Video Treasures).

HOLLYWOOD STRANGLER MEETS THE SKID ROW SLASHER, THE (1979) ★½ One sleazy slasher flick, trying to pass itself off as a psychological study of a serial killer who photographs prostitutes and then strangles them. The strangler (Pierre Agostino) is searching for a "pure" woman. Meanwhile, the Skid Row Slasher kills winos and then runs to cleanse the spirit. It's one murder after the other, each unconvincingly staged, providing elongated glimpses at nude bodies. Although direction is credited to Wolfgang Schmidt, Ray Dennis Steckler has admitted he made this in rundown sections of L.A. It's thoroughly depressing, and you want to take a shower after seeing it. Carolyn Brandt. (Mascot; Program Releasing Corp.; from Regal as *The Model Killer* and Active as *Hollywood Strangler*)

HOLOCAUST 2000. Video version of *The Chosen* (Vestron).

HOLY TERROR. Video version of *Alice, Sweet Alice* (FHS).

HOMECOMING NIGHT. See *Night of the Creeps.*

HOMEGEIST. Video of *Boarding House* (Air).

HOMEWRECKER (1992) ★★½ After his attempt to create a nuclear-weapons-system computer ends in disaster, scientist Robby Benson decides to reprogram Star Shield with a woman's personality named "Lucy" (voice by Kate Jackson). Gradually, "she" falls in love with Benson and gets so jealous when he reestablishes a relationship with his estranged wife that she turns homicidal. This TV-movie, written by Eric Harlacher and director Fred Walton, works neither as a sensitive love story between man and machine nor as a sci-fi horror story about technology gone awry. Sarah Rose Karr. (Paramount)

HONEY, I BLEW UP THE KID (1992) ★★★½ This follow-up to *Honey, I Shrunk the Kids* is a rollicking delight bringing back Rick Moranis' daffy inventor Wayne Szalinski, who is working on a secret project that results in the enlargement of his two-year-old son. The kid reaches a height of 50 feet and walks down Glitter Gulch in Las Vegas with his brother and his girlfriend in his pocket. The oversized effects are marvelous and the film unfolds at an amusing clip under the direction of Randal Kleiser. Lloyd Bridges, Ken Tobey, John Shea, twins Daniel and Joshua Shalikar, Marcia Strassman, Robert Oliveri. (Video/Laser: Disney)

HONEY, I SHRUNK THE KIDS (1989) ★★★ Wacky Walt Disney fantasy-comedy that shows the comic side to *The Incredible Shrinking Man* and his household milieu. Rick Moranis portrays a nerdy but lovable inventor who can't get his electromagnet shrinking machine to work. And when it does, it's pointed at a group of youngsters, who are made so small they can't be seen floating in a bowl of Cheerios. The children have to make their way across the grassy backyard to home so fumbling dad can restore them to human size. Their adventures are highlighted by a ride on a bumblebee, a friendly and heroic ant, a killer scorpion and other things too large and small to mention. It's a joyous, innocuous adventure that scripters Ed Naha and Tom Schulman make palatable for young and old. Directed by Joe Johnston. Matt Frewer, Marcia Strassman, Kristine Sutherland. (Laser/Video: Disney)

HONEYMOON HORROR (1982) ★½ Clone of *Friday the 13th,* amateurish in its effects—so bad, in fact, when an ax sinks into a human's brain, it falls out before the cut. At Honeymoon Cove, on Lover's Island in Texas, a husband finds his wife with another man and is trapped in a fire. Later, three pairs of newlyweds stop at the rundown resort to frolick, but meet bloody demises at the hands of a badly burned maniac. William F. Pecchi steals the movie (a mean achievement) as a potbellied redneck sheriff who chomps on an old cigar. No honeymoon, this. Directed by Harry Preston. (Sony)

HONEY, WE SHRUNK OURSELVES (1997) ★★ If you count the "Honey" amusement attraction at the Epcot Center, this makes the fourth effort in the Disney comedy franchise about an absentminded, utterly nerdy inventor (Wayne Szalinski, as played by Rick Moranis) who always succeeds in either reducing or increasing the size of human beings, depending on how his atomizer machine control is set. First came *Honey, I Shrunk the Kids,* created by Stuart Gordon, Brian Yuzna, and Ed Naha (a triumvirate of horror aficionados), followed by *Honey, I Blew Up the Kid.* Now, under the direction of Dean Cundey, we have Moranis getting moronic with brother Stuart Pankin and reducing his Tiki-god statute to miniature size. But, of course, screenwriters Karey Kilpatrick, Joel Nell Scovell, and Joel Hodgson rig it so the fellas also get reduced to near nothingness, then they contrive to have the wives (Eve Gordon and Robin Bartlett) reduced, too. Now the four miniaturized adults go through the expected misadventures of somehow telling the kids (who have taken over the house for a wild-party weekend) what's happened. Among those kids are Allison Mack, Jake Richardson, and Bug Hall. This is about as lightweight as the characters as they take a roller-coaster ride, climb up a wicker chair, hide in a roach motel box from an attacking cockroach, and make friends with a benevolent daddy longlegs spider. If it has one funny scene, it's when Moranis and Pankin fall into a dish of gooey onion dip while the kids are dunking their potato chips into the white mess. Another kind-of-funny scene has the spider climbing up a wall while the two wives hang onto one of its threads, exchanging ingredients for a recipe. In short, it's a harmless way to spend 75 minutes. And thanks to the Disney guys for keeping it as mercifully short as they did . . . but beware: you may be mortally shocked when Morans refers to that awful-looking thing on the living floor as a "roach turd." In a Disney movie? (Touchstone)

HOOK (1991) ★★★ Steven Spielberg's paean

to J. M. Barrie's *Peter Pan* finds Robin Williams portraying Pan as an adult who has forgotten his adventures in Neverland and doesn't know how to fly anymore. It's overflowing with warmth, sentiment and comedy-adventure as Williams forsakes his business as a financial "pirate" to return to Neverland to recover his kidnapped son and daughter from Captain Hook. As the blustering pirate, Dustin Hoffman so well submerges himself into the part that one forgets it's Hoffman. Williams is perfect for this child-adult role, because what is he but a grown-up kid. A brightly lit, opulent production that really comes to life when Williams flies, and when young pirates do battle with adult pirates aboard Hook's ship. Julia Roberts is an okay Tinkerbell and Bob Hoskins is a standout as the pirate Smee. Maggie Smith, Caroline Goddall, Amber Scott, Charlie Korsmo. (Video/Laser: Columbia TriStar)

HORRIBLE DR. HICHCOCK, THE (1962) ★★★½ There was a time when the subtlety of suggestion earmarked good horror films, and such attributes as music, atmosphere and the unseen played as big a role as monsters and mad doctors. In this Italian thriller (which reeks with a morbid atmosphere and a hint of depravity beneath the face of Robert Flemying, a strange doctor of London 1885) Barbara Steele is the lovely innocent in constant peril once inside the decaying mansion of Dr. Hichcock. More is suggested than shown, although we know early on that the doctor once gave his first wife blood transfusions, and has kept her coffin inside his locked laboratory. Steele, in the kind of role that earned her the title Queen of Horror, is delicious to watch as a haunted, terrorized beautiful woman, flitting through dank corridors and pursued by wind, lightning and something always just out of the frame. Scripted by Julyan Perry, it was directed by Riccardo Freda (as Robert Hampton for the U.S.) with a grand appreciation of Gothic style and heightened hysteria. Roman Vlad provided a chilling music score. The sequel was *The Ghost.* Aka *The Frightening Secret of Dr. Hichcock, The Horrible Secret of Dr. Hichcock, The Terrible Secret of Dr. Hichcock, Raptus, The Secret of Dr. Hichcock,* and *The Terror of Dr. Hichcock.* Teresa Fitzgerald, Montgomery Glenn, Harriet White. (Republic; S/Weird; Sinister/C; Filmfax)

HORRIBLE HORROR (1986) ★★★ Hosted by the great TV host Zacherley, this contains clips from 50 "vintage" examples of "the best and the worst in horror and sci-fi." Included are *Santa Claus Conquers the Martians, Glen or Glenda?, The Snow Creature, King of the Zombies,* etc. (Goodtimes)

HORRIBLE HOUSE ON THE HILL. See *Devil Times Five.*

HORRIBLE ORGIES OF COUNT DRACULA. See *Reincarnation of Isabel.*

HORRIBLE SECRET OF DR. HICHCOCK, THE. See *The Horrible Dr. Hichcock.*

HORROR! (1963). See *Children of the Damned.*

HORROR AND SEX. See *Night of the Bloody Apes.*

HORROR CHAMBER OF DR. FAUSTUS, THE (1958) ★★★ Mad doctor Pierre Brasseur believes he can restore his daughter's marred beauty by grafting on the faces of kidnapped lasses. This French film, directed by Georges Franju, who collaborated with mystery writers Pierre Boileau and Thomas Narcejac, has numerous plot holes, as do the faces of victims when the doc gets through. The grafting sequences have an overabundance of hideous detail but that's what gives this cult favorite its charm. Aka *House of Dr. Rasanoff.* (Sinister/C; S/Weird; Filmfax; from Interama as *Eyes Without a Face*) (Laser)

HORROR CONVENTION. Video version of *Nightmare in Blood* (Imperial).

HORROR CREATURES OF THE LOST PLANET. See *Vampire Men of the Lost Planet.*

HORROR CREATURES OF THE PREHISTORIC PLANET. See *Vampire Men of the Lost Planet.*

HORROR CREATURES OF THE RED PLANET. See *Vampire Men of the Lost Planet.*

HORROR EXPRESS (1972) ★★★ All aboard for terror and destruction! Cataclysmic evil emanates from the remains of a prehistoric monster being railed to Moscow via the trans-Siberian Railroad. The will of the monster invades the minds of the passengers because it needs to build a starship to return to its own galaxy. British-Spanish chiller with superior production values and gory effects. Directed by Eugenio Martia. Christopher Lee is an archeologist, Peter Cushing a scientist and Telly Savalas a Hungarian cop. Aka *Panic in the Trans-Siberian Train.* (Media; Sinister/C; S/Weird; Goodtimes; Prism; Interglobal; Worldvision; Filmfax)

HORROR FARM. Video version of *Daddy's Deadly Darling* (HQV).

HORROR FROM BEYOND, THE. See *Blood Thirst.*

HORROR HOSPITAL (1973) ★★½ Emergency! Acting coach needed in Ward B to restrain Michael Gough from going bonkers in a fright mask as he tampers with patients' brains and cuts off their heads. Gory British import (aka *Computer Killers*) written-directed by Anthony Balch, produced by Richard Gordon. Calling all film doctors . . . (MPI; Gorgon; from Bingo as *Doctor Bloodbath*)

HORROR HOTEL (1960) ★★½ British thriller reeking with atmosphere in crisp black-and-white photography. The setting is a New England community taken over by a witches' coven. Into the sinister town come a young man and woman seeking one of the coven's victims. Aka *City of the Dead*, this was directed by John Llewellyn Moxey from a George Baxt script. Patricia Jessel, Christopher Lee, Betta St. John, Valentine Dyall. (United; S/Weird; Amvest; Filmfax; Sinister/C) (Laser: Elete)

HORROR HOTEL MASSACRE. See *Eaten Alive*.

HORROR MAN, THE. See *The Tell-Tale Heart*.

HORROR OF DEATH. See *The Asphyx*.

HORROR OF DRACULA (1958) ★★★½ Hammer shocker, scripted by Jimmy Sangster and directed by Terence Fisher, was responsible for reviving Bram Stoker's classic vampire villain. This Gothic production brought international acclaim (and box office receipts) to the British studio, which continued in the same vein for 20 years. Christopher Lee captured the more subtle nuances of the Transylvanian count and the film is punctuated by its own miasma of Gothic mistiness. Peter Cushing essayed the Van Helsing role. Sometimes known as *Dracula 1958*. Michael Gough, Melissa Stribling, Carol Marsh. (Video/Laser: Warner Bros.)

HORROR OF FRANKENSTEIN (1970) ★★ Writer-director Jimmy Sangster, who cowrote with Jeremy Burnham, demonstrates less subtlety and more black comedy in this lowbrow entry in the Hammer Frankenstein series. Ralph Bates, as the industrious Baron, is no replacement for Peter Cushing and David Prowse (Darth Vader's body in *Star Wars*) is no surrogate for Christopher Lee as the Monster. The least effective of the Hammer outpourings. Veronica Carlson, Kate O'Mara, Dennis Price. (HBO)

HORROR OF PARTY BEACH, THE (1964) ★★½ Bikini beach girls are ruthlessly attacked, the flesh ripped from their succulent bodies, by *Black Lagoon*-style amphibians created from radioactive waste dumped in the ocean. Wonderfully inept as the creatures crash a slumber party and carry the girls away—from the Neanderthal production values to the Stoned Age cast headed by John Scott and Alice Lyon to the nondirection of Del Tenney. A classic of superior ineptitude. Aka *Invasion of the Zombies*. (Prism)

HORROR OF THE BLOOD MONSTERS. Video version of *Vampire Men of the Lost Planet* (VidAmerica; Republic; Super).

HORROR OF THE ZOMBIES (1973) ★★ Third entry in the Spanish "Blind Dead" series, aka *The Ghost Galleon*, with writer-director Amando De Ossorio at the helm, features the long-dead Templar priests returning as rotting, cloaked corpses aboard a Spanish galleon that floats in a mysterious "other dimensional" fog, trapping seafarers. The victims are two buxom babes adrift in a motorboat, soon engulfed by the flesh-munching skeletal knights. Next comes

a wealthy sporting goods magnate, a goofball scientist and more dames—fodder for the flesh fondlers. Effects are cheesy, but De Ossorio does inject atmosphere. Maria Perschy, Jack Taylor, Barbara Rey, Carlos Lemos. (Super; World's Worst Video/VidAmerica; Video Tours)

HORROR ON SNAPE ISLAND. Video version of *Tower of Evil*.

HORROR PLANET (1981) ★ Awful British ripoff of *Alien*, with touches of *Friday the 13th* and *Dracula* thrown in. On a research lab on a far-flung planet in some faraway galaxy, a bug-eyed monster impregnates researcher Judy Geeson. With superhuman strength she vampirizes her research workers, pausing to give birth to mini-monsters. A bloody mess, literally, with plenty of weird electronic noises to keep you on edge. Nick Maley, who cowrote with Gloria Maley, also did the sickening gore effects and creatures. Directed by Norman J. Warren. Robin Clarke, Jennifer Ashley, Stephanie Beacham, Victoria Tennant. Also called *Inseminoid*. (Embassy) (Laser: Image)

HORROR SHOW, THE (1989) ★★ Made as *House III* by producer Sean Cunningham, then strangely retitled, this is a minimally effective tale, weak on all levels and built with poor foundations. L.A. cop Lucas McCarthy (Lance Henriksen) helps to put serial killer Max Jenke (the growling Brion James) into the electric chair, but Jenke's spirit returns to terrorize McCarthy with hallucinations. Jenke's target is the policeman's family—wife Rita Taggart and daughter Deedee Pfeiffer. An unending series of fumbled setups, anticlimactic and uninvolving. The film finally hits rock bottom when a turkey on a platter comes to life with Jenke's face on it. Directed by James Isaac. Aron Eisenberg, Matt Clark, Lawrence Tierney, Alvy Moore. (New World; MGM/UA)

HORRORS OF BLOOD ISLAND. See *Beast of Blood*.

HORRORS OF THE RED PLANET. Video version of *The Wizard of Mars* (Star Classics; Genesis; Republic).

HORROR STAR. See *Frightmare* (1981).

HOSPITAL MASSACRE (1982) ★★★ Like *Halloween II*, this is set entirely in a city hospital in which a mad slasher is on the loose, murdering without discrimination. Director Boaz Davidson's stylishness is weakened by a chamberpot of clichés plotted by Marc Behm. Still, there's a greater sense of fun than in most slasher flicks, thanks to a cast overemphasizing hysteria and paranoia. A flashback shows a 1961 Valentine's Day murder witnessed by an adolescent girl. Flash forward to Barbi Benton entering "massacre hospital" for a check-up—and the body count climbs. There are effective images of horror and death, and Davidson captures an eerie ambience that takes one's attention off the story holes. Barbi does well with her characterless role and is the only non-suspicious character. Chip Lucia, Jon Van Ness, Guy Austin, Lanny Duncay and John Warner Williams always look and sound as if one of them is the killer. Nice music by Arlon Ober, even if it is all clichés. Aka *Be My Valentine, or Else, X-Ray* and *Ward 13* (MGM/UA; Embassy).

HOSPITAL OF TERROR. Video version of *Beyond the Living* (World's Worst; Super Sitters).

HOSTAGE—DALLAS. See *Getting Even*.

HOUND OF THE BASKERVILLES, THE (1939) ★★★ First film to team Basil Rathbone and Nigel Bruce as Sherlock Holmes and Dr. Watson is not a masterpiece but still a good attempt to recapture the flavor of Sir Arthur Conan Doyle's novel. Setting is the foggy moors surrounding Baskerville Hall and the curse that taints its inhabitants. Directed by Sidney Lanfield. Richard Greene, Lionel Atwill, John Carradine, Wendy Barrie. (Video/Laser: CBS/Fox)

HOUND OF THE BASKERVILLES, THE (1959) ★★★ Hammer's version of the Conan Doyle classic stars Peter Cushing as the Baker Street sleuth, Sherlock Holmes, and Andre Morell as the winsome Watson. This is more effective than the Rathbone-Bruce treatment and will grip your interest with its hellish hound, mist-bound swamps and devious characters, even if the story about a family living under a dreaded curse is familiar. Directed by Terence Fisher. Christopher Lee is Baskerville. Miles Malleson, David Oxley. (CBS/Fox; Magnetic; United Artists)

HOUND OF THE BASKERVILLES, THE (1983) ★★★ British remake of the classic Conan Doyle horror novel set on the English moors, with Sherlock Holmes (Ian Richardson) and Dr. Watson (Donald Churchill) hurrying to the aid of Sir Henry Baskerville, plagued by a family curse and a "hound from Hell" that stalks the bogs, tearing out human throats. Martin Shaw portrays Baskerville, Denholm Elliott is Dr. Mortimer and Ronald Lacey is Inspector Lestrade. Directed by Douglas Hickox. Nicholas Clay, Brian Blessed, Glynis Barber. (Laser: Japanese)

HOUNDS OF ZAROFF. See *The Most Dangerous Game* (from the producers of *King Kong*).

HOURGLASS (1995) ★★½ This low-budget direct-to-video feature, produced by Steven Paul, has a lot of ragged edges, but it is also an unusually gritty portrait of the psychology of revenge, with mild slasher-killer overtones. C. Thomas Howell, who directed and cowrote the script with Darren Dalton, also stars as the owner of a fashion design company who is seduced by sultry-and-strange Sofia Shinas. He is completely suckered by this woman and sinks ever deeper into a drug-dazed, lust-filled abyss. A couple of knife murders are thrown into the plot of intrigue and deception but the real thrust is the downfall of Howell and how he finally becomes a total basket case. What's missing is more details about the underlying motive, which would have developed more interesting characters, but *Hourglass* still flows. Ed Begley Jr. (as a suspicious cop), Keifer Sutherland (in a cameo as a doctor), Timothy Bottoms, Terry Kiser, Anthony Clark. (Live)

HOUR WHEN DRACULA COMES, THE. See *Black Sunday* (1960).

HOUSE AT THE END OF THE WORLD (1964). See *Tomb of Ligeia*.

HOUSE AT THE END OF THE WORLD, THE (1965). See *Die, Monster, Die*.

HOUSE: DING DONG, YOU'RE DEAD (1986) ★★ Sean S. Cunningham's production blends supernatural and horror but can't decide whether to play it straight or zoom into camp. Hence, it unwinds with a troubled sense about its own soul. William Katt is mystery writer Roger Cobb, so haunted by his Vietnam experiences that he moves into a sinister Gothic house (where his aunt committed suicide) to write his memoirs. He relives his 'Nam experiences in flashbacks, a bug-eyed monster is coming out of a closet to get him, and he's off into another dimension in search of his long-missing son. The film, directed by Steve Miner, vacillates between stark thrills and comedic laughs played straight-faced by George Wendt (as a neighbor), Kay Lenz (as Katt's ex-wife, who still loves him) and Richard Moll as a soldier returned from the dead. *House* is a mood piece of loosely knit vignettes, vague characters and a sense of displacement. Call it weak foundations. (New World) (Laser: Image)

HOUSE II: THE SECOND STORY (1987) ★★ Inferior sequel in no way related to the first *House*. Director Ethan Wiley's script is neither funny nor scary as it takes on overtones of a stupid teenage comedy when Jesse MacLaughlin, dead 60 years, is dug up by his great great nephew. Royal Dano, in "dead man" makeup, plays it cantankerous and ornery as malevolent forces of the dead pursue a priceless Aztec crystal skull with magical powers. The protagonists are nerds who run around with a friendly worm with the face of a dog and a baby pterodactyl. Arye Gross, Jonathan Stark, Bill Maher, Lar Park Lincoln, Amy Yasbeck (the mermaid in *Splash Too*). (New World) (Laser: Image)

HOUSE III. See *The Horror Show*.

HOUSE IV: HOME DEADLY HOME (1991) ★★ William Katt is back from the original *House* as Roger Cobb, who refuses to sell his old family manor because it was built over a sacred Indian spring. Cobb's soul is trapped there after his death in a car accident, and it's up to wife Terri

Treas and crippled daughter Melissa Clayton to protect the spring from evil brother Scott Burkholder. Sean Cunningham's production, directed by Lewis Abernathy, vacillates between a sensitive portrayal of Cobb's wife and daughter coping with his death and a kitchen-sink horror thriller with an abundance of special effects. Ned Romero stands out as a wise old Indian. Denny Dillon, Dabbs Greer, Ned Bellamy. (New Line) (Laser: Image)

HOUSEBOAT HORROR (1989) ★★ Lake Infinity, where a crew is photographing a music video, is the setting for a series of slasher killings in this Australian imitation of *Friday the 13th*. Directed by Kendal Flanagan. Alan Dale, Christine Jeston.

HOUSEKEEPER, THE (1985) ★★★ This adaptation of Ruth Rendell's novel *A Judgment in Stone* is a tour de force for Rita Tushingham: Under Ousama Rawi's direction, she superbly portrays a psychotic woman who suffocates her cruel father, then moves to America to become a maid for a wealthy family. She captures the antisocial traits of a sexually repressed woman who disintegrates into a diabolical murderess. Ross Petty, Tom Kneebone, Shelly Peterson. (Lorimar; from Cineplex Odeon as *A Judgment in Stone*) (Laser: Image)

HOUSE OF BLOOD. See *Mansion of the Doomed*.

HOUSE OF CRAZIES. TV version of *Asylum*.

HOUSE OF DARK SHADOWS (1970) ★★ Daytime serial *Dark Shadows* prompted producer Dan Curtis to make two features, of which this is the first. (*Night of Dark Shadows* was a sequel.) Jonathan Frid re-creates Barnabas Collins, who rises from the grave and does the Dracula bit, turning residents of the family mansion into "blood brothers." Joan Bennett is Elizabeth, a fellow Collins. Barnabas ages to 150 years in one sequence, an effect achieved by Dick Smith. Produced-directed by Curtis, scripted by Sam Hall and Gordon Russell. Grayson Hall, Kathryn Leigh Scott, Roger Davis, John Carlen. (Video/Laser: MGM/UA)

HOUSE OF DEATH (1981) ★★ This slasher flick, made in and around Shelby, NC, depicts teen-agers frolicking at a carnival, then telling stories in Sunset Cemetery. That's when the machete-wielding killer attacks. You get a girl with an arrow in her shoulder who is decapitated on a merry-go-round, a double decapitation in a truck, a guy trapped in a grave whose hands are cut off, and other stabbings, slittings and torso penetrations. Also, two dead bodies floating down a river. Not a bad body count. And let's not forget the creamy breasts of the girls. Directed by David Nelson with total indifference. Susan Kiger, William T. Hicks. (Video Gems; Virgin Vision)

HOUSE OF DIES DREAR, THE (1984) ★★★ Quasisupernatural TV-movie, produced by the Children's TV Workshop and directed by Allan Goldstein, depicts the plight of young Howard E. Rollins Jr. when he and his family move into an old rural Ohio home once owned by a Dutchman who helped slaves escape through the pre–Civil War underground. The house's reputation for being haunted results in a spectral-like image scaring the black family half to death on a stormy night as well as the appearance of an old man, Pluto, who could be a ghost too. Based on a Virginia Hamilton novel, this is distinguished by a climax that spoofs *Night of the Living Dead*. Joe Seneca, Clarence Williams III, Moses Gunn (as cantankerous River Lewis Darrow). (Home Vision/Public Media; Pied Piper)

HOUSE OF DOOM (1934). See *The Black Cat*.

HOUSE OF DRACULA (1945) ★★★★ Sequel to *House of Frankenstein*, in which Universal amalgamated its popular monsters for maximum box-office potential. You get Lon Chaney Jr. as the Wolf Man, John Carradine as Dracula and Glenn Strange as the Frankenstein Monster. There's a hunchbacked nurse, Lionel Atwill as a police inspector, and an assortment of creepy characters. This romp was to mark the finale to the studio's pseudoserious monster movies, and paved the way for Abbott and Costello horror comedies. Directed by Erle C. Kenton, written by Edward T. Lowe. Jane Adams, Martha O'Driscoll, Ludwig Stossel, Skelton Knaggs, Dick Dickinson. Makeup by Jack Pierce. Aka *The Wolf Man's Cure*. (Video/Laser: MCA)

HOUSE OF DREAMS (1964) Robert Berry gets writer's block and then sees into a future that appears to have many unpleasantries waiting. Berry also directed. Pauline Elliott, Charlene Bradley, Lance Bird, David Goodnow. (LSVideo)

HOUSE OF DR. RASANOFF. See *The Horror Chamber of Dr. Faustus*.

HOUSE OF EVIL (1968) ★ One of four low-budget features made with Boris Karloff two years before his death. The film was caught up in courtroom battles after the death of producer Luis Vergara. The Jack Hill screenplay centers on a castle equipped with a torture chamber, and "torture" is exactly what this Mexican-financed movie is. Karloff plays sinister piano music when relatives gather for the reading of the will. It turns out he's a toy maker whose playthings are endowed with a homicidal spirit. Directed by Juan Ibanez and Hill. (Sinister/C; Filmfax; from MPI as *Dance of Death* and Unicorn as *Macabre Serenade*)

HOUSE OF EVIL. Video version of *The House on Sorority Row* (Dura Vision).

HOUSE OF EVIL. TV title for *The Evil*.

HOUSE OF EXORCISM (1976) ★ What's needed here is a priest to exorcise awful imitations of *The Exorcist*, of which this Italian film is one. Excellently curved Elke Sommer brings sensuousness to her role as a possessed woman who spits out frogs! And there's Telly Savalas, doing an imitation of Kojak in search of Kolchak. Re-edited version of *Lisa and the Devil*, with new footage of Robert Alda as a priest. Aka *The Devil and the Dead*. Directed by Mario Bava. Alida Valli, Sylva Koscina. (Maljack; Amvest; from MPI as *The Devil in the House of Exorcism*)

HOUSE OF FRANKENSTEIN (1944) ★★★★ This followed *Frankenstein Meets the Wolf Man* and marks Universal's first attempt to unite its money-making monsters. For price of admission you get Lon Chaney Jr. as the Wolf Man, John Carradine as Dracula and Glenn Strange as the Frankenstein Monster. Boris Karloff is Dr. Niemann, who escapes prison with hunchback killer J. Carrol Naish to restore supernatural creatures to life. This was such a hit, it was followed by *House of Dracula*. Lionel Atwill as the inspector, Elena Verdugo as the gypsy and George Zucco as a showman. Directed by Erle C. Kenton, scripted by Edward T. Lowe. Early titles: *The Devil's Brood* and *Doom of Dracula*. (Video/Laser: MCA)

HOUSE OF FRANKENSTEIN 1997, THE (1997) ★★★ This TV-movie attempt to remold the 1945 Universal horror classic, which featured the Frankenstein Monster, the Wolf Man and Dracula, into a modern monster marathon is an oddball, very loose interpretation by telewriter J. B. White. The creatures are all there, morphing, and digitalizing themselves into familiar horror images, though in a Los Angeles setting that gives the gothic trappings a modern sensibility. "The Midnight Raptor" is what the media is calling a killer that leaves horribly mutilated bodies scattered around the City of Angels, but supernatural lore expert Dr. Shauna Kendall (played by CCH Pounder in a sex-change twist on vampire-hunting Professor Von Helsing) knows it's a "master vampire" doing the dirty work. If only practical-minded, plodding cop Vernon Coyle (Adrian Pasdar) would listen. No, he's too busy protecting (or chasing after) beautiful blonde Teri Polo, who may or may not be turning into a werewolf after she's been bitten by a wild wolf-like creature (in human form played by Richard Libertini). He could care less during the scene when they jump into bed together and do PG-rated lovemaking. The four-hour, two-parter starts at a night club–museum complex called The House of Frankenstein, where owner-curator Christian Grimes (Greg Wise, looking evil in every scene) pretends to be human when he's really a vampire, even though he looks more like a demon from hell as he flies above the city's skyscrapers on his missions of noctural death. Meanwhile, Wise's expedition to the Arctic Circle (with Miguel

Sandoval playing the henchman in charge) has found the original Frankenstein Monster in an icefield and brought the revived creature back. That creature (the facial makeup by Greg Common spins off from the Boris Karloff version) escapes into the city to be befriended by a derelict character patterned after the blind beggar in *The Bride of Frankenstein*. This is the only moment when the film has a sense of humor about itself and turns playful. Then it gets a little silly when the derelict and monster ride around the city on a bus and nobody pays much attention except one little black kid who smiles at the monster, evoking memories of the *Frankenstein* original when the monster throws a small child into a lake. Directed by Peter Werner, *The House of Frankenstein 1997* goes on and on in this vein, depicting chases through buildings and elevators, sudden attacks and violent deaths, and blending images of horror movies past with images of movies present. It's never boring but the clichés abound and one never really cares much for the characters, whether they are human or monster. However, it's all quite watchable.

HOUSE OF FREAKS. See *Dr. Frankenstein's Castle of Freaks.*

HOUSE OF FRIGHT (1960). See *Black Sunday.*

HOUSE OF FRIGHT (1961). See *The Two Faces of Dr. Jekyll.*

HOUSE OF HORRORS (1946) ★★ Rondo Hatton, who suffered from a disease of the pituitary gland and needed no makeup for his elongated, fearful face, was featured in a handful of pictures as the Creeper. In this, the first of the short-lived Universal series, Hatton is saved from death by a sculptor (Martin Kosleck) who sends him out to commit revenge murders. Hatton was an inept actor badly exploited in these shockers, which included *Pearl of Death* and *The Brute Man*. He died the year this was released. Directed by Jean Yarbrough. Made as *Joan Medford Is Missing*. Virginia Grey, Robert Lowery, Kent Taylor, Alan Napier, Bill Goodwin. (MCA)

HOUSE OF INSANE WOMEN. Video of *Exorcism's Daughter* (Sinister/C; S/Weird; Filmfax).

HOUSE OF MADNESS. See *Dr. Tarr's Torture Dungeon.*

HOUSE OF MYSTERY (1942). See *Night Monster.*

HOUSE OF SECRETS (1993) ★★★ A TV-movie remake of Clouzot's *Diabolique*, reset in New Orleans with voodoo and the walking dead—touches not found in the novel by Pierre Boileau and Thomas Narcejac, *The Woman Who Was No More*. In that thriller a man and woman plot to kill another woman. But Clouzot switched it around to two women killing one man—a more perverse idea that appealed to the French director, to those who helmed the 1974 TV remake *Reflections of Murder*, and to the makers of this low-key piece of suspense. Bruce Boxleitner, the sadistic owner of a sanitarium, becomes the target of his weak-of-heart wife (Melissa Gilbert) and former mistress (Kate Vernon), who feed him spiked lemonade and drown him in a tub. But it soon appears that his restless, vengeful spirit has returned from the grave to haunt the wife. More cannot be revealed. This version is told as a flashback by voodoo priestess Cicely Tyson to investigating cop Michael Boatman. *House of Secrets*, except for a couple of by-now classic set pieces borrowed from the Clouzot film, is handled without much style by director Mimi Leder. Originally called *Conspiracy of Terror*.

HOUSE OF SEVEN CORPSES (1972) ★ Low budgeter with a decent cast forced into a wasteland of shoddy material. John Ireland, John Carradine and Faith Domergue wander through a feeble plot about the making of a horror film in a mansion (shades of *Frankenstein '80*). A resurrected ghoul knocks off a movie producer, a couple of performers and anyone else who wanders through the script. Maybe the ghoul didn't like producer-writer-director Paul Harrison's dialogue. (Video Gems; Hollywood Home Theater)

HOUSE OF THE DAMNED (1996) ★★½ Routine possessed/haunted house melodrama from producer Roger Corman with the stars being a plethora of spectral special effects even though Greg Evigan and Alexandra Paul headline as new owners of a rural mansion taken over by supernatural forces once they move in. Their daughter (Briana Evigan, Greg's real-life daughter) reminds one a lot of *Poltergeist* and hence Brendan Broderick's script, which includes a team of ghostchasers, can't be called exactly original. Scott Levy directs it with all the traditional spooky stuff in the obvious places. Mary Kate Ryan, Eamon Draper. (New Horizons)

HOUSE OF THE DARK STAIRWAY. See *A Blade in the Dark.*

HOUSE OF THE DEAD. Video version of *The Alien Zone* (Dig that unreal estate!) (JLT Films).

HOUSE OF THE LONG SHADOWS (1983) ★★ Couched in Gothic imagery, this updated version of George M. Cohan's mystery-comedy play, *Seven Keys to Baldpate*, was based on an original novel by Earl Derr Biggers, creator of Charlie Chan. Director Peter Walker assembled Vincent Price, Christopher Lee, Peter Cushing and John Carradine to portray weirdos in the eerie mansion Bllyddpaetwr (the setting is now Wales) on the same night American writer Desi Arnaz Jr. settles into the house to write a novel within 24 hours to win a $20,000 wager with publisher Richard Todd. Thrills are played tongue-in-cheek and the violence suggestive

rather than overt. Sheila Keith is the blonde in the "long shadows." (MGM/UA)

HOUSE OF THE SEVEN CORPSES. Video version of *House of Seven Corpses.*

HOUSE OF THE YELLOW CARPET (1984) ★ The aura of a knife killer rises up from the surface of a Persian rug. Shag on you, murderer. Erland Josephson, Beatrice Romand. Directed by Carlo Lizzani. (Lightning)

HOUSE OF USHER (1960) ★★★★ Originally shot as *The Mysterious House of Usher*, Roger Corman's adaptation of Edgar Allan Poe's short story "The Fall of the House of Usher" makes excellent use of color to convey a sense of foreboding horror. Vincent Price essays Roderick Usher, a demented aristocrat who unwittingly entombed his sister alive. He spits out the scenery while the rest of the cast creeps along passageways, stares at degenerate Usher paintings and breathes Victorian decay. Scripted by Richard Matheson. (From Warner Bros. on video and laser as *The Fall of the House of Usher*)

HOUSE OF USHER, THE (1988) ★★ Unfaithful adaptation of Edgar Allan Poe's "The Fall of the House of Usher," turned into a cheapjack damsel-in-distress thriller with clichés of the "old dark house" genre. Oliver Reed, as the super-sensitive Roderick Usher, holds back none of the histrionics when Romy Windsor falls into his clutches, nor is Donald Pleasence guilty of under-restraint when he appears as a demented degenerate with a killer-drill on his hook-hand. The sickening and unnecessary murder of a child would have offended Mr. Poe—a final insult to the memory of that great writer, whose uncopyrighted material serves producer Harry Alan Towers, director Alan Birkinshaw and irreverent screen adapter Michael J. Murray. Rent Roger Corman's 1960 version—that remains the definitive movie adaptation. Rufus Swart, Norman Coombes, Anne Stradi. (Video/Laser: RCA/Columbia)

HOUSE OF WAX (1953) ★★★★ Superb remake of *Mystery of the Wax Museum*, horror in the Grand Guignol tradition, with Vincent Price as a "mad wax" museum curator/sculptor who covers victims with wax and displays them in his Chamber of Horrors. The setting is turn-of-the-century New York City, from fogbound streets to gaslit morgues. The 3-D composition lends maximum effect and there is an excellent fire sequence, as well as a memorable chase through dark streets. And, of course, the great paddle-ball scene. Frank Lovejoy is the concerned policeman, Phyllis Kirk and Carolyn Jones are among potential victims. Watch for Charles Buchinsky as the mute assistant—he later became Charles Bronson. Directed by one-eyed Andre de Toth (short in vision but long in de Toth?) and written by Crane Wilbur. Paul

Picerni, Roy Roberts. (Video/Laser: Warner Bros.)

HOUSE ON HAUNTED HILL (1959) ★★★ William Castle's best gimmick flick with Vincent Price as a sophisticated madman who invites five guests to Haunted Hill with the offer of $10,000 to anyone who can spend the night and still collect in the morning. Floating sheets, ghostly faces, skeletons, bubbling pits, doors and windows that fly open mysteriously, etc. etc. It's really great fun . . . Robb White's script even has a few genuinely frightening moments. Castle directed with his usual lack of subtlety, but here it worked. Richard Long, Elisha Cook Jr., Carol Ohmart, Carolyn Craig. (Key) (Laser: CBS/Fox, with *Attack of the 50-Foot Woman*)

HOUSE ON HAUNTED HILL (1999) ★★½ This remake of the 1959 low-budgeter directed by William Castle and starring Vincent Price starts with the original premise and its principal character but then takes off on new flights of fancy, and hence falls somewhere into a fuzzy middle ground. Not a classic, not a complete flop. Mildly entertaining, but still helplessly mediocre. Because it doesn't establish interesting characters but delights in throwing buckets of blood all over everything, it misses every opportunity to rise above its genre and only wallows in its own crudities. Geoffrey Rush, who resembles Vincent Price in some ways, portrays the leading role: Steven Price, an entertainment-world entrepreneur who provides thrill-seekers hair-raising rides on a roller coaster and in an elevator attraction. He's sleazy but he knows a good scare. Price and faithless wife, Famke Janssen, throw a party in a mansion that was once a mental asylum, better known as the Vannacutt Psychiatric Institute for the Criminally Insane. Nowadays, the Institute is infamous for the fact the patients took it over one night in 1931 and slaughtered the chief doctor (Jeffrey Combs in a cameo) and his staff. (A graphic black-and-white film of the bloodletting has survived.) Price makes an offer to his guests: Spend the night in the asylum without going mad. And if you should be alive in the morning, you can pick up your check for one mill. The guests (trapped caretaker Chris Kattan, doctor Peter Gallagher, baseball player Taye Diggs, movie producer Ali Larter and would-be TV talk host Bridgette Wilson) turn out to be descendants of staff members who died in '31 and a malevolent spirit has brought them here for revenge. It's amazing how freely these dopy characters wander the huge estate, not bothered at all by poorly lit rooms, eerie corridors and other creepy things. And how quickly they want to shoot off the .45 automatics each has been given for self-defense. The 1959 script by Robb White was a lot simpler, cleaner and clearer about who was doing what to whom, as nothing was as it

seemed with Vincent Price in charge of events. In this new version, things get very messy with all the human deception onto which is heaped a lot of messy supernatural events. Screenwriter Dick Beebe uses the Kitchen Sink approach to plotting, tossing in whatever keeps the movie going. He's written in a black supernatural cloud with tentacle-like arms that seeps through the cracks and sucks you away or explodes your body, a revolving sensory chamber that creates illusions for its occupant, a vat of thick gooey blood, and other little goodies scattered throughout the mansion of madness and mayhem. Be sure to sit through the credits, as there is a scene at the very end showing the final fate of Mr. Price and his bitchy wife. (Video/DVD: Warner Bros.)

HOUSE ON SKULL MOUNTAIN (1973) ★ It's the old *Ten Little Indians* theme with touches of voodoo and black magic when heirs gather in a weird house outside Atlanta. Directed by Ron Honthaner, written by Mildred Pares. Mike Evans, Victor French, Ella Woods, Janee Michelle. (CBS/Fox) (Laser: CBS/Fox, with *Attack of the 50-Foot Woman*)

HOUSE ON SORORITY ROW, THE (1983) ★ Yet again, another slasher terrorizer in which sorority sisters, on the night of a grad party, are murdered one by one. This marked the writing-directing debut of Mark Rosman, who filmed at an old house in Baltimore. Special effects by Rob E. Holland. Aka *House of Evil* and *Seven Sisters*. Kathryn McNeil, Eileen Davidson. (Vestron; from Dura Vision as *House of Evil*) (Laser: Vestron)

HOUSE ON THE EDGE OF THE PARK (1984) ★ Despicable Italian film, shot in America, depicts razor-wielding murderer David A. Hess slicing up women's bodies, bashing in a man's head and performing disgusting acts of rape when he and an equally sadistic accomplice terrorize a number of hostages. This is an awful, gratuitous film to endure, even though it tries to pull off a moralistic ending. Annie Belle, Cristian Borromeo, Lorraine DeSelle. Directed by Ruggero Deodato. (Vestron)

HOUSE ON TOMBSTONE HILL, THE (1992)★½ He/She/It is knocking them off—a number of buyers, one at a time, in the house atop the ghostly hill. Mark Zobian, Victor Verhaeghe, Doug Gibson, Naomi Kooker. (Action International)

HOUSE THAT DRIPPED BLOOD, THE (1971) ★★★★ Good Amicus horror film (produced in Britain) written by a prestigious master of horror tales, Robert Bloch. The macabremeister interweaves four stories to recount a strange mansion's history. The main thread is an investigator, searching for a missing film star, who checks out previous tenants. Story one: A horror writer (a chip off the old Bloch?) is haunted by his creations. Story two: Ghostly figure haunts a wax museum managed by a lunatic. Story three: Witchcraft and voodoo dolls with Nyree Dawn Porter and Christopher Lee. Story four: The investigator discovers what happened to that missing star—and wishes he hadn't. Directed by Peter Duffell. Peter Cushing, Ingrid Pitt, Denholm Elliott. (Prism)

HOUSE THAT MARY BOUGHT, THE (1995) ★★★½ Unusually literate psychological suspense tale (made for cable TV) with pseudosupernatural overtones, based on Tim Wynne Jones' award-winning novel *Odd's End*. The adaptation by director Simon MacCorkindale and Chris Bryant captures all the subtle nuances and quirky characterizations of four people caught up in a mystery. Is a ghost at work when painter Susan George (also co–executive producer) and businessman husband Ben Cross move into a new home in a small French town and begin experiencing weird things? Or is someone terrorizing her? Is it Cross, who is on the verge of having an affair with his secretary? Or does George's old friend Maurice Thorogood have something to do with all the scary stuff? Who's the strange old man living nearby? Intriguing and delicious, the stuff that gives whodunits a good name, this is enhanced by on-location photography. Vernon Dobtcheff, Jean-Paul Muel, Charlotte Valandrey.

HOUSE THAT SCREAMED, THE. See *The Boarding School*.

HOUSE WHERE DEATH LIVES, THE. See *Delusion*.

HOUSE WHERE EVIL DWELLS, THE (1982) ★★ Lackluster, predictable "haunted teahouse" tale begins in Japan in 1840 and depicts a cuckolded samurai chopping up his wayward wife and her lecherous lover. Heads roll, arms fly, legs gambol and blood spatters. So much for the prologue. Cut to modern times as Edward Albert and Susan George move into the house, aided by U.S. Ambassador Doug McClure, an old family friend. Susan is haunted by three Japanese spirits superimposed over the footage, leaving nothing to the imagination. Gradually (as certain as death and taxes), the Americans are caught up in a love triangle and restage the samurai violence with karate and swingin' swords. Very unscary, even when Susan's daughter is attacked by crawling spider creatures (where did they come from?). Uninspired except for torrid love scenes in which bare-breasted Susan gives all she has—which is considerable. Directed by Kevin Connor. (MGM/UA)

HOWARD THE DUCK (1986) ★★ Expensive flop that never makes a duck character from another planet, trapped on Earth, believable. For one, the duck costume and makeup are phony— Howard looks like a midget in a Halloween costume. For another, the duck is stupid, when he should have been played seriously, in contrast to the ridiculous premise. Yes, the effects are stupendous . . . but without a story they produce only yawns. Howard, a quacker living on a parallel Earth, is sucked into an astronomical beam and swept across the Universe to Earth, where he falls for musician Lea Thompson and thwarts an alien overlord from conquering our planet. A monumental fowl-up for producers George Lucas and Gloria Katz, and director Willard Huyck. Duck, you suckers. (MCA)

HOWLING, THE (1981) ★★★★ Outrageous werewolf film based on the lousy paperback by Gary Brandner, which director Joe Dante threw away for a tongue-in-cheek narrative by John Sayles and Terence H. Winkless, reinforced by Rob Bottin's great state-of-the-art effects. Transmutation of man into werewolf is one of the most harrowing ever filmed—done with special masks and apparatus that permit us to see jaws growing into shape (complete with dripping teeth). Dante has loaded his yarn with visual in-jokes (Roger Corman and Forrest J. Ackerman have cameos). Dee Wallace, Patrick Macnee, Elizabeth Brooks, John Carradine, Slim Pickens, Kenneth Tobey howl it up. (Video/Laser: Embassy)

HOWLING II: YOUR SISTER IS A WEREWOLF (1986) ★★ Not a sequel, just crass exploitation. Psychic investigator/occult practitioner/wolf expert Christopher Lee is hot on the spoor of werewolves and subsidiary monsters, aided by Anne McEnroe (her sister was murdered by beasts) and boyfriend Reb Brown. The bloody trail leads to Transylvania and the Queen of the Werewolves (Sybil Danning). Just to watch her rip off her robe, or grow hair when she makes love to her male werewolf, makes this worth seeing. Grrrrrrrrr. A noisy morsel, loaded with effects, transmutating wolves and a gargoylelike monster. Philippe Mora directs with emphasis on the action and Ms. Danning's spectacular body, no doubt hoping to shore up the weak story coscripted by Gary Brandner, creator of the *Howling* books. (HBO; Republic) (Laser: Image)

HOWLING III (1987) ★★ Somewhere in this third attempt to deal with the werewolves created by novelist Gary Brandner is a kitchen sink—just watch for it. What a mess: There's a town called Flow (wolf backwards); scenes from a movie, *It Came From Uranus*; footage of Aborigines taken in 1905; three goofy nuns who turn into werewolves, and a movie director who looks like Hitchcock making *The Shape Shifters Part 8*. What's it really about? A tribe of werewolf people living in Australia and a runaway girl who gives birth to a marsupial human and stuffs it into her stomach pouch. Writer-director Philippe Mora makes this *Return of the Wilderness Wolf Family*. *Howling III* is not even a howl—it simply defies description. Barry Otto, Max Fairchild, Imogen Annesley, Frank Thring, Michael Pate. (IVE; Vista) (Laser: Image)

HOWLING IV: THE ORIGINAL NIGHTMARE (1988) ★★ At least the first three *Howling* films weren't dull! This boring thudder, made in South Africa and L.A. by producer Harry Alan Towers, is set in a town called Drago—where howling can be heard from the woods. Only in the last minutes is there any action, and the special effects—except for a man melting down to his skeletal components—are shoddy. Romy Windsor suffers through as the innocent misunderstood heroine. Directed by John Hough, without his heart in it. Michael T. Weiss, Susanne Severeid. (IVE) (Laser: Image)

HOWLING V: THE REBIRTH (1989) ★★★ Decent entry in this erratic series based on the novels by Gary Brandner, shaped as a whodunit occurring in a castle outside Budapest. The castle has been closed since the 15th century because of a family curse, but one of several visitors is a hideous werewolf (a descendant of the family) that is killing guests in the secret chambers of the eerie place. Trying to figure out who is the hairy one is the game to be played. Directed with appropriate focus on suspense by Neal Sundstrom. Philip Davis, Citoria Catlin, Elizabeth Shé, Ben Cole. (IVE) (Laser: Image)

HOWLING VI: THE FREAKS (1990) ★★★ Sharp improvement over previous sequels in this catch-all series, various elements having been borrowed from three books by Gary Brandner. The centerpiece is Harker's World of Wonders, a carnival of freaks and misfits featuring an alligator boy, a half-man/half-woman combination and assorted vagaries of nature. It unfolds under Hope Perello's direction with surprises and twists. Effects and monster makeup are better than competent and there's one good monster that resembles Nosferatu. Brendan Hughes, Michele Matheson, Carlos Cervantes, Antonio Fargas, Carol Lynley. (Live) (Laser: Image)

HOWLING [7]: NEW MOON RISING, THE (1994) ★ This strange little homemade movie is a real anomaly in the series, being set in Pioneertown in Yucca Valley, CA (near Barstow). Using characters and situations from *Howling IV* and *Howling V*, as well as a little werewolf footage to spice up a film noticeably lacking good special effects and believable gore thrills, this sequel depicts folks in Pioneertown singing and playing country/western music (including "Keep the Wolf Away From the Door") and square dancing—inexpensive padding to lengthen this into a feature. The unnecessarily convoluted plot has Australian wanderer Clive Hunter (who also wrote, produced and directed) suspected of several ripped-throats murders, which baffle analytic cop John Ramsen (an associate producer)

and God-fearing priest John Huff, who has been tracking the werewolves from the previous pictures. Perhaps the real star of this failed film is Pappy and Harriet's Pioneertown Palace, a saloon where much of the action (and nonaction) occur. Claude "Pappy" and Harriet Allen portray themselves and do a pretty good job, considering all the cast is amateurs. *The Howling* series, based on novels by Gary Brandner, started to sink long ago but it sure hit its nadir with this goofy movie, which in final analysis makes no sense whatsoever. Elizabeth Shé, Jacqueline Armitage, Jim Lozano. (New Line)

HOW TO MAKE A MONSTER (1958) ★★ Herman Cohen horrifier bravely dares to mock its own genre, making its weak script (which producer Cohen wrote with Kenneth Langtry) and mediocre makeup effects worth enduring. Hollywood makeup man Robert H. Harris, working at American-International Studios, is told monster movies are passé and his services no longer needed. An ingredient mixed into his cosmetics turns young actors into monsters—enabling Cohen to use all the fright masks from his earlier horror flicks. Targets of these monstrous murderers are studio bosses; they couldn't have picked a more deserving bunch. Gary Conway portrays the werewolf. Directed by Herbert L. Strock. Paul Brinegar, John Ashley, Gary Clarke, Morris Ankrum, Walter Reed, Robert Shayne. (RCA/Columbia)

HUMAN DUPLICATORS, THE (1965) ★ Unsubstantiated rumors have it this was financed by Xerox . . . Richard Kiel, ET humanoid Kolos, dispatched to conquer Earth, is so ridiculously stilted that his ineptitude is topped only by blond sexpot Barbara Nichols portraying an undercover woman. Then there's the automaton-like performance of George Nader as the most wooden secret agent since Pinocchio the Spy. George Macready tries to make his mad scientist tolerable. One film you won't want to copy. Directed by Hugo Grimaldi from an Arthur C. Pierce script. Richard Arlen, Hugh Beaumont. Aka *Space Agent K 1*. (IVE; Thrillervideo; from Star Classics as *Jaws of the Alien*)

HUMAN EXPERIMENTS (1980) ★★ Prison doctor believes that shock treatment will make criminals go straight. Crooked thinking, for sure. Sleaze-bag stuff directed by J. Gregory Goodell. Experiment ultimately fails. Linda Haynes, Jackie Coogan, Aldo Ray, Geoffrey Lewis, Lurene Tuttle. Aka *Beyond the Gate*. (VidAmerica)

HUMAN FEELINGS (1978) ★★ The only reason to watch this simply awful TV-movie, directed stylelessly by Ernest Pintoff, is to see a young Billy Crystal do what he can with a hopeless telescript by Henry Bloomstein. It's one of those misconceived comedies set in Heaven, with Nancy Walker playing God and Crystal as an angel she dispatches to Earth to find six decent people living in Las Vegas. Otherwise, she'll destroy the city just like she destroyed Sodom and Gomorrah. Crystal has little to work with as he falls in love with Donna Pescow and outsmarts casino crook Armand Assante, knocking down waiters and waitresses as he constantly runs through the casinos and streets of the city. This is one you won't have any human feelings for except pity. Squire Fridell, Richard Dimitri, Jack Carter, Pat Morita, Pamela Sue Martin.

HUMAN MONSTER, THE (1940) ★★★ Bela Lugosi in a dual role could double your pleasure. On one hand, he is Professor Dearborn, proprietor of the Dearborn Institute for the Blind. On the other, he is Dr. Orloff, who tortures the blind and electrocutes them to collect insurance. Directed by Walter Summers in England as *Dark Eyes of London*. Summers, John Argyle and Patrick Kirwin based their script on an Edgar Wallace novel. Remade in 1961 as *The Dead Eyes of London*. (Thunderbird; VCI; Kartes; Filmfax; Sinister/C)

HUMANOID DEFENDER. Retitled video version of *J.O.E. and the Colonel* (MCA).

HUMANOIDS FROM THE DEEP (1980) ★★ Grotesque zombiemen from the depths answer the mating call by sexually attacking young women. Originally this was a less-violent film directed by Barbara Peeters (and written by Frederick James), but producer Roger Corman shot new footage emphasizing amorous amphibians ripping clothes from wriggling sexpots. Starring Doug McClure, Vic Morrow and Ann Turkel, this climaxes (excuse me!) with a battle at a dockside carnival. Aka *Monster* and *Monsters*. (Warner Bros.)

HUMANOIDS FROM THE DEEP (1995) ★★ A by-the-numbers recycling of the 1980 Roger Corman exploitation thriller, remade for Showtime and then released to video. It's nothing much more than a lot of boring above-sea level scenes involving the pollution of waters with a chemical called Synestin and a few underwater sequences depicting a race of ugly fishmen abducting beautiful young maidens and storing them in a subterranean chamber until such time as they can impregnate them and create little baby fish monsters. Robert Carradine, affecting a rugged, unshaven Chuck Norris look, gets a little upset when his own daughter (Danielle Weeks) is kidnapped from the waterfront community of Harbor Shores. Again, a dockside event (a salmon festival) is the site for an outright attack on human beings as sheriff Kaz Garas and deputy Clint Howard look on wide-eyed. Explaining how the government caused all this mayhem through an experiment to create amphibious supersoldiers that went awry is scientist Emma Samms. There's little in the way of good special effects, and writer-director Jeff

Yonis, working with Martin B. Cohen's original premise, is clearly out of his depth. Mark Rolston, Season Hubley, Justin Walker, Bert Remsen. (New Horizons)

HUMAN PETS, THE. See *Josh Kirby... Time Warrior!*

HUMONGOUS (1982) ★★ Teenagers accidentally sink their yacht off a strange island where, back in 1946, a pretty woman was raped. The shipwrecked clods find the island deserted, but one by one are knocked off by a hairy wild man. There's nothing surprising or special about the "creature," and the characters are cannon fodder, without personalities. From director Paul Lynch and writer William Gray. Janet Julian, David Wallace, Janet Baldwin. (Embassy; Sultan; New Line)

HUNCHBACK. Video version of *The Hunchback of Notre Dame* (1981) (Vidmark).

HUNCHBACK OF NOTRE DAME, THE (1923) ★★★ Lon Chaney is Quasimodo, the deformed bellringer who falls in love with gypsy girl Esmeralda. This features the sequence in which the misshapen freak is publicly whipped on a turntable. For mastery of makeup and acting, this was Chaney's finest midnight hour. Directed by Wallace Worsley. Chaney closely followed Victor Hugo's description of the humped man and wore a device so he could not stand erect. Ernest Torrence, Patsy Ruth Miller. (Blackhawk; Kino; Nostalgia) (Laser: Republic; Image)

HUNCHBACK OF NOTRE DAME, THE (1939) ★★★★ As the hunchback Quasimodo, the misshapen bellringer of Paris, Charles Laughton is more hideous than the stone gargoyles. Directed by William Dieterle from a script by Sonya Levien and Bruno Frank, this second film version of Hugo's tumultuous tale of 15th-century France explores the murky medieval mind in a Gothic setting. High production makes this a masterpiece. Maureen O'Hara is the beautiful Esmeralda; Sir Cedric Hardwicke is the villainous Frollo and Walter Hampden is the Archbishop. Thomas Mitchell, George Zucco, Edmond O'Brien, Fritz Leiber, Rondo Hatton. (Nostalgia Merchant; RKO; Media; Vid-America) (Laser: Image)

HUNCHBACK OF NOTRE DAME, THE (1957) ★★ Anthony Quinn is the bellringing gnome in this French adaptation lacking the classical elements of the 1939 version. Quinn portrays Quasimodo as though he were a Mongoloid idiot—mumbling and slobbering à la Brando. Provocative Gina Lollobrigida is Esmeralda, the beauty Quasimodo hides in the cathedral. Directed by Jean Delannoy. Alain Cuny, Jean Danet. (Laser: Japanese)

HUNCHBACK OF NOTRE DAME, THE (1976) ★★ BBC-TV version of Hugo's novel, directed by Alan Cooke and written by Robert Muller, is an early experiment in tape-to-film techniques. Warren Clark is the titular freak, Kenneth Haigh is Archdeacon Frollo and Michelle Newell is Esmeralda.

HUNCHBACK OF NOTRE DAME, THE (1982) ★★★ Distinguished TV version of Hugo's tale of the bellringer Quasimodo, and his search for love in a world of hate. Writer John Gay etches fine characterizations and period dialogue that isn't stilted. Anthony Hopkins brings warmth to the misshapen human-gargoyle. Derek Jacobi, John Gielgud, Robert Powell, Lesley-Anne Down. Directed by Michael Tuchner. (From Vidmark as *Hunchback*)

HUNCHBACK OF NOTRE DAME, THE (1996) ★★★★ This is a brilliantly visualized cartoon feature from Disney, with stunning, life-like animation, and an adaptation of Victor Hugo's classic story that deals with good vs. evil in an unusually dark fashion (at least for Disney). Directed by Kirk Wise and Gary Trousdale with a three-dimensional quality, this umpteenth remake of the 1831 novel is a thrilling version that breathes new life into old material as the deformed Quasimodo (voice: Tom Hulce) meets the beautiful Esmeralda (voice: Demi Moore) during a festival in medieval Paris but is thwarted from normal human contact by the evil Frollo (voice: Tony Jay), a villain of the slimiest (dis)order. As with other recent Disney cartoon films, the soundtrack is loaded with effective songs (by Alan Menken and Stephen Schwartz) as heroic captain of the guard Phoebus (voice: Kevin Kline) tries to save the day for Quasi. Portions might be too intense for the very young, but there's little else to quibble about. (Video/Laser: Disney)

HUNCHBACK OF THE MORGUE, THE (1972). See *The Rue Morgue Massacres*.

HUNCHBACK OF THE RUE MORGUE, THE. See *The Rue Morgue Massacres*.

HUNCHBACK OF UCLA. See *Big Man on Campus*.

HUNDRED YEARS TO COME, THE. See *Things to Come*.

HUNGER, THE (1983) ★★★★ Bizarre, offbeat vampire tale, directed with razzle-dazzle by Tony Scott, brother of Ridley. While the shots are boggling and the ambience effective, this Ivan Davis–Michael Thomas adaptation of Whitley Strieber's novel has enigmatic characters in search of a plot. At times the narrative disintegrates into eye-zapping images and effects. The outré story deals with two vampires (Catherine Deneuve, David Bowie) living off human blood—until Bowie's aging accelerates and Deneuve needs a new partner. She picks Susan Sarandon, a researcher in human longevity, and seduces her in a tasteful lesbian sequence. The "makeup illusions" are by Dick Smith and Carl Fullerton. Dave Allen and Roger Dicken did the monkey effects. Cliff De Young,

Beth Ehlers, Dan Hedaya. (Video/Laser: MGM/UA)

HUNGRY PETS. See *Please Don't Eat My Mother!*

HUNGRY WIVES. See *Season of the Witch*.

HUNK (1987) ★★★ Charming fantasy-comedy in which nerdy Steve Levitt makes a pact with Satan's emissary (beautiful Deborah Shelton) to be turned into a beach bum with a body women can't resist (John Allen Nelson, some hunk indeed). Director Lawrence Bassoff's script is also nicely developed, emphasizing that beauty is only skin deep, etc. There are beautiful women to ogle and James Coco turns up as the Devil, assuming assorted disguises and, since he can travel back and forth in time, making amusing historical references to tragedies past and present. Robert Morse does a parody of Robin Leach as a TV personality named Garrison Gaylord. (Video/Laser: RCA/Columbia)

HUNTER'S BLOOD (1987) ★★ Father-son Clu Gulager and Samuel Bottoms take three pals on a hunting trip on the Arkansas border, encountering murderous rednecks who operate the Razorback Meat Co. A bloodbath ensues. Missing the characters, poetry and deeper themes of *Deliverance*, this is a senseless retread. Directed by Robert C. Hughes. Kim Delaney, Ken Swofford, Joey Travolta. (Video/Laser: Embassy/Nelson)

HUNTERS OF THE GOLDEN COBRA (1982) ★★★ Italian adventure-fantasy in the Indiana Jones style . . . not as classy but still rousing good action as a British Intelligence officer and an American soldier (David Warbeck) pursue the precious Golden Cobra, a relic containing supernatural destructive powers. Warbeck meets a tribe of blowgun-packin' natives, ruled by a white woman, but is wounded and passes out. Later, he and the English spy undergo adventures in the Philippines with a native cult called the Awoks. Directed by Anthony Dawson. Rena Abadesa, Almanta Suska. (Vestron)

HUSH, HUSH, SWEET CHARLOTTE (1964) ★★★ Following the success of *What Ever Happened to Baby Jane?*, producer-director Robert Aldrich duplicated the formula of daffy old crones played by one-time Hollywood greats. Bette Davis is a demented spinster, haunted by a 30-year-old murder and seeing dead bodies all over the old family mansion. It's treated by Aldrich, working with a script by Lukas Heller and Henry Farrell, as a macabre joke and you'll see through the red herrings without much difficulty. What makes this memorable is the decaying Southern plantation and decadent characters to match. Joseph Cotten, Olivia de Havilland, Agnes Moorehead, Victor Buono, Bruce Dern, Mary Astor, William Campbell. Aka *Cross of Iron* and *What Ever Happened to Cousin Charlotte?* (Video/Laser: CBS/Fox)

HYDRA. Variant video version of *Attack of the Swamp Creatures* (Lettuce Entertain You).

HYPER SAPIEN: PEOPLE FROM ANOTHER STAR (1986) ★★★ Innocuous, pleasant sci-fi fantasy-comedy for children. Humanoid aliens (Sydney Penny as Robyn and Rosie Marcel as Tavy) teleport to Earth to prove that their Taros is a good planet, taking with them a furry, three-eyed creature called the Tri-Lat Kirbi—which provides this Canadian film with its best comedy when Tri-Lat is befriended by Keenan Wynn as a cantankerous grandfather. (It was Wynn's last role.) British director Peter Hunt took over this heart-warming project from Michael (*Wolfen*) Wadleigh. Talia Shire, who appears in the cast, was also a producer. Ricky Paul Goldin, Dennis Holahen, Gail Strickland, Chuck Shamata. (Video/Laser: Warner Bros.)

HYSTERICAL (1983) ★ Pathetic parody of horror movies, with dumb jokes coming fast but never attaining wit. In a lighthouse in Hell-view, Oregon, the Hudson Brothers (Bill, Mark, Brett) investigate a long-dead lighthouse keeper (Richard "Jaws" Kiel), whose corpse is restored to life by his also-long-dead wife (Julie Newmar). Half the cast walks with zombie death faces and the other half grimaces at the non sequiturs and weary sight gags. Supporting players helpless to support even themselves are Franklyn Ajaye, Keenan Wynn, Charlie Callas, Richard Donner, Murray Hamilton and Clint Walker. They're as much at sea as the lighthouse keeper. Let's hear it for gross incompetence for director Chris Bearde and the Hudsons, who wrote this mess with Trace Johnston. (Embassy) (Laser: Image)

his ice-age soul. A gallant attempt, ably directed by Fred Schepisi. Danny Glover, Josef Sommer, David Strathairn. (Video/Laser: MCA)

ICE PIRATES, THE (1984) ★★★ Rollicking parody of space adventures in which warp-drive buccaneer Robert Urich and spaced-out laser-bucklers Michael D. Roberts, Anjelica Huston and John Matuszak embark to the only planet in the galaxy having water to battle the evil Templar Empire. The funniest elements are (1) a castrating assembly line complete with gay "barber"; (2) the grungiest looking robots in any universe and (3) a time warp sequence in which the action is speeded up as the characters age at accelerated pace. Credit the stylishness to director Stewart Raffill, who co-wrote with Stanford Sherman. For a switch, Urich is a sometimes-cowardly hero. Mary Crosby, as the kidnapped Princes Karina, is so beautiful, she alone is reason to keep your eyes glued to the foolishness. (Video/Laser: MGM/UA)

I CHANGED MY SEX. See *Glen or Glenda?*

I COME IN PEACE (1990) ★★½ The cliché of buddy cops trying to crack a drug case is given a science-fictional twist in this brutally graphic, unsettling urban tale. An alien drug king lands in L.A. and drains vital fluids from victims—on his planet they make for a great "high." A good alien is tracking the bad one while cop Dolph Lundgren and ill-matched pal Brian Benben crack the crack E.T. A series of violent, bloody encounters with nary an ounce of restraint on the part of director Craig R. Baxley. Betsy Brantley, Matthias Hues, David Ackroyd. Also called *Dark Angel.* (Media) (Laser: Image)

ICY DEATH. Video version of *Death Dimension* (Lettuce Entertain You; Bennu).

IDAHO TRANSFER (1973) ★★½ Well-intended but emotionally flat message film directed by Peter Fonda. Keith Carradine and other young scientists invent a time machine that carries them ahead into a post-catalysmic world. (MPI; from Satellite as *Deranged*)

IDENTITY CRISIS (1984) ★★ Robin Ward portrays twins. One crucified his girl and is in fruitcake prison. But when he escapes, he takes over his brother's girl (Wendy Crewson) with evil intentions: to split her into two—just like his personality. Directed by Bruce Pittman. Deborah Grover, Anthony Parr. (Command; from Metropolitan as *The Mark of Cain*)

IDENTITY CRISIS (1990) ★★ At the incantational demands of a witch with a perverted sense of humor, the body of a white fashion designer and a black rapper musician are switched, causing "identity crisis" with racial overtones. Directed by Melvin Van Peebles, this oddball comedy was written by and stars Melvin's son, Mario. Ilan Mitchell-Smith, Nicholas Kepros. (Academy)

I DISMEMBER MAMA (1972) ★★ Screenwriter William Norton comments on the sexual perversions of contemporary society when a psycho

I BURY THE LIVING (1958) ★★★ Weird graveyard chiller with Richard Boone as a cemetery curator who thinks he has power over life and death by shifting stickpins in a cemetery map. Superior tombstone mood established by director Albert Band and "plotter" Louis Garfinkle, although the film is marred by a cop-out ending. Theodore Bikel, Herbert Anderson, Peggy Maurer, Russ Bender. (Goodtimes; S/Weird; Sinister/C; Filmfax)

ICEBOX MURDERS, THE (1986) ★ Fiendish killer chases beauties through a maze of corridors, then stuffs their freshly-slain corpses into his deep freeze. Give it the cold shoulder. Jack Taylor, Mirta Miller. (Mogul)

ICED (1988) ★½ An "Ice Crusher," snow country equivalent to Jason Voorhees, breaks the ice at Snow Peak Resort by (1) killing a guy with a snowplow; (2) thrusting a ski pole through a man's chest; (3) driving an icicle through a woman's heart; (4) electrocuting a woman in a hot tub; (5) catching a guy's foot in a bear trap and (6) plunging a butcher knife into a pie-eating skier's chest. While the ski blades are sharp, this is a dull variation on the slasher flick, turgidly scripted by Joseph Alan Johnson, who also plays a skier. Director Jeff Kwitny slips on the slopes of this slushy saga. Doug Stevenson, Debra DeLiso, Ron Kologie, Alan Johnson. (Prism)

ICEMAN (1984) ★★★½ This starts as a fascinating, pseudoscientific examination of how Arctic anthropologists uncover a 40,000-year-old Neanderthal Man. The film loses its impetus when the Iceman is placed in an artificial environment for study. Although John Lone is excellent as the primitive man, and Timothy Hutton and Lindsay Crouse compassionate as his befrienders, the story moves into muddled quasi-religious ideas. One wants to feel more for the Iceman, a good guy trapped in a world he can't understand, but he never develops beyond case flips out and wants to kill his mother. First he goes after another older mother, slaughtering her and befriending her daughter. But this attempt at pathos amidst bloodletting is feeble, misguided sentimentality. This guy is a psychokiller and deserves to be put away! Zooey Hall is the "I" of the title, a freaked-out killer living in Movieland, but it's Greg Mullavey as a hard-nosed cop who's far more interesting. Aka *Poor Albert and Little Annie*. Directed by Paul Leder. (AstroVideo; Video Gems)

IDLE HANDS (1999) ★ Here's what you get in the name of rollicking, joy-filled comedy entertainment: a teenager's head cut off by a flying circular saw blade; a broken bottle shoved into a teenager's forehead; a cat hurled through an open window by its tail; a knitting needle through a cop's neck; a cop electrocuted with lightning charges penetrating his writhing body; a teenager's hand cut off at the wrist on a chopping block; a hand microwaved to a crisp and exploding in a shower of blood; fingertips of the severed hand being honed to fine points in an electric pencil sharpener; and several teenagers killed by the severed hand in unexplained ways, with bursts of blood splattering against walls and windows. All its violence aside, *Idle Hands* deserves The Finger. This failure of a movie was designed to be a tongue-in-cheek parody of *The Beast with Five Fingers* and other horror classics and we're supposed to laugh at all the mirth-filled mayhem and lavish lampoonery. That might have happened had there been something that resembled a story line, but screenwriters Terri Hughes and Ron Milbauer fail to provide the slightest coherence. Exposition? The Hughes/Milbauer team would never resort to such a mundane device. What one might gather from its chaotic narrative is that the devil is loose, taking possession of various people and using their hands to strangle, maim, and kill. So teenager Devon Sawa smokes a joint made with oregano and nutmeg and suddenly his hands are possessed by the devil. Then, when he kills his two best friends with his evil hands, they return to life. What this has to do with the devil's plan is never explained. Why clutter up a movie with logic when you can sum it all up with the old axiom "Idle hands are the devil's playground." Very profound. The characters? They all suffer from hormone imbalance: the guys all want to get laid and the girls have only sex on their minds. (Or is it the other way around?) *Idle Hands* is what happens to idle Hollywood producers with too much time on their hands and no creativity in their empty minds. In turning out crap they think is cute, they end up insulting even the feebleminded whom they think they're making the film for. Here's news for you guys and gals: nobody is that feebleminded. Director Rodman Flender? It would be wise not to allow this individual anywhere near a movie camera again. (Video/DVD: Columbia TriStar)

I DON'T WANT TO BE BORN. Video version of *The Devil Within Her* (Intra; Axon).

I EAT YOUR SKIN (1964) ★½ Reedited version of *Zombies*, a 1961 feature written-produced-directed by Del Tenney which still turns up on TV in its original form under that title. (It is also known as *Voodoo Blood Bath*.) *I Eat Your Skin* was a new version that was released in 1971 with *I Drink Your Blood*. See *Zombies* for a full report. William Joyce, Heather Hewitt. (Wizard; Sinister/C; Rhino; S/Weird; Filmfax)

IF ALL THE WOMEN IN THE WORLD. See *Kiss the Girls and Make Them Die*.

IGOR AND THE LUNATICS (1985) ★ Simply awful—no other way to describe this Troma mess that appears originally to have been a mild-mannered movie (written by Jocelyn Beard and director Billy Parolini) about a religious sex cult à la Charles Manson. It was reedited into a graphic gore thriller with new footage written-directed by Tom Doran and Brendan Faulkner featuring "horror, action and suspense scenes." These "horror" scenes include death by buzzsaw, hacksaw, claw hammer, icepick, crossbow, pitchfork and a routine kitchen knife or two as the titular madmen go on a murder spree. Sleazy and cheap, and completely unwatchable. Forget Igor and don't be a lunatic and watch. Joseph Eero, Joe Niola, Mary Ann Schacht, T. J. Michaels. (Troma; Lightning; Live)

I HAVE NO MOUTH BUT I MUST SCREAM. This is an alternate title for *And Now the Screaming Starts* and has nothing to do with a famous short story by Harlan Ellison. Maybe Harlan should sue.

I KNOW WHAT YOU DID LAST SUMMER (1997) ★★★½ This slasher-genre special spends adequate time to build the characters who will ultimately be in jeopardy and face the wrath of the killer, and hence it's a little better than most. It also benefits from excellent casting: Jennifer Love Hewitt (of TV's *Party of Five*) and Sarah Michelle Gellar (of TV's *Buffy the Vampire Killer*) are the two femmes in peril and they do a nice job of conveying the fear of the trap in which they feel caught. Freddie Prinze Jr. (as the nice guy next door and the closest thing to a hero this movie has), and Ryan Philippe (as an obnoxious, unlikable catalyst for the group) round out the foursome of students who accidentally hit a man walking on the roadside and decide to cover it up rather than report the incident to police. It's the Fourth of July in a sleepy fishing village on the eastern seaboard and all four have plans to escape their small-town environment and make their fortunes in the world. But the cover-up includes finding out the victim is still alive just before they dump his body into the bay, and a year later all four are wallowing in angst and guilt, failures all. Kevin Williamson's script came after the success of *Scream*, and rather than tongue-in-cheek, he opted for a somber tale in which the four find themselves stalked by someone who knows what happened. The killer, wearing a fisherman's slicker and armed with a deadly hook he's stolen from an icehouse, comes after them in a series of cat-and-mouse sequences. Each is tormented by the killer but left alive—he's waiting for the next Fourth of July, when he will wreak his final vengeance. In developing the characters, Williamson has done a good job, but his plot suffers from more than a few lapses in logic. For one, the identity of the killer is almost an afterthought when it might have been cleverly integrated into the tale. Also, the killer strikes openly in the middle of town, but there's never anyone else around to witness his dastardly feats. Streets are always empty and nobody responds to the screaming heroines. This might have been better set up by director Jim Gillespie, who otherwise creates an oppressive atmosphere for his characters and offers a rousing climax aboard a fishing boat. Gillespie obviously spends time with his cast, for smaller roles by Anne Heche, Bridgette Wilson, and Johnny Galecki are well handled. The ending is ambiguous, leaving it open for the sequel *I Still Know What You Did Last Summer*. (Video/ DVD: Columbia TriStar)

I LED TWO LIVES. See *Glen or Glenda?*

ILLICIT DREAMS (1995) ★★★ Well-written, tastefully directed erotic thriller with unexplained ESP overtones. Abused rich wife Shannon Tweed dreams about a secret lover, and the secret lover (Andrew Stevens, who also directed) dreams about her. When a key materializes in her hand during a dream, Tweed seeks help from friend Michelle Johnson and psychic reader Stella Stevens (Andrew's mom). Karen Kelly's script is a taut, compelling tale in which Joe Cortese is excellent as the bad-guy husband. Rochelle Swanson, Brad Blaisdell.

ILLUSTRATED MAN, THE (1968) ★★½ A major disappointment, for producer Howard B. Kreitsek's script fails to capture the poetry or imagination of Ray Bradbury's famous collection. Jack Smight is too conventional a director to give this the technique it screams out for. Three tales are linked by Rod Steiger, a stranger tattooed from head to foot except for a bare place on his back. In this space weird images appear: "The Veldt" is about children living in a playroom with a holograph-projected African setting; "The Long Rains" is about a rocket crew stranded on a rain-pelted Venus and trying to make its way to safety; "The Last Night of the World" depicts a family of the future which beds down in anticipation of Armageddon.

Claire Bloom, Jason Evers, Robert Drivas, Don Dubbins, Tim Weldon. (Warner Bros.)

I, MADMAN (1989) ★★ Dig Malcolm Brand, a demented '50s writer whose prose makes Stephen King read like fairy tales. He was so crazy he carved off his ears, nose and mouth. Now it's modern L.A. and bookstore employee Jenny Wright picks up a copy of Brand's opus, *I, Madman*. Suddenly Brand is back in all his hideous disfigurement, murdering. This supernatural thriller has moments of weird mood, but the script by David Chaskin is formula and clichéd. There's a good stop-motion monster—created by Randall William Cook (he also plays Brand)—but it's a device that doesn't belong in this film. Directed by Tabor Takacs. Clayton Rohner, Steven Memel, Stephanie Hodge. (Media) (Laser: Image)

I MARRIED A MONSTER (1998) ★½ This Stu Segall–produced TV movie, first shown on the UPN network, is a mediocre update of 1958's *I Married a Monster From Outer Space*, which starred Tom Tryon and Gloria Talbott. In fact, Tryon and Talbott are featured in a brief TV clip from the original, which could be one of the few exciting moments in Duane Poole's script-by-the-numbers. He's turned Louis Vittes's old script for the cult favorite into a grade-B exercise in paranoia and hohum alien-invasion clichés. This is your standard "body snatcher scenario," where a human being is replaced by an alien-driven clone and the real body is placed on a hook within an alien spacecraft. Inside the new clone is the extraterrestrial life-form which occasionally pops out looking like a body turned inside out, with glaring red eyes that shoot out electrical lightning bolts. Gee, how unique and exciting. One poor guy gets zapped and stuffed down a toilet (after being compressed somewhat). That's how mean these E.T.s are. All of the computerized effects are cheesy and the film never regains its momentum (not that it ever had any) after a transparent pulsating bubbly time-space continuum spaceship machine (or whatever the hell it is) plunks down in a forest outside the rural town of Blue Falls. About-to-be-married Richard Burgi (TV's *The Sentinel*) is quickly turned into a zombielike jerk. On the honeymoon, sweet warm wifey Susan Walters (TV's *Melrose Place*) begins to suspect something is wrong when Burgi goes into a rape mode, but what the hell, maybe he's just a little excited about being on his honeymoon. So what if he glares hatefully at her during the quieter interludes. Hey, marriage can do that to a guy. Walters, portraying one dumb sweet warm wife, only gets wise after girlfriend Barbara Niven (the buxom blonde who played Marilyn Monroe in *The Rat Pack* TV movie) marries Tim Ryan and gives birth prematurely to an ugly alien embryo. (Does it come as any surprise that Ryan is a clone, too?) Then all B-movie hell cuts loose. It's a wasted role for Burgi, who keeps rolling his eyes and making odd sounds when he twists his neck. Like he's crunching a bone. All Walters can do with her helpless role is look puzzled, suspicious, or yell and scream when she finds out the local sheriff and his deputies are also alien-driven. Niven comes off best in her low-cut blouses and she frequently bends over to reveal her deeply curving bosom. Nancy Malone directed with all the compassion and artistry of a schlockmeister. And Richard Herd helps out as an avuncular doctor who finally leads the armed citizens of Blue Falls against the alien hordes. Instantly forgettable genre crap. (Paramount)

I MARRIED A MONSTER FROM OUTER SPACE (1958) ★★★½ Superior bug-eyed monster material from director Gene Fowler Jr. and writer Louis Vittes focuses on newlyweds Gloria Talbott and Tom Tryon when an alien inhabits Tryon's body. Gloria suspects something is wrong—Tom acts emotionless—and by sticking to her viewpoint the film builds as a satisfying mystery. Sexual implications, unfortunately, are barely dealt with. The story is more concerned with conspiracy (à la *Invasion of the Body Snatchers*). Limited effects are good for their time. Ken Lynch, John Eldridge, Valerie Allen, Maxie Rosenbloom. (Video/Laser: Paramount)

I MARRIED A VAMPIRE (1981) ★ Down-on-her-luck Rachel Golden finally encounters the man of her dreams—a century-old vampire (Brendan Hickey)—in this low-budget first feature from writer-director Jay Raskin. Ted Zalewski, Deborah Carroll. (Prism)

I MARRIED A WITCH (1942) ★★★★ Classic René Clair comedy full of bitchy battle-of-the-sexes dialogue and "ghostly" effects by Gordon Jennings. Witch spirit (Veronica Lake) is freed from imprisonment and haunts the descendant (Fredric March) of a witch hunter who sent her to the stake 300 years before. Adapted from the Thorne (*Topper*) Smith novel. Robert Benchley, Susan Hayward, Cecil Kellaway, Chester Conklin. (Lightning) (Laser: Warner Bros.; Vestron)

I'M DANGEROUS TONIGHT (1990) ★★½ Based on a tale by Cornell Woolrich in name only, this TV-movie projects dollops of sex and violence, conveying neither the anguish nor torture that dominates the source material. A cursed red Aztec cloak, after it's removed from a sacrificial altar-sarcophagus, contains powers that turn its wearers evil, and among those who don it (converted into a sexy red dress) are Madchen Amick, Corey Parker and Dee Wallace Stone, the latter as a morgue attendant turned serial murderess. Only Anthony Perkins,

as an oddball professor, and R. Lee Ermey as Captain Akman, an even odder cop, bring character to this ineffectual effort. A low-water mark for director Tobe Hooper. Mary Frann, Natalie Schafer, William Berger. (MCA)

IM-HO-TEP. See *The Mummy* (1932).

IMMORTAL COMBAT (1993) ★★★ Your basic martial arts actioner with a few dollops of sci-fi, and a fair albeit mindless entertainment for the undemanding. Cops Sonny "J. J." Chiba and Roddy Piper (after the death of a partner) venture to a Caribbean isle where they join forces with photojournalist Deron McBee to uncover a biological warfare plot by the Hybrico Corp. to create superhuman warriors with the help of an adrenaline drug (or some nonsense). There's a mildly interesting romance between Piper and McBee in the Daniel A. Neira–Robert Crabtree script, and even Chiba goes dramatic when he has to reveal secrets to his adopted daughter, but this is basic karate-kicking stuff. The best thing about it is Meg Foster's over-the-top portrayal of a demented Hybrico rep. Slam bam, thank you, ma'am. Tiny Lister Woon, Lara Steinick, Roger Cudney, Kim Morgan Greene. (A-Pix Entertainment)

IMMORTALIZER, THE (1989) ★½ Crazed plastic surgeon, charging a fee that would make your skin crawl from your neck to your thighs, transfers the brains of the old to the bodies of the young. Ron Ray, Chris Croner, Melody Patterson. Script by Mark Nelson; direction by Joel Bender. (Video/Laser: RCA/Columbia)

IMP, THE. See *Sorority Babes in the Slimeball Bowl-O-Rama*.

IMPULSE (1984) ★★½ When Meg Tilly's mother tries to blow out her brains, Meg and husband-doctor Tim Matheson journey to her small rural hometown, where people are acting strangely; something is not allowing them to censor out their own unacceptable, antisocial urges. Soon the whole town is going crazy. Director Graham Baker emphasizes compelling ambience and mystery and a conspiratorial air. The visual and verbal clues are given early on; see if you can figure it out. Hume Cronyn, John Karlen, Bill Paxton. (Video/Laser: Vestron)

IN A GLASS CAGE (1982) ★★★½ This notorious Spanish import, written and directed by Agustin Villaronga, is the controversial portrait of a sex pervert, accomplished in a sickening, non-entertaining fashion. A Nazi war criminal, who sexually abused and murdered children in a concentration camp, carries his unnatural desires into civilian life, but a youth he corrupted stalks him for revenge. Had the youth merely used irony for that revenge, this might have been bearable. But because the lad himself is a killer, twisted as the war criminal is twisted, his vengeance is merely disgusting. The murders include a graphic hanging, the slitting of a young boy's throat, and acts of fornication between males. Gunter Meisner, Marisa Paredes. (Cinevista with subtitles)

IN BETWEEN (1991) ★½ Turgid morality tale in which Wings Hauser, Robin Mattson and Alexandra Paul wake up in a strange house from which they cannot escape. As they bicker, Heavenly messenger Robert Forster shows up to tell them that one has to return to the land of the living, and asks them to reexamine their lives to decide which one. Writer-producer-director Thomas Constantinides fails to bring any humor or charm to the situation. And with no unusual special effects, it's a monumental yawner. (Monarch)

INCREDIBLE HULK, THE (1977) ★★★ Adult approach to a popular green-tinted comic book hero results in a better-than-average TV-movie starring Bill Bixby as scientist David Bruce Banner, conducting experiments that enable test subjects to perform superhuman feats in times of anger and duress. Through gamma rays and ire, Bixby is transformed into a giant brute, primitive and uncontrollable (the creature is Lou Ferrigno). Teleplay by producer-director Kenneth Johnson deals with Bixby's anguish and romance with lab assistant Susan Sullivan. Jack Colvin, Susan Batson. (MCA) (Laser: Image)

INCREDIBLE HULK RETURNS, THE (1988) ★★ This will go down in history as the TV-movie that introduced Mighty Thor, a Marvel Comics superhero, into the thick of action with the Hulk. While the Hulk (Lou Ferrigno in green paint) is a visceral anti-hero, all brawn and no brain, Thor (Eric Kramer) is a dunderhead with a stylish sense of amusement. The comic-book plot, scripted by director Nick (Nicholas) Corea, has David Banner (the Hulk's alter ego) taking a new identity as a scientist at the Joshua Lambert Institute and developing the Gamma Transponder, a laser that could keep him from turning into the Hulk whenever he gets angry. Meanwhile, a quasi-nerd friend of Banner's has found the Viking tomb of Thor in a fjord agency, and with his hammer brings him magically back from Valhalla. Joining forces, Thor and the Hulk fight thugs who've kidnapped Banner's girl (Lee Purcell, in a thankless imperiled-female role). None of the action is inspired (with the slow-motion cliché overused once again). Charles Napier, John Gabriel, Jack Colvin, Tim Thomerson. (Video/Laser: New World)

INCREDIBLE INVASION, THE (1968) ★ Jack Hill assisted Juan Ibanez in directing this U.S.-Mexican film (aka *Alien Terror*) which historically is the last Boris Karloff made. Hill also wrote the script. Karloff portrays the inventor of a machine that destroys with radioactive powers. Extraterrestrial entities, in the bodies of unsavory humans, infiltrate Mayer's home, attacking his daughter (Christa Linder). Karloff was ill and his movements are restricted. (From Unicorn and Sinister/C as *Sinister Invasion*; from Sony and MPI as *Alien Terror*)

INCREDIBLE MELTING MAN, THE (1978) ★★ Makeup specialist Rick Baker creates a hideous countenance stripped of human flesh—eyeballs are exposed and atilt, ears are ready to drop off and the face is oozing with bubbly goo. Unfortunately, writer-director William Sachs does nothing exciting with the melter. Alex Rebar, only survivor of a flight to Saturn, is infected with radiation poisoning and becomes a Frankenstein Monster bashing everyone in sight and throwing their body parts around while he decomposes at an alarming rate. A throwback to the sci-fiers of the 1950s. Myron Healey, Jonathan Demme, Burr DeBenning. (Vestron; Orion)

INCREDIBLE PETRIFIED WORLD, THE (1957) ★½ Incredible petrified script by John Steiner creates wooden acting and a director, Jerry Warren, who is "stumped" by the material. John Carradine, Robert Clarke, Phyllis Coates and other B players are trapped in a diving bell in a submerged world (the bottom of a goldfish bowl, maybe?). (Sinister/C; S/Weird; Nostalgia; Filmfax)

INCREDIBLE PREYING MANTIS, THE. See *The Deadly Mantis*. (And now, let us prey.)

INCREDIBLE SHRINKING MAN, THE (1957) ★★★★ A special-effects classic, brilliantly designed by Universal-International's Clifford Stine and featuring a 15-foot mousetrap, an 18-foot pencil, a four-foot pin and a 40-pound pair of scissors. Thus is Grant Williams dwarfed and made to appear shrinking at the rate of an inch a week. Based on a Richard Matheson novel, and adapted by Matheson, Albert Zugsmith's production transcends the limitations of the fantasy thriller to deal with the metaphysical aspects of a shrinking human. It begins when Williams is inundated in a strange cloud while at sea and follows him "down" until a house cat, a spider and water drops are staggering nemeses in his miniaturized world. Jack Arnold directed it beautifully. Randy Stuart (the wife), William Schallert, Billy Curtis. (Video/Laser: MCA)

INCREDIBLE SHRINKING WOMAN, THE (1981) ★★★½ Delightful parody combining slapstick and satire. Lily Tomlin portrays a housewife (among several roles) exposed to chemical products that shrink her to minuscule size. In one scene she literally stands on a soap box to deliver a tirade to her long-suffering (but talllll) husband, Charles Grodin; in another she is (again, literally) washed down the drain. Finally she's kidnapped by corporation boss Ned Beatty, who wants to learn her secret so he can shrink anyone who stands in the way of company progress. Lily and a gorilla (makeup man Rick Baker) bring the film to a hysterical conclusion. Photographed in pastel shades by Bruce Logan. Effects by Baker and Roy Arbogast. Intelligently directed by Joel Schumacher; Jane Wagner's script works on several levels. A treat for big and little people. Henry Gibson, Maria Smith, Mike Douglas. (Video/Laser: MCA)

INCREDIBLE TORTURE SHOW, THE (1977) ★★ A Grand Guignol show presented by Sardu the Great. But offstage he's performing the real thing. Yes, fans, see a woman's brains popped out of her cranium, see eyeballs eaten before your very . . . eyeballs? See . . . yuch! The mastermind behind this blood-and-gore thriller is writer-producer-director Joel Reed. Seamus O'Brien, Louie de Jesus, Niles McMaster. (From Vestron as *Bloodsucking Freaks* and *Heritage of Caligula*)

INCREDIBLE TWO-HEADED TRANSPLANT, THE (1971) ★ Stomach-churning nonsense about the head of a homicidal maniac being grafted onto the body of a thorough idiot by crazy doctor Bruce Dern. What's incredible about this movie is that it was ever produced. Directed by Anthony Lanza. John Bloom, Pat Priest, Casey Kasem, Berry Kroeger. Aka *The Incredible Transplant*. (TransAtlantic; Vintage)

INCREDIBLE WEREWOLF MURDERS, THE. See *The Maltese Bippy.*

INCREDIBLY MIXED UP ZOMBIE, THE. See *The Incredibly Strange Creatures Who Stopped Living and Became Mixed-Up Zombies.*

INCREDIBLY STRANGE CREATURES WHO STOPPED LIVING AND BECAME MIXED-UP ZOMBIES, THE (1964) ★★ Madame Estrella, a fortune teller at a sleazy carnival, gets angry at customers if they mock her prophecies, throws acid in their faces and has her Igor assistant toss their bodies into a pit. So much for the zombies. Along comes a shiftless bum (Cash Flagg) who falls prey to her influences, becoming a knife murderer. Meanwhile, back at the midway, hapless audiences are subjected to outrageous production numbers, some featuring talentless stripper Carmelita. It's the work of producer-director Ray Dennis Steckler, obeying the script by Gene Pollock and Robert Silliphant. Meanwhile, the Theater Marquee Dressers of America complain about this movie—every time it plays, they run out of letters. Atlas King, Carolyn Brandt. (Oh yeah, Cash Flagg is an alias for Steckler. A Steckler for details?) Aka *Diabolical Dr. Voodoo*, *The Incredibly Mixed Up Zombie* and *The Teenage Psycho Meets Bloody Mary*. (Mascot; Camp)

INCREDIBLY STRANGE R. D. STECKLER. ★★ Documentary of the life and career of horror director Ray Dennis Steckler. Others in this series: *Steckler Interviews* and *Carolyn Brandt: Queen of Cult*. (Mascot)

INCUBUS (1982) ★★ John Hough (*Legend of Hell House*) helms this grisly Canadian horror-charger in which the town of Galen is terrorized by an invisible, sex-starved demon that materializes during the dreams of a man whose mother was once a witch. Or so it seems . . . Trying to solve the mystery is doctor John Cassavetes, cop John Ireland and newspaperwoman Kerrie Keane. Not an outstanding terrorizer, but it has enough oddball characters and screams to sustain attention. Scripted by George Franklin from Ray Russell's novel. Helen Hughes, Dirk McLean. (Video/Laser: Vestron)

INDEPENDENCE DAY (1996) ★★★★½ Whatever your carps about the silliness of its characters, who serve as symbols for heroic acts to come, there is no denying the power and awesomeness of this $70 million sci-fi epic, the ultimate depiction of an alien invasion of Earth by an E.T. race bent on taking over the entire Milky Way. Dwarfing TV's *V* and such features as *Earth vs. the Flying Saucer* and *War of the Worlds*, this Fox release skillfully blends the fiery spectacle of a catastrophe movie with the action elements of a space sci-fi adventure to make a pure popcorn movie. Its immediate appeal is to our fascination of watching worldwide destruction and our visceral thrill of seeing a hideous enemy destroyed in the name of patriotism and self-preservation. For starters, a mothership a quarter of the size of the moon glides into our atmosphere and dispatches smaller (15-mile-across) sister ships into attack positions. Director Roland Emmerich captures the magnitude of these events while introducing various (if stereotyped) characters. It isn't long before New York, Washington D.C. and Los Angeles are under simultaneous attack in a breathtaking fireball sequence—one of the best disaster-movie gimmicks yet. The magnitude of the destruction, as thousands of Americans sit helplessly in their cars and watch their death approaching, is stunning. How survivors like alcoholic pilot Randy Quaid, jet pilot Will Smith, military advisor Robert Loggia and computer scientist Jeff Goldblum (and his father Judd Hirsch) gather in Area 51 (a secret Nevada installation where Brent Spiner portrays a semi-crazed research scientist) under President Bill Pullman to instigate a retaliatory attack is one of the film's better sequences, and includes an autopsy of a captured alien (only the alien isn't quite dead). The script (by Emmerich and Dean Devlin) uses modern UFOlogy to good advantage, but eschews traditional alien-intruder appearances in favor of a more grotesque *Alien*-like alien. Then it's pure *Star Wars*–style action as Goldblum proposes a way of destroying the evil E.T.s and all races cooperate in one final battle royal punctuated by patriotic speeches (à la World War II propaganda movies) and acts of heroic sacrifice. *Independence Day* is a special-effects extravaganza you won't soon forget. Mary McDonald, Margaret Colin, James Rebhorn, Harvey Fierstein, Adam Spiner, James Duval. (Video/Laser: Fox)

INDESTRUCTIBLE MAN, THE (1956) ★½ Bottom-of-the-barrel pulper with Lon Chaney Jr. as an electrocuted criminal restored to life (yeah, one of those plots) who goes around town knocking off guys who sent him up the river. Said to be a remake of *Man-Made Monster*, but don't believe it. So poorly scripted (by Sue Bradford and Vy Russell) and directed (by Jack Pollexfen) it's bad enough to be entertaining. Robert Shayne, Marian Carr, Ross Elliott. (Sinister/C; S/Weird; Filmfax)

INDIANA JONES AND THE LAST CRUSADE (1989) ★★★★ This third (and final?) installment in the series from Steven Spielberg and George Lucas is a wonderful lark—as good as the first film for its ingenuity of plot and action. The opening is a classic example of visual storytelling, without the need of exposition, as we meet a young Boy Scout named Jones (River Phoenix) pursuing a Spanish artifact. The adventure in this prolonged sequence cleverly blends a bag of action-tricks with a visual explanation of all the gadgets and phobias of the Indiana Jones character (leather jacket, hat, whip, fear of snakes, etc.). Especially memorable is a chase aboard a circus train. Cut to the 1930s and we're now with Jones as he leaps into a new adventure—the search for the Holy Grail. A major twist in *The Last Crusade* is the introduction of Sean Connery as Dr. Henry Jones, Indy's father, who has been kidnapped by Nazis. The interplay between Harrison Ford (as Indy) and Connery is delightful. Highlights include a Nazi rally complete with Adolf Hitler, motorcycle and speedboat chases, a ride on a dirigible, a search through a tunnel beneath Venice, and the finding of the Grail. It is then that the film takes on mythical proportions that zoom Indiana into pure fantasy. Screenwriter Jeffrey Boam makes it all work, and director Spielberg never allows the pace to let up. Denholm Elliott returns as the bumbling museum curator Marcus Brody and Alison Doody provides the minimal love interest. (Video/Laser: Paramount)

INDIANA JONES AND THE TEMPLE OF DOOM (1984) ★★★½ A rousing cliffhanger that sweeps one headlong into the second screen adventure of soldier-of-fortune/archeologist Indiana Jones. And because the "thrill ride" is nonstop, one has no time to consider the absurdities and excesses screenwriters Willard Hyuck and Gloria Katz pump into George Lucas' original idea. Like *Raiders of the Lost Ark*, it's a fast-paced, exciting saga produced by Lucas and Steven Spielberg, with Spielberg directing. The action is tongue-in-cheek, but there are also moments of severe intensity. The madcap plot begins in Shanghai 1935 with Jones and

dancer Kate Capshaw and the kid Shortround (homage to the orphan in Samuel Fuller's *The Steel Helmet*) fleeing from insidious Asians. After a great night club dance sequence, the three escape via a wild airplane ride that leads them to a hair-raising parachute jump (but without a parachute), a ski ride and a "white rapids" excursion. Then the trio winds up in India where they help recover a magical glowing rock from a Kali cult. There's a fiery pit, secret caverns, torture chambers, creepies and crawlies, a variation on a roller coaster ride, a tidal wave and a suspension bridge with Indy trapped and crocodiles snapping below. Harrison Ford leaps and jumps and runs through it all, always managing to recover his hat and whip. Ke Huy Quan is cute as the Chinese youth and Amrish Puri and Roshan Seth make for good cardboard villains. Don't miss the eating scene—it's the funniest gross-out ever. (Video/Laser: Paramount)

INDIAN IN THE CUPBOARD, THE (1995) ★★½ Screenwriter Melissa Mathison, in adapting the award-winning book by Lynn Reid Banks, strived mightily to recapture the sense of youthful wonder that made *E.T.—The Extraterrestrial* so memorable. But she and director Frank Oz tried *too* hard. The results, though well-intended, are mixed. A wonderful young actor, Hal Scardino, is excellent as Omri, who discovers that a wooden cabinet in his room has the magic to turn toys into miniaturized beings. He begins a relationship with an Indian (Litefoot) and a rootin' tootin' cowboy (David Keith). There is a heavy-handed adult side to this fantasy premise, as racism, selfishness, respect, friendship, and the need of survival in one's own culture become themes that affect Omri and his less-than-likable friend Patrick (Rishi Bhat). This is a sincere effort, produced by Kathleen Kennedy and Frank Marshall, that leaves you wanting more than it delivers. Lindsay Crouse and Richard Jenkins have thankless roles as Omri's parents. (Video/Laser: Paramount)

IN DREAMS (1998) ★★★ Long ago Hollywood set up the formula for the lady-in-peril plot. Create a woman viewers can sympathize with, make her seem crazy even though she isn't, contrive things so nobody believes her, make each character seem suspicious so the woman's paranoia builds (and viewers can guess at the true identity of the culprit), and finally isolate her so the menace/killer/unseen thing can close in for the *coup de grâce*. Then have the climactic, wrenching action and revelations that turn a fogbound mystery into a crystal-clear resolution. *In Dreams*, based on the novel *Doll's Eyes* by Bari Wood, follows that tradition but then deviates from it and plunges its lady in peril into a less reassuring formula. Annette Bening goes on that traditional roller-coaster ride as Claire Cooper, illustrator of dark children's stories and living in a small Massachusetts town. She is like Alice slipping away into a Wonderland of horror when she begins to have nightmares—and gradually the nightmares come true. She sees only images and flashes, so has no way of putting together what they mean until it's too late. When her own daughter dies at the hands of a serial killer, *In Dreams* begins to look like a remake of *Snake Pit*, Olivia de Havilland's classic mental-breakdown movie. Screaming that the killer is inside her head, she writes a nursery rhyme on the walls of her home and stuffs apples into the garbage disposal. What can headshrinker Stephen Rea do but put her in a padded cell. There she freaks out, screaming that her husband (Aidan Quinn, playing a 747 pilot) is being attacked by a dog in a deserted hotel. Nobody listens. Certainly not the psychiatrist or the plainclothesman working the case (Paul Guilfoyle). Bening is all set up for maximum terrorizing. But then *In Dreams*, which was scripted by Bruce Robinson and director Neil Jordan, breaks all the rules by having the serial killer (who ultimately becomes Robert Downey, Jr.) doing unbelievable things. *In Dreams* disintegrates (before your very eyes, yes) and becomes a wretched grade-B psychokiller movie. Jordan, who directed *Interview with the Vampire* and *The Butcher Boy*, allows Downey to run wild and the character completely loses his narrative connection. Yes, there are striking images in *In Dreams*, especially some underwater sequences of a submerged town, but they are linked only marginally to the story. It is its disjointed, arbitrary nature that ultimately does not allow the film to work. Only in your dreams, Neil, only in your dreams. (Video/DVD: DreamWorks)

INFERNAL IDOL, THE. See *Craze*.

INFERNO (1980) ★★★ Italy's Dario Argento, famed for *Deep Red*, is up to his usual writing-directing scare tactics in this tale of witchcraft, suspended animation and other supernatural delights set in a New York apartment where a gloved killer stalks. Mario Bava was credited with some effects. Irene Miracle, Leigh McCloskey. (Key)

INFINITY OF HORRORS, AN. See *Galaxy of Terror*.

INFRA-MAN (1975) ★★★½ Kids will cheer the wonderful menagerie of extraterrestrial creatures, the kung fu fighting and other comic book elements of this Asian mishmash. Adults may become fascinated watching this awfulness carried to ultra-ludicrous extremes as a superpowerful hero in funny clothing (he's a bionic man!) fights a dragon lady (Dragon Mom) who sends these boggling creatures—Octopus Man, Beetle Man, etc.—out from her headquarters in the bowels of the Earth to do battle. It Came From Hong Kong. Directed by Hua-Shan. Hsiu-

Hsien portrays Infra-Man. Aka *Infra Superman* and *The Super Inframan*. (Prism; S/Weird)

INFRA SUPERMAN. See *Infra-Man*.

INHERITOR (1990) ★★ When her twin sister dies in Windsor Lake, Lisa McGuire turns up to investigate with local cop John Rice. Seems an old Indian curse might have done in the girl—as a bloodlusting minotaur. Directed by Brian Kendal-Savegar. Barnaby Spring, Dan Haggerty, John Russo. (Vidamerica)

INITIATION, THE (1982) ★★★ Unusual slasher film with more meat than usual: In addition to members of a sorority pulling pranks during Hell Week, there is a member (Marilyn Kagan) undergoing nightmares of a childhood trauma when she saw her mother in bed with another man, and a man burst into flames. There's an odd relationship with her mother (Vera Miles) and father (Clu Galager). Meanwhile, seven inmates escape from an insane asylum. The climactic bloodbath comes during a night in a shopping mall when the killer strikes with bow and arrow, hatchet, crossbow, speargun, etc. Directed by Larry Stewart. (HBO; Starmaker)

INITIATION OF SARAH, THE (1978) ★½ Undistinguished TV-movie ripoff of *Carrie*, complete with girl-being-hazed scenes. Shy, reticent Kay Lenz attends college only to come into conflict with a rival sorority to which her more outgoing sister belongs. Kay has strange psychic powers, you see, so on the night of the initiation who should urge her to utilize them but batty sorority mistress Shelley Winters. Directed by Robert Day. Tony Bill, Kathryn Crosby, Morgan Fairchild (as a great bitch), Tisa Farrow. (Worldvision)

INITIATION: SILENT NIGHT, DEADLY NIGHT 4. See *Silent Night, Deadly Night 4: Initiation.*

INNER SANCTUM 2 (1994) ★★½ Fred Olen Ray, who once threatened cinema as the potential new Ed Wood and then went on to become a better-than-competent low-budget producer-writer-director, is back in action with this mixture of erotic thriller and the plot about the psychologically disturbed young woman being driven crazy by nightmares . . . or could it be there is a well-planned conspiracy preying on her paranoia? The Sherman Scott–Steve Armogida screenplay is a compendium of clichés as poor Tracy Brooks Swope keeps dreaming about a corpse with a hideous face, while all the guests in her household (including Margaux Hemingway, Michael Nouri, Sandahl Bergman, Jennifer Ciesar and John E. Coleman) behave suspiciously. David Warner gets to play Swope's friendly doctor, Joe Estevez and James Booth are cops on the case, and Robert Quarry has a brief appearance. The "shock ending" is totally predictable. Ray certainly turned out better than Ed Wood. (Columbia TriStar; one unrated version has some steamy love-making sequences)

INNERSPACE (1987) ★★★ Shades of *Fantastic Voyage* with touches of *The Incredible Shrinking Man*: Space astronaut Dennis Quaid is miniaturized and injected into the buttocks of a nerdish supermarket cashier (Martin Short), who is then chased by the hired killer of mad scientists Kevin McCarthy and Fiona Lewis, in pursuit of the microchip that permits the shrinkage. This Steven Spielberg production is played for comedy and while director Joe Dante injects his usual in-jokes, it's too long to sustain its light themes. Dennis Muren and Rob Bottin contributed the effects. Vernon Wells, Robert Picardo, Orson Bean, Henry Gibson, Dick Miller, Kenneth Tobey. (Video/Laser: Warner Bros.)

INNOCENT BLOOD (1992) ★★★½ Offbeat vampire comedy-thriller starring Anne Parillaud as a sexy bloodsucker who feasts on gangsters and makes it appear that the underworld did it. She chews their necks ravenously, her eyes glowing red and green, but the vicious tearing turns victims into vampires. Gang boss Robert Loggia decides to take over the rackets by turning his gang into vampires. Realizing her mistake, Parillaud joins cop Anthony LaPaglia to wipe out the fanged hoods. Director John Landis emphasizes the comedy of Michael Wolk's script with homages to vampire and monster movies. Made in Pittsburgh, *Innocent Blood* is refreshing, with Frank Oz, Sam Raimi and other Landis cronies popping up. And Don Rickles gives a lively performance as Loggia's mouthpiece. David Proval. (Video/Laser: Columbia TriStar)

INNOCENTS, THE (1961) ★★★★★ Superior cinematic version of Henry James' "The Turn of the Screw," produced-directed with unbearable tension by Jack Clayton, scripted by Truman Capote and William Archibald with insight, and capturing the decay, depravity and haunted possession which reek in the novel. Deborah Kerr is the prim governess dispatched to a country mansion to tend the children of ice-cold baron Michael Redgrave. Beneath the serene exterior are undercurrents of menace. Are the children possessed by a former governess and valet who were sadistic lovers before their deaths? Or is it all in Kerr's imagination? Much of the horror is only suggested. One of the best ghost movies ever made. Martin Stevens, Pamela Franklin.

INNOCENTS FROM HELL. Video version of *The Nuns of Saint Archangelo* (Showcase).

INN OF THE DAMNED (1974) ★★★ This Australian horror Western (set in Gippsland, 1896) is worth seeing for Dame Judith Anderson as a crazed, homicidal Austrian innkeeper who murders her guests with her demented husband. The first half, however, moves with the agility of a wombat with two Achilles' tendons cut as no one has the wits to figure out why all the travelers are checking in but not checking out. Finally, lawman Alex Cord uses his wits against the pair in a hair-raising cat-and-mouse sequence. Produced-written-directed by Terry Bourke. Michael Craig, Joseph Furst, Robert Guilte. (Paragon)

INN OF THE FLYING DRAGON, THE. See *Sleep of Death.*

INQUISITION (1976) ★★ This Spanish torture-chamber melodrama, in which a lustful inquisitioner cuts off the nipple of a "witch" and stretches several beautiful nubile bodies on the rack, is one oddball movie from writer-director Jacinto Molina, who also stars under the name Paul Naschy as the sadistic fanatic who makes the mistake of falling in love with the daughter of a warlock, whom he has sentenced to death. She makes a pact with the Devil to get even, and does Molina/Naschy get burned up about it. Why is this oddball? On the one hand, *Inquisition* deals graphically with the terrors and indignations imposed on the Spanish people by the Church; on the other, it portrays real witches and demons, suggesting that perhaps the Church was slightly justified in burning witches at the stake. Can you have your torture and beat it too? Hmm. Daniela Giordano, Monica Randall, Tony Isbert, Juan Luis Galiardo, Ricardo Merino. (Video City)

IN SEARCH OF OZ (1994) ★★★ Good British TV documentary traces the literary history of L. Frank Baum, the early movie versions of the Oz books that he produced himself in the 1910s, and the ultimate MGM film version, with rare footage of Judy Garland's screen test. Salman Rushdie, Martha Coolidge, Gore Vidal and Ray Bradbury offer on-camera commentary about what Oz meant to them as children, and why the Oz stories are so enduring. This special also reminds that in the '50s the Oz books were briefly banned in some U.S. libraries. Directed by Brian Skeet.

INSECT. Video version of *Blue Monkey* (Winson Entertainment).

INSECT WOMAN. See *The Wasp Woman.*

INSEMINOID. See *Horror Planet.*

INSPECTOR GADGET (1999) ★★ Originally the title character was a bumbling TV cartoon detective from 1982–'85 with the voice of Don Adams and the ineptitude of Adams's *Get Smart* secret agent or Peter Sellers's Inspector Clouseau. In this Disney revival, which retells the original story, the crimefighter has been updated to the computer age but he's such a dumbed-down character, designed purely for slapstick antics, that it's doubtful even kids will find much appeal here. If there's any novelty, it's to be found in the ridiculous devices Inspector

Gadget uses in his ongoing battle with his arch-nemesis, Claw. First you have to understand how the inspector came to be. In the opening, he is an ineffectual security guard John Brown ("a geek from Kansas") played by Matthew Broderick as a nerd as well as a geek. He dreams about rescuing kids and being a hero. When Broderick attempts to pursue the inventor-scientist who will become Claw, his body is badly damaged and he undergoes an operation, during which a benevolent scientist separates the body pieces and rejoins them with all kinds of "gadgets" inside, controlled by voice-activated robotic chips and software. (Says police chief Dabney Coleman: "Columbo and Nintendo rolled into one.") His head, for example, now springs upward on a long coil. His legs have long stilts that pop out and enable him to bound down a street while rising 50 feet in the air. All Inspector Gadget has to do to make these devices work, once clad in his trench coat and soft hat, is cry, "Go go Gadget," and the name of the thing he needs, and out it pops. In one scene, a helicopter blade pops out of his head and he flies through the city after the villains. Meanwhile, villain Rupert Everett, who loses a hand and names himself Claw, steals the gadget technology and creates a look-alike called RoboGadget who goes around the city of Riverton destroying everything the Inspector is trying to save. The special effects by Stan Winston and the direction by David Kellogg are passable; it's the idiotic script by Kerry Ehrin and Zak Penn that defeats this condescending kiddie movie. A beautiful redhead named Joely Fisher gets to play a scientist's daughter as well as an evil look-alike, RoboBrenda, but her talents are wasted too. So are those of Michell Trachtenberg, Cheri Oteri, Andy Dick, and Rene Auberjonois. (Video/DVD: Disney)

INTERFACE (1984) ★ Silly, poorly conceived computer-theme fantasy, made in Dallas by regional filmmakers (dare we call them hackers?). Its saving grace is a couple who play it strictly for laughs as they search for the secret to a group of masked, costumed computerites ("We are the interpreters of the Master Process") who sit around their consols speaking with metallic voices and killing by remote-control devices. The ending falls apart. Maybe director Andy Anderson forgot his modem operandi. John Davies, Laura Lane. (Vestron)

INTERVIEW WITH THE VAMPIRE (1994) ★★★★ One of the most intriguing vampire movies ever made, based on the popular novel by Anne Rice, who wrote her own adaptation. Be prepared for a very nontraditional vampire yarn that drips with gore, its veins coursing with perversity. There is nothing romanticized or typically Gothic in this variation on a theme as reporter Christian Slater listens raptly as the vampire Louis (Brad Pitt) relates his 200-year-history as a bloodsucker. In flashbacks, Louis shows us how he was introduced to vampirism by Lestat (Tom Cruise, in a departure from his pretty-boy roles) with none of the gory details spared. You live and feel the desperation these men feel as they nightly prowl through society, looking for fresh victims, and eventually turning the child Claudia (Kirsten Dunst) into one of their kind. But *Interview* improves in character quality and insight into a vampire's psyche with the sequences involving Paris' Theater of Vampires, where a coven of creatures stage, for the public, their lavish rites of sacrifice. Director Neil Jordan directs it with a sure but unintrusive hand, showing little style as he lets the stark, dark atmosphere and chilling situations speak for themselves. This will be disturbing to squeamish individuals, but beneath its sanguinary, flesh-crawling surface are brilliant observations about man's behavior. Thus, *Interview* becomes a metaphor for our daily struggle to survive in a hostile world, and our never-ending search for mentors to show us the correct way out of the darkness. Antonio Banderas, Stephen Rea, Domiziana Giordano, Thandie Newton. (Video/Laser: Warner Bros.)

INTERZONE (1988) ★ In a post-Armageddon society, human survivors must battle mutants. So what else is new after the Apocalypse? Directed by Deran Sarafian. Bruce Abbott. (Media)

IN THE CASTLE OF BLOODY LUST. See *Castle of the Creeping Flesh.*

IN THE DEVIL'S GARDEN. See *Assault.*

IN THE GRIP OF THE MANIAC. See *The Diabolical Dr. Z.*

IN THE GRIP OF THE SPIDER. See *Web of the Spider.* (A well-spun yarn?)

IN THE MIDNIGHT HOUR (1985) ★★★½ Violent TV-movie vacillating between graveyard humor and shock thrills in telling its satirical tale of the town of Pitchfork Cove, where teenagers on Halloween night violate the graveyard to enact a ritual that unleashes scores of corpses. These walking dead are ghouls who crash a teen party and go for yocks; the vampires go for the jugular; others are werewolves. A lively affair, full of laughs and thrills. Dick Van Patten has fun as a silly dentist and Kevin McCarthy is the drunken judge who gets his comeuppance. Lee Montgomery, Shari Belafonte-Harper, LeVar Burton. Directed by Jack Bender. (On TV as *The Midnight Hour* and from Vidmark under that title)

IN THE MOUTH OF MADNESS (1994) ★★★½ One of John Carpenter's most accomplished works as a director, and one of the strangest of horror films to examine the fine dividing line between fact and fiction, reality and nightmare. Although the script by exec producer Michael De Luca is an original, there are overtones of

H. P. Lovecraft's "Elder Gods" tales and Stephen King's best-selling novels. This bizarre movie begins in an insane asylum where straitjacketed Sam Neill tells his story to visiting psychodoc David Warner. Flashback to Neill as a hard-nosed insurance investigator who is hired by publisher Jackson Harglow (Charlton Heston) to locate a missing writer, Sutter Cane, an equivalent to Stephen King in today's book market. It is suggested that an outbreak of violence and ax murdering is caused by the evil in Cane's books. Neill's odyssey to uncover a publicity-stunt fraud, in the company of Cane's editor Linda Styles (Julie Carmen), leads to Hobb's End, a weirdo town in the King style where monstrous beings are being kept from invading Earth until the hiding Cane can finish his novel, which in reality will spell the end for all of mankind. All these crazy ingredients are blended into a thinking man's horror film which Carpenter directs with an auteuristic style. Stark, horrific images are skillfully blended with intriguing ideas about horror writing, good vs. evil, etc. Jurgen Prochnow (as Cane), John Glover, Bernie Casey. (Video/Laser: New Line)

IN THE NICK OF TIME (1991) ★★ Lloyd Bridges dons the garb of old St. Nick and rushes to New York to find a replacement for himself—or else there will be no Christmas. You see, he's up for mandatory retirement after 300 years. Walt Disney production directed by George Miller. Michael Tucker, Cleavon Little.

IN THE SHADOW OF KILAMANJARO (1986) ★★★ Dramatization of a true incident that took place in Kenya during the drought of 1984, when 90,000 starving baboons went on a killing spree, terrorizing natives and settlers alike. Director Raju Patel treats this topic as though it were a remake of *Jaws*, emphasizing gore and building suspense each time the critters amass in the darkness. Well done, with interesting characters, good photography. Timothy Bottoms, Michele Carey, Don Blakely, John Rhys-Davies, Irene Miracle. (IVE)

IN THE SPIRIT (1990) ★★ Oddball supernatural comedy in which Marlo Thomas and Elaine May portray the guests of a nutty psychic who lives next door to a murderer. Peter Falk, Olympia Dukakis, Melanie Griffith. Directed by Sandra Seacat. (Academy)

IN THE STEEL NET OF DR. MABUSE/IN THE STEEL CABINET OF DR. MABUSE. See *The Return of Dr. Mabuse* (1961).

INTO THE BADLANDS (1991) ★ Macabre TV-movie (possibly inspired by *Grim Prairie Tales*) is a failed anthology, all mood and little substance. The trilogy features unsatisfactory twist endings as bountyman-narrator-storyteller T. L. Barston (Bruce Dern) roves the West in search of outlaw Red Roundtree. In the first yarn, an outlaw flees a lawman and takes up with a prostitute; in the second, two women rivals for the same man are snowbound in an isolated cabin and attacked by wolves; and in the third Barston closes in on Roundtree. Director Sam Pillsbury pumps sardonic touches into the creaky old wagon, but ultimately it groans. Helen Hunt, Dylan McDermott, Lisa Pelikan, Andrew Robinson. (MCA)

INTO THE DARKNESS (1986) ★★ Beautiful models are knocked off in this blood-splasher, enhanced by the menacing presence of Donald Pleasence. Ronald Lacey, Polly Pleasence. Double your Pleasances? Directed by Michael Parkinson. (Video Pictures; Westernworld)

INTO THE WEST (1993) ★★★ A touching, mature children's adventure with metaphysical and supernatural overtones, beautifully directed by Mike Newell from a sensitive, insightful script by Jim Sheridan. Two Irish youths, disturbed that their father (Gabriel Byrne, who doubles as associate producer) has turned into a drunken bum following the death of their mother, run away on the back of a white horse, believed to be a mythical being named Teinerno, hailing from "The Land of Eternal Youth." Or is the horse possessed by the spirit of the dead mother? The youths' odyssey is a picturesque one, inspired by such bits as the horse having popcorn and punch in a movie theater, and watching scenes from *Back to the Future III*. By maintaining an ambiguity toward the horse, *Into the West* is a ride worth taking. Ellen Barkin, Ruaidhri Conroy, Ciaran Fitzgerald. (Video/Laser: Touchstone)

INTRUDER (1989) ★★★ Better-than-average "trapped with a slasher" genre flick thanks to writer-director Scott Spiegel's clever use of camera angles and point-of-view shots. His ironic juxtaposing of images holds one's interest while story and characters do not. This time the human fodder is trapped in a supermarket at night with a crazed killer who uses tools of the produce-butcher trade to commit his murders. Bodies on meat hooks, sliced on meat cutters, cracked open with butcher knives, hatchets, axes—if your butcher has it, Spiegel uses it. Spiegel taints his story meat with a forced ending that speaks poorly of our police—a disturbing element unnecessary in a gory, spoofy entertainment. Elizabeth Cox, David Byrnes, Sam Raimi. (Video/Laser: Paramount)

INTRUDERS (1992) ★★★½ True-life UFO abduction cases documented in Budd Hopkins' book have been blended into a dramatization in this four-hour TV-movie directed by Dan Curtis. Richard Crenna is a disbelieving psychiatrist who comes to realize these bizarre cases cannot be explained in traditional psychiatric terms; he takes up the cause of helping abductees find inner peace. What emerges from the Barry Oringer–Tracy Torme teleplay is a convincing, chilling study of a phase of UFO-ology that is little understood. Mare Winningham and Susan Blakely portray sisters who have been terrorized by strange aliens since they were children. What is shockingly revealed through G. D. Spradlin's cynical Air Force general is the government's contemptuous attitude of keeping the truth hidden from the public while their own researchers carry out a clandestine study of abductions. Daphne Ashbrook, Alan Autry, Ben Vereen, Steven Berkoff. (Fox)

INTRUDER WITHIN, THE (1981) ★★ Okay TV-movie, but too imitative of *Alien* to generate its own unique suspense. Chad Everett is a "tool-pusher" on an oil rig for the Zorton Oil Company, who drills to 19,000 feet to uncover a hideous creature from our ecological past, a spawn that implants reproductive sperm within a human being. When that man goes crazy and attacks a woman crew member, she is destined to give birth to . . . you know what, don't you? The monster passes through evolutionary stages before becoming a man in a glistening fright suit. Directed by Peter Carter, written by Ed Waters. Joseph Bottoms, Jennifer Warren. Aka *The Lucifer Rig*. (Transworld)

INVADER (1992) ★★★½ Exciting, high-tech sci-fi thriller jam-packed with ambitious computerized effects and model work ranging from mediocre to excellent. Although an adventure, the film manages to comment on wasted government spending, if subtext is your thing. An alien entity (in the form of a miniaturized flying saucer) takes over the military and plans nuclear war, with only three standing in its way: a wisecracking reporter for a scandal sheet, a Defense Department investigator, and an Air Force general. The pacing is swift under writer-director Philip J. Cook as the trio faces giant robot HAR-V (Heavily Armed Rampaging Vaporizer) and jet fighters equipped with ASMODS (Automated System Managing Offense & Defense Strategies). Hans Bachmann, A. Thomas Smith. (Video/Laser: Vidmark)

INVADER, THE (1997) ★★½ Set your brain at zero as this HBO-produced sci-fi adventure unfolds at hyperspace-jump warp-drive speed. A saucer pops out of a mother ship and skims to Earth with humanoid alien Ben Cross at the controls. You know he's a good guy because he's wearing a white robe. Swooping out of the clouds surrounding Earth is another alien craft, much bigger and purely evil, what with another humanoid alien (Nick Mancuso) at its controls dressed in metallic black. After a dogfight, both ships crashland on Earth in rugged Canadian terrain. Cut to small-town school teacher Sean Young, who is breaking up with sheriff Daniel Baldwin. She meets Cross in a bar—he kisses her. Wham bang, thank you, alien. The next day Young is pregnant and kidnapped. Cross, whose

alien is named Rem Atti Dar, says he hails from a planet in a "white nova system," and needs the baby, which will be born in just three days, to save his species. Why is never made clear, but you have to admit that Cross makes Speedy Gonzalez look like a molasses salesman. This movie moves so fast it doesn't have time to explain any of the important details. Mancuso assumes the guise of a bounty hunter and goes after Young to kill her and the baby, because for some reason (also unexplained) it would endanger the existence of his species. Director-writer Mark Rosman prefers to keep his nonstop plot moving across the Canadian countryside as one faction chases another. Young, naturally, starts to fall in love with her impregnator and they look at the developing fetus in a laser holograph. Maternal warmth creeps into the picture just long enough for one sequence, then the chase is on again, with many deputies getting blasted by the terminating Mancuso, who stops at nothing to blast everybody in sight with, handguns and automatic weapons. Finally everyone important to the plot arrives at the top of a ski lift where Cross and Mancuso have their final showdown and an alien ship lands, out of which step the good guys. You know they're good guys because they emerge from a glowing white light in uniforms. What happens after that will warm the maternal cockles of your heart, even if you don't like your sci-fi actioners cluttered up with weepy stuff. (Live Home Entertainment)

INVADERS, THE (1995) ★★½ This reprise of the 1967–68 TV series starring Roy Thinnes as David Vincent, who singlehandedly fought off E.T. invaders within a conspiracy plot touching the most responsive parts of our paranoia and suspicion, is a four-hour TV-movie that starts off pretty good and then deteriorates into standard boob-tube stuff. Thinnes only appears in one scene (call it a guest cameo) with attention shifting to just-released convict Scott Bakula, who is taken over by aliens, but escapes their control with the help of his young son and a nurse (Elizabeth Pena). James Dott's telescript seems unnecessarily convoluted, with more characters than needed, but does highlight one exciting sequence wherein we get to see how the aliens take over our bodies. In the second half, Bakula must save a presidential hopeful aboard an out-of-control metro train in L.A., and it's pretty routine from then on. Directed by Paul Shapiro. Richard Thomas, DeLane Matthews, Terence Knox, Shannon Kenny. (Fox)

INVADERS FROM MARS (1953) ★★★ A cult following has built over the years because this touches a sensitive cord in people, who remember those things which first frightened them, and the gap between youth and adults. Jimmy Hunt wakes up one night to spy an E.T. craft submerging itself in a hill outside his house, but no one will believe him, not even when aliens take over humans in a widespread conspiracy. It's the ultimate in paranoia-for-kids. Director William Cameron Menzies, who directed *The Maze*, brings abstract styles to the strange sets, giving this a surreal touch. While Richard Blake's script cops out at the end, the story does have wonderful moments. Arthur Franz, Helena Carter, Leif Erickson, Morris Ankrum, Milburn Stone. Remade in 1986. (Nostalgia Merchant; Media) (Laser: Image)

INVADERS FROM MARS (1986) ★★★ Sincere remake of Menzies' 1953 cult favorite, with writers Dan O'Bannon and Don Jakoby sticking to the original story and director Tobe Hooper trying to recapture what made the original so memorable to the young. In ways they do a better job in capturing the paranoia of a lad who sees everyone being turned into zombies but whom nobody will believe. This excels with its effects by John Dykstra and its Stan Winston–designed monsters. Wonderful cave and spaceship interiors too as Hunter Carson and Karen Black lead the Marines in an exciting old-fashioned rescue. The film is simple and fast-moving with cliff-hangers and visual delights: soldiers being sucked into the sand, Louise Fletcher swallowing a frog whole, and a machine that bores needles into humans being zomboided. Jimmy Hunt, who played the boy in the original, is back as the town's police chief; as he walks up to the hill toward the sandpit, he remarks, "I haven't been up here since I was a kid." Timothy Bottoms, Laraine Newman, James Karen, Bud Cort. (Cannon) (Laser: Image)

INVASION (1966) ★★★ Atmospheric British chiller in which an alien "Lystrian" craft crashes near a country hospital, with the E.T.s aboard being a policewoman and prisoner. When they're taken to the hospital, a force field pops up around the building. A peculiar ambience is generated by director Alan Bridges, who bolsters Roger Marshall's script considerably. Edward Judd, Yoko Tani, Tsai Chin, Valerie Gearon. (S/Weird; Movies Unlimited)

INVASION BY THE ATOMIC ZOMBIES. See *City of the Walking Dead*.

INVASION EARTH: THE ALIENS ARE HERE (1988) ★★½ When insectlike aliens invade a small town, the creatures have a close encounter with an audience watching clips from monster movies, ranging from *The Blob* to *War of the Worlds* to *Them* to *The Giant Claw* to *Fiend Without a Face*. These scenes, including a few from Japanese monster flicks, give the kids in the audience what they need to fight the hideous invaders. Directed by George Maitland. Janice Fabian, Christian Lee. (New World) (Laser: Image)

INVASION EARTH 2150 A.D. (1966). See *Daleks—Invasion Earth 2150 A.D.*

INVASION FORCE. TV version of *Hangar 18* with a different ending.

INVASION FROM INNER EARTH (1977) ★ Filmed in the snow wastes of Wisconsin, this low-budget cheapie depicts stranded travelers being knocked off by red-glowing death rays generated by off-camera aliens. The plot plods as often as the snowbound characters, and director Ito Rebane's idea of an E.T. is to have a heavy-handed voice boom over a radio receiver. The effects are awful and the film lumbers to an incomprehensible ending. (VCI; from Platinum as *Hell Fire*)

INVASION OF CAROL ENDERS, THE (1974) ★★ Meredith Baxter, after almost being killed by a mugger, awakens from a coma with the personality of a woman killed in an "accident" in this TV-movie produced by Dan Curtis, written by Gene Raser Kearney and directed by Burt Brinckeroff. Chris Connelly, Charles Aidman, John Karlen, George Dicenzo. (Thrillervideo; MPI)

INVASION OF MARS. See *The Angry Red Planet*.

INVASION OF PLANET X. See *Godzilla Vs. Monster Zero*.

INVASION OF THE ASTRO MONSTERS. See *Godzilla Vs. Monster Zero*.

INVASION OF THE BODY SNATCHERS (1956) ★★★★★ The political ramifications of director Don Siegel's classic have been well expounded on (it was produced during the McCarthy hysteria of the 1950s and its subtext is rooted in fear of conspiracy) but it can be enjoyed strictly for its thrills. First made as *They Came From Another World*, and aka *Sleep No More*, this is a tale of mounting suspicion and horror as Kevin McCarthy, resident of Santa Mira, discovers an alien race (creatures encased in strange pods which froth and crack open) is creating duplicates of the townspeople and turning them into zombies. The literate Daniel Mainwaring–Sam Peckinpah script (from Jack Finney's novel) and the supporting cast (Dana Wynter, Carolyn Jones, King Donovan) contribute fine work, but it is Siegel's direction that makes it a classic. Remade in '78 under this title and in '93 as *Body Snatchers*. (RCA/Columbia; Republic has a colorized version) (Laser: Republic; Criterion; Voyager)

INVASION OF THE BODY SNATCHERS (1978) ★★★★ Inspired by Jack Finney's novel and first produced in 1956, this has undergone so many changes in W. D. Richter's adaptation that it stands apart from Don Siegel's version. This time we are introduced to alien spores as they leave their home planet and drift through space; it's a striking sequence. The spores settle in San Francisco near victims-to-be: Donald Sutherland, Brooke Adams, Leonard Nimoy, Jeff

Goldblum, Veronica Cartwright. Slowly the humans are replaced by pod creatures, but we're still not sure how much is conspiracy and how much is paranoia and hysteria. The pod effects are revoltingly good and there are several startling scenes, including a mutation dog, that makes this Philip Kaufman–directed film memorable. Don Siegel turns up in a cameo as a cab driver, and Kevin McCarthy plays his character from the original. (Video/Laser: MGM/UA)

INVASION OF THE BODY STEALERS (1969) ★★ Subtitled Thin Air . . . describing what the Mike St. Clair's–Peter Marcus plot went into. A sci-fi belly flop in which parachutists keep disappearing in a strange reddish mist. Agents George Sanders and Neil Connery leap into this vaporous mystery to find out why. Maurice Evans (believe it or don't) appears as an alien. What will director Gerry Levy and producer Tony Tenser think of next? Aka *The Body Stealers*. Robert Flemyng, Patrick Allen. (USA; Live; Vestron).

INVASION OF THE FLESH HUNTERS (1980) ★ Italian-Spanish "zombies on the loose" flick from director Anthony M. Dawson (aka Antonio Margheriti), with gore by Gianetto De Rossi, who splashed blood in *Zombie*. The flesh-eaters are Vietnam veterans in downtown Atlanta led by John Saxon and John Morghen. Aka *Cannibal Massacre, The Cannibals Are in the Streets, Savage Apocalypse, The Slaughterers* and *Virus*. (Vestron; from Midnight Video in an uncut version as *Cannibal Apocalypse*)

INVASION OF THE FLYING SAUCERS. See *Earth Vs. the Flying Saucers*.

INVASION OF THE GARGON. See *Teenagers From Outer Space*.

INVASION OF THE HELL CREATURES. See *Invasion of the Saucermen*.

INVASION OF THE SAUCERMEN (1957) ★★ American-International double-biller slanted for teenagers and featuring wonderful bug-eyed, head-bulging Martians. The film, first made as *Invasion of the Hell Creatures*, has a reputation for being so-bad-it's-good. The Robert Gurney Jr.–Al Martin mishmash of a plot (from a Paul Fairman story, "The Cosmic Frame") has teeners being injected with alcohol by the aliens in an attempt to have them arrested for drunk driving. The hero is Lyn Osborne, Cadet Happy on TV's *Space Patrol*. Frank Gorshin, Steve Terrell, Gloria Castillo, Russ Bender, Ed Nelson. Directed by Edward L. Cahn. Would you call this a Cahn Job? Remade as *The Eye Creatures*. Aka *Spacemen Saturday Night* and *Hell Creatures*. (Columbia TriStar)

INVASION OF THE SPACE PREACHERS (1990) ★★ An asinine accountant and a dumb dentist—pale imitations of Bill & Ted—head for West Virginia for a vacation and nerd their way through pallid misadventures when they encoun-

ter a lizardlike alien from a far-off planet, on Earth to capture a fugitive from her own world posing as a preacherman. Lash of God, who wields a whip in barrooms to convert the sinners, has an insidious plan to hypnotize his radio-show listeners into obeying his orders, but our insipid heroes save the day with the help of a militant gun nut. Writer-director Daniel Boyd stages one flop sequence after another, and not a single gag for 100 minutes is funny. Pray this movie goes away. Jim Wolfe, Gary Nelson, Elisha Hahn. Musician Jimmy Walker plays himself. Aka *Strangest Dreams*. (Rhino) (Laser: Image)

INVASION OF THE TRIFFIDS. See *Day of the Triffids*.

INVASION OF THE ZOMBIES. (1964). See *The Horror of Party Beach*.

INVISIBLE AGENT (1942) ★★★ Cigarettes floating in air and Gestapo agents being kicked in the seat of their pants by an unseen presence are high points of this propagandistic comedy-adventure in which Jon Hall is rendered "unsightly" by taking a drug intravenously. Traveling to Nazi Germany, he gives the Führer what for. Curt Siodmak's script is preachy and preposterous and director Edwin L. Marin glorifies mock heroics as Hall indulges in espionage situations, but it's great fun. Peter Lorre overplays a Japanese baron and Ilona Massey slinks through Berlin as a femme fatale. Cedric Hardwicke, Keye Luke, John Litel, Holmes Herbert. (MCA)

INVISIBLE AVENGER (1958) ★★ "The Shadow," the invisible crimefighter (real name: Lamont Cranston) of pulps and radio, is the hero in this Republic film made in New Orleans (originally as *Bourbon Street Shadows*) and directed by cameraman James Wong Howe and John Sledge. Cranston ("who clouds men's minds so they cannot see him") uses his hypnotic cloak of invisibility to thwart a political assassin while also investigating the murder of a jazz figure. Richard Derr is the playboy investigator in the script by George Bellak and Betty Jeffries. Marc Daniels, Helen Westcott, Jeanne Neher. (Sinister/C; S/Weird; Filmfax; Rex Miller)

INVISIBLE BOY, THE (1957) ★★★ A vehicle designed for Robby the Robot following *Forbidden Planet*, with Richard Eyer as a likable youth who puts Robby back together. As a reward, Robby (voice by Marvin Miller) turns the boy invisible. Unfortunately, the robot comes under the spell of a central computer, Univac, which plans world conquest. Nice special effects and refreshing comedy sparkle throughout Cyril Hume's screenplay. Philip Abbott, Diane Brewster, Harold J. Stone. Directed by Herman Hoffman. Aka *S.O.S. Spaceship*. (MGM)

INVISIBLE CLAWS OF DR. MABUSE, THE. See *The Invisible Dr. Mabuse*.

INVISIBLE DR. MABUSE, THE (1961) ★★ Mediocre German revival of the super archvillain created by Norbert Jacques and made famous by Fritz Lang in the 1920s. Dr. Mabuse (Wolfgang Priess) schemes to steal a formula for invisibility and take over the world. His nemesis is government man Lex Barker. Karin Dor, Werner Peters. Directed by Harald Reinl, written by Ladislas Fodor. Aka *The Invisible Claws of Dr. Mabuse* and *The Invisible Horror*. (S/Weird)

INVISIBLE GHOST, THE (1941) ★★ Monogram mess produced by Sam Katzman with Bela Lugosi as confused, mixed-up Charles Kessler, who is hypnotized by his wife into committing murders. Directed by Joseph H. Lewis; barely written by Helen and Al Martin. Betty Compson, John McGuire, Polly Ann Young. Aka *The Phantom Killer*. (Video Yesteryear; Nostalgia; Sinister/C; United American; Moore; Filmfax) (Laser)

INVISIBLE HORROR, THE. See *The Invisible Dr. Mabuse*.

INVISIBLE INVADERS, THE (1959) ★ Here's one that would have warmed the heart of Ed Wood Jr. It's a riotously inept low budgeter, each scene a treat for buffs who take perverse delight in watching celluloid disasters. Invisible aliens, hiding on the moon, fly to Earth and, changing molecular structure, take possession of corpses to become an army of walking dead. They start with Dr. Noymann (John Carradine). Bad special effects and terrible acting by John Agar, Jean Byron and Robert Hutton provide a laugh a minute, as do the solemn narrator and documentary footage. Director Edward L. Cahn has a style as stiff as a zombie, and writer Samuel Newman must have been in a walking-dead state behind the typewriter. By all means, see it and revel in its absolute ineptitude, and consider how it might have influenced George Romero. (Laser: MGM/UA)

INVISIBLE KID, THE (1987) ★½ Nerdish teenage scientist Jay Underwood, searching for the formula of invisibility once sought by his late father, creates a greenish, gloopy goo that, when combined with pigeon shit, renders him unseeable. Getting revenge on the jerks at Valleyville High, spying on naked, large-breasted girls in the shower and evoking gasps from dumbbell mom Karen Black are Underwood's applications of his formula in this vapid excuse for a fantasy-comedy, in which pigeon shit is the most compelling commodity. The invisibility effects are impoverished, the acting is pitiful and a curse of invisibility should be wished on writer-director Avery Crounse. Wally Ward, Chynna Phillips, Brother Theodore. (Media; Video Treasures) (Laser: Image)

INVISIBLE MAN, THE (1933) ★★★★ The irony of Universal's adaptation of H. G. Wells' novel about scientist Jack Griffin (who discovers monocaine, a drug that renders him invisible) is that it made a star of Claude Rains, even though he is seldom seen, only heard, while swathed in bandages and wearing black goggles. Because of the formula, he is turned into a power-mad killer. "Suddenly I realized the power I had, the power to rule, to make the world grovel at my feet," he proclaims. James Whale's direction and the effects are marvelous. So are character bits by Una O'Connor, John Carradine, Dwight Frye, E. E. Clive and Gloria Stuart. Adapted by R. C. Sherriff and Philip Wylie. (Video/Laser: MCA)

INVISIBLE MANIAC (1990) ★½ A pubescent attitude hangs over this semi-comedic stab at the *Invisible Man* formula, making it a tasteless variation on the dumb-teenager slasher flicks. Numerous nubile, naked female bodies dominate the shower and locker rooms of a high school where a brilliant but insane physics professor (Noel Peters) is hiding from the law, posing as a physics teacher. The cackling madman (and he cackles a lot) turns himself invisible with a "molecule reorganization" serum and pinches bare fannies and titties before a rampage of destruction, first by killing the nymphomaniacal principal and then the students. Gore effects are substandard, writer-director Rif Coogan doesn't know how to bring out the humor in his script, and it fails as a gorefest. Shannon Wilsey, Melissa Moore. (Republic)

INVISIBLE MAN RETURNS, THE (1940) ★★★ Sequel to *The Invisible Man* stars Vincent Price as the brother of scientist Jack Griffin. Price is seldom seen but often heard once he takes a duocaine inoculation and is rendered unseeable. Escaping prison (where he has been unjustly sent), he searches for Jack's real killer. The effects are startling as Price wraps and unwraps himself and as objects float. Quite enjoyable. Joe May directed the Lester Cole–Curt Siodmak script. Nan Grey, Cedric Hardwicke, John Sutton, Alan Napier, Cecil Kellaway. (MCA)

INVISIBLE MAN'S REVENGE, THE (1944) ★★★ Sequel to a sequel has little to do with Wells' fantasy, or with the two films preceding it. Scientist John Carradine discovers a formula for invisibility via injection, which he gives to wrongly accused Jon Hall so he can escape pursuers and track down the culprits who cheated him out of a diamond mine. More floating objects and invisible man trickery, but producer Ford Beebe's direction is lackluster. Written by Bertram Millhauser. Evelyn Ankers, Alan Curtis, Gale Sondergaard, Ian Wolfe. (MCA)

INVISIBLE MONSTER, THE (1950) ★★★ A 12-chapter Republic serial depicting an incredibly inept madman (Stanley Price) who calls himself the Phantom Ruler and intends to conquer the world with an army of invisible warriors. Wearing a cloak chemically treated with a magical formula, he makes himself disappear while standing in the beam of a light ray, but the Phantom Idiot rarely uses this device effectively in his capers to steal money or equipment. Seems that insurance investigator Lane Carson (square-jawed Richard Webb) always outsmarts him. And then there's his assistant Carol Richards (Aline Towne), who runs around the hills of Hollywood in her high heels, occasionally pulling a pistol from her oversized purse and taking potshots at bad guys she can never hit. But no matter how naive it gets, this is nonstop fun. Directed by Fred C. Brannon. Lane Bradford, John Crawford, Marshall Reed. The TV edited version is *Slaves of the Invisible Monster*. Aka *Phantom Ruler*. (Republic)

INVISIBLE RAY, THE (1936) ★★★ Boris Karloff is scientist Janos Rukh, who captures light rays from the past and finds an ancient meteor in the Carpathians imbued with "Radium X," a substance that infects Karloff with a luminous radioactivity that kills anything he touches. On the expedition is Bela Lugosi as Dr. Felix Benet, a sympathetic scientist. The effects are innovative in this unusually lively Universal horror thriller directed by Lambert Hillyer and written by John Colton. Frances Drake, Frank Lawton, Beulah Bondi. (Video/Laser: MCA)

INVISIBLE STRANGLER (1984) ★½ Produced in 1976 as *The Astral Factor*, this remained unreleased for years—for obvious reasons. It's a muddled mess as an imprisoned murderer learns the art of making himself invisible and escapes to knock off those who sent him up. Robert Foxworth plays the stupefied cop and nice-looking ladies pop in and out (Elke Sommer, Mariana Hill, Leslie Parrish, Sue Lyon, Stefanie Powers). The awful script is by Arthur C. Pierce; the bland direction is by John Florea. Insignificant cameos by Alex Dreier, Percy Rodrigues, John Hart. (Trans World)

INVISIBLE: THE CHRONICLES OF BENJAMIN KNIGHT (1993) ★★★ This sequel to *Mandroid* requires that you see the original first to get the drift. This picks up the adventures of how Benjamin Knight (Michael Dellafemina) turns invisible when he takes "Super-Com Crystal" tablets designed by scientist Jennifer Nash, and how wheelchair-bound inventor Brian Cousins controls a robot warrior through a headpiece now reduced to a pair of dark glasses. Nash (as Zanna) becomes a kind of female Rambo when she battles Eastern European police and a gang of misfits and cutthroats led by the ugly Drago (Curt Lownes). Written by Earl Kenton and directed by Jack Ersgard, *Invisible*

was produced in Romania by Charles Band and is notable for its "Invisible Man" special effects if not coherence. (Paramount) (Laser: Full Moon)

INVISIBLE WOMAN, THE (1940) ★★★ No connection to *The Invisible Man* outside of the title. John Barrymore, in one of his last roles, invents a machine that renders fashion model Virginia Bruce invisible. Foreign spies pursue the machine and Miss Bruce. The usual invisible sight gags predominate over the script by Robert Lees, Fred Rinaldo and Gertrude Purcell, but it's worth watching for its cast: Shemp Howard, John Howard, Charles Ruggles, Oscar Homolka, Maria Montez, Margaret Hamilton. Directed by A. Edward Sutherland. (MCA)

INVITATION TO HELL (1984) ★★ Wes Craven–directed TV-movie inspired by *Poltergeist* in which inventor Robert Urich arrives at a strange corporation, Micro Digitech, to begin experiments on a new spacesuit (designed for a Venus expedition) that has laser weaponry built into its sleeves and a helmet that detects nonhuman lifeforms. Meanwhile, a seductive demon from Hell (Susan Lucci) is luring everyone through the portals of her country club into the depths of Hell to seize control of their souls. When Urich's wife (Joanna Cassidy) and children are mind-zapped, he dons the spacesuit for his descent into Hell. Silly premise never convinces. (Sony)

IO. Original title for *Outland*.

IRON GIANT, THE (1999) ★★★½ Can a 100-foot-tall robot creature that hails from another world, and is programmed to destroy planetary life as thoroughly as Gort in *The Day the Earth Stood Still*, be a charming character for a full-length animated feature? Thanks to a thoughtful script by Tim McCanlies and director Brad Bird (who adapted the book by Ted Hughes), the answer is a rousing "Yes, Yes!" Without any of the songs or cutie-pie characters that nowadays dominate the Disney cartoon movies, *Iron Giant* is a straightforward sci-fi adventure told in a simplistic animation style that seems inspired by Japanese cartoons. The robot (voice by Vin Diesel) lands on Earth in 1957, at a time when Americans are very paranoid about the threat of a Russian invasion and kids are seeing a classroom film, *Duck and Cover*, about how to hide under a desk during an atomic attack. The metal-eating man and a 9-year-old boy (Hogarth Hughes, voice by Eli Marienthal) bond after the youth bravely saves the life of the giant, and their relationship is reminiscent of Spielberg's *E.T.* as Hogarth hides the giant's existence from his mother and others. (As in *E.T.* our young hero has no father figure.) That relationship is filled with warmth as the boy teaches the creature how to speak English and the creature shows a gentle side, reacting to the loss of life with compassion. What's refreshing is that the villain of this movie looks like anything but a villain: he's a handsome, almost comedic government agent named Kent Mansley (voice by Christopher McDonald) who gradually turns into a total dastard and betrayer of all of our values. One of the nice supporting characters is the owner of a scrap-metal shop (voice by Harry Connick, Jr.) who creates iron sculptures and helps Hogarth to conceal the giant. Mom is your typical fifties housewife mom (voice by Jennifer Aniston), but her love for Hogarth is a moving part of the film. What makes *The Iron Giant* work so well is its underlying theme that you can become whatever you want to be—you don't have to conform to what others expect of you—and the satiric portrayal of life in the late 1950s that eventually becomes very serious when a nuclear sub launches a missile at the Iron Giant. At a time when many youth-oriented movies express many wrong values, *The Iron Giant* says all the right things in a style that is exciting, moving, and pleasing to the eye. (Video/DVD: Warner Bros.)

IRON MAN. See *Tetsuo: The Iron Man.*

IRONMASTER (1982) ★★½ Despite its simple-mindedness, this French-Italian caveman saga set "20,000 years ago" (in the style of *One Million B.C.*) has a few good moments as an evil warrior named Vor (George Eastman) discovers the secret of forging steel from a volcano lava flow and makes swords to attack the tribe that expelled him for his homicidal ways. The script makes some interesting comments on man's warlike nature and, although it's often violent in its depiction of men being slaughtered by cold steel, makes a pitch for disarmament and more peaceful ways among men. It also features muscular, beautiful bodies as the heroic Sam Pasco and beautiful girlfriend Pamela Field race through a buffalo field in Custer, South Dakota, and try to convince a benevolent tribe it must fight to save itself from Vor. Elvire Audray, William Berger, Jacques Herlin, Brian Redford. Directed by Umberto Lenzi. (Prism; ANE)

IRON WARRIOR (1986) ★ This sequel to *Ator the Fighting Eagle* and *Blade Master* in the easily forgettable Ator series stars that Poor Man's Conan, Michael O'Keefe, on the island of Malta as he does battle with monsters and assorted villains to protect Princess Janna (Savina Gersak). Directed by Italian potboiler king Al Bradly. Tim Lane, Elizabeth Kaza. (Media; Video Treasures)

I SAW WHAT YOU DID (1965) ★★½ Gimmicky William Castle–directed potboiler in which two teenage babysitters phone at random, exclaim "I saw what you did and I know who you are!" and hang up. One man they call (John Ireland) has just finished slaughtering his wife (Joan Crawford) in a shower scene inspired by *Psycho.* William McGivern's script (from an Ursula Curtiss novel, *Out of the Dark*) has mysteriously opening and closing doors and windows as the mad killer stalks the teeners. A minor film that satisfies more for its campiness than its outdated thrills. Leif Erickson, Sarah Lane, Pat Breslin, John Archer.

I SAW WHAT YOU DID (1988) ★★ This TV-movie remake of the 1965 William Castle feature is the medium at its worst—plodding direction by Fred Walton, a mediocre script by Cynthia Cidre (from *Out of the Dark,* the Ursula Curtiss novel) and a sincere cast in need of all the help it can get. Castle's work had a tongue-in-cheek endearment, but this lacks it all. The plotline has been shifted around so the killer is now film-music composer Adrian Lancer (Robert Carradine), who goes berserk. He loves to tie you up and set you on fire. Out of tune, isn't he? The teenagers who becry "I saw what you did and I know who you are!" are a wearisome lot, and the whole thing unfolds predictably. Shawnee Smith, Tammy Lauren, Candace Cameron, David Carradine.

ISLAND, THE (1980) ★ This Zanuck-Brown production of Peter Benchley's novel proposes a solution to the Bermuda Triangle mystery: All those boats and people are vanishing because modern descendants of 17th-century pirates are still flying the skull and crossbones. An exciting premise, but Benchley's script is insipid and the characterizations are atrocious. Magazine researcher Michael Caine and son seek an answer to the mystery by acting as decoys. David Warner and his pirates are supposed to have a code all their own, but it's a ridiculous life they lead, plunging the film into laughability. Director Michael Ritchie's worst. Angela McGregor, Frank Middlemass. (Video/ Laser: MCA)

ISLAND AT THE TOP OF THE WORLD (1974) ★★ Inferior Disney adventure-fantasy with poor effects and a horribly mangled story—a cinematic massacre of Ian Cameron's *The Lost Ones* by John Whedon and Harry Spalding. David Hartman, hardly the stuff movie heroes are made of, leads an expedition to the polar regions in the airship Hyperion in 1908. The team discovers a long-forgotten kingdom ruled by bloodthirsty Vikings. This "adventure epic" misses by miles, turning its potential fun into turgidity. Directed by Robert Stevenson, this does feature a good music score by Maurice Jarre. Donald Sinden, Mako, Jacques Marin. (Video/Laser: Disney)

ISLAND CITY (1994) ★★½ Mediocre TV pilot for a sci-fi series set in a futuristic, fortified city where the last remnants of the human race struggle against roving "Recessives," mutant monsters (created by a drug gone bad) with superhuman, superpsychotic strength. The pacing of director Jorge Montesi is sluggish, and the teleplay by Jonathan Glassner is strangely lacking in excitement as commando Kevin Conroy heads up a team assigned to rescue one of their numbers lost in the desertlike wilderness that is the world outside the city. There are, however, some interesting "Virtual Reality" touches, a fascinating good-guy Recessive, and a clever use of a clone character who has several lookalike brothers. Brenda Strong, Eric McCormack, Pete Koch, Constance Marie.

ISLAND CLAWS (1982) ★★★ Old-fashioned giant-monster-on-the-rampage flick, enhanced by Florida photography and the personas of Robert Lansing and Barry Nelson. A research team is experimenting with crustaceans when an atomic energy malfunction creates one huge monster crab killer and forces the little crabbers to turn against mankind, with a taste for People Thermidor. Thrills are minimal until the monster crab attacks. The story (by Jack Cowden and underwater stuntman Ricou Browning) is predictable. Herman Cardenas directs. Jo McDonnell, Nita Talbot. Aka *Night of the Claw*. (Vestron)

ISLAND OF DEATH. See *Island of the Damned*.

ISLAND OF DR. MOREAU, THE (1977) ★★★½ Effective adaptation of H. G. Wells' novel (by John H. Shaner and Al Ramrus) with Burt Lancaster as the demented albeit earnest doctor who converts animals into half-men through vivisection. The "creative makeup" is excellent, resulting in a menagerie of "manbeasts" led by Richard Basehart as the Sayer of the Law. The tropical rain forests near St. Croix in the Virgin Islands are a superb location for director Don Taylor. Michael York and Barbara Carrera as the lovers confronted with Moreau's horrors make for a sympathetic couple. *Island of Lost Souls* was the 1933 version starring Charles Laughton, and that was a good one too. Watch for Nick Cravat as M'Ling. Nigel Davenport, Fumio Demura. (Warner Bros.)

ISLAND OF DR. MOREAU, THE (1996) ★★★ This is an unusual remake of the H. G. Wells horror tale about a mad scientist who creates a society of half-man, half-animal creatures (first made as *Island of Lost Souls* in 1933 with Charles Laughton, and then again in 1976 as *The Island of Dr. Moreau* with Burt Lancaster). The eccentric standout in this John Frankenheimer–directed version is Marlon Brando as a British-accented Moreau, who paints himself white to avoid the sun's rays, wears robes over his corpulent body, and shows a wacky intellectual side to his madness. His Dr. Moreau is only a half-complete performance (Moreau is a crazed scientist trying to improve the human species by eliminating destructive impulses through DNA splicing) in a role that's far too short, considering its needs to the story.

That leaves it up to his insane henchman (Val Kilmer) and shipwrecked innocent David Thewlis (who is totally miscast as the hero) to carry the moral weight of the tale, which they cannot do. *Island* ends up being an overdone statement about man's inhumanity to himself. The script by Richard Stanley and Ron Hutchinson is mostly action, with far too little characterization to give it balance. Stan Winston's makeup for the creatures, on the other hand, is terrific and finally steals the show, even from Brando. Fairuza Balk, Ron Perlman, Neil Young. Charles Laughton is still the best Moreau. (Video/DVD: New Line)

ISLAND OF LIVING HORROR, THE. See *Brides of the Beast*.

ISLAND OF LOST SOULS (1933) ★★★★★ One of the most chilling horror films of the 1930s, a repellant though intriguing adaptation of H. G. Wells' novel about the mad Dr. Moreau, who grafts animals into men in his "House of Pain" to change the process of evolution. Charles Laughton, as the vivisectionist who presides Godlike over his creatures, is on the hammy side, but his overplaying is what makes Moreau seem above the affairs of ordinary men, destined to change science. Bela Lugosi as the Sayer of the Law has a grotesquely satisfying role. Not for the squeamish as the beast-men scamper about in mental and physical anguish. Written by Philip Wylie and Waldemar Young, directed by Erle C. Kenton and starring Richard Arlen as the shipwrecked hero. Remade in 1977 as *The Island of Dr. Moreau*. (Video/Laser: MCA)

ISLAND OF MUTATIONS. See *Screamers*.

ISLAND OF TERROR (1967) ★★★ An isolated community is under attack from man-produced silicate monsters that suck human bone marrow. Director Terence Fisher and writers Alan Ramsen and Edward Andrew Mann infuse tongue-in-cheek with the macabre to avoid the humdrum in this sickening nightmare. Silicates are snakelike tentacles that slither around corners when you least expect them. They'll have you jumping as they wriggle up stairways and latch onto human flesh. There's a great sequence where Peter Cushing has to cut off his own hand to save himself. Niall MacGinnis, Edward Judd, Eddie Byrne. Also known as *The Creepers, The Night the Creatures Came, Night of the Silicates* and *The Night the Silicates Came*. (Sinister/C; S/Weird; MCA)

ISLAND OF THE ALIVE. See *It's Alive III: Island of the Alive*.

ISLAND OF THE BURNING DAMNED. See *Island of the Burning Doomed*.

ISLAND OF THE BURNING DOOMED (1967) ★ Produced in Britain as *Night of the Big Heat*, and known as *Island of the Burning Damned*, this is a simmering adaptation of a John Lymington novel by Ronald Liles in which Christopher Lee, Peter Cushing, Patrick Allen, Sarah Lawson and Jane Merrow are attacked by aliens capable of burning measly humans to death with a heat wave. But the film, unlike the characters, never catches fire. Directed by Terence Fisher. (New Star)

ISLAND OF THE DAMNED (1976) ★★★ Spanish horror thriller is an exciting exploitation film in which a pregnant wife and her husband visit a pleasure island to find all the adults dead and homicidal children eager to slaughter more. On a less obvious level, it points out how children become victims of adult madness through civil war and strife. Hence, their revenge! Luis Perafiel's script is food for thought and explicitly violent as the children close in on the couple, forcing them to commit acts of mayhem. Directed by Narciso Ibanez Serrador. Also known as *Who Can Kill a Child?*, *Would You Kill a Child?*, *Death Is Child's Play* and *Island of Death*. Lewis Fiander, Prunella Ransome.

ISLAND OF THE DEAD/ISLAND OF THE DOOMED. See *Man-Eater of Hydra*.

ISLAND OF THE FISHMEN. See *Screamers*.

ISLAND OF THE LAST ZOMBIES, THE. See *Dr. Butcher M.D. (Medical Deviate)*.

ISLAND OF THE LIVING DEAD. See *Zombie* (1979).

ISLAND OF THE SNAKE PEOPLE. See *The Snake People*.

ISLAND OF THE TWILIGHT PEOPLE. See *The Twilight People*.

ISLE OF THE DEAD (1945) ★★★★ Arnold Boecklin's painting, "Die Todinsel," inspired this low-key Val Lewton horror chiller, which was written by Ardel Wray and Josef Mischel. It is strongly atmospheric but strangely slow under Mark Robson's direction. One of Boris Karloff's strangest roles—he portrays a tyrannical Greek general in the year 1912 (the Balkan War is raging) who believes in "vrykolakas," Greek vampires. When a sinister plague infects the island, Karloff quarantines everyone and, one by one, the assorted characters meet their doom. Ellen Drew, Jason Robards Sr., Alan Napier, Marc Cramer. (Fox Hills; Media; Facets Multimedia; Nostalgia Merchant; Turner) (Laser: Image; Turner)

ISLE OF THE FISH MEN. See *Screamers*.

ISLE OF THE LIVING DEAD. See *The Snake People*.

ISLE OF THE SNAKE PEOPLE. See *The Snake People*.

I SPIT ON YOUR GRAVE (1979) ★★ The epitome of rape-woman's revenge pictures, a cult favorite written-directed-edited by Meir Zarchi. A bloody tale (aka *Day of the Woman*) about four men who gang-bang vacationing Camille Keaton. After a second go-around of debasement, the chauvinistic pigs are wasted/castrated by the avenging angel, who uses every weapon at hand from butcher knife to hangman's rope to woodman's ax to . . . not for the squeamish. Eron Tabor, Richard Pace, Anthony Nichols. (Wizard; VidAmerica) (Laser: VidAmerica; Image)

I STILL KNOW WHAT YOU DID LAST SUMMER (1998) ★★½ If characterization was the strength of Kevin Williamson's screenplay for *I Know What You Did Last Summer*, it is not the strength of Trey Callaway's for this lackluster sequel, which creates the dumb characters associated with the slasher genre. On the other hand, Callaway stacks the cards for some climactic surprises that at least make the final payoff a bit enjoyable. It isn't saying much, since getting there should be half the fun. It isn't. This gory movie, in which the fisherman killer with the hook is back stalking new victims, epitomizes the clichés of its genre: sudden "stings" (a blast of music to punctuate a visual surprise or an anticlimax), a woman screaming at the top of her lungs whether she's in danger or not, lengthy scenes of a woman in peril creeping around in the darkness, and drawn-out sequences in which the killer never runs but always walks steadily and determinedly toward his victim while the victim tries to extricate herself/himself from some trap or cliffhanger situation. Jennifer Love Hewitt and Freddie Prinze, Jr., the only survivors of the 1997 box-office success, are both back in their seaport town when Hewitt's best friend Karla (played by music star Brandy) wins a free trip to the Bahamas through a radio contest. (The fact that they answer incorrectly should have tipped them off that the killer might have a hand in the free vacation, but our characters aren't that smart.) While Prinze is attacked by the slasher, the two ladies and their boyfriends (Mekhi Phifer as the loudmouthed, obnoxious pal of Brandy and Matthew Settle as a shy, retiring type who has the hots for Hewitt) arrive on an isolated island, which is quickly cut off from the rest of the world by a tropical storm. Who's running the resort? A sassy-mouthed manager played by onetime horror star Jeffrey Combs, so you know this is going to be paradise hell. Other goofy characters—a voodoo baggage handler, a sexy bartender, and a pot-smoking fat man—become body count for the wrath of the fisherman. Chaotic, disconnected scenes pass for a plot, but that doesn't bother director Danny Cannon (*Judge Dredd*), who just keeps the bloody murders coming, with the hook always penetrating through the brain or torso of the victims, and the victims being carried away on the point of the hook with blood smeared all over the sets. The only reason this was made was because of the $100 million-plus box office of *I Know What You Did Last Summer*, a cynical thought but the bottom line. (Video/DVD: Columbia TriStar)

IT! (1966) ★★ The Golem is the Jewish Avenger, a creature of clay wreaking havoc on desecrators. Roddy McDowall is a batty museum curator keeping the mummified body of the Golem as an exhibit who finally misuses the creature for evil revenge. The thing goes berserk, destroying Hammersmith Bridge and kidnapping Jill Haworth. Written-produced-directed by Herbert J. Leder. Aka *The Curse of the Golem* and *Anger of the Golem*. Paul Maxwell, Aubrey Richards, Ernest Clark.

IT (1958). See *It! The Terror From Beyond Space*.

IT! (1990). See *Stephen King's It!*

IT CAME FROM BENEATH THE SEA (1955) ★★★½ Collaboration between producers Charles Schneer and Sam Katzman and stop-motion animator Ray Harryhausen resulted in a historic monster flick about a giant octopus awakened by an atomic blast and attracted to San Francisco Bay. The creature (with only six tentacles, due to Katzman's insufficient budget) attacks the Golden Gate Bridge and Embarcadero. This has its fun moments as directed by Robert Gordon from a George Worthington Yates–Hal Smith script. Donald Curtis and Kenneth Tobey still have time to woo scientist Faith Domergue during the mayhem. Ian Keith, Harry Lauter, Del Courtney. Aka *Monster From Beneath the Sea*. (RCA/Columbia; Goodtimes) (Laser: Columbia TriStar)

IT CAME FROM HOLLYWOOD (1982) ★★★ Compilation of the best "worst" scenes from genre movies, emphasis on monsters, horror and drugs, put together under the direction of Malcolm Leo and Andrew Solt, and unwritten by Dana Olsen. Comedians appear in camped-up cameos covering specialized themes. Gilda Radner does Gorillas and Musical Memories; Cheech and Chong cover (naturally) Getting High, Giants, and Animal Kingdom Goes Berserk; Dan Aykroyd deals with Brains, Aliens and Troubled Teenagers. There's a salute to Edward D. Wood Jr. (*Plan 9 From Outer Space*) and Prevues of Coming Attractions and Technical Triumphs. The guest hosts are superfluous—the clips can stand alone. Anyway, fans, you'll see scenes from *White Gorilla, The Brain That Wouldn't Die*, etc. Hollywood at its funniest—and dumbiest. (Video/Laser: Paramount)

IT CAME FROM OUTER SPACE (1953) ★★★★★ One of the finest science-fiction thrillers of the 1950s, inspired by a Ray Bradbury outline that was modified for Universal-International by Harry Essex, and originally released in 3-D. Essex's screenplay, while being among the first to portray benevolent aliens, is also a plea for better understanding between races. This is Jack Arnold's best directorial work, for he captures a desert eeriness as bug-eyed aliens crash land their ship near astronomer Richard Carlson's isolated home. The E.T.s, dubbed Xenomorphs, are giant eyeball creatures capable of assuming human forms. A "fish-eye" lens is used to simulate the point of view of the creatures. Barbara Rush provides love interest, Charles Drake is the disbelieving sheriff, and Russell Johnson and Joe Sawyer are possessed telephone linemen. Known in the early stages as *The Meteor, Atomic Monster* and *Strangers From Outer Space*. (Video/Laser: MCA)

IT CAME FROM OUTER SPACE II (1995) ★★ To purposefully set out in the nineties to make a cheapjack sequel to a science-fiction classic of the fifties is beyond comprehenshion, beyond the pale, beyond the stars. Yet here it is, a low-budget, lowbrow rehash of events first depicted in the 1953 Jack Arnold–directed Universal-International hit that starred Richard Carlson as a scientist who comes in contact with aliens stranded in the Arizona wilderness. In this updated mishmash of the Ray Bradbury story, photographer Brian Kerwin, living in an isolated desert community of social misfits, discovers that a multidimensional craft from space has assumed the shape of a rock that grows as it sucks up all the water as well as a few wandering folks. These include single mother Elizabeth Peña, who provides barely a modicum of love interest for Kerwin, and her estranged son Jonathan Carrasco. While the bug-eyed aliens in the original were benevolent and incapable of harming Earthlings, the extraterrestrial presence here is capable of violence, but never materializes as anything more than a glowing blue color. The special effects are genuinely cheesy, the script by Ken and Jim Wheat is strictly threadbare, and producer-director Roger Duchowny does nothing to disguise a lack of enthusiam for this doomed project. There's little for Bill McKinney, Adrian Sparks, Howard Morris, and Lauren Tewes (as residents of the desert town) to do; at least you have the option of ignoring this time waster. (Universal)

IT CAME UP FROM THE DEPTHS. Alternate title for the TV-movie *The Bermuda Depths*.

IT CAME . . . WITHOUT WARNING. See *Without Warning* (1980).

IT CONQUERED THE EARTH. See *It Conquered the World*.

IT CONQUERED THE WORLD (1956) ★★★ "It" does nothing of the sort—"it" is one sad-looking Venusian hiding in a cave that blows its invasion because "it" is dumb enough to rely on Lee Van Cleef to carry out "its" evil bidding. And dumb enough to send a squad of bat creatures to kill Beverly Garland, thereby tipping off Peter Graves to what is happening. This Roger Corman produced-directed quickie (remade as *Zontar, the Thing From Mars*) ranks as one of his all-time worst, yet fans continue to enjoy its campiness, to which writer Lou Rusoff made a considerable contribution. Dick Miller, Russ Bender, Sally Fraser, Jonathan Haze, Charles B. Griffith, Paul Blaisdell. Aka *It Conquered the Earth*. (RCA/Columbia)

IT FELL FROM THE FLAME BARRIER. See *The Flame Barrier*.

IT FELL FROM THE SKY. See *The Alien Dead*.

IT HAPPENED AT LAKEWOOD MANOR (1977). See *Ants*.

IT HAPPENED AT NIGHTMARE INN (1970) ★★ Spanish horror flick, written-directed by Eugenio Martin, is set in a hostelry of hostility on the Mediterranean coast, where two batty sisters murder tourists when they fail to live up to moral standards. The bodies, with gaping knife wounds in vital organs, are dumped into wine vats before the wine is served to the guests. Meanwhile, innocent Judy Geeson arrives looking for her missing sister and notices how strange it is guests disappear without checking out. Accommodations must be poor. Don't make a reservation. Aka *Nightmare Hotel, A Candle for the Devil* and *Nightmare Inn*. Aurora Bautista, Esperanza Roy, Victor Alcocer. (Sinister/C; S/Weird).

IT HAPPENS EVERY SPRING (1949) ★★★★½ For fantasy fans, baseball lovers, romanticists and scientists. Professor Ray Milland invents an anti-wood substance. Think what that could mean if applied to a baseball. So, as his spitball curves around every swinging bat in the majors, he becomes a big league pitcher and carries a losing team to the World Series. It's the whimsical side to *The Natural*, a marvelous comedy starring Jean Peters as the love interest and Paul Douglas as a blustering manager. A film like this should happen every spring. A hit directed by Lloyd Bacon from a clever script by Valentine Davies and Shirley Smith. Alan Hale Jr., Ray Collins, Ed Begley, Ray Teal, Gene Evans. (Fox)

IT LIVES AGAIN. Video version of *It's Alive II* (Warner Bros.).

IT LIVES BY NIGHT. See *The Bat People*.

IT'S ALIVE (1968) ★ Credit writer-producer-director Larry Buchanan for botching this one thoroughly. A crazy rancher who collects snakes and crawlies has also found a "lizard amphibian" in a cave, so he feeds it passersby. Along comes paleontologist Tommy Kirk plus another couple, and they're all thrown to the Masasaurus. The most exciting thing is not the creature—it's a rubber-suited fake—but watching blond Shirley Bonne walk around in a yellow miniskirt. (S/Weird; Nostalgia; Loonic)

IT'S ALIVE (1974). See *The Bat People*.

IT'S ALIVE (1975) ★★★ Larry Cohen wrote-directed this gruesome shocker about an infamous infant who slides from the womb with claws, fangs and sharp teeth and kills doctors and nurses before they even have time to spank his spiked behind. While it sounds like the ultimate nightmare, rolling birth and death into one act, Cohen creates the ambience of an abnormal world tainted by birth control pills, poisonous chemicals, smoggy air and atomic fallout. Your skin will crawl as the bloodthirsty bambino (created from the nightmares of Rick Baker) lurks around every corner. Cohen keeps his monster out of camera range most of the time, thereby building suspense and shocks. John Ryan, Sharon Farrell, Guy Stockwell, Andrew Duggan, Michael Ansara. Original title: *Baby Killer*. (Warner Bros.)

IT'S ALIVE II (1978) ★★ Larry Cohen's *It's Alive* was a powerful indictment against our misuse of atomic power and drugs, but this sequel fails in the delivery room. Call it stillborn. Cohen's writing and directing are utterly off the mark in depicting another baby-faced killer sliding from a womb with claws and teeth to kill. Parents Frederic Forrest and Kathleen Lloyd flee with the mutant to an incubation hideout where other baby-monsters are under study by scientist Andrew Duggan and the father from the first film, John Ryan. (Duggan believes the babies are "the next step in evolution so we can survive the pollution of our planet.") Credit Rick Baker for the hideously fanged creatures infrequently shown during Cohen's hide-and-seek direction. John Marley, Eddie Constantine. (From Warner Bros. as *It Lives Again*)

IT'S ALIVE III: ISLAND OF THE ALIVE (1986) ★★ An unusual performance by Michael Moriarty earmarks this second sequel to writer-director Larry Cohen's 1975 hit. A wave of baby monsters is hitting society and Moriarty decides that love and not death is the way to deal with the teethy tykes when their fate must be decided in a court of law. Judge MacDonald Carey decrees they be sent to a desert island. Moriarty goes a little paranoid, turned cynical by how society exploits the mutant monsters through the media, and he returns to the island with an expedition to help the freaks. Moriarty's nuttiness and the social issues touched on by Cohen's script make this above-average. The monsters are depicted with live action and stop-motion animation. Karen Black, Laurene Landos, Gerrit Graham, James Dixon. (Warner Bros.)

IT'S ALIVE! THE TRUE STORY OF FRANKENSTEIN (1994) ★★★ A two-hour TV special (originally broadcast on the A&E network) tracing, in literate, fascinating fashion, the history of Mary Shelley's *Frankenstein* novel, from the origin of how she came to write it, her personal history as a 19th-century author, on through the cinematic interpretations ranging from Universal's 1932 version to Mel Brooks' *Young Frankenstein* to Kenneth Branagh's 1994 extravaganza. Among those interviewed are Brooks, David J. Skal, Sara Karloff (daughter of Boris), makeup man Rick Baker and Branagh. This documentary by Richard and Zora Brown, loaded with historic movie stills, trailers and film excerpts, is hosted by Roger Moore and narrated by Eli Wallach.

IT'S A WONDERFUL LIFE (1946) ★★★★★ Capra-corn as Hollywood's producer-director Frank Capra indulges in whimsical nostalgia to present a slice of unforgettable Americana. Guardian Angel Clarence (Henry Travers) is dispatched to a small Wisconsin town to show Jimmy Stewart, a disillusioned young man, what might have happened had he never been born. A touch of *A Christmas Carol* makes this an exceptionally penetrating slice of life, which Capra scripted with Frances Goodrich and Albert Hackett (under the original title of *The Greatest Gift*). Donna Reed, Lionel Barrymore, Thomas Mitchell, Gloria Grahame, Ward Bond. Wonderful music by Dimitri Tiomkin. (Hal Roach; Republic; Nostalgia Merchant; a colorized version also exists) (Laser: Republic; Criterion)

IT'S GROWING INSIDE HER. TV title for *The Devil Within Her*.

IT STALKED THE OCEAN FLOOR. See *Monster From the Ocean Floor*.

IT! THE TERROR FROM BEYOND SPACE (1958) ★★★ Epitome of the sci-fi monster movies of the 1950s, more bearable than its title would suggest thanks to a decent script by Jerome Bixby. Ray "Crash" Corrigan dons the rubber suit to play a vampire-style Martian which stows away on a rocketship and then, when deep in space, develops a thirst that can't be quenched at the snack bar. That's when astronauts Marshall Thompson, Shawn Smith, Ann Doran and Kim Spalding get it in the neck. Frequently compared to *Alien*. Directed by "quickie master" Edward L. Cahn. Aka *It! The Vampire From Outer Space*. (Video/Laser: MGM/UA)

IT! THE VAMPIRE FROM OUTER SPACE. See *It! The Terror From Beyond Space*.

IVANNA. See *Scream of the Demon Lover*.

I'VE BEEN WAITING FOR YOU (1998) ★★★ This TV-movie imitation of the slasher genre, in the vein of *Scream* and *I Know What You Did Last Summer*, is well done for its type, and comes complete with a surprise ending that might even fool a few fans. Sarah Chalke portrays a teenager who settles in Pinecrest, MA, only to be haunted by dreams of a witch who was burned at the stake 300 years before. Sarah's fellow students, descendants of those who burned the witch, are then attacked by a robed fiend with the face of a hag and a four-pronged knife, and the descendants think Sarah's hexing them with her supernatural powers. There's nothing believable in Duane Poole's script (based on Lois Duncan's novel *Gallows Hill*), it's all contrived to be a slasher movie, remember? Christopher Leitch directs with a sure understanding of the genre, with all the clichés in the right places. Soleil Moon Frye, Ben Foster, Christian Campbell, Maggie Lawson, Chad Cox, Tom Dugan, Markie Post. (Video/ DVD: PM Entertainment)

I WALKED WITH A ZOMBIE (1943) ★★★★ RKO low budgeter is producer Val Lewton's classic, a loose adaptation of *Jane Eyre* (scripted by Curt Siodmak and Ardel Wray) in which nurse Frances Dee is brought to a Caribbean island to care for a woman in a zombielike state, victim of mental paralysis. Hauntingly directed by Jacques Tourneur, with a Calypso-inspired score by Roy Webb. J. Roy Hunt's cinematography is punctuated by striking visuals, such as a voodoo native (Darby Jones) with a cadaverous face stalking two women through a canefield. James Ellison, Tom Conway, Edith Barrett. (Nostalgia Merchant; Media; RKO; Turner) (Laser: Turner)

I WAS A TEENAGE BOY. See *Something Special*.

I WAS A TEENAGE CAVEMAN. See *Teenage Caveman*.

I WAS A TEENAGE FRANKENSTEIN (1957) ★★ Herman Cohen's sequel to *I Was a Teenage Werewolf*, with Whit Bissell reappearing as a mad doctor, relative of the infamous Baron. Ludicrous as its title, with severed limbs graphically offered up for their shock value (and severed limbs in 1957 were an onscreen rarity). Despite its trend-setting virtues, and the fact it was an early proponent of black-macabre humor, Kenneth Langtry's script is hopelessly laughable, often in the wrong places. You, too, will be a teenage zombie if you sit through this. Phyllis Coates, Gary Conway. Aka *Teenage Frankenstein*. (RCA/Columbia)

I WAS A TEENAGE SEX MUTANT (1989) ★ Poor Billy Jacoby. Every time a tubular, humming creature pops out of his head all the women rip their clothes off and claw his body. It's worse than acne. That creature got there because of alien Judy Landers, a biology teacher in miniskirt and high heels who's on Earth to conduct experiments in human (and inhuman) behavior. Kenneth J. Hall's kitchen-sink script (with emphasis on sex rather than mutant) is pretty dumb, with nerdy Jacoby turning into a rock star, an excuse for a musical number. Directed by David DeCoteau. Olivia Barash, Stuart Fratkin, Bobby Jacoby, Arlene Golonka, Edy Williams. (From Paramount as *Dr. Alien*)

I WAS A TEENAGE WEREWOLF (1957) ★★★
An American-International classic (written by
Ralph Thornton) with Michael Landon as a troubled youth etched in the style of James Dean.
When he falls under the control of wicked doctor Whit Bissell, Landon regresses to a primitive, animalistic state (make that werewolfian)
on a rampage of killing. The suspense is minimum under Gene Fowler Jr.'s direction, but the
point of view of the story's young people, the
depiction of adults, and the time-lapse transformation special effects, although dated, now
seem nostalgic and quaint. For decades Landon
disavowed this film, then came to Arkoff in the
1980s and asked permission to use some footage
for an episode of *Highway to Heaven* he called
"I Was a Middle-Aged Werewolf." Yvonne
Lime, Guy Williams, Robert Griffin. Aka *Blood
of the Werewolf.* (RCA/Columbia)
I WAS A TEENAGE ZOMBIE (1987) ★ An amateurish, almost unwatchable piece of crapola.
Better it should have been called *I Was a Teenage Nerd.* Some jerks hanging around Woodbridge High discover that a drug dealer named
Mussolini (Moose for short), whom they killed

and threw in the bay, has been brought back to
life by high-energy radioactive contamination
from the Mohawk Nuclear Power Plant. Mix the
contamination with "kinetic energy" and presto—
a dreaded zombie killer. Director John Elias
Michalakis tries to shock by having a tongue
pulled out of a man's mouth and a young
woman bent in half while she's being raped by
"Moose," but these effects leave everything to
be desired. Michael Ruben, George Seminara.
(Video/Laser: Charter)
I WAS A ZOMBIE FOR THE FBI (1984) ★ An
alien monster presented in stop-motion animation, a silver ball that turns humans into zombies, the secret formula for a soft drink,
Unicola—these are the bizarre ingredients that
make this an offbeat sci-fi spoof played straight
by writer-director Marius Penczner. The time is
the 1950s when the criminally inclined Brazzo
brothers survive a plane crash, stumble across
an alien plot and involve the FBI in a kidnapping—and that's only the beginning. Refreshing
oddity; unusual in that it was produced at Mem-
phis State University. John Gillick, James Rasberry, Larry Rasberry. (Cinema Group;
Continental)

JACK AND THE BEANSTALK (1952) ★★½
Fantasy-comedy written by Nat Curtis with Lou
Costello as a babysitter reading the famed fable
to an obnoxious brat. Presto: Costello becomes
Jack and Bud Abbott plays the village butcher
"boy." Buddy Baer is the ogre—ferocious but
appealing enough not to scare the kids for whom
this fluff was intended. Directed by Jean Yar-
brough from a script by Nat Curtis. William
Farnum, Dorothy Ford. (MGM/UA; Amvest;
VCI; Burbank; Alpha; Video Treasures; from
Goodtimes with *Africa Screams*)

JACK FROST (1999) ★★ This film about a dead
father who returns to life in the shape of a snowman with stick arms tries to melt your heart, but
if you are not a mild-mannered sentimentalist
who likes sappy movies designed to tug shamelessly at your heartstrings, it may just give you
a cold shoulder. I wanted to throw snowballs at
screenwriters Mark Steven Johnson, Steve
Bloom, Jonathan Roberts, and Jeff Cesario for
their lack of imagination. If you're going to
have a dead man return from the land beyond
and reincarnate a snowman, how about some
wild and crazy explanation, or some funny logic
(or illogic; hell, it's a movie) about how man
and snow could blend into a living entity that
walks and talks. This creative vacuum extends
beyond just a lack of a colorful fantasy concept.
It includes a clichéd relationship between father
and son: Mark Addy is this obnoxious, unbearable kid who gets mad at dad Michael Keaton
because he's never around. Dad is always off
with his rock-and-roll band, trying to make it
big in show business instead of showing his son
how to play hockey. It doesn't seem to matter
that dad is dedicated and working his butt off to
make a good home for the kid and wife Kelly
Preston. Such selfishness in a child is horrible
to see on the screen, given the deteriorating state
of the American family and the fact this is intended as a children's picture. Filmed during
snow season in and around Medford, CO, *Jack
Frost* features live-action special effects created
by Jim Henson's Creature Shop, but the snowman is such a curiously unexciting design, these
sequences are as lackluster as everything else.
Laszlo Kovacs remains one of the best cinematographers in the business, but his talents are
wasted on this kiddie-oriented hogwash, as are
those of director Troy Miller, who struggles to
inject excitement into his hopelessly limp story.
Supporting players Henry Rollins, Joseph Cross,
Mika Borrem, and Andy Lawrence do what they
can with underwritten characters. Only the boy's
dog, Mr. Chips, seems to have any charm.
(Video/DVD: Warner Bros.)

JACK-O (1995) ★★ A cheesy Fred Olen Ray
production, poorly directed by coproducer Steve
Latshaw, and featuring sexy scream queens
(Linnea Quigley, Brinke Stevens, Dawn Wildsmith, etc.) in nothing roles. The setting is Oak-
moor Crossing, where "The Pumpkin Man"
stalks innocent folks on Halloween eve. Pumpkin Man is a two-bit fright job—a glowing
pumpkin head with a crummy-looking scythe in
his gnarly hands. Not as scary as the L.A. Freeway system at rush-hour time. Ray dug up some
leftover footage from previous films of John
Carradine and Cameron Mitchell, but they add
nothing to the nothing script by another coproducer, Patrick Moran. The gore effects are not
convincing, so this excuse for a movie just flops
around for 90 minutes, dying every second.
Gary Doles, Ryan Latshaw (Steve's son), Catherine Walsh, Rachel Carter. (Triboro) (Laser:
Image)

JACK'S BACK (1987) ★★★ Intriguing update
to Jack the Ripper is set in L.A. where a slasher-
killer is duplicating the infamous 1888 crimes
and the city is in a grip of terror. There's a psychic link between twin brothers John and Rick
Wesford (James Spader) and when John is
found hanged, and assumed to be the Ripper,
Rick comes forth to clear his name. Nice plot
twists involve a police hypnotist, a short-
tempered doctor and a brute named, naturally,
Jack. The script by director Rowdy Herrington
is above average. Cynthia Gibb, Rod Loomis,
Rex Ryon. (Video/Laser: Paramount)

JACK'S WIFE. See *Season of the Witch*.

JACK THE GIANT KILLER (1962) ★★★ Director Nathan Juran (who cowrote the script with
Orville Hampton) and actors Kerwin Mathews
and Torin Thatcher reteamed again after *The
Seventh Voyage of Sinbad*, but this fantasy-
adventure sorely needs the Harryhausen touch.
While Don Beddoe is effective as a leprechaun,
the giants, sea serpents, gryphons and flying
witches leave something to be desired. Mathews
is brave of heart, Thatcher is treacherous as Pendragon the Sorcerer and Judi Meredith is enchantingly beautiful. Youngsters will enjoy. The
special effects are by Jim Danforth. (Video/La-
ser: MGM/UA)

JACK THE MANGLER OF LONDON. See *Jack the Ripper of London* (1971).

JACK THE RIPPER (1958) ★★ Boris Karloff anthology of four mild tales, each introduced by Karloff, who also has roles in three. These studio-bound yarns rely on dialogue and acting, and hence are of minimal impact. "Jack the Ripper" (made in London) is the best, with a clairvoyent aiding Scotland Yard's Inspector McWilliams in solving the Whitechapel murders. "Summer Heat" has Harry Bartell as a man with precognition powers who witnesses the murder of a blonde—before it happens. Karloff is the police psychiatrist. "Vision of Crime" involves rival brothers whose father returns from the grave. Karloff is the family attorney. "Food on the Table" features Karloff as a scheming sea captain who poisons his wife, only to have her return as a mischievous spirit. Michael Plant wrote the Ripper segment; no other writing credits given. The only director's credit is David MacDonald. These episodes were produced by Hal Roach Jr. for the series *The Veil*, but it was a flop and sold into syndication as three anthologies. The others are *The Veil* and *Destination Nightmare*. Paul Bryar, Gretchen Thomas, Robert Griffin, Niall MacGinnis. (S/Weird)

JACK THE RIPPER (1971). See *Jack the Ripper of London*.

JACK THE RIPPER (1976) ★ This Jack tears it! A totally inaccurate German-Swiss depiction of the infamous London murders, with facts discarded by screenwriter-director Jesus Franco for exploitation. Klaus Kinski portrays the sexual brute as a despicable freako who stops at nothing to murder-fornicate. Clinically sickening in details. Josephine Chaplin, Herbert Fux. (Vestron)

JACK THE RIPPER (1988) ★★★½ Engrossing and intense TV-movie that offers a solution to the unsolved Jack the Ripper case. This dramatization of the five horrendous slasher-crimes covers the investigation, political intrigue and near-rioting of citizens. At the heart of the film's power is Michael Caine as Inspector Frederick George Abberline, who heads the investigation with Sergeant George Godley (Lewis Collins). Producer-director David Wickes' script takes on a whodunit aspect as suspects are established, among them the Queen's grandson (Marc Culwick), a psychic (Ken Bones), a vigilante leader (Michael Gothard), American actor Richard Mansfield (Armand Assante), even members of the police. The last half-hour is especially fascinating as Caine's behavior rises to a fever pitch as he closes in on the Ripper. Ray McAnally, Jane Seymour, Susan George, Harry Morgan, Edward Judd. (MPI; Vestron)

JACK THE RIPPER GOES WEST. See *Silent Sentence*.

JACK THE RIPPER OF LONDON (1971) ★★ Modernized treatment of the infamous Whitechapel murders, showing the killer to have cannibalistic instincts. An unsavory Spanish-Italian version that is beneath contempt. Cowritten by the film's star Paul Naschy (as Jacinto Molina) and director Jose Luis Madrid. Patricia Loran. Aka *Jack the Ripper* and *Jack the Mangler of London*.

JACOB'S LADDER (1990) ★★★★ Intriguing cinematic puzzle that offers numerous clues to its surprise conclusion but only if you're watching carefully, and can see where screenwriter Bruce Joel Rubin is headed. In Vietnam in 1971, a platoon is attacked under odd circumstances. Flash ahead to the present as Tim Robbins, a GI wounded in the assault, undergoes visions, in which it appears demons are determined to kill him. We also flash back to his life before Vietnam, and elements from all three realities intermingle, and we are adrift in Robbins' mind. Directed by Adrian Lyne in brilliant style. Elizabeth Pena, Danny Aiello, Matt Craven. (IVE) (Laser: Image)

JACULA (1973) Variant title for an X-rated horror film directed by Jesus Franco that was recut into *Erotikill*. Aka *The Last Thrill, The Bare-Breasted Countess* and *Sicarius—The Midnight Party*.

JADE (1995) ★★★ Basic instincts should tell you that if the script is by Joe Eszterhas you are in for a sleazy, sex-riddled time as a killer strikes with a battle ax and an African face mask, leaving the blood-drenched victim pinioned to the wall. Cop David Caruso (looking lost during the entire film) discovers the governor (Richard Crenna) is involved, as is an old girlfriend (Linda Fiorentino) who enjoys sex with strange men. This twisted, convoluted and messy tale is saved only by the artful direction of William Friedkin, who photographs his unsavory but beautiful people on elegant sets, and a car chase over the hilly streets of San Francisco and through Chinatown during a New Year's parade. An ugly movie, lacking believable motivations, but challenging to the eye and the ear with its creepy James Horner score and smashing sound effects. Chazz Palminteri, Michael Biehn, Donna Murphy, Kevin Tighe, Kenny King (a real S.F. cop). (Video/Laser: Paramount)

JANE AND THE LOST CITY (1986) ★★½ "Jane" was first a comic strip in the London *Daily Mirror* about a blonde whose clothes were always falling away to reveal her shapely form in panties and bra—she alone kept up the morale of British troops during World War II. This film version, with Kirsten Hughes playing Jane, is a takeoff on the adventures of Indiana Jones, with Jane venturing into Africa in 1940 to find a lost city's diamond fortune. With Jack Buck or "Jungle Jack" (a square hero dumbly played by Sam Jones) she fights a Nazi beauty (Maud Adams) and her inept henchmen. There's a leopard queen with a British accent, a British colonel and his butler, and tribes of lizard and water warriors. A bland spoof at best. Jasper Carrott, Robin Bailey. Directed by Terry Marcel. (New World)

JAR, THE (1984) ★ For 90 minutes little happens while Gary Wallace sits and looks either blank or frightened. Following an auto accident (filmed so darkly one can barely see it), Wallace finds a bottle containing a demon that proceeds to drive him out of his mind. This attempt at surrealism and horror (also called *Carrion*) with very few visuals (corpse rising out of tub of blood; slaughter of American troops in Vietnam) isn't worth one's time. Directed by Bruce Toscano. (Magnum)

JASON AND THE ARGONAUTS (1963) ★★★★½ Superb mythological fantasy, directed by Don Chaffey, with stop-motion animation by the incomparable Ray Harryhausen. A recounting of the adventures of Jason and his warriors who dare the dangers of a bronze giant named Talos, the winged harpies, the seven-headed Hydra and sword-wielding skeletons to claim the Golden Fleece. Todd Armstrong is a superb Jason, watched from on high by the gods of Mt. Olympus. The link between mortal and immortal becomes a compelling element to the Jan Read–Beverly Cross script. As a picturesque, picaresque fantasy, this is hard to top. Nancy Kovack is Medea, Honor Blackman and Niall MacGinnis are goddess and god, Nigel Green is the brave Hercules. A great score by Bernard Herrmann enhances this British-U.S. effort. Aka *Jason and the Golden Fleece*. (Columbia TriStar) (Laser: Columbia TriStar; Criterion)

JASON AND THE GOLDEN FLEECE. See *Jason and the Argonauts*.

JASON GOES TO HELL: THE FINAL FRIDAY (1993) ★★★ Is this really the last of the *Friday the 13th* flickers? Yes . . . until Hollywood decides to make a few million more from the Jason-Voorhees-in-a-hockey-mask-formula. In this, the ninth series entry, directed by Adam Marcus, Jason is back as a supernatural entity transferring his evil soul from body to body by injecting a piece of his heart into a new recipient's mouth. Hot on his trail: bounty hunter Creighton Duke (Steven Williams), the only man on Earth who knows that only a descendant of Jason can kill him, if equipped with a magical sword that Duke just happens to carry. This remains a relatively unimaginative blood-and-violence fest, with the usual variety of death devices to dispatch the cannon-fodder charac-

ters. Nobody in the cast is memorable—only Kane Hodder as the hockey-masked Jason. According to the script, Jason murdered a total of 83 people in the preceding films. Not bad. Not great, but not bad. Jon D. LeMay, Karl Keegan, Steven Culp, Erin Gray. (New Line)

JAWS (1975) ★★★★★ Box-office smash based on the so-so albeit best-seller by Peter Benchley. Under Steven Spielberg's direction, this becomes a classic adventure saga, ingeniously mounted to evoke our primeval fears as a Great White Shark (25 feet long) attacks the New England community of Amity. After episodes in which humans are bait or narrowly escape the superfish, sharkfighters Robert Shaw, Richard Dreyfuss and Roy Scheider set out aboard the *Orca* to kill the monster. In addition to taut action sequences and great shark effects, there are subtle horrors too, such as when Shaw, a survivor of the sinking of the USS *Indianapolis* in 1945, describes how men were eaten alive. Carl Gottlieb and Spielberg hashed out the final story. This all-time fish whopper did for public beaches what *Alien* did for space travel. The great "shark machine" music is by John Williams. Lorraine Gray, Murray Hamilton, Jeffrey Kramer. (Video/Laser: MCA)

JAWS 2 (1978) ★★½ This sequel to the smasheroo inspired by Peter Benchley's novel is afloat in too-familiar waters and lacks the bite of the original. Director Jeannot Szwarc imitates Spielberg in shameless style, but captures none of the visceral terror. Bruce the Mechanical Shark looks exactly that as he "attacks" youngsters trapped on the high seas. Surely a colossal case of overbite. Carl Gottlieb coscripted with Howard Sackler. Returning are Roy Scheider as the sheriff, Lorraine Gary as his wife and Murray Hamilton as the obnoxious mayor. Jeffrey Kramer, Collin Wilcox. (Video/Laser: MCA)

JAWS 3 (1983) ★★ What could have been gnashing thrills, Bruce the Shark in 3-D, is a disappointment when a baby Great White and 35-foot-long mother enter the lagoon of a Florida seaworld park and attack swimmers and the underwater observation rooms and corridors. Except for scenes where the behemoth swallows a man, or bumps its snout against plucky heroine Bess Armstrong, *Jaws 3* strangely lacks excitement. It's hard to understand why some scenes are underlit, the stupid characters (did Richard Matheson and Carl Gottlieb really write this dribble?), and the juvenile, almost *Porky's* approach. A few 3-D effects are fine (such as a floating severed arm), but stereovision adds little to the dimensions of this mediocre attempt. Production designer Joe Alves directed. Lou Gossett Jr., Dennis Quaid, Lisa Mauer, Simon MacCorkindale, Barbara Eden. (Video/Laser: MCA)

JAWS 3-D. See *Jaws 3.*
JAWS 4. See *Jaws: The Revenge.*
JAWS OF DEATH (1976). Video version of *Mako: The Jaws of Death* (King of Video; Paragon; United American)
JAWS OF SATAN (1983) ★ Terrible killer-snake movie: a King Cobra (the film's original title) on a rampage is a demon serpent sent from Hell to terrorize priest Fritz Weaver. If that sounds absurd, consider the awful Neanderthal special effects, the absurd screenplay by Gerry Holland and the unskilled direction of Bob Claver. The cobra commands other poisonous creatures (asps, rattlers, cottonmouths, water moccasins) to carry out its biting, so the coiled critters are everywhere, harassing Gretchen Corbett and Jon Korkes, both of the Wimp School of Acting. A wretched wreck filmed in Alabama. (Wood Knapp)
JAWS OF THE ALIEN. Video version of *The Human Duplicators* (Star Classics).
JAWS: THE REVENGE (1987) ★★ Anyone who has been to Universal Studios' tour knows that Bruce the Great White Shark rises out of the water to scare everyone on the tourist tram. Well, that's exactly how Bruce looks when he/she/it goes on the attack in this third sequel in the *Jaws* series. With that all-important illusion shattered, *Jaws: The Revenge* is a waste of viewing time. Bruce is now endowed with a supernatural ability to single out members of the Brody family: Lorraine Gary's two sons, and Gary herself during the climactic encounter. Producer-director Joe Sargent gives away the shark's presence prior to each attack, so no tension builds. Michael de Guzman's script defies all credibility, and not even Michael Caine as a pilot helps much. Mario Van Peebles, Karen Young. (Video/Laser: MCA)
J.D.'S REVENGE (1976) ★★★ Well-acted supernatural tale in which law student/cabbie Glynn Turman (in an excellent performance) is possessed by the spirit of a razor-wielding black lowlife murdered in 1942. Turman undergoes transformation, becoming the deceased J. D. Walker. Motivation for the possession is a nightclub hypnosis act—a weakness in Jaison Starkes' otherwise compelling story. Produced-directed by Arthur Marks. Lou Gossett Jr., Joan Pringle, David McKnight. (Orion)
JEKYLL AND HYDE (1990) ★★★ Elaborate sets and period costumes enhance this British TV-movie version of Robert Louis Stevenson's classic tale of dual personality, written-directed by David Wickes. Michael Caine is Dr. Henry Jekyll, whose experiments have turned him into a monstrous murderer terrorizing London. The effects of the metabiological transmutation are familiar though well done. Caine's performance captures the doctor's psychic pain. His Jekyll is a doomed man, and really tears apart the scenery. A new element is the doctor's romance with Cheryl Ladd, which leads to a startling conclusion. Wickes and Caine previously collaborated on a *Jack the Ripper* TV-movie. Joss Ackland. Lionel Jeffries.
JEKYLL AND HYDE... TOGETHER AGAIN (1982) ★ Comedian Mark Blankfield creates a white powder that, when sniffed, brings out an alter ego. It's a "beast of the '80s" that sprouts kinky hair and jewelry (yes, jewelry). And then this hybrid Hyde grows platform heels (yes, platform heels) and a gold tooth with "Love" inscribed on it (yes...). This is a self-respecting monster? Blankfield's talent could not salvage this mess from writer-director Jerry Belson, who demonstrates no taste or respect for "an audience of the '80s." Bess Armstrong, Tim Thomerson, George Chakiris. (Paramount)
JEKYLL'S INFERNO. See *The Two Faces of Dr. Jekyll.*
JENNIFER (1978) ★★½ Thinly disguised copy of *Carrie*, about withdrawn Lisa Pelikan, who possesses supernatural powers in time of jeopardy. Jennifer is harassed by the campus bitch at Green View School for Girls but, because she once reached into a box of poisonous serpents without being bitten, she can call upon the Winds of Fury. That's when the snake gods attack. "Give me the vengeance of the viper," she demands. You should say, "Give me the Power to resist imitation B-movies." Nina Foch, John Gavin. Directed by Brice Mack. Aka *Jennifer: The Snake Goddess.* (Vestron)
JENNIFER: THE SNAKE GODDESS. See *Jennifer.*
JERICHO FEVER (1993) ★★ In the vein of *Outbreak* and *Virus*, this minor TV-movie depicts the efforts of disease doctors Stephanie Zimbalist and Branscombe Richmond in stopping a new strain of virus that is killing people coming up from Jericho, Mexico, where a gang of terrorists have just blown up an armored car. I. C. Rapoport's script is more concerned with how an FBI Navajo Indian and Israeli secret police track the mercenaries into Texas. Directed by Sandor Stern, *Jericho Fever* is a momentary diversion, quickly forgotten, which in no way approaches the major disease movies it brashly imitates. Alan Scarfe, Ari Barak, Perry King, Elysa Davalos, Kario Salem, Don Harvey.
JESSE JAMES MEETS FRANKENSTEIN. See *Jesse James Meets Frankenstein's Daughter.*
JESSE JAMES MEETS FRANKENSTEIN'S DAUGHTER (1966) ★ Outré oater with monster motifs, a blend of cowboys and mad doctor. Result: A laughable disaster that bites the dust. This abomination depicts a pardner of fast-drawing Jesse transmutated into a cactus-chewing Monster dubbed "Igor" when the daughter of the title implants Dr. Frankenstein's brain in his cranium. Directed by William Beaudine. John Lupton, Nestor Paiva, Narda Onyx,

Jim Davis. Originally made as *Jesse James Meets Frankenstein*. (Embassy; Nostalgia; Sultan)

JIGSAW MURDERS, THE (1989) ★★ Mild horrific overtones (mad killer is leaving body parts of a beautiful model all over L.A.) are all that will appeal to horror lovers in this low-budget police procedural. Emphasis is on cops Chad Everett (a drunk unable to control his petulant daughter) and Paul Kent (a likable partner on the verge of marriage) who build a vendetta against the killer (Eli Rich). Since the murderer's identity is no secret, there's no suspense, nor does director Jag Mundhra give it a hard edge. Yaphet Kotto stands out as a medical examiner. Michelle Johnson, Dena Drotan. (MGM/UA)

JIMMY, THE BOY WONDER (1966) ★★ This has been described as the one time the king of movie gore, Herschell Gordon Lewis, set out to make a family movie (!?). A youth sets out to find out why time has stopped, meeting a bizarre assortment of characters. (Movies Unlimited; Tapeworm)

JITTERS, THE (1989) ★★ Kyonshee, the Chinese walking dead, become trapped on Earth and are sought by Marilyn Yokuida and boyfriend Sal Viviano, plus some magicians who know a few incantations of the undead. It's pretty silly, played for laughs, and has minimal impact. A brick falling on your head from 12 stories—that has impact. Produced-directed by John M. Fasano. James Hong, Frank Dietz, Handy Atmadja. (Prism)

JOAN MEDFORD IS MISSING. See *House of Horrors*.

J.O.E. AND THE COLONEL (1985) ★★★ "Project Omega" creates a superperfect human by a recombining of molecules in a controlled environment. The result is "J-type Omega Elemental," a perfect soldier. This comic-book idea is improved by producer-writer Nicholas Corea by allowing J.O.E. to have compassion for the scientists who created him. The rest is formula action as J.O.E. carries out dangerous missions to satisfy a need for excitement. Directed by Ron Satlof. Terence Knox, Gary Kasper, Aimee Eccles, William Lucking, Marie Windsor. (From MCA as *Humanoid Defender*)

JOE VS. THE VOLCANO (1990) ★★ John Patrick Shanley wrote-directed this parable (with overtones of fantasy and comedy) in which Tom Hanks, diagnosed as having a terminal illness, agrees to jump into a South Pacific volcano to appease the angry island gods. Why he wants to sacrifice himself and why Lloyd Bridges hires him are just two cloudy issues surrounding this eccentric movie. Shanley errs by not letting us know this is a fantasy until the climax. Meg Ryan portrays half-sisters, each diametrically opposed to the other (as well as a third role),

Ossie Davis shines as a philosophical chauffeur, and Robert Stack is authoritative and sinister as Hanks' doctor, who diagnoses that Hanks has a "brain cloud." But it still doesn't jell. (Video/Laser: Warner Bros.)

JOHN CARPENTER PRESENTS "BODY BAGS" (1993) ★★★ Acting if he were an out-of-control Crypt Keeper, with "blab on the slab," John Carpenter portrays a ghoulish morgue keeper who introduces three tales. In "Gas Station," directed by Carpenter, Alex Datcher is an attendant at an all-night service booth who is terrorized by a serial killer. Standard slasher, woman-in-peril stuff, with only a clever tag line to set it apart from the zillion other slashers. In "Hair," also directed by Carpenter, Stacy Keach learns the hard way that his phobia about growing bald, and his deal with hair-restoring Dr. Locks (David Warner), are terrible prices to pay. And in "Eye," directed by Tobe Hooper, Mark Hamill plays a guy who loses his right eye in a car accident and has it replaced with the eye of a serial killer. Roger Corman has a cameo in this one. Carpenter's tongue-in-cheek gore gags are the best thing this has to offer. In short, he puts hip zip in the flip trip to the prop shop. (Video/Laser: Republic)

JOHNNY MNEMONIC (1995) ★★★ An overabundance of high-impact violence, much of which is gratuitous at best, undermines this Canadian adaptation of William Gibson's cyberpunk sci-fi adventure, which he himself scripted. What it needed more of is its imaginative computer animation, which attempts to simulate the inner look of the Internet, if one could somehow be within that mazework of abstract pathways. Instead, Gibson relies on the grossest kind of man's inhumanity to man, with assorted killers (Takeshi as a yakuza hitman, Dolph Lundgren as a religious fanatic) using futuristic weapons (such as a kind of laser garroting wire) as they pursue the titular character, whose severed head is wanted by the underworld. As played on a one-note level of anger by Keanu Reeves, Johnny Mnemonic is a courier with a computer chip in his brain that allows him to upload and download vital information that could expose the corruption of the corporations that ruthlessly rule the world in the year 2021. Mnemonic's odyssey takes him through a half-destroyed world where Ice-T's freedom movement in Newark helps him to fight attackers with a dolphin used to transmit information (?). A lot of powerful visual material ultimately seems wasted on an unpleasant tale populated purely by unpleasant characters. Conceptual artist Robert Longo directed with some style, but the drab, dark photography and the total lack of humanity and warmth never allows the viewer to feel close to the protagonists. (Video/Laser: Columbia TriStar)

JOHNNY ZOMBIE. See *My Boyfriend's Back.*

JOHN TRAVIS—SOLAR SURVIVOR. See *Omega Cop.*

JOSH KIRBY . . . TIME WARRIOR! (1995) This is a six-part cliff-hanger serial from producer Charles Band depicting the juvenile sci-fi/fantasy adventures of 13-year-old Corbin Allred as he is swept through hyperspace with kooky professor Irwin 1138 (Barrie Ingham) and a furball named Prism from A.D. 2420. In pursuit is Dr. Zoetrope (Derek Webster), a madman in a weird spacesuit who also travels the time zones in search of six parts of the Nullifier Component, a device from the Milky Way that could destroy the Universe if it falls into Zoetrope's hands.

JOSH KIRBY: PLANET OF THE DINO-KNIGHTS (CHAPTER 1) ★★½ This adventure finds all parties in medieval England, where Azabeth, an adventuress from the future (Jennifer Burns), has fallen into the hands of evil Lord Henry (amusingly played with weasely evil by Spencer Rochfort), who is in cahoots with Zoetrope and a T.-Rex monster. The Ethan Reiff/Cyrus Voris/Paul Cassini script was directed by Ernesto Farino (with help from Frank Arnold). (Video: Paramount) (Laser: Moonbeam)

JOSH KIRBY . . . TIME WARRIOR! THE HUMAN PETS (CHAPTER 2) ★★ This second in the series completes the action in *Dyno-Knights* with a battle between two dragons (poorly done model work), then moves through time and space to a goofy world of A.D. 7000 where giants rule Earth and all the characters (miniaturized) fall into the hands of a precocious kid who misuses them in his bedroom as toys. At Josh's side from now on is adventuress Burns. Added to the mix are a German flyer, a cowboy and a caveman. Pretty silly stuff, a comedown after the first episode. Corbin Allred, Derek Webster, John De Mita, Richard Lineback. Script by Ethan Reiff, Cyrus Voris and Paul Callisi; directed by Frank Arnold (with help from Ernest Farino). (Video: Paramount) (Laser: Moonbeam)

JOSH KIRBY . . . TIME WARRIOR! TRAPPED ON TOYWORLD (CHAPTER 3) ★½ This third chapter is a complete bore. Toyworld is on a burned-out planet where the only human, Japetto (Buck Kartalian), makes good-spirited toys to amuse himself, including Annie (Sharon Lee Jones), a bubbly thing that would like to lay Josh (Corbin Allred) if he wasn't such a conceited time-traveling jerk. The nothing script was by Nick Paine and the direction by Frank Arnold is negligible. The only good thing is Robert Band's theme music. But will it never end? (Video: Paramount) (Laser: Moonbeam)

JOSH KIRBY . . . TIME WARRIOR! EGGS FROM 70 MILLION B.C. (CHAPTER 4) ★★ This is a decided improvement over the Toyword fiasco, with the gang turning up on Asabeth's home planet, which is under attack from Dreadnaught, who wants to conquer her world. One still wonders how producer Charles Band gets away with some awful special effects (the furry critter Prism is absolutely unbelievably bad). Oh well, the Patrick Clifton script deals with cute little worm creatures that thrive on eating metal after they hatch from their eggs. Director Mark Manos tries to make it all cutesy-pie, but he should get a custard in the face for it. Steve Wilder, Gary Kasper. (Video: Paramount) (Laser: Fullmoon)

JOSH KIRBY . . . TIME WARRIOR! JOURNEY TO THE MAGIC CAVERN (CHAPTER 5) ★★½ Great jumping ions! This adventure in the time continuum takes Josh and gang to a world of mushroom people called "shrooms," and is enhanced by tongue-in-cheek touches in the Ethan Reiff–Cyrus Voris script (the ruler, for example, is Lord Truffle). When Azabeth is poisoned, the gang rushes to "Nightmare Hollow" in search of Puffball for an antidote. They encounter Colonel Damon (Matt Winston, doing a take-off on a confederate officer) and his Intergalactic Circus. It appears that Irwin 1138 may be evil and Zoetrope a good guy, thereby giving a much needed lift to this lethargically developed "serial," which seems to have little forward thrust even though Josh keeps saying "I must save the Universe from total destruction." Directed by Ernest Farino. Nick De Gruccio, Cindy L. Sorenson. (Video/Laser: Paramount)

JOSH KIRBY . . . TIME WARRIOR! LAST BATTLE OF THE UNIVERSE (CHAPTER 6) ★★ Some battle. In this last (and merciful) chapter, Josh, Azabeth and Professor Zoetrope wind up back at Josh's home in 1980 and stand around talking most of the time—yak yak yak gibberish about time travel, continuums, warp anomalies, etc. Instead of coming to an exciting resolution, this alleged cliffhanger series fizzles out and dies. Writers Ethan Reiff and Cyrus Voris had no idea what to do with all the stuff that had gone before, so director Frank Arnold dozes at the camera. Yawn. Jonathan Charles Kaplan, Stacy Sullivan, Michael Mahon, Johnny Green. (Video/Laser: Paramount)

JOURNEY BENEATH THE DESERT (1961) ★★ French-Italian actioner finds a triumvirate of directors (Edgar G. Ulmer, Frank Borzage and Giuseppe Masini) struggling with an arid script (based on Pierre Benoit's *L'Atlantide*) and coming up lost in the middle of story desolation. An atomic explosion reveals an entrance to the Lost City of Atlantis, ruled by the wicked queen Antinea (Haya Harareet), who gives nosy explorer Jean-Louis Trintignant a bad time. Georges Riviere, Rod Fulton, Gabriele Tinti. Aka *Queen of Atlantis, Lost Kingdom, Atlantis, City Beneath the Desert.* (Sinister/C; S/Weird; Filmfax)

JOURNEY BEYOND THE STARS. Early title of *2001: A Space Odyssey*.

JOURNEY INTO THE UNKNOWN. See *The Wizard of Mars*.

JOURNEY THAT SHOOK THE WORLD, THE. See *Blast Off* (1967).

JOURNEY TO PLANET FOUR. See *The Angry Red Planet*.

JOURNEY TO THE BOTTOM OF THE SEA. Original production title for *Voyage to the Bottom of the Sea*.

JOURNEY TO THE CENTER OF THE EARTH (1959) ★★★ Bernard Herrmann's music sets the mood for this spirited version of Jules Verne's novel about an expedition into the bowels of our planet, directed by Henry Levin with style. The light-hearted touches in the script by producer Charles Brackett and Walter Reisch (aka *Trip to the Center of the Earth*) contribute to the entertainment. The underground sets are stunningly imaginative, the adventures replete with giant lizards and an erupting volcano and the cast colorful: James Mason and Pat Boone lead the expedition while Arlene Dahl keeps her lips well painted to lessen our fears she might be too far from civilization. Diane Baker, Alan Napier. (Video/Laser: CBS/Fox)

JOURNEY TO THE CENTER OF THE EARTH (1987) ★ Youngsters fooling around in a Hawaiian cave drop through a hole into a subterranean world containing the lost continent of Atlantis. A mess of a movie, worked over by two directors (Rusty Lemorande and Albert Pyun), written by Lemorande with Kitty Chalmers, and pasted together into something that only vaguely resembled a feature film. It sounds strangely similar to *Alien From L.A.*, which was also directed by Pyun around the same time as this film. (Anyone out there know about a connection?) Nicola Cowper, Ilan Mitchell-Smith, Kathy Ireland. (Video/Laser: Cannon)

JOURNEY TO THE CENTER OF THE EARTH. See *Where Time Began*.

JOURNEY TO THE CENTER OF THE EARTH (1993) ★★★ Jules Verne might want to strangle those responsible for this TV-movie, so far is it removed from his 1863 fantasy novel about explorers descending into a beautiful but deadly subterranean world. That criticism aside, this is an over-the-top sci-fi extravaganza depicting a bullet-shaped vessel, the Adventure, which is fired into volcanic molten lava and "swims" to the center of the Earth, a world of alien creatures, a race of wise Yetis (as represented by 7-foot Carel Struycken, who plays Lurch in the Addams Family movies), a humanoid shape in a life-support unit, and prehistoric cavemen. It gets ridiculous at times, yet it has a thrusting vitality. Aboard the ship is a woman's head floating in a bubble (a computer nicknamed "Devin," short for Digital Electro-Plastic Virtual Intelligence Navigation) and several stereotypes. Directed by William (*Harry and the Hendersons*) Dear. David Dundada, Farrah Forke, Kim Miyori, Jeffrey Nordling, Tim Russ, Fabiana Undenio. Standouts are John Neville as an eccentric expert on inner world myths and F. Murray Abraham as a professor who goes nuts.

JOURNEY TO THE CENTER OF TIME (1968) ★★½ Back and forth in time—centuries into the future when mutants battle a dictatorship, centuries into the past when dinosaurs are savage—keeps this fantasy clipping along, even if it fails to come to grips with logic. Directed by David L. Hewitt from a David Prentiss script. Scott Brady, Gigi Perreau, Anthony Eisley, Lyle Waggoner. (Academy; Genesis; also from American as *Time Warp*)

JOURNEY TO THE FAR SIDE OF THE SUN (1969) ★★ The Doppelgänger theory, that there is a parallel world matching our own detail for detail, is put to the test in this commendable space thriller, directed by Robert Parrish and written by Gerry and Sylvia Anderson and Donald James. European Space Exploration Center uncovers a planet on the other side of the sun and sends a manned vehicle with Roy Thinnes. The film is also a study in conspiratory paranoia. Made as *Doppelganger*. Herbert Lom, Ian Hendry, Lynn Loring. (MCA)

JOURNEY TO THE MAGIC CAVERN. See *Josh Kirby . . . Time Warrior! Journey to the Magic Cavern (Chapter 5)*.

JUDAS GOAT. See *Xtro*.

JUDAS PROJECT, THE: THE ULTIMATE ENCOUNTER (1995) ★½ The only reason, and I do mean the only reason, to watch this retelling of the Jesus Christ legend in a contemporary setting is for the cosmic, zappy special effects by Richard Edlund, who at one point turns the spirit of Jesus into a ball of light not unlike Tinkerbell. Otherwise, you can forget this turgid, didactic tract of religious clichés and Biblical teachings, which score a big Scripture Zero for entertainment value. John O'Banion plays the neoJesus in cowboy boots and Ramy Zara is Jude, who naturally betrays J. C. for 30 pieces of silver. Overacting to the point of disbelief is Jeff Corey as Ponerous, who represents the evil government with designs to misuse Jesus' popularity. Richard Herd and Gerald Gordon costar. It all came from the fundamentally muddled mind of one James H. Barden, who wrote and directed. (Hemdale)

JUDGE DREDD (1995) ★★★★ An imaginative, over-the-top rendering of the famous British comic-book series created by Pat Mills, Mike McMahon and Brian Bolland, this is technically superior in capturing the essence of a futuristic world (A.D. 2139) in which mankind has formed into Mega-Cities. The world outside is "The Cursed Earth," an uninhabitable region fit for neither man nor beast. The depiction of Mega-City One is awesome with its complex use of computerized graphics. Law and order is maintained by Judges, and those bizarre shoulder pads of Judge Dredd couldn't have been filled by a better choice than Sylvester Stallone, who has the perfect sneer for the dirty job of acting as cop, judge and executioner in one laser blast. This is how audiences like their Stallone served up—without subtlety. Stallone and comedy sidekick Rob Schneider escape going to prison to return to Mega-City One to prevent Rico (Armand Assante, showing not the least restraint, with a plan to destroy the Judges and their system of law and order) and his Mean Machine (a killer robot with great personality). Helping out is fellow cop Diane Lane and a sympathetic Judge (Max von Sydow) who trained Dredd. There's little story in the William Wisher–Steven E. deSouza script but plenty of action with a variety of superweapons, supercycles and other equipment. Director Danny Cannon blends it all into one satisfying action sci-fi flick that is frequently stunning, and always exciting. Joan Chen, Jurgen Prochnow. (Video/Laser: Buena Vista)

JUDGMENT DAY (1989) ★★ Video flick is an uneven supernatural thriller set in the village of Santana, where once a year the Devil and disciples drop in from Hell to claim souls. There's good dialogue by writer-director Ferde Grofe Jr. and a professional air lent by Monte Markham, Peter Mark Richman and Cesar Romero; and yet, elements are muddled, and Kenneth McLeod and David Anthony Smith, portraying wanderers trapped in the village, range from good to poor. Grofe captures an eeriness in some ruins in the Philippines, and there are chilling scenes of marching demons, but one wishes it could be better than it is. (Magnum)

JUDGMENT IN STONE, A. Video title for *The Housekeeper.*

JULES VERNE'S MYSTERIOUS ISLAND. See *Mysterious Island* (1961).

JULES VERNE'S ROCKET TO THE MOON. See *Blast Off.*

JUMANJI (1995) ★★★★ As a special-effects extravaganza and thrilling adventure with a light comedic touch, this is a winner from director Joe Johnston, who worked from an imaginative script by Jonathan Hensleigh, Greg Taylor and Jim Strain, who in turn had the children's novel by Chris Van Allsburg to inspire them. Although Robin Williams headlines as a wildly hairy jungle man who has survived 26 years in a fantasy wilderness, and is now back in real time to face new adventures, the true star is Animaltronics, a computer graphics technique. (The team was headed by Ken Ralston, of Lucas' Industrial Light and Magic.) Animaltronics creates an army of African beasts on the rampage through a New England town, an overgrown and somewhat amusing crocodile, a man-eating plant with lengthy tendrils, a roaring lion, and a small army of gremlin-like chimpanzees. This thundering herd has been unleashed by a supernatural board-game called Jumanji, which uses Mother Nature to unleash perils on any and all who dare to play. The underlying sense of comedy to the action helps this film along immensely, and makes it more palatable for the children for whom it was largely intended. Still, adults will enjoy its unending series of surprises, and discover a fine cast that includes Jonathan Hyde as a British big game hunter, Bonnie Hunt as Williams' grown-up childhood sweetheart, and Kirstein Dunet and Bradley Pierce as the kids who are drawn into the game with Williams. It's a jungle in there! (Video/Laser: Sony)

JUNGLE CAPTIVE (1945) ★★ Universal's third and final entry in its hairy apewoman series (see *Captive Wild Woman* and *Jungle Woman*) is campish fun from the typewriters of Dwight V. Babcock and M. Coates Webster in which Otto Kruger (mad doctor) and Rondo Hatton (mad doctor's mad assistant) revive an apewoman from the twilight of death and monkey around with her ancestral genes. Vicky Lane endures the ape makeup. Aka *Wild Jungle Captive*. Directed by Harold Young. Amelita Ward, Jerome Cowan, Eddie Acuff. (MCA)

JUNGLEGROUND (1995) ★★★ Although on the surface your basic urban action thriller, this is recommended to horror fans for its surreal sense of brutality and pain, its stylized gory violence and its use of *The Most Dangerous Game* theme. Roddy Piper (in what could be his best performance) plays an undercover cop trapped in a big-city crime zone taken over by rival drug gangs. He is forced to play a game of eluding his captors until dawn, whereupon he would be released—maybe. All the while knowing his girlfriend is being held prisoner by a gang. How Piper uses whatever weapon he can lay his hands on, and how some of his enemies meet their ends, is mesmerizing in the hands of director Don Allan, who knows how to stage a good action picture. Michael Stokes's script constantly offers twists and turns and a tension is established through the speedy pacing. Peter Williams, J. R. Bourne, Nicholas Campbell, Torri Higginson. (Triboro)

JUNGLE HEAT (1983) ★★ First made as *Dance of the Dwarves,* from a novel by Geoffrey Household, this faltering adventure is set in the Philippines, where anthropologist Deborah Raffin hires drunken helicopter pilot Peter Fonda to locate a scientist investigating a tribe of reptilemen. However, the hideous monsters (designed by Craig Reardon) are too small a part of this adaptation by producer Michael Viner: the story is devoted to bickering and jokes about Fonda's drinking and chauvinism. A drawn-out affair under Gus Trikonis' direction. John Amos is wasted as a snake-loving witch doctor.(Tans World)

JUNGLE HOLOCAUST (1976) ★★★ A classic of the Italian school of cannibal movies; completist horror fans should see it to understand what this genre is about. Originally written as *The Last Survivor,* the script by Tito Carpi, Gianfranco Clerici and Renzo Genta is allegedly based on a true story in which a white man fell into the hands of a "Stone Age tribe on Mindanao" and underwent torture and ordeals of survival. Director Ruggero Deodato spares none of the gory rituals of these natives, including ants feeding on a native's open wound, the ceremonial slicing open of a crocodile and acts of cannibalism when explorer Massimo Foschi falls into the tribe's clutches. Frontal male and female nudity and genital fondling are among its near-pornographic ingredients, although Deodato, to his credit, never allows his film to become titillating for its own sake. It's raunchy but never sexy and has an edge of unrelenting, grimy realism. It will take a strong stomach to watch some of these scenes, but one has to admire how Foschi struggles to survive his ordeal with native girl Me Me Lai and fellow explorer Ivan Rassimov. There's nothing squeamish about this movie. It's a bitch. Lamberty Bava worked as script consultant. Aka *The Last Cannibal World.* (Video City; from AIR as *Cannibal*)

JUNGLE RAIDERS (1985) ★★ Expedition searches for a cursed jewel (the Ruby of Gloom) in the verdant thick. Aka *Captain Yankee.* Lee Van Cleef, Christopher Connelly, Marina Costa. Directed by Anthony M. Dawson. (MGM/UA)

JUNGLE WOMAN (1944) ★★ Sequel to *Captive Wild Woman* continues the adventures of Acquanetta, an unfortunate who keeps transmutating into a gorilla woman when doctor J. Carrol Naish fools around with her genes (and we don't mean Levi's, gang). Occasionally the she-creature reverts to type and kills. Either you will view this as a stilted, turgid mess or you will find it nostalgically pleasing, reflecting the values of Universal horror movies of the '40s. Reginald Le Borg directed the lurid script by Henry Sucher, Bernard Schubert and Edward Dein. Third and final film in this series: *Jungle Captive.* Evelyn Ankers, Lois Collier and Milburn Stone are all competent, but Acquanetta walks through her role in a trance. (MCA)

JUNIOR (1985) ★★ Two busty hookers just released from prison start a new life on an abandoned riverboat but are terrorized by a low-I.Q. pervert and his equally crazed mother. The best moment is when Junior (Jeremy Ratchford) cuts apart their house with his chainsaw; another so-cially redeeming scene has Junior fondling one of the girl's privates. A movie with a contradiction: It depicts the women as gutsy and liberated, yet exploits their sexuality. Strictly for intellectuals and (lame)brains. Directed by Jim Hawley. Suzanne De Laurentis, Linda Singer. (Starmaker; Prism)

JUNIOR (1994) ★★★½ Arnold Schwarzenegger as the world's first pregnant man? It doesn't sound like a promising premise, yet Schwarzenegger delivers the goods (excuse the phrase) because he underplays the comedy in the Kevin Wade–Chris Conrad script and lets Danny DeVito (as a sassy gynecologist) and Emma Thompson (as a klutzy research scientist) do the clowning around. Arnie plays a brainy type perfecting a new drug to guarantee pregnancy, Expectane, which he decides to try himself along with an embryo implant. Presto—Arnie is heavy with child and begins behaving like your traditional expectant mother, trying to keep it a secret from rival doctor Frank Langella. And he loves pickles. An amusing, strangely satisfying fantasy-comedy handled with taste by director Ivan Reitman. Pamela Reed, Judy Collins. (Video/Laser: MCA)

JUNIOR G-MEN (1940) ★★ Twelve-chapter Universal serial, directed by Ford Beebe and John Rawlins, depicts a youth group (Billy Halop, Huntz Hall, Gabriel Dell, etc.) working with a real-life G-Man (Philip Terry) to stop a band of baddies called the Order of the Flaming Torch from stealing some newfangled inventions. The sequel was *Junior G-Men of the Air.* (Rhino; Video Connection; Video Yesteryear; Nostalgia)

JUNIOR G-MEN OF THE AIR (1942) ★★ A 13-chapter cliffhanger from Universal, a sequel to *Junior G-Men,* in which some of the Bowery Boys (Huntz Hall, Gabriel Dell, David Gorcey, Frankie Darro) work as undercover kids against a fifth columnist group called the Order of the Black Dragonfly, which is out to destroy American values with a number of newfangled Axis inventions. Directed by Ray Taylor and Lewis D. Collins. (Sinister/C; Media; Nostalgia)

JURASSIC PARK (1993) ★★★★½ One of the most important movies in the technological use of computers, proving that nothing is impossible in the world of film as long as artists have the imagination to pull it off. This adaptation of Michael Crichton's best-seller is a fascinating example of how electronic technology can be blended with live-action footage to produce an ultimate thrill-adventure movie. In this case, we are taken to an amusement park on a small island off the coast of Costa Rica where Richard Attenborough has established a zoo-park for prehistoric creatures. (He's extracted DNA from ancient fossils and bred several species.) Unfortunately, he didn't reckon on everything going wrong when paleontologists Sam Neill and Laura Dern visit the island with scientist Jeff Goldblum. The script by David Koepp, from an adaptation by Crichton and Malia Scotch Marmo, spends little time on characterizations, as this was designed to thrill us with dinosaur footage unlike any dinosaur footage you've seen before. Under Steven Spielberg's direction, this marvelous shocker features a thundering Tyrannosaurus rex attacking two amusement park vans; angry Velociraptors chasing two children through a kitchen; a herd of galloping Triceratops bounding across a meadow past three human figures; and a poison-spitting Bilophosaur trapping a human during a rainstorm. Dennis Muren headed the staff of special-effects workers that included Phil Tippet, Stan Winston and Michael Lantieri. Every trick was paraded out and blended into a seamless whole. *Jurassic Park* made box-office, and technological, history. (Video/Laser: MCA)

JURASSIC 2. See *Lost World: Jurassic Park, The.*

JUST BEFORE DAWN (1982) ★★ Youthful campers, with a deed to a section of wilderness, ignore warnings of forest ranger George Kennedy not to go into the woods. They go anyway, only to be terrorized by evil mountain men. Director Jeff Lieberman (*Squirm, Blue Sunshine*), with a script by Mark Arywitz and Gregg Irving, creates suspenseful moments but has nothing new to offer. Kennedy gives a good limited performance, and Deborah Benson is the best of the teen-agers, proving in the climactic struggle that a woman can be effective in the most terrifying of situations. Chris Lemmon, Gregg Henry, Mike Kellin. (Paragon)

JUST CAUSE (1995) ★★★ Those who admired Anthony Hopkins' performance as Hannibal Lecter in *The Silence of the Lambs* will equally appreciate and enjoy Ed Harris' performance as serial killer Blair Sullivan, who figures prominently in this murder mystery with psycho-terror-suspense overtones. Harris brings just the right amount of psychotic madness to the role in this superior adaptation of John Katzenbach's novel by screenwriters Jeb Stuart and Peter Stone. The setting is the Florida Everglades as retired attorney turned law professor Sean Connery takes one last case—proving the innocence of a black man (Blair Underwood) accused of a heinous rape and murder of an 11-year-old child. Involved is a tough cop (Laurence Fishburne) and Connery's wife (Kate Capshaw). Director Arne Glimcher walks a fine line between a police procedural–trial story and the eventual terror sequences, never quite tipping his hand as to what is coming next. Christopher Murray, Ruby Dee, Daniel J. Travanti, Ned Beatty, Kevin McCarthy, Hope Lange, Chris Sarandon. (Video/Laser: Warner Bros.)

JUSTIN CASE (1988) ★★ This Walt Disney TV-movie from writer-director Blake Edwards is a dreary mystery-comedy in which Molly Hagan (as an out-of-work dancer) teams up with the ghost of a newly deceased private eye (George Carlin, in a wasted role) to find his murderer, a beautiful "Lady in Black." He materializes in and out, permitting Edwards to vent tired Invisible Man gags. And since only Hagan sees/hears Carlin, everyone wonders why she's talking to herself, why she's kissing empty air, ad nauseam. Timothy Stack, Kevin McClarnon. Music by Henry Mancini. Watch this Justin A. Pinch.

KARATE COP (1991) ★★½ Lowbrow sci-fi actioner—set in a ravaged futuristic world in
which "Scabs" are roving gangs of sadists and
"Freebies" are the good survivors of atomic holocaust—has the advantage of nonstop action,
with few words coming out of the mouth of
martial arts hero Ron Marchini. A good idea,
since Ron, of the stone-faced school of antiheroes, isn't the world's greatest actor. (His
companion, Mick the Dog, does better in that
department.) But Marchini does provide excellent fights and the action is well choreographed
for director Alan Roberts. Marchini, portraying
cop John Travis on locations in and around
Stockton, CA, helps lovely Carrie Chambers
find a crystal for a teleporter device and destroys
a gang of baddies that includes a barkeep named
Dad (David Carradine in a cameo) and an overweight leader named Lincoln. The Denny Grayson–Ronald L. Marchini–Bill Zide script hardly
strives for literacy, but it gets a C for its plentiful action. Michael Bristow, D. W. Lan-
dingham, Michael M. Foley. (Imperial) (Laser:
Image)

KARNSTEIN. See *Terror in the Crypt.*

KARNSTEIN CURSE, THE. See *Terror in the
Crypt.*

KEEP, THE (1983) ★★ When writer-director
Michael Mann adapted F. Paul Wilson's vampire novel, he dropped all references to vampires—and took himself so seriously he fell flat
on his egg-covered face. So there is Mr. Mann,
face down in the mire over this solemnly pretentious affair. The only saving grace are the
special effects, light-show extravaganzas with
thick white beams of light. An immortal guardian, Glaeken Trismegestus (Scott Glenn), arrives
in a Rumanian village in 1941 after Nazi troops
have unleashed a demonic power (Molasar)
from a castle. Jewish language expert Ian
McKellen and daughter Alberta Watson are
brought to the Keep to translate runes for Wehrmacht officer Jurgen Prochnow and SS major
Gabriel Byrne. McKellen believes Molasar to be
a savior of the Jews (a Golem?) but the Nazis
believe it to be only evil. The vampire that's
never called a vampire rips asunder the crummy
Nazis and is ready for a showdown with that
Glaeken guy, eyes glowing like emeralds, and
squares off in a battle of Killer Zap Rays, music
by Tangerine Dream swirling around them with
the fog. Figure it out and give us a call. (Video/
Laser: Paramount)

KEEPER, THE (1976) ★★ Canadian film
written-directed by Tom Drake, with Christopher Lee as an insane asylum director who has
a plan to insure his patients and murder their
heirs, giving him the dough he needs to conquer
the world à la Dr. Mabuse. Lee accomplishes
this with a hypnosis machine. A private detective, Dick Driver, acting melodramatic to the
max, is hired by a man whose brother is an inmate and to whom he is psychically linked.

There are strange twists and turns, plus a police
chief who falls under Lee's spell and acts as if
he's in a comedy and not a horror film. Tell
Schrieber, Sally Gray. (Interglobal; Trans
World)

KEEPERS, THE/KEEPERS OF THE EARTH. See
The Brain Eaters.

KEMEK (1970) ★ Minor cautionary tale about
the misuse of modern drugs. Kemek is a pharmaceutical company using people as guinea pigs
to test a new concoction that affects one's memory and brings on bursts of violence. David
Hedison portrays a man misused by an unscrupulous gang of opportunists and killers. The
writing-direction by Theodore Gershuny and
Don Ray Patterson is so convoluted and the editing so choppy, it's impossible to tell what's
going on. This movie was a drug on the market.
Diagnosis: Don't take it. Mary Woronov, Cal
Haynes, Alexandra Stewart. (Genesis; from
Neon as *For Love or Murder*)

KID IN KING ARTHUR'S COURT, A (1995)
★★★ A pleasant if not overly exciting time-
travel comedy adventure in the Disney tradition
(but obviously based on Mark Twain's *A Connecticut Yankee in King Arthur's Court*), with
baseball-playing youngster Thomas Ian Nicholsen dropping through a time tunnel to end up
on the outskirts of Camelot, guided in his misadventure by Merlin the Magician (Ron Moody
appears in this role as nothing but a head in a
pool of water). He's soon known as Calvin of
Reseda and is the talk of the Round Table (mi-
nus pizzas), impressing King Arthur (Joss Ackland, in a role he sometimes seems awkward in)
and wooing the King's younger daughter (Pal-
oma Baeza). The evil Belasco (Art Malik) has
a plot going to take over the court, and before
long Nicholsen is introducing skates and bicy-
cles to the culture, while a mysterious "Black
Knight" is always hanging around the fringes of
Camelot. There isn't much fire to the standard,

292 - CREATURE FEATURES

oft-predictable script by Robert L. Levy and Michael Part, and director Michael Gottlieb can't even inject much excitement into the jousting tournament sequence. Still, *A Kid* makes you feel good with its upstanding moral values, and you'll come away feeling swell for a short while. Daniel Craig, Kate Winslet, David Tysall. (Video/Laser: Buena Vista)

KIDS OF THE ROUND TABLE (1995) ★★½ A good performance by Malcolm McDowell as Merlin the Magician can't save this Canadian TV-movie which attempts to make a poignant drama out of a young boy's encounter with magic to teach him a few object lessons about life. Johnny Morina's search for himself, after he pulls Excalibur out of a rock, is destroyed by the introduction of a silly hold-up man (Michael Ironside, in a wasted part) and his two equally incompetent cronies. David Sherman's telescript is all over the Montreal landscape, but without a sharper focus director Robert Tinnell is at a disadvantage. Rene Simard, Roc Lafortune.

KILL AND GO HIDE. Video version of *The Child* (Monterey; Paragon).

KILL, BABY, KILL (1966) ★★★ One of director Mario Bava's great gothic supernatural thrillers, revealing his power in the use of color for psychological effect. Coroner Giacomo Rossi-Stuart arrives in a 19th-century village to conduct an autopsy, and soon realizes that the ghost of a child, murdered by the citizens, is haunting the town. Erica Blanc, one of Bava's beautiful heroines, is Rossi-Stuart's assistant who discovers that witch Fabienne Dali is also spinning diabolical magic. But the real dread remains unseen, punctuated by the dead girl's laughter. And there are fine scenes of Rossi-Stuart and Blanc trapped in eerie rooms. Aka *Curse of the Dead, Curse of the Living Dead, Don't Walk in the Park* and *Operation Fear*. (Sinister/C; S/Weird; Filmfax) (Laser: Polygram)

KILLBOTS. See *Chopping Mall*.

KILLER, THE. Video title for *Daddy's Deadly Darling*, also in video under that title. Original title was *Pigs*. It's a porker under any snout.

KILLER BAT. Video version of *The Devil Bat* (Kartes).

KILLER GRIZZLY. See *Grizzly*. (Grrrrrrrr!)

KILLER INSTINCT, THE (1981) ★★½ This hillbilly horror saga set in Tennessee is distinguished by a ferocious performance by Henry Silva as a murderous, sadistic redneck who goes completely out of control, torturing and murdering to protect the good name of rednecks everywhere. Interesting death devices are used (watch for the TV antenna sequence) as well as the usual explosions, hot tar, feathers and other homicidal methods common in the Deep South. This Canadian effort, of minimal consequence, was directed by William Fruet. Nicholas Campbell, Barbara Gordon. (Cineplex Odeon; VEC; Pan-Canadian)

KILLER KLOWNS FROM OUTER SPACE (1988) ★★★ Hilarious spoof of sci-fi alien invader movies finds the town of Santa Cruz invaded by E.T. humanoids who dress up as clowns and use "funny" props to zap humans into cocoonlike containers. The funnymen are never explained but it doesn't matter as the movie clips along with a blend of thrills and laughs. The only way to kill a killer "klown" is to shoot it in the nose, which sends it off into another dimension. The effects are zany and the characters memorable, especially John Vernon as a paranoid cop. About those clowns: While they seem funny at first glance, they're really quite ugly and their laughter is the stuff of dark comedy. Grant Cramer, Suzanne Snyder, John Allen Nelson, Royal Dano. Directed by Stephen Chiodo. (Video/Laser: Media)

KILLER NERD (1991) ★½ Toby Radloff, a face in MTV spots, portrays a maniac with a mother complex who gets over it by burying the hatchet—in mom's head. He also turns his ire on fire by sticking it to his adversaries with TNT sticks. Written-produced-directed by Mark Steven Bosko. (Hollywood Home)

KILLER PARTY (1986) ★★ April Fool's Day saga only for fools: When three pledges in the Sigma Alpha Phi sorority undergo initiation on "Ghost Night," real horrors begin at a costume party when a killer in a diving suit (isn't this synopsis incredible?) kills with electricity, hammer, guillotine, pitchfork and standard kitchen knife, then stuffs body parts into a fridge. Then this slasher flick turns into supernatural hogwash when a spirit takes over a live body. Paul Bartel (as a nerdy professor), Martin Hewitt, Ralph Seymour. Directed by William Fruet. (Key)

KILLER'S CURSE. Video version of *Beyond the Living* (Iver).

KILLERS FROM SPACE (1954) ★★ Humanoids with bulging eyeballs and jumpsuits resurrect Peter Graves from the dead as part of their plot to take over Earth. Don't they know hundreds of other E.T.s have tried without success? Some aliens just never get the message. Dull sci-fi directed by W. Lee Wilder (brother of Billy Wilder) from a Bill Raynor script. Barbara Bestar, James Seay, Frank Gerstle. (VCI; Sinister/C; S/Weird; Rhino; Filmfax)

KILLER SHREWS, THE (1959) ★ This is not about ugly wives going on a murderous rampage. According to Jay Simms' script, shrews are the tiniest of rodents, but some crazy scientist has enlarged them to 100 pounds each. Strange how these giant killer shrews resemble Irish setters in blackface. Maybe they'll bark the hero (James Best) or his Norwegian girlfriend (Ingrid Goude) to death. There's such a wonderful sense of ineptitude to Ray Kellogg's direction that this is fun to watch. Producer Ken Curtis doubles as a victim, proving he's a "shrewed" guy. Baruch Lumet, Gordon McLendon. (Sinister/C; S/Weird; Filmfax)

KILLERS OF THE CASTLE OF BLOOD. See *Scream of the Demon Lover.*

KILLER TOMATOES. It started with *Attack of the Killer Tomatoes,* continued with *Return of the Killer Tomatoes,* went to *Killer Tomatoes Strike Back* and then splattered again with *Killer Tomatoes Eat France.*

KILLER TOMATOES EAT FRANCE (1991) ★½ Another squishy sauce of mirth and gory madness, the fourth in the series, when those rolling homicidal love fruits take to the French landscape to squash humans anew. Wow, those are some tomatoes! Marc Price, Angela Visser, I. M. Seedless, Steve Lundquist. Directed by John DeBello. Question: Where are the "Killer Tomato" movies shot? Answer: At Hollywood on vine. (Video/Laser: CBS/Fox)

KILLER TOMATOES STRIKE BACK (1990) ★½ The murderous love fruits are on another roll, squashing mankind into oblivion and making a lot of people stew. Directed by John DeBello. John Astin, Rick Rockwell, Steve Lundquist, Crystal Carson, John Weatherspoon. (Video/Laser: Fox)

KILLER WHALE, THE. See *Orca: The Killer Whale.*

KILLER WORKOUT (1986) ★ A serial killer is on the loose again (*not again!!!*) in this typically bloody but boring intellectual treatise on man's inhumanity to his fellow man in the form of murdering them in a gym. As strained as the face of Arnold Schwarzenegger when he lifts a weight too heavy even for him. Directed by David A. Prior. David James Campbell, Ted Prior. Aka *Aerobicide.* (Academy)

KILL FACTOR, THE Video version of *Death Dimension* (Academy).

KILLING BOX, THE (1995) ★★★ This most unusual TV-movie, set in 1862, is an odd breed of supernatural tale which depicts how a unit of Confederate soldiers is possessed by the "Makers," an undead bunch that wants to stop the senseless killing on both sides by killing Rebs and Yankees fighting the Civil War. These zombie killers (the original "Makers" are from the previous century, and reside in a hole in the ground) enjoy crucifying their victims and performing sadistic tortures. But what makes Matt Greenberg's telescript memorable is its surreal depiction of the real horrors of the Civil War as well as those imagined here. This flavor of the battlefield, so well captured by director George Hickenlooper, gives *The Killing Box* a compelling quality, as do the performances by Corbin Bernsen, Adrian Pasdar, Ray Wise, Dean Cameron and Martin Sheen (redoing his General Lee from *Gettysburg*), all which capture a sense of doomed men caught up in a maelstrom of madness. Roger Wilson, Alexis Arquette, Josh Evans.

KILLING HOUR, THE (1982). Video version of *The Clairvoyant* (Clair who?) (CBS/Fox)

KILLING MAN (1994) ★★★ Hired hit man Jeff Wincott, after being terribly burned in a fire, undergoes plastic surgery and a reprogramming to become a government assassin for sinister Michael Ironside (who's good in anything) in this Canadian-produced thriller with mild psychological overtones. Good martial-arts sequences and suspenseful shoot-outs in the script by director David Mitchell and producer Damien Lee highlight this nihilistic portrait of a murderer when Wincott falls in love with an AIDS researcher (Terri Hawkes) and can't murder her to keep her discoveries a secret from the public. The AIDS subplot is an interesting one, giving the film's conspiracy background a decidedly sinister twist. David Bolt, Jeff Pustil. (Video/DVD: Simitar)

KILLING OF SATAN, THE (1983) ★½ Filipino supernatural fantasy in which "The Prince of Magic" (a wizard in a red jumpsuit) calls forth Satan (with a tail and a pitchfork) to do battle with "Coronado," a parolee who has inherited superpowers from the dead village shaman and runs around in Levi's and tennis shoes. Bolts of magic zap juice are fired, seductive women turn into killer snakes, snakes turn into serpent-tongued succubi and on it goes, with the supernatural magic accomplishing little excitement, especially when "Coronado" blows one of his adversaries over a cliff using just his breath. Directed without wit or style by Efron C. Pinon. Ramon Revilla, Elizabeth Oropesa. (Paragon)

KILLING SPREE (1990) ★★ Man reads diary by wife, unaware that it's fiction, and thinks she's dallying with other men and flips out, killing in the worst ways: Gutting human torsos, decapitating them and removing scalps. Then the corpses come to life and return for revenge. Overdone by producer-writer-director Tim Ritter. Asbestos Felt, Courtney Lercara. (Twisted Illusions)

KILLING TOUCH, THE. See *Fatal Games.*

KILL THE BEAST. See *The Beast Must Die.*

KINDRED, THE (1986) ★★ Ripoff of *Alien,* without an original thought, and an embarrassment for Rod Steiger. He's a nutty scientist on the fringes of an experiment in gene-splicing that results in "Anthony," a tentacled monster hiding in subterranean chambers underneath a doctor's country home. What are catacombs and deep pits doing under the floorboards? Just one of the many dumb aspects of this goo movie. From Jeffrey Obrow and Stephen Carpenter, the schlockmeisters who gave us *The Dorm That Dripped Blood*. One critic thought the title referred to a benevolent Communist. No, it stands for trash of the sleaziest kind. David Allen Brooks, Talia Balsam, Kim Hunter. David Newman wrote the eerie music. (Video/Laser: Vestron)

KING APE. Early proposed title for *King Kong.*

KING COBRA. Original title of *Jaws of Satan.*

KINGDOM, THE (1994) ★★★ Reedited version of a four-hour Danish TV miniseries that, on the surface, is an entertaining horror story that brilliantly combines supernatural thrills with a dark, morbid sense of humor. (Underneath, *The Kingdom* is a controversial indictment of Denmark's bureaucratic hospital system.) The setting is a Copenhagen hospital complex (built over a strange marshland) that is haunted by the spirit of a little girl murdered back in 1919, pipes that spit blood, a dog that roves the eerie corridors and X-rays that reveal strange things. The characters are excellently conceived, from an arrogant doctor (Ernst-Hugo Jaregard) trying to cover up a malpractice case; a hypochrondriac (Kirsten Rolffes) who communicates with the dead; an amusing CEO concerned with all the wrong things in his hospital; two psychic retards who do nothing but wash dishes all day; and a pregnant woman who shouldn't be pregnant. This is the masterpiece of director Lars von Trier, and is superior to most American TV. (Evergreen).

KINGDOM OF THE SPIDERS (1977) ★★★½ Several thousand tarantulas, bola, crab, wolf and funnel-web spiders attack an Arizona community to get even for man's misuse of insecticides. Director John "Bud" Cardos, taking cues from the script by Richard Robinson and Alan Caillou, makes this absurdity work with the help of William Shatner in one of his better movie roles as a veterinarian who joins up with bug expert Tiffany Bolling, who's really bug-eyed over Captain Kirk. The effect of 5,000 spiders swarming over everything (and everybody) is chilling and will have you watching where you step for days afterward. Woody Strode, Nancy Lafferty, Natasha Ryan. (United; VCI)

KING KONG (1933) ★★★★★ The granddaddy of giant-ape movies, so skillfully conceived by producers-directors Merian Cooper and Ernest B. Schoedsack that it has lost little of its charm and suspense. Willis O'Brien's stop-motion effects are still startling for their time, ingeniously depicting the 50-foot-tall gorilla presiding over prehistoric Skull Island. A filmmaking expedition headed by Carl Denham (Robert Armstrong) and an adventurer (Bruce Cabot) pursues the creature after it abducts Fay Wray. The chase includes battles with dinosaurs, a marauding pterodactyl, a giant snake and other monstrous spectacles. Captured and

returned to civilization as a stage display, mighty Kong breaks free to provide this unbridled fantasy with a grand climax atop the Empire State Building. It features a great Max Steiner score and its cast includes Wray as Ann Darrow, the woman Kong rips the clothes from, Frank Reicher as Captain Englehorn, Noble Johnson as the native chieftain, and Sam Hardy as Charles Weston. The script was begun by British mystery writer Edgar Wallace and finished after his sudden death by Ruth Rose (Schoedsack's wife) and James A. Creelman. David O. Selznick was executive producer. Dino De Laurentiis remade it in 1976 but this remains the definitive giant ape movie. Early proposed titles include *The Beast*, *King Ape* and *Kong*. (RKO; Turner; Media) (Laser: Criterion; Image, with *Son of Kong*)

KING KONG (1976) ★★★ Producer Dino De Laurentiis proclaimed this $24 million remake a "cinema event"—and while it is undeniably an event, it is far from recommendable cinema. The Lorenzo Semple Jr. screenplay calls on the TV *Batman* traditions of high camp and emerges a mishmash of satire, thrills, fantasy and spectacle under John Guillermin's direction. This leaves only the special effects to marvel at, and while some of them are good, there is no sense of tradition, balance or proportion. The hairy paw picking up screaming Jessica Lange, so deftly handled in the 1933 original, is so overdone here it becomes ludicrous. No stop-motion animation—it was all done with men in monkey suits or with unconvincing giant mock-ups. It finally topples from its own weight. Jeff Bridges, Charles Brodin, John Randolph, John Agar, Rene Auberjonois, Ed Lauter. Rick Baker wears the monkey suit. Made as *King Kong: The Legend Reborn*. (Video/Laser: Paramount)

KING KONG ESCAPES! (1968) ★★ More Toho Studio mass destruction (special effects by Eiji Tsuburaya) as the hairy desecrator of Tokyo battles Gorosaurus, a relative of Godzilla, plus an exact replica of himself, Mechanikong, the work of a nutty scientist (dubbed Dr. Who). American footage featuring Rhodes Reason was appended. You really have to like these Japanese things to enjoy. Aka *The Revenge of King Kong* and *King Kong's Counterattack*. Directed by Inoshiro Honda. Mie Hama, Linda Miller.

KING KONG LIVES (1986) ★★ How the mighty have dropped with a leaden thud since Kong plummeted from the Empire State Building in Dino De Laurentiis' 1976 remake. Here Dino offers a sequel wherein dedicated doctor Linda Hamilton keeps Kong in the world's biggest animal hospital to give him a heart transplant. Who should adventurer Brian Kerwin find on Kong Island—just when Linda needs a transfusion for Kong—but a Young Chick Kong with the hots for the hairy guy. The most hilarious scene comes when Kong is operated on, the surgical tools like props from *The Incredible Shrinking Man*. Kong and his Chick thunder across the plains, stomping everything in sight, in some of the funniest scenes imaginable. The idea of trying to take a romance, complete with mother's love, and turn it into a thundering-plundering-blundering Kong movie is the most ludicrous thing imaginable—yet director John Guillermin (who helmed the 1976 adaptation) does it with a straight face. So bad it's not even good. (Lorimar) (Laser: Image)

KING KONG'S COUNTERATTACK. See *King Kong Escapes!*

KING KONG: THE LEGEND REBORN. See *King Kong* (1976).

KING KONG VS. FRANKENSTEIN. See *King Kong Vs. Godzilla.*

KING KONG VS. GODZILLA (1963) ★★ Clash of the century between "two world-shaking monsters" is in reality a Japanese thud as loud as Kong's footfall. The hairy ape of Skull Island battles a king-sized octopus and Godzilla in a seemingly endless series of fisticuffs and body bashings. Additional footage with Michael Keith was shot for the U.S. by Thomas Montgomery. Directed by Inoshiro Honda. Based on an idea by animator Willis O'Brien. James Yogi, Tadao Takashima. Aka *King Kong Vs. Prometheus* and *King Kong Vs. Frankenstein*. (Goodtimes) (Laser: Japanese)

KING OF KONG ISLAND (1968) ★ With remote-control devices, giant gorillas become robot killers. A descendant of the King himself happens along and decides enough is enough already and starts crunching skulls—and remote-control devices. Left to its own devices, this Spanish-produced job (made as *Eve the Wild Woman*) would fall flat on its ugly kisser. Directed by Robert Morris. Brad Harris, Marc Lawrence. (VCI)

KING OF THE CONGO (1952) ★★ Based on the Thunda comic strip, this 15-chapter Columbia serial from producer Sam Katzman stars Buster Crabbe as a jungle warrior who encounters rock people and other fantastic elements in the jungle. Directed by Spencer G. Bennet and Wallace Grissell. Gloria Dee, Leonard Penn, Jack Ingram, Rick Vallin. Aka *Thunda*. (Mike Lebell's)

KING OF THE DEAD. See *The Mummy* (1932).

KING OF THE JUNGLELAND. See *Darkest Africa.*

KING OF THE MOUNTIES (1942) ★★★ Action-packed 12-chapter Republic serial, directed by cliffhanger master William Witney, stars Allan Lane as "King of the Royal Mounted" as he fights Axis agents who intend to bomb America with a new kind of aircraft. Gilbert Emery, Russell Hicks, Peggy Drake, Duncan Renaldo.

KING OF THE ROCKET MEN (1951) ★★★ Republic serial, all 12 chapters, in which Tris Cof-

fin, a member of Science Associates, dons a jet-propelled flying suit to become "Rocket Man," a high-flying hero who soars against Mr. Vulcan, an evil nerd trying to steal the Sonutron (a rock disintegrator) and wreak havoc on the world. Instead, he should have concentrated on disintegrating the rocks in his head—he and his henchmen bungle the job so badly. Straight out of the comic books, and lively directed by Fred C. Brannon. Don Haggerty, Mae Clarke, House Peters Jr. Released to TV in a shortened version as *Lost Planet Airmen*. (Video/Laser: Republic)

KING OF THE STREETS. See *Alien Warrior.*

KING OF THE ZOMBIES (1941) ★ Not king of the zombie movies, for sure. Horridly hoary and ingratiatingly insipid "walking dead" melodrama in which mad doctor Henry Victor creates zombies for the Axis. Mantan Moreland rolls his eyes and runs at the slightest sign of a "spook." As dated as whalebone corsets and Easter bonnets. Dick Purcell, Joan Woodbury. Directed by Jean Yarbrough from an Edmund Kelso script. (Video Archive; Sinister/C; Video Yesteryear)

KING ROBOT. See *My Son, the Vampire.*

KING SOLOMON'S MINES (1985) ★★★ This has such a spirited sense of light-hearted adventure, and moves at such a lightning clip, that one is almost willing to overlook the fact it has nothing to do with H. R. Haggard's novel and everything to do with Indiana Jones. The exciting action sequences are almost direct steals, right down to the line "Trust me." Richard Chamberlain proves a virile, rugged Quartermain helping feisty heroine Sharon Stone find her lost father and a diamond mine in Africa prior to World War I. Full of derring-do and mock heroics in a tongue-in-cheek vein, with the villains (Herbert Lom as a German officer, John Rhys-Davies as a Turkish adventurer) more caricature than menace. There's an hysterical cannibal pot sequence, a madcap flying chase, a strange tribe of tree-hanging Africans, a couple of village massacres and one lengthy cave sequence that features a wicked witch, a giant spider and death devices à la *Temple of Doom*. Production values are grand, with half the tribes of Africa working as extras. Directed by J. Lee Thompson. (MGM/UA)

KING SOLOMON'S TREASURE (1978) ★★½ Light-hearted, minor fantasy-adventure based loosely on H. R. Haggard's novel (from a script by Colin Turner and Allan Prior) about Allan Quartermain, a Great White Hunter searching for a lost fortune in the wilds of Africa. John Colicos makes for a different Quartermain, but equal emphasis is put on comedy relief: naval officer Patrick Macnee and David McCallum, who help in rescuing a young woman from a prehistoric monster and in finding a lost Roman-style city ruled by a Cleopatra-like Britt Ekland.

Harry Alan Towers' production, directed by Alvin Rakoff. Wilfrid Hyde-White, Ken Gampu. (VCI)

KIRLIAN EFFECT, THE/KIRLIAN FORCE, THE. See *Psychic Killer*.

KISS, THE (1988) ★★ Felice (Joanna Pacula) is a witch after the daughter of her sister. When the sister dies in an auto accident right out of the *Omen* series, the beguiling witch moves in on the daughter (Meredith Salenger) and father (Nicholas Kilbertus), and begins murders that involve a catlike familiar, solidified from Felice's mumbo-jumbo incantations and curses. The climax is such an unbelievable series of actions that it becomes laughable. The hero is Mimi Kuzyk, a friendly neighbor who comes to the daughter's rescue. Unclarified story points and unexplained reasons for a monster emerging from Felice's mouth are just two unexplained things this film poses. Directed by Pen Densham. (Video/Laser: RCA/Columbia)

KISS AND KILL (1968) ★★ Christopher Lee essays the insidious Fu Manchu role for the fourth time with sadistic glee. This time Fu's plot to rule the world involves hypnotized women who transfer a deadly poison to anyone who touches their passionate lips. Call it the Hacks Factor application. Richard Greene portrays the Scotland Yard pursuer Nayland Smith and Shirley Eaton is chief among the "black widows." Producer Harry Alan Towers wrote as Peter Welbeck. Aka *Against All Odds*, *Blood of Fu Manchu*, *Fu Manchu and the Kiss of Death*, and *Fu Manchu and the Keys of Death*. Directed by Jesus Franco. Preceded in the series by *The Face of Fu Manchu*, *The Brides of Fu Manchu* and *Vengeance of Fu Manchu* and followed by *The Castle of Fu Manchu*. (Trans Atlantic; Moore; American; from Republic as *Against All Odds* and from Bingo as *Kiss of Death*)

KISS DADDY GOODBYE (1981) ★½ Brother and sister with ESP powers resurrect their father after he's been killed by a motorcycle gang, and the dead parent goes after people whom his children consider "bad guys." Strangle strangle mangle mangle. Meanwhile, social worker Marilyn Burns and county deputy Fabian Forte Bonaparte (former teen idol Fabian) try to solve the mystery and have a little G-rated sex but both are slow on the uptake and remain mentally behind while a predictable plot flows like molasses, and with about as much excitement as watching molasses flow. Director Patrick Regan's kids, Nell and Patrick III, portray the adorable let's-get-revenge-kids. Jon Cedar, Marvin Miller. (Monterey; Twilight; from Premiere as *The Vengeful Dead* and from IVE and Genesis as *Revenge of the Zombies*—a misnomer since there is only one zombie in the movie)

KISSED (1996) ★★★ No way is a movie about a necrophiliac, a kinky cat who enjoys making love to corpses, ever going to be a rollicking entertainment. Dress it up any way you want, make it a musical comedy even, but count me out. Even when a good filmmaker like Lynne Stopkewich chooses to study this twilight abnormal human behavior, no amount of good intentions and poetic voice-over narration is going to lighten the load or make the sky look blue instead of dark gray. This unusual movie about a classic taboo subject not surprisingly shook up audiences in Toronto and Sundance when it was first screened; the controversy helped it to land a deal with Orion Home Video, but its appeal, to be sure, remains confined to those who enjoy climbing into a box of another kind. According to Sandra Larson (played by Molly Parker), who works as a mortician in a funeral home, each body has its own "grief" and "wisdom" and "innocence." And making love to the dead is like "looking into the sun without going blind. I'm consumed." Matters really turn kooky when Sandra meets Matt (Peter Outerbridge), a would-be medical student who becomes obsessed with Sandra's obsession, and wants her to pretend that he's a dead body and make love to him. She refuses, which causes Matt to go goofy and do some bizarre things. Apparently somebody named Barbara Goudy wrote an article, "We So Seldom Look on Love," and that's where Stopkewich got the idea and wrote her script with the help of Angus Fraser. To her credit, Stopkewich deals with Sandra's childhood (with Natasha Morley playing an adolescent Sandra) and shows her early obsession with dead birds and mice and dissecting frogs in science class—an honest attempt to deal with her twisted psychology. You can still count me out. (Orion)

KISS ME DEADLY (1955) ★★★½ What's a Mike Hammer thriller by Mickey Spillane doing in this book? Because Ralph Meeker, as the blood-and-guts private eye, is in pursuit of a suitcase that could have a holocaustic effect on anyone who opens it. Director Robert Aldrich, with A. I. Bezzerides' script, has fashioned one of the strangest of film noir thrillers. Albert Dekker, Paul Stewart, Cloris Leachman, Leigh Snowden, Strother Martin, Jack Elam, Robert Cornthwaite. (Video/Laser: MGM/UA)

KISS MEETS THE PHANTOM OF THE PARK (1978) ★★½ Outrageous TV vehicle for the rock group Kiss, its title giving away the storyline about mad doctor Anthony Zerbe trying to turn the musicians into sideshow freaks who're so far out, it's hard to distinguish them from rockers. They end up a menagerie of monsters (Frankenstein Monster, werewolf, Dracula) under Gordon Hessler's direction. Our advice: Kiss it off. Peter Criss, Ace Frehley, Gene Simmons, Paul Stanley. Aka *Kiss in Attack of the Phantoms, Attack of the Phantoms.* (Worldvision) (Laser: Image)

KISS ME GOODBYE (1982) ★★ If you set your brain on zero, this could be a mildly charming comedy with supernatural overtones. This is a fluffy throwback to the light-hearted comedies of the 1960s. Broadway choreographer Jolly Villano (James Caan), dead these past five years, turns up to pester ex-wife Sally Field, who is about to marry an Egyptologist (Jeff Bridges). The Charlie Peters script has Jolly invisible to all but Sally, who keeps saying something dumb and then something even dumber to cover up for the first dumb statement. This leads to pointless conversations, confusions and other devices that barely move the story. Too, Bridges is stuck with a nerdish character no one would want to marry, and you wonder why Sally is bothering. You also wonder why producer-director Robert Mulligan picked this project. Mildred Natwick, Claire Trevor, William Prince, Maryedith Burrell. (CBS/Fox)

KISS OF DEATH. Video of *Kiss and Kill* (Bingo).

KISS OF EVIL. See *Kiss of the Vampire.*

KISS OF THE BEAST (1990) ★★ This variation on *Beauty and the Beast* is a rich-looking production, having been filmed on Italian locations. But the Dennis Paoli script is a mess of stuff about the owner of a castle (Sherilyn Fenn) who encounters a traveling "World of Wonders" sideshow that brings distress into her life. She discovers there's a beast living in the walls who materializes in and out of her reality-fantasy reveries. Meanwhile, the statues on the castle grounds are actually the frozen spirits of those who have sinned and other family secrets are contained in a painting. There's a lot of R-rated sex between beautiful woman and ugly beast but producer-director Charles Band never brings the elements together. Malcolm Jamieson, Hilary Mason, Alex Daniels, Phil Fondacaro. (On video and laser from Paramount as *Meridian: Kiss of the Beast*)

KISS OF THE TARANTULA (1972) ★★★ A lonely, misunderstood child, befriended by her undertaker father but hated by her unfaithful mother, realizes mom is committing adultery with dad's brother and unleashes a tarantula spider into her bedroom. It's the beginnings of a spider murderess. This independent low budgeter, directed by Chris Munger from a Warren Hamilton Jr. script, does for spiders what *Willard* did for rats. You'll shudder as scores of tarantulas scurry up the arms and legs of a pair of kissers in Lover's Lane when the demented Suzanne Love unleashes her pretty pets as eight-legged avengers. She cackles such commands as "Spin faster" and "Scuttle, you creepers" as they scurry into the night to spread their web of hor-

ror. A strange subplot involves a rural policeman who falls in love with Suzanne (as though she were a hypnotic spiderwoman) and covers up her crimes, but his faith/fate is a chilling one. Eric Mason, Patricia Landon. Aka *Shudder.* (Monterey; Gorgon; United)

KISS OF THE VAMPIRE (1962) ★★★ Heavily reedited for the U.S. market and retitled *Kiss of Evil* when released, this was released on video in 1995 by MCA. It was produced by Hammer during that long period when Christopher Lee refused to don the cape of Dracula, and the British studio was forced to cast a surrogate count, in this case Noel Willman, who portrays Dr. Ravna. The good doc invites an English couple honeymooning in Bavaria to his château, where he and his disciples practice the black arts and drink plenty of blood to keep their strength up. A professor resembling Van Helsing turns the tables on the vampire gang with the help of a squadron of bats. One of the better Hammer offerings. Directed by Don Sharp and scripted by producer Anthony Hinds (as John Elder). Clifford Evans, Edward De Souza, Isobel Black. (Video/Laser: MCA)

KISS THE GIRLS AND MAKE THEM DIE (1967) ★★ Lightweight spoof of the James Bond genre, made by Dino De Laurentiis in Rio de Janeiro. Although a pale copy of 007's exploits, it has a sparkle to its comedy, gorgeous women in figure-flattering wardrobes, and scenic action set against picturesque Rio. The villain is industrialist Ardonian (Raf Vallone), who intends to bombard the U.S. with emissions of "cordize" to "kill the sex drive in men" and allow Chinese hordes to invade America. For his own sexual amusement, Ardonian has a bevy of beauties in suspended animation. Michael Connors walks somnambulistic through his role as super agent Kelly who has minipistols hidden in his clothing and is always eating bananas. A standout is Terry-Thomas as a chauffeur secret agent. Directed by Henry Levin and Dino Maiuri. Dorothy Provine portrays Connors' charming, sexy contact. Beverly Adams, Marilu Tolo, Margaret Lee, Sandro Dori. Aka *Operation Paradise* and *If All the Women in the World.*

KNIFE FOR THE LADIES, A. See *Silent Sentence.*

KNIFE IN THE BODY. See *The Murder Clinic.*

KNIGHT IN CAMELOT, A (1998) ★½ This Disney version of Mark Twain's is no better or worse than other TV-movie and feature-film attempts to have some fun with a classic piece of satirical literature. Like all the others, it, too, fails. Even with Whoopi Goldberg as its time-traveling star, *A Knight in Camelot* is mediocre, undistinguished grist for the video mill. As a modern computer programmer, Whoopi finds herself transported back to West Cornwall, 589 A.D., where the evil knight Sir Sagramour (Robert Addie) brings her before King Arthur (Michael York) and Queen Guinevere (played, surprisingly, as a really devious bitch by Amanda Donohoe). Appearing to be a magician who outwizards even Merlin, Whoopi becomes the darling of the king's court. In a totally unbelievable sequence, she does battle with the bad wicked knight and in other dreary sequences she introduces rock-and-roll music to the Camelot crowd as well as other modern customs that totally corrupt the witless British characters. (Disney)

KNIGHT RIDER 2000 (1991) ★★½ TV-movie revival of the popular 1982–86 series with David Hasselhoff as the crime-fighting driver of a computerized car. Typical TV action stuff when he takes on crooked cops in the year 2000 and befriends crusading policewoman Carmen Argenziano. Directed by Alan J. Levi. Megan Butler. Edward Mulhare returns as assignment chief Devon Miles. William Daniels returns as the voice of KITT.

KNIGHTS (1992) ★★★ Does the world need another cyborg movie? Hardly, but writer-director Albert Pyun brings such kinetic energy to the feeble plot that one cannot help but enjoy the flying bodies and mindless action. Once you get past the absurd idea of Kris Kristofferson playing a cyborg warrior named Gabriel, you've got clear sailing into Armageddon land ("another age, another place") where evil cyborg Lance Henriksen (chewing scenery, growling under his breath and waving a mechanical arm) searches for fresh humans so that he might feast on their blood, a "fuel" for him and his machinemen. Kickboxing champ Kathy Long makes for a believable warrior as she takes on Henriksen's fighters in the butte country around Moab, Utah. The film's conclusion suggests a sequel. Scott Paulin, Gary Daniels, Nicholas Guest. (Paramount)

KNIGHTS OF THE DRAGON, THE. Theatrical title for *Star Knight.*

K-9000 (1991) ★★ Compendium of cops-and-robbers clichés: high-speed car chases; shootouts; bodies crashing through windows; punches that would destroy an average human. Providing a fantasy twist to this TV-movie is "Niner," a German shepherd (experimental model K-9000) cybernetically able to communicate mentally with cop Chris Mulkey. Scientist Catherine Owenberg's Piper Institute has developed the dog as a peaceful weapon, but bad guy Judson Scott and gang want it for a wartime weapon. You've seen it B4–1000 times. Directed by Kim Manners. Dennis Haysbert, Danna Gladstone. (Fries)

KOLCHAK PAPERS, THE/KOLCHAK TAPES, THE. See *The Night Stalker* (1972).

KONG. Early proposed title for *King Kong.*

KONGA (1961) ★½ Herman Cohen production, unconscionably made as *I Was a Teenage Gorilla.* Biologist Michael Gough is raising man-eating plants when he branches out into bigger things. Twenty-five feet bigger: that's the size of a chimp-turned-killer-gorilla injected with a New Scientific Serum That Will Advance Mankind Into a New Epoch. Gough also has an ogling eye for Claire Gordon, a bouncy young thing who wears tight sweaters, much to the jealousy of lab assistant Margo Johns. The gorilla comes off looking all right, but you can't say the same for Gough when Konga picks up the hapless doctor and carries him into the London street to do an imitation of King Kong. Quite terrible, but its high incompetency level makes it fun. John Lemont directed and Cohen coscripted with Aben Kandel. Jess Conrad, Austin Trevor, Jack Watson.

KRONOS (1957) ★★★ A different kind of alien invasion thriller, even if it is hampered by a low budget, and average direction by producer Kurt Neumann. A UFO deposits a towering hunk of computerized machinery on Earth, which then pistons its way across the landscape, sucking up energy and squashing everyone who gets beneath its size 45 sneakers. Jeff Morrow, John Emery and Morris Ankrum are experienced hands with this kind of material, but it's that gigantic mechanical block that steals the show. Written by Lawrence Goldman. Barbara Lawrence, Robert Shayne. Aka *Kronos, Destroyer of the Universe.* (Nostalgia Merchant) (Laser: Image)

KRONOS. See *Captain Kronos—Vampire Hunter.*

KRONOS, DESTROYER OF THE UNIVERSE. See *Kronos.*

KRUG AND COMPANY. See *The Last House on the Left.*

KRULL (1983) ★★★½ A fairy-tale quality instills this sword-and-sorcery adventure with a sense of childlike wonder, making it more palatable for the young than the grittier Conan sagas. Emphasis is on dazzling effects and innovative designs on the planet Krull, where a rock-fortress spaceship commanded by the Beast unloads an army of Slayers. Warrior Ken Marshall is separated from his lovely princess (Lysette Anthony) and joins forces with Ergo the Magician and a band of thieves to challenge the Beast in his Black Fortress. The odyssey unfolds with a deadly bog, two murderous changelings, a cavern of webs housing the Widow of the Spider, a herd of sky-riding Firemares and assorted quest perils. Final assault on the Beast is a rousing one—plenty of thunder, fire and clashing steel—and there's an opulent score by James Horner. *Krull* is fine matinee material, blazing with color and action. Peter Yates' direction is first-rate, giving Stanford Sherman's script a sense of the majestic. Freddie

Jones is the wise man, Ynyr; Francesca Annis is the Widow of the Web; Bernard Bresslaw is the one-eyed Cyclops; David Barttley is Ergo the Magician and Alun Armstrong is Torquil, bandit leader. Aka *Dragons of Krull, Dungeons and Dragons, The Dungeons of Krull* and *Krull: Invaders of the Black Fortress.* (Video/Laser: RCA/Columbia)

KRULL: INVADERS OF THE BLACK FORTRESS. See *Krull.*

KWAIDAN (1965) ★★★★ Japanese anthology film by Masaki Kobayashi plunges into the shadowy valley of Lafcadio Hearn's ghost stories, once described as "permanent archetypes of human experience." Yoko Mizuki's script masters the paradox of being horrifying and beautiful with its four-part, two-and-a-half-hour format. The first tale is the surrealistic vignette of a defeated Samurai warrior who leaves his wife for a wealthy highborn who turns out to be an unbearable bitch. "In the Cup of Tea" deals with a man who peers into his teacup one morning and finds the reflection of a stranger gazing back. "Koichi, the Earless" is the most ghostly of the yarns, depicting a man summoned by ancient spirits to serve as their storyteller. "The Woman of the Snow" is about a secret whispered by one friend to another which must never be repeated. A color film of lush composition featuring superb dreamlike special effects. Excellent cast headed by Renato Mikuni, Michiyo Aratama and Tatsuya Nakadai. Aka *Ghost Stories* and *Weird Tales.* (S/Weird; Video Yesteryear; Filmfax; Sinister/C; Nostalgia) (Laser: Criterion)

KULL THE CONQUEROR (1997) ★★ This is such familiar sword-and-sorcery fantasy, with a plot that has been used so frequently, it is an instant video movie. On its surface *Kull the Conqueror* would seem to have promise. It stars Kevin Sorbo, who is internationally known as Hercules from his syndicated TV series produced by Sam Raimi. It's based on a heroic-fantasy character created by Robert E. Howard, the famous pulp-magazine writer of the early 20th century who also created Conan the Barbarian. Actually, Kull was nothing more than a carbon copy of Conan so Howard could expand his writing markets, yet Howard knew how to flesh out the character and make him interesting. That's something Charle Edward Pogue's screenplay does not achieve with its use of the deposed king fleeing on an odyssey to find "The Breath of Vulka," a burst of flame that will destroy the evil sorceress queen Akivasha, she who rules the kingdom of Acheron. Insert several sword fights and hand-to-hand combat among large numbers and that's about all you get. Although Karina Lombard is acceptable as the tarot-card-reading palace slave whom Sorbo yearns after, Tia Carrera as the wicked Akivasha is not. She doesn't quite have the fire and brimstone and anger to pull off her written material, even though her skimpy palace costumes do pull your eyes across the woven material. Why director John Nicolella couldn't find a little more energy and care to put into his action scenes remains a bigger mystery than anything Pogue offers in the script. To his credit, Nicolella does make one shipboard fight seem exciting, and there's some rousing action in a cave of frozen men wherein the Breath of Vulka resides. The mediocre special effects are by Kit West and Richard Malzahn. Thomas Ian Griffith, Litefoot, Roy Brocksmith, and Sven Ole Thorsen struggle with underwritten roles. Only Harvey Fierstein as a gay tavern owner named Jabu seems to have any fun in this movie. Second-rate all the way—something the critics never said about Robert E. Howard. (Video/DVD: Universal)

LABORS OF HERCULES. See *Hercules* (1959).

LABYRINTH (1986) ★★★ Curious mixture of Muppet humor, *The Wizard of Oz* and *Alice in Wonderland*: Obnoxious teenager Jennifer Connelly is plunged into the kingdom of the King of Goblins (David Bowie) as she pursues gremlins who whisked away her baby brother. The premise is weak (the infant is never in any real danger) and not even a 13-hour time limit imposed on Connelly adds suspense as she has adventures with fairies, goblins and dwarves. While Brian Froud's designs and Jim Henson's creatures are amusing (especially a shaggy dog with eyepatch, a clumsy dwarf named Hoggle and a dimwit fuzzball called Bluto), there is an air of ersatz to the thrills in Terry Jones's script, and Bowie is much too charming. Produced by George Lucas and directed by Jim Henson. (Embassy/Nelson) (Laser: Embassy/Nelson; New Line has a wide-screen version)

LADY AND THE MONSTER, THE (1943) ★★½ This screen adaptation of Curt Siodmak's novel *Donovan's Brain* (written by Danie Lussier and Frederick Kohner), in which a financial genius's brain is preserved after his death and takes over others by telepathic communication, is inferior to the 1953 version. The classic idea was misshaped by Republic into an ordinary horror flick. Directed by George Sherman, the film is a dated atmosphere piece, chiefly memorable for John Alton's *noir* lighting. Vera Ralston is miscast as the heroine. Erich von Stroheim, Richard Arlen, Sidney Blackmer. Aka *The Monster, The Monster's Castle, The Monster and the Lady* and *The Tiger Man*.

LADY DRACULA (1973). See *Lemora—The Lady Dracula*.

LADY FRANKENSTEIN (1971) ★★ Women's Lib comes to the laboratory! Smock-wearing femme fatale Sara Bey (as evil as her father) is a cut-up as she switches brains in two bodies to create a new Frankenstein Monster, copying Daddy's techniques. Daddy is Joseph Cotten, who wanders through this European Hammer clone looking a bit lost. The monster is a frightful makeup job but Bey is well built, exposing her beautiful breasts in sizzling love scenes. Mel Welles (real name: Ernst von Theumer) forgot to direct Mickey Hargitay, who stands around looking very brawny—and also lost. Aka *The Daughter of Frankenstein* and *Madame Frankenstein*. Herbert Fux, Paul Muller. (Sinister/C; Embassy; S/Weird; Filmfax; Horizon; Sultan)

LADYHAWKE (1985) ★★★½ Top-notch fantasy adventure filled with derring-do and swashbuckling; it's also a pleasing fairy-tale romance in which gallant knight Rutger Hauer turns into a wolf at night, and beautiful princess Isabeau (Michelle Pfeiffer) transmutes into a hawk by day. This means they can never fulfill their love—until there happens along a flippant squire (Matthew Broderick), who conspires with old Imperius (Leo McKern) to undo the evil spell imposed by evil bishop John Wood. The Italian castles and ruins lend authenticity to this gritty costume drama with high-energy performances. Directed by Richard Donner for producer Harvey (*The Omen*) Bernhard. (Video/ Laser: Warner Bros.)

LADY IN WHITE (1988) ★★★★ A movie for your Top Ten list. Writer-producer-director Frank LaLoggia, who showed promise in 1981's *Fear No Evil*, has fashioned a supernatural tale. that captures the "sense of wonder" Ray Bradbury often speaks of. LaLoggia blends life in a small Eastern Seaboard town in 1962 (in the nostalgic style of Spielberg) with ghost and gothic elements. Lukas Haas is superb as Frankie Scarlotti, 10, who encounters the spectral spirits of a girl who was violently murdered and her mother, a legendary "Lady in White" who haunts the environs of Willowpoint Falls. The story is told as a voice-over memory—that and its racial subplot are reminiscent of *To Kill a Mockingbird*. While adults might think its menacing qualities will be frightening to children, it is this very quality that will attract youngsters. Len Cariou, Alex Rocco, Katherine Helmond. (Virgin Vision) (Laser: Image)

LADYKILLERS (1988) ★★★ A male-strippers' club is the setting for this unusually steamy TV-movie in which guys are slashed to death by a psychokiller during their act, before legions of lust-driven lady spectators. The killing device is made of four razorblades welded together. Greg Dinallo's script only touches lightly on the velvet underground milieu of male strippers and focuses on the investigation by cops Marilu Henner and Thomas Calabro. Susan Blakely gives a sexually intense performance as a wealthy nymphomaniac who hangs around the guy dancers. This variation on *Stripped to Kill* is a reversal of clichés, so that it's the males who are in peril and a woman who comes to their rescue. A solid entertainment directed by

Robert Lewis. Lesley-Anne Down, William Lucking, Alexandra Borrie, Mark Carlton, David Correia. (Prism)

LADY OF THE SHADOWS. See *The Terror* (1963).

LADY TERMINATOR (1989) ★★½ An evil queen's reincarnation—a student on an anthropological quest—goes on a rampage, killing half the population of Indonesia. Barbara Anne Constable, Christopher J. Hart, Claudia Raedmaker, Joseph McGlynn. Directed by Jalil Jackson. (Studio Entertainment)

LAIR OF THE WHITE WORM, THE (1988) ★★★ Writer-director Ken Russell takes a standard horror-movie plot and gives it his usual bizarre twists and sense of perversity. The result: a decadent, perplexing mixture of campy one-liners, absurd visuals and unapproachable characters. The setting is the mansion of Lady Sylvia Marsh (Amanda Donohoe), the head of a snake cult preparing virginal sacrifices to the Worm God, who lives in a deep pit and only emerges for fresh munchies. Lady Marsh claims her victims, sways to music like a cobra, and sharpens her fangs for the next attack. With hysteria and garish style, Russell again proves he's one of the wildest filmmakers in the world. Hugh Grant, Catherine Oxenberg, Peter Capaldi. (Vestron) (Laser: Image)

LAKE PLACID (1999) ★★½ Of those films that qualify for the giant-monster-in-a-lake, this is the only one with a happy ending for the creature. The 50-foot behemoth Asian-Pacific crocodile, which somehow swam into Roostock County, ME, is presumably on its way to a safe habitat to be studied by scientists. It will be well fed and cared for, if the music tells us anything. Gee, did I give away the surprise ending? Gosh, what are horror movies coming to when a monster, after devouring at least 33.3 percent of the cast in the grossest manner possible, is given such humane treatment? Is there no justice in the screen battle of man against mutated nature? Have giant-monster-movie writers had a change of heart? Certainly the screenwriter of *Lake Placid*, David E. Kelley, has some odd ideas about this genre that appealed to director Steve Miner. For example, he creates a paleontologist (Bridget Fonda) working for a natural-history museum in New York City and has her behave so bitchily when she reaches the shores of Lake Placid that you hope the croc will rise up out of the water and eat her, just to shut off her endless antimale prattling. Then there's a crocodile expert named Hector (Oliver Platt) who is twice as obnoxious and offensive as Fonda. Platt has no respect for the law and treats sheriff Brendan Gleeson with total disdain. For 75 minutes one hopes and prays the nauseous Platt will be eaten. No, not just eaten. Bitten in half. Head chomped off in one bite. Each arm and leg separately de-

voured. But does anything good like that happen? No, instead the horrible eating things happen to nice characters. Like the underwater diver in the opening sequence who is cut in two—no legs when he comes out of the boat. Or the friendly sheriff's deputy who's leaning over the side of the boat, just doing his job, when the croc rises out of the water and separates head from neck in just one "g*n*a*s*h." Writer Kelley's sense of twisting all the clichés around continues with the Bill Pullman character. He's from the Department of Fish and Game and you would think he's supposed to be the hero. He looks like a hero, the virile way he climbs in and out of vans and boats. But does he do anything heroic? Not hardly, not in this giant-monster-in-a-lake movie. He fires his service pistol into the creature a number of times, but so what? Anyone who's seen these movies knows a few rounds of pistol fire never hurt anything monstrous. Then he fires a tranquilizer gun, but hell, even Fonda could have done that, if only she had stopped screaming all the while. Fonda? Well, she does get treated like your mundane clichéd heroine. She keeps falling in the water and the croc keeps coming after her. In the final scenes, she falls in a third time and gets trapped underwater with the jaws of the beast chomping away, but never quite slashing into her lovely skin and voluptuous body parts. No way you can fool us, Kelley. We know that girl heroines never get eaten in giant-monster-in-a-lake movies. On the other hand, when you write the sequel, *Lake Placid: The Birth of the Baby Crocs,* you might think about getting rid of Fonda's character in the first reel. Chomp chomp chomp glug glug bubble bubble. Now then, that leaves Betty White, who plays a half-crazed woman who feeds her livestock to the croc in the lake. This shows you what happens when even a Golden Girl gets beyond her prime and has to take eccentric character roles. (Video/ DVD: Fox)

LAKE OF THE LIVING DEAD. See *Zombie Lake*.

LAMP, THE. See *The Outing*.

LAND BEFORE TIME, THE (1988) ★★★ Outstanding cartoon feature from the team of Don Bluth (director), Gary Goldman and John Pomeroy, produced by Steven Spielberg and George Lucas. It's a warm, thrilling account about a young dinosaur named Littlefoot who survives a prehistoric cataclysm and leads young survivors on a trek to a promised land. The terse 66 minutes have some wonderful set pieces and are reminiscent of the best Disney cartoons of yore. Youngsters might be frightened when the band is imperiled by the carnivorous Sharptooth, but that is counterbalanced by wonderful characters and a warm humor. Voices by Pat Hingle (narrator and Rooter), Helen Shaver (Littlefoot's mom), Candice Houston (Cera), Judith Barsi

(Ducky), Will Ryan (Petrie), Burke Barnes (Daddy Topps). (MCA; Applause) (Laser: MCA)

LAND OF DOOM (1985) ★★★ As *Mad Max* imitations go, this one is pretty good. Set in a post-holocaust desert world, it follows the adventures of two survivors: Harmony (Deborah Rennard), a crossbow-packing, man-hating blond who trusts no man, and Anderson (Garrick Dowhen), a good-hearted, reformed biker warrior on a trek to a mystical land called Blue Lake. They reluctantly join up to undergo harrowing ordeals at the hands of a cannibal gang, plague victims, little people in robes, and a biker gang led by sadist Daniel Radell. It's almost wall-to-wall action with crazy vehicles and zap guns. Director-coproducer Peter Maris gets okay performances out of his cast (including Frank Garrett, Richard Allen and Aykut Duz) and milks Craig Rand's script for nuances of character. Action fans should be pleased. (Lightning)

LAND OF FARAWAY, THE (1987) ★★ Limited special effects by Derek Meddings and tedious stretches make for a fair children's fantasy spun as a sword-and-sorcery fairy tale. Stockholm orphan boy Nicholas Pickard is carried away on the white beard of an old man to a kingdom ruled by benevolent king Timothy Bottoms. But to earn happiness the boy (renamed Mio) decides to venture with Jum-Jum (Christopher Bale) to the Land Outside, to kill evil knight Kato (Christopher Lee). Aided by a magical sword and a cloak of invisibility spun by Susannah York, the youths close in on Kato for a showdown, the film's one exciting moment. Directed by Vladimir Grammatikov. (Prism; Starmaker)

LAND THAT TIME FORGOT, THE (1975) ★★★ First in a series of Edgar Rice Burroughs adventure-fantasy yarns produced by John Dark and directed by Kevin Connor in England. When a British merchant is sunk by a U-boat during World War I, the survivors (Doug McClure, Susan Penhaligon) seek refuge on an uncharted island forgotten by time. All the monsters (dragon, pterodactyl, etc.) are full-scale mock-ups moved mechanically, and sometimes it shows. Yet a spirit of rousing adventure makes the script by James Cawthorne and Michael Moorecock enjoyable. Others in this series: *At the Earth's Core, The People That Time Forgot* and *Warlords of Atlantis*. John McEnery, Anthony Ainley. (Vestron)

LAND UNKNOWN, THE (1956) ★★★ This forerunner to *Jurassic Park* is an interesting if sometimes corny special-effects extravaganza from Universal-International at a time when the studio was making state-of-the-art sci-fi/horror films. It's a "lost world" variation set near the South Pole where a helicopter carrying a handful of explorers crash-lands in a "tropical hot spot" in the middle of nowhere, encountering flying pterodactyls, an angry T.-Rex, battling lizard creatures, assorted sea serpents, and a plant with more tentacles than an octopus. Clifford Stine's effects are dated by today's standards, but if you can put your mindset on 1956, it's an intriguing reminder of how far special effects have come since then. Jock Mahoney and Shawn Smith are a handsome couple and adequately carry their limited roles as they run through the potted jungle. Directed by Virgil Vogel from a script by William Robson and Laszlo Gorog, this costars Douglas Kennedy, Henry Brandon and William Reynolds. Originally produced as *The Hidden Valley*. (Video/Laser: MCA)

LANGOLIERS, THE. See *Stephen King's The Langoliers*.

LASERBLAST (1978) ★★ Teenager Kim Milford discovers a laser cannon in the desert (dropped during a war between alien armies) and uses it for revengeful purposes. This low-budget quickie from producer Charles Band is one zap after the other, with Milford turning green whenever he blows up cars and buildings. There's some nice stop-motion work of the aliens by Dave Allen—it's the story that's nonanimated. Keenan Wynn and Roddy McDowall are wasted in stupid cameos. Directed with a one-track mind to blow everything up by Michael Raeburn, from an ammo-laden script by Franne Schacht and Frank Ray Perilli. (Media) (Laser: Shadow Entertainment)

LASER MAN, THE (1988) ★★★ Chinese-American filmmaker Peter Wang wrote-directed this offbeat tale that makes a statement about our misguided development of technology, in this case a laser weapon that an industrial firm intends to use in an assassination. Wang stars as New York cop Lt. Lu (a blend of Judge Dee and Charlie Chan) who investigates a laser technician (Arthur Weiss) being manipulated into the plot. It's a curious mix of cultural interchange, Zen philosphy, action and artistic direction. The results are interesting and well-intended. MarcHayashi, Maryann Urbano, Tony Ka-Fei Leung.

LASER MISSION (1990) ★★ A U.S. agent is assigned to destroy a Soviet superweapon and the scientist who invented it. Brandon Lee, Ernest Borgnine, Debi Monahan. Directed by Beau Davis. (Turner) (Laser: Image)

LASER MOON (1992) ★★ A crazed doctor, in possession of a laser Death Ray to do in his victims, plays a cat-and-mouse game with a radio disc jockey, proclaiming his next kill on the air and forcing authorities to send in a ringer (Traci Lords) to capture him. One zapped movie. Crystal Shaw, Harrison Leduke. Directed by Bruce Carter. (Hemdale)

LAST ACTION HERO (1993) ★★★ An $80-million misfire for Arnold Schwarzenegger, who parodies his screen persona in a mishmash of ingredients. There is promise in the Shane Black–David Arnott script, but it's buried within worthless debris and a sense of chaos evoked by producer-director John McTiernan, whose dark style doesn't match this comic-book material. Austin O'Brien portrays a youth who loves Schwarzenegger's Jack Slater movies, and is watching the latest (*Jack Slater IV*) when a magical ticket (given to him by old projectionist Robert Prosky) transports him into the film. Now he lives Slater's adventures against gang boss Anthony Quinn, hit man Charles Dance and crooked cop F. Murray Abraham. Look at this mess: in-parody with references to Hollywood movies; violent action and sudden death; spectacular fireworks and choreography; and a host of secondary characters, including police captain Frank McRae, obligatory girl Mercedes Ruehl and cameos by Jim Belushi, Chevy Chase, Little Richard, Art Carney, Sharon Stone, Jean-Claude Van Damme. Only Dance seems to be having any fun. How do you sum up this movie? As Slater would say, "Big mistake!" (Video/Laser: Columbia TriStar)

LAST BROADCAST, THE (1996) ★★★ Hopefully the producers of *The Blair Witch Project* and *The Curse of the Blair Witch* (the latter being a psuedo-documentary about the first) are sending over a few of their residuals checks to the makers of this remarkably clever film. There can be no doubt that *The Last Broadcast* inspired the *Blair Witch* projects, so similar are the subjects and the producing techniques. This is a "mockumentary" of a "true" incident of 1995 known as either "The Jersey Double Murders" or "The Pine Barrens and the Jersey Devil." Using interviews, television-program footage, still photographs, and computer images, the film documents how two access TV-show hosts (Stephen Avkast and Locus Wheeler of *Fact or Fiction*) hired soundman Rein Clacker and alleged psychic Jim Suerd and ventured into a desolate region of New Jersey known as the Pine Barrens, where perhaps the Jersey Devil might be lurking. Two of the filmmaking team were found horribly mutilated and Suerd, after a courtroom trial where he maintained his innocence to the end, was sent to prison for the murders, the blood of all three (including the missing man) having been found on his clothing. A year later Suerd died mysteriously while in prison, and a week later a mass of unwound recording tape was found at the doorstep of producer David Leigh, who is now putting together *The Last Broadcast*. Among those telling this fascinating crime story from Baroarke County are forensic pathologist Dr. Vann K. Waller, video editor Clair DeForest, psychologist Dr.

Dale Orstall, one-time soap opera director Sam Woods, Web-page designer Jay McDowell, Detective Anthony Rosi, data-retrieval specialist Michelle Monarch, and documentary filmmaker David Leigh. Much of the footage is what the filmmakers shot on their ill-fated venture, later recovered by investigating officers and used at the trial. This is all done in an "unsolved mysteries" style that was to be copied in *The Curse of the Blair Witch*. But where *The Last Broadcast* differs is that during its final ten minutes it suddenly drops the pseudo-documentary approach and becomes a well-photographed feature film with a shocking new murder (performed in vivid detail) and a final explanation for the mystery. *The Last Broadcast* was produced, written, and directed by Stefan Avalos and Lance Weiler for a reported $900 (some of that going for chow) and was awarded a Silver Prize at the Chicago Underground Film Festival. It made the low-budget rounds for a while, but never caught on like *The Blair Witch Project*. After the success of that film, it was revived and given video distribution. A fascinating must-see for anyone interesting in how our ever-changing technology is being used to make movies in novel ways. (Video/DVD: Wavelength)

LAST CANNIBAL WORLD, THE. See *Jungle Holocaust*.

LAST DANCE (1991) ★½ A chintzy, clichéd, poor ecdysiast slasher movie, obviously inspired by *Stripped to Kill* and set almost entirely in a topless club where five pretty but cheap chicks are preparing for a TV dance championship when suddenly a slasher killer strikes, killing each in a different fashion. Each male character is a suspect (creepy janitor, womanizing club owner Kurt T. Williams, jilted bartender) but Emerson Bixby's script is totally predictable as it narrows down to just dance novice Cynthia Stanton running through the club screaming as more characters are knifed to death. The motives are so unbelievable as to make this one of the worst of its type. Produced-directed by Anthony Markes. Low Markes at best. Elaine Hendrix, Kelly Poole, Allison Rhea. (Prism) (Laser: Image)

LAST GASP (1995) ★★½ A dark, *Twilight Zone*-like supernatural terror tale allowing Robert Patrick to give one of his sinister, tight-lipped performances à la T-1000 in *Terminator 2*. And because Pierce Milestone's script is set on such a grim note, and Scott McGinnis's direction is unrelenting in its depiction of a nihilistic world, it's hard to find much entertainment in all the starkness. Patrick is an unscrupulous, homicidal building designer who slaughters a tribe of Mexican Indians for their land, and is possessed by the spirit of a warrior at the moment of the attacker's "last gasp." His face covered with paint, Patrick turns into a primitive savage, murdering intruders with his knife and guarding his secret against nosy Joanna Pacula, who is searching for her missing husband. Mimi Craven, a gorgeous blond in a minidress, is the one pleasing element in this otherwise depressing tale, but her part is superceded by Pacula's. Vyto Ruginis, Alexander Enberg, Nan Martin, Shashawnee Hall.

LAST HORROR FILM, THE (1982) ★★★ Amusing satire on horror movies with Joe Spinell as neurotic New York cabbie Vinny Durand, who has the hots for actress Jana Bates (Caroline Munro) and imagines himself a movie director making *The Loves of Dracula.* He follows her to France's Cannes Film Festival, where this was filmed, so there's a rich amount of moviedom detail to intrigue buffs. A series of gory murders begins with Durand hanging around the edges, taking films of Jana and making love to her projected image. And dig those hilarious scenes between Spinell and his little old Jewish mother (played by his real mom, Mary). A wayout derivative of slasher flicks directed and coproduced by David Winters. Aka *The Fanatic.* (Media; Video Treasures)

LAST HOUSE ON THE LEFT, THE (1972) ★½ Pandering effort of producer Sean S. Cunningham and writer-director Wes Craven, made to shock in the grossest manner with its tale of retribution. Aka *Sex Crime of the Century, Night of Vengeance* and *Krug and Company*, this depicts a family under attack from sadists: rape, castration, buzzsaw killings, crucifixions, torture. Craven leaves out nothing. And yet this has an unrelenting power that makes it compelling despite crudities. You'll still need a strong stomach. Believe it or not but Cunningham and Craven have claimed they were inspired to make this film by Bergman's *The Virgin Spring.* David Alex Hess, Lucy Grantham. (Vestron; CIC offers the complete version) (Laser: CIC; Vestron)

LAST HOUSE ON THE LEFT II. See *Carnage.*

LAST MAN ON EARTH, THE (1964) ★★★ First adaptation of Richard Matheson's classic novel, *I Am Legend*, is far more faithful than the second, *The Omega Man.* Filmed in Italy by director Ubaldo Ragona (with U.S. insert shots by Sidney Salkow), it stars Vincent Price as the only nontainted survivor of a worldwide plague; all others are walking corpses, a mutated form of vampirism. Price burns their bodies during the day and, with the coming of dusk, rushes to his fortress to fight off the nocturnal marauders. Cowritten by Matheson (under the name Logan Swanson). Emma Danieli, Giacomo Rossi Stuart. Various early titles: *The Night Creatures, Night People, Naked Terror* and *Wind of Death.* (Sinister/C; S/Weird)

LAST OF PHILIP BANTER, THE (1987) ★★ The manuscript of alcoholic writer Scott Paulin seems to predict events to come. Tony Curtis, Kate Vernon, Gregg Henry. Directed by Herve Hachuel. (Republic)

LAST OF THE WARRIORS. Video title of *Empire of Ash III* (AIP).

LAST PREY OF THE VAMPIRE, THE. See *Curse of the Vampire.*

LAST RITES. See *Dracula's Last Rites.*

LAST RITES (1999) ★★★½ A tightly made thriller that keeps you entertained and still has something to say when it's all over. Intelligence and good filmmaking—a tough combination to find in a B movie, but here's one that has it. Thanks to a terrific acting job by Randy Quaid, superior scripting by Tim Frost and Richard Outten, and some flashy directing by Kevin Dowling, this Universal TV movie seems ripped out of the headlines, what with the way it deals with capital punishment and isn't afraid to take swipes at the liberal-minded people who release sex offenders from prison when those criminals are clearly far from rehabilitated. Quaid is Jeremy Dillon, a serial killer facing electrocution. It comes quickly and you know he deserves it—but a freakish accident (a lightning bolt hits the prison's transformer) staves off Dillon's death. His brain gets fried, though, and when he recovers, he can't remember his past and is a totally different person with ESP powers that enable him to prevent some terrible crimes. Should he be executed or has he been rehabilitated by nature's unusual act? It's a compelling question that plagues prison warden Clarence Williams III, FBI man A. Martinez, psychologist Embeth Davidtz, and civil-rights activist Tracey Ellis. The finale is a classic piece of cat-and-mouse suspense and several cinematic tricks are employed, so watch closely and don't reach any conclusions too quickly. If you sense electricity flowing through this review, good. You'll get several jolts from this excellent flick. (Universal)

LAST SLUMBER PARTY, THE (1987) ★ This ripoff of *The Slumber Party Massacre* series depicts the usual slasher killer with horrible murder instruments (and we mean instruments) attacking a bevy of young beauties gathered for an all-night romp. Directed by Stephen Tyler. Joann White, Jan Jensen, Nancy Meyer. (VCI)

LAST STARFIGHTER, THE (1984) ★★★½ Superior space adventure with excellent effects and an interesting love story fleshed out by writer Jonathan Betuel. Lance Guest is living a bleak existence in a trailer park and excelling only at video games when he is picked by humanoid alien Robert Preston (portraying lovable conman Centauri) to help the Star League of Planets fight off a flotilla of invaders. Guest is trained by Dan O'Herlihy as Grig, the only remaining E.T. who knows intergalactic warfare. Designers Ron Cobb and James D. Bissell give this fairy tale a glossy look, but it is the sensitive love between Guest and Catherine Mary Stewart that makes this work. Directed by Nick Castle. (Video/Laser: MCA)

LAST SURVIVOR, THE (1976) Original title of the (in)famous Italian cannibal movie better known in America as *Jungle Holocaust* (Video City) and *Cannibal* (AIR). See *Jungle Holocaust.*

LAST THRILL, THE. See *Erotikill.*

LAST TOMB OF LIGEIA. See *Tomb of Ligeia.*

LAST VAMPYRE, THE (1993) ★★★ Fascinating 2-part British TV adaptation of Sir Arthur Conan Doyle's "The Sussex Vampire," with Jeremy Brett as Sherlock Holmes and Edward Hardwicke as Dr. Watson involved in a most singular adventure with a caped man (Roy Marsden) who seems to have strange powers over others, and who believes in the vampire-bat legend. Jeremy Paul's telescript deals with the psychological aspects this strange fellow has over others, and even upon himself, and you must decide if the supernatural impinges itself into Holmes's world or not. Watson, at one point, talks about a ghost he met in India, and asks Holmes, "Do vampires exist within your philosophy?" Holmes replies, "In human terms, perhaps." Hmm, the game is decidedly afoot, my dear viewer. Directed by Tim Sullivan. Keith Barron, Maurice Denham, Elizabeth Spriggs, Freddie Jones. (MPI)

LAST VICTIM OF THE VAMPIRE. See *The Playgirls and the Vampire.*

LAST WARRIOR, THE. See *The Final Executioner.*

LAST WAVE, THE (1978) ★★★ Australia's Peter Weir directs an intriguing if mystifying tale of prophecy and doom. The symbolism is fascinating, though, and the atmosphere of pending death heavy as Sydney-based attorney Richard Chamberlain defends Aborigines accused of murder, but he is plagued by visions of horrors to come. A film that works on several levels, and which challenges the intellect as well as pleases the eye. Olivia Hamnett. (Warner Bros.; Rhino) (Laser: Japanese)

LAST WILL OF DR. MABUSE, THE. See *The Testament of Dr. Mabuse.*

LATE FOR DINNER (1991) ★★★ Surprising mixture of genres from director W. D. Richter, who helmed *The Adventures of Buckaroo Banzai.* Scripted by Mark Andrus, this opens in 1962 as 2 innocents—Brian Wimmer and Peter Berg—are caught up in a land swindle. They fall into the hands of a doctor doing a cryonics experiment—and wake up 29 years later without aging a day. The film then abandons sci-fi gimmicks and deals with what happens when the boys return to their New Mexico home and resume old relationships. This odd movie maintains a sense of freshness. Marcia Gay Harden, Colleen Flynn. (New Line) (Laser: Image)

LATIN QUARTER. See *Frenzy.*

LAUGHING DEAD, THE (1989) ★★ Travelers in Mexico participate in a "festival of the dead" celebration, only to become some of the dead when Mayans decide it's sacrifice time. Zombies run amok, pulling off body parts (credit special effects man John Buechler for that). Produced-written-directed by J. P. Somtow. Tim Sullivan, Forrest J. Ackerman (as a dead body).

LAWLESS LAND (1988) ★★ Another post-holocaust world à la *Mad Max,* depicting the arid adventures of two young people who try to escape from a totalitarian ruler of the devastated landscape, and their predictable adventures staying ahead of a bad guy called Road Kill. Directed by Jon Hess. Leon Berkeley, Xander Berkeley, Nick Corri. (MGM/UA)

LAWNMOWER MAN, THE (1992) ★★★ That tired plot about the dimwit who's turned into a genius gets virtual reality technology in this overblown adaptation of a story from Stephen King's *Nightshift.* Jeff Fahey is a simpleminded gardener-grasscutter who falls into the clutches of scientist Pierce Brosnan, whose experiments with computers turns Fahey into a psychic superman. The Shop, a secret organization behind Brosnan's research, wants Fahey to carry out evil deeds. Only the computerized nightmare sequences stand out from the myriad clichés in the script by the husband-and-wife team of Brett Leonard (who also directed) and Gimel Everett (who also coproduced). Jenny Wright, Mark Bringleson, Geoffrey Lewis, Jeremy Slate. (Video/Laser: Columbia)

LAWNMOWER MAN 2: BEYOND CYBERSPACE (1995) ★★½ If Stephen King hasn't sued, he should. This sequel to the 1992 film adaptation of his short story is a mishmash of undistinguished virtual reality special effects, muddled story line (you can thank director Farhad Mann for that) and characters that never have the emotional depth needed to make you care about what's happening. Instead of Jeff Fahey (who must have read the script and considered it virtually unreal), we now have Matt Frewer as a legless man who transmits himself into a universe of his own with the help of a computer chip stolen from inventor Patrick Bergin and marketed by evil electronics bigwig Kevin Conway and his cold-as-icicles assistant Camille Cooper. Jobe plans to interface with the entire world and then evilly control transmission, and it's up to Bergin, Austin O'Brien (back from the original film) and a sympathetic computer lady (Ely Pouget) to thwart the plan. With the plot always being told to you by the characters, there's no suspense and the film just fizzles out with a half-hearted climax of special effects. (Video/Laser: Turner)

LAW OF THE LAND (1976) ★★ This Quinn Martin TV-movie, oddly enough, is a slasher whodunit set in a Western town where sheriff Jim Davis and deputies Cal Bellini, Don Johnson and Charles Martin Smith pursue clues to the identity of a saber-wielding maniac slaughtering prostitutes at Dutch Annie's place. Eerie lighting gives some scenes the quality of a horror film, but too much of this cowtown tale is wasted on subplots and endless dialogue, so it's a minor item that buffs could easily pass on. Scripted by John Wilder and Sam Rolfe and directed by Virgil W. Vogel. Andrew Prine, Moses Gunn, Glenn Corbett, Nicholas Hammond, Barbara Parkins, Darleen Carr. (Worldvision)

LEATHERFACE: THE TEXAS CHAINSAW MASSACRE III (1989) ★★★ This second sequel to the 1974 trendsetter in U.S. Grand Guignol comes close to being a remake. The script by "splatter punk" writer David J. Schow (heavily tampered with by producer Robert Engelman and director Jeff Burr) has desert travelers Kate Hodge, William Butler, Toni Hudson and Ken Foree falling prey to Leatherface Sawyer and his new surrogate family of all-American perverts, murderers and sadists. Finally it's Hodge who is subjected to one horror after the other as she is captured, tortured and escapes—only to find herself in a bog of bubbling yuck. The black humor is suitably gruesome but the sum total is less than expected. The film was extensively cut for an R rating, and Schow says many of his set pieces (such as a man being cut down the middle) were as brutally mutilated as his characters. R. A. Mihailoff (Leatherface), Viggo Mortensen. (Video/Laser: RCA/Columbia)

LEECH. See *The Leech Woman.*

LEECH WOMAN, THE (1960) ★★½ Coleen Gray, seeking eternal life, learns from Africans that a brain secretion can restore the aging body. One murder, however, leads to more before she and the plot turn to powder. Edward Dein directed the David Duncan screenplay. Gloria Talbott, Grant Williams, John Van Dreelan. Produced under the title *Leech.* (Video/Laser: MCA)

LEGACY OF BLOOD. See *Blood Legacy.*

LEGACY OF HORROR (1978) ★ Primary primer in how not to make a movie—a masterpiece of choppy editing, poor lighting, camera noise, uneven acting and rank cinematography. Credit tacky Andy Milligan the exploitationer—he wrote-directed this mess about 3 silly sisters who spend a night on Haney Island with their inane husbands to collect an inheritance. A slouch-hatted slouch leaves a head on a platter, shoves a pitchfork into a fat stomach and saws a man in half. Elaine Boies, Chris Broderick. A remake of Milligan's *The Ghastly Ones.* Ghastly is right! (Vidcrest; Gorgon; MPI)

LEGEND (1985) ★★★ Ridley Scott's fairy-tale fantasy is in a never-never land rendered in au-

tumnal detail, all falling leaves, mysticism and magic. So beautiful is the scenery that exquisite detail overshadows the weak story. Peasant Tom Cruise and Princess Lili (Mia Sara) seek the last unicorn in the kingdom, unaware that Darkness (Tim Curry, excellent as a world-weary demon) is using them to set a trap for the horned creature (designed by Rob Bottin). A disappointment because the script by William Hjortsberg lacks humor or clever development, and the romantic leads are real wimps, hardly the stuff of quest-fantasy. Billy Barty, Alice Playten, David Bennett. (Video/Laser: MCA)

LEGENDARY CURSE OF LEMORA. See *Lemora—The Lady Dracula.*

LEGEND LIVES, THE. See *Madman.*

LEGEND OF BIGFOOT, THE (1976) ★ Did naturalist Ivan Marx capture "exclusive" footage of hairy beasts lunching in an unidentified swamp? Or are they Screen Actors Guild extras in monkey costumes? Burning questions to ask as you watch this "documentary." Marx, who claims the creatures are genuine, follows the trail of Bigfoot from Arizona to the Arctic Circle and has interesting travel footage, if nothing else. There is a strange scene of a bright light moving across the twilight landscape, as if an old Indian legend is coming true. Or is it a Volkswagen lost on the tundra? More burning questions . . .

LEGEND OF BLOOD CASTLE, THE (1972) ★½ Another sanguinary variation on the Countess Bathory myth, with Lucia Bose bathing in the blood of victims and husband Esparatco Santoni becoming a vampire. Jorge Grau directed this Spanish-Italian effort, considered one of the better interpretations of the Bathory legend. Aka *Lady Dracula, Bloody Ceremony, Countess Dracula and The Female Butcher.* Ewa (Candy) Aulin, Ana Farra, Franca Grey. (Simitar; CVC; also in video as *Blood Castle)*

LEGEND OF BOGGY CREEK, THE (1973) ★★★ Producer-director Charles B. Pierce uses pseudodocumentary techniques to tell this allegedly true story of a Bigfoot haunting the Arkansas swamp. Pierce uses local residents who claim to have seen the monster and reenact close encounters with such veracity, you almost believe them. Earl E. Smith's script is told in voiceover, as though it were a misty memory. Willie E. Smith, John Hixon. The sequel was *Return to Boggy Creek.* (Lightning; Vestron)

LEGEND OF GATOR FACE, THE (1996) ★★ Predictable children's morality tale, the old "cry wolf" story respun in an Everglades setting, where two obnoxious kids find a monster costume and pretend to be a legendary half-alligator, half-man creature. Looking like an extra from *The Alligator People,* the "monster" goes around scaring aging swamp expert Paul Winfield and others. Then the real thing shows up—a benevolent being that looks like an extra from *The Alligator People*. Needless to say, you will not be convinced. The telescript by David Covell, coproducer Alan Mruvka and Sahara Riley is a compendium of clichés, and director Vic Sarin is simply stuck with that crummy-looking creature suit. John White, Dan Warry-Smith, Gordon Michael Woolvett, Kathleen Laskey, C. David Johnson.

LEGEND OF HELL HOUSE (1973) ★★★★ In adapting his own novel *Hell House*, Richard Matheson eschewed garishness and gory imagery for unseen grotesqueries. Hell House, accursed estate of the perverse Emeric Belasco, has been haunted by psychic phenomena since his death years before. A dying millionaire hires psychist Clive Revill to prove the existence of life after death and Hell House becomes the proving ground. Members of Revill's team are wife Gayle Hunnicutt, mental medium Pamela Franklin and medium Roddy McDowall, sole survivor of an earlier attempt to exorcise Hell House. This atmospheric film (in the league of *The Haunting*) is tense under John Hough's direction. Watch for Michael Gough. (Video/Laser: CBS/Fox)

LEGEND OF HILLBILLY JOHN (1972) ★★½ "One Step Beyond" TV host John Newland directed this version of Manly Wade Wellman's book *Who Fears the Devil?* (scripted by Melvn Levy), a collection of supernatural stories about a guitarist, Silver John, who roves the Appalachians, warding off evil with his guitar's silver strings. Hedge Capers, Denver Pyle, Susan Strasberg, Percy Rodriguez, R. G. Armstrong. Aka *My Name Is John*. (New World) (Laser: Image)

LEGEND OF THE BAYOU. See *Eaten Alive*.

LEGEND OF THE FRANKENSTEIN MONSTER, THE (1993) ★★ A two-cassette packaging from Simitar consisting of old movie trailers that, when compiled, trace a history of Mary Shelley's classic novel as interpreted by filmmakers. "Part One: The Creature Is Born" ranges from Edison's 1910 version (featuring some long-lost footage depicting the Monster's creation) through the '50s. "Part Two: The Creature Lives On" is notable for the previously unreleased footage from the British TV pilot "Tales of Frankenstein," starring Anton Diffring (as the doctor), Don Megowan (as the Monster) and Helen Westcott. Similar in structure to Ted Newsom's *Frankenstein: A Cinematic Scrapbook*. Narrated by Jeffrey Lee, written by Jeff Bottcher. (Simitar)

LEGEND OF THE OVERFIEND (1989) ★★★ Controversial Japanese animated feature that wildly, imaginatively mixes graphic sex with supernatural events, although the U.S. version has been heavily edited. Set in a futuristic society, the normal human world overlaps with the World of Manbeasts and the World of the Monster Demons. The Overfiend ("the God of Gods") has been prophesied to return every 3,000 years to destroy all existing creatures and begin a new world of peace, and now is the time. If you're tired of bland mainstream cartoon movies, and don't mind having your sensitivities blasted by sex, violence and hideous creatures, this is when the phrase "mind boggling" is an appropriate term. Directed by Hideki Takayama. (Anime 18)

LEGEND OF THE SEVEN GOLDEN VAMPIRES (1973) ★★★ Coproduction between Hammer and the Shaw Brothers of Hong Kong results in satisfying sukiyaki—an East-West blending of martial arts, kung fu and vampire bloodletting. In 1804, Count Dracula inhabits the body of a Chinese priest in order to resurrect vampire corpses in Samurai armor who terrorize villagers. Flash ahead to 1904: Peter Cushing, as Van Helsing, joins his heroic son, Swedish beauty Julie Ege (in low-cut gowns, blouses and high-heeled boots) and a troupe of Chinese warriors to destroy the demons. The action is nonstop, the fights are tremendous jobs of choreography and the monster makeup effective. A rousing entertainment. Directed by Roy Ward Baker from an imaginative script by Don Houghton. Aka *Dracula and the Seven Golden Vampires* and *The Seven Brothers Meet Dracula*. Robin Stewart, David Chiang, John Forbes Robertson. (Sinister/C; 21st Genesis; from Media and Electric as *The Seven Brothers Meet Dracula*)

LEGEND OF THE WEREWOLF (1975) ★★ British horrorizer in the Hammer mood, with Gothic atmosphere, superior direction by Freddie Francis and a fine cast headed by Peter Cushing as an investigating medical examiner and David Rintoul as a man plagued by lycanthropy, who goes on murder sprees when the moon is full. (He was raised by a wolf pack.) Anthony Hines scripted as John Elder, his plot reminiscent of *Curse of the Werewolf*. Aka *Plague of the Werewolves*. Ron Moody, Hugh Griffith. (Interglobal; VCL; Moore)

LEGEND OF THE WHITE HORSE (1985) ★★ A faraway fantasy kingdom is the setting for this children's adventure directed by Jerzy Domaradski and Janusz Morganstern. Allison Dalson, Dee Wallace Stone, Christopher Lloyd.

LEGEND OF THE WOLFWOMAN (1977) ★ A degenerate, lowbrow Spanish horror film with helpings of sadism, violence and sex as Ann Borel, reincarnation of a wolf creature from a previous century, rips, tears and slashes her way to oblivion. Directed-written by Rino di Silvestro. Frederick Stafford, Dagmar Lassander. Aka *The Wolf Woman, Werewolf Woman* and *Daughter of a Werewolf*. (United; VCI; VIP; from VBG as *She Wolf* and from Mogul as *Terror of the She Wolf*)

LEGEND OF WITCH HOLLOW. See *The Witchmaker*.

LEGEND OF WOLF MOUNTAIN (1992) ★★ Children's outdoor adventure in which the spirit of a wolf comes to the aid of three children being held captive by escaped criminals. Directed by Craig Clyde. Mickey Rooney, Bo Hopkins, Vivian Schilling, Don Shanks. (Video/Laser: Hemdale)

LEMON GROVE KIDS MEET THE GREEN GRASSHOPPER AND THE VAMPIRE LADY FROM OUTER SPACE, THE (1967) ★ If you guess by its lengthy title that this was probably made by Ray Dennis Steckler, go suck a lemon and eat a green grasshopper. You are right. In this rare cult classic in which Steckler appears as Cash Flagg (as he did in his own terrorizer with a long title, *The Incredibly Strange Creatures Who Stopped Living and Became Mixed-up Zombies*), a band of squareheads meets up with an insect creature and a bloodsucking dame (Carolyn Brandt) who have dropped in on Earth from a faraway planet. Mike Kannon, Coleman Francis. The script (if you dare to call it that) is by one E. M. Kevke and the direction is by Ted Rotter. Aka (for those short of breath) *The Lemon Grove Kids Meet the Monsters*. (Mascot)

LEMORA—THE LADY DRACULA (1973) ★★ Surrealistic vampire flick with arty overtones—some scenes pretentious as hell, others traditionally imitative of *Dracula*. A young girl's odyssey through a nightmarish landscape is filled with grotesque people and maintains curiosity if you don't take it literally. Cheryl Smith carries the picture as the 13-year-old girl. Written by producer Robert Fern and directed by Richard Blackburn, who wrote *Eating Raoul*. Aka *The Legendary Curse of Lemora* and *Lemora—A Child's Tale of the Supernatural*. Lesley Gilb, William Whitton, Hy (Monte) Pyke, Maxine Ballantyne. (Demonique; Fright; Moore)

LEMRO, PRIVATE EYE. See *Alien Private Eye*.

LENSMAN (1989) ★★★ Computer animation enhances this Japanese cartoon based on the cosmic adventures written by Edward E. (Doc) Smith, in which war breaks out between the Galactic Alliance (good guys) and the Bosconian War Lords (bad guys). Painstakingly drawn, with ample battles to hold one's attention. Directed by Yoshiyuki Kawajiri and Kazuyuki Hirokawa. (Streamline; Fusion) (Laser: Lumivision)

LEOPARD MAN, THE (1943) ★★★½ Cornell Woolrich's novel *Black Alibi* was adapted by screenwriter Ardel Wray for producer Val Lewton. It emerges a superb low-budget, high-thrills masterpiece of "quiet horror." Director Jacques Tourneur provides memorable sequences greater than the sum total—including one in which a gypsy girl's blood flows under a door after she is locked outside and attacked by an unseen force. That force is believed to be an escaped leopard, but all is not what it seems. Minimal focus is placed on hero and heroine (Dennis O'Keefe, Jean Brooks) as they track down the source of evil. (Fox Hill; Media) (Laser: Image; Turner)

LEPRECHAUN (1992) ★★ This low-budget quickie turns the fun-loving elf of Irish lore into a serial murderer who makes nasty quips in the style of Freddy Krueger. Short on cinematic stature, just like the titular entity, who is played on a one-dimensional mean and ugly note by Warwick Davis. The minuscule plot revolves around a family that settles in a rural shack where the leprechaun's sack of gold is hidden. Written-directed by Mark Jones, whom the Irish should sue. Jennifer Aniston, Ken Olandt, Mark Holton, Robert Gorman. (Video/Laser: Vidmark)

LEPRECHAUN 2 (1994) ★★ In the same vile vein of its predecessor, this slap against Irish folk legend stars Warwick Davis (again) as a shortish but effectual imp seeking a new bride. Directed by Rodman Flender. Charlie Heath, Shevonne Durkin, Sandy Baron, Clint Howard. (Video/Laser: Vidmark)

LEPRECHAUN 3 (1995) ★★½ What a strange mixture of stuff: First they take a leprechaun (Warwick Davis, in all that makeup again) and totally besmirch its good Irish character by having the devilish one attack an Indian pawnshop owner, biting off an ear and a big toe and killing the poor fellow in the most ghastly manner. Then we meet an innocent kid (John Gattins) and a magician's assistant (Lee Armstrong, who does the entire picture in a sexy stage costume) as they have good luck with the leprechaun's good-luck gold coin in a Las Vegas casino. Then the leprechaun dude is killing various people to get his coin back (including casino owner John DeMita), enlarging Caroline Williams's buttocks and breasts, and reciting all his dialogue in rhyme. Scriptwriter David Dubos is quite the elfin one himself. Somehow, director Brian Trenchard-Smith keeps it from totally falling apart. Yes, a strange mixture of stuff, indeed. Marcelo Tubert, Michael Callan, Tedia Gabriel. (Vidmark)

LEPRECHAUN 4: IN SPACE (1996) ★ If this was intended to be so-bad-it's-good, plant a pliant kiss on the Baloney Stone in dubious honor of this fourth in a series starring Warwick Davis as a mean-spirited, wisecracking elf of Irish folklore. With no explanation, Leprechaun is suddenly in the distant future on a far-flung planet, seducing Princess Zarina (Debbe Dunning, the "Tool Time" girl on TV's *Home Improvement*), whom he has kidnapped from the planet Daminian. Along comes a rocket loaded with space marines and a blond biologist (Jessica Collins) to rescue the royal dame. Leprechaun gets blown to pieces but, back on the ship, regenerates himself through the penis of one of the dumber space troopers. (And just when he thought it was safe to unzip.) Now the screenplay by Dennis Pratt, who had to be in an enlightened, heightened state of mind when he cranked this one out, really gets good: Dr. Mittenhand (Guy Siner) exists from the chest up only, the torso attached to a computer machine, and he orders his men to eliminate the destructive Leprechaun while he injects himself with Zarina's rejuvenating DNA. Unfortunately, since Leprechaun can work magical spells and keeps coming back to life each time he's eviscerated, nobody stands a chance, not even heroic Brent Jasmen. Finally, through the DNA injection, the German doc gets turned into a giant spider (now you can call him Dr. Mittenspider). Then Leprechaun eliminates the troopers one by one for command of the ship, while a computer voice does a countdown to a time bomb that will destroy the spaceship. Meanwhile, Zarina bares her wonderful breasts, explaining for a minute or so (with the camera never looking away) that anyone who sees these nifty knockers is going to get knocked off (an old custom on Damianian). This is certainly the most pleasant moment in this film, since director Brian Trenchard-Smith focuses mostly on exploding bodies and other forms of mutilation to human flesh while Leprechaun makes puns and sings "Danny Boy." Yes, you have to see it to believe that this movie ever got produced. Tim Colceri, Miguel A. Nuñez, Jr., Gary Grossman, Rebekah Carlton. (Vidmark-Trimark)

LESBIAN VAMPIRES/LESBIAN VAMPIRES—THE HEIRESS OF DRACULA. See *The Heritage of Dracula.*

LET'S SCARE JESSICA TO DEATH (1971) ★★★ Director John Hancock and screenwriters Norman Jonas and Ralph Rose are to be congratulated for a multilayered horror film with frightening visuals. There isn't much logic to the story yet the overall effect is unsettling. Zohra Lampert, newly released from an asylum, never knows if she's hallucinating or something weird is happening on her Connecticut farm. Are those spaced-out inhabitants in town vampires or zombies? The film has a dreamlike quality in depicting her nightmares. Gretchen Corbett, Barton Heyman, Kevin O'Connor. (Paramount)

LEVIATHAN (1989) ★★½ Whatever possessed director George P. Cosmatos to make a demeaning imitation of *Alien* is more mysterious than anything in the David Peoples–Jeb Stuart script. Emerging in the wake of *Deepstar Six*, this is inferior underwater horror-action set on a mining station two miles deep. The crew discovers a sunken Russian ship and the genetic-experiment infection that killed the Soviets begins to kill the Americans, one of them turning into an amphibian-fishman, a Stan Winston accomplishment. Peter Weller and Richard Crenna (as the boss and doctor of the crew) fare best with the underwritten roles, while Amanda Pays, Daniel Stern, Ernie Hudson, Michael Carmine, Hector Elizondo and Lisa Eilbacher are mere monster fodder. It never gels, even with composer Jerry Goldsmith and designer Rob Cobb contributing. (Video/Laser: MGM/UA)

LIANA, JUNGLE GODDESS (1956) ★★ A long-obscure movie, now available on home video, in which a female version of Tarzan is found romping through the foliage of Africa (mainly to keep her naked breasts concealed from the rest of the world) and brought back to England (shades of *Greystoke*) to meet a nobleman. Marion Michael, Hardy Kruger. (Sinister/C)

LIAR LIAR (1997) ★★½ This is one of those silly, contrived comedies designed for a specific talent, and fashioned to reach a wide mainstream audience, so unless you are a solid Jim Carrey fan who can't wait to see him acting as goofy as possible, don't exactly rush out for this empty-headed mess directed by Tom Shadyac. Too bad, the premise is a good one: a wish-come-true fantasy (never explained—just used by screenwriters Paul Guay and Stephen Mazur), makes Carrey unable to lie for 24 hours. And since he's a constantly lying attorney, this becomes a problem when he tries to help Jennifer Tilly in divorce court, and when he must face the domestic crises in his life, involving his estranged wife (Maura Tierney) and neglected adolescent son (Justin Cooper). They milk the father-kid plot for all the tears it's worth, while Carrey mugs, overacts, screams, and behaves in a way contrary to any known mortal being. Oh well, it's just a fantasy comedy, right? Yeah, sure. Swoosie Kurtz, Amanda Donahoe, Jason Bernard, Mitchell Ryan. (Video/DVD: Universal)

LICENCE TO KILL (1989) ★★★½ Superior entry in the James Bond series (marking Timothy Dalton's second portrayal and the fifth time that John Glen directed) has 007 going after the gang that tries to assassinate agent Felix Leiter (David Hedison). The stunts are spectacular, the fantastic gadgets kept to a minimum, and Dalton brings a no-nonsense verisimilitude to Bond, who races through Florida and South America in search of a drug operation commanded by Robert Davi and Frank McRae. Carey Lowell, Talisa Soto, Anthony Zerbe, Wayne Newton. (Video/Laser: CBS/Fox)

LIFE FOR A LIFE. See *Necromancy.*

LIFEFORCE (1985) ★★★ Colin Wilson's intellectual novel *Space Vampires* becomes an uneven but still recommended space-horror film by director Tobe Hooper and adaptors Dan O'Bannon and Don Jakoby. Hooper helms macabre scenes of corpses popping to life—these horrific visuals will have you shivering. A spaceship discovers an alien vessel harboring batlike creatures and three incubated humanoids. One of them, a big-busted female, sucks energy from Earthlings, turning them to cadavers. The gripping and eerie fascination builds as inspector Peter Firth and astronaut Steve Railsback attempt to solve the soul-transference, lifeforce-energy mystery. It is when London is ablaze, and half the population turns into zombies, that the film falls apart, its effects too metaphysical and its ending too ridiculous to live up to earlier thrills. Frank Finlay, Mathilda May, Patrick Stewart. Music by Henry Mancini; effects by John Dykstra and John Gant. (Vestron) (Laser: Image; MGM)

LIFEFORM (1995) ★★½ After a Viking space probe of 1983 to Mars mysteriously returns to Earth under alien control, it's taken to a secret laboratory, where scientists go to work trying to explain the spacecraft's return. Out of its innards pops your anticipated alien entity, which soon has the research team and a small band of soldiers fighting for their lives as the E.T. keeps changing size and intelligence by using corridors and viaducts to conduct its reign of terror. Writer-producer-director Mark H. Baker attempts to inject some different touches into this all-too-familiar sci-fi thriller, including a twist ending that doesn't really work. The cast (Cotter Smith, Deirdre O'Connell, Robert Wisdom) struggles with their underwritten roles. Strictly fodder for the guts-and-gore/monster-entity market. (Live)

LIFEPOD (1993) ★★★½ This "stranded in space" adventure, with a script by M. Jay Roach and Pen Densham that was inspired by Alfred Hitchcock's film *Lifeboat*, is an exciting, fast-moving TV-movie directed by Ron Silver, who is also in the cast. On Christmas Eve, 2169, a civilian space cruiser (the *Lutrania*) is returning from Venus ("across an ocean of 10 billion light years") when it's sabotaged. A handful of survivors escapes aboard an emergency "lifepod." But from the start, things go wrong and it's obvious there is a traitor in the ranks, as well as social issues to be discussed. This is a pure genre film done with style by Silver, who uses claustrophobic tricks to good advantage. The outer-space effects and hardware are excellent, twists come frequently, and the characters (including a dwarf called Q-3) are interesting enough to warrant caring about the whodunit aspect. Robert Loggia, Jessica Tuck, Stan Shaw, Adam Storke, Ted Gale, CCH Pounder. (Cabin Fever) (Laser: Image)

LIFT, THE (1983) ★★★½ Fascinating Dutch import (aka *Goin' Up*), a cross between an exploitation shocker and an art film. A new elevator system in a high rise reprograms its organic microchips to kill passengers in grisly ways—at least that's what writer-director Dick Maas intimates as his tale tersely unfolds. Maas conveys a sense of classy horror and then lapses into graphic slayings—including one hair-lifting sequence in which a security guard is decapitated. The mystery involves a conspiracy between the elevator designer and the electronics programmer as a lift repairman (Huub Stapel) searches for the truth. Gripping stuff, "up-lifting." Willeke Van Ammelrooy, Josine Van Dalsum. (Media) (Laser: Image)

LIGEIA. See *Tomb of Ligeia*.

LIGHT BLAST (1985) ★★ Mad physicist with a ray machine (it resembles a prop from a Buck Rogers serial) burns the flesh right off your bones when he terrorizes San Francisco by demanding $10 million in ransom money. It's up to homicide cop Erik Estrada and his partner (comedian Michael Pritchard) to stop the madman. This kicks in with a gritty, pseudodocumentary feeling with its scenic locations, fast editing and dynamic camera angles. But writer-director Enzo G. Castellari and cowriter Titus Carpenter have too feeble a story and too vapid a set of characters to sustain what is finally an empty-headed action film with interminable chases with cars, trucks, motorboats and anything that moves. Thomas Moore, Peggy Rowe, Bob Taylor, Nancy Fish. (Lightning)

LIGHTNING FIELD, THE. See *The Lightning Incident*.

LIGHTNING INCIDENT, THE (1991) ★★★ Intriguing story about a mother-to-be (Nancy McKeon) who undergoes strange incidents before the baby's birth, which suggest her aging mother (Polly Bergen) is haunted by a Central American devil-worship cult that will place the baby in jeopardy. Daughter and mother are led into a labyrinth of horror involving a killer snake, a tattoo of a lizard, and a field of pillars that attracts lightning bolts. Directed by Michael Switzer from a Michael J. Murray telescript. Elpidia Carrillo, Miriam Colon, Tim Ryan. (Paramount)

LIGHT YEARS (1987) ★★★★½ Superb French animated feature from Rene Laloux (*Fantastic Planet*) showcasing his impression of the human experience through science fiction. In this parable of good vs. evil, based on Jean-Pierre Andrevan's "Robots Against Gondohar," Laloux deals with the kingdom of Gondohar, a playground where man and organic life live in peace. But something begins turning men into stone, so Queen Ambisextra sends her handsome son, Sylvain, to investigate. Accompanied by a beautiful, bare-breasted woman, Airelle, Sylvain is led into a world of chaos, meeting killer robots called Men of Metal, a race of mutants called the Deformed (who speak only in past or future tense), a godlike brain, the Metamorphis, and a mystery involving the time-space continuum. A thinking man's action cartoon about the paradoxes of time, the misuse of power and science, the impersonalization of machines, the poisoning of our atmosphere, and the danger of peace without vigilance. "Adapted" into English by Isaac Asimov. (Vidmark) (Laser: Image)

LIKE FATHER LIKE SON (1987) ★★ A stuffy heart specialist (Dudley Moore) and his wild teenage son (Kirk Cameron) undergo personality transference via an Indian brew mistakenly put in a Tabasco bottle. The youth attends school with all the knowledge of the doctor and the father attends to his hospital rounds with zero knowledge. The situations and gags fall pretty flat, with director Rod Daniel unable to bring much oomph or merriment to the lackluster premise. Sean Astin as the boy Trigger, inadvertently responsible for the change of souls, Catherine Hicks as a sympathetic nurse, and Patrick O'Neal as the snobbish head of the hospital all do their best, but it fizzles. Margaret Colin as a sexpot adds a sizzle, then dissipates and dies. (RCA/Columbia) (Laser: Image)

LILIOM (1930) ★★ Ferenc Molnar's play served as the basis for this updated account of a carnival barker who commits suicide and goes to Hell, where he must confront his past to determine if he should have a future. Directed by Frank Borzage from a script by S. N. Behrman and Sony Levien. Charles Farrell, Rose Hobart, Estelle Taylor, Lee Tracy.

LILIOM (1934) ★★ In this version of the Ferenc Molnar play, a carnival spielsmeister kills himself and goes to Heaven (not Hell, as in the 1930 film version) and must face a court of inquiry as to his worthiness. This was Fritz Lang's first film (made in France) after he fled Nazi Germany and it stars Charles Boyer, Roland Toutain and Madeleine Ozeray. Director of photography was Rudolph Maté, who went on to Hollywood with Lang to become a film director. (Sinister/C; Discount; Horizon)

LIMIT UP (1989) ★★★ Nancy Allen shines in this amusing fantasy-comedy as a soybeans commodity trader at Chicago's Midwest Grain Exchange, working her way up from runner to the cover of *Time* as saleswoman. However, she has to make a deal with Danitra Vance, a rep for Lost Souls Inc. ("You sin, we win") who will claim Allen's soul some day. (Her license plate: CU-N-HELL). However, the thrust of the script by director Richard Martini and Lu Anders is on Allen's positive qualities and her warm relationship with Brad Hall. There's a neat surprise ending with Ray Charles as a street musician. Dean Stockwell is good as Allen's hard-driven boss. (Video/Laser: MCEG/Virgin)

LINK (1986) ★★ Offbeat suspense thriller with horror overtones—an oddity from Australian producer-director Richard Franklin and writer Everett DeRoche. Terence Stamp, specialist in the behavior of chimpanzees, brings student

Elizabeth Shue to his isolated mansion where she meets a superintelligent chimp named Link, who dresses like the family retainer, smokes cigars and watches her take a bath with a lecherous look. Franklin mounts the suspense during the siege portion, but a weak character for the woman and a small role for Stamp create an unsatisfying, unfocused film. (HBO; Republic)

LINK, THE (1982). See *Blood Link*.

LINNEA QUIGLEY'S HORROR WORKOUT (1991) ★½ The queen of the B horror flicks, star of such sophisticated fare as *Creepozoids*, headlines this parody of exercise videos in which she leads assorted monsters and fright characters through aerobics. Directed by Kenneth J. Hall. (Cinema Home)

LION MAN (1980) ★★½ Get beyond the turgid beginnings of this swashbuckling Greek production and you'll discover a campy action flick with ridiculously choreographed battles as the Son of Solomon does combat with evil. Having been raised by lions, this son of a witch has clawlike hands that penetrate into enemies' bodies like knives and kills them. Later on, when his hands are destroyed by acid, he dons appendages to wipe out a hundred soldiers (no kidding) in one encounter. Get into a mood for a great awful movie and you'll groove. Directed by Natuch Baitan. Steve Arkin, Barbara Lake. (Best Film & Video)

LIQUID DREAMS (1991) ★★★½ Offbeat mystery thriller with sci-fi overtones, set in a futuristic society, where Candice Daly searches for her sister's killer in a surreal nightclub world where a mad doctor conducts experiments on beautiful strippers. He is searching for an extract that recaptures the ultimate sexual climax—just one of several bizarre elements in the Zack Davis–Mark Manos script that capture an intriguing perverse atmosphere. Its only downfall is a threadbare production look. Also directed by Manos. Richard Steinmetz, Barry Dennen, Tracey Walter, Juan Fernandez, Paul Bartel. (Academy offers rated and unrated versions) (Laser: Image)

LIQUID SKY (1983) ★★½ New wave/punk rock/heavy metal/western decadence flick depicting freaked-out androgyne Margaret whose penthouse rooftop is visited by a flying saucer. Once she's been infected by an alien organism, her orgasms result in the deaths of her partners. What a way to go in the land of debauchery. Sardonic and funk punk bunk, with video graphics and reverse polarity taking the place of sexual encounters of the closest kind. More MTV than movie as Anne Carlisle (as the borderline man-woman) writhes through her torrid affairs with Manhattan lowlife. Smartly produced-directed by Russian emigre Slava Tsukerman, who cowrote with wife Nina Kerova. (Video/Laser: Media)

LISA, LISA. See *Axe!*

LITTLE MATCH GIRL, THE (1987) ★★★
Comedienne-actress Maryedith Burrell wrote
this TV-movie based on Hans Christian Andersen's tale about a beam of light that falls to
Earth and turns into an 8-year-old girl (Kesiah
Knight Pulliam) who sells matches to bring
magical happiness to others. Burrell, who also
has a featured role, sets it during the Depression
around the forced eviction of poor people at
Christmas and a rich man's conflict with his two
sons. Pulliam pulls off her role with just the
right touch. Directed with a nice touch by Michael Lindsay-Hogg. Jim Metzler, John Rhys-
Davies, William Youmans, Rue McClanahan.
(Academy)

LITTLE MERMAID, THE (1989) ★★★★½
Hans Christian Andersen's classic fairy tale is
excellently rendered in this animated Disney musical feature directed by John Musker and Ron
Clements. A mermaid named Ariel (voice by
Jodi Benson) lives with her father, Triton, in an
underwater kingdom. After she saves a handsome prince from drowning, she trades her singing voice to an evil octopus to live on land and
marry him. Her companion is a crab named Sebastian, and his plight in the kitchen of a French
chef is one of the most charming sequences in the
film. Great songs and music by Howard Ashman
and Alan Menken. (Video/Laser: Disney)

LITTLE MONSTERS (1989) ★★ Fred Savage
stars in this vicious fantasy comedy about a
kid's encounter with Maurice, a warthog creature (Howie Mandel). They venture into a realm
of monsters—inspired by *Beetlejuice*, perhaps?
This film has a mean edge and is offensive without being funny. Directed as if it were a Halloween special for kids by Richard Alan
Greenberg. Ben Savage (Fred's brother), Daniel
Stern, Margaret Whitton. (Video/Laser: MCA)

LITTLE NEMO: ADVENTURES IN SLUMBERLAND
(1992) ★★★ Winsor McCay's comic strip
character, conceived for the screen by Ray
Bradbury, is a superior example of Japanese animation, with the youthful Nemo being carried
off to Slumberland to be the playmate of Princess Camille, daughter of King Morpheus. The
Chris Columbus–Richard Outten script was directed by Misami Hata and William T. Hurtz.
Voices by Gabriel Damon, Mickey Rooney,
Rene Auberjonois. (Video/Laser: Hemdale)

**LITTLE PRINCE AND THE EIGHT-HEADED
DRAGON, THE** (1963) ★★ This Japanese animated cartoon will be of limited appeal to U.S.
audiences, its story riddled with cultural peculiarities. A young boy who has lost his mother
to death ventures forth on an odyssey to find
her, engaging in a series of adventures only
moderately exciting. Scripted by Ichiro Ikeda
and Takashi Jima, and directed by Yugo Seri-

kawa, *Little Prince* was redesigned for the U.S.
by writer-director William Ross. Aka *Prince in
Wonderland* and *Rainbow Bridge*.

LITTLE SHOP OF HORRORS, THE (1960)
★★★★ Producer-director Roger Corman's
macabre comedy parodies horror-monster flicks
with a vengeance. Jonathan Haze is in a daze as
Seymour Krelboing, a flower shop clerk who
raises a giant plant that repeatedly burps "Feed
me, I'm hungry!" Seymour does—human food.
Belch! Mel Welles is shop owner Gravis Mush-
nik, Jackie Joseph is the love interest and Dick
Miller is a customer. Jack Nicholson has a crazy
cameo in a dentist's chair. Scripted as *The Passionate People Eater* by Charles Griffith, who
wrote the story around a set Corman had seen
in a studio. The film developed a cult following
and became a stage musical and then was remade as a film in 1986. This 1960 version is
available in home video in a colorized edition.
(Hollywood Home Theatre; Vestron; Filmfax)
(Laser: Japanese)

LITTLE SHOP OF HORRORS (1986) ★★★ Corman's B film and intimate musical were turned
into an overinflated horror musical, following
the music and story line of the play but much
darker and crueler in depicting how a nerd falls
in love with a bimbo and feeds human body
parts to a man-eating, talking plant. What was
once a charming comedy becomes an uncomfortable experience, for the screen over-
emphasizes the slum area of Mushkin's Floral
Shop and the monstrousness of the plant, Audrey II, as it sways humans with its Svengali-
like hold. Especially unfunny are Steve Martin
as a sadistic dentist and Bill Murray as his mas-
ochistic patient, carrying to extremes what in the
original film was a funny moment. Director
Frank Oz was escaping his G-rated Muppet image—even Warner Bros. had to lighten up the
unpleasantries before the film was released.
(Video/Laser: Warner Bros.)

LITTLE WITCHES (1996) ★★ Young seniors in
an all-girl Catholic school rebel against the system when they find a secret well in a sealed-off
section of the rectory as well as a book of spells,
with which, after dressing up like witches, they
try to summon He Who Comes, a demon from
hell. The horned entity arrives for a less-than-
exciting climax, preceded by less-than-exciting
events in which some of the girls become possessed and turn evil, and little Zelda Rubinstein
does her weird stuff as a "guardian" nun. Written tediously by Brian DiMuccio and Dino Vindeni, and directed lethargically by Jane
Simpson, this is strangely lacking in special effects or thrills, and demeans females by having
the girls strip down to the buff for no good reason. Even the overweight girls strip. And one of
them does an unnecessary striptease for some

construction workers gathered below her window. Sometimes less is better. Jennifer Rubin, Sherri Rappaport, Melissa Taub, Zoe Alexander. (Video: Unapix/DVD: Image)

LIVE AND LET DIE (1973) ★★★½ Roger Moore's first time out as British spy 007, James Bond . . . He attempts the droll indifference and sophisticated snobbery of the licensed-to-kill superagent, but he's a connoisseur strictly for philistines. The series had begun to deteriorate to the point that screenwriter Tom Mankiewicz here resorts to a stereotyped Southern sheriff, J. W. Pepper. The plot centers around drug king Kananga (Yaphet Kotto) and Bond tracking him to his lair in the Louisiana swamps. It features a wild motorboat chase, an alligator pit and other jeopardy devices. Director Guy Hamilton maintains the visual standards he established in *Goldfinger*. Jane Seymour, David Hedison. (CBS/Fox) (Laser: MGM)

LIVER EATERS, THE. See *Spider Baby*.

LIVING DAYLIGHTS, THE (1987) ★★★½ Timothy Dalton's first outing as James Bond proved that he could carry off the role with a more serious demeanor than his predecessor, Roger Moore, and a greater sense of depth. The fantasy-weapon elements are minimal as everyone tries harder for suspenseful realism, without sacrificing the visual qualities of previous 007 adventures. The Richard Maibaum–Michael G. Wilson script has Bond involved with Soviet defectors, KGB agents, gunrunners and a beautiful Czech concert cellist (Maryam d'Abo). The climactic fight aboard a cargo plane is a stunning action piece that puts this with the best of the Bonds. Directed with an adventurous flair by John Glen. Jeroen Krabbe, Joe Don Baker, John Rhys-Davies, Art Malik, Caroline Bliss (Miss Moneypenny). (CBS/Fox) (Laser: MGM/UA; CBS/Fox)

LIVING DEAD, THE (1934) ★★ Antiquated British mystery mellow-drama (based on a play by Wallace Geoffrey) in which a Scotland Yard dick invents a serum that induces a death-like condition—part of a scheme to collect insurance money. Only he has the antitoxin when he kidnaps his partner's daughter and puts her into a coma. You too will slide into catatonia. Directed by Thomas Bentley from a Frank Miller script. Aka *Scotland Yard Mystery*. Gerald Du Maurier, George Curzon. (Thunderbird; Filmfax; Sinister/ C; Discount)

LIVING DEAD, THE See *Psychomania* (1973).

LIVING DOLL (1990) ★ Medical student Mark Jax, working part-time in a morgue, collects the corpse of flower girl Katie Orgill and takes her home to study her beauty, his romantic fantasies blinding him to her rotting condition. Even though his landlady is Eartha Kitt, this low-budget, New York–based horror flicker is nothing to sing about as Jax fantasizes that the corpse is talking to him. For necrophiliacs only. Directed by George Dugdale and Peter Litten. (MGM)

LIVING HEAD, THE (1959) ★ Mexican horror importer K. Gordon Murray jazzed up this Abel Salazar flicker for U.S. consumption. This abomination is head but not shoulders above others of its (stereo)type. When a tomb is opened by an archeological expedition, its members find the head of an Aztec warrior, who's been waiting centuries to fulfill a curse. Directed by Chano Urueta. German Robles, Ana Luisa Peluffo. (Sinister/C; Video Yesteryear; S/Weird; Filmfax)

LOBSTER MAN FROM MARS (1989) ★★★ Sci-fi buffs of '50s movies will find this parody a treat—a movie-within-a-movie that starts when sleazy producer Tony Curtis (as J. P. Sheildrake) sits down in his screening room to see *Lobster Man from Mars*, a schlocker in which a flying saucer crash-lands and regurgitates an alien invader accompanied by flying bat-creatures. In pursuit of the monsters go private eye Tommy Sledge (the stand-up comic), a young couple (Deborah Foreman and Anthony Hickox), and scientist-professor Patrick Macnee. Directed with the right touch by Stanley Sheff. Billy Barty, Dean Jacobsen, Fred Holiday, Dr. Demento. (Video/Laser: IVE)

LOCH NESS HORROR, THE (1982) ★½ One sorry monster movie, filmed at Lake Tahoe, CA, by writer-director Larry Buchanan. A papier-mâché neck and head, with rows of serrated teeth, is more a lovable toy than a ferocious sea beast. Buchanan throws in subplots (Nazi plane that crashed in 1940 has cargo of dangerous bombs aboard; nut tries to kidnap beautiful girl; dynamite expert is blackmailed by military to perform a dangerous dive) but the harder he tries the sillier it gets. And some of the Scottish accents are not to be believed! What an embarrassment to the real-life Nessie. Sandy Kenton, Miki McKenzie, Barry Buchanan. (Monterey)

LOCK UP YOUR DAUGHTERS (1956) ★★ A collection of scenes from cheap Bela Lugosi movies, thrown together by producer Sam Katzman, who hired Lugosi to narrate shortly before the actor died. Footage includes scenes from *The Ape Man* and *The Voodoo Man*.

LOCK YOUR DOORS. See *The Ape Man*.

LODGER, THE (A STORY OF THE LONDON FOG) (1926) ★★★ Alfred Hitchcock's first major thriller and the film that many critics feel is seminal to the horror and suspense sound films on which he would sharpen his teeth in later years. This was the first of several versions of the 1913 Marie Belloc-Lowndes novel about Jack the Ripper, thinly disguised here as the Avenger, a knife-wielding madman who specializes in murdering women with blond tresses. Tilted angles and an influence of German expressionism earmark this effective chiller. Ivor Novello, Marie Ault, Malcolm Keen. Aka *The Case of Jonathan Drew*. (Video Yesteryear; Video Image; Nostalgia; Grapevine)

LODGER, THE (1944) ★★★★★ Atmosphere and performance are everything in this fogbound, eerie version of Marie Belloc-Lowndes's novel depicting fear-stricken London during the horrendous Jack the Ripper rippings in Soho. Laird Cregar, a superb heavy of the early 1940s, provides an undercurrent of menace and smouldering psychosis in a fine portrayal of a heinous villain. Barre Lyndon's adaptation is brooding with Victorian ambience. Merle Oberon is the music hall dancer who becomes Cregar's target; George Sanders is her compassionate lover. Congratulations to director John Brahm, cinematographer Lucien Ballard and composer Hugo Friedhofer for haunting contributions to this horror classic. This remake of a 1926 Alfred Hitchcock thriller was in turn remade by Fox in 1953 as *The Man in the Attic*. Sir Cedric Hardwicke, Sara Allgood, Doris Lloyd.

LOGAN'S RUN (1976) ★★ MGM's version of the William Nolan–George Clayton Johnson novel (adapted by David Zelag Goodman) was thoroughly botched into a bastardization of glaring inconsistencies, peopled by uninteresting characters and often ineptly directed by Michael Anderson. The setting is a subterranean future society where everyone is brainwashed into going to their deaths at age 30; if they try to "run" they are cut down by Sandmen. Sandman Michael York rebels and escapes to the outside world. Peter Ustinov lives in the ruins of the nation's capital, Roscoe Lee Brown plays a robot named Box, Jenny Agutter is the love interest, and Farrah Fawcett-Majors delivers an appalling performance. Richard Jordan is also in the cast. (Video/ Laser: MGM/UA)

LONE WOLF (1988) ★★ While the police fumble around like buffoons, intelligent and sensitive high school teens use a computer to track down a werewolf monster murdering people in Denver, CO. Directed by John Callas from a script by coproducer Michael Krueger, *Lone Wolf* is a minor thriller offering too few thrills and suspense, and only one sequence involving special effects that by 1988 were standard horror movie stuff. Dyann Brown, Kevin Hart, Jamie Newcomb, Ann Douglas. (Prism)

LONG DARK NIGHT, THE. Condensed TV version of *The Pack*. (A dogged film!)

LONG HAIR OF DEATH (1964) ★★ Italian shocker, in the vein of *Black Sunday*, in which Barbara Steele, the daughter of a witch burned at the stake, dies and returns from the dead after her tomb is opened by a burst of lightning. Directed by Anthony Dawson (Antonio Margheriti). Robert Bohr's script is based on J. Sheridan

Le Fanu's *Carmilla*. Giorgio Ardisson, Robert Rains. (Sinister/C; S/Weird; Filmfax)

LONG HARD NIGHT, THE. See *The Pack*.

LONG NIGHT OF TERROR, THE. See *Castle of Blood*.

LONG, SWIFT SWORD OF SIEGFRIED (1971) ★ U.S.–West German fantasy adventure (aka *Erotic Adventures of Siegfried* and *The Terrible Quick Sword of Siegfried*) with plenty of sex, depicting the heroic knight in pursuit of the fire-eating dragon. Long all right, but not too swift. Originally directed by Adrian Hoven in German, with English scenes written-directed by sex exploitationer David F. Friedman. One of Sybil Danning's first films . . . now she's swift—if you get our drift. Raymond Harmstorf, Heidi Bohlen. (From Private Screenings as *Maidenquest*)

LOOKER (1981) ★★ Michael Crichton wrote-directed this strange mixture of sci-fi, suspense and horror, never quite finding the right blend. It's gimmicky and tricky, about a TV-commercial production company that has an artificial way of creating laser projections of beautiful models. But first the company must eliminate the real women on whom these clone lovelies are patterned with a strange time-continuum blaster. Sinks into utter confusion at times but the set designs are outstanding and the cast (Albert Finney as the hero, James Coburn as the heavy, Susan Dey and Leigh Taylor-Young as love interests) is accomplished. (Video/Laser: Warner Bros.)

LOONIES ON BROADWAY. See *Zombies on Broadway*.

LORCA AND THE OUTLAWS. See *Starship*.

LORD OF ILLUSIONS (1995) ★★★★ It's as if Clive Barker went to Hell, saw horrific things burning before his eyes, and returned to Earth determined to share his Hellbent images with all of us. This is the best of the horror films Barker has directed, and although he has learned since *Hellraiser* and *Nightbreed* that a modicum of cinematic restraint can go a long way, by no means has he turned into a sissy. *Lord of Illusions*, based on Barker's short story "The Last Illusion," is a terrific genre film that will please horror buffs with its imaginative special effects and unique morphing, blood-and-gore graphics (done with a surer hand this time) and intriguing story set within the world of magic practitioners. In Barker's version/vision of this world, some "illusions" are real, performed by a select few who have tapped into supernatural powers. Private eye Harry D'Amour (Scott "Quantum Leap" Bakula), a recurring character from Barker's fiction, is on the trail of an evil cult spiritualist leader (Daniel Von Bargen), who is soon incapacitated inside a metal encasing and buried away. New private-eye adventures at Magic Castle (the L.A. magic center) involve D'Amour with beautiful Famke Janssen, illusionist Swann (Kevin J. O'Connor) and assorted evildoers. Barker's script is sometimes too unfocused and convoluted to allow us to follow the narrative totally, but the horror sequences are superb and Barker is clearly a masterful director as horrendous events lead to an effects-riddled climax between Von Bargen and Bakula in the deteriorating cult center. Vincent Schiavelli offers a fascinating cameo (all too brief) as a magician. Barry Del Sherman, Sheila Tousey, Joel Swetow. (Video/Laser: MGM/UA)

LORD OF THE FLIES (1963) ★★★ On the eve of atomic holocaust, English schoolboys crashland on a tropical island. The youths splinter into bands and deteriorate into practitioners of cruel barbarism. This strange allegory on social and political behavior, based on the novel by William Golding, has uneven acting and suspense, but still yields a high rate of cinematic symbolism. A good effort from screenwriter-director Peter Brook. James Aubrey, Tom Chapin. (Home Vision; Fusion; Diamond; King of Video) (Laser: Criterion)

LORD OF THE FLIES (1990) ★★★ This version of William Golding's novel is superior to the 1963 film in that it has a better cast and a slicker production, but generally it tells the same allegorical tale about British schoolboys stranded on a tropical island and how they break into groups, one representing the thoughtful side of man, the other man's primitivism. The obvious symbolism doesn't detract from this compelling object lesson about human behavior. Directed by Harry Hook. Balthazar Getty, Badgett Dale. (Video/Laser: Nelson)

LORDS OF MAGICK (1989) ★★ Two young magicians from the 10th century (Jarrett Parker and Mark Gauthier) travel through time to the future (our present day) to battle an evil power named Saladin and save a princess (Ruth Zackarian) from harm. David Marsh produced and directed and cowrote the script with Sherman Hirsch. Brendan Dillon Jr., David Snow, John Clark. (Prism)

LORDS OF THE DEEP (1989) ★ You can hear producer Roger Corman's mind turning over: "Hey, guys, underwater lab movies are in; let's churn out a quickie to cash in." So Howard Cohen and Daryl Haney crank out a potboiler script set in 2020 about an underwater lab crew trapped with a creature that looks like a swimming bat. This isn't even as good as the science-fiction pastiches Corman used to produce in the early '80s—it's a throwback to the '50s with its antiquated set design, costumes and stilted dialogue, all with a Buck Rogers look. Not even the monster is interesting—*Deep* is a shallow way to spend your time. Directed without an ounce of flair by Mary Ann Fisher. Corman appears in a cameo role as a corporate official.

Bradford Dillman, Priscilla Barnes, Daryl Haney, Ed Lottimer. (MGM/UA)

LORELEI'S GRASP, THE. See *When the Screaming Stops*.

LOST BOYS, THE (1987) ★★★ Premise with promise is never exploited to its max: In a coastal town (Santa Cruz, Calif.) a punk gang is made up of vampires who terrorize newcomer kids. This launched the career of Kiefer Sutherland and is full of effects and rock music that should appeal to a young audience, but it fails to render a strong payoff. Directed by Joel Schumacher, written by Janice Fischer, James Jeremias and Jeffrey Boam. Jason Patric, Corey Haim, Dianne Wiest, Barnard Hughes, Ed Herrmann. (Video/Laser: Warner Bros.)

LOST CITY, THE (1935) ★ Mascot's 12-chapter serial (aka *Lost City of the Ligurians*) is nonstop jungle action as electrical engineer Kane Richmond discovers Magnetic Mountain, hideaway of Zolok (stage actor William Boyd), who plans to take over the world with his earthquake-making machine. Watch for George "Gabby" Hayes as the slave trader. Fun if you overlook outmoded acting and filming techniques. Directed by Harry Revier. (Foothill; Sinister/C; Nostalgia; Filmfax offers the serial and a feature version, which is known as *City of Lost Men*)

LOST CITY, THE (1982) ★ Robert Dukes directed this imitation of *She*, featuring a long-undiscovered metropolis, a queen with a headdress, crumbling ruins and a quest for romance and riches. Bernadette Clark, David Cain Haughton, Margot Samson.

LOST CITY OF THE JUNGLE (1946) ★★★ Historically this was the last serial Universal produced. Although it is short on action, and moves at the pace of a sluggish, sickly snail suffering from arthritis, it has an unusually literate script with emphasis on nefarious double crosses and characterizations. The cliff-hangers seem to come as afterthoughts. The slim fantasy premise is that warmonger Lionel Atwill (appearing in his last role, and replaced by a double in some shots) is after an atomic substance, Meteorium 245, hidden away in a Ceylon jungle. This is a curiosity piece serial fans will enjoy for its offbeat approach and production values. Russell Hayden, Jane Adams, John Miljan, Keye Luke. (VCI)

LOST CITY OF THE LUGARIANS. See *The Lost City* (1935).

LOST CONTINENT, THE (1951) ★★★ Robert L. Lippert fantasy adventure has atmospheric production values, a memorable score by the excellent but underrated Paul Dunlap, and a strong performance by Cesar Romero as a flight commander looking for a rocket that crashed on a high plateau of a lost island. His flight crew (John Hoyt, Hugh Beaumont, Sid Melton) is surrounded by man-eating dinosaurs. Surprisingly good for a low-budget quickie. Hillary Brooke, Acquanetta, Whit Bissell, Chick Chandler. Directed by Sam Newfield from a good Richard Landau screenplay. (Weiss Global; Moore)

LOST CONTINENT, THE (1968) ★★ Michael Nash's adaptation of a Dennis Wheatley novel, *Uncharted Seas*, has touches of William Hope Hodgson splashed in for added monster moisture, and it was produced and directed by Michael Carreras (and briefly by Leslie Norman) for Hammer. A freighter is jeopardized by a cargo of high explosives. Survivors of this ordeal face another: a Sargasso Sea of Lost Ships, menaced by seaweed serpents, colossal crabs and shipwrecked Spanish nuts who worship a wriggling octopus god. This pulp adventure with middling effects goes dead in the water. Eric Porter, Hildegard Knef, Suzanna Leigh. Aka *Lost Island* and *The People of Abrimes*.

LOST EMPIRE, THE (1985) ★½ As dumb as this is, it has moments to please oglers, for producer-writer-director Jim Wynorski has made a male sexual fantasy first, an adventure second. Unlikely L.A. cop Angel Wolfe (buxom Melanie Vincz) is out to avenge a fellow cop's death and find the Eye of Avatar, an energy-packed gem belonging to a lost race of Lemurians. Her adversary is Dr. Sin Do (hammily rendered by Angus Scrimm, the Tall Man from *Phantasm*) who runs an island called Golgotha, where Angel goes with Raven de la Croix, an endowed woman on a white charger, and karate-kicking Angela Aames. It's the bouncing breasts that will make you say: So who wants subtlety? Bob Tessier is superawful as Scrimm's toady. Linda Shayne, Angelique Pettyjohn, Kenneth Tobey, Garry Goodrow. (Lightning)

LOST HORIZON (1937) ★★★★★ James Hilton's romantic fantasy set in Shangri-la, a luxuriant valley hidden in the Tibetan mountains, is given poetic, sensitive interpretation by producer-director Frank Capra. Shangri-la, where aging, greed and brutality are nonexistent, is an idyllic symbol for everything man searches for. Ronald Colman was never more appealing than as Robert Conway, brought to the valley with other stranded airline passengers aboard a pilotless plane. Jane Wyatt is Conway's sweetheart, H. B. Warner is wise old Chang, Sam Jaffe is the High Lama, and Edward Everett Horton is a fussy paleontologist. Thomas Mitchell, Noble Johnson, Margo. (Video/Laser: RCA/Columbia)

LOST HORIZON (1973) ★★★ Although Ross Hunter's musical version of the James Hilton book was severely panned (Rex Reed called it "*Brigadoon* with chopsticks"), it is not nearly as static or plastic as you might fear. True, its musical sequences are absurd within the framework of such a time and place, yet this version (directed by Charles Jarrott) follows the spirit of Capra's 1937 film. Charles Boyer as the High Lama, John Gielgud as wise old Chang, Peter Finch and Michael York as the stranded travelers. Olivia Hussey, Sally Kellerman, George Kennedy, Liv Ullmann. (Laser: Pioneer)

LOST IN SPACE (1998) ★★★½ This $90 million spin-off from Irwin Allen's popular 1965–'68 CBS-TV series is at its nostalgic best when the voice of Dick Tufeld booms from the metallic body of the robot ("It does not compute, Will Robinson . . . Danger! Danger!")—which is kind of sad when you consider all the expensive resources that went into this sci-fi extravaganza. Tufeld's voice is the one major surviving connection to the TV series that featured the *Jupiter II* on a three-year quest in the deepest reaches of the universe after a certain Dr. Zachary Smith (Jonathan Harris) sabotaged the ship. In this version, Smith is played less interestingly by Gary Oldman, but he's still the chatty source of evil to the Robinson family (father William Hurt, terribly miscast for this role; mother Mimi Rogers; daughters Heather Graham and Lacey Chabert; and computer-nerd whiz kid Jack Johnson as the irrepressible Will Robinson). *Lost in Space* has a fabulous space-battle opening when hotshot fighter pilot Matt LeBlanc (soon to be the *Jupiter II*'s Major Don West) takes on a conspiracy group trying to stop Earth forces from going into space at a time (2058 A.D.) when the human race is threatened with famine and extinction. There is a continuous stream of complex cliff-hangers as the Robinsons blast off into space only to be attacked by a malfunctioning robot and shifting into hyperdrive to keep from being burned up by the sun. After some exciting stuff on an abandoned space station involving an army of killer spiders and a cutesy creature nicknamed "Blawp," the film's script (by producer Akiva Goldman) bogs down in incomprehensible plot twists involving time warps and other gadgets and concepts that spin crazily out of control. While the effects and technology maintain center spotlight, the characters and their relationships are unbelievably hokey, of which a modern audience is undeserving, especially if they fondly remember the TV show. Director Stephen Hopkins always keeps *Lost in Space* brimming with visual delight (the sets are never short of magnificent) but can do nothing to spice up the lousy dialogue and oft-confusing plot. The *Jupiter II* is always bouncing through time and space without suffering a scratch. Sorry, Will Robinson, but it doesn't compute. Guest appearances by Angela Cartwright, June Lockhart, Marta Kristen, and Mark Goddard, who all appeared in the original TV series. Edward Fox appears briefly as Oldman's traitorous spy boss. (Video/ Laser: New Line)

LOST IN TIME (1977) ★★ Reedited episodes of TV's "Fantastic Journey," a short-lived Bruce Lansbury–produced series in which yacht travelers through the Bermuda Triangle are enveloped in a strange green cloud and end up on an unknown island broken into time zones. In the pilot episode, directed by Andrew V. McLaglen, the survivors meet a band of British buccaneers; in the second, directed by Barry Crane, they are taken to the city of Atlantium, where an evil brain called the Provider plans to misuse them to recharge its thinking cells. Routine TV science fiction, pulp magazine hokum resorting to threadbare production values. Already seems dated. Scott Thomas, Susan Howard, Jared Martin, Carl Franklin, Karen Somerville, Leif Erickson, Scott Brady, Gary Collins, Mary Ann Mobley, Jason Evers.

LOST ISLAND. See *The Lost Continent* (1968).

LOST ISLAND OF KIOGA (1938). Feature version of Republic's *Hawk of the Wilderness*.

LOST JUNGLE, THE (1934) ★★ Feature version of Mascot's serial with animal trainer Clyde Beatty as an African explorer looking for his fiancée's missing father. He crashes his dirigible on an island and stumbles across a subterranean metropolis that has everything but Rapid Transit. It's poorly directed by Armand Schaefer and David Howard and the acting is atrocious but if you like serials, it's a must. Warner Richmond, Cecelia Parker, Syd Saylor, Mickey Rooney. (Nostalgia; Video Connection; Video Dimensions)

LOST KINGDOM. See *Journey Beneath the Desert*.

LOST PLANET, THE (1953) ★ One of the worst serials Sam Katzman produced for Columbia during his cliff-hanger days. It's utterly inept, having none of the campiness that made some Columbia serials from this period at least endurable. *The Lost Planet* is set on the ersatz Ergro, where the incompetent Dr. Grood (Michael Fox, who never rises to the occasion) plots to conquer Earth with various fantastic devices he forces a scientist to create for him. Who should land on the planet but newsman Judd Holdren and the scientist's dense daughter (Vivian Mason). Directed without an ounce of concern by Spencer Bennet. Ted Thorpe, Forrest Taylor, Gene Roth. Aka *Planet Men*. (Heavenly Video)

LOST PLANET AIRMEN (1949). Feature version of Republic's *King of the Rocket Men*.

LOST PLATOON, THE (1989) ★ Four dead soldier-vampires wander the battlefields from the Civil War to Vietnam, their presence spotted by a combat cameraman who's wise to their eternal wanderings. Directed by David A. Prior. William Knight, David Parry, Stephen Quadros, Lew Pipes. (Action International)

LOST TRIBE, THE (1983) ★★ Writer-director John Laing attempts to tell a metaphysical tale about an anthropologist in the jungle of New Zealand searching for a missing race of Indians and becoming missing himself. His twin brother (both roles by John Bach) is suddenly possessed with weird tendencies, including a yen for his brother's wife. The characters' behaviors are irritating rather than compelling and this evolves into an inexplicable mystery never satisfactorily resolved. Darien Takle, Emma Takle, Terry Connolly. (Thrillervideo; Fox Hills; Media)

LOST VALLEY, THE. See *The Valley of Gwangi*.

LOST WOMEN (1952) ★ Turgidly written, directed and acted sci-fi thriller about a mad scientist (Jackie Coogan) who creates a race of superwomen (hah!) injected with the emotions of spiders. So incompetent you won't believe your eyes. A lost cause for Richard Travis, Lyle Talbot, Allan Nixon, Tandra Quinn. Directed by writer Herbert Tevos and Ron Ormond. Aka *Lost Women of Zarpa*. (On video from Sinister/ C as *Mesa of Lost Women*)

LOST WORLD, THE (1925) ★★★ Silent milestone, first major feature to spotlight the stop-motion work of special effects pioneer Willis O'Brien, the man who moved King Kong. It's the Sir Arthur Conan Doyle story about explorers, led by Professor Challenger, who find a prehistoric world of brontosauruses and *Tyranosaurus rex*es. Wallace Beery, Bessie Love, Lewis Stone. Directed by Harry Hoyt. Some video versions have the original theatrical trailer and some restored footage. (Video Yesteryear; Nostalgia) (Laser: Lumivision)

LOST WORLD, THE (1992). See *Return to the Lost World*.

LOST WORLD: JURASSIC PARK, THE (1997) ★★½ There is nothing wrong with a special-effects movie produced purely for action content, but when it's a movie directed by Steven Spielberg, and it goes nowhere beyond the bounds of a special-effects action movie, one cannot help but feel a waste has occurred. David Koepp's screenplay, based on the novel by Michael Crichton, is nothing more than a series of situations contrived to lead from one cliffhanger to another, with characters doing some of the dumbest things ever seen in movies. This is unfortunate, because the original *Jurassic Park*, a rousing adventure of man creating new strains of dinosaur monsters from DNA, suggested rich possibilities for a sequel. The same old Tyrannosaurus rex attacks (not one monster but two) and the same old raptors assault as human beings struggle to escape the snapping, slavering jaws of said creatures. The setting is Isla Sorna, or Site B, a place where the dinosaurs were originally created before they went to Site A (Isla Nublar, where the first film occurred). Venturing to Isla Sorna, where the creatures have the run of the land, Dr. Ian Malcolm (Jeffrey Goldblum) searches for his love, Sarah

Harding (Julianne Moore), who is blithely checking out the creatures as if there's no cause for alarm. This careless, indifferent behavior for her own safety in the most dangerous place on earth is the first warning bell that the film is headed in the wrong direction. Bam, along comes a squad of helicopters, dumping a large army of dinosaur chasers on the island who behave like big-game hunters and display a callous indifference to the largest creatures on earth, another dumb kind of behavior. Where is some respect for a behemoth that could crush you with one footfall? Hell, for that matter, where is the awe and wonder we felt in the first film? You know instantly that the hunters (led by Pete Postlethwaite) are nothing more than human food for the monsters when they finally close to the attack. Sure enough, they succumb in droves, dying the horrible deaths they no doubt deserve for being such jerks. It finally boils down to Goldberg, Moore, and Vanessa Lee Chester (playing Goldberg's daughter from a failed interracial marriage, which has nothing to do with the plot but gives Spielberg the opportunity to hire a black actress) dodging raptors. Yes, the special effects by Dennis Muren, Stan Winston, and Michael Lantieri are just as good as in the original. So what? Not even taking the film to San Diego, where an irate T-Rex in search of its kidnapped baby stomps through the city and causes a *Gorgo* kind of panic (among those fleeing are Japanese businessmen, Spielberg's idea of a *Godzilla* joke, perhaps), has any sense of originality. Only John Williams's excellent score seems to hold its own in this misguided, sadly disappointing project. Richard Attenborough, Arliss Howard, Vince Vaughn, Peter Sotrmare, Harvey Jason, Richard Schiff. (Video/DVD: Universal)

LOU COSTELLO AND HIS 30-FOOT BRIDE. See *The 30-Foot Bride of Candy Rock.*

LOVE AT FIRST BITE (1979) ★★★★ New wrinkles are painted onto the 800-year-old face of Dracula in this funny satire on movie monsters. George Hamilton is marvelous as the Transylvanian shut-in who yearns for the 20th century so much that he jets to New York to claim a fashion model. Dracula is an anachronism adapting to 20th-century Manhattan, and the gags are fast and furious. Classic scenes: the disruption of a funeral in a Harlem chapel, a midnight raid on a New York blood bank, Dracula disco dancing. Susan St. James is the lovely fashion model hypnotically falling for Hamilton's charms, and Richard Benjamin is the whacky psychiatrist who gets his monster lore scrambled. Robert Kaufman's script is a delight and director Stan Dragoti pulls it wonderfully together. Dick Shawn is a zany cop and Arte

Johnson is Drac's Igor. (Warner Bros.) (Laser: Vestron)

LOVE AT STAKE (1986) ★★ *Mad* magazine–styled slapstick comedy about the Salem witch trials, consisting of sexual innuendos and anachronisms of a dumb nature. The Terry Sweeney–Lanier Laney script never rises above such yuks as a baker named Sara Lee and the appearance of Dr. Joyce Brothers as an expert trial witness. The witch is Barbara Carrera, who uses her sexual aura and black magic to trick and mislead our forefathers in puritanical New England. John Moffitt was cursed to be director. Patrick Cassidy, Kelly Preston, Bud Cort, David Graf. (Video/Laser: Nelson)

LOVE EXORCIST. See *Daddy's Deadly Darling.*

LOVE FACTOR, THE. Video version of *Zeta One.*

LOVE MANIAC. See *The Man with the Synthetic Brain.*

LOVE POTION NO. 9 (1992) ★★★ The Jerry Leiber–Mike Stoller song inspired this amusing fantasy comedy in which nerdy biochemists Tate Donovan and Sandra Bullock discover an aphrodisiac and become the worms that turn. Writer-producer-director Dale Launer brings cute twists to the battle of the sexes. Mary Mara, Dale Midkiff, Anne Bancroft (as fortune teller Madame Ruth). (Video/Laser: Fox)

LOVERS BEYOND THE TOMB. See *Nightmare Castle.*

LOVESICK (1983) ★★ Psychiatrist Dudley Moore falls for playwright patient Elizabeth McGovern—which so irritates the ghost of Sigmund Freud that he appears as Alec Guinness. Only Moore can hear Guinness's pearls of couched wisdom, so characters keep wondering why Moore talks into thin air (into which this ridiculous movie evaporates). John Huston is a shrink warning Moore about his infidelity. Alan King, Renee Taylor, Ron Silver, Gene Saks. You won't love *Lovesick* but you may get sick, luv. Directed by Marshall Brickman. (Video/Laser: Warner Bros.)

LOVES OF COUNT IORGA. See *Count Yorga—Vampire.*

LOVES OF IRINA, THE. Reedited version of *Erotikill* that eliminates the supernatural element.

LOVE TRAP (1977). See *Curse of the Black Widow.*

LUCIFER COMPLEX, THE (1978) ★ Mountain hiker enters a cave where a computer is stored with tapes of man's history. For 20 minutes he watches footage of warfare and moralizes in stream-of-consciousness dribble. Jump to 1986 as spy Robert Vaughn uncovers a Nazi plot to clone Hitler. The Vaughn footage (directed-written by David L. Hewitt) appears to be an unsold pilot added to James T. Flocker's cave junk. And Kenneth Hartford also shot some footage. An editor's nightmare. Keenan Wynn, Aldo Ray. (VCI; United)

LUCIFER PROJECT, THE. See *Barracuda (The Lucifer Project)*.

LUCIFER RIG, THE. See *The Intruder Within*.

LUCKY STIFF (1988) ★★★ Anthony Perkins directed this comedy about a rejected fat man (Joe Alaskey) picked out by cannibals to be the main course at Christmas dinner. Donna Dixon seduces him at Lake Tahoe and takes him to the family spread, where sex gags and visual tom-foolery unfold. Alaskey makes wise-guy jokes as he tries to avoid becoming an entrée. Better than it sounds; a sleeper. Jeff Kober, Elizabeth Arlen, Charles Frank, Barbara Howard, Leigh McCloskey, Bill Quinn. Aka *That Shamrock Touch*. (Video/Laser: RCA/Columbia)

LUGOSI MEETS A BROOKLYN GORILLA. See *Bela Lugosi Meets a Brooklyn Gorilla*.

LUGOSI: THE FORGOTTEN KING (1985) ★★ Modestly produced 45-minute TV documentary hosted by Forrest J. ("Welcome to Grisleyland") Ackerman, wearing Bela Lugosi's Dracula cape as he narrates the life story of the Hungarian actor who made a career out of playing horror roles. The numerous film clips are supplemented by interview footage with Ralph Bellamy, John Carradine, Carrol Borland and Alex Gordon. It's an honest look into the actor's troubled life and career and gets an A for Accuracy. Written, produced and directed by Mark S. Gilman, Jr. and Dave Stuckey. (MPI)

LUNATIC (1991) ★ A homicidal madman, recently escaped from a nearby insane asylum (how convenient), preys on a group of high school students who just happen to be yukking it up in the woods. Written-directed by James Tucker. Rocky Tucker, Ondrea Tucker, Brian D'Lawrence, Cameron Derric. (Coast to Coast)

LUNATICS—A LOVE STORY (1991) ★★★ Cute comedy with light fantasy overtones in which Theodore Raimi portrays a nerdish agoraphobiac who, locked in his apartment, imagines spiders crawling in his brain and a mad doctor with a hypo chasing him. Yeah, he's a lunatic. Deborah Foreman runs around Pontiac, MI, also fantasizing her worst fears. She's a lunatic too. They finally meet and face their fears together. Director Josh Becker's script includes a stop-motion giant spider. Produced by Bruce Campbell, who is also in the cast. A production from Sam Raimi/Robert Tapert. (Video/Laser: SVS/Triumph)

LUNCH MEAT (1987) ★½ Sickening ripoff of *The Texas Chainsaw Massacre*, written-directed on a shoestring by Kirk Alex. It's full of cut-up bodies as it depicts a demented family that slaughters humans for meat and sells these unkindest cuts of all to a hamburger stand. Garden tools are used to hack the cast to pieces. Kim McKamy, Chuck Ellis, Elroy Wiese. (Tapeworm)

LURKERS (1988) ★★ Study in abnormal psychology (what other kind is there in a horror movie?) from director Roberta Findlay, focusing on a young girl tormented during her childhood who grows up to be a tormented cello player. The woman's dead mother keeps coming back to torment her more in visions. Totally abnormal. Christine Moore, Gary Warner. (Media)

LURKING FEAR (1994) ★★ The only element of H. P. Lovecraft's short story retained by writer-director C. Courtney Joyner is family in-breeding and how it creates a family of ghouls living beneath a cemetery in Arkham County, MA. For this Full Moon–Charles Band production, Joyner has enjoined gangsters looking for buried money, a plot to blow up the cemetery, a normal member of the ghoul family searching for identity, and two women who fight it out in a muddy graveyard in pouring rain. *Lurking Fear* is loaded with graphic violence, monsters and gore, so fans of this fare will not be disappointed. And the cast is good: Jon Finch as the head of the gangsters who loses his head over money (ahem), Ashley Lauren as a Rambo-style participant, Jeffrey Combs as a crazed doctor (again?), Alison Mackie, Paul Mantee, Blake Bailey. And Vincent Schiavelli plays undertaker Skelton Knaggs. It's a gas. (Paramount)

LUST FOR A VAMPIRE (1970) ★★★ In the wake of the success of *The Vampire Lovers*, a blatant amalgam of lesbian love and vampirism, Hammer produced this sequel in the Karnstein series, utilizing characters created by J. S. Le Fanu, although any relationship to the original book was abandoned for commercial shock and gore-horror. A girls' finishing school next door to Karnstein Castle provides the perfect setting for dozens of nubile women exercising in flowing white robes and some exercising lesbian contact with a girl named Mircalla (Yvette Stensgaard). Jimmy Sangster directed Tudor Gates's script without subtlety, which forced U.S. distributors to cut heavily. Ralph Bates, Mike Raven, Pippa Steel, Suzanna Leigh. Originally shot as *To Love a Vampire*. (HBO) (Laser: Image, with *Die, Monster, Die*)

LUTHER THE GEEK (1989) ★ Director Carlton J. Albright (*The Children*) spins a tale of a guy who likes to bite off the heads of chickens (an old carnival geek act he saw as a kid) and slaughter people. Gore fans should derive satisfaction from watching the body-maiming mayhem. Edward Terry, Joan Roth, Tom Mills. (Quest)

LYNN HART, THE STRANGE LOVE EXORCIST. See *Daddy's Deadly Darling*.

M (1930) ★★★★ Fascinating portrait of abnormal sexuality, years ahead of its time in technique and psychological insight. This trend-setting German film was directed by Fritz Lang, who cowrote the unique crime study with Thea von Harbou. Lang employed real Berlin underworld characters in small but pivotal roles. Peter Lorre made his screen debut as a perverted child murderer who wants to stop but can't resist his homicidal impulses. The role made Lorre famous but typecast him for life. Lang was an imaginative filmmaker, a fact reflected in every frame of this innovative work. Ellen Widmann, Inge Landgut, Herter von Walter. There was an American remake in 1951 that has never appeared on tape. (Budget; Kartes; Crown; Embassy; Sinister/C; Nostalgia)

M3: THE GEMINI STRAIN. See *The Plague*.

MACABRA. TV title for *Demonoid*.

MACABRE (1958) ★★★ The first of producer-director William Castle's gimmicky shriekers: Audiences were insured by Lloyds of London against death by fright. Based on *The Marble Forest*, a novel by 15 mystery writers, and adapted by Robb White, it tells of a doctor (William Prince) with just five hours to find his daughter, who has been buried alive. Delightful closing credits. Castle was off and running for the next 15 years as a purveyor of horrifying and pleasing hokum. Jim Backus, Ellen Corby, Christine White, Susan Morrow.

MACABRE SERENADE. Video version of Karloff's *House of Evil* (Unicorn).

MACABRO (1980). Video version of Lamberto Bava's *Frozen Terror* (CIC).

MAC AND ME (1988) ★★½ A rip-off of *E.T.*, depicting a space probe landing on a moon of Saturn and accidentally sucking a family of four aliens aboard. On Earth, alien tyke Mac is separated from his parents and moves in with a suburban family. This retread finally comes to life when the aliens are reunited with the help of the Earth youngsters but even then the outcome is predictable, since writers Steve Feke and Stewart Raffill (also the director) swipe again from *E.T.* The Alan Silvestri music is a plus, as is the cast: Christine Ebersole (as the struggling widowed mom), Jonathan Ward, Katrine Caspary. (Orion) (Laser: Image)

MACISTE AND THE NIGHT QUEEN. See *Mole Men vs. the Son of Hercules*.

MACISTE IN THE LAND OF THE CYCLOPS. See *Atlas Against the Cyclops*.

MACISTE, STRONGEST MAN IN THE WORLD. See *Mole Men vs. the Son of Hercules*.

MACISTE VS. THE CYCLOPS. See *Atlas Against the Cyclops*.

MACISTE VS. THE VAMPIRES. See *Goliath and the Vampires*.

MADAME FRANKENSTEIN. See *Lady Frankenstein*.

MAD AT THE MOON (1991) ★ Ssslllooowww-moving, pretentious werewolf Western that doesn't even deliver a werewolf—just a guy with a little hair on his hands and face. In fact, this "supernatural tale of the Old West" directed by Martin Donovan doesn't even have much of the supernatural. What we do have is a frontierswoman with hot pants (Mary Stuart Masterson) getting married to a man for name and prestige when she really loves gunfighter Hart Bochner. A ponderous, pretentious and enigmatic movie. Fionnula Flanagan, Cec Verrell, Stephen Blake. (Video/Laser: Republic)

MAD BUTCHER, THE (1972) ★★★ Italian black-comedy variation on Sweeney Todd with Victor Buono as Otto Lehman, a crazed Viennese meat-cutter who is released from an asylum to resume his practice . . . of strangling people and grinding them into delicious sausages he sells to the police. Director John (Guido) Zurli goes for laughs with a lilting Viennese waltz in the background. Buono brings a charm to his madman who calmly does his thing while newspaperman Brad Harris and frustrated cop John Ireland try to solve the mystery. There's no blood or gore—the horror underlying this whimsically macabre tale is implied. "Buono appetito!" Karin Field, Carl Stearns. Aka *The Mad Butcher of Vienna*, *The Vienna Strangler* and *Meat Is Meat*. (Magnum; Star Classics; Genesis)

MAD BUTCHER OF VIENNA. See *The Mad Butcher*.

MADDENING, THE (1995) ★★ In its depiction of violence to children, this psychothriller is a disturbing and unpleasant viewing experience, especially since it seems to be contrived solely to shock. Based on the novel *Playmates* by Andrew Neiderman, the script by producer Leslie Greif and Henry Slesar depicts beautiful Mia Sara and her daughter (Kayla Buglewicz) trapped in the rural house of horrors belonging to crazed roadside mechanic Burt Reynolds. Adding to the vulture stew is Reynolds's deranged wife (Angie Dickinson) and her equally nutty child (Candace Hutson, who is just as cruel to Buglewicz as Reynolds). Seems Reynolds smothered his young son to death and is constantly haunted by the memory of his dead father—who appears as wheelchair-bound William Hickey. Sara's husband (Brian Wimmer) and the cop working the case (John Mostel in an offbeat performance) finally find their way to the fruitcake house, and it's then that director Danny Huston (son of John Huston) skewers all your expectations. Hickey is also interpreted more as a ghost than a figment of Reynolds's imagination, but who can say. Without so much child abuse, *The Maddening* might have been a more acceptable shocker. (Vidmark-Trimark)

MADDEST STORY EVER TOLD, THE. See *Spider Baby.*

MAD DOC CLICK. Director's cut of *The Thrill Killers* (Mascot).

MAD DOCTOR OF BLOOD ISLAND (1969) ★ Sanguinary companion to *Beast of Blood* (same monster appears in both), shot in the Philippines with John Ashley and Angelique Pettyjohn. In this sequel to *Brides of the Beast*, a monster of chlorophyll turns green every time it sees a fresh victim. Directed by Eddie Romero and Gerardo (Gerry) De Leon. Aka *Tomb of the Living Dead* and *Blood Doctor.* (Magnum; in video as *Revenge of Dr. X*; Regal issued a tape under this title but it's actually *The Double Garden*)

MADE IN HEAVEN (1987) ★★★ Poetic, lyrical fantasy that is a hallmark in the career of director Alan Rudolph. This remarkable film touches on human destiny, love at first sight and our purpose for being—without infringing on personal religious concepts. Timothy Hutton is charming as a heroic young man who dies in his prime and finds that Heaven is an idyllic region where there is room for romance and the better emotions of man. He and angel Kelly McGillis fall in love, but she's reincarnated in a new life and Hutton is given 30 years to find her by heavenly boss man Emmett. (He is really a she—Debra Winger in disguise.) How McGillis and Hutton live new lives on Earth, and unwittingly search for each other, touches the heartstrings. Maureen Stapleton, Don Murray, Marj Dusay, Ray Gideon, Mare Winningham. Music figures Neil Young, Tom Petty, and Tom Robbins do cameos. (Lorimar) (Laser: Image)

MAD GHOUL, THE (1943) ★★ David Bruce is a laughable walking monster when George Zucco (a mad scientist, cackling with sadistic glee) discovers a poisonous vapor that forces Bruce, with strange lighting falling on his face, to kill at Zucco's bidding. Robert Armstrong, Evelyn Ankers, Turhan Bey, Milburn Stone and Charles McGraw work hard with the feeble idea. James P. Hogan directed this helping of tasteless ghoulish ghoulash written by Brenda Weisberg

and Paul Gangelin. Made as *Mystery of the Ghoul.* (MCA)

MADHOUSE (1972) ★ Sleazy spooker filmed in London (aka *The Revenge of Dr. Death, Deathday,* and *The Madhouse of Dr. Fear*) about a hammy actor (Vincent Price) suspected of committing gore murders during the filming of a TV series. As written by Greg Morrison from Angus Halls's novel *Devilday,* the climax is so unbelievable and forced even horror fans will wonder what's happening. Made by the kind of mentality that thinks the sight of a spider is the height of horror. Eeeekkkkk! Directed by Jim Clark. Adrienne Corri, Linda Hayden, Robert Quarry, Peter Cushing. (HBO)

MADHOUSE MANSION (1974) ★★★ Ghost story in the M. R. James tradition, so damn bloody British that Americans might find it too fey and slow-moving when a sexually repressed young man shows up at a baronial house in the 1920s. He's haunted by a doll that inflicts him with psychic images of a hundred years ago when the mansion was next door to Borden's Insane Asylum and plots were afoot to incarcerate an innocent woman. The minimum gore scenes are forever in coming and one must look for subtleties within the excellent period milieu. Produced-directed by Stephen Weeks at Penhow Castle. Marianne Faithfull, Leigh Lawson, Barbara Shelley. Aka *Ghost Story.* (Comet; Cinema Group)

MADHOUSE OF DR. FEAR. See *Madhouse* (1972).

MAD JAKE. Video of *Blood Salvage* (Malo).

MAD LOVE (1935) ★★★★ Peter Lorre brilliantly conveys madness and compassion as Dr. Gogol in this excellent adaptation of Maurice Renard's *The Hands of Orlac,* screenscripted by John L. Balderston and P. J. Wolfson. It's the classic story of how the hands of a murderer, recently guillotined, are grafted onto the wrists of a musical pianist whose own hands have been crushed in an accident. Lorre, the surgeon who has a fatal obsession for the lovely star of a Grand Guignol show in Paris, descends ever deeper into madness, yet retains a sense of the pathetic. Karl Freund's direction is ahead of its time for atmosphere and camera angles. Ted Healy is intrusive as a comic-relief reporter but he does not interfere with the scenes between Lorre and the actress (Frances Drake) or the pianist (Colin Clive). Gregg Toland photographed it beautifully and Dimitri Tiomkin wrote the score. Definitely a must-see. (MGM/UA)

MAD MAGICIAN, THE (1954) ★★★ Inspired by *House of Wax,* this has remained an appreciated thriller in which Vincent Price hams it up as a stage illusionist's assistant who kills his employer and takes his place. John Brahm directed Crane Wilbur's script, which features among its death devices a crematorium designed for stage work and a buzz-saw trick that isn't a trick. Patrick O'Neal portrays the hero. Not as good as *House of Wax* but still compelling. Jay Novello, Corey Allen, Eva Gabor, Mary Murphy.

MADMAN (1981) ★★ Old "Madman Marz," a farmer (Paul Ehlers) who dangled from a rope after murdering his family, is said to prowl the woods at night. Children around the campfire are warned not to speak his name or he may come back to murder again. Sure enough, Marz goes on a marvelous murder march, knocking off the characters of writer-director Joe Giannone as fast as possible. Tony Fish, Alexis Dubin. Aka *The Legend Lives* and *Madman Marz*. (HBO)

MADMAN MARZ. See *Madman*.

MAD MAX (1979) ★★★ Australian landmark film that instigated a new trend in futuristic fantasies set in an anarchistic world of roving warrior bands. Mel Gibson portrays a policeman after industrial collapse who foresakes his badge to pursue cutthroats who wiped out his family. The car chases and crashes are spectacularly staged, establishing a new state of the art for breathless pursuits and grinding collisions. And the brutality is extreme. After *Mad Max*, action movies were never the same. The mastermind was George Miller, who codirected with Gibson. Two wildly successful sequels followed: *The Road Warrior* and *Mad Max Beyond Thunderdome*. (Vestron; Goodtimes) (Laser: Vestron; the Orion/Image version is letterboxed but from a U.S. print that has an overdub of Gibson's voice)

MAD MAX II. See *The Road Warrior*.

MAD MAX BEYOND THUNDERDOME (1985) ★★★½ Third action-packed saga in the career of Mad Max, from the rip-roaring imaginations of directors George Miller and George Ogilvie, who give full vent to the fantasy of a post-holocaust world in which a roving warrior (Mel Gibson) fights daily to survive. Max (played with greater sensitivity by Gibson this time) meets Aunty Entity (Tina Turner), dictatorial champion of Bartertown, and squares off against a brute named Blaster in a gladiatorial arena of bone-cracking action. Ever-changing scenery and creative plot twists keep one enthralled as Max faces not only Thunderdome but a wheel of fortune, a blistering desert crossing, a society of youngsters that keeps old traditions alive, and a climactic train-and-car chase that includes the chief villain (Ironbar, played by Angry Anderson) and the zany pilot Jedediah (Bruce Spence) from the second film. Totally satisfying action fantasy. (Video/Laser: Warner Bros.)

MADMEN OF MANDORAS. See *They Saved Hitler's Brain*.

MAD MISSION 3 (1984) ★ Rotund Harold Sakata (Oddjob of *Goldfinger*) and Richard Kiel (Jaws of the Bond films) harass a bumbling Japanese agent who is tricked by James Bond and Queen Elizabeth lookalikes to steal the Star of Fortune from a well-guarded security system. Madcap parody, vigorous but dumb, with Peter Graves doing a gag on his own "Mission: Impossible" TV series. Directed by Tsui Hark. (HBO)

MAD MONSTER, THE (1942) ★ PRC quickie, directed by Sam Newfield and written by Fred Myton, has scientist George Zucco (what, again?) as a madman mainlining a transfusion of wolf's blood into a farmer's bloodstream. And guess what that turns him into—Fangs McDonald. Zucco whips the hairy creation into submission and sends him on errands of revenge. And don't forget a quart of milk on the way home. Rock-bottom material, so bad it fascinates. Glenn Strange, who was to play the Frankenstein Monster at Universal, is the wolf creature. Anne Nagel, Johnny Downs, Mae Busch, Sarah Padden. Made as *The Mad Monsters*. (Video Archive; Loonic; Sinister/C; Nostalgia; Filmfax)

MAD MONSTERS, THE. Original title of *The Mad Monster*.

MAD PEOPLE, THE. See *The Crazies*.

MAFU CAGE, THE. Video version of *My Sister, My Love*. (Wizard; Ontario, a version missing 20 minutes of film)

MAGIC (1978) ★★½ Low-key version of William Goldman's novel depicting a demented ventriloquist whose dummy Fats overpowers his personality. The slasher aspects are minimized as director Richard Attenborough focuses on the warped character of Anthony Hopkins. Ann-Margret delivers a laid-back performance as a childhood sweetheart whom Hopkins returns to during his descent into madness. Goldman adapted from his own novel. Ed Lauter, Burgess Meredith. (Video/Laser: Nelson)

MAGIC BUBBLE, THE (1991) ★★ Modest urban fairy tale about a woman (Diane Salinger) turning 40 who is granted a magical wish for youngness and mentally becomes a teenager with new sexual vitality—a change that shakes up hubby John Calvin and gets her into new relationships. Eventually Salinger's attitude affects the lives of all those troubled people around her in a positive way, and brings newfound awareness to her husband. This obvious morality lesson was written by Meredith Baer and Geof Prysier and was directed by Alfredo and Deborah Taper Ringel. George Clooney (in a small role), Wallace Shawn (as a psychiatrist), Priscilla Pointer (as Salinger's unhappy, dying mother), Shera Danese, Colleen Camp. (Monarch)

MAGICIAN, THE (1958) ★★★ Genuinely chilling moments dominate this Swedish mystery from writer-director Ingmar Bergman about a mesmerizing legerdemain expert who travels the countryside, claiming ESP powers. It's a dark mood that Bergman projects, and he does it brilliantly. Ingrid Thulin, Bibi Anderson, Max von Sydow. Aka *The Face*. (Video/Laser: Nelson)

MAGICIAN OF LUBLIN, THE (1978) ★★★ Fascinating portrait of a Jewish entertainer who rises to the top of Warsaw society as a magician/escape artist, then throws it all away to greed, ego and lust. Alan Arkin's portrayal is unusually anachronistic for a turn-of-the-century drama, but the German locations, period costumes and coperformances (Louise Fletcher, Valerie Perrine, Lou Jacobi, Shelley Winters) make it work. Yasha (the magician) believes he can fly and this fantasy element provides this adaptation of Isaac Bashevis Singer's "The Magician" with some startling moments and a supernatural climax. Directed by Menahen Golan. (HBO/Cannon)

MAGIC IN THE WATER (1995) ★★★ The recovery of one's inner youth, and an appreciation for simpler ways in a complex world, is the theme behind this children's fantasy set in the lakeside community of Glenorky (actually Kaslo in British Columbia), where beleaguered businessman Mark Harmon brings his daughter and son for vacation. The Loch Ness–type lake serpent alleged to roam local waters, and known as Orky, turns out to be a cutesy-pie, Oreo cookie–loving, benevolent creature harassed by nosy Japanese scientists, toxic pollution and mean guys who want to exploit it/him/her for tourism. The script by first-time director Rick Stevenson and Icel Dobell Massey works best when dealing with Harmon's transformation into a goofy, fun-loving guy (Orky has the power to get into men's minds and change them into simpler beings) who tries to dig his way to China and behaves sillily. There are a few heartwarming moments at the end, but too many undeveloped subplots dilute the message and effect. A good cast, though, helps to save the day, if not the lake beast. Harley James Wozak, Sarah Wayne, Willie Nark-Orn. Aka *Glenorky*. (Video/Laser: Sony)

MAGIC ISLAND (1995) ★★ Lackluster Moonbeam Entertainment production from Charles and Albert Band, in which a 13-year-old kid (Zachery Ty Bryan) ignored by his mother is whisked away through the pages of a magical book to a Caribbean island where he encounters Blackbeard the Pirate (Andrew Divoff), silly cutthroats, a benevolent prince of pirates (Edward Kerr) and a mermaid. The only highlight in the Neil Ruttenberg–Brent V. Friedman script is a stone statue coming to life via stop motion. Even Richard Band's score seems uninspired as this video movie made for kids tediously unfolds under Sam Irvin's direction. The only treasure adults will find is treasured sleep. French Stewart, Lee Armstrong, Jessie-Ann Friend, Os-

car Dillon, Abraham Benrubi, Sean O'Kane. Guest voices by Isaac Hayes and Martine Beswicke. (Video/Laser: Paramount)

MAGIC RIDDLE, THE (1991) ★★★ This Australian animated feature doesn't have the clout of a Disney hit, but it does have many satisfying ingredients in the Disney tradition that will make it pleasurable watching for young and old. It's an odd mixture of the Cinderella story with assorted elements from "classical folklore" (the Three Little Pigs, Pinocchio, the Seven Dwarfs, Prince Charming, etc.). The story by Yoram Gross, Leonard Lee and John Palmer evolves around Cindy (a variation on Cinderella) as she joins with the Seven Dwarfs and Phillippe (her lover) to find a lost will. Added enjoyment comes from grotesque but very funny portrayals of Cindy's "evil stepsisters," some charming musical numbers, and a visit to the Castle of 1,000 Doors. Voices by Robyn Moore and Keith Scott. The Brothers Grimm, Carlo Lorenzini and Hans Christian Andersen are credited for inspiration. Gross also produced and directed.

MAGIC SWORD, THE (1962) ★★★ Bert I. Gordon fantasy-adventure yarn for the young set, based on the St. George–dragon legend and written by Bernard Schoenfeld. Basil Rathbone is a chilly sorcerer, Estelle Winwood a maladroit witch, Gary Lockwood the heroic St. George, Anne Helm the fair Helene. Also on hand: an ogre, a bubbling pond that dissolves flesh, a French shepherdess who turns hag, and assorted magic. Above average, capturing the quality of a rousing fairy tale. Richard Kiel is a giant. Aka *St. George and the Seven Curses* and *St. George and the Dragon*. (Sinister/C; S/Weird; Video Yesteryear; MGM/UA; Filmfax)

MAGNETIC MONSTER, THE (1953) ★★½ Producer Ivan Tors and director Curt Siodmak teamed to write this low budgeter dealing with sci-fi theories difficult to depict—which makes this more oriented to ideas than visuals. The "monster" is a new isotope sucking up energy and giving off radiation as it grows in size. The good cast makes up for the intangible monster: Richard Carlson, King Donovan, Strother Martin. (Monterey) (Laser: MGM/UA)

MAIDENQUEST. Video version of *The Long, Swift Sword of Siegfried* (Private Screenings).

MAIDSTONE (1971) ★★ Offbeat, obscure feature directed and written by Norman Mailer and set in a near future when all political leaders have been eliminated and the world teeters on the brink of anarchy. Rip Torn, Joy Bang, Ultra Violet and Harris Yulin all costar with Mailer. Music by Isaac Hayes.

MAID TO ORDER (1987) ★★★ Get past an awkward beginning and a clumsy Cinderella premise, and this evolves into a funny, warm comedy that takes satirical jabs at Hollywood. Beverly Hills philanthropist Tom Skerritt, angry at spoiled daughter Ally Sheedy, wishes her out of his life—a wish Good Fairy Beverly D'Angelo grants him. Homeless, Sheedy takes a job as a housecleaner with a wealthy Malibu Beach family. Director Amy Jones balances the hokeyness with amusing characters: Dick Shawn's music entrepreneur, Valerie Perrine's whacky Lotusland wife, Michael Ontkean's chauffeur and Merry Clayton's maid. (Video/ Laser: IVE)

MAJIN II. See *The Return of Giant Majin.*

MAJIN, MONSTER OF TERROR (1966) ★★ Well-produced Japanese supernatural actioner with fine destruction effects when a legendary "golem" of Asia (a stone statue imbued with a warrior's spirit) comes to life for revenge against an evil chamberlain. Before the rampage, when villains are crushed underfoot or swallowed up by gaping holes in the earth, the film is a Samurai warrior saga with ample sword action. Aka *The Devil Got Angry, The Vengeance of the Monster* and *Majin, the Hideous Idol.* Directed by Kimiyoshi Yasuda. Follow-ups were *The Return of Giant Majin* and *Majin Strikes Again.* (S/Weird)

MAJIN STRIKES AGAIN (1966) ★★ You've heard of rock 'n' roll idols—here's a rock idol who rolls with the punches when fighting evil. Yes, it's Rock Head himself, that legendary warrior statue imbued with a soul who does for the Japanese what the golem did for the Hebrews in this third entry in Japan's Majin series. Directed by Issei Mori and Yoshiyuki Kuroda. See *Majin, Monster of Terror* and the sequel, *Return of Giant Majin,* to find out you can't keep a stoned guy down.

MAJIN, THE HIDEOUS IDOL. See *Majin, Monster of Terror.*

MAJORETTES, THE (1987) ★ John Russo, co-writer of *Night of the Living Dead* with George Romero, scripted this variation on the slasher theme (also known as *One by One*) with a "broad" mixture of uncovered breasts and sliced up body organs in depicting the slaughter of cheerleaders by a maniac killer. Directed by Bill Hinzman. Kevin Kindlin, Terrie Godfrey. (Vestron)

MAKE THEM DIE SLOWLY (1983) ★★ Italian cannibal shocker stars Lorainne de Selle as an anthropologist who wants to prove that cannibalism doesn't exist and goes to South America. She's wrong—or there wouldn't be a movie. One stomach-churning atrocity after another as members of her expedition are put to death. The most appalling device is a head-holder that allows a machete-wielding native to slice off a scalp and pluck out the brains for a feast. Allegedly banned in 31 countries, but don't believe it. Written-directed by Umberto Lenzi. John Morghen, Robert Kerman. Aka *Cannibal Ferox.* (Thrillervideo without Elvira)

MAKING CONTACT (1986) ★★★ Well-produced, well-directed fantasy from German filmmaker Roland Emmerich is filled with Spielbergisms: the weird lights and moving toys of *Close Encounters,* the telepathy and scientific teams of *E.T.,* the supernatural voice from Beyond on the phone of *Poltergeist,* etc. Joshua Morrell, after his father's death, makes contact with a voice that turns out to be that of a turn-of-the-century magician, represented by a devil doll. *Making Contact* never connects. Tammy Shields, Eva Kryll. (New World)

MAKING MR. RIGHT (1987) ★★ Well-intended but tedious fantasy comedy in which nerdy professor John Malkovitch creates android Ulysses in his own image for Chemtec Corporation. When PR expert Ann Magnuson is called in to hype him, she teaches the naive robot the art of romance—causing him to short circuit. This tries to make comments about love, loneliness and the human condition, but it's full of dumb humor (mistaken identities, people falling into swimming pools) that leaves director Susan Seidelman with Mr. Wrong. Polly Bergen, Ben Masters. (Video/Laser: HBO)

MAKING OF JURASSIC PARK, THE (1995) ★★★ A 1-hour documentary written and directed by John Schultz, which neatly chronicles the filmmaking history of Steven Spielberg's dinosaur epic, featuring fascinating interviews with all the special effects wizards who assisted him. (MCA)

MAKO: THE JAWS OF DEATH (1976) ★★ In this oceanic thriller inspired, one has no doubt, by *Jaws,* sea-life trainer Sonny Stein (Richard Jaeckel) makes friends with killer Mako sharks and learns to communicate. When the sharks are borrowed by marine biologists for inhumane experiments, Stein flips out and turns the formerly friendly fish into underwater attackers. Produced-directed by William Grefe. Jennifer Bishop, Harold Sakata, John Davis Chandler. (Video Media; from King of Video, Paragon and United America as *Jaws of Death*)

MALENKA THE VAMPIRE. See *Fangs of the Living Dead.*

MALIBU BEACH VAMPIRES, THE (1991) ★ Three guys living in a beach house have girlfriends who are really vampires. Directed by Francis Creighton. Angelyne, Becky Le Beau, Joan Rudelstein, Marcus A. Frishman.

MALTESE BIPPY, THE (1969) ★ Made as *The Incredible Werewolf Murders* and/or *The Strange Case of . . . !#★%* at the height of the popularity of TV's "Laugh In," this is an awful vehicle for Dan Rowan and Dick Martin. Norman Panama is responsible for writing-directing this outrageous turkey, which depicts the boys as witless wonders exchanging dumb banter as they enter a Yonkers house haunted by werewolves from next door. Aka *Who Killed Cock*

Rubin? Julie Newmar, Fritz Weaver, Dana Elcar, Carol Lynley, Robert Reed. This was a bomb, so *Son of the Maltese Bippy* was abandoned. Thank your lucky bippy.

MAMBA. See *Fair Game.*

MAMMA DRACULA (1980) ★★ French-Belgian effort with Louise Fletcher as a vampire (unaffected by daylight or religious symbols) who must periodically bathe in the blood of virgins. But did you know there's a short supply? Society is so perverted, you see. Maria Schneider portrays a policewoman and the whole thing, as the title indicates, is played for broad farce by farcical broads. Cowritten-produced-directed by Boris Szulzinger. Jimmy Shuman, Alexander Wajnberg. (Trans World; RCA/Columbia)

MAN AND HIS MATE. See *One Million B.C.*

MAN CALLED SLOANE, A. See *Death Ray 2000.*

MANCHURIAN CANDIDATE, THE (1962) ★★★★★ One might interpret that the intriguing premise to this Howard Koch production—Communists brainwash a loyal American and turn him into an assassin—came true when Lee Harvey Oswald assassinated John F. Kennedy. George Axelrod's adaptation of Richard Condon's novel will have you outraged and entertained as it depicts Laurence Harvey as a brainwashed GI conditioned to murder—and the murder is to be a U.S. candidate for the presidency. Audacious theme is handled brilliantly by director John Frankenheimer, even if it defies credulity. Frank Sinatra, Janet Leigh, Angela Lansbury, James Gregory, Henry Silva, Leslie Parrish, John McGiver, Whit Bissell, James Edwards. (Video/Laser: MGM/UA)

MANDRAKE THE MAGICIAN (1939) ★★★ This 12-chapter Columbia serial stars Warren Hull as a popular stage magician and comic-strip character created by Lee Falk and drawn by Phil Davis. In this adventure Mandrake is after the Wasp, an insidious villain trying to get his claws on a superradium zap machine. Assisting Mandrake is his assistant Lothar (Al Kikume), a professor (Kenneth MacDonald) and a beautiful woman (Doris Weston). Directed by Sam Nelson and Norman Deming. (Heavenly)

MANDROID (1993) ★★★½ On-location filming in Romania enhances this above-average Charles Band–Full Moon production, in which a Supercon plant-spore process leads to the creation of a metal warrior piloted by a human soul. The Earl Kenton–Jackson Barr screenplay focuses on the intrigue surrounding the selling of Mandroid to the West and the attempts by the Russians to wrest it away. There's plenty of action and special effects as the parties outfox each other and as Mandroid gets into the fray. Well directed by Jack Ersgard, whose brother Patrick Ersgard portrays an Interpol agent in need of a shave. Brian Cousins, Jane Caldwell, Michael Dellafemina, Curt Lowens. The sequel: *Invisible: The Chronicles of Benjamin Knight.* (Video/Laser: Paramount)

MAN EATER. See *The Grim Reaper.*

MAN-EATER OF HYDRA (1966) ★★★ "My beauties," chortles insane baron Cameron Mitchell to mutant plants—carnivorous cacti, fiendish fronds and terror tendrils. And the crazy count loves earthworms! A collection of upper-crust Europeans, gathered at his estate, are murdered one by one by an unseen presence while the baron blithely shows off his cross between a Venus flytrap and a century plant. Beg pardon, sire, but something in the garden is eating the guests. Spanish-German production is crudely photographed and acted, and plays almost like a stereotyped whodunit, yet has a compulsion in the way the decadent characters behave, setting themselves up for the slurping green creepers and wriggling branches. Aka *The Bloodsuckers, Island of the Dead, Death Island* and *Island of the Doomed.* Directed by Mel Welles from a script by Ira Meltcher and E. V. Theumer.

MANFISH (1956) ★★ Colorful tale in which adventurers John Bromfield, Victor Jory and Lon Chaney, Jr., sail the South Seas in search of treasure and other action-packed quests. Joel Murcott's script is said to be based on Edgar Allan Poe's *Tell-tale Heart* and *The Gold Bug,* although the adaptations are very loose. Produced-directed by W. Lee Wilder. Barbara Nichols, Vincent Chang. (S/Weird; Sinister/C; Nostalgia)

MAN FROM PLANET X, THE (1951) ★★★ Scientist Raymond Bond informs newspaperman Robert Clarke a new planet is heading toward Earth. . . . Sure enough, on a foggy moor in Scotland, a spaceship lands to spearhead an invasion. The twist here is that a human, for his own evil ends, captures the bubble-headed alien and tortures it for information. This sci-fier was directed in only a week by Edgar G. Ulmer. The script by producers Aubrey Wisberg and Jack Pollexfen is unusual. Margaret Field, William Schallert, Roy Engel, Charles Davis. (Laser: MGM/UA)

MANGLER, THE (1995) ★★★ Tobe Hooper has always been an off-the-wall filmmaker who delights in giving you the bizarre, and with this adaptation of Stephen King's short story he reaches his zenith in esoteric horror. Would you believe an industrial laundry machine that folds sheets is an entity of evil? Yes, it seems that the ugly piece of machinery (wonderfully created by William Hooper) is the embodiment of the Devil, and those willing to feed in a leg or finger are given unlimited power in return. And by the way, if your daughter is a virgin and 16, you feed her in on her birthday. So in the town of Riker's Valley, at the Blue Ribbon Laundry, you've got some really weird stuff. Such as a haunted refrigerator that literally blows its top and spurts out supernatural forces; an aging crime photographer named Pictureman who uses a Speed Graphic (Jeremy Crutchley); a burned-out, angry cop (Ted Levine); and a 16-year-old (Vanessa Pike) who just happens to be working at the Blue Ribbon. One gets the feeling, however, that Hooper makes a lot of stuff weird just to be weird. Such as taking a young man (Robert Englund) and putting a lot of makeup on him so he can play an old cripple (the main villain). Or giving the laundry machine legs so it can walk and pursue the hero and heroine in a rousing, if improbable, climax. In short, you gotta come clean and see this one. It's a pressing matter. You just gotta. Coproduced by Harry Alan Towers. Hooper cowrote with Stephen Brooks and Peter Welbeck. (Video/Laser: New Line)

MANHATTAN BABY (1984) ★★½ Ancient Egyptian curse blinds archeologist Christopher Connelly and gives his daughter ESP. Italian film made in New York and Egypt by Lucio Fulci. Aka *Eye of the Evil Dead* and *The Possessed*. Martha Taylor, Brigitta Boccolli. (Lightning)

MANHUNTER (1986) ★★★ Offbeat crime thriller with baffling twists, based on Thomas Harris's *Red Dragon*, the book that introduces Hannibal (Cannibal) Lecter, who figured more prominently in *The Silence of the Lambs*. Retired FBI operative William Petersen has the psychic ability to enter the minds (or dreams) of the serial killers he pursues. He's brought back by his former chief Dennis Farina to pursue a madman (known as "the Tooth Fairy") who is slaughtering entire families. Director Michael Mann gives this the glitz and pop appeal of a "Miami Vice" episode, and further enhances it with startling violence and death. Kim Greist, Brian Cox. (Karl/Lorimar) (Laser: Karl/Lorimar; Warner Bros.)

MANHUNT IN THE AFRICAN JUNGLE (1943) ★★★★ Originally made as *Secret Service in Darkest Africa*, this superb Republic serial is nonstop action featuring great choreographed fights. Cliff-hanging situations, skullduggery among spies, Death Ray beams, wonder drugs, a forged legendary scroll and the Dagger of Solomon are among its rousing ingredients. Rod Cameron is heroic Rex Bennett, undercover man who infiltrates the Gestapo. This is said to be the serial that inspired Steven Spielberg to create Indiana Jones. Directed by Spencer Bennet. Joan Marsh, Duncan Renaldo, Kurt Kreuger. The sequel was *G-men vs. the Black Dragon* with Cameron returning. The feature TV version is "The Baron's African War." (Video/Laser: Republic)

MANHUNT OF MYSTERY ISLAND (1945) ★★★★ Outstanding 15-chapter Republic serial with Roy Barcroft as a bloodthirsty buccaneer who uses a zingy electric chair (the Atomic Power Transmitter) to change into one of four owners of Mystery Island—but which one? Guessing Captain Mephisto's true identity is but one fun element of this wonderful serial. Linda Stirling, queen of the cliff-hangers, and Richard Bailey, a square-jawed hero, search for her kidnapped father (a scientist with a Death Ray machine) and fight Mephisto's pirate gang led by Kenne Duncan. Plenty of chuckles and thrills, and some of the finest speedboat chases and fistfights ever staged by the studio. Barcroft, Republic's ubiquitous villain, is superb in the role of Captain Mephisto. Directed with flair by stunt specialist Yakima Canutt, Spencer Bennet and Wallace Brissell. The shortened TV version is "Captain Mephisto and the Transformation Machine." (Republic; Nostalgia Merchant) (Laser: Republic)

MANIAC (1963) ★★½ Hammer psychothriller has several plot twists as Kerwin Mathews, an artist living in France, is pursued by his girlfriend's husband and faces death by blowtorch. Startlingly good shocker in the Hitchcock tradition, directed by Michael Carreras and written by producer Jimmy Sangster. Nadia Gray, Donald Houston, Justine Lord. (RCA/Columbia)

MANIAC (1980) ★★ Penultimate "sicko" movie about a depraved murderer with a mother fixation who scalps his victims and nails their hair onto mannequins. Makeup specialist Tom Savini lets the blood flow from severed throats, decapitated heads and body cavities as psycho-killer Frank Zito (Joe Spinell) kills with knives, shotgun, garroting wire and other delicate instruments. This movie sinks pretty low in its exploitation of schizophrenic, psychopathic bloodletting: it is so obsessed with scenes of death that director William Lustig doesn't even bother to titillate us with nudity when he has ample opportunity. Caroline Munro appears as a curvaceous fashion photographer. The killer rattles on with a stream-of-consciousness dialogue, but there is no insight into a fiendish sex murderer. This is ultimately more sickening for what it implies than what it graphically depicts. Gail Lawrence, Kelly Piper. (Media) (Laser; Elete)

MANIAC COP (1988) ★★★ Lively psychokiller flick, inspired a little by *The Phantom of the Opera* in depicting the murder spree of a crazy cop terrorizing a city. He was once a good cop who was wronged by the department, sent to Sing Sing and murdered by inmates. However, he returns from the dead with a vengeance, murdering with a long knife built into his nightstick. Despite plot holes and deck stacking, producer Larry Cohen's script is full of twists, and director William Lustig keeps the action moving. Bruce Campbell is a cop accused of the crimes, Laurene Landon is a cop in love with Campbell, Richard Roundtree is a dense-headed commissioner, William Smith is bald cop Captain Ripley, Sheree North is a cripple with an odd relationship with Maniac Cop, and Robert Z'Dar is the uniformed fruitcake. (RCA/Columbia; Star Classics)

MANIAC COP 2 (1990) ★★★ Effective sequel brings back dead policeman Matt Cordell (Robert Z'Dar) as a supernatural entity who perversely keeps turning up at crime scenes to aid the criminal, not the victim. Producer-writer Larry Cohen demonstrates a knack for blending cops-and-robbers action with slasher-horror elements and director William Lustig brings a *noir* style to the revengeful mayhem. The carchase material and action sequences are spectacular, culminating in an exciting incident in Sing Sing. An amusing song has Maniac Cop proclaiming: "You have the right to remain silent . . . forever!" Robert Davi, Claudia Christian, Michael Lerner, Bruce Campbell, Laurene Landon, Clarence Williams III, Charles Napier. (Live) (Laser: Image)

MANIAC COP 3: BADGE OF SILENCE (1992) ★★★ Another energetic, violence-prone study in mayhem from beyond the grave when that dead cop Matt Cordell is resurrected by voodoo magic on the day of his funeral and returns with a new vengeance to get even again. Robert Z'Dar is back as Cordell with a messed-up, rotting face, and Robert Davi is good cop Sean McKinney, trying to protect a female cop who's been shot and is bordering on death. Coproducer Larry Cohen's script is an imaginative array of action set pieces, concluding with a great ambulance-car chase with Cordell's body engulfed in flames behind the wheel. Directed by William Lustig and Joel Soisson. Caitlin Dulany, Gretchen Becker. (Academy) (Laser: Image)

MANIACS ARE LOOSE, THE. See *The Thrill Killers.*

MANIAC WARRIORS. Video version of *Empire of Ash II* (AIP; Movies Unlimited).

MAN IN THE SANTA CLAUS SUIT, THE (1979) ★★★ Seasonal TV-movie with a yuletide warmth. Fred Astaire is an elfin character in a dozen roles (chauffeur, cabbie, hot dog salesman, on and on) but mainly runs a costume shop. Each customer who dons his Santa suit undergoes a crisis. Zany pacing keeps this moving as if Donner and Blitzen were yanking the team. Among the likable people: a destitute restaurateur (John Byner) pursued by gangsters, an unhappily married senator's aide (Bert Convy) and Gary Burghoff as a nerd trying to land a beautiful model. Nanette Fabray and Harold Gould are memorable as a couple reenacting their old vaudeville routines. Directed by Corey Allen. (Media)

MAN IN THE WHITE SUIT, THE (1952) ★★★½ Rollicking, irreverent satire on British big business and labor. Research chemist Alec Guinness discovers, in his bubbling laboratory, a formula for indestructible suit fabric. He's hailed, then hated when it dawns on England's textile industry that this discovery could put it out of business. Directed by Alexander Mackendrick, who cowrote the script with Roger MacDougall and John Dighton. Joan Greenwood, Michael Gough, Ernest Thesiger, Cecil Parker. (HBO)

MANIPULATOR, THE (1971) ★ Mickey Rooney has a powerful range, but not even he can carry this avant-garde study in psychological disintegration. Using distorted camera angles to capture bewilderment, this experiment in madness (aka *B. J. Lang Presents*) is set in a loft of props and mannequins, where Rooney imagines he is directing movies in 1947. His captive audience is actress Luana Anders tied to a chair. Lang imagines all kinds of oddball scenes, allowing director-writer Yabo Yablonsky to escape total claustrophobia with crowds of weirdo people at orgies and hippie parties. (The only other character is a janitor played by Keenan Wynn.) It's like a dream, enhanced by slow motion and other tricks, but what could have been a tour de force becomes overindulgence. Coproduced by Burt Sugarman. (Vestron)

MANITOU, THE (1978) ★★★ A 400-year-old Indian medicine man spirit, Misquamacus, is reborn in the body of Susan Strasberg and bursts from her back in a harrowing birth sequence. Sound absurd? It is, and yet this adaptation of Graham Masterson's novel (directed by William Girdler, who cowrote with Jon Cedar) transcends its own ridiculousness by virtue of its cinematic power. Mechanical effects by Gene Grigg and Tim Smythe and horrific makeup by Tom Burman are superb and will have your own skin crawling. Also a far-out special effects ending by Dalt Tate and Frank Van Der Veer. Tony Curtis as a charlatan mystic heads the cast: Ann Sothern, Stella Stevens, Paul Mantee, Michael Ansara (as exorcist Indian Singing Rock) and Burgess Meredith. (CBS/Fox; Charter) (Laser: Nelson)

MAN-MADE MONSTER (1942) ★★★ Excellent effects and Jack Pierce's makeup lend class to this B production from Universal which was Lon Chaney, Jr.'s first monster role. Sole survivor of a bus crash, he emerges an anomaly of glowing electricity. He joins a carnival as Dynamo Dan the Electrical Man and is experimented on by evil Dr. Rigas (Lionel Atwill) who foresees a race of walking electric men, their mere touch lethal. Deemed a killer, Chaney is sent to the electric chair, but all that does is add to the glow in his cheeks. The sympathetic, misunderstood monster finally goes berserk and decides to light up everyone's life. A "shock-ing" ending. Directed by George Waggner from a Joseph West script, based on a story called "The Electric Man." Aka *Mysterious Dr. R* and *The Atomic Monster*. Anne Nagel, Frank Al-bertson. (MCA)

MANNIKIN (1977) ★★ Half-hour adaptation of Robert Bloch's short story about a singer ob-sessed by the Devil. Directed by Donald W. Thompson. Ronee Blakley, Keir Dullea. (Learn-ing Corp. of America)

MAN OF A THOUSAND FACES (1957) ★★★ Universal's biography of Lon Chaney, Sr., the pliable actor who specialized in grotesque mon-ster roles during the Silent Era. As a melodrama about Chaney's marital strife it's on the hokey side, but the studio atmosphere and re-created scenes from Chaney's classics are ably captured by director Joseph Pevney from the script by Ivan Goff, Ben Roberts and R. Wright Camp-bell. James Cagney is a feisty, memorable Cha-ney, Dorothy Malone and Jane Greer provide teary love interests, Roger Smith appears as Chaney Jr. and Robert Evans is studio honcho. (Video/Laser: MCA)

MAN'S BEST FRIEND (1993) ★★ Better this should have been called *Man's Beast Friend* or *Man's Best Fiend*. Yes, Alpo salespeople, it's another "killer dog" movie, this time with a big, lovable pooch called Max 3000, who's being groomed as a powerful weapon in lab experi-ments conducted by Dr. Paul Jarret (Lance Hen-riksen). Along comes snoopy TV newswoman Ally Sheedy, who ends up taking Max 3000 home with her, unaware in her own inept way that on occasion Max becomes a drooling killing machine, with a penchant for cookie snacks. (Cookies, in this case, being human.) There isn't much more to the dog-eared script by director John Lafia. Robert Costanzo, Fredric Lehne, John Cassini, J. D. Daniels, William Sanderson. (Video/Laser: New Line)

MANSION OF MADNESS, THE. See *Dr. Tarr's Torture Dungeon*.

MANSION OF THE DOOMED (1975) ★ Unqual-ified revulsion is generated by this crude horror film . . . certainly it demeaned the careers of Richard Basehart and Gloria Grahame. Basehart portrays Dr. Chaney, an eyeball transplant ex-perimenter. When his daughter is blinded, he stops at nothing to restore her sight, including the taking of eyeballs from others. Not only does this Charles Band production show the op-erations graphically, but victims are depicted by director Michael Pataki in all their sightless mis-ery. The bloody, shocking ending of eyeless vic-tims avenging themselves remains one of the sickest in memory. Vic Tayback, Arthur Space. Aka *Eyes*, *Eyes of Dr. Chaney*, *House of Blood* and *The Terror of Dr. Chaney*. (Bingo)

MANSTER, THE (1959) ★★★ This U.S.-Japanese coproduction (aka *The Split*) epito-mizes the thrills in the monster-horror movies of the '50s: pseudoscientific explanations, cheesy effects and hammy acting. And that's exactly why it's so fun. American accountant Peter Dy-neley is turned into a two-headed creature by a Japanese doctor experimenting with new body-altering drugs, who also keeps his deformed wife locked in a cell. Made in Japan with a mixed cast. Directed by G. P. Breakston and Kenneth G. Crane from a Walter Sheldon script based on Breakston's story "Nightmare." Aka *The Manster—Half Man, Half Monster*. (J & J; Sinister/C; S/Weird; Filmfax)

MAN THEY COULD NOT HANG, THE (1939) ★★★ Prophetic horror thriller has a fascinat-ing sequence in which Boris Karloff, on trial for murder, pronounces that body transplants will one day become a vital field of science. In this Columbia scientific thriller, Karloff is Dr. Sa-vaard, whose experiments to arrest the body's metabolism, so transplants can be carried out, causes a patient's death. Sentenced to hang, Sa-vaard is resurrected by a loyal lab assistant. Then all those responsible for sending Savaard to prison are gathered in a mansion and mur-dered one by one. Directed by Nick Grinde from a Karl Brown script. Roger Pryor, Lorna Gray, Ann Doran, Don Beddoe, James Craig. (RCA/Columbia; Goodtimes)

M.A.N.T.I.S. (1993) ★★★ Rousing special-effects superhero TV-movie in which M.A.N.T.I.S. (Mechanically Augmented Neuro-Transmitter System), a crippled black man in a metallic suit who flies around Ocean City in a futuristic air machine, wages war against a crooked politico who is pitting black gangs against each other as an excuse to use excessive, dictatorial force on the streets. Produced by Sam Raimi, Robert Tapert and Sam Hamm (the lat-ter, of *Batman* recognition, also wrote the tele-script), this is pure gourmet genre that action fans will dig—from the technological hardware to the groovy supersuit to the pyrotechnics. Di-rected by Eric Laneuville. Carl Lumbly, Bobby Hosea, Gina Torres, Steve James, Obba Basa-tunde. After this pilot, "M.A.N.T.I.S." became a weekly series on Fox.

MAN WHO CAME FROM UMMO, THE. See *As-signment Terror*.

MAN WHO CHANGED HIS MIND, THE. See *The Man Who Lived Again*.

MAN WHO COULD WORK MIRACLES, THE (1937) ★★★ Alexander Korda's version of H. G. Wells's story about George McWhirter Fotheringay, an Essex draper's clerk endowed with miraculous powers, is a playful blending of the cosmic and the comic. Roland Young as Fotheringay performs minor miracles at first, then graduates to bigger stuff. Directed by Lo-thar Mendes, scripted by Wells. Beautifully arresting film with pleasing effects for their time. Ralph Richardson, Ernest Thesiger, George Zucco, Torin Thatcher. (Embassy) (Laser: Image)

MAN WHO FELL TO EARTH, THE (1976) ★★★½ Enigmatic Nicolas Roeg sci-fi film is complex and will be indecipherable to some—but a rich mosaic of study to others. David Bowie, in his screen debut, conveys the asexual manner and features of an E.T. humanoid from a dying planet who crash-lands on Earth. Using a scientific formula, he establishes a corporate empire and raises money to build a rocket ship so he can return to his family. But he becomes a victim of a corrupt society, dwindling away to a hopeless alcoholic. An unusually sensitive film, beautifully photographed (Roeg began as a cinematographer) with offbeat effects. Claudia Jennings, Buck Henry, Bernie Casey, Candy Clark, Rip Torn. (Video/Laser: RCA/Columbia)

MAN WHO HAUNTED HIMSELF, THE (1970) ★★★½ Roger Moore undergoes surgery after an auto accident and suddenly doctors can hear two heartbeats. After recovery, Moore realizes he has an exact double—a doppleganger conspiring to take his place. The ending is extremely weird; in fact, the Michael Relph–Basil Dearden script is very original. Dearden also directed. Hildegard Neil, Olga Georges-Picot, Anton Rodgers. (HBO)

MAN WHO LIVED AGAIN, THE (1936) ★★★ Boris Karloff is the creator of a brain transference machine. Unfortunately, Dr. Laurience goes bonkers when his financial backer stops funding the project, and he sets out to exchange his mind with that of John Loder, with whom his lab assistant Anna Lee is in love. A British film directed by Robert Stevenson from a script by Sidney Gilliat and L. DuGarde Peach. Cecil Parker, Lynn Harding, Donald Calthrop. Aka *The Man Who Changed His Mind, The Brainsnatcher* and *Dr. Maniac*. (Sinister/C; Nostalgia; Filmfax)

MAN WHO SAW TOMORROW, THE (1981) ★★★ Orson Welles narrates (on and off camera) this fascinating pseudodocumentary that reexamines the predictions of Michel de Nostradame, the 16th-century French physician who jotted down thousands of quatrains, all of which are believed to be forecasts of history, right down to one that predicts a tyrant named "Hister" will terrorize the world. The latter part of the film deals with predictions of a nuclear war in 1999—following which there will be a 1,000-year peace. Welles's voice (if nothing else) will hold you riveted. Much of the footage was staged by director Robert Guenette. (Warner Bros.)

MAN WHO WASN'T THERE, THE (1983) ★ Abysmal attempt to create a mystery comedy à la *Foul Play* with *The Invisible Man* blindly thrown in. Director Bruce Malmuth and writer Stanford Sherman give this a teenage mentality that will make you evaporate. The sexual jokes are a leering slap against women; the 3-D is pointless; and the plot so incomprehensible that the twists only irritate. State Department official Sam Cooper finds an egg-shaped device loaded with vials of green serum that renders its drinkers invisible. An invisible criminal has three dumb henchmen à la the Three Stooges running around Washington, D.C., after Cooper and girlfriend (Lisa Langlois, who has some silly scenes making love to empty air). The only member of the woe-begone cast who makes anything funny of this is Jeffrey Tambor as a Soviet official. (Paramount)

MAN WITH NINE LIVES, THE (1940) ★★★½ Premonitory glimpses at cryonics, the science of freezing bodies into suspended animation, long before it was called that. Boris Karloff stars as Dr. Kravaal, whose intentions are far from mad when he entombs a dying patient. A drug accidentally knocks out everyone in the cave and when the good doc awakens 10 years later, he has a cancer cure but goes bonkers, forcing scientists Roger Pryor and JoAnn Sayers to become guinea pigs. Directed by Nick Grinde, scripted by Karl Brown and Harold Shumate. Hal Taliaferro, Charles Trowbridge. Aka *Behind the Door*.

MAN WITH THE GOLDEN GUN, THE (1974) ★★★ Ninth in the James Bond series, with Christopher Lee as the $1-million assassin Scaramanga. Bond and Scaramanga fight over a solar energy laser beam on a Pacific island but it's not very exciting stuff, with Roger Moore (as 007) seeming fatigued and indifferent. Reintroduction of a Southern sheriff during a car chase indicates writers Richard Maibaum and Tom Mankiewicz were running low on ideas. Britt Ekland and Maud Adams are lovely to behold but this still needs more attractions. One of the villain's aides, Nick Nack, is Herve Villechaize, who went on to "Fantasy Island." Directed by Guy Hamilton. Clifton James, Richard Loo, Marc Lawrence, Bernard Lee. (CBS/Fox) (Laser: MGM/UA)

MAN WITH THE SYNTHETIC BRAIN. (1972) ★ In the beginning, producer-director Al Adamson hacked out *Psycho a Go-go* in 1965. When that was a no-go-go he shot new footage and called it *Fiend with the Electronic Brain*. When that short-circuited, he went back and filmed Kent Taylor, John Carradine and buxom, curvaceous blond Regina Carroll in revised footage, calling it *Blood of Ghastly Horror*. And when that emerged a ghastly horror, he retitled it *Man with the Synthetic Brain*. And at some time during all this retitling, the industrious Adamson threw in the titles *Love Maniac* and *The Fiend with the Atomic Brain*. So what's it all about? You tell us. A murder in an alley leads to a flashback about a diamond robbery, which leads to a flashback about mad doctor Carradine with a high-pitch voltage machine, who creates a man with an electronic brain. The man's father (Taylor) kidnaps Carradine's daughter and holds her hostage while cop Tommy Kirk chases the robbers in the hills near Lake Tahoe. Filmed in "Chill-O-Rama." (From Movies Unlimited as *Blood of Ghastly Horror*.)

MAN WITH THE X-RAY EYES, THE. Video version of *X—The Man with the X-ray Eyes*.

MAN WITH TWO BRAINS, THE (1983) ★★★ That wild and crazy guy, Steve Martin, in a wild and crazy picture— make that wild and uncontrolled. It's a hodgepodge of mad-doctor clichés and tongue-in-cheek Frankenstein jokes, a roller-coaster ride with laugh peaks and non-guffaw valleys too. And yet, it's enchantingly watchable, with a barrage of sex jokes downright hilarious. Carl Reiner directed with an eye for colorful visual parody. Martin falls in love with a brain floating in a solution created by doctor David Warner and can't get sexy wife Kathleen Turner to make love to him. Paul Benedict, Peter Hobbs, James Cromwell, Merv Griffin. (Video/Laser: Warner Bros.)

MAN WITH TWO HEADS (1972). See *The Thing with Two Heads*.

MARCH OF THE MONSTERS, THE. See *Destroy All Monsters*.

MARCH OF THE WOODEN SOLDIERS. Video version of *Babes in Toyland*.

MARDI GRAS FOR THE DEVIL (1993) ★★★ Effective supernatural thriller set in New Orleans at Mardi Gras time when cop Robert Davi tangles with the Devil (Michael Ironside). Satan killed Davi's father 20 years before and now wants to destroy everything that Davi loves— ex-wife Lesley-Anne Down, girlfriend Lydia Denier and partner Mike Starr. There's ample pyrotechnics and stunt work and cross-cutting between the Devil making love to a sadistic prostitute and Davi and Denier coupling. The script by director David A. Prior captures the emotional involvement of the characters and offers well-defined roles for police chief John Amos and voodoo expert Margaret Avery (as Sadie), who provides background that the Mardi Gras holiday began in Europe 800 years ago to celebrate the rites of spring and involved bloody sacrifices by the Church. Made as *Night Trap*. (Prism) (Laser: Image)

MARK OF THE BEAST. See *Fear No Evil*.

MARK OF THE BEAST. Video version of *Fertilizing the Blasphemizing Bombshell* (Rhino).

MARK OF THE CLAW. Original title of *The Giant Claw*.

MARK OF THE DEVIL (1970) ★ Sickening German-British gore bore about 17th-century witchhunter Herbert Lom and his ghastly torture methods. Features the jolly sight of a woman's tongue being cut out of her head, and other nubile desirables with their blouses ripped open undergoing heinous forms of sadism. This revolting material went over with the public, for a sequel was also embraced by viewers. Directed by Michael Armstrong (real name: Sergio Cassner). Udo Kier, Reginalf Nalder. Aka *Austria 1700*, *Satan* and *Burn, Witch, Burn!* (Vestron; Lightning)

MARK OF THE DEVIL PART II (1972) ★ Blood flows in gushing streams from broken, twisted bodies and ripped-asunder flesh as alleged witches and heretics are tortured by fun-loving purveyors of the Inquisition (what a sedate period in history!). Producer Adrian Hoven leaves his devilish mark by writing and directing. Anton Diffring, Erica Blanc. (Video Dimensions; Vidmark)

MARK OF THE DEVIL PART III. Video version of *Sisters of Satan* (Fame Entertainment).

MARK OF THE VAMPIRE (1936) ★★½ Tod Browning's horror thriller sets itself up as a graveyard-vampire chiller, its script by Guy Endore and Bernard Schubert closely following the silent film *London After Midnight*. However, too soon it turns into a whodunit with preposterous premises, certain to disappoint fans expecting supernatural thrills. Bela Lugosi duplicates his Dracula image as Count Mora, Carol Borland is his "Bride" who flaps him across the dungeons, Lionel Barrymore appears as the vampire chaser and Lionel Atwill, for the umpteenth time, is the probing policeman. Elizabeth Allen, Jean Hersholt, Donald Meek. Aka *Vampires of Prague*. (MGM/UA)

MARK OF THE WOLFMAN, THE See *Frankenstein's Bloody Terror*.

MARK TWAIN CLASSICS: THE MYSTERIOUS STRANGER. Video version of *The Mysterious Stranger* (MCA).

MARKUS 4 (1996) ★½ On "a distant plant," in 2047 A.D., the half-human, half-cyborg miners are revolting—but that isn't the only revolting thing about this sorry excuse for an action movie disguised paper-thinly as a sci-fier: there's the alleged plot by Nick Spagnoli, which has practically no legitimate sci-fi in it, and the alleged direction by John Shepphiro, and the alleged acting by Bentley Mitchum in a dual role as twin brothers. When evil corporate boss John Savage kills Brother No. 1, Brother 2 (a government agent specializing in dangerous assignments) seeks revenge on the mining world of Markus 4, proving to be totally unsympathetic as he and partner Sherrie Rose go gunning for the baddies, showing no mercy. Then there's the revolting acting of Robert Carradine as the leader of the revolting miners. Adults and minors will be equally revolted by this time waster. It ends with Brother No. 2 being assigned to solve some new problems on Markus 3. The idea of a sequel is positively revolting. Joseph Culp, Paul Ben-Victor, Paul Williams, Gary Wolf, Roxana Zal.

MARS ATTACKS (1996) ★★★ Chew on this one for a moment: a major science-fiction movie based on popular bubblegum cards? Since it's the infamous, once-controversial Topps cards featuring hideous-looking alien monsters destroying Earth babies and dogs, not to mention buildings and other earthly dwellings, why not? But in the hands of oddball director Tim Burton, who was obviously inspired by the kind of madness that permeated *Dr. Strangelove,* does this audacious idea work? Sometimes . . . but not always. British playwright Jonathan Gems's original screenplay (developed in tandem with Burton) treats the concept of Earth's invasion as a parody of sci-fi-movie styles of the 1950s, and even Danny Elfman's memorable score copies Bernard Herrmann's *The Day the Earth Stood Still* to improved perfection. The whacked-out script is also a platform for satirical comments on the stupidity of government and military officials and Las Vegas moguls. But, and it's a big but, the comic-book look of the evil invaders and the cartoonish special effects (by Industrial Light & Magic) seem better suited to a full-length animated version, and never quite jibe with the live action. What might have blended, had the characters not been so stupidly written, instead becomes an uneven, dumb exercise in comedy-action often excruciating to watch. One keeps waiting for one brilliant Burton touch to pull it all together, but it never arrives. Burton has always been unique and quirky in his choices, and here he goes not only over the top but completely out of sight. The silly characters are endless: Jack Nicholson doubles his fun as a conservative president (who never stops making an ass of himself) and as the cowboy owner of Las Vegas's new Galaxy Hotel; Glenn Close is an insufferably snobbish first lady; Pierce Brosnan underplays his foolishly passive expert on Martian life, falling in love with TV hostess Sarah Jessica Parker in the strangest of ways. Others involved in the oft-dull proceedings are hawkish general Rod Steiger, press secretary Martin Short (who has one funny scene with a Martian disguised as a busty Martian), Michael J. Fox, Tom Jones (in a send-up of his own singing stardom), Annette Bening, Danny DeVito, Sylvia Sidney, James Brown. (Video/DVD: Warner Bros.)

MARS ATTACKS THE WORLD (1938). Feature-length version of *Flash Gordon's Trip to Mars;* available in all 12 chapters on video, too.

MARS INVADES PUERTO RICO. See *Frankenstein Meets the Space Monster.*

MARS PROJECT. See *Conquest of Space.*

MARSUPIALS: THE HOWLING III. See *Howling III.*

MARTIAN CHRONICLES, THE (1979) ★★★ Ray Bradbury's classic novel of Mars colonization (a loose-knit collection reprinted from pulps) arrived as a 6-hour miniseries with Rock Hudson as John Wilder, the one character who links the disjointed narratives. Bradbury's book is poetic style and atmosphere, difficult qualities for film. Occasionally director Michael Anderson works well with the limited sets and skimpy effects, but he cannot prevent the meager budget (for so huge an undertaking) from showing. Richard Matheson has written a thoughtful teleplay recounting man's colonization of the Red Planet, the chameleon qualities of the Martians, and other fantasy premises that make Bradbury's work one of the finest of the 20th century. Darren McGavin, Gayle Hunnicutt, Bernadette Peters, Fritz Weaver, Roddy McDowall, Maria Schell, Barry Morse, Jon Finch, Chris Connelly. Available in a 3-set video series: Vol. I: "The Expeditions" (IVE); Vol. II: "The Settlers" (USA); Vol. III: "The Martians" (USA) (Laser: Image)

MARTIANS GO HOME (1990) ★ Composer Randy Quaid is writing a score for a sci-fi movie when the music is piped into space. As a result, Martians invade Earth, showing up as green-skinned beings in green clothing who behave like obnoxious stand-up comedians. This adaptation of Fredric Brown's popular novel, written by Charlie (*Gremlins II*) Haas, is a misfire that is excruciatingly unfunny. Haas's every attempt at something original is either destroyed by director David Odell or just doesn't work in the hands of Quaid, Margaret Collin (as his love interest), the sexy Anita Morris (as an insufferable talk show psychologist) and Barry Sobel (doing his fast patter stand-up shtick). (IVE) (Laser: Image)

MARTIN (1976) ★★★ Portrait of an 18-year-old vampire, directed-written by George A. Romero (*Night of the Living Dead*), who de-mythologizes the living-dead legend. Martin (John Amplas) imagines he is a descendant of Nosferatu but in reality he uses a razor blade to slash victims' wrists, and he is bothered by neither garlic cloves nor Christian crosses. There are two outstanding sequences—the assault of a woman in her train compartment and the snaring of two lovers in a large home—and as a black comedy of exploitation, *Martin* comes off nicely. Romero's most thoughtful work. Makeup man Tom Savini costars with Lincoln Maazel and Christine Forrest. (HBO) (Laser: Image)

MARY REILLY (1996) ★★★½ As grim as a slaughterhouse's wall decor and as bleak as a neglected gothic graveyard at midnight, this unique and atmospheric variation on Robert

Louis Stevenson's Dr. Jekyll/Mr. Hyde classic is an unusually effective (and disturbing) revisionist's look at the tale of dual identity, as seen through the eyes of repressed housemaid Julia Roberts. Against her better judgment, she falls in love with Hyde, in this version a younger (though still handsome) mutation of the aging Dr. Jekyll. Both men are played with effectiveness by John Malkovich, who captures the perversity of Hyde and the cynical intellect of Jekyll. Roberts, in a restrained, almost catatonic role, somehow makes the abused Miss Reilly come to life in a strange, lethargic way. If there is any one thing working against director Stephen Frears, screenwriter Christopher Hampton (basing his script on a novel by Valerie Martin) and producer Iaian Smith, it is the unrelenting darkness and fog that shuts out every glimmer of hope for any of the characters. If this was intended to be a love story, it is a depiction of romance at its darkest and most twisted, and it can only leave you feeling cold and empty. But the craftsmanship that went into achieving that is remarkable. George Cole, Michael Gambon, Kathy Staff, Glenn Close (as a madame running a brothel, she is brilliantly bitchy and nasty in a secondary role). (Video/Laser: Columbia Tri-Star)

MARY SHELLEY'S FRANKENSTEIN (1994) ★★★½ Don't be put off by some of the critical rejection that attached to this Francis Ford Coppola production (a companion piece to his *Bram Stoker's Dracula*). Director Kenneth Branagh brings an incredibly energetic, frenetic style to Shelley's classic novel, which is followed more faithfully than by most adaptors. Screenwriters Steph Lady and Frank Darabont (Lady wrote the script on spec, Darabont enhanced it) give Branagh a distillation of the complex novel that allows him to go over the top in his overwrought, but powerful, style as director. Branagh's camera is constantly moving through the imagery of a gothic nightmare, as dizzy and crazy as many of the characters. Branagh doubles as Victor von Frankenstein and is a dynamic monster maker, obsessed in a way that no mad scientist before him has been obsessed. As the Monster, Robert De Niro stretches his acting legs to provide a new slant on the creature: articulate, burning with a passion of his own for his "Bride"-to-be, and cognizant of the ironies in which he is trapped. Yes, it's overdone and gory and funky, but who would want a Frankenstein movie to be otherwise. The great supporting cast includes Tom Hulce, Helena Bonham Carter as Elizabeth, Aidan Quinn as North Pole explorer Walton and Ian Holm as Victor's father. It's a great version, not to be missed. (Video/Laser: Columbia TriStar)

MASK, THE (1961) ★ A hokey but mildly fun Canadian horror film (aka *The Eyes of Hell* and *The Spooky Movie Show*) with segments shot in 3-D; viewers are forewarned to put on their glasses each time psychiatrist Paul Stevens starts to have one of his hallucinations. These stereovision bits are full of arbitrary horror images (witches, misty swamps, killer snakes, corpses coming to life, evil spirits reaching out for you, etc.). The story line is like a "Twilight Zone" episode with "Outer Limits" lighting as Stevens comes into possession of a South American art treasure—a mask that brings out homicidal tendencies in its wearer. Produced-directed by Julian Roffman. Claudette Nevins, Bill Walker. In 1982 a version was released to TV with the 3-D segments in red-and-green tinting, introduced by magician Harry Blackstone. (From Rhino in 3-D) (Laser: Image)

MASK, THE (1994) ★★★★ A live-action comedy that pays tribute to the zany style of Tex Avery and other Warner Bros. animators from the Golden Age of cartoons. There's a touch of *Roger Rabbit* at work here, although it never quite becomes an animated film. The effects appear to have been computer generated. It's an ideal vehicle for the daffy Jim Carrey, who portrays the worm that turns. He's an ineffectual banker and ladies' man, searching for his own identity, when he finds a magical mask (allegedly the property of the Viking god Loki) and can fulfill his wildest fantasy by turning into a superhero with the capabilities of behaving just like an Avery character: moving with the speed of a whirlwind; popping his eyeballs and changing other parts of his anatomy in cartoonish style; producing wild and crazy props at the blink of an eyelid; changing costumes and characterizations at will; and practicing a form of wild abandon found only in the world of Bugs Bunny. Set in the metropolis of Edge City, *The Mask* has a nominal plot (by Mike Webb) about a gangster trying to get the facepiece for his own evil designs, but it's all just an excuse that's a mile high and three miles wide for Carrey to go bonkers as only he can go bonkers. Director/co-producer Chuck Russell gives this unusual novelty piece just the right comic book touches. Peter Riegert, Peter Greene, Amy Yasbeck, Richard Jeni, Nancy Fish. (Video/Laser: New Line)

MASKED MARVEL, THE (1943) ★★★ A 12-chapter Republic serial with a switch: Instead of the mastermind villain's identity being withheld, the identity of the heroic Masked Marvel is kept secret—you only know it has to be one of four insurance cops. Superexplosives and superpowerful weaponry are used as the Marvel prevents Japanese saboteurs from blowing up America. Yet another excursion into wonderfully staged nonstop action. Just marvel-ous, darling. Directed by Spencer G. Bennet. Tom Steele, William Forrest. The TV-feature version is *Sakima and the Masked Marvel*. (Republic; Video Treasures)

MASK OF FU MANCHU, THE (1965). See *The Face of Fu Manchu*.

MASK OF SATAN, THE. Heavily edited version of *Black Sunday*.

MASK OF THE DEMON. See *Black Sunday*.

MASKS OF DEATH (1984) ★★★ Stylish British TV-movie, bringing Peter Cushing back as the Baker Street sleuth, with a rather sedate John Mills portraying Dr. Watson. Parallel plots unfold: the finding of several corpses with twisted, hideous expressions, and a mystery involving the Home Secretary. The setting is London 1913, on the eve of World War I—a clue to a diabolical scheme involving English and German associations. Directed by Roy Ward Baker. The cast is enhanced by Anton Diffring as German royalty, Ray Milland as the secretary under fire and Anne Baxter as Irene Adler. Aka *Sherlock Holmes and the Masks of Death*. (Warner Bros.; Lorimar) (Laser: Image)

MASQUE OF THE RED DEATH, THE (1964) ★★★★ Edgar Allan Poe's allegory about aristocrats who hold a costume ball at the height of a virulent plague to keep away Death has been strongly adapted to a full-length horror thriller. Produced-directed by Roger Corman and written by Charles Beaumont and R. Wright Campbell, this stars Vincent Price as Prince Prospero, a sadistic Italian nobleman of the 12th century, surrounded by decadence and deceit in the form of Hazel Court (she makes a deal with the Devil) and Patrick Magee in an ape's outfit. One of the best in Corman's Poe series. Nigel Green, Jane Asher, David Weston. (Lightning; Live) (Laser: Image, with *The Premature Burial*)

MASQUE OF THE RED DEATH (1989) ★★ It's hard to understand why producer Roger Corman would take one of his best movies, American-International's superb 1964 version, and turn it into this inferior remake. Adrian Paul as the sadistic Prince Prospero is no match for Vincent Price, nor is Larry Brand (who cowrote the script with Daryl Haney) half the director that Corman is. The production values are woeful, as is most of the acting. Only Patrick Macnee as the Red Death brings any professionalism to this wrong movie. Clare Hoak, Jeff Osterhage, Tracy Reiner. (Video/Laser: MGM/UA)

MASQUE OF THE RED DEATH (1990) ★★ Frank Stallone, Brenda Vaccaro, Herbert Lom and Michelle McBride star in this unfaithful adaptation of Poe's tale, in which a dying millionaire invites folks to his mansion, where they are murdered by a slasher-basher. Directed by Alan Birkinshaw. (RCA/Columbia)

MASSACRE AT R.V. PARK. See *Alien Predator(s)*.

MASSACRE IN DINOSAUR VALLEY (1985) ★ Despite its title this foreign-produced adventure film has no fantasy elements, but rather falls into the category of the "jungle holocaust" genre, being filled with gruesome torture effects, killer piranha fish, spears, blowguns and machete body chops. Michael Sopkiw is an adventurer in the Indiana Jones vein, a dinosaur-bone hunter forced to land in the South American jungle with other travelers. An odd mixture of adventure, explicit violence and sex (including a torrid lesbian number) without being much fun, with the morbid elements taking hold. The dubbing is pretty terrible, and the acting without subtlety. Susane Carvall, Milton Morris, Martha Anderson. Written-edited-directed by Michael E. Lemick. (Lightning; Live)

MASTER KEY, THE (1945) ★★ A 15-chapter Universal serial that is typical for the studio's output during World War II: Its emphasis is on a strong cast of B-picture players, a lot of plot that doesn't require more than an occasional outburst of action, and fistfights that can't compare to those in the Republic cliff-hangers. In short, expect plenty of story and dialogue as government agent Tom Brant (Milburn Stone, who went on to become Doc on "Gunsmoke") fights a gang of Nazis in 1938 America that is out to use the Orotron machine to turn seawater into gold. Helping Stone in his multichapter quest are fellow agent Dennis Moore and girlfriend Jan Wiley. Directed by Ray Taylor and Lewis D. Collins. (VCI)

MASTER OF EVIL. Video version of *Demon Lover* (Premiere).

MASTER OF TERROR (1965) See *Die, Monster, Die!*

MASTER OF THE WORLD (1961) ★★ A mingling of Jules Verne's *Master of the World* and *Robur the Conqueror* results in an uneven fantasy adventure. What is good is the *Albatross*, a marvelous Victorian craft kept aloft by whirling blades and electrical current. Also good: the decorative staterooms and 19th-century costumes. What isn't so good is Richard Matheson's adaptation: Robur is portrayed as just another mad genius who hates war but inflicts it on others. Also not so good is the hammy acting of Vincent Price. Also not so good is the presence of Charles Bronson as the hero. A hero in this kind of movie he is not. A mixed bag of air directed by William Witney. Henry Hull, Mary Webster, Wally Campo. (Warner Bros.; MGM/UA)

MASTERS OF THE UNIVERSE (1987) ★★★ A live-action version of TV's animated "He-Man and the Masters of the Universe." What we have are wind-up characters fighting a cosmic battle to save the universe. (You expected less?) An obvious clone of *Star Wars* and other fantasy-quest films, yet it has a life of its own, unfolding at a feverish pitch, with imaginative costume and set designs. Dolph Lundgren as He-Man is some hunk as he pursues the Cosmic Key, a device that holds the power of good over evil. His adversary is Frank Langella as Skeletor, who sends his ugly minions after He-Man and pals: Man-at-War (Jon Cypher), his daughter Teela (Chelsea Field), and a dwarf-alien named Gwildor (Billy Barty in a lot of costume and makeup). Ultimately, *Masters* suffers from David Odell's campy dialogue, the superficially glittering direction of Gary Goddard, and mock heroics of monumental proportion as He-Man takes on armies of laser-armed robots. Bill Conti's music is a ripoff of *Star Wars* and *Superman*. Meg Foster is Evil-Lyn, James Tolkan is the cop Lubic, and Courteney Cox and Robert Duncan McNeil portray Earthlings caught up in the war when it shifts to Earth through a time-space continuum. (Video/Laser: Warner Bros.)

MASTERS OF THE UNIVERSE II: THE CYBORG. TV title for *Cyborg* (1989).

MASTERS OF VENUS (1954) ★½ This British equivalent of U.S.-produced cliff-hanger serials just can't compare. An 8-chapter sci-fi story, it ineptly depicts teenagers Amanda Coxell and Robin Stewart ending up aboard a rocket to Venus, where they and other Earth beings encounter a militant culture descended from Atlantis. The special effects are shabby beyond belief, Michael Barnes's script is not to be believed for its naïveté, and Ernest Morris directs it all as if he wouldn't know a cliff-hanger if it walked up to him at Piccadilly Circus and tapped him on the shoulder. Norman Wooland, Ferdy Mayne, Arnold Diamond. (Sinister/C; Vidmark; Filmfax)

MATANGO, THE FUNGUS OF TERROR. See *Attack of the Mushroom People*.

MATERNAL INSTINCTS (1995) ★★★ Can a hysterectomy turn a sweet, God-loving woman into a homicidal bitch who displays all the seven deadly sins? With Delta Burke in the title role, you bet. This campy, classic TV-movie is a delight as Burke (who was also executive producer) seeks bittersweet revenge against her husband (who gave the order without her consent), the doctor (Beth Broderick) who performed the operation, and the doctor's architect husband. All are lured into scheming traps laid by the eyeball-rolling Burke. Even one of her best friends gets pushed off a tall building. Coproduced and written by Lisa Friedman Bloch and Kathy Kirtland Silverman, this twisted portrayal of mother's love will have you rolling in the aisles as director George Kaczender presents Burke as the new Queen of Mean. Roll 'em, Delta baby, you are wonderful in this role! Garwin Sanford, Tom Mason, Sandra Nelson, Gillian Barber.

MATILDA (1996) ★★★★ Quirky in the way that *Edward Scissorhands* was quirky, and twisted in the way of the fairy tales by Roald Dahl, this adaptation of Dahl's story by Nicholas Kazan and Robert Swicord is a delightfully skewed urban morality fable about the gifted but mentally abused Matilda Wormwood (Mara Wilson) who is mistreated by parents Danny DeVito (who also directed) and Rhea Perlman. Poor little Matilda is sent to a horrible school (Crunchem Hall) run by the wicked Miss Trunchbull (Pam Ferris), where the child's telekinetic powers become full-blown as she avenges herself on all the terrible people who have neglected and abused her. Also helping Matilda through this learning experience is sympathetic teacher Miss Honey (Embeth Davidtz, portraying the epitome of goodness). This statement about how American society misunderstands youth never becomes unduly heavy-handed, and because DeVito allows everyone to play the script farcically, it comes off as quite funny and occasionally touching. Assisting in small roles are Paul Reubens, Tracey Walter, Brian Levinson. (Video/DVD: Columbia TriStar)

MATINEE (1993) ★★★★½ Director Joe Dante and producer Michael Finnell (the *Gremlins* team) are back for this homage to moviegoing that is set in a Florida town in 1962 at the height of the Cuban Missile Crisis. Producer Lawrence Woolsey (John Goodman), molded after the gimmick king William Castle, arrives with his latest exploitation horror flick *Mant!* to be shown in Atomo-Vision and Rumble-Rama. Much of the black-and-white *Mant!* is shown during the matinee, and it's a wonderful send-up of sci-fi/monster movies of the '50s ("Half Man, Half Ant, All Terror!"), starring Kevin McCarthy, William Schallert and Robert Cornthwaite, who actually appeared in these things. The rest of Charles Haas's plot focuses on a family and its reaction to the crisis. All the teenagers attend the matinee and become caught up in the gimmicks of the afternoon. Haas also deals with the bomb scare of the day, the craze for bomb shelters and other nostalgia of the 1960s. It's a satisfying comedy, enhanced by Cathy Moriarty's performance as a jaded actress and mistress of Goodman's, who attends the screening dressed as a nurse. Simon Fenton, Omri Katz, Lisa Jakub, Jesse Lee, Lucinda Jenney, James Villemaire. Jesse White, Dick Miller and John Sayles make brief appearances. (Video/Laser: MCA)

THE MATRIX (1999) ★★★★½ Movie science fiction has traditionally been behind literary science fiction, primarily because there wasn't the technology to create the imaginative worlds described so well on paper, and producers have always been afraid of inundating sci-fi audiences with too many complex ideas, lest they lose the plot. However, with computerized special effects (now any kind of sci-fi world can be created on a desktop) and a hipper audience tuned into cyberspace, DNA, and scientific breakthroughs, the gap between the printed page and the motion-picture frame is narrowing—witness this superlative combination of compelling ideas and stunning visual action. *The Matrix,* written and directed by Larry and Andy Wachowski (called "The Wachowski Brothers" in the credits), is a mind-blowing adventure with a never-slowing pace, blazing action, and several layers of story. It becomes a metaphor for life and death, the eternal struggle of man to reach greater heights, and a comment on our society's overemphasis on the governmentally controlled. And yet for those wanting just a good time, there's an abundance of marital-arts fights, shoot-outs, and other standard forms of visceral movie excitement. Keanu Reeves is a computer hacker in a futuristic world who gets caught up in a battle between rebel forces and government agents (the latter wear dark suits and sunglasses). Suddenly "Neo" (Reeves) wakes up in a tank of fluid, connected to a thing called "The Matrix," a machine-created survival system that feeds an artificial world in which everyone thinks they live and work. With the help of gurulike rebel Morpheus (Laurence Fishburne) and his companion Trinity (Carrie Anne Moss), Reeves escapes his tank and goes through a symbolic kind of birth experience as he slides down a tunnel into the real world. Then he's taken to a spaceship, where he finds other escapees making up the team of rebel forces. Fishburne thinks Reeves is the Messiah who will somehow overcome the Matrix and return mankind to its former glories, and begins a quasi-religious education that includes the use of weapons and hand-to-hand combat. There are some splendid karate fights and some startling scenes of human bodies floating through space and performing acts that defy gravity. Reeves's main adversary is "Agent Smith" (Hugo Weaving), who is able to place himself in another body when he's pursuing Reeves, and hence can suddenly be standing next to him at the drop of a keyboard. The dual realities of *The Matrix* make for a multilayered series of plots and action set pieces, and the mechanical octopus monsters that control the Matrix program are a fascinating new kind of alien creature. If the film falters at all, it is in the climactic action sequences in which everything is too easily resolved after such a complex setup. But even those action pieces are astounding. There is a firefight in an office-building lobby unlike any you've seen before, and there's a grand duel between Reeves and Weaving. *The Matrix* is exciting stuff, indeed. Joe Pantolpano, Marcus Chong, Julian Arahanga, Matt Doran. (Video/DVD: Warner Brothers)

MATT RIKER. See *Mutant Hunt.*

MAUSOLEUM. See *One Dark Night.*

MAUSOLEUM (1982) ★★ Minor supernatural tale with hokey effects. Would you believe dry-ice mist in the family crypt with rats in the shadows and thunder and lightning outside? Totally devoid of thrills since we know from the outset that sexy Bobbie Bresee, member of the cursed Nomed family, is possessed by a demon that forces her to act like a nymphomaniac and slaughter her lovers. None of these bloody deaths is particularly exciting, nor are the gore effects believable. John Buechler's makeup and fright masks are only fair. Bresee is the highlight, frequently baring her wonderful breasts with wild abandon. Too bad her acting isn't as magnificent. Marjoe Gortner is wasted as Bresee's dumb husband and La Wanda Page has an embarrassing cameo as a maid whose feet don't fail her when it's time to run. Directed by Michael Dugan from a script by Katherine Rosenwink. Norman Burton, Maurice Sherbanee. (Video/Laser: Nelson/Image)

MAX HEADROOM, THE ORIGINAL STORY (1985) ★★ High-tech British black comedy fantasy with imaginative computer graphics and TV transmissions. In a near-future world, a crusading investigative TV reporter for the 23rd Network discovers a conspiracy to telecast a subliminal "blip" commercial that will cause viewers to overload and literally explode. A check of network officials and the adolescent genius who created the "blips" leads to weird confrontations and chases through a depressed industrialized England as an entity named Max Headroom is sent over the airwaves. Success of this TV-movie led to TV specials and a network series starring Max, who also became featured in U.S. commercials. Life imitates art. Directed by Rocky Morton and Annabel Jankel. Matt Frewer, Amanda Pays, Nickolas Grace. (Karl/Lorimar) (Laser: Warner Bros.)

MAXIMUM OVERDRIVE (1986) ★ Stephen King's debut as a director tells us he should stick to writing. He's taken a story from *Night Shift,* the one about killer semitrailers trapping travelers in a roadside diner, and added sci-fi overtones. Seems a comet passing Earth has affected electrical and gas machines and instilled in them a homicidal urge to wipe out mankind. So trucks run people down, lawn mowers mow and Walkmans strangle. King falls back on the old cliché siege story, but his characters are unbelievable and unsympathetic, and one ends up laughing at, and not gasping with, this hapless bunch. Lacking suspense, a human villain and any sense of form, *Maximum Overdrive* delivers minimum underthrust. Emilio Estevez, Pat Hingle, Laura Harrington. (Video/Laser: Lorimar)

MAXIMUM THRUST. See *The Occultist* (Urban Classics).

MAXIM XUL (1991) ★ Professor of ancient lore

(Adam West) discovers nine demons that he believes are responsible for all evil on Earth, but policeman Jefferson Leinberger isn't convinced as he tries to solve a series of murders. Filmed in Baltimore by director-producer Arthur Egeli. Mary Shaeffer, Billie Shaeffer. (Magnum)

MAXWELL SMART AND THE NUDE BOMB. See *The Nude Bomb.*

MEAT IS MEAT. See *The Mad Butcher.*

MEDICAL DEVIATE. See *Dr. Butcher M.D.* (*Medical Deviate*)

MEET JOE BLACK (1998) ★★★★ This intelligent study of fascinating, articulate people that blends in a supernatural element is based on a stage play of the 1930s by Alberto Cassella, *Death Takes a Holiday.* It was filmed twice before, first as a Fredric March vehicle in 1934, then as a TV movie in 1971 with Monte Markham. It is a parable about Death personified, coming to Earth to experience human emotion. Although this new version scripted by Ron Osborn, Jeff Reno, Kevin Wade, and Bo Goldman changes many elements, it is still a fascinating extension of Cassella's original concept, delving in far greater depth into the characters and changing Death from his princely image of the stage to a young man (blond, handsome Brad Pitt) of modern New York. At the core of this film's success is a beautiful performance by Anthony Hopkins as a communications-company chairman who realizes he is about to die and prepares to get his life in order. Every scene in which he appears sparkles with character and polished dialogue. Pitt first plays a young man who meets Hopkins's daughter (Claire Forlani) in a coffee shop; there is almost instant love between them. But Pitt is killed crossing a street, and hours later, his body now occupied by Death, turns up (as "Joe Black") in Hopkins's mansion to make a deal: allow Death to learn the ways of man, and Hopkins's life will be extended so he can clean up some pressing matters. Obviously, Death has chosen Pitt's body so he can also be near Forlani, and a romance develops that brings about conflict between Death and Hopkins. Others connected to this strange relationship are Jake Weber as a diabolical and devious manipulator in company affairs; Jeffrey Tambor as a loyal and thoroughly likable employee of the company married to Hopkins's second daughter; Marcia Gay Harden as that unhappy, neurotic daughter; and Lois Kelly-Miller as a dying Jamaican woman. Pitt offers a strange performance, often talking in riddles, acting emotionless most of the time, and yet showing a smile that indicates he knows everything. (One wonders why Death wouldn't know about mortal man.) Forlani is an exceptional actress, conveying a vulnerability that is rare in movies. If *Meet Joe Black* has a problem, it is its 178-minute running time. Yet it is still a moving experience with beautiful background music by Thomas Newman that includes popular thirties tunes during the gala-birthday-party sequence that concludes the film. Produced-directed by Martin Brest (*Scent of a Woman*) with sensitivity and understanding, *Meet Joe Black* works on so many levels and is done in such excellent taste that it should please almost everyone, fantasy fan or not. (Video/DVD: Universal)

MEET THE APPLEGATES. See *The Applegates.*

MEET THE GHOSTS. See *Abbott and Costello Meet Frankenstein.*

MEET THE HOLLOWHEADS (1989) ★ Makeup specialist Tom Burman made his directing debut with this comedy set in a futuristic society that resembles a parody of a TV sitcom as it focuses on the Hollowhead family (John Glover, Nancy Mette, Matt Shakman, Juliette Lewis and Lightfield Lewis) coping with tomorrow's world. (Video/Laser: Media)

MEET THE INVISIBLE MAN. See *Abbott and Costello Meet the Invisible Man.*

MEET THE KILLER. See *Abbott and Costello Meet the Killer.*

MEET THE MUMMY. See *Abbott and Costello Meet the Mummy.*

MEGAVILLE (1990) ★ Overdone, unconvincing futuristic tale in the "Big Brother" mold with J. C. Quinn as a brainwashed cop for a corporate-ruled society who is assigned by boss Daniel J. Travanti to infiltrate a gang offering uncensored TV shows to the public, including one that shows the President being strangled to death. Quinn's programming is unstable and he keeps short-circuiting and undergoing weird hallucinations and illnesses. Why anyone would pick him for a spy is a major weakness in the script by director Peter Lehner and Gordon Chavis. Billy Zane, Grace Zabriskie, Hamilton Camp. (IVE)

MEMOIRS OF AN INVISIBLE MAN (1992) ★★ Disappointing adaptation of H. F. Saint's novel about an average working man rendered invisible when a scientific experiment goes awry at a research plant. Its failure is all the more distressing because John Carpenter directed and Chevy Chase starred and neither rises to the occasion. Chase underplays Nick Halloway, failing to engage us on a comedic or a dramatic level. The script by William Goldman, Dana Olsen and Robert Collector stresses a routine chase as Halloway is pursued by maverick agents of the CIA led by Sam Neill. And where's the romantic spark between Chase and Daryl Hannah as the girlfriend who agrees to help him escape his pursuers? (That they meet and have a quickie in the ladies' room doesn't help the relationship.) Some of the invisible-man effects are interesting but it's not enough to recommend this tired failure. Michael McKean, Jim Norton, Patricia Heaton. (Video/Laser: Warner Bros.)

MEMORIAL VALLEY MASSACRE (1988) ★½ Ax-wielding madman plagues campers who thought they were getting a holiday, and instead get a hollow slay. Directed by Robert C. Hughes. William Smith, Cameron Mitchell, John Kerry, Lesa Lee. (Video/Laser: Nelson)

MEN IN BLACK (1997) ★★★★ Out of the annals of UFO reporting has evolved an urban legend about strange men in black suits, presumably government agents, who "investigate" flying-saucer sightings and other phenomena and try to convince witnesses they haven't seen what they think they've seen. Known as "men in black," these sinister figures are treated strictly as tongue-in-cheek comedy fodder in this very funny, cleverly crafted sci-fi spoof that features hilarious special effects and stars Tommy Lee Jones and Will Smith as members of MIB-6, a secret government unit that controls an estimated 1,500 aliens from various planets in the galaxy that have come to Earth under a policy of political asylum. They live among us disguised as humans and nobody must know of their existence. Based on the Marvel comic book by Lowell Cunningham, Ed Solomon's screenplay gets off to a good start when an alien bug makes its way through space to Earth only to end up splattered on a windshield. Street-wise cop Smith is recruited by cool MIB operative Jones and told the unit's motto by assignment boss Zed (Rip Torn): "Your image is crafted to leave no lasting memory . . . you are rumor, recognizable as only déjà vu and dismissed just as quickly. You don't exist, you were never even born. Anonymity is your name, silence your native tongue. You are no longer part of the system, you are above the system, over it, beyond it. We are Them, we are They, we are the Men in Black." The wild, crazy plot has something to do with a race of bugs on Earth secretly planning to take over the planet, while another race, the Arcillians, are trying to prevent the conquest. Jones trains wisecracking Smith in the ways of keeping the aliens' presence a secret from the masses with the use of a neurolyzer (it zaps away all memories of seeing what you shouldn't have seen), a series-4 deatomizer rifle and a "midget cricket" hand weapon. Rick Baker created the alien life forms sprinkled throughout this hilarious movie (there's a giant bug-like bug-eyed-monster that is delicious) and Lucas' Industrial Light & Magic did the flying saucers and various alien spaceware. Full of chases with amazing acrobatics, lots of I've-been-slimed jokes, and scads of in-gags (a bulletin board of "aliens disguised as humans" includes Sylvester Stallone and Newt Gingrich), *Men in Black* costars Linda Fiorentino as a dedicated though sometimes necrophiliac mortician and Vincent D'Onofrio as a bug exterminator whose outer skin is taken over and worn by a bug monster. Smith is very funny as he incredulously walks through the outrageous adventures and Jones plays it coolly indifferent, as if nothing is out of the ordinary, remarking "There's always an alien battle cruiser or a Corellian Death Ray or a plague that's about to wipe out life on this miserable little planet." None of it, he adds, is worth getting upset about. It's that satiric tone that director Barry Sonnenfeld establishes and maintains so beautifully throughout *Men in Black*. If you want to get the real lowdown about men in black check out Jenny Randles's *The Truth Behind Men in Black*. Tony Shalhoub, Siobhan Fallon, Mike Nussbaum, Jon Gries, Carel Struycken. (Video/DVD: Columbia)

MENNO'S MIND (1996) ★★½ Is this a mindless Showtime TV-movie? Almost. Set in a futuristic fascist society where a "virtual reality" center called The Resort provides escape into fantasy cyberworlds for unhappy citizens, its blazing action scenes are unbelievably one-sided (a large portion of the evil regime's security force is slaughtered by just one submachine-toting woman rebel), and characters sneak in and out of guarded facilities with too much ease. But the cast of B players is good and makes Mark Valenti's bad scriptwriting seem better than it is. Credit Bill Campbell as an almost nerdy computer expert for giving it a little charm, thank Corbin Bernsen as a security chief with evil designs to take over the presidency, and honor Stephanie Romanov as a rebel Rambo for killing fascist troops without the slightest remorse. She knifes them, strangles them, bullet-riddles them, and even engages in fierce hand-to-hand combat. Yet she never stops looking beautiful. You might even congratulate Robert Vaughn for getting paid for doing nothing more than sitting in a chair and looking mean, Michael Dorn for removing his Worf makeup long enough to play a worm that turns, and Bruce Campbell for managing to stay alive (after he's officially dead) inside a computer program. Try it sometime, it's not easy dodging cyber-terrors. Director Jon Kroll never allows a modicum of subtlety to slow down the explosive action scenes, nor does he slacken off to let a little meaningful characterization creep in for the benefit of intellectually leaning viewers. Hell, this is a barrage-of-bullets-in-your-face and that's all that counts. Marc McClure, Phil Proctor, Robert Picardo. (Showtime/Two Left Shoes)

MEN WITH STEEL FACES. Feature-length version of the Gene Autry serial *The Phantom Empire*.

MERIDIAN: KISS OF THE BEAST. Video/laser version of *Kiss of the Beast* (Paramount).

MERLIN (1992) ★★½ Fantasy adventure with a reincarnation theme, in which counterparts to characters from the King Arthur legend are still warring against each other in modern times in a California mining community. Standouts in the cast are Richard Lynch as Pendragon, a black-magic sorcerer; James Hong as Leong Tao, "Guardian of the Sword" Excaliber; and Rodney Wood as the titular magician ("older than time, older than stars"). Made in England under the title *October 32nd, Merlin* is an ambitious if sometimes poverty-stricken production that was directed vigorously by coproducer Peter Hunt (John Stewart directed the action sequences). Nick McCarthy's script vacillates between poetic passages, "mumbo jumbo" as Pendragon calls up his demons and magic, and standard action stuff. Peter Phelps, Nadia Cameron, Robert Padilla, Ted Markland, Desmond Llewelyn. (Hemdale)

MERLIN (1998) ★★★½ "Once upon a time there were dragons, elves, griffins, and magic" ... so begins this excellent TV-movie retelling of the Arthur legend, with emphasis on the boy born of no earthly father (under the magical manipulations of Mab the Witch, played with refreshingly evil relish by Miranda Richardson). *Merlin* is presented in a mythical context that includes computerized special effects (there's a great fire-breathing dragon), plenty of pain and suffering, and scads of action, some of it quite bloody. Sam Neill brilliantly portrays the grown Merlin, capturing all his angst and zest for life. The David Stevens–Peter Barnes script—which always remains epic in proportions, unfolding to Trevor Jones's vibrant score—follows the familiar legendary characters with some degree of faithfulness but still gives the tale new twists along the way. This was directed with a strong dramatic sense by Steve Barron. The cast includes Rutger Hauer as the evil Lord Vortigern, Isabella Rossellini as Merlin's great love Minue, Martin Short as the servant Frik (a wicked companion to the already wicked Mab), Helena Bonham Carter as Morgan Le Fey, Jeremy Sheffield as Lancelot, and Lena Headey as Guinevere and Paul Curran as King Arthur. Filmed on location in Wales and England, the two-part TV movie captures a medieval sense of desolation. (Video/DVD: Hallmark)

MERLIN AND THE SWORD (1983) ★★½ Just seeing Candice Bergen in a fright wig in her pre–Murphy Brown days, playing a mean witch-bitch, makes this TV-movie worthwhile. This retelling of the Arthurian legend (originally *Arthur the King*) has an outstanding cast (Malcolm McDowall as King Arthur, Edward Woodward as Merlin), action, intrigue and an occasional magic trick or monster. Dyan Cannon is visiting Stonehenge when she's transported to an ice cave where Merlin has been imprisoned, and he relates in flashback the legend. Directed by Clive Donner, this is not a superepic, but its good acting carries it over its low-budget rough

spots. Joseph Blatchley, Rupert Everett, Liam Neeson, Michael Gough. Narrated by John Smith. (Vestron)

MESA OF LOST WOMEN. Video version of *Lost Women* (S/Weird; Filmfax).

METALLICA. Variant video title for *Star Odyssey*.

METALSTORM: THE DESTRUCTION OF JARED-SYN (1983) ★½ Blatant rip-off of *Road Warrior* from producer-director Charles Band and writer Alan J. Adler, jam-packed with grim-jawed, steely-eyed characters and overacting. Some effects are unusual for a 3-D movie, and production is occasionally ambitious, but this has no heart. "Peacekeeping Ranger" Jeffrey Byron is sent to quell an uprising on Lemuria and arrest head insurrectionist Jared-Syn. It plays like a cowboys-and-Indians nonsaga, with Western clichés creeping into the imbecilic dialogue. The dusty auto chases are routine, the zap gun shoot-outs are dumbly staged and the climax never happens—Jared-Syn simply vanishes into another dimension with promise of a sequel. *Metalstorm II* never happened. Richard Moll, Mike Preston, Tim Thomerson. (Video/Laser: MCA)

METAMORPHOSIS (1990) ★★½ Genetic engineer Gene Le Brock, in experiments designed to control cellular aging, is hounded by the college paying his way to produce results quickly—so he zealously injects himself as a guinea pig and turns into assorted murderous mutations, going back millions of years on the evolutionary scale until he's a "living fossil" (whatever that is). This sci-fi thriller, made in Norfolk, Virginia, has a good musical score by Pahamian, effective location footage, and competent direction by screenwriter G. L. Eastman, but some members of the cast are less than great, the effects are just so-so and the end result is only mildly satisfying. Harry Cason, David Wicker, Jason Arnold, Stephen Brown. (Imperial) (Laser: Image)

METAMORPHOSIS: THE ALIEN FACTOR (1990) ★★ This is a hoot of a monster movie, but only monster fans will appreciate its otherwise absurd and sometimes comedic excesses. An orange Alien-type thing—with saliva dripping off its hundreds of fangs, tentacles with suckers that shoot out of its body and mushy furballs that fly out of its gaping mouth—is the result of a genetic experiment with E.T. creatures at the Talos Research Lab in Newark, New Jersey. All hell breaks loose when doctors experiment once too often with tissue samples of an E.T. in their top-security laboratory, and one of the docs (George Gerrard), after being bitten on the hand, turns into a monster big enough to require occasional stop-motion animation as it cavorts the hallways, chasing pretties Tara Leigh, Katherine Romaine and Dianne Flaherty. Derivative script by writer-director Glenn Takakjian has clichéd evil doctors and opportunists, but they get theirs in the end. Takakjian gets an A for giving the monster the most closeups. Tony Gigante, Allen Lewis Rickman. (Video/Laser: Vidmark)

METEOR, THE. Early title for *It Came from Outer Space*.

METEORITE MONSTER, THE. Rejected title for *The Blob* (1958).

METEOR MAN, THE (1993) ★★ Excellent cast is wasted in this lightweight albeit well-intended parody of Superman. Writer-director-star Robert Townsend is a pleasant personality but the funniest moments are too infrequent, and come too late, to save the premise. This Tinsel Townsend production stars Townsend as an ineffectual schoolteacher who is hit by a meteor and absorbs a gooey green ball into his body. Before you can spell kryptonite, he's transformed into . . . *Meteor Man*, and going up against the vicious Golden Lords street gang. That excellent cast has James Earl Jones as Mr. Moses (a silly guy wearing funny wigs), Bill Cosby as a street bum, Nancy Wilson, Sinbad, Lawanda Page, Eddie Griffin, Don Cheadle and rap artists Biz Markie, Big Daddy Kane and Bobbie McGee. (Video/Laser: MGM)

METEOR MONSTER (1957) ★★½ Aka *Teenage Monster* and *Monster on the Hill*, this uses the clichés of the Western. A mysterious ray shoots out of an asteroid and infects the body of a young boy. Slowly he turns into a monster who commits outrages against a desert community. Produced-directed by James Marquette. Gilbert Perkins, Anne Gwynne. (Monterey; Sinister/C)

METROPOLIS (1927) ★★★★ Silent German classic, directed by Fritz Lang, is an expressionistic view of a city in 2026, a complex skyscraper system built for slavery. The enslaved population's only hope is a woman messiah, so the totalitarian rulers plot to substitute her with a robot. Revolt and destruction follow. This landmark classic is viewed in modern times with mixed reactions: some feel it is naive and outdated; others feel it is a masterpiece of political sci-fi and a forerunner of the special-effects picture. In 1984 a reconstructed version was released (scenes missing since the film was cut for the U.S. market in the '20s were restored) with new sound effects, color and a score by Giorgio Moroder. A controversy developed over whether or not a new score was suitable for an old picture. Within the score were eight new songs, with many lyrics by Pete Bellotte. Karl Freund was one of the cinematographers. Brigitte Helm, Alfred Abel, Gustav Froehlich, Fritz Rasp, Rudolf Klein-Rogge (Vestron; Kino; Cable; Video Yesteryear; with *Things to Come* from Goodtimes; Critic's Choice) (Laser: Vestron)

MIAMI GOLEM. See *Miami Horror*.

MIAMI HORROR (1987) ★★ E.T. force controls Earthlings with psychic energies but TV reporter David Warbeck fights the alien invaders as well as John Ireland's gang of thugs. Aka *Miami Golem*, this was directed by Martin Herbert. Lawrence Loddi, Laura Trotter, George Favretto. (Action International; Panther)

MICHAEL (1996) ★★★ This has to be the most eccentric fairy tale about an angel visiting Earth ever made, consisting of a series of non sequiturs rather than a thought-out story. First off, John Travolta's unshaven winged entity, constantly shedding feathers, is different from any previous movie angel. Behaving like he didn't have a care in the universe, he guzzles beer, feeds his face with sugar-laced breakfast cereal, seduces several young beauties, and engages in a barroom brawl, all the while enjoying himself in a happy-go-lucky style. He also loves pie, takes credit for writing Psalm 85, and insists he invented the notion of standing in a line. First showing up in a rural Iowa town to cause a local bank to collapse suddenly (a comment on man's crass love of money?) for Jean Stapleton, he soon appears to be as "lost" as three reporters from a sleazy Chicago tabloid (the *National Mirror*, edited by a brash Bob Hoskins) looking for a story about Michael in the company of a national dog icon, Sparky. They are down-and-out newspaperman William Hurt, an "angel expert" played by Andie MacDowall, and Sparky's master, Robert Pastorelli. They set out together for Chicago on a series of unrelated events, but slowly it becomes apparent that Michael will regain his purpose in life and in turn behave like a reformed angel to help his companions find romance and happiness. It's an oddball love story, really fuzzy around the edges, that was directed by Nora Ephron, who cowrote the script with Delia Ephron, Peter Dexter, and Jim Quinlan. Teri Garr puts in a guest appearance as a rural judge and MacDowall sings a few country-western songs. (Video/Laser: Turner)

MICROSCOPIA. Early title for *Fantastic Voyage*.

MICROWAVE MASSACRE (1979) ★ Comedian Jackie Vernon, playing a construction worker, chops up his wife (Claire Ginsberg) and stuffs the tidbits into the freezer. He develops a taste for those morsels and stockpiles human flesh—the coldest cuts of all in Thomas Singer's "tasteless" script. Director Wayne Berwick plays this rancidly macabre meatloaf for laughs; if you find cannibalism funny, you'll guffaw up an appetite. Loren Schein, Al Troupe, Lou Ann Webber. (Rhino; Select-A-Tape; Midnight)

MIDNIGHT (1980) ★★ John Russo, who coauthored *The Night of the Living Dead* with George Romero, wrote-directed this horror effort (based on his novel) in the vein of *The Texas Chainsaw Massacre*. A teenager runs away from home and falls into the hands of a family of demented killers who worship the

Devil. It's familiar territory enlivened by the makeup of Tom Savini. Lawrence Tierney is a drunken cop who attempts to molest the teenager sexually in the opening scenes and later comes to her rescue—an odd morality. Melanie Verlin, John Amplas, Greg Besnak. (Vidmark; from Midnight as *Backwoods Massacre*)

MIDNIGHT (1989) ★★ Lynn Redgrave goes over the top as a shrill, bitchy TV horror-movie hostess named Midnight, and Tony Curtis goes with her as a TV producer conniving to get the copyright to her character. This is more an indictment of Hollywood than a horror film, with the scary stuff coming toward the end when a mysterious killer knocks off Midnight's associates. Producer-writer-director Norman Chaddeus Vane allows the cast to overindulge and you end up with unpleasant profiles, hardly the stuff of a riveting movie. Frank Gorshin stands out as an actor turned agent. Steve Parrish, Karen Witter, Rita Gam, Wolfman Jack, Gloria Morrison. (Sony) (Laser: Image)

MIDNIGHT CABARET (1990) ★ Devil-worship cult plots for a young actress to become impregnated with the child of Satan, using a New York nightclub as the base of operation. Directed by Pece Dingo. Michael Des Barres, Thom Mathews, Carolyn Seymour. (Warner Bros.)

MIDNIGHT HOUR, THE. Video version of the TV-movie *In the Midnight Hour* (Vidmark).

MIDNIGHT KISS (1992) ★★½ Unusual urban cops-and-vampire thriller with undercover cop Michelle Owens being bitten by a modern-type blond bloodsucker (Gregory A. Greer, playing the creature with cute one-liners) and slowly turning into a blood-lusting creature . . . but never quite all the way. Gore fans will find plenty of bloody special effects and ravaging murder sequences. Scripters John Weidner and Ken Lamplugh have included subplots involving Owens versus her chauvinistic boss and in an adversarial relationship with partner stakeout cop Michael McMillan. Given all that extra jazz, *Midnight Kiss*, as directed and edited by Joel Bender, doesn't get the kiss-off. It's worth seeing. Robert Miano, B. J. Gates, Michael Shawn, Celeste Yarnall. (Academy) (Laser: Image)

MIDNIGHT MOVIE MASSACRE (1986) ★★ Producer Wade Williams made this spoof of 1950s sci-fi movies at the Granada Theater in Kansas City, MO. Set in 1956, it depicts an audience of freaks, nerds, nuts, misfits and rejects watching *Sweater Girl from Mars* and *Space Patrol: Guardians of the Universe*. Williams uses the "kitchen sink" principle as he insults you, shocks you, tickles your funny bone and reminds you why you enjoy bad movies. *Space Patrol* (directed by Larry Jacobs) features Robert Clarke and Ann Robinson as heroic types. Meanwhile, an alien monster lands near the the-

ater and closes in, killing the ticket-office gal and moving toward the snack bar. Will the beast get the obese popcorn eater, the back-row smoochers, the trio of stupid tough guys, the girl who keeps dropping snotty rags into a sex-crazed cowboy's beer cup? Stand by for more dripping gore. Mark Stock directed the script by David Houston, John Chadwell, Roger Branit (also the editor) and Williams. David Staffer, Mary Stevens, Tom Hutsler, Margie Robbins. (VCI; United)

MIDNIGHT'S CHILD (1992) ★★ Subtitle this derivative mixture of *Rosemary's Baby* and *The Hand That Rocks the Cradle* as "The Nanny from Hell." Olivia D'Abo, possessing a red crystal pendant with powers to sway men's minds, portrays a Swedish disciple of Satan ("the Prince") who picks the daughter (Elissabeth Moss) of a young L.A. couple (Marcy Walker and Cotter Smith) to be the Devil's next bride. David Chaskin's TV script is obvious and Colin Bucksey's direction of this Victoria Principal production lacks surprises. You'll be calling the shots long before Ms. Walker wises up. Jim Norton, Judy Parfitt, Roxann Biggs.

MIGHTY JOE YOUNG (1949) ★★★★½ *King Kong* mentors Merian C. Cooper and Ernest B. Schoedsack teamed to spoof their giant ape with this mighty adventure showcasing the stop motion of Willis O'Brien, Hollywood's screen-magic pioneer. (O'Brien received a much-deserved Oscar.) Mighty Joe Young, a friendly giant gorilla raised in Africa by Terry Moore, is brought to the states by promoter Robert Armstrong (repeating his role from *Kong*) where the creature is an attraction in a Hollywood nightclub, the Golden Safari. While Moore plays "Beautiful Dreamer" on her piano, Joe goes bananas, demolishes the place and escapes. It's up to sympathetic cowhand Ben Johnson and Moore to rescue the hapless Joe. A fire in an orphanage climaxes the script by Ruth Rose (Mrs. Schoedsack). John Ford, although he received no credit, directed some second unit. Ray Harryhausen assisted O'Brien. Remarkably well made if old-fashioned picture produced by Cooper and directed by Schoedsack. Frank McHugh, Regis Toomey, Nester Paiva, Primo Camera, Douglas Fowley. Aka *Mr. Joseph Young of Africa*. (Nostalgia Merchant; Turner) (Laser: Image, also in a tinted version)

MIGHTY JOE YOUNG (1998) ★★★ After the great success of *King Kong* and *Son of Kong*, RKO producers Meriam Cooper and Joseph Schoedsack wanted to make more movies about giant creatures that challenged moviegoers' imaginations, and finally saw that dream come true in 1949 with *Mighty Joe Young*. If anything extended Joe's personality beyond the usual chest-pounding gorilla, it was the magical stop-motion work of the man who had also moved

King Kong, Willis O'Brien, who was aided in this new effort by a fledgling named Ray Harryhausen. Willis would win a special-effects Oscar and Harryhausen would go on to fame as a monster animator that finally surpassed even O'Brien's. But all that movie history seems quaint now that Hollywood has computerized graphics, animaltronics, and other visual tricks up its sleeve for a *Mighty Joe Young* remake. All the technical improvements have turned Joe into the most lovable ape of the movies. As designed by Rick Baker, you want to hug the 15-foot-tall, 2,000-pound hirsute lug and give him big slurpy kisses—well, sort of. Yet screenwriters Mark Rosenthal and Lawrence Konner, working with the '49 version by Ruth Rose (wife of director Schoedsack), remembered that Joe should still have his wild, animalistic side. Which allows him to seem primitive and uncontrollable, even though we know he wouldn't harm a tsetse fly. And so a lumbering, thundering Joe is on the loose. Crashing (literally) a cocktail party, bellowing his way through the entrance to a carnival, crossing the busy Hollywood Freeway, climbing the front of Grauman's Chinese Theater, and hanging around the Hollywood sign. How did he get into the heart of Movieland? It all starts in Africa, where Joe has been tamed and raised by Charlize Theron, orphaned daughter of a Diane Fossey–like zoologist who was killed by poachers while studying gorillas in their natural habitat. Along comes zoologist Bill Paxton to save Joe from poachers and take him (and the beautiful Theron) to a California "conservancy." But the misunderstood gorilla is never safe for long, especially when a former poacher (Rade Sherbedgia), now selling animal body parts illegally, seeks revenge for the finger Joe bit off his hand when the ape was a wee 10-foot-tall baby. It's the bad guy who's responsible for Joe's pseudo-violent behavior, so you never stop rooting for the big ape. Another key to this film's success as a pleasing entertainment is director Ron Underwood, who paces it with plenty of action, comedy, and menace, just as he did with *Tremors*. Another plus is James Horner's African-oriented score. Others who contribute characterizations without getting too much in the way of the lightweight story are Lawrence Pressman, Naveen Andrews, David Paymer, Peter Firth, and Regina King. Gail Katz was executive producer. (Video/DVD: Disney)

MIGHTY MORPHIN POWER RANGERS: THE MOVIE (1995) ★★★ They might have made a fast cheapie to exploit the popular TV series, but Fox went all out to make this a movie, even if it is designed for the kid audience. So while the mentality of Arne Olsen's script is on the level of TV, the action is technically superior, using computerized animation to produce monsters and the flying hardware known as Zords. And the stunt choreographers stage some fine hand-to-hand fights in which the Power Rangers (teenagers who turn into fighting superheroes with the help of magical equipment) take on villain Ivan Ooze (Paul Freeman in purple makeup and costuming) and his assorted spider monsters and wisecracking minions. While there's little for the mind, there's plenty for the eye, including an opening skydiving sequence that's a real leap of faith. Directed with style by Bryan Spicer, *Power Rangers: The Movie* is a kick in the face. Karan Ashley, Johnny Yong Bosch, Steve Cardenas, Jason David Frank, Amy Jo Johnson, David Yost, Jason Narvy, Paul Schrier. (Video/Laser: Fox)

MIGHTY THUNDA, THE. See *King of the Congo.*

MIKEY (1991) ★★ Weak retread of *The Bad Seed* with Brian Bonsall as a ten-year-old murderer who diabolically slaughters his real parents (mom is electrocuted in the bathtub; dad is beaten to death with a baseball bat) and then is adopted by new parents who soon become new victims (mom, in a mundane moment, is electrocuted in the bathtub; dad, in a moment of brilliant inspiration, is blown to bits by a Molotov cocktail). Writer Jonathan Glassner tries to give Bonsall cute one-liners à la Freddy Kroeger but they fall as flat as the boy's victims, who die by arrow and other gruesome (but homicidally effective) weapons, such as a ball bearing to the forehead. Director Dennis Dimster-Dink blows it all low key, forgetting to give the movie any suspense or surprises. Josie Bissett, Lyman Ward, John Diehl, Ashley Lawrence, Mimi Craven. (Imperial)

MILLENNIUM (1989) ★★★ John Varley adapted his short story "Air Raid" into this feature that seems to be two separate movies welded together. It opens with a grim depiction of two airliners colliding and investigator Kris Kristofferson examining the wreckage. This portion is uncannily realistic. Suddenly Varley introduces time travelers from 1,000 years in the future, led by Cheryl Ladd. It is then the plot gets bogged down in an unconvincing love story, many scenes of which are repeated when Ladd messes with time, jumping from time zone to time zone. Seems that in the distant future mankind will be faced with the danger of becoming sterile, and must mate with people from the present day to procreate the race. And that's Ladd's job. Ultimately, the time-travel/Armageddon plot is too full of holes to take seriously and the picture crashes as grimly as those jetliners. Directed by Michael (*Logan's Run*) Anderson. Daniel J. Travanti, Robert Joy, Lloyd Bochner. (IVE) (Laser: Image)

MILLENNIUM (1996) ★★★ This pilot episode for a Chris Carter–created series for the Fox TV network was a followup to the success of "The

X-Files," and those who groove on Fox Mulder and Dana Scully adventures will appreciate much of this somber, dark portrait of an ex-FBI man (Lance Henriksen) with extrasensory powers that psychically link him to the hideous serial killers he pursues. The title of the series refers to a secret band of men like Henriksen who track down killers who are part of the coming Apocalypse. Much about the Millennium group and the murderers is purposely left unclear. Henriksen is a one-note actor on whom this series must rely, and how Carter develops his personality and paranoias will play a key role in the success or failure of this unusual show. Co-executive producer David Nutter directed the script by Carter. Megan Gallagher plays Henriksen's wife. Terry O'Quinn, Bill Smitrovich, Paul Dillon. (Fox)

MILPITAS MONSTER, THE (1975) ★½ After being the brunt of jokes by Steve Allen and Jack Benny, the Bay Area community of Milpitas, CA, pulled a joke on the public by producing a horror film. The town of 32,500 helped in the production, which took two years and cost $11,000 in 16mm. The titular titan is a creature with batlike wings and a gas-mask face, spawned in the embryo of pollution. "Milpy" rises from the ooze to wipe out a town drunk and ends up atop a TV transformer tower. Quite amateurish, from Robert L. Burrill's direction to Davie E. Boston's script to the acting of half of Milpitas. Ben Burtt, who went on to win an Oscar for his sound effects in *Star Wars*, contributed to the effects. Paul Frees narrates. And Milpitas lives! (United; VCI)

MIMIC (1997) ★★★½ Subtitle this *A Bug's Life of Horror*. It's one helluva thrill ride that follows the familiar formula of a handful of humans trapped in some hellish place with monsters/aliens/creatures/ghosts they must destroy in the blood-drenched process. Mira Sorvino plays a genetics engineer who takes termite and mantis DNA and mixes it into a "Judas Breed," a new six-legged species that can disguise itself as a cockroach and then kill all the cockroaches it can eat. This is necessary to stop a new disease that has stricken children in Manhattan. Set loose in the sewer systems of New York, the Judas Breed insects kill off the infected roaches and the disease is stopped. These new bugs have been engineered to die off soon, but there's a bug in the bug plan. The creatures mutate and become giant mantises and termites, with the ability to camouflage themselves as humans. (That is one nice touch that Matthew Robbins and director Guillermo del Toro throw into the mix of this horror/sci-fi shocker, which was inspired by a Donald A. Wollheim short story.) Not surprisingly, the set piece for the action becomes the subway system beneath Manhattan, where Sorvino and husband Jeremy Northam

lead the search to find the nest and destroy it. Don't think you are totally inured by now to dark tunnels, monsters that leap into frame, and gooey special effects. You will be startled by del Toro's direction and the intensity he brings to otherwise familiar genre clichés. There's graphic gore, several harrowing cliffhangers, narrow escapes, and subterranean atmosphere galore, with the monster design—by Rob Bottin and Tyruben Ellingson—seemingly all too real at times. Assisting in the search is Giancarlo Giannini (a simple shoeshine man looking for his lost son), Josh Brolin as the missing boy, F. Murray Abraham (as Sorvino's fellow experimenter in bug life), and subway security expert Charles S. Dutton (who goes through hell when he and the others are besieged in an abandoned subway car). (Video/DVD: Dimension)

MIND BENDERS, THE (1967). See *Five Million Years to Earth*.

MIND, BODY & SOUL (1992) ★★ A woman who witnesses a satanic ritual becomes the target for horrendous supernatural events. Directed by Rick Sloane. Wings Hauser, Ginger Lynn Allen, Jay Richardson, Tami Bakke, Jesse Kaye, Ken Hill. (Action International)

MINDFIELD (1989) ★★ In this Canadian production, an experiment with LSD to turn men into mindless murderers has left Michael Ironside living a nightmarish existence. Doctor Christopher Plummer is in on the plot. Directed by Jean-Claude (*Visiting Hours*) Lord. Lisa Langlois, Stefas Wodoslowsky, Sean McCann. (Magnum) (Laser: Image)

MIND GAMES (1979) ★★½ Mildly compelling psychological thriller told subtly, in the vein of *The Servant*. Lone traveler Maxwell Caulfield is befriended by vacationers Edward Albert, wife Shawn Weatherly and son Matt Norero, but manipulates each for devious purposes—corrupting the innocent youth, seducing the unhappy wife and making life miserable for angst-ridden Albert. The film has its most ironic moment when Albert reads the deranged hitchhiker's diary, which lucidly describes the family's psychological needs and hang-ups. But Kenneth Dorward's script is without enough depth or horror to make this worthy of a fan's attention. Directed by Bob Yari. (CBS/Fox)

MIND KILLER (1988) ★ Threadbare, sloppily produced video feature, with unpleasant graphics that are not backed up by a strong story or good acting. Joe McDonald is a nerdy librarian whom the girls ignore—until he finds an old manuscript that gives him the secret to controlling the will of others. But the one librarian (Shirley Ross) whom he would like to get his hands on is too smart for him. The script by Dave Sipos, Curtis Hannum and director Michael Krueger has the final twist of McDonald producing a creature within his exploding brain.

A real mind-numbing experience. Christopher Wade, Kevin Hart, Tom Henry. (Prism)

MIND OF MR. SOAMES, THE (1970) ★★★½ Amicus version of Charles Eric Maine's novel (adapted by John Hale and Edward Simpson) is a thoughtful psychological study of a young man in a coma since birth who, awakened by electrical stimulation, must be taught like a newborn child. Terence Stamp is excellent as the bewildered young man, Robert Vaughn has one of his finest roles as a sympathetic scientist, and Nigel Davenport is coldly clinical as the project boss who has no compassion. This maintains a high level of intelligence and avoids a contrived climax, leaving some problems unresolved. Sensitively directed by Alan Cooke.

MIND RIPPER. See *Wes Craven Presents Mind Ripper.*

MIND SNATCHERS, THE (1972) ★★★½ Should science tamper with those parts of the human mind that control our emotional levels and personality traits, in an effort to create happy people? Or do we need to be individuals, even if we are plagued by neuroses and other unstable traits? This literate film explores that issue by establishing a clandestine military laboratory in Germany, where doctor Joss Ackland inserts steel fibers into men's brains to improve their health and eliminate disobedient traits. Fine direction by Bernard Girard and excellent performances by two of the guinea pigs, Ronny Cox and Christopher Walken, keep Rony Whyte's screenplay (based on Dennis Reardon's play, *The Happiness Cage*) on a heightened edge, as does the presence of sinister army officer Ralph Meeker. Filmed in Denmark. Tom Aldredge, Marco St. John. (Congress; Prism; from Ace as *The Demon Within*)

MINDSWEEPERS, THE. See *The Clones.*

MIND TWISTER (1992) ★★ Minor, almost insignificant psychothriller from director Fred Olen Ray, in which sex therapist Gary Hudson and his perverted wife (Erika Nann) kill beautiful young women and photograph them for their personal tape collection. Sexy Suzanne Slater, working undercover for cops Telly Savalas and Richard Roundtree, poses as a troubled psychic to get the goods on the gang. Routine slasher-killer stuff, halfheartedly scripted by Mark Thomas McGee. Except for a passionate lesbian scene between Slater and Nann, this is an easy one to forget. Maria Ford, Angel Ashley, Nels Van Patten, Robert Quarry. (VCI)

MIND WARP. Alternate video version of *Grey Matter* (Academy).

MINDWARP (1990) ★★★½ The first of several horror movies produced by the Fangoria publishing empire, this post-holocaust actioner is a sci-fi *Alice in Mutantland*. It opens in Inworld, where Judy (Marta Alicia) is hooked up to Infinisynth, a "happiness system" that provides a pleasant dream-state for human survivors. But being a rebel, she's unhappy in her vegetating state and is granted permission by the Overseer (Angus Scrimm) to venture into Deadland, an area of the Outer World where Stover (Bruce Campbell, in an excellent action role) roves as a Mad Max wannabe hero, armed only with a crossbow. Alicia doesn't know the surface has been nuked and consists of an Ice Age-like terrain inhabited by cannibal mutants living in tunnels (and led by Scrimm in an alter ego role). When Campbell and the girl are taken prisoner, this entertaining sci-fier gets good and gory and is a barrel of fun if you're willing to take it as tongue-in-cheek, especially Scrimm's madness. The set design is unusually good for this genre. Well directed by Steve Barnett from a well-shaped Henry Dominick script. Elizabeth Kent, Mary Becker, Wendy Sandow. (Video/Laser: RCA/Columbia)

MINDWARP: AN INFINITY OF TERROR. See *Galaxy of Terror*

MINISTER'S MAGICIAN, THE. See *Harlequin.*

MIRACLE BEACH (1991) ★½ Not a single effects shot graces this time killer about a beautiful green-eyed genie (Ami Dolenz) sent by a heavenly assignment chief (Allen Garfield) to an L.A. beach to help a nerdy guy (Dean Cameron) find true love with Felicity Waterman at the same time he's throwing a beauty contest attended by big-busted babes. Pat Morita and Vincent Schiavelli are wasted in this grant-my-wish comedy directed by Skott Snider. Ample nudity (the T&A kind) is all there to keep one awake. Alexis Arquette, Brian Perry, Martin Mull. (Video/Laser: RCA/Columbia)

MIRACLE MILE (1988) ★★★ Offbeat cautionary tale (call it pre-Armageddon) that scores for mood and unpredictable plot. What would you do if you had 70 minutes to react to pending nuclear attack? That's the situation for musician Anthony Edwards who answers a phone outside Johnnie's Restaurant in L.A. and learns the horrible truth. This second feature from writer-director Steve (*Cherry 2000*) de Jarnatt is an intriguing study in mass hysteria that builds unrelentingly as Edwards plans an escape route. Be forewarned this is a downer, with no cop-out ending. Denise Crosby is exceptionally good as a stockbroker who represents the intellectual side of man in dealing with a life-and-death crisis. Compelling viewing. John Agar, Lou Hancock, Mykel T. Williams, Kelly Minter. (HBO) (Laser: Image)

MIRACLE RIDER, THE (1935) ★★ Cowboy star Tom Mix came out of semiretirement to make this, his final screen appearance. It's a lengthy 15-chapter serial composed mainly of standard Western action but with a slight sci-fi touch: a powerful explosive, dubbed X-94, is sought by both villain Zaroff (Charles Middleton, better known as Ming the Merciless in the *Flash Gordon* serials) and Mix, who portrays a special ranger. There are a few oddball flying contraptions thrown in. As directed by Armand Schaefer and B. Reeves Eason, *The Miracle Rider* has its moments of hard-riding and action, and the script by John Rathmell is sympathetic to the American Indian even though it portrays those Indians as rather backward and slow. Not a great serial, but one that's worth revisiting one more time. Joan Gale, Jason Robards, Edward Earle, George Chesebro. (Grapevine; Video Connection; VCI; Burbank)

MIRROR, MIRROR (1990) ★★ *Carrie* meets *The Gate* swept open by *Demon Wind*. So goes this compendium of clichés enhanced only by Rainbow Harvest as a shy teenager turned into a force of vengeful evil when she falls under the spell of a cursed mirror through which monsters pass to the earthly plane. Such pros as Karen Black (as a self-centered mother), William Sanderson (as a science teacher) and Yvonne De Carlo (as a furniture dealer) cannot salvage a movie as dreary as this. MTV director Marina Sargenti makes her feature debut, and while she does a creditable job, there's no freshness to this endless series of scenes you've seen before, and before, and before. Kristin Dattilo, Ricky Paul Goldin. (Academy) (Laser: Image)

MIRROR, MIRROR II: RAVEN DANCE (1992) ★★★ A sequel in name only, this features the haunted bureau and the mirror that "draws its power from innocent wishes of youth," but with new characters. Attractive Tracy Wells is a ballerina whose earthly goods are sought by simpering, spoiled sister Sally Kellerman and corrupt doctor Roddy McDowall. The oddball setting is a nunnery where Wells, recovering from a fall, dances dreamily through a wide-open room while the mirror wreaks new forms of evil, turning a nun blind and setting loose a raven that causes death for evil people. Kellerman has some good scenes, especially when she goes bonkers when the mirror sends her into a speeded-up aging process. This is a one-man tour de force for Jimmy Lifton, who wrote, produced, directed, and created the music score. Producer Virginia Perfili helped out with the minimal story. William Sanderson, Sarah Douglas, Veronica Cartwright, Lois Nettleton (the latter two as nuns). (Academy) (Laser: Image)

MIRROR OF DEATH (1987) ★ How can you take a movie seriously when one character says, "Who knows how to deal with evil spirits floating out of mirrors?" and another says, "Why don't we just look in the yellow pages!" What makes it worse: they do hire an exorcist through the phone book, who rides to the exorcism on a bike. This minimally developed tale of witchcraft and possession focuses on a battered wife who seeks revenge by creating a doppelgänger

that leaves her body and, in sexy outfits, kills off the men she picks up. Directed by Deryn Warren as *Dead of Night*, the film's initial TV title. Julie Merrill, Kuri Browne, John Reno, J. K. Dumont. (Video)

MISERY (1990) ★★★½ Rob Reiner's triumphant adaptation of Stephen King's best-seller with Kathy Bates winning an Oscar for her crazed Annie Wilks, any writer's ultimate nightmare of a fan gone mad. James Caan, in one of his best roles in years, brings numerous nuances to novelist Paul Sheldon, injured in a car accident during a snowstorm and cared for secretly by the infatuated Ms. Wilks—infatuated, that is, until her insanity takes over and he becomes her prisoner. The scene with the sledgehammer is guaranteed to evoke a scream, and to Reiner's credit is a most effective shock-violence sequence. One wishes to see more of Richard Farnsworth's homespun sheriff, Buster, but that is a minor flaw. Frances Sternhagen, Lauren Bacall, Graham Jarvis, J. T. Walsh. (Video/Laser: MCA)

MISS DEATH. See *The Diabolical Dr. Z.*

MISS DEATH AND DR. Z. See *The Diabolical Dr. Z.*

MISSILE BASE AT TANIAK (1953). Reedited TV version of the Republic serial *Canadian Mounties vs. Atomic Invaders.*

MISSILE MONSTERS (1951). Feature version of Republic's *Flying Disc Man from Mars.*

MISSING LINK (1989) ★½ Set "one million years ago," this oddity from producers Peter Guber and Jon Peters depicts an ape-man (*Australopithecus robustus*) wandering the African veldt, observing wild animals, finding his family slaughtered by lions, and wondering how he can put a stone ax to good use. There's very little in it that will appeal to fantasy fans. Peter Elliott plays the hairy guy, with makeup by Rick Baker. Written-directed-photographed by David and Carol Hughes. (MCA)

MISSION GALACTICA: THE CYLON ATTACK. TV version of the 1978 TV pilot for "Battlestar Galactica" (Video/Laser: MCA).

MISSION MARS (1968) ★ Laughable kiddie stuff with Darren McGavin and Nick Adams as hysterically incompetent astronauts on Mars I, the first manned probe to the Red Planet. Their ship looks like an inverted Campbell's soup can, the alien life form (called a Polarite) resembles Gumby and an E.T. sphere is a golf ball magnified. Directed by Nicholas Webster. (Unicorn)

MISSION STARDUST (1968) ★ Spacecraft from Earth is forced down on the Moon, where robots lead astronauts to an alien craft. Medical help is needed to overcome a disease. Spanish–Italian–West German effort is based on the Perry Rhodan book series. Directed by Primo Zeglio. Lang Jeffries, Essy Persson. Aka *Mortal Orbit, Operation Stardust* and *You Only Live Once.* (Rhino)

MISS MUERTE. See *The Diabolical Dr. Z.*
MISTRESSES OF DR. JEKYLL. See *Dr. Orloff's Monster.*
MODEL KILLER, THE. Video version of *The Hollywood Strangler Meets the Skid Row Slasher* (Regal).
MODEL MASSACRE. Video version of *Color Me Blood Red* (BFPI).
MOLE MEN VS. THE SON OF HERCULES (1962) ★ Mark Forest grunts and groans as Maciste, a musclebound he-man fighting through an underground city. All brawn and no brain in this Italian sword-and-sandal scandal directed by Antonio Leonviola. Moira Orfei, Paul Wynter, Gianna Garko. Aka *Maciste, Strongest Man in the World; Strongest Man in the World* and *Maciste and the Night Queen.* (Sinister/C; S/Weird)
MOLE PEOPLE, THE (1956) ★★★ John Agar leads a Tibetan expedition underground, where it encounters mutant human-moles. But the mole moles aren't the bad guys—they're dirt slaves to the Sumerians, a white race dwelling in a typical Hollywood Underground Lost City. This pulp adventure tale is made acceptable by good mole makeup and rubber suits. In a laughable prologue, Dr. Frank Baxter discusses the possibilities of life in the core of the Earth, which is as bogus as the plot by Laszlo Gorog. Dig it! Directed by Virgil Vogel. Cynthia Patrick, Hugh Beaumont, Alan Napier. (Video/Laser: MCA)
MOLTEN METEOR, THE. Original title for *The Blob* (1958).
MOM (1989) ★★ Dreary direct-to-video flop predicated on the idea that a sweet old mother turned into a flesh-eating monster makes an intriguing concept. Maybe so, but the guys who made *Flesh-Eating Mothers* did it better. This limps along in depicting serial-killer Brion James taking refuge in the home of sweet Jeanne Bates and turning her into a demon who looks for bums to murder and eat. Mom's son (Mark Thomas Miller) is a TV newscaster who figures out what's going on. Stella Stevens appears as an aging whore, dressed in an outrageous costume, and is the only relief from tedium. Directed-written without flair by Patrick Rand. Mary McDonough, Art Evans. (Video/Laser: RCA/Columbia)
MOM AND DAD SAVE THE WORLD (1991) ★★★ Imagine a blatant spoof of sci-fi serials of the '30s and you've got the basis for this parody in which a planet of "idiots" plots to blow up Earth with a Death Ray laser. Led by Lord Tod (Jon Lovitz) of the planet Spengo, the aliens transport an Earth couple (Jeffrey Jones and Teri Garr) to their world. How the witless Earthlings (Jones is a couch potato, Garr is the ultimate loving mother) outsmart the more witless aliens, with the help of a tribe of cave-dwelling natives who are the most witless of all, is the basis for the Chris Matheson–Ed Solomon script

(they also created *Bill & Ted*). Directed by Greg Beeman. Thalmus Rasulala, Tod's wise old sage, died after the film was finished. Kathy Ireland, Dwier Brown, Wallace Shawn, Eric Idle. (Video/Laser: HBO)
MOMMA'S BOY. See *Night Warning.*
MOMMY (1994) ★★½ Mystery writer Max Allan Collins raised the money for this psychological suspense thriller in his hometown of Muscatine, Iowa, and filmed it on location, bringing in a professional cast that included Jason Miller, Brinke Stevens, Majel Barrett, Sarah Jane Miller and Mickey Spillane (in a cameo as a tough-talking lawyer). However, it is Patty McCormack who steals this movie away with her chilling, disturbing performance as a homicidal mother. Her story is told through the eyes of her daughter (Rachel Lemieux)—an ironic twist since McCormack played Rhoda in *The Bad Seed* in the 1956 version. Collins avoids most of the clichés of this genre to carry his twisted yarn (originally called "Fear Itself" as a short story); if the film suffers, it is from slow pacing and lousy lighting. (Eagle Entertainment)
MONDO LUGOSI: A VAMPIRE'S SCRAPBOOK (19??) ★★½ Compilation of interviews with horror-film star Bela Lugosi and clips from his movies. (Rhino)
MONGREL (1983) ★ Its bite is worse than its bark—so conclude the men and women living in Aldo Ray's rural boardinghouse when, one by one, they are killed off by a "killer animal" heard roving the hallways at night. Filmed in Austin, Texas, this cheap horror flick is of little consequence. Writer-director Robert A. Burns found himself in the doghouse when it was finished. Terry Evans, Catherine Malloy, Mitch Pileggi. (Paragon)
MONITORS, THE (1969) ★★ Misguided satirical misfire, involving Chicago's Second City comedy troupe, in which benevolent humanoids called the Monitors take over an American city, but an underground movement called SCRAG threatens peaceful order. This adaptation of a Keith Laumer novel is played in a dumb, farcical manner that never engages the viewer and meanders all over the landscape. Myron J. Gold's script was directed by Jack Shea with mimimal production values and the good cast is swamped by the material, including Guy Stockwell, Susan Oliver, Larry Storch, Avery Schreiber, Keenan Wynn, Shepperd Strudwick and Sherry Jackson. Appearing in cameos are Alan Arkin, Stubby Kaye, Xavier Cugat and Jackie Vernon. Don't bother to monitor.
MONKEY BOY. Condensed video version from Prism of the 4-hour British TV-movie reedited to *Chimera.*
MONKEY BUSINESS (1952) ★★★★½ Hilarious comedy classic written (under the title *Be Your Age*) by Ben Hecht and I. A. L. Diamond

and directed by Howard Hawks. It's a screwball affair with Cary Grant, as the epitome of the Absentminded Professor, searching for a youth formula for industrialist Charles Coburn. Inadvertently, a chimpanzee mixes into the lab's drinking water chemicals that regress one's mental state to a puberty level. Grant is aptly aided by Ginger Rogers as his jealous wife (she also portrays a mischievous juvenile to hilarious effect) and Marilyn Monroe as a leggy secretary who amply and unabashedly displays a pair of Grant's latest creation, nonrun stockings. A delight of comedy and satire, one of the greats of the '50s. Hugh Marlowe, Robert Cornthwaite, Larry Keating, Douglas Spencer, George Winslow. (Video/Laser: CBS/Fox)

MONKEY PLANET. See *Planet of the Apes*.

MONKEY SHINES (1988) ★★★ With George Romero directing, one might assume this would be filled with horrible graphics—but such is not the case. And yet the film (scripted by Romero, from a novel by Michael Stewart) is an unpleasant experience, for it depicts a capuchin monkey as a bloodthirsty killer. Jason Beghe portrays a paraplegic trying to adjust to his situation when Melanie Parker brings him a well-trained monkey to serve as aide. But mad scientist John Pankow injects the monkey with a serum that turns him rabid. There's an unexplained psychic link between the creature and Beghe during the murders. Not for the psychologically squeamish. Joyce Van Patten, Christine Forrest, Stephen Root. Aka *Monkey Shines: An Experiment in Fear*. (Orion) (Laser: Image)

MONOLITH See *The Monolith Monsters*.

MONOLITH (1993) ★★★ Eyeballs that shoot off Great Balls of Fire belong to zombie men who are part of a covert government operation involving flying saucers and related "Blue Book" projects. What gives this rather tired idea an explosive shot in the butt are Bill Paxton and Lindsay Frost as cops always bickering with each other and John Hurt as a cold, unnerving heavy in charge of the secret operation. Stephen Lister's script keeps the pacing up with some nice action pieces, and uses Lou Gossett, Jr., to good effect in a small cop role. Directed by John (*Shadowchaser; Armed and Deadly*) Eyres with an eye for good camera angles and vigorous, believable fights. (Video/Laser: MCA)

MONOLITH MONSTERS, THE (1957) ★★★ A meteor, after crashing near a town in Death Valley, expands and grows when touched by water. Different pieces form into rocklike monsters that turn humans into solid stone. Grant (*Incredible Shrinking Man*) Williams and Lola Albright struggle to evacuate a town in danger of the titular entities. John Sherman directed the script by Robert Fresco and Norman Jolley, originally cranked out as *Monolith*. Les Tre-

mayne, William Schallert. Effects by Clifford Stine. (Fright; MCA) (Laser: MCA)

MONSTER (1975). See *The Devil Within Her*.

MONSTER (THE LEGEND THAT BECAME A TERROR) (1979). K-Tel's, Genesis's and Premiere's video versions of *The Toxic Monster*.

MONSTER/MONSTERS (1980). See *Humanoids from the Deep*.

MONSTER AND THE APE, THE (1945) ★★ Fifteen-chapter Columbia serial (directed by Howard Bretherton) in which a new robot is sought after by foreign agents. George Macready portrays the villain, Ernst, and Ralph Morgan is the inventor, Professor Arnold. Carole Mathews is the traditional girl for the cliffhangers. Robert Lowery is the U.S. agent who must face not only human foes but that monkey creature of the title. (Heavenly)

MONSTER AND THE GIRL, THE (1941) ★★ Vengeful criminal swears to knock off the scoundrels who framed him, is knocked off himself in the electric chair. His brain is transferred into an ape's skull and the ape begins the Simian Shamble, killing scoundrels. Nostalgic material of the '40s, directed by Stuart Heisler from a script by Stuart Anthony. George Zucco essays a mad scientist while Ellen Drew is the hapless heroine and Rod Cameron the square-jawed hero. Gerald Mohr, Paul Lukas, Onslow Stevens, Philip Terry. Aka *D.O.A.* and *The Avenging Brain*. (MCA)

MONSTER CLUB, THE (1981) ★★★½ Fun-filled British horror flick has bizarre elements: a conversation between Vincent Price (portraying a vampire) and John Carradine (portraying horror writer R. Chetwynd-Hayes); the Monster Club, a disco hangout for freaks and ghoulies dancing hard-rock musical numbers; and a trilogy of tales told by Price, based on Chetwynd-Hayes stories (and adapted to screen by Edward and Valerie Abraham). One concerns a monster called a "shadmock," whose silent whistle is fatal to mortals; the second features Donald Pleasence leading a band of vampire chasers who keep their stakes in violin cases; and the third is about a village of "humgoos," who put the whammy on movie director Stuart Whitman. Roy Ward Baker directed with tongue in his cheek. A must for buffs for its in-jokes. Richard Johnson, Britt Ekland, Simon Ward, Patrick Magee, Anthony Steel. (Thrillervideo) (Laser: Image)

MONSTER DOG (1985) ★★½ Rock star Vince Raven (played by rock star Alice Cooper) returns to his old family mansion to make a music video. Wild dogs surround the place, killing the sheriff and his deputy, while inside Raven raves about an old legend that his father was a werewolf who commanded the killer canine corps. There's nice atmosphere to this thriller that makes up for mediocre acting. Even Cooper comes off looking good, and Victoria Vera is a beautiful heroine. Written-directed by Clyde Anderson. (Trans World)

MONSTER FROM BENEATH THE SEA. Original title for *It Came from Beneath the Sea*.

MONSTER FROM GALAXY 27, THE. See *Night of the Blood Beast*.

MONSTER FROM MARS. See *Robot Monster*.

MONSTER FROM THE MOON. See *Robot Monster*.

MONSTER FROM THE OCEAN FLOOR (1954) ★★ One of the very first films from Roger Corman in which we don't see the titular monstrosity until the climax. Showing it any sooner (octopus with a giant eye in the center of its head) would have destroyed the minimal mood and suspense. The setting is the coast of Mexico where a village is being terrorized by the—dare we say it?—Devil Fish! The worst aspect of this E.C. (Early Corman) film is the dubbing—the voices are clearly in an echo chamber. The cast of unknowns (Stuart Wade, Dick Pinner and Anne Kimball) remained unknowns. And whatever happened to that oddly named director, Wyott Ordung? And who was William Danch, who, according to Hollywood legend, cranked out the script in one night? Aka *It Stalked the Ocean Floor* and *Monster Maker*. (Vidmark)

MONSTER FROM THE SURF. See *The Beach Girls and the Monster*.

MONSTER FROM THE UNKNOWN WORLD. See *Atlas Against the Cyclops*.

MONSTER HIGH (1988) ★★ A certain Mr. Armageddon from another world lands on Earth in pursuit of two goofballs who stole an explosive device and are threatening to blow up the Green Planet. Sophomoric mentality mars this feeble attempt at parody. Directed by Rudiger Poe. David Marriott, Dean Iandoli, Diana Frank, Robert M. Lind, Sean Haines. (Video/Laser: RCA/Columbia)

MONSTER HUNTER. (1982) ★★ This bloodthirsty Italian sequel to *The Grim Reaper* (known as *Anthropophagus II* and *Absurd* in Europe) was written by John Cart and marketed in America with the name Peter Newton as director. He's really Aristide Massaccesi (aka Joe D'Amato) and this is purely Italian spaghetti dripping with blood. George Eastman is back as the cannibalistic monster with superhuman strength who is chased by priest Edmund Purdom. Annie Belle, Ian Danby. Meanwhile, Eastman's real name is Luigi Montefiore. (Lightning; Wizard)

MONSTER IN THE CLOSET (1986) ★★ Outright parody of the monster movies of the '50s. In this case it's an E.T. beast with gaping mouth that shambles through Chestnut Hills, CA, murdering people in their closets, places from which the creature draws unexplained energy. ("Destroy your closets," one of the characters pleads.) Donald Grant as a nerdy newspaperman is aided by Claude Akins as the sheriff who thinks the monster is a giant snake, Howard Duff as a priest who feels all beings are God's children, Henry Gibson as a scientist who wants to study the thing rather than kill it, Donald Moffat as a crazy Army general, Jesse White as a cranky news editor, Stella Stevens as a woman named Crane taking a shower, Paul Walker as a boy genius nicknamed "the Professor," and Denise DuBarry as the heroine. Writer-director Bob Dahlin allows you to participate in the satire without being slammed over the head. (Lorimar) (Laser: Japanese)

MONSTER IN THE NIGHT. See *Monster on the Campus*.

MONSTER MAKER. See *Monster from the Ocean Floor*.

MONSTER MEETS THE GORILLA, THE. See *Bela Lugosi Meets a Brooklyn Gorilla*.

MONSTER OF LONDON CITY, THE (1964) ★★★ Well-produced West German psycho-thriller whodunit based on an Edgar Wallace novel and set in modern London, where the "New Jack the Ripper" stalks prostitutes in the foggy streets. A Ripper play is being performed at an Edgar Allan Poe theater and it appears its producer could be the killer. Belongs to the "clutching hand" school of horror, with touches of mild nudity. Directed by Edwin Zbonek from a Robert Stemmle script. Hansjorg Felmy, Marianne Koch, Hans Nielsen. (Sinister/C; S/Weird; Filmfax)

MONSTER OF MONSTERS—GHIDORAH. See *Ghidrah, the Three-Headed Monster*.

MONSTER OF PIEDRAS BLANCAS, THE (1959) ★ A thing from the sea resembling a "Black Lagoon" reject hangs out near a lighthouse. The lighthouse keeper puts food out for the visiting thing. That's when a series of murders occurs. Fans are still laughing their heads off at this mess directed by Irvin Berwick. Les Tremayne, John Harmon, Jeanne Carmem, Don Sullivan. (Video Dimensions; Republic; Vidmark)

MONSTER OF TERROR. See *Die, Monster, Die!*

MONSTER OF THE MARSHES. One of Ed Wood, Jr.'s early titles for *Bride of the Monster*.

MONSTER OF THE WAX MUSEUM. See *Nightmare in Wax* (Beware waxy build-up!).

MONSTER ON THE CAMPUS (1958) ★★ Director Jack Arnold flunked out on this Neanderthal man thriller for Universal-International, falling below standards he established in *Creature from the Black Lagoon* and *It Came from Outer Space*. The blood from a prehistoric fish is used by college professor Arthur Franz to concoct a coelacanth serum that creates a mutant dragonfly and dog. When Franz cuts himself on the fish, he reverts to primeval barbarism and goes on a rampage. Script by David Duncan gets a C-minus. Eddie Parker, Whit Bissell, Joanna Moore, Troy Donahue. Aka *Monster in the Night* and *Stranger on the Campus.* (Video/Laser: MCA)

MONSTER ON THE HILL. See *Meteor Monster.*

MONSTERS ARE LOOSE, THE. See *The Thrill Killers.*

MONSTERS FROM AN UNKNOWN PLANET. See *Terror of Mechagodzilla.*

MONSTERS FROM THE MOON. See *Robot Monster.*

MONSTER SHARK. See *Devilfish.*

MONSTERS INVADE EXPO '70. See *Gamera vs. Monster X.*

MONSTERS OF FRANKENSTEIN. See *Frankenstein's Castle of Freaks.*

MONSTERS OF THE NIGHT. See *The Navy vs. the Night Monsters.*

MONSTER SQUAD, THE (1987) ★★★½ A cute idea nicely executed: Count Dracula rises from his tomb to gather the Mummy, the Frankenstein Monster and the Gillman to go after a magical amulet that will give them power to control the world. The only thing blocking their way is a group of kids—the Monster Squad! Director Fred (*Night of the Creeps*) Dekker has fashioned a gothic horror comedy with cowriter Shane Black that is amusing and quaint, lambasting viewers with special effects. While it's derivative, Dekker pulls it off with charm and style. Duncan Regehr portrays Dracula in a hammy style, while Tom Noonan is a benevolent Frankenstein creature who grows on you. And the kids are great: Andre Gower, Robby Kiger, Brent Chalem, Ryan Lambert, Ashley Bank. Stephen Macht does what he can with the thankless role of a disbelieving cop. Effects by Stan Winston and Richard Edlund. (Vestron) (Laser: Image)

MONSTER THAT CHALLENGED THE WORLD, THE (1957) ★★ Uninspired formula "giant monster created by radiation" nonthriller. This time the monstrosity is a giant caterpillar (would you believe a mutant mollusk?) rising from the depths to terrorize Tim Holt, Audrey Dalton and Hans Conried. Or is Hans Conried terrorizing us? Poorly done, from the effects to Arnold Laven's direction to Pat Fielder's script. Milton Parsons, Barbara Darrow, Jody McCrea, Casey Adams. (Fright; MGM) (Laser: MGM/UA)

MONSTER VARAN, THE. See *Varan the Unbelievable.*

MONSTER X. See *Godzilla vs. Monster Zero.*

MONSTER YONGKARI. See *Yongary, Monster from the Deep.*

MONSTER ZERO. See *Godzilla vs. Monster Zero.*

MONSTROSITY. Video version of *The Atomic Brain.*

MOON 44 (1990) ★★★½ Expensive adventure in the vein of *Star Wars* is set in 2038, when galactic mining colonies are controlled by corporations. Internal affairs agent Michael Pare is sent by company president Roscoe Lee Browne to Moon 44 in the Outer Zone to find out why shuttlecraft are disappearing. Action centers around uncovering company turncoats and fighting off a robot-controlled spaceship. Script by producer Dean Heyde and director Roland Emmerich for this German production is weak but the set designs are realistic. Lisa Eichhorn plays the love interest and Malcolm McDowell is commander of the mining station. Brian Thompson, Dean Devlin, Stephen Geoffreys. (Live) (Laser: Image)

MOON IN SCORPIO (1987) ★★ Psycho killer whodunit in which 3 couples embark on a Pacific voyage aboard a yacht; one of the passengers is a murderer who first sticks a butcher knife into the victim's stomach, then cuts his or her throat with a multibladed spear-gun. Robert S. Aiken's script attempts to limn the characters—three of whom are Vietnam War buddies—but fails to provide motivation for the killings. Best sequence has John Phillip Law struggling in the water with a half-rotted corpse. Now that's a macabre image. Otherwise, cinematographer-director Gary Graver treats it without much style, and Britt Ekland seems uncomfortable in this genre. Fred Olen Ray coproduced this direct-to-video release. William Smith, Louis Dan Bergen, April Wayne, Robert Quarry, Jillian Resner. (Trans World)

MOONRAKER (1979) ★★★★ Eleventh James Bond adventure, depicting 007's attempt to stop master villain Drax (Michael Lonsdale) from starting a totalitarian colony in space. There's an excellent space station battle, a gondola chase through Venice, motorboat action, ample fistfights and sexual encounters of the closest kind. Richard Kiel repeats his Jaws role. One of the more fun-to-watch Bonds, although Roger Moore walks indifferently through it all. Lois Chiles costars as Mary Goodhead. Directed by Lewis Gilbert, scripted by Christopher Wood. Brian Keith, Bernard Lee. (Video/Laser: CBS/Fox; MGM/UA).

MOONSHINE MOUNTAIN (1967) ★½ Undistilled Herschell Gordon Lewis in which an ape killer stands vigilance over an infamous Kentucky still, knocking off dirty revenooers who chance along. Chuck Scott, Adam Sorg, Jeffrey Allen, Bonnie Hinson. Aka *White Trash on Moonshine Mountain.* Lewis directed the script by Charles Glore. (Sinister/C)

MOONTRAP (1988) ★★ Hardware sci-fi actioner, directed by Robert Dyke, involving a moon-landing expedition that finds a civilization of mechanical robots with murderous intent. The astronauts also find a lone woman alien and this provides for a romance that can only be described as feeble. The Tex Ragsdale script isn't much, and the cast (headed by Walter Koenig of "Star Trek" fame) isn't exceptional, but the special effects provide a few thrilling moments in what amounts to a mild diversion. Unfortunately, exposition is never provided for the 14,000-year-old race of machines or how its technology was developed. Bruce Campbell, Leigh Lombardi, Robert Kurcz, Reavis Graham. (Shapiro Glickenhaus; Movies Unlimited) (Laser: Image)

MORNING TERROR. See *Time Troopers.*

MORONS FROM OUTER SPACE (1985) ★★★ Witty British spoof of sci-fi movies and the British classes in which a crew of hapless humanoid aliens bumbles to Earth, crash-landing on a freeway in a hysterically funny sequence. Pompous leaders and the media assume these maladroit fools are superintelligent and make efforts to display them to the world as superiors. Directed by Michael Hodges, scripted by Mel Smith and Griff Rhys Jones, a comedy team portraying the aliens Bernard and Graham Sweetley. James B. Sikking, Dinsdale Landen, Joanna Pearce. (Cannon; HBO)

MORTAL FEAR (1994) ★★½ If you've seen *Coma* and other medical horror-suspense thrillers, this adaptation of Robin Cook's novel will prove to be a predictable, rather tedious lady-doctor-in-danger story. It mixes in a little genetic, molecular biological, controlling-diseases science fiction to make it mildly intriguing, but even those themes never quite pay off. Nor does the TV-movie's attempt to inject an erotic, sensual element seem compatible with the tale. Anyway, doctor Joanna Kerns is baffled when patients receiving care in her big-city hospital begin to age suddenly and die from heart attack–style deaths. It has something to do with growth hormones, but even with pseudoscience to give it a shot in the arm, *Mortal Fear* is empty of many scares as Kerns, troubled over the recent accidental death of her husband, copes with personal problems and deals with investigating cop Max Gail and hospital honcho Gregory Harrison. Director Larry Shaw nods to the film's horror-movie antecedents by casting Robert Englund as a research specialist, and there are unusual scenes in a strip café on the seedy side of the city. Adaptation by Rob Gilmer and Roger Young. Tobin Bell, Katherine Lanasa, Judith Chapman, Rebecca Schull.

MORTAL KOMBAT (1995) ★★★ If there is any good reason to see this film version of the popular video game, it is to savor the wily performance of Christopher Lambert as the God of Electricity, Rayden, who comes out of his cloud to help a small band of Earthling warriors (an egotistical Hollywood actor, a young Asian grieving over his brother's death, a black with self-doubts, etc.) "chosen" by demon sorcerer Shang Tsung (Cary-Hiroyuki Tagawa) to fight his bad guys to see who will rule the universe. Nothing like having the cosmos on the betting table to beef up interest . . . but unless you're a terrific fan of the martial arts vidgame, *Mortal Kombat* isn't much more than a wearisome series of whomp and chop suey nonsense with special effects, morphing and a noisy sound track of grunts and groans. Many elements of Kevin Droney's script will have you groaning along with the wrestlers and strong-arm types (often in Asian warrior garb). Although director Paul Anderson has good choreographers and stuntmen to help him out, there isn't much believability he can inject into the characters, and this becomes simply an excuse for violence. So see it just to groove on Lambert's performance. Robin Shou, Linden Ashby, Bridgette Wilson, Talisa Soto, Trevor Goddard. (Video/Laser: New Line)

MORTAL KOMBAT: THE JOURNEY BEGINS (1995) ★★½ A direct-to-video animated feature version of the arcade computer game featuring all the usual warriors in "motion capture" and "3-D computer animation." This cassette also contains "The Making of Mortal Kombat the Movie." (Turner/New Line)

MORTAL ORBIT. See *Mission Stardust.*

MORTAL SINS (1990) ★★ Psycho-killer thriller with religious overtones when a TV evangelist of the Divine Church of the People is caught up in a series of murders that implicate him in sinful doings. Brian Benben, Debrah Farentino, Anthony LaPaglia. Directed by Yuri Sivo. (Academy; Fox) (Laser: Image)

MORTAL SINS (1992) ★★½ A serial killer who gives his female victims the last rites as they are dying confesses to Christopher Reeve in the St. Mary's confessional one day, and Reeve must hold to the Catholic Church's edict that this information is privileged. The moral issues are about all this TV-movie has going for it. Director Bradford May tries to keep it moving by allowing Reeve to be determined, likable, confused all in one satisfying whole. Roxann Biggs, Francis Guinan, Weston McMillan, Philip R. Allen, Lisa Vultaggio. (Video/Laser: Fox)

MORTUARY (1981) ★★ All of us will have our day with the mortician (or cremator) sooner than we hope, so why watch a madman mortician thrust blunt instruments into bodies and tube out their blood? A wretched excuse for a movie from writer-producer-director Howard Avedis, with Christopher George as an uptight mortician. But is he or his morbid son (Bill Paxton) the caped, pasty-faced killer who stalks Lynda Day George with a skewering device? It's a moot point—you'll only want to divert your eyes when the embalming techniques are dragged out in their bloody horrification. And you'll cringe as a still-living body (Mary

McDonough's) is about to be skewered alive and the killer cackles, "This way, heh heh, we'll be together forever." Morbid City with Paul Smith helping out. (Vestron)

MORTUARY ACADEMY (1988) ★★½ Grimm Mortuary and Academy is inherited by Paul Bartel and Mary Woronov and they set out to reanimate a dead heavy-metal band in order for the group to perform one last gig to save the funeral home. Directed by Michael Schroeder. Perry Lang, Tracey Walter, Christopher Atkins, Lynn Danielson, Cesar Romero. (RCA/Columbia) (Laser: Criterion)

MOSQUITO. See *Bloodlust* (1976).

MOST DANGEROUS GAME, THE (1932) ★★★½ Richard Connell's story was perfect for producers Ernest Schoedsack and Merian C. Cooper, who were themselves adventurers and must have felt rapport with great white hunter Rainsford (Joel McCrea) and evil hunter Count Zaroff (Leslie Banks). In its day this was hard-hitting and explicit (and originally entitled *The Hounds of Zaroff*) but time has blunted its undercurrents of perverted sex and made apparent its cinematic crudities. Still, one can sense the genius of Schoedsack (who codirected with Irving Pichel) and Cooper in depicting a madman and how he hunts people for the greatest thrill of all, the human trophy. Remade as *A Game of Death, Run for the Sun* and *Bloodlust*. Robert Armstrong, Fay Wray. (Cable; Sinister/C; Media; Kartes)

MOTEL HELL (1980) ★★★★ Outrageous black comedy–horror film that will make you laugh in spite of your good taste. Rory Calhoun is a good ol' country boy operating the roadside Motel Hello (the *O* burned out on the neon sign) and a sausage-packing plant next door. Seems Farmer Smith and his sister have decided smoked people're better'n smoked pig, so to fatten 'em up they bury their still-living human guinea pigs up to their necks in a field. (Occasionally Rory, bein' a humane sorta guy, goes out there and snaps their necks.) Calhoun's nonchalance, Kevin Connor's witty direction and the script by Robert and Steven-Charles Jaffe make this in-bad-taste film palatable, right up to the bloody climax featuring a duel with chainsaws and a tied-down heroine heading toward a buzz saw. Wolfman Jack, Dick Curtis, Paul Linke, Nancy Parsons. (Video/Laser: MGM/UA)

MOTHER RILEY IN DRACULA'S DESIRE. See *My Son, the Vampire.*

MOTHER RILEY MEETS THE VAMPIRE. See *My Son, the Vampire.*

MOTHER RILEY RUNS RIOT. See *My Son, the Vampire.*

MOTHER'S BOYS (1993) ★★★½ Not since *The Bad Seed* has there been a story of genetic evil as skillfully woven, and as bloodcurdling,

as this wicked tale about a sociopath (Jamie Lee Curtis in a tour de force performance). Having earlier deserted hubbie Peter Gallagher and his three children, Curtis wants her family back, but Gallagher has fallen in love with the decent Joanne Whalley-Kilmer. Here's where the Barry Schneider–Richard Hawley script gets good: Curtis brainwashes her older son (Luke Edwards) to plot against the family, and their union results in two portraits of evil working in delicious if disturbing harmony. (There's a third portrait of evil involving Curtis's mother, played by Vanessa Redgrave.) The ending gets a little contrived, but the payoff has an exciting cliffhanger. Directed by Yves Simoneau, *Mother's Boys* captures Curtis as one evil mom from Hell as she vents her fury on Whalley-Kilmer. Joss Ackland, Paul Guilfoyle. (Video/Laser: Buena Vista/Miramax)

MOTHER'S DAY (1980) ★★ Offshoot of *The Texas Chainsaw Massacre*—macabre humor mixed with bloody, excruciatingly painful attacks on women. Mother (Rose Ross, the epitome of matriarchal love) is training her perverted backwoods sons in the art of attack and rape. Holden McGuire and Billy Ray McQuade are the slobbering oafs who eat their breakfast from swill buckets. The demented lads have their fun with three campers. How two turn against the boys makes for a hair-raising climax that involves a can of Drano and a TV set as murder weapons. Oh, almost forgot the electric carving knife. You'll cheer the girls in spite of yourself. Nancy Hendrickson, Deborah Luce and Tiana Pierce turn in good performances. Produced-written-directed by Charles Kaufman. (Media; Video Treasures)

MOTHRA (1962) ★★½ Two Asian girls called the Peanut Sisters, each 6 inches high, help a giant caterpillar hatch from its egg. When the girls are kidnapped by a contemporary P. T. Barnum, Mothra goes wild, destroying Tokyo Tower and spinning a cocoon. The usual massive destruction results as it rescues the helpless girlettes. Mothra is not a man in a rubber suit but a mock-up controlled by wires. Directed by Inoshiro Honda, with effects by his pal Eiji Tsuburaya. Frankie Sakai, Hiroshi Koizumi, Ken Uehara. (RCA/Columbia; Goodtimes) (Laser: Japanese)

MOTHRA VS. GODZILLA. See *Godzilla vs. Mothra.*

MOUNTAIN OF CANNIBAL GODS. See *Slave of the Cannibal God.*

MOUNTAINTOP MOTEL MASSACRE (1983) ★ Taking her cue from Norman Bates about motel management, proprietor Anna Chappell kills her daughter in a fit of rage, then attacks unsuspecting roomers (black carpenter, drunken preacherman, newlyweds, two bimbos and an ad man) with a sickle or throws bugs and snakes on their sleeping bodies. Utterly bad gore effects. Guests check in but don't check out in this sleazy slasher flick poorly shot in Louisiana. Directed by Jim McCullough, Bill Thurman, Will Mitchel. (New World)

MOUSE THAT ROARED, THE (1959) ★★★★ It's the audience that roared—that's how this British satire comedy (conceived as *The Day New York Was Invaded*) was received around the world. In the fictional principality of Grand Fenwick the grand duchess declares war on the U.S. (solely for rehabilitation funds). An attack expedition sets out for America and becomes embroiled in slapstick with the deadly Q-bomb. Peter Sellers plays three roles (the prime minister, a soldier in arms and the grand duchess) and is ably assisted by Jean Seberg, daughter of the bomb's creator. Directed by Jack (*The Creature from the Black Lagoon*) Arnold. The screamingly funny screenplay was by Stanley Mann and Roger MacDougall. The sequel was *Mouse on the Moon*. Leo McKern, William Hartnell. (RCA/Columbia)

MOVINI'S VENOM. See *Night of the Cobra Woman*.

MR. CORBETT'S GHOST (1990) ★★ John Huston made his last on-camera appearance in this TV-movie directed by his son Danny Huston. It's your traditional deal-with-the-Devil plot and it costars Burgess Meredith, Paul Scofield and Mark Farmer. (Monterey; Kartes)

MR. DESTINY (1990) ★★★½ Entertaining variation on *It's a Wonderful Life*, sublimely directed by James Orr, who collaborated on the heartfelt script with Jim Cruikshank. James Belushi portrays an unhappy executive with a baseball bat manufacturing company who wishes things could have gone better . . . and presto! up pops Michael Caine as the embodiment of destiny. Belushi is projected into a parallel universe where he now has the best of everything, but quickly learns that the best can be superficial and that he has lost more than he has gained. This parable is delightfully developed with a subtle sense of humor and with Caine in peak form in an effective if limited role. This is one fantasy the whole family can enjoy. Linda Hamilton, Jon Lovitz, Hart Bochner, Bill McCutcheon, Rene Russo, Maury Chaykin. (Video/Laser: Touchstone)

MR. FROST (1990) ★★★ Intellectually fascinating study of good vs. evil and the ironic corruption of good in order to fight evil. This French-British production stars Jeff Goldblum as an incarnation of the Devil—or so he claims when he's arrested for 24 heinous murders he confesses to. Psychiatrist Kathy Baker thinks she's dealing with a serial killer until others around her are cursed by Mr. Frost and arresting-cop Alan Bates convinces her of the man's true identity. The war of nerves and wits

between Goldblum and Baker, similar to that between Jodie Foster and Anthony Hopkins in *Silence of the Lambs*, becomes the core of this unusually thoughtful study of man and his ambiguously evil ways. Directed by Phillipe Setbon, who cowrote with Brad Lynch. Roland Giraud, Jean-Pierre Cassel, Daniel Gelin. (Sony) (Laser: Image)

MR. JOSEPH YOUNG OF AFRICA. See *Mighty Joe Young*.

MR. SARDONICUS (1961) ★★★½ Enjoyable gimmick film from William Castle, in which the audience is given the opportunity to decree the villain's fate during the closing minutes. While critics could argue that this impeded the film's pacing, it's a historic moment in the Castle canon that, unfortunately, has been dropped from TV prints. This ironic, perverse horror story (scripted by Ray Russell, from his own short story) is about a Transylvanian count with a problem: his face has frozen into a hideous smile and he must wear a mask. Oscar Homolka is the one-eyed, sadistic Krull. Several cuties pass through, for Sardonicus is obsessed by beauty, the thing he cannot have. Offbeat. Ronald Lewis, Guy Rolfe, Audrey Dalton, Erika Peters, Lorna Hanson. Aka *Sardonicus*.

MR. SCIENCE FICTION'S FANTASTIC UNIVERSE (1988) ★★ A guided tour through the home/museum of Forrest J. Ackerman. Artwork, magazines, books, masks, props and everything else this prominent figurehead in the world of science-fiction has amassed during this career as a gadfly for fantasy. (VC)

MR. WRONG. See *Dark of the Night*.

MS. .45 (1980) ★★★½ Disturbing avant-garde exploitation film made in Manhattan is fascinating in its surrealistic depiction of an "angel of vengeance." Zoe Tamerlis is a mute Garment District worker brutally raped twice in the same day. She kills her second attacker, cuts up his body and stores the pieces in her fridge. With the dead rapist's .45, she is turned into a cold-blooded murderess, her targets any men she meets on the street. It's not so much a revenge movie as the portrait of a woman driven insane by life's pressures. Zoe is coolly beautiful and frightening, conveying the madness of Nicholas St. John's script. Abel Ferrara has a real sense of stylized direction, ending on a ritualistic touch of symbolism as Zoe, dressed as a nun at a masquerade party, becomes a black image of Death. Also known as *Angel of Vengeance*, this is a knockout, gritty movie, unpleasant but enthralling. Steve Singer, Jack Thibeau, Peter Yellen. (Fries; IVE)

MUCH ADO ABOUT MURDER. See *Theater of Blood*.

MULTIPLICITY (1996) ★★★½ This comedy variation on Ray Bradbury's short story "Marionettes Inc." (man gets cloned so his double can help to make his life happier) is a tour de force for Michael Keaton, who plays four variations of the same character, each emerging with a distinct personality. He portrays an overworked construction worker who gets cloned by Harry Yulin (a scientist who disappears once the first duplicate is made) so he can have more time for wife Andie MacDowall and kids. But in this morality tale (scripted by Mary Hale, Lowell Ganz, Babaloo Mandel, and Chris Miller, from a story accredited to Miller), Keaton comes to learn he's not in control of his other selves, who entangle his life far beyond its former complications. The film is sublimely funny until sex rears its beautiful head (MacDowall gets horny one night and mistaken identity prevails) and the fourth clone turns out to be an idiot à la Jerry Lewis (each copy of a copy, you see, is slightly more inferior). Then it turns riotously funny. Director Harold Ramis directs the silliness in such a clever way that one accepts Keaton's topsy-turvy world. Richard Masur, Eugene Levy, Ann Cusack, John de Lancie. (Video/DVD: Columbia TriStar)

MUMMY, THE (1932) ★★★★ This Universal horror feature (written by John L. Balderston) inspired four sequels and numerous imitations, but this has best withstood the Egyptian sands of time. It holds up thanks to cinematographer Karl Freund, making his directorial debut. Freund often relied on the unseen to convey horror, and this approach has assured Stanley Bergerman's production an immortality of its own. Boris Karloff, in Jack Pierce's superb makeup, portrays Im-Ho-Tep, a 3,700-year-old high priest of Egypt resurrected by an archeological expedition. Disguising himself in yet another kind of Pierce makeup, wizened Karloff walks through modern Egypt carrying the Scroll of Thoth in an effort to find his long-dead love, reincarnated in the modern body of Zita Johann. Edward Van Sloan, David Manners, Noble Johnson, Bramwell Fletcher. Aka *King of the Dead, Cagliostro* and *Im-Ho-Tep*. The sequels were *The Mummy's Hand, The Mummy's Tomb, The Mummy's Ghost* and *The Mummy's Curse*. (Video/Laser: MCA)

MUMMY, THE (1959) ★★★½ Unlike many Universal *Mummy* sequels of the '40s, in which Kharis shambled around pathetically, this Hammer version (original title: *Terror of the Mummy*) captures the murderous ferocity of the gauze-enwrapped high priest as he stomps across foggy 19th-century England, seeking the reincarnation of a princess related to archeologist Peter Cushing, the man who desecrated Kharis's tomb. It's Christoper Lee in the makeup of Roy Ashton, and he's wonderfully unstoppable. The scene of Lee rising from a bog is especially striking. Directed by Terence Fisher, written by Jimmy Sangster. Yvonne Fur-

neaux, Eddie Byrne, Felix Aylmer, George Pastell, Michael Ripper. (Video/Laser: Warner Bros.)

MUMMY, THE (1999) ★★★★ Rarely does a successful effects-laden horror extravaganza also have blazing action, larger-than-life characters, and a sense of humor. Thanks to the tongue-in-cheek attitude of writer-director Stephen Sommers, who was assisted in story by Lloyd Fonvielle, Kevin Jarre, and John L. Balderston (the latter wrote the 1933 Boris Karloff classic from which Sommers takes his inspiration), *The Mummy* provides one helluva fun roller-coaster ride through the pyramid district of Egypt. It's a cross between Indiana Jones, H. Rider Haggard, and Hammer mummy flicks. So what if it's ultimately mindless sound and fury? It's a trip and a half to the Nile, background music by Jerry Goldsmith, and that's what counts. Add to that an excellent production design by Allan Cameron (dig that crazy reddish desert and all those pastels) and dazzling camerawork and lighting by Adrian Bittle and you've got a rollicking camel-hawing experience, even if some of the sights along the sandy pathway are grotesque and ugly. Spirit, and that's meant as a term of enthusiasm, is everything as we open in 1290 B.C. in Hamunapra, "the city of the dead," where pharoahs are mummified. Being mummified at this very moment are Princess Anck-su-Namun (Patricia Velazquez) and her murderous lover Imhotep (Arnold Vosloo), with a curse placed on anyone who should dare desecrate their burial sites. Industrial Light & Magic's special effects set the note for a whirlwind of effects to come. Cut to 1923 as French legionnaire Brendan Fraser survives an Arab attack and finds himself in the ruins of Hamunapra, where thousands of beetles consume human bodies alive, a pharoah's face forms in the sand, and other Egyptology horrors abound. Three years later Fraser's still alive but a prisoner in Cairo, where he is befriended by perky, gorgeous Rachel Weisz and her goofy British brother John Hannah. They set out to find the treasure of Hamunapra, encountering a band of hapless adventurers (including Corey Johnson), a cowardly but larcenous Egyptian guide (Kevin O'Connor, who provides the film with its comedy relief) and a guardian of the city (Oded Fehr) sworn to protect the world from the ten curses of the Pharoahs. More comedy relief is thrown in by Bernard Fox as Winston, a stiff upper-lip Brit with a biplane. An army of Egyptian soldiers rising up as corpses is reminiscent of the skeleton army in *Jason and the Argonauts*. In fact, Sommers provides a lot of homage, with a major nod going to Indiana Jones. Also to John Woo, what with the way Fraser is always firing away at human targets with two revolvers. *The Mummy* is what makes going to the movies a fun and flippant pastime. (Video/DVD: Universal)

MUMMY AND THE CURSE OF THE JACKALS, THE (1969) ★ Archeologist Anthony Eisley showing a 4,000-year-old Egyptian princess how to hook up a modern bra is about as good as it gets in this amateurish attempt to recapture the spirit of Universal's *Mummy* series. The injection of John Carradine as an Egyptologist to explain how the curse works only underscores how pathetic this monsterthon is. And the scenes of a werewolf (described also as a "jackal man") fighting with a mummy in a casino in downtown Las Vegas is hilariously incompetent, causing any incredulous viewer to wonder just what director Oliver Drake had in mind—it couldn't have been an exciting movie. (Drake was also an associate producer on *The Mummy's Curse*, unless the name is being used here as a pseudonym.) Robert Allen Browne, Marlita Pons, Maurine Dawson, Saul Goldsmith. (Academy)

MUMMY'S CURSE, THE (1945) ★★★ The last of Universal's four "Kharis the Mummy" films, which had so deteriorated that the hulking high-priest-in-bandages was a laughing, not a screaming, matter. The Bernard Schubert–Dwight V. Babcock–Leon Abrams script picks up where *The Mummy's Ghost* left off—as the swamp is drained and the bodies of Princess Ananka and Kharis are recovered. Soon Kharis (shabbily played by Lon Chaney, Jr.) is footloose on a diet of tana leaves, chasing a beautiful woman who can't quite flee the slow-moving shambler. Virginia Christine, Peter Coe, Martin Kosleck. Directed by Leslie Goodwins. (Video/Laser: MCA)

MUMMY'S CURSE OF THE JACKAL. See *The Mummy and the Curse of the Jackals*.

MUMMY'S GHOST, THE (1944) ★★★ Third in Universal's "Kharis the Mummy" series, coming on the heels of *The Mummy's Tomb*, with Lon Chaney, Jr., stumbling around New England to discover that Ananka, his beloved princess, is reincarnated in the shapely form of Ramsay Ames. John Carradine takes over as high priest to force-feed the tana leaves. Makeup by Jack Pierce. George Zucco appears briefly to send Carradine on his mission. Barton MacLane, Robert Lowery. Reginald Le Borg directed the script by Griffin Jay, Brenda Weisberg and Henry Sucher, which was written as *The Mummy's Return*. Followed by *The Mummy's Curse*. (Video/Laser:MCA)

MUMMY'S HAND, THE (1940) ★★★½ This entertaining sequence to Universal's *The Mummy* started a series of low-budget programmers (four in all) featuring a bandaged high priest named Kharis, who forsakes the Scroll of Thoth for tana leaves. They are all quite similar, with a mummy slowly shambling along, while no one else can ever quite get away from its clutches. The role of the long-dead Egyptian went to former cowboy actor Tom Tyler—his only appearance as a monster. Dick Foran and Wallace Ford provide romantic and comedy relief as a pair of down-and-out archeologists trying to finance an expedition to the Hill of the Seven Jackals through magician Cecil Kelloway and daughter Peggy Moran, who is mistaken by the Mummy for his long-lost love, Princess Ananka. A historic film moment occurs when the High Priest of Karnak (Eduardo Ciannelli) instructs George Zucco in the art of tana leaf cooking, and footage from *The Mummy* is repeated. This is solid B-picture material and better than the three films that followed. Directed by Christy Cabanne from a Maxwell Shane–Griffin Jay script. Followed by *The Mummy's Tomb*, *The Mummy's Ghost* and *The Mummy's Curse*. (Video/Laser: MCA)

MUMMY'S RETURN, THE. Original title of *The Mummy's Ghost*.

MUMMY'S REVENGE, THE (1973) ★ Spanish stew of supernatural curses and Egyptian walking dead is strictly meat and potatoes—basic to the horror viewer's diet, without any rich calories. Ultimately inedible. Directed by Carlos Aured, scripted by Jacinto Molina. Paul Naschy portrays the Nile Valley drifter in bandages. Aka *The Vengeance of the Mummy*. (Unicorn)

MUMMY'S SHROUD, THE (1967) ★★★ Despite the clichés that riddle its plot like holes in ancient bandages, this Hammer horror thriller is well done in the acting department. After a cumbersome beginning in Egyptian times, as we're inundated with exposition about a gauze-enwrapped entity, we flash to present day as an expedition desecrates the tomb and removes mummy Eddie Powell to a museum to be resurrected by He Who Possesses an Accursed Blanket. Intense murders follow. John Phillips is exceptional as the head of the expedition, a spoiled millionaire. Stylishly done with individual details often outshining the sum total. Maggie Kimberley portrays an unlikely archeologist, what with all those flimsy nightgowns and low-cut blouses. Best of the cast is Catherine Lacey as a decaying soothsayer who reads crystal balls. John Gilling wrote and directed. Produced and plotted by Anthony Nelson-Keys (John Elder).

MUMMY'S TOMB, THE (1942) ★★★ Third Universal feature in its Mummy series (begun by Karloff in 1932) and the second in a row of "Kharis" sequels, with Lon Chaney, Jr., inheriting the gauze from Tom Tyler in *The Mummy's Hand*. Again it's George Zucco as the High Priest, who turns the evildoing over to Turhan Bey, who then dispatches Kharis to kill archeologist–tomb defiler Dick Foran, but not until we've seen footage from *The Mummy's Hand* and the angry villagers from *Franken-*

stein. In this one Elyse Knox is the reincarnated beauty who is carried away by Kharis. Directed by Harold Young. Makeup by Jack Pierce. Followed by *The Mummy's Ghost* and *The Mummy's Curse*. (Video/Laser: MCA)

MUMMY STRIKES, THE. See *The Aztec Mummy*.

MUNCHIE (1992) ★★ A sequel in name if not spirit to *Munchies*, this depicts a mischievous but not murderous alien (with the jolly face of a pig and the voice of Dom DeLuise) wisecracking his way through a comedy misadventure with youth Jaime McEnnan, his beautiful mother Loni Anderson and her simpering boyfriend, a total nerd as played by Andrew Stevens. There are cute moments in the script by R. J. Robertson and director Jim Wynorski, especially when nutty inventor Arte Johnson gets into the fun. Strictly family viewing without the campy sex and violence that are Wynorski's usual trademarks. The third in the series: *Munchie Strikes Back*. (New Horizon)

MUNCHIES (1987) ★★ This rank imitation of *Gremlins* has nothing to recommend it—not even deep philosophical values. Archeologist Harvey Korman and son Charles Stratton find an alien in a South American cave and bring it back to civilization, where it multiples into several mischievous, murderous Munchies. The creatures are unconvincing, and so the film doesn't even work as high camp. Director Bettina Hirsch fails to bring crunch to this bunch . . . but why go on. Two sequels involving just one silly creature followed: *Munchie* and *Munchie Strikes Back*. Nadine Van Der Velde, Alix Elias, Charles Phillips. (MGM/UA)

MUNCHIE STRIKES BACK (1994) ★½ Watered-down kiddie fantasy from the Roger Corman factory, coming in the wake of the success of Munchie in home video. This time the phonylooking puppet (with the voice of Howard Hesseman) is sent by Kronos, the Master of Time and Space (Angus Scrimm), back to Earth to care for a mother (Lesley-Anne Down) and her son (Trenton Knight) when they need $20,000 to keep their home. Andrew Stevens provides silly slapstick antics as a media mogul who decides to use Munchie's magical powers for his own ends. Otherwise there is very little happening in the script by R. J. Robertson and Jim Wynorski. The latter directed with incredible restraint, considering the usual campy sex and violence that dominate his exploitation films. John Byner, Steve Franken, Natalyn Ross and Ace Mask contribute bits, as do Wynorski cronies Linda Shayne and Fred Olen Ray. (New Horizons)

MUNSTER, GO HOME! (1966) ★★½ Okay feature, barely a notch above the weekly TV series, "The Munsters," on which it was based, with Fred Gwynne, Yvonne De Carlo, Al Lewis and Butch Patrick recreating their video roles. The Munsters inherit a haunted house in England and all its problems, which include a counterfeiting ring led by Hermione Gingold, Terry-Thomas and John Carradine (as an amusing butler). And there's a roadster race with minimal impact. The only reason to see this thing today is for the cast and a quaintly humorous quality that belongs strictly to '60s TV. Directed by Earl Bellamy, written by George Tibbles, producer Joe Connelly and producer Bob Mosher. (MCA)

MUNSTERS' REVENGE, THE (1981) ★★★ Reviewed in the context of the '90s, this Universal TV-movie revival of "The Munsters," the popular series of the '60s, has a charm it seemed to lack in its own time. Is it just nostalgia, or is there something quaint this captures? At the core of its charm are Fred Gwynne as Herman Munster and Al Lewis as Grandpa Munster, with Yvonne De Carlo (as Lily Munster) taking a backseat to the action. The silly Dr. Diabolic (Sid Caesar, in a funny role) instills robotic life in the monsters of a Hollywood wax museum and arranges for them to steal the jewels from a mummy's sarcophagus. Memorable scenes have Gwynne and Lewis in drag as coffee shop waitresses fighting off male customers, Lily decorating a Christmas tree with horror symbols, and Caesar doing characters that include his crazed German scientist. The Arthur Alsberg–Don Nelson script was directed by Don Weis without much enthusiasm, but time has been good to this minor effort, as if a Beverly Hills plastic surgeon had given it a face-lift. K. C. Martel, Jo McDonnel, Bob Hastings, Gary Vinson, Charles Macaulay, Howard Morris, Ezra Stone. (MCA)

MUPPETS FROM SPACE (1999) ★★★ In all fairness, have you ever asked yourself where a Muppet comes from? It doesn't take much of a stretch to imagine that a critter like Gonzo (voice by Dave Goelz) might hail from a distant planet, and is trapped here on Earth, the only kind of his species and hence deprived of a meaningful sex life. At least that's why Gonzo, he/it with the hooked nose, dreams that Noah won't let him on the Ark, and why after being struck by lightning he takes a trip through the Universe (à la Jodie Foster in *Contact*) to be told by superintelligent fish-creatures that he should mow his lawn. Well, whoever said the world of Muppets was easy to explain? Cut to the chase: COVNER, a secret government project seeking the presence of aliens on Earth, thinks Gonzo is an alien and sends him/it to have his/its brain sucked out of his cranium, while Rizzo (voice by Steve Whitmire) is sent into the "lab rat" pact. Meanwhile, Ms. Piggy (playing a wanna-be news investigative reporter with Frank Oz's voice) and Kermit (the only sane-acting Muppet in this outing of the franchise) join with the rest of the critters to save Gonzo from a death worse than his fate and allow him to have a rendezvous with a gleaming spaceship carrying a pack of music-happy aliens from his home planet. There's a lot of heartfelt enjoyment in this spoof of *Men in Black* and *Close Encounters of the Third Kind* and it's got some wonderfully funny moments: Jeffrey Tambor is pleasingly goofy as K. Edgar Singer (an incompetent J. Edgar Hoover wanna-be mismanaging COVNER), the gang of rats running through a maze is cute, and there's diverting cameos by F. Murray Abraham (as Noah), Rob Schneider (as a greedy TV producer), Andie MacDowell (as a UFO investigator), Ray Liotta (as a security guard) and Pat Hingle (as a stern general). Hulk Hogan is thrown into the mix, too. A lot of zippy one-liners are sprinkled throughout the script by Jerry Juhl, Joseph Mazzarino and Ken Kaufman, and director Tim Hill allows some warmth to creep into the nonsense without it ever getting sticky and prickly. Other Muppet voices by Bill Barretta, Jerry Nelson, Brian Henson and Kevin Clash. (Video/DVD: Columbia TriStar)

MURDER BY MAIL. See *Schizoid* (1980).

MURDER BY MOONLIGHT (1989) ★ Watching Brigitte Nielsen climb out of a spacesuit to reveal she's in a push-up bra makes one realize it's a crying shame there isn't any gravity on the moon to give her a helping hand. This scene is the high point of this otherwise static, talkative TV-movie set on a moon station where U.S. and Soviet personnel argue over how to carry out a murder investigation, and Brigitte and a blond Russian strip off their moon gear to make love. The story, set in 2015, 10 years after a near-nuclear war on Earth, was directed by Michael Lindsay-Hogg with a sagging feeling. Gee, did we say sagging? Sorry about that, Brigitte. Julian Sands, Jan Lapotrire, Brian Cox, Gerald McRaney. (Vidmark)

MURDER BY NIGHT (1989) ★★ Average TV-movie, produced in Canada, centers on the "Claw Hammer Killer," a serial murderer terrorizing people who once ate at the Puzzles Restaurant. During one murder, Robert Urich is exposed to a car explosion and wakes up with amnesia. Is he the killer or only a passerby? Detective Michael Ironside and police psychologist Kay Lenz manipulate Urich to remember. Tepid whodunit, in which the killer's identity is easily spotted in advance. Directed by Paul Lynch. Richard Monette, Jim Metzler. (MCA)

MURDER BY PHONE (1980) ★★★ A literately written Canadian horror film, best for its clever dialogue between ecology advocate Richard Chamberlain and telephone company advisor John Houseman, who meet in Toronto during a save-the-environment convention. Meanwhile, certain citizens are answering their phones only to have blood shoot from their ears, nose, eyes and mouth because of a terrible vibrating force. Then a killer bolt of electricity pours through the receiver and throws them against the wall as if Zeus had struck.

Chamberlain, when he isn't dating mural painter Sara Botsford, is hot on the trail of the killer. Slickly directed by Michael Anderson. Hell's bells, this is pretty good stuff. Barry Morse, Robin Gammell, Gary Reineke. Aka *Bells, The Calling* and *Hell's Bells*. (Warner Bros.)

MURDER CLINIC, THE (1966) ★★★½ Black-robed fiend (with a cowl yet) stalks the halls of an isolated hospital for weirdos, slashing victims with a razor blade. A young nurse arrives on the Gothic scene to serve as the heroine of this Italian-French horror tale that is overacted but compellingly presented with its period ambience, costumes and baroque settings. William Berger stars as a misunderstood doctor who keeps an ugly secret in one of the upstairs rooms, from which weird sounds emanate. Plenty of gore (some was cut for TV) and creeping around to create tension and suspense. Produced-directed by Michael Hamilton (Elio Scardamaglia). Françoise Prevost, Mary Young, Barbara Wilson. Aka *A Knife in the Body, The Blade in the Body, Night of Terrors, The Murder Society* and *Revenge of the Living Dead*. (VCI)

MURDERERS' KEEP. Video version of *The Butcher* (Genesis; Star Classics).

MURDERERS' ROW (1966) ★★½ A sequel to *The Silencers*, this is the second in the Matt Helm series with Dean Martin as the superspy who walks indifferently through bizarre adventures. Brimming with succulent women, gleaming gadgets, ingenious weapons and flippant dialogue, it never for a moment takes itself seriously. You'll enjoy Karl Malden as a villain with a killer ray who hopes to destroy the White House. Stylishly directed by Henry Levin and flashily written by Herbert Baker, they allow you to set your brain on "idle" and enjoy. Follow-ups: *The Ambushers* and *The Wrecking Crew*. Ann-Margret, Camilla Sparv, Beverly Adams, James Gregory. (RCA/Columbia)

MURDER IN LAW (1989) ★★½ This slap against mother's love might have given new depths of horror to the phrase "mother-in-law" were it not for the fact that its unfolding is far more ludicrous than it is scary. Still, Marilyn Adams is rather deviously delightful as a daffy old bat who spears an orderly to death and escapes from Silver Oak Asylum, in Louisiana, to take up residence later with her son Joe Estevez in his stately San Francisco home. Joe refuses to believe Mom might be crazy even though she (1) slaughters the family cat, (2) trashes the bedrooms and (3) pushes an iron into the face of the family's Mexican maid. Talk about denial! Anyway, he finally puts murderous Mother away, but she escapes and chases Joe's wife and daughter with a butcher knife. Adams really goes over the top as a total nut. Sandy Snyder, Darrel Guilbeau, Debra Lee Giometti, Rebecca Russell. Directed by Tony Jiti Gill. (Monarch)

MURDER ON LINE ONE (1990) ★★ British horror flick opens with an eyeball being left on the doorstep of Emma Jacobs by a murderer who slaughtered an entire family. A whodunit unfolds. Written-directed by Anders Palm. Peter Blake, Simon Shepherd, Allan Surtees. (Academy)

MURDEROUS VISION (1991) ★ Unimpressive TV-movie with Bruce Boxleitner as a demoted cop trying to restore his honor by tracking down a mad doctor-killer who skins the faces of his victims. He achieves this with the help of a psychic. Directed by Gary Sherman. Laura Johnson, Joseph D'Angerio, Robert Culp. (Paramount)

MURDERS IN THE RUE MORGUE (1932) ★★★½ The title is the only Poe you'll find in this Universal thriller starring Bela Lugosi as a carnival spielman with a gorilla act. The early promising atmosphere and odd sexual overtones are not sustained as master detective Dupin (Leon Ames billed as Leon Waycroft) tracks Dr. Mirakle to put a stop to his crazy theory that mating ape with virgin will result in a perfect union between man and animal. Directed by Robert Florey, from a script by Tom Reed and Dale van Avery that swings like a pendulum from good to bad. The camera of Karl Freund lingers sadistically on the scenes in which the Darwin-crazed Lugosi tortures prostitutes. (Video/Laser: MCA)

MURDERS IN THE RUE MORGUE (1971) ★★★ Strangely compelling thriller of the Grand Guignol school, though it has nothing to do with Poe's story. The offbeat Henry Slesar–Christopher Wicking script features bizarre relationships, flashbacks within flashbacks and dreams within dreams. Maniac Herbert Lom commits ghastly acid murders while Jason Robards, Jr., and Christine Kaufman stage a horror play in Paris's finest theater. Gordon Hessler directed. Adolfo Celi, Lilli Palmer, Maria Perschy, Michael Dunn. (Orion) (Laser: Japanese)

MURDERS IN THE RUE MORGUE, THE (1986) ★★★½ Well-produced TV-movie with George C. Scott as French detective Auguste Dupin, who comes out of retirement to solve two bloody murders and prove his daughter's fiancé is not guilty of the crimes. Paris locations are cleverly used, and Scott is fine, but the pacing is slow. Directed by Jeannot Szwarc. Val Kilmer, Rebecca De Mornay, Ian McShane. (Video/Laser: Vidmark)

MURDERS IN THE ZOO (1933) ★★½ Lionel Atwill so overacts as a philanthropist/big game hunter that what should be horrifying is ludicrous. Because he's insanely jealous of his unfaithful wife, he sews up the mouth of her paramour and leaves him to die in the jungle. The next lover is killed by a mamba snake. And on it goes, involving lions, tigers and a house of pythons. While today it might seem mild, it was hard-hitting in its day and frequently censored because of Atwill's suggested depravity. Directed by A. Edward Sutherland with a relish for the distasteful, the best word to describe the screenplay by Philip Wylie and Seton Miller. Randolph Scott, Gail Patrick, John Lodge. (MCA)

MURDER SOCIETY, THE. See *The Murder Clinic*.

MUTANT (1982). See *Forbidden World*.

MUTANT (1983) ★★ This time the zombies are on the march (to the music of Richard Band) because of exposure to toxic refuge, but a zombie is still a zombie with only an appetite for human flesh. Same old "walking dead" clichés with Wings Hauser, Bo Hopkins and Jennifer Warren fighting off monsters. Directed by John "Bud" Cardos. Aka *Dark Shadows* and *Night Shadows*. (Video/Laser: Vestron)

MUTANT II. See *Alien Predator(s)*.

MUTANT HUNT (1986) ★½ Made-for-video sci-fi–horror combination, with emphasis on hand-to-hand fighting and depressed New York City locations. Writer-director Tim Kincaid does a creditable job with this tale of Delta VII cyborgs out of control after they've been given a drug, Euphoran, that turns them into psychosexual killers. Rick Gianasi is Matt Ryker, mercenary for hire who sets out with a stripper and a martial arts dude to track the mindless killers. There are nifty scenes of a cyborg pulling his face apart and a lot of drippy, gooey effects, all done in a less-than-serious style. One character says it all with: "Total carnage, uncontrolled fury, what else could you ask for?" Mary Fahey, Ron Reynaldi, Tawnie Vernon. Aka *Matt Riker*. (Wizard; VCI)

MUTANT ON THE BOUNTY (1989) ★★ Kyle T. Heffner, a mutated saxophone player, gets beamed into the year 2048 aboard the spacecraft USS *Bounty*. Ha ha ha. Then he tries to make it with Deborah Benson. Ha ha ha. And other crew people, such as a humanoid robot, a female doctor and a fat captain. Directed by Robert Torrance. Ha ha ha. And ha ha ha to John Roarke, John Furey and Victoria Catlin. (South Gate; Hemdale)

MUTANTS IN PARADISE (1987) ★ Lamebrained comedy that parodies TV's "The Six Million Dollar Man" without an ounce of wit. Nitwit scientist "Oscar Tinman" (Robert Ingham) creates a genetically superior superman named "Steve Awesome" out of a nerd (Brad Greenquist). Mad doctor Edith Massey also creates a female counterpart, "Alice Durchfall," played by Anna Nicholas. The only plot has a gang of Russian agents out to kidnap the pair. The dumb jokes are nonstop and there isn't a laugh in the carload. Stylelessly written-directed by Scott Apostolou, who filmed in Charlottesville, VA. Skip Suddeth, Ray Mancini. (Transworld)

MUTANT SPECIES (1995) ★★★ The first half

of this suspenseful monster movie written by William Virgil and director David A. Prior deals with a Special Forces squad that parachutes into unknown territory to retrieve a cannister from the crashed rocket ship *Icarus*. They are unaware their assignment boss (government man Powers Booth) is using them as guinea pigs to test a new strain of DNA (a blend of human and predator animal) that creates a viral infection, and transmutes man into killer beast monster. Soon, squad leader Leo Rossi turns into one ugly, slavering creature that kills numerous soldiers. It's up to squad survivor Ted Prior and local farmgirl Denise Crosby to defeat the thing. Back at headquarters central, army guy Wilford Brimley tries to correct Booth's conspiracy. Certain to please fans with its mix of action, suspense and special effects. (Live)

MUTATION, THE/MUTATIONS (1974). See *The Freakmaker*.

MUTATION (1979). See *The Plague*.

MUTATOR (1990) ★ This A Cut Above production is barely that, being a familiar "genetics gone amok," "man shouldn't tamper with nature" horror tale with mediocre hairy monster effects. Directed by John R. Bowey, the cast works hard with the meager characterizations. Tigen Inc. is a chemical engineering corporation that must seal itself off one night when genetically engineered beings (caused by an experiment gone awry) cut loose with homicidal intent. Trapped in the huge plant-laboratory are Brion James (in an unusual role as hero), the miniskirted Carolyn Ann Clark, Milton Raphael Murrill and Brian O'Shaughnessy. (Prism) (Laser: Image)

MUTE WITNESS (1995) ★★★½ The first half of this British-German-Russian coproduction plays like a slasher movie when a young special effects artist (Marina Sudina) incapable of speech is trapped in a Moscow film studio after witnessing a woman's bloody murder during the filming of a "snuff" movie. The suspenseful cat-and-mouse techniques of writer-director Anthony Waller are stylish as Sudina flees the Reaper (the "snuff" killer) and his cameraman. The second half of the film turns into intrigue and double-dealing with a heavy spylike atmosphere when Russian police enter the picture. And then *Mute Witness* becomes a remake of *F/X* with its tricky ending. Still, it's above average as a genre piece and many of its chase sequences would warm the heart of Alfred Hitchcock. Fay Ripley as Sudina's sister, Evan Richards as a rather stupid horror-movie director, and Oleg Jankowski as a special investigator of the porno ring add sparkle to this mystery of concealed identities. (Video/Laser: Columbia TriStar)

MUTILATED. See *Shriek of the Mutilated*.

MUTILATOR, THE. Video version of *The Dark* (1979) (Impulse; Simitar).

MUTILATOR, THE (1983) ★ Below-average slasher flick (aka *Fall Break*) bespeckled with weak characterizations and only moderately sickening gore. After a clumsy prologue in which a youngster accidentally shoots his father, the story jumps to the present day to follow six teenagers to a seaside condominium, where they are stalked and slaughtered by the father, a big game hunter. Death by drowning, chainsaw slicing, machete chopping, pitchfork plunging, hook impalement, and battle-ax bleeding. Also for your viewing pleasure: a body severed in half, another body beheaded, still another delegged. My, my, ain't we got fun. Filmed near Atlantic Beach in a dismal coastal location. Buddy Cooper wrote and directed. Matt Mitler, Frances Raines, Morey Lampley. (Video/Laser: Vestron)

MY BEST FRIEND IS A VAMPIRE (1987) ★★½ Mildly amusing, but never hysterically hilarious or fabulously funny, comedy in which Robert Sean Leonard slowly turns into a vampire. But this is a world of benevolent families, similar to the world of benevolent werewolves in *Teen Wolf*, so our sympathy is always with Leonard as he faces two misguided vampire hunters, Professor Leopold McCarthy (David Warner, in a parody of the bat hater he played in *Nightwing*) and Grimsdyke (an Igor type played by an amusing character actor, Paul Willson). The funniest bit is the title of a vampire book: *A Practical Guide to an Alternative Lifestyle*. Directed by Jimmy Huston. Cheryl Pollak, Rene Auberjonois, Evan Mirand, Fannie Flagg. (HBO)

MY BLOODY VALENTINE (1981) ★★★½ Roses are red / Violets are blue / *My Bloody Valentine* / Is absolute grue." . . . Heart-to-heart Canadian horror film of the slasher school is strangely compelling despite lack of characters and logic. It hinges on grabby visuals as a deranged killer—wearing a miner's uniform and face mask—attacks citizens of Valentine Village with a pickax. Photography and stunt work are excellent as the murderer stalks partygoers in a coal mine. Without getting pickie, we enjoyed it. Sorry, no miners allowed. Directed by George Mihalka from a John Beaird script. Effects by Tom Burman. Paul Kelman, Cynthia Dale. (Video/Laser: Paramount)

MY BOYFRIEND'S BACK (1992) ★★½ Lamebrain teenage supernatural comedy (aka *Johnny Zombie*) from producer Sean S. Cunningham that's one joke: Johnny Dingle (Andrew Lowery), shot while trying to save girlfriend Traci Lind from a robber's bullet, ends up dead. When he returns from the grave, everyone takes him for granted, even though he is turning into a flesh-craving zombie creature. Dean Lorey's screenplay vacillates all over the cemetery but nothing much takes hold until Lowery arrives in Heaven and the gatekeeper (Paxton Whitehead) tries to straighten out the books. Directed by actor Bob Balaban, who deserves better material than this. Danny Zorn, Bob Dishy, Paul Dooley, Edward Herrmann, Mary Beth Hurt, Cloris Leachman. (Video/Laser: Buena Vista)

MY DEMON LOVER (1987) ★★ This mindless supernatural comedy could have been a total disaster, but screenwriter Leslie Ray wisely injected a sense of the old Saturday matinee into his tale about a young man (Scott Valentine) "po-zassed" by the "Rumanian Blue Balls Curse"—which turns him into a different kind of monster, or "Pazosky," each time he tries to make love. Valentine must perform a "noble deed" to exorcise himself, and he does it with the help of nerdy blond Michelle Little. Meanwhile, there's a killer called the Mangler and it appears Valentine is that killer. Good performances by Arnold Johnson (as the Fixer), Robert Trebor (as Little's dunderhead suitor), Gina Gallego (as a sexy newswoman) and Alan Fudge (as the cop), plus that sense of cliff-hanger derring-do, make this enjoyable. Directed by Charles Loventhal. (Video/Laser: RCA/Columbia)

MY FAVORITE MARTIAN (1999) ★★★ This Walt Disney spinoff of the CBS-TV 1964–66 sitcom is a reminder of just how strong the memories of our youth can be. The very fact that the Bill Bixby–Ray Walston sitcom has not been forgotten by a generation of kiddies who are now executives and filmmakers in Hollywood says it all. The original TV premise was quaintly presented, with a kind of twinkle in the eye, and that's what gave the show its initial charm. Because those pleasant memories live on, we now have this motion picture version with Christopher Lloyd in the Walston role as "Uncle Martin," the Martian who lands on Earth in a rocketship and is befriended by newspaper reporter Tim O'Hara, and Jeff Daniels in the Bixby role as a new version of O'Hara—not a reporter but a TV newscast producer. Walston has been brought back to play a sinister government agent, or so it seems. (Don't look for Bixby—he died in 1992 at the age of 58.) This new film is loaded with computerized special effects, overplayed characters who are without charm or wit, and a pie-in-the-face approach to each scene. Director Donald Petrie, whose earlier comedic efforts included *Grumpy Old Men* and *Richie Rich*, goes for slapstick and raucous, ridiculous behavior, and strangely blends humor slanted for kids with an occasional adult zinger that seems a bit out of place. Lloyd delivers his usual manic performance, Daniels becomes the straight man to all the visual and verbal gags, Daryl Hannah is the most repressed cast member as a TV-camera lady with a secret passion for Daniels, Elizabeth Hurley plays a spoiled, devious TV reporter you love to hate, and Wally

Shawn goes berserk as a goofy scientist who wants to believe in aliens on earth. On the TV show, "Uncle Martin" wore a special metallic suit that gave him some of his magical powers. Here the suit (called a "polymorphic suitenex 3000") walks and talks on its own (special effects by Phil Tippett) and it's one of the film's more creatively funny features. Most of the script by Sherri Stoner and Deanna Oliver goes for the juvenile laugh, with a little toilet humor thrown in. (Video/DVD: Disney)

MY GRANDFATHER (GRANDPA) IS A VAMPIRE (1991) ★★½ Al Lewis has a ball as a jovial, fun-loving, 280-year-old vampire who never harms a single neck in this New Zealand production for children. It's spun as a fairy tale when the old man dies and returns from the dead to enter into adventures with his grandson, most of them centered around the efforts of Lewis's sister's aging suitor coming after Lewis as a vampire killer. A light-hearted quality runs throughout Michael Heath's script and David Blyth's direction. Justin Gocke, Milan Borich. (Republic)

MY MOM'S A WEREWOLF (1988) ★★★ Silly Crown-International comedy along the lines of *Teen Wolf*, but with sexually frustrated mother Susan Blakely the member of the family who turns into a hairy beast after she meets Harry Thropen (John Saxon) in his pet shop. The visual gags don't extend much beyond long fangs and hirsute legs. Little fire is added by director Michael Fischa to this weak kettle of guffaw grue, although Saxon gives a menacing performance given the inanities loping around him. Katrina Caspary, John Schuck, Diana Barrows, Ruth Buzzi, Marilyn McCoo. (Prism) (Laser: Image)

MY NAME IS JOHN. See *Legend of Hillbilly John.*

MY SCIENCE PROJECT (1985) ★½ Boring teenage fantasy comedy in which an inept science student, poking around an abandoned Air Force installation, discovers a force-field gadget left over from a flying saucer discovered by the military in 1959. The device sucks up all the energy in sight and becomes a time tunnel, out of which emerge monsters and warriors of the past. John Stockwell, Danielle Von Zerneck and Fisher Stevens are the hapless teens, but the picture goes to a freaked-out performance by Dennis Hopper as a science teacher who regresses to his hippie habits when he's sucked into the space-warp continuum. Jonathan Betuel, who wrote *The Last Starfighter*, wrote-directed but no amount of effects can save his sci-fi project. (Video/Laser: Touchstone)

MY SISTER, MY LOVE (1979) ★★ Intriguing psychological study of two sisters living in a cluttered mansion, where they keep an ape in a "mafu cage" belonging to their late father, a noted jungle explorer. Lee Grant tries to stay afloat while her sister, Carol Kane, sinks into barbarism, torturing apes and humans alike. Produced largely by women, this low-budget effort is strangely compelling and offbeat, with lesbian overtones. Directed by Karen Arthur. Will Geer, James Olson and Badur the Orang. Aka *The Mafu Cage*. (Wizard; VCI; Magnum)

MY SON, THE VAMPIRE (1952) ★★ Made in England as *Old Mother Riley Meets the Vampire*, this was released in the U.S. as *Vampires over London*. This present version was rereissued in 1964 and is part of the Mother Riley series popular for many years in Great Britain. Arthur Lucan appears in drag, capturing a music hall lowbrow humor for which he was famous. Bela Lugosi is Baron Van Housen, who thinks he's Dracula and wears all the regalia and sleeps in a coffin. Produced-directed by John Gilling from a Val Valentine script. Kitty McShane, Dora Bryan. Aka *Mother Riley in Dracula's Desire, Mother Riley Meets the Vampire, Old Mother Riley Meets the Vampire, Mother Riley Runs Riot* and *The Vampire and the Robot*. (From Sinister/C as *Vampire over London*)

MY STEPMOTHER IS AN ALIEN (1988) ★★ Kim Basinger's sex appeal is the saving grace of this labored sci-fi comedy in which the blond beaut portrays an E.T. life form (some form!) who hooks up with scientist Dan Aykroyd to save her planet from destruction. She has a great time learning about sex—so good, in fact, that Aykroyd becomes her straight man (in more ways than one). If you take this for the parody that it was intended, you might have a good time despite a less-than-great alien that looks like a cross between a sick cobra and a malfunctioning flute, and rather pedestrian direction by Richard Benjamin. Jon Lovitz, Alyson Hanigan, Joseph Maher. (Video/Laser: RCA/Columbia)

MYSTERIANS, THE (1959) ★★ Cockroach-headed aliens from Mysteroid, their eyes shooting blue flames, wear uniforms that strangely resemble Asian styles and have a bearing that smacks of Shinto etiquette. Despite these indications that you're watching a Japanese movie, *The Mysterians* is a visual delight with ample special-effects destruction. Sympathy is engendered for the Mysterians who claim their planet has been destroyed by Strontium-90 and they have come to Earth to procreate with our beautiful women. From that indomitable *Godzilla* pair, director Inoshiro Honda and effects pioneer Eiji Tsuburaya. Kenji Sahara, Yumi Shirakawa. Aka *Earth Defense Force*. (VCI; United; Star Classics) (Laser: Japanese import)

MYSTERIOUS DR. R. See *Man-Made Monster*.

MYSTERIOUS DR. SATAN, THE (1940) ★★★ Republic serial directed by cliff-hanging masters William Witney and John English. Dr. Satan (Eduardo Cinnelli) is an archfiend who has invented a robot to terrorize the world. But he needs C. Montague Shaw's remote control device to make it work. That's when a man in a copper mask steps in to thwart the evil gang. Nonstop action and nonstop nonsense will have you alternately gasping and chuckling—it never stops moving along its ludicrous, fun-filled pathways. Robert Wilcox is the hero, Ella Neal the heroine. The feature version is *Dr. Satan's Robot*. (Republic; Nostalgia Merchant)

MYSTERIOUS HOUSE OF USHER, THE. See *House of Usher* (1960).

MYSTERIOUS ISLAND (1951) ★★ This 15-chapter Sam Katzman Columbia serial, subtitled "Captain Harding's Fabulous Adventures," is one sorry excuse for a cliff-hanger—and don't you believe it when the credits say it's based on Jules Verne's famous novel. But you do get a lot of intriguingly goofy stuff in this inept adventure: Karen Randle as Rulu, a woman from Mercury who visits the isle in search of a precious metal that will help her take over Earth; two Rulu henchmen who carry ray guns and look like early versions of Spider-Man; a tribe of natives called the Volcano People (because they worship a volcano); and a mysterious presence in a weird helmet. Plus you have Richard Crane as a Civil War hero stuck on the island with some other guys (Ralph Hodges, Hugh Prosser, Bernard Hamilton) who just walk around most of the time looking for cutthroat pirates (led by Gene Roth) and a crazy, bearded castaway (Terry Frost) whose actions never are explained. Directed by Spencer G. Bennet, and loaded with phony-looking special effects, *Mysterious Island* is fun to watch but for all the wrong reasons. (Heavenly Video)

MYSTERIOUS ISLAND (1961) ★★★★ Visually exciting adaptation of Jules Verne's book with effects by Ray Harryhausen and outstanding music by Bernard Herrmann. The John Prebble–Daniel Ullman–Wilbur Crane script (aka *Jules Verne's Mysterious Island*) is the weakest element of this Charles H. Schneer production filmed in Spain and England, for the characters are treated as stereotypes and the situations often deteriorate into shopworn thrills. Three Yankee prisoners of war escape Richmond Prison during a storm and make their getaway in an observation balloon to an unexplored Pacific island where they establish a Swiss Family Robinson life-style. The Yanks are joined by shipwreck survivors and all are under attack from giant monsters: an overgrown chicken, a prehistoric Phororhacos, a nautiloid cephalopod and other Harryhausen marvels. Michael Craig, Michael Callan, Gary Merrill and Joan Greenwood are among the stranded, while Herbert Lom emerges from the foamy brine as Captain

Nemo. Stylishly directed by Cy Endfield. (Columbia TriStar) (Laser: Columbia TriStar with Harryhausen interview; Voyager)

MYSTERIOUS ISLAND OF CAPTAIN NEMO (1973) ★★ French-Spanish production, an adaptation of Jules Verne themes, is sorely lacking in imagination and exciting effects. Omar Sharif portrays the *Nautilus*'s sailing captain, but it is a portrayal inferior to James Mason's in Disney's 1954 *Twenty Thousand Leagues under the Sea*. Directed by Henri Colpi and Juan Antonio Bardem. Philippe Nicaud, Gerald Tichy, Jess Hann. Aka *Jules Verne's Mysterious Island of Captain Nemo* and *Jules Verne's Mysterious Island of Dr. Nemo*.

MYSTERIOUS MR. M, THE (1946) ★★ Thirteen-chapter Universal serial in which a submarine inventor, under the spell of the drug Hyponotrene, falls into the hands of evil agents out to steal his underwater devices. Running the motley gang of nefarious gangsters is a strange bird named Mr. M. (It's less sinister than being called Mr. X.) Kirby Walsh and Shirley Clinton go after the baddies under the direction of Lewis D. Collins and Vernon Keays. Dennis Moore, Jane Randolph.

MYSTERIOUS PLANET (1982) ★ Ambitious but incompetent attempt to blend matte paintings, stop-motion animation creatures and space hardware effects into a grand adventure, allegedly based on a novel by Jules Verne. A spaceship carrying some unconvincing galaxy jockeys crash-lands on a life-sustaining planet inhabited by a bikini-clad girl with healing powers and a lost race of superintelligent beings. The actors are too amateurish to create interesting characters, the photography is slapdash and the monsters all look like cute pieces of clay (which is what they are). Technically this is a nightmare, with some of the sound unintelligible and other portions containing an unwanted echo effect. Produced and directed (if you can call it that) by Brett Piper and "starring" Paula Tauper, Boyd Piper, Michael Quigley and Bruce Nadeau. (Video City)

MYSTERIOUS STRANGER, THE (1982) ★★★ Delightful adaptation of a Mark Twain fantasy, a companion piece to his *Connecticut Yankee in King Arthur's Court*, in which a printer's apprentice (Chris Makepeace) imagines he is back in Guggenheim's day, helping print Bibles. He conjures up a freewheeling youthful spirit from the future named No. 44 (Lance Kerwin) who works magical spells over striking printers and confounds an alchemist (a wonderful character essayed by Fred Gwynne). An amusing period fantasy, rich in character and detail, superbly directed by Peter H. Hunt. (From MCA as *Mark Twain Classics: The Mysterious Stranger*)

MYSTERIOUS TWO (1979) ★★ Alan Landsburg TV-movie stars John Forsythe and Priscilla Pointer as white-robed emissaries from another planet or dimension who hypnotically gather followers and then lead them away to . . . where? Not even you, the viewer, will find out in this allegorical tale inspired by the Jonestown massacre of 1978. Here the lambs to the slaughter believe that "He and She" (as the aliens are called) will provide and make a blissful world. Originally made as *Follow Me if You Dare*, then shelved before coming to the network in 1982. Director-writer Gary Sherman captures a weird quality with his glaring white lighting. Great buildup to a nonpayoff. James Stephens, Robert Pine, Noah Beery, Jr., Vic Tayback. (USA; IVE)

MYSTERY MEN (1999) ★★½ This two-hour adaptation of the Dark Horse comic-book series by Bob Burden is one giant battle as a handful of funny one-liners and clever ideas try to break through and overpower a megaton of unfunny scenes, stupid dialogue and overblown special-effects visuals. The one-liners and ideas, as good as they are, are finally overpowered and pummeled into nothingness in the resulting morass and mess that is this movie. The promising premise—a band of incompetent, wanna-be superheroes in a place called Champion City must overcome their constant bickering and inner weaknesses to find the strength and courage to rescue their imprisoned idol Captain Amazing—becomes lost almost immediately. Screenwriter Neil Cuthbert has no sense of what works or what is just mindless sound and fury, and director Kinka Usher, a wunderkind known for his peppy TV commercials, perpetuates the mistake by presenting it with a bombastic excitement when maybe some quieter attitudes and fewer characters might have saved the day. Stupidity mingled with sparks of genius is the mixture as we meet The Blue Raja (Hank Azaria throwing spoons and forks and talking like a British avenger-hero), The Shoveler (William C. Macy in a miner's hat and equipped with a steel shovel) and Mr. Furious (Ben Stiller just angry all the time, and hence ineffectual) being shown up by Amazing (Greg Kinnear) in an opening battle of good vs. evil. Amazing, who looks like an Indy 500 driver with all the endorsement patches on his crime-fighting uniform, is declining in popularity because of a lack of nemeses, so he arranges to have his archenemy Casanova Frankenstein (Geoffrey Rush) released from prison. Instantly, Casanova proves he's no lover as he begins a new plot to blow up Champion City, a cross between *Batman*'s Gotham and the metropolis of *Bladerunner*. Casanova also succeeds in kidnapping the very naive Captain Amazing and tying him to a machine of massive destruction—it disintegrates molecular structure and leaves things and people charred to death. To rescue him, the incompetents add new superheroes to the dubious team: Spleen (Paul

Reubens), who knocks his enemies over with powerful farts, The Bowler (Janeane Garofalo), who has a ricocheting bowling ball empowered by the skull of her late father, and The Invisible Boy (Kel Mitchell, who fails to disappear even once). Of all these, Macy is the only one who is constantly funny, although why he is married to a black woman raises an interracial theme that seems strangely out of place in a superhero comic-book movie. Added to the soup are Wes Studi as Sphinx, a masked avenger who talks in metaphors and conundrums and trains the wanna-bes into a fighting unit, and a weapons expert (Tom Waits as Dr. Heller) who refuses to allow any of his firepower to be lethal. Instead, he offers a "blame thrower" (everyone starts blaming everyone else when exposed to its invisible blast), a "dry-cleaning gun" that shrinks clothing, and a tornado-whirlwind in a can. The film's funniest scene is when the superheroes hold auditions to recruit new members: Paraded before them are Ballerina Man, PMS Avenger, Pencil Man and other absurd though funny misfits trying to be heroic. The destruction and sci-fi special effects are excellent but they ultimately only add to the chaotic confusion of this satire with more characters than it can comfortably manage. Less would have been better. (Video/DVD: Universal)

MYSTERY OF RAMPO, THE (1994) ★★★★ A beautifully photographed mystical fantasy from director Kazuyoshi Okuyama about a Japanese mystery novelist (Masahiro Motoki) who finds that the characters from his latest book, *The Appearance of Osei*, have come to life and he can no longer distinguish fact from fiction. A woman accused of leaving her husband to die in a locked trunk (a story told in animated form as the film opens) takes up with a perverted marquis in a cliffside castle, and Edogawa Rampo's detective character, Akechi, poses as a parachute tester to find out if she is planning also to murder the marquis for his fortune. This is a lyrical, slow-moving and cerebral mystery, but it's fascinating and full of striking images—including black-and-white footage from one of Rampo's movie adaptations (*The Phantom with 20 Faces*), and a graphic sex film used by the depraved marquis. Naoto Takenaka, Michiko Hada. (Video: Hallmark) (Laser: Image)

MYSTERY OF THE GHOUL. See *The Mad Ghoul*.

MYSTERY OF THE WAX MUSEUM (1932) ★★★½ One of the first films made in the two-strip Technicolor process; it also served as the model for the 1953 3-D remake, *House of Wax*. Lionel Atwill has one of his finest roles as museum curator Ivan Igor, a genius wax sculptor disfigured in a fire. Now he is a madman, killing his enemies and encasing their corpses in wax to serve as his "horror displays." Has the famous scene in which Fay Wray pounds away at Atwill's face until it cracks to reveal a terribly scarred countenance beneath. Michael Curtiz directed the Don Mullaly–Carl Erickson script. Glenda Farrell, Frank McHugh, Holmes Herbert, Gavin Gordon. Aka *Wax Museum*. (Video/Laser: MGM/UA)

MYSTERY OF THUG ISLAND. See *The Snake Hunter Strangler*.

MYSTERY SCIENCE THEATER 3000 (1995) ★ This dud of a turkey-flop sat on the shelf for a year before being minimally released to alleged art theaters. It is even worse than the Comedy Central series that spawned it, for nobody tries to do anything different or fresh with the now-stale idea of two cutesy-pie robots (Tom Servo and Crow T. Robot) and a bland blond guy (Michael J. Nelson) sitting in a movie theater watching an old bad movie and making stupid wisecracks the whole time. Bad movie? The movie they watch in this is *This Island Earth*, which in some quarters is considered a classic or a still-okay sci-fi effort for its time and place. The production values are those of the TV show (the setting, a space station above Earth, keeps the concept totally confined when it needs to crash out of its stuffy environment) and no creative attempt is made by any of the principals. Blame producer-director Jim Mallon and about 10 writers for this unwatchable travesty and utter fiasco which has not a single funny moment in it. Trace Beaulieu appears as the crazed Dr. Forrester, hoping to drive Murphy and the robots mad with old movies and then taking over the world. Pathetic! (Polygram)

MY UNCLE THE VAMPIRE. See *Uncle Was a Vampire*.

NADJA (1994) ★★ You really have to be into avant-garde vampire movies, ones with unusual twists on standard genre clichés, to get with this black-and-white feature written and directed by Michael Almereyda and produced by David Lynch (who appears in a brief scene as a disheveled morgue attendant). Romanian actress Elina Lowensohn portrays a modern version of Dracula's daughter living in Manhattan with long-haired Peter Fonda (in one of the strangest roles of his oddball career) serving as the von Helsing pursuer. There's every opportunity here for something unique, but *Nadja* is strangely lacking in energy and for the first half is nothing but a series of close-ups of unhappy, angst-riddled characters (living and dead) with out-of-focus Pixelvision shots that add nothing to an already murky theme. Visuals pick up considerably once the story moves to Transylvania and the weird castle of Dracula, but the characters are so aloof and unsympathetic, there's nothing to relate to and hence nothing to care about. Inspired by the 1928 surrealistic novel by Andre Breton. Suzy Amis, Galaxy Rage, Martin Donovan, Jared Harris. (Evergreen)

NAIL GUN MASSACRE (1987) ★½ Helmeted avenger takes to Texas streets to slaughter construction workers who gang-banged his girl. The only novelty here is the murder weapon, subtly referred to in the title, which is used in a variety of ways so you'll bite your nails. Written-directed by Terry Loftin and Bill Leslie. Rocky Patterson, Michelle Meyer, Ron Queen. (Magnum)

NAKED JUNGLE, THE (1954) ★★★ Cancel your picnic plans to see this grand version of Carl Stephenson's classic story, "Leiningen vs. the Ants." It's slow going at first—what with all those smoochy embraces between mail-order bride Eleanor Parker and plantation owner Charlton Heston—until the killer ants mobilize and march on the plantation's crops. Those little ravenous carnivores will scare the hell out of you as men are eaten alive. Directed by an antsy Byron Haskin, written by Philip Yordan and Ronald MacDougall with ants in their pants. Great thrills in this George Pal production co-starring William Conrad. (Video/Laser: Paramount)

NAKED LUNCH (1991) ★★★½ Written and directed by David Cronenberg, this adaptation of William S. Burroughs's cult novel is a nightmarish descent into the drugged-out world of a novelist (Peter Weller) who hallucinates reality into a twisted spy adventure where giant centipedes and other monstrous creatures (created by Chris Walis) control him. It's a metaphor of homosexuality that will baffle some, sicken others and intrigue those who appreciate Cronenberg's intepretation of what was generally considered an unfilmable book. Judy Davis, Julian Sands, Roy Scheider. (Fox)

NAKED SOULS (1995) ★★½ The only good reason to watch this low-budget soul-transference thriller is for the love-making scenes with blond bombshell Pamela Anderson, as you will see the talents of the "Baywatch" star in all their glorious magnitude. Otherwise you have your basic mind-switch melodrama when dying millionaire David Warner transfers his soul with that of genetic scientist Brian Krause, unaware Krause has been infected with the memory cells of a serial killer that now turn Warner into a killer. But all this stuff in Frank Dietz's script pales alongside the undulating, uncovered body of Anderson, pouty lips and all, as director Lyndon Chubbick does all he can to expose her lovely flesh to the world. Clayton Rohner, Justina Vail, Dean Stockwell. (WarnerVision)

NAKED SPACE. See *Spaceship.*

NAKED TERROR. See *The Last Man on Earth.*

NAME FOR EVIL, A (1973) ★★ Pretentious, esoteric allegory, in which Robert Culp resigns his architectural firm by throwing his TV out the window and moving to Canada to restore his great-great-grandfather's mansion, haunted by a ghost on a white charger. The ghost sleeps with wife Samantha Eggar while Culp seeks solace with a mountain girl. Ambiguous as hell. Written-directed by Bernard Girard from a novel by Andrew Lytle. Aka *The Grove, The Face of Evil* and *There Is a Name for Evil.* (Premiere; Paragon)

NAME IS BLACULA, THE. See *Scream, Blacula, Scream.*

NATHANIEL HAWTHORNE'S TWICE-TOLD TALES. See *Twice-told Tales.*

NATURE OF THE BEAST, THE (1994) ★★★½ Bodies are being chopped into little pieces by "Hatchet Man," a serial killer working out of Reno, Nevada. And an embezzler just lifted $1 million from a casino. That's when two disparate strangers begin a tense relationship as they travel through desert country. Call this *The Odd*

Couple of the Horror Set. Eric Roberts is a druggie drifter, sleazy and cruel, and Lance Henriksen is a nervous businessman with a suitcase filled with—ho, that would be giving it away. In addition to its horrific elements, and excellent set pieces of suspense, this is a well-written character development of the two travelers as written by director Victor Salva (*Powder*), who has a good grasp on the psychology of his people. Brion James, Sasha Jenson, Ana Gabriel, Eloy Casados. (Video/Laser: New Line)

NAVIGATOR: AN ODYSSEY ACROSS TIME, THE (1988) ★★★★ New Zealand filmmaker Vincent Ward has created a minimasterpiece of fantasy with this offbeat, beautifully photographed tale of 14th-century England, when the Black Plague is sweeping the land. In an isolated village, miners are impressed with visionary dreams of young Griffin, who leads select followers on a journey through time and space. Ward's viewpoint is of a stranger in a strange land, so that modern technology to a man from the past looks life-threatening. This unlikely time travel movie is filled with symbolism and layers of meaning as it weaves in and out of dreams and reality in a wondrous way. The film won 19 awards. Bruce Lyons, Chris Haywood, Hamish McFarlane. (Trylon)

NAVY VS. THE NIGHT MONSTERS, THE (1966) ★ Director Michael Hoey's script, based on Murray Leinster's *Monster from the Earth's End*, depicts plant creatures with acid in their veins who stalk forth and "stump" Anthony Eisley before launching their invasion against Earth. Mamie Van Doren breaths heavily to push the biggest night monsters of all against the thin material of her blouse, thereby revealing the roundness of the Gargantuas concealed beneath. Bobby Van, Billy Gray, Pamela Mason, Russ Bender. Aka *Monsters of the Night* and *The Night Crawlers*. (Paragon)

NEAR DARK (1987) ★★★★ The Bonnie and Clyde of horror films, shirking clichéd gothic trappings to take on the look of a rural gangster movie, and photographed against a stark Americana landscape and peopled by grubby killers who resemble Depression-era migrant workers. They're really vampires and there's nothing fastidious about these Texas clod kickers. Director Kathryn Bigelow and cowriter Eric (*Hitcher*) Red create a disturbing, violent, bloody story that many may find too gory to watch. Genre buffs, however, will dig this modern Western in which Jenny Wright hooks Adrian Pasdar with a neck bite and he reluctantly joins the gang. A parable of innocence exposed to evil, with Lance Henriksen and Bill Paxton as fascinatingly grotesque gang members. Offbeat and worth catching—the film, not vampirism. Tim Thomerson. (HBO) (Laser: Image)

NECROMANCER: SATAN'S SERVANT (1988) ★★ Slow-moving, predictable horror flick underplays its violence and bloodletting. A demon called from Beyond carries out revenge murders by taking possession of a witch, or necromancer. This happens after drama student Elizabeth Cayton is raped by three fellow students but is afraid to tell authorities, and calls on Lisa the Avenger (Lois Masten) to wreak havoc. Softcore sex scenes reveal that Cayton has a fine body, but that's the only appeal this offers. Russ Tamblyn is wasted as a lecherous drama coach. Directed by Dusty Nelson. John Tyler, Rhonda Durton. (Forum) (Laser: Image)

NECROMANCY (1971) ★ Terror tale written-produced-directed by Bert I. Gordon with Orson Welles as toy manufacturer Cato, boss man of a witchcraft cult restoring life to Cato's dead son. Into the community of Lilith comes Pamela Franklin, unwitting (or is it witless?) heroine subjected to tortures from Mr. Cato's so-called toys. For lovers of dead movies only. Lee Purcell, Michael Ontkean. Aka *A Life for a Life* and *The Toy Factory*. (From Paragon as *The Witching* and Magnum as *Rosemary's Disciples*)

NECROMANIAC. Video version of *Graveyard of Horror* (All American).

NECROPHAGUS. See *Graveyard of Horror*.

NECROPOLIS (1986) ★½ Sleazy, kinky R-rated supernatural flick, so nihilistic there's nary an entertaining moment in its 77 minutes. After an opening set in 1686 New Amsterdam, where it's revealed Leeanne Baker runs a devil cult, she turns up reincarnated as a blond sex kitten in black miniskirt and nylons in modern Manhattan. Wearing the Devil's Ring, she uses mind control over the street trash and fights a psychological battle with a black priest, a former adversary who has also been reincarnated. She has three sets of breasts that leak this white gooey stuff, a substance her zombies suckle on. Yes, it's pretty weird stuff coming from writer-director Bruce Hickey. Jacquie Fitz, Michael Conte. (Vestron) (Laser: Japanese)

NEEDFUL THINGS (1993) ★★★½ This adaptation of Stephen King's sprawling, dark novel (one of his most complex) combines black comedy and bloody thrills, a mixture that prevents the film from being ultimately satisfying. However, to the credit of writer W. D. Richter and director Fraser Heston (son of Charlton), it's loaded with filmmaking artistry and sports a fine cast. To Castle Rock, Maine, pure Stephen King territory, comes the Devil in the form of Leland Gaunt (Max von Sydow, in a fine performance), who opens a shop (Needful Things) and offers items for sale to lure buyers into pacts. Now in the clutches of evil, these townspeople carry out acts against each other until the town explodes—figuratively and literally. Ed Harris plays Sheriff Alan Pangborn, the film's only heroic figure, and Bonnie Bedelia is outstanding as a café proprietress suffering from arthritic pain. Amanda Plummer's Nettie Cobb is an ultimate portrayal of sexual oppression, and J. T. Walsh as the crazed Buster carries madness to cartoonish proportions. This film is so stark, and so deeply disturbing in commenting on man's inhumanity, that it is missing one needful thing: more rays of hope to counteract its too-effective darkness. (Video/Laser: Columbia TriStar)

NEMESIS (1992) ★★★½ Slam-bang action thriller set in A.D. 2027, when a movement is afoot to replace human beings with mechanical clones. Oliver Gruner, doing an impression of Jean-Claude Van Damme, portrays Alex Rain, L.A. cyborg cop who undergoes harrowing adventures in his quest to reach the Red Army Hammerheads, a terrorist group that could help prevent evil clone-cop Tim Thomerson from fulfilling the conspiracy. Director Albert Pyun brings such kinetic energy to the rousing battle sequences—filled with acrobatic bodies, explosions and incredibly intense firepower—that the film grabs on and won't let go. Cary-Hirdyuki Tagawa, Merle Kennedy, Deborah Shelton, Brion James, Marjorie Monaghan, Thom Mathews. (Imperial) (Laser: Image)

NEMESIS 2: NEBULA (1995) ★★½ This is pure action movie, with not enough dialogue to fill a 2-minute phone conversation. That's not necessarily good if the action is all mindless, and *Nemesis 2*, believe me, is mindless. The baby daughter of Alex Rain (the hero in the first film) travels through time and ends up in East Africa, where she grows into a muscle-bound warrior in the form of Sue Price. Meanwhile, from A.D. 2077 comes a force field–enwrapped cyborg warrior (codename: Nebula) to destroy her, as she will affect the future. Sounds like *Terminator*, you say? Well, Nebula (played by Chad Stahelski) looks like the Hunter from *Predator*. Writer-director Albert Pyun offers nothing for the brain and a lot of explosions in the Arizona desert for the eye, and not enough plot to bury one body. And that's it. This Gary Schmoeller–Tom Karnowski production promises another in the series, *Nemesis 3: Time Lapse*, but one hopes they will reconsider. Tina Cote, Earl White, Jahi J. J. Zuri, Traci Davis, Karen Studer. (Imperial) (Laser: Image)

NEMESIS 3: TIME LAPSE (1996) ★ Another incoherent sci-fi adventure from writer-director Albert Pyun using the very same plot from *Nemesis 2: Nebula*. While the Terminator-styled time traveler to the Arizona desert (standing in for East Africa) used to be called "Nebula," this time he's named "Farnsworth 2" and played by Tim Thomerson (who played a cyborg cop named Farnsworth in the first *Nemesis*). The robot-humanoid (he keeps shifting from metallic form to human) is accompanied from 2077 A.D.

to 1998 by two sex kittens with white wigs (or blond, depending on the lighting) and glowing green eyes. With their ray guns and wisecracking patter, the sexually activated creatures run around trying to capture "Alex," a human mutant with "a unique molecular structure" that holds the key to the cyborgs' continued control of Earth in the 21st century. Or so it is subtly suggested in the written prologue. Alex is played by muscle-bound Sue Price, a colorless actress who keeps encountering guys who might or might not help her, since the desert is full of spies, traitors, and turncoats. She kicks a lot of butt, bedevils baddies with barrages of bullets, turns down any form of sexual advance (even ones from nice guys), and keeps on pushing through explosions, traps, and bullet-riddled double crosses. While avoiding capture at every turn, Alex still finds time to search for her missing sister who has a necklace that could hold the key to something else grandiose . . . who knows and who cares? The only interesting special effect is a time-shift dune buggy that looks like a rolling, shimmering opal as it speeds around the desert, but what significance it's supposed to have is as lost as everything else. Aka *Nemesis 3: Prey Harder.* Followed, unfortunately, by *Nemesis 4: City of Angels.* Norbert Weisser, Xavier Declie, Sharron Bruneau, Debbie Muggli, Ursula Sarcev. (Warner/Imperial Entertainment)

NEMESIS 4: CITY OF ANGELS (1999) ½ This is one awful, unwatchable movie. It seems that writer-director Albert Pyun, who got off to a decent start with the first *Nemesis* in 1992, becomes worse with each passing year. Everything about this waste of 83 minutes is ugly and detestable. Gone is Tom Thomerson, who at least was fun in the beginning, and back is muscle-bound Sue Price, whose voluptuous body is more a turnoff than a turn-on, with bulging muscles that give her a masculine appearance. That body is naked most of the time as we visit the ruins of a city in 2080 A.D., when global crime syndicates rule a world of fighting cyborgs and humans. Cyborg Price, her giant breasts threatening to smash into the camera lens in almost every scene, is a hit woman for syndicate underling Bernardo (Andrew Divoff) and is set up to kill the wrong syndicate boss. Everyone comes after Price (playing Alex Sinclair again) but she keeps killing them—but only after she bores them to death with meaningless, never-ending dialogue. Ever watch two cyborgs get it on in the front seat of a car? Watch *Nemesis 4* and you'll see just that—a disgusting depiction of substitute sex organs (cyborg instead of human) coming together for a wild climax. Simon Poland turns up as Alex's lover, Johnny Impact, and Nicholas Guest is the cyborg named Earl Typhoon. Then there's a woman (Blanka Copikova) who might be "The Angel of Death" but turns out instead to be an underworld character nicknamed Mother. Even a Catholic priest gets slaughtered by Alex's electrical jolts in the opening minutes of this fiasco. Norbert Weisser, Michael Gucik. (Avalanche)

NEON CITY (1991) ★★★½ Sci-fi version of *Stagecoach* set in Mad Max country—an enjoyable action derivation masterminded by Monte Markham, who cowrote (with Buck Finch and Jeff Begun), directed and stars as a corrupt sheriff ranger in a post-holocaust world of A.D. 2053. While there's plenty of action, there's also good ensemble acting led by Michael Ironside (as ex-ranger Harry M. Stark) and Vanity (as a fugitive who becomes Stark's bounty). They're with motley passengers traveling in a futuristic funky bus across a dangerous desert zone ruled by "Skins." Lyle Alzado, Valerie Wildman, Mick Klar. Shot on the salt flats of Utah. (Vidmark)

NEON MANIACS (1985) ★★ "When the world is ruled by violence, and the soul of mankind fades, the children's path shall be darkened by the shadows of the . . . Neon Maniacs." That prologue doesn't make much sense, but neither does this exercise in excessive gore effects. The premise—that a gang of grotesque killer monsters live within a tower of the Golden Gate Bridge in San Francisco—is never developed; instead we're subjected to teenagers who are disbelieved by police when they tell of the slimy creatures they've seen slithering around the bridge, killing their buddies. Director Joseph Mangine manages some harrowing suspense (especially a runaway streetcar sequence) and the monsters are ugly enough, but the story sucks. Just a lot of gooey mayhem as the Samurai, Bowman and Hangman monsters stalk their prey. Donna Locke, Allan Hayes. (Lightning; Vestron)

NEO-TOKYO (1986–91) ★★★ This trilogy of excellent Japanese animation, commissioned for a futuristic exposition in Japan many years ago, opens with Rin Taro's "Labyrinth," the story of a little girl who lives in a surreal city with her big house cat. Suddenly she's pulled through a mirror into another dimension. Things pick up considerably with Yoshiaki Kawajiri's "Running Man," the depiction of the world's greatest race-car driver and his disintegration as he races toward oblivion. (An edited version of this once ran on MTV.) Katsuhiro Otomo's "The Order to Stop Construction" depicts an executive sent to the jungles of South America where he finds that the robot workers have taken over. (Streamline)

NEST, THE (1987) ★★ There's the flavor of a '50s "creatures on a rampage" flick to this adaptation of Eli Cantor's novel about an island community being attacked by a swarm of genetically jazzed cockroaches. Scripter Robert King and director Terence H. Winkless bring to this Julie Corman production a mixture of straight thrills and comedy. The roaches are the result of unauthorized testing by the company INTEC. The best moments come when the roaches take on the shape of life-forms they've ingested, including humans, giving the special effects team the opportunity to create man and cat monsters. Robert Lansing, Lisa Langlois, Franc Luz and Terri Treas bring a sense of fun to the picture. (MGM/UA)

NESTING, THE (1981) ★★½ Robin Groves, a neurotic writer suffering from agoraphobia, seeks refuge in a haunted house and is driven to madness by ghostly specters in this blending of supernatural shocks and psychological terrors. It's a valiant try by writers Daria Price and Armand Weston (the latter, a one-time porn maker, produced-directed) on a limited budget, but it's a strong supporting cast (John Carradine and Gloria Grahame in pivotal roles; for Grahame it was her last) that finally gives convincing clout to an otherwise predictable horror story. Christopher Loomis, Michael David Lally, David Tabor. Originally made as *Phobia*. (Warner Bros.)

NETHERWORLD (1991) ★★ A quieter-than-usual Full Moon production from producer Charles Band, enhanced by New Orleans locations. Michael Bendetti arrives at his father's Louisiana mansion where a cult of bird lovers uses winged creatures as a means of restoring the dead to life. The best effect by Steve Patino is the Hand of Satan, a severed human paw that floats through the mansion's corridors (shades of *Phantasm*!) and thrusts its claws into your eyeballs. A hint of sexual decadence hangs over the script by Billy Chicago (pseudonym for director David Schmoeller, who appears as bartender Billy Chicago). Excellent performances by Denise Gentile, Anjanette Comer, Holly Floria and Alex Datcher add up to one interesting video movie. (Paramount) (Laser: Full Moon)

NEVER CRY DEVIL. See *Night Visitor* (1989).

NEVERENDING STORY, THE (1984) ★★★ Offbeat fairy tale told in striking details by German filmmaker Wolfgang Petersen. A youth, reading a book given to him by a strange shop owner, is projected into the land of Fantasia, which is about to be destroyed by the Nothing. He must find a cure for the dying empress in her Ivory Tower, and he sets out on his episodic quest. The lad meets a racing snail, a rock-eating stone man, a wise old colossal turtle, statues with laser-beam eyes and other charming creatures. But when the film tries to be philosophical with a form of doublethink, it is a letdown. Tami Stronach, Moses Gunn, Patrick Hayes. (Video/ Laser: Warner Bros.)

NEVERENDING STORY II: THE NEXT CHAPTER, THE (1990) ★★ Weak follow-up to Wolfgang Petersen's popular film of 1984, its fantasy elements appealing mainly to the young because of a sanitized script by Karin Howard, who adapted new parts of Michael Ende's novel. However, its visuals are again a delight to behold as youngster Jonathan Brandis, reading a magical book given to him by Mr. Koreander (Thomas Hill), is propelled into the kingdom of Fantasia. Evil empress Xayide (Clarissa Burt) tries to trick Brandis into using up all the wishes granted by Orin, the magic medallion, for then he will become her slave. The creatures Falkor and Rock Biter are back, as well as Atreyu, a birdlike entity. John Wesley Shipp, of TV's "The Flash," figures into the story minimally as he reads the narrative from the book. Director George Miller is not the same George Miller who made *Mad Max*. Kenny Morrison, Alexandra Johnes, Martin Umbach. (Video/Laser: Warner Bros.)

NEVERENDING STORY III: THE ESCAPE FROM FANTASIA, THE (1994) ★★★ Although this is nothing like the Wolfgang Petersen original of 1984, it is nevertheless a satisfying children's movie (again spinning off from the book by Michael Ende) with enough adult touches to make it a palatable family comedy-adventure, emphasis on comedy. Jim Henson's Creature Shop rendered the fairy-tale creatures of the kingdom of Fantasia. That overgrown flying doglike being Falkor, once described as a "Luck Dragon," returns to carry the characters to and fro on its back and projects a lovable quality that sets the tone for the other Muppet-inspired creatures. There is Rockbiter Jr., a bumbling hunk of granite, two arguing ma-and-pa gnomes named Urgl and Engywook (who accidentally get sent to Nome, AK), and Barky, a fussy tree complete with branches and roots. They all turn up in our world with the Orin, the medallion that grants any wish, to help young Bastian Balthasar Bux (Jason James Richter, of *Free Willy*) recover a library copy of *The Neverending Story* taken by a gang of juvenile toughies called the Nasties, an act that is causing catastrophes at the Crystal Palace of Fantasia. Since nothing is ever at stake in Jeff Lieberman's script, director Peter MacDonald takes a playful attitude toward the nonsensical proceedings and lets everyone be either sincere or silly, depending on the needs of the moment. Melody Kay is good as Jason's sister, who goes on a shopping spree (her wish to have all the merchandise free is granted) and Julie Cox is the childlike empress who runs the Crystal Palace. Jason's mom and dad, who touch lightly on certain morality issues, such as daughter Melody's greed over the shopping spree, are played by Tracey Ellis and Kevin McNulty. Among the Nasties—who provide more laughs than threats—are Carole Finn, Jack Black, Ryan Bollman, and Nicole Parker. Shot in a German studio, *Neverending Story III* is an instant video movie, the kind best seen between major kiddie releases from Disney. (Touchstone)

NEVER PICK UP A STRANGER. Video version of *Bloodrage* (Live; Best Film & Video).

NEVER SAY NEVER AGAIN (1983) ★★★½ Sean Connery's return as James Bond after he forsook the part for 12 years is a loose remake of *Thunderball* (producer Kevin McClory ended up with story rights after a legal battle; this is not part of the official series). It's a return to adventurous derring-do as British secret agent 007 tries to thwart Largo from detonating two atomic warheads he's stolen from U.S. missiles as part of a SPECTRE plot. The gadgetry, action and sexy ladies are abundant—everything you expect in a Bond thriller. Barbara Carrera is a sadistic SPECTRE assassin, as exotic as she is deadly; Kim Basinger is the innocent (though well-rounded) young thing saved by Bond; Max von Sydow is the insidious SPECTRE chief with the white cat; Klaus Maria Brandauer is one of the best Bond villains yet, giving Largo such human traits as a sense of humor, joviality and jealousy. There are jokes about Bond growing old, but Connery still has the looks to pull it off. Irvin Kershner's direction is slick and unobtrusive. (Video/Laser: Warner Bros.)

NEW ADVENTURES OF BATMAN AND ROBIN, THE. See *Batman and Robin*.

NEW ADVENTURES OF TARZAN, THE (1935) ★★ A 12-chapter serial starring Herman Brix (later to become Bruce Bennett) independently produced by Edgar Rice Burroughs in Guatemala, which provides colorful jungle and old-ruins footage. The jungle hero has left Africa for South America to find a friend kidnapped by villainous Mayans. Tarzan locates a valuable artifact that also contains the formula for a revolutionary explosive. The acting is dreadfully passé. Directed by Edward Kull and W. F. McGaugh. Ula Holt, Frank Baker, Dale Walsh, Harry Ernest. In 1938, it was rereleased in feature form as *Tarzan and the Green Goddess*. Known at various times as *Tarzan in Guatemala, Tarzan and the Lost Goddess* and *Tarzan's New Adventure*. (The complete serial is available from Rhino.)

NEW BARBARIANS, THE. Video version of *Warriors of the Wasteland* (Impulse).

NEW CRIME CITY: LOS ANGELES 2020 (1994) ★★ A rip-off mixture of *Mad Max* and *Escape from New York*, from producer Roger Corman, in which L.A. has been turned into a penal colony and prisoner Rick Rossovich is assigned by military officer Stacy Keach to infiltrate the crime-infested inner city to prevent a madman named Ironhead Wilks from releasing a killer virus created by a chemist called the Wizard.

(Got all that?) Rossovich, in the company of hard-bitten Sherrie Ross, has just 48 hours to track down these fruitcakes in an urban nightmare landscape of roving killer bands and other freak-out oddball deals. A very terrible movie without a single original idea. (New Horizons) (Laser: Image)

NEW EDEN (1994) ★ *Mad Max*-styled futuristic actioner in which Stephen Baldwin leads a ragtag team against "sand pirates" in a desert world ruined by man's catastrophic behavior. Lisa Bonet costars as a waiflike wanderer. (MCA)

NEW GLADIATORS, THE (ROME, 2072 A.D.) (1987) ★ "Kill Bike" is the highest-rated show on the World Broadcasting System, in which men fight on "machines of death." It's the greatest in "pain, brutality and human cruelty." But along comes a new show, "Battle of the Damned," in which the best bikers are given old-fashioned gladiatorial weaponry and told to rip each other apart. It's "live until the death." Meanwhile, there's a scheme afoot involving corporate crooks, computers and a distant satellite to gain control of the world, and only the gladiators can stop the nefarious plot. Yes, gang, it's one of those Italian futuristic action films, directed by Lucio Fulci, loaded down with zap guns, storm troopers, exploding bikes and beheadings. Jared Martin, Fred Williamson, Howard Ross. (Media)

NEW HOUSE ON THE LEFT. See *Carnage* (1983).

NEW KING KONG, THE. See *A*P*E*.

NEWLYDEADS, THE (1988) ★ A very poor walking corpse supernatural nonthriller set at the Newlywed Hotel, where the owner once murdered a homosexual in drag. Now, 15 years later on the day of his wedding, the ghost of the slain man turns up to slaughter all the newlywed couples staying at the lakeside hotel, sticking knifes, icepicks and poles into torsos and cutting off one head with a bandsaw. Joseph Merhi directed this slasher-revenge mess that is more boring than shocking, what with its phony monster makeup, lack of suspense or shock and a pace that plods thanks to an empty script by Merhi and Sean Dash that lacks everything. Merhi's partner Richard Pepin was cameraman. Scott Kaske, Jim Williams, Jean Levine, Jay Richardson, Roxanne Michaels. (City Lights)

NEW YEAR'S EVIL (1982) ★★★ Roz Kelly, a sexy chick-emcee for a punk-rock radio special, is the target for a knife killer calling himself Evil (Kip Niven). She tries to act as a psychiatrist for the police, but the killer continues to knock off beautiful women, moving ever closer to the station. Footage is devoted to punk-rock numbers while the plot waits in the wings, so don't anticipate breathtaking pace. Writerdirector Emmett Alston supplies some surprise twists. Chris Wallace, Grant Cramer, Louisa Moritz. (Paragon; Cannon)

NEW YORK RIPPER (1981) ★★ Italy's horror writer-director Lucio Fulci is up to his usual graphic close-ups of human flesh being ripped apart in this Manhattan melodrama of murder, in which a knife-wielding killer, who cackles like a duck, slaughters prostitutes. Fulci has added a whodunit element in the Dario Argento vein, so there are many suspects to suspect. But when it comes to scenes of a woman's stomach and breast being opened by a razor blade, Fulci returns to his primitive level. Jack Hedley, Almanta Keller, Howard Ross, Andrew Painter. (Vidmark)

NEXT. U.S. theatrical title for *Blade of the Ripper*.

NEXT ONE, THE (1982) ★ Weak, tedious Greek-produced fantasy with supernaturalreligious overtones, about as exciting as Zorba the Greek on crutches. Adrienne Barbeau and her young son are living in a villa on the isle of Mykonos when a stranger (Keir Dullea) washes ashore. He's someone from the time-space continuum, the brother of Jesus Christ, although what significance this has remains a mystery in the hands of writer-director Nico Mastorakis. Dull and slow-moving. Peter Hobbs, Jeremy Licht. (Vestron)

NEXT VICTIM. Alternate video version of *Blade of the Ripper* (Video Gems; Dominique).

NICE GIRLS DON'T EXPLODE (1987) ★★★½ An amusing and unusual premise (teenager Michelle Meyrink causes objects to burst into flames whenever she makes love) is reduced to screwball cases of mistaken identity and daffy misunderstandings in this fantasy comedy shot in Lawrence, Kansas. Meyrink's mother (Barbara Harris) tries to prevent the fires from breaking out—literal flames as well as passionate ones. Paul Harris's script deals with sexual themes, although this element is kept on a cutesy level. William O'Leary portrays the bewildered boyfriend and Wallace Shawn is a would-be paramour of Harris, named "Ellen." Directed with a light touch by Chuck Martinez. Irwin Keyes, Belinda Wills, James Mardini. (New World) (Laser: Image)

NICK KNIGHT (1989) ★★★ A clever idea— L.A. cop Knight is a good-guy vampire who can only work at night—is witlessly carried out in this TV-movie starring Rick Springfield as the detective investigating a series of killings in which the blood of the victims is drained. Knight's old rival, another eternal vampire, is out to get a sacrifical Mayan globe, the key to becoming mortal again. Meanwhile, Knight has a romance with museum curator Laura Johnson that lacks conviction. The level of violence is unusually grim for a TV-movie. There's never a sense that Springfield is a cop, and the premise becomes anemic. John Kapelos, Robert Harper, Michael Nader. (Starmaker) (Laser: Image)

NIECE OF THE VAMPIRE. See *Fangs of the Living Dead.*

NIGHT ANDY CAME HOME, THE. See *Dead of Night* (1974).

NIGHT ANGEL (1990) ★½ An evil spirit, assuming the shapeliness of a modern female, seduces men to kill them for power. It's the Lilith legend retold in modern gory story terms by scripter Joe Augustyn and director Dominique Othenin-Girard. Isa Anderson, Karen Black, Linden Ashby. Narrated by Roscoe Lee Browne. (Fries) (Laser: Image)

NIGHTBREED (1990) ★★½ In the wake of *Hellraiser*'s success, Clive Barker returns as writer-director with a rip-roaring monster flick, all the stops out and pumping with imagination. Based on Barker's novel *Cabal*, this is the story of Midian, where monsters dwell after they die. And there are scores of beasts, creatures and "things" so don't miss this if you love effects and monster makeup. Craig Sheffer is a human monster who joins their ranks after his death is set up by a psychiatrist hoping to learn secrets of eternal life. That psychiatrist, in a brilliant bit of twist-casting, is David Cronenberg, the Canadian director. Anne Bobby, Charles Haid, Malcolm Smith, Catherine Chevalier. (Media) (Laser: Image)

NIGHT BRINGS CHARLIE, THE (1990) ★ Low-budget effort, from Orlando, FL, in which a psycho killer (a tree surgeon who has been disfigured) with power tools goes after women at a slumber party. Be careful you don't fall asleep yourself. Directed by Tom Logan. Kerry Knight, Wally Parks, Paul Stubenrach, Joe Fishback, Monica Simmons. (Quest)

NIGHT CALLER. See *The Night Caller from Outer Space.*

NIGHT CALLER FROM OUTER SPACE, THE (1965) ★★ Low-budget British effort, in which an egg-shaped object sent to Ganymede (a moon of Jupiter) and back is discovered by scientist John Saxon, working at an astronomy station. The egg transfers matter for a monster sent here to (1) frighten Patricia Haines half to death and (2) kidnap pretty women by posing as a girly magazine editor. John Gilling's direction achieves a dreary look distinctively British with a stiff-lipped cast: Maurice Denham, Alfred Burke, Aubrey Morris, Warren Mitchell. Script by Jim O'Connally from Frank Crisp's novel *Night Callers*. Aka *Blood Beast from Outer Space* and *The Night Caller*. (Sony) (Laser: Image)

NIGHT CHILD (1973). See *What the Peeper Saw.*

NIGHTCOMERS, THE (1972) ★★★ Prequel to Henry James's *Turn of the Screw*, written by Michael Hastings, reveals how evil valet-gardener Quint (Marlon Brando) and governess Miss Jessel (Stephanie Beacham) engage in brutal, voyeuristic bedroom techniques that turn two innocent children into little monsters. Directed by Michael Winner. Harry Andrews, Anna Palk, Thora Hird. (RCA/Columbia; Nelson; Charter) (Laser: Image)

NIGHT CRAWL (1988) ★ When the Japanese build an amusement park in the Australian desert, dedicated to the Robotman cartoon hero, a graveyard of Vietnam dead is disturbed and shambling corpses arise from their resting places to bounce around like kangaroos and lust for the blood of Japanese tourists. Written-produced-directed by Carmelo Musca and Barrie Pattison. John Moore, Khym Lam, Geoff Gibbs, Adam A. Wong. Aka *Zombie Brigade*. (Alliance/MCA)

NIGHT CRAWLERS. See *The Navy vs. the Night Monsters.*

NIGHT CREATURE (1977) ★★½ Metaphysical link between big game hunter Axel McGregory (Donald Pleasence) and a killer leopard provides an odd ambience to this strangely compelling tale of cowardice and bravery, photographed in exotic Thai locations. Pleasence brings the black cat to his private island for a showdown, but unexpected visitors foul up his plans. Good dialogue and mood make up for an ambiguous, unresolved script by Hubert Smith. Directed by Lee Madden. Ross Hagen, Nancy Kwan, Jennifer Rhodes. Aka *Cat, Out of the Darkness, Devil Cat* and *Fear*. (VCI).

NIGHT CREATURES, THE (1964). See *The Last Man on Earth.*

NIGHT DANIEL DIED, THE. See *Bloodstalkers.*

NIGHTDREAMS (1981) ★ Lightly pornographic fantasy, from the makers of *Cafe Flesh*, in which a pair of scientists observes a woman, jolting her with stimulating electrons so she will undergo erotic dreams. Directed by F. X. Pope from a script by Herbert W. Day and Rinse Dream. Dorothy LeMay, Loni Sanders, Jennifer West, Ken Starbuck (as the Devil).

NIGHT EYES. See *Deadly Eyes.*

NIGHTFALL (1988) ★ Night doesn't fall fast enough in this Julie Corman production of Isaac Asimov's famous short story about a race of people faced with losing all sunlight every thousand years and coping with the psychological terror of darkness. All the robed characters act like tragic figures from Shakespearean drama, but without poetry or pentameter it plays more like a soap opera made for Julius Caesar. Paul Mayersberg wrote the misguided script, which is a travesty against sci-fi literature, and also directed the dullish events on Arizona desert locations. David Birney is awful in a fright wig as the leader of a cult. Sarah Douglas, Alexis Kanner, Andra Millian, Starr Andreeff. (MGM/UA)

NIGHT FIEND. TV title for *Violent Blood Bath*.

NIGHTFLYERS (1987) ★★ In adapting George R. R. Martin's novella, screenwriter Robert Jaffe and producers Robert and Herb Jaffe had good intentions to produce a space adventure combining literary and cinematic techniques. Unfortunately, the effects are uneven, the plot is unnecessarily convoluted, and the characters so abrasive that *Nightflyers* annoys more than it intrigues. In the 21st century, Catherine Mary Stewart and a group of scientists set out on an old space freighter, *Nightflyer*, only to discover that the ship's computer is controlled by the essence of an evil woman, who created a male clone (Michael Praed) before her death. Now she wants the clone, Captain Royd, for herself and kills the intruders one by one. Director Robert Collector had his name replaced with the alias T. C. Blake, so unhappy was he with the results. John Standing, Lisa Blount, Glenn Withrow, James Avery, Michael Des Barres. (IVE) (Laser: Pioneer)

NIGHT FRIGHT (1968) ★½ Low-budget schlock, filmed in the South and strictly from hunger. A rocket sent into space with hundreds of animals (Operation Noah's Ark) is subjected to radiation, mutating the animals. The ship (now a UFO) lands near Satan's Hollow, and a creature attacks stupid teenagers making out in a convertible. This monster (with the body of Robot Monster and the face of It! The Terror from Beyond Space) runs through the woods after sheriff John Agar and deputy Bill Thurman, pipe-smoking scientist Roger Ready and more stupid teenagers led by Carol Gilley. Deadly dull, without a whit of imagination from director James A. Sullivan or writer Russ Marker. Based on a previous film called *The Demon from Black Lake*, this is aka *The Extraterrestrial Nasty*. (Sinister/C)

NIGHT GALLERY (1969) ★★★½ Rod Serling's collection of horror stories, *The Season to Be Wary*, was adapted by him for Universal into a trilogy that became the pilot for a popular series. Stories are hung together by the theme of surrealistic paintings in a creepy art gallery, presided over by host Rod Serling, who introduces each tale. In the first, directed by Boris Sagal, Roddy McDowall speeds along the death of a relative, then realizes he is being haunted by a painting. In the second, directed by Steven Spielberg (making his directorial debut), Joan Crawford is a blind woman who buys the eyes of a beggar so she might see again. And in the third, directed by Barry Shear, Richard Kiley is a one-time Nazi butcher seeking refuge from Israeli avengers (and his conscience) by hiding in a painting hanging in an art gallery. (MCA)

NIGHT HAIR CHILD. See *What the Peeper Saw*.

NIGHT IN THE CRYPT. See *One Dark Night*.

NIGHTKILLERS, THE. See *Silent Madness*.

NIGHT LEGS. See *Fright* (1971).

NIGHT LIFE (1989) ★★½ Teenage mortician's assistant Scott Grimes is in for one gory zombie attack on the night when a bolt of lightning turns dead teenagers into flesh-munching shamblers. The blood, severed limbs and torn throats are abundant in this *Night of the Living Dead* mixture of macabre comedy and shocks. As the mean old mortician who browbeats Grimes, John Astin has the film's best scenes, especially the one in which his stomach is pumped to enormous size with embalming fluid. You'll laugh, cry and scream at this revolting gore flick written by Keith Critchlow and directed by David Acomba. Cheryl Pollak, Anthony Geary, Lisa Fuller, Alan Blumenfeld. (Video/Laser: RCA/ Columbia)

NIGHTLIFE (1990) ★★ Quirky vampire love tale with satirical overtones: a century-old vampire beauty (Maryam D'Abo) is resurrected and wants nothing to do with former vampire flame Ben Cross, falling instead for a doctor (Keith Szarabajka) willing to treat her disorder as a "disease." Szarabajka and D'Abo making love in a coffin, Camille Saviola as a superstitious Mexican woman who looks after D'Abo, and Cross as a star-crossed lover all contribute to the atmosphere of this straight-faced, but funny-underneath TV-movie directed by Daniel Taplitz. Jesse Cori, Oliver Clark, Glenn Shadix. (Video/Laser: MCA)

NIGHTMARE (1964) ★★½ Teenager Jennie Linden has terrifying dreams in which she hears the voice of her crazed mother. Seems the old bat went berserk and stabbed a man to death; and now Jennie fears she has Mom's madness. A phantom figure in a nightmare haunts her until her birthday, when Jennie flips out and stabs the woman to death. This Hammer suspense thriller has an intriguing script by producer Jimmy Sangster, but if you're sharp, you'll spot the red herrings and figure out what's happening. Directed by Freddie Francis. David Knight, Moira Richmond, Brenda Bruce. (Video/Laser: MCA)

NIGHTMARE (1981) ★★ Cinematic sleaze scuzz recommended to splatter fans only. A homicidal maniac keeps reliving an incident from childhood during which he axed to death his mother and father while they were engaging in sadistic sexual pleasure. Despite its morbidity and grisly effects, *Nightmare* has a fascination that holds and repels you. Written-directed by Romano Scavolini. Sharon Smith, Baird Stafford. (New Star; Planet; from Platinum as *Blood Splash* and Continental as *Nightmares in a Damaged Brain*)

NIGHTMARE ALLEY (1947) ★★★★★ William Lindsay Gresham's novel was a shocker in depicting a maladjusted young man who joins a carnival and rises to become a successful nightclub mind reader and then a bilker of million-airesses via a spiritualism racket. The movie code allowed only portions of the book into Jules Furthman's screenplay, but Fox still made an earnest attempt to capture Gresham's psychological portrait. Tyrone Power is powerful as Stan Carlisle, repelled when he first sees the geek—the half-man, half-beast of the midway who tears off heads of chickens. This deterioration of an ambitious man into a dipsomaniac is more shivery than any alleged "monster" movie. Directed by Edmund Goulding. Coleen Gray, Joan Blondell, Helen Walker, Ian Keith.

NIGHTMARE AT NOON (1988) ★★★ Outstanding photography of Utah desert locations and well-staged action highlight this adventure. Travelers Wings Hauser, Kimberly Beck and Bo Hopkins stop in Canyon Land only to find that everyone has gone crazy from the water and is on a homicidal rampage, their bodies full of green blood. It seems that APE (the Agency for Protection of the Environment), under the guidance of albino Brion James, is conducting an unauthorized experiment, the details of which are never explained. Director Nico Mastorakis includes a well-staged helicopter chase. George Kennedy is Sheriff Hanks and Kimberley Ross is his sexy daughter. (Republic)

NIGHTMARE AT SHADOW WOODS. See *Blood Rage.*

NIGHTMARE BEFORE CHRISTMAS (1993) ★★★★ A unique and wonderfully imaginative feature that employs 3-D models in telling the story of Halloweentown, a kingdom of freakish characters ruled by Jack Skellington, a lean, unmean figure who discovers there's also a Christmastown and decides to bring the macabre spirit of his land to the Real World of children by posing as Santa Claus—with disastrous results. This is the dark side to Disneyesque cartoons and while its frequently grotesque images contradict the usual spirit of cartoons, it still captures a sense of warmth and humanity. The idea was Burton's, the adaptation is by Michael McDowell and Caroline Thompson, and San Francisco–based animator Henry Selick directed with an inspired touch. This is a one-of-a-kind experiment in stop motion, which took three years to produce, and features several songs. Danny Elfman wrote the music. Aka *Tim Burton's Nightmare Before Christmas.* (Video/ Laser: Buena Vista)

NIGHTMARE CASTLE (1966) ★★½ Standard Italian gothic chiller distinguished by Barbara Steele in two roles, as a wife cheating on her scientist husband and as a cousin. You've seen it before: mad doctor utilizes electrical impulses in experiments with human blood; murder victims rise from grave to wreak vengeance. Directed-written by Mario Caiano (aka Allen Grunewald). Paul Miller, Helga Line, Laurence

Clift, Rik Battaglia. Music by Ennio Morricone. Aka *Night of the Doomed, Orgasmo, The Faceless Monster* and *Lovers Beyond the Tomb.* (Hollywood Home Theater; Sinister/C; Filmfax; S/Weird; Budget)

NIGHTMARE CIRCUS. Video version of *Terror Circus* (Regal).

NIGHTMARE CITY. See *City of the Walking Dead.*

NIGHTMARE HOTEL (1970). See *It Happened at Nightmare Inn.*

NIGHTMARE IN BLOOD (1976) ★★★ Low-budget horror film depicts the world of fantasy comic book fandom. While its humor is hip and droll, it's still a genre suspense shocker featuring macabre murders. Jerry Walter brings new facets to the screen vampire as Malakai, an actor specializing in vampire films and guest of honor at a San Francisco convention. Elements of fandom (horror writer, Sherlock Holmes fan, comic book store owner) band to track Malakai when he turns out to be a real vampire. Malakai's henchmen are publicity men who turn out to be Burke and Hare, infamous body snatchers. The John Stanley–Kenn Davis screenplay incorporates a censor of comic books named Unworth and an Israeli avenger searching for Malakai since the Nazi atrocities. Stanley, host of TV's "Creature Features" in San Francisco for six years, directed and coproduced with Davis. Kerwin Mathews has a cameo in a swashbuckling sequence. Barrie Youngfellow, Hy Pyke, Ray K. Goman, Drew Eshelman, Morgan Upton, Justin Bishop. (Video City; from Imperial as *Horror Convention*)

NIGHTMARE IN WAX (1969) ★★½ Variation on the *House of Wax* theme but as limp as a piece of melting candle. Cameron Mitchell is good as Rinaud, disfigured curator of a wax museum who showcases his victims as exhibits. Rex Carlton's story is so ludicrous and sleazy, it's fascinating to watch. The ending, unfortunately, is a cop-out. Directed by Bud Townsend, from a script by executive producer Rex Carlton, in the Movieland Wax Museum in Los Angeles. Anne Helm, Berry Kroeger, Scott Brady. Aka *Crimes in the Wax Museum* and *Monster of the Wax Museum.* (United; VCI)

NIGHTMARE ISLAND. See *The Slayer.*

NIGHTMARE MAKER. See *Night Warning.*

NIGHTMARE NEVER ENDS, THE (1980) ★ In the vein of *The Omen*, this blends biblical prophecy with horror, and with its sense of hysteria emerges a strange film defying description. The script can be accredited to Philip Yordan, but the production is hampered by uneven cinematography, atrocious sound and unrestrained performances. Jewish avenger Abraham Weiss, in search of the SS officer who murdered his family during Hitler's reign, discovers that musician Robert Bristol is the son of Satan, on Earth to create havoc. Cops Cameron Mitchell and Marc Lawrence, after much soul-searching, believe Weiss. Meanwhile, surgeon Faith Clift is married to Nobel prize–winning author Charles Moll, whose book *God is Dead* becomes a center for controversy. Whew! This can also be seen in truncated form in *Night Train to Terror.* The erratic nature of *The Nightmare Never Ends* might be explained by three directors: Tom McGowan, Greg Tallas and Philip Marsak. Also known as *Satan's Supper.* Maurice Grandmaison, Klint Stevenson, T. J. Savage. (Nite Flite; Simitar; Premiere; Video BanCorp; from Genesis under its original title, *Cataclysm*)

NIGHTMARE OF TERROR. Video version of *Demons of the Mind* (Odds and Ids?).

NIGHTMARE ON ELM STREET, A (1984) ★★★★ A box-office hit with Robert Englund as maniacal killer Freddy Krueger, who wears a glove with long knives at the fingertips. Krueger is a supernatural entity in a slouch hat who turns up in the dreams of teenagers and proceeds to murder them. Director Wes Craven's script is weak on exposition and logic, but it didn't bother audiences, as he focuses in on suspenseful murders and bloody special effects, with atmosphere and spooky shadows abounding. This led to five sequels and a TV series. John Saxon, Heather Langenkamp, Ronee Blakley, Johnny Depp. (Media) (Laser: Image)

NIGHTMARE ON ELM STREET, PART 2: FREDDY'S REVENGE, A (1985) ★★★ In some ways this is better than the original, being capably directed by Jack Sholder and having more character development. On the other hand, it doesn't have as many scares and it barely walks the twilight nightmare world of dreams as the first film did. Anyway, what we have is the return of Freddy Krueger in the dreams of Mark Patton, who moves into the sinister house on Elm Street. Father Clu Gulager and mother Hope Lange, having not seen the original movie, have no idea their son is being taken over by Freddy. It becomes not a symbolic battle but a literal one as the external Mark Patton cracks open and Robert Englund (as Krueger, wearing the knives-for-fingernails device) pops out. This battle of wills is the film's primary strength, with a climactic confrontation in a boiler factory. However, the film's best sequence comes at the beginning as a runaway bus is perched on a precipice—that is straight out of a terrifying nightmare. (Media) (Laser: Image)

NIGHTMARE ON ELM STREET 3: DREAM WARRIORS, A (1987) ★★★ Another solid follow-up to the Wes Craven box-office hit, exploring new "nuances" of the Freddy Krueger character for shock exploitation. This time youngsters terrorized by Krueger in their dreams take part in a controlled experiment using a new drug. The last 30 minutes are exciting as they link together in the same dream and fight Krueger with various combative techniques. Imaginative surprises and creative effects are in store, though as usual the story remains slender and the characters of minimal interest. Directed by Chuck Russell. Heather Langenkamp, Patricia Arquette, Priscilla Pointer, John Saxon, Craig Wasson, Robert Englund. (Media) (Laser: Image)

NIGHTMARE ON ELM STREET 4: THE DREAM MASTER, A (1988) ★★ The lousiest entry in the Freddy Krueger series—this hodgepodge of horror effects, Krueger's witty one-liners and teenage tomfoolery never makes any sense, and lacks a premise. There is no set of rules as Freddy pops in and out of nightmares and reality, wreaking the same old havoc, by now boring. Director Renny Harlin does a good job capturing the ambience of the series, and accolades to the set designers for creating the Elm Street house. Robert Englund is wonderful as the character, but he sorely needs new business. Rodney Eastman, Andras Jones, Tuesday Knight, Danny Hassel. (Media) (Laser: Image)

NIGHTMARE ON ELM STREET 5: THE DREAM CHILD, A (1989) ★★ Audiences seem to love these disjointed plots with little (if any) logic as child murderer Freddy Krueger invades the dreams of intended victims. Under the direction of Stephen Hopkins, this s-s-s-s-sequel becomes graphic shock heaped on graphic shock when Freddy decides to be reborn through the pregnancy of archenemy Alice Johnson (Lisa Wilcox). Robert Englund has his usual throwaway lines, and repeats all the clichés as prescribed by writers Sara Risher and Jon Turtle. It's really time to do something new with Freddy—like cast him as the antagonist in *Nemo in Slumberland.* Danny Hassel, Whitby Hertford, Kelly Jo Minter, Erika Anderson, Nick Mele. (Media) (Laser: Image)

NIGHTMARE ON ELM STREET 6, A. See *Freddy's Dead: The Final Nightmare.*

NIGHTMARE ON ELM STREET 7, A. See *Wes Craven's New Nightmare.*

NIGHTMARE ON THE 13TH FLOOR, THE (1990) ★ Below-average TV-movie in which something weird is happening on the 13th floor of the Wessex Hotel, where travel writer Michelle Greene is doing an article about the hotel's history. She's soon the hapless girl in peril, having witnessed a murder on the supposedly nonexistent 13th floor that involves a devil cult, a fire-ax murderer, and a staff of conspirators. The teleplay by Dan Distefano and Frank De Felitta is a premise that doesn't stand scrutiny. Greene is merely irritating as the heroine, and James Brolin's role is all too obvious. But there are stand-out performances by John Karlen as an ulcer-suffering cop and Lucille Fletcher as a sassy hotel employee. Director Walter Grauman does not seem suited to this genre, as all surprises are telegraphed, and the horror images repetitive, not frightening. (Paramount)

NIGHTMARES (1983) ★★★ Anthology of eerie tales, directed by Joseph Sargent, without any bonding theme. "Terror in Topanga" is derivative of the slasher genre with a murderer threatening housewife Cristina Raines, who has to go out for cigarettes one night. This is the weakest of the lot, so the film builds with "The Bishop of Battle," detailing how Emilio Estevez, obsessed with video games, challenges a 13-level, 3-dimensional war game. "The Benediction" is a chilling narrative about a man of the cloth (Lance Henriksen) and his lack of faith prior to his encounter with a sinister truck. "Night of the Rat" is the biggest crowd-pleaser, in which a giant demon rodent from German mythology terrorizes a suburbanite family. Suspense mounts as the unhappily married husband and wife (Richard Masur and Veronica Cartwright) face a horrific onslaught. The first three yarns were written by Christopher Crowe, the fourth by Jeffrey Bloom. (MCA)

NIGHTMARES IN A DAMAGED BRAIN. Video version of *Nightmare* (1981) (Continental).

NIGHTMARE SISTERS (1987) ★ Made under the guise of a sex-fantasy comedy, this sequel to *Sorority Babes in the Slimeball Bowl-O-Rama* ranks as one dumb "dumb teenagers on the loose" flick. It's the mindless concoction of producer-director Dave DeCoteau and writer Kenneth J. Hall as they retread those nerdy Tri Eta Phi gals from *Sorority Babes* who turn into sexpots during a séance with a crystal ball in which fortune-teller Omar is trapped. The curvaceous threesome proceeds to turn into vampy vampires while sucking on the bodies of three macho guys from the campus. Much of this is softcore raunch as Linnea Quigly, Brinke Stevens and Michelle McClellan pop in and out of their lingerie. A monster doesn't appear until the nonclimax when an exorcist shows up. Hitless and witless. Richard Gabai, Marcus Vaughter, William Dristas. Omar is billed as Dukey Flyswatter. (Trans World)

NIGHTMARE VACATION. See *Sleepaway Camp*.

NIGHTMARE WEEKEND (1986) ★½ Evil computer scientist Debbie Laster uses software (and soft wear?) to warp human minds and turn college girls into "mutantoids." How? By firing a silver ball into the brain, which turns its owner into a drooling, slavering walking dead shambling rambling zombie freako monster ghoul killer. Directed by Henry Sala. Dale Midkiff, Debra Hunter, Lori Lewis. (Lightning; Live)

NIGHT MONSTER (1942) ★★★ Metaphysical theme concocted by screenwriter Clarence Upson Young rescues this Universal potboiler from cinematic mediocrity. Ralph Morgan portrays a legless madman who creates new limbs through sheer willpower. He behaves in standard crazy-man style by stalking into the night to murder the doctors responsible for his double amputation. Bela Lugosi and Lionel Atwill are present but contribute little. Ford Beebe directed in the style of an "old, dark house" thriller comedy. Nils Asther, Irene Harvey. Aka *House of Mystery*. (MCA)

NIGHT OF ANUBIS. See *Night of the Living Dead*.

NIGHT OF A THOUSAND CATS (1974) ★½ Meow-ish Spanish exploitationer with comely pussycat Anjanette Comer for catnip, but you won't buy the canned goods director René Cardona is selling: a crazed nobleman lives in an old Mexican castle with his Igor-type aide and a kennel of hungry cats, to whom nutty Hugo Stiglitz feeds human flesh. Meanwhile, Hugo flies around in a helicopter looking for women in bikinis and has a trophy room where he keeps the heads of beauties with whom he has had sex. The climax hardly lives up to its title, with only a few dozen tomcats rushing through the castle. The film finally tucks its tail and ducks into an alley. Zulma Faiad, Gerardo Cepeda. (Paragon; from Academy as *Blood Feast*)

NIGHT OF DARK SHADOWS (1971) ★★½ "Dark Shadows," TV's daytime serial with supernatural creatures, led to *House of Dark Shadows*, which in turn led to this sequel which doesn't have Jonathan Frid as Barnabas the Vampire, even though it still deals with the infamous Collins family. David Selby plays Quentin Collins, a painter haunted by the spirit of an ancestor once involved with witches. Evil spirits pop up in his studio in the Collinwood mansion, making wife Kate Jackson think he's cheating. The setting—the Jay Gould estate in Tarrytown, NY—should have been an imposingly menacing location but it isn't, the humor is unintentional and the plot (by Sam Hall) unfolds in haphazard fashion, as though producer-director Dan Curtis was still grinding out mindless TV fodder. Lara Parker, Nancy Barrett, Grayson Hall, John Karlen. Aka *Curse of Dark Shadows*. (Video/Laser: MGM/UA)

NIGHT OF HORROR (1981) ★ Visitors to an old Civil War battlefield are haunted by voices and spirit images of the dead. So watch out for the dead to "rise again." Produced-directed in Baltimore by Tony Malanowski, who specializes in making horror movies with Confederate themes. (Also see—or don't see might be better advice—*The Curse of the Screaming Dead*.) Steve Sandkuhler, Gae Schmitt. Johnny Reb Malanowski also wrote this thing with the help of (actress) Rebecca Bach and Gae Schmitt. (Genesis)

NIGHT OF TERROR (1987) ★ Renee Harmon, Henry Lewis, Frank Neuhaus and Lauren Brent star in this gore-flow in which a family of psychos conducts brain operations, and a woman seeks revenge for acts committed against her in the name of science. Directed by Felix Gerard. (Image)

NIGHT OF TERRORS. See *The Murder Clinic*.

NIGHT OF THE BIG HEAT. See *Island of the Burning Doomed*.

NIGHT OF THE BLIND DEAD. See *The Blind Dead*.

NIGHT OF THE BLOOD BEAST (1958) ★ Astronaut passing through Earth's radiation belt is infected by an alien spore and returns a "blood beast." Scientists are trapped in a space center with the creature, allowing scripter Martin Varno and director Bernard L. Kowalski (working for producers Gene and Roger Corman) to imitate scenes from *The Thing*. Ed Nelson, Jean Hagen, Angela Greene, Michael Emmet. Aka *The Creature from Galaxy 27* and *The Monster from Galaxy 27*. (Sinister/C; S/Weird; Filmfax)

NIGHT OF THE BLOODY APES (1971) ★ Brunette in shocking red tights and a catlike face mask wrestles other women while her boyfriend, a police inspector, watches. Meanwhile, a goofy scientist transfers a gorilla's heart into his dying son but the young man turns into an ape-man who crashes through Mexican streets on a rampage. Mostly, the simian-man tears clothing off women and mauls them, revealing large bare breasts and creamy thighs. The gore effects are crude and sickening, the wrestling scenes dull and the acting and dubbing pathetically bad. And the title is wrong—there's only one ape. Directed by René Cardona, who cowrote with son René Cardona, Jr. Armand Silvestre, Norma Lazareno, José Elias Moreno. Aka *Horror and Sex* and *Gomar the Human Gorilla*. (MPI; Gorgon)

NIGHT OF THE BLOODY TRANSPLANT (1970) ★ A cacklingly insane physician, who follows an oath of hypocrisy, moves hearts from body to body in hopes of saving lives, but instead he creates gory death scenes. Directed by David W. Hanson. Dick Grimms grimly stars. Aka *The Transplant*. (VCI)

NIGHT OF THE CLAW. See *Island Claws*.

NIGHT OF THE CLONES/ESCORT TO DANGER (1978). Two episodes of the "Spiderman" TV series.

NIGHT OF THE COBRA WOMAN (1972) ★★½ In a Filipino setting, beautiful Marlene Clark transmutes into a deadly snake whenever she doesn't get her formula—a mixture of sex and serum. Some fix. This U.S.-Philippines venture, written-directed by Andrew Meyer under the title *Movini's Venom*, was defanged for U.S. consumption and is less "striking." Features the subtle acting of Joy Bang and Slash Marks. Audiences hissed back. The pits. (Embassy)

NIGHT OF THE COMET (1984) ★★ A juvenile mentality permeates this low-budget horror fantasy, written-directed by Thom Eberhardt, in which the end of the world is trivialized as a visit by teenaged survivors to a clothing store, where they run wild. It begins when a passing comet sends out deadly rays that either kill people or turn them into zombies. There are bits and pieces from so many other movies, it's impossible to keep tabs on the pasted-together plot. There's also some indecipherable business with scientists in an underground lab who hope to find a serum to combat lethal cosmic rays. Geoffrey Lewis, Mary Woronov, Sharon Farrell, Catherine Mary Stewart, Kelli Maroney. (CBS/Fox)

NIGHT OF THE CREEPING DEAD, THE. Rejected title for *The Blob* (1958).

NIGHT OF THE CREEPS (1986) ★★★½ Low-budget sci-fi horror thriller derivative of everything: *The Thing, Night of the Living Dead, Friday the 13th, Alien* and any other innovative special effects movie. It was a promising debut for director-writer Fred Dekker. Made as *Homecoming Night*, it begins in 1959 when an alien probe is launched to Earth, just when an ax maniac is about to murder a couple of college students. Cut to 1986 as Tom Atkins (Detective Cameron) tries to solve a series of murders involving walking corpses, wormlike creatures that leap into your mouth and take over your body, and that old ax killer. Atkins is very good as the unorthodox cop. Jason Lively, Lene Starger, Steve Marshall, Jill Whitlow. Above average for its type. (HBO) (Laser: Image)

NIGHT OF THE DEATH CULT (1975) ★★ Dead knights thirsting for virgins' blood ride through a small village, terrorizing superstitious folks. It takes a newly arrived doctor (Victor Petit) and his wife to find a way to stop them in this sequel to *The Blind Dead* from writer-director Amando De Ossorio. Maria Kosti, Sandra Mozarosky. Aka *Night of the Seagulls*. (Sony; also on tape as *Terror Beach*)

NIGHT OF THE DEMON. TV title of *Curse of the Demon*.

NIGHT OF THE DEMON (1979) ★ Cheesy "Bigfoot" gore flick, overloaded with bloody, violent deaths, amateurish under James C. Watson's direction, who's stuck with Paul Cassey's script. Five colorless explorers go in search of "Crazy Wanda," a legendary woman of the backwoods who was raped by a beast and gave birth to a malformed hairy infant. When they dig up the baby's grave to prove the story, the hirsute one with bad body odor goes on a rampage. Climactic siege features death by routine saw cut, ordinary broken glass, standard strangulation, typical throttling, mundane disembowelment, and predictable pitchfork. And that doesn't include other deaths revealed in flashbacks-within-the-flashback. For blood-and-guts fans only. Mike Cutt, Joy Allen. (VCII; Gemstone)

NIGHT OF THE DEMONS (1988) ★★★ On Halloween night, insufferable teenagers party in an abandoned mortuary. Sexy chicks Linnea Quigley and Mimi Kinkade unleash demons from Hell and, before you can pull the arms and legs off a human torso, are turned into monsters. The teeners are knocked off in hideous ways, until a miniarmy of zombies hulks around the digs. Director Kevin S. Tenney (*Witchboard*) creates a spirit of fun in a carnival house of horror, but never is any of this juvenilia designed seriously. Alvin Alexis, Allison Barron, Lance Fenton. (Video/Laser: Republic)

NIGHT OF THE DEMONS 2 (1994) ★★★ That demonic bride Angela is back at Hull House to terrorize a few students from St. Rita's Academy, who are dumb enough to pay her a visit on Halloween night. This time for your money you get a lot of dark sex humor and visual horror with (1) a spiked bat through a human brain; (2) breasts that turn into hands that kill; (3) a snake that crawls into a woman's vagina; (4) a nun's head chopped off with a sword; (5) a priest who turns into a pile of goo and gore; (6) a head that's used as a basketball; and (7) a snake-lady monster. Well, that's a few of the more enlightening moments in this special-effects extravaganza that might upset the Catholic Church but which is certain to please diehard fans of monster-zombie flicks that spare no expense to splash blood. Directed by Brian Trenchard-Smith, *Night of the Demons 2* is a real chomp, klomp, ker-flonk romp. Christi Harris, Darin Hearnes, Bobby Jacoby, Merle Kennedy, Amelia Kinkade, Zoe Trilling. (Video/Laser: Republic)

NIGHT OF THE DOOMED. See *Nightmare Castle*.

NIGHT OF THE EAGLE. See *Burn, Witch, Burn*.

NIGHT OF THE FLESH EATERS. See *Night of the Living Dead*.

NIGHT OF THE GHOULS (1958) ★★ While *Plan 9 from Outer Space* and other Edward D. Wood, Jr., films have a warped perspective and garishness that make them high camp, this supernatural horror tale has only brief flashes of Woodmania, and is mainly dreary. Criswell's narration helps, but Wood's story plods. Undercover cop Duke Moore (described as a "ghost chaser") enters the house on Willows Lake to find old cowboy actor Kenne Duncan (as Dr. Acula) holding phony séances. Nothing quite makes sense as Duke wanders the house, a comic-relief cop does a Stepin Fetchit parody and a couple of women shamble like Vampira. Tor Johnson stomps around as Lobo, and there are suggestions this could be a sequel to *Bride of the Atom*. Maybe. John Carpenter, Paul Marco, Valda Hansen, Bud Osborne. Aka *Revenge of the Dead*. (Rhino; Nostalgia Merchant; Sinister/C; S/Weird; Filmfax)

NIGHT OF THE HUNTER (1954) ★★★★★ Visually artistic film directed by Charles Laughton, surrealistic and macabre in recounting Davis Grubb's hair-raiser about a psychotic, Scriptures-quoting preacher (Robert Mitchum) who has "love" tattooed on one hand, "hate" on the other. He's in pursuit of two children who know where a stash of stolen money is kept, and there's no doubt of his homicidal intentions. Literate screenplay by James Agee; Stanley Cortez's cinematography is outstanding. Shelley Winters, Peter Graves, James Gleason, Lillian Gish, Don Beddoe. (MGM/UA) (Laser: Voyager; Criterion)

NIGHT OF THE LIVING BABES (1987) ★ Jon Valentine directed this sex-horror comedy in which two guys looking for a brothel find more than they bargained for in the form of female zombies. Michelle McClellan, Connie Woods, Andrew Nichols, Louie Bonanno. (Magnum)

NIGHT OF THE LIVING DEAD (1968) ★★★★★ Pittsburgh's George Romero shot this low-budget horror film on weekends, with a cast of unknowns, for $150,000. The result (aka *Night of Anubis* and *Night of the Flesh Eaters*) was a classic that built one of the strongest reputations in the horror genre, and it set a trend. It's a miniclassic of eerie proportions due to its black-and-white photography, its clever use of documentary techniques to lend verisimilitude, its imaginative editing and its horribly ironic ending. A space probe returning to Earth introduces into our atmosphere a form of radiation that affects dead bodies, bringing them to life. Soon the countryside is crowded with armies of walking dead. Untainted humans seek refuge in a farmhouse—and the horror is unrelenting as the zombies attack, often munching on human flesh. John A. Russo wrote the script for Romero, who got great mileage out of Duane Jones, Judith O'Dea, Karl Hardman, Marilyn Eastman. Rereleased to TV in 1986 in a colorized form. There were two sequels: *Dawn of the Dead* and *Day of the Dead* as well as a 1990 remake. (Republic; Media; United; Nostalgia Merchant; S/Weird; Filmfax; Vestron; Spotlite) (Laser: Republic; 3M; Collectible Classics; Image; Landmark) (Note: Elite's Laser is made from the original 35mm negative in a special edition with running audio commentary.)

NIGHT OF THE LIVING DEAD—THE REMAKE (1990) ★★★ Yes, this is a remake of George Romero's 1968 classic, but there are new elements, as if Romero decided that since you already know how the old movie came out, you should be thrown a few surprises. The first half hour is identical to the original, with Barbara (Patricia Tallman) taking refuge in a deserted farmhouse after she's been attacked by the living dead. The same band of characters are introduced . . . then scripter Romero plays revisionist, changing Barbara from a comatose broad into a female Rambo, tampering with how characters are killed off, and eliminating exposition about why the dead are back to life (elements that made the original work so well). This isn't as effective as the original (the gore effects, for one, don't have the impact after years of imitative exploitation), but it does stand on its own merits, thanks in part to Tom Savini's direction. It just ain't the classic you made the first time, George. John Russo, who wrote the original 1968 script with Romero, coproduced with Russ Streiner. (Video/Laser: RCA/Columbia)

NIGHT OF THE LIVING DEAD, 25TH ANNIVERSARY DOCUMENTARY (1993) ★★★½ The behind-the-scenes story of how George Romero, cast and crew made the low-budget classic of 1968. (MTI Home Video)

NIGHT OF THE SCARECROW (1995) ★★½ A cruel and ludicrous gore-thriller in the *Friday the 13th* tradition, this depicts how the spirit of a 17th-century warlock (John Lazar), buried in the middle of a cornfield, is transferred by lightning to the body of a scarecrow and sets out on a murderous rampage, killing minor characters with a thrashing machine, hooks, spears, swords and knives, and anything else that makes a pointed statement. Adopting the motto "Hay there!" in the script by Reed Steiner and Dan Mazur, the scary scarecrow is searching for a magical book that others could use to destroy him. But nothing destroys this "straw boss" as he sews a preacher's mouth shut and inserts roots and other organic growth into his erupting victims. Director Jeff Burr uses every cliché of the genre to make this one strictly for buffs who like plenty of gore and guts. Elizabeth Barondes, John Mese, Stephen Root, Gary Lockwood, Dirk Blocker, Bruce Glover. (Video/Laser: Republic)

NIGHT OF THE SEAGULLS (1975) Alternate title for an entry in the *Blind Dead* series better known as *Night of the Death Cult*.

NIGHT OF THE SILICATES. See *Island of Terror*.

NIGHT OF THE WEHRMACHT ZOMBIES. See *Night of the Zombies* (1983).

NIGHT OF THE WEREWOLF. See *The Craving*.

NIGHT OF THE ZOMBIES (1983) ★ Wretched Italian steal of *Dawn of the Dead*: New Guinea is exposed to a gas (unleashed during secret experiments) and turned into a landscape of walking dead. The whole thing is ludicrous as SWAT-team types set out on a mission (the purpose is never clear) by blasting through the undead. Even though the yokels know to shoot the creatures in the head, they repeatedly waste ammo by firing into bodies, and behave like the Three Stooges. Director Vincent Dawn goes to extremes to make this bloody, with exploding heads, maggot-infested bodies, ghouls munching on human organs and intestines. Not a single frightening moment, it's simply repulsive and unwatchable. Aka *Zombie Creeping Flesh, Zombie Inferno, Cannibal Virus,* and *Hell of the Living Dead.* Frank Garfield, Margit Evelyn Newton, Selan Karay. (Vestron)

NIGHT OF THE ZOMBIES (1983) ★½ This is not to be confused with the *Night of the Zombies* above. Writer-director Joel M. Reed, the intellectualizing sentimentalist of *Bloodthirsty Freaks,* is up to his blood-gushing tricks in this walking-dead tale of World War II soldiers who have been kept in suspended animation with nerve gas Gamma 693 and are now terrorizing civilians on a former battlefield in Germany. Sleazy stuff with cheap makeup and effects. Jamie Gillis is an investigating CIA agent, Ryan Hilliard is the doctor and Samantha Grey is the obligatory love interest. And Reed, ever so shy, turns up as a modern-day Nazi. Aka *Gamma 693* and *Night of the Wehrmacht Zombies.* (Prism)

NIGHT OF VENGEANCE. See *The Last House on the Left.*

NIGHT OWL (1993) ★★★ A literate quality hangs over this TV-movie about an evil "feminine power of the universe"—a sirenlike "witch voice" that arrives with the full moon of the autumn equinox and lures lonely, unhappy men to their doom. This "collective rage of all women who have been ridiculed by men" picks on jazz musician James Wilder, whose wife Jennifer Beals ends up trying to solve the mystery with the help of Dr. Matthews (Jackie Burroughs), an expert in understanding "female vengeance" and the invisible seductress entity. The fine writing by producers Rose Schacht and Ann Powell, and the atmospheric direction of Matthew Patrick, shape this into something different. Allis Hossack, Justin Louis.

NIGHT PEOPLE. See *The Last Man on Earth.*

NIGHT RIPPER (1986) ★ Fiendish killer stalks and slashes fashion models. Directed by Jeff Hathcock. James Hansen, April Anne. (Magnum; International)

NIGHTSCARE (1993) ★★★½ A knockout of a British horror picture that is chilling and disturbing in the style of *Silence of the Lambs.* A serial killer à la Hannibal Lector (played effectively by Keith Allen) is undergoing a drug experiment designed to eliminate his psychotic tendencies, at the Institute for Neurological Research. He suddenly has the power to create hallucinations in the minds of cop Craig Fairbrass and his girlfriend Elizabeth Hurley—hallucinations designed to prey on guilt. Reality and mind games blend until you can't tell if what is happening is real or not, and *Nightscare* gets really scary. Robert Walker's script holds back none of the fright potentials of this idea as Fairbrass and Hurley stalk the serial killer in a creepy hospital. And director Vadim Jean visually fulfills the horrific images with style and punch. Anita Dobson, Craig Kelly, Georgina Hale. (Video/Laser: Live)

NIGHT SCHOOL (1980) ★★ Although atmospherically directed by Kenneth Hughes, this slasher-gasher has a silly premise: the headhunter rituals of New Guinea and how they're applied to ghastly killings at a Boston college. After each beheading, the motorcyclist-murderer throws the head into liquid. The killings are repetitive (woman victim screams, slasher closes fast with a knife) and moments of depraved sexuality are gratuitously thrown in. Rachel Ward looks great in a shower strip scene, but is hopelessly lost with her dialogue. You'll spot the killer's identity early on. Aka *Terror Eyes*. (Key)

NIGHT SCREAMS (1987) ★ Football hero holds a party for friends just when two psycho killers escape from an asylum. Guess who crashes the party. Joe Manno, Ron Thomas, Randy Lundsford. Directed by Allen Plone. (Prism)

NIGHT SHADOWS. See *Mutant* (1983).

NIGHT SLASHER. Video version of *Night After Night (He Kills)* (Unicorn).

NIGHTS OF TERROR. See *Twice-Told Tales*.

NIGHT STALKER, THE (1972) ★★★★½ Dan Curtis's production made history as the highest-rated TV-movie of its day as it took a fresh, novel approach to the vampire theme. Kolchak, an impetuous, fast-talking newspaperman (Darren McGavin), believes Las Vegas murders are being committed by an ageless bloodsucker (no, not a slot machine). After frustrating politics with police and city officials, Kolchak faces the creature (Barry Atwater) in a hair-raising showdown. Superbly directed by John Llewellyn Moxey. Full of moxie and wonderfully scripted by Richard Matheson, from Jeff Rice's story. Carol Lynley, Ralph Meeker, Kent Smith, Claude Akins, Simon Oakland (as Kolchak's city editor). The concept resulted in a sequel, *The Night Strangler*, and a short-lived series. The series ran down, but not Kolchak. He's forever incorrigible. Based on ideas by Jeff Rice originally conceived as *The Kolchak Papers* and *The Kolchak Tapes*. (Magnetic; CBS/Fox)

NIGHTSTALKER (1979) ★ Two 20,000-year-old flesh eaters (i.e., cannibals) move to L.A., hearing that the meat there is fresh daily. Molar-moving melodrama, aka *Curse of the Living Dead*. Directed by Lawrence D. Foldes. And what the hell is Aldo Ray doing in this mess? (Live)

NIGHT STALKER, THE (1986) ★ The only outstanding aspect of this "killer-on-a-spree" shoot-'em-up is Charles Napier as unsympathetic alcoholic cop J. J. Stryker. That aside, this movie defies credulity as a Vietnam vet, adher-

ent to Eastern philosophies that involve worshipping cattle, makes himself impervious to police bullets. The "boogeyman"-style killer is murdering prostitutes in L.A. and painting gibberish on their foreheads. How the criminal is tracked is without imagination and the climactic shoot-out is unnecessarily bloody, with scores of good guys getting slaughtered. Director Max Cleven gives the film a tough, gritty feel by shooting in city slums. Michelle Reese, Katherine Kelly Lang, Robert Z'Dar, Gary Crosby. (Lightning; Vestron)

NIGHT STRANGLER, THE (1973) ★★★★ Fascinating sequel to *The Night Stalker* (originally called *The Time Killer*) stars Darren McGavin as aggressive newsman Kolchak, stalking mysteries that lead him into the supernatural. Richard Matheson's teleplay has Kolchak in Seattle, trailing a "walking corpse" killer who slaughters women. With research help from librarian Wally Cox, Kolchak realizes he is dealing with a 100-year-old madman who needs a serum to stay alive. Jo Ann Pflug is the heroine and Simon Oakland re-creates the harassed assignment editor. Directed by Dan Curtis. Richard Anderson, Scott Brady, Margaret Hamilton, John Carradine.

NIGHT TERROR (1989) ★½ Dreams plague a man who keeps waking up to discover his worst nightmares are real. Directed by Michael Weaver and Paul Howard. Lloyd B. Mote, Jeff Keel, Guy Ecker, Jon Hoffman. (Magnum)

NIGHT THE CREATURES CAME, THE. See *Island of Terror*.

NIGHT THE SILICATES CAME, THE. See *Island of Terror*.

NIGHT TRAIN TO TERROR (1985) ★★ White-haired God (billed as Himself) and Satan (billed as Lu Sifer) are on a celestial/hellbound train debating good vs. evil and ownership of three souls: hence, three stories made up of parts of unreleased features. "The Case of Harry Billings" is a surreal nightmare in a hospital where the bodies of patients are cut up and sold. John Philip Law wanders through this dream-of-horrors, surrounded by crazy doctors and naked, sexy women. "The Case of Gretta Connors" is about a Death Club, where members subject themselves to dangers for thrills—there's an electrocution sequence, a winged beetle of death (stop motion) and a wrecking-ball torture device. "The Case of Claire Hanson" is footage from *Cataclysm*, with Cameron Mitchell and Marc Lawrence as cops in pursuit of the Son of Satan. This features amateurish stop-motion monsters. Several directors are credited: John Carr, producer Jay Schlossberg-Cohen, Philip Marsak, Tom McGowan, Gregg Tallas. (Prism)

NIGHT TRAP. See *Mardis Gras for the Devil*.

NIGHT VISION (1987) ★★ Stolen VCR machine provides visions of demon worship and allows watchers to predict the future. Stacy Carson, Shirley Ross, Tony Carpenter. Directed by Michael Krueger. (Prism)

NIGHT VISION (1990) ★★★ Maniacally paced TV-movie directed and cowritten (with Thomas Baum) by Wes Craven. A burned-out, vicious cop (James Remar in a high-energy role) and a sweet psychologist (Loryn Locklin) join forces to find "the Spread-Eagle Killer." Despite the clichés, Remar and Locklin bring so much energy to this oddball serial-killer-vs.-cops yarn that the film rushes like a firetruck to the scene of the arson. Dr. Sally Powers (Locklin) is capable of absorbing psychic impressions and thoughts, turning into a dual personality: half normal cop, half innocent-woman-about-to-be-victimized-and-enjoying-it. It's weird. Remar grows to like her so much he destroys half of L.A. to save her. Penny Johnson, Bruce MacVittie, Francis X. McCarthy.

NIGHT VISITOR, THE (1971) ★★★½ Many Ingmar Bergman regulars star in this Mel Ferrer production—a horror thriller set in an insane asylum from which Max von Sydow escapes each night to carry out a gruesome murder, returning before morning. Directed by Laslo Benedek in Sweden, from a Guy Elmes script. Trevor Howard, Liv Ullmann, Per Oscarsson, Andrew Keir, Rupert Davies. Aka *Salem Come to Supper*. (United; VCI)

NIGHT VISITOR (1989) ★ Below (wayyyyyy belowwwww) average urban horror thriller too technically inferior to be taken seriously by today's demanding audiences. An attempt by director Rupert Hitzig to turn elements of the weak plot into sardonic comedy doesn't work either. Derek Rydall portrays a failing student who becomes infatuated with a sexy neighbor (Shannon Tweed as a sexpot/whore/tease). One night he sees his teacher killing her in a devil-cult ritual, but then nobody believes him because he's always crying wolf. Allen Garfield and Michael J. Pollard as a pair of demented brothers are never convincing, even as campy cutups, and Elliott Gould is wasted as a former cop who comes out of retirement to help track the killers. Just as wasted is Richard Roundtree as a plainclothes cop who just stands around. Not even garbled portions of the soundtrack were redubbed. An absolute loser. Aka *Never Cry Devil*. (MGM/UA)

NIGHT WALK. See *Dead of Night* (1972).

NIGHT WALKER, THE (1965) ★★★ William Castle gimmick horror film, written by Robert Bloch and prefaced with gobblydygook about dreams, making producer-director Castle seem as though he is seriously dealing with the subconscious. Of course, Castle was a master showman and movie-world huckster just making another buck. After her husband dies in a mysterious explosion, Barbara Stanwyck has bizarre dreams about a walking man (Lloyd Bochner). Numerous thrills follow, with at least a dozen red herrings and a climax in a "room of death" more hilarious than frightening. Robert Taylor, Judith Meredith, Rochelle Hudson, Hayden Rourke. Aka *The Dream Killer*. (MCA)

NIGHT WARNING (1981) ★★★ Susan Tyrrell's performance as a demented, getting-battier-by-the-minute broad is the saving grace of this exploitation shocker—and we mean exploitation. This low-budget film (aka *Nightmare Maker; Momma's Boy; Butcher, Baker, Nightmare Maker* and *Thrilled to Death*) rakes homosexual haters over the coals in the form of prejudiced cop Bo Svenson, who wants to nail Tyrrell's nephew (Jimmy McNichol) for murder and for hanging around a homosexual basketball coach. The situation in Stephen Breimer's script is contrived and denigrates the film's more honorable intentions, leaving only Ms. Tyrrell to go bonkers in her wonderfully unsubtle way. She knifes nearly all the cast to death with unrestrained glee. Directed by William Asher. Marcia Lewis, William Paxton. (HBO)

NIGHT WARS (1988) ★ Vietnam War memories plague the dreams of buddies Brian O'Connor and Cameron Smith. Dan Haggerty is a headshrinker who tries to figure it all out. Written-directed by David A. Prior. Steve Horton, Chet Hood, Jill Foor. (Sony) (Laser: Image)

NIGHTWATCH (1998) ★★★ Rarely does a horror-genre film effectively tap into the "fear factor," that thing within each of us that arouses our greatest feelings of unease and sets us on edge in the worst way. *Nightwatch* does that by being fresh in the way it unfolds its seemingly traditional slasher-killer tale. It really gets into the head of its characters, and in turn they get into your head. The settings are also creepily presented when law student Ewan McGregor takes a job as night watchman in the city's morgue. A couple of scenes will have you ready to spring from your seat as he makes his nightly rounds, trying to be cool with all those corpses covered by white sheets. The tension between McGregor and his oddball college pal Josh Brolin grows as they are caught up in sex games Brolin chooses to play, and then the tension erupts when they are prime suspects in a series of slasher murders in which a necrophiliac killer removes the eyes of his victims. Patricia Arquette adds to the unusual quality of this film as McGregor's girlfriend, who is drawn into the murders as a witness. Equally effective is Nick Nolte as the local homicide plainclothesman working the case—his soft-spoken cop is one of his best roles. Also in unusual parts are Lonny Chapman (as a freaked-out retiring night watchman), Lauren Graham (as Brolin's girlfriend), and Brad Dourif (playing one of his quirky guys—a medical examiner). Based on a short film by Ole Bornedal, *Nightwatch* was directed by Bornedal, who collaborated with Steven Soderbergh on the strange screenplay. This one is definitely worth seeing. (Dimension)

NIGHT WATCH (1973) ★★ Cat-and-mouse suspense thriller based on a play by Lucille Fletcher and adapted to the movies by Tony Williamson. Elizabeth Taylor thinks she's seen the moving figure of a dead man in the house next door. Has she? Or is she crazy? Or is some diabolical plot afoot? Husband Laurence Harvey isn't telling. Brian G. Hutton's direction keeps you guessing. Billie Whitelaw. (Fox Hills; Media)

NIGHTWING (1979) ★★ Columbia adaptation of Martin Cruz Smith's novel starts as a study of the plight of American Indians—then shifts to bat exterminator David Warner showing up with a "bat mobile" loaded with scientific tracking equipment. Next, bats attack out of the night, claiming victims. Then the search for the bat cave. A muddled mess because of the meandering screenplay by Steve Shagan, the uninspired direction of Arthur Hiller, and the mediocre bat effects. Nick Mancuso, Strother Martin, George Clutesi, Steven Macht, Kathryn Harrold. (RCA/Columbia) (Laser: Image)

NIGHTWISH (1989) ★★ Director-cum-actor Jack Starrett is a doctor conducting experiments in deep-sleep nightmares with four sexy gals who include Elizabeth Kaitan and Alisha Das. His Igor-type assistant is Robert Tessier. Written-directed by Bruce R. Cook Jr., Artur Cybulski, Tom Dugan, Brian Thompson. (Vidmark; Vestron)

976-EVIL (1989) ★★½ Robert Englund, who portrays Freddy Krueger in the *Nightmare on Elm Street* films, made his directorial debut with this slow-moving supernatural tale. A high school tough (Patrick O'Bryan) lives with his nerdy cousin (Stephen Geoffreys) and religious, kooky aunt (Sandy Dennis, who turns out to be the best thing in the picture). But all too soon the story deteriorates into a standard "the-worm-turns" plot in which Geoffreys, by calling a "horrorscope" hot line, meets a hell-ish guy named Mark Dark (Robert Picardo) who gives the nerd the powers of evil to destroy his tormentors. The ending is a steal from the *Poltergeist* movies, and the makeup effects by Kevin Yagher and the supernormal action are never overwhelmingly exciting—just routine. The video contains footage cut from the theatrical release. Jim Metzler, Maria Rubell. (Video/Laser: RCA/Columbia)

976-EVIL II: THE ASTRAL FACTOR (1992) ★★½ It's the usual "kitchen sink" blend of horror and comedy from director Jim Wynorski as he spins this sequel in which "the Slate River Serial Killer" (Rene Assa, playing a high school principal) terrorizes citizens, with help from Satan, by turning up as an astral projection of himself. The effects are pretty good (body splattered by truck, a talking mouse's head, an icicle through the chest, fiery crashes, etc.) and there's a bizarre sequence in which a victim is trapped inside a black-and-white movie combining elements of *Night of the Living Dead* and *It's a Wonderful Life*. It's pure Wynorski although the script was written by one Eric Anjou. Debbie James makes for an attractive heroine and Patrick O'Bryan (from the original) serves as a kind of antihero. Brigitte Nielsen guest stars as a sexy occult-shop owner. Paul Coufos, Leslie Ryan, Karen Mayo Chandler, Buck Flower, Phil McKeon. (Vestron)

1984 (1956) ★★★ If George Orwell intended his 1949 novel to be a frightful warning, this British film version of its contents isn't even an old-fashioned "boo." The main fault lies in its limited budget: it is imperative that the atmosphere of the future totalitarian state of Big Brother be realistically conveyed, that the paranoia of everybody under surveillance in a grim world be felt. That grimness is lost here. The workload falls on Edmond O'Brien and Jan Sterling as the defiant lovers and on Michael Redgrave as the ruthless leader who subjects Winston Smith (O'Brien) to the ultimate terrors in physical and psychological torture. A well-intended film that just didn't come off. Directed by Michael Anderson from a William P. Templeton–Ralph Bettinson script. Donald Pleasence, Michael Ripper, Patrick Allen. Two versions exist, with different endings.

1984 (1983) ★★★ George Orwell's world of Big Brother—a dictatorship in which men are enslaved by tricks of government—today seems more a parable than a possible future. If ever a movie grimly portrayed an unbearable society, this is it in all its depression. The cast resembles concentration camp victims—gaunt, closely shaven, empty-eyed, traumatized—and there isn't a single humorous moment. The superb acting plays second to the blemishes, bleak settings and somber tone of director Michael Radford. Hence, John Hurt as the trammeled Winston Smith (who has love for his fellow man despite dehumanization) and Richard Burton (as the interrogator who has neither love nor hate, just obedience) are not pleasant to watch. Orwell's message comes through strong: that once man has lost his freedom, he is totally subservient to propaganda, and will believe what isn't true, and disbelieve what is. In conveying a frightening image, this British film succeeds, but in terms of entertainment, it is depressing. (IVE) (Laser: Image)

1990: THE BRONX WARRIORS (1983) ★★ Vic Morrow, in one of his last roles, portrays Hammer the Exterminator, a policeman of the future who infiltrates the Bronx, a battleground for gang wars between Trash (whites) and Ogre (blacks). Inspired by *The Road Warrior*, this Italian production will be of interest to archeologists, for it was filmed in the ruins of the Bronx and affords a depressing look at a major U.S. city. Directed by Enzo G. Castellari. Christopher Connelly, Fred Williamson, Mark Gregory. Aka *Bronx Warriors*. (Media)

NINTH CONFIGURATION, THE (1979) ★★½ Oddball study in schizophrenia by writer-producer-director William Peter Blatty, who adapted his novel *Twinkle Twinkle, Killer Kane*. In this portrait of madness without heroes or easy answers, several U.S. soldiers (including an astronaut) suffering from breakdowns gather in a castle to act out their fantasies for psychiatrist Stacy Keach. But there is a secret behind Keach's behavior that wrenches the narrative. Not an easy film to endure, but sincere and literate, and well acted. Jason Miller, Scott Wilson, Robert Loggia, Moses Gunn, Tom Atkins, Neville Brand. (New World) (Laser: Image)

NO END (1984) ★★ Polish supernatural drama in which the ghost of an attorney returns to see his wife and son struggling to make it alone. Directed by Krzysztof Kieslowski, who cowrote the script with Krzysztof Piesiewicz. Starring Grazyna Szapolowska and Jerzy Radziwilowicz. (New Yorker; Facets Multimedia)

NO ESCAPE (1994) ★★★½ A rousing first-rate action movie with futuristic overtones, enhanced by rugged, scenic Australian locations, the frenetic, stylish work of director Michael Campbell (working with producer Gale Anne Herd) and Ray Liotta as an antihero trapped in the penal world of A.D. 2022. A Rambo of tomorrow, Liotta is sentenced to maximum security prison, only to be transferred by sadistic warden Michael Learned to an island where two convict factions are at war—a band of primitive warriors led by Kevin Dillon and a more peaceable bunch guided by the Father (Lance Henriksen). Campbell stages the numerous action scenes with impact, and Liotta emerges a durable action star thanks to a Michael Gaylin–Joel Gross script (based on Richard Herley's *The Penal Colony*) that allows him to develop a dimensional character. Stuart Wilson, Ernie Hudson, Kevin J. O'Connor. (Video/Laser: HBO)

NOMADS (1985) ★★½ Avant-garde supernatural tale in which nurse Lesley-Anne Down is bitten by a raving patient (Pierce Brosnan) and is possessed by images of the man's past. Through psychic flashes she learns he is an anthropologist who just moved into a home once frequented by "nomads," evil spirits in human form who wander the deserts of the world. Cross-cutting between Pierce's persecution at the hands of the nomads (who take on the persona of a punk motorcycle gang) and the images haunting Down, the film unfolds enigmatically.

Written-directed by John McTiernan. Anna-Maria Montecelli, Adam Ant, Hector Mercado, Mary Woronov. (Paramount) (Laser: Image)

NO PLACE TO HIDE (1981) ★★★ With Jimmy Sangster as telewriter, you know this suspense TV-movie will have plenty of twists and turns as a masked tormentor keeps popping up to threaten Kathleen Beller. No one believes her story, so it appears she's a fruitcake case. But if someone is trying to kill her, where does stepmother Mariette Hartley fit in? Double deception is everywhere and director John Llewellyn Moxey milks this cat-and-mouser for all its worth with psychiatric double-talk, disbelieving cops, etc. The possibility of ghosts, stalkers and serial killers will hold you rapt even if you see through the gossamer plot. Arlen Dean Snyder, Gary Graham, Keir Dullea. (Prism)

NORMAN'S AWESOME EXPERIENCE (1989) ★★ Science lab assistant Tom McCamus is transported through time to the Roman Empire with cutie Laurie Paton and photographer Jacques Lussier. The threesome engages in witticisms as they fight off a barbarian horde. Written-directed by coproducer Paul Donovan. Lee Broker, David Hemblen. Aka *A Switch in Time*. (South Gate; Hemdale)

NOSFERATU (1922) ★★★ German filmmaker F. W. Murnau changed the names and incidents in Bram Stoker's *Dracula* and foisted it on the public as an original story about a bloodsucker living in Bremen in 1838. Stoker's widow recognized the similarities and sued Murnau. All prints were ordered destroyed but a few survived the purge and *Nosferatu* has taken its just place among silent vampire classics. There's no doubting the Stoker influence in these chronicles of the nocturnal affairs of Count Orlock (Max Schreck), but the film warrants attention as a historical conversation piece. Aka *Nosferatu, a Symphony of Horror*; *Nosferatu, a Symphony of Terror*; *Nosferatu the Vampire* and *Terror of Dracula* (Kino; Goodtimes; Foothill; Discount; Republic; Sinister/C; Video Yesteryear; Critic's Choice) (Laser: Image; Republic)

NOSFERATU, A SYMPHONY OF HORROR/ TERROR. See *Nosferatu*.

NOSFERATU DIARIES, THE. Original working title of *Embrace of the Vampire*.

NOSFERATU—THE VAMPIRE (1979) ★★★ Decidedly offbeat remake of F. W. Murnau's 1922 pirated version of *Dracula*, written-produced-directed by Germany's Werner Herzog. But the pacing is so leisurely, the film plods along when it should leap out at you. Yet, the heavy atmosphere and unnerving makeup on Klaus Kinski in the title role gives this lengthy (124 minutes) West German production a compelling attraction-repulsion. Isabelle Adjani. (Crown) (Laser: Japanese)

NOSTRADAMUS ★★ This title adorns the Bargain Video cassette box, but the film inside is actually *Prophecies of Nostradamus*, an Australian TV documentary. (See that entry.)

NOSTRADAMUS (1994) ★★½ This dramatic biography of Michel de Nostradame (1504–1566), the prophet who wrote hundreds of quatrains predicting events to come, is a dark, brooding portrait of 16th-century life. There is something stark and challenging in its re-creation of that time, but it is also impenetrable and so full of angst and enigmas that it becomes unreachable. Where director Roger Christian succeeds best is in depicting the anguish Nostradamus went through each time he was overwhelmed by a vision of horrible things to come. The emphasis of these visions is Nazi Germany, for the rise of Hitler is one of the most famous of the visionary's predictions. Nostradamus's life was a tumultuous one, with plague, the Inquisition and the deaths of his wife and children among the tragic events he faced. A worthy project, based on a script by Knut Boeser and Piers Ashworth, that is recommended despite its shortcomings. Tcheky Karyo (in the title role), Amanda Plummer, Julia Ormond, Assumpta Serna, Rutger Hauer (as a mystic monk), F. Murray Abraham. (Orion)

NOT AGAINST THE FLESH. See *Vampyr*.

NOTHING BUT TROUBLE (1991) ★★★ Madcap, Monty Python–esque comedy with horrific overtones in which financial advisor Chevy Chase and companion Demi Moore are picked up for speeding in a small town and subjected to death traps and other cliff-hanging situations at the hands of a crazed justice of the peace (Dan Aykroyd, who also directed), his assistant John Candy and other whacky characters, including two human piglet twins. This exercise in disguises (Aykroyd and Candy play other characters in dense makeup) quickly turns to slapstick. The funky set design and crazy gadgets are terrific. (Video/Laser: Warner Bros.)

NOT LIKE US (1995) ★★★½ An unusually hilarious gorefest TV-movie produced by Roger Corman, in which two alien scientists (disguised as humans) settle into the rural region of Tranquility to experiment on humans in an underground lab. In a "black macabre" vein, writer Daniella Purcell plays the blood and guts and graphic effects strictly for laughs and director Dave Payne holds back none of the campy opportunities for sexual humor and bare skin exposure. Not a serious moment on the slab in the lab, so expect to be amused in a morbidly pleasant manner. Rainer Grant, Joanna Pacula, Peter Onorati, Billy Burnette, Morgan Englund, Gabrielle Gurwitch, Paul Bartel, Clint Howard. (New Horizons)

NOT OF THIS EARTH (1956) ★★½ Paul Birch, alien humanoid from the planet Darvana, generates Death Rays whenever he removes his dark glasses and concentrates his gleaming, blank orbs. He's on Earth to send specimens of mankind back to his home planet, and he's aided in his vampiric mission (they need blood, you see) by a bat monster. Produced-directed by Roger Corman from a script by Charles Griffith and Mark Hanna. Beverly Garland, Jonathan Haze, Dick Miller, Gail Ganley.

NOT OF THIS EARTH (1988) ★★★ Entertaining remake of Roger Corman's 1956 cult favorite, opening with a main title with scenes from Corman's horror and sci-fi favorites. This self-homage is appropriate to the pleasing campiness that follows. The story again focuses on a strange man in dark glasses (Arthur Roberts) whose eyeballs zap you to death. The alien is from planet Darvana to check out human blood. If it works in the alien's veins, then Darvana (where inhabitants are dying, and need blood) will invade Earth. Ex–porn movie star Traci Lords (in her first "straight" role) is a nurse assigned to take care of the alien. Other odd characters include a blond chauffeur (Lenny Juliano), a uniformed policeman (Roger Lodge), a doctor (Ace Mask), a silly vacuum salesman (Michael Delano) and assorted big-busted bimbos. Lords is good, especially in a blue bikini. Directed by Jim Wynorski. Followed by a 1995 TV-movie remake. (MGM/UA)

NOT OF THIS EARTH (1995) ★★★½ This second remake of Roger Corman's 1956 cult favorite is superior to the 1988 redo, and is a sci-fi fan's delight, full of groovy monsters and special effects. Made for TV, this version offers an amusing performance by Michael York as the humanoid alien with the blazing eyeballs (usually covered by dark glasses, unless he wants to hypnotize you or zap you into a fireball). York is one quirky alien (he calls the glasses "optical blockers" and clicks his neck when he turns his head). The new script, by Charles Philip Moore, has York on Earth to find a cure for a blood disease on his dying planet. Leggy Elizabeth Barondes is the nurse hired to give blood transfusions to York; Mason Adams is the doctor forced to help York find a cure; Parker Stevenson is the motorcycle cop; Richard Belzer is the sleazy chauffeur. Director Terence H. Winkless contributes stylistic touches and uses the film's best-remembered imagery (dark glasses, blazing eyes) to good advantage, adding in hideous E.T. beasts and monsters, and a teleporter device ("cosmic cable"). (New Horizons)

NOT QUITE HUMAN (1987) ★★ Two-part Disney TV-movie is undistinguished fodder for the video mill, with dense-brained scientist Alan Thicke creating an android (Jay Underwood, from *The Boy Who Could Fly*) named "Chip" that is programmed to take everything he's told literally—the main source of humor in Alan Ormsby's script, based on books by Seth

McEvoy. Steven Hilliard Stern produced-directed. Joseph Bologna, Robyn Lively, Robert Harper. (Disney)

NOT QUITE HUMAN II (1989) ★★★ A charming improvement over part I in this series based on the novels by Seth McEvoy and produced by Disney. Alan Thicke returns as the scientist who created the android Chip Carson. In this misadventure Chip goes to college where he overcomes his built-in naïveté, meets a female android and falls in love for the first time, and outsmarts robotic scientists. Good fun, with yuks provided by writer-director Eric Luke. Greg Mullavey, Robyn Lively, Katie Barberi. (Disney)

NOT QUITE HUMAN III. See *Still Not Quite Human*.

NO TRESPASSING. See *The Red House*.

NOWHERE MAN (1995) ★★★ In this two-hour TV-pilot a famous photographer (Bruce Greenwood) steps out of the men's room in a restaurant to find he suddenly no longer has his old identity—his wife (Megan Gallagher), his mother and everyone else in his life no longer recognize him or acknowledge his existence. It's a classic nightmare of suspicion, paranoia and conspiracy; Greenwood is placed in a mental institution and slowly comes to realize people are manipulating him, but how and why remain a mystery, even when this concludes—purposely being left up in the air for a continuing series. Well directed by Tobe Hooper from a telescript by the show's creator-producer Lawrence Hertzog. Ted Levine, Bernie McInerney, Michael Tucker. (Paramount)

NUDE BOMB, THE (1980) ★ Feature version of TV's "Get Smart," about CONTROL agent 86, Maxwell Smart, who fights CHAOS in his delightfully inept style. Don Adams is no different from his TV days as he fights for the freedom, liberty and clothing of all by preventing a plot that would strip us bare-ass nude. Clive Donner directs this compendium of spy gags (by Arne Sutton, Bill Dana and Leonard B. Stern) with monumental indifference. Bomb indeed. Sylvia Kristel, Rhonda Fleming, Dana Elcar, Pamela Hensley. Aka *Maxwell Smart and the Nude Bomb* and *The Return of Maxwell Smart*. (Video/Laser: MCA)

NUKIE (1989) ★ U.S.-German coproduction is really a children's movie trying to cash in on the success of *E.T.* as it depicts two "lightballs" that land on Earth. Out of these energy fields emerge two aliens from across the universe: Nukie finds itself in Africa, befriended by two African tribal children and accosted by a ruthless poacher. Niko ends up in the hands of a research team where he reprograms a computer in an effort to find Nukie. Adults will find this movie cloying and unwatchable as it ineffectively delivers its message of brotherly love. Benjamin

Taylor's script is a big bore. Directed with unrelenting tedium by Slas Odendalt and Michael Pakleppa. Glynis Johns is wasted as a nun stationed in Africa. Ronald France, Steve Railsback, Siphiwe and Sipho Mlangeni. (Video/Laser: Vidmark)

NUKIE . . . IN SEARCH OF AMERICA. See *Nukie*.

NUMBERED DAYS. See *Cycle Psycho*.

NUN AND THE DEVIL, THE. See *The Nuns of Saint Archangelo*.

NUNS OF SAINT ARCHANGELO, THE (1971) ★★ French-Italian horror film set in the 16th century, directed by Paolo Dominici, who co-scripted with Tonino Cervi. Anne Heywood, Martine Brochard, Muriel Catall, Ornella Muti. Aka *The Nun and the Devil*. (From MPI as *Sisters of Satan*; from Showcase as *Innocents from Hell*)

NURSE SHERRI. See *Beyond the Living*.

THE NURSE (1996) ★★★ Lisa Zane (brother of actor Billy Zane) portrays the title role in this low-budget direct-to-video slash-'em-up with such deliciously bitchy villainy and sweet deception she should be given a year's supply of free surgical gowns, white nylons, and white work shoes. At a time when it's hard to get good help, along comes Lisa to take care of Michael Fairman, who's just had a stroke that's left him completely paralyzed and speechless. He'd be speechless even without the stroke if he knew that Zane was the daughter of his business partner, who recently shot himself after killing his wife and son. Dad would have shot Zane, too, except she was at the hospital doing her humanitarian thing. And we know one thing Zane doesn't—that dad was guilty of embezzlement, which makes Fairman totally innocent of any wrongdoing. Pretty ironic, the fact that Zane has vowed vengeance by killing all the members of Fairman's family while he helplessly watches. *The Nurse* is great for horror freaks who savor high body counts. Zane's first victim is a nurse into whose neck she thrusts a long needle, all the while smiling as she pushes it deeper and deeper. Then she bashes in the head of a snoopy investigative reporter with a tire iron. Smiling, of course. Then she pushes Fairman's wife down the stairs (she's played by Nancy Dussault, who used to be on Ted Knight's TV show). Then she shoots two other family members, slashes the throat of a security cop, and breaks into the family mansion to shoot Fairman's brother (John Stockwell), with whom she recently had sex. Then Zane has a lively catfight with Fairman's daughter (Janet Gunn) in the kitchen, with butcher knives and a revolver figuring prominently in the action. Although director Rob Malenfant keeps the blood and gore to the barest minimum, you have to give scripter Richard Brandes credit for keeping the corpse rate as high as he dared in 90 minutes without sacrificing plot construction and social relevance. Technical credits, especially the cinematography, are all top-notch. William R. Moses, Sherrie Rose, Jay Underwood. (Live)

NUTRIAMAN: THE COPASAW CREATURE. See *Terror in the Swamp.*

NUTTY PROFESSOR, THE (1963) ★★★½ Even those who normally eschew Jerry Lewis comedies have found this fulfilling in exploring the Jekyll/Hyde theme. Lewis portrays clumsy professor Julius F. Kelp, a myopic, marmottoothed scientist who discovers a concoction that turns him into an aggressive alter ego, Buddy Love. Lewis also directed and cowrote the clever script with Bill Richmond. Stella Stevens, Del Moore, Kathleen Freeman, Howard Morris. Aka *Dr. Jerkyll and Mr. Hyde.* (Video/Laser: Paramount)

NUTTY PROFESSOR, THE (1996) ★★★ Diehard Eddie Murphy fans will rollick over this remake of the 1963 Jerry Lewis comedy classic, but those expecting it to come up to the level of its inspiration will be disappointed when Murphy completely goes over the top and misses some of the more poignant touches Lewis gave to the Buddy Love character. Murphy excels in creating a terribly obese college professor, Sherman Klump, and gives him a touching, sad quality aided by Rob Bottin's remarkably effective makeup job. But when Klump, who holds himself in low esteem, takes a serum that alters his DNA structure and transforms into svelte, woman-chasing Love, Murphy plays the womanizer like his *Beverly Hills Cop* character and some points are lost within this raucous, misguided performance. Murphy also overindulges by playing Klump's father, mother, brother and grandmother in a dinnertable scene that doesn't belong in the story. A lot of the flatulation humor is also out of place. Ultimately it's Murphy as Klump, and the great computerized morphing techniques when Klump transmutates into Love, that save this remake from disaster. Directed by Tom Shadyac from a script he reworked and updated from the original with David Sheffield, Barry W. Blaustein and Steve Oedekerk. Jada Pinkett, James Coburn, Larry Miller, Dave Chappelle, John Ales. (Video/Laser: Sony/Columbia)

NYMPHOID BARBARIAN IN DINOSAUR HELL, A (1990) ★ If this were only half as good as its title . . . a superlow-budget novelty set in a post-Armageddon world where Linda Corwin (in the briefest of animal skins) fights mutation cavemen, stop-motion giant dinosaurs and other prehistoric evils. Most of the unconvincing action is inarticulate, no doubt a matchup to the mentality of writer-director Brett Piper and producer Alex Pirnie, who doubles as actor. Paul Guzzi, Marc deShales, K. Alan Hodder.

NYOKA AND THE TIGERMEN (1942) ★★★★ Rousing, fun-packed 15-chapter Republic serial (made as *Perils of Nyoka*) stars Kay Aldridge as the comic-book jungle girl searching for her missing father and the Tablets of Hippocrates, said to record long-lost secrets of the ancient Greeks—and the cure for cancer. Evil, sexy high priestess Vultura (Lorna Gray, later Adrian Booth), is also after the tablets and it's one cliffhanger after another, including an encounter with a giant gorilla, Satan. One of the most action-packed, energetic serials ever produced. Gray's slit skirts, which reveal her beautiful legs when she sits on her throne, indicate this was made for an audience other than mere juveniles. Directed with nonstop excitement by serial whiz William Witney. Clayton Moore, Tris Coffin, William Benedict, Charles Middleton. A TV feature version is *Nyoka and the Lost Secrets of Hippocrates.* (All 15 chapters from Republic) (Laser: Republic)

OASIS OF THE ZOMBIES (1981) ★ Adventurers searching for Rommel's treasure in North Africa face a legion of walking Nazi corpses. Manuel Gelin, Frances Jordon, Jeff Montgomery, Myriam Landson. Directed by A. M. Frank (aka Marius Lasoeur), who borrowed footage from Jesus Franco's *Grave of the Living Dead*. Aka *The Treasure of the Living Dead*. (United American; Lightning; Wizard; Filmline; Gemstone; from Trans World as *Bloodsucking Nazi Zombies*)

OBLIVION (1994) ★★★ A curious blend of sci-fi and western clichés, this comedy spoof is set on a far-flung desert planet in a town not unlike Dodge City. It even boasts a saloon called Kitty's, run by Julie Newmar. A strange mixture of frontier types and aliens live in this bizarre cow town: Meg Foster is a cyborg deputy sheriff who whirs when she walks, Isaac Hayes is a bartender, George Takei is the silly, drunken Dr. Valentine, Irwin Keyes is the town idiot and Carel Struycken is the tall, tall mortician Gaunt. All of these colorful characters surround a cowardly sheriff's son (Richard Joseph Paul) out to prove his honor. Up against him is a whip-and-leather sexpot and a lizard-man villain, and on his side is a Tonto-like Indian. Made in Romania for Charles Band's Full Moon Productions, *Oblivion* was written by Peter David and directed by Sam Irvin. For a movie with a lot going for it, including some stop-motion scorpionlike monsters created by David Allen, this moves rather slowly and has only intermitten success as a comedy. Shot simultaneously was a sequel: *Oblivion 2: Backlash*. Jackie Swanson, Andrew Divoff, Jimmie F. Skaggs. (Video/Laser: Paramount)

OBLIVION 2. See *Backlash: Oblivion 2.*

OBLONG BOX, THE (1969) ★★ "Far worse things are known to mankind," says Vincent Price, possibly referring to other American-International pics exploiting Edgar Allan Poe titles. Pretty gory stuff, with depravity and bawdiness thrown in by producer-director Gordon Hessler who worked from a script by Laurence Huntingdon. Price's brother was disfigured by an African witch doctor and buried alive, only someone dug him up and now he's alive, on a rampage of lustful murder. Alastair Williamson, Christopher Lee, Sally Geeson, Rupert Davies. Original title: *Dance, Mephisto*. Aka *Edgar Allan Poe's The Oblong Box*. (Key; HBO) (Laser: Japanese)

OBSESSIONS. See *Flesh and Fantasy.*

OCCULTIST, THE (1988) ★ Private eye Rick Gianasi goes to the voodoo island of San Caribe to fight zombies. Written-directed by Tim Kincaid. Joe Derrig, Jennifer Kanter, Mizan Nunes, Richard Mooney. (Unicorn; from Urban Classics as *Maximum Thrust*)

OCTOBER 32ND. Original theatrical title for *Merlin*.

OCTOPUSSY (1983) ★★★ The 13th James Bond adventure and sixth with Roger Moore as the indefatigable 007. There are the usual su-

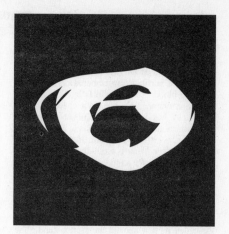

perweapons and the action sequences are among the liveliest for the series. His adversary is Afghan prince Kamal Khan (Louis Jourdan), who operates a palace in India with henchman Gobinda (Kabir Bedi). Kamal plots with power-hungry Russian general Steven Berkoff to explode an atomic bomb in Germany and bring chaos to N.A.T.O. Titular character is an octopus-loving dragon lady (Maud Adams) heading an all-women's smuggling ring. The derring-do is frequently exciting, thanks to high production standards. Especially fun is a fight aboard a speeding train and Bond clinging to the fuselage of a plane in flight. Directed by John Glen, who helmed *For Your Eyes Only*. Script by George MacDonald Fraser, Richard Maubaum and Michael G. Wilson. Music by John Barry. Lois Maxwell, Kristina Wayborn. (CBS/Fox) (Laser: CBS/Fox; MGM/UA)

OFFERINGS (1989) ★ Writer-producer-director Christopher Reynolds borrows heavily from *Halloween* in spinning this Oklahoma-based production about a cannibalistic youth who grows up to escape the insane asylum in which he has been incarcerated, terrorizing teenagers and murdering with chainsaw and other body-penetrating weaponry. *Offerings* offers nothing new—even the music is swiped from Carpenter. Loretta Leigh Bowman, Elizabeth Greene. (South Gate)

OFFICE KILLER (1998) ★ Downsizing and termination are the theme of scripters Elise MacAdam and Tom Kalin in this "office noir." Mousy office worker Dorine Douglas enjoys slaughtering her fellow workers and taking their stiffening corpses home to her front room, where she wallows in the gore. Upstairs, bedridden mother has no idea what's happening. Given that Dorine is played by Carol Kane, you know that she is a freaked-out psychopathic murderer, because nobody plays freaked-out psychopathic murderers better than Kane. What great bats that actress has in her belfry. From the moment she stuffs a dead mouse down the garbage disposal until she stalks her final victim with a butcher knife in her cellar of horrors, Kane holds the picture together. Yeah sure, like a mortician who sews severed limbs back onto a horribly dismembered corpse. However, the blood-and-guts effects by Bob Benevides are crummy. Take the open chest cavity. It looks icky but it isn't frightening. And when Kane covers the wound with plastic and sprays it with Windex, it isn't macabre. Just good housecleaning. *Office Killer* is a nothing moment in the career of Molly Ringwald, who plays the only woman who suspects Kane of her terrible deeds. But her screaming is as incoherent as her acting. And Jeanne Tripplehorn may be the sexiest office employee but she's so stupid as to be unbelievable. As for director Cindy Sherman, I suspect she called in sick and let the janitor handle the setups. Pray Sherman doesn't give up her day job (she's a well-known still photographer who specializes in self-portraits) and goes back to taking more pictures of herself. Barbara Sukowa, Michael Imperioli, David Thornton, Mike Hodge, Alice Drummond (Dimension)

OFFICIAL DENIAL (1993) ★★★ A thoughtful, well-intention thriller written by Bruce Zabel that blends UFOs, "gray" aliens, and abductions, originally produced for the Sci-Fi Channel and well directed by Brian Trenchard-Smith. Dirk Benedict portrays a sensitive greenhouse keeper trying to deal with abduction memories with wife Erin Gray when the U.S. Air Force shoots down an E.T. craft. Through officer Chad Everett, Benedict is brought into the top-secret project (but only after signing an "official denial" document) to make contact with the single surviving alien, who uses telepathy to communicate. This functions well on the level of a TV movie and projects a positive spirit about man and alien contact, with some of its plot elements reminiscent of Spielberg's *Close Encounters*. Parker Stevenson assists. (Paramount)

OFFSPRING, THE (1986) ★★★ Oldfield, TN, is the setting for horror stories reflecting the evil people and activities of the community. Aka *From a Whisper to a Scream*, it stars Susan Tyrrell as a reporter who witnesses the execution of a madwoman (Martine Beswick) by lethal injection and visits Vincent Price in his musty library to learn the town's history. The first yarn stars Clu Gulagher as a sexually suppressed clod who kills women, only to have one of them return from the grave to haunt him. This is the weakest segment, memorable only for Gulagher's odd albino makeup. The second story is about a swamp witch doctor who has the secret to eternal life, and the efforts of a criminal to find the elixir. A nice twist ending here. The third yarn is set at Lovecraft's Traveling Carnival, where a snake woman uses her voodoo powers to control the Amazing Arden, who eats razor blades and glass. The Civil War tale that follows is the film's most

chilling, reminiscent of *Lord of the Flies* when Union stragglers fall into the hands of youngsters who have formed their own religion based on the horrors of the war. Finally, the Tyrrell-Price footage has its own surprise ending. *The Offspring*, shot in Georgia, has good direction by Jeff Burr, who coscripted with C. Courtney Joyner and Darin Scott. Terry Kiser, Harry Caesar, Rosalind Cash, Cameron Mitchell, Lawrence Tierney. (Video/Laser: Live)

OF UNKNOWN ORIGIN (1983) ★★★ Strangely compelling war of cunning erupts in a Manhattan apartment when advertising exec Peter Weller duels with an intelligent mutant rat. Hence, the film becomes a metaphor for man's never-ending war against vermin, and the history of how rats have plagued mankind is graphically described and depicted in this adaptation of "The Visitor" by Chauncey G. Parker III. Director George P. Cosmatos captures a surreal element as Weller is obsessed and sinks into insanity. This psychological exploration in Brian Taggert's script also insightfully deals with Weller's professional life, giving the film a rich subtext. Supporting cast is good (Jennifer Dale, Shannon Tweed, Lawrence Dale) but ultimately the rat and Weller's obsession dominate. (Warner Bros.)

OGRE, THE (1988) ★ Italy's Lamberto Bava helmed this psychological horror tale about a sexually mixed-up author of horror novels (Virginia Bryant) haunted by childhood memories when she moves into a mansion. Out of her disturbed mind emerges the titular entity of evil. (Video Mania)

OH, GOD! (1977) ★★★ Thought-provoking allegorical story in which a supermarket manager (John Denver) is asked by the Almighty (George Burns) to tell the human race to straighten up. Denver is judged part of the Lunatic Fringe but finds notoriety on Dinah Shore's TV show. This leads to a courtroom hearing, where Burns appears to prove God's existence. The laughs are gentle, the message obvious, the acting restrained. Director Carl Reiner makes it work without piousness. Ralph Bellamy, Donald Pleasence, Teri Garr, William Daniels, Barnard Hughes, Paul Sorvino, Barry Sullivan. (Video/Laser: Warner Bros.)

OH, GOD! BOOK TWO (1980) ★★★ In the beginning there was *Oh, God!* and lo, it came to pass there was a sequel directed by Gilbert Cates, and audiences looked at it and said it was fair to middling. And God, who does resembleth George Burns with a cigar, said, "I shall choose a child to carry My Word to the people," and the child was Louanne. And she was good. Worldly wickedness was challenged by universal goodwill, and box office keepers did say, "Receipts, thou art beautiful." And Suzanne Pleshette, David Birney, Howard Duff, Wilfrid Hyde-White, Conrad Janis and Hans Conried were hence employed. (Warner Bros.)

OH, GOD! YOU DEVIL (1984) ★★★ Third film in the series with George Burns (cigar and all) as the Lord is a whimsical, entertaining allegory about good vs. evil, decency vs. greed, etc. Podunk musician Ted Wass unwittingly signs a pact with the Devil (also Burns) to be metamorphosed into rock star Billy Wayne (Robert Desiderio), only Billy realizes success isn't so great and just wants his wife back. He calls on God for help, and at a poker table in Las Vegas, God and Satan determine the fate of all. Low-key and amusing with Paul Bogart directing unobtrusively. Eugene Roche is especially good as Wayne's record agent. Roxanne Hart, Eugene Roche, Ron Silver. (Video/Laser: Warner Bros.)

OH HEAVENLY DOG (1980) ★★★ Joe Camp, creator of *Benji*, puts the pooch to a new use in directing this fantasy comedy in which private eye Chevy Chase, while investigating a murder, is stabbed to death and winds up in Heaven. He's ordered to return to Earth to solve his own homicide but the only body available is a dog's. So he goes down on all fours, wags his tail and tracks Omar Sharif and other suspects through rainy London streets. Inoffensive fun, with several plot surprises and a good performance by Benji. Jane Seymour, Robert Morley, Donnelly Rhodes, Alan Sues. (CBS/Fox) (Laser: Japanese)

OLD DARK HOUSE, THE (1932) ★★★ Following *Frankenstein*, director James Whale made this version of J. B. Priestley's *Benighted*, creating a terror-satire subgenre (with the help of Benn Levy's script) that persisted for years. A violent thunderstorm (what other kind are there in horror films?) forces travelers to spend the night in a weird mansion inhabited by butler Boris Karloff, a 102-year-old lunatic, a fire-loving brother and a God-fearing sister, all suffering from assorted psychoses, neuroses and halitoses. Tons of fun in an atmosphere of musky decay. Ernest Thesiger, Charles Laughton, Raymond Massey. Inadequately remade by William Castle in 1963.

OLD MOTHER RILEY MEETS THE VAMPIRE. See *My Son, the Vampire*.

OLIVIA (1983) ★★ German filmmaker Ulli Lommel (*Boogeyman*) cast his wife Suzanne Love as a British woman who previously witnessed her mother murdered by a GI, and who now murders her lovers. She meets an engineer (Robert Walker, Jr.) in the process of dismantling the London Bridge and moving it to Arizona. Four years later Walker turns up at the relocated bridge, seeing a realtor who resembles Love but who now speaks without a British accent and doesn't recognize him. This *Vertigo*-like twist is about the only interesting thing going in an otherwise slow-moving, would-be suspense thriller. Producer-director Lommel also cowrote the shadowy script. Bibbe Hansen, Jeff Winchester, Nicholas Love, Amy Robinson.

Aka *A Taste of Sin, Faces of Fear, Beyond the Bridge, Double Jeopardy*. (Astral; VCII)

OMEGA COP (1990) ★ Stuart Whitman, Adam West and Troy Donahue enliven this derivative future-cop action yarn starring martial arts fighter Ron Marchini, who's after a gang of slave traders. Pretty ho-hum stuff otherwise. Directed by Paul Kyriazi. (South Gate; Hemdale)

OMEGA DOOM (1995) ★ To attempt to explain an Albert Pyun cyborg movie is like trying to pluck a piece of atomic cloud out of a mushrooming explosion and carry it away in your robopack. Shot on location in a ruined town in Slovakia, this dreary sci-fi exercise is set during the nuclear winter of "The Dark Epoch" after man and robots had a great war and nobody won. His prime directive destroyed, cyborg Omega Doom (Rutger Hauer) discovers two warring factions of machine people—the Roms and the Droids—submitting to a truce while they attempt to locate a "treasure": a cache of hidden weapons. In what appears to be a steal of *Yojimbo*, for Omega Doom walks a neutral line between the factions, testing one against the other, the film never leaves its single location as various characters talk to each other in a pseudo-futuristic lingo. Pyun casts with an eye for the unusual, and his actors are visually interesting if their characters are not. Pyun also selects colorful names: Zed for Shannon Thirry (the R-rated gal doesn't show either one of her magnificent breasts, if you can believe that), Blackheart for Tina Cote, Bartender for Anna Katarina, Zinc for Jill Pierce, Marko for Jahi Zuri, Ironface for Cynthia Ireland, Head for Norbert Weisser. The latter is the film's failed comedy relief, a droid who keeps losing his head, and struggling to get it reattached to his hapless torso. Ed Naha helped or hindered Pyun with the script, it's impossible to know. The location appears to have been used again by Pyun in his fourth entry in the *Nemesis* series. Pyun is in a category all by himself, and one can only ponder what abomination he will create next. (Largo Entertainment; Columbia Tristar)

OMEGA FACTOR, THE. See *Silent Madness*.

OMEGA MAN, THE (1971) ★★ Richard Matheson's *I Am Legend* was first adapted as *The Last Man on Earth*, an Italian cheapie that was faithful to the book, blending mythical vampirism with science fiction. This Charlton Heston vehicle (adapted by John William and Joyce H. Corrington) is less faithful. The year is 1975 and Heston would appear to be the sole survivor of a plague. Gone are the vampires of *I Am Legend*; gone is the one-man battle to survive against blood-drinking zombies. A new plot line has Anthony Zerbe heading religious mutants wishing to kill Heston because he represents the knowledge that poisoned mankind. Then comes a real clunker: Heston finds other untainted survivors and has a miscegenational romance with Rosalind Cash. Director Boris Sagal has made a sow's ear out of a silk purse. (Video/Laser: Warner Bros.)

OMEN, THE (1976) ★★★★ Screenwriter David Seltzer borrowed a prophecy from the Book of Revelation, which foredooms the coming of Armageddon, and fashioned the premise for a horror trilogy, of which this is the first. It's a supernatural terror tale of sensational proportions: the Antichrist child, the son of Satan, is reborn and walks among us, destined to rise up through politics and turn "man against his brother . . . till man exists no more." A whopper of a tale—from Jerry Goldsmith's suspenseful score to Gil Taylor's low-key lighting to John Richardson's bloody effects to Richard Donner's taut direction. This features grisly, imaginative murders as Gregory Peck sets out with photographer David Warner to prove the Antichrist exists. There's a ghastly beheading, a hanging, an attack by the Hounds of Hell and other demonic horrors. While sequels (*Damien: Omen II* and *The Final Conflict*) never fully lived up to the premise, this carries it too well. Produced by Harvey Bernhard. Leo McKern, Lee Remick, Billie Whitelaw, Harvey Stephens, Martin Benson, Sheila Raynor. Aka *Birthmark* and *The Antichrist*. (Video/Laser: CBS/Fox)

OMEN II. See *Damien—Omen II.*

OMEN III. See *The Final Conflict*

OMEN IV: THE AWAKENING (1991) ★★ Loose remake of *The Omen*, with producer Harvey Bernhard recycling ingredients of his 1976 hit. This TV-movie has a few exciting moments when a female counterpart to Damien is adopted by a U.S. politician, unaware that "Delia" ("Always Visible" in Greek) is the spawn of Satan. A sequence at a psychic fair is especially effective. But the teleplay by Brian Taggert (from a story by Taggert and Bernhard) has the beheading sequence, the evil devil dog that causes a death, and other familiar "horrible deaths," without exploring new territory. Composer Jonathan Sheffer uses Jerry Goldsmith's themes. Faye Grant, Michael Woods, Michael Lerner, Madison Mason. Directed by Jorge Montesi and Dominique Othenin-Girard. (Video/Laser: CBS/Fox)

ONCE BITTEN (1985) ★★★ Teenage sex comedy with supernatural overtones, not as dumb as some but still kind of dumb. Lauren Hutton is the Countess, a 400-year-old vampire living in an L.A. mansion. She needs three fixes from a male virgin or she'll show her away, so she picks Jim Carrey, who is also frustrated because his girl (Karen Kopins) won't dish out. The women fight for Carrey's attention while Carrey is dumbfounded. There's funny chase stuff through the Countess's mansion with her manservant, a gay vampire (Cleavon Little), leading the monster followers. Finally fizzles under Howard Storm's direction. They deserve a transfusion for trying, anyway. (Video/Laser: Vestron)

ONCE UPON A FRIGHTMARE. Video version and TV title for the British-made *Frightmare II* (Monterey).

ONE BY ONE. See *The Majorettes.*

ONE DARK NIGHT (1982) ★★ Writer-director Thomas McLoughlin borrows the bobbing corpses of *Poltergeist* as 154 zombies (designed by Tom Burman) shamble through a shadowy mausoleum, smothering the panicked characters to death. But instead of being macabre, the sequence has the effect of a funhouse of horrors, and shock value is minimized. On the plus side is an underlying premise of telekinesis. Karl Raymar has developed the power to rob young girls of their bioenergy and becomes a psychic vampire. His corpse is placed in the mausoleum, and then a teenage sorority forces a plebe to spend the night there. Rest in pieces. Aka *Night in the Crypt, Rest in Peace, Mausoleum* and *Entity Force*. Adam West, Robin Evans, Melissa Newman, Meg Tilly, Leslie Spreights. (Thorn EMI/HBO)

ONE MAGIC CHRISTMAS (1985) ★★ Harry Dean Stanton as an angel named Gideon? That's one of many oddities in this dark parable (from Walt Disney yet!) in which he is assigned (by God?) to convince a certain mother the values of the yuletide season. That mother, Mary Steenburgen, has lost her seasonal spirit because (1) hubby was just shot by a bank robber, (2) her kidnapped children have drowned and (3) she's been fired from her supermarket job. Stanton (who looks more like a sinister character than an angel) sends Mary's daughter to the North Pole to meet Santa. A sentimental tearjerker that doesn't have the strength of its schmaltz to pull it off. Gary Basaraba, Elizabeth Harnois, Arthur Hill (playing a white-haired grandfather), Wayne Robson. Directed by Phillip Borsos. (Video/Laser: Disney)

ONE MILLION B.C. (1940) ★★★ Hal Roach's production depicting men vs. dinosaurs makes for whopping good adventure. Aka *Cave Man, Cave Dwellers, Man and His Mate* and *Battle of the Giants*, this tribute to the Stone Age is filled with visual thrills, not the least of which is Carole Landis in antelope pelt. The Rock People are a crude, meat-eating tribe lorded over by grunting Tomack (Lon Chaney, Jr.), who kicks Victor Mature out into the cold. Jutting-jawed Mature goes to the Shell People, a less boorish tribe that savors vegetables and practices manners. Eventually the tribes become gregarious, but not before battles with brontosaurus, trachodons and other beasts. There's a climactic volcanic eruption. A classic, directed by Roach, Roach Jr. and D. W. Griffith; scripted by Mickell Novak, George Baker and Joseph Frickert. Remade with Raquel Welch in 1967 as *One Million Years* B.C. (Media; Nostalgic Merchant; Fox Hills) (Laser: 3M)

ONE MILLION YEARS B.C. (1967) ★★★ Hammer's remake of Hal Roach's 1940 miniclassic, with Raquel Welch (fetching in animal skins) as the Shell People gal who meets a Rock Tribe guy (John Richardson). Michael Carreras wrote-produced for Hammer, with Don Chaffey directing. A must-see for Ray Harryhausen's stop-motion animation. Like its predecessor, this is grand entertainment. Martine Beswick.

ONE MINUTE BEFORE DEATH. See *The Oval Portrait.*

ONE NEVER KNOWS. See *You Never Can Tell.*

ONE OF OUR DINOSAURS IS MISSING (1975) ★★★ Amusing Disney fantasy comedy spoofs British behavior (nannies, stiff upper lip, that sort of thing, old chap) and monster films. Lotus X is a Chinese secret hidden in the tibia of a museum dinosaur, which restores life into the ancient creature. Fighting over possession of Lotus X are Peter Ustinov (Hnup Wan, of Chinese Intelligence) and Helen Hayes (nanny and backbone of the Empire). Made in England with Robert Stevenson directing. (Disney)

ONE THOUSAND CRIES HAS THE NIGHT. See *Pieces.*

ON HER MAJESTY'S SECRET SERVICE (1969) ★★★ George Lazenby replaces Sean Connery in this, the sixth in the James Bond series. Lazenby has neither the diction nor the finesse of Connery, nor does he appear comfortable in the arms of Diana Rigg and other beauties. To take up the slack, director Peter Hunt works extra hard with action. Villain Ernst Stavros Blofeld (Telly Savalas) is masterminding a takeover of the world by concealing in women's cosmetics allergies that will result in sterility. Richard Maibaum adapted the Fleming novel, providing a love affair between Bond and Rigg (daughter of an international bad guy) that is the best aspect of this spy adventure. Connery would return in *Diamonds Are Forever.* Julie Ege, Bessie Love, Catherina Von Schell. (Video/Laser: MGM/UA; CBS/Fox)

ON THE BEACH (1959) ★★★ Stanley Kramer's plea for peace is a classy version of Nevil Shute's novel (adapted by John Paxton) in which mankind has dropped the Bomb and Australia is the only continent yet untouched by radiation. The story pivots on a submarine commander (Gregory Peck), his affair with Ava Gardner and their subsequent acceptance, and rejection, of doom. Kramer's direction emphasizes the gloom of inexorable death. "Waltzing Matilda" is used to haunting effect. Anthony Perkins, Fred Astaire, Donna Anderson. (CBS/Fox) (Laser: Image)

ON THE TRAIL OF ED WOOD (1990) ★★ Documentary on the career of Ed Wood, Jr., responsible for *Plan 9 from Outer Space* and other schlocky flicks. Actor Conrad Brooks is the host of this excursion into the dark side of an unhappy creative artist and his botched attempts at cinema. Directed by Michael Copner. (Videosonic Arts)

ON TO MARS. See *Abbott and Costello Go to Mars.*

OPEN HOUSE (1987) ★★ Routine slasher flick with routine gore murders when the Open House Killer—angered by rising costs of homes in Beverly Hills—slaughters sexy realtors and their clients. Joseph Bottoms portrays radio psychologist Dr. David Kelly, who hosts "The Survival Line," and the killer calls him up during a broadcast, drawing him and his girl, Adrienne Barbeau, into the mystery. Director Jag Mundhra handles the bloody murders well, spicing them up with kinky sex and nudity. Rudy Ramos, Mary Stavin. (Prism)

OPERA. See *Terror at the Opera.*

OPERATION FEAR. See *Kill, Baby, Kill.*

OPERATION MONSTERLAND. See *Destroy All Monsters.*

OPERATION PARADISE. See *Kiss the Girls and Make Them Die.*

OPERATION STARDUST. See *Mission Stardust.*

ORACLE, THE (1985) ★★ The spirit of a murdered businessman (Willliam Graham) is contained in an ancient form of Ouija board that seduces beautiful Caroline Capers Powers and causes her to see visions of his murder. Directed by Roberta Findlay, Roger Neil, Pam LaTesta, Victoria Dryden. (USA; IVE)

ORCA: THE KILLER WHALE (1977) ★★ To whales what *Jaws* was to sharks—but hardly a whale of a movie. Seafaring Richard Harris, after harpooning Orca's mate, is attacked by the superwhale, which also rams its snout into a seacoast town, almost sinking it. Touches of *Moby Dick* don't do much to improve the silly story, nor do gratuitous touches of gore false to the nature of killer whales. Among potential whale bait are Bo Derek, Keenan Wynn, Charlotte Rampling and Will Sampson. Munchy munchy. Michael Anderson directed this in the wake of *Jaws* from a script written by producer Luciano Vincenzoni. Aka *The Killer Whale.* (Video/Laser: Paramount)

ORGASMO. See *Nightmare Castle.*

ORGY OF BLOOD. See *Brides of the Beast.*

ORGY OF THE BLOOD PARASITES. See *They Came from Within.*

ORGY OF THE DEAD (1965) ★★★ Campy send-up of horror movies, but whether director A. C. Stephens knew that is debatable. Based on a novel by Edward Wood, Jr., and said to be a loose sequel to *Plan 9 from Outer Space,* this hysterically funny anomaly is set in a cemetery where the Devil (Criswell) and Ghoulita (Fawn Silver) watch exotic dancers perform their stuff in the buff. Criswell and Silver are hilarious as they stumble through their lines as a pair of innocents watch while tied to stakes. Also hanging around the graveyard are a mummy and a werewolf who crack jokes about Cleopatra. The dancers are lovely, making this nudie a girl watcher's delight. The color is good and the dry ice swirls dramatically. A must for Wood aficionados and flesh peddlers. Aka *Revenge of the Dead* and *Orgy of the Vampires*. (Rhino)

ORGY OF THE VAMPIRES. See *Orgy of the Dead*.

ORIGINAL FABULOUS ADVENTURES OF BARON MUNCHAUSEN (BARON PRASIL), THE (1961) Video/laser variations on *Fabulous Adventures of Baron Munchausen* (American Video) (Laser: Image).

ORIGINAL FLASH GORDON COLLECTION. Boxed set of four condensations of the Flash Gordon serials under the titles *Spaceship to the Unknown, Deadly Ray from Mars, Peril from Planet Mongo* and *Purple Death from Outer Space*. (Questar)

ORLANDO (1992) ★★★ One of the strangest reincarnation (or is it time-travel?) tales ever spun for the movies—and if you can make total sense out of it, please send in your explanation. One thing for certain: this British film is a beautiful and opulent adaptation of Virginia Woolf's novel about a human spirit (first man, then woman) who lives for 400 years, beginning with the court of Elizabeth I in 1600 and proceeding through the present day. There is a muddled quality to the script (by director Sally Potter) that appears intended, as if one is not to make sense of it but rather be swept along with an offbeat tale that favors angst and ruffled period costumes over clarity. Tilda Swinton is superb in the title role, and Quentin Crisp has a ball playing Elizabeth I. The excellent cast includes Billy Zane, Lothaire Bluteau, John Wood and Heathcote Williams. (Video/Laser: Columbia TriStar)

ORPHAN, THE (1979) ★ Mixed-up youth undergoes traumas as a prelude to graphic murders. Children shouldn't play with dead adults. John Ballard wrote-directed; allegedly inspired by Saki's short story "Sredni Vashtar." Mark Owens, Joanna Miles. Aka *Don't Open the Door* and *Friday the 13th . . . The Orphan*. (Rhino; Prism)

ORPHEUS (1949) ★★★ Intriguing, baffling, perplexing, irritating, pleasing—all these describe French director Jean Cocteau's retelling of the ancient Greek legend of Orpheus, a dead poet who descended into Hell after being returned to life by a personification of Death. In this modernized version, Jean Marais portrays the poet and Maria Casares is the entrancing, mysterious woman in black. Rather than trying to follow a coherent story line, Cocteau chose a surreal approach with stark black-and-white photography and a range of special effects that are startling. This is a dizzying treat for the eye and the intellect, and a cinematic challenge for anyone who enjoys unusual filmmaking. Music by Georges Auric. Francois Perier, Juliette Greco, Maria Dea. (Embassy; Video Yesteryear; Sinister/C; Sultan)

ORSON WELLES'S GHOST STORY (1953) ★★★★½ Originally produced by Welles as a 30-minute short subject in 1951 under the title *Return to Glennascaul: A Story That Is Told in Dublin*, this was nominated for an Oscar as Best Two-Reel Short Subject. Welles, who collaborated with his friends Hilton Edwards and Micheal MacLiammoir to make the film, stars as himself who, driving home from a rehearsal one dark night, picks up stranded motorist Michael Laurence, who proceeds to tell him a tale of the supernatural. The MPI home video version has an introduction featuring director Peter Bogdanovich.

OSA (1985) ★ Pointless *Mad Max* rip-off, poorly written and stylelessly directed by Oleg Egorov. In a vague future society where water is a precious commodity, and anarchy rules in the desert, a gang of cutthroats led by Mr. Big murders a young girl's family. She grows up under the tutelage of Trooper, who teaches her how to use a crossbow so that she might wreak her vengeance on Big's baddies. The climax is a game to the death called Bird Hunt. For the birds is right! Kelly Lynch, Peter Walker, Etienne Chicot, Daniel Grimm. (HBO Cannon)

OTHER, THE (1972) ★★★ Thomas Tryon's best-selling novel (which he adapted), heavy with religious symbolism, is such ingenious storytelling it is difficult to describe without giving away its jolting surprises. Under Robert Mulligan's direction, it unfolds on a Connecticut farm in 1935 and shows the strangest abnormal psychology in children since *The Bad Seed*. In spite of visual gimmicks Mulligan never cheapens the story, only enhances it with his clever manipulations. We refuse to say anything else—except see it! Chris and Martin Udvaronky, Uta Hagen, Diana Muldaur, John Ritter, Victor French, Christopher Connelly. (CBS/Fox)

OTHER HELL, THE (1980) ★ A blasphemous Italian slap at Catholicism, set in a nunnery where women are slaughtered by supernatural forces, the "work of the Devil." But an ecclesiastical detective thinks it's a human murderer and investigates. Jesus, is he in for a surprise. Included are scenes of a dead body having its vagina ripped out, a child stabbed several times, a baby scalded in a cauldron of boiling water, and a priest knifed in the groin at least twice. Sit all the way through this and you'll need a few Hail Marys yourself. Directed by Stefan Oblowsky, who must never go to church on Sunday. Franca Stoppi, Carlo Demejo. (Vestron; Prism; Lettuce Entertain You)

OUTBREAK (1995) ★★★★½ A fabulous medical action thriller directed by Wolfgang Petersen with panache and a search for constantly exciting visuals and characters, from a suspense-laden script by Laurence Dworet and Robert Roy Pool that stresses high-concept hardware. A mutated virus, brought into America via a small monkey from Zaire, Africa, infects the California town of Cedar Creek, invoking conflict at the U.S. Army Medical Research Institute for Infectious Diseases, where commanding generals Morgan Freeman and Donald Sutherland set out to prevent dedicated officer Dustin Hoffman from discovering top secrets surrounding the outbreak. Involved in this, as a search is conducted for an antidote, is Hoffman's estranged wife (Rene Russo) and closest associate (Cuba Gooding, Jr.). The action includes the destruction of an African village, a bombing threat to Cedar Creek, a theater sequence that shows how the airborne disease is spread mouth to mouth, aerial action and chilling sequences of martial law befalling the town. Patrick Dempsey, Kevin Spacey, Zakes Mokae, Malick Bowens. (Video/Laser: Warner Bros.)

OUTING, THE See *Scream* (1985).

OUTING, THE (1986) ★ Nothing amusing about the Aladdin's lamp in this low-budget quickie—it's inhabited by an ugly demon who exerts supernatural powers in *Omen*-like revenge murders (spear impales man, rattlesnake crawls up man's trouser leg, cobra attacks woman in bathtub, man is broken in half). The lamp is first taken from an Old Hag by crooks disposed of by green rays of death, then it goes into an anthropology museum. The murders occur when stupid teenagers have an all-night party (an "outing") in the museum. Fans will dig the gory murders but not groove so much on the demon-monster. Deborah Winters (also associate producer) plays the Old Hag as well as modern woman Eve Farrell. Written-produced by Warren Chaney, directed by Tom Daley. James Huston, Andra St. Ivanyi, Danny D. Daniels. Aka *The Lamp*. (IVE)

OUTLAND (1981) ★★★★ Superbly crafted action mystery from writer-director Peter Hyams that depicts a farflung world (Io, a moon of Jupiter) where Earthmen mine trinium. The full-scale interior sets are complex, the exterior models mind-boggling and the pace unrelenting as marshal Sean Connery tracks down a company conspiracy to feed its workmen a dangerous drug to improve their output. When Connery won't knuckle under, company boss Peter Boyle imports two hired gunmen. There's even swinging doors for those who want to compare this to *High Noon*. Frances Sternhagen, James Sikking. Originally made as *Io*. (Video/Laser: Warner Bros.)

OUTLAW OF GOR (1987) ★★★½ Entertaining if corny sequel to *Gor*, continuing the adventures of Tarl Cabot (a square-jawed square played by Urbano Barberini) who, with a ruby-red magical ring, returns to the harsh, sandy world where the high priest Xenos (Jack Palance) rules with bitchy Lara (Donna Denton). Before you can plunge a sword into the nearest guard, she's usurped the throne, Cabot is her avowed enemy and she's thrown Cabot's love Talena (Rebecca Ferrati) into the dungeon. Cabot, his stupid friend Watney (Russel Savadier) and the dwarf Hup (Nigel Chipps) fight back. Denton steals the show with her hysterical portrayal of a totally evil bitch-queen, while Palance brings little conviction to his role (being stuck with dialogue by Rick Marx and Peter Welbeck, who adapted the novels by John Norman). Director John "Bud" Cardos holds it all together rather well. (Warner Bros.)

OUTLAW PLANET, THE. See *Planet of the Vampires*.

OUTLAWS (1986) ★★★ Above-average TV-movie blending time travel and the traditional Western. Outside Houston, Texas, in 1899, an outlaw gang is trapped by lawman John Grail (Rod Taylor), and just as the shoot-out begins, a bolt of electricity propels them into the 1980s, where they learn the ways of modern man without giving up their own code of the West. The parable element of Nicholas Corea's script is well done, and the characters (William Lucking, Charles Napier, Patrick Houser, Richard Roundtree) appealing. Director Peter Werner permits the action to get wild and woolly.

OUT OF SIGHT, OUT OF HER MIND (1989) ★ Horror director Greydon Clark is back with a tale of the Kabuki Killer and how this antisocial guy terrorizes Susan Blakely after he burns her daughter alive. Wings Hauser plays Blakely's husband and Edward Albert is the cop. Lynn-Holly Johnson, Richard Masur. (Prism) (Laser: Image)

OUT OF THE BODY (1988) ★★ In Sydney, Australia, a killer is knocking off beautiful women and removing their eyeballs. Musician Mark Hembrow foresees the crimes but police won't believe him. Turns out there's more than meets the eyes—a supernatural monster is afoot. Directed by Brian Trenchard-Smith. Tessa Humphries, Carrie Zivetz, Shane Briant. (Sony) (Laser: Image)

OUT OF THE DARK (1989) ★★½ An office of young women (call girls?) who specialize in faked orgasms on the phone for a "sex talk" business, Suite Nothings (the boss is Karen Black), becomes target for a pervert who dresses as Bobo the Clown and bludgeons or strangles the cuties. The issue this movie raises—do sex-by-phone businesses contribute to the sickness of America?—is never touched on, only exploited with smutty talk. Director Michael Schroeder treats *Out of the Dark*, red herrings and all, as a cheapo slasher flick. Paul Bartel makes a cameo appearance along with Tab Hunter, Divine and Geoffrey Lewis. Black has little to do but look worried and scream—a waste of her talents. Also wasted is Bud Cort as a suspect. Sorry, but we kept hearing a wrong number on this one. A lot of Suite Nothings in our ear? Cameron Dye, Lynn Danielson, Starr Andreeff. (Video/Laser: RCA/Columbia)

OUT OF THE DARKNESS. See *Teenage Caveman*.

OUT OF THE DARKNESS. See *Night Creature*.

OUT OF TIME (1988) ★★ Light-spirited, sometimes satirical TV-movie in the vein of *Back to the Future*, in which future cop Bruce Abbott, tracking a criminal in the year 2088, is transported to modern times in the time-chopper of baddie Adam Ant. He meets his silly great-grandfather (Bill Maher) and begins to shape his ancestor's future as a great cop-hero and inventor. Robert Butler directed in typical TV style, with the time-travel effects being a shaky, out-of-focus picture. Did they run out of time on the set? Leo Rossi, Kristan Alfonso.

OUTRAGE, THE (1964) ★★★ Remake of the Japanese classic *Rashomon*, reshaped into a Western by director Martin Ritt, but a pretentious misfire, overacted by Paul Newman as a greasy Mexican bandit who may have raped a woman and murdered her husband. The same story is told from different points of view with an Indian witch doctor spinning the dead man's side from beyond the grave. Heavy-handed outrage against Japan's Akira Kurosawa. Others who overact are Clair Bloom as the wife, Laurence Harvey as the husband and William Shatner as the disillusioned priest. Faring better are Howard Da Silva as the narrator and Edward G. Robinson as the philosophical peddler who best understands the dark side of human nature.

OUT THERE (1995) ★★½ Mildly amusing, lightweight comedy making fun of supermarket tabloids, UFOs, government cover-ups and alien abductions. Bill Campbell is a prize-winning photographer who buys an old camera and discovers a roll of undeveloped film containing photos of a 1969 alien abduction case. He and Wendy Schaal (whose father disappeared that year) are off on a trail of bizarre characters (June Lockhart, Paul Dooley, Rod Steiger, Bobcat Goldthwait, Jill St. John, Julie Brown) that eventually leads to a trailer camp and an underground flying saucer. This is a slow, droll film that never gathers much steam, with the Thomas Strelich–Alison Nigh script content with wisecracks rather than a clever plot. Sam Irvin does a competent job as director, but there isn't much in the way of special effects or aliens, so fans will come away slightly disappointed. (Video/Laser: Paramount)

OVAL PORTRAIT, THE (1972) ★★★ As corny and overwrought as this "woman in peril" period thriller is, it has a sense of fun about itself that makes it palatable. Set in an isolated mansion during the Civil War, with a thunderstorm always breaking out and the cast walking in bulky costumes, this "premature burial" tale stars Wanda Hendrix as a wealthy lady who falls down the stairs and is cast into a catatonic state. As she lies there motionless, greedy family members fight over her inheritance and say nasty things about her. Hendrix comes to realize these folks are no good (her husband is two-timing her and her sister cares only about jewels). Deception and murder propel producer Enrique Torres Tudela's teleplay, and director Rogelio Gonzales, Jr., maintains the suspense with zooms and carooms as the film vacillates between a walking-dead interpretation and a plot-to-drive-humans-mad possibility. Gisele MacKenzie is a catty, bitchy member of the family. Poe had nothing to do with any of this. Barry Coe, Pia Shandel, Ty Haller, Maray Ayres. (Parade; from Platinum Productions; Front Row; Tenth Avenue; on video from Parade as *Edgar Allen Poe's One Minute before Death*)

OVERDRAWN AT THE MEMORY BANK (1983) ★★★ Good sci-fi tale based on a John Varley story set in a totalitarian society ruled by a giant corporation, Novicorp. Raul Julia stars as Aram Fingal, a "processor third class" who discovers the existence of movies and projects himself into a new reality based on *Casablanca*. Julia does a fair impression of Bogart as Rick Blaine but the key to this story is the clever use of dual universes and alternate realities as programmer Linda Griffiths (as Appolonia James) helps Fingal restore his true identity and overcome the dictatorial Mr. Big, who takes on the persona of Sydney Greenstreet from *Casablanca*. Director Douglas Williams does a remarkable job, given his limited budget. Wanda Cannon, Donald C. Moore, Louis Negin, Jackie Burroughs, Maury Chaykin. (Starmaker/New World) (Laser: Image)

OVER MY DEAD BODY. See *The Brain* (1962).

OZONE (1993) ★★ A new street drug called "ozone" is turning its users into walking killer zombies, and eventually will take them to a new evolutionary state as toad creatures, in this semiprofessional shocker made for the less-discriminating gore/special effects crowd. Promising director J. R. Bookwalter (who co-wrote the script with David Wagner) has a good story but inadequate funds (he couldn't even afford blanks for the revolvers, and the dubbed gunshots are terrible) pretty much defeat his purpose. Cop James Black runs around the city fighting off the zombies and their leader (a toadman who looks like Jabba the Hutt) while everyone else in the cast turns into one of the ozone creatures. That's about it. Tom Hoover, Bill Morrison, Michael Cagnoli, Lori Scarlett. (Tempe)

PACK, THE (1977) ★½ Schweinhund of dog-slasher movies as psycho poodles, demonic dachshunds, terror terriers and horror hounds seek human hydrants. A "We're surrounded and got to find a way out" plot with Joe Don Baker as chief canine-kicker. Robert Clouse wrote-directed. "Dogs' worst enemies" are R. G. Armstrong, Richard B. Shull, Richard O'Brien, Hope Alexander-Willis. Aka in some pounds as *Killers Who Wore Collars*—heh heh, just kidding. Aka *The Long Dark Night*. (Warner Bros.; Vestron)

PAGEMASTER, THE (1994) ★★★ This is a moderately entertaining use of live action and animation by producer David Kirschner to use historical literature for themes. In the live-action opening, directed by Joe Johnston, Macaulay Culkin, son of Ed Begley, Jr., and Mel Harris, is a nonadventurous kid who stops in a huge library one rainy afternoon to be confronted by head librarian Christopher Lloyd. Culkin enters a literary fantasy kingdom (animated) where three books (Adventure, pirate voice by Patrick Stewart; Fantasy, voice by Whoopi Goldberg; Horror, voice by Frank Welker) take him on odysseys to: Horrorland, where Dr. Jekyll (voice by Leonard Nimoy) provides terrors; Pirateland, where he encounters Long John Silver (voice by George Hearn) on Treasure Island; and Fantasyland, where Culkin fights a fire-breathing dragon. Scripted by David Casci, Kirschner and Ernie Contreras, *The Pagemaster* never flames fiery hot, and the animation (directed by Maurice Hunt) is just average. Kids, nonetheless, should enjoy its traditional cartoon images. (Video/Laser: Fox)

PALE BLOOD (1990) ★★★½ Offbeat, stylized vampire thriller with clever twists and a bravura performance by Wings Hauser. The Hong Kong team of writer Takashi Matsuoka and director V. V. Dachin Hsu have concocted a vampire named Michael Fury (George Chakiris), hired to solve the Vampire Killer murders. Chakiris, his face pale and drawn, is sinister in his antiheroic role as a supernatural entity. Ultimately, though, it is Hauser's vampire hunter and his maniacal acting that sets this apart. Pamela Ludwig, Diana Frank, Darcy DeMoss. (Video/Laser: RCA/Columbia)

PANDEMONIUM (1982) ★★★ This now seems one of the funniest of the *Friday the 13th* parodies that came in that film's wake. A Jason-styled killer, who skewered five girls on a very long spear in 1963, is back in black stalking the ridiculous men and women undergoing cheer-leader training at It Had to Be U. In an *Airplane*-like compendium of parodies and sketches, Debralee Scott, Carol Kane and Candy Azzara are subjected to nonsense. The film sparkles with surprise cameos by Tom Smothers, Pee-wee Herman, Tab Hunter, Kaye Ballard, Donald O'Connor and Eve Arden. Enough of the hodge-podge works thanks to the polished direction of

Alfred Sole and the amusing script by Richard Whitley and Jaime Klein. Originally produced as *Thursday the 12th*. (MGM/UA)

PANGA. See *The Curse III: Blood Sacrifice*.

PANIC (1960). See *The Tell-tale Heart*.

PANIC AT LAKEWOOD MANOR. See *Ants*.

PANIC IN THE TRANS-SIBERIAN TRAIN. See *Horror Express*.

PANIC IN YEAR ZERO (1962) ★★½ Hydrogen holocaust is upon us and so is anarchy—rape, murder and other human reactions to Armageddon. A family fights off pillagers and rapists to survive. Cheap production values, a vague screenplay (by Jay Simms and John Morton) and the indifferent direction by Ray Milland (who also portrays Harry Baldwin, average father) make this a weak "end of civilization" yarn. When a doctor comments, "If we scrape the scabs off, and apply disinfectant, civilization might recover," one wishes American-International had applied disinfectant to the script's botched complexion. Milland's family: Jean Hagen, Mary Mitchell, Frankie Avalon. Others in the cast: Scott Peters, Russ Bender, O. Z. Whitehead. Music by Les Baxter. Aka *Survival* and *End of the World*. (Fright; Orion)

PANTHER GIRL OF THE KONGO (1955) ★ One of the last of the cliff-hangers from Republic, and only a shadow of the great '40s serials. After realizing how good Phyllis Coates looked in khaki shorts and tight blouse in *Jungle Drums of Africa*, she was cast in the Nyoka mold as an African adventurer, thereby increasing the heart-beats of young viewers. But Coates performed without emotion and it's a poorly produced serial. Her adversary is Dr. Morgan (Arthur Space) who turns crawfish into monsters, and uses these mutations to chase away African natives from a diamond mine. The serial, inspired by *Them*, is salvaged by Myron Healey as great white hunter Larry Sanders. When seen as 12 chapters there's a certain inept charm that makes you want to forgive director Franklin Adreon and writer Ronald Davidson. Not a lot, just a little. Archie Savage, Mike Ragan. Feature version: *The Claw Monsters*. (Video/Laser: Republic)

PAPERHOUSE (1987) ★★★½ Poignant psychological fantasy, expertly directed by Bernard Rose, about an 11-year-old (Charlotte Burke) who escapes her unhappy world by dreaming herself into her drawings. Burke finds herself on a windy coastline in front of a strange house and meets a young boy—she also encounters her worst fears in a frightening horror sequence. But basically this is about her internal struggles to find herself, to reconcile her differences with her parents (Glenne Headly and Ben Cross) and to discover first-time love with the boy (Elliott Spiers). The excellent script by Matthew Jacobs was adapted from a Catherine Starr novel. (Vestron) (Laser: Image)

PARANOIAC (1963) ★½ Despite Jimmy Sangster's clever plot and the sure hand of director Freddie Francis, this Hammer mystery is dull, lacking the wallops of a good psychological terror film. Oliver Reed, who killed his brother, is stunned when the brother returns alive. Things get tricky after that, so pay attention. Janette Scott, Alexander Davion, Maurice Denham. (Video/Laser: MCA)

PARASITE (1982) ★★½ Released to theaters in 3-D, this low-budget sci-fi–horror cheapie takes place in a post-Armageddon world where men are equipped with laser guns. A monster runs around burrowing into people and leaping at the camera. Stan Winston's creature effects are average, the gore is gratuitous. The stuff wrapped around the violence is lethargic as Robert Glaudini discovers there's a worm in his abdomen that could spread to mankind. Produced-directed by Charles Band, from an Alan J. Adler–Michael Shoob–Frank Levering script. Of passing interest, perhaps, as one of Demi Moore's first films. Luca Bercovici, Cherie Currie, Vivian Blaine. (Wizard; Paramount; Embassy) (Laser: Shadow)

PARASITE MURDERS, THE. See *They Came from Within* (Intestional subterfuge required).

PARDON ME, BUT YOUR TEETH ARE IN MY NECK. See *The Fearless Vampire Killers*.

PARENTS (1989) ★★★½ This stark, disturbing psychological horror tale set in suburbia in the atomic age of the 1950s can be viewed in three ways: (1) as a grim study of a youth who discovers his parents are cannibals; (2) as a hallucination of a manic-depressive child who only imagines the meat on the table is human flesh; (3) as a metaphor for the childhood trauma many go through when well-meaning parents force some awful food down their throats. Director Bob Balaban has done a good job of delivering the goods in Christopher Hawthorne's

script. Superb as the Laemle family are Randy Quaid, Mary Beth Hurt and Bryan Madorsky; the latter goes through the film without a single change of expression, and yet reflects the script's needs. Sandy Dennis is good as a flighty psychologist. Graham Jarvis, Juno Mills-Cockett, Kathryn Grody. (Vestron) (Laser: Image)

PARTS—THE CLONUS HORROR. Video version of *The Clonus Horror* (Catalina).

PASSIONATE PEOPLE EATER, THE. Original title for Corman's 1960 *Little Shop of Horrors*.

PASSION FLOWER HOTEL. See *Boarding House*.

PAST MIDNIGHT (1991) ★★½ Psychological horror tale of slight consequence, classically structured by screenwriter Frank Norwood in the Hitchcock tradition, but it's still slight stuff. Social worker Natasha Richardson falls for ex-con Rutger Hauer, refusing to believe he murdered his wife with a butcher knife and took 8mm movies while committing the crime. However, the finger of suspicion points toward him and Richardson is on the horns of a dilemma, especially when she realizes she's pregnant. The film only comes to life during the climatic revelations, but it's a long wait, and the direction by Jan Eliasberg is only occasionally flashy, with too many lengthy, lethargic stretches. Clancy Brown portrays Richardson's former boyfriend, who provides her with an essential plot device: a pump-action shotgun. (Video/Laser: Columbia TriStar)

PAST TENSE (1994) ★★★ If you enjoy putting together complicated jigsaw puzzles, you should enjoy this psychological suspense thriller that's treated as a schizophrenic nightmare by screenwriters Scott Frost and Miguel Tejada-Flores. Nothing is what it seems when you are introduced to cop–mystery novelist Scott Glenn (maybe) who meets new beautiful neighbor Lara Flynn Boyle (maybe) and becomes involved in a could-be murder. Sort of. It's a challenging mystery in which past, present and future are blended, and which director Graeme Clifford treats with some neat mysterious touches. The ending is routine, but getting there is all the fun. Anthony LaPaglia, David Ogden Stiers, Sheree Wilson, Marita Geraghty. (Video/Laser: Republic)

PEACEMAKER (1990) ★½ Sci-fi action in which two humanoid aliens end up on Earth fighting it out—each claiming to be the good "lawman." Figuring out which is which is no fun the way writer-director Kevin S. Tenney has it laid out. The aliens crash through windows, leap over walls, fall through trees, crash cars, trucks and bikes, shoot at each other with pistols, rifles, shotguns and submachine guns, and sock each other on the jaw repeatedly. But since they can rejuvenate themselves, so what? You'd think one of them would figure out a way to kill the other. Robert Forster and Lance Edwards (the latter talking like a Russian) run all over L.A. with medical examiner Hilary Shepard. Seems the aliens got to Earth through a black hole. They should send this movie back through it. (Charles Fries) (Laser: Image)

PEARL OF DEATH (1944) ★★★½ Sherlock Holmes feature in the Basil Rathbone–Nigel Bruce Universal series, featuring Rondo Hatton as the Creeper, a character whose origins are detailed in *The Brute Man*. Updated Holmesian adventure, above average for the series, based on Arthur Conan Doyle's "The Adventure of the Six Napoleons." Evelyn Ankers, Dennis Hooey, Ian Wolfe. Directed by Roy William Neill from a terrific script by Bertram Milhauser. (CBS/Fox)

PEEPING TOM (1960) ★★★★ Director Michael Powell's unrelenting portrait of a psychopathic young man (who photographs the women he murders with a 16mm camera) was ahead of its time and resulted in Powell's ostracism from Britain's film industry. "Shovel it up and flush it down the sewer," wrote one critic. Yet this has no blood or gore, maintaining an implicit viewpoint toward sex and violence. What disturbed Powell's contemporaries was Leo Marks's screenplay focusing on sexual perversion through metaphor and symbolism. Thus, the film asks viewers to become voyeurs and this evoked negative response. Carl Boehm is superb as the filmmaker. Moira Shearer, Anna Massey, Shirley Anne Field. Aka *Face of Fear*. (Admit One) (Laser: Image; Voyager/Criterion)

PENALTY OF DEATH. See *Violent Blood Bath*.

PENDULUM. See *The Castle of the Walking Dead*.

PENTAGRAM. See *The First Power*.

PEOPLE, THE (1972) ★★★ Sensitive adaptation (by James M. Miller) of Zenna Henderson's *Pilgrimage: The Book of the People*, morality parables about humanoids stranded on Earth, living in an isolated rural community. Their dormant telepathic and levitation abilities are reactivated with the help of new schoolteacher Kim Darby, who gains their trust along with doctor William Shatner. John Korty directs this offbeat Francis Ford Coppola TV production with a gentle, poetic touch. Dan O'Herlihy, Laurie Walters, Diane Varsi. (Prism)

PEOPLE OF ABRIMES, THE. See *The Lost Continent* (1968).

PEOPLE THAT TIME FORGOT, THE (1977) ★★★ Third in a series of Edgar Rice Burroughs adventures produced in Britain—the others being *The Land That Time Forgot* and *At the Earth's Core*. Patrick Wayne and explorers find Doug McClure (star of the previous adaptations) in a kingdom of dinosaurs, pterodactyls and Neanderthal brutes. The effects (mechanized mock-ups) aren't always convincing, but a spirit of adventure makes up for shortcomings. Directed by Kevin Connor from a Patrick Tilley script. Dana Gillespie, Thorley Walters, Sarah Douglas, David Prowse. Next in the series: *Warlords of Atlantis*. (Embassy)

PEOPLETOYS. See *Devil Times Five*.

PEOPLE UNDER THE STAIRS, THE (1991) ★★★½ Satisfying romp through a house of horrors—one of writer-director Wes Craven's best efforts. It's an unusual horror fairy tale about a youth (Brandon Adams) who, because his mother needs an operation, breaks into his landlord's home to steal gold coins. But the mansion is inhabited by a homicidal husband-wife team, zombies kept in a dungeon, a killer rottweiler, trapdoors, secret corridors with death traps, a kitchen of cannibal terror and a pit of corpses. The violence and ghastliness is counterbalanced by humorous portrayals of the adult killers by Everet McGill (he runs around in a black leather outfit, blasting everything with a shotgun) and Wendy Robie, who insists they say their prayers before retiring. This avoids the moral ambiguities of Craven's earlier works and has a whimsical conclusion to its subplot about poor ghetto conditions. Ving Rhames, A. J. Langer, Sean Whalen. (Video/Laser: MCA)

PERCY (1971) ★ Would you believe the first male sex organ transplant? Performed by that stiff-mannered, upright surgeon Sir Emmanuel Whitbread? Smutty British joke, erected from a novel by Raymond Hitchcock and inserted into a screenplay by Hugh Leonard. Director Ralph Thomas tries to pump energy into this flaccid project, but it's limp. There isn't even a climax, offhand. Oh, the film has spurts but suffers from self-abuse and withdrawal symptons as Hywel Bennett, Denholm Elliott, Elke Sommer and Britt Ekland end up rubbing you the wrong way. In the final analysis, sterile and impotent. Call it emasculated. But don't call it irresistible. The sequel was *It's Not the Size That Counts* (aka *Percy's Progress*).

PERFECT BRIDE (1990) ★★ Female counterpart to Terry O'Quinn's "Stepfather" is essayed by Sammi Davis as she goes from family to family, killing those who suspect she's a murderess with a hypo. John Agar, Kelly Preston. Directed by Terrence O'Hara. (Media)

PERFECT VICTIMS (1988) ★ Originally made as *Hidden Rage*, this presents a serial killer who has AIDS and is out to humiliate and kill women. His first targets are two models whom he drugs and rapes. Then this demented guy goes after the models' boss—a beautiful woman with a boyfriend who owns a Malibu mansion—and in his spare time sets fire to a guy and knifes a woman in the belly. The cop on the case is Clarence Williams III. While the Academy video retains the AIDS angle, the TV version drops it completely so it appears the guy is just another slasher killer. Whichever way you see it, *Perfect Victims* is undistinguished. Leading lady Deborah Sheldon was also exec producer and director Shuki Levy also wrote the music. Lyman Ward, Tom Dugan, Nikolete Scorsese. John Agar appears briefly as a neighbor walking his dog. (Academy)

PERIL FROM THE PLANET MONGO. Reedited footage of *Flash Gordon's Trip to Mars* (Questar).

PERILS OF GWENDOLINE: IN THE LAND OF THE YIK YAK (1985) ★★ Tongue-in-cheek erotic-bondage adventure based on the lesbian-oriented French comic strip by John Willie, with director Just Jaeckin adding Indiana Jones touches. This light-hearted male fantasy has happy-go-lucky Brent Huff reluctantly leading Tawny Kitaen into jungle dangers to find her father and a priceless butterfly. The Kiop kingdom of cannibals and a forbidden city of breast-plated (ha ha!) beauties pulling chariots are among the points of interest, not to mention the two naked points on most of the women in the cast. Filmed in the Philippines. (Video/Laser: Vestron)

PERILS OF NYOKA. See *Nyoka and the Tigermen.*

PERILS OF PAULINE, THE (1933) ★★ Although it's hampered by old-fashioned, corny acting and some pretty stiff filmmaking, this 12-chapter serial is still worth going back for a look, what with Evalyn Knapp's performance as the hapless heroine, some Egyptology elements, a lot of old cars tearing around city streets, and many attempts to inject horrific elements into a story about a search for a poison-gas formula. It's a kick. Ray Taylor directed it on some interesting locations. (Video/Yesteryear; Nostalgia)

PERSECUTION. Video version of *The Graveyard* (Electric).

PERSONALS (1990) ★★★ This TV-movie is notable for Jennifer O'Neill's performance as a homicidal knife killer (her blade is enscribed with "Aloha") who performs her misdeeds in a blond wig with a cool detachment made all the more terrifying by her sexuality and beauty. Unfortunately for O'Neill, who is suffering from a mother problem, one of her victims is a writer doing a story on lonely women and the man's wife (Stephanie Zimbalist) decides to avenge his death. Has twists that make it above average. Directed by Steven H. Stern. Robin Thomas, Gina Gallego, Rosemary Dunsmore. (Video/Laser: Paramount)

PETER BENCHLEY'S THE BEAST (1996) ★★★ Putting aside the fact that Benchley must suffer from creative deprivation (for this is nothing more than a very obvious rewrite of *Jaws*), this two-part TV-movie adaptation of his popular novel *Beast* is a well-done if predictable sea ad-

venture. The substitution to make here is a giant squid monster (60 feet long, with 30-foot tentacles) for the Great White Shark of *Jaws*. So you get an island community being terrorized by the hungry sea monster, an expert about sealife who gives you all the data, assorted humans who become food for the rampaging beast and the inevitable boat expedition to kill the creature in its home depths, with fisherman William Petersen leading the group. Director Jeff Bleckner even copies Steven Spielberg's underwater shots of legs kicking through water as the killer monster approaches from below. J. B. White's teleplay suffers from extraneous subplots, but when the telefilm (shot in Australia) gets around to special effects and seabound thrills, it ain't too bad. Karen Sillas, Charles Martin Smith, Ronald Guttman, Missy Crider, Sterling Macer Jr.

PETER BENCHLEY'S CREATURE (1998) ★★½ Rockne S. O'Bannon, stealing every monster-movie cliché from Benchley's novel, which had already swiped those clichés from Hollywood, struggles to spin a horror tale that should have pleased hard-core fans of the genre. Instead, the telewriter makes everything obvious, clumsy, and laughable. Part of the problem is the four-hour length that ABC chose for this miniseries. The concept just can't sustain, even though director Stuart Gillard has beautiful West Indies locations in which to set the ugly tale. The titular creature is a cross between shark and man, a hybrid created years earlier during a U.S. Navy experiment (to develop amphibious fighters for Vietnam's rivers and jungle) that went awry. Cut to sharkologist Craig T. Nelson, ex-wife Kim Cattrall, and a son (Matthew Carey) who become embroiled in the monster's attacks while researching a cure for cancer that involves shark components. Helping them out is a local nicknamed Werewolf (Giancarlo Esposito), who was secretly involved in the creation of the hybrid beast and now acts totally nutty. The inconsistency of characterizations is only one problem as Nelson battles the monster almost single-handedly—until a group of navy commandos arrives, trying to clean up the mess they left in a hidden laboratory back in '72. Which means there's plenty of personal conflicts and more fodder to fit between the teeth of the creature. Stan Winston created the monster, which is better than Swamp Thing but not as good as the Creature from the Black Lagoon. The word "ugly" totally describes this effort, which co-stars Colm Feore, Cress Williams, Michael Reilly Burek, and Michael Michele. Parts were filmed in Vancouver, B.C.

PETE'S DRAGON (1977) ★★★½ Superb Disney musical comedy, blending live action and animation to tell the hilarious saga of Elliott the Dragon, a fire-breather from Fantasy World, on

Earth to help children in trouble. He flies, turns invisible and has a sense of humor, snarling at disbelievers and throwing frightening shadows on walls. His lovableness ultimately wins you over. Elliott meets 9-year-old Pete (Sean Marshall), a runaway pursued by the nasty Gogans. Setting is Passamaquoddy, where lighthouse keeper Mickey Rooney and daughter Helen Reddy befriend the boy and dragon. Jim Dale pops up as a medicine show man, Dr. Terminus, with Red Buttons as his assistant, Hoagy. Shelley Winters is grotesquely hilarious as Ma Gogan. Don Chaffey directed with a masterful touch. Jim Backus, Jane Kean, Jeff Conaway. (Video/Laser: Disney)

PET SEMATARY (1989) ★★★½ Based on one of Stephen King's most intriguing novels, this film is rooted in pessimism, and so dark in its statement about life that one comes away with a deep sense of dread. It is set in a landscape of evil where an old Indian burial ground restores life to anything buried in it, and at no time does director Mary Lambert allow a ray of hope to penetrate the doom-laden atmosphere. Its plot roots are borrowed from W. F. Jacob's "The Monkey's Paw," but King (who wrote the screenplay too) imbues it with his own unique vision. The story revolves around a doctor and his family who have just moved into an old house in the country, and what happens to these four decent people will depress you to the core of your soul. Adding a strong presence is Fred Gwynne as an old farmer who knows all the secrets of the graveyard and becomes the catalyst for the dire events. (Video/Laser: Paramount)

PET SEMATARY II (1992) ★★ A mean-spiritedness hangs so triumphantly over this sequel to the popular 1989 Stephen King movie that, rather than being classically morbid, this horror tale is grossly sickening and nihilistic in its statement about man's inhumanity to animals—not to mention man himself. Once again the setting is the rural community of Ludlow, Maine, where new veterinarian Anthony Edwards and son Edward Furlong settle to start over following the death of Edward's wife (a "scream queen" movie actress electrocuted while making *Castle of Terror*). Before long Furlong and his friend Jason McGuire are burying McGuire's dead dog in the cursed Pet Sematary. This sets into motion horrific events, exploited to their maximum bloodletting by director Mary Lambert, who shows us such sights as a cageful of torn-apart kittens, rabbits being ripped apart, and a bully (Jared Rushton) having his face chopped up in a spinning motorbike wheel. It's a thoroughly unpleasant viewing experience with its touches of physical abuse to children and a scene of deputy sheriff Clancy

Brown shooting his stepson's dog in cold blood. Sarah Trigger, Lisa Watty, Darlene Fluegel. (Video/Laser: Paramount)

PET SHOP (1994) ★★½ Charles Band's Moonbeam Entertainment makes cute "family fantasy" comedies, but like the *Prehysteria* series that predates and inspired this, *Pet Shop* suffers from one major flaw: Mark Rappaport's creatures are not believable. If Band had been more demanding, and the creatures more articulated, this bit of whimsy might have made it. *Sigh . . .* a family under the government's protection program ends up in Cactus Flats, AZ, where two aliens dressed in cowboy outfits and named Mr. and Mrs. Zip (Jeff Michalski and Jane Morris) run the local (p)et shop (get it?). The zany Zips give away human pets, but these pets turn themselves into cutesy-pie aliens and the pets get involved when gangsters come to town looking for Terry Kiser. A lot of nonsensical business goes on in the Mark Goldstein–Greg Suddeth–Brent Friedman script, and younger audiences (really younger) might be satisfied. It was directed by Hope Perello without style. Leigh Ann Orsi, Spencer Vrooman, Joanne Baron, David Wagner, Shashawnee Hall. (Video/Laser: Paramount)

PHANTASM (1979) ★★★½ Little logic dominates this macabre tale set at Morningside Cemetery, U.S.A., as the sinister Tall Man (Angus Scrimm, shouting "BOOOYYYYY!") sends human victims into another dimension where they are reduced to dwarves and exploited as slaves. This hogwash is a crowd pleaser thanks to the stylish direction-photography by Don Coscarelli, who has included a severed hand and finger, .45 slugs plowing into flesh and a floating silver sphere that thuds into heads and drills out brains and blood. Coscarelli's only concern is to shock us into our early tombstones. A pleasing supernatural thriller. Just lean back into your casket and enjoy. Bill Thornbury, Michael Baldwin, Reggie Bannister. (Embassy; CBS/Fox) (Laser: Nelson; Vestron)

PHANTASM II (1988) ★★★½ The original 1979 hit horror flick remains writer-director Don Coscarelli's crowning achievement, as he attempts nothing new in this sequel. Instead, he relies on the Tall Man (sneeringly revived by menacing Angus Scrimm), the steel ball with knives and drills, the dwarves from another dimension and the portals into that other dimension. Mike (played this time by James Le Gros) and Reggie (repeated by Reggie Bannister) are after Scrimm, who is sucking the souls out of the graveyards of America. They meet up with a couple of chicks (Paula Irvine, Samantha Phillips) who really add nothing to the plot. It's the steel ball that reigns and rains (blood, that is) as it burrows into a man's back, chews up his insides and comes out his mouth. At times this has the feel of the graveyard and mausoleum to it. (Video/Laser: MCA)

PHANTASM III: LORD OF THE DEAD (1993) ★★★½ By now the Tall Man (none other than Angus Scrimm), the flying steel ball with the knives and brain drill, and the threesome of Reggie (again, Reggie Bannister), Mike (A. Michael Baldwin) and Jody (Bill Thornbury) have become minor icons of Hollywood horror. It's always a kind of perverse pleasure to live again in the mausoleumlike world of writer/producer/director Don Coscarelli, who has the *Phantasm* formula down to perfection. So here we are again in graveyard land, where Scrimm ("It's time now, Boy!") and his army of killer dwarves are out to destroy community after community, with only Reggie and his four-barrel shotgun to stop them. This time the lovable guy is joined by a new kid (Tim, played by Kevin Connors) and a karate fighter (Rocky, played by Gloria Lynne Henry) while Mike and Jody remain strangely trapped in other dimensons—or something like that. It's better not to try making any sense of the plot (what plot?) and just kick back and let things happen in the wild Coscarelli way as reality and fantasy impinge on each other in unexpected ways and there's no such thing as a dull (or unfunny) minute as yellow blood squirts, dead people attack, and countless surprises are thrown at you. Ah, the bloody glory of it all. Cindy Ambuehl, John Chandler, Brooks Gardner. (Video/Laser: MCA)

PHANTASM IV: OBLIVION (1998) ★★★ The *Phantasm* series has become a cult favorite that die-hard fans have supported primarily because of its four recurring characters. Foremost of these is Angus Scrimm as the Tall Man, with his wonderfully threatening walk and his "boy, it's time!" dialogue, delivered with all the dripping evil you could ask for in a despicable villain. He's still traveling from town to town, killing everybody and shipping their souls into another dimension in the bodies of demonlike dwarves. Then there's the three guys fighting this evil: bald-headed Reggie (Reggie Bannister) is still traveling alone across country with a four-barrel shotgun, seeking to blow away the dwarves. Mike (Michael Baldwin), the youngest of the characters, who dominated the original *Phantasm* with his adolescent vulnerability, is also out there searching for the Tall Man as well as his brother Jody (Bill Thornbury), the character who got killed off in a car-crash explosion in the original and therefore we can never be sure if he's really alive or he's one of the walking dead the Tall Man is always creating. A fifth figure to be reckoned with is writer-director Don Coscarelli, who continues to write plots that cannot be thoroughly fathomed and that defy logical description: characters pop in and out of dimensions; Scrimm conducts ugly experiments in the halls of his large mausoleum; dwarves turn up unexpectedly to attack Reggie; the infamous steel balls with the knifes that pop out to drill your brains from your head keep floating into view and have to be destroyed by a tuning fork. *Phantasm IV: Oblivion* seems to have something to do with the origins of the Tall Man, who in another time and place was a scientist named Jedidiah Morningstar, who invented time-travel rods. Mike wants to go back in time to stop him from making his invention, thinking that will restore the world order. Foolish boy. Meanwhile there's Jody, who by all rights should be dead. He keeps turning up looking sinister and making strange remarks, so you can pretty much figure his image is an illusion created by the Tall Man. But is it? Coscarelli photographs his characters against a desert background in a style that gives the film an eerie atmosphere, and eeriness has always been a plus for this franchise. As expected, there's some very revolting violence: a dying demon vomits green bile directly into Reggie's open mouth; a woman (Heidi Marnhour) has her breasts drilled away by two of the steel balls; assorted demon dwarves are blown away with shotgun blasts, etc. Yet *Phantasm* would not be *Phantasm* without such visuals. There's every reason to believe there'll be another sequel, as Reggie is last shown passing through the portals to another dimension, shotgun at the ready. Keep that gooey stuff flowing and the green gore flowing, Don. We can't wait for the next horrific but fun-loving installment. (MGM)

PHANTOM. See *Phantom of the Paradise*.

PHANTOM, THE (1996) ★★★½ This full-scale adaptation of Lee Falk's long-running comic-strip adventure about a masked man in a purple jump suit (aka *The Ghost Who Walks*) is a rousing action movie jammed with special effects, exciting stunt work and a '30s ambience that recaptures the days of the China Clipper. While Jeffrey Boam's script is shopworn with its use of three magical masks (the Skulls of Zuganda) that will give their possessor unlimited power to rule the world, and characters are etched in the simplest of black-and-white terms, there's a joy in the pacing from director Simon Wincer that propels this movie at breathless speed, and which David Newman's pounding music helps immensely. Billy Zane is amusing as the masked avenger who lives on Bengalla Island in 1938 with his wolf dog Devil, and who faces evil businessman Treat Williams when he kidnaps Kristy Swanson. This is a satisfying adventure produced by Joe Dante, Alan Ladd Jr. and Robert Evans. James Remar, Patrick McGoohan (as the Phantom's spectral father), Samantha Eggar, Cary Hiroyki Tagawa, Zeta Jones. (Video/Laser: Paramount)

PHANTOM BROTHER (1988) ★ Orphaned teenager is haunted by the spirit of his brother, who was killed in a car crash, in this whimsical spoof on the supernatural. Directed by William Szarka. Jon Hammer, Patrick Molloy, John Gigante, Mary Beth Pelshaw. (South Gate; Hemdale)

PHANTOM CREEPS, THE (1939) ★★★ Campy Universal serial starring Bela Lugosi as Dr. Alex Zorka, an insane inventor who in the first chapter creates an 8-foot robot with an evil face, invents a belt that turns him invisible, sends mechanical killer spiders after his enemies, and plots the overthrow of the world through the powers of a meteor fragment. Captain Bob West (Robert Kent) is Zorka's adversary, accompanied by a pretty newspaperwoman (Dorothy Arnold) in frilly skirts. A bit dated but still an enjoyable serial when viewed with an eye toward Lugosi's over-the-top performance as the mad doctor, and the incompetence of his number-one henchman Monk (Jack C. Smith). Directed by Saul Goodkind and Ford Beebe without a trace of subtlety. Edward Van Sloan, Regis Toomey, Eddie Acuff. Aka *The Shadow Creeps*. (Kartes; Captain Bijou; VCI; Nostalgia; Video Connection)

PHANTOM EMPIRE, THE (1935) ★★★ Gene Autry serial blending an underground lost city with cowboy action. Autry sings on the air from Radio Ranch then rushes off with his Thunder Riders to prevent subterranean tyrants from destroying civilization with Death Rays, disintegrator units, sonar devices and atom-smashing smasheroos. For loyal Autry fans only—it's very crude toil. Frankie Darro, Smiley Burnette. Directed by action specialists B. Reeves Eason and Otto Brewer. Aka *Gene Autry's Phantom Empire*, this was shortened to feature-length versions called *Radio Ranch* and *Men with Steel Faces*. (MCA; Rhino; Nostalgia Merchant; Sinister/C; Video Yesteryear; Filmfax; the feature version, *Radio Ranch*, is also in video)

PHANTOM EMPIRE, THE (1989) ★★ Schlockmeister producer-director Fred Olen Ray, who believes in throwing in the kitchen sink just in case, has concocted a yarn (with collaborator T. L. Lankford) that features cannibalistic mutant cavemen, a secret underground world, a race of women in animal skins, Robby the Robot, stop-motion dinosaurs, and an expedition of idiots. Wow, gang, that's exciting. Actually, gang, it's campy, as only Ray can make them campy. And we're talking master of the camp grounds. Sybil Danning hits an all-time silly high as the queen of the underground chicks, Russ Tamblyn is laughable as an aging prospector, Robert Quarry bumbles his way around caves, Susan Stokey and Michelle Bauer look sexy and Ross Hagen and Jeffrey Combs look tough. (Prism)

PHANTOM FIEND (1961). See *The Return of Dr. Mabuse*.

PHANTOM KILLER, THE. See *The Invisible Ghost*.

PHANTOM MEETS THE RETURN OF DR. MABUSE, THE. See *The Return of Dr. Mabuse* (1961).

PHANTOM OF DEATH (1987) ★★½ Psychological portrait of a brilliant concert pianist (Michael York) who has a rare disease called protaria, or premature senility, that turns him into a psycho killer. Cop Donald Pleasence takes on the case and develops a vendetta when the pianist harasses him with phone calls, taunting him to solve the murders. Despite its intriguing premise, this Italian production directed by Ruggero Deodato never builds excitement or suspense. The disease prematurely ages York, so by the end he's turned into a wrinkled monster. Edwige Fenech, Mapi Galan. (Vidmark)

PHANTOM OF THE CIRCUS. See *Circus of Horrors*.

PHANTOM OF THE FILLMORE. See *Phantom of the Paradise*.

PHANTOM OF THE MALL: ERIC'S REVENGE (1989) ★★½ Modernized variation on *The Phantom of the Opera*, in which a wronged young man, burned in a fire started by an unscrupulous land developer, wears a metallic face mask as he wreaks revenge on the occupants of Midwood Mall and protects his one-time girlfriend from harm. All that's missing is the falling-chandelier scene. With its shopper's spree of genre clichés and motley collection of mediocre murders under the direction of Richard Friedman, the film fails to generate suspense. Kari Whitman, Derek Rydall, Jonathan Goldsmith, Morgan Fairchild (as a mayor yet—some politics). (Fries; United America issued *Making of Phantom of the Mall*) (Laser: Image)

PHANTOM OF THE OPERA, THE (1925) ★★★ Appreciation for the silent screen helps but isn't mandatory for enjoying this oldie with makeup genius Lon Chaney as an acid-scarred madman living beneath the Paris Opera House who frightens the sopranos out of their tenors. Based on a Gaston Leroux novel, this Universal classic has marvelous makeup and imagery that would inspire filmmakers for decades. Despite outdated acting techniques and staginess, this is a must-see. Directed by Rupert Julian. Mary Philbin, Norman Kerry. Rereleased in 1930 with sound. (Kino; Video Yesteryear; Kartes; Critic's Choice) (Laser: Lumivision; Image)

PHANTOM OF THE OPERA, THE (1943) ★★★ Second screen version of Gaston Leroux's novel is one of the few horror films in Technicolor from the 1940s. Stylized, beautifully photographed by Hal Mohr and very entertaining despite some hokum. Claude Rains portrays a misused-abused composer whose face is scarred by acid and who, in pain-riddled madness, seeks refuge in sewers beneath the opera house. In revenge, he commits outrages against the establishment he once so loved. Enduring favorite with great sets and costumes and a flamboyant cast: Nelson Eddy, Susanna Foster, Leo Carrillo, Fritz Leiber, Edgar Barrier. Directed by Arthur Lubin from a script by Eric Taylor and Samuel Hoffenstein. (Video/Laser: MCA)

PHANTOM OF THE OPERA, THE (1962) ★★★½ Hammer's filmization of Gaston Leroux's novel is comparable to the 1943 version in story and opulence. Herbert Lom is the Phantom in a one-eyed mask, Michael Gough is the music pirate and Heather Sears is the beautiful soprano. Polished under Terence Fisher's direction, romantically mysterious and set in London instead of Paris, with the underground chambers of the Phantom now connected with the slimy blimey sewers. Adaptation by producer Anthony Hinds (as John Elder). Thorley Walters, Edward De Souza, Miles Milleson, Michael Ripper. (Video/Laser: MCA)

PHANTOM OF THE OPERA, THE (1983) ★★ TV-movie version of Leroux's novel is set in turn-of-the-century Budapest. Maximilian Schell's singing wife is beautiful but incompetent, and commits suicide, driving Schell to the brink of insanity. He is disfigured and, with an accomplice, flees underground into the labyrinth of the city, there to heal his body and scheme revenge. Five years later he reemerges as the Phantom to terrorize American singer Jane Seymour, British opera director Michael York and other hapless figures in the musical landscape. Though this has the ambience of Budapest, it remains inferior to earlier sound versions and unfolds in a most peculiar way. Directed by Robert Markowitz. Jeremy Kemp, Diana Quick, Philip Stone.

PHANTOM OF THE OPERA, THE (1989) ★★ Despite opulent Budapest settings (standing in for Paris), costumes and sets, producer Menahem Golan still manages to turn Gaston Leroux's gothic horror classic into an exploitation shocker that cashes in on the use of Robert (Freddy Krueger) Englund in the title role. Unlike the actors who have faced this part before, Englund brings little sympathy to Erik, who is no longer an unfortunate victim of circumstances, but a man who exchanges his soul for supernatural powers. Director Dwight H. Little brings ambience and pace to this, the bloodiest version of all the film and TV adaptations. Jill Schoelen, Alex Hyde-White, Bill Nighy, Stephanie Lawrence. (Video/Laser: RCA/Columbia)

PHANTOM OF THE OPERA, THE (1990) ★★★ Opulent, splendidly rendered variation on Gaston Leroux's novel, originally a 4-hour TV-movie made at the Paris Opera and Paris Caves of Mello. Arthur Kopit adapted his own play, which depicts Erik the Phantom not as a menacing mystery but as a tragic figure who falls in love with a costume girl "who sings like an angel." The sets, costumes and cast are exquisite, and despite its theatrical origins, director Tony Richardson does a masterful job. Burt Lancaster stars as the benefactor of Erik; Charles Dance is a poetic, reachable Phantom; and Teri Polo is the delicate waif turned into Paris's newest diva. The first half is a comedy send-up, but when Erik is wronged the story line turns serious. The opera sequences are splendid. One of the best adaptations in the series, even if it does stray quite far from the original material. Andrea Ferreol, Adam Storke, Jean-Pierre Cassel. The above-average score is by John Addison.

PHANTOM OF THE PARADISE (1975) ★★★½ Bizarre Brian De Palma film satirizes *Phantom of the Opera* and comments on our music-oriented rock 'n' roll youth and the debased values of the business world. De Palma's script is a retelling of the Faust legend, with crazed songwriter William Finley entering into a blood pact with rock impresario Paul Williams (who wrote music and lyrics). Climactic rock concert is a masterpiece of hysteria, but clarity of plot is often sacrificed for wild visuals. Williams is brilliant as the satanic force of depraved sexuality. For the "turned on" generation(s); squares may find it hard going. Aka *Phantom* and *Phantom of The Fillmore*. (Key) (Laser: CBS/Fox)

PHANTOM OF THE RITZ (1988) ★★½ This variation on *Phantom of the Opera* is less successful as a horror movie than it is a study of eccentric and bizarre characters remindful of the Hippie era. The Phantom (Joshua Sussman) is a wisecracking brute (in 1958 he was almost burned alive in a teenage car-racing crash) who now haunts a rundown porno theater that Peter Bergman buys and turns into a showcase for live musical acts that include The Coasters. A wisecracking Jewish secretary (Cindy Vincino), a perky and sexy brunette (Deborah Van Valkenburgh), a black bodyguard who talks like a rocket scientist (Russell Curry) and a plethora of other unusual personalities make this bearable if not exactly exciting. Filmed in Ybor City, Florida, the film features a few mildly interesting murders committed by the Phantom but mainly seems an excuse for extended musical performance pieces. It was written by Tom Dempsey and directed by Allen Plone. (Prism) (Laser: Image)

PHANTOM RULER, THE. Original title of the Republic serial *The Invisible Monster.*

PHANTOM 2040: THE GHOST WHO WALKS (1994) ★★★ Full-length animated version of Lee Falk's famous comic strip, set in the futuristic city of Metropia, where young Kit Walker, Jr., discovers his destiny as the newest in a line of crime fighters known as the Phantom (or the Ghost Who Walks). The wife and son of Maxwell Madison, the Phantom's old nemesis, plot to build Cyberville, a city of machines that will rule the world, and they use cyborg warriors and a phony projection of the Phantom to achieve their nefarious ends. A well-produced cartoon with ample story and a good cast of voices: Scott Valentine, Margot Kidder, Ron Perlman, Mark Hamill and Carrie Snodgrass.

PHANTOMS. See *Dean Koontz's Phantoms.*

PHARAOH'S CURSE, THE (1956) ★★ Slow-moving, poor man's version of *The Mummy*, with pedestrian direction by Lee Sholem and inferior monster makeup for the wizened face of the creature in this bit of desert turgidity written by Richard Landau (first called *Curse of the Pharaoh*). In 1902 a British patrol led by Mark Dana encounters a strange priestess (Ziva Shapir) of a cat cult linked to an Egyptian tomb desecrated by explorer Ben Wright and his archeologists. Members of the expedition die one by one from a curse. If you like old '50s horror movies in black and white you might enjoy some of its old-fashioned touches, but by modern standards this, like the mummy Ra-Hatib, should be kept under wraps. Diane Brewster, Alvado Guillot. (J & J)

PHASE IV (1974) ★★★ Saul Bass, famed film-title designer, directed this bizarre sci-fi–horror thriller (a prizewinner at Trieste) depicting a war between scientists in a desert outpost and an army of intelligent killer ants that drench their enemies in a sticky yellow substance. The ants, a result of pollution, are diabolical adversaries as they chew their way into the installation and demonstrate hypnotic powers. The excellent cinematography, the special ant documentary footage, Mayo Simon's unusual script and John Barry's art direction enhance this offbeat tale with a way-out metaphysical ending. Michael Murphy, Nigel Davenport, Lynne Frederick, Alan Gifford. (Video/Laser: Paramount)

PHENOMENA (1985). Japanese laser title for *Creepers.*

PHENOMENAL AND THE TREASURE OF TUTANKAMEN (1984) ★ The curse of King Tut strikes again in this inept French-Italian super-hero adventure as a masked hero pursues a golden relic with mystical powers and stops the blundering of a tomb. Slam bam, crash boom. Directed by Ruggero Deodato. Maura Nicola Parenti, Gordon Mitchell, Lucretia Love, Mauro Parenti. (Wizard; VCI)

PHENOMENON (1996) ★★★½ John Travolta gives a touching performance as an average auto mechanic living outside a rural California town who is suddenly endowed with superior intelligence after he's exposed to a beam of light from space (although the question of why and how is never explored). How his enhanced thinking

leads to problems with government agents, his own townspeople and girlfriend Kyra Sedgwick (a widow with two kids) is the thrust of Gerald DiPego's script, and director Jon Turtletaub keeps the material fittingly low key, opting for character development over plot. *Phenomenon* becomes a series of morality lessons about human needs and trust, and although it ends on a downbeat note, it is warm and touching. You will be moved by Travolta, by Sedgwick, by Forrest Whitaker as Travolta's best friend; and by Robert Duvall as the wise, understanding town doctor. Minimum special effects and little exploration of the story's sci-fi premise might disappoint genre fans; this is for those who dig people stories. Richard Kiley, Brent Spiner (in a cameo as a psychologist), Bruce Young. (Video/Laser: Buena Vista)

PHILADELPHIA EXPERIMENT, THE (1984) ★★★ Since 1943 unsubstantiated legends have swum through the annals of "unsolved mysteries" about the U.S. Navy conducting experiments with an invisible force field that caused ships to turn invisible. This builds an exciting time-travel story around that legend: two sailors in the radar experiment (Michael Pare, Bobby Di Cicco) are catapulted to the present to face fish-out-of-water adventures. This sensitively deals with the problems of a young man finding that the woman he loved in 1943 is now beyond his reach. But director Stewart Raffill also emphasizes action and weird effects, balancing plot and adventure. Eric Christmas, Nancy Allen, Miles McNamara. (Thorn EMI/ HBO) (Laser: Image)

PHILADELPHIA EXPERIMENT II (1993) ★★★ This picks up nine years after the end of *Philadelphia Experiment* with "monolithic vortex machine" time traveler Brad Johnson (from 1943) being sent into an alternative universe where Hitler won World War II because he got his grubby hands on a Stealth fighter equipped with atomic weaponry that went through a time anomaly. It's up to Johnson to go back and change history and prevent a totalitarian world from happening. This is a taut, well-produced action fantasy written by Kevin Roch and Nick Paine and directed by Stephen Cornwell. Marjean Holden, Gerrit Graham, John Christian Graas, Cyril O'Reilly. (Video/Laser: Vidmark)

PHOBIA. See *The Nesting.*

PHOENIX THE WARRIOR (1988) ★★★ Welcome to a post-Armageddon world, following bacteriological war and plague, in which only men have survived to rove the wastelands. Kathleen Kinmont is a warrior of the future who befriends a woman who gives birth to a new male—and then the evil Reverent Mother (an ugly mutant) and her henchwoman (Persis Khambatta) are after the child, a symbol of power. It's a series of male-fantasy clichés: dune buggies racing in the desert, a bevy of beauties in bikini outfits, and the attractive Kinmont repeatedly stirring one's libido. Despite the hackneyed script by Robert Hayes and Dan Rotblatt, the film unfolds (under Hayes's direction) in a competent, fast-moving way, and lacks that element of incompetence that makes bad movies better. Peggy Sands, James H. Emery, Sheila Howard. (Sony) (Laser: Image)

PHOENIX 2772. See *Space Firebird 2772.*

PHOTOGRAPHER, THE. See *Double Exposure.*

PIANO LESSON, THE (1995) ★★★ This CBS-TV "Hallmark Hall of Fame" production is based on the Pulitzer prize–winning play by August Wilson. While on the surface it's about a number of family members fighting over possession of a piano in Pittsburgh 1936, when the Depression is at its worst, this is an insightful study in people at a time in American history when some were trying to escape the "ghosts" of their cultural past to strike out in fresh directions. The "ghosts" become literal when one keeps appearing before the characters at different times, influencing how they will behave in the future. Charles Dutton is superb recreating his Broadway role as Boy Willie, whose appearance, and demand for the piano, shakes up the family household. This bit of literate TV was coproduced by Wilson and directed by Lloyd Richards. Alfre Woodard, Carl Gordon, Courtney B. Vance, Lou Myers.

PICKING UP THE PIECES. See *Bloodsucking Pharaohs in Pittsburgh.*

PICKLE, THE (1993) ★★★½ In this amusing satire on Hollywood moviemaking and its assorted personalities by writer-producer-director Paul Mazursky, everything is kosher as movie director Harry Stone (Danny Aiello) undergoes a midlife/career crisis because he's made a movie about a pickle that flies into outer space to the planet Cleveland, where Ally Sheedy and other midwestern farm types meet a race of humanoids all wearing black suits. But this is less about the movie-within-a-movie than about Stone remembering his childhood (black-and-white flashbacks), considering suicide, and finally recovering his self-esteem with mother Shelley Winters, ex-wife Dyan Cannon and French girlfriend Clotilde Courau. This work is filled with colorful characters and stylish filmmaking, not to mention a wonderful special-effects pickle. Never a dill moment. Barry Miller, Jerry Stiller, Griffin Dunne, Isabella Rossellini, Little Richard. (Video/Laser: Columbia TriStar)

PICTURE OF DORIAN GRAY, THE (1945) ★★★½ Oscar Wilde's morality horror story, about an evil man (Hurd Hatfield) whose decadence is embodied in a painting that reflects his degradation while he remains young, becomes literate, fascinating cinema in the hands of writer-director Albert Lewin, with George Sanders memorable as the Englishman who introduces Dorian Gray to debauchery. The original release prints contained some Technicolor footage. Angela Lansbury (she was nominated for an Oscar), Donna Reed, Peter Lawford, Bernard Gorcey. Narration read by Sir Cedric Hardwicke. (Video/Laser: MGM)

PIECES (1983) ★½ Repulsive chainsaw-killer flick, in which a madman dismembers beautiful women, taking "pieces" back to his freezer locker to complete a human "jigsaw puzzle." As degrading as it is absurd, and humiliating to women. Filmed in Boston by writer-director Juan Piquer Simon, who apparently went all to pieces behind the camera, this is awful awful sleazy trash. Christopher George plays an unlikable cop, Lynda Day is an unlikely undercover woman, Edmund Purdom is the campus dean and Paul L. Smith provides red herrings. Aka *One Thousand Cries Has the Night.* (Vestron) (Laser: Japanese)

PIGS. Video of *Daddy's Deadly Darling* (Simitar; Home Cinema; Paragon; Studio One).

PIN (1988) ★★★ Subtitled "An Unexpected Visit to a Most Terrifying Place," this adaptation of a popular novel by Andrew Neiderman is a fascinating study of abnormal sexual psychology in depicting a paranoid schizophrenic played by David Hewlett. Country doctor Terry O'Quinn uses a mannequin nicknamed Pin (short for Pinocchio) to teach his son and daughter sex education, and uses ventriloquist talents to project the voice. Hewlett believes Pin is real and sinks ever deeper into his own soulful terror, making life miserable for his sister (Cyndy Preston) and her boyfriend (John Ferguson). Writer-director Sandor Stern not only makes it seem plausible by eliciting good performances, but captures an understanding of mental illness too often lost in "mind thrillers." (New World) (Laser: Image)

PINK CHIQUITAS, THE (1986) ★½ This has all the elements of a campy takeoff on sci-fi flicks, but falls flatter than a discarded banana peel. After a pink meteor falls near Beansville, sexy gals are turned into nymphomaniacs. Meanwhile, dumb private eye Tony Mareda, Jr., (Frank Stallone, brother of Sylvester) tries to outwit the alien force (symbolized by the voice of Eartha Kitt). It's played for farce (especially by John Hemphill as a mayor, Bruce Pirrie as a nerdy TV weatherman and Don Lake as a deputy sheriff) but it's so erratically zany that it never fulfills its promises. Written-directed by Anthony Currie. Elizabeth Edwards, Claudia Udy, McKinlay Robinson. (Starmaker; Prism)

PIRANHA (1978) ★★★½ On the surface an exploitation "eat 'em alive" picture, but more a fantasy satire thanks to John Sayles's script and Joe Dante's whimsical direction. A mutant strain of piranha is fed into U.S. waterways and the teeny waterdemons feast on the feet of Keenan Wynn and the facial tissues of Bradford Dillman. Barbara Steele fans will enjoy her as a conspiratorial military officer. There's also unusual stop-motion footage of strange creatures in a laboratory. And some dialogue is wonderfuly witty. (Warner Bros.)

PIRANHA (1995) ★★ This is Roger Corman's TV-movie remake of his 1978 cult favorite and it proves the old adage: if the original is good, don't bother trying to remake it because it never comes out as good as, or better than, the original. Okay, it's competent, and Alex Simon's new script follows John Sayles's old one faithfully, but it's missing Barbara Steele's character and in no way has Corman tried to improve on the look of the flesh-eating water creatures. The plot follows private investigator Alexandra Paul as she and guide William Katt look for a resort owner's missing daughter in lonely country. The trail leads to an old U.S. military installation where Operation Razorteeth produced a strain of superpiranha killer fish, designed for dumping into Russian rivers in the case of war. Meanwhile, resort owner Monte Markham plans to open his country hotel, ignoring Katt's warning: "The piranha are coming!" Directed by Scott Levy, the cast includes Darlene Carr as a crazed scientist, Soleil Moon Frye, James Karen, Kaz Garas and Mila Kunis. (New Horizons)

PIRANHA II: THE SPAWNING (1981) ★★ Loose sequel to *Piranha* is set at a Caribbean resort where underwater diving coach Tricia O'Neil is in conflict with chief of police Lance Henriksen (her estranged husband) and tourist Steve Marachuk, a member of a research program that has created a mutant—a cross between a piranha and a flying fish. These winged monsters are munching on hotel guests. It's hard to get suspense out of tiny creatures and the effects are standard blood and gore, with one *Alien*-style attack when a minimonster pops from a victim's stomach. Director James Cameron is strongest in allowing his cast to create believable characters. Cameron went on to make *Terminator* and *Aliens*, two superior thrillers. Aka *Piranha II: Flying Killers*. (Video/Laser: Embassy/Nelson)

PIRATE'S HARBOR. See *Haunted Harbor*.

PIT, THE (1981) ★½ Horror movie twice as bad as its title—hence, the pits. A perverted look at a perverted kid (Sammy Snyders) who peeps on his sexy baby-sitter and talks to his friend Teddy, a toy bear who talks back, planting salacious ideas in his "innocent" head. Sammy is also the friend of Trogs, gnarly beasts with blazing yellow eyes in a pit outside town. To keep them fat, Sammy feeds them his friends. The perversity and gore never really gel, with Sammy's abnormal sexuality shallowly ex-

plored. The story picks up steam once the beasties escape the pit and reign munching terror on delicious humans. Filmed around Beaver Dam, WI. Directed by Lew Lehman. Laura Hollingsworth, Jeannie Elias. First entitled *Teddy*. (Embassy; Starmaker)

PIT AND THE PENDULUM, THE (1961) ★★★★ Excellent adaptation of Edgar Allan Poe's tale starring Vincent Price, but Poe's narrow story line about a prisoner tortured by a razor-edged pendulum swinging closer and closer to his restrained body has been expanded by Richard Matheson into a gothic masterpiece of horror. Nobleman John Kerr arrives at a creepy seacoast castle to face Price, playing a Spanish count haunted by the fact his father was an executioner for the Inquisition. "Am I not the spawn of his depraved blood?" cries out Price. Producer-director Roger Corman was at his inspired height making this AIP masterwork. Barbara Steele, Luana Anders, Anthony Carbone. (Vestron; Warner Bros.) (Laser: Image, coupled with *The Fall of the House of Usher*; Japanese)

PIT AND THE PENDULUM, THE (1990) ★★ This Charles Band production, filmed in Giove, Italy, depicts the sadism of the Spanish Inquisition. One is subjected to torture scenes and dungeon bloodletting when breadmaker Rona De Ricci is accused of being a witch and taken captive by the cruel monk Torquemada. (Lance Henriksen, in another of his villain roles, holds back nothing.) While the Dennis Paoli script has its antecedents in Poe (touches are borrowed from "The Cask of Amontillado," "The Premature Burial," and the title tale), it is director Stuart Gordon having his excesses, such as cutting out a woman's tongue, exploding an old hag being burned at the stake, cutting a swordsman in half with the swaying pendulum, grinding a skeleton to powder, and pouring water down a woman's throat. Oliver Reed appears as a cardinal who remarks, "The good Lord wants us to love our neighbor—not roast him." A roasting is certainly in order. Jonathan Fuller, Frances Bay, Mark Margolis, Jeffrey Combs, Tom Towles. (Paramount) (Laser: Full Moon)

PITCH BLACK (2000) ★★★ After making a good time-travel adventure (*Grand Tour: Disaster in Time*) and an effective alien-invasion paranoia thriller (*The Arrival*), David Twohy takes a slight step backward with this mixture of horror and science-fiction that takes its inspiration from the *Alien* school. Writing an original script with Ken and Jim Wheat, Twohy gets mixed results in the way of plot and characters . . . only the unwashed and the undemanding will be satisfied with the imitation scary monsters. Ironically, director Twohy demonstrates an advanced sense of style that surpasses his earlier films of the fantastic, and yet this time out his characters are less interesting and the plot foolishly contrived to include artistic touches that seem unnecessarily artsy-fartsy for what is basically your down-and-dirty sci-fi adventure tale set on a farflung planet in some farflung galaxy. Twohy opens with a spectacular disaster-in-space sequence when a cargo/passenger spaceship is struck by meteor fragments that penetrate the hull and kill the captain and others sleeping in cryonic chambers. Rocket jockey Fry (Radha Mitchell trying to be the latest Sigourney Weaver of the spaceways set) crashlands the ship—after a harrowing ordeal to regain control—on a desert planet that has three suns beating down on its arid, bleached surface. The model work here is excellent and the landing is thrilling, and the premise seems at first compelling: Everything appears to be dead on this world, including an Earth geological survey team that landed 22 years earlier. However, the characters are far less interesting than the extraterrestrial terrain. Vin Diesel is a cold-blooded convict, sentenced to life for murder, who escapes his shackles and threatens the safety of the others; Cole Hauser appears to be the heroic type but turns wormy when the chips are down (a shift in character that is not adequately set up by the writers) and Keith David plays the leader of a band of Islamic pilgrims (a strange choice that the script only shallowly deals with). Mitchell emerges as the strongest of the characterizations. The other people are minor and hang around mainly as food for a breed of alien lifeform that exists in dark tunnels beneath the planet's surface. The creatures, an offshoot of the hungry killing machines of *Alien*, are kept at bay until suddenly the three suns align into an eclipse (this only happens every 22 years, which explains what happened to that geological team) and now they can rush to the surface and track down and kill the survivors. Redemption becomes Twohy's theme as everyone struggles with their consciences, but such high-handed character writing is sadly out of place in a movie about men destroying monsters, or monsters destroying men, depending on whose side you're on. Rhiana Griffith, Lewis Fitz-Gerald, Claudia Black. (USA Films)

PLAGUE, THE (1979) ★★ Scientist working on a mutant bacterium, M3, to nourish plants and provide food for millions causes a leakage to the outside world, where bacteria infect children. The epidemic snowballs as a researcher seeks a virus to counteract the acetylcholine created by the bacteria. Kate Reid, who fought the Andromeda Strain, is a loyal scientist battling the killer disease. Canadian production, written-produced-directed by Ed Hunt. Aka *Plague M3: The Gemini Strain* and *Mutation*. (VidAmerica; Avid)

PLAGUE OF THE ZOMBIES (1966) ★★★½ Director John Gilling has fashioned a stylish gothic Hammer horror thriller set in the last century that builds tension with superior production values. Peter Bryan's story line touches on British hierarchy and its indifference to the working class when a doctor and his daughter come to visit an old friend in an eerie Cornish village and uncover a sadistic squire who turns men into voodoo zombies to work an old tin mine beneath his plantation. Especially memorable are scenes in which corpses slither and wriggle out of their graves. One of Hammer's best. Jacqueline Pearce, Andre Morell, Diane Clare, Michael Ripper. Aka *The Zombies*.

PLANETA BURG (1962) A Soviet sci-fi film that Roger Corman recut into *Voyage to a Prehistoric Planet*. Later, footage was used in *Voyage to the Planet of Prehistoric Women*. In its U.S.S.R. version it is also known as *Planet of Tempests, Storm Planet, Cosmonauts on Venus* and *Planet of Storms*. The original was directed and cowritten by Pavel Klushantsev. Gennadi Vernov, Ladimir Temelianov, Yuri Sarantsev. (Sinister/C)

PLANET MEN. See *The Lost Planet*.

PLANET OF BLOOD. Video version of *Queen of Blood* (Star Classics; Sinister/C; S/Weird).

PLANET OF DINOSAURS (1978) ★★ Despite its crude shortcomings, there is an earnestness behind this low-budget attempt at a sci-fi *One Million Years B.C.* When the spaceship *Odyssey* explodes in space, survivors aboard a shuttlecraft land on a prehistoric planet ruled by dinosaurs. Their various attitudes toward survival become a microscopic look at mankind. It has stop-motion animation work by Douglas Beswick (in the Harryhausen vein) and interesting matte paintings by Jim Danforth. Of the cast members, James Whitworth is most effective as he persuades others that to survive they must become the hunters and not the hunted. Produced-directed by James K. Shea, who shows occasional flair. Ramela Bottaro, Louie Lawless, Harvey Shain. (Active; Star Classics)

PLANET OF HORRORS. Made as *Mindwarp: An Infinity of Terror*, but released as *Planet of Horrors*, then retitled *Galaxy of Terror* (see that entry) for cable TV. Call it what you will.

PLANET OF INCREDIBLE CREATURES. Video version of *Fantastic Planet* (Vidcrest).

PLANET OF STORMS (1962). See *Planeta Burg*.

PLANET OF TEMPESTS. See *Planeta Burg*.

PLANET OF TERROR, THE (1965). See *Planet of the Vampires*.

PLANET OF TERROR (1966). See *Queen of Blood*.

PLANET OF THE APES (1968) ★★★★ Based loosely on the Pierre Boulle novel, this is a mixture of action, suspense and satire, although the latter element tends toward parody and cheapens the effect, though only in a minor way—this is still an exciting, oft eerie movie. Charlton Heston is a U.S. astronaut caught in a time warp and thrown into the future. He crash-lands on a desolate planet ruled by chimpanzees, orangutans and gorillas, where man is a mute slave. There is much ape talk about man's warlike nature and his downfall. John Chambers's makeup is imaginative, Franklin J. Schaffner's direction is brilliant and there is a visually rewarding punch line to the Rod Serling–Michael Wilson script. Jerry Goldsmith's music is excellent. Kim Hunter, Roddy McDowall, James Whitmore, James Daly and Maurice Evans are among many stars who appear in makeup and costumes. Aka *Monkey Planet*. Four sequels followed. (Video/Laser: CBS/Fox)

PLANET OF THE APES REVISITED. See *Beneath the Planet of the Apes*.

PLANET OF THE DAMNED, THE. See *Planet of the Vampires*.

PLANET OF THE DINO-KNIGHTS. See *Josh Kirby . . . Time Warrior!*

PLANET OF THE DINOSAURS. See *Planet of Dinosaurs*.

PLANET OF THE MEN. See *Beneath the Planet of the Apes*.

PLANET OF THE VAMPIRES (1965) ★★★ Italian space opera (originally made as *The Demon Planet*) directed by Mario Bava combines elements of the supernatural with sci-fi when rocket jockey Barry Sullivan investigates the planet Aura to discover inhabitants are disembodied spirits. Aura resembles a Transylvanian moor more than a foreign world. Aka *Planet of Blood, The Haunted Planet, Planet of Terror, Terror in Space, The Outlaw Planet, Space Mutants* and *The Planet of the Damned*. (HBO; Orion) (Laser: Image, with *Queen of Blood*; Polygram).

PLANET OF VAMPIRES. See *Queen of Blood*.

PLANET OUTLAWS (1939). Reedited version of the 1939 serial *Buck Rogers* (Thunderbird).

PLAN 9 FROM OUTER SPACE (1956) ★ Ranks with *Fire Maidens from Outer Space* and *Cat Women of the Moon* in sinking to new, inspired depths of cinematic ineptitude. Words such as amateurish, crude, tedious and *aaarrrggghhhh* can't begin to describe this Edward D. Wood film with Bela Lugosi in graveyard scenes made shortly before his death. Other footage has Lugosi coming out of a drab house. Lugosi died before the film was finished and an obvious double was used. Wood's unplotted plot (first known as *Vampire's Tomb* before becoming *Grave Robbers from Outer Space*) has San Fernando Valley residents troubled by UFOs of the worst encounter. Humanoid aliens Dudley Manlove (a famous radio voice) and Joanna Lee land their cardboard ship with a ninth plan to conquer the world (the first eight failed, you see). They resurrect corpses, including Vampira, Tor Johnson and Lugosi's double. The results are un-

viewable except for masochists who enjoy a good laugh derived from watching folks making fools of themselves. Psychic Criswell introduces the film with typical Wood nonsense. Lyle Talbot, Tom Keene, Mona McKinnon. (Nostalgia Merchant; Sinister/C; S/Weird) (Laser: Image)

PLAY DEAD (1985) ★ Yvonne De Carlo has a satanic pact with a devil dog, who murders members of her family for revenge. One is strangled, another electrocuted; even an investigating cop dies after the canine pours him a lye-laced cocktail. Pretty well acted and produced, but lacking sufficient exposition and characterizations to give it substance. In short, it finally rolls over and . . . Directed by Peter Wittman. Stephanie Dunnam, David Cullinand. (Academy; from Video Vision as *Satan's Dogs*)

PLAYGIRLS AND THE VAMPIRE, THE (1960). See *Curse of the Vampire*.

PLAYMAKER (1994) ★★★½ This psychological plunge into the mind of a likable aspiring actress (Jennifer Rubin) who is turned into a cold-blooded, amoral murderess makes for a gripping tale of deceit, deception and homicide—with horrific overtones. This could be a parable for how Hollywood chews up talent and spits it out, and it's certainly an indictment against those who manipulate and control others for personal gain. Based on ideas by Michael Schroder, the script by director Yuri Zeltser gives Rubin such a perverse coldness that this film is strangely compelling. Colin Firth, John Getz, Jeff Perry, Arthur Tanier, Dean Norris.

PLAY NICE (1992) ★★★½ Excellent psychosexual thriller with a grandiose performance by Ed O'Ross as L.A. cop Jack "Mouth" Peducci, a serial-killer specialist pursuing a murderess who shoots her male victims in the mouth with a pistol after kinky bedroom antics. The Luigi Cingolani production examines the cop's own psychological hang-ups in a fascinating fashion, and O'Ross is a compelling performer who rises several levels above the material written by Michael Zand (coproducer and the actor who portrays Peducci's partner), producer Chuck McCollum and director Terri Treas. It's a *Basic Instinct* rip-off but it works on its own level. Bruce McGill, Ron Canada, Ann Dusenberry, Angel Ashley, Mark Carlton. (Video/Laser: Vidmark, in rated and unrated versions)

PLAYROOM (1990) ★★ Variation on the Mummy tales, in which an archeologist (Christopher McDonald) opens a tomb and releases the spirit of a long-buried demon prince. Directed by Manny Coto. Lisa Aliff, Aron Eisenberg, James Purcell, Jamie Rose, Vincent Schiavelli. (Video/Laser: Republic)

PLEASANTVILLE (1998) ★★★★ This thoughtful, sensitive comedy is presented as a parable about our present-day world but mainly explores the good and bad sides of human nature in a tender, gentle way. It starts off with the framework of a comedy fantasy: teenager Tobey Maguire, whose father has deserted his unhappy mother and sister Reese Witherspoon is sexually promiscuous, is all set to escape into a marathon of his favorite sitcom of the 1950s called *Pleasantville* which depicts a totally happy way of life à la *Ozzie and Harriet* or *Father Knows Best.* But a strange TV repairman (Don Knotts) gives him a remote control that allows him and his sister to enter the black-and-white world of the show, where values are blandly identical to those of the sitcom. The modern teenagers are now children of the fifties sitcom, in which Dad is smiling William H. Macy (his "honey, I'm home" will become a dramatic refrain) and Mom is Joan Allen in full skirt and high heels, with a hearty breakfast ready for everybody. In this unimaginative world of conformity, nobody goes to the bathroom, marrieds sleep in twin beds (sex?—no such thing), and basketball players never miss a hoop. Gradually, Maguire and Witherspoon make the citizens realize there is more humanity inside them than they know, and those who allow themselves to experience new things become colorized. In a delightful role reversal, Mom is introduced to the ways of masturbation by daughter and she sets a tree in front of the house on fire when she tries it in the bathtub. The owner of the town's soda shop (Jeff Daniels) is introduced to the world of painters by Maguire and goes color, too, and realizes he's in love with Allen. Symbolism runs rampant in the excellent script by writer/producer/director Gary Ross (*Big*), such as the red apple Maguire bites into after his new girlfriend plucks it from a tree. There's the sign NO COLOREDS that leads to a riot, and a book-burning sequence to remind us of what happens when people cling tenaciously to old ways. The theme of conformity vs. freedom is played out as the people of Pleasantville put Maguire on trial for helping Daniels to paint a tableau on his building that depicts the turmoil of Pleasantville. The staunchest believer in the status quo is town manager J. T. Walsh (appearing in his final role), who leads the witch-hunt against the coloreds and imposes a "pleasant music only" edict. This is a beautifully shaped movie in which characters actually learn lessons and emerge as different people. To find that in a Hollywood movie is a rarity. Consider *Pleasantville* a classic. (Video/DVD: New Line)

PLEASE DON'T EAT MY MOTHER! (1973) ★★½ Revoltingly titled exploitationer—an alleged comedy about a plant that devours human flesh à la *Little Shop of Horrors*, only with a lot of bare female flesh on the premises. Produced-directed by Carl Monson. Rene Bond, Flora Wisel, Buck Kartalian. Aka *Glump, Hungry Pets, Please Release My Mother, Please Not My Mother.* (S/Weird; Movies Unlimited; Video Dimensions)

PLEASE NOT MY MOTHER. See *Please Don't Eat My Mother!*

PLEASE RELEASE MY MOTHER. See *Please Don't Eat My Mother!*

POE'S TALES OF TERROR. See *Tales of Terror.*

POINT OF TERROR. Video version of *The Bird with the Crystal Plumage* (United).

POISON (1990) ★★★½ A prizewinner at the 1991 Sundance Film Festival, this surreal story of a boy who kills his father is broken into three parts intercut into a confusing, bizarre mosaic. "Hero" is in the style of a "60 Minutes" documentary, consisting of pseudointerviews with people who know the incarcerated youth, trying to explain the killing. "Horror" is a black-and-white account of a doctor (Larry Maxwell) who has isolated the hormone of the sex drive ("the molecular coagulation theory") but turns into a leper-monster when he drinks his own serum. This is spun in a nightmarish Frankenstein fashion with satirical overtones. "Homo" depicts the disturbing, graphic adventures of a man trapped in the homosexual environment of prison, and features notorious sex sequences. Writer-director Todd Haynes was inspired by the novels of Jean Genet and uses quotations from *Miracle of the Rose, Our Lady of the Flowers* and *Thief's Journal.* This enigmatic, moody art film will not be for everyone. Edith Meeks, Susan Norman, Scott Renderer. (Fox Lorber).

POLISH VAMPIRE IN BURBANK, A (1988) ★ Failed foreign-produced parody of *The Addams Family* with barely a laugh in a coffinload. A family of Dracula clones suffers from a son (writer-producer-director Mark Pirro) who doesn't want to drink blood, so a sexy member of the family introduces them to throat-biting and bloodsucking with lovely Lori Sutton. And then the creepo's brother, also a family outcast, turns up as a walking skeleton. Ugh. The cute title never pays off because we're never given any sense of the L.A. milieu, and the juvenile level to which Pirro resorts ultimately buries him alive. Bobbi Dorsch, Hugh O. Fields, Eddie Deezen. (Simitar)

POLTERGEIST (1982) ★★★★ Smash winner from Steven Spielberg, who gave the directorial reins to Tobe Hooper. Spielberg's goal, with fellow writers Mark Grais and Michael Victor, is one of contrasts: to tell a suburban haunted-house story and throw in all the ESP and parapsychology tricks in the books on haunting. It's a child's nightmare as unseen entities enter a tract home through the TV and inspire grosser phenomena. Along the supernatural path the daughter is trapped in another dimension, the son is attacked by a tree, and coffins and corpses pop up from the ground to terrorize the housewife. Edge-of-the-seat movie comes complete with a monstrous demon from beyond and glaring white lights. Outstanding effects by Industrial Light and Magic. Heather O'Rourke as the daughter, Craig T. Nelson as the average father, JoBeth Williams as the typical housewife and Zelda Rubinstein as the petite but powerfully weird clairvoyant. (Video/Laser: MGM/UA)

POLTERGEIST II: THE OTHER SIDE (1986) ★★ Inferior sequel to *Poltergeist* never captures the intensity of the original, no matter how many monsters or supernatural effects director Brian Gibson throws at the camera. The Freeling family (victims of that first Cuesta Verde haunting) are now staying with JoBeth Williams's mother. This time the evil spirits are members of a religious sect that sought refuge in a cave (the one under the tract home) with their maniacal leader back in the 1800s. But ol' man Kane (Julian Beck) is trapped in Purgatory, and must out-magic Indian medicine man Will Sampson who chants and smokes demons up his nose. There's no logic within the logic-of-the-supernatural, just disconnected events with ill-defined characters. (Only Beck comes off well, looking genuinely satanic as the brimstone preacher.) Richard Edlund's effects are up to standard, but without a strong story, they float in limbo. Craig T. Nelson is back as the father, Zelda Rubinstein reprises her role as the diminutive, squeaky-voiced psychic investigator and Geraldine Fitzgerald is the dead mother who dons angel's wings in an unintentionally comic scene. (Video/Laser: MGM/UA)

POLTERGEIST III (1988) ★★ With each sequel this series becomes more disappointing, considering how good the original was. This time Carol Anne (Heather O'Rourke) is living in a New York skyscraper that her uncle designed. Nathan, that bad old dead man in a black hat, needs Carol Anne for reasons never made clear, but instead of taking her away to the dead zone, he plays horror games by breaking mirrors, shafting elevators, turning the swimming pool into an iceberg and trapping people in other dimensions. There's hardly any plot to the screenplay by Brian Taggert and producer-director Gary Sherman, so it's a tedious series of supernormal incidents. Tom Skerritt and Nancy Allen have thankless roles as the surrogate parents, Zelda Rubinstein seems a parody of the former Tangina character, and O'Rourke almost has to carry the picture herself. Unfortunately, she died not long after the film was finished, adding to the legendary stories about a curse stalking the series. Lara Flynn Boyle, Richard Fine, Kip Wentz. (Video/Laser: MGM/UA)

POLTERGEIST: THE LEGACY (1996) ★★★ A rousing, effects-filled, imaginative pilot for the Showtime supernatural series about the Luna Foundation, an organization run by Derek Raine (Derek De Lint), head of a team of ghostchasers called The Legacy. Using computer technology and ancient incantations, Raine and team track the fifth of five evil-filled trunks that, when unlocked in unison, will unleash a skeletal monster on the world that will reign over "the dark time." This is a swiftly paced dazzle for the eyes as ghosts, goblins and assorted supernatural beings blow open your mind, and landscapes in Ireland are blasted apart by beams of ethereal energy. *Poltergeist: The Legacy* is a piece of filmmaking to seek out, and a series not to be missed. Martin Cummings, Robbi Chang, Patrick Fitzgerald, Helen Shaver, Jordan Bayne, William Sadler. Teleplay by Brad Wright, direction by Stuart Gillard.

POOR ALBERT AND LITTLE ANNIE. See *I Dismember Mama.*

POOR PRETTY EDDIE (1977) ★★ See this redneck's version of a horror film and you'll understand why Leslie Uggams never had much of a film career. As a famous singer stranded in the South, Uggams is trapped in a nightmare of human monsters that include a rape-hungry degenerate named Eddie Collins (Michael Christian), a former movie star turned to fat and histrionics (Shelley Winters) who runs Bertha's Oasis, a slobbering sheriff (Slim Pickens), a perverted barkeep (Dub Taylor), and a mentally retarded giant named Keno (Ted Cassidy). Don't miss the dog-for-dinner sequence, frontseat fellatio scene, assorted rapes and the climactic shotgun shootout in slow motion. A horror in more ways than one. Written by B. W. Sandefur and produced-directed by Richard Robinson. Aka *Black Vengeance, Redneck County* and *Heartbreak Motel.* (Star Classics)

POPCORN (1991) ★★★½ A must-see for movie genre buffs. A film class at UC at Oceanview, taught by Tony Roberts, decides to hold a horrorthon at the Dreamland Theater, showing films with William Castle–type gimmicks: "Mosquito!" is a 3-D epic satirizing monster flicks of the '50s; "Attack of the Amazing Electrified Man" (in Shock-a-Rama) is a spoof on electric killing machines; and "The Stench" (in Aroma-Rama) is a pastiche of a Japanese horror flick à la *The H-Man.* Portions are shown as the horrorthon unfolds and takes on elements of *The Phantom of the Opera* when a masked killer stalks the committee. The film (scripted by Alan Ormsby as "Tod Hackett") goes merrily whacky with death devices, a woman (Jill Schoelen) having dreams about her past, and mysterious filmmaker Lanyard Gates, who once made the film *The Possessor.* This mixture of send-up and thrills is delightful under Mark Herrier's direction despite a skewered sense of story. Ray Walston is a movie-memorabilia shop owner (Dr. Mnesyne) who helps the committee set up the theater. Tom Villard, Dee Wallace Stone, Derek Rydall, Elliott Hurst, Freddie Marie Simpson. (Video/Laser: RCA/Columbia)

PORTRAIT IN TERROR. Yugoslav horror film reedited into *Track of the Vampire*.

POSED FOR MURDER (1989) ★ Playboy pinup Charlotte Helmkamp imitates life by playing a model for *Thrill* magazine in an effort to get a major part in the film *Meat Cleavers from Mars*. Meanwhile, a killer stalks her with tools of dismemberment. Directed by Brian Thomas Jones. Carl Fury, Rick Gianasi, Michael Merrins. (Academy)

POSSESSED (1947) ★★★ One of the weirdest of A movies produced by Warner Bros. when many of that studio's vehicles were designed solely for their female stars. In this oddball blending of film noir, dark psychology and scenes designed for Joan Crawford to go bonkers in her inimitable style, one can only admire the high levels of atmospheric filmmaking and casting the studio once had among its many resources. Crawford is a psycho case in this one, a split personality chewing up Van Heflin and Raymond Massey in her numerous fits of madness and hysteria. It's difficult to make much sense out of all the mayhem conjured up by writers Ranald MacDougall and Silvia Richards, but director Curtis Bernhardt sure has a field day with this bizarre picture, punctuated so wonderfully by the music of Franz Waxman. Geraldine Brooks, Douglas Kennedy, Stanley Ridges. (Video/Laser: MGM)

POSSESSED, THE (1982). See *Manhattan Baby*.

POSSESSED BY THE NIGHT (1993) ★★ A strangely structured supernatural thriller (by writer Maria Thomas McGee) with two plots that only mesh during the climax. The main story is about novelist Ted Prior, who comes into possession of an old Chinese relic in a bottle—a brainlike thing with a huge eye that has a hypnotic hold on folks à la *Donovan's Brain*. Prior makes rough love with wife Sandahl Bergman and later to secretary Shannon Tweed while under the control of the thing—and then it taps into Tweed's evil for a bloody good time. The second story concerns gangster Henry Silva and his soft-hearted collector (Frank Sivero). Oddball roles are filled by Turhan Bey and Chad McQueen. This unusual erotic horror thriller, from director Fred Olen Ray, strives to be different but it's strained, and there are no special effects or exposition to jazz up the thing in the bottle. (Vision)

POSSESSION OF JOEL DELANEY, THE (1972) ★★★ Tense, unsettling supernatural thriller in which socialite Shirley MacLaine realizes her brother's soul is possessed by voodoo in downtown Manhattan. Black magic in squalid tene-

ments? This contrast of imagery is nicely depicted by director Waris Hussein. The climax of the Matt Robinson–Grimes Grice script (from Ramona Stewart's novel) is set in a lonely beach cottage and offers (a) a severed head and (b) a twist ending that might surprise you. Perry King, Michael Hordern, Lovelady Powell. (Paramount)

POSSESSION OF MICHAEL D, THE (1995) ★★★ Occasionally frightening demonic possession TV-movie (allegedly based on true accounts) with a good performance by Stephen Lang as the title character, an average man who is suddenly plagued by spirit possession and frequent outbursts of fire. Long-suffering wife Sheila McCarthy (who also gives a good and believable performance) seeks the help of paranormal investigator Michael Riley, psychiatrist Phylicia Rashad and hypnotist Roger Rees before the psychological secrets of Michael D are unlocked and horrors of his childhood lead to at least a pseudoexplanation of the phenomena that haunt him and his family. This is a thoughtful study of possession and exorcism that doesn't rely on exploitation for its effect; rather, telewriter Ronald Parker provides much food for thought. Directed with equal taste by Michael Kennedy.

POSSESSION: UNTIL DEATH DO YOU PART (1987) ★ Another despicable example of how movies demean womanhood as nothing more than an object for male desire—and murder. John R. Johnston is a wide-eyed babbling idiot with a mother fixation who kills indiscriminately, using blunt screwdrivers, stakes, shovels, axes and other implements, apparently to make up for the one major tool he's lacking. An excuse for scenes of beautiful women taking baths and showers, dressing and undressing, and behaving like sex objects as they attend drunken orgies and male strip clubs. There isn't an ounce of entertainment as Johnston, his face painted like a wild Indian, goes on his bloody spree. Directed by Lloyd A. Simandl and Michael Mazo. Melissa Martin, Cat Williams. (Marathon; Cinema Group)

POSSESS MY SOUL. See *Abby*.

POSTMAN, THE (1997) ★★★½ Kevin Costner is a serious filmmaker who has worthwhile things to say (*Dances with Wolves* proved that) and who stretches for something refreshingly new. Perhaps in the case of *The Postman*, which can be hailed as a thinking man's adventure epic, he stretched too hard, or became too pretentious, in this offbeat, sometimes fascinating portrait of a postapocalytic world in which small bands live within the broken-down United States. Contrasting with the need for peace in the wake of a major nuclear war is an army of warriors led by an intellectualizing sadist called General Bethlehem (Will Patton). Costner, who directed the project and coproduced it with Jim

Wilson and Steve Tisch, portrays a roving pac-
ifist who performs Shakespeare in exchange for
food and drink—a loner who tries to look away
from the evil and hardships of his time . . . until
he is reluctantly conscripted into Patton's
harshly militant Holnists. Patton, symbolizing
man's intellect and cruelty housed in the same
body, becomes a challenging foe for Costner,
the thinker who abhors violence. Costner escapes, assumes the identity of a dead postman,
and delivers a lost bag of mail in exchange for
food and drink, and suddenly becomes a symbol
for man's new search for order in a world of
chaos. When the Eric Roth–Brian Helgeland
script (based on a 1985 David Brin novel) slows
down for a romance with Olivia Williams, *The
Postman* bogs down and suffers badly from
bloat. But Costner the director perks up his personalized epic with bursts of action and gets the
film back on track. The symbols and messages
are delivered with frequency in the three-hour
running time, yet there's a naive sincerity to it
all that turns *The Postman* into an inspiring, uplifting morality play. The film is full of memorable moments: Williams proving to be a fierce
warrior, Costner taking up arms in a worm-turns
sequence, the birth of a new kind of Pony Express. There is no doubt that *The Postman* is the
most thoughtful of the post-Armageddon movies
(a genre that has proliferated in recent years
with bad flicks), but its lengthy running time and
heavy-handedness made it inaccessible to the
majority. However, true-blue movie lovers will
find food for thought and enough pathos to
make this a memorable viewing experience. It's
just too bad Costner couldn't have been more
economical and disciplined. James Russo, Daniel Von Bargen, Tom Petty. (Video/DVD: Warner Bros.)

POSTMORTEM (1997) ★★★ After the awful
Nemesis series, director Albert Pyun redeems
himself with this atmospheric, psychological
serial-killer thriller shot on location in and
around Glasgow, Scotland. Pyun does justice to
the screenplay by John Lowry Lamb and Robert
McDonnell, which is the story of an alcoholic
detective who once specialized in tracking child
killers for the LAPD and writing books about
them. But he became so depressed and disillusioned with life that he left his family behind to
live alone in a coastal mansion. As etched by
Charles Sheen, the ex-cop has become a hopeless dispomaniac when a necrophiliac serial
killer sends him an obituary notice with clues to
the identity of his next victim. After the young
woman is found stripped naked and dead outside
his front door, Sheen realizes his book has set
off the killer and he comes out of his drunken-
ness to help Glasgow police work the case. The
cat-and-mouse games that follow, similar to the
plot of *The Bone Collector,* force Sheen to come

to grips with his personal problems. The script
also allows us to get into the head of the killer,
whose identity only becomes important when
the film deals with the world of undertakers and
embalmers. Certain elements of this story are
definitely distasteful, but Sheen's performance
and Pyun's restrained direction make it palatable. The Scottish cast, although their accents are
sometimes difficult to decipher, is solidly professional and includes Michael Halsey, Ivana
Milicevic, Stephen McCole, and Gary Lewis.
(Video/DVD: Sterling)

POTTSVILLE HORROR, THE. See *The Being.*

POWDER (1995) ★★★½ This emotion-
wracked fantasy film about a social misfit explores, in startling ways, the dark side of the
human heart and man's search to understand and
control his violent nature. It is difficult to watch,
but it can have its rewards if you are willing to
endure its pain. Written and directed by Victor
Salva, it depicts a young man (Sean Patrick Flanery) who has spent his childhood in seclusion
as he is emerging into society. A hairless albino
(makeup by Thomas and Bari Drieband Burman), he looks unappealingly different but has
the greatest intellect in the world. When he enters a school for troubled youths run by Mary
Steenburgen, and meets teacher Jeff Goldblum,
he is shy and repressed and struggling to understand the world, but harassed by those who
don't understand him. He can move objects tele-
kinetically, attract bolts of electricity, explode
windows in a fit of anger, touch a sick woman's
forehead and read thoughts, etc. He uses his
magical powers to help the local sheriff (Lance
Henriksen, who gives a moving performance)
communicate with his dying wife, and connects
a hunter to a dying deer so he can "feel" what
death is like. And ultimately his superpower carries him to a surprising ending. Heavy stuff,
heavy stuff. Susan Tyrrell, Brandon Smith, Ray
Wise, Bradford Tatum. (Video/Laser: Buena
Vista)

POWER, THE (1968) ★★½ Producer George
Pal took the gourmet novel by Frank Robinson
and turned it into a plate of scrambled eggs.
John Gay's screenplay is undernourished, and
Byron Haskin's direction unfulfilling, as George
Hamilton realizes that one of several men in a
research project has a terrible "power" to move
objects, to blot out entire memories and to kill
by telekinesis. In short, one of the finest novels
of the '50s emerged as one of the most disappointing films of the '60s. Offbeat music by
Miklos Rozsa. Suzanne Pleshette, Michael Rennie, Nehemiah Persoff, Earl Holliman, Richard
Carlson, Aldo Ray, Ken Murray, Barbara Nichols, Yvonne De Carlo. (Paramount)

POWER, THE (1984) ★ Not an original idea in
this low-budget hunkajunk from Jeffrey Obrow
and Steve Carpenter, who also concocted *The*

Dorm That Dripped Blood. A clay Aztec figurine (housing evil powers of the god Destacatyl) levitates a man and pinions him on a spike, drops a ton of steel on a night watchman and harasses a reporter for a tabloid as sleazy as this movie. The exploding arms and throbbing armpits have been done before and the climax is a monster terrorizing Susan Stokey and teenagers in an ordinary house. They even had the audacity to drop the original title of *Evil Passage* and blatantly steal the title of Frank Robinson's sci-fi classic. Shameful. (Vestron)

POWER MAN. See *The Power Within.*

POWER WITHIN, THE (1995) ★★★ Another well-made if predictable martial-arts action film from producers Joseph Merhi and Richard Pepin, with Ted Jan Roberts as a shy high school student incapable of fighting, who comes into possession of an "ancient ring of power" that gives him karate skills to fight off school bullies and the gang that's out to steal the ring for ultimate power. Gerald Okamura portrays the wise old sage who gives the ring to Roberts and tells him it is "the doorway to the power of the will." The script by Jacobsen Hart offers interesting characters (benevolent cop John O'Hurley, sympathetic mother Karen Valentine as a one-time child TV actress) and director Art Camacho keeps it moving with nice action sequences, a guest appearance by Don "the Dragon" Wilson and teenager love stuff with lovely Tracy Lindsey. Keith Coogan, P. J. Soles, Irwin Keyes, Ed O'Ross, Jacob Parker, William Zabka. (PM Entertainment) (Laser: Image)

PRACTICAL MAGIC (1998) ★★★½ As sibling sisters of the Owens family, a Massachusetts clan whose women have been cursed with a talent for black magic since the days of the Salem witch trials, Sandra Bullock and Nicole Kidman dominate this comedy. The adaptation of Alice Hoffman's novel by Robin Swicord, Akiva Goldsman, and Adam Brooks remains lighthearted and whimsical, yet at times *Practical Magic* is a realistic portrayal of sisters who alternately love and hate each other but who are always there for the other when it gets rough. At other times it turns into an outrageously funny witchcraft movie. Helping to stir the witches' cauldron are the sisters' aunts—Dianne Wiest and Stockard Channing, a delightful pair of cutups older and wiser in the ways of casting spells and yet who don't always make things easier for the sisters. When these four characters get together at the kitchen table and pass around a bottle of mind-bending formula, the movie soars like a witch taking a midnight ride on a broomstick. Griffin Dunne's direction takes an adult attitude toward material normally portrayed on the screen as juvenile. Especially toward the lovers of the sisters, who are all

doomed one way or another. Kidman plays a fun-loving slut you always sympathize with because invariably the guy she chooses is the wrong one for her. And one of her lovers (Goran Visnjic) turns out to be a serial killer who begins to physically abuse her, so she and sister Bullock—the more levelheaded of the two—devise a way to eliminate him. Then decide to bring him back to life—a mistake the aunts have always warned them about. Naturally, the cop investigating Visnjic's disappearance, Aidan Quinn, falls under the sisters' spell in what turns out to be a very strange cop/suspect relationship. This is a beguiling, off-the-wall brew of character and comedy that produces gentle laughs and guffaws, but it becomes a feel-good movie, too, when the right kind of justice (as perceived by vengeful witches, of course) prevails. Chloe Webb and Evan Rachel Wood provide strong support. (Video/DVD: Warner Bros.)

PRANCER (1989) ★ Mawkish, unappealing children's fantasy, about a little girl's love for a reindeer she believes to be Santa's. As the centerpiece for a sentimental movie, the reindeer is without charm or warmth and one can only wonder what possessed producer Raffaella de Laurentiis. An unbelievable mess, with the girl's mean old wicked father (Sam Elliott) undergoing an unconvincing character change. Even Cloris Leachman's crotchedy old woman, who's supposed to be sympathetic, isn't. The ad proclaims "something magical is about to happen," but it never does. Also forgettable: John Hancock's direction and Maurice Jarre's score. Abe Vigoda, Michael Constantine, Rutanya Alda. (Orion) (Laser: Nelson)

PRANKS. See *The Dorm That Dripped Blood.*

PRAYER OF THE ROLLERBOYS (1991) ★ Despite its pseudofuturistic setting and scads of extras on roller skates, this is not part of the *Rollerball* series. Set in a society that is breaking down, this depicts undercover agent Corey Haim penetrating a gang of extortionists called "Rollerboys" to uncover a plot to sterilize the population. Fantasy elements are minimal—this plays more like a crime thriller. Directed perfunctorily by Rick King, who only wrings a few moments of excitement during roller-skate chase sequences employing a mobile camera. Patricia Arquette, Christopher Collet, Julius Harris, Devin Clark. (Academy) (Laser: Image)

PREACHER'S WIFE, THE (1996) ★★★½ This Samuel Goldwyn, Jr., remake of his father's beloved 1947 comedy *The Bishop's Wife* (originally conceived by Robert E. Sherwood and Leonardo Bercovici) was directed by Penny Marshall with an all-black cast and a new script (by Nat Mauldin and Allan Scott) that resets the feel-good fantasy in a New York Baptist church. This gives Whitney Houston (in the Loretta

Young role) a good excuse to sing a number of excellent hymns and songs. The writing is still sharp and the characters warmly conceived: Courtney B. Vance (in the David Niven role) conveys well the alternating moods of a man losing faith in his God and flock; Denzel Washington (who was instrumental in getting the film produced) plays the angel named Dudley originally etched by Cary Grant, and plays him with soft-spoken subtlety; Gregory Hines plays the only villain of the piece with good-natured charm; and newcomer Justin Pierre Edmund is good as the preacher's son. The chemistry and music are what ultimately make this bit of old-fashioned hokum work, as there are virtually no special effects or tricked-up situations. (Video/Laser: Touchstone)

PRECIOUS FIND (1996) ★★½ This seems like an unusually good space adventure—and then wham! One suddenly realizes it is a rip-off of *The Treasure of the Sierra Madre*, with its three mineral-seeking adventurers all patterned on the characters in the 1948 John Huston classic. Greedy, half-crazed Rutger Hauer is the equivalent of Humphrey Bogart's Fred C. Dobbs, sincere young guy Harold Pruett is the Tim Holt copy and thus the hero, and colorful Brion James, as the owner of a space garbage scow, takes on characteristics of Walter Huston's grizzled but wise prospector. This unlikely threesome ventures out of Moon City to mine for "precious," a futuristic equivalent to earthly gold, on an asteroid identified as AU-79. Unfortunately, screenwriter Lenny Britton knows nothing about character consistency, and their behavior is more than a bit bizarre. Throw in Joan Chen and her claim-jumping pal and a samurailike warrior who also crashes the party (equivalent to Alfonso Bedoya's Mexican bandido, maybe?) and *Precious Find* emerges less precious than it might have been, and only a find if you're looking for something that imitates classic movies poorly. Philippe Mora goes by the numbers directing this unusual but ultimately failed project. Morgan Huton, Don Stroud. (Republic)

PREDATOR (1987) ★★★★ Tense, action-packed, high-tech sci-fi–horror adventure, forever moving under John McTiernan's direction as Arnold Schwarzenegger and his commando team move into a South American jungle to retrieve a cabinet member held hostage by rebel forces. What Arnie and his men don't know, once they've completed their mission in a blaze of pyrotechnics, is that they are being stalked by an alien creature, on Earth to claim human trophies. Finally it's just Arnie against the alien as he uses his wits *Rambo*-style. Early scenes of the alien using camouflage techniques (by Stan Winston) are effective, the tension sustains and the film ends on a satisfying, uplifting note after an intense bashing match. Carl Weathers, Elpida Carrillo, Bill Duke, Jesse Ventura, R. G. Armstrong. (Video/Laser: CBS/Fox)

PREDATOR 2 (1990) ★★★ A relentless, driving pace, gory action and a futuristic setting (1997 L.A.), in which drug gangs are making life miserable for police, provide an unusual background for this sequel movie about the semi-invisible hunter from another planet who stalks human beings for his trophy room. The script by Jim and John Thomas has lapses but director Stephen Hopkins keeps it moving. Danny Glover stars as the cop Harrigan who is forced to work with creepy FBI agent Gary Busey when drug dealers start turning up dead— victims of the alien offspring of the creature from the first film. Alan Silvestri's score is an enhancement. Seven-foot-tall Kevin Peter Hall is back as the monster. Ruben Blades, Maria Conchita Alonso, Bill Paxton, Kent McCord, Calvin Lockhart, Morton Downey, Jr. (Video/Laser: CBS/Fox)

PREHISTORIC BIMBOS IN ARMAGEDDON CITY (1993) ★ After World War III, a roving band of shapely nymphs and liberated, buxom blonds roves the ruins of Old Chicago City, hoping to destroy a dictator named Nemesis and his evil cyborg warriors. Yeah, sure. Directed with a bimbo mentality by Todd Sheets. Robert Vollrath, Charles Monroe, Tonia Monahan, Deric Bernier. (Tempe)

PREHISTORIC PLANET. See *Queen of Blood*.

PREHISTORIC PLANET WOMEN. See *Women of the Prehistoric Planet*.

PREHISTORIC WOMEN (1966) ★★★ Voluptuous brunettes and fair-skinned blonds in animal-skin bikinis are the primary (and primordial?) reason to watch this Hammer delight primevally produced-directed by Michael Carreras in the wake of his other seminude girly-revue triumphs: *She* and *One Million Years B.C.* Big game hunter Michael Latimore is magically transported through time to prehistoric days when evil ruler Martine Beswick (captivating, shall we say?) holds sway over her fair-haired slaves, among them pouty-lipped, ravenous Edina Ronay and buxom Carol White. This girl-watcher's delight, made in England as *Slave Girls*, is utter nonsense, but nonsense men enjoy as the acres of undulating flesh parade past the camera and bevies of babes perform ritual dances that might have been choreographed by Busby Berkeley. And dig that phallic-symbol nose on the rhino, a deep intellectual comment on the primitive urges that motivate mankind. Stephanie Randall, Alexandra Stevenson. (Increase)

PREHISTORIC WORLD. See *Teenage Caveman*.

PREHYSTERIA! (1993) ★★★ To cash in on the

Jurassic Park dinosaur hysteria of 1993, Charles Band and his father Albert coproduced and co-directed this light-hearted video comedy in which dinosaur eggs hatch five cutesy-pie creatures (pterodactyl, *T-Rex*, brontosaurus, etc.) that proceed mischievously to plague a household that includes a couple of nice, affectionate kids. David Allen's special effects and Richard Band's sublime musical score are the highlights of this adolescent, feel-good romp. Brett Cullen, Colleen Morris, Samantha Mills, Austin O'Brien, Tony Longo. (Video/Laser: Paramount)

PREHYSTERIA! 2 (1994) ★★★ Those cutesy-pie little critters known as minisaurs are back for more cuddly, coo-filled fun and games under the special-effects tutelage of David Allen, in this warm, silly and satisfying Full Moon production directed by Albert Band, from a script by Brent Friedman and Michael Davis. In this series of misadventures with Elvis, Hammer, Paula, Jagger, and Madonna, the dino-mites get trapped in a crate of raisins and end up in the hands of spoiled rich kid Kevin R. Connors. The setting becomes a mansion ruled by mean old Bettye Ackerman, who does all she can to make life miserable for the lovable critters. And along come two zany exterminators, Ketchum and Killum, to do the same. Jennifer Harte, Alan Palo, Larry Hankin, Greg Lewis, Michael Hagiwara. (Video/Laser: Paramount)

PREHYSTERIA! 3 (1995) ★★ A comedown from the second film in the series, these continuing misadventures of five minidinosaurs who do sweet things to good people and silly, mildly nasty things to bad people is really wearing thin. The tiny ones, cooing, oohing and aahing but looking unrealistic and clumsy in close-ups, show up at a miniature golf course to help a struggling father and daughter to fight off the efforts of a villainous golf pro who wants to tear down the amusement center to make way for his own super golf course with a Japanese promoter. With its silly sound effects and half-baked script by Michael Davis and Neil Ruttenberg, and static direction by David De-Couteau (as Julian Breen), *Prehysteria! 3* plays like a feeble sitcom episode from the '60s, and sputters when it should ignite. It's time to retire the little critters or get better special effects to make them more believable. Fred Willard, Whitney Anderson, Pam Matteson, Dave Buzzotta, Bruce Weitz, Matt Letscher, John Fujioka. (Video/Laser: Moonbeam/Paramount)

PRELUDE TO A KISS (1992) ★★★½ It's the old "soul transference" theme again, this time with an aging man taking over the body of a young woman after he kisses her during her wedding ceremony. Craig Lucas's 1988 Broadway play was adapted by Lucas for director Norman Rene with a sensitive, sophisticated touch that keeps events on a spiritual, moving level. Alec Baldwin, who starred in the play, is back as the husband who realizes bride Meg Ryan is not a woman but a man, and Sydney Walker is the old man whose kiss starts it all. Kathy Bates, Ned Beatty, Patty Duke, Richard Riehle, Stanley Tucci. (Video/Laser: Fox)

PREMATURE BURIAL, THE (1962) ★★★ One of the best in Roger Corman's Edgar Allan Poe series, reeking with decay and desolation as nobleman Ray Milland, who lives in a weird house isolated on a foggy moor, is obsessed with the fear of being buried alive. Ray Russell and Charles Beaumont concocted an intriguing if frequently corny story line that, combined with Daniel Haller's set design and Corman's direction, is a winner. Hazel Court, Richard Ney, Heather Angel, Alan Napier, John Dierkes. (Vestron; MCA) (Laser: Image)

PREMONITION, THE (1975) ★★★ Despite a ponderous beginning, this emerges an offbeat tale of ESP, with supernatural overtones, in the hands of writer-producer-director Robert Allen Schnitzer. It unfolds like a mystery story as crazed mother Ellen Barber seeks to reclaim the baby she gave away for adoption, aided by a crazy carnival clown (Richard Lynch). Sharon Farrell, the new mother, experiences flashes of things to come and other phenomena as the kidnapping plot unfolds, thickened by the appearance of a female doctor experimenting in telepathetic dreams. Some elements don't blend smoothly, but the film gallops to a rapid conclusion, with policeman Jeff Corey helping out. Filmed in Mississippi. (Embassy)

PRESENCE, THE. See *Witchtrap*.

PREY. See *Alien Prey*.

PREY, THE (1980) ★★ A man in the woods is beheaded by his own ax. Along come three guys and three gals, and guess who are "the prey." A lot of footage of bugs, insects, snakes, spiders, raccoons and other creatures preying on each other, as well as gushing blood, severed throats and detached heads. Someone tells "The Monkey's Paw" at a campfire. Minor slasher movie—very minor. Directed by Edwin Scott Brown. Debbie Thureson, Steve Bond. (Thorn EMI/HBO; Starmaker)

PREY FOR THE HUNTER (1992) ★★ Another variation on "The Most Dangerous Game," with some prankster-type guys going on a "hunt" with paint pellet weapons, but deciding to substitute bursts of eggshell white with real lead, all aimed at a newspaperman with a camera. Directed by John H. Parr. Todd Jensen, Andre Jacobs, Evan J. Klisser, Michelle Bestbier. (Columbia)

PRICELESS BEAUTY (1989) ★½ Better this should be called *Highlander Dreams of Jeannie*. Christopher Lambert plays a rock star who feels responsible for his brother's motorcycle death and retires to Italy's coast to become angst-riddled. When he finds China—a "small genie" in an ancient urn who materializes as shapely Diane Ladd—life improves but he still refuses to return to the music world. Lambert's search for love amidst personal pain gets in the way of any enjoyment this minor Italian production might have had. With its ponderous pacing, lengthy shots in which nothing happens, and Lambert's overwrought performance, writer-director Charles Finch should be put in a bottle. Francesco Quinn, J. C. Quinn. (Video/Laser: Republic)

PRIMAL RAGE (1990) ★★½ The bite of a monkey undergoing lab experiments causes a student to feel basic urges manifesting in strange ways. A reporter uncovers the cause as a mad scientist on a college campus. Special effects by Carlo Rambaldi. Directed by Vittorie Rambaldi. Patrick Lowe, Bo Svenson, Cheryl Arutt, Mitch Watson. (Warner Bros.)

PRIMAL SCREAM (1987) ★ Imitation of *Blade Runner* with elements of the private-eye thriller tossed in. A new power source, Hellfire, is being developed by a corporation with questionable values. When a space colony near Saturn is destroyed, Earthbound PI Corby McHale (Kenneth J. McGregor) gets involved with a beautiful dame (Sharon Mason as Samantha Keller) and others (including Nicky Fingers, played by Joseph White) in an incomprehensible plot ill-conceived by director William Murray. This low-budget effort has moments of sheer energy, but then so do panty hose. Mickey Shaughnessy, Jon Maurice. (Magnum; Nova)

PRIME EVIL (1988) ★★ Lackluster and tedious bit about a devil cult formed in the 14th century, at the time of the Black Death, so the Parkman family will have eternal life and carry out acts of "prime evil" for Lucifer. The supernatural elements are boring rather than stimulating, the monster that oversees the sacrificial rites is not convincing, and there's predictable business about beauties in white robes about to be sacrificed. The whole enterprise, directed by Roberta Findlay, is without inspiration. William Beckwith, Christine Moore. (New World) (Laser: Image)

PRINCE IN WONDERLAND. See *The Little Prince and the Eight-Headed Dragon.*

PRINCE OF DARKNESS, THE (1987) ★★★½ Writer-director John Carpenter creates an above-average supernatural thriller reminiscent of his *Assault on Precinct 13* in that the story is in a single setting where main characters are trapped. It's an abandoned L.A. church watched over by a sect called the Brotherhood of Sleep. A weird container of swirling fluids is a doorway for the Devil to return to Earth. Scientists, led by Victor Wong, and priest Donald Pleasence study the phenomenon only to fall prey to zombies. Old superstitions vs. computers is an exciting element, and one wishes Carpenter had focused more on that than on the gory murders he overuses to keep the plot moving. Carpenter directs with a sense of doom (enhanced by his synthesized score). Jameson Parker, Lisa Blount, Dennis Dun, Susan Blanchard. Alice Cooper has a small role as a street bum. (Video/Laser: MCA)

PRINCESS BRIDE, THE (1987) ★★★½ This gallant attempt by director Rob Reiner to capture the whimsical qualities of an old-fashioned fairy tale (actually a short novel by William Goldman, who wrote the adaptation too) is a refreshing treat with only occasional moments of fizzle. Cary Elwes must rescue his princess lover (Robin Wright) from kidnappers. On his odyssey, he meets villain Christopher Guest, talkative kidnapper Vizzini (Wallace Shawn in the film's funniest role), lovable brute Fezzik (Andre the Giant), Miracle Max (Billy Crystal, unrecognizable in makeup), old witch Valerie (Carol Kane, also unrecognizable), and a Spanish swordsman (Mandy Patinkin) seeking the six-fingered murderer of his father. For monster lovers there are giant killer eels, a huge muskrat in the Fire Swamp and the Machine, a contraption that sucks its victim's life away. Peter Falk portrays the grandfather who reads bedridden Fred Savage the tale from an old book. (Nelson) (Laser: Nelson; Criterion)

PRINCESS WARRIOR (1990) ★ One sorry excuse for a low (make that "nonexistent") budget fantasy, and one miserably acted and directed flicker. It opens on Vulkara, a planet of sexy bubbleheaded blonds in negligees. Among them are sisters vying with Queenmother (Cheryl Janecky) for power. A teleporter carries several of them to Earth where the queen partakes in a wet T-shirt contest, meets a motorbike guy (Mark Pacific) and two L.A. cops (Tony Riccardi and Augie Blunt) who are as dumb as the blonds. These antics go on forever. Only funny thing is the name of one Vulkarian: Bulemia. Ha ha ha! Lindsay Norgard directed without revealing talent. Dana Fredsti, Sharon Lee Jones.

PRISON (1987) ★★★½ There's a tough, brutal edge to this supernatural tale set within Wyoming State Penitentiary, in which the spirit of an electrocuted prisoner, William Forsythe, returns from the dead as an energy field. Inanimate objects become very animated as they kill off the prisoners and guards, with a barbed-wire death being quite effective. Charles Band's production has a strong sense of doom and grittiness, provided by director Renny Harlin. Lane Smith, Viggo Mortensen, Chelsea Field, Lincoln Kilpatrick. (New World) (Laser: Image)

PRISONER OF THE CANNIBAL GOD. See *Slave of the Cannibal God.*

PRISONERS OF THE LOST UNIVERSE (1983) ★★ Fantasy adventure on the level of a Saturday matinee. TV personality Kay Lenz and workaday electrician Richard Hatch are propelled into another dimension, a medieval world where evil tribesman Kleel (John Saxon) rules with an iron gauntlet. Hatch, who just happens to be an expert kendo swordsman, and Lenz, who has a spicy tongue and liberated attitude, do in the heavies with the help of a comedy-relief thief (Peter O'Farrell) and a Green Man (Ray Charleson). There are moments when director Terry Marcel captures a spirit of fun and action, but otherwise it's colossally stupid. Effects are mediocre. Kenneth Hendel, Myles Robertson. (VCL)

PRISON PLANET (1992) ★★ The setting is the year 2200, and Earth has fallen into the clutches of a bad-guy king, but rebels are roving the devastated landscape searching for truth, justice and the new American way. Written-directed by Armand Gazarian. James Phillips, Jack Willcox, Michael Foley. (Columbia)

PRISON SHIP STAR SLAMMER. See *Starslammer*.

PRIVATE LIFE OF SHERLOCK HOLMES, THE (1970) ★★★½ Must-see fare for Baker Street Irregulars and Holmesphiles . . . a minor masterpiece written by Billy Wilder and I. A. L. Diamond and directed by Wilder, with excellent music by Miklos Rozsa. Robert Stephens makes the London sleuth a much likable man with a sense of humor and a self-effacing manner. Almost at once the game is afoot when Holmes helps an attempted suicide . . . a plot involving marvelous Jules Verne–style gadgets, Queen Victoria, and Holmes's supercilious brother Mycroft (Christopher Lee). Lush, expensive production handsomely mounted, which unfortunately died at the box office and has been brutally edited. Colin Blakely offers an intelligent Dr. Watson. The film was heavily cut before release and Wilder was never happy with this version. Genevieve Page, Clive Revill. (Key; MGM/UA) (Laser: Image, featuring restored footage, original shooting script, interview with editor Ernest Walter)

PRIZE OF PERIL, THE (1983) ★ Futuristic "death game" movie (based on a short story by Robert Sheckley) in which men must match their skills against each other for cash money in a life-and-death competition that is televised to the public (shades of *The Running Man*). French film directed by Yves Boisset. Gerard Lanvin, Michel Piccoli, Marie-France Pisier. (Astral).

PROBABLE CAUSE (1994) ★★★½ Paranoia and suspicion are cleverly developed by screenwriter Hal Salwen in this serial-killer slasher film, one of the strangest, and darkest, of its genre. Someone is killing cops in Edmonton, Canada, and tired, beaten homicide cop Michael Ironside (in one of his better roles) suspects

partner Kate Vernon as a sleepwalking killer. Several clever twists are in this macabre, psychological tale of murder and deception. Directed by Paul Ziller, it costars Craig T. Nelson as chief of homicide, M. Emmet Walsh as a psychologist in sleepwalking, and Kirk Baltz as a fellow cop. (Live)

PROFILE OF TERROR, THE. See *The Sadist*.

PROGRAMMED TO KILL (1987) ★★½ Competently made action thriller combining blazing Uzis in Israel with a new cyborg technology the U.S. government uses to create a superassassin. Their model is a PLO-style terrorist (Sandahl Bergman) brought back alive from a kidnapping plot by supercommando Robert Ginty, and turned into the perfect killing machine. When Bergman malfunctions and starts killing those in the government who created her, Ginty swings back into action to stop her. What this film lacks is a sense of cyborg technology and a personality for Bergman, who goes through the picture with few lines. True, she is supposed to lack emotion, but this prevents the grudge between her and Ginty to develop emotionally. And the film just moves slowly under the direction of producer Allan Holzman and Robert Short, who also wrote the script. James Booth, Alex Courtney, Louise Caire Clark, Paul Walker, Peter Bromilow. Aka *The Retaliator*. (Media)

PROJECT: ALIEN (1990) ★★★ Set in central Norway, but shot in Yugoslavia as *The Fatal Sky*, this thriller blends every "unsolved mystery" imaginable: UFOs, mutilated cattle, meteor showers, humanoid forms in spacesuits, a disease that poxes its victims and kills them, weird black helicopters, a military conspiracy, a top-secret medical installation, etc. Michael Nouri plays a photojournalist tracking an explosion over Norway with sexy pilot Darlene Fluegel. The script by Anthony Able plays off our phobias about government secrets and reinforces them with the cliché army general essayed by Charles Durning. It moves at a brisk clip and its characters are colorful, but genre fans may be disappointed by the clean resolution of the mysteries. Director Frank Shields gets good performances out of Maxwell Caulfield (as a pretty-boy news broadcaster from a news superstation), Dereen Nesbitt and Ray Charleston. (Video/Laser: Vidmark)

PROJECT: GENESIS (1993) ★★ Andy McNeill directed this sci-fi adventure set in the 23rd century and written by Philip Jackson. It's set on a far-flung planet where shipwrecked women set out to make a new world for themselves. David Ferry, Olga Prokhorova. (Prism) (Laser: Image)

PROJECT METALBEAST (1994) ★★★ Scary monster fans will groove on this well-crafted werewolf thriller (produced by Lamar Card, Barry Collier and Penny Karlin) in which Operation Lycanthropus, in the year 1974, uncovers a Hungarian wolf-man whose blood is used to carry on secret government experiments under the guidance of demented Barry Bostwick. Skin tissue expert Kim Delaney carries on more experiments 20 years later in a bioferal lab, only to face the wrath of a rampaging werewolf monster whose makeup (that's Kane Hodder beneath all the hairy stuff) is quite convincing. A rocket launcher with shells made from silver is one of the more unusual aspects of the script by director Alessandro de Gaetano and coproducer Timothy E. Sabo. Good atmospheric photography, that hirsute creature and a good cast (including John Marzilli, Musetta Vander, Dean Scofield and Lance Slaughter) make for one satisfying monster movie. (Prism)

PROJECT SHADOWCHASER (1992) ★★★½ Subtitle this "Hospital Diehard Meets Cyborg Man Under Siege." All flippancy aside, it's a rousing high-tech sci-fi action thriller starring Martin Kove as a criminal brought out of suspended animation to infiltrate a high-rise hospital that's been taken over by terrorists led by Romulus (Frank Zagarino), a billion-dollar android ("a perfect synthetic warrior") turned renegade against his ruthless government-backed creator (Joss Ackland). Kove's aided by the President's daughter (Meg Foster in a miniskirt) while FBI guy Paul Koslo assists from control center. Stephen Lister's script has so many twists and surprises that this plays better than some of the big-budget actioners it imitates. And it's well directed by John Eyres. (Prism) (Laser: Image)

PROJECT SHADOWCHASER 3000 (1994) ★★★ The only carryover from *Project Shadowchaser* (the second entry in this series appears to have been titled *Armed and Dangerous*) is the killer android played by white-haired Frank Zagarino, who is found aboard an abandoned Russian spaceship (the *Siberia*) after it collides with Comstat-5 space station. It's up to underpaid astronauts Sam Bottoms, Musetta Vander, Christopher Atkins and Christopher Neame to escape a number of suspenseful situations, destroy the android and somehow get off the doomed ship before it blows. John Eyres is a fine action director and he struts his stuff with Nick Davis's exciting, never-a-dull-moment script. Definitely a must for action fans, as it's loaded with space special effects, explosions and assorted tumult and shouting. Ricco Ross, Bill Kirchenbauer. (Turner/New Line)

PROJECT VAMPIRE (1992) ★ "Resurrection by injection" is the tag line for this zero-budget horror thriller with sci-fi overtones, in which crazed German Dr. Klaus and his blond nurse, who decidedly has the hots for his perverted Teutonic profile, carries out Project Alpha with cackling, hand rubbing and predictions of world conquest. This daffy duo wants to turn the world

into blood-drinking vampires by injecting everyone with a secret-formula serum. Most of the action is of the chase variety, with little linking logic—a technique of writer-director Peter Flynn. Myron Natwick, Brian Knudson, Mary-Louise Gemmill. (Video/Laser: Action International)

PROMISE OF RED LIPS, THE. See *Daughters of Darkness.*

PROM NIGHT (1980) ★★ In a moment of moppets' malice, four youngsters cause the death of a fifth.... Years later, an ax-packing, black-masked killer turns up at the school prom to wreak revenge. This gore thriller features one harrowing chase through the campus, but is otherwise predictable slasher fare. You'll feel stood up. Directed by Paul Lynch from a script by William Gray. Jamie Lee Curtis, Leslie Nielsen, Robert Silverman, Antoinette Bower. (Pioneer Artists; MCA) (Laser: MCA)

PROM NIGHT II. See *Hello Mary Lou: Prom Night II.*

PROM NIGHT III: THE LAST KISS (1990) ★★ Following through on the supernatural elements inherent in the second *Prom Night* film, this is an undistinguished rehash of clumsy clichés and stupefying stereotypes that are moldy hat. Beauty queen Mary Lou Mahoney (Courtney Taylor) is back from the dead to hypnotize student Tim Conlon into helping her carry out murders, with death devices seemingly stolen from *Phantasm.* Since it's all been done before, there's not much pizzazz in Ron Oliver's directing or writing. Cyndy Preston, David Stratton. (IVE) (Laser: Image)

PROM NIGHT IV: DELIVER US FROM EVIL (1991) ★★★ Better-than-average slasher flick, despite clichés and predictable twists, primarily because the Richard Beattie script spends time setting up four characters for the climactic kill. The murderer is a Catholic priest kept locked up since 1957, when he viciously murdered prom-nighters for performing sex. In 1991 he escapes his captors and closes in on the four celebrating students gathered in a country manor for fun and sex. The customary association between sex and death in these slasher things is utilized to the utmost as the bloody events unfold. Directed by Clay Borris with the usual POV shots of the killer spying on his victims and an array of religious symbolism. If anyone shines in this bloodbath it is Nikki de Boer, who undergoes harrowing near-death experiences—barefoot yet. Alden Kane, Joy Tanner. (Video/Laser: Live)

PROPHECIES OF NOSTRADAMUS (1979) ★★ Packaged in video under the title *Nostradamus,* this Australian TV documentary is a study of the 16th-century prophet Michel de Nostradame, who wrote hundreds of quatrains that might have predicted the future. Of special interest are his quatrains referring to three Antichrists, two of whom were Hitler and Napoleon, and a description of what would appear to be an atomic war that will occur no later than 1999. The third Antichrist, if you believe the soothsayer, has yet to rise to power. Speculative but intriguing. (Bargain)

PROPHECY (1979) ★★ Director John Frankenheimer fails to come to grips with making an effective horror thriller. Scriptwriter David Seltzer disguises this tale with ecological themes and social "significance," but none of it helps to make the monster plot cohesive. Tom Burman's grotesque creatures, created by pollution, are frightening at first, but then become grotesque as the film turns into a chase-action film. Armand Assante, Talia Shire, Robert Foxworth, Richard Dysart. (Paramount)

PROPHECY, THE (1995) ★★★ You'll either dig this bizarre tale about evil renegade angels from Heaven (named Simon and Gabriel, and not a harp or wing showing) as they battle it out on Earth, or you'll consider this a hopelessly ludicrous mess. Writer-director Gregory Widen surrounds his neoreligious duel of saintly titans with doom-laden chanting and Deeply Significant Narration from the mouth of cop Elias Koteas, who gave up the cloth years ago after a glimpse into the bowels of Hell and who now finds himself caught between the less-than-angelic forces. Love or hate the movie, you'll have to admit that Christopher Walken delivers an unusual performance as the sardonic, wisecracking Gabriel, on Earth to procure the soul of an evil army general that has been placed inside a young girl by another angel. For a film depicting an apocalyptic battle between forces of unlimited power, *The Prophecy* is strangely ambiguous, pretentiously poetic and, except for one scene of several skewered souls in Hell, is strangely lacking in the Armageddon/Doomsday special effects one would expect from so ambitious a project. It's difficult to give a literal quality to Biblical concepts and maybe that's why this succeeds or fails based on your personal values. Virginia Madsen, Eric Stoltz (as Simon), Amanda Plummer. (Dimension)

PROPHECY II, THE (1997) ★ Be sure to pop plenty of antidepressants (the more the merrier) before you sit through this incomprehensible, godawful (excuse the pun) excuse for another good-angels-vs.-evil-angels direct-to-video movie, coming in the wake of the 1995 original that featured a striking performance by Christopher Walken as the sociopath archangel Gabriel who always had a wisecrack no matter how horrible his deeds. In this sequel, Walken tries to blow his horn again, but the dialogue of screenwriter Matthew Greenberg (abetted by director Greg Spense) is so meaningless and lacking in wit that the film just flaps in the wind. It is nothing

but depressing as Walken kills "good" angels by ripping their hearts out. It seems there's a civil war of angels raging in heaven and a lot of the winged ones have taken human form to settle matters in an American city that just happens to be the former site of "Eden." You know, Paradise. Now it's nothing but factories belching out pollutants. So much for man's legacy. Russell Wong, a literally "fallen angel" because he drops out of nowhere onto the hood of Jennifer Beals's car, is described as a Nephilim, a son of God who has made an emergency landing to impregnate Beals. Not because she's a good flashdancer or has a supple body but because her offspring will fulfill a prophecy and end the war among the angels. Meanwhile, Walken hypnotizes a suicide-bent woman named Izzy (Brittany Murphy) to act as his gofer, and she walks around in a daze helping him with a computer problem, stealing cars, and holding his automatic when he isn't firing it. In one scene she succeeds in shooting herself, but the bullet has no effect. Gabriel can do that. There's a lively sex scene for the impregnation bit, but afterward Beals runs an emotional range of A to B as she is pursued by Walken, who throws her around a lot but can never kill her, even though he's killing everyone else. There are no logical rules to this game of rebel angels. When Wong gets impaled, he just gets up and walks away. When Walken gets impaled, he can't get up. Go figure. You will be further depressed by the waste of Eric Roberts in this movie as an angel named Michael. He just talks a lot, and says nothing. Even if Lucifer himself was hell-bent on amassing video movies, I strongly doubt he would have this one in his collection. He would say, "Oh, the hell with it." Steve Hytner, Bruce Abbott, William Prael, Glenn Danzig. (Video/DVD: Dimension)

PROTECTORS, BOOK #1, THE. See *Angel of H.E.A.T.*

PROTOTYPE (1983) ★★★½ Thinking man's sci-fi TV-movie, written with dignity by Richard Levinson and William Link in dealing with the dilemma a scientist faces when his creation is used for ill purposes. The new design is a humanoid (David Morse) perfected by scientist Christopher Plummer. When the Pentagon intervenes, Plummer steals his creation and hides him away. Levinson and Link concentrate on the cerebral, intellectual aspects. Arthur Hill, as a Pentagon general, is restrained and sympathetic, indicating that the writers feel there are two sides to every weapon. David Greene directs with a sure, restrained hand. Frances Sternhagen, James Sutorius, Stephen Elliott. (King Bee; Live) (Laser: Live)

PROTOTYPE X29A (1992) ★★★½ Good computer graphics and a strong story about the merging of man's soul into the metal body of a programmed robot make this special-effects sci-fi actioner above average. In A.D. 2057, cybernetic humans (Omegans) are hunted down by killer cyborgs (Prototypes) and intrigue surrounds one scientist's attempt to alter the program. Writer-director Phillip Roth captures a nihilistic landscape and the sadness of humans/machines caught up in the bleakness of a shattered society. But despite its interesting subtext, it's still your basic actioner. Lane Lenhart, Robert Tossberg, Brenda Swanson. (Video/Laser: Vidmark)

PROWLER, THE (1981) ★★★½ One of the better slasher bloodbaths that flowed in the wake of *Friday the 13th*, with just enough tantilizing mystery to go with Tom Savini's bloodily graphic makeup. The bloodletting begins in 1945 when two prom attendees are impaled on a pitchfork, presumably by a crazed GI just returned from combat. Jump to 1980, when a menacing figure in fatigues and helmet, his face hideously scarred, stalks the campus on prom night, shoving his bayonet through the head of a male victim and impaling a naked woman in a shower with his thematic pitchfork. This is an intense murder sequence and ranks as one of the best in the slasher canon. Director Joseph Zito maintains a gloomy, suspenseful atmosphere in the stalking sequences. Vicky Dawson is credible as the heroine who accompanies sheriff Christopher Goutman. Lawrence Tierney and Farley Granger add touches of professionalism to this cut above the average, if you'll excuse the pun. Aka *The Graduation*. (VCII; Direct; from VCI as *Rosemary's Killer*)

PSYCHIC, THE (1977) ★★ Jennifer O'Neill's performance as a woman who suffers visions of violent deaths that have happened or will happen elevates this Italian psychothriller from director-writer Lucio (*Zombie*) Fulci, who unfortunately lingers too long on O'Neill's face and zooms the landscape like a maniacal cinematographer, distracting from the suspense of O'Neill's discovery of a body entombed in a country estate. The most effective sequence has O'Neill as a child visualizing her mother's suicidal plunge from a cliff as her face scrapes against the shale and rips to shreds. Gabriele Ferzetti, Marc Porel, Gianni Garko. (Catalina; Lightning)

PSYCHIC (1991) ★★★ Taut, Hitchcockian cat-and-mouse TV-movie thriller with ESP overtones. College student Zach Galligan has prophetic visions of a serial killer in dark glasses but becomes a suspect when he tries to help disbelieving police. Thin characterizations (including a villain that needed fleshing out) and a few slasher-movie clichés are deficiencies director George Mihalka tries valiantly to overcome. Catherine Mary Stewart, Michael Nouri, Albert Schultz. (Video/Laser: Vidmark)

PSYCHIC KILLER (1975) ★★ Convicted murderer Jim Hutton learns astral projection through a strange medallion and, when released, uses his power against those who wronged him. The revenge killings foreshadow techniques in slasher films to come. Despite inspired moments, this is hampered by an inadequate budget and ordinary direction by Ray Danton, who cast then-wife Julie Adams as a psychiatrist heroine, Paul Burke and Aldo Ray as bewildered cops, Nehemiah Persoff as a believer in ESP and Neville Brand as a butcher. Rod Cameron, Della Reese, Whit Bissell. Aka *The Kirlian Effect* and *The Kirlian Force*. (Embassy)

PSYCHO (1960) ★★★★★ The ultimate in horror thrills, a genuine genre classic. It's a series of cinematic tricks allowing director Alfred Hitchcock to indulge his unique, impactful techniques. The shower sequence, the most famous movie murder of all time, demonstrates the fine art of editing, and there are at least three other sequences that will have you leaping once Hitchcock focuses on Norman Bates, a reclusive young man who runs a motel and lives in a weird house with his domineering mother. But first there's Janet Leigh embezzling money from her boss and taking it on the lam. Later, her lover John Gavin and her sister Vera Miles search for her, as does investigator Martin Balsam. Then comes the sequence when Miles dares to enter the Bates's cellar and—But we can't reveal more without spoiling the many thrills this adaptation of Robert Bloch's famous novel delivers. (It was scripted faithfully by Joseph Stefano.) This ultimate horror in schizophrenia isn't as farfetched as it might seem—Bloch claims his descent into a killer's warped mind is based on a true-life case. The great score is by Bernard Herrmann. Simon Oakland, John McIntire, Frank Albertson. (Video/Laser: MCA)

PSYCHO (1998) ★★★ Remembering the first time you saw Alfred Hitchcock's 1960 classic—the name of the theater, the time of day, how the popcorn tasted—ranks alongside remembering where you were when Pearl Harbor was attacked or John F. Kennedy was assassinated. *Psycho* remains one of the most reputable horror films, so it takes a lot of guts to remake it. Why anyone would want to remake the movie is obvious. Box office. All the fans will come to see if it's better than the original. Aesthetically, however, how do you improve on a masterpiece? Hell, how do you even do a remake that's just as good? Forget about being better. Who can be better than Hitchcock? All these questions must have plagued director Gus Van Sant, who is not an exploitation moviemaker but a dedicated craftsman who genuinely cares about his work. Obviously, he had the courage of his convictions, so he plunged ahead in spite of all the demons in his head screaming at him to stop. So, how does it stack up? Well, Van Sant tried to be as faithful as he could to Stefano's screenplay, which in turn had been faithful to Robert Bloch's novel. Some dialogue sequences have been expanded a little, but the major scenes are all there. The first of several problems is the use of color, when *Psycho* cries out for black-and-white, which always gives a psychological edge to a thriller or a horror film. Especially *Psycho*. Just citing the fact that a bright orange dress is worn by Marion Crane just prior to the shower sequence should be enough. There is also the problem of casting, for each actor brings different nuances and shadings to a character, no matter how hard he or she might try to capture the original. Hence, none of the players seem quite right. They're competent, but they're not quite right. Too much identity factor here. Anne Heche, in the Marion Crane role, is totally different from Janet Leigh. Heche conveys vulnerability and guilt, yes, but not the way Leigh did it. By 1960 Leigh had enjoyed 13 years as a leading Hollywood actress. She knew her craft. Heck, Heche is just getting started. An even bigger problem is the casting of Vince Vaughn as Norman Bates. He is nowhere the actor that Anthony Perkins was. He attempts to convey Bates's quirkier traits, but it doesn't seem natural. Notice the scenes where he gives a nervous little laugh to punctuate his dialogue. It's forced. Julianne Moore, as Marion's sister, seems full of too much anger and fire when she should be worried and concerned, as Vera Miles so well conveyed. Viggo Mortensen as Marion's lover, Sam Loomis, has a kind of indifference toward the missing Marion, as if he is trying to make his character suspicious or sinister. John Gavin, as the original Sam, was just a concerned, sincere, square kind of guy you trusted. The one good piece of casting was selecting William H. Macy to portray the nosy investigator Arbogast, a role originated by Martin Balsam. Macy in 1998 is a pro on the same level as Balsam was in 1960, and his interpretation is flawless. And what about the historic shower sequence, which in its time was the most graphic murder ever portrayed on screen? Van Sant stayed to Hitchcock's storyboard, scene for scene. But . . . but more about that later. The music is one thing that remains unchanged, for it is virtually the same score. Pure Bernard Herrmann, reproduced and readapted faithfully to the picture (frame by frame, I suspect) by Danny Elfman and Steve Bartek. On the music, there is absolutely nothing to quibble about. Ultimately, Hitchcock was a master of detail and nuance, and created a tension in the way he directed his scenes. Van Sant is a fine director (*Drugstore Cowboy, My Own Private Idaho, Even Cowgirls Get the Blues*) but he's better at telling different kinds of stories than *Psycho*. Horror movies, especially a classic like *Psycho*, calls for a touch that perhaps nobody else but Hitchcock had. The shower sequence illustrates that. Van Sant copied the original almost frame for frame, but something is missing. The horror of it all. The impact of it all. Maybe part of the failure is that we're so familiar with this scene, we know what to expect, there are no surprises left. Oh yeah? Wanna bet? Go back and see the original. The shower sequence is still one of the all-time great horror sequences. To try to emulate a master of the cinema is a noble deed, and my hat is off to Van Sant for trying. However, he should stick to the kind of movies he understands best. And maybe with classics like *Psycho*, they should leave well enough alone. (Video/DVD: Universal)

PSYCHO II (1983) ★★★½ Is it possible to follow in Hitchcock's footprints and successfully make a sequel to the great macabre classic? Sort of . . . at least this is not a failure, even if it can't reach the heights of that which inspired it. Richard Franklin, an Australian who had barely distinguished himself with *Patrick* and *Roadgames* before being picked to direct Norman Bates's return 23 years later, seems an unlikely choice. But he was a Hitchcock disciple; the director advised him in the art of German expressionistic cinema. With writer Tom Holland, Franklin fashions a homage to the themes and characters of Robert Bloch's novel (although, alas, Bloch was not involved) and strives for a film that spins off from, but doesn't copy, the original. Now it is Bates (declared sane and released from Atascadero Hospital) being terrorized by someone dressing up like Mother and murdering with a butcher knife. Behavior of the characters is often confusing, but the shocks keep one's mind off script deficiencies. The macabre ending, comedic one moment and horrifying the next, comes as a jolt. Anthony Perkins is oddly vulnerable as Bates; Vera Miles returns as Lila, fighting to keep Bates institutionalized; Robert Loggia is the sympathetic psychiatrist; and Meg Tilly is Norman's confused love interest. (Video/Laser: MCA)

PSYCHO III (1986) ★★ Call it "Daze of His Lives: The Continuing Love Story of Norman Bates." That infamous mother-lover is back in the phantom house on the hill next door to the motel, welcoming travelers in his inimitable style. This time the callers include a defrocked nun on the run from her haunted past and a lowlife vagabond with kinky sex habits (not the nun's). Anthony Perkins doubles as director of this offshoot of Robert Bloch's famous novel, bringing unusual touches to Charles Pogue's script. Gore murders liven up the pace, but this lacks the intensity of its predecessors. Just run-of-the-kill. Jeff Fahey, Diane Scarinid, Roberta Maxwell. (Video/Laser: MCA)

PSYCHO IV: THE BEGINNING (1990) ★★★½ Unexpectedly good follow-up to the original themes established in Hitchcock's 1960 classic based on the equally classic Robert Bloch novel, with screenwriter Joseph Stefano again dealing with Norman Bates, this time as a youngster growing up in that sinister house on the hill. It opens with a radio show discussion of matricide (children murdering their mothers) with one of the callers turning out to be Bates (Anthony Perkins). In flashbacks, we see the aberrant sexual psychology of Mrs. Bates (wonderfully limned by Olivia Hussey) that led to Norman's character makeup. The murder sequences, in which young Norman (played by *E. T.*'s Henry Thomas) murders the girls he meets, are so realistic as to be unsettling, and the double homicide-by-poison of Norman's mother and lover is painful to watch. Director Mick Garris does a remarkably good job on this one. (Video/Laser: MCA)

PSYCHO A GO-GO! See *The Man with the Synthetic Brain*.

PSYCHO BOY AND HIS KILLER DOG. See *A Boy and His Dog*.

PSYCHO CIRCUS (1966) ★★ Christopher Lee's lean figure graces this Harry Alan Towers production designed to follow in the bloody footprints of *Circus of Horrors*, but it's a weak whodunit with only mildly horrific overtones, based on the Edgar Wallace novel of 1928, *Again the Three Just Men*. Stolen money is the motive behind a series of murders surrounding the traveling Barberini Circus, and John Llewelyn Moxey's direction plays up the cops-and-robbers elements far more than the horror fans might be expecting. Leo Genn gives a good performance as a Scotland Yard cop, Heinz Drache portrays the ringmaster, Anthony Newlands is the Big Top owner, Cecil Parker is amusing as the blubbering Yard supervisor, Suzy Kendall and Margaret Lee provide beauty, and Victor Maddern is a robber. (From Sinister Cinema and Saturn as *Circus of Fear*)

PSYCHO COP (1988) ★★ Pseudopoliceman Joe Vickers (played with ghoulish delight by Bobby Ray Shafer) kills for his satanic cult, the blood needed for rituals. Semi-illiterate teenagers figure prominently among his many victims. Written-directed by Wallace Potts. Jeff Qualle, Palmer Lee Todd. (South Gate)

PSYCHO COP 2 (1994) ★ That crazed, Satan-loving policeman Joe Vickers (Bobby Ray Shafer, delivering such wisecracks as "You have a right to remain silent—you're dead!") is back in blue, and seeing red, as he drives his squad car around L.A., its interior stuffed with severed body parts and organs. What a messy guy. When some nerdy and stupid joes hold a bachelor party/orgy in their office, Joe drops in unannounced to gouge out a security guard's eyeball, throw a prostitute from a rooftop into a garbage bin, and behave in other antisocial ways, such as shooting people in the head with his revolver. You might say the fit hits the Shafer. Directed by Rif Coogan (real name: Adam Rifkin) from an alleged script by Dan Povenmire, who didn't work overtime to come up with a plot. Double-threat Shafer also acted as associate producer. There's nudity and simulated sex, including lesbian behavior. The cable-TV prints identify the film as *Psycho Cop Returns*. Barbara Lee Alexander, Julie Strain, Roderick Darin, Dave Bean, Nick Vallelonga, Alexandria Lake Wood. (Columbia TriStar)

PSYCHO FROM TEXAS (1981) ★ Although copyrighted in 1981, this was shot in Texas in 1974. It finally reached the screen with the impact of a redneck's double-barreled shotgun missing both firing pins. It's not Southern Comfort as John King III portrays a wild man who kidnaps an oilman for ransom, murdering an innocent girl to keep her quiet and committing general mayhem. Watch this to ogle Linnea Quigley stripped naked by King III in the middle of an empty barroom; she jiggles her breasts while he pours a pitcher of beer over her head. Watch for Jack Collins as the stereotyped sheriff, Joann Bruno as a screaming maid, and Tommy Lamey as a demented Southerner named Slick who spends half the film chasing the overweight oilman through the swamp. Written-directed by Jim Feazell. Also known as *Evil + Hate = Killer*. (Paragon; from Bronx as *The Butcher*)

PSYCHOMANIA (1963) ★ Girls' school is always a suitable setting for a bloody horror movie—so many lovely young bodies for a sadistic killer to choose from, and the camera can linger on the gory details as the madman hacks and hews. This will turn your stomach as well as it turned a profit when first released. A Del Tenney production directed by Richard Hilliard, it stars Dick Van Patten as a cop, Lee Philips as the killer, James Farentino, Sylvia Miles and Sheppard Strudwick. Aka *Black Autumn* and *Violent Midnight*. (Sinister/C; Filmfax)

PSYCHOMANIA (1973) ★★ Upper-crust Britishers George Sanders and Beryl Reid make a pact with a Frog Demon so when their son (Patrick Holt), the leader of a motorcyclist gang called the Living Dead, kills himself in a crash, they resurrect him and he roars out of his grave aboard his hog. He urges his buddies to kill themselves too. So the riders set out to commit suicide in spectacular ways (running their bikes into stone walls and off cliffs, like that). What a bizarre British horror film, especially when the grand dame, Reid, turns into a frog. Defies description. Directed by Don Sharp. Aka *The Living Dead, The Frog* and *The Death Wheelers*. (King of Video; Media; Goodtimes; United; Western World)

PSYCHOPATH, THE (1968) ★★ Klaus Kinski lends his special screen madness to this European-produced tale about a psychiatrist who discovers that his girlfriend's ex-husband is a murderer. Directed by Guido Zurli. George Martin, Ingrid Schoeller. (Lightning)

PSYCHO PUPPET. Video of *Delirium* (Viz).

PSYCHO RIPPER. See *New York Ripper*.

PSYCHOS IN LOVE (1987) ★ Black humor predominates in this gory thriller in which a bartender and manicurist kill people just for laughs. Finally they turn their attention on a topless dancer. This film has been compared to *Eating Raoul*, but it isn't as tasty. Produced-edited-directed by Gorman Bechard. Debi Thibeault, Frank Stewart. (Wizard; VCI)

PSYCHO SISTERS (1972) ★★ Psychologically troubled weakling Susan Strasberg screams in the shower and behaves neurotically after her husband dies in a flaming car crash (or does he?) in this crude exploitation cheapie, a poor off-shoot of the imperiled-woman suspense genre. She's consoled, or so it appears, by her sweet young sister Faith Domergue, yet keeps fainting. She thinks she sees snakes crawling in her bed and hears her dead mother's voice, and she screams every time the slavering handyman walks by carrying his ax (seems he murdered someone with it once, but let's let bygones be bygones, shall we). A couple of cops on stakeout complicate Tony Crechales's hackneyed script, and one of them (Charles Knox Robinson) pretends to fall for Strasberg, but you'll see through the deception. John Howard, Sydney Chaplin, Steve Mitchell, Biff Yeager, Kathleen Freeman, Ben Frank. Directed haphazardly by Reginald LeBorg. Aka *So Evil My Sister*. (Prism)

PSYCHOTRONIC MAN, THE (1980) ★ Slow-moving, ponderous independent feature shot in Chicago by writer-director-cameraman Jack M. Sell, with long stretches where very little happens. A barber (Rocky Foscoe) is possessed with what a scientist calls "psychotronic energy" (submerged power in the subconscious mind) and he wills people to die. One man splatters on the sidewalk in slow motion, others are engulfed by wind and go bonkers. (Unicorn)

P. T. BARNUM'S ROCKET TO THE MOON. See *Blast Off.*

PULSE (1988) ★★★½ Surprisingly good science-gone-amok thriller with effective close-up work on household appliances, wiring systems and other modern technology. The premise of director Paul Golding's script is that our electrical system is being invaded by bursts (or "pulses") caused by an alien force, although that force is never fully explained. Cliff DeYoung and son Joey Lawrence are trapped in their home and under attack from anything being fed electrical power. The film never overexploits its theme and accomplishes chilling moments when wires and plugs turn quite menacing. Myron Healey, Charles Tyner, Matthew Lawrence, Dennis Redfield. (Video/Laser: RCA/Columbia)

PUMA MAN, THE (1980) ★ Superpoor super-hero Italian fantasy adventure: An ancient Aztec legend claims that aliens descended to Earth at the dawn of time, giving superpowers to a race of men. Now conquest-hungry Donald Pleasence wants those powers and steals a golden mask that enables him to put people under hypnotic spells and perhaps knock off Pumaman. Who is Pumaman? Glad you asked. He's a wimpy guy working as a paleontologist in a museum, who is befriended by a South American Indian named Vadinho. Suddenly Pumaman is wearing this cheap cape and can fly. The special effects shots are terrible, the acting even worse. Misconceived by director Alberto De Martino, this stuff gives comic books a rotten reputation. Walter George Alton is Pumaman, Miguelangel Fuentes the Indian, and Sydne Rome the heroine. (Prism; Parade)

PUMPKINHEAD (1988) ★★★½ This first directorial effort by special effects genius Stan Winston has the flavor of an old morality horror tale from an E.C. comic. Young Ed Harley witnesses a demon finishing off his prey. Flash ahead to Harley as an adult (Lance Henriksen), living a lonely life in the backwoods with his son. Odd circumstances lead Harley to seek the help of an old crone to resurrect Pumpkinhead (the vengeful monster) so he can kill off a band of irresponsible dirt bikers. Pumpkinhead is a powerful, and awesome, creature and the plot has several twists as the murders are carried out one by one. Genre fans will appreciate the ambience that Winston pumps into every scene. Above average and highly recommended. Jeff East, John DiAquino, Kimberly Ross, Joel Hoffman. (Video/Laser: MGM/UA)

PUMPKINHEAD II: BLOOD WINGS (1993) ★★★½ Monster fans will enjoy this bloody, high-energy beastbash when that vengeful demon (who resembles *Alien* more than a little) is brought back to life in a burial ground ritual carried out by carousing teenagers after they've run over the thing's poor old crone of a mother. Director Jeff Burr gives the numerous monster attacks style and ambience, which is really what this sequel to the 1988 Stan Winston film is all about. The story (by Ivan and Constantine Chachornia) is just an excuse for the mayhem and bloodletting. Andrew Robinson as the town sheriff is pretty good, and so is Ami Dolenz as his errant daughter. Femme fatale fans will enjoy the appearance of Linnea Quigley. Steve Kanaly, J. Trevor Edmond, Caren Kaye, Lilyan Chauin, Roger Clinton, Soleil Moon Frye. (Video/Laser: Live)

PUPPET MASTER (1989) ★★★½ One of producer Charles Band's better horror offerings, enhanced by the fine puppet trickery of David Allen, who uses every effects device in the book. Director David Schmoeller also demonstrates style, especially in an opening sequence in which a little creature scurries around the lobby of the Bodega Bay Inn in 1939 as Gestapo agents come to murder William Hickey, a puppet master considered an enemy of the Third Reich. Jump to the hotel during modern times, when psychics (each with a different power) investigate the suicide of Hickey's son. But the son is still alive, using the minimonsters to commit murders, and the horror is on as Drillhead (has a drill for a pate) and other homicidal creatures, each with a murder shtick, attack and the gore gets thick. Schmoeller's camera is effective in making the puppets plausible, often by having his Steadicam sweeping at floor level. Paul Le Mat, Irene Miracle, Matt Roe, Kathryn O'Reilly, Jimmie F. Scaggs, Barbara Crampton. A topnotch choice. (Paramount) (Laser: Full Moon)

PUPPET MASTER II (1990) ★★ The Attack of the Doll People is on again when investigators from the Office of Paranormal Claims turns up at the Scarab Hill Hotel at Bodega Bay, CA, dying one by one at the bloodied hands of the murderous marionettes of Andre Toulon, the phantomlike puppet master with a formula for giving life to his wired folk. Stop-motion specialist David Allen directed this Charles Band production and his workshop provided the effects. While this sequel never reaches the heights of the original, it is not without interesting points, the large breasts of pinup gal Charlie Spradling among them. The puppets are a varied lot, including Drillhead, Death Face, and a Darth Vader–like character with a fire extinguisher arm. And Steve Welles has a ball portraying the evil Toulon, whose face is covered by bandages and weird goggles. Toulon's origins story is revealed in a 1912 Cairo flashback, a plot element expanded on in the third film. Toulon imagines that psychic investigator Elizabeth MacClellan is his long-dead wife and saves her for an amusing transformation sequence. Gregory Webb, Nita Talbot, Jeff Weston. (Paramount) (Laser: Full Moon)

PUPPET MASTER III: TOULON'S REVENGE (1990) ★★★ Set in 1941 Germany, this traces the origins of how Andre Toulon (Guy Rolfe in an effective role) came to discover the secrets of animating inanimate objects with the souls of victims of the Hitler regime. Major Krauss (Richard Lynch, in one of his sneering roles) is heading the Death Corps Project—a perverted attempt to restore life to dead German soldiers so they can be used to kill again—and murders Toulon's wife. This forces Toulon to seek his revenge and he accomplishes it in a most hideous way, his Nazi adversaries dying most unpleasantly. Charles Band's *Puppet Master* series continues to show a sense of intelligence and sardonic wit with this amusing entry written by C. Courtney Joyner (from an idea by Band) and directed by coproducer David DeCoteau. David Allen pulled the strings for the puppets, which this time include a five-gun cowboy. Sarah Douglas, Walter Gotell, Ian Abercrombie, Kristopher Logan. (Paramount) (Laser: Full Moon)

PUPPET MASTER 4 (1993) ★★★½ Another lively entry in Charles Band's popular series depicting the puppet creations of German scientist Andre Toulon (Guy Rolfe), who now directs his creatures to help scientist Rick Myers (Gordon Currie) fight the Totem monsters. These alien-like minicreepies, commanded by the ancient Egyptian warrior monster Sutek, trap Currie, Chandra West and Teresa Hill in deserted Bodega Bay Inn to prevent them from discovering the secret of life. Pinhead, Drillhead and others, in a resurrection scene out of *Frankenstein*, animate Toulon's latest puppet, Decapitron, which has interchangeable heads, one of them a bank of weapons. And the war between little monsters rages with Richard Band's music accentuating the combat. This lively piece (puppets by the real puppet master, David Allen) was directed by Jeff Burr. Jason Adams, Felton Perry. (Video/Laser: Paramount)

PUPPET MASTER 5 (1994) ★★ You really have to have dug the previous entries in this Charles Band series to get the full drift right away. Scientist Rick Myers (Gordon Currie) is back from the fourth film, accused of murdering all those dead folks at Bodega Bay Inn. He and Chandra West return to the inn for another showdown in which lines dividing good and evil are sometimes difficult to discern. Decapitron is resurrected from the mechanical dead again to fight off an evil spirit sent by warrior monster Sutek, who wants control of the puppets. Decapitron gets some help from the other puppets: Pinhead, Drillhead, the six-armed gunslinger, etc. Meanwhile, bad guy Ian Ogilvy invades the inn with evil henchmen (Willard Pugh, Duane Whitaker) to take control of the puppets, but of course the puppets give it to them instead. Occasionally the head of Andre Toulon (Guy Rolfe) pops up to philosophize about the power of the puppet master, which is eventually passed on to Myers for this alleged conclusion to the series. It took five writers to come up with this hodgepodge of plot.

The real heroes of this piece are special effects wizard David Allen and director Jeff Burr, who have the unenviable task of making all those toy models look real. Teresa Hill, Nicholas Guest, Kaz Garas. (Video/Laser: Paramount)

PUPPET MASTERS, THE (1994) ★★★★ An excellent Canadian adaptation of Robert A. Heinlein's sci-fi novel, with Donald Sutherland giving a good performance as the chief of the Office of Scientific Intelligence, which has the task of stopping an alien race from taking over Earth. The aliens are squishy-looking flat things that attach themselves to the backs of humans and bore tentacles into their hosts' brains to take control of the nervous system. OSI agent Eric Thal and exobiologist Julie Warner lead the investigation to Ambrose, Iowa, where the E.T. invasion begins before spreading throughout the state. Heightened action sequences under Stuart Orme's direction, fine special effects and a sense of paranoia give an unusual spin to this top-notch effort scripted by Ted Elliott, Terry Rossio and David S. Goyer. Keith David, Will Patton, Richard Belzer, Yaphet Kotto, Andrew Robinson, Marshall Bell, Tom Mason. (Video/Laser: Hollywood Pictures)

PURPLE DEATH FROM OUTER SPACE (1940). Video version of the serial *Flash Gordon's Trip to Mars* (Questar).

PURPLE MONSTER STRIKES, THE (1945) ★★½ Fifteen-chapter Republic serial (aka *The Purple Shadow Strikes*) is distinguished (and made a bit laughable) by Roy Barcroft's campy performance as an alien in tights who intends to steal a rocket engine so he can then invade our planet. The Purple Monster (so-called because he came to Earth on a meteor that trailed a purple stream) can make himself invisible and take possession of another body and appear to be that person. Dennis Moore plays the intrepid hero who stands alone against the invasion, with tall, leggy Linda Stirling helping out. Serial king Barcroft utters plenty of purple prose, but it's hardly his best villain. The fights are well staged and there are such sci-fi devices as the Electro Annihilator. Codirected by Spencer Bennet and Fred C. Brannon. James Craven, Mary Moore. The TV-feature version is *D-Day on Mars*. (Republic; Nostalgia Merchant)

PURPLE PEOPLE EATER (1988) ★★ "We've thrown in everything about the 1950s that might trigger nostalgic memories," writer-director Linda Shayne says of this family movie in which an alien entity (inspired by Sheb Wooley's 1958 hit song) joins a young rock 'n' roll band led by Neil Patrick Harris. The creature, a cutesy-pie E.T. type with a yellow horn on its head that plays musical notes, proceeds to thwart evil landlord John Brumfield from evicting lovable oldsters Ned Beatty and Shelley Winters, while Chubby Checker and Little Richard show up for a benefit concert. Wooley appears briefly as a circus manager. Shayne (with an assist from Jim Wynorski) has concocted an innocuous entertainment for the young. Peggy Lipton, James Houghton, Molly Cheek. (Media) (Laser: Image)

PURPLE SHADOW STRIKES, THE. See *The Purple Monster Strikes*.

Q: THE WINGED SERPENT (1982) ★★★½
Satisfying monster movie written-produced-directed by Larry Cohen, with stop-motion effects by David Allen. Decapitation of a window washer on the Empire State Building is the first in many claw crimes committed by a feathered flying serpent, known in Aztec mythology as Quetzlcoatl. Q, for affectionate brevity, lives atop the Chrysler Building and brings daily terror to residents by skinning them alive. Bizarre sacrificial killings by a believer in Aztec legends has led to the "rebirth" of the bird—that's the theory of cop David Carradine, who has a hard time convincing fellow cops Richard Roundtree and James Dixon. Outstanding is Michael Moriarty as a hood who knows where the bird is hiding. Good score by Richard O. Ragland. Aka *Serpent* and *The Winged Serpent*. Candy Clark, Lee Louis. (MCA)

QUARANTINE (1989) ★★½ Eccentric, offbeat Canadian TV-feature set in a futuristic society wracked by plague. A dictatorial state has seized power and its Gestapo-styled police subject anyone related to a victim of disease to an area of quarantine. Rebels (represented by Beatrice Boepple) try to assassinate a senator, in the process meeting a computer expert programming a way of tracking the disease. One finds a parallel to AIDS in Charles Wilkinson's script (he also produced-directed) but the message is muddled and the film fails to reach a resolution. Garwin Sanford, Jerry Wasserman, Tom McBeath, Michelle Goodger. (Republic)

QUATERMASS AND THE PIT (1958) Remade in the '60s as *Five Million Years to Earth*, but here's the original British three-hour, six-chapter TV series starring Andre Morell as Professor Quatermass. (Sinister/C; S/Weird)

QUATERMASS CONCLUSION, THE (1979) ★★★
This final chapter in Nigel Kneale's scientific adventures about Professor Bernard Quatermass is not as compelling as the three previous (*The Creeping Unknown, Enemy from Space, Five Million Miles to Earth*) but is still arcane enough that it should satisfy series followers. John Mills is a less believable scientist than his earlier incarnations but still effective, with a crazed look in his eye, as he roves an England on the verge of anarchy, looking for a missing niece. A strange power is attracting thousands of people to Stonehenge, where they are "beamed up" to an unknown planet. The dialogue and characters all have the Kneale twist so nothing is ordinary about this TV-movie made for the BBC, with Piers Haggard directing. Simon MacCorkindale, Barbara Kellerman, Margaret Tyzack, Brewster Manson. (Thorn EMI/HBO)

QUATERMASS II. Original British theatrical version of *Enemy from Space* (Laser: Image).

QUATERMASS II: ENEMY FROM SPACE. Video of the British version of *Enemy from Space* (Corinth; Sinister/C).

QUATERMASS EXPERIMENT. Original British

theatrical version of *The Creeping Unknown.* (Dark Dreams; Sinister/C; S/Weird) (Laser: Japanese)

QUEEN OF ATLANTIS (1961) See *Journey Beneath the Desert.*

QUEEN OF BLOOD (1966) ★★★ Writer-director Curtis Harrington, to make up for a small budget, utilizes color to good advantage and emphasizes character rather than effects in telling of an expedition sent into space in 1990 to a dying planet. Astronauts John Saxon, Judi Meredith and Dennis Hopper find a green-colored woman (Florence Marly), sole survivor of her race, and one by one fall victim to her vampirism. Harrington throws a surprise into the climax. Basil Rathbone in one of his final roles. Forrest J. Ackerman guest stars. Rocket footage was lifted from a Soviet sci-fi movie. Aka *The Green Woman, Prehistoric Planet, Flight to a Far Planet, Planet of Vampires, Planet of Blood* and *Planet of Terror*. (Star Classics; from Sinister/C and S/Weird as *Planet of Blood*) (Laser: HBO)

QUEEN OF EVIL. Alternate title for Oliver Stone's first effort, *Seizure.*

QUEEN OF OUTER SPACE (1958) ★★ Spaceship crew discovers life on Venus—and what life! Beautifully stacked babes in silk stockings, miniskirts and high-heel stiletto boots. And wearing Earth-type lipstick and mascara yet! Their queen (Laurie Mitchell) cuts down on the divorce ratio by issuing no-men-allowed decrees. She then turns her Beta Disintegrator Ray on Earth. Space heroes Eric Fleming, Paul Birch, Dave Willock and Patrick Waltz keep their jaws jutting and crack chauvinistic jokes about the well-rounded dolls while scientist (!?) Zsa Zsa Gabor—who can't resist men—gads about helping them. Edward Bernds, who directed Three Stooges vehicles, was at the helm. Script by Charles Beaumont from a one-joke outline by Ben Hecht. Laurie Mitchell, Lynn Cartwright. Aka *Queen of the Universe*. (Fox)

QUEEN OF THE CANNIBALS. See *Dr. Butcher M.D.* (*Medical Deviate*).

QUEEN OF THE GORILLAS. See *The Bride and the Beast* (Bride-and-seek in the bush?).

QUEEN OF THE JUNGLE (1935) ★★ A 12-chapter serial, which featured stock footage from a 1922 cliff-hanger, *Jungle Goddess*. It's set in the lost land of Mu, where a killer ray emanates from the eye of an idol. The usual collection of motley natives (posing as leopard men) comes up against the great white hunter, and so on. Directed by Robert Hill. Reed Howes, Mary Kornman, Dickie Jones, Marilyn Spinner. (A feature-length version under this title is on tape from Nostalgia and Mike Le-Bell's.)

QUEEN OF THE UNIVERSE. See *Queen of Outer Space*.

QUEST. See *Galaxy of Terror*.

QUEST, THE (1984) ★★★ Offbeat Australian quasi fantasy (also known as *Frog Dreaming*) blending metaphysical overtones with coming-of-age object lessons when inquisitive youth Henry Thomas probes the mystery behind a legendary creature living in a lake of Devil's Knob, an area shrouded in frog mysteries. Thomas's meeting with an Aborigine, steeped in the region's legends, leads him deeper into the meaning of life (and lake) until the climax, where the explanation behind the monster offers insight into Thomas's learning process. Beautifully photographed and acted. Tony Barry, Rachel Friend, John Ewart. Written by Everett de Roche, directed by Brian Trenchard-Smith. (Charter)

QUEST FOR FIRE (1982) ★★★½ Gritty, realistic look at Neanderthals, showing how man discovered not only fire but a sexual position other than the standard missionary grope. Nothing glamorous about these people, who dress in rags and paint their faces with mud. Mammoths and saber-toothed tigers harass them, and their guttural language was created by Anthony Burgess. Directed by Jean-Jacques Annaud from a script by Gerard Brach. Everett McGill, Rae Dawn Chong, Ron Perlman. (Video/Laser: CBS/Fox)

QUEST FOR LOVE (1971) ★★★ Unusually sensitive, literate British fantasy romance, dealing with an outré form of time travel. Scientist Tom Bell awakens in a different time stream, where he is now a novelist unhappily married to Joan Collins. Time "split" back in 1938 into two different parallel courses, and he's trapped in his alter ego, a man who has many traits he despises. He falls in love with Collins, but their newfound relationship is—But that would be spoiling it. Handsomely directed by Ralph Thomas, intelligently scripted by Bert Batt, from John Wyndham's "Random Quest." Simon Ward, Denholm Elliott, Laurence Naismith. (Independent United)

QUEST FOR THE LOST CITY (1990) ★ Independent, low-budget Canadian adventure film none too convincing in depicting how a young man (Christian Malcom) tracks his missing father to a place called Xeon where a devil cult is headed by a demonic guy named Satoris. Made as *The Final Sacrifice*, this cheapie has little to recommend. Brice Mitchell, Shane Marceau. Produced-directed in Alberta by T. Jardus Greidanus. (Action International) (Laser: Image)

QUEST FOR THE MIGHTY SWORD (1989) ★ Another pathetic entry in the Italian-produced Ator series, this time with the son of Ator (Eric Allen Kramer) on the march to free his mother Dejanira from a magical spell that has entrapped her within the Flame of Thorn, the devious work of an evil wizard who is assisted by dwarf creatures. But first, Ator must find the Treasure of the Kingdom of the West and destroy skeleton warriors as well as an unconvincing fire-breathing dragon that oozes different colors of blood when sliced by Ator's Mighty Sword of Sacred Thrall. Feeble direction by David Hills. Also known as *Ator III: The Hobgoblin*, although that title is incorrect since this is actually the fourth *Ator* movie. Margaret Lenzey, Donald O'Brien, Dina Morrone, Chris Murphy, Laura Gemser, Melissa Mell. (Video/Laser: RCA/Columbia)

QUEST FOR THE SEVEN CITIES. Video version of *Gold of the Amazon Women*. (Euro Scan)

QUEST OF THE DELTA KNIGHTS (1993) ★★ Sword-and-sorcery adventure in which the titular heroes fight a supernatural ruler with the help of secrets that can only be found in ruins of Atlantis. Directed by James Dodson. David Warner, Olivia Hussey, Corbin Allred, David Kriegel. (Hemdale)

QUIET EARTH, THE (1985) ★★★ Provocative, compelling morality tale that explores the end of civilization in a vein reminiscent of *The World, the Flesh and the Devil*. At 6:12 one Sunday morning everyone vanishes from the planet except Zac Hobson (Bruno Lawrence), a scientist working on Operation Flashlight, which apparently has altered and made unstable the fabric of the universe. The implication is that Zac refused to will himself to go to the Great Beyond with everyone else, and is now faced with the final destruction of Earth. But he's not alone—he finds a woman (Alison Routledge) and another man (Peter Smith) and a volatile relationship begins. This New Zealand film, based on the novel by Craig Harrison, was directed by Geoff Murphy. (Video/Laser: CBS/Fox)

RABID (1977) ★★½ Porn queen Marilyn Chambers has a wardrobe in this shocker (aka *Rage*) written-directed by Canadian horror king David Cronenberg. She's carrier of a blood disease that compels her to inject poison into victims through a phallic syringe in her armpit. Deodorant companies, take note. The mad-dog disease sends victims screaming and biting into the world. It's an epidemic of monumental proportions in downtown Montreal! Graphic effects are enough to make you foam at the mouth. Morbidly compelling, with unpleasant ending. Frank Moore, Joe Silver, Patricia Gage. (Warner Bros.)

RABID GRANNIES (1988) ★★★ Although released as a Troma film, this is a French-Belgian-Dutch production dubbed by a British cast. It's wild black comedy poking fun at the hypocrisy of the Catholic Church and human greed when a family gathers to celebrate the birthday of 2 grannies and ponders who will receive the family fortune. Retribution against the greedy ones comes when "grannies" become "whammies," bloodthirsty demons with claws. Family members, trapped in rooms of the estate, are murdered in horrendous ways while survivors bicker and seek escape. Writer-director Emmanuel Kervyn treats the demons with humor. One gets the feeling he's making a statement about gory American films. Whatever he's up to, it works. Catherine Aymerie, Caroline Braekman, Danielle Daven, Raymond Lescot. (Media) (Laser)

RACE WITH THE DEVIL (1975) ★★½ Only Jack Starrett's direction injects life into this chase chiller. Starrett, working with a script by Lee Frost and Wes Bishop, keeps the film keen with excitement when two married couples—vacationing in a trailer—accidentally witness a sacrificial murder during a satanic cult meeting. It's a hair-raising, tire-squealing pursuit with a large-scale conspiracy going down. But not even Starrett salvages the lousy ending. Warren Oates, Loretta Swit, Peter Fonda, Lara Parker, R. G. Armstrong. (CBS/Fox/Key)

RADAR MEN FROM THE MOON (1952) ★★★ Hero in a flying suit—Commando Cody, Sky Marshal of the Universe—jet-packs to the moon to discover a dictator (hammily played by Roy Barcroft, the great serial villain) using atomic weapons against Earth, in this rollicking 12-chapter Republic serial. George Wallace runs around in the rocket suit (first worn in *King of the Rocketmen*) against adversary Retik and his incompetent henchmen. If Commando Cody is your idol, see another serial in which he appears, *Zombies of the Stratosphere*, and *Commando Cody*, a compilation of episodes from a 1953 TV series. Directed by Fred C. Brannon, this is corny but wonderful campy fun. Aline Towne, Clayton Moore, Tom Steele. The TV-movie feature is *Retik, the Moon Menace*. (Republic; Burbank; Filmfax) (Laser: Republic)

RADAR PATROL VS. SPY KING (1949) ★★★

Slam-bang action serial, 12 chapters of it, from Republic cliff-hanger director Fred C. Brannon. The evil Baroda and his sexy accomplice, Nitra, sabotage radar defenses along the U.S. border, bringing into play the Electro Annihilator and death-producing Gamma Ray. Kirk (*Superman*) Alyn stars as government guy Chris Calvert. Chapter-play regulars Jean Dean, Anthony Warde, John Merton, Tristram Coffin, John Crawford. (Republic)

RADIOACTIVE DREAMS (1986) ★★ Somewhere in this mess is an idea for a movie that hasn't been made yet. It's the attempted funny side to *Mad Max* when missile-site watchmen Michael Dudikoff and John Stockwell dig to the surface on April 1, 2010 (a joke on us all?) to play private eyes Philip and Marlowe (detective stories being all they've read for years) in a post-holocaust world. What follows is a mishmash in which mutants, little boys in white suits (who keep saying "fuck"), and other grotesque survivors chase after two keys that will launch the only remaining atomic missile. Dudikoff and Stockwell run around Edge City in their BVDs while sexy Miles Archer (Lisa Blouton, a Sybil Danning rival) attempts to seduce the keys from them, and a dude named Dash Hammer pursues with a zap gun. Directed by Albert Pyun. George Kennedy and Don Murray have ridiculous roles. (Vestron) (Laser: Image)

RADIO FLYER (1992) ★★★ This grimly depicts children exposed to physical abuse from their stepfather, but concludes on a mystical twist that allows one battered youth to escape his pain. It's a wonderful movie about golden moments of adolescence and discovery of new marvels during a summertime of wide-eyed enchantment. Granted, these are difficult elements to reconcile, abuse and fantasy, and yet director Richard Donner and cinematographer Laszlo Kovacs capture the importance of a belief in the impossible, and David Mickey Evans's script (based on experiences as an abused child) is a delicate masterpiece. Lorraine Bracco portrays a single mother who takes her sons Joseph Mazzello and Elijah Wood to the California town of Novato in 1969. *Radio Flyer* has moments when the narration (read by Tom Hanks), the color photography and Hans Zimmer's music combine into moviemaking at its most powerful. The excellent cast includes Adam Baldwin as the drunken stepfather and John Heard as a sympathetic lawman. (Video/Laser: Columbia TriStar)

RADIOLAND MURDERS (1994) ★★★★½ Unfortunately a box-office flop, this is a bravura piece of zany filmmaking that captures the old-fashioned values that earmarked Hollywood's best movies during the '30s and '40s. It's a whacky one-night depiction of events in Chicago in 1939 when radio station WBN presents a premiere evening of programming, while a murderer runs wild through the studios killing off the station personnel, each dying in a new, bizarre way: poison, electrocution, shooting, etc. It has the craziness of a Howard Hawks movie, the slapstick of Laurel and Hardy and the crazed ingenuity of an Agatha Christie whodunit. These diverse elements are comedically blended by writers Willard Huyck, Gloria Katz, Jeff Reno and Ron Osborne, from an idea by producer George Lucas. And director Mel Smith establishes a wonderfully nonstop madcap pacing as characters rush to and fro, interspersed by parody bits of dramatic and musical radio of the period. A flashy cast has fun with the satirical material, starting with estranged husband-and-wife producing team Mary Stuart Masterson and Brian Benben, and cutting to goofy sound man Zoltan (Christopher Lloyd), station owner General Whalen (Ned Beatty), sexy showgirl Anita Morris (in her last role), Michael Lerner (as the hard-talkin', cigar-chompin' investigatin' cop) and Brion James as the growling sponsor. Don't miss this grand fun movie, with special effects by Lucas's Industrial Light & Magic. Guest appearances by Bo Hopkins, George Burns, Michael McKean, Corbin Bernsen, Harvey Korman and Bobcat Goldthwait. (Video/Laser: MCA)

RADIO PATROL (1937) ★★★ A new kind of steel is sought by a gang of criminals but a "radio cop" (Grant Withers) and a gal named Molly (Catherine Hughes) strut forward in boots and high heels or speed across the terrain in a "radio car" with a kid named Pinky (Mickey Rentschler) to prevent assorted dastardly deeds. This 12-chapter Universal serial was directed by Ford Beebe and Cliff Smith. Adrian Morris, Max Hoffman, Jr., Frank Lackteen. (Nostalgia; Vidmark; Mike Lebell's)

RADIO RANCH (1935). Feature-length video version of the serial *Phantom Empire* (Video Yesteryear).

RAGE. See *Rabid*.

RAGE (1984) ★ Italian *Mad Max* imitation offering brainless action and stupid plotting. Captain Rage is a survivor of nuclear apocalypse who goes into the "forbidden land" (nuked New Mexico?) to Alpha Base to find uranium to save mankind. His adversary, Sergeant Flash, pursues him into the "Land of the trembling rocks" where they fight it out in a climactic train chase. Styleless and witless, with inane dialogue that runs to such lines as "It won't be easy building up a new world, but there's no harm in trying." Wanna bet? (Un)directed by Anthony Richmond. Conrad Nichols, Steve Eliot.

RAGE (1995) ★★★ Terrific chase sequences, stunt work, and karate fights—the hallmarks of many Richard Pepin–Joseph Merhi films—highlight this exciting, edge-of-your-chair adventure with a *Fugitive*-like plot in which schoolteacher Gary Daniels is accidentally taken to a cloning laboratory (Westech Industries) as a guinea pig. In escape after thrilling escape, the innocent Daniels is pursued by government conspirators and crooked police, the action blazing all the while. Daniels harrowingly clings to the wall of a skyscraper; drives a big rig through police cars and thick traffic; fights it out with FBI guys in a video store in a shopping mall; and endures hair-raising adventures that incorporate spectacular stunts. A TV newsman (Kenneth Tigar) tries to help Daniels prove his innocence, and this adds to the suspense and tension of this fast-paced tour de force of filmmaking. Credit screenwriters Joseph John Barmettler and Jacobsen Hart, director Joseph Merhi, and a no-nonsense cast that continually gives this film bite. Don't miss it! Fiona Hutchison, Jillian McWhirter, Peter Jason. (PM Entertainment) (Laser: Image)

RAGE: CARRIE 2, THE (1999) ★★ *Carrie* was Brian De Palma's classic of 1975, one of the best movie adaptations of a Stephen King novel. It launched the careers of several newcomers and set new standards of visual shock effects as it spun the weird tale of teenager Carrie White, who possessed powers of telekinesis and used them lethally when she got ticked off at her high-school prom. So you have to ask yourself, why did they bother to make a sequel with such a lousy script by Rafael Moreu? The single element that carries over from the original is Amy Irving, the only woman in Hollywood who can say she *used* to be married to Steven Spielberg. In the original, she was a teenager sympathetic to Carrie's cause, and the only survivor of the violent prom-night attack. Now she's one of the adminstrators of Bates High School, where she suspects that a newcomer to the classrooms, Rachel Lang (played by Emily Bergl), might possess Carrie's terrible powers. You see, Rachel's father is the same dude who sired Carrie. That Bergl fails to bring any sense of the genuine fear that made Sissy Spacek's Carrie so compelling is just one element missing in this misguided follow-up. Moreu stacks the deck against Bergl by having her humiliated by a gang of high-school guys who take campus virgins to bed and then dump them. Director Katt Shea, an alumnus of the Roger Corman School of Filmmaking (how about *Hollywood Hot Tubs* and *Stripped to Kill*?), isn't all the rage handling this flick. She allows Bergl to behave so stupidly you want to scream at the screen. Where the original Carrie had some brains and class, this gal is brainless and classless. Of course, there is the climactic retribution sequence, when all the veins in Bergl's torso and arms expand and crisscross her flesh like dark rivulets. When her powers erupt, heads get sliced off, wriggling torsos are penetrated by jagged pieces of flying glass, and blood spills everywhere. A spear pinions two bodies to a door. A body burns. A cheerleader has her eyeballs burned to a crisp. The meanest guy in school gets his deserts in the gym swimming pool. The body count goes on, but in the vein of a slasher flick, not in the vein of a classic like *Carrie*. Will they never learn? Jason London, Dylan Bruno, J. Smith-Cameron. (Video/DVD: MGM)

RAGEWAR. See *The Dungeonmaster*.

RAGING ANGELS (1994) ★★½ Diane Ladd as a "Discerner" (one who sees angels and demons) is the only highlight of this otherwise boring and pointless supernatural rock drama. Watching her even in a silly role has its payoff. But the rest of this tale by Kevin Rock, David Markov and Chris Bittler is a boring series of musical numbers with added scenes of a burned-out musician (Sean Patrick Flanery) trying to save a pretty girl singer (Monet Mazur) from a fate worse than death from evil spirits. Costarring is Michael Pare, an evil evangelist type (and rock singer) for the Coalition for World Unity. The elements never really fit together. And the demon is your typical monster guy with glowing eyes who has a ridiculous sword battle with a good angel with flowing blond hair. I mean, really! Even the director took his name off and substituted the traditional "Alan Smithee." Arielle Dombasle, Shelley Winters (as Flanery's sweet old grandma who has prophetic dreams). (Vidmark)

RAIDERS OF ATLANTIS (1983) ★★★ Satisfying U.S.-Italian actioner, full of blazing machine-guns, exploding grenades, Molotov cocktails, and bodies falling from parapets. The salvaging of a Russian sub causes lost Atlantis to rise from the ocean just when Chris Connolly

and other soldiers of fortune are passing by. Out of nowhere appear mercenaries to restore Atlantis to its full glory. From then on the action is nonstop under the direction of Roger Franklin (Ruggero Deodato?). Mike Miller, Ivan Rassimov, John Blade, Bruce Baron. (Prism; Video Treasures)

RAIDERS OF THE LOST ARK (1981) ★★★★★ Dynamite team George Lucas (producer) and Steven Spielberg (director) created this homage to the cliff-hangers of yesteryear, accomplished with the flashy, dazzling production and effects expertise of the '80s. Lawrence Kasdan's script has all the clichés, and yet, since they have been unused for so long, they are like newfound gems. The excitement begins with archeologist-adventurer Indiana Jones (Harrison Ford) stealing a sacred stone from temple ruins in South America (actually Hawaii) and escaping death traps and angry natives before flying off in an airplane with a boa constrictor in the cockpit. Then the pacing really picks up when he and the heroine—tough chick Karen Allen—search for the lost Ark of the Covenant, which has a sinister power the Nazis covet. (This takes place in the 1930s.) There's a great snake-chamber sequence, a wild-and-woolly chase with Ford single-handedly battling a German truck convoy, and climactic special-effects hoopla when the Ark is opened and Pandora's demons are unleashed. The raw spirit of adventure is beautifully punctuated by John Williams's music. Ronald Lacey, John Rhys-Davies, Denholm Elliott, Paul Freeman. Sequels are *Indiana Jones and the Temple of Doom* and *Indiana Jones and the Last Crusade*. (Video/Laser: Paramount)

RAIDERS OF THE SUN (1992) ★½ Another one of those *Mad Max* rip-offs by a man who seems to have made a career out of them, Filipino director Cirio H. Santiago. In this one, Earth has undergone another biological Armageddon and so people have nothing better to do than ride around in oddball vehicles and fire superzap guns at each other. Richard Norton, Rick Dean, Blake Boyd. (New Horizons)

RAINBOW BRIDGE. See *The Little Prince and the Eight-Headed Dragon*.

RAIN KILLER, THE (1990) ★★½ A serial murderer strikes when it's raining, viciously slashing women who are ex–drug addicts. ("Round up the usual perverts," remarks a cop.) The twists and turns involve alcoholic cop Ray Sharkey and federal agent David Beecroft as they form an uneasy alliance to track the knife-wielding killer. Directed by Ken Stein. Michael Chiklis, Tania Coleridge, Woody Brown. (Video/Laser: RCA/Columbia)

RAISING CAIN (1992) ★★★½ One of Brian De Palma's better films—an unpredictable work that will have you hooked from the moment you meet Dr. Carter Nix, a schizophrenic madman (John Lithgow). There's no denying that De Palma is manipulative, but he pulls off this experiment in terror with such outrageous panache, you can only admire him for his creative gall. Lithgow gets to play Nix, Nix's evil alter ego, Nix's father and a female nurse. Produced by Gale Anne Hurd, *Raising Cain* uses all the gimmicks in the cinematic book and overcomes disturbing themes of serial murder, child kidnapping and a plethora of abnormal behavior to remain an entertainment designed to scare the daylights out of you. It will. Lolita Davidovich, Steven Bauer, Frances Sternhagen. (Video/Laser: MCA)

RAPTURE, THE (1992) ★★★ Fascinating if baffling parable about man's never-ending search for God, his belief in the hereafter and his salvation. This cosmic tale by writer-director Michael Tolkin uses an unhappy telephone operator (Mimi Rogers, in a tour de force performance) as a metaphor for that search. She's a woman who's wasted her life, indulged in group sex in her quest for love, and now, on the verge of becoming manic-depressive, "sees the light" and embraces Jesus. But her confusion reaches new heights when her husband is killed by a crazed gunman and she takes her daughter to Vasquez Rocks, there to wait for Christ's Second Coming. The Horsemen of the Apocalypse are soon on the horizon. This oddball movie, since it questions fundamental beliefs and depicts group sex as well as a murder, is a shocker, and certainly will not be to everyone's liking. Gutsy stuff. David Duchovny, Patrick Bauchau, Kimberly Cullum. (Video/Laser: Columbia TriStar)

RAPTUS, THE SECRET OF DR. HICHCOCK. See *The Horrible Dr. Hichcock*.

RASHOMON (1951) ★★★★ Japanese director Akira Kurosawa's masterpiece. Set in 8th-century Japan, it tells of 3 men (priest, woodchopper, servant) who take refuge from a storm under the gate of Rashomon, in the ruined city of Kyoto, where they discuss the recent murder of a Samurai warrior and the seduction of his wife by a bandit. In flashbacks, we see 5 versions of the same tragedy, including one told by the dead warrior through a medium. A compelling study of objective/subjective truth, of man's lust, greed and prejudice. Toshiro Mifune is the grunting, animalistic bandit and his performance is unforgettable. Hollywood remade this as *The Outrage*. (Embassy) (Laser: Voyager)

RASPUTIN (1996) ★★★½ An opulent, beautifully photographed TV-movie biography of Gregori Rasputin, the pseudopriest from Siberia who is brilliantly recreated by Alan Rickman in a tour de force performance, aided immensely by a literate Peter Pruce script. Director Uli Edel captures the rich palace atmosphere of the Czar's lifestyle and all the contradictions of Rasputin's wild and raucous character when he plunges into the world of power to help the ruler's sick son Alexei (who narrates the story in voiceover). Pruce suggests that Rasputin had minimal hypnotic and prescience powers, but was really a master of human psychology who misused his limited abilities to get what he wanted. If Rasputin was capable of hypnotism, Rickman is also hypnotic in his intense, crazed performance. The supporting cast (Greta Scacchi as the vulnerable Czarina, Ian McKellen as the confused Czar and David Warner as his aide de camp) give compelling performances. John Wood, James Frain, Ian Hogg, Sheila Ruskin.

RATBOY (1986) ★★½ This honorable attempt by actress-turned-director Sondra Locke, produced by Clint Eastwood's Malpaso company, is an American fairy tale about a human freak living in a garbage dump befriended by a journalist (Ms. Locke) who wants to exploit him. It's about our media-hungry culture, our penchant for exploitation and our lack of compassion for what is different. Whatever the good intentions, however, it remains an anomaly, trapped in a twilight zone of its own making. It's tough to sympathize with a half-rat person, no matter how cute Rick Baker has designed him. The story is finally self-defeating. Robert Townsend, Larry Hankin, Christopher Hewett. (Warner Bros.)

RATS, THE. See *Deadly Eyes*.

RATS. See *Rats: Night of Terror*.

RATS: NIGHT OF TERROR (1983) ★★★ Above-average Italian-French post-holocaust shocker starts in a *Mad Max* vein, then shifts to horror. In 225 A.B. (After the Bomb) the world is divided into an underground society and "primitives" roving the surface. A motorcycle gang led by Kurt (a Jesus Christ lookalike—this whole movie has a strange Biblical connection) finds a food cache in a desert town taken over by rats. How the rodents devour the characters (often from within, chewing their way to the surface) is the focus while the bikers go hysterical. A surprise ending works nicely. Director Vincent Dawn was going for something different in the genre. Richard Raymond, Richard Cross. (Lightning)

RATTLED (1996) ★★★ Veteran genre director Tony Randel does a fang-up job with this adaptation of Joseph Gilmore's novel *Rattlers* (scripted by Ken and Jim Wheat) by using every manipulative snake-and-mouse trick to make your skin crawl. When a blasting operation in the California foothills disturbs a huge den of rattlesnakes, the angry critters head for civilization, settling into the home of William Katt and Shanna Reed, among other domestic places. Randel puts the bite on you repeatedly in this thrilling TV-movie, enhanced by Ian Abercrombie's performance as a snake expert. It will strike you in all the right places. Ed Lauter, Bib Besch, Monica Creel, Clint Howard. (MCA)

RAVAGED. See *Blood Rose*.

RAVAGER (1997) ★★½ Although this direct-to-video sci-fi thriller has only mediocre special effects of spacecraft in flight, and a B-movie cast, *Ravager* sports an unusual script by director James D. Deck and Donald J. Loperfido that attempts, within its narrow scope, to deal with the state of mind of characters living in 2034 A.D. who are faced with moral decisions. The setting is a sunbaked region of Asia called Edmonds Wasteland, a secret U.S. government dumping grounds for a failed virus experiment called Ravager. A cargo shuttle rocketship crash-lands and one of the crew members (Yancy Butler) is exposed to the virus, which turns him into a homicidal killer. However, the murders and the bloody aftermath are minimal, with director Deck focusing strongly on his characters and using the voice-over technique to good effect. Robin Sachs adds an unusual twist as a synthetic being called a "Spare," created to be nothing more than a donor of organs to sick humans. It is her interactions with ship's captain Bruce Payne and copilot Juliet Landau that provide more substance than usual. Hard-core fans of gory action movies may be disappointed by Deck's less bloody approach to this genre; on the other hand, let's credit Deck with at least trying to expand the horizons of low-budget movies. Actor Robert Patrick is credited as a coproducer. Salvator Xuereb, David Stratton, Stanley Kamel. (Paramount)

RAVEN, THE (1935) ★★★ This has nothing to do with Poe's poem, but it does owe inspiration to Edgar Allan for torture devices used by mad doctor Bela Lugosi, a Poe-phile who turns to the master's literature to wreak vengeance. Boris Karloff has a sympathetic role playing a criminal disfigured by Lugosi as a form of blackmail. Unusually sadistic; a Universal period piece you want to see. Directed by Louis Friedlander, who later became Lew Landers, and written by David Boehm. Irene Ware, Samuel Hinds, Ian Wolfe. (Video/Laser: MCA, with *The Black Cat*)

RAVEN, THE (1963) ★★★★ The chemistry of Peter Lorre, Vincent Price and Boris Karloff results in a delightful horror parody. Price portrays a queasy magician who hears someone tapping, tapping, tapping at his 15th-century chamber door . . . yes, it's Poe's famous black bird with the refrain "Nevermore," but this bird has a quirk: it keeps transmuting into Lorre (or is it the other way around?). Producer-director Roger Corman winds up with a Duel of the Wizards—a classic piece of comedy and effects. Kudos to screenwriter Richard Matheson. Hazel Court, Jack Nicholson, Olive Sturgess. (Warner Bros.) (Laser: Image)

RAVEN DANCE. See *Mirror, Mirror II: Raven Dance*.

RAW FORCE (1982) ★½ Martial arts action thriller, in which adventurers set sail for Warriors' Island, where kung fu zombies await. Once Cameron Mitchell, Geoff Binney and Jillian Kessner are in action, it's shoot-outs and skull crashings. Directed-written by Edward Murphy. Jennifer Holmes, Robert Dennis. Aka *Shogun Island*. (Media)

RAWHEAD REX (1987) ★★½ On the surface, a "monster on a rampage" movie, depicting a creature that rises from the ruins of a fertility cult site and kills. However, this being set in Ireland and involving a church leads one to believe that screenwriter Clive Barker was saying something about the current religious war there. For example, in one scene the demon urinates on his disciple in a church graveyard. Barker has disavowed this film, probably because the monster design is less than exciting, and it pulls down the imaginative writing. David Dukes portrays the American yanked into the adventure with wife Kelly Piper and children while investigating "sacred sites" near Dublin. Many of the bloody murders are effective, and good cat-and-mouse sequences help build tension. Niall Toibin, Ronin Wilmot, Hugh O'Connor, Cora Luinny. Directed by George Pavlou. (Vestron) (Laser: Image)

RAW NERVE (1991) ★★ Serial killings performed in a room of mirrors cause Ted Prior to have nightmare visions, but policemen Glenn Ford and Jan-Michael Vincent pooh-pooh the information. The only sympathetic ear is reporter Sandhal Bergman's. Filmed in Mobile, Ala., this features Traci Lords and Randall "Tex" Cobb and Red West. Directed by Ted's brother, David A. Prior. (Video/Laser: Action International) (Laser: Image)

RAZORBACK (1983) ★★★ Australian import is one of the better imitations of *Jaws*, capturing a shivery element of fear. Here the ruthless predator is a killer boar stalking the Outback, so huge it crashes through walls and drags away victims into the desert. Gregory Harrison plays the husband of a TV reporter researching kangaroo poachers who is attacked by the razorback. Harrison and a big game hunter, whose baby was dragged off by the beast, join ranks to track the killer. Director Russell Mulcahy uses desert locations to great advantage, employing lights and shadows to capture an eeriness similar to the mood in *It Came from Outer Space*. Disturbing symbolism enhances the psychology of the horrors Harrison encounters, and the film makes a statement about man's inhumanity through the uncouth kangaroo hunters. Scripted by Everett De Roche. Bill Kerr, Chris Haywood, John Howard, David Argue. (Warner Bros.) (Laser: Japanese)

R.C.M.P. AND THE TREASURE OF GENGHIS KHAN (1948). TV-feature version of the Republic serial *Dangers of the Canadian Mounted*.

REACTOR. Video version of *War of the Robots* (Mogul).

RE-ANIMATOR (1985) ★★★★ Top-notch gore flick—disgustingly sickening as it panders terribly on one hand and amuses cleverly on the other. Smart filmmakers give us a send-up while satisfying vicarious, visceral needs. Although based on H. P. Lovecraft's stories about Herbert West, a resurrector of the dead, this is really George Romero–Herschell Lewis–Lucio Fulci in one. The Dennis Paoli–William J. Norris–Stuart Gordon script is outrageous: An intense, nerdish medical student (Jeffrey Combs) discovers a green serum that brings corpses to life. His main adversary is a sadistic, perverted doctor (David Gale) who has eyes only for Barbara Crampton, even after his head is severed. There are graphic encounters with the dead come-to-life, a scene where the doctor's head makes love to the heroine while she's strapped to a table, and a final crescendo of morgue black humor when cadavers attack, their intestines popping out and enwrapping the hero like a vengeful serpent. If it sounds grotesque, blame makeup men Anthony Doublin, John Naulin and John Buechler, and credit director Gordon. You'll "ugh" and "ahh" but you'll love it, perverted viewer that you are. (Vestron) (Laser: Image; Vestron)

REASON TO DIE (1989) ★★ Another slasher thriller in which cop Wings Hauser sets up his own girlfriend to trap the razor-wielding killer. Isn't that what girlfriends are for? Directed by Tim Spring. Liam Cundill, Anneline Kriel. (Video/Laser: Vidmark)

REBELLION OF THE DEAD WOMEN, THE. See *Vengeance of the Zombies*.

REBEL STORM. See *Rising Storm*.

RECKLESS KELLY (1993) ★★ This is Yahoo Serious's follow-up to *Young Einstein*, in which the Australian comedy actor–filmmaker, who has a penchant for the weird and the bizarre stretched to cartoonish slapstick extremes, portrays the spirit of outlaw Ned Kelly, now living on an island off Australia. He heads a band of good-guy outlaws who rob from evil bankers to give to the poor. Kelly is able to absorb bullets without injury—one of many silly premises on which this parody of Australian, British and American characters picks away at without subtlety. Serious sets out for Hollywood, Las Vegas and other points American on an odyssey of adventure to raise $1 million. If you like 'em whacky and out of control, by all means. Serious wrote-directed, seriously. Melorie Hardin, Alexei Sayle, Kathleen Freeman, Hugo Weaving, John Pinette. (Video/Laser: Warner Bros.)

RED BLOODED AMERICAN GIRL (1990) ★★ Heather Thomas's uninhibited role as a guinea pig (in an experiment to find a cure for AIDS) who is turned into an insatiable vampire is the only offbeat thing in this Canadian film with Christopher Plummer as an obsessed doctor in charge of Life Reach Foundation. Andrew Stevens is Dr. Owen Augustus Urban II, an expert in the unscrambling of the genetic code. Screenwriter Alan Moyle ends this scientific adventure on an upbeat note and director David Blyth sustains interest by focusing on the attractive body of Ms. Thomas in a torrid love scene with Stevens. Kim Coates, Lydie Denier (she in an all-too-brief sex scene). (Prism) (Laser: Image)

RED DAWN (1984) ★★★½ On a visceral level, this John Milius film is a patriotic depiction of U.S. guerrilla youths killing Soviet and Cuban troops who have invaded America. You'll be caught up in the mock heroics as the teenage Wolverines fire machine guns and rocket launchers, blowing away the Ruskie army. However, the politics of this movie are so scrambled, and the explanation of how the U.S. is invaded in a war of conventional weapons so unconvincing, the story falls apart when it attempts to justify its own militarism. Patrick Swayze heads the freedom fighters guided by blind hate, while enemy forces are commanded by William Smith, whose guile suggests an updated Fu Manchu. Powers Boothe is a downed jet pilot and Harry Dean Stanton and Ben Johnson are among captured Americans tortured or mowed down by firing squads. This will kick you in the guts or leave you cold with incredulity. (Video/Laser: MGM/UA)

RED DRAGON. See *Manhunter*.

REDEEMER, THE (1976) ★ Homosexual actor, lesbian bitch, unscrupulous attorney, athlete, rich woman, louse of a lover—these 1967 graduates of Stuart Morse Academy turn up at the creepy school to be imprisoned by a fiend who uses flamethrower, shotgun, swords and washroom basin to kill. It's never clear why this is happening and it's covered over with pseudo-religious overtones. Director Constantine S. Gochis offers nothing redeeming in *The Redeemer*. Nick Carter, T. G. Finkbinder, Jeanette Arnette, Michael Hollingsworth. Subtitled *Son of Satan!* (Genesis; from Continental and VCI as *Class Reunion Massacre*)

RED HANGMAN, THE. See *Bloody Pit of Horror*.

RED HOUSE, THE (1947) ★★★★½ Thanks to screenwriter-director Delmer Daves, and the theremin of composer Miklos Rozsa, this ranks as a superentertaining horror mystery. True, there are no ghosts or goblins, but the film reeks with a cursed atmosphere and Rozsa's music evokes dreaded things that not even the script suggested. (It is a score that should be listened to, and studied, by aficionados of film music.) Never has Edward G. Robinson been so tormented by the horrors of the past, and never have "the haunted woods" been filled with such foreboding. Lon McCallister, Judith Anderson, Rory Calhoun, Julie London. Based on a novel by George Agnew Chamberlain. Aka *No Trespassing*. (Goodtimes; Crown; Kartes; Congress; Filmfax; Sinister/C)

RED LIPS. See *Vampyres—Daughters of Darkness*.

RED MARK OF MADNESS. See *Hatchet for the Honeymoon*.

REDNECK COUNTY RAPE. See *Redneck Zombies*.

REDNECK ZOMBIES (1988) ★ Beer infected with radioactivity turns ale-swilling patrons into walking dead. What? Again? In "Entrailvision" yet. Directed by Pericles Lewnes. Lisa De Haven, W. E. Benson, William Decker. (Trans World)

REDNESS OF THE LIPS, THE. See *Vampyres—Daughters of Darkness*.

RED SIGN OF MADNESS, THE. See *Hatchet for a Honeymoon*.

RED SONJA (1986) ★★½ Sword-wielding heroine of Conan creator Robert E. Howard is brought to life by Danish model Brigitte Nielsen, who had never acted before. She does a creditable job under Richard Fleischer's direction. The plot is odyssey stuff (by Clive Exton and George MacDonald Fraser) as Red Sonja and a male counterpart (not Conan, but played by Arnold Schwarzenegger as if he were) seek a green crystal with destructive powers. Fantasy elements include a pet spider that purrs like a kitten and a viewing screen manipulated by a wizard as wicked as the way Nielsen handles her sword. Could have used more romance between Brigitte and Arnold, but they went for a PG rating. Sandahl Bergman, Paul Smith, Ronald Lacey. Music by Ennio Morricone. (Video/Laser: CBS/Fox)

RED TIDE, THE. See *Blood Tide*.

REFLECTING SKIN, THE (1991) ★★★ Philip Ridley, award-winning British painter and playwright of the macabre, wrote-directed this disturbing study of an 8-year-old (Jeremy Cooper) whose world is a compendium of horrors: a serial killer stalks his playmates, his mother and father are manic-depressives with suicidal tendencies, and a neighbor could be a vampire. This cold, indifferent universe is beautiful on the surface, but dark as a trip down a rabbit hole into Hell. It is a contrast of lovely cinematography and graphic horrors, and a film that taps into one's primal fears as it depicts a loss of innocence. Viggo Mortensen, Lindsay Duncan. (Video/Laser: Live)

REFLECTIONS OF MURDER (1974) ★★ TV-movie reworking of *Diabolique*, the French horror thriller directed by Henri-Georges Clouzot and based on the Pierre Boileau–Thomas Narcejac novel. In this version, which follows the major changes from the book Clouzot introduced, Joan Hackett and Tuesday Weld plot to kill cruel Sam Waterston, then face the wrath of his vengeful spirit—or so it seems. Directed by John Badham and written by Edward Hume and Lewis John Carlino. Remade as *House of Secrets* in 1993. (Republic)

REFRIGERATOR, THE (1991) ★★ Although this low budgeter produced in Ohio suffers from a crude style and nondescript production, it has a rather intriguing allegorical flavor, as if something deep is going on here (though you suspect it really isn't). It would appear that an apartment manager is Satan himself, renting a run-down flat to newlyweds David Simonds and Julia McNeal. They soon discover, to their horror and yours, that their refrigerator-freezer unit is actually the door leading to Hades, for occasionally it opens up to swallow a person whole, drip blood and create horrific hallucinations. The characters (including Juan the Plumber) are just eccentric enough to add to the strange appeal of this offbeat, metaphorical movie. Phyllis Sanz, Angel Caban. Written-directed by Nicholas Tony Jacobs. (Monarch)

REINCARNATION, THE. See *The Crimson Cult*.

REINCARNATION OF ISABEL, THE (1973) ★ Mickey Hargitay, one-time muscleman-husband of sex symbol Jayne Mansfield, stars in this Italian chiller about a castle where satanic monks resurrect a witch burned at the stake 400 years before. She has a strange appetite, this beautiful woman: she thrives on virgins' blood. From director Ralph Brown and writer Renato Polselli, the team that collaborated on *Delirium*. Aka *The Ghastly Orgies of Count Dracula, The Horrible Orgies of Count Dracula* and *Black Magic Rites—Reincarnations*. Whew! Rita Calderoni, Max Dorian, Consolata Moschera.

REINCARNATION OF PETER PROUD, THE (1975) ★★½ Faithful adaptation of Max Ehrlich's best-seller (Max did the script himself), but what works on paper doesn't always translate to screen. The climax is predictable and the pacing is slow under J. Lee Thompson's direction. Michael Sarrazin stars as a man suffering from nightmares who discovers he lived a former life in New England. He tracks down his heritage only to fall in love with his daughter from the previous lifetime. It gets a mite kinky at that point, with a masturbation scene that is erotic but tasteful. Margot Kidder, Jennifer O'Neill, Cornelia Sharpe, Debralee Scott, Steve Franken. (Vestron) (Laser: Image)

REJUVENATOR, THE (1988) ★★★ A perverse quality hangs over this twisted tale (aka *Rejuvenatrix*) of the search for eternal youth, in which screenwriters Simon Nuchtern and Brian Thomas Jones (the latter also directed) remind us we are better off to accept ourselves for what we are. Another asset to this grotesque but hypnotic film is John MacKay's performance as a misguided doctor searching for a youth serum. Jessica Dublin portrays an aging actress who finances MacKay's lab tests in hopes she can start a new movie career. But the serum creates a brain-eating monster and Jones indulges in disgusting effects of the gooey kind. An odd film that fascinates as it repels. James Hogue, Katell Pleven, Marcus Powell. (Sony) (Laser: Image)

REJUVENATRIX. See *The Rejuvenator*.

RELENTLESS (1989) ★★★ Intriguing psychokiller thriller in which Judd Nelson is "the Sunset Killer," who selects victims with his own last name who live on Sunset Boulevard and kills them at sunset. The murders are graphically unappealing (kitchen knife into stomach, piano wire around neck, gunshots to the chest, etc.) but the search by cops Robert Loggia and Leo Rossi is fascinating. Rossi is a New Yorker transplanted to the L.A. milieu and Loggia is the toughened old-timer. Nelson is portrayed as "the mundanity of death"—a wimpy-looking but well-trained killer. Director William Lustig does justice to the script by Jack T. D. Robinson. Meg Foster, Patrick O'Bryan, Mindy Seeger, Angel Tompkins. (Video/Laser: RCA/Columbia)

RELENTLESS II: DEAD ON (1991) ★★★ This sequel is up to the quality of the original, with Michael Schroeder taking the directorial reins. It's a hard-hitting tale of horror, murder and conspiracy. Driven, out-of-control cop Sam Dietz (again played by Leo Rossi), who solved the case of "the Sunset Killer" in *Relentless*, is on the trail of another serial killer—or so it appears. His manic behavior leads him into trouble: conflicts occur with ex-wife Meg Foster, FBI agent Ray Sharkey and hired assassin Miles O'Keefe. The murders are in slasher-movie style and supporting cast is strong. Dale Dye, Marc Poppel. (Video/Laser: Columbia TriStar)

RELENTLESS III (1992) ★★ This has all the makings for a bang-up third entry in the unrelenting *Relentless* series, again with maverick cop Sam Dietz (Leo Rossi, back for his third outing) in search of a diabolical serial killer. There's never any mystery about whodunit—these films are about cat-and-mouse games the killers play with Dietz, who instigates personal vendettas against his adversaries. This time the "repeater" is a charming snake played by William Forsythe. While there are twists during the unfolding, and writer-director James Lemmo brings tension to the characters, examines the emptiness of Dietz's personal life, and creates a sense of nihilistic inevitability, the film fails because of a miserably unsatisfactory ending. Robert Costanzo, Edward Wiley, Tom Bower, Savanah Smith Boucher. (Video/Laser: New Line)

RELENTLESS IV: ASHES TO ASHES (1994) ★★★ One of the best in this series, with Leo Rossi (also a coproducer) further exploring the character of self-styled cop Sam Dietz (harddriven but likable, and trying to be honest with his treatment of the law). This time he's got a female partner who gives him a hard time as he tracks a serial killer whose victims all have undergone near-death experiences. Dietz himself has such an experience—when he's stalked by the killer. But all for a reason that will keep you enthralled. The excellent script by Mack Sevi (which delves into Dietz's personal life) was directed by Oley Sassone. A nice build of mystery and character. Colleen Coffey, John Scott Clough, Christopher Pettiet, Ken Lerner.

RELIC, THE (1996) ★★★½ This is pure monster movie, with director Peter Hyams having a ball parading out all the material to fulfill fan expectations. Yes, the screenplay by Amy Jones, John Raffo, Rick Jaffa, and Amanda Silver (based on the Douglas Preston–Lincoln Child novel) does get awfully muddled at times with its pseudo-scientific explanations, but who cares when the monster is overwhelmingly good and the action nonstop? Even the setting is unusual: Chicago's Museum of Natural History, where a genetically altered creature is on a rampage, and what a rampage. Hundreds of characters are wiped out (and some die horrible deaths) as the gigantic thing storms around on the night of a museum gala that has brought the mayor (Robert Lesser) and dignitaries. It ends in disaster, with the partygoers trapped inside. Also trapped are evolutionary biologist Penelope Anne Miller; her father, scientist James Whitmore; cynical cop Tom Sizemore; and curator Linda Hunt. Escape via water-filled tunnels is enhanced by low-key lighting, and when the action erupts, it's spectacular. The scary monster effects, by Stan Winston, are capped by a memorable fire sequence. This is one to be savored and seen more than once. Clayton Rohner, Chi Muoi Lo, Thomas Ryan. (Video/DVD: Paramount)

REMARKABLE ANDREW, THE (1942) ★★★ A literate and entertaining World War II Paramount propaganda piece, handsomely directed by Stuart Heisler. Although it possesses the sensitivities of another time, the values that the film stands for still hold up and are worth reliving. William Holden, a whiz of a bookkeeper, discovers that his bank is up to fraud and wants to expose the bad-doers, but he's fired instead. Holden is helped by Andrew Jackson's ghost (Brian Donlevy in a role of gusto) to maintain integrity and fight corruption, as well as a jury panel of historic figures (à la *The Devil and Daniel Webster*). Ironically, this was adapted by Dalton Trumbo (from his own novel), who in later years was blacklisted. Ellen Drew is sweet as Holden's girl. Rod Cameron, Richard Webb. Aka *At Good Old Siwash*.

REMEMBER ME (1995) ★★★ As a psychological study of a woman who thinks she's going bonkers, this TV-movie adaptation of the Mary Higgins Clark supernatural-suspense novel (by Michael Norell and Robert Lenski) has a few good scenes that give Kelly McGillis the opportunity to play a real bitchy housewife. She and long-suffering hubby Cotter Smith have just moved into a small coastal town, into a mansion alleged to be haunted. But it's standard TV material, with its supernatural elements, unfortunately, playing second fiddle to a madness plot. Director Michael Switzer gets good mileage from his cast (especially from Shanna Reed as a realtor, Michael T. Weiss as a local resident accused of murdering his wife, and Stephen McHattie as the suspicious cop on the case).

REMOTE (1993) ★★½ Call this Charles Band video production "*Home Alone* Meets the *Remote-Control* Kid in *E.T.* Suburbia." Chris Carrara portrays a remote-control expert (he's great controlling toy helicopters, planes and other airborne craft) trapped in a model tract home with three bumbling hold-up men (John Diehl, Tony Longo, Stuart Fratkin). The kid uses his skills to outwit the foolish outlaws and win the heart of girlfriend Jessica Bowman. A yodeling puppet named Gunther, whom Carrara uses to good comic effect, is reminiscent of a creature from *Puppet Master*. A pleasant family picture written by Mike Farrow and directed with style by Ted Nicolaou. Richard Band provides a light-hearted score. (Paramount)

REMOTE CONTROL (1987) ★★ There's this new "sci-fi" video movie out on the market, *Remote Control*, supposedly made in the '50s, that depicts a wife slaughtering her husband with a futuristic sewing machine. However, anyone playing this hot flick on a VCR is instantly turned into a maniacal killer. Video store employee Kevin Dillon gets wise and with girlfriend Deborah Goodrich tracks the filmmakers to a studio where employees are under the control of alien invaders. This comment on video and what it's doing to minds and libidos is from writer-director Jeff (*Squirm*) Lieberman. Christopher Wynne, Jennifer Tilly. (Video/Laser: IVE)

REMO WILLIAMS: THE ADVENTURE BEGINS (1985) ★★½ Loose adaptation of the Warren Murphy–Richard Sapir "Destroyer" novels, scripted by Christopher Wood and directed by Guy Hamilton. Despite an incredible premise (one-time New York cop undergoes plastic surgery to assume new identity to work for clandestine government operation that fights evil forces), this is an engaging fantasy adventure. As Remo Williams (a name selected off a bedpan), Fred Ward portrays a dour, slightly likable

hunk who trains with 80-year-old Chiun, a Korean played by Joel Grey. Chiun teaches Remo to dodge bullets, scale walls, climb the Statue of Liberty and other feats of derring-do (would you believe walking on water?). Plot: Industrialist Charles Cioffi misappropriates U.S. funds for a "Star Wars" spaceware program. The action is rousing (especially the Statue of Liberty sequence) and there are mock heroics aplenty. Wilford Brimley and J. A. Preston are secretive government men and Kate Mulgrew the minimal love interest. (Video/Laser: HBO)

REPO MAN (1984) ★★★½ Outré blending of punk rock imagery and surrealistic sci-fi by British writer-director Alex Cox. Emilio Estevez is a punker wandering through industrial sections of L.A., searching for meaning to his nihilistic existence, when he teams with Harry Dean Stanton, a cynic who repossesses cars. Meanwhile, there's a 1964 Chevy Malibu driven by a crazed nuclear scientist who has stolen alien corpses from a government lab and hidden them in the trunk. Cox blends the seamy slice of life with metaphysical fantasy into this offbeat meringue of genres. Produced by "Monkee" Michael Nesmith. Tracey Walter, Sy Richardson, Jennifer Balgobin. (Video/Laser: MCA)

REPOSSESSED (1990) ★★ Freewheeling, uninhibited parody of *The Exorcist* with Linda Blair playing a comedy counterpart to her vomit-spewing Regan. Either you'll enjoy this olio of non sequiturs, visual puns, regurgitation gags and other juvenile comedy or you'll find it hopelessly lame-brained. Probably the latter as the genuinely funny bits are far between in director Bob Logan's anything-goes script. However, Blair and Leslie Nielsen (he as the exorcising priest) enjoy themselves, especially Nielsen as he hams it up singing and dancing. Ned Beatty seems less certain as a TV evangelist. Jennifer Daniel, Noel Willman, Ray Barrett. In cameos are Jack LaLanne, Wally George, Army Archerd. (Live) (Laser: Image)

REPULSION (1965) ★★★★ Director Roman Polanski's masterpiece of psychological horror will unmercifully grip you. For the entire movie you are in the mind of Catherine Deneuve, a demented woman on a killing spree in her apartment. The reasons are not explained, only visually hinted at. Catherine is possessed by a frightening form of madness—you sympathize with her, even after she commits heinous crimes. The detail is realistic, the setting is stark, the music by Chico Hamilton and Gabor Szabo captures a mood of mental aberration. This is about the horrors of the mind. Polanski wrote the script with Gerard Brach. (Studio Entertainment; Video Dimensions; Film Classics; Global Media) (Laser: Voyager/Criterion)

REST IN PEACE. See *One Dark Night*.

REST IN PIECES (1987) ★★ After daffy aunt

Dorothy Malone commits suicide by taking cyanide while performing her will on a tape, young marrieds Loren Jean Vail and Scott Thompson Baker inherit her mansion and $8 million in missing money. At the estate, they discover everyone—from the maid to a minister—is homicidal, having joined Malone's zombie cult by committing suicide in exchange for eternal life. This tale takes too long to get going, but once the murderous creepos go into action, and Ms. Vail runs through corridors going bonkers, it's not bad. Directed by Joseph Braunstein with a penchant for showing off the shapely form of Ms. Vail as she sinks ever deeper into paranoia. Jack Taylor, Patty Shepard, David Rose. (Video/Laser: IVE)

RESURRECTED, THE (1992) ★★★ A dandy horror film and one of the better adaptations of H. P. Lovecraft. Screenwriter Brent V. Friedman borrows from "The Case of Charles Dexter Ward" and in the hands of director Dan O'Bannon it's a winner. Providence, R.I., private eye John March (John Terry) is hired by beautiful Jane Sibbett to find out why hubby Chris Sarandon is behaving so strangely. What March finds is that an ancestor of Sarandon, a wicked wizard, has taken over his body and is conducting experiments in giving life to dead beings. Todd Masters's effects depict half-decayed cadavers that are very much alive; one scene features the flesh being stripped off one body and reapplied to another; and the subterranean pit sequence is memorable. Good music score by Richard Band. Robert Romanus, Laurie Briscoe. Aka *Shatterbrain*. (Video/Laser: Live)

RESURRECTION (1980) ★★★ Ellen Burstyn is a Kansan who almost dies in an auto crash, undergoing an out-of-body experience in which dead figures beckon for her. Back among the living she is endowed with healing powers. Lewis John Carlino's script deals with faith healing without copping out, and Daniel Petrie directed with conviction. Even though this was nominated for several awards, it died at the box office. Sam Shepard, Eva Le Gallienne. (Video/Laser: MCA)

RESURRECTION (1999) ★★★ After *Adrenalin: Fear the Rush*, undoubtedly the lowest point in the career of Christopher Lambert, it's a relief to see him returning to the league of good B movies. And this is a good one, an intense serial-killer gorethriller not for the faint of heart. Lambert is a powder keg always about to explode, a whirlwind of emotional anguish as Chicago cop John Prodhomme, who with partner Leland Orser is hot on the trail of "The Numbers Killer," a fiend who takes one body part from each of his victims and leaves lamb's blood smeared all over the murder scenes. The screenplay by Brad Mirman (with story assist from Lambert) is a direct steal of *Seven*, but it smartly goes off on its own grisly pathways through the Windy City. Lambert, who is recovering from the auto-accident death of his son, and has rejected God and almost seems suicidal, must use his knowledge of the Bible to piece together the clues that lead him to believe the killer is planning to assemble a whole body from all the severed parts in time for Easter. (Director David Cronenberg pops up in a cameo as Lambert's priest.) The clues are cleverly designed and director Russell Mulcahy captures Lambert's chaotic state of mind with a constantly moving camera and frequent cutting. The stark cinematography is perfect for the bloody murder scenes where little graphic detail is spared. The identity of the killer (Robert Joy) is revealed halfway through, so the latter half of the film deals with the cops trying to get the evidence to hold him and a chase through a Chicago train depot. Also partly filmed in Toronto, *Resurrection* certainly resurrects the career of Lambert and Mulcahy. Let's hope it's not too big a cross to bear. Rick Fox, Barbara Tyson, Peter MacNeill, Jonathan Potto, James Kidnie, Philip Williams. (Columbia TriStar)

RETALIATOR, THE. See *Programmed to Kill*.

RETIK THE MOON MENACE. Feature version of the serial *Radar Men from the Moon*.

RETRIBUTION (1987) ★★½ The spirit of a man brutally shot and set on fire inhabits the body of a quiet, depressed hotel resident just as he leaps to suicidal death. Dennis Lipscomb returns to life, unaware his body is possessed, and that the spirit goes on nocturnal jaunts to avenge the fiery, bloody murder. This supernatural thriller almost reaches a point of total revulsion when a victim is cut down the middle by a meat saw. *Retribution* never recovers after that, and distances itself from empathy, producer-writer-director Guy Magar allowing his story to remain nihilistic. Leslie Wing is okay as a psychologist, but Hoyt Axton is wasted as a cop. Suzanne Snyder, Jeff Pomerantz, George Murdock. (Virgin Vision) (Laser: Image)

RETROACTIVE (1997) ★★★ This is a smooth blend of sci-fi time-travel paradoxes and suspenseful desert action from director Louis Morneau. He has a firm grip on the intriguing screenplay by Michael Hamilton-Wright, Robert Strauss, and Phillip Badger, who aren't afraid to play around with some fascinating ideas within the framework of a pure thriller. Police psychiatrist Kylie Travis is traveling down a lonely road in Texas when her car breaks down and she reluctantly accepts a ride with hostile redneck James Belushi (who gives a good bad-ol'-boy performance) and wife Shannon Whirry, who appears to be a manic-depressive. Witness to Belushi flipping out and murdering Whirry in cold blood, Travis flees for her life and ends up in an underground installation (the Texas Super-

Collider Accelerator Project) where nerdy scientist Frank Whaley is conducting time-travel experiments. To see if she can't alter events by tampering with time flow, Travis goes back 20 minutes in time—but in taking steps to prevent Whirry's homicide, she only makes things worse when Belushi and two accomplices in a computer-chip smuggling operation (store owner Walsh and local Hispanic Borrego) muck things up and cause the death of an intervening highway cop (Sherman Howard). Through a series of convoluted events, Travis ends up back in the government center and convinces Whaley to let her go through the time portal twice more. Each time the outcome of the situation is altered by newly introduced death and destruction. How Travis, after fumbling the ball so terribly, resolves the dire situation once and for all makes for a cool, flip action movie that never lets up for a moment during its jam-packed 91 minutes. Filmed on desert locations around Palmdale and Lancaster in Southern California, *Retroactive* has a polished, slick look and features excellent car crashes and explosions. Special note should be made of Belushi's performance. Although he's asked to portray a heavy without subtleties, he does an outstanding job. And Travis is always believable in a role that demands she blast away with a semiautomatic pistol on several occasions and take a lot of falls and rolls. She conveys an intensity that you can really get into, and it helps to make the movie whiz along. (Orion)

RETURN, THE (1980) ★★ UFO hovers over a desert community, bathing a boy and girl in eerie light and fog. Years later he's a deputy marshal, she's a satellite research expert. Man meets woman in town while she's investigating strange emanations from rocks. There's also a crazed prospector responsible for cattle mutilations with his laser-beam killer gun. Low-budgeter from producer-director Greydon Clark lacks high-tech clout. Jan-Michael Vincent (deputy), Cybill Shepherd (research expert), Raymond Burr (Cybill's scientist dad), Vincent Schiavelli (crazy miner), Neville Brand (sarcastic rancher), Martin Landau (stupid marshal). Aka *Earthright* and *The Alien's Return*. (Thorn EMI)

RETURN FROM THE PAST (1966) ★ Dreadful anthology of stories about vampires, werewolves, walking dead, etc.—in short, scrapings from the dregs in the bottom of the horror barrel. This cheapie, directed by David L. Hewitt from stories by Gary Heacock, David Prentiss and Russ Jones, looks like it was performed by a fourth-rate acting troupe with props and wardrobe left over from a school play. Released as *Dr. Terror's Gallery of Horrors* and aka *Alien Massacre, The Blood Drinkers* and *The Blood Suckers*. Should be returned to the past under any title. John Carradine, Lon Chaney, Jr., Ro-

chelle Hudson, Roger Gentry. (S/Weird; from Academy as *Gallery of Horrors*)

RETURN OF BATMAN. See *Batman and Robin*.

RETURN OF BLACKENSTEIN. See *Blackenstein*.

RETURN OF CAPTAIN AMERICA. See *Captain America* (1944).

RETURN OF CAPTAIN MARVEL. Feature-length version of the Republic serial *The Adventures of Captain Marvel*.

RETURN OF CAPTAIN NEMO, THE. See *The Amazing Captain Nemo*. (Boggling, not amazing!)

RETURN OF CHANDU (THE MAGICIAN), THE (1934) ★ Serial with Bela Lugosi as Chandu the Magician (popular radio hero of the '30s) who goes up against the black magic cult of Ubasti on the isle of Lemuria. Dreary, outdated material in need of action, pacing and decent acting. Directed by Ray Taylor, scripted by Barry Barringer. Maria Alba, Clara Kimball Young. Feature versions are *The Return of Chandu* and *Chandu on the Magic Island*. Aka *Chandu's Return*. (On video in serial form from Captain Bijou and Sinister/C; from Rhino as *The Return of Chandu the Magician*)

RETURN OF COUNT YORGA, THE (1971) ★★★ The success of *Count Yorga—Vampire* dictated this sequel, Robert Quarry again portraying the bloodsucker who runs amok in California. Now there's better acting thanks to Mariette Hartley, Roger Perry, Walter Brooke, Yvonne Wilder (as a deaf mute) and George Macready. And director Bob Kelljan has greater control, providing frightening moments when corpses attack an orphanage near San Francisco. Bill Butler's cinematography is high-class. Once again Michael Macready (George's son) produced. Screenplay by Kelljan and Wilder. Aka *The Abominable Count Yorga* and *Curse of Count Yorga*. (Orion)

RETURN OF DR. MABUSE, THE (1961) ★★★ Well-produced Italian-French-German sequel to Fritz Lang's films of the '30s and the 1960 *The Thousand Eyes of Dr. Mabuse*, depicting an ingenious madman bent on conquering the world. Inspector Lohmann (Gert Frobe) and FBI man Lex Barker join reporter Daliah Lavi to prevent the archvillain (Wolfgang Preiss) from infiltrating a nuclear plant and controlling employees' minds. Interesting, but not up to Lang's originals or the books by Norbert Jacques. Directed by Harald Reinl. Fausto Tozzi, Werner Peters. Aka *Phantom Fiend, In the Steel Net of Dr. Mabuse, In the Steel Cabinet of Dr. Mabuse* and *The Phantom Meets the Return of Dr. Mabuse*. Next came *The Testament of Dr. Mabuse, Dr. Mabuse vs. Scotland Yard, The Secret of Dr. Mabuse* and *The FBI vs. Dr. Mabuse*. (Sinister/C; S/Weird; Filmfax)

RETURN OF FRANKENSTEIN, THE. Early title for *The Bride of Frankenstein*.

RETURN OF GIANT MAJIN, THE (1966) ★★

Clomping time again for that ancient god of war who inhabits a stone statue and goes around crushing the worst offenders in a medieval feud. In this sequel to *Majin, Monster of Terror*, production values are good and the action is well staged. Directed by Kenji Misumi and Yoshi-yuki Kuroda. Third film in the series was *Majin Strikes Again*. Kojiro Hongo, Shiho Fujimura. Aka *The Return of Majin*.

RETURN OF GODZILLA. See *Gigantis, the Fire Monster*.

RETURN OF JAFAR, THE (1994) ★★★ This sequel to Walt Disney's 1992 animated hit *Aladdin*, made for home video, brings back the same character lineup and whacky sense of humor, but no matter how hard this cartoon tries, it lacks the comedic impact of its predecessor. *Return of Jafar* has many visually clever moments, but without Robin Williams as the voice of the zany genie, it falls short. In this adventure, the evil wizard Jafar escapes from his bottled imprisonment and plots his revenge against Aladdin. Voices by Jonathan Freeman, Gilbert Gottfried, Jason Alexander and Liz Callaway. Directed by Toby Shelton, Tad Stones and Alan Zaslove. (Video/Laser: Walt Disney/Image)

RETURN OF MAJIN, THE. See *The Return of Giant Majin*.

RETURN OF MAXWELL SMART. See *The Nude Bomb*.

RETURN OF MR. H. See *They Saved Hitler's Brain*.

RETURN OF SWAMP THING, THE (1989) ★★ Another comic-book movie from Jim Wynorski, one-time PR man for Roger Corman. The tragic qualities of the original Berni Wrightson–Len Wein comic-book character are forsaken as the creature is used as a springboard device for a tongue-in-cheek comedy. Managing a straight face, Louis Jourdan reprises his role as Dr. Arcane from the 1981 Wes Craven vehicle, conducting new genetic experiments à la H. G. Wells's Dr. Moreau in his antebellum mansion. There's talent here—lovely, sexy Heather Locklear, attractive, exotic Sarah Douglas, Ace Mask as a silly doctor, and Joey Sagal as a security guard. What passes for a story has Swamp Thing (stoically played by Dick Durock in a rubber suit) always at the site of trouble, ready to rescue someone. The attempt at a romance between Swampy and Heather is ludicrous. . . . If only this had tried to equal the melancholic, tragic feel of the comics. (Video/Laser: RCA/Columbia)

RETURN OF THE ALIEN'S DEADLY SPAWN (1983) ★★ An E.T. monster, ripped out of *Alien*, crash-lands on Earth in a meteor and proceeds to a dank cellar where it opens its toothsome mouth and swallows up the first person it sees. It's an ugly creation, surrounded by smaller mouths, with tadpolelike babies on the rafters and swimming through greasy puddles. Pretty soon the mother ejects a half-eaten head, which the infants swarm over, devouring with (hamburger?) relish. The only intelligent cast member is a kid who loves horror movies, so he figures out a homemade weapon to combat the gobbling mouth-thing. Very grotesque and poorly shot in 16mm. Obscure is writer-director Douglas McKeown. Aka *The Deadly Spawn*. (Continental)

RETURN OF THE APE MAN (1944) ★ Not that it matters, but this is not a sequel to *The Ape Man*. Bela Lugosi and John Carradine bring a prehistoric Neanderthal out of its deep freeze—a hairy caveman who loves to run amok, a non-social trait they exorcise by giving him the brain of George Zucco. The result is a cultured, refined gentleman who plays "Moonlight Sonata" . . . and then goes on a rampage. All-time low for the cast. Sam Katzman and Jack Dietz produced for Monogram; Phil Rosen directed the script by Robert Charles. (Media; on a "Double Bill" Nostalgia Merchant video with *Fog Island*)

RETURN OF THE BLIND DEAD (1973) ★★ Spanish sequel to *The Blind Dead* (aka *Tomb of the Blind Dead* and *Attack of the Blind Dead*) directed by Amando de Ossorio, with Tony Kendall. This "walking dead" series includes *Horror of the Zombies* and *Night of the Seagulls* (aka *Night of the Death Cult*). (Genesis; from JEF and Bingo as *Return of the Evil Dead*)

RETURN OF THE EVIL DEAD. Video version of *Return of the Blind Dead* (Bingo; JEF Films).

RETURN OF THE FAMILY MAN (1990) ★ Another interpretation of *The Stepfather*'s theme, with Ron Smerczak as a man who wipes out families whenever the mood strikes him. Made in South Africa, this was directed by John Murlowski. Liam Cundill, Terence Reis, Debra Kaye. (Raedon)

RETURN OF THE FLY (1959) ★★★ Underrated sequel to *The Fly*, with a scientist's son (Brett Halsey) picking up the experiment in teleportation where dead old Dad left off. With stark black-and-white photography by Brydon Baker, director Edward L. Bernds evokes some horrifying moments in a mortuary and keeps things buzzing. George Langelaan's story gimmick—transposition of body parts on human and fly, so tiny fly has human head and huge human has huge fly's head—is repeated by Bernds (he also scripted), indicating there was nothing new to be achieved in this sequel. But it's still a nice low-budget film. Vincent Price, Dan Seymour, John Sutton. (Video/Laser: CBS/Fox)

RETURN OF THE GIANT MONSTERS, THE. See *Gamera vs. Gaos*.

RETURN OF THE JEDI (1983) ★★★★½ Third in the *Star Wars* series, culminating the middle trilogy of George Lucas's proposed 9-part saga. *Jedi* resolves the cliff-hangers in *The Empire Strikes Back* and moves faster than Imperial fighters as Luke Skywalker, Princess Leia, Chewbacca, Lando Calrissian and that Laurel-and-Hardy team in space, R2D2 and C3PO, penetrate the fortress of vile bandit Jabba the Hutt (a giant toad creature) to rescue Han Solo's carbonized body. After a marvelous opening, featuring a menagerie of E.T.s and a hair-raising battle aboard Jabba's land barge, our heroes are off to fight the Empire, personified by Darth Vader and the Emperor (looking like a wicked wizard) and several thousand storm troopers. Ken Ralston's team at Industrial Light & Magic perfected its equipment so that the effects are great. There's mind-boggling space hardware whizzing past the camera, and a fabulous chase on air bikes through a forest. Phil Tippett's otherworldly beings are a delight to terrestrial eyes. In addition to nonstop action, die-hard fans will be intrigued by Luke's quest for his heritage. It's a mythological duel of good vs. evil in its purest form and elevates Lawrence Kasdan's script, often guilty of banal dialogue and indifference to the characters. Director Richard Marquand goes for the glossy and bright; hence, this doesn't have the pessimism Irvin Kershner brought to *Empire*, and it ends on an upbeat note in the camp of the Ewoks, a race of cuddly creatures who help fight the Empire. A superexciting superpicture. Mark Hamill, Carrie Fisher, Harrison Ford, Peter Mayhew, Billy Dee Williams, David Prowse, Anthony Daniels. (Video/Laser: CBS/Fox)

RETURN OF THE KILLER TOMATOES (1988) ★★★ This sequel to the 1979 sci-fi farce, remembered more for its title than its content, is quite dumb—and a lot of fun. It's played for broad comedy and spends more time satirizing TV commercials and advertising than malevolent love apples. This silly romp, directed by John DeBello, has a thin story built around mad Professor Gangreen (John Astin) who turns a tomato into a sexy woman (Karen Mistal) by exposing it to music. Mistal gets mixed up with the hero of the first movie (Anthony Starke), now a pizza parlor owner, and with the help of an investigator in a cowboy suit, a scuba diver, a guy parodying John Belushi from Spielberg's *1941* and a benevolent little tomato nicknamed "F. T.," they race around San Diego like stooges. Somehow a charming little film emerges from the hodgepodge. George Clooney, Steve Lundquist, Charlie Jones. (New World) (Laser: Image)

RETURN OF THE LIVING DEAD, THE (1985) ★★★ Dan O'Bannon, author of *Alien* and *Dead and Buried*, makes his directorial debut with this spin-off from *Night of the Living Dead*

and spoofs the genre without sacrificing shocks, making this superior black-comedy horror (O'Bannon scripted too). In a warehouse for the world's oddities are U.S. military cannisters rumored to contain corpses inflicted with a plague from space (there are references to George Romero's 1967 movie). A malfunction frees a corpse and causes a toxic rain to fall on Resurrection Cemetery. Next, the walking dead are everywhere. Absolutely hysterical (if you have a morbid sense of humor) with thrills in the Romero tradition. O'Bannon is to be commended. And thanks also goes to Clu Gulager, James Karen, Beverly Randolph, Thom Mathews and Don Calfa for giving verisimilitude to the wild, woolly fun. (HBO; Hemdale) (Laser: Image)

RETURN OF THE LIVING DEAD PART II (1987) ★★½ This isn't half as much fun as part I. It duplicates the effects of the first film without exploring the themes in any novel ways, and it never builds up steam. No suspense, no surprises. This time one of those deadly cannisters falls out of an Army truck (Toxic and Hazardous Waste Unit), spreading its gas to a graveyard. Out of the ground pops an army of shambling dead people, eager for "Brains! More brains!" It's finally a small band of survivors escaping in a cherry-red Chevy. The cast standout is Philip Bruns as a goofy doctor who has the funniest lines in the picture and mugs for all he's worth, knowing there is no better way to play this material. Written-directed by Ken Wiederhorn. James Karen, Thom Mathews, Michael Kenworthy, Marsha Dietlein, Dana Ashbrook. (Lorimar) (Laser: Image)

RETURN OF THE LIVING DEAD III (1993) ★★★½ Not since *Re-Animator* has a gore-horror film had the impact and the style of this masterpiece of grisliness. The credit must go to producer-director Brian Yuzna as he maintains an unrelenting pace and builds the horror in calculating steps, taking the graphic effects to new heights as this bloody spine-chiller unfolds. J. Trevor Edmond portrays a young man whose military father (Kent McCord) is involved in the latest experiments with Trioxin, the gas that brings the dead to life. In a secret lab, the new horrors unfolding are witnessed by Edmond and girlfriend Mindy Clarke. Soon, both are caught up in the ghastliness of events, trapped in an old sewer as the walking dead (who must dull the terrible pains they feel by eating human brains) close in. The last 20 minutes feature a gallery of human corpses on the move, and the effect is riveting. This is one gore flick that really pays off, thanks also to a well thought-out script by John Penney. Sarah Douglas assists as an uptight militarist who wants to use the living corpses as combat troops. James T. Callahan,

Sal Lopez, Mike Moroff, Basil Wallace. (Video/Laser: Vidmark)

RETURN OF THE TEXAS CHAINSAW MASSACRE. See *Texas Chainsaw Massacre: The Next Generation*.

RETURN OF THE TIME TRAVELERS, THE. See *The Time Travelers*.

RETURN OF THE WOLFMAN, THE. See *The Craving*.

RETURN OF THE ZOMBIES. Video version of *Beyond the Living Dead* (Wizard).

RETURN OF WALPURGIS. See *Curse of the Devil*.

RETURN TO HORROR HIGH (1987) ★★½ Because unsolved murders occurred at Crippen High in 1982, a film crew uses the abandoned institution to make a horror pic. This is not a sequel to *Horror High* but rather another belabored spoof of *Friday the 13th*, with a penchant for thinking that buckets of spattering blood is something to laugh about. The story is told within a flashback framework and the plot mixes reality with movie fantasy, which might have been amusing had it all fit together, which it doesn't. Vincent Edwards portrays a biology professor dissected like one of his frogs. Alex Rocco has a few funny moments as a sleazy producer but this is a series of juvenile, unscary gore gags with mediocre characters. Bill Froehlich wrote-directed. George Clooney, Scott Jacoby, Pepper Martin, Panchito Gomez. (New World) (Laser: Image)

RETURN TO OZ (1985) ★★★½ Admirable attempt by Disney to recapture the flavor of the adventures of Dorothy in Oz (as originally conceived by L. Frank Baum) was a box-office failure, which critics decried for its somber tone and its failure to be as charming and appealing as the 1939 MGM musical. All that aside, it's an imaginative if slow-paced sequel, following Dorothy as she is subjected to the electrical machine of a doctor (Nicol Williamson) and nurse (Jean Marsh) trying to cure her of insomnia caused by her first adventure in Oz. She awakens in the fanciful kingdom with a talking chicken named Billina and joins with Tik Tok, a mechanical robot, Jack Pumpkinhead and a moose head named Gump. They must free the Emerald City inhabitants, frozen into marble statues by the evil gnome king and his queen, Princess Mombi (also played by Marsh). Memorable sequences include the Wheelers, cackling jokers who move about on wheels, and a chamber where the princess keeps heads encased behind glass. The effects are good, especially Will Vinton's Claymation, a process of animating the rock faces. There's more production quality than zip to Walter Murch's direction, but don't be put off by the bad word of mouth. Fairuza Balk is a good Dorothy, Piper Laurie appears as Aunt Em, and Matt Clark is Uncle Henry. The dark side to *The Wizard of Oz*. (Video/Laser: Disney)

RETURN TO SALEM'S LOT, A (1987) ★★★½ Enjoyable vampire-horror sequel (unofficial) to Stephen King's *Salem's Lot*, directed by Larry Cohen, who collaborated on the script with James Dixon. Anthropologist Michael Moriarty resettles in the New England vampire community with estranged son Ricky Addison Reed and their relationship is at the core of this film—each is a loser in life, lured too easily into the world of the vampires, and each recognizes the other's fragilities. Another unusual treat is the presence of filmmaker Samuel Fuller, who plays Van Meer, a Nazi hunter turned vampire killer who has some wonderfully esoteric dialogue as he rushes through the town, staking monsters to death. Leading the vampire coven is Andrew Duggan aided by June Havoc, Evelyn Keyes and Ronee Blakley. (Warner Bros.)

RETURN TO THE HORRORS OF BLOOD ISLAND. See *Beast of Blood*.

RETURN TO THE LOST WORLD (1992) ★★★½ Very good adaptation of the famous Professor Challenger fantasy adventure by Sir Arthur Conan Doyle, with John Rhys-Davies giving a vigorous performance as Challenger and David Warner equally effective as his rival. They join ranks in this Canadian film (made in Zimbabwe by producer Harry Alan Towers) with reporter Eric McCormic, photographer Tamara Goeski, young stowaway Darren Peter Mercer and native girl Nathania Stanford to discover prehistoric life on a plateau in Africa. Peter Welbeck's telescript is slanted for family viewing and has modern save-the-species overtones. Directed by Timothy Bond. Aka *The Lost World*. (Worldvision)

REUNION (1996) ★★★ An intense psychological study of a young mother's deterioration and descent into morbidity highlights this TV-movie based on Linda Gray Sexton's novel *Points of Light*. The adaptation by Ronald Bass and John Pielmeier zeros in on the mental illness of Marlo Thomas after her five-year-old son suffocates, and she begins seeing his ghost. Obsessed with being with her dead son, Thomas's happiness with hubby Peter Strauss and their two surviving children is threatened, and she is eventually led to the brink of suicide. This has less to do with ghosts, per se than with how they affect our state of mind. Good writing, fine acting, and a desire to explore the human mind more than ghostly special effects carry this odd tale into a realm of reality. Frances Sternhagen, Courtney Chase, Matthew Kelly.

REVENGE (1986) ★½ Here's a blood cult flick that goes to the dogs: In Tulsa, Okla., some of the best citizens are members of the Kaninas Cult, which worships a demon hound. Patrick

Wayne and a farmer lady track down the culprits in a video cheapie described as a sequel to *Blood Cult*. Among the delights: an ax in a farmer's forehead, a coed's severed foot, deskinned heads and charred bodies. Written-directed by Christopher Lewis. John Carradine. (United/VCI)

REVENGE OF DRACULA (1958). See *Dracula—Prince of Darkness*.

REVENGE OF DRACULA (1971). Video version of *Dracula vs. Frankenstein* (Duravision).

REVENGE OF DR. DEATH. See *Madhouse* (1972).

REVENGE OF DR. X. Video version of *The Double Garden* (Regal).

REVENGE OF DR. X (1969). This is a video version of *Mad Doctor of Blood Island*. See that entry.

REVENGE OF FRANKENSTEIN, THE (1958) ★★★★½ Sequel to *The Curse of Frankenstein* and one of the best in Hammer's Frankenstein series, permeated with a satanical sense of humor (thanks to scripter Jimmy Sangster) that does not distract from horrific elements. Peter Cushing returns as the baron, working in a hospital in Carlsbruck for access to organs and limbs so he might give his hunchback assistant a new body. It's warped (the story, not the body) but that's what makes these British fright flicks so bloody good, old man. Directed by Terence Fisher with a lust for macabre humor. Michael Gwynn replaces Christopher Lee as the Monster, with Lionel Jeffries as a body snatcher. (Video/Laser: Columbia TriStar)

REVENGE OF GODZILLA. Japanese laser title for *Godzilla's Revenge*.

REVENGE OF KING KONG, THE. See *King Kong Escapes!*

REVENGE OF MECHAGODZILLA. See *Terror of Mechagodzilla*.

REVENGE OF THE BLOOD BEAST. See *She-Beast*.

REVENGE OF THE COLOSSAL MAN. See *War of the Colossal Beast*.

REVENGE OF THE CREATURE (1955) ★★★★ *The Creature from the Black Lagoon* was too big a hit just to float away, so director Jack Arnold and producer William Alland reteamed for this exciting sequel recapturing the superb underwater photography and brain-bashing thrills of the original. Martin Berkeley's story is nonstop action when the Gill-Man is rediscovered in his Black Lagoon, captured and brought to a sea world park in Florida. Eventually the primeval creature goes on a rampage—mainly to carry Lori Nelson away to his marshy hideaway in the Everglades. John Agar and John Bromfield fight over the girl, but it's just a half-hearted subplot. Originally produced in 3-D, but few patrons saw it that way in the '50s. In 1982 the film resurfaced on TV in a special 3-D presentation. Nestor Paiva, Clint Eastwood (in his

debut as a lab technician), Robert B. Williams, Dave Willock. (Video/Laser: MCA)

REVENGE OF THE DEAD. See *Night of the Ghouls*.

REVENGE OF THE DEAD. See *Orgy of the Dead*.

REVENGE OF THE DEAD (1984) ★★ By Italian horror standards, one of the tamest spaghetti-shockers ever produced. This TV-movie (aka *Zeder—Voices from Beyond* and *Zeder—Voices from Darkness*) is about an unsold novelist who discovers letters written on his typewriter ribbon that refer to "K zones," areas where the dead return to life. Writer and wife set out for Necropolis and an oracle of the dead. Unfortunately, the emphasis of director-producer Pupi Avati is on dialogue and literacy with a modicum of visual shocks. The film's 100 minutes cannot sustain interest. Gabriele Lavia, Anna Canovas, Bob Tonelli, John Stacy. (Lightning; Wizard; Live)

REVENGE OF THE JEDI. George Lucas announced the third film in his *Star Wars* series under this title, but changed his mind before the release date, retitling the project *Return of the Jedi*. Some posters and prerelease material carry the *Revenge* title.

REVENGE OF THE LIVING DEAD. See *The Murder Clinic*. (Feeling lifeless? See a doctor!)

REVENGE OF THE LIVING DEAD (1972). Video version of *Children Shouldn't Play with Dead Things* (True World).

REVENGE OF THE LIVING ZOMBIES (1989) ★★ Bill Hinzman, who appeared in George Romero's *Night of the Living Dead* as a zombie, produced-directed this homage to Romero, and it's strictly for cultists, with bloodletting, gore effects and nihilistic attitude. In one respect, you wish Hinzman (who appears as Flesh Eater) was more original in depicting walking zombies—on the other hand, you have to respect his respect for Romero. But there are libel laws and there's little (if any) originality—even the ending is a rip-off. Made near Pittsburgh, in the same area where Romero made the original. Recommended to those who appreciate this sort of bloody thing. John Mowod, Leslie Ann Wick, Kevin Kindlin. Aka *Flesh Eater*. (Magnum)

REVENGE OF THE RADIOACTIVE REPORTER (1990) ★ In the satiric (and yes, dumb) vein of *Toxic Avenger*, this Canadian spoof set in Toronto depicts reporter David Scammell's attempts to investigate a nuclear power plant leak, only to be pushed into a contaminated vat by his nemeses and emerge . . . a freak who goes on a rampage. Produced-directed by Craig Pryce. Derrick Strange, Randy Pearlson. (Magnum)

REVENGE OF THE RED BARON (1993) ★★½ Roger Corman's answer to those lightweight Full Moon video movies blending comedy and fantasy, but without some of the intrinsic charm that Charles Band can bring to the genre. This walks a fine line between tragedy and farce when young Tobey Maguire, coming from a split home, goes to live with his father (Cliff De Young), a jerk of the first order, and a wheelchair-bound grandfather (Mickey Rooney), the World War I aviation hero who shot down the Red Baron. A bolt of electricity strikes Rooney's remote-controlled model of Richtofen's warship, giving life to the miniplane and doll pilot in the form of a reincarnated Richtofen. The doll delivers quips in the style of Chucky the Killer Doll while Maguire has to prove he's innocent of murder and isn't insane. The contrast between comedy and real-life tragedy gives this film a difficult balance, and makes it impossible for director Robert Gordon to make the film work. Ronnie Schell, Don Stark, Joe Balogh, Laraine Newman. (New Horizons) (Laser: Image)

REVENGE OF THE VAMPIRE. See *Black Sunday*.

REVENGE OF THE ZOMBIES (1981). Video version of *Kiss Daddy Goodbye* (Genesis; IVE).

REVOLT OF THE DEAD ONES. See *Vengeance of the Zombies*.

REVOLT OF THE HUMANOIDS. See *Creation of the Humanoids*.

REVOLT OF THE ROBOTS. See *Aelita*.

REVOLT OF THE TRIFFIDS. See *Day of the Triffids*.

RIDERS OF THE STORM (1986) ★★½ Politically radical, cinematically bizarre satire set in the near future when Willa Westinghouse is leaning way to the right in her effort to become the first woman president, assisted by an advisor named McCarthy. Meanwhile, Dennis Hopper, Michael J. Pollard and other Vietnam aviation vets are flying around in the democratic skies in an old beat-up bomber, broadcasting S&M-TV, a pirate station projecting a non-Establishment view and a "psy-ops" technique of mind control. The military, in cahoots with Westinghouse, plans to blow Hopper's superstation out of the sky while he manipulates to destroy Westinghouse's career. This is a pillhead's nightmare and contains a few swift kicks at the electronic pulpit. Directed by Maurice Phillips. Eugene Lipinski, James Aubrey, Nigel Pegram. Aka *The American Way*. (Nelson; New Line) (Laser: Nelson)

RIFT, THE. See *Endless Descent*.

RIPPER, THE. See *New York Ripper*.

RIPPER, THE (1985) ★½ Amateurish, low-budget regional thudder shot on tape in Tulsa, Okla. A college instructor teaching Famous Crimes on Film finds a ring worn by Mary Kelly, a Jack the Ripper victim. At night he has nightmares in which he sees old Jack slaughtering women and ripping out their intestines.

Lumbering, cumbersome hunkajunk with tediously repetitious murders and downright bad acting—not to mention crummy dialogue (by Bill Groves) and slow direction (by Christopher Lewis). An excruciating viewing experience. Robert Brewer and David Powell did the makeup effects. Famed makeup man Tom Savini plays Jack the Ripper by twirling the ends of his mustache and chuckling with fiendish glee. (VCI; United)

RISING STORM (1989) ★★★ Set in A.D. 2099, this satirical adventure (aka *Rebel Storm*) depicts a tyrannical society run by Reverend Jimmy Joe II, who controls the Oval Office with a hypocritical, dictatorial hand. This film's best moments are in its comments about religion and government not mixing, and in the humorous personalities of its four main characters. Zach Galligan, a totally naive young man, and his hard-boiled brother Wayne Crawford join freedom fighters June Chadwick and Elizabeth Keifer to find a lost radio station in the desert, and their fresh characterizations give this tired genre retread a shot in the arm. The rest is mock heroics as the rebels close in on Jimmy Joe II for a blazing climax. Director Francis Schaeffer filmed in South Africa. John Rhys-Davies, William Katt, Graham Clark, Gordon Mullholland. (Academy)

RITES OF DRACULA, THE. Video version of *The Satanic Rites of Dracula* (Gemstone).

RITUALS (1978) ★★★ Engrossing performance by Hal Holbrook, struggling against the wilderness and his fellow man, holds together this Canadian picture, which vacillates between *Deliverance* and a slasher theme. Five physicians take a fishing trip into the Cauldron of the Moon, a beautiful but isolated region of Ontario, to be terrorized by an unseen madman. The explanation to the mystery is weak, and never gets worked into the dialogue by writer Ian Sutherland, and Peter Carter is perhaps too introspective to be directing an action picture; but there is a raw energy that works through the mundanities. Not for the squeamish, however. Lawrence Dane, Robin Gammell, Ken James. Aka *The Creeper*. (Embassy)

ROADGAMES (1982) ★★★½ Well-crafted though eccentric thriller in the Hitchcock vein, cleverly conceived by writer Everett De Roch and intelligently directed by Richard Franklin. Patrick Anthony Quid (Stacy Keach) is a trucker on his way to Perth with pig carcasses when he suspects the driver of a green van is a Jack the Ripper–style murderer whose game is chopping women's bodies—and Quid suspects carcasses in his rig might be human. Quid is an independent, good-humored driver who talks to his dingo companion, Boswell. Jamie Lee Curtis turns up as a runaway heiress and joins Quid in his "game" to track the killer. Franklin never compromises the story for shocks and shows insight into screen suspense. (Embassy; Charter)

ROAD GANGS. See *Spacehunter: Adventures in the Forbidden Zone.*

ROAD WARRIOR, THE (1981) ★★★★ Sequel to *Mad Max* is George Miller's masterpiece of the Cinema of the Bizarre, ten times better than its predecessor, with Mel Gibson repeating his role as a lone warrior in a post-Armageddon society where gas and oil are the richest commodities and survivors of industrial collapse fight to claim them. Max, in the tradition of the roving gunslinger aiding the underdog, befriends a benevolent band to keep precious fuels from falling into the hands of a vicious gang led by Humungus. The chase sequences are among the most exciting ever filmed. Characters are often grotesque and unlikable, but you'll be rooting for the good guys and booing the bad. Miller coscripted with Terry Hayes and Brian Hannant. Bruce Spence, Vernon Wells, Kjell Nilsson, Mike Preston. Aka *Mad Max 2*. (Video/Laser: Warner Bros.)

ROBBERS OF THE SACRED MOUNTAIN (1982) ★★ Pulp adventure with mild sci-fi overtones: a chunk of meteorite holds the key to laser power, and various governments are after the secret of its destructiveness. The action is slambang and there's little time to consider the story holes and absurdities. Simon MacCorkindale, Louise Vallance and John Marley star. Directed by Bob Schulz. First released to cable TV as *Falcon's Gold*. (Prism)

ROBIN COOK'S MORTAL FEAR. See *Mortal Fear.*

ROBIN COOK'S TERMINAL (1996) ★★½ Routine TV-movie version of Cook's conspiratorial medical thriller, set at a clinic where doctors working under Michael Ironside appear to have a cure for cancer. However, young doctor Doug Savant and nurse Nia Peeples discover it is a plot to infect rich men so they can be "cured" and then donate to Ironside's research program. Nancy Isaak's teleplay is lacking in any subtleties, and hence the suspense is minimal. However, director Larry Elikann keeps it all moving at such a furious rate you may not notice. Roy Thinnes, Jenny O'Hara, Khandi Alexander, Gregg Henry, James Eckhouse.

ROBIN COOK'S VIRUS. See *Virus* (1995).

ROBINSON CRUSOE OF CLIPPER ISLAND (1936) ★★★ Polynesia is the setting for this action-packed tropical 14-chapter Republic cliffhanger. Mala, an imitation of Sabu the Jungle Boy, is an undercover agent for U.S. Intelligence, sent to an island where the villain Porotu is trying to erupt a volcano with the help of a Volcano Eruption Machine. A big canine named Buck the Wonder Dog and a gallant steed named Rex help Mala to save the island. Mamo

Clark, William Newell. Directed by Mack V. Wright and Ray Taylor. Aka *S.O.S. Clipper Island*. (Republic; Nostalgia; Sinister/C; Video Connection offers the TV-feature version *Robinson Crusoe of Mystery Island*) (Laser: Republic)

ROBINSON CRUSOE OF MYSTERY ISLAND. TV-feature version of the serial *Robinson Crusoe of Clipper Island*. (Video Connection)

ROBINSON CRUSOE ON MARS (1964) ★★★½ Fascinating sci-fi version of Daniel Defoe's novel of survival, written by Ib Melchior and John C. Higgins. Astronaut Paul Mantee is ejected from Gravity Probe One when his missile almost collides with a meteor. Landing on the Red Planet, he undergoes incredible hardships, finding a means of breathing and overcoming nightmares in which dead partner Adam West returns alive. Mantee meets an escapee humanoid slave whom he dubs Friday. Aliens with heat rays seek Friday, allowing for exciting space opera with zappy (for their time) effects. Elements of this were borrowed for 1985's *Enemy Mine*. Directed by Byron Haskin. (Laser: Voyager, featuring running commentary and production design sketchbook)

ROBO-C.H.I.C. (1989) ★ An incomprehensible movie mess about a Computerized Humanoid Intelligence Clone (blond Kathy Showers, one-time intellectual pinup), who drives her Robocar to defeat a silly guy who goes around planting bombs in the city, a gang of extortionists, and ridiculous city hall politicos and policemen. *C.H.I.C.* is W.E.A.K. The action is so poor, one wonders what director Jeff Mandel (who cowrote the script with Ed Hansen) was thinking about (maybe he wasn't thinking at all). Wasted roles for Burt Ward, Kip King (as mad Dr. Von Colon), Jack Carter (as another crazed inventor) and Phil Proctor (who could use a script doctor). The funniest gag in this waste-of-timer is a newscaster for KAKA-TV named Bambi Doe. Ha ha. Aka *Cyber Chic*. (Action International)

ROBOCOP (1987) ★★★★½ Glossy, high-tech comic-book action, superior in photography and design and featuring excellent stop-motion work by Phil Tippett, who contributed so much fine material to the *Star Wars* trilogy. In a futuristic society controlled by an evil corporation, dedicated cop Peter Weller is blasted by a gang of sadists in a gory death scene. Weller is resurrected as a cyborg, but this is a six-million dollar man with only half a heart; the other half is ruled by computerized directives and a penchant for violence against lawbreakers. It's wall-to-wall action, with Tippett's activation of an "enforcement droid" the high point. What's contradictive about Paul Verhoeven's direction is the stark violence, which is unsuitable for the young people this was intended for. In this slam-bang superhero superflick, Weller's partner is Nancy Allen, with Ronny Cox as a corporate villain of the slimiest order. Two sequels followed. (Orion) (Laser: Image)

ROBOCOP II (1990) ★★½ Colossal action film that ends in colossal frustration for the viewer, with horrible lapses of taste on the part of writers Walon Green and Frank Miller (he of the *Batman* comic books). A youth gang led by adolescent Gabriel Damon is one of the most dubious choices for violent material, and mars whatever good intentions director Irvin Kershner had. This is mindless action from beginning to end, with Peter Weller back to portray the half-man/half-android without the humanity of the first box-office success. Phil Tippett is back with his superb stop-motion model effects, but nothing can save this excessive case of screen mayhem. Nancy Allen, Daniel O'Herlihy, Belinda Bauer, Tom Noonan, Felton Perry. (Orion) (Laser: Image)

ROBOCOP 3 (1993) ★★★ This is a vast improvement over the second film, and returns to the central themes that made the first *Robocop* such a hit. Robert Burke replaces Peter Weller in the title role as we return to a futuristic Detroit where the evil corporation, Omni Consumer Products, hires thugs to keep disorder so it can carry out nefarious plans. Robocop fights a Japanese cyborg assassin, undergoes trauma when his human/mechanical psyches clash, and even flies to defeat lawbreakers. Nancy Allen returns as Robocop's partner. Well directed and written by Fred Dekker. (Video/Laser: Orion)

ROBO MAN (1974) ★★★ Originally shot as *Who?* and based on Algis Budrys's novel of the same title, this intriguing, unusually intelligent spy thriller stars Elliott Gould as cynical FBI man Sean Rogers, assigned to find out if American scientist Lucas Martino (well played by Joseph Bova), after being cared for by the Soviets following a car crash, is really the man beneath a metal head unit (cybernetic surgery having reconstructed him after the accident). The John Gould script uses flashbacks to the Soviet point of view (with Trevor Howard as a Russian intelligence officer) to suggest that Robo Man is really a plant, designed to penetrate the top-secret Neptune Project. Director Jack Gold filmed this fascinating psychological study in Germany and Florida for producer Barry Levinson, and saves the final surprise for the last few moments. James Noble, Ed Grover, John Lehne, Kay Tornborg, Ivan Desny. (Ace; MNTEX).

R.O.B.O.T. See *Chopping Mall.*

ROBOT HOLOCAUST (1985) ★½ Video sci-fi that is so bad, camp followers might get a chuckle out of this megamess. The plot is indecipherable. On New Terra, following the Robot Rebellion of '33, a band of Earthlings

(stupid heroes, whiney broads in halter tops and a Conan lookalike) faces forces of the Dark One and a chick in spike heels (Angelika Jager, a wonderfully incompetent ham actress) by defying the Cave of Sewage Worms, the Room of Questions, the Pleasure Machine and the Vault of Beasts. Everyone looks like a refugee from an Edward D. Wood, Jr., movie. Unbelievably poor effects, to boot. Speaking of boots, give one to director-writer Tim Kincaid and the cast: Nadine Hart, Norris Culf, Joel von Ornstein. (Vestron; VCI)

ROBOT JOX (1990) ★★½ Popular sci-fi novelist Joe Haldeman scripts a rousing tale of futuristic gladiators who take to controlling giant robots that fight it out in special arenas. The idea of monstrous upright walking machines controlled by their pilots, or jox, is a novel one but never reaches maximum effectiveness, perhaps because director Stuart Gordon (of *Re-Animator* fame) was hampered by a limited budget. Gary Graham is the robot jox who goes through personal trauma before he accepts the ultimate challenge from his archrival. Originally released as *Robojox.* Anne-Marie Johnson, David Koslo. (Video/Laser: RCA/Columbia)

ROBOT MONSTER (1953) ★½ Reportedly produced-directed by Phil Tucker in less than a week and written in 30 minutes by Wyott Ordung. Exec producer Al Zimbalist even decided to contribute to the Arts by filming in 3-D. As the hero, George Nader looks as mechanical as the extra in an ape suit (with a fishbowl over his head) called Ro-Man, who lands on Earth with his Bubble Communications Machine to kill the only 6 human beings left after a zap ray has wiped out mankind. Once those six are dead, it will be safe for 268,000 Martians to carry out a landing. Meanwhile, in Bronson Canyon, Ro-Man chases Nader, Claudia Barrett and Selena Royle in the funniest footage ever. Must be seen to be (dis)believed. Marvelously incompetent. Yes, see it! Aka *Monster from Mars* and *Monster from the Moon.* (Sony; Rhino offers a 3-D version) (Laser: Image)

ROBOT NINJA (1990) ★★ An actor playing a costumed superhero turns into a real superhero to fight the forces of evil. Michael Todd, Burt Ward, Michael Shea, Bogdan Pecic, Maria Markovic. Written-produced-directed by J. R. Bookwalter. (Cinema Home; Phoenix)

ROBOTS. See *War of the Robots.*

ROBOT VS. THE AZTEC MUMMY, THE (1959) ★ Third and final entry in the Mexican *Aztec Mummy* series, preceded by *The Aztec Mummy* (aka *Attack of the Mayan Mummy*) and *The Curse of the Aztec Mummy.* Directed by Raphael Portillo from an Alfredo Salazar script, this depicts Dr. Krupp wandering into a crypt with a clanking robot, which he has given a brain so it won't bump into any sarcophaguses. Krupp wants to loot Aztec treasure, but standing guard is that hulking package of bandages, that walking commercial for plastic strips, that swathed slob . . . the Aztec Mummy. Crash! Bang! Thunk! Boom! Bash! Mangle! Thud! Crunch! Wallop! Repackaged for U.S. tastes by K. Gordon Murray. Ramón Gay, Rosita Arenas. Aka *The Aztec Mummy vs. the Human Robot.* (Admit One; Goodtimes; Sinister/C; S/Weird; also in video as *Aztec Mummy Double Feature*)

ROBOT WARS (1993) ★★★ Dave Allen has created a wonderful stop-motion battle between the upright walking robot warrior (reprised from *Robot Jox*) and a spiderlike walking robot (inspired by the Imperial Walkers from *The Empire Strikes Back*?) in this Charles Band adventure. It's set in A.D. 2041 when Earth is divided into zones and America is selling "robotic security systems" to foreign powers. An Asian general (Danny Kamekoni), representing the "Centros," schemes to steal a Mega Robot, disrupting rebel robot jock Marion Drake (Don Michael Paul) and his girl Barbara Crampton. Peter Haskell is the boss at control central always in conflict with Drake and James Staley is comic-relief hero Stumpy. Albert Band, father of Charles Band, directed this loose sequel to *Robot Jox*. Lisa Rinna, Kuji Okumoto. (Paramount) (Laser: Full Moon)

ROCKET AND ROLL. See *Abbott and Costello Go to Mars.*

ROCKETEER, THE (1991) ★★★★ This $40 million-plus spin-off from Dave Stevens's popular comic book is a gem of a Disney adventure movie as a young pilot of 1938 (Bill Campbell playing Cliff Secord) battles machine gun–toting gangsters, stoic FBI men and devious Nazis. They're all after Secord for possession of a rocket-propelled jet pack that enables the pilot to streak through the sky at fantastic speeds, in the style of Commander Cody of *Radar Men from the Moon*. The flying sequences (created by George Lucas's Industrial Light & Magic) are superexciting, director Joe Johnston (creator of Yoda and other *Star Wars* ingredients) captures the art-deco ambience of L.A. of the '30s, and the script by Danny Bilson and Paul De Meo always maintains a clear-cut distinction between good and evil. The cast is great: Campbell as the naive, unstoppable hero; Jennifer Connelly as his sexy girlfriend Jenny; Alan Arkin as the absent-minded mechanic Peevy; Timothy Dalton as a suave Hollywood movie star; Paul Sorvino as the chief hoodlum, and Ed Lauter as the glib FBI agent. There's a character named Lothar (7-foot Tiny Ron) who's made up to look like Rondo "the Creeper" Hatton. (Disney) (Laser: Image)

ROCKET SHIP. See *Flash Gordon* (1936).

ROCKETSHIP X-M (1950) ★★★½ Producer Robert L. Lippert rushed this low-budgeter (first written as *Expedition Moon*) into production to beat *Destination Moon* into theaters, and some consider this B effort superior to the more expensive George Pal production. The first rocketship blasting off for the moon malfunctions and lands instead on Mars, where astronauts Lloyd Bridges, Ona Massen, Noah Beery, Jr., John Emery and Hugh O'Brian find the atomized remains of a once-great civilization. The remnants are primitive cavemen, blinded by radiation. An unhappy ending is an unexpected twist to this film directed-written by Kurt Neumann. Good production values and a fine score by Ferde Grofe, with effective use of the theremin. (Media; Nostalgia Merchant; a different video version, *Rocketship X-M: Special Edition*, features new special-effects footage and tinted sequences) (Laser: Image)

ROCKET TO THE MOON (1954). See *Cat Women of the Moon.*

ROCKET TO THE MOON (1967). See *Blast Off.*

ROCK 'N' ROLL NIGHTMARE. Video version of *Edge of Hell* (Academy).

ROCK 'N' ROLL WRESTLING WOMEN VS. THE AZTEC APE. Video of *Wrestling Women vs. the Aztec Ape*, with rock and roll track. (Rhino)

ROCKTOBER BLOOD (1986) ★ "Heavy metal" horror flick in which a psycho singer comes back from the dead to kill members of his former band. Directed by Beverly and Ferd Sebastian. (Vestron)

ROCKULA (1990) ★★ Every 22 years, centuries-old vampire Dean Cameron meets a reincarnated version of a former lover and rescues her from a gang of pirates who always show up to murder her. If that isn't hard enough to swallow, Cameron also has a running dialogue with his mirror reflection, which has a life (and dress) of its own, and he forms a vampire rock 'n' roll band. This mess from director Luca Bercovici (who ground out the script with producer Jeffrey Levy and Christopher Vernel) has occasional charming moments (Susan Tyrell as a sassy bartender, Bo Diddley as a band member, a cute animated main title) but it overstretches itself with too many whacky premises. Tawny Fere, Nancy Ferguson, Kevin Hunter. (Video/Laser: Warner Bros.)

ROCKY HORROR PICTURE SHOW, THE (1975) ★★★★ Like Richard O'Brien's London stage musical on which it is based, this film is slanted for the freak-rock crowd. It satirizes Frankenstein, haunted-house mysteries, sci-fi movies and our penchant for sexual-identity confusion. Naive newlyweds Barry Bostwick and Susan Sarandon stumble onto a foreboding castle where aliens from Transsexual are creating the perfect he-man stud under the scientific (and loving) care of Dr. Frank N. Furter (Tim Curry). Full of bizarre props, musical numbers and strange cutting techniques, it has become a successful midnight movie and continues to play in major cities with attendees dressed as the characters. Those who relate to a mixture of depravity and satire will find this diverting. Directed by Jim Sharman, who cowrote with Richard O'Brien, who also appears in the cast. Jonathan Adams, Charles Gray, Meatloaf, Little Nell, Patricia Quinn, Peter Hinwood. (Video/Laser: CBS/Fox)

RODAN (1956) ★★★ Made in the wake of *Godzilla—King of the Monsters* by Japan's leading director, Inoshiro Honda, this Japanese sci-fi epic reflects the Asian predilection for superludicrous effects in depicting a giant pterodactyl with a 250-foot wingspan and a destructive nature that allows it to do in several metropolises. Emphasis is on rousing catastrophe, while the dwarfed humans stand in awe or run screaming in terror. Eiji Tsuburaya is responsible for the destruction. Better than later Japanese monster movies, with more care lavished on the spectacle. But the dubbing is atrocious and acting styles hard to take. Kenji Sawara, Yumi Shirakawa, Akihiko Hirata. Aka *Rodan the Flying Monster*. (Vestron; Video Treasures; Gateway/Paramount) (Laser: Vestron)

RODAN THE FLYING MONSTER. See *Rodan*.

ROGER CORMAN'S FRANKENSTEIN UNBOUND. See *Frankenstein Unbound*.

ROGUES' TAVERN (1936) ★★ Old-fashioned thriller in which a group of people gather under one roof only to be terrorized by an unseen entity of evil. In this oldie, the victims are ripped apart by something with fangs built into it by what is described as a bad-guy scientist. Directed by Bob Hill from an Al Martin script. Wallace Ford, Barbara Pepper, Joan Woodbury, Clara Kimball Young. (Nostalgia; Discount; Horizon)

ROLLERBABIES (1976) ★★ In the wake of *Rollerball* came this imitative sci-fi population satire in which a future society passes an antilovemaking law. Instead, folks fornicate live to satisfy the vicarious needs of the masses. This sex exploitation piece was produced-directed by Carter Stevens. Robert Random, Suzanne McBain, Yolanda Savalas, Alan Marlo.

ROLLERBALL (1975) ★★★ Title refers to a futuristic, bloodied version of Roller Derby that takes the place of warfare—controlled by 6 cartels merged to form a world government. Director Norman Jewison creates a sterile picture when depicting the robotlike people of tomorrow—but an exciting, bloody one when depicting the awesome-awful sport. Chief player is Jonathan E. (James Caan), who rebels in one final orgy of Rollerball bloodlust. William Harrison's story was a terse metaphor—millions were expended to give the sport specific rules and bring it to life, as conceived by Harrison in his script adaptation. John Houseman, Maud

Adams, Pamela Hensley, Ralph Richardson, John Beck. (MGM/UA) (Laser: Image)

ROLLER BLADE (1986) ★ Unbelievably bad *Mad Max* imitation, so incompetent one wonders to what new low Donald G. Jackson (cowriter, producer, photographer, director) will sink next (see below). Set in the post-holocaust Second Dark Age, this portrays a cult of "Holy Rollers"—religious women of the Cosmic Order of Roller Blade who wear skates, fight with knives and take orders from Mother Speed, who talks with a lisp. They're looking for a magic crystal but so is the masked villain Saticon, who commands a hand puppet cackling with lustful glee as it strips cellophane off a nude woman. It's hard to imagine a society that runs on skates and skateboards, but here it is in all its vast stupidity, including a marshal who talks with "thee" and "thou." The action is phony, the attempts at religion blasphemous, the effects laughable and the acting hitting rank amateurism. Has to be seen to be believed. Suzanne Solari, Jeff Hutchinson. (New World)

ROLLER BLADE WARRIORS: TAKEN BY FORCE (1988) ★ Holy rollers! You can't say photographer-director Donald G. Jackson isn't consistent: The bad acting he allowed in *Roller Blade* is permitted in this new adventure on skates set in a post-holocaust world where Mother Speed (Abby Dalton) reigns over women warriors ("Go forth," she proclaims, "and skate the paths of righteousness.") This time the wheeled wenches are protecting a psychic virgin from falling into the hands of evildoers who feed beautiful women to a monster in an energy plant. Little sense is to be made from Lloyd Strathen's script (from a Jackson idea), what with tongue-in-cheek characters, exaggerated swordplay and sappy dialogue. Example: One woman says, "What's a man like?" and another replies, "Like soup on a cold night." And yet the direction has a strange kinetic energy and sincerity of purpose, suggesting Jackson is a dedicated schlock filmmaker. You should see at least one of these things—they defy description. Kathleen Kinmont, Jack Damon, Elizabeth Kaitan, Rory Calhoun (in a cameo), Norman Alder, Suzanne Solari. (Raedon)

ROME, 2072 A.D.—THE NEW GLADIATORS. See *The New Gladiators*.

ROSEMARY'S BABY (1968) ★★★★★ Congratulate William Castle for buying Ira Levin's book in galley form (before it became a bestseller) and for realizing he needed Roman Polanski (and not himself) to direct and write the adaptation. The results became the high point of Castle's career. This is a quiet exercise in the supernatural that builds gradually, often providing only a suspicion of evil, and sometimes a doubt, that newlywed Mia Farrow is the victim of a conspiracy plot in modern Manhattan. She suspects neighbors Sidney Blackmer and Ruth Gordon are witches, joined in a bloodpact with her husband-actor John Cassavetes. Is it possible he has formed a union with the Devil? Is the baby in her womb spawned by Satan during one of her nightmares? She becomes the perfect Hitchcockian foil: a misunderstood, sympathetic, vulnerable young woman whose bizarre story is disbelieved by everyone, including doctor Ralph Bellamy. Maurice Evans, Patsy Kelly, Charles Grodin, Hope Summers, Castle (as the man in the phone booth). (Paramount; RCA/Columbia) (Laser: Paramount)

ROSEMARY'S DISCIPLES. Variant video version of *Necromancy* (Magnum).

ROSEMARY'S KILLER. Variant video version of *The Prowler* (VCI).

ROSWELL: THE ALIENS ATTACK (1999) ★★ Jim Makichuk's teleplay for this UPN TV movie so strains credulity that its one interesting element is overshadowed and canceled out. We are expected to believe that a strange-behaving alien humanoid (Steven Flynn) can penetrate a top-security army-air-force base (at Roswell, NM) and be shown an atomic bomb in a secured facility. Then we're expected to believe that a sexy babe (Heather Hanson) dressed like a prostitute and acting like one could pose as a government official with a security clearance, and be shown around the secret installation without anyone asking questions. The interesting subplot is a burgeoning romance between Flynn and a lonely, widowed military secretary (Kate Greenhouse), but it comes too late in this hogwash sci-fi interpretation of the Roswell crash of 1947. Seems the humanoid aliens (they don't look like us, we look like them) are here to destroy Earth by setting off that atomic bomb at Roswell, with Flynn having a change of heart because he falls in love with Greenhouse. Director Brad Turner makes up for a total lack of special effects by enhancing the styles and music of the forties to create a sense of time, and making the atmosphere and troops of the base as sinister as possible to create a sense of place. Definitely no cigars for this movie, with Canada standing in for the New Mexican desert. Brent Stait, Sean McCann, Donnelly Rhodes. (Paramount)

ROSWELL: THE UFO COVER-UP (1994) ★★★★ A fascinating TV-movie account of what has come to be known as one of the best-documented cases of a crashed UFO, based on a well-researched nonfiction book by Kevin D. Randle and Donald R. Schmitt, *UFO Crash at Roswell*. At Roswell, New Mexico, in July 1947, the U.S. Army Air Force base reported that a UFO had crashed nearby in the desert. However, the military immediately changed its story and began a massive cover-up that involved hundreds of civilian and military person-nel. What was suppressed was the discovery of 4 or 5 alien corpses, and 1 extraterrestrial that was still alive. This adaptation by Arthur Kopit follows the intelligence officer (played by Kyle MacLachlan) who was one of the first to the crash site, and who had to bear the burden of silence, and of not knowing the full truth, for many years. Told through the device of a 30-year reunion at the Air Force base, *Roswell* unfolds as a mystery jigsaw, many of the pieces fitting into place, but others remaining lost. Finally, through a strange character played by Martin Sheen, MacLachlan learns of an alleged cover-up that extended all the way to the White House, and of subsequent events and encounters between the U.S. government and UFOs. It gets wild and woolly, but you can't deny it's engrossing. And director Jeremy Kagan photographs many portions of this eerie "true tale" with odd camera angles, slightly out-of-focus lenses, and a real sense for the shivery quality such a story produces in all of us. Charles Martin Smith, John M. Jackson, Dwight Yoakum, Bob Gunton, Xander Berkeley, Kim Greist, Peter MacNichol. (Republic)

R.O.T.O.R. (1987) ★ Amateurish rip-off of *Robocop*, made by regional filmmakers in Dallas in dire need of a good director and stunt coordinator. The film appears to have been dubbed, as if the producers lost the sound tracks or decided the voices weren't right. Dallas cop Barrett Coldyron, with the help of Dr. Steel from Houston, pursues #222, a runaway cop named R.O.T.O.R. (Robotic Officer Tactical Operation Research) programmed "to judge and execute." There's behind-the-scenes political shenanigans going on (a senator is backing the project so he can get into the White House, that kind of stuff) but it's all deadened by the acting. Coldyron has discovered an "unknown alloy" that contains molecular memory and enables a metal man to learn by moving its joints. An unbelievably bad flick directed by Cullen Blaine. Richard Gesswein, Margaret Trigg, Jayne Smith, James Cole. (Imperial; Laser:Image)

ROTTWEILER. See *Dogs of Hell* (Some bark!).

ROUGE (1987) ★ Pedantic Hong Kong supernatural love story in which a newspaperman is sought out by the spirit of a courtesan, who wants him to help her find her lover, who is still on the mortal level. Directed by Stanley Kwan. Anita Mui, Leslie Cheung. (Facets Multimedia Inc.)

ROUGH MAGIC (1997) ★★ This throwback to the screwball comedies of the thirties is a misfire that doesn't create much magic on any level—as a comedy, as a romance, as a fantasy, as a south-of-the-border adventure. A talented actress who is wasted in this rabbit that never comes out of a top hat, Bridget Fonda plays a strong-willed, feisty magician's assistant who flees to Mexico after her senator-fiancé (D. W. Moffett playing a real jerk) accidentally shoots Ivan the Terrific (a man of legerdemain and sleight-of-hand played by Kenneth Mars) and she vows to find a magical elixir on an island where old ladies sit around and drink the stuff that makes them giggle and act silly. If that isn't puzzling enough, wait until you see the scene where Fonda turns a sadistic Mexican (Paul Rodriguez) into a tiny "fat sausage" that is swallowed whole by a pet terrier. Or the scene where she lays a blue egg. How about the one where she's upchucking into a toilet and spits out a valentine. It's her heart, and now she's a cold, empty woman who cannot love until she gets it back. Investigator Russell Crowe (assigned by Moffett to track Fonda through Mexico) is a fine actor who tries to bring touches of "film noir" to this misguided project, but even he cannot breath magic into the flaccid script by Robert Mundy, William Brookfield, and director Clare Peploe (who got all this mixed-up stuff from a book by James Hadley Chase entitled *Miss Shumway Waves a Wand*). What might have been told as a quaint modern-day fairy tale with Cinderella overtones falls apart. All the magicians in Hollywood couldn't possibly have put it back together again. Jim Broadbent, Andy Romano, Richard Schiff, Michael Ensign, Euva Anderson. (Video/DVD: Columbia TriStar)

RUBY (1977) ★★ Weakly directed Curtis Harrington horror film, with Piper Laurie as the former moll of a deceased gangster; the hood returns from the dead and leaves the bodies of victims all over a drive-in theater specializing in old horror movies. Harrington was reportedly fired during production and replaced by Stephanie Rothman. Janet Baldwin, Stuart Whitman, Roger Davis, Fred Kohler. Original title was *Blood Ruby*. (VCI; United)

RUE MORGUE MASSACRES, THE (1973) ★★★ Paul Naschy stockpiles dead women in his cellar, fighting off hungry rats and keeping company with a mad scientist and his monster (a head floating in liquid) in this, the seventh outing in the Waldemar Daninsky series produced in Spain (aka *The Hunchback of the Morgue*). Previously there were *Frankenstein's Bloody Terror, Nights of the Werewolf, The Werewolf vs. the Vampire Women, Assignment Terror* and *Fury of the Wolfman*. It's the Movie Theme That Never Dies costarring Rossana Yanni, Maria Perschy, Vic Winner. Directed by Javier Aguirre (Naschy?). Next in the series: *Dracula's Great Love*. (All Seasons)

RUNAWAY (1984) ★★★½ Exciting, imaginative sci-fi action mystery from writer-director Michael Crichton, set in a near future when mankind is served by robots, which occasionally go haywire. Tom Selleck and Cynthia Rhodes are members of the "runaway squad," designed to put amok metal out of commission. Villain Gene Simmons, armed with a zap gun that fires guided-missile bullets around corners, is after microcomputer chips that will give him control of the robots and he sics an army of mechanical spiders on Selleck in a rousing, outrageous climax. Kirstie Alley, Stan Shaw. (Video/Laser: RCA/Columbia)

RUNESTONE, THE (1990) ★★★ Rip-roaring old-fashioned monster movie in which a 6th-century Norse runestone is uncovered during a dig in west Pennsylvania and brought to Manhattan. A tall, hairy creature with long, scary fingers escapes the stone and kills half the New York City police force, since bullets cannot stop it—only a legendary Viking battle ax can do that. Despite plenty of graphic murders and an eerie atmosphere, the film is loaded by writer-director Willard Carroll (working from a novella by Mark B. Rogers) with pretentious, cryptic crap that keeps slowing down the excitement, especially scenes of Alexander Godunov sitting in a cuckoo clock shop. Standouts in the solid cast are Peter Riegert and Lawrence Tierney as hardened Manhattan cops. William Hickey, Mitchell Laurance, Tim Ryan, Dawan Scott. (Video/Laser: Live)

RUNNING AGAINST TIME (1990) ★★★ A straight-faced variation on *Back to the Future*, in which university professor Robert Hays discovers that campus scientist Sam Wanamaker has designed a "transdimensional physics machine" capable of moving objects through time and space. Hays "transdimensionalizes" himself to Dallas in 1963 to prevent the assassination of President John F. Kennedy—only the beginning of the time continuum screwups in this daffy, gassy TV-movie written by Robert Glass and Stanley Shapiro (based on a novel by Shapiro) and directed by Bruce Seth Green. Hays sometimes seems to be in a comedy rather than a serious time-travel drama but since the absurdities are too many to list, it doesn't make much difference. Fun in a zany way, though meant to be a thriller. Catherine Hicks, Wayne Tippit, Juanita Jennings. (MCA)

RUNNING MAN, THE (1987) ★★★ While this is a vehicle for the biceps and physique of Arnold Schwarzenegger, it is really Richard Dawson who steals the picture as Damon Killian, the host of a futuristic TV series. The twist is that in 2017, Schwarzenegger is a political undesirable thrown into prison. Following his exciting escape, he grabs the attention of Killian, who wants Schwartzy for his game show in which participants are pursued by assorted killers, and awarded grand prizes if they survive the "contest." All too soon Schwartzy is the guest of honor, and must fight Sub-Zero (Prof. Taru Tanaka), Buzzsaw (Gus Rethwisch), Dynamo (Erland Van Lidth), Captain Freedom (Jess

Ventura) and Fireball (Jim Brown). It's rough, tumble action, well staged by director Paul Michael Glaser, but contrived for its shocking deaths and the quippish lines Arnold tosses after his victims. ("He had to split," he says in reference to Buzzsaw, who's just had a whirring blade shoved up his gonads). Schwartzy promises Killian "I'll be back" (a line from *The Terminator*) but their final showdown is anticlimactic after so many violent confrontations. Stephen E. de Souza's script is based on the novel by Richard Bachman (Stephen King) and it never comes to grips with the pseudopolitical backgrounds to make the action plausible or the characters sympathetic. Supporting cast is good (Maria Conchita Alonso, Yaphet Kotto, Mick Fleetwood) but ultimately it's Dawson you want to run with. (Vestron) (Laser: Image)

RUNNING SILENT. See *Silent Running*.

RUSH (1984) ★ Super-chintzy Italian *Mad Max* rip-off, relying on action as Rush (Conrad Nichols), a Rambo-style survivor of nuclear war, roves the desert's "forbidden zone." In this world you're either a prisoner in tattered rags or a well-armed soldier working for villain Gordon Mitchell. . . . Rush rushes to support the former by blasting the latter to pieces in poorly staged, unbelievable action sequences directed by Anthony Richmond. The video version is enhanced by an introduction and closing that feature Sybil Danning, clad in a camouflaged bra and little else, carrying a wicked machine gun and making cracks about her .38s and the guys' "big barrels." Now that's worth seeing. (USA)

RUSH WEEK (1989) ★ Generic slasher film is lacking in both gory special effects and a plot clever enough to avoid giving away who the killer is. A robed figure carrying an executioner's ax roves the hallways of Tambers College, slicing up sexy coeds posing for girlie photos. This vacillates between slasher scenes and unfunny prankster gags being pulled on the campus folks by the Beta Delta Beta. In short, a stupid "kill the teenagers" movie with Pamela Ludwig as a reporter with an inquiring mind, Gregg Allman as her journalism instructor (?) and Roy Thinnes as Dean Grail. Bob Bralver's direction is pretty lousy. Courtney Gebhart, Don Grant, David Denney. (Video/Laser: RCA/Columbia)

graveyard. Reggie Nalder is the vampire Barlow in the Lugosi tradition, with James Mason portraying Barlow's aide-de-vamp. David Soul tries to stop the pair with the help of Lance Kerwin. Written by Paul Monash, directed by Tobe Hooper, the mild-mannered sentimentalist who gave us *Texas Chainsaw Massacre*, and produced by Richard Kobritz (*Christine*). Originally 4 hours but cut to a shorter version for cable TV. Some scenes are stronger than those shown on the network. (The European version, also stronger, is in video/laser from Warner Bros. as *Salem's Lot—The Movie*; from On Line Cinema as *Blood Thirst*)

SALUTE OF THE JUGGER. See *The Blood of Heroes*.

SAMSON VS. THE VAMPIRE WOMEN (1961) ★★½ This entry in the Mexican-produced series about a wrestling hero who fights the supernatural on the sidelines (known as Santo, the Silver Maskman) is a potboiler reedited for the U.S. by producer J. Gordon Murray and director Manuel San Fernando. These flicks from the Churubusco-Azteca studio resemble old Universal horror movies in production and music, and this has good sets, beautiful women and an intriguing visual design, though the wrestling sequences are mundane in comparison. A Mistress of the Night resurrects an army of women vampires and uses hypnosis to disguise how ugly they really are. Santo, Maria Duval, Lorena Velazquez, Jaime Fernandez, Augusto Benedico. Original Mexican director was the dis-grunted Alfonso Corona Blake. Aka *The Saint Against the Vampire Women*. (Sinister/C; S/Weird; Filmfax)

SANDMAN, THE (1996) ★★★ Given the skimpy budget he had to work with, and the semiprofessional status of writer-director J. R. Bookwalter and his cast of unknowns, this independent video horror flick is a creditable job, suggesting Bookwalter has a future in genre moviemaking. A. J. Richards portrays a writer living in a house trailer whose neighbors are dying of a "sleeping disease." Actually it's the hideously hooded Sandman (Stan Fitzgerald), a monster with glowing red eyes, a skeleton hand and whisking scythe who intrudes into your dream and gives you enough nightmares that you die of fright. Bookwalter benefits from good special effects and colorful secondary characters, such as a sweet old lady and a kooky Vietnam War veteran. For monster buffs, for sure. Rita Gutowski, Terry J. Lipko, James Viront. (Tempe)

SANTA CLAUS CONQUERS THE MARTIANS (1964) ★★★ Given this was designed as a children's sci-fi fairy tale by screenwriter Glenville Mareth, and given it's played like a Dr. Seuss fractured fable, *Martians* fulfills its limited expectations and is not as awful as some critics say. Because the green-faced children on Mars are distracted by the TV shows beaming in from

SABRE TOOTH TIGER. See *Deep Red*.

SABRINA THE TEENAGE WITCH (1996) ★ One dumb, boring TV-movie about a Riverside High School student (Melissa Joan Hart) who learns she and her mother have witchcraft powers. Based on characters in Archie comic books, *Sabrina* is a prolonged ordeal that lacks special effects, excitement or any sense of comedy. Put the whammy on writers Barney Cohen, Kathryn Wallack and Nicholas Factor. And why is Tibor (*The Gate*) Takacs directing this stuff, when he could be out making a self-respecting monster movie? Would eating have something to do with it? Sherry Miller, Charlene Fernetz, Ryan Reynolds, Michelle Beaudoin.

SADIST, THE (1963) ★★★ Surprisingly good shocker never resorts to exploitation in telling the taut tale of a serial killer and girlfriend holding waylaid travelers as hostages in a wrecking yard. Blond, blue-eyed Arch Hall, Jr., is excellent as the cackling killer who talks like Richard Widmark and taunts victims with cat-and-mouse threats. Writer-director James Landis throws in nifty twists of plot and brings prestige to a story that in lesser hands would be schlock. Excellent photography by William Zsigmond. Richard Alden, Don Russell, Marilyn Manning, Helen Hovey. Aka *The Profile of Terror*. (Rhino; Sinister/C)

SAGA OF THE VIKING WOMEN AND THEIR VOYAGE TO THE WATERS OF THE GREAT SEA SERPENT. Move over, Ray Dennis Steckler! It's Roger Corman's grab at the longest title of all time! See *Viking Women and the Sea Serpent*.

SAINT AGAINST THE VAMPIRE WOMEN, THE. See *Samson vs. the Vampire Women*.

SAKIMA AND THE MASKED MARVEL (1943). TV-feature version of *The Masked Marvel*.

SALEM'S LOT (1979) ★★★½ TV adaptation of Stephen King's best-selling vampire novel—the shuddery tale of how a European bloodsucker turns an East Coast community into a

Earth, the grand ruler Kemar orders his men to kidnap Santa Claus from the North Pole and use him as a propaganda weapon to cheer up the canal kids. Accompanying the invaders on their mission is a Tobor-type robot, Tog. Two Earth children are also kidnapped, and of course they and Santa teach the Martians a few lessons. As a curiosity piece, this production isn't half bad. Directed by Nicholas Webster. John Call plays a jovial Santa and somewhere among the green-faced kids is Pia Zadora. Leonard Hicks, Vincent Beck. (Nelson; S/Weird; Filmfax; from Valley Star as *Santa Claus Defeats the Aliens*)

SANTA CLAUS DEFEATS THE ALIENS. See *Santa Claus Conquers the Martians.*

SANTA CLAUSE, THE (1994) ★★★½ This is a mildly pleasant Disney film designed for family viewing that tugs at your heartstrings by making average guy Tim Allen (separated from wife Wendy Crewson, but still having custody rights to visit his son) take over the role of St. Nicholas when the real McNicholas falls dead at his feet after sliding off a roof one Christmas Eve. How Allen's physique gradually changes into that of Kris Kringle, and how his solid relationship with son Eric Lloyd is adversely affected, are the high points of the script by director John Pasquin. This reminds one of William Dear's episode about Santa Claus from Spielberg's "Amazing Stories" series. Judge Reinholt is Crewson's new boyfriend, a psychiatrist who naturally thinks Allen is a fruitcake, and Peter Boyle is barely in the film as Allen's nonunderstanding boss. There are seasonal special effects (flying reindeer and sled, an armada of flying elves out to rescue Santa) so this is suitable for a holiday viewing. (Video/Laser: Disney)

SANTA CLAUS—THE MOVIE (1985) ★★★ Enchanting family movie depicts how a big-hearted Earthling and wife are picked by Father Time to be Mr. and Mrs. Santa Claus, destined to live at the North Pole where elves led by Dudley Moore make the toys. This portion is charming, with elaborate sets to give Santa Claus verisimilitude. Then the film switches to modern times and trivializes the spirit of Christmas by focusing on two kids and one evil toy manufacturer (John Lithgow). It's still successful enough that you should put this on your Christmas list. David Huddleston is an excellent Santa. Burgess Meredith, Judy Cornwell. Directed by Jeannot Szwarc. (Media) (Laser: Image)

SATAN. See *Mark of the Devil.*

SATANIC RITES OF DRACULA. This Hammer horror thriller was retitled in the U.S. as *Count Dracula and His Vampire Bride.* Liberty Entertainment offers a complete tape version under its original title; UAV also offers a version, *The Rites of Dracula.* For a critique see *Count Dracula and His Vampire Bride.*

SATANISM AND WITCHCRAFT. See *Scream Greats II: Satanism and Witchcraft.*

SATAN KILLER, THE (1993) ★½ Poorly lit and photographed in Norfolk, Va., incoherently edited and inanely acted, and cruel in its violence toward women, this is a waste-of-time serial killer chase in which cop Steve Sayre goes on a bloody vendetta after his lovely fiancée is murdered. Director Stephen Calamari should be chopped up and served in a ketchup sauce. Billy Franklin, James Westbrook, Belinda Creason, Cindy Healy. Aka *Death Penalty.* (Action International)

SATAN'S BLOODY FREAKS. See *Dracula vs. Frankenstein.*

SATAN'S CHEERLEADERS (1976) ★ Writer-director Greydon Clark intermingles *The Omen* with *I Was a Rah Rah Boom Girl* in this cheer-y tale of a witch cult headed by John Ireland and Yvonne De Carlo that terrorizes big-busted, miniskirted cheerleaders from Benedict High. Remarks a cult member, "Some townspeople feel the Prince of Darkness might desire that the blood of a maiden flow tonight." Incompetently handled, in a bemusing way, with Jack Kruschen and John Carradine on the sidelines. Let's hear it for Satan: Give me an . . . E—X—P—L—O—I—T—A— T—I—O—N. . . . Give me an . . . F—I—L—M. . . . Give me . . . Aw hell, give me a raincheck. (United; Interglobal; VCI)

SATAN'S CLAW. See *The Blood on Satan's Claw.*

SATAN'S DAUGHTERS. Video version of *Vampyres—Daughters of Darkness* (Majestic).

SATAN'S DOGS. Video version of *Play Dead* (Video Vision).

SATAN'S MISTRESS. See *Demon Rage.*

SATAN'S PRINCESS (1989) ★★½ This witchcraft movie presents a little of everything to titillate you (lesbian love scenes, heterosexual love scenes, cops-and-robbers shoot-outs, a strangling, an icepick-in-the-back scene, a blowtorch job, etc.) but only adds up to exploitation material from producer-director Bert I. Gordon. Robert Forster portrays a burned-out ex-cop searching for the missing daughter of a friend. The girl is making love with beautiful French actress Lydie Denier while Forster runs around having bad dreams, kicking and hitting people to learn the truth, being nasty to his girl and trying to take care of his handicapped son. Caren Kaye, Philip Glasser, M. K. Harris, Ellen Geer, Jack Carter. (Video/Laser: Paramount)

SATAN'S SATELLITES (1952). Feature version of *Zombies of the Stratosphere* (Admit One).

SATAN'S SISTER. See *The She-Beast.*

SATAN'S SKIN. See *The Blood on Satan's Claw.*

SATAN'S SUPPER. Variant video version of *The Nightmare Never Ends* (Academy).

SATURDAY NIGHT SHOCKERS VOL. I. Video

combo of *The Creeping Terror* and *Chained for Life* (Rhino).

SATURDAY NIGHT SHOCKERS VOL. II. Video combo of *Manbeast* and *Human Gorilla* (Rhino).

SATURDAY NIGHT SHOCKERS VOL. III. Video combo of *Murders in the Red Barn* and *Face at the Window* (Rhino).

SATURDAY NIGHT SHOCKERS VOL. IV. Video combo of *The Monster of Piedras Blancas* and *The Mesa of Lost Women* (Rhino).

SATURDAY THE 14TH (1981) ★ Blame producer Julie Corman, wife of Roger, for this flubbed comedy spoof directed childishly by Howard R. Cohen. A couple (Richard Benjamin, Paula Prentiss) moving into a haunted house are confronted by aliens, vampires and other monsters and things. Many folks worked on the effects, but men in rubber monster suits still look like men in rubber monster suits and most of the jokes fall as flat as corpses. The only funny sequence is when a shark fin appears in a bathtub. Rosemary DeCamp, Jeffrey Tambor, Severen Darden. (Embassy; Sultan)

SATURDAY THE 14TH STRIKES BACK (1988) ★ This sequel to Julie Corman's 1981 horror spoof is not an improvement on the original but another series of weak gags written-directed by Howard R. Cohen and produced by Corman with the poorest of effects. A weird family living in a strange L.A. house is again the target of a bevy of monsters, unleashed when a crack opens under the mansion. Neither a quintet of sexy young women nor footage lifted from Corman action films can save this fluff, and a good cast (Ray Walston, Avery Schreiber, Patty McCormack, Julianna McNamara, Jason Presson, Leo Gordon) is wasted. (MGM/UA)

SATURN THREE (1980) ★★½ Astonishing sets and futuristic hardware mean very little when the plot is one big story hole in blackest space. The star here is Hector the Demigod Robot, a masterpiece of technology, blending human features with robotic traits. The less successful human stars are Kirk Douglas and Farrah Fawcett as space dwellers on Titan, a moon of Saturn, living an idyllic Adam-and-Eve existence until Harvey Keitel drops by to malprogram the robot to lust after Farrah's body. This mess of contrivance and confusion never reaches a suitable conclusion. Based on an idea by production designer John Barry, who died before the film was completed, it was finished by Stanley Donen. Douglas Lambert, Ed Bishop. (Video/Laser: CBS/Fox)

SAVAGE ABDUCTION. Variant video version of *Cycle Psychos* (King of Video; Paragon).

SAVAGE APOCALYPSE. See *Invasion of the Flesh Hunters.*

SAVAGE DAWN. Video of *Stryker* (Media; Bingo).

SAVAGE LUST (1989) ★★ Weakly plotted "dark old house" mystery in which 6 teenagers and a fugitive seek shelter in a deserted mansion, where in the front yard a demolished automobile has been enshrined. Suddenly, a knife-wielding maniac in a white mime mask starts knocking them off. The explanation behind the almost nonexistent mystery provided by writer-director José Ramon Larraz is barely enough to hold this clichéd picture together, and there is only 1 torrid lovemaking sequence to justify a title that implies this film is an "erotic thriller" when it is not. Jennifer Delora, William Russell. (Action International)

SAVAGE PLANET, THE. See *Fantastic Planet.*

SAWBONES (1995) ★★½ A companion piece to *Dr. Giggles*, this routine Roger Corman TV movie depicts a totally crazed would-be doctor (Don Harvey) kidnapping people in order to operate on them—without painkillers! While Sam Montgomery's script lacks the sardonic, morbid humor of *Dr. Giggles*, it does focus on some gory sequences that, if you hate surgical probes, will have your flesh crawling the walls of the OR. Adam Baldwin, Luis Antonio Ramos, and Don Stroud are cops working the case, but the real hero is Nina Sipmaszko, who follows a trail of clues to the bad doctor's home, there to undergo horrors as the doctor operates on the buttocks of Barbara Carrera (!). Unfortunately, why Sipmaszko is dumb enough to do some of the things she does doesn't concern director Catherine Cyran—just the bloody acts themselves. Ugh! (New Horizons)

SCALPEL (1978) ★★½ First feature effort of Joseph Weintraub and John M. Grissmer (aka *False Face*) could have used a finer edge in depicting a psychopathic plastic surgeon (Robert Lansing) who creates a "dead ringer" lookalike for his missing daughter (Judith Chapman) so he can collect a $5 million inheritance. Ample twists and turns in director Grissmer's screenplay; a minor suspense melodrama with a surprise ending. Go ahead, take a stab at *Scalpel*. (Charter; Embassy)

SCALPS (1983) ★½ Juvenile gore thriller poorly written and sloppily directed by Fred Olen Ray, with a terrible sound track and an amateurish cast, which at least makes for a few unintended laughs. Archeology students on an expedition to the Black Trees Indian Burial Ground disturb the spirit of the renegade Black Claw (also known as Tom A. Hawk), who scalps the kids, shoots arrows into them and otherwise behaves abominably. Cancel his reservation. Kirk Alyn (one-time serial Superman) appears briefly as an absentminded dig specialist, Forrest J. Ackerman has a pointless cameo as Professor Trentwood and Carroll Borland pops up as Dr. Reynolds, with nothing to do. Jo Ann Robinson, Roger Maycock, Richard Hench,

Frank McDonald. (Imperial; Marquis; on Planet video with *Slayer*)

SCANNERCOP (1993) ★★★ This fourth entry in the *Scanners* series is a riveting, well-produced cop thriller in which scanner Daniel Quinn, a member of the LAPD, uses his powers to track down a mad scientist (Richard Lynch) who is using a brainwashing technique to turn innocent people into cop killers. Good effects, suspense and a honed script by George Sanders and John Bryant make this one a winner. Directed by Pierre David. Darlanne Fluegel. (Republic)

SCANNERCOP II: VOLKIN'S REVENGE. See *Scanners: The Showdown*.

SCANNERS (1981) ★★★ Contrived but fascinating film written-directed by David Cronenberg. Psychics (scanners) have disrupted a government investigation of their powers and gone underground to wage a war of conquest. Scientist Patrick McGoohan sends a scanner into their secret ranks to spy . . . intrigue and violent death follow. Cronenberg achieves a weird atmosphere and the special effects (including an exploding human head) shook up audiences and gave the film word of mouth. If Cronenberg had avoided his muddled plot, he might have scanned better. Four interesting sequels followed. Stephen Lack, Jennifer O'Neill, Michael Ironside, Lawrence Dane. Aka *Telepathy 2000*. (Embassy; CBS/Fox) (Laser: CBS/Fox)

SCANNERS II: THE NEW ORDER (1990) ★★★ Although David Cronenberg didn't return to make this sequel to his 1981 hit, it's a fair follow-up depicting new adventures of scanners—those with power to control others via mental forces, and even explode heads on occasion. The Canadian film, scripted by B. J. Nelson and directed by Christian Duguay, depicts scanner David Kellum (David Hewlett) preventing crooked elements in Toronto's government from taking over with evil scanners. The gory scanner duels are handled well and 3 sequences stand out: the destruction of a video arcade; the demolition of a mannequin warehouse; and a mental battle between Hewlett and bad-guy scanner Raoul Trujillo. Yvan Ponton, Deborah Raffin, Isabelle Mejias, Tom Butler. (Media/Fox) (Laser: Image)

SCANNERS III: THE TAKEOVER (1991) ★★ Liliana Komorowska's campy performance as a sweet scanner who takes an experimental drug from her father and turns into a purely evil woman is the high point of this Canadian film directed by Christian Duguay. She all but chews the sets as she sways the masses through TV, kills dear old Dad in a hot tub and seduces a young executive during her ruthless climb to the top. The only person in her way is wayward brother Steve Parrish, who returns from a Thai monastery to give Liliana's henchmen a piece

of his scanner mind, resulting in mayhem and pyrotechnics. Call this one *Kung Fu Meets Videodrome*. Valerie Valois, Daniel Pilon, Collin Fox, Claire Cellucci. (Video/Laser: Republic)

SCANNERS IV. See *Scannercop*.

SCANNERS: THE SHOWDOWN (1994) ★★★ This direct sequel to *Scannercop*, originally produced as *Scannercop II: Volkin's Revenge*, is a pretty worn-out follow-up, given that little is new in Mark Sevi's script—just the same old tired scenes in which a mean old bad scanner (Patrick Kilpatrick) screws up his face and looks real mean as he mentally makes people do awful things to themselves. And it's all just so he can get even with good cop–scanner Staziak (Daniel Quinn). John Carl Buechler contributes good effects (heads pulsating and cracking open, that kind of stuff) as Kilpatrick sucks the energy out of his victims, leaving behind dehydrated corpses, but there's little here to challenge the mind, or to increase your desire to see more movies about scanners. Produced by Pierre David and directed by Steve Barnett, this fifth *Scanners* movie makes it pretty clear that, creatively speaking anyway, there's no need for a sixth. Fat chance. Khrystyne Haje, Stephen Mendel, Robert Forster, Jewel Shepard, Brenda Swanson, Jerry Potter. (Video/Laser: Republic)

SCARECROWS (1988) ★★★ Above-average video horror flick which, despite derivative plotting devices and typical grisliness, is fascinating as conceived by Richard Jefferies and co-writer-editor-producer-director William Wesley. In the Florida jungle, paramilitary robbers, after pulling off an army payroll heist, find themselves the hunted when they get mixed up with scarecrows endowed with homicidal tendencies (exactly how is alluded to in some shallow exposition). It's your basic "walking dead" story with mildly interesting characters and not too many genre clichés. Gang member Ted Vernon was also executive producer. Victoria Christian, Richard Vidan. (Forum) (Laser: Image)

SCARED STIFF (1987) ★★ Slave master of the 1850s comes back to a Southern mansion to terrorize a psychiatrist and his wife and child who apparently have been cursed. Director Richard Friedman cowrote the script with Mark Frost and producer Daniel F. Bacaner. David Ramsey, Nicole Fortier, Andrew Stevens, Mary Page Keller. (Video/Laser: Republic)

SCARED TO DEATH (1946) ★★ The only color film Bela Lugosi ever worked in—a skid-row programmer narrated by a dead girl, her report coming in flashback from the morgue. A stiff, boring plot has several characters coming together under one roof and behaving ridiculously. Slow moving and talkative, with minimal horror elements. Directed by Christy Cabanne from a W. J. Abbott script. George Zucco, Nat Pendleton, Joyce Compton, Douglas Fowley. (Nostalgia Merchant; Sinister/C; Filmfax; Admit One offers this with *Dick Tracy's Dilemma*) (Laser: Lumivision, with *Devil Bat*)

SCARED TO DEATH (1980) ★★★ *Alien* lookalike called a Syngenor (Synthesized Genetic Organism), created in a lab DNA experiment, hides in L.A.'s sewers, sucking marrow from victims by inserting its tongue into the mouth. Ugh. Under the direction of Bill Malone, who also wrote the script (aka *The Aberdeen Experiment*), the first half is slow going, alternating trapped humans undergoing attack and the domestic life of ex-cop John Stinston and secretary Diana Davidson. The last half picks up in the sewers, where Stinston and scientist Toni Jannotta are pursued by the thing. Climax takes place in a factory and finally the film becomes harrowing. The characters, unfortunately, are all contrived and boring. (Media)

SCAREMAKER, THE. See *Girls Nite Out*.

SCARLET CLAW, THE (1944) ★★★½ Phosphorescent ghost haunts the moors, ripping out throats of victims with a bloody claw and fleeing—a white, glittering specter etched against foggy swampland. Who should pick up a glow of his own as he cries "The game is afoot!" but Sherlock Holmes, visiting Canada with the good Dr. Watson. Jolly good item, with thrilling and scary moments, in the Universal series with Basil Rathbone and Nigel Bruce. A fine chap, that producer-director Roy William Neill. And that writer Edmund L. Hartman, now there's a good fellow, eh what? Aka *Sherlock Holmes and the Scarlet Claw*. (Key)

SCARLET EXECUTIONER, THE. See *Bloody Pit of Horror*.

SCARLET HANGMAN, THE. See *Bloody Pit of Horror*.

SCARLET JUNGLE, THE. See *Dr. Mabuse vs. Scotland Yard*.

SCARLET SCORPION, THE (1986) ★★ A Brazilian adaptation of a popular radio serial "The Adventures of the Angel," in which a cloaked villain known as the Scarlet Scorpion does battle with the Angel, a millionaire playboy (shades of the Shadow!) Directed by Ivan Cardoso. Herson Capri, Leo Jaime, Felipe Falcao. (S/Weird)

SCARS OF DRACULA (1970) ★★★ Popular Hammer production in the Christopher Lee/Dracula series—written by John Elder (alias for producer Anthony Hinds), directed by Roy Ward Baker, scored by James Bernard. Lee, resurrected when his ashes are covered with bat's blood, begins his reign of terror and fights off a revenge seeker. Blood and sadism (lots) have been added to the formula. Dennis Waterman, Christopher Matthews, Jenny Hanley, Michael Gwynn, Michael Ripper. (HBO; Republic) (Laser: Republic with *The Horror of Frankenstein*)

SCHIZO (1976) ★★★ Graphic British psy-

chothriller with a top-notch cast, good direction by Peter Walker and a mildly intriguing script by David McGillivray. It's a bloody thing, though, highlighting a darning needle through an eyeball socket, a sledgehammer into a human brain, a body run over by a truck, and a few standard knife slashings. Lynne Frederick portrays a pretty ice-skating star pursued by a strange man (John Leyton) and a memory of maternal homicide. Nice twist ending. Stephanie Beacham adds her charms to the tense tale. John Fraser, Jack Watson. Aka *Amok* and *Blood of the Undead*. (Media; VCI)

SCHIZO (1990) ★★ Lisa Aliff's 30-minute ordeal to escape the horrors of a Yugoslavian monastery, where a slavic spirit-demon takes over archeologist Aron Eisenberg, is the best thing about this offbeat tale of Eisenberg's search for a lost tomb. Keaton Jones's script gets skewered at times before the focus falls on Eisenberg's possession and the horrors he performs in a chamber of torture. Director Manny Coto succeeds in capturing a claustrophobic and oppressive feeling amidst the Yugoslav locations and emphasizes the obsessed behavior of Eisenberg as he gradually goes bonkers. Vincent Schiavelli has an unusual role as a mental patient. Coto went on to make the superior *Dr. Giggles*. Christopher McDonald, Maja, James Purcell. (Media; VCI)

SCHIZOID. See *The Psychopath*.

SCHIZOID (1980) ★★ Psychiatrist Klaus Kinski's group-therapy patients are knocked off one by one by a scissors-wielding maniac while gossip columnist Marianna Hill investigates. Cheap and tasteless, although some scenes of Kinski capture an eerie quality whenever director-writer David Paulsen tries to upgrade this sleazy material. Aka *Murder by Mail*. Craig Wasson, Richard Herd, Christopher Lloyd, Flo Gerrish. (MCA)

SCHLOCK (1973) ★★★ John Landis's first feature (he wrote-directed) is a refreshing change of pain for horror fans, depicting a Neanderthal man (Landis) thawed from his prehistoric haven and on a rampage in an average U.S. city. It's played as a satire on movie monsters. Forrest J. Ackerman and Don Glut guest with Saul Kahn and Joseph Piantodosi. (Lightning; Wizard; from Westernworld as *Banana Monster*, an a-peeling title)

SCHOOL THAT ATE MY BRAIN, THE. See *Zombie High*.

SCIENCE CRAZED (1990) ★ Instantly forgettable claptrap set in Shelley Institute where "the Fiend" attacks women. Produced in Canada in 1987, this amateurish effort was written and co-produced, -directed and -edited by Ron Switzer. Cameron Klein, Tony Dellaventura, Robin Hartsell. (Interamerica Entertainment)

SCIENCE FICTION: A JOURNEY INTO THE UNKNOWN (1994) ★★★ Sponsored by the Museum of Television and Radio, this historical 2-hour study of TV science fiction from the early '50s through "Star Trek: Deep Space Nine" is hosted by William Shatner, Leonard Nimoy, Dean Cain and Carrie Fisher. The themed segments include "Time Travel," "Nightmare Worlds," "Other Dimensions and Fantasies," "Man and Machine" and "Outer Space." Running commentary by producer-director Scott Goldstein and Mary Wallace is intelligent and the choice of clips—from such shows as "The Outer Limits," "The Invaders," "Alien Nation," "Star Trek," "Lost in Space," "Space: 1999," "Robocop" and "The Prisoner"—is superb.

SCOTLAND YARD HUNTS DR. MABUSE. See *Dr. Mabuse vs. Scotland Yard.*

SCOTLAND YARD IN PURSUIT OF DR. MABUSE. See *Dr. Mabuse vs. Scotland Yard.*

SCOTLAND YARD MYSTERY. See *The Living Dead.*

SCOTLAND YARD VS. DR. MABUSE. See *Dr. Mabuse vs. Scotland Yard.*

SCREAM (1985) ★ Originally shot in 1981 as *The Outing,* this was released 4 years later and hailed as the worst horror movie of all time. Hopelessly written-directed by Byron Quisenberry with the pacing of a snail, this follows uninteresting, never-developed hikers to a deserted Western town where a killer strikes with hatchet and ax. Minimal gore scenes and hardly any explanation about the killer is given. Woody Strode turns up mysteriously on horseback. One long series of dull panning shots with people who act contrary to human nature. Pepper Martin, Hank Worden, Alvy Moore, Gregg Palmer. (Vestron)

SCREAM (1996) ★★★ Wes Craven is one of the few horror-genre directors to search for new twists within stereotyped forms, as *Wes Craven's New Nightmare* demonstrated. In this recycled vision of the *Friday the 13th* and *Halloween* series, Craven—using an original script by Kevin Williamson—mixes standard terror thrills with spoofs of the formula. This blurring of distinctions is summed up by one of the characters: "It's all one great big movie." Craven/Williamson even remind us of the three rules a character in a horror movie should always follow: 1) Never have sex. 2) Never drink or take drugs. 3) Never say, "I'll be right back." Do any one of them and you're dead for sure. All that aside, *Scream* is, in many ways, a scream and a half when Craven trowels on the shocks and thrills. A knife-wielding killer with a startling ghost mask attacks and corners Drew Barrymore in the film's opening, and best, set piece. Now the rural community of Woodsboro is beset by the fiendish killer, complicating the lives of heroine Neve Campbell, her boyfriend Skeet Ulrich, TV reporter Courteney Cox, high-school principal Henry Winkler, deputy David Arquette, and assorted horror-movie-happy teenagers. The twist ending, designed to poke fun at the plotting of horror-slasher movies and the whole issue of motive for murder, is slam-bang crazy if totally implausible, but then that's the point. *Scream,* which is frequently gory and has several stalking-followed-by-death scenes, is designed to satisfy and yet tinker with hardcore buffs. Matthew Lillard, Rose McGowan, Lawrence Hecht. (Video/DVD: Buena Vista)

SCREAM 2 (1997) ★★★ Kevin Williamson's screenplay for the first *Scream* was so clever in making fun of the slasher genre, with its characters' awareness of the existence of horror movies and the clichés that drive them, that it's a tough act to follow. Obviously, this was made to cash in on the enormous success of the 1996 box-office smash, and once again Wes Craven directs with a keen sense of satire without sacrificing any of the thrills. The film opens with a memorable set piece that exploits what the genre is all about: college students have filled a movie theater to see the premiere of *Stab,* a horror flick (in "Stab-O-Rama" yet) that is based on *The Woodsboro Murders,* a book by investigative journalist Gale Weathers about all the crimes committed in the first *Scream.* As horrible things unfold on the screen (young women trapped in house with killer), the real fiend is at work in the theater committing a double murder—the final victim dying in front of the screen before the entire audience. Cut to the nearby college, where the distressed Sidney Prescott (Neve Campbell) is still getting over the horrors of the first *Scream,* surrounded by characters who ultimately become "the usual suspects." Anyone could be the killer. There's the horror-genre expert Randy Meeks (Jamie Kennedy) who informs us that what is unfolding is a real-life sequel; therefore the rules, as laid out in movie-movies, are 1) the body count has to be higher, 2) the death scenes have to be more elaborate, and 3) there must be more blood and gore—"carnage candy." And so it is, and so are there other characters to ponder on the clever way Williamson lays out his tale: there's onetime deputy Dewey Riley (David Arquette) who's always hanging around like an investigator; Sidney's well-intended boyfriend Derek (Jerry O'Connell); Cotton Weary (Liev Schreiber), who spent a year wrongly incarcerated because Sidney made a mistaken identification of the killer; and that bitchy newswoman Gale Weathers (Courteney Cox) who wrote that damn book and her cameraman Joel (Duane Martin). How about the film student Mickey (Timothy

Olyphant) and another reporter Debbie Salt (Laurie Metcalf)? Which one is it? As crafty as Williamson's script is, and it is full of delightful dialogue and startling revelations, you might figure out what's going on—or you may just become absorbed in the suspenseful murder sequences, which are, of course, more elaborate than in *Scream 1*. One interesting point: there is a classroom discussion among the characters about the effect violent movies have on us. Since *Scream 2* features some very graphic and disturbing acts of criminal behavior toward young women, and then discusses the ramifications of audiences seeing these terrible acts, the movie is questioning its own values in an articulate and honest manner. When Williamson and Craven do that, suddenly what looked like a simple entertainment is not simple at all. (Video/ DVD: Dimension)

SCREAM 3 (1999) ★★★ Wes Craven continues to spoof himself and the content of slasher movies and other types of horror flicks in this final (well, maybe final) entry in the series he began in 1996 with boffo box office. Once Craven has established the central rule—that when you make the third film in a trilogy "all bets are off"—you know you're in for a fair number of graphic and grisly surprises. And he doesn't let you down, although he is unable to rise to the heights of the first feature, either visually or story-wise. (The script by Ehren Kruger in no way matches Kevin Williamson's original.) The setting is the Sunrise Studios of Hollywood, where schlockmeister producer Lance Henriksen (with Roger Corman assisting) is making *Stab 2*, a sequel re-creation of the Woodsboro murders depicted in the original *Scream*. Only trouble is, someone has donned the mask of the killer for the third time and the body count is climbing again, beginning with the slaughter of Cotton Weary (Liev Schreiber). Back to be terrorized by the masked murderer are Neve Campbell as Sidney Prescott (who will become the central and ultimate intended victim), Courteney Cox Arquette as TV anchor-woman Gale Weathers (being her usual bitchy, you-love-to-hate-her self) and David Arquette as Dewey Riley, the hero who is forever hapless in helping others. There's a lot of red herrings and background exposition to clutter the landscape with possibilities as to the killer's true identity, but this time there isn't quite enough interest built so that you really care whose face is beneath the mask. Rather, it's a tried-and-true formula that Craven follows, so what you really get are the shock moments and the violent set pieces of cat-and-mouse pursuit/escape excitement. Also a lot of "stinger" pieces of music to punctuate dozens of ersatz surprises. Since that's all you probably care about anyway, being jolted, jarred and stunned, *Scream 3* has to be deemed a better-than-adequate follow-up. Will there be a fourth *Scream?* This one made $33 million on its opening weekend, so go figure. (Video/DVD: Dimension)

SCREAM . . . AND DIE. Video version of *The House That Vanished* (Lightning).

SCREAM AND SCREAM AGAIN (1970) ★★★½ Stomach-churning thrill piece from director Gordon Hessler and writer Christopher Wicking, who bring to this British luridness a touch of allegory. Vincent Price is a scientist creating superhumans through fiendish surgical anomalies, mutilating bodies in sickening ways to acquire transplants. That's when Hessler and Wicking get a little carried away . . . again and again. Peter Cushing is an ex-Nazi and Christopher Lee is a British secret agent. Judy Huxtable is a screaming victim. Based on a Peter Saxon novel, *The Disorientated Man*. Alfred Marx, Uta Levka. Aka *Screamer*. (Vestron; Orion)

SCREAM, BLACULA, SCREAM (1972) ★★★ Sequel to the box office smash *Blacula*, a sometimes amusing, often chilling portrait of vampirism with William Marshall again "bringing to life" the aristocratic black vampire. This time his bones are used in voodoo rituals, and he reappears in human form to do battle with priestess Pam Grier. Marshall, with his authoritative presence and booming, rich voice, creates a sympathetic vampire. Directed by Bob Kelljan of *Count Yorga—Vampire* fame. Don Mitchell, Richard Lawson, Bernie Hamilton. Aka *Blacula II, The Name Is Blacula, Blacula Lives Again!* and *Blacula Is Beautiful*. (Filmways; Orion) (Laser: Japanese)

SCREAM DREAM (1990) ★½ Carol Carr portrays a rock singer whose body is possessed by a witch/demon that turns her screaming fans into screaming maniacs who commit bloody murders. Cheap effort in the gore tradition, shot by writer-director Donald Farmer in Tennessee. Melissa More, Nikki Riggins, Jesse Raye. (American; Interamerican Entertainment/New Image)

SCREAMER (1970). See *Scream and Scream Again*.

SCREAMERS (1978) ★★ Roger Corman purchased an Italian flick, *The Fish Men*, added 12 minutes of new footage and rereleased it on an unsuspecting world. Mad doc Richard Johnson creates gill guys, and daughter Barbara Bach reluctantly cooperates until the shipwreck survivor Claudio Cassinelli helps her escape the volcanic island as it sinks. Special monster makeup by Chris Walas. Italian footage was shot by Sergio Martino, U.S. inserts by Dan T. Miller. Aka *Island of Mutations, Something Waits in the Dark* and *Isle of the Fishmen*. Joseph Cotten, Mel Ferrer, Cameron Mitchell, Beryl Cunningham. (Embassy)

SCREAMERS (1995) ★★★½ Grim and gritty to

the extreme, this Charles Fries–produced amalgam of science fiction, suspense and horror is based on Philip K. Dick's short story "Second Variety" and is a hard-hitting and effective shocker/mood piece as screenwriter Dan O'Bannon has interpreted it. Call it "sci-fi *noir*." Set in deep space in A.D. 2078 on the planet Sirius 6B, it involves the intrigue and deception surrounding a war between Earth-based factions who are fighting over a new mineral called Berynium; they are also faced with a new nemesis in the form of a mechanical killing machine called a Screamer that has developed an intelligence of its own to replicate human beings. The warring sides join forces to fight the common enemy, a burrowing death machine that attacks humans not wearing a protective armband. (Though seen only briefly, the design is chilling.) Peter Weller and Jennifer Rubin are cynical foes who must find faith in each other, and Roy Dupuis, Andy Lauer and Ron White portray wary, almost paranoid soldiers. It's good screen high-tech science fiction that will please lovers of both genres, and a feather in the cap of Canadian director Christian Duguay, who previously made two *Scanners* sequels.

SCREAM FOR HELP (1984) ★★★ Swift pacing and thrill piled on thrill make this a lively suspense mystery, scripted by Tom Holland and directed by Michael Winner. Teenager Rachael Kelly suspects her stepfather of trying to kill her mother for the family fortune but no one in town (including the police commissioner) will believe her, even though it's apparent from the outset there is a conspiracy afoot. The climax is ludicrous and grossly violent yet you will be compelled to watch. David Brooks, Marie Masters. (Lorimar) (Laser: Warner Bros.)

SCREAM GREATS I (1986) ★★★ Documentary on makeup/special effects man Tom Savini, featuring quotes by Savini and interviews with George Romero and various actors on the set of *Day of the Dead*. Fascinating look into low-budget movies. Footage features many films Savini has labored on, with emphasis on his working relationship with Romero. First in a series from *Fangoria* magazine. Directed by Damon Santostefano. (Video/Laser: Paramount)

SCREAM GREATS II: SATANISM AND WITCHCRAFT (1986) ★★★ Second video in a series produced by *Fangoria* magazine, this volume tracks real-life devil cults, witches and other satanic elements in the world of black arts. Directed by Damon Santostefano from a Richard Lawton script. (Video/Laser: Paramount)

SCREAMING DEAD, THE (1971). Video version of *Dracula vs. Dr. Frankenstein* (VCI; Wizard).

SCREAMING STARTS, THE. See *And Now the Screaming Starts*.

SCREAM OF FEAR (1961) ★★★ Favorite Hammer production in the "let's scare the lovely woman to death" genre, written by producer Jimmy Sangster and directed by Seth Holt. Susan Strasberg is haunted by the corpse of her father, who turns up in the swimming pool. Decorum dictates we reveal nothing further, lest your enjoyment of this labyrinthine thriller be marred. Take nothing for granted, and be prepared to be jolted by the "haunting" scenes. Aka *A Taste of Fear*. Christopher Lee, Ronald Lewis, Ann Todd. (CBS/Fox; RCA/Columbia)

SCREAM OF THE DEMON LOVER (1971) ★★★ Spanish-Italian programmer with an all-too-familiar plot (beautiful woman comes to eerie gothic castle, where sinister nobleman holds sway) is well photographed and acted, suggesting exciting things that never arrive. He's a part-time doctor experimenting with rejuvenating dead flesh, she's a biochemist falling for the baron even though he's suspected by the villagers of heinous crimes against women. There's a decayed hand that crawls over her supple body and a fiend in the cellar—and would you believe a servant named Igor? Directed by J. L. Merino (Jacinto Molina) from an E. Colombo screenplay. Jennifer Hartley and Jeffrey Chase do what they can as the odd couple, but are ultimately defeated by an unsatisfying, illogical ending. Aka *Altar of Blood* and *Killers of the Castle of Blood*. (Charter; from Lightning as *Blood Castle*)

SCREAMS IN THE NIGHT. See *The Awful Dr. Orlof*.

SCREAMS OF A WINTER NIGHT (1977) ★★★ Effective attempt to deal with the fear that mounts to a crescendo if we listen to one horror story too many, told with a minimum of gory effects or monstrous visuals—emphasis is on suggestion. The setting is Lake Durant (called Coyote Lake by the Indians) where young vacationers settle in a cabin for the weekend. Half the script by coproducer Richard H. Wadsack deals with Chataba, a legendary evil spirit of the wind that wreaks havoc. The other half is made up of stories the kids tell each other on a dark night. "Moss Point Man" deals with a Yeti creature stalking two kids; "Green Light" depicts fraternity students spending the night in a hotel haunted by a green light; and "Crazy Annie" is the psychological study of a young woman who kills with a knife. The framework story is most effective as director James L. Wilson builds to the horrifying climax. Filmed in Natchitoches Parish, La., this features William Ragsdale (*Fright Night*) in a bit part. Matt Borel, Gil Glasgow, Patrick Byers, Mary Anne Cox. (VCI; United)

SCREAMTIME (1983) ★★ Anthology of 3 British TV episodes with wraparound footage shot in New York City of two small-time hoodlums watching the episodes on cassettes they've stolen. The first is about a maladjusted puppeteer who brings his dummies to homicidal life. The second depicts a woman in a mansion who keeps seeing a child playing in the yard and a man rushing about the house with a butcher knife. In "Garden of Blood" (the only title given to any of the chapters) dirt bikers invade the home of two old ladies to rob them but a spirit in a painting comes to life to wreak revenge. Below par for TV production. The hoods get their comeuppance in the dumbest ways. Produced and directed by Al Beresford, written by Michael Armstrong. Vincent Russo, Robin Bailey, Dora Bryan. (Lightning; Live)

SCROOGE (1935) ★★½ As British adaptations of Dickens's *A Christmas Carol* go, this is now a pretty creaky, slow-moving affair, the quality of available prints being poor. Too many better versions (especially the 1951 rendition with Alastair Sim) have weakened its impact. However, its attention to period detail is rather interesting and the cast, while overwrought at times, has that "typically British" quality Americans love to watch. Sir Seymour Hicks does an excellent job capturing the unlovable, miserly Ebenezer Scrooge. Hicks also cowrote the script with H. Fowler Mear. Directed by Henry Edwards. Donald Calthrop, Robert Cochran, Philip Frost, Mary Glynne, Oscar Asche. (Video Yesteryear; Discount)

SEA CREATURES. See *Beyond Atlantis*.

SEARCHERS OF THE VOODOO MOUNTAIN. See *Warriors of the Apocalypse*.

SEASON OF THE WITCH (1973) ★★ Writer-director George Romero's attempt to deal with witches in modern suburbia functions better as a psychology study of sexually frustrated, alcoholic housewives. This has the unorthodox editing of early Romero but it's a tedious ordeal, without sympathetic characters or a plot structure. Virginia Greenwald, Ray Laine. Aka *Hungry Wives* and *Jack's Wife*. (Vidamerica; Vista)

SECONDS (1966) ★★★★½ Multitiered John Frankenheimer film, adapted by Lewis John Carlino from David Ely's novel, is an allegory about our search for identity and a fresh start, and a whopper of a horror tale, photographed surrealistically by James Wong Howe. A secret organization supplies clients with new identities and faces so they can escape to a new milieu. John Randolph, disillusioned New York banker, emerges from his operation as Rock Hudson. But the "new man" cannot adjust to the artificial world the organization provides and he demands yet another identity. The climax is absolutely shocking; Rock Hudson was never better. Salome Jens, Will Geer, Jeff Corey, Murray Hamilton. A neglected film deserving to be rediscovered.

SECRET ADVENTURES OF TOM THUMB, THE (1993) ★★★ A totally off-the-ball fairy tale blending jerky, live-action footage with stop-motion animation and other filmic trickery to tell the whacked-out life story of a miniature baby in a world of giant adults who grunt, coo and chuckle without ever saying a distinguishable word. This weird time and place is populated by scurrying spiders and other unidentifiable species of insects that are always buzzing about—when they are not being eaten by adults. Smashing, startling sound effects enhance the track as the clay figure of Tom Thumb tries to find a place in a society of misfits and social freaks. This 1-hour "cartoon" was made in Bristol by the Bolex Bros., with Dave Borthwick writing, designing, directing and editing. Nick Upton, Deborah Collard, Frank Passingham. (Tara Releasing)

SECRET BRIDE OF CANDY ROCK, THE. See *The 30-Foot Bride of Candy Rock*.

SECRET LIFE OF WALTER MITTY, THE (1948) ★★★★ Wonderful adaptation of James Thurber's story (by Ken Englund and Everett Freeman) about a meekish gent who escapes into fantasies, ideally slanted for the comedic talents of Danny Kaye. Mitty, a Milquetoast working for a pulp-magazine publisher, fantasizes numerous whimsical adventures, then he's pulled into a real one when he comes into possession of a secret formula that spy Boris Karloff is seeking. Frothily directed by Norman Z. McLeod. Virginia Mayo, Ann Rutherford, Fay Bainter. (Nelson; Goldwyn) (Laser: Nelson)

SECRET OF DR. ALUCARD. See *A Taste of Blood*.

SECRET OF DR. MABUSE, THE (1964) ★★ One of several West German sequels to Fritz Lang's films of the '20s about a mastermind criminal with plans to conquer the world. The mad doctor (Wolfgang Preiss) is a math genius who turns his brilliance to evil with the use of a Death Ray. Peter Van Eyck, Werner Peters, Leo Genn, Yvonne Furneaux and Yoko Tani drudge drearily through Western Europe, looking like refugees. Directed by Hugo Fregonese from a Ladislas Fodor script. Aka *Death Rays of Dr. Mabuse, The Death Ray Mirror of Dr. Mabuse* and *The Devilish Dr. Mabuse*. Other entries in this series: *The Thousand Eyes of Dr. Mabuse, The Return of Dr. Mabuse* and *Dr. Mabuse vs. Scotland Yard*.

SECRET OF DR. ORLOFF, THE. See *Dr. Orloff's Monster*.

SECRET OF NIMH, THE (1982) ★★★½ Splendid adaptation of Robert C. O'Brien's novel about a family of mice seeking a new home and mother mouse searching for mythical characters because a son is sick with pneumonia and needs medicine. A fanciful odyssey with wonderful animal characters, this is stylish, old-fashioned animation by producer-artist Don Bluth. The film was not a big success, perhaps because audiences were asked to accept rats as heroic figures. Too bad—the film deserved better with its bursts of vivid imagination. Voices by Elizabeth Hartman, Dom De Luise, Hermione Baddeley, Peter Strauss, Paul Shenar, Derek Jacobi, John Carradine, Aldo Ray. (Video/Laser: MGM/UA)

SECRET OF ROAN INISH, THE (1994) ★★★★ Irish mythology and legend are lyrically examined by writer-director John Sayles in this adaptation of Rosalie K. Fry's novel *Secret of the Ron Mor Skerey*. Jeni Courtney plays a sweet adolescent who, in 1946, learns of strange beings through stories told to her—stories about a half-seal, half-woman creature who looks after souls lost at sea, and a youth floating in a bassinet, who survives with the help of seals. The latter she sees for herself—but how to convince disbelieving adults? Filmed by Haskell Wexler in Ireland's County Donegal, this unusual film has lovely footage of the country's rugged coastline. It's slow moving with minimal plot, but what an atmosphere Sayles and Wexler create. And Mick Lally is wonderful as the God-fearing, story-telling grandfather. John Lynch, Eileen Colgan, Richard Sheridan, Lillian Byrne. (Video/Laser: Columbia TriStar)

SECRET OF THE GOLDEN EAGLE, THE (1991) ★★ The statue of an eagle has the power to age people prematurely, and this strange object is sought by a pair of adventurers. Brandon McKay, Michael Berryman. Directed by Cole McKay. (Western)

SECRET OF THE MUMMY, THE (1982) ★★ Eight parts of a map, when put together, will reveal the tomb of Runamb the Mummy in Egypt. But the owners of the pieces are being murdered in this Brazilian horror thriller directed by Ivan Cardoso. José Mojica Marins, Anseimo Vasconceilos, Wilson Grey. (S/Weird)

SECRET SERVICE IN DARKEST AFRICA. See *Manhunt in the African Jungle*.

SECRETS OF THE UNKNOWN. Five-volume video set of the ABC documentary series about unnatural phenomena, including reports on UFOs, the *Titanic*, the pyramids, Jack the Ripper, and dreams. (MPI)

SECRET WORLD OF DR. LAO, THE. See *The Seven Faces of Dr. Lao*.

SECT, THE. See *The Devil's Daughter* (1991).

SEDUCED BY EVIL (1994) ★★ Hackneyed TV-movie offers nothing new in the supernatural department when magazine writer Suzanne Somers encounters a strange healer living in the desert near Tucson, who turns out to be a *brujo* (shape-shifter) from the 17th century. As if he's seen too many of Universal's *Mummy* movies, he thinks Somers is the reincarnation of the lover who deserted him a few centuries before. Raven and wolf icons supply the special effects of this tedious, gee-I've-seen-it-all-before offering. It was written by Bill Svanoe, from a book by Ann Arrington Wolcott, and directed on Arizona locations by Tony Wharmby in routine

fashion. James B. Sikking, John Vargas, Mindy Spence, Nancy Moonves, Julie Carmen. (Paramount)

SEDUCTION: THREE TALES FROM THE INNER SANCTUM (1992) ★★½ This is a tepid revival of Himan Brown's classic "creaking door" horror series for radio, in which a ghoulish chap in a crypt introduced horror tales. However, for this TV-movie they dropped the ghoulish chap and just let three film noir–type mysteries unfold, with little of the radio show's shock values. The gimmick here is that Victoria Principal portrays the lead women in the yarns. In "Temptation" (written by Barrow Brown) she's a femme fatale luring a man into a trap; in "Sacrifice" (written by Barry Brown and Robert Glass) she's the wife of a tormented painter; and in "Ecstasy" (written by Robert Glass and Steven Whitney) she plays another beauty luring a man into her web via computer games. The twist endings are weak, to say the least, and director Michael Ray Rhodes has too little to work with. John Terry, Jon O'Hurley, Richard Herd, W. Morgan Sheppard, Andreas Katsulas.

SEED OF TERROR. See *Grave of the Vampire*.

SEEDPEOPLE (1992) ★★ Producer Charles Band's video movie borrows heavily from *The Invasion of the Body Snatchers* for its premise: In Comet Valley, where a meteorite struck centuries before, alien spores scatter to turn folks into hideous killer monsters with long fangs and terrible-looking mouths covered with drippy slime. The beings change back and forth from monster to human, and when they're humans they are without emotion. Gee, that is familiar. Sam Hennings and Bernard Kates lead the fight to stop the alien takeover in this paranoia thriller flick. Directed by Peter Manoogian. Andrea Roth, Dane Witherspoon, David Dunard, Holly Fields. (Paramount) (Laser: Full Moon)

SEIZURE (1974) ★★ Gore murders galore when a demented writer (Jonathan Frid of "Dark Shadows") creates characters who spring to life: Martine Beswick is the Queen of Death, Henry Baker plays an executioner and Herve Villechaize is Shorty the Slicer. Director Oliver Stone coscripted with Edward Mann. Troy Donahue, Mary Woronov. Being that it's Stone's first effort, this is worth seeking out. Aka *Queen of Evil*. (Prism; Starmaker)

SENDER, THE (1982) ★★★ Thought-provoking sophisticated horror film dealing with the psychological traumas of a young man (Zeljko Ivanek) suffering from amnesia. He's placed under the care of psychiatrist Kathryn Harrold, who experiences the mental images of his nightmares. Low-key handling by director Roger Christian and the taut screenplay by Thomas Baum make for a decent shocker. Shirley Knight appears as an apparition (or ghost?) of the boy's domineering mother, who fights Harrold for her son's love. Paul Freeman, Sean Hewitt. (Video/Laser: Paramount)

SENSATION (1994) ★★★ A lot of weird shit is going down in this erotic whodunit psycho-thriller that is moody to the extreme under the direction of Brian Grant. Psychic Kari Wuhrer is hired by university professor Eric Roberts to take part in experiments in psychometry, the receiving of sensory impressions from inanimate objects. What Wuhrer doesn't know is that the objects once belonged to a young woman who was murdered, and the professor, having had an affair with her, remains a suspect for investigating cop Ron Perlman. The eroticism and nudity work to the film's advantage, as the whole thing is kinky from the start. How Wuhrer becomes obsessed by the dead woman, taking on her characteristics, becomes the thrust of Doug Wallace's script, which has a punchy payoff. Paul Le Mat, Claire Stansfield, Tracy Needham, Kieran Mulroney, Ed Begley, Jr.; producer John Morrissey plays a cop. (Video/Laser: Columbia TriStar)

SENSELESS (1998) ★ The title says it all for this tasteless, smutty failure of a comedy starring Harlon Wayans as a business student flubbing his way to success. Call it a 'hood fantasy, a black man's daydream. This ain't the way it happens, baby. Wayans, short of cash just when his grades are failing, volunteers to test crazy doctor Brad Dourif's new Protocol 563, a drug that intensifies the senses. The main problem with the Greg Ebb–Craig Mazin script is that Wayans is strangely brilliant one minute and a complete idiot the next. With no consistency of character to work with, director Penelope Spheeris is totally lost in trying to make Wayans funny. Wayans tries to be another Eddie Murphy but misses by miles. For some reason, there's nothing funny about making sport of handicapped people or having a woman reaching into Wayans's pants to feel his crotch. That and other unfunny sex gags are enough to gag anyone. Rip Torn does okay as the business executive thinking about hiring Wayans as an intern, but the rest of the cast is as tasteless as Wayans: David Spade, Matthew Lillard, Tamara Taylor, Richard McGonagle. (Video/DVD: Dimension)

SENTINEL, THE (1977) ★★½ Attempt at a classy demonic film in the league of *The Omen* or *The Exorcist* falls short in the hands of director Michael Winner, who allows the climax to deteriorate into a freak sideshow. Too many important events in Jeffrey Konvitz's story (scripted by Konvitz and Winner) are unexplained and characterizations are muddy as a river bottom when fashion model Cristina Raines settles in a New York City brownstone, where priest John Carradine maintains a singular vigil at an upstairs window. One scary sequence has the model confronted with the terrors of her childhood but the film as a whole never gels, this despite a plethora of interesting characters: Eli Wallach as the cop on the case, Ava Gardner as a strange realtor; Sylvia Miles and Beverly D'Angelo as lesbian lovers; Burgess Meredith as a sinister man with a cat; Christopher Walken as a cop; Chris Sarandon as Cristina's lover; and Jose Ferrer and Arthur Kennedy as men of the cloth. (MCA)

SERIAL KILLER (1995) ★★★ Inspired by *Silence of the Lambs*, this above-average genre movie depicts an intriguing duel of wits between serial killer Tobin Bell (who gives a tour de force performance as an intellectual madman) and FBI "mindwalker" profilist Kim Delaney (who specializes in getting into the heads of murderers), while cop Gary Hudson is buffeted about by both forces. William Lucian Morrano (Bell), a former taxidermist, is one helluva crafty murderer but has a problem: he hates Delaney for getting into his mind and he escapes immune-system experimentation in a hospital to terrorize her by attacking everyone she knows. The script by Mark Sevi is full of twists and surprises and producer-director Pierre David milks the cat-and-mouse stalking for all it's worth. A tense if derivative movie, enhanced by performances by Pam Grier (as the cop boss), Andrew Prine (as Morrano's biographer), Cyndi Pass, Joel Polis, Marco Rodriguez, Lyman Ward. (Video/Laser: Republic)

SERIAL MOM (1994) ★★★ A very amusing satire from writer-director John Waters as he pokes fun at murder in America and how it turns some individuals into media stars. At the core of this movie's success is Kathleen Turner as a sparkling, happy mother and housewife who seems to stand for grand family traditions—until someone insults those sensitivities and transforms her into a raving murderess who kills with her car, a knife, a leg of roast, a spear, and other objects just lying about the house. Turner commits all this mayhem with a smile, and smiles are what you'll have when the trial portion adds to, and enhances, Waters's amusingly blunt take on American justice. The excellent cast includes Ricki Lake (as a daughter), Sam Waterston (as the husband), Mathew Lillard, Mary Jo Catlett, Patricia Dunnock, Justin Whalin, Patricia Hearst and Suzanne Somers (as herself, signed to do the TV miniseries version). (Video/Laser: HBO)

SERPENT. See *Q: The Winged Serpent.*

SERPENT AND THE RAINBOW, THE (1988) ★★★½ Wade Davis is an anthropologist-adventurer who in 1982 went to Haiti in search of a legendary "zombie poison"—a toxic substance that could explain the existence of zombies in the voodoo netherworld. He came back with a sample of a drug (tetrodotoxin) that might explain "voodoo death." This film borrows the concept liberally and turns Davis's quest into a horror tale. Craven, who made the film in Haiti under dangerous conditions, mixes dreams and reality effectively. As long as you understand this is a Hollywood interpretation, and not a literal rendering of Davis's book, watch and enjoy. It has great visual thrills, a creepy Haitian atmosphere and a superb drum-music sound track (by Brad Fiedel) authentic to the island's culture. Bill Pullman, Cathy Tyson, Zakes Mokae, Paul Winfield. (Video/Laser: MCA)

SERPENT OF DEATH (1990) ★★ A cursed statue brings instability into the life of an archeologist. Directed by Anwar Kawadiri. Jeff Fahey, Camilla More, Peiros Fous. (Prism; Paramount) (Laser: Image)

SERPENT WARRIORS (1986) ★★ Eartha Kitt as a snake goddess? Clint Walker as a zoologist? You bet your fangs. An ancient curse by a snake-loving tribe is plaguing a construction site, so Walker, Anne Lockhart and Chris Mitchum fight off wriggling warriors and sinuous slammers. Hundreds of snake extras were needed by director Niels Rasmussen to satisfy Martin Wise's hissing script demands. Coil up and go to sleep.

SERPENT'S LAIR (1995) ★★½ Shot in Bucharest, Romania, this poor man's spin on *Rosemary's Baby*—but with a male being terrorized by a devil-worship cult instead of a female— stars Jeff Fahey as a real-estate agent in love with Heather Medway. They take a large apartment, where a short time before a man committed suicide after scratching strange writing on a wall, but don't expect domestic bliss. As soon as sexy, sultry Lisa Barbuscial happens on the scene, Fahey is seduced and sucked dry of his strengths in more ways than one. Lisa, you see, is a hypnotic succubus surrounded by cats, surviving on Fahey's semen, with which she intends to make little baby demons. Fahey does a good job as a man pulled under by feminine wiles, although director Jeffrey Reiner does little to prepare you for the moment when the realtor has to strike back against her seducer and the strange guy next door (Patrick Buchau), who seems to be in cohoots with the witch babe. A lot of sizzly sex scenes, with panting and "oohs and aahs" is about all this film offers for visual stimulation, since Marc Rosenberg's script is woefully short on action and special effects. Anthony Palermo, Kathleen Noone, Jack Kehler, Taylor Nichols. (Republic)

SERUM. See *Dr. Black and Mr. Hyde*.

SERVANTS OF TWILIGHT, THE (1991) ★★★ Chillingly effective variation on *The Omen* theme, in which private eye Bruce Greenwood is hired to protect young Jarrett Lennon and his mother Belinda Bauer from zealots from the Church of Twilight. Led by kooky fanatic Grace Zabriskie, the group believes the boy to be the

Antichrist and will stop at nothing to kill him. Although it's a lengthy chase, with ambushes, fistfights and murders, it maintains a strong supernatural flavor thanks to the fine direction of coproducer Jeffrey Obrow and the sharp-edged script by Obrow and Stephen Carpenter, who based it on Dean R. Koontz's novel *Twilight*. Carel Struycken is effective as one of the religious nuts with homicidal tendencies, and Richard Bradford stands out as one of Greenwood's associates. (Vidmark)

SEVEN (1995) ★★★★ A stylish serial-killer movie à la *Silence of the Lambs*, heavy on film noir ambience and characterizations. Cops Morgan Freeman (intelligent, controlled, about to retire) and Brad Pitt (headstrong, violent, trying to climb in his profession) team to track a sadistic but intellectual killer (Kevin Spacey, delivering a chilling performance) who uses the 7 deadly sins as themes for his graphic, sickening murders (gore effects by Rob Bottin). And they are sickening: a fat man is forced to eat until he bursts (Gluttony); a man is tied to a bed for a full year and tortured (Sloth); a prostitute is horribly cut up in full view of a man tied up (Envy); etc. The deterioration of Pitt's disturbed plainclothesman, the growth of Freeman (who thought he already knew it all) and how Pitt's wife (Gwyneth Paltrow) fits into this strange jigsaw puzzle of murder are at the heart of Andrew Kevin Walker's script, which David (*Alien 3*) Fincher directs to perfection. The climax, even if you see it coming, still has considerable impact. Richard Roundtree and R. Lee Ermey appear in supporting roles. (Video/Laser: New Line)

SEVEN BROTHERS MEET DRACULA, THE. Video version of *The Legend of the Seven Golden Vampires* (Electric; Media; American).

SEVEN CITIES OF ATLANTIS. See *Warlords of Atlantis*.

SEVEN FACES OF DR. LAO (1964) ★★★½ Producer-director George Pal's egg roll captures the Confucius charm of Charles Finney's novel, thanks to most honorable Charles Beaumont script. Tony Randall, playing a Chinese circus owner who turns up in Abalone, Arizona, also essays Merlin the Magician, seer Appolonius of Tyana, Pan, Medusa, the Abominable Snowman, and a mustachioed serpent. Frank Tuttle won an Oscar for his makeup. Unscrupulous businessman Arthur O'Connell is buying up property because a railroad is coming through and things must be set right by the philosophical (but never insidious) Dr. Lao. Barbara Eden, Noah Beery. Jim Danforth provided animation. Aka *The Secret World of Dr. Lao*. (Video/Laser: MGM/UA)

SEVEN MAGNIFICENT GLADIATORS, THE (1983) ★★★ Sword-and-sandal remake of *Seven Samurai*, but playing more like *The Magnificent*

Seven, a remake in itself. Bandit leader Dan Vadis, endowed with supernatural powers by his sorceress mother, yearly attacks a village, but the town's women have had enough and, armed with a magical sword, seek a gladiator who can wield it without burning his hands. That warrior is Han (Lou Ferrigno) who joins with Sybil Danning (as a good-natured swordplayer) and 5 other heroes to fight to the death with Vadis. Entertaining for its rousing battles and Danning's performance. Directed by Bruno Mattei. Brad Harris, Carla Ferrigno, Mandy Rice-Davies (one-time prostitute involved in the British Parliament scandals of the 1960s). (MCA)

SEVEN SECRETS OF SU-MARU, THE. See *Future Women*.

SEVEN SISTERS. See *The House On Sorority Row*.

SEVENTH SIGN, THE (1988) ★★ The Bible predicts God will give 7 signs to tell us the end is here, that it's time to go out with a bang. In this apocalyptic thriller—a kind of *Omen* without the Antichrist—a stranger (Jurgen Prochnow) appears with a parchment in hand, breaks its seal, and drops it to the earth. Dreadful things happen, such as all the fish in the ocean turn up dead, and an Arab village where Sodom once stood turns to ice. The end of the world is trivialized when average housewife Demi Moore becomes the seventh sign, the only thing that can prevent Armageddon. Heaped on that absurdity is the idea that the Roman soldier who refused Christ water on the way to crucifixion has been damned to walk the Earth, and is here, garbed as a Catholic priest, to make certain the end of the world happens on cue. What the religious symbolism and heavy-handed music from Heaven means could only be explained by Hungarian director Carl Schultz. What makes it all the more appalling is that nobody wanted to make a pseudoreligious turkey. But they did. And got gobbled up. Michael Biehn, Peter Friedman, Manny Jacobs, John Heard. (RCA/Columbia) (Laser: Image)

SEVENTH VICTIM, THE (1943) ★★★½ Esoteric Val Lewton production for RKO, when he was turning out memorable low-budget horror films. Kim Hunter (in her screen debut) plays a meek student at a strict girls' academy, who ventures to New York City to find her missing sister. Hunter is befriended by a strange private eye who turns up dead on a subway. Then she meets Hugh Beaumont, once married to her sister, who introduces her to an Italian café called Dante's, inhabited by disillusioned poets. The sister, acting as one in a trance, is part of a cult worshipping the Devil, and she must die for betraying the cult's code of silence. An allegorical conclusion to the DeWitt Bodeen–Charles O'Neal script has the sister entering a flat that has a hangman's rope dangling from the ceiling.

Director Mark Robson, in his debut, never compromises the dark pessimism. Tom Conway, Jean Brooks, Isabel Jewell, Evelyn Brent. (RKO) (Laser: Turner; RKO)

SEVENTH VOYAGE OF SINBAD, THE (1958) ★★★★½ Fruitful collaboration between producer Charles Schneer, director Nathan Juran, writer Kenneth Kolb and stop-motion animator Ray Harryhausen—an enchanting adventure tale, its acting and dialogue appropriately stylized, its creatures often sympathetic and its story capturing the magic of the Arabian Nights. Kerwin Mathews is a robust, romantic Sinbad forced by evil magician Torin Thatcher (who has shrunk princess Kathryn Grant to minuscule size) to seek the egg of a roc on an island dominated by a cyclops. Harryhausen's effects (including an ingenious sword duel with a skeleton) were to improve in subsequent films but the sheer art of his talent is all here: the dancing snake woman, a two-headed roc, a fire-breathing dragon, and more, all beautifully enhanced by Bernard Herrmann's score. An absolute must for fantasophiles. Richard Eyer appears as the genie from "the land beyond beyond." (RCA/Columbia) (Laser: RCA/Columbia; Pioneer)

SEVERED TIES (1991) ★★★ Produced by the filmmaking arm of the *Fangoria* magazine empire, this horror-gore extravaganza attempts to capture the macabre, sickening humor of *Re-Animator* and the *Basket Case* sequels, and pretty much succeeds. Billy Morrissette portrays a crazed scientist trying to regenerate diseased organs through a genetic engineering experiment. When his arm is severed from his body, a new one grows back, but it's half-human, half-reptilian. And it scuttles away on a pathway to gore and mayhem. Elke Sommers (as Morrissette's evil mom) and Oliver Reed (as her unscrupulous lover trying to sell the limb-rejuvenation formula to the government) give campy performances as the human villains in the John Nystrom–Henry Dominic script. Directed by Damon Santostefano (with "additional scenes" by Richard Roberts), *Severed Ties* is outrageous and bizarre with its icky body parts, and it features an army of reptilian arms running around choking innocent folks. It is aided considerably by lively performances from Garrett Morris as a one-legged war veteran, Johnny Legend as a freaked-out preacher, and Denise Wallace as a beautiful mute in love with Morrissette. (Columbia TriStar)

SEX AND THE SINGLE ALIEN (1993) ★½ Sexually frustrated topless-bar owner (whose UFO-obsessed wife is frigid and hires the sexy strippers for the show) is about to explode when a flying saucer abducts him and his body is occupied by an alien who is capable of making women undergo immediate orgasm of the most intense kind. Ridiculous sex comedy has special effects of the unmemorable kind but is enhanced by big-busted dancers, women masturbating while under the alien's hypnotic spell, and a lot of softcore sex. Eric Kohler, Melanie Rose, Michelle Hess. Written by director Peter Daskalof and Frank Fowler (the latter also turns up in the cast).

SEX CRIME OF THE CENTURY. See *The Last House on the Left*.

SGT. KABUKIMAN N.Y.P.D. (1995) ★★ A parody of superhero movies, this Troma film comedy actioner directed by producers Lloyd Kaufman and Michael Herz depicts the bumbling misadventures of cop Hank Griswald, who turns into a Japanese superhero equipped with heat-seeking chopsticks, flying sandals, bulletproof fan and magic parasol. A sexy Asian woman, Lotus, teaches him the martial arts to fight a supernatural evil. (Troma)

SHADEY (1985) ★★★½ Fascinating study in human eccentricities and madness, a parable of good vs. evil told with biting satire. Anthony Sher portrays a garage mechanic who can transfer thoughts onto film. For giving this "talent" to the government, Shadey wants a sex-change operation, but he's betrayed by doctor Billie Whitelaw when his ESP is used by the military. A secondary plot has Shadey involved with financier Patrick Macnee, his daughter (Leslie Ash) and crazy mother (Katherine Helmond). Several acts of violence are effective under Philip Saville's direction, and Sher's performance is a tour de force. The over-the-edge script is by Snoo Wilson. Bernard Hepton, Larry Lamb. (Key)

SHADOW. Variant video version of *Tenebrae*.

SHADOW, THE (1940) ★★★½ Columbia's 15-chapter cliff-hanger, based on a dark-avenger character who was popular in pulp magazines and on radio during the '30s and '40s, offers little of the eerie horror mystery for which the series was best known. This is more in keeping with the traditional serial plot of the day, as "eminent scientist and good citizen" Lamont Cranston goes against a supervillain known only as the Black Tiger. This guy is an invisible being who is unseen because he walks in a beam of light, a gimmick later used by Republic in its serial *Invisible Monster*. The Black Tiger is after "supreme financial power" so he can take over the world with his Death Ray and other sophisticated weaponry. Victor Jory assumes the disguise of Chinese gentleman Lin Chang to fool the underworld when he isn't assuming the guise of the Shadow, a caped figure who laughs menacingly each time he pops up suddenly to thwart the criminals. (There are many plot parallels between this and *The Spider's Web*, another vigorous, action-packed cliff-hanger.) James W. Horne was good at directing these,

and may be one of the best serial makers of the period. Veda Ann Borg is Margot Lane, Frank La Rue is Commissioner Weston, Philip Ahn is Cranston's faithful servant, and Jack Ingram heads up the baddies. (Available on video from serial specialty houses.)

SHADOW, THE (1994) ★★★½ The famous pulp-magazine antihero of the '30s, and a radio staple throughout the '40s, comes to the screen full-blown in the style of *Batman*, with great emphasis on "the look" and "the feel" of a world in which Lamont Cranston, a wealthy playboy, assumes the guise of a masked avenger who has the power "to cloud men's minds so they cannot see him," and goes after a descendant of Genghis Khan (John Lone), who intends to conquer the world with a pre–World War II nuclear device. Alec Baldwin is enormously powerful as Cranston/the Shadow, and Penelope Ann Miller makes for a very sexy and adorable Margo Lane ("the only person who knows to whom the voice of the Shadow belongs"). Although there are campy elements that give *The Shadow* a sense of fun, and David Koepp's screenplay is stuffed with the clichés of the "dark avenger" genre, the spectacle of the production design remains overpowering and is key to this movie's success. So is the fluid direction of Russell Mulcahy. A totally satisfying adventure. Ian McKellen, Tim Curry, Jonathan Winters, Andre Gregory. (Video/Laser: MCA)

SHADOW CREEPS, THE. See *The Phantom Creeps*.

SHADOW DANCING (1988) ★★ Ballet dancer Nadine Van der Velde, while rehearsing for *Medusa*, takes on the personality of another dancer. Plenty of dancing, too few shocks. Directed by Lewis Furey. Christopher Plummer portrays the leader of the troupe. James Kee, Gregory Osborne, John Colicos. (SGE) (Laser: Image)

SHADOWHUNTER (1991) ★★★½ Taut chase-actioner that blends with the supernatural as angst-ridden cop Scott Glenn is assigned to an Arizona Indian reservation to bring back cold-blooded killer Twobear (Benjamin Bratt). Twobear is a "coyote man," a shaman capable of creating "ghost sickness" in enemies, and Glenn undergoes ordeals on a physical and spiritual level as he pursues his quarry across the rugged landscape with Indian guide Angela Alvarado. Writer-director J. S. Cardone (*Shadowzone*) brings an intelligent balance between action and the metaphysical in this above-average thriller. Robert Beltran, Tim Sampson, George Aguilar, Beth Broderick. (Video/Laser: Republic)

SHADOW OF CHIKARA (1977) ★★★ What begins as an adventure Western, as Confederate survivors of the last battle of the Civil War set out to find a treasure, shifts into a moody, strange tale of the quasi supernatural. Is a hidden cache of diamonds in a cave watched over by demon hawks or hawk spirits in human form? Writer-producer-director Earl E. Smith fashions his macabre yarn with dandy surprise twists and creepy ambience. Joe Don Baker, Sondra Locke, Ted Neeley, Slim Pickens, John Davis Chandler, Joy Houck, Jr. Aka *The Ballad of Virgil Cane* and *The Curse of Demon Mountain.* (New World; from Mintex as *Wishbone Cutter*; from High Desert Films as *Thunder Mountain*) (Laser: New World)

SHADOW OF DEATH. TV title for *Brainwaves.*

SHADOW OF FEAR (1973) ★★ Low-budget, impoverished Dan Curtis TV-movie production dealing with a schizophrenic personality (Anjanette Comer) suddenly attacked one night by someone who appears to have a vendetta against her or her husband (an electronics bigwig played by Jason Evers). Larry Brody's teleplay takes several unexpected twists, and has some good dialogue (if a few too many convoluted points) when ex-cop/security guard Claude Akins joins plainclothesman Philip Carey in solving the psychological mystery behind the attack and a subsequent murder. Tom Selleck has a brief role as Comer's innocuous boyfriend. Directed statically by Herbert Kenwith. (MPI offers this as part of its home video "Dan Curtis series.")

SHADOW OF THE WEREWOLF. See *The Werewolf vs. the Vampire Women.*

SHADOWS RUN BLACK (1984) ★ Bouncing naked titties, bare asses and other female anatomy men generally find provocative are the most intriguing features in this drearily directed slasher whodunit in which a serial killer, "the Black Angel," murders sexy coeds. Chief suspect is Kevin Costner in an uncredited role. It's nothing his fans would want to bother seeing. Meanwhile there's plenty of pubic hair from a frontal view as the killer in a black jumpsuit and mask murders cuties, always when they just happen to be undressed. The dialogue is clichéd and vacuous, the killer's motive is pure baloney and director Howard Heard is stuck with a cast as dreary as the locations. William J. Kulzer, Shea Porter, George J. Engelson. (Lightning)

SHADOW VS. THE THOUSAND EYES OF DR. MABUSE, THE. See *The Thousand Eyes of Dr. Mabuse.*

SHADOWZONE (1989) ★★★ "Scientific horror" best describes this Charles Band production, which blends bits of *Alien, The Thing* and *Dreamscape* to spin its claustrophobia nightmare. Investigating officer David Beecroft arrives at an underground lab where Operation Shadowzone is under way: experiments in extended deep sleep, as part of a space program. But the subconscious mind of a subject (bigbreasted Maureen Flaherty) opens a portal to another dimension and a monster (code name: John Doe) slips in—one that assumes shapes

and identities. The lab personnel (Cutter the obese cook, Shivers the jittery maintenance man, Kidwell the beautiful technician, Von Fleet the Asian scientist) are soon stalked by the shape-changing creature. Louise Fletcher, always rubbing Chap Stick on her lips, becomes the key to reopening the dimension-portal. Good script by director J. S. Cardone has surprise twists. James Hong, Shawn Weatherly, Miguel Nunez, Lu Leonard. (Paramount) (Laser: Full Moon)

SHAGGY D.A., THE (1976) ★★★ Sequel to Disney's *The Shaggy Dog* is missing its original cast, but it does have the original scarab ring, once owned by the Borgia family, inscribed with the Latin phrase *Intra Kapori Transmuto.* This is the device that turns lawyer Dean Jones into a Bratislavian sheep dog capable of speech and thought, and it happens at a bad time, since Jones is running for D.A. against crooked Keenan Wynn. Directed by Robert Stevenson. Tim Conway, Suzanne Pleshette, Vic Tayback, Jo Anne Worley. (Disney)

SHAGGY DOG, THE (1959) ★★★ Scarab ring of the Borgias, combined with the proper incantation, turns the son of mailman Fred MacMurray into a Bratislavian sheep dog—at the most embarrassing moments. Endearing Disney comedy, capturing the nostalgia of a Saturday matinee. A frustrated policeman ("Follow that dog!") and spies add to this fluffy innocuousness directed by Charles T. Barton and written by producer Bill Walsh and Lillie Hayward. Tommy Kirk, Jean Hagen, Annette Funicello. The sequels were *The Shaggy D.A.* and *Return of the Shaggy Dog.* In 1995 Disney produced a loose TV remake, *The Shaggy Dog.* (Video/Laser: Disney)

SHAGGY DOG, THE (1995) ★★ This is a loose remake of the 1959 Disney classic, updated for modern sensibilities by Tim Doyle (working off the original script by Bill Walsh and Lillie Hayward) but that doesn't make it better than its inspiration. Still, it's a pleasant piece of family viewing with the Borgias' ring curse turning another young man into a Bratislavian (or English) sheep dog, this time via improved computerized special effects. A thief plans to steal a valuable diamond from a museum and our shaggy guy gets involved. There's some cute comedy involving a pair of inept dogcatchers, and one almost wishes there had been more of this to spice up the tired idea of a human turning into a dog. Directed by Dennis Dugan. Sharon Lawrence, Ed Begley, Jr., Jon Polito, James Cromwell, Jeremy Sisto. Comedian Bobby Slayton has a cameo as a frustrated driving instructor. (Disney)

SHAKER RUN (1985) ★★ Although a science-horror theme sets this New Zealand film into motion (deadly virus is sought by the military), this is mainly car chases and action sequences that go on too long. Director Bruce Morrison doesn't know when to slow down. Peter Weller, Sam Elliott, Antonio Fargas, Blanche Baker. (Video/ Laser: Embassy/Nelson)

SHAKMA (1990) ★★½ In Roddy McDowall's research lab, experiments with a baboon result in a berserk creature named Shakma, who escapes during a Dungeons and Dragons–type game called Nemesis, played by immature scientists in a closed-off high rise. It becomes a different game when Shakma attacks and kills the participants in gory cat-and-mouse situations. The only unusual thing about Robert Engle's script, besides substituting a baboon for a slasher-killer, is that the heroines don't come out of the horror situation as well as you might suspect. Christopher Atkins finally faces the hairy onslaught one-on-one. Codirected by producer Hugh Parks and Tom Logan. Amanda Wyss, Ari Meyers, Robb Morris, Greg Flowers. (Quest)

SHALLOW GRAVE (1987) ★★ Frustrating, unresolved suspense thriller that owes its allegiance to Alfred Hitchcock. In addition to parodying the *Psycho* shower sequence (which has no business in this movie), it borrows its premise from the "innocent person caught up in mysterious circumstances" genre. Four teenage students driving to Florida are caught up in the murder of a waitress. Innocent, trying to convince others of the truth, the girls die one by one. It's disturbing when evil wins and a movie ends before it should. This has decent acting and camera work but screenwriter-producer George E. Fernandez digs a deep grave for himself. Directed by Richard Styles. Tony March, Tom Law, Lisa Stahl. (Prism)

SHALLOW GRAVE (1994) ★★★★ Ingeniously plotted Scottish psychological horror thriller offering black comedy and suspenseful surprises as 3 prank-oriented roommates in a Glasgow flat rent to a 4th party, who immediately dies with a fortune in money in his room. They form an unholy union to dispose of the body (by cutting it to pieces so it can't be identified) but when the underworld comes after them, their friendship disintegrates and each descends into greed and madness. From a script by Glasgow doctor John Hodge, TV director Danny Boyle, in his feature debut, brings a frenetic pacing to this bloody, disturbing tale. Kerry Fox, Christopher Eccleston, Ewan McGregor, Keith Allen. (Hodge, by the way, appears as a strange cop working the case, just one of many unusual elements in his offbeat script.) Nothing shallow about it. (Video/Laser: Polygram)

SHAPE OF THINGS TO COME, THE. See *Things to Come.*

SHARAD OF ATLANTIS (1936). Reedited feature version of the Republic serial *Undersea Kingdom.*

SHARON'S BABY. See *The Devil Within Her.*

SHARON'S SECRET (1995) ★★½ Half-baked psychothriller that appears to deal with a psychotic schizophrenic 16-year-old (Candace Cameron) accused of shotgunning her mom and dad to death and then mutilating their bodies. But police psychologist Mel Harris believes the teenager didn't do it. So how come someone is stalking the doctor now, and tries to run her over? Mark Homer's script barely makes any sense as its convolutions and contrivances unwind in predictable (and less-than-satisfying) fashion. This weak flick was conventionally directed by Michael Scott and costars Alex McArthur, Paul Regina, Gregg Henry and James Pickens, Jr. (MCA)

SHATTERBRAIN. See *The Resurrected.*

SHATTERED (1991) ★★★½ San Francisco and Marin County provide scenic locations for this suspense thriller with psychological overtones, which writer-director Wolfgang Petersen adapted from a novel by Richard Neely. Tom Berenger portrays an architect whose face is severely damaged when his sports car goes over a cliff, and who undergoes psychogenic amnesia, the inability to remember anything from his personal life. He suspects he murdered his wife's lover on the night of the crash, and seeks the help of colorful private eye Bob Hoskins, who almost steals this movie with his performance. Surprises and plot twists give this the flavor of a Hitchcockian shocker, and much of it is treated by Petersen as a nightmare in which Berenger is trapped. Produced by David Korda, Petersen and John Davis. Greta Scacchi, Joanne Whalley-Kilmer, Corbin Bernsen. (Video/Laser: MGM)

SHATTERED MIND (1996) ★★★ Better-than-average TV-movie starring glamorous Heather Locklear in a non-glamorous role as a young mother who suffers from multiple personality syndrome, brought on by the sexual abuse of her doctor-father. Producer-director Stephen Gyllenhaal captures the confusion, madness and fear of housewife Suzie, who also turns into a weepy little kid, a sassy prostitute, a sharp-tongued intellect and other types too numerous to count as Thomas Baum's intriguing teleplay unfolds. Locklear shows she can do more than "Melrose Place" and is ably supported by Brett Cullen as her trying-to-understand husband. Richard Herd, Kevin Dunn, Carolina Kava and Edward Edwards.

SHE (1982) ★★ Sandahl Bergman portrays the ruler of a lost kingdom, but this Italian film strays markedly from Haggard's novel, incorporating parody and sci-fi to create a hybrid. In this city of the Urech people, the ruler can levitate his enemies, and mutants can clone themselves each time an arm falls off. Writer-director Avi Nesher (an Israeli) has written a black-comedy adventure of anachronisms. David Goss, Quin Kessler, Harrison Muller, Gordon Mitchell. (Vestron; Lightning)

SHE-BEAST, THE (1965) ★★★ One of the few works of director Michael Reeves, who attracted a cult following after his premature death in 1968 of a drug overdose. Originally made as *The Revenge of the Blood Beast*, and later known as *Satan's Sister* and *The Sister of Satan*, this stars Barbara Steele as a woman possessed by an ancient witch. She goes on a murderous rampage, while husband Ian Ogilvy searches Transylvania for her. The rampage allows Reeves some interesting juxtaposing of images. He was working with a limited budget (and not the greatest script by Michael Byron) yet he brings it off well. (Gorgon; Rhino; S/Weird; Filmfax; MPI)

SHE DEMONS (1958) ★ Ludicrous, grade-Z Arthur Jacobs abomination suffering from diarrhea of the jungle, but don't let that stop it—this is wickedly entertaining. Whip-cracking sadistic Nazis dominate a Pacific island where a fiendish doctor strips the beauty off assorted lasses and tries to transfer their good looks to his ugly frau. You'll need a sense of humor to sit through this. Richard E. Cunha directed, if you can call it directing, and cowrote the script with H. E. Barrie, if you can call it writing. One historical highlight is Irish McCalla as a shipwrecked traveler—that same year she appeared on TV as Sheena the jungle girl. Tod Griffin, Victor Sen Young, Gene Roth. (Media; Rhino; VCI; Sinister/C)

SHEENA—QUEEN OF THE JUNGLE (1984) ★★½ The major mistake in bringing the comic-book Queen of the Jungle to the screen was to present her as a naive innocent rather than as a hip modern woman. Thus, as sexy as she may be in her leopard skins, Tanya Roberts doesn't convince. Instead, writers David Newman, Leslie Stevens and Lorenzo Semple, Jr., spinning off from the character created by Will Eisner and S. M. Eiger in the '30s, concoct a campy adventure, which John Guillermin directs with a straight face. Ted Wass and Donovan Scott are newsreel cameramen in Tigorda (an African kingdom) involved in political intrigue and picturesque adventures with Sheena, who bounces along (in more places than one) on a horse painted like a zebra. It becomes a chase with soldiers, trucks, helicopters and other gimmicks. Sheena can talk to the animals and has mystical powers as the silly story unfolds. If you can get into the spirit, you might have fun watching this turkey. Elizabeth of Toro costars. (RCA/Columbia; Goodtimes) (Laser: RCA/Columbia)

SHE-MONSTER OF THE NIGHT. See *Frankenstein's Daughter.*

SHER MOUNTAIN KILLINGS MYSTERY (1990). See *The Cursed Mountain Mystery.*

SHE'S BACK (1989) ★★★ Carrie Fisher plays a Queens housewife murdered by robbers who returns from the dead. But only husband Robert Joy sees her as she encourages him to get revenge. (Sound a little like *Ghost*?) Directed by Tim Kincaid. Matthew Cowles, Sam Coppola. (Vestron) (Laser: Image)

SHE WOLF. Video version of *Legend of the Wolf Woman* (VBG).

SHINING, THE (1980) ★★★½ Stanley Kubrick's uneven adaptation of Stephen King's best-seller set in the Overlook, a haunted hotel in the Rockies, and featuring a boy with powers of telepathy and prophecy. Kubrick's camera is fluid and creates brilliant sequences: Jack Torrance (Jack Nicholson) and family haunted by a moldy corpse; wife Shelley Duvall discovering a weird manuscript by her husband; a chase through a hedgerow maze; Torrance meeting ghostly bartender Joseph Turkel; and the deterioration of Torrance as he chases his wife with an ax. But director Kubrick and cowriter Diane Johnson have erringly and frequently deviated from King's masterful plot and neglected important exposition; scenes are enigmatic and frustrating when they should be thrilling and enlightening. Scatman Crothers plays a man who, like Torrance's son, has "the shining," but it's another misinterpreted role. (Warner Bros.; RCA/Columbia) (Laser: Warner Bros.)

SHIP OF ZOMBIES. See *Horror of the Zombies.*

SHIVERS. See *They Came From Within.*

SHOCK (1946) ★★★ Nifty suspense thriller is frugal on budget but frenetic on technique when psychiatrist Vincent Price murders his wife, unaware that a young woman has seen the ghastly crime and gone into shock. When he finds out she knows too much, he and his nurse set out to keep her quiet by using drugs and hypnosis. Lynn Bari, Reed Hadley, Anabel Shaw, Frank Latimore, Charles Trowbridge. Directed by Alfred Werker from a script by Eugene King. (Kartes; Cable; Sinister/C; Filmfax)

SHOCK. See *Beyond the Door II.*

SHOCK 'EM DEAD (1990) ★ Repugnant, horribly acted horror film depicting a nerd (Stephen Quadros) losing his job in a pizza parlor and striking up a deal with voodoo woman Tyger Soope: his soul for a chance to be a great rock 'n' roll musician. Only problem is, he has to kill with magical daggers as a source of energy to stay alive. This stupid premise, concocted by director Mark Freed with writers David Tedder and Andrew Cross, makes for one insufferable movie that will shock no one, so incompetent are its effects and bloodletting. Its emptiness only makes the appearances of Traci Lords (as the group manager), Troy Donahue (as the rock promoter) and Aldo Ray (as the pizza parlor owner) all the more pathetic. Tim Moffet, Gina Parks. (Academy) (Laser: Image)

SHOCKER (1989) ★★½ Writer-director Wes Craven creates a new variation on Freddy Krueger through the Family Killer—a wisecracking ugly guy named Horace Pinker who terrorizes a city as a serial murderer. Pinker is too unappealing and doesn't have the campiness of Freddy as he is propelled through horrific adventures that turn into outright parody, in sharp contrast to sincere attempts to terrify. Craven also borrows the device of the dream (as in *Nightmare on Elm Street*, pick any number) to provide impetus—in this case Peter Berg dreams of Pinker and where he's committing crimes, so Berg and his policeman father (Michael Murphy) can track him. Pinker is electrocuted, but he's made a deal with the evil gods of TV and passes in and out of TV screens at will. Mitch Pileggi, Cami Cooper, Richard Brooks, Theodore Raimi, John Tesh, Dr. Timothy Leary. (Video/Laser: MCA)

SHOCKING DARK (1989) ★★½ Set in a not too distant future, a commando squad called Mega Force enters a viaduct system beneath Venice, where a purification of foul water project is underway. But a "genetic mutation" has resulted in monstrous creatures that attack and kill off the squad members. One member of the team (named Samuel Fuller!) is from the Tubular Corp., and you know that means trouble. It ends up a time-travel story with touches of *Terminator*. While this is pure horror movie, designed for fans who will probably groove on it, it so closely follows portions of *Aliens* that it has remained unavailable in America for fear of copyright infringement laws. This Italian production was largely directed by Vincent Dawn in underground tunnels and factories. Cristoffer Ahrens, Haven Tyler, Geretta Giancarlo. (A Japanese laser version is entitled *Alienators*.)

SHOCK (TRANSFER SUSPENSE HYPNOS). See *Beyond the Door II*.

SHOCK WAVES (1970) ★★★½ Low-budget horror favorite with SS officer Peter Cushing creating an underwater corps of Aryan zombies, who rise from the depths as blond figures wearing goggles. Brooke Adams ends up on Cushing's Nazi-happy island after surviving the sinking of a yacht captained by John Carradine. Directed by Ken Wiederhorn, who cowrote with John Harrison and Ken Pare. Jay Maeder, Luke Halpin. Aka *Death Corps* and *Almost Human*. (Prism; Starmaker; American)

SHOGUN ISLAND. See *Raw Force*.

SHORT CIRCUIT (1986) ★★★★ Sparkling comedy with cute touches, this spoof on hardware movies stars Robot #5, designed by Syd Mead and activated by Eric Allard. The cutest damn robot in any movie, #5 is part of a line of laser-equipped metal warriors called Saints, created by scientist Steve Guttenberg, who works for Nova Laboratories. During a lightning storm, #5 takes on human characteristics and is befriended by Ally Sheedy. Afraid of being dismantled, #5 flees into madcap, hilarous misadventures during which he is inspired by John Wayne, the Three Stooges and John Travolta, among others. Wonderfully directed by John Badham from the script by S. S. Wilson and Brent Maddock. Don't miss it. (Video/Laser: CBS/Fox)

SHORT CIRCUIT 2 (1988) ★★★½ This sequel to the wonderful *Short Circuit* again presents the amusing Johnny-Five robot, but cannot sustain the charm of the original. This time #5 (with the darling voice of Tim Blaney) turns up in the big city where he helps Fisher Stevens (as the malapropism-speaking Ben Jahrvi) and con man Michael McLean mass-produce a slew of tiny Johnny-Fives for toy marketer Cynthia Gibb. Along the way the gullible J-5 is misused by crook Jack Weston for a bank heist, flies through the sky on a hang glider and helps street crooks rip off car stereos. Kids will love its action scenes and morality lessons, but the film ultimately becomes an endurance test. Directed by Kenneth Johnson, written by J-5's originators, S. S. Wilson and Brent Maddock. (RCA/Columbia) (Laser: Image)

SHREDDER ORPHEUS (1989) ★★ A TV signal beamed from Hell is destroying people on Earth who have survived the Apocalypse and are living in the Grey Zone. As if the world wasn't already in bad enough shape, society is now controlled by TV stations that specialize in punk rock. Written-directed by Robert McGinley, who also stars as band leader Orpheus. Stephen J. Bernstein, Megan Murphy. (Action International)

SHRIEKING, THE (1974) ★★ Filmed in the hills of South Dakota as *Hex*, this oddball movie produced by Max L. Raab offers many promises but fails to pay off. Keith Carradine, Gary Busey and Scott Glenn portray well-decorated World War I aviation heroes traveling on motorcycles (the first biker gang?), searching for whatever the Lost Generation searched for in those days. They meet sexy sisters who appear to be witches—at least, one of them sews shut the mouth of a frog. Nothing is made explicit by screenwriters Leo Garen (also the director) and Steve Katz. There's absolutely zero excitement as this fizzles out. Hilarie Thompson, Dan Haggerty, Robert Walker. (Prism) (Laser: Image)

SHRIEK OF THE MUTILATED (1974) ★ Amateurish low budgeter in which a peculiar Dr. Prell (Alan Brock), alleged to be the survivor of an expedition in search of the legendary Yeti, returns to Boot Island with researchers. They are murdered one by one by a creature in a white suit. Also involved is a crazy mute Indian named Laughing Crow and a cannibal-devil cult and the worst acting you've ever seen. The real shrieks came from mentally mutilated theater patrons who wanted their money back after exposure to this bad cheapie. Jennifer Stock, Tawn Ellis, Michael Harris. Directed by Mike Findlay from an Ed Adlum–Ed Kelleher script. Aka *Mutilated*. (Lightning; Live)

SHRINKING CORPSE, THE. See *Cauldron of Blood*.

SHRUNKEN HEADS (1994) ★★½ A rather disgusting premise undermines this minor Charles Band–Full Moon horror comedy: the severed (and shrunken) heads of three comic book–reading teenagers, under the control of a voodoo master, float around the city killing young gang juveniles and turning them into zombie monsters. There are only two reasons to watch this half-hearted, failed effort—for the performance of Meg Foster in drag as a heavyset gangster named Big Moe (you will barely recognize her), and for the zesty performance of Julius Harris as ex–Haitan cop Sumatra, who uses magic dust, incantations and a cauldron of bubbling goo to control the avenging heads. The effects are less than startling and the cast screams most of its lines under the control of director Richard Elfman. A. J. Damato, Aeryk Egan, Becky Herbst, Bo Sharon, Darris Love, Bodhi (son of Richard) Elfman, Troy Fromin. Dim-witted script by Matthew Bright. (Paramount) (Laser: Full Moon)

SHUDDER. See *Kiss of the Tarantula*.

SHUTTERED ROOM, THE. See *Blood Island*.

SICARIUS—THE MIDNIGHT PARTY (1973). This was an X-rated horror film directed by Jesus Franco that was heavily cut into *Erotikill*. It's also been called *The Last Thrill, Jacula* and *The Bare-breasted Countess*.

SIGHTINGS (1995) Repackaged episodes from the TV series chronicling real-life weird mysteries, hosted by Tim White. Much of these shows are pseudoscience at best, but they are nevertheless intriguing reports with alleged eyewitnesses and historic footage. There are three video releases: "The UFO Report," "The Ghost Report" and "The Psychic Experience." (Paramount)

SIGN OF THE VAMPIRE, THE. See *The Heritage of Dracula*.

SILENCE OF THE HAMS (1993) ★★ In the style of the *Naked Gun* parodies, this "30th Century Fox" film (produced by Julie Corman and Ezio Greggio) attempts to spoof *Psycho* and *Silence of the Lambs* with concurrent story lines involving FBI agent Jo Dee Fostar searching for a killer with the help of imprisoned Dr. Animal Cannibal Pizza (Dom DeLuise). There's an occasionally funny sight gag or visual pun, but most of the gags are enough to make you gag. Producer Greggio also stars as the Norman Bates character and wrote-directed. There's a good cast here (Billy Zane, Joanna Pacula, Charlene Tilton, Martin Balsam, Stuart Pankin, John Astin, Phyllis Diller, Bubba Smith, Larry Storch, Rip Taylor, Shelley Winters) but they fall on their faces as flat as the jokes.

SILENCE OF THE LAMBS, THE (1991) ★★★★★ Dynamite adaptation (by Ted Tally) of Thomas Harris's novel about an FBI woman's efforts to track down the serial killer Buffalo Bill—the nickname he's earned by skinning his victims. Helping her is imprisoned serial murderer Dr. Hannibal Lecter, who eats his victims. Lecter becomes one of the screen's most electrifying fiends thanks to Anthony Hopkins. Under Jonathan Demme's direction, this is a masterful blend of psychological horror and physical violence. "Hannibal the Cannibal," incidentally, appeared in Thomas's novel *Red Dragon*, which was produced by Michael Mann in 1986. Jodie Foster is great as FBI agent Clarice Starling; the drama between her and Hannibal is unforgettable. Scott Glenn, Ted Levine, Anthony Heald, Brooke Smith, Diane Baker. Roger Corman and George Romero appear in cameos. (Orion) (Laser: Orion/Image; Orion/Voyager; Criterion, with commentary by stars and director)

SILENT DEATH. See *Voodoo Island*.

SILENT FLUTE, THE. See *Circle of Iron*.

SILENT MADNESS (1983) ★★ Unsavory slasher thriller with *Coma*-like subplot (concocted by producer William Milling) as Belinda Montgomery, deserving of better material, portrays a nurse in Cresthaven Mental Hospital who discovers that through a computer error a homicidal maniac (who committed the "Sororiety Slaughter") was released by mistake. Montgomery tracks the killer (Solly Marx), who is murdering with sledgehammer, drill press, vice, crowbar and whatever device is handy. Meanwhile, sinister doctors at the hospital dispatch their own killers to clean up mistakes. Producer-director Simon Nuchtern handles action sequences clumsily, and gore effects are minimal (or edited from the TV prints, which are poorly scanned off the 'scope original). Sharp instruments are always being thrust at the camera because this was shot in grainy 3-D. Viveca Lindfors, Sydney Lassick. Aka *The Nightkillers, The Omega Factor* and *Beautiful Screamers*. (Media)

SILENT MOBIUS (1990) ★★★ A fascinating account, told through Japanese animation, about the Abnormal Mystery Police, women of the future with psychic powers who fight monsters that break through another dimension to invade Earth. Their chief adversary is Lucifer Hawke, one of the key characters from the famous comic strip on which this cartoon feature is based. Directed by Michitaka Kikuchi. (Streamline)

SILENT NIGHT, DEADLY NIGHT (1984) ★★ Controversial (when released) bloodthirsty slasher flick about a killer in a Santa Claus suit. Controversy also flowed from its less-than-lovely portrait of a Catholic school for orphans, operated by a starkly stern Mother Superior who delights in sadistic spankings. All that aside, it's a slasher-genre entry, undeserving of attention. A shallow psychological history of the murderer is presented when, as a youngster, he watches his mother and father being murdered on Christmas Eve by a Santa Claus lookalike. He grows into a tall, muscular teenager (Robert Brian Wilson) who thinks Santa punishes those who aren't good during the year. When he's forced to don a St. Nicholas outfit by his boss, he's primed for a rampage of yuletide destruction: a beheading, an impaling and assorted ax penetrations. Directed by Charles E. Sellier. Lilyan Chauvan, Toni Nero, Danny Wagner. (Paragon; USA) (Laser: Image)

SILENT NIGHT, DEADLY NIGHT PART II (1986) ★★ Anyone who saw the first entry in this slasher series about a killer in a Santa Claus suit will feel ripped off watching the first half of this sequel: most of it is footage from the original as the killer's brother, locked up in an asylum, tells his family history in flashback to a head-shrinker. All viewers will feel ripped off watching the second half as the brother begins killing. There's a reprehensible sequence in which he walks down a suburban street, killing residents with a pistol, and commits other sickening crimes while clad as St. Nick, including an attack on a deformed nun. Director-editor Lee Harry succeeds in making this one of the most mean-spirited slasher films ever made. Eric Freeman, James L. Newman, Elizabeth Cayton. (IVE) (Laser: Image)

SILENT NIGHT, DEADLY NIGHT III: BETTER WATCH OUT! (1989) ★★★ Third entry in the once-controversial Santa Claus killer series is an improvement over the wretched second entry, but . . . it's okay to pout because this is still a tedious affair that parades out every cliché, without panache or energy. What's equally depressing: it was directed by Monte (*Two-Lane Blacktop*) Hellman. The plot (by Carlos Laszlo, Hellman and producer Richard Gladstein) concerns a blind woman (Samantha Scully) psychically linked to the Santa Claus killer (played without menace by Bill Moseley), who has been restored to life by mad scientist Richard Beymer. Not even the refreshing Robert Culp can

bring much vitality to his cop role. Eric Da Re, Laura Herring, Elizabeth Hoffman. (IVE) (Laser: Image)

SILENT NIGHT, DEADLY NIGHT 4: INITIATION (1990) ★★ Since there's no killer Santa Claus to terrorize Christmas lovers, here's another crass example of using a title solely for exploitation purposes. All that aside, it's more unpleasant and disgusting than scary in the hands of director Brian Yuzna. Neith Hunter portrays a writer for the L.A. *Eye*, whose investigations of a woman's fatal fiery leap off a building lead her to a Daughter of Isis witch cult led by Maud Adams. Cockroaches, slugs and giant leeches (created by Screamin' Mad George) figure prominently in how the cult terrorizes Hunter, who is needed as a witch replacement. Clint Howard appears in one of his grotesque-evil roles, and commits a sickening murder in Hunter's flat. (He's the only memorable thing.) One hopes that lovely Adams and Allyce Beasley (of TV's "Moonlighting") can get their careers back on track, as this nowhere movie is a bottoming out. Tommy Hinkley, Reggie Bannister, Jeanne Bates, Laurel Lockhart. (Live) (Laser: Image)

SILENT NIGHT, DEADLY NIGHT 5: THE TOY MAKER (1991) ★★★ At least a killer Santa Claus, missing from the fourth film in this mediocre series, is on the prowl again in this horror whodunit in which a killer produces toys that come to life through an electrical charge and kill their recipients. Among the toy tinglers are a ball with snakelike arms, a snail monster, rollerskates with jet propulsion, a severed hand, and a flying superhero. Among the suspects is Mickey Rooney as toy-store owner Joe Petto (and that name is a joke, son), his weirdo son and a department store Santa who's behaving strangely around a certain mother and mute child. Out of this olio scripting by producer Brian Yuzna and director Martin Kitrosser comes an adequate twist climax and opportunities for makeup guy Screamin' Mad George to show off his special effects. Jane Higginson, Brian Breyer, Tracy Fraim, William Thorne, Neith Hunter, Clint Howard. (Live)

SILENT NIGHT, EVIL NIGHT. Originally *Black Christmas*, then *Stranger in the House*.

SILENT RUNNING (1972) ★★★★ "A" for effort to special effects maestro and director Douglas Trumbull, who first found favor through his effects in *2001: A Space Odyssey*. Trumbull repeats his spectacular space images: awesome ships floating between planets, exploding suns and a solar storm. A floating space station (the last garden of a defoliated Earth) is manned by Bruce Dern and three "drone" robots, Huey, Dewey and Louie. Dern goes psychotic when ordered to destroy his forest, and he mutinies. The effects are won-

derful and Dern's demented attitude is justified by the Deric Washburn–Michael Cimino–
Steve Bochco script. Adult sci-fi worthy of repeated viewings. Originally called *Running Silent*. (Video/Laser: MCA)

SILENT SCREAM (1980) ★★½ Writer-director
Denny Harris pays homage to Hitchcock's *Psycho* with this tale of a demented household
where innocent roomers are murdered by a
knife-happy kook daughter (played without restraint by Barbara Steele). Gore murders provide
shocks, but the plotting (or is it plodding?) of
the Ken and Jim Wheat script (with W. C. Bennett helping) is predictable, and characterizations without depth. A moment of silence,
please, while we scream for Harris. Yvonne De
Carlo, Cameron Mitchell, Avery Schreiber, Rebecca Balding. (Media)

SILENT SENTENCE (1973) ★★½ Heavily edited TV version of the feature *A Knife for the
Ladies*. Not quite a Western, not quite a horror
flick. Call it an oater-bloater. A Jack the Ripper–
style killer is stalking saloon girls while sheriff
Jack Elam and investigator Jeff Cooper stalk the
murderer. Made in Old Tucson, this has Gene
Evans, Joe Santos, John Kellog and Ruth Roman in interesting character roles, but it's a minor stab at best. Directed by Larry G. Spangler.
Aka *Jack the Ripper Goes West*.

SILENT TONGUE (1992) ★½ You'd require a
battery of psychiatrists and assorted head doctors and shrinks to figure out what writer-
director Sam Shepard was trying to prove in
creating this twisted tale of the Old West (1873)
in which sideshow medicine man Alan Bates
goes absolutely raving loony on the prairie.
Then there's Richard Harris, who wants to buy
Bates's half-breed Indian daughter because the
first daughter he bought from Bates just died
and Harris's son (River Phoenix) will go crazy
if he doesn't get the second sister. Then there's
the first dead Indian daughter, only she isn't
dead. Her spirit comes back with white paint
stripes down her face to haunt Phoenix (who is
as bonkers as Bates) and appear as assorted apparitions on the plains. Then there's Tim Scott
as an old prospector pushing around a basket
that makes him look like a modern bag lady.
Then there's two medicine show stand-up comics doing frontier humor. If this movie is about
"the fever of the Demon Prairie" (as Shepard
writes) then one must assume that fever ravaged
Shepard's brain as he cranked out the script.
There isn't a single ounce of coherence in the
whole messy morass. Dermot Mulroney, Sheila
Tousey, Jeri Arrendondo, Tim Scott, Bill Irwin.
(Video/Laser: Vidmark)

SILHOUETTE (1990) ★★ Unconvincing, preposterous "woman in peril" TV-movie starring
Faye Dunaway in a role way beneath her dignity. She plays an architect stranded in a small
Texas town who witnesses a knife murder, only
she can't prove it and the local sheriff is pow-
erless to help her. Thinking she can identify
him, the killer tries to kill her time and again,
succeeding only in frightening her half to death
and boring the audience. The holes in the Jay
Wolf–Victor Buelle script are bigger than the
shotgun wounds, and director Carl Schenkel telegraphs every ersatz surprise. David Rasche,
John Terry, Carlos Gomez. (MCA)

SILVER BULLET (1985) ★★★½ Well-
produced adaptation of Stephen King's novelette, "Cycle of the Werewolf," which proves to
be a slight story. King adapted his own book,
emphasizing life in a small North Carolina town,
Tarker's Mills, and how it is plagued by brutal
werewolf killings. The focus is on crippled
Corey Haim (his motorized wheelchair is
dubbed Silver Bullet) and his relationship with
sister Megan Follows and alcoholic uncle Gary
Busey. How they learn the werewolf's identity
and set a trap builds to an unexceptional climax.
Carlo Rambaldi's werewolf is effective; the
moon stalker just needs a stronger story. Daniel
Attias directs well, especially a sequence in the
swamp when the wolf-man stalks his stalkers
through nocturnal mist. Everett McGill, Terry
O'Quinn. (Video/Laser: Paramount)

SINBAD AND THE EYE OF THE TIGER (1977)
★★★ Packed with the visual stop-motion
thrills only animator Ray Harryhausen can bring
to romantic fantasies, this adventure in the land
of Arabian Nights lore is abroil with mythical
monsters, exciting duels between man and beast,
wizardry and witchcraft. Patrick Wayne is a mediocre Sinbad, as wooden as the dialogue, so it's
a showcase for Harryhausen's memorable creations: a chess-playing baboon, three ax-
swinging jinnis; a troglodyte; a giant tiger; a
king-size walrus and a metal giant called Min-
aton. What, no Caroline Munro? Directed by actor Sam Wanamaker, scripted by Beverly Cross.
Taryn Power, Jane Seymour, Margaret Whiting,
Patrick Troughton. Harryhausen also coproduced with Charles Schneer. Aka *Sinbad at the
World's End*. (Video/Laser: RCA/Columbia)

SINBAD AT THE WORLD'S END. See *Sinbad and
the Eye of the Tiger*.

SINBAD OF THE SEVEN SEAS (1989) ★ Alleged
to be based on Edgar Allan Poe's "The Thousand and Second Tale of Scheherazade," this
emerges as a children's fantasy adventure with
Lou Ferrigno as the muscular hero he established in the *Hercules* films, although he has a
sense of humor this time. There's thrill after
thrill (hah!) as the evil vizier is busier than usual
flinging the Sacred Gems of Basra to the four
corners of the world, forcing Sinbad and his adventurers (the son of a king, a Viking warrior,
a dwarf, a bald cook and a Chinese soldier of
fortune) to fight the Legions of Death, the War-

rior Women (or Amazons) of the Enchanted Island, the Army of Ghost Warriors and the Stone Man with a Shining Face. All manner of magic and wizardry is employed. Produced-directed by Enzo G. Castellari, who cowrote with Tito Carpi, from a Lewis Coates idea. John Steiner, Leo Gullotta, Teagan Clive, Haruhiko Yamanouchi. (Video/Laser: Cannon)

SINBAD'S GOLDEN VOYAGE. See *The Golden Voyage of Sinbad*.

SINGLE WHITE FEMALE (1992) ★★★½ Provocative study of two women living in a New York flat and how one takes control, until this unusually classy psychothriller explodes into the violence you find in slasher bashers. Bridget Fonda is superb as a computer businesswoman whose shaky existence is shaken further when she chooses Jennifer Jason Leigh as her roommate. Leigh turns into an unforgettable murderess, endowing this study of depression and madness with rich character not quickly forgotten. Don Roos based his script on John Lutz's novel *SWF Seeks Same*, and director Barbet Schroeder proves he's top-notch. Steven Weber, Peter Friedman. (Video/Laser: Columbia Tristar)

SINISTER INVASION (1968). Video of *The Incredible Invasion* (UIV; Sinister/C; S/Weird; Filmfax).

SIR ARTHUR CONAN DOYLE'S THE LOST WORLD (1999) ★★½ This attempt by Ted Turner's TNT to cash in on the *Jurassic Park* craze, with John Landis listed as a coproducer, is yet another spin on an old Doyle sci-fi adventure that was first made as a silent film in 1925 and then as an Irwin Allen saga in 1960, in which harmless lizards were photographed in macro to look like giant monsters. Neither of those versions, even with the lizard trickery, came anywhere near being the campy nonsense that Australian director Richard Franklin, working with a laughable script by Jim Henshaw and Peter Mohan, has made of this refried hash of movie clichés. Professor Challenger is one of Doyle's more endearing adventure characters, who in the original "Lost World" tale took a small band to a plateau in South America to prove the existence of prehistoric beasts. In this made-for-TV version, Peter McCauley is the leader of the band of adventure seekers that includes an intrepid journalist, an old disbelieving scientist, a shrewd woman who is paying the professor's travel expenses, a superstitious native guide, and a great-white-hunter type. If that isn't already bad enough, wait until a beautiful blonde in an animal-skin bikini, who calls herself Veronica yet, drops out of the trees and warns the expedition that they're headed for trouble. Director Franklin, however you may want to knock the man's work in this T-Rex turkey, must be complimented for the way he photographs Veronica.

He captures her leaning far forward, he captures her sprawled out like she's posing for *Playboy*, and he is forever focusing on her lithe body as the safari presses ever forward toward danger. *The Lost World* gets so bad, in fact, that ultimately, when the ape monsters attack, it starts to get howlingly good. That's when the blonde in the bikini attracts the eye of a T-Rex creature and makes it chase her. That she and her male companion should be able to outrun this monster when it can cover fifty feet to their ten is by far the funniest moment in what amounts to many chortles, chuckles, and guffaws. Even if it means embarrassing the cast, here are the other names: Rachel Blakely, William De Vry, William Snow, Jennifer O'Dell, Mikel Sinel Nikoff. (Turner)

SISTERHOOD, THE (1988) ★★ Women of a voluptuous nature fight to stay alive in a *Mad Max* kind of post-holocaust world. Directed in the Philippines by Cirio H. Santiago. Rebecca Holden, Chuck Wagner, Lynn-Holly Johnson, Barbara Hooper. (Media) (Laser: Image)

SISTER OF SATAN, THE. See *The She-Beast*.

SISTERS (1973) ★★★½ Director Brian De Palma's homage to Hitchcock (aka *Blood Sisters*) is black comedy and biting satire, but confused by erratic editing, strange juxtaposing of scenes and lack of logic. Because De Palma's intentions are fuzzy, *Sisters* is an intriguing mess. The director (who cowrote with Louisa Rose) examines one of two Siamese sisters (both played by Margot Kidder) who keeps splitting her personality—not to mention a few heads. Jennifer Salt, an irascible reporter, sets out to prove the sister committed murder. True, the suspense is considerable and there is excellent use of split screen but it's ultimately a bumble of a jumble. Bernard Herrmann wrote the music. Charles Durning, Barnard Hughes. (Warner Bros.)

SISTER, SISTER (1987) ★★★ Moody, heavily gothic horror melodrama, strong for its ambience and miasma of the decaying swamp and decadent spirit of the South. In the bayou country, in an antebellum mansion dubbed the Willows, the Bonnard sisters (Jennifer Jason Leigh and Judith Ivey) go bonkers because of past and present stimuli. Director Bill Condon (who cowrote with Joel Cohen and Ginny Cerrella) has the advantage of a real location (the Greenwood Plantation in Napoleonville, La.) as his tale unfolds with all the hysterics and histrionics of a fire-and-brimstone damnation preacher sermon. It doesn't make a lot of sense but the atmosphere makes it compelling. Dennis Lipscomb, Eric Stoltz, Anne Pitoniak. (New World) (Laser: Image)

SISTERS OF DEATH (1978) ★★½ Sleazily made albeit entertaining low-budget thriller stars young Claudia Jennings as one of 5 women lured to the Hacienda del Sol outside Paso Robles. They're former members of a cult group called the Sisters, and one of them harbors a dark secret. They're soon trapped by madman Arthur Franz, who loads bullets for his Gatling gun and plays the flute. Even though it's shoddily directed by Joseph A. Mazzuca, this has a fascination that most movies of this kind miss by miles. The explanations and surprise ending make no sense—it's in the unfolding. Cheri Howell, Sherry Boucher, Paul Carr. (United; VCI)

SISTERS OF SATAN (1971). Video version of *The Nuns of Saint Archangelo* (MPI).

SIX DESTINIES. See *Flesh and Fantasy.*

SIX INCHES TALL. See *Attack of the Puppet People.*

SIX MILLION DOLLAR MAN, THE (1973) ★★★ While the Lee Majors TV series denigrated into a kiddie-oriented *Superman*, this pilot is an exciting thriller that does justice to Martin Caudin's novel, *Cyborg* (also the series's original title). Majors is a test pilot horribly mutilated in a plane crash; the U.S. government spends $6 million to restore him with greater speed, strength, X-ray vision and other superhuman talents. Richard Irving directed the adaptation by Henri Simoun. Barbara Anderson, Martin Balsam, Darren McGavin, Robert Cornthwaite, Olan Soule. (In video as *Cyborg: The Six Million Dollar Man*)

SIX WOMEN FOR THE MURDERER. Video version of *Blood and Black Lace.*

SIXTH SENSE, THE (1999) ★★★★ An invisible world around us of wandering souls is an image that must have visited writer-director M. Night Shyamalan during his worst nightmares; at least it is a notion that preoccupied him in his previous film, *Wide Awake*, which depicted a young boy with a connection to the world of the dead as he mourned his deceased grandfather. It preoccupies Shyamalan again in *The Sixth Sense*, but on a grander and more compelling scale. In fact, this is among the best films to explore the world of ghosts seriously, and it even creates "rules" the ghosts have to follow. It is also two movies in one, for there is a twist to Shyamalan's plot in the tradition of the best of O. Henry's trick endings. See it once and it's one movie with a jolting surprise (assuming you don't see it coming, and most people don't). See it a second time and it becomes a different tale, for you will view each scene from a new perspective. Bruce Willis is child psychiatrist Malcolm Crowe, who, on the eve of being honored by the mayor of Philadelphia for his fine work with kids, is faced with the failure of a patient he treated years earlier. To redeem himself the "next fall," he sets out to help youngster Cole Sear (Haley Joel Osment). Cole is an intelligent boy who lives with his divorced

mother (Toni Collette) and carries within him a secret talent. As Crowe builds Sear's trust, he learns that secret—that Cole can see "dead people." Not in coffins or graves. "Dead people" who walk around his apartment at night. Ghosts who open the drawers and cabinets in the kitchen. Ghosts capable of inflicting wounds on his skin. And when these ghosts get mad, the temperature drops. When it starts to get cold, Cole knows it's time to watch out. Meanwhile, Crowe is trying to rebuild his relationship with wife Olivia Williams, and wants deeply to help Cole, and in turn suggests that perhaps Cole can help the ghosts resolve their problems, Cole remarks, "They want me to do things for them." One ghost is a young girl who has been poisoned, and Cole helps to "solve" her murder. It is one of the few times in a "ghost story" that a ghost elicits sympathy instead of dread and there is a rare rapport between the world of the living and that of the dead. How Willis resolves his personal problems is something you will have to find out for yourself. *The Sixth Sense* is a solemn, dark movie and yet it is subtle and underplayed, with only a few quick glimpses of the ghosts. Ghosts, in this case, seem to be ordinary people—except for the fact that they still carry the wounds that killed them. There are none of the razzle-dazzle special effects that usually mark this genre. Shyamalan wants this to be a psychological ghost story that deals with the state of mind of people who have the unwanted talent to see ghosts. This is Bruce Willis's best attempt at acting—at least he demonstrates a greater range. Osment's performance is also remarkable, considering he is so young. He convincingly conveys a sense of abject fear. The relationship between Cole and his mother is a positive one and bridges a generation gap most movies don't want to show. What is finally most remarkable about *The Sixth Sense* is its sense of reality and its depiction of human emotions within its supernatural frame. The film is honest and heartfelt even if ultimately it becomes a trick of storytelling. (Video/DVD: Hollywood Pictures)

SKEETER (1993) ★★½ That old sci-fi standby, the mutated creature of nature (first made popular in such '50s fare as *Them*), is recycled in this desert-based action thriller that blends too many characters and subplots for its own good, and fails to generate a sense of building suspense. A "skeeter" is a flesh-munching mosquito monster, a few times bigger than it should be. Young sheriff's deputy Jim Youngs, corrupt sheriff Charles Napier, a crazed man in a limousine (Jay Robinson), another crazed character played by Michael J. Pollard and screaming Tracey Griffith all figure in this olio of special effects, mystery and mosquito attacks. Director

Clark Brandon cowrote the derivative script with Lanny Horn. (Video/Laser: New World)

SKULLDUGGERY (1983) ★★★ Stylish, imaginative glimpse at role-playing games and how they cross from fantasy into reality. This fascinating tale begins in Canterbury in 1382 when the Warlock claims the soul of an unborn child and curses a royal family. Flash ahead to Trottelville, U.S.A. in 1982 as a group meets to play life-and-death games, unaware Diabolus has dealt himself into the contest. A phantom archer is involved in the deadly play and the murders are cleverly fashioned by director Ota Richter. Thom Haverstock, Wendy Crewson, Clark Johnson, Kate Lynch. (Media; from Paragon as *Warlock*)

SKY CALLS, THE (1959) This is included so we can make reference to the fact that footage from this Russian production was used in *Battle Beyond the Sun*. Its U.S.S.R title is *Niebo Zowiet*.

SKY PIRATES (1986) ★★★ In 1945, John Hargreaves flies into a time warp near Easter Island and crash-lands in the ocean . . . flash ahead to his court martial where we learn he and other explorers are involved with a stone of magical powers brought to Earth by aliens. Indiana Jones–style Australian adventure, directed by Colin Eggleston. Meredith Phillips, Max Phillips, Bill Hunter. (CBS/Fox) (Laser: Japanese)

SLASH. See *Blood Sisters* (1986).

SLASH DANCE (1989) ★★ When young dancers turn out to audition for a musical show, a killer goes into action, knocking them off one by one—perhaps because of their questionable acting abilities? Lots of dancing, few thrills. Written-directed by James Shyman. Cindy Maranne, James Carrol Jordan, Jay Richardson. (Glencoe; Simitar)

SLASHER . . . IS THE SEX MANIAC, THE (1976) ★★★ Well-structured Italian psycho-killer thriller enhanced by Farley Granger as a cop after the Avenger, a knife murderer who targets unfaithful wives of prominent men. The script by director Robert Montero, I. Fasant and Lou Angeli builds tensely to the bloody climax and throws in surprise twists. Aka *So Sweet, So Dead*; an X-rated version was called *Penetration*. Sylva Koscina, Susan Scott, Jessica Dublin. (Monterey)

SLAUGHTER. TV title of *Dogs*.

SLAUGHTERERS, THE. See *Invasion of the Flesh Hunters*.

SLAUGHTER HIGH (1985) ★★½ Derivative slasher flick, opening at Doddsville County High, where nerdy Simon Scuddamore is the brunt of a practical joke when he's photographed nude by callous peers and dumped headfirst down the toilet. Further victimized in a fire-acid scarring accident, Simon is carried away on a stretcher. Flash ahead to modern times as model Caroline Munro and others who participated in the sick joke are lured to a fake reunion where, in the hallowed halls, they are hollowed out or slaughtered one by bloody one: crucifixion to door, stomach blown up to spill out intestines, knife through seat of car pinioning driver, acid bath in tub, submersion in sump hole, crushing under weight of car. Finally it's just Caroline in a virginal white pantsuit, discovering all the bodies as she flees the killer who wears a court jester's mask. George Dugdale, Mark Ezra and Peter Litten double as writers-directors. Munro fans get to see their sweetie in sexy poses. Carmine Iannoccone, Donna Yaeger. Originally released as *April Fool's Day*. (Vestron)

SLAUGHTER HOTEL (1973) ★★ An exposé of a popular hotel chain, as some business critics have claimed? Or just another beastly Italian horror film? Viewers will have to ponder subtleties and allegorical overtones for the answer . . . if they can stand the bloodletting and beheadings. The setting is an asylum run by Klaus Kinski. Directed by Fernando Di Leo. Margaret Lee. Aka *Cold-blooded Beast* and *The Beast Kills in Cold Blood*. (MPI; Gorgon; from Amvest as *Asylum Erotica*)

SLAUGHTERHOUSE (1987) ★★ Slasher sleaze bottoms out with this reprehensible, repugnant, repulsive movie. A companion piece to *Daddy's Deadly Darlings*, and just as unfit for swine, *Slaughterhouse* depicts a degenerate butcher-knife killer and his evil father (Bacon & Son) murdering people as if they were so many pigs and hanging them on hooks in a dilapidated factory. Writer-director Rick Roessler treats teenagers as dumb fodder and treats hogs with more affection than people. No matter how you slice it, this comes up a porker. Sherry Bendorf (as Lizzie Borden, the sheriff's daughter), William Houck, Don Barrett, Joe Barton, Eric Schwartz. (Embassy; Charter)

SLAUGHTERHOUSE FIVE (1972) ★★★★½ Contemporary *Pilgrim's Progress*, based on Kurt Vonnegut's novel and directed by George Roy Hill, depicting the firebombing of Dresden in 1945. But that is only one episode in the life of Billy Pilgrim, who is "unstuck" in time and leaps from time period to time period—or is he "traveling" in his mind? He and Hollywood starlet Montana Wildhack (Valerie Perrine) are captured by invisible beings and placed in a zoo on the planet Tralfamador. Wry commentary on the absurdity of human existence is presented in disjointed fashion by screenwriter Stephen Geller, but cleverly edited to produce a philosophical shrug of the shoulders. Michael Sacks, Ron Leibman, Perry King, Holly Near, John Dehner, Eugene Roche, Sorrell Booke. (MCA) (Laser: Image; MCA)

SLAUGHTERHOUSE ROCK (1987) ★★ Alcatraz Island in San Francisco Bay once again serves as the site for murderous, monstrous mayhem in another hard-to-sit-through horror flick. Nicholas Celozzi is suffering from horrible dreams caused by the one-time commandant of Alcatraz who turned into a cannibal and formed a pact with the Devil. When Celozzi and friends visit the Rock they meet the spirit of a rock musician (Toni Basil) who solicits Celozzi's help to destroy the forces of evil. It's a muddled mess as people die, souls transfer bodies, etc. All the horror-genre clichés are dragged out by writer Ted Landon and director Dimitri Logothetis. Tom Reilly, Donna Denton, Hope Marie Carlton. (Sony) (Laser: Image)

SLAUGHTER OF THE INNOCENTS (1993) ★★★ An unusual serial-killer movie combined with a police-procedural plot, culminating with one lengthy sequence of pure horror set in a cave of visual horrors that will rattle the hardest of gore and shock fans. That's one way to pay tribute to writer-director James Glickenhaus, who spins a dark tale about a top FBI agent (Scott Glenn) and his computer-bright 11-year-old son (Jesse Cameron-Glickenhaus) who join forces to track down the crazed killer of 2 children. The trail leads to the Cleveland Zoo and finally to Monument Valley, Utah, where the scenic sites of John Ford movies become the backdrop to this tale of murder and madness. Glickenhaus flings one surprise after the other at you as this bizarre adventure unfolds. Sheila Tousey, Darlanne Fluegel, Zitto Kazann, Zakes Mokae, Kevin Sorbo. (Video/Laser: MCA)

SLAVE GIRLS. See *Prehistoric Women.*

SLAVE GIRLS FROM BEYOND INFINITY (1987) ★ From the garbage pits of the universe comes this unbelievably bad sci-fi remake of "The Most Dangerous Game," the classic Richard Connell story filmed many times. This is pandering at its worst by producer-director Ken Dixon when shapely women land on a jungle planet where hunter Zed and his robots torture them and use them for sport. The 3 gals run around in bikini bottoms and bras, dodging killer ray guns, zombies and "phantazoid warriors." "It's a cold cosmos," remarks Zed. It was an even colder time when this hit the shelves. One of the worst. Cindy Berl, Elizabeth Cayton, Don Scribner, Brinke Stevens. (Urban Classics) (Laser: Full Moon; Shadow Entertainment)

SLAVE OF THE CANNIBAL GOD (1978) ★★ A cross between Italian cannibal movies and jungle adventure à la *King Solomon's Mines,* with the former genre overpowering the latter and the film becoming distasteful (pardon the pun). Ursula Andress and her weak-willed brother want to find her missing husband, and she solicits big-game hunter Stacy Keach. The Cesare Frugoni–Sergio Martino script degenerates into cannibals munching on snakes, lizards and human flesh; a mummified corpse with a Geiger counter in its open stomach; a lizard being sliced open and its blood being poured on natives' hands; a native spiked to death in a tree trap; a man eaten by a crocodile. The high point comes when the Pukahs strip Andress and rub red paint over legs and thighs—a scene her one-time husband, John Derek, borrowed for his Tarzan movie with Bo Derek. But the scene is a long time arriving. Martino also directed. Antonio Marsina, Claudio Cassinelli. Aka *Mountain of Cannibal Gods* and *Prisoner of the Cannibal God.* (Wizard; Video City; Vestron)

SLAVES OF THE INVISIBLE MONSTER (1950). TV-feature version of *The Invisible Monster.*

SLAYER, THE (1982) ★★ On Georgia's Tybee Island, an actress who has nightmares and her friends stay in an old house, soon to be stalked by a diabolical killer. Director J. S. Cardone, who wrote this as *Nightmare Island,* brings an unusual intensity to this slash-bash and creates an eerie electrical storm atmosphere. He also builds up the gore murders—a man decapitated by a trapdoor, a derelict battered with a ship's oar and a woman pitchforked through the breasts. The skimpy plot deals with the actress's childhood phobias. Sarah Kendall, Frederick Flynn, Carol Kottenbrook, Alan McRae, Carl Kraines. (Planet; Marquis; on a Continental video with *Scalps*)

SLAYRIDE. See *Silent Night, Deadly Night.*

SLEAZEMANIA STRIKES BACK (1987) ★★★ More previews of coming attractions of some of the worst sex and horror films ever made. Rollick to the rhythm of *Beach Blanket Blood Bath, Two Thousand Maniacs, Blood Feast, Gorilla Woman* and *The Girl from S.I.N.* Subtitled "The Good, the Bad and the Sleazy!" And "coming soon to a theater or cesspool near you." Don't miss it if you can. (Rhino)

SLEAZEMANIA: THE SPECIAL EDITION (1986) ★★★ Captivating compilation of previews of coming attractions for assorted sex films, nudies and softcorn pornies stretching from the '30s through the '80s, with no redeeming social values. See all the good scenes without having to sit through the bad films. Listen to bombastic announcers recite lurid come-ons ("an orgy overweight with immorality!") and see that wonderful "Explosive Thrills"–type lettering lurch across the screen. While the emphasis is on sex (would you believe "Pin Down Girls" and "Curfew Breakers"?), there are horror trailers, starting with *Last of the Pentinent,* an obscure exploitationer of the '30s, proceeding to *Orgy of the Dead,* incorporating *The Psychic* and winding up with Fred Olsen Ray's *Prison Ship,* a women-in-space sci-fi schlocker. Take yourself to the lower depths of depravity with these siren-screaming, bullet-blazing, thriller-diller "trailers for sailors." (Rhino)

SLEAZEMANIA III: THE GOOD, THE BAD AND THE SLEAZY (1988) ★★★ Here Rhino goes again, this time with previews of coming attractions that highlight *Dance Hall Racket, Teenage Zombies* and other cruddy goodies. (Rhino)

SLEDGE HAMMER (1984) ★ Below par slasher thriller made on videotape about a hammer slammer who kills mom and lover at an early age and grows up to be an adult basher smasher when teenagers come to the family home one weekend. Writer-director David A. Prior hammers home his point, nailing down the characters. Consider this critic a hammer damner. Ted Prior, Linda McGill, John Eastman. (Western World)

SLEEPAWAY CAMP (1983) ★ Weak-kneed slasher flick, without flair for gore. Oh, there are murders galore at Camp Arawak (sex pervert is scalded in vat of boiling water, boy drowns in overturned rowboat, youth is stung to death by angry bees, another kid is knifed in the shower) but they're clumsily staged homicides. Mike Kellin runs the dilapidated camp, covering up the killings so his reputation won't suffer. Written-directed by Robert Hiltzik with no understanding of what makes a horror film work. He should be sent to camp to sleep away his career. Felissa Rose, Karen Fields. (Media)

SLEEPAWAY CAMP 2: UNHAPPY CAMPERS (1988) ★ Thoroughly despicable slasher film carried to tasteless extremes with rock and roll yammering on the sound track. Pamela Springsteen, sister of Bruce, portrays a counselor at Camp Rolling Hills who meticulously murders each and every vacationer—including her senior male counselor. When she stuffs one poor victim into a latrine, flies buzzing around a face covered with human excrement, you know moviemaking has reached an all-time low. Murders occur by every device imaginable—not a single one original to Fritz Gordon's pathetic excuse for a script. Directed by coproducer Michael A. Simpson. Brian Patrick Clarke, Renee Estevez, Walter Gotell. (Nelson)

SLEEPAWAY CAMP 3: TEENAGE WASTELAND (1989) ★ Another gratuitous exercise in gross bloodletting and terrible taste, all directed at teenagers. Michael J. Pollard gets to act crazy again as a supervisor when the killer of part 2 returns to kill again and again and again. Twice was bad enough—3 times is unforgivable. Written by Fritz Gordon and directed by coproducer Michael A. Simpson. (Video/Laser: Nelson)

SLEEPING CAR, THE (1989) ★★★ College student David Naughton has hallucinations of ghastly-ghostly manifestations in a sleeping car converted into a rural rental unit after it was recovered from a railroad collision. Naughton resembles the man responsible for causing the accident so the spirit of the train's engineer (turned into a serial killer as a result) comes back as a decaying corpse to murder Naughton's fellow students and journalism instructor. These ghastly gore murders highlight Greg O'Neill's script, which attempts to deal with Naughton's difficulties in adjusting to a new life—and with a practitioner of "white magic" (played by Kevin McCarthy), the eccentric wife of the dead engineer, and the engineer (played by monster creator John Carl Beuchler). Should satisy genre fans. Produced-directed by Douglas Curtis. Judie Aronson, Jeff Conaway, Dani Minnick, Steve Lundquist. (Vidmark) (Laser: Image)

SLEEPLESS NIGHTS. See *The Slumber Party Massacre.*

SLEEP NO MORE. See *Invasion of the Body Snatchers* (1956).

SLEEP OF DEATH (1978) ★★ Slow-paced costume horror melodrama produced in Britain/Ireland and set in France, 1793, when nobleman Per Oscarson sets out for Paris, after his father dies, to learn about the world. Unfortunately, he meets a sinister gentleman (Patrick Magee) and other unsavory characters before it's apparent he's mixed up with vampires who will stop at nothing to put him into a deathlike trance. Magee steals the movie with his slimy performance but producer-director Calvin Floyd (who cranked out the script with his wife Yvonne, basing it on a Joseph Sheridan Le Fanu story) never builds the momentum to make this compelling. Marilu Tolo, Brenda Price, Curt Jurgens. Aka *Inn of the Flying Dragon*. (Prism)

SLEEPSTALKER: THE SANDMAN'S LAST RITES (1995) ★★★½ A pure horror movie in the sense that it was constructed by screenwriters Al Septien (also a coproducer) and director Turi Meyer as a vehicle for digital special effects (by Chris Walker), monstrous makeup (by Gary J. Tunnicliffe), blood and gore, trick camera work, and a monster villain with personality—the Sandman, played with a sardonic sense of glee by Michael Harris. (Would you call this a whodune-it?) The Sandman is a droll, underplayed type who sings lullabies to his victims and who turns into streams of sand, sliding through keyholes and under doors and flying up light fixtures. Nothing is predictable in this stylishly presented tale—even the hero, Griffin (Jay Underwood), is different from the usual monster stalker, as he spends most of his time fleeing from the serial killer Sandman and undergoing traumatic memories of his childhood. Life is a real beach sometimes. Kathryn Morris (as screaming heroine), William Lucking (as the cop working the case), Kathleen McCartin, Michael D. Roberts. (Turner)

SLEEPWALKERS (1991) ★★½ The script, a Stephen King original, was hailed as "the first King story written expressly for the screen," but it is minor King, depicting 2 shape-changing monsters who have assimilated themselves into society as humans but who face discovery when the "boy" falls in love with a mortal, much to the chagrin of his distraught "mother." They also have the power to make themselves and objects (such as cars) invisible, so this dark tale is all over the map, and director Mick Garris is stuck with the wavering narrative. King and some of his pals (Clive Barker, Joe Dante, John Landis) have cameos but it's an in-joke that falls flatter than the film's attack victims. What with cats coming to the rescue, *Sleepwalkers* is a disappointment. Brian Krause, Alice Krige, Mädchen Amick, Ron Perlman. (Video/Laser: RCA/Columbia)

SLEEPY HOLLOW (1999) ★★★½ Heads up! That thundering steed galloping out of the fog-bound New England countryside carries a rider who promises in advance, with the lengthy sword swirling over his head, to decapitate you without mercy. How ironic, and curious, that the horseman has no head himself. It's Tim Burton bringing Washington Irving's classic "The Legend of Sleepy Hollow" to cinematic life. As a film of atmosphere and period detail, *Sleepy Hollow* creates a sunless world of desolation and decay, forever trapped within mists and fogs. The brightest color is red, which is freely splattered about this world of supernatural ambience. Its citizens often appear as portraits by the old masters in costumes rich in period detail. Time and place are everything to Burton, and he captures them masterfully with the help of production designer Rick Heinrich, cinematographer Emmanuel Lubezki, and costume artist Colleen Atwood. The screenplay by Andrew Kevin Walker, who wrote *Seven* (from an idea by Kevin Yahger, special-effects artist of the *Nightmare on Elm Street* films and *Child's Play* series), is more about modern horror and mystery-movie traditions, with the viewer always uncertain when the murderous rider will strike next, and who the next victim will be. The beheadings are graphic, none of the details spared. And Burton fills the film with rousing action sequences in which brave souls battle the well-armed headless horseman, who may or may not be supernatural, depending on your beliefs. It is fashioned as a whodunit with Perry Mason–like overtones and some touches of Sherlock Holmes thrown in for added flavor. And there is a lot to savor here. If there is a major problem, it is the inconsistency of Johnny Depp's forensic investigator Ichabod Crane (in Irving's story he was a schoolteacher, but what the hey), who has been sent into the Hudson River country of 1799 to find the cause of three decapitation-murders. Depp vacillates from being a driven professional with his eccentric forensic tools to a bumbling buffoon who, at one moment, performs a bloody autopsy on one of the victims, and at another moment passes out at the sight of some new

horror. And he's so terrorized by his first one-on-one meeting with the Horseman that he retreats to his bed, quivering. Later, using Holmesian deductive reasoning, he figures out convoluted conspiracies involving complicated family trees and inner-village relationships. However, Depp plays Crane with such charming naïveté and presence that he ultimately wins you over, no matter how many times he is asked to pass out or fumble the ball. Gradually, Crane comes to realize that the "Hessian Horseman"— a German swordsman (Christopher Walken) who worked for the British during the Revolutionary War and slayed many a local resident before he himself was killed, beheaded, and buried outside the town—has been resurrected by someone who possesses his head. That unknown person uses an incantation to bring the Horseman back to kill enemies, and hence has secret motives that Crane must uncover. Burton's cast is peerless in bringing the period characters to life: Christina Ricci is beautiful in her low-cut bodices; Miranda Richardson and Michael Gambon portray the rich hosts who invite Crane to stay; Jeffrey Jones is whimsical as the village reverend; Richard Griffiths is the magistrate; Ian McDiarmid is the country doctor; and Michael Gough (one eye clouded white) is the sinister notary. Christopher Lee and Martin Landau appear in surprise cameos. *Sleepy Hollow* is like a strong ale, with a very good head . . . if you will pardon the expression. (Video/DVD: Paramount)

SLIME CITY (1988) ★★ The "slime" refers to what people turn into when they live in a New York apartment—but what's so strange about that? Written-directed by coproducer Gregory Lamberson. Robert C. Sabin, Mary Hunter, T. J. Merrick, Dick Biel. (Camp)

SLIPPING INTO DARKNESS. Video version of *Crazed* (Genesis).

SLIP SLIDE ADVENTURES. TV title for *The Water Babies*.

SLIPSTREAM (1989) ★★★½ This starts out as a seemingly clichéd imitation of the *Mad Max*, post-Armageddon genre, depicting an outlaw of the future (Bill Paxton) kidnapping a fugitive with a price on his head from lawman Mark Hamill and his partner Kitty Aldridge. However, the film—produced by Gary Kurtz, who also produced the first two *Star Wars* films—turns into something quite different (and special) as it depicts Paxton's flight into the "slipstream," a current of air flowing above Earth that "washes the planet clean." The characters take on dimension as Hamill realizes his charge is an android and capable of healing the sick. The dialogue by Tony Kayden becomes unusually poetic and intriguing, and the performances are sensitive as the excitingly photographed adventures unfold. Director Steven M. Lisberger captures an affinity for soaring in aerial footage, enhanced by the score of Elmer Bernstein. Eleanor David, Ben Kingsley, F. Murray Abraham. (Virgin Vision)

SLITHIS (1978) ★★ There's no way for us feeble humans to stop this hulking, antisocial monster—a mixture of radioactivity and organic mud from the Imperial Energy Plant off the L.A. coast. Now the slimy humanoid is stalking folks around Venice and Marina Del Rey, tearing them limb from limb, chomping hungrily on their tasty flesh and slashing their faces to pulp. The monster (ex-Olympic swimmer Win Condict in a rubber suit) is a nice try by fledgling writer-producer-director Stephen Traxler. On TV as *Spawn of the Slithis*. (Media)

SLUGS: THE MOVIE (1988) ★★ It's a familiar plot: Toxic waste infects a rural community's slugs and snails until they turn into monster-sized killers in the local sewers. Health inspector Michael Garfield investigates and has to deal with not only marauding mollusks but pesty bureaucrats. Despite the clichés, director Juan Piquer Simon does a credible job with a cast that plays it straight, enhancing the routine script by Ron Gantman, based on a novel by Sharon Houston. Kim Terry, Philip Machale, Alicia Moro, Santiago Alvarez, John Battaglia. (New World) (Laser: Image)

SLUMBER PARTY MASSACRE (1982) ★★ Call it *Son of Driller Killer*. A murderer escapes from an asylum and terrorizes L.A. teenagers (well-stacked ones) with his portable battery-operated drill. The unusual aspect about an otherwise not-unusual slasher film: it was written by female activist Rita Mae Brown and produced-directed by Amy Jones. Yes, when it comes down to the wire, women as well as men exploit bare asses and titties and gobs of violence to make a buck. This features the ubiquitous drill churning through eyeballs, brains, shoulder blades and chest cavities, and slashing open an occasional throat or stomach. What is really sickeningly depressing is that once an innocent character is forced to pick up a weapon for defense, he or she seems to enjoy using it as much as the frenzied, drooling killer. Michele Michaels, Robin Stille. (Embassy)

SLUMBER PARTY MASSACRE II (1987) ★ Not that *Slumber Party Massacre* was any great shakes, but at least it was made by women who wanted to take pokes at the Establishment, using the slasher theme as its foundation. This sequel is just stupid, and in its own inept way condescendingly puts down rock and roll music and its entertainers, probably without realizing it. The main killer (Atanas Ilitch) is a singer-guitarist in black with an electrical guitar that is also a giant drill, and that drill penetrates several nubile, teenage bodies when a female rock group gets together for a party. Disintegrating flesh, far-flung gore and a pillow fight with fly-ing feathers are the high points of the script by director Deborah Brock. A genuinely terrible movie in every respect. Crystal Bernard, Kimberly McArthur, Juliette Cummings, Patrick Lowe, Heidi Kozak. (Video/Laser: Nelson)

SLUMBER PARTY MASSACRE 3 (1990) ★ A repeat of the drill-killer attacks of the first two entries in this pitiful series. Strictly boring from top (head) to bottom (ass). Directed by Sally Mattison. Keely Christian, Brittain Frye, M. K. Harris, David Greenlee. (MGM/UA)

SMALL SOLDIERS (1998) ★★½ The Commando Elite—soldier toys manufactured by a glib, cynical toy company called Globotech with computer chips purchased from the U.S. military—literally smashes its way to life in the interior of a toy store as fully dedicated warriors, ready to do battle. Motivated by macho emotions and a racial hatred of their programmed nemeses, another line of Globotech toys called Gorgonites, the warped GIs swing into blazing action, although none too soon for the viewer. Not only is the Commando Elite against the Gorgonites but against "traitorous" mankind as well, when several small-town folks decide to help the adorable if somewhat ugly Gorgonites escape their show-no-mercy pursuers. This premise by Gavin Scott, Adam Rifkin, Ted Elliott, and Terry Rossio, which on the surface makes a powerful if obvious statement about man's warlike nature, might have worked better for director Joe Dante's intended audience of youngsters had the film been less violent and had the warriors been less mean-spirited. *Toy Story* it ain't. This violent aspect seems at odds with the film's satirical side, and where the comedy in *Gremlins* worked for Dante, in *Small Soldiers* it fails. That is not to say the film doesn't have its intriguing Commando characters. Major Chip Hazard (voice by Tommy Lee Jones), Butch Meathook (voice by Jim Brown), Brick Bazooka (voice by George Kennedy), Link Static (voice by Bruce Dern), Nick Nitro (voice by Clint Walker), Archer (voice by Frank Langella), Slamfist/Scratch It (voice by Christopher Guest), Insaniac (voice by Michael McKean) and Kip Killagin (voice by Ernest Borgnine) are an imaginative band of destruction-happy dog-faces. Less effective are the girl dolls turned into commandos via some strange Frankenstein-like operation performed with computer chips—this strains the credibility of even Dante's weird little world, and brings a sexism to the film that is terribly out of place. The human cast struggles with the uneven tones, including Gregory Smith as a misunderstood small-town teenager, Kevin Dunn as his abusive father, Phil Hartman as a more gentle dad living in the neighborhood, and Denis Leary as the mean Globotech CEO (who, surprisingly, never gets his comeuppance). Stan Winston deserves four stars on his shoulder for designing the toy soldiers, and Jerry Goldsmith's sublime music score is full of musical references to previous movies. (Video/DVD/Laser: Universal)

SMALL TOWN MASSACRE. Video version of *Strange Behavior* (Scorpio).

SNAKE HUNTER STRANGLER, THE (1966) ★★ Originally called *Mystery of Thug Island*, this Italian-produced thriller stars Guy Madison as an adventurer involved with a cult of snake worshippers. Directed by Luigi Capuano.

SNAKE PEOPLE, THE (1971) ★★ One of 4 Boris Karloff movies made in 1968, but unreleased for several years due to legal complications. In this undistinguished fare, aka *Isle of the Snake People* and *Isle of the Living Dead*, Karloff portrays Karl Van Molder, a landowner whose daughter (Julissa) is kidnapped by a snake cult on Coaibai Island. Codirected and cowritten by Jack Hill and Juan Ibanez. (Gemstone; Unicorn; Sinister/C; S/Weird; Filmfax; from MPI as *Cult of the Dead*)

SNAKE PIT, THE. Video version of *The Castle of the Walking Dead* (Magnum).

SNAKE PIT AND THE PENDULUM, THE. Another title for *The Castle of the Walking Dead*.

SNAKE WOMAN, THE (1960) ★½ As torpid as a serpent trapped in an arctic blizzard, this low-budget British film was directed with the bite of a fangless black mamba. In a corny style, thanks to an outdated script by Orville H. Hampton, George Fowler's production depicts a "legendary" event in 1890 in North Cumberland, England. A crazed herpatologist injects his wife with snake poison to cure her mental illness. She gives birth to a baby with characteristics of a reptile, who grows up as sexy Susan Travers, the only appealing element of this unwatchable mess. It was directed by Sidney J. Furie with assistant director Douglas Hickox, who would go on to make many horror pictures. John McCarthy, Geoffrey Denton, Elsie Wagstan. Aka *Terror of the Snake Woman*. (Cinemacabre)

SNAPDRAGON (1993) ★★★ Offbeat psychological serial killer thriller in which police psychologist Steven Bauer falls in love with a mysterious young woman whom he begins to suspect is slitting the throats of men with "the dragon's tongue," a Chinese razor concealed in her mouth, under her tongue. This low-key cop-vs.-killer drama is strangely compelling and underplayed all the way by director Worth Keeter, who treats Gene Church's script with respect. Chelsea Field, Pamela Anderson, Matt McCoy, Rance Howard. (Prism) (Laser: Image)

SNAP-SHOT. See *Day Before Halloween*.

SNOW CREATURE, THE (1957). See *The Abominable Snowman of the Himalayas*.

SNOW WHITE: A TALE OF TERROR (1998) ★★★ Set design, costumes, and atmosphere are everything in this imaginative, clever reinterpretation of the Grimm fairy tale, but in a much grimmer fashion. In a perverse bit of casting against type, Sigourney Weaver weaves a superbly evil performance as the wicked stepmother (or wicked witch, for she has supernatural powers) who wages a war of power against her stepdaughter Lilli (Taryn Davis, who is the purest of driven Snow). Apparently Weaver's Claudia has made a deal with the devil, for she marries land baron Sam Neill (who was forced to cut Lilli from her mother's stomach after she was attacked by wolves with gleaming eyes) and is quickly casting magical spells and various forms of evil to bring forth the son of Satan as part of her unholy pact. (Some elements in the Showtime TV-movie script by Tom Szollosi and Deborah Serra are not always crystal clear.) What's fun is finding the parallels to the Snow White legend and seeing how the writers and director Michael Cohn twist them with delightful creativity. Such as when the runaway Lilli (substitute Snow White) encounters seven foul men (only one is a true dwarf) in a hut in the woods, and is held prisoner for ransom. They don't sing "Heigh-ho," for they are an unkempt, unruly bunch, more threatening than cutesy. Or when the ugly, wicked witch looks into her mirror and finds a beautiful Weaver gazing back. There's also the coma-inducing bite of the apple, and a parallel to the Prince Charming kiss (delivered as artificial respiration by Gil Bellows, the one sympathetic member of the mine-working woodsmen). But it's really Peter Russell's art direction, Gemma Jackson's production design, and Marit Allen's costumes that capture the medieval feeling in this distorted fairy tale. Made on locations in the Czech Republic, *Snow White: A Tale of Terror* is certain to please horror fans and those who like their traditional stories skewered more than a bit. David Conrad, Brian Glover, Monica Keena. Aka *Snow White in the Black Forest* and *Snow White in the Dark Forest*. (Video/DVD: PolyGram)

SOCIETY (1989) ★★★½ Taken literally, *Society* is a horror movie about a secret band in Beverly Hills that feasts on "outsiders" at orgies. The bodies of these creatures, when sexually aroused, turn into a puttylike substance, absorbing victims "body and soul." Figuratively, it's an allegory about what society does to us if we are vulnerable—it monstrously feeds on us. Whichever way you view *Society*, it is one of the oddest films of its day, the Woody Keith–Rick Fry script functioning on several tiers. Billy Warlock portrays a 17-year-old teen haunted by hallucinations and caught up in the hysteria of paranoia as he realizes his mother, father and sister are part of the incestuous sex cult. The film's reputation rests largely on its orgy sequence in which the "surrealistic makeup" of Screamin' Mad George depicts grotesque, twisted bodies oozing in and out of each other, faces where vaginas and buttocks should be, and a woman who walks on her hands. Themes of racism, corruption of law and order, and ostracization are part of the rich mosaic that Brian Yuzna directed with a sure hand. Devin Devasquez, Evan Richards, Ben Meyerson, Charles Lucia. (Video/Laser: Republic)

SO EVIL MY SISTER. See *Psycho Sisters.*

SOLARBABIES (1986) ★★★ In the post-Armageddon year 41, the world has been nuked into a desert where children are indoctrinated by a dictatorship, the Protectorate, which allows young ones to act out aggression with skateball teams. In Orphanage 43, ruled by benevolent Charles Durning and showcasing violent arena action similar to that in *Rollerball*, a group of youths finds Bohdi, a glowing white ball that possesses an alien life force. As Bohdi changes hands we meet Nazi-like policeman Richard Jordan, a gang called the Scorpions, "eco-warriors," and tribes of survivors. Action on roller skates, with futuristic equipment (such as a robot named Terminec), dominates the plot. *Mad Max* clichés make you wish *Solarbabies* had more solar energy. Effects by Richard Edlund. Directed by Alan Johnson, scripted by Walon Green. Jami Gertz, Jason Patric, Lukas Haas, Claude Brooks, Sarah Douglas. Music by Maurice Jarre. (Video/Laser: MGM/UA)

SOLAR CRISIS (1992) ★★ High-tech sci-fi adventure with ample space hardware in which astronauts are sent into the sun to set off an antimatter bomb to prevent a megaflare that will destroy Earth. But back on Earth, corporate magnate Peter Boyle schemes to sabotage the project by reprogramming the ship's half-android crew member. And there's another plot involving military commander Charlton Heston and his missing grandson Tim Matheson. In fact, too many plots causes confusion and spoils this expensive Japanese-financed project, which underwent enough reshooting for the original director to assume the pseudonym of Alan Smithee. Based on a novel by Takeshi Kawata, and adapted by Joe Gannon and Crispan Bolt, this ambitious project sports Jack Palance as an old desert rat, Annabel Schofield as the android, Michael Berryman, and Paul Koslo. Musical score by Maurice Jarre, effects by coproducer Richard Edlund. Its production problems aside, there's enough good stuff here to satisfy fans. (Video/Laser: Vidmark)

SOLAR FORCE (1994) ★★★ As cyborg movies go, this one, directed by cyborg expert Boaz (*American Cyborg*) Davidson, is pretty good. At least it has a little humanity, and action hero Michael Pare, unlike many of his contemporary counterparts, projects sympathy in his role as a superagent living on the moon (Earth is allegedly uninhabitable) who is assigned to track down a substance on Earth called "amarinth" before it falls into the wrong hands. Earth is a desert land where small communities fight off gangs of sadistic bikers (led by Billy Drago, delivering one of his over-the-top fruitcake performances). Some action sequences seem to go on forever, and death is plentiful—but all this is counterbalanced in Terrence Pare's script with an interesting love story between the lunar agent and a beautiful Earth woman. Well, it boils down to being a pretty good B action movie. Walker Brandt, Robin Smith. Aka *Lunar Cop* (Hallmark) (Laser: Image)

SOLDIER (1998) ★★★½ This highly entertaining mixture of combat action, science fiction, and human psychology—produced by Jerry Weintraub—stars Kurt Russell as Todd 3465, a soldier of the 21st century taught to kill from the day he was born as part of the then-new "Adam Project." Even his name and blood type have been tattooed onto his face. Raised to be an automaton without emotions, Todd fights in the War of the Six Cities, the Moscow Incident, and the Battle of the Argentine Woods before he is pitted against an improved version of himself (better DNA choices, etc.) known as Caine 607 (Jason Scott Lee). When Todd loses, he is literally dropped at the age of 38 into a scrap heap on a far-flung planet (#234) in the Arcadia System. It's there on this godforsaken, windswept world that the battle-scarred wreck of a man must find the humanity he never had and help a band of settlers who befriend him. But being human doesn't come easy to Todd 3465, who struggles with the simplest of emotions and day-to-day customs while living with a settler's family (Connie Nielsen and Sean Pertwee). There are subtle hints that a blunted sexual desire in Todd is finally working its way to the surface, and that deep within him he would like to be a father and have a family. The script by David Webb Peoples (his previous works have included *Blade Runner* and *Unforgiven*) never descends into sentimentality or mock emotions for Todd, and Russell maintains a hard edge to the character. When the film is not working its psychological arenas, it's in the gladiatorial arena of battle where an evil commander (Jason Isaacs) brings his new breed of trooper to Arcadia #234 along with Todd's old battle-wise commander (Gary Busey). It's then that Todd reverts to his Rambo-like training and sets out single-handedly to destroy the invading force that treats the settlers as "hostiles." Naturally, there comes the final showdown between Todd 3465 and Caine 607. With Paul Anderson directing (his previous work includes *Mortal Kombat* and *Event Horizon*), the action is stylishly presented with futuristic weaponry and science-fictional trappings that help create a very dark and sometimes disturbing vision of man's inhumanity and a sense that Armageddon is always just an atom blaster away. (Video/ DVD: Warner Bros.)

SOLE SURVIVOR (1982) ★★½ Offbeat supernatural horror thriller, thinking fan's fare that is too mystifying to bring total satisfaction. Aging actress Anita Skinner has a premonition that her TV producer (Caren Larkey) will survive a catastrophic plane crash—and she does. Why is never made clear by writer-director Thom Eberhardt, but it is intimated she was "overlooked" and weird forces of the undead are coming to claim her. Walking corpses turn up. Eberhardt, in not providing exposition, creates a murky tale as he goes for ambience over visual shocks. Watch for death symbolism. (Vestron)

SOLO (1996) ★½ Does the world need another android movie about a "perfect-soldier fighting machine"? Probably not, but Mario Van Peebles (who helped to produce this thing) must think so, for he also stars as the half man, half machine being called "Solo" by its creator (Adrien Brody). Solo is assigned to an operation he bungles, gets wise to a plan by military redneck Barry Corbin to terminate him, and escapes to Mexico, where he helps villagers fight off Bill Sadler and other mercenaries assigned to wipe them out. This empty-headed action movie written by David Corley (from the Robert Mason novel *Weapon*) is given a little flash by director Norberto Barba and by Van Peebles's stoic portrayal, but no amount of pyrotechnics or arty camerawork could possibly salvage this formula genre movie. Seidy Lopez, Abraham Verduzco, Jaime Gomez. (Video/DVD: Columbia TriStar)

SOMBRA THE SPIDER WOMAN (1947). Feature version of *The Black Widow*.

SOMEONE'S WATCHING ME! (1978) ★★★ This TV-movie, which owes much to Alfred Hitchcock's *Rear Window* for its voyeurism and persecution paranoia, was written-directed by John Carpenter, who again distills the finest essences of the suspense-horror story. Lauren Hutton portrays a likable TV director who takes an apartment in an L.A. high rise, only to become the target for a long-range Peeping Tom who harasses her with calls, letters and eventually the promise of death. Hutton makes for a resourceful heroine-in-peril who is willing to go after the killer instead of vice versa. David Birney plays her ineffectual boyfriend (a USC philosophy instructor) and Adrienne Barbeau is a fellow office worker who also becomes prey for the killer, whose identity is less important than his tactics. This also works as a parable about modern-day hazards of city living, but just taken for what it is, it's a better-than-average effort for TV with fine music by Harry Sukman. Aka *High Rise*.

SOMETHING IS OUT THERE (1977). Video version of *Day of the Animals* (Action Inc.)

SOMETHING SPECIAL (1987) ★★★ The

"something" of the title is a male sex organ, grown on the body of young teenager Pamela Segall by magical means. While that might sound raunchy, screenwriters Carla Reuben and Walter Carbone (working with the Alan Friedman short story "Willy Milly") make this a thoughtful teen comedy, dealing with teenage behavior on a satirical level. The Milly who becomes an overnight Willy takes on the guise of a male, encouraged by her father to box and curse to be "one of the boys." How she/he learns about the sexes is clever story-telling, enhanced by the sensitive direction of Paul Schneider. Eric Curry, Mary Tanner, Seth Green, Taryn Grimes, John Glover, Patty Duke. Alternate titles: *Willy Milly* and *I Was a Teenage Boy*. (Continental)

SOMETHING WAITS IN THE DARK. See *Screamers* (1978).

SOMETHING WICKED THIS WAY COMES (1983) ★★★½ Ray Bradbury's 1962 best-seller reached the screen as a Disney production, with Bradbury writing his own screenplay and picking his own director, Jack Clayton, and star, Jason Robards. The result, alas, is not a classic (even Bradbury, apparently, has a hard time adapting Bradbury) but still recaptures the melancholy "dandelion wine" mood of Bradbury's youth in Illinois in 1932 and his poetic imagery. Two boys (one representing the daring side of Bradbury's schizophrenic soul, the other the conservative intellectual) encounter a sinister carnival operated by Mr. Dark, a delicious personification of evil. Dark and his midway freaks steal the youth of victims to replenish themselves (a theme explored in Bradbury's "The Dark Ferris") and it's up to the boys (aided by Robards as a librarian father) to resist the temptations of the insidious Dark, well etched by Jonathan Pryce. While the effects are dazzling and offbeat, the relationship between the intellectual youth and the father doesn't build the fire it needs to consume the viewer. Great character bits by Royal Dano as the Electric Man and Pam Grier as a witch. (Video/Laser: Disney)

SOMETIMES THEY COME BACK. See *Stephen King's Sometimes They Come Back*.

SOMETIMES THEY COME BACK... AGAIN (1995) ★★ For those who grooved on 1991's *Stephen King's Sometimes They Come Back*, here's a minimal blood-drenched body count: one beautiful big-busted slut-babe whose ears are cut off and sent to her best friend; one nice young lady whose body is surrounded by a giant pool of blood after she's been sliced in numerous places (including her forehead) by flying tarot cards with razor-sharp edges; a lawnmowing man whose face gets in the way of his whirling blades; a priest who cuts off his thumb while building a pentagram because that's what the Great Giant Book with Frayed Pages told him to do... but why go on with this lineup of gratuitous gore. Let's get to the more intellectual plot by director Adam Grossman and Guy Riedel: Michael Grossman, a psychiatrist taking care of freaked-out patients, returns to his home in the small town where *Sometimes They Come Back* happened after he learns his mother has died (under mysterious circumstances involving moving objects that shouldn't be moving). Accompanying him is his sweet young daughter Hilary Swank (and boy is she sweet, even a little swank). Whom does she meet but one of the dead teenagers from the original movie, a handsome guy who sweet-talks everybody until he turns into a friggin' freako demon with a face that could only pop up in a Stephen King nightmare. Grossman grosses himself out with a dream about his daughter having sex with a demon with a snakelike tail and confronts the village priest (the one who'll eventually cut off his thumb) so they can talk about pentagrams and other demon-killing devices that will be needed for the denouement. Then there's the retarded grass-mowing young guy who eventually gets his face turned to mulch. Well, you can see that there isn't much coherence to the plot, but that never stops director Grossman from grossing out on electrocuted corpses, pools of blood six inches deep, and other visual delights designed to please empty-headed gore buffs. Milton Subotsky, who once produced British horror movies, is included in the credits as a producer. Sometimes the good ol' boys do come back again, but not always for the right reasons. Alexis Arquette, Jennifer Elise Cox, W. Morgan Sheppard, Patricia Renna, Bojesse Christopher. (Video/DVD: Vidmark)

SOME VIRGINS FOR THE EXECUTIONER. See *Bloody Pit of Horror.*

SOMEWHERE IN TIME (1980) ★★★½ Sensitive adaptation of Richard Matheson's time-travel novel, *Bid Time Return.* Christopher (*Superman*) Reeve is a romantic playwright fascinated with a turn-of-the-century stage actress (Jane Seymour). So intense is this fascination that he overcomes time flow and travels back through the years to Michigan's Mackinac Island where he finds the actress and conducts a bittersweet love affair. Matheson adapted his book, Jeannot Szwarc directed. Teresa Wright, Christopher Plummer. (Video/Laser: MCA)

SONG SPINNER, THE (1995) ★★★ This U.S.-Canadian TV-movie, written by Pauline Le Bel, is a fairy-tale allegory about the suppression of the human spirit and the fight to keep it free. Set in an Elizabethan-styled kingdom called Shandrilan, Le Bel's unusual fantasy depicts a society in which "silence is golden" and music is outlawed (even tap dancing is forbidden), all because the benevolent king (John Neville) once lost the love of his singing Zantalalia (Patti Lupone) and now forces the Quiet Police to keep

the people tightly controlled. How adolescent Meredith Henderson as Aurora restores order with Zantalalia's help (she's thought to be a witch, and maybe she is) is the "geist" of this unusual parable made in Nova Scotia. Directed by coproducer Randy Bradshaw, it also features Wendel Meldrum, David Hemblen, Julia Richings and Brent Carver. (Video/Laser: Hallmark)

SONNET FOR THE HUNTER, A. See *Witchfire.*

SON OF BLOB (1971) ★★½ This sequel to *The Blob*, produced by Jack H. Harris, written by Jack Woods and Anthony Harris, and directed by actor Larry Hagman, is a poor horror film trying to be satirical without much success. Robert Walker, Jr., Richard Webb, Godfrey Cambridge, Carol Lynley; Shelley Berman and Burgess Meredith appear in cameos, becoming Blob food. Without redeeming social values, and with mediocre effects, beware! The Blob is a slob. Aka *Here Comes the Blob, Beware of the Blob, Beware! The Blob* (Video Gems)

SON OF DARKNESS: TO DIE FOR 2. See *To Die For 2: Son of Darkness.*

SON OF DRACULA (1943) ★★★ Universal's second sequel to *Dracula* (after *Dracula's Daughter*) focuses on Count Alucard (check that spelling, fans), a cloaked entity in Louisiana country who hypnotically draws Louise Albritton into vampirism. Loads of atmosphere, good makeup by Jack Pierce, nifty man-to-bat transitions (done with animation) and a sense of fun, with Lon Chaney, Jr., enjoying his role. Directed by Robert Siodmak, written by Eric Taylor from a Curt Siodmak story. J. Edgar Bromberg, Evelyn Ankers, Robert Paige. (Video/Laser: MCA)

SON OF FLUBBER (1963) ★★★ Disney's sequel to *The Absent-minded Professor* revives Fred MacMurray as the forgetful scientist who invents a "flubber gas" that allows him to control the weather (imagine an impromptu rainstorm inside a station wagon). Keenan Wynn is again the bad guy trying to steal the gas, Nancy Olson is suffering Mom and Tommy Kirk is the son. Visually witty fantasy prevails. Directed by Robert Stevenson and written by producer Bill Walsh. Ed Wynn, Charles Ruggles, William Demarest, Paul Lynde, Stuart Erwin. (Disney)

SON OF FRANKENSTEIN (1939) ★★★★ The third and final time Boris Karloff played the Monster—and the last time the Monster evoked viewer sympathy. Director Rowland V. Lee, imitating James Whale, captures a surrealistic aura—Germanic in its expressionism—and there's a literate ring to the script by Willis Cooper, a famous radio writer (*Lights Out, Quiet Please*). Bela Lugosi's Ygor the Shepherd is one of his more menacing roles—he escapes his own hamminess and type-casting. Basil Rathbone as the good doctor chews the scenery, but his histrionics are appropriate to the story. Lionel Atwill is unforgettable as the police chief with an artificial hand that clicks and jerks like a mechanical monster. Superior effort in the series, one no true-blooded horror fan should miss. (MCA; RCA/Columbia) (Laser:MCA)

SON OF GODZILLA (1968) ★★★ Bringing up junior can be trying, as this Japanese study in parenthood shows. Out of a giant egg pops a baby Godzilla, Minya. The monster tyke has a slight disadvantage: he has harmless breath and blows only smoke rings. Minya is slapped around by father a bit until he learns good manners—such as how to hulk with style, shamble with grace and crush and maim with finesse. And then a giant praying mantis flies by, challenging the moppet monster to a duel. Children will find this delightful; adults will wonder if the Japanese are putting them on with inept charm. Directed by Jun Fukuda. Tadao Takashima, Akira Kubo, Beverly Maeda. (Hollywood Home; Prism; Budget; Video Treasures) (Laser: Japanese)

SON OF KONG, THE (1934) ★★★★ *King Kong* creators Merian C. Cooper and Ernest B. Schoedsack concocted this sequel, panned by critics and disowned by its stop-motion animator, Willis O'Brien, who resented Ruth Rose's tongue-in-cheek script. That didn't stop it from making money, but it has never attained classic status, remaining in Kong's shadow. Still, it now plays like a film of historic importance with ample comedy and adventure (and that wonderful music by Max Steiner) as Carl Denham (Robert Armstrong) returns to Skull Island to pay off debts incurred from Kong's destructive rampage through New York City. (Can you imagine the bill the Empire State Building owners handed him?) The offspring of Kong is a lovable albino creature. Helen Mack replaces Fay Wray as the heroine, but returning are Frank Reicher, Noble Johnson and Victor Wong. Cooper produced while Schoedsack directed. (Nostalgia Merchant; Media; Fox Hills) (Laser: Image, with *King Kong*)

SON OF SATAN (1976). See *The Redeemer.*

SON OF SINBAD (1955) ★★½ Made in 3-D but released flat—you might use that same word to describe the impact this Howard Hughes–RKO release had on viewers. Dale Robertson as Sinbad, with a Texas accent? Yech. More at home in this Hollywood-esque fantasy nonsense are Vincent Price (as poet Omar Khayyam) and the stimulating Mari Blanchard, who fills her scanty harem costumes with considerable pulchritude. Other women doing the same are Sally Forrest and Lili St. Cyr. The plot (by Aubrey Wisberg and Jack Pollexfen) has to do with the secret of Green Fire, a forerunner to TNT, but the only fire this picture needed was under director Ted Tetzlaff. Arabian music by Victor Young. (United; VCI; Republic)

SORCERESS (1982) ★★★ High-camp sword-and-sorcery actioner produced by Jack Hill with the subtlety of a cauldron-stirring, cackling witch and directed by Brian Stuart with the finesse of an axman hacking through brambles. Dialogue by Jim Wynorski will have you howling as two sisters, endowed with supernatural strength as well as healthy chests (which they reveal often), search for the wicked wizard who murdered their mother. There's a satyric character who bellows like a goat, a Viking swordsman and a beefcake who introduces the twins to nightly pleasures. Plus an army of zombie swordsmen and effects by John Carl Buechler, added by producer Roger Corman to save the picture. Leigh Harris, Lynette Harris, Bob Nelson. (HBO)

SORORITY BABES IN THE SLIMEBALL BOWL-O-RAMA (1988) ★ The title is the only thing distinctive about this purely pathetic attempt at campy comedy. First you have lowlife Peeping Tom nerds who crash a campus house for dames to watch their sorority rites, such as having bare fannies spanked and chests squirted with whipped cream. Then you have the broads playing a joke on the guys by having them break into a bowling alley. Gee, really exciting so far, right? Then you have a stupid hand-puppet imp from another dimension that turns the asinine teens into homicidal killers. The monster is as unbelievable as the cast, and the lowest common denominator is always sought by director David DeCoteau. Linnea Quigley, Andras Jones, Robin Rochelle, Hal Havins, Brinke Stevens. Aka *The Imp.* (Urban Classics) (Laser: Full Moon/Shadow)

SORORITY GIRLS AND THE CREATURE FROM HELL (1990) ★ This bears no relationship to David DeCoteau's "Sorority Babes" series, which at least had sophomoric hum. This is unfunny and dumb as unappealing gals and guys rendezvous at a mountain cabin and are torn apart by a man with a Neanderthal face turned killer by a giant skull statue in a secret cave. The stone-age script by producer-director John McBrearty makes no more sense than that. A rank amateur production, stricken by poverty. Len Lesser, Stacy Lynn, Eric Clark, Dori Courtney. (Complete Entertainment)

SORORITY HOUSE MASSACRE (1985) ★ Eternal fraternal is internal and infernal when a cackling knife killer, foaming at the mouth and wide of eyeballs within their sockets, slaughters daughters of the rich and seeks to make dead coed Angela O'Neill, who's been dreaming about an escaped psycho case. Written-directed by Carol Frank. (Warner Bros.)

SORORITY HOUSE MASSACRE 2 (1990) ★★ Five babes, their bodies barely covered by Frederick's of Hollywood lingerie, rush about a house of horror pursued by a killer who apparently is the ghost of a demented madman who slaughtered his family in the residence years before. As dumb as it sounds, it's fun to watch how director Jim Wynorski poses the babes for ultimate sexploitation, and how overweight Orville Ketchum is used as a red-herring handyman. Melissa Moore, Robyn Harris, Stacia Zhivago, Dana Bentley. The barely-a-sequel sequel was *Hard to Die*. (New Horizons)

SORORITY SISTERS. See *Nightmare Sisters*.

SO SAD ABOUT GLORIA. See *Visions of Evil*.

S.O.S. CLIPPER ISLAND. See *Robinson Crusoe of Clipper Island*.

S.O.S. COAST GUARD (1937) ★★★ A 12-chapter Republic serial in which Bela Lugosi portrays a scientist (Boroff) who creates a deadly gas capable of disintegrating objects (in case you're wondering, the gas is composed of Arnaltite and Zanzoid, got it?). His opponent is Ralph Byrd (later to play Dick Tracy) as a Coast Guard undercover man. Directed breathlessly by William Witney and Alan James. Maxine Doyle, Carlton Young, Thomas Carr. There's a feature version under the same title. (Video/Laser: Republic)

S.O.S. SPACESHIP. Foreign release title for *The Invisible Boy*.

SO SWEET, SO DEAD. See *The Slasher . . . Is the Sex Maniac*.

SOULTAKER (1990) ★★ Evil entity comes to Earth to take souls. Written by Vivian Schilling, who also stars, and directed by Michael Rissi. Joe Estevez, Gregg Thomsen, David Shark and Robert Z'Dar as the Angel of Death. (Action International) (Laser: Image)

SOUND STAGE MASSACRE. See *Stagefright*.

SOYLENT GREEN (1973) ★★★½ Big-budgeted version of Harry Harrison's *Make Room, Make Room* that graphically, and depressingly, depicts life in 2022. A curious blending of the private-eye genre with glimpses of a world to come, scripted by Stanley Greenberg without much faith to Harrison's story. Earth has become a smog-shrouded planet, hopelessly populated, and near-anarchy is at hand as Manhattan cop Charlton Heston investigates a series of murders—perpetrated to protect a secret. This was Edward G. Robinson's last film, and ironically he portrays a dying man who seeks a pleasant form of suicide in this downbeat world of tomorrow. Leigh Taylor-Young, Chuck Connors, Joseph Cotten, Brock Peters. Tautly directed by Richard Fleischer. (Video/Laser: MGM/UA)

SPACE AGENT K1. See *The Human Duplicators*.

SPACE AMOEBA, THE. See *Yog—Monster from Space*.

SPACE AVENGER. See *Alien Space Avenger*.

SPACEBALLS (1987) ★★★ Another "babbling Brooks" production. In spite of himself, writer-producer-director Mel Brooks manages to sprin-

kle funny one-liners and puns throughout this spoof of *Star Wars*. It begins with "Once upon a time warp . . ." with rolling credits, then introduces Dark Helmet (villain), Lone Starr (young hero), Barf (dog-man, his own best friend), Princess Vespa (heroine), Yogurt (wise old sage with knowledge of that ethereal power, the Schwartz) and Pizza the Hut (monster). Helmet and his Spaceballs try to steal the oxygen from planet Druidia's atmosphere, the lampoonery being of the broadest kind. Not all the characters work and the spoofery comes too late after the success of *Star Wars* to seem relevant. (Didn't *Hardware Wars* do it better?) Still, the cast is bright: John Candy, Rick Moranis, Daphne Zuniga, Bill Pullman, Dick Van Patten, George Wyner. Brooks doubles as Yogurt and a human villain, President Skoorb. Joan Rivers provides the voice of a female golden robot who "wants to talk." Brooks cowrote with Ronny Graham and Thomas Meehan. (Video/Laser: MGM/UA)

SPACED INVADERS (1990) ★★ A kiddie sci-fi parody of "alien invaders attack Earth" movies—midget E.T.s who speak in English idioms idiotically are fighting an interstellar war when their radio picks up a broadcast of Orson Welles's "War of the Worlds." Thinking Earth is a rendezvous point for their space fleet, the aliens land in a rural town on Halloween night and are taken by townspeople to be simple "treat-or-treaters." It's lowbrow action and comedy juvenilely directed by Patrick Read Johnson. Douglas Barr, Royal Dano, Ariana Richards, J. J. Anderson, Gregg Berger. (Video/Laser: Touchstone)

SPACE FIREBIRD 2772 (1980) ★★★ Japanese animated feature is a creative exercise in space adventure as heroic Godoh and sexy robot Olga rocket into the void to circumvent the destructive activities of a monster. Written-directed by Taku Sugiyama. Aka *Phoenix 2772*. (Celebrity)

SPACE FREAKS FROM PLANET MUTOID (1988) ★ This Troma pickup defies description. Rock 'n' roll singer Tyler Upshaw (played by rock 'n' roll singer Denis Adam Zervos), after appearing in miles of boring rock 'n' role footage, meets sexy blond alien Lazer (Tamela Glenn) and, ending her 212-year search for Upshaw (?!), "melds" with him, even though they retain their respective bodies and souls. Then an ugly alien humanoid monster freak (yes, from the planet Mutoid) shows up to prevent Upshaw/Lazer from broadcasting his rock 'n' roll music into the Soviet Union, otherwise the Soviets will sue for peace and all troubles in the world will end. (Yeah, you read it right.) It ends with more boring rock 'n' roll footage. What can you do but avoid seeing this worthless, ridiculous movie (originally called *Herculean I*)? To make matters worse, Zervos also directed, a task he knows nothing about. Henry Coleman, Harry Sando, Gregory Harvey. (Troma)

SPACEHUNTER: ADVENTURES IN THE FORBIDDEN ZONE (1983) ★★ A $12 million space saga released in 3-D with few "comin' at ya!" thrills. In the 22nd century, interstellar mercenary Peter Strauss diverts his scow to the plague-riddled planet Terra 11 to rescue tourists in the clutches of villainous Overdog (Michael Ironside), a half-machine entity who soaks up psychic power of beautiful women (without bothering with physical contact). Production design is messy and funky with an eclectic assortment of costumes, weapons and vehicles. The script never develops Strauss's Wolff character or his "Odd Couple" relationship with waif Molly Ringwald. Ernie Hudson is wasted as the sidekick, Washington. Lamont Johnson directs with an eye to continuous action, and there's a conflagration with Overdog. Andrea Marcovicci. Aka *Adventures in the Creep Zone* and *Road Gangs*. (Video/Laser: RCA/Columbia)

SPACE IS THE PLACE. See *Sun Ra & His Intergalactic Arkestra: Space Is the Place.*

SPACEMAN AND KING ARTHUR, THE. See *The Spaceman in King Arthur's Court.*

SPACEMAN IN KING ARTHUR'S COURT, THE (1980) ★★★ Juvenile-minded time-travel fantasy (obviously inspired by Mark Twain's *A Connecticut Yankee in King Arthur's Court*) starring Dennis Dugan as a nerdy inventor who creates a lookalike humanoid robot of himself (named Hermes) and travels aboard the spaceship *Stardust* back to the days of King Arthur, where he uses modern wizardry to defeat a coup to overthrow the king. This pleasant, innocuous bit of whimsy (a U.S.-British production) is enhanced by a British cast headed by Kenneth More (as Arthur), Jim Dale and Ron Moody. Don Tait wrote the telescript directed by Russell Mayberry, who gives this the same kind of spoofy touch that enhanced *Pete's Dragon*. Aka *The Spaceman and King Arthur*, *UFO* and *Unidentified Flying Oddball*. (Disney)

SPACEMAN SATURDAY NIGHT. See *Invasion of the Saucermen.*

SPACE MARINES (1995) ★★½ This Showtime original cable-TV movie is your basic commandos-in-space action adventure with elements of your basic siege plot, so file it under derivative stuff. Edward Albert heads a team of hard-boiled space troopers tangling with a warped "space pirate" and his gang of cutthroats, and helping space diplomat James Shigeta pull off a hostage-for-money exchange. It highlights a plethora of galactic hardware, plenty of explosions, and blazing zap guns, but the telescript by Robert Moreland is weak on character and plot, and director John Weidner doesn't always succeed in making the derring-do look believable. Comic-book fodder at best.

Billy Wirth, John Pyper-Ferguson, Cady Huffman, Sherman Augustus. Only Meg Foster, as a commander-made-of-steel, stands out. (Republic)

SPACE MISSION TO THE LOST PLANET. See *Vampire Men of the Lost Planet.*

SPACE MONSTER DAGORA. See *Dagora, The Space Monster.*

SPACE MUTANTS. See *Planet of the Vampires.*

SPACERAGE: BREAKOUT ON PRISON PLANET (1985) ★★★ Bank robber Michael Pare is sentenced to imprisonment on Proxima Centauri 3, in New Botany Bay's Penal Colony #5, in the 22nd century. While that may sound like sci-fi, this turns into a basic action film with Pare leading a major breakout. The factions race through the desert in *Road Warrior*–style dune buggies, blasting away with ordinary pistols and machine guns. Screenwriter Jim Lenahan attempts to inject human elements into the mock heroics by focusing on "escaper hunter" John Laughlin, his gorgeous red-headed wife Lee Purcell, ex-LAPD cop Robert Farnsworth, and redneck planet governor William Windom. Farnsworth, a one-time stunt man turned actor, portrays the sagacious, laconic Western hero who straps on his 6-guns at the finale, so it's easy to compare this to Hollywood's action Westerns. Despite its mindlessness, this film moves at a fast clip. Directed by Conrad E. Palmisano. (Lightning)

SPACE RAIDERS (1983) ★★ What might have been a classic kind of *Treasure Island in Space*, with a castaway youth joining star-roving renegades and mercenaries, is a leaden nonadventure in tedium, as characterless as the space pirates it depicts. Roger Corman's film is lacking in style and pace, unfolding mechanically, without heart, under writer-director Howard R. Cohen. Not one of the alien creatures looks like anything more than an actor wearing a rubber face mask, and the space battles are staged without excitement, often consisting of outtakes from earlier Corman space movies. When gang leader Vince Edwards (tough on the outside, all marshmallowy inside when it comes to the kid) goes against the Robot Death Ship, you root for the bad guys. Thom Christopher, Patsy Pease, David Menderhall, Dick Miller. Aka *Star Child*. (Warner Bros.)

SPACESHIP (1983) ★★ Abominable attempt to satirize *Alien* in the vein of *Airplane* (hence the title) as the *Vertigo*, a phony-looking rocket, streaks through space carrying a ridiculous crew commanded by Leslie Nielsen. An alien, as phony as the rocket, sings and dances a little ditty called "I Want to Eat Your Face." Whatever charm this might have had is obliterated by overacting (including Ron Kurowski as the monster), flat direction and utterly dumb writing. The major blame can be put on Bruce Kimmel, who wrote, directed and plays one of the crew. Eject it through the airlock, quick! Gerrit Graham, Cindy Williams, Patrick Macnee (as wild-eyed Dr. Stark). Aka *The Creature Wasn't Nice* and *Naked Space*. (Vestron)

SPACESHIP TO THE UNKNOWN (1936). Newly reedited version of the first half of the *Flash Gordon* serial from Universal. See *Flash Gordon*.

SPACE SOLDIERS. See *Flash Gordon* (1936).

SPACE SOLDIERS CONQUER THE UNIVERSE. See *Flash Gordon Conquers the Universe*.

SPACE SOLDIERS' TRIP TO MARS. See *Flash Gordon's Trip to Mars*.

SPACE VAMPIRES (1981) Video version of *Astro Zombies*.

SPASMS (1983) ★★ *Death Bite*, a chilling novel by Michael Maryk and Brent Monahan, depicted the horrible attacks of a 19-foot taipan snake, a serpent from the island of Narka-Pintu whose bite kills in 3 minutes. This Canadian adaptation alters the taipan to a demon serpent from the Gates of Hell. Oliver Reed, a hunter once bitten by the supernatural reptile, has an ESP link to the demon and undergoes visions (in black and white) of its vicious, gory, "cold-blooded" attacks. Peter Fonda is the snake expert who talks about "viral telepathy" and Kerrie Keane is the obligatory female. Al Waxman is the uncouth villain who goes out with 3 "strikes" against him. Screenwriter Don Enright also introduces a pointless snake cult; his adaptation should have been exciting (the book certainly was) but it generates little suspense and uncoils lethargically to an anticlimax. Tangerine Dream provides a "serpent's love theme." Minimum effects footage of the supernatural serpent—director William Fruet doesn't have the bite. (Thorn EMI/HBO)

SPAWN (1997) ★★½ This cinematic version of Todd MacFarlane's comic-book series, with a script by Alan McElroy, features one of the most repugnant, physically ugly superheroes ever conceived—secret agent Lieutenant Colonel Al Simmons, a good guy fighting evil who is set up by assignment boss Jason Wynn (Martin Sheen) and his sadomasochist accomplice-in-black Jessica Priest (Melinda Clarke) and seared into barbecued flesh in a roaring fire. This is all part of Wynn's sociopathic scheme to cooperate with the devil and take over the world and run it for Satan. Williams (Michael Jai White in hideous fire-burn makeup) wakes up five years later in a slum area called "Rat City," not realizing he has agreed to help the devil (in the shape of a monstrous dragon) lead an army of evil souls against heaven and throw God into chains—this in exchange for vengeance against his destroyers, and a chance to visit his wife (Theresa Randle), now married to one of Wynn's toadies (D. B. Sweeney). Urging the newly formed being "Spawn" to carry out this diabolical plan is

his watchdog, a toad of a man named Clown (John Leguizamo), a thoroughly unlikable guy who cracks terrible puns, farts blue smoke, and demonstrates he's a shape-shifter by turning into other characters or becoming a lizard creature that battles Spawn for supremacy. Standing around on the sidelines and uttering enigmatic lines in a floppy hat and cape is good angel Cogliostro (Nicol Williamson), who thrusts Spawn into a moral dilemma and shows him how to use his superpowers for good. This includes the ability to throw up a metallic suit of armor when he's attacked, and the talent to thrust out wicked-looking chains that kill enemies or stick into walls so he can leap around like a circus acrobat. Spawn also features a billowing red cape that seems to whirl through his adversaries as it settles around him. While all of this is darkly depressing as hell, style is everything to special-effects-artist-turned director Mark A. Z. Dippe, who goes for dazzling visuals, such as Spawn spiraling through a cyclone of burning fire to reach hell, and Spawn in a multilayered hell where thousands of souls wriggle in pain and suffering. These visuals are by effects master Steve "Spaz" Williams, who presents one dark apocalyptic vision after another as the battle for the looming Armageddon is fought out on various planes. Unpleasant but compelling material, where everyone is definitely trying hard to push the envelope. You'll love its graphic portrayal of Satan's hell and man's self-made forms of hell-on-earth but you may hate yourself in the morning for being so perverse. (Video/DVD: New Line)

SPAWNING, THE. Video version of *Piranha II: The Spawning* (Video/Laser: Embassy).

SPAWN OF THE SLITHIS. See *Slithis*.

SPEAK OF THE DEVIL (1989) ★★ Belabored comedy in which a lecherous, phony evangelist (Robert Elarton) and his equally phony but quite nymphomaniac wife (Jean Miller) buy a haunted house in L.A. and convert it into "Church of Latter Day Sin"—motto being "Sin today without guilt." The greedy wife, meanwhile, makes a pact with the Devil. The script by producer-director Raphael Nussbaum and Bob Craft is all over the place with subplots: innocent girl threatened with "learning about sin"; rabbi subjected to castigation by a foul-mouthed Christian. The satanic rituals are attended by unconvincing demons and there are weak-willed attempts to have the reverend get religious. But to what avail? Bernice Tamara Goor, Walter Kay, Louise Sherill. (Action International)

SPEAR OF DESTINY, THE. See *Future Hunters*.

SPECIAL BULLETIN (1983) ★★★ Controversial TV-movie (by producer Don Ohlmeyer and writer-director Marshall Herskovitz) is a pastiche of a network news special. Scenes of an anchor team at a network studio are interspersed with footage shot by "live" cameras on the scene. Suspense is ever-building and the effect of realism ever-numbing as antinuclear protestors hold hostages in Charleston, S.C. These well-intended but warped radicals have an atomic device and threaten to set it off. The ending is a stunner. Ed Flanders, Kathryn Walker. (Karl Lorimar; Kartes; RCA/Columbia)

SPECIAL EFFECTS (1984) ★★★ Unusual psychopathic murder-mystery written-directed by Larry Cohen. Eric Bogosian is a legendary pornographic filmmaker who puts angst into his work—and secretly murders the women in his life, photographing their deaths with a camera hidden in his decorative bedroom. After killing a talentless model, he wins the confidence of cop Kevin O'Connor and plans to make a film about her murder, using her husband as an actor. Bogosian's cat-and-mouse games with the cops and the husband make for a compelling film with surprising twists. Zoe Tamerlis, Brad Rijn. (Embassy)

SPECIES (1995) ★★★½ Despite a grossly engaging alien-monster design by H. R. Giger (the Swiss artist who designed the creature in *Alien*), swiftly paced direction by Roger Donaldson, and shocking effects by Richard Edlund and Steve Johnson, this is strictly a B thriller, albeit a good one. It never rises above its thriller antecedents as a team of specialists (hit man Michael Madsen; empath Forest Whitaker; molecular biologist Marg Helgenberger and anthropologist Alfred Molina) overseen by DNA scientist Ben Kingsley track "Sil," a young woman–E.T. creature combination that has escaped from a laboratory. The result of an experiment between an alien culture and ours (via mixing DNAs), Natasha Henstridge has superpowers (frequently turning into an alien creature to murder humans) and is eager to mate, allowing for R-rated sexual passages. The script by Dennis Feldman (who coproduced with Frank Mancuso, Jr.) is loaded down with clichéd movie tricks but they work rather well and should satisfy the sci-fi moviegoer. (Video/Laser: MGM/UA)

SPECIES 2 (1998) ★★★½ Unpretentiously designed to satisfy the visceral needs of the horror- or monster-movie buff, *Species II* is a nonstop gorefest with H. R. Giger's hideously designed monster spinning off rather luridly from the already lurid 1995 box-office smash that starred Natasha Henstridge as a half-human, half-alien destroyer who ravenously coupled with her hapless male victims and murdered them horribly to raise cuddly little alien baby killers. In this sequel, Henstridge is back as a cloned version of her previous self, held captive in a laboratory where scientist Marg Helgenberger is conducting experiments to find a way to control the sexually dangerous if beautiful creature. Mean-while, an expedition to Mars with astronauts Justin Lazard, Mykelti Williamson, and Myriam Cyr returns to Earth with a container of elements of the Species Monster, which have been passed on to Lazard and Cyr. That means it doesn't take long for the Chris Brancato script (based on the original by Dennis Feldman) to show us gory deaths as Lazard turns into a serial killer, murdering woman after woman and taking their fast-to-grow offspring to a hiding place. Hot on Lazard's bloody trail are Colonel Burgess (played crudely but effectively by George Dzundza with damaged-eye makeup), Michael Madsen as the warrior Press Lennox (returning from the original), and astronaut Williamson, who turns semiheroic. The gory deaths compose most of the action, although there is a minor subplot involving Lazard and his senator father (James Cromwell), and Helgenberger's sympathy for Henstridge's desire to help earthlings while her alien half is psychically connected to Lazard and desperately desires to mate with him. The inevitable lab escape and chase are trotted out by the numbers. It's gooey and gory and just what monster fans love. An old pro at movie and TV sci-fi, Peter Medak helms it all with a sure hand. (Video/DVD: MGM)

SPECTERS (1987) ★★ Tedious Italian horror job that makes a specter-acle of itself when archeologist Donald Pleasence, digging in the catacombs beneath Rome, uncovers a crypt that contains the spirit of a demon that looks like Nosferatu in silhouette. The film is stretched beyond human endurance, offering nothing frightening. It took three Italians to think up the story and four to write the script for director Marcello Avallone. They do not add up to the Magnificent Seven. John Pepper, Katrine Michelsen, Massimo de Rossi. (Imperial)

SPECTRE, THE. See *The Ghost*.

SPELLBINDER (1988) ★★ L.A. lawyer Timothy Daly is so many steps behind the viewer in figuring out this supernatural mystery that he grows into a tedious hero long before the climax to Tracy Torme's script. Without Daly's Jeff Mills to care about, there's little director Janet Greek can bring to this tale of a satanic cult that sets up sacrifices for the full moon. There is Kelly Preston to watch when she seduces Daly in a sizzling bedroom scene, there's the menacing presence of Anthony Crivello and there's Cary-Hiroyuki Tagawa's portrayal of a cop—but this wizened witchcraft tale is bereft of effects, gore or anything else to hold one's interest. Rick Rossovich, Audra Lindley. (CBS/Fox)

SPELLBOUND (1945) ★★★★ Alfred Hitchcock walks "the dark corridors of the human mind," probing into guilt, fantasy, schizophrenia, paranoia and persecution complexes, but never forgetting this is a psychothriller. What a screenplay Ben Hecht has adapted from Francis

Beeding's novel, *The House of Dr. Edwardes*. You're in for a couchful of tricks as headshrinker Ingrid Bergman attempts to unlock the brain of amnesia victim Gregory Peck. Watch how the "master of suspense" gradually reveals the Freudian clues, and see how he toys with the audience, leaving doubt if Peck is a murderer or not. The dream sequences were designed by Salvador Dali and include blank, staring eyes, mouthless-noseless faces, bizarre landscapes. Miklos Rozsa's music, employing the eerie-sounding theremin, is the best "psychoanalytic" score ever written. Donald Curtis, Leo G. Carroll, Wallace Ford, Rhonda Fleming. (Video/Laser: CBS/Fox)

SPELLCASTER (1988) ★★ Unreleased until 1992, this Charles Band production made under his Empire logo is half-horror, half-comedy that unfolds in Bracciano's Castle outside Rome, where a motley collection of contest winners gathers to find a million-dollar check hidden on the premises. A drunken rich-bitch rock star, a fat guy, an Italian crook, a blond floozy and a TV video-jock are the greedy characters offset by a nice couple from Cleveland. Adam Ant is the host and castle's owner, named Diablocyril St. Michaels but obviously the Devil incarnate. The Dennis Paoli–Charles Bogel script (from a story by Ed Naha) has such a cop-out ending that the film falls on its pie-studded face in spite of rich production values, good monsters by John Buechler and satisfying gory murders staged by director Rafael Zielinski. It's a case of the film never taking itself seriously enough. Richard Blade, Gail O'Grady, Harold "P" Pruett. (Video/Laser: RCA/Columbia)

SPELL OF THE HYPNOTIST. See *Fright* (1957).

SPIDER, THE. See *Earth vs. the Spider*.

SPIDER BABY or THE MADDEST STORY EVER TOLD (1964) ★★★ Peculiar and fascinating blend of black humor and macabre horror, designed with a tongue-in-cheek attitude that still does not lessen the impact of chilling moments. The bizarre plot revolves around the Merrye family, which is stricken by Merrye's Syndrome, a "progressive age regression" disease that takes victims "beyond prenatal to a level of savagery and cannibalism." Two sisters, demented beyond description, live in an "old dark house" with their crazy brother and family chauffeur Bruno, played by Lon Chaney, Jr., with conviction. Relatives, with a lawyer named Schlocker (a nice touch, that), come to the house to win the family inheritance and must face the death games, designed by the children in an air of naïveté. There's a great dinner-table scene and crazy dialogue that keeps the film working as shock and satire. One of Chaney's best low-budget roles, with director Jack Hill keeping everything in balance despite the wild nature of his script. Carol Ohmart, Quinn Rebeker, Man-

tand Moreland. Aka *The Liver Eaters, Attack of the Liver Eaters* and *Cannibal Orgy*. (Loonic; Dark Dreams; S/Weird; Filmfax; Admit One)

SPIDER RETURNS, THE (1941) ★★½ Feature version of the 15-chapter Columbia serial of the same title, based on a once-popular pulp magazine character who wore a mask and fought supercriminals. The Spider is out to stop the Gargoyle, a foreign saboteur seeking to subjugate mankind with a TV spying gadget called the X-Ray Eye. Directed by James W. Horne. Warren Hull, Mary Ainslee. (Heavenly)

SPIDER'S WEB, THE (1938) ★★★★ One of the best, and most exciting, of the serials produced by Columbia. There's a breathless sense to the pacing uncommon to most Columbia chapter plays, and directors Ray Taylor and James W. Horne keep it bouncing along with energetic stunts, explosive special effects and a strong cast headed by Warren Hull (as the Spider; his alter ego, "famed criminologist" Richard Wentworth; and a disguised underworld figure named Blinky McQuade) and Kenneth Duncan as faithful companion Ram Singh. The Spider (based on a "dark avenger" character from a popular pulp magazine series) is after the Octopus, a villain in a white sheet who plans to disrupt American society through sabotage and take over with his own government. It's neat how the Spider swings on ropes and drops numerous villains with a volley of pistol fire, and follows a vigilante doctrine in stopping the bad guys. Iris Meredith, Richard Fiske, Marc Lawrence. Aka *The Spider—Master of Men*. (Videos available from mail-order serial specialists)

SPIES COME FROM HALFCOLD. See *Dr. Goldfoot and the Girl Bombs*.

SPIRIT OF '76 (1990) ★★ Roman Coppola, son of Francis Ford Coppola, produced. Lucas Reiner, son of Carl Reiner, wrote-directed. Susan Landau, daughter of Martin Landau, also produced. Call it *All in the Family*. This is a rip-off of *Back to the Future* and *Bill & Ted's Excellent Adventure* in which nitwits from the future (where recorded history is lost because the records were "degoused") land in 1976 to learn the ways of modern men (rock 'n' roll dancing, fast cars, self-identity groups) while trying to repair their busted time machine. The gags are lame and the cast can do little with the threadbare script. In short, a waste of time unless you like to watch celebrity offspring. David Cassidy, Olivia d'Abo, Carl Reiner, Leif Garrett, Rob Reiner, Julie Brown, Moon Zappa, Don Novello, Iron Eyes Cody, Barbara Bain, Geoff Hoyle. (Video/Laser: Columbia TriStar; Sony)

SPIRIT OF THE DEAD (1968). See *The Curse of the Crimson Altar*.

SPIRIT OF THE DEAD (1972). Video version of *The Asphyx* (VCL).

SPIRITUALIST, THE. See *The Amazing Mr. X.*

SPLASH (1984) ★★★★ This comedy hits the water just right—a Disney release that is a gainer and a half. Released under the Touchstone banner, it was that studio's first film with a glimpse of female nudity. Mermaid Daryl Hannah leaves Bermuda waters for Manhattan, where on dry land she falls for Tom Hanks and creates hysterical scenes gnawing on lobsters in a restaurant and screeching fish notes that shatter a dozen TV screens. Ron Howard's direction never jackknifes and the Lowell Ganz–Babaloo Mandel–Bruce Jay Friedman script is a series of charming vignettes. John Candy as Hanks's produce-district brother, Eugene Levy as the nerd trying to expose Hannah's secret and Richard Shull as Dr. Ross contribute wonderful characterizations. And love those scenes of Hannah, tail and all, floating in a bathtub. Dody Goodman and Shecky Greene also contribute bits. (Video/Laser: Touchstone)

SPLATTER. See *Future Kill.*

SPLATTER . . . ARCHITECTS OF FEAR (1986) ★★★ Special-effects artists run wild on a movie location, creating mutants, zombies and Amazon women for the sake of cinema art. Interesting, informative; better than the movies the effects guys are working on, that's for sure. Directed by Peter Rowe. (Synchron)

SPLATTER PACK. Video compilation of three Herschell Gordon Lewis gore flicks: *Blood Feast, 2000 Maniacs* and *The Wizard of Gore.*

SPLIT, THE (1959). See *The Manster.*

SPLIT SECOND (1992) ★★★½ Outstanding aspects of this monster-and-effects extravaganza are the manic performances of Rutger Hauer as the maverick cop Stone and Neil Duncan as a serial-killer specialist who takes on aspects of Hauer's crazed personality when they are assigned to track down a 10-foot-tall *Alien*-like monster in a futuristic London plagued by rats and flood waters caused by a thermal thaw. Hauer, an anxiety-stricken paranoiac who lives on coffee and chocolate, plays the psychic Stone to maximum effectiveness as the monster turns out to be unkillable and flits about the sewers, ripping the hearts out of victims. The ambience of a deteriorating city is excellently captured in Tony Maylam's direction, and the characters are vividly grotesque. Kim Cattrall plays the heroine and Michael J. Pollard is the rat catcher. (Video/Laser: HBO)

SPONTANEOUS COMBUSTION (1989) ★★★ What appears to be a steal of Stephen King's *Firestarter* turns into an intense sci-fi paranoia thriller involving a 1955 A-bomb test and how an experiment leads to a man capable of human combustion—the art of setting his fellow man on fire. Brad Dourif brings a strong intensity to the role, and one gets the feeling that writer-director Tobe Hooper (who crafted the script with Howard Goldberg) was expressing his personal anger against Hollywood. The cast (Cynthia Bain as the girlfriend, William Prince as the sinister mastermind and Jon Cypher as the strange doctor) brings to this work a sense of conspiratorial fear. The fire effects by Stephen Brooks (with John Dykstra as consultant) are good. Dey Young, Melinda Dillon. (Media) (Laser: Image)

SPOOKIES (1985) ★ Two horror movies (one of them *Twisted Souls*) are joined with Elmer's glue to (1) tell the tale of travelers trapped in a mansion with zombies and inhuman monsters and (2) spin the tale of a ghoul who resembles a "Creature Features" TV host and his minions as they terrorize innocent folks. The "kitchen sink" approach should please undemanding fans. It took 3 directors (Eugenie Joseph, Thomas Doran, Brendan Faulkner) to make nothing out of something. Felix Ward, Dan Scott. (Sony) (Laser: Image)

SPOOKY MOVIE SHOW, THE. See *The Mask.*

SPRING, THE (1990) ★★ Archeologists Dack Rambo and Gedde Watanabe search for Ponce De Leon's Fountain of Youth in Florida jungles. Also searching for eternal youth is industrialist Steven Keats and guarding the secret are voodoo sirens Virginia Watson and Shari Shattuck. Directed by John D. Patterson. (Quest)

SPUTNIK. Video version of *A Dog, a Mouse and a Sputnik* (Ingram).

SPY FROM THE SEMI-COLD. See *Dr. Goldfoot and the Girl Bombs.*

SPY SMASHER (1942) ★★★★ Spy Smasher was a character in Fawcett comic books during the 1940s; in this 12-chapter serial from Republic, which stands out for its glossy production values and is one of Republic's best, the superhero is portrayed by Kane Richmond. He battles valiantly against the Mask, a German dastard heading a sabotage ring in America. Ongoing cliff-hangers feature zap guns, supersonic skyplanes, and advanced forms of TV electronics. Directed by serial specialist William Witney. Marguerite Chapman, Tris Coffin, Sam Flint, Hans Schumm, Frank Corsaro. Feature version is *Spy Smasher Returns.* (Republic)

SPY WHO LOVED ME, THE (1977) ★★★★ One of the best James Bond adventure fantasies following Sean Connery's retirement from 007 activities. Bond (Roger Moore) is assigned to prevent the builder of an underwater city (Curt Jurgens) from stealing atomic subs and turning their missiles on the free world—an impossible mission made possible with the help of Soviet spy Barbara Bach. The action sequences are terrific, the full-scale freighter sets are impressive and overall the film brims with stylish action. The sex jokes are leeringly sophomoric and the

Christopher Wood–Richard Maibaum script typically far-fetched, but you won't be bored. Richard Kiel almost steals the film as the indefatigable villain Jaws, who survives catastrophes without disrupting a hair on his head. The character, in fact, returned in *Moonraker.* Lewis Gilbert directed the action and mayhem. Caroline Munro is featured in a bikini, chasing Bond in her helicopter. (RCA/Columbia) (Laser: MGM/UA)

SQUIRM (1976) ★★ Just try to worm out of watching this one: electrically charged earthworms, sandworms and bookworms (not to mention such bilateral invertebrates as acanthocephalans, nemertines, gordiaceans and annelids) wriggle, wiggle and squiggle into huge lumps prior to dawn, attacking dumb clucks (Don Scardino, Patricia Pearcy and Jean Sullivan) who drop by the swamp. Yep, it's the early worm that gets the bird. Made in Georgia by writer-director Jeff Lieberman with tongue in cheek. Ludicrous but fun cinema, allegedly populated by 250,000 real-life worms. Glow, worms, glow.... (Video/Laser: Vestron)

STAGE FRIGHT (1983) ★★ Demented actress (Jenny Neumann) gets cold feet before the curtain rises, the first of several things that turn frigid during this British horror movie-within-a-movie, aka *Nightmares.* Drop your drapes! (VidAmerica)

STAGEFRIGHT (1987) ★★★ Aka *Deliria, Bloody Bird* and *Aquarius,* this is out of the *Friday the 13th* mold, with escaped killer Irving Wallace (a demented actor who went berserk and killed 16 people) amok in a theater in an owl's costume, murdering a musical-play troupe: egotistical director, lecherous producer, bitchy actress, gay extra, rejected actress, etc. There are gore murders with chain saw, ax, power drill—one body is literally pulled in half. The film takes a turn for the better once the killer is pitted against one actress, a resourceful type who has Wallace hanging by his thumbs. Slasher-gore fans will be satisfied, but the nihilistic mood may unsettle sentimentalists and crybabies. David Brandon, Barbara Cupisti, Don Fiore, Robert Gligorov, Directed by Michael Soavi. (Imperial)

STAND, THE (1994) ★★★ Stephen King's colossal novel of an Apocalyptic showdown between good and evil in a world ravaged by disease (a man-made virus that has killed millions) is a difficult one to translate to film. After years as a possible movie property, it finally came to the TV screen as a 6-hour epic directed by Mick Garris, and it sports many good performances, including Ruby Dee's as the sweet old woman who gathers the forces of good around herself, and Jamey Sheridan's as Randall Flag, who symbolizes the Devil. Other distinguished performers: Rob Lowe, Ray Walston,

Miguel Ferrer, Ed Harris, Kathy Bates. This is a long one, though, and requires a lot of patience to get through as it skips around to different parts of the country as the opposing forces join ranks to face the Armageddon to come. For King fans, though, it's a must. (Video/Laser Republic)

STANLEY'S DRAGON (1994) ★★½ Pleasant albeit minor British TV movie in which nerdy guy Judd Trichter climbs down into a pothole and discovers a prehistoric dragon's egg, which he takes home and puts into the bathtub. Out pops a baby dragon that quickly grows into a big dragon breathing fire. It's a benevolent, cooing creature (pretty good special effects for a low-budgeter) but it's misunderstood and flees for its life, pursued by the law. Trichter and girl reporter Mia Fochergill hurry after it. A morality tale about man's penchant for destruction produced and directed by Gerry Poulson, perhaps inspired by such American fare as *Dragonworld,* which it resembles in some ways. (Family Home Entertainment)

STARBEAST. Original working title for *Alien.*

STARCHASER: THE LEGEND OF ORIN (1982) ★★★ Full-length 3-D cartoon feature has breathtaking space battles and weapons of tomorrow, and many stereovision effects are outstanding. But characters and story line smack of *Star Wars.* It's certainly no Disney-esque film Steven Hahn produced-directed from a script by Jeffrey Scott: Orin is a slave digging for power crystals in Mineworld, ruled by the tyrant Zygon and robots with electric whips. Orin breaks out to the land above, undergoing adventures with an obligatory female, a blind youth, a roughish adventurer à la Han Solo and a spaceship operated by Arthur the Computer. Parts of the film, however, move at warp factor 5, making up for technical and story defects. One of the best scenes has Orin manhandled by scraggly "mandroids," half-machine creatures. A must-see for 3-D addicts. Voices by Joe Colligan, Carmen Argenziano, Noelle North, Les Tremayne. (Video/Laser: Paramount)

STAR CHILD. See *Space Raiders.*

STARCRASH (1979) ★★ A return to the delightfully campy dialogue and plot lines of old-fashioned serials. The universe is in the grip of the evil Count Zarth Arn (Joe Spinell) and only Stella Starr, a space pilot who wears high-heeled boots in warp drive, can stop him with the help of alien navigator Akton and Elle the Robot, who speaks like a mentally deficient Texan. As played by Caroline Munro, wearing black leather underwear, Stella stops the starshow. Marjoe Gortner is her partner and Christopher Plummer is the Emperor of Space. A galactic wreck for adults, but kids 6 to 18 will shriek with delight. Flash Gordon never had a girl like Stella.... Directed by Lewis Coates, an Italian better known as Luigi Cozzi. Aka *Stella Star*. Music by John Barry. (Charter; Embassy) (Laser: New Line)

STAR CRYSTAL (1985) ★★★ High-tech sci-fi with good effects and spaceship interiors. It begins as a horror-mystery film in the vein of *Alien* when astronauts discover a crystal in Mars's Olympus Mons crater. Later, when a crew is trapped aboard a shuttlecraft with a life-form from the rock, director Lance Lindsay brings out the clichés: tentacles that wrap around victims, drained corpses, and so on. But after the creature taps into the computer and gets Bible religion, it/him/she emerges a cute E.T. copy. This never makes up its mind what it is, and turns into an anomaly. John W. Smith, Faye Bolt, C. Jutson Campbell. (New World)

STARGATE (1994) ★★★★ This sweeping cosmic sci-fi adventure opens with a superb first half as eccentric but ingenious Egyptologist James Spader helps scientists (working in an underground laboratory under the watchful eyes of the U.S. military) solve the mystery behind a time-and space-traveling device found in 1927 near the Great Pyramids of Giza. Spader joins with tough army officer Kurt Russell and other adventurous soldiers to cross the universe through the Stargate (a name borrowed from Kubrick's *2001: A Space Odyssey* and hence a homage to that classic movie). This unusual film is spellbinding up to the point where the team winds up on a far-flung planet that is not unlike Earth when its own pyramids were under construction, but then it turns into a *Star Wars* clone involving a race of aliens that also once visited Earth. Not that the film isn't beautifully made and acted. It's just that you wish producers wouldn't compromise so much. Still, the script by Dean Devlin and director Roland Emmerich is clever in taking Egyptian lore and turning it into sci-fi. Jaye (*The Crying Game*) Davidson gives an odd performance as a humanoid alien named Ra. One of the film's best achievements is its depiction of what it might feel and look like to be sent across the universe at the speed of light. For that scene alone, this handsomely made film (with great art direction yet) should be seen. Viveca Lindfors, Mili Avital. (Video/Laser: Live)

STARGATE SG-1 (1997) ★★★ Surprisingly, this TV-movie sequel to the '94 box-office hit *Stargate*, made to kick off a Showtime series and subtitled *Children of the Gods*, stands as a solid adventure piece as Richard Dean Anderson is sent back through the Stargate to the planet Abidoz when a Ra look-alike threatens Earth with invasion through the time-space portal. The script by producers Jonathan Grassner and Brad Wright is pure pulp-magazine fodder and a spirit of adventurous fun is achieved and maintained by Canadian director Mario Azzopardi as long as you don't take any of it too seriously. The best scene has a snakelike monster popping out of a woman's stomach and making love to a shapely Earthling woman. It'll make you shudder. Otherwise, it's good slam-bang action and suspense. Amanda Tapping, Michael Shanks, Christopher Judge, Don S. Davis, Jay Acovone, Vaitiare Bandera, Robert Wisen, Peter Williams, Alexis Cruz. Jerry Goldsmith wrote the score. (Orion)

STAR HUNTER (1995) ★ This is a decent idea (imagine *Predator Meets the Most Dangerous Game*) but it is amateurishly executed by screenwriters R. J. Robertson, M. B. Dick, and Mark Litton and just as amateurishly produced by struggling low-budget would-be filmmakers headed by directors Cole McKay and Sherman Scott II (aka Sam Newfield II). Two "Star Hunters," described as "intergalactic predators" who consider all species in the universe to be "game," escape imprisonment on some far-flung planet, and rocket to Earth, setting up their equipment in an American city for the hunt. Their prey is a broken-down busload of teenagers and one adult supervisor (Stella Stevens) who seek refuge in the home of blind Roddy McDowell, unaware that he is one of the deadly hunters. An area of the city is cordoned off with an invisible force field and the band is given firearms to fight against a superior robot creature impossible to destroy. One by one, the kids get knocked off while the survivors fight back and try to find ways of outfoxing the robot, while McDowell controls its actions back at a master computer, which displays futuristic information about the robot. Into the foray pops a "tracker," another alien being in pursuit of the escapee "hunters." It enters one of the teenagers in an effort to fight back but gets slowed by the human emotional system. The action sequences are poorly staged (not even the gunshots are realistic and should have been redubbed) and the whole thing has a hokey, ill-produced quality. Among the kids are Kenn Scott, Zack Ward, Sean Donahue, Wendy Schumacher, and Greg Brazzel. Helping out in small roles are two well-known B-movie makers: Steve Barkett and Fred Olen Ray. Roger Corman picked this one up and distributed it. (New Horizons)

STAR KNIGHT (1986) ★★½ Any film with Klaus Kinski, Fernando Rey and Harvey Keitel has to arouse curiosity, but in this case one can ignore the triple billing. This turns out to be an oddball Spanish film (released as *Knights of the Dragon*) set in the days of knights rescuing damsels from fire-breathing dragons. Kinski is a benevolent magician for a foolish ruler who surrounds himself with a plotting priest (Rey) and bodyguard knight (Keitel). An alien in a space suit lands in a Spielberg-esque UFO and communicates to the king's daughter (Marie Lamor) telepathically, while comedy relief with a bumbling "Green Knight" sets a light-hearted mood that predominates the direction by producer Fernando Colombo. (Video/Laser: Vidmark)

STARLIGHT SLAUGHTER. See *Eaten Alive*.

STARMAN (1984) ★★★★ One of the few sci-fi movies of the '80s with as much heart and emotion as effects—not quite as triumphant as *E.T.* but trying hard. When a ship crash-lands on Earth, its pilot transforms into deceased Jeff Bridges, whose wife (Karen Allen) must accompany him on his odyssey to safety. Starman has the powers of resurrection, and there's a Christ parable in the Bruce A. Evans–Raynold Gideon screenplay. What builds is a love between Earthling and alien, which culminates in her impregnation—the first joining of two races. On their trail is sympathetic scientist Charles Martin Smith and a ruthless government agent, Richard Jaeckel. John Carpenter directed with a feeling for his characters, injecting as much comedy as the serious theme allowed. A commendable effort, with Dick Smith, Stan Winston and Rick Baker contributing top-notch effects. (Video/Laser: RCA/Columbia; Pioneer)

STAR ODYSSEY (1978) ★★ In this Italian potboiler, aka *Metallica*, aliens auction off "insignificant" planets, with Earth going for the highest price. The inheritors show up over the Green Planet in a death ship, blasting away. The only man who can save us is a psychic professor surrounded by adventurers, misfits and comedic robots, who seek to destroy the alien ship's metal, Indirium. The humanoids wear metallic suits and blond wigs, props left over from *War of the Robots*, a spaghetti import also directed by Al Bradly. Screen sci-fi at its worst, with inane dialogue and a music track that is a joke. The funniest scenes involve a fight between a human and an android boxer and stupid antics between man-and-wife robots. You have to see one of these to believe they exist. Yanti Somer, Gianni Garko, Sharon Baker. (From Mogul as *Captive Planet*)

STAR PORTAL (1997) ★ Roger Corman prides himself on making movies for a buck, but not even this exploitationer comes up to one's minimum expectations of the master schlockmeister. Imagine a half-dazed film editor taking all the outer-space action scenes from Corman's past mini-epics and running them together to provide a mishmash opening. It's a space war designed to bring an alien named Quad Rona to Earth, where it takes possession of the body of a big-breasted sex object (played by Athena Massey). Suddenly the buxom babe, after having R-rated sex with some of her male victims, fires red laser blasts from her eyeballs, knocking down her targets. Then she hangs them up by their feet and drains the blood from their bodies. She drinks the blood to suspend a disease in her body, and then experiments to find a cure for the disease in order to take it back to her home planet. If this sounds familiar, it's a rehash with switched sex roles of Corman's 1955 *Not of This Earth*, in which Paul Birch played the alien with the glazed-over eyeballs. (Corman also remade this thing in 1988 with Arthur Roberts as the male body for the alien and threw in onetime porn queen Traci Lords to make it a little livelier.) Although no mention is made of *Not of This Earth* in the credits, the story idea is credited to Mark Hanna and Charles B. Griffith, who did indeed crank out the original screenplay. Steven Bauer (who has made B movies since debuting in 1983's *Scarface*) portrays a ridiculous doctor who falls in love with Massey. Along comes a guy wearing a black helmet who confronts Massey and Bauer and says he's here to take Quad Rona back to space. A cop gets shot and there's some stupid action and suddenly it's over. Director-writer Jon Purdy shot the whole thing in Ireland for a song—probably "My Foolish Heart." (New Horizons-Concorde)

STARQUEST (1994) ★★★ This above-average Roger Corman production features a surprise twist ending, so all is not what it seems. An international crew of seven aboard a United Federation starship awakens in midflight (hundreds of years from Earth) to find the captain dead in his suspended animation unit. As other crew members die mysteriously, it's suspected there is a killer on board. But there are more surprises yet in Mark Evan Schwartz's script, which includes a few virtual reality sequences. Rick Jacobson directed without giving away too many clues as to the story's true nature. The fine cast includes Steve Bauer, Brenda Bakke, Alan Rachins, Cliff De Young, Ming-Na Wen, Emma Samms and Gregory A. McKinney. Steve Railsback served as second-unit director. (New Horizons)

STAR QUEST: BEYOND THE RISING MOON (1989) ★★ Outer-space, effects-laden adventure set in the next century starring Tracy Davis as Pentan, an artificially created bionic woman who fights evil when an alien spaceship is sought by vying factions on Earth. She teams with space trader Hans Bachmann to fight the bad guys. Written-produced-edited by Philip L. Cook. Aka *Beyond the Rising Moon* and *Space 2074*. (VidAmerica) (Laser: Image)

STARSHIP (1986) ★★ Convoluted Australian sci-fier in the *Star Wars* vein, set on a mining station on Ordessa in the 21st century. It's the Empire vs. the Rebels again as renegades uncover a plot to kill 600 miners and try to take over the starship before the massacre happens. Director Roger Christian has a hard-edged style but the script he and Matthew Jacobs wrote is lacking in humor, clarity and sharply defined characters. You know a film is in trouble when robots are more interesting than humans, and that's the case here with a droid named Grid, whose face resembles a Noh mask. The most exciting moments occur during a hand-to-hand battle aboard a mining truck. John Tarrlant, Donough Rees, Deep Roy, Ralph Cotterill. Aka *Lorca and the Outlaws*. (Cinema Group; Magnum)

STARSHIP INVASIONS (1977) ★ Christopher Lee, playing humanoid alien Captain Ramses in a silly costume, battles another race of E.T.s in order to invade Earth. Robert Vaughn is equally wasted as a UFO expert investigating sightings followed by mass suicides. No one seems to be trying very hard to raise this above the level of a juvenile Z movie. A tax shelter deal for writer-director Ed Hunt? Daniel Pilon, Victoria Johnson. Aka *War of the Aliens*. (Live)

STARSHIP TROOPERS (1997) ★★★★ This adaptation of the novel by Robert Heinlein goes beyond that modest book (about camaraderie among young soldiers) to become a spectacular war-in-space adventure, enhanced by special effects by Phil Tibbett, George Lucas's ILM, and assorted computer animation artists. The adaptation by Ed Neumeier has the strange flavor of an old-fashioned propaganda film with a "gung ho" attitude about going into combat, and depicts a neofascist government training young troopers for battle against Klendathu, a planet inhabited by a culture of bug monsters. Every war-movie cliché is methodically paraded out in a tongue-in-cheek style by Neumeier and co-writer/director Paul Verhoeven, who admitted that this movie is his catharsis for having lived through the carnage of World War II. Verhoeven holds nothing back in depicting the horrors of war (torn-up corpses often without heads and limbs, men being consumed alive by flames, bodies being torn apart in hand-to-hand combat) and those not prepared for these visuals will find them disturbing. On the other hand, they make for a fascinating glimpse into the ultimate destruction of war, a glimpse that is softened somewhat by the fact this is, after all, just a fanciful, imaginative science-fiction movie. Also brilliantly depicted by Verhoeven and his teams of movie tricksters are two space-battle sequences depicting colliding ships. If there is anything that runs afoul in the script, it's the utter lack of explanation for how a race of bug monsters, without any noticeable technology, could be threatening Earth and causing war. Oh well, it's just a sci-fi extravaganza, so don't ask. The cast of young relative unknowns (Casper Van Dien, Denise Richards, Jake Busey, Neil Patrick Harris, and Clancy Brown) is adequate to excellent, but always overpowered by Verhoeven's deft directorial touch and the oft-astounding special effects. (Video/DVD: Columbia TriStar)

STARSLAMMER (1986) ★ Hilariously bad Jack H. Harris misfire produced-directed by Fred Olen Ray, blending the "women behind bars" theme with a Roger Cormanish space adventure. Sandy Brooke, a miner on Arous, is captured by Ross Hagen, a psycho bad guy with spiked hands, and sent to Vehement, a women's prison in space where female guards dress like sado-masochists and behave like raving lesbians. Sandy and pal Susan Stokey endure adventures with the Sovereign, a space tyrant; the Inquisitor (Aldo Ray in fright makeup); the Deadly Spawn (an awkward Alien-like mess); the Jagger Rat (a rodent with sharp teeth) and assorted depraved freakos. Ray plays it for laughs at times but Michael D. Sonye's script is torturous torture. The film is broken into chapters ("Death on Planet Arous," "Jail Break 3000") and promises Taura will be back in *Chain Gang Planet*. So far it hasn't happened. Mary Gant, Dawn Wildsmith, John Carradine, Bobby Bresee. Aka *Starslammer: The Escape* and *Prison Ship Star Slammer*. (Video/Laser: Vidmark)

STAR TIME (1992) ★★ A complete social misfit/fruitcake named Henry Finkel (Michael St. Gerard), because his favorite sitcom is cancelled, turns into a sociopath with homicidal tendencies when a figment of his twisted imagination turns up as Sam Bones (John P. Ryan), who encourages the sick hick to pick a face mask and stick an ax into human flesh in order to become a celebrity. Social worker Maureen Teefy becomes his target after he's already murdered one young woman by slicing open her neck. This is a confusing avant-garde experimental film (written, produced, directed by Alexander Cassini) with almost zero entertainment value, and is made bearable only by Ryan, a worthy actor who deserves better. Only for those who like slasher flicks with pretentious overtones and very little gore or effects. (Monarch)

STAR TREK—THE MOTION PICTURE (1979) ★★★½ First movie version of the popular TV series was a $40 million epic. But did director Robert Wise pull off an epic? "Trekkies" came away disappointed, feeling it was talkative and handicapped by weak concepts. Harold Livingston's screenplay—combining the TV episodes "The Changeling" and "The Doomsday Machine"—depicts a cloudlike object on a collision course with Earth and the USS *Enterprise* speeding from dry dock to intercept. Attempts are made to rise above the mock heroics of *Star Wars* but it still falls short of being a *2001: A Space Odyssey* with its lack of a living villain and its cloudy characters. The effects are uneven—ranging from excellent (when depicting the cloud's interior) to less-than-adequate (when depicting a San Francisco shuttleport.) The original cast is here: William Shatner, Leonard Nimoy, DeForest Kelley, James Doohan, George Takei, Walter Koenig, Nichelle Nichols and Grace Lee Whitney. Stephen Collins and Persis Khambatta are nonregulars. Despite its flaws, this was a worldwide box-office success and began a series of sequels and spawned several new TV series. (Paramount; RCA/Columbia) (Laser: Paramount)

STAR TREK II: THE WRATH OF KHAN (1982) ★★★★ Rejoice! This is truer to the TV series than the first film. A 1967 episode, "Space Seed," serves as the springboard, with villainous Khan (Ricardo Montalban, playing a superintelligent Earthman) wreaking revenge on Captain Kirk for stranding him on a God-forsaken planet. The crew is back (Shatner, Kelley, Doohan, Koenig, Takei, Nichols), but it's Leonard Nimoy who commands center stage with his death scene and burial in space. It was a brilliant gimmick by writer Jack B. Sowards that beamed up a sequel, *Star Trek III: The Search for Spock*. An enormous success for Paramount, producer Harve Bennett and director Nicholas Meyer. Nonregulars included Kirstie Alley, Bibi Besch, Paul Winfield and Ike Eisenmann. The one individual shoved into the background was creator Gene Roddenberry, who reportedly did not get along with Paramount during the making of the first film. *Wrath of Khan* is not a classic but its clean-lined effects (by Ken Ralston and the Industrial Light & Magic team) and its unpretentious space-opera yarn make it an A effort worth going to the end of the universe to see. (Video/Laser: Paramount)

STAR TREK III: THE SEARCH FOR SPOCK (1984) ★★★ This begins where *Star Trek II* left off—with the Enterprise returning to Earth, its crew members grieving over the death of science officer Spock. But while *Wrath of Khan* was classic in its depiction of the "Star Trek" regulars, this smacks of TV writing. So it finally resembles an overinflated 1-hour show, brimming with effects you wish they could have done on TV in the '60s. Before he died, Spock transferred his soul's essence to Dr. McCoy, so they must return to Genesis (a planet undergoing an accelerated evolutionary cycle), recover Spock's corpse while fighting off Klingons, and get back to Vulcan. Leonard Nimoy does a fine job directing—one wishes the script by producer Harve Bennett had contained more emotion and sharper dialogue. Ken Ralston again heads the Industrial Light & Magic team, creating effects that reflect the state-of-the-art level to which this series had ascended. Guest appearances by Mark Lenard as Spock's father, Dame Judith Anderson as the High Priestess of Vulcan, Christopher Lloyd as the Klingon commander. At hand are regulars William Shatner, Leonard Nimoy, DeForest Kelley, Jimmy Doohan, George Takei,

Nichelle Nichols, Walter Koenig. (Video/Laser: Paramount)

STAR TREK IV: THE VOYAGE HOME (1986) ★★★★ Unquestionably the best of the *Star Trek* features, a satisfying blend of story and characters. Picking up where *The Search for Spock* ended, this depicts the regulars returning to Earth aboard the Klingon Bird of Prey, while Earth is under siege from an alien space probe. To save Earth, Kirk and crew travel back to the 20th century to kidnap 2 humpback whales. This action takes place in San Francisco and the scenes of Kirk, Spock and others adjusting to modern times are hilarious. A charming idea, beautifully directed by Leonard Nimoy, and a family film in the truest sense, with an ecology message to boot. Catherine Hicks appears as a whale conservationist. William Shatner, Leonard Nimoy, DeForest Kelley, George Takei, James Doohan, Nichelle Nicholas, Walter Koenig. (Video/Laser: Paramount)

STAR TREK V: THE FINAL FRONTIER (1989) ★★★ The *Enterprise* goes in search of God in this fifth series contender, and under the direction of William Shatner, Captain Kirk himself, it emerges an average but enjoyable adventure containing comedy, action, metaphysical dialogue, even the deeper meanings of life, if superficially. Laurence Luckinbill is at the core of the film's strength as a Christ-like figure named Sybok (hailing from Vulcan) who converts disciples for a trek to find the meaning of the universe. After a burst of action on a planet in the Neutral Zone, Sybok commandeers the *Enterprise* and heads for the Great Barrier, beyond which lies the legendary Sha Ka Ri, the home of . . . ? The Kirk-Spock-McCoy interplay is here, there's a romance between Uhuru and Sulu, and Scotty gets to camp it up as comedy relief. The ending is ambiguous and you might say that Shatner, producer Harve Bennett and screenwriter David Loughery copped out about the final meaning of life, but you can't expect to learn everything from a *Star Trek* adventure. Leonard Nimoy, DeForest Kelley, James Doohan, George Takei, Nichelle Nichols, Walter Koenig, David Warner. (Video/Laser: Paramount)

STAR TREK VI: THE UNDISCOVERED COUNTRY (1991) ★★★★ Outstanding entry in the series, tightly written-directed by Nicholas Meyer, produced efficiently by Leonard Nimoy and starring the world-famous cast in its swan song. It is a darker *Star Trek* with less bantering between cast regulars and none of the buffoonery that tinged the fifth film. There are Shakespearean touches in the dialogue and a sense of tragic doom about its characters that even reaches out and touches Captain Kirk, forced to face his prejudice against Klingons. With a plot paralleling world events at the time, *The Undiscov-*

ered Country depicts the *Enterprise* assigned to establish contact with Klingon leader David Warner, who wants to make peace with the Federation. (The Klingon Empire faces collapse after the explosion of a mining moon, in a close parallel to the Chernobyl disaster in the Soviet Union.) The story unfolds with Kirk and Dr. McCoy on trial for murder and sentenced to an ice planet while Spock, in command of the *Enterprise*, encounters treachery and duplicity as loyalties are divided by peace proceedings. Sulu turns up as captain of his own starship, the *Excelsior*. The film was released only weeks after the death of series creator Gene Roddenberry. A standout in the cast is Christopher Plummer as a Klingon warrior, Chang. DeForest Kelley, James Doohan, Walter Koenig, Nichelle Nichols, George Takei, Kim Cattrall, Mark Lenard, Grace Lee Whitney, Brock Peters, John Schuck, Christian Slater. (Video/Laser: Paramount)

STAR TREK: FIRST CONTACT (1996) ★★★
This feature-film spinoff of TV's *Star Trek: The Next Generation* is a far different "final frontier" from that established by the original *Star Trek* gang. But if you are a fan of the sequel series, then this second feature offering with the TV cast was programmed to fulfill all your expectations. In this, the eighth overall entry in Gene Roddenberry's creation, Captain Jean-Luc Picard (British classical actor Patrick Stewart, doing a bang-up job as usual) and his crew (Jonathan Frakes, Brent Spiner, Michael Dorn, LeVar Burton, Gates McFadden, Marina Sirtis) helm the USS Enterprise back in time to Earth in the 21st century to prevent The Borg (led by Queen Borg, played with oozing menace and sexuality by Alice Krige) from conquering Earth. Then there's a subplot about the Earthman who discovered Warp Drive (played by James Cromwell in a most singular manner.) Producer Rick Berman opted to keep the series firmly grounded in the attitudes and style of the TV series, and hence this suffers from limitations of scope and clarity—a problem that Frakes, doubling this time out as director, can't always overcome in working with the script by Brannon Braga and Ronald D. Moore. Quibblings include Sirtis seeming out of character and difficult to relate to, and Picard's link to The Borg (it was all explained in the TV series long ago) a bit too convenient. Ah, well. Fans will "engage"; nonfans won't be in the theater, anyway. (Video/DVD: Paramount)

STAR TREK GENERATIONS (1994) ★★★★
The title is apropos, for this seventh film in the *Star Trek* series is "generational" in the sense that a new generation of filmmakers has taken over the bridge command chair from the Gene Roddenberry generation. This 2-hour space adventure is quite similar in themes and tone to the "Star Trek: The Next Generation" TV series.

It opens with Captain James T. Kirk (William Shatner) coming out of retirement to help christen a new starship commanded by a young crew that includes Sulu's daughter. The nostalgia and history of *Star Trek* makes this sequence very sentimental and memorable. Kirk, Scotty (James Doohan) and Chekov (Walter Koenig) are quickly launched on an adventure that leads to a time-space continuum problem, allowing the 2 "generations" to merge into 1 story. Captain Jean-Luc Picard (Patrick Stewart) and the newer *Enterprise* crew come into play with an evil character named Dr. Soran (played snarlingly by Malcolm McDowell) who wants to tap into an energy source floating through space that brings one's most wanted fantasies to reality. The main thrust of the script by Ronald D. Moore and Brannon Braga is to bring the two starship captains together to prevent the destruction of a solar system and the *Enterprise* crew commanded by Picard. This is the heart of the film, and in that respect *Star Trek Generations* is something of a letdown when the film resorts to simplistic action. However, there's still enough good writing and directing (by David Carson) and cinematography (by John A. Alonzo) and special effects (by Lucas's Industrial Light & Magic) to make this worthwhile. All the TV regulars are here: Brent Spiner (as Data, who gets an "emotion chip"), Jonathan Frakes (as Commander Riker), LeVar Burton (as Geordi La Forge), Michael Dorn (as the Klingon Lt. Worf), Gates McFadden (as Dr. Crusher), Marina Sirtis (as Counselor Troi) and Whoopi Goldberg (as Guinan). TV producer Rick Berman helmed the project. (Video/Laser: Paramount)

STAR TREK: INSURRECTION (1998) ★★★ It's surprising that Paramount allows its precious science-fiction franchise to be treated as if it were still a TV series, never permitting the writing and producing to break out of the confines that characterized *Star Trek: The Next Generation* during its lengthy though excellent run. The characters are still intact and interesting in their expected ways, but one wishes for more movie-epic sparkle from producer Rick Berman. An attempt is made by screenwriter Michael Piller (story by Piller and Berman) to inject some romance for Captain Jean-Luc Picard (the always excellent Patrick Stewart) but even that is treated like a throwaway subplot for a TV episode. And although there's some playing around with the Prime Directive and the fact that Picard and crew actually revolt against the Federation (hence the title), the cards are so stacked in their favor that there's little concern for the outcome of their insubordination. After all, the crew of the USS *Enterprise* is always on the side of good and you know they'll come out clean on the far end of the star system. Keeps getting back to that TV mentality, doesn't it? Anyway, this depicts an idyllic planet in the "Briar Patch" solar system where the Bu'ka, a race of peace-loving folks (numbering only 600), enjoy immortality, which comes to them from "metaphasic radiation," a source of power generated by the rings around their peaceful world. Another race, the Son'a (aliens with skin that stretches), want to see the Bu'ka destroyed because of a past blood feud (they are united by DNA structure) and have entered into a "benign" conspiracy with the Federation to move the Bu'ka off the planet so the "Calvinate" (a metal that stops the aging process) can be refined and used throughout the universe. But secretly the Son'a plot to kill the Bu'ka. The issue of resettlement and sacrifice of a race (Picard compares it to the moving of the American Indians off their reservations) is at the heart of this otherwise average entry in the series, and it finally seems a concocted excuse for some typical sci-fi action with spacecraft, phasers, flying troll machines that transport you elsewhere, etc. Brent Spiner has a chance for his Data to run amok and do some destruction (it's called a "phase variance" in his "postironic matrix"), LeVar Burton gets new cornea implants so you see what he looks like without his eyeball visor; Jonathan Frakes (who also directed in a clean if not superexciting style) and Marina Sirtis get it on in a bathtub with glasses of champagne yet; and Michael Dorn has trouble with acne (or the Klingon equivalent). Gates McFadden does the usual doctor exposition and stands around looking concerned. F. Murray Abraham conveys pure evil as the Son'a commander (call him a Son'a bitch if you like) and Donna Murphy does one wet-blouse number during her brief fling with Picard. Anthony Zerbe stands out as a misguided Federation officer in conflict with Picard and meets a most unpleasant demise. Speaking of the captain . . . Mr. Stewart, please tell the producers and writers to give you and the other regulars more epic glitter next time. Since they gave you a coproducer's credit on *Insurrection,* use your power. Use your influence. Use your force. Insist. Make it so. (Video/DVD: Paramount)

STAR WARS (1977) ★★★★★ Director-writer George Lucas's masterpiece of space-opera adventure. Plotwise, it's nothing more than a rehash of *Flash Gordon* narratives, but Lucas treats the material with $10 million of respect. Every penny shows in dazzling effects, futuristic gadgets and costumes. There are laser gun battles; a planet called Tatoonie; hairy space freighter pilot Chewbacca the Wookiee; a spaceship squadron attack on the Death Star satellite; Darth Vader, villainous Dark Lord of the Sith; ships moving at the speed of light; robots and more robots; and a spaceport bar sequence featuring a menagerie of grotesque alien life.

Laurel-and-Hardy robots (R2D2 and C3P0) provide comedy relief, in some ways becoming more human than the humans. A close look reveals Lucas has a penchant for objects (call them "toys") and this is like an adolescent fantasy, wrought by adult technology. Lucas wisely chose refreshing unknowns (Mark Hamill as Luke Skywalker, Harrison Ford as Han Solo, Carrie Fisher as Princess Leia Organa) and added pros Alec Guinness as an aging space warrior and Peter Cushing as Darth Vader's right-hand henchman. John Dykstra supervised vast teams of effects artists; the popular music is by John Williams. Followed by *The Empire Strikes Back* and *Return of the Jedi.* Aka *Star Wars: Episode IV*; *Star Wars: Episode IV–A New Hope* and first written as *Adventures of the Starkiller.* (CBS/Fox)

STAR WARS: EPISODE I—THE PHANTOM MENACE (1999) ★★★ The old saying "You can't go home again" is as true for movies as it is for life: what's magical one year could be dreck the next. While *Star Wars* set the style for state-of-the-art special effects and dazzling, breathlessly paced storytelling, there have been inspired filmmakers who have succeeded in surpassing Lucas's visions and carrying comic-book style movies to loftier heights. Thus, *The Phantom Menace,* no matter how overpowering in outer-space and otherworld special effects, is not the magical experience of *Star Wars: Episode IV–A New Hope.* Not that writer-director Lucas doesn't try with all his moviemaking might. The story, a "prequel" that begins years before the first *Star Wars,* ranges across a galaxy of worlds, involving many alien races and mind-boggling technologies of spaceships, robots, and cities of tomorrow. If the characters seem heavy-handedly and shallowly written, it is because *Star Wars* movies were intended to be enjoyed for their breathtaking visuals and Lucas's consistent need to push for new science-fictional experiences. This is never going to be Shakespeare. On the other hand, it is a movie with very little humanity or heart, and yes, the alien Jar Jar Binks is an utter buffoon, pandering to the youngest of the viewers who buy most of the toys and merchandising. Let's not forget that commercialism is what some (if not all) of this franchise is about. *The Phantom Menace* introduces one fascinating character—Jedi Master Qui-Gon Jinn, played by Liam Neeson with perfect nobility and agility of mind and body. He brings the kind of intelligence that the series needs. Then there are those characters from the earlier films but in younger guises: Obi-Wan Kenobi (created by Alec Guinness) is now Qui-Gon's young apprentice, played by Ewan McGregor, and Darth Vader is the boy Anakin Skywalker, played by Jake Lloyd. Yes, Yoda (voice by Frank Oz) is back to spout his expected puzzling philosophies and predictions of events to come in later *Star Wars* movies, and so is R2-D2, the friendly droid. In this intergalactic adventure, the evil Trade Federation plans to invade the planet Naboo (Jar Jar's home) and take control of the Galactic Republic. Naboo's teenage queen Amidala (Natalie Portman, who plays two different versions of the character) joins Qui-Gon and Obi-Wan in an odyssey that takes them to Tatooine, where they meet young Skywalker, whom Qui-Gon recognizes as "The Chosen One," a boy destined to be a Jedi Knight (and other things not so noble). After a rousing Pod-racer chase featuring bizarre futuristic variations on racing cars, and broadcast by a two-headed E.T. "sports announcer," the action returns to Naboo, where the evil Darth Sidious (Ian McDiarmid) and Darth Maul (stunt specialist Ray Parks) plan an invasion of droids against the planet's alien races, who join forces for an exciting land battle sprinkled with Jar Jar comedy bits. The climax is Lucas at his best—three pieces of concurrent action: the hand-to-hand ground fighting, the palace takeover coup in which Qui-Gon and Obi-Wan face Darth Maul for a climactic light-saber battle, and an attack on the spaceship controlling the droid ground forces. Given the box-office success of *The Phantom Menace*, Lucas has inspired the future for this spearheading science-fantasy series. Whatever its story weaknesses, *Star Wars* lives as a visual tour de force. (Video/DVD: Fox)

STAY AWAKE, THE (1987) ★★ This South African monster flick is inferior work more aptly titled *The Go to Sleep*. It's a steal of *The Slumber Party Massacre* only instead of a human killer it sports an unconvincing red-eyed, green-hued demon, the Angel of Darkness, that descends on nubile pretties at the St. Mary's School for Girls as they hold an all-night party. As created by screenwriter-director John Bernard, the Angel is the reincarnated spirit of a serial killer who knocked off 11 women before he was executed and vowed to return and kill again. Now he's back, gang, and ready to slaughter with windy demonic powers. Uninspired and clichéd, a depressing way to kill 88 minutes. Shirley Jane Harris, Tanya Gordon, Jayne Hutton, Heath Potter. (Video/Laser: Nelson)

STAY TUNED (1992) ★★★½ Entertaining, whacked-out supernatural comedy that parodies TV by sending couch potato John Ritter and wife Pam Dawber into TV Hell where they have just 24 hours to escape various cliff-hanging situations or their souls will be claimed by the Devil (Jeffrey Jones). The ambitious Tom S. Parker–Jim Jennewein script offers pastiches of MTV, *Star Trek, Wayne's World*, film noir and cat-and-mouse cartoons as Ritter and Dawber leap from program to program. Director Peter Hyams obviously had a good time directing the frisky cast made up also of Bob Dishy, David Tom, Eugene Levy and Don Calfa. (Video/Laser: Warner Bros.)

STECKLER INTERVIEWS. Film historian John Roberts interviews horror director Ray Dennis Steckler about his life and career. Do you have the fortitude to take it? Other tapes in this seres: *Incredibly Strange R. D. Steckler* and *Carolyn Brandt: Queen of Cult*. (Mascot)

STEEL AND LACE (1990) ★★½ Fair mixture of gory horror and cybernetics sci-fi in which mad doc Bruce Davison, to avenge the suicide of his sister (she was raped but the five guilty men went free), creates a humanoid robot that knocks off the men (now unscrupulous businessmen) by tearing off their heads, drilling holes in their stomachs or doing naughty things to their ding-dongs. On the trail is a cop and his girlfriend artist. The Joseph Dougherty–Dave Edison script is predictable after the first half hour, although Ernest Farino directs in a fast-moving style. Clare Wren, David Naughton, Stacy Haiduk. (Fries) (Laser: Image)

STEEL DAWN (1987) ★★½ Patrick Swayze is at the center of this film's modest success, for he brings intensity and a sense of mystery to Nomad, a swordsman in the Mad Max tradition who roves the deserts of a nuked-out world. Doug Lefler's screenplay has a parallel to *Shane* and countless Samurai warrior flicks when Nomad stops wandering to help a mother (Lisa Niemi, Swayze's real-life wife) and son (Brett Hool) protect their water purification station from land baron Anthony Zerbe. Contributing minor but interesting characters to the action are Brion James, John Fujioka and the Namib Desert of southwest Africa. It's been done before in the post-holocaust genre, so director Lance Hool, given inferior material, fights a gallant if losing battle. (Vestron) (Laser: Image)

STEEL FRONTIER (1995) ★★★½ Although this unusual action movie is set in a post-Armageddon America, where the terrain has been turned into desert and men ride around in souped-up dune buggies, it is really a sci-fi spaghetti Western. Joe (*American Cyborg*) Lara does an impression of Eastwood's Man With No Name, portraying a gunslinger named Yuma. He appears in the town of New Hope where dictator Brion James and his cutthroat killers have taken the populace hostage. With a few touches of *Yojimbo* and *A Fistful of Dollars* thrown in, Lara proves to be a bounty hunter with a moral code that makes for an interesting time in this actioner from producers Richard Pepin and Joseph Merhi, which is directed by Paul G. Volk and Jacobsen Hart with a strong feeling for heavy-duty firepower, the ambivalent character of Yuma and his romance with Stacie Foster. Thrown into this maelstrom of morality and action are truck-highway stunts and an intellectual

Bo Svenson, whose intriguing character should have been developed more. All in all, a bang-up job. (PM Entertainment) (Laser: Image)

STEEL JUSTICE (1992) ★★ Two-hour pilot for a proposed but dropped TV series is set in the 21st century, when a future society suffers from overcrowding and roving lawlessness within the city structure. Future cop Robert Taylor is plagued by dreams of his son's death at the hands of a gunrunning syndicate and the images of a beckoning black man (J. A. Preston) and a toy in the shape of a dragon. How producer-director Christopher Crowe (writing with John Hill) resolves this with a wish-granting time traveler from the future and the toy turning into a giant fire-breathing monster (a "robosaurus") is absurd and unfitting to the film's seriously intended themes. Roy Brocksmith, John Finn, Neil Giuntoli, Geoffrey Rivas, Joan Chen.

STELLA STAR. See *Starcrash.*

STEPFATHER, THE (1986) ★★★½ Above-average portrait of a serial killer, played well by Terry O'Quinn and compellingly written by Donald E. Westlake, who concocted this tale with fellow mystery writer Brian Garfield and Carolyn Lefcourt. O'Quinn's madman is a schizophrenic who needs the family structure in his life, until the urge to massacre overtakes him. Then he moves on, setting up a new identity in a new town, seeking out a new fatherless family. The implications are chilling and director Joseph Ruben never allows the unexpected twists to become too nihilistic—there's always hope that fate will intervene. Shelley Hack, Jill Schoelen, Charles Lanyer. (Video/Laser: Nelson/Embassy)

STEPFATHER II: MAKE ROOM FOR DADDY (1989) ★★ This sequel to the video hit is another example of a premise that should not be resurrected. This picks up with O'Quinn in a mental institution in Puget Sound—but it doesn't take him long to escape and establish a new identity as a headshrinker living near realtor Meg Foster, with whom he soon sets up housekeeping. Director Jeff Burr is handicapped by John Auerbach's script and directs indifferently, injecting too little suspense into the sluggish events. *Stepfather II* ends up being another slasher flick. Caroline Williams, Jonathan Brandis, Henry Brown, Mitchell Laurance. (HBO) (Laser: Image)

STEPFATHER III: FATHER'S DAY (1992) ★★½ Another inferior sequel that attempts to retread the irony of a psychotic serial killer posing as the perfect family man, and then exploding into homicidal action when his cover is blown. Here the paradox is reduced to Robert Wightman (taking over the Terry O'Quinn role by undergoing plastic surgery in the opening sequence) acting like an automated suburbanite when he resettles in Deer View, Calif., to marry Priscilla

Barnes, and making wisecracks ("Father knows best . . . come to Daddy!") whenever he's just killed—usually with a sharp instrument that allows for blood squirting and dollops of gore splattering on walls. The script by director Guy Magar and Marc B. Ray fails to explore a subplot in which Wightman's new stepson suspects him and uses his home computor to investigate. The use of a leaf mulcher does provide this excursion into bloody violence with a memorably sickening climax. Sickening? Make that disgusting. David Tom, John Ingle, Season Hubley. (Video/Laser: Vidmark)

STEPFORD CHILDREN, THE (1988) ★★★ This TV-movie is the third go-around to work with material from Ira Levin's novel, *The Stepford Wives.* (The second effort was a worthless 1980 TV-film, *Return of the Stepford Wives.*) This Paul Pompian production fares better as Don Murray and Barbara Eden settle in the New England community that seems conservative and peaceful, but that harbors a lab where human substitutes are created by crazy doctor Richard Anderson. Murray lived in the village 20 years ago and had a robot wife, so he knows what idyllic bliss this can be. Where the film falls short is in credulity: Murray's behavior is never really dealt with, and all the husbands in town (members of the Men's Association) are so obviously evil, it's hard to believe they could have gotten away with malprogrammed robots for so long. James Coco appears in his final role as the school's cooking teacher. Bill Bleich adapted and Alan J. Levi directed. Randall Batinok, Tammy Lauren, Debbie Barker, Dick Butkus.

STEPFORD HUSBANDS, THE (1996) ★★½ Back to Connecticut we go—back to that quiet community where conformity is everything and turning people into programmed zombies is a given. Usually the wives get lobotomized and turned into men-pleasing freaks, but in this TV-movie, written by Ken and Jim Wheat and directed by Fred Walton, the hubbies are taken into a sinister clinic and transformed into shells of men. Donna Mills is the loving wife who gets wise to the lab experiments of Sarah Douglas and Louise Fletcher and sets out to free her husband (Michael Ontkean as an angry, frustrated novelist) from his mental bondage. Nothing special in this routine retread. Cindy Williams, Caitlin Clarke.

STEPFORD WIVES, THE (1975) ★★★★ Superior horror film with an intelligent William Goldman script (from Ira Levin's fine novel) and thoughtful direction by Bryan Forbes. This says more about our obsession with mechanical things than dozens of so-called relevant movies, and it says it in a frightening way: In a complacent upper-crust community in New England a conspiracy is afoot among men to replace their wives with robot-controlled humanoid imitations. And the mastermind is a former employee of Disney (think about that one). Katharine Ross discovers her friends (Paula Prentiss and Tina Louise, among others) are automated replacements and the suspense builds to a finish right out of *Frankenstein*. Owen Roizman's cinematography adds to the atmosphere of this scary piece. Patrick O'Neal, Nanette Newman, Peter Masterson. Sequels: *Return of the Stepford Wives* and *The Stepford Children*. (Embassy)

STEPHEN KING'S CAT'S EYE. See *Cat's Eye*.

STEPHEN KING'S GOLDEN YEARS (1991) ★★½ Originally a 7-part TV miniseries, this is one of Stephen King's more eccentric creations, though ultimately a failed one. A top-secret experiment at Falco Plains Agriculture Testing Center results in an explosion set off by a crazed doctor. Exposed to the blast is an aging janitor who comes under the scrutiny of government guys when he starts to grow younger, and glows a bright green. Intrigue, suspicion and double-dealing abound. An assassin from "the shop" is out to kill anyone who knows the secret, and another agent is out to save the janitor. These various factions provide for a lively chase and intriguing characters, but where the script goes wrong is in not developing the fantasy elements. While the payoff is a disappointing one, especially after a 4-hour duration, the individual moments make up for some of the letdown. Keith Szarabajka, Felicity Huffman, Frances Sternhagen, Ed Lauter, R. D. Call, Bill Raymond. Directed by Kenneth Fink. (Worldvision) (Laser: Image)

STEPHEN KING'S GRAVEYARD SHIFT. See *Graveyard Shift* (1990).

STEPHEN KING'S IT! (1990) ★★★½ Four-hour TV-movie adaptation of the imaginative, nerve-wracking best-seller about an entity in the sewer of the town of Derry that wreaks havoc every 30 years. This unseen entity appears in human form as Pennywise the Clown (Tim Curry, in a bravado performance), feeding off the fear of locals and manifesting illusions and fantasies. Seven of the town's adolescents band to destroy it, then return 30 years later to redo the job. It takes nearly two hours just to establish characters and premise, and repeats the same illusions over and over. The characters are interesting and the cast labors valiantly but director Tommy Lee Wallace (writing with Lawrence D. Cohen) provides an unsatisfying ending. John Ritter, Harry Anderson, Annette O'Toole, Richard Thomas, Dennis Christopher, Richard Masur, Tim Reid. (Video/Laser: Warner Bros.)

STEPHEN KING'S NIGHT SHIFT COLLECTION. (1978) ★★ Video exclusive containing 2 half-hour adaptations from King's 1978 collection, *Night Shift*. "Woman in the Room," written-directed by Frank Darabont in 1983, is the simple story of an attorney whose mother is dying, and who contemplates euthanasia. This is a strong mood piece. "Boogeyman," written-directed by Jeffrey C. Schiro, is about a father (Michael Reid) who suspects a "boogeyman" murdered his children and put his wife into a nuthouse. He goes to a psychiatrist (Bert Linder) for help. Nice twist ending. Again heavy on ambience. Latter produced in 1982 at the N.Y. University School of Undergraduate Film. (Granite)

STEPHEN KING'S NIGHT SHIFT COLLECTION II. (1989) ★★ This 1989 video consists of 2 more short films made by students based on stories from King's anthology. "Disciples of the Corn" (1983) was made before *Children of the Corn* and, because it is succinct and faithful to the original material, is better than the feature. Jonah, "the nicest little town in Oklahoma," is taken over by homicidal children who worship a crow god and attack travelers passing through. Writer-director-editor John Woodward displays a talent for atmosphere and action. "The Night Waiter" (1987) was made as a student project at San Diego State by writer-director-producer-editor Jack Garrett and is reminiscent of ideas expanded in *The Shining*. To the Bay View Hotel comes new room service waiter Brian Caldwell, who's in immediate conflict with night clerk Ray Adamski. Again, good atmosphere prevails, although the ending is abrupt. (Karl James Associates)

STEPHEN KING'S SILVER BULLET. Video version of *Silver Bullet*. (Hiyo, King, away!)

STEPHEN KING'S SLEEPWALKERS. See *Sleepwalkers*.

STEPHEN KING'S SOMETIMES THEY COME BACK (1991) ★★★ Supernatural TV-movie, based on a story by the King of horror, is a macabre tale of revenge from beyond the grave. Tim Matheson portrays a schoolteacher who returns to his hometown, where 27 years earlier his brother was knifed to death by teenage hoodlums. A train killed all but one of the attackers . . . and now those dead youths have returned in a phantom car that spits fire to kill Matheson's students and make his life a living nightmare. Matheson stumbles through his hallucinations and dreams conveying a deep sense of dread. Why the dead boys can be seen by everyone else, but their car cannot, makes for a disconcerting ghost story that doesn't stay consistent within its own rules. But it's still engrossing work, nicely directed by Tom McLoughlin and ably adapted by Mark Rosenthal and Lawrence Konner. Brooke Adams, Robert Rusler, Robert Hy Gorman, William Sanderson. Sequel: *Sometimes They Come Back . . . Again* (Video/Laser: Vidmark)

STEPHEN KING'S STORM OF THE CENTURY (1999) ★★★★ This original six-hour, three-part TV miniseries represents one of King's finest creations. Not only is it riveting, spinning a chilling narrative that blends elements of a pure horror story with those of the natural-disaster epic, but it makes an extremely disturbing comment about human behavior. King has also created a handful of memorable and vivid characters. The cast, under the direction of Craig R. Baxley, is excellent, especially Tim Daly as the constable of a small, tight-knit community on an island off the coast of Maine (pure Stephen King territory). Equaling Daly in intensity and impact is Colm Feore as a sinister and evil presence that invades the people of Little Tall Island. With only a modicum of makeup and special-effects trickery, Feore etches one of the most frightening figures in modern movies. Even when he is sitting isolated in a cell, staring through the bars, you feel a tingle along the spine. Here's the tale: Residents of the island, in the year 1989, are battening down the hatches for a looming hurricane when a lone figure (Feore) enters an old woman's home, bludgeons her to death with his cane (an object that is endowed with supernatural powers), sits down in front of her TV set, and finishes off her cup of tea. Incarcerated by Daly (who also runs the town's major grocery store, hence he is not the best trained of law officers), the killer, Andre Linoge, knows everyone's sins, often expressing them to that person's face, and begins to manipulate the residents through mind control. Several commit suicide, others are exposed for what they are and begin to fall apart, while outside a blizzard blankets the town and a tidal wave destroys the island's lighthouse. Linoge's repeated refrain, "Give me what I want and I'll go away," soon haunts the town, and eventually the citizens, despite Feore's evil, must come to grips with his demand. The showdown between the town and Linoge is stunning, as is the sequence that depicts what happens to Daly after he abandons the island. Among other standouts in the cast are Debrah Fiorentino as Daly's wife, Casey Siemaszko as Daly's inexperienced deputy, Dyllan Christopher as Daly's adolescent son, and Jeffrey DeMunn as the town administrator, always at odds with procedures. (Video/DVD: Vidmark/Trimark)

STEPHEN KING'S THE LANGOLIERS (1995) ★★★ One of the strangest of time-travel yarns, this 2-part TV-movie adaptation of a Stephen King novella (from his anthology *Four Past Midnight*) depicts 10 members of an airliner flight who find themselves alone in midflight, after passing through a rift in the time continuum. It's largely a low-key, cerebral mystery (solved in part by Dean Stockwell's mystery writer character) with only one sequence in which the titular monsters (huge furry balls with thousands of teeth) show up to devour the past, literally. Despite its talky telescript (by director Tom Holland), it's still interesting how these oddball passengers figure out how to save themselves, and it's full of fascinating premises about the conduct of past, present and future. Patricia Wettig, David Morse, Mark Lindsay Chapman, Frankie Faison, Baxter Harris, Kimber Riddle, Christopher Collet, Kate Maberly, Bronson Pinchot (as the only human villain). (Video/Laser: Republic)

STEPHEN KING'S THE NIGHT FLIER (1997) ★★★ This is one of the better adaptations of a King vampire story, and one strange story it is. Miguel Ferrer portrays a cynical, unlikable investigator reporter for *Inside View*, a lowbrow tabloid (a "diary of the deranged") where fledgling newswoman Julie Entwistle hopes to learn the ropes. Ferrer pursues a serial killer of a different kind—a demon vampire who flies in and out of airports in his single-engine plane, killing those in or near the landing site for nourishment. Though taken off the story by editor Dan Monahan, Entwistle follows Ferrer into the thick of the mystery, still hoping to make the grade. The demon, who calls himself Dwight Renfield (after Dwight Frye, who played the character of Renfield in the original *Dracula* movie), knows Ferrer is after him and enters into mind games with the sleazy investigator. The demon's face, not revealed until a gory climax, is truly frightening and director Mark Pavia (who cowrote the script with Jack O'Donnell) has included a chilling black-and-white sequence that pays homage to *Night of the Living Dead* as numerous corpses close in on Ferrer in an airport lobby. Michael H. Moss appears very briefly as the human face of the monster that flies from murder site to murder site. Definitely worth seeing for its atmosphere and its well-done grisliness. (Video/DVD: HBO)

STEPHEN KING'S THE TOMMYKNOCKERS. See *The Tommyknockers.*

STEPHEN KING'S THINNER (1996) ★★★ This adaptation of a "Richard Bachman" novel has more meat on its bones than it first seems, thanks to an unpredictable script by Michael McDowell and director Tom (*Fright Night*) Holland. After King establishes good old American corruption in a small town as his theme, and you know you're in darkening King territory, the tale becomes that of a traditional "curse" picture, with a 109-year-old gypsy (Michael Constantine, in heavy makeup and conveying a venomous attitude) putting a weight-loss whammy on a sleazy small-town attorney (Robert John Burke) after the latter accidentally runs down and kills Constantine's daughter. And Burke does go through an incredible drop in pounds, threatening to turn into skin and bones despite constant eating. But then this dark, nihilistic tale takes another dramatic twist to depict Burke's revenge on his cheating wife (Lucinda Jenney) and boyfriend. This kind of heavy morality, trailing clouds of paranoia, almost overshadows the film's original story of curse-followed-by-revenge. Thus, you will either groove on the surprise ending or wonder what the hell went wrong. In any event, Holland has done better. If anyone really stands out in this macabre morbidity, it is Joe Mantegna as a Mafia hooligan who decides to help Burke get his revenge against Constantine. He's one mean dude. Watch for Stephen King in a cameo as Dr. Bangor (ha-ha). (Video/DVD: Republic)

STEPHEN KING'S TRUCKS. See *Trucks.*

STEPMONSTER (1992) ★★½ A Roger Corman production, from a story by Fred Olen Ray, in which a hideous creature known as a Tropopkin assumes the human form of a sexy young woman (Robin Riker) to trick Alan Thicke into marrying her. But Thicke's son George Gaynes is wise to the monster and its gargoyle batlike companion and sets out to stop the nefarious plan. Because the special effects are not convincing, there's little reason to see this exercise in comedy-thrills half-heartedly achieved by director Jeremy Stanford. Ami Dolenz, Edie McClurg, John Astin (as a coughing preacher). (New Horizons) (Laser: Image)

ST. GEORGE AND THE DRAGON/ST. GEORGE AND THE SEVEN CURSES. See *The Magic Sword.*

STIGMATA (1999) ★★½ This is such a doom-and-gloom exercise in special effects and kinetic editing (so fast is the cutting that you sometimes can't tell what the hell is happening) that you would have to be part manic-depressive to sit through all of it. This falls into *The Exorcist* school of heaven-vs.-hell horror, with a few touches of *The Omen* thrown in to keep you full of the devil. It opens in South America, where Vatican investigator Gabriel Byrne is in a church checking out a marble statue of the Virgin Mary that bleeds warm blood from its eye sockets. In a coffin next to the statue is a dead priest. A string of rosary beads and a cross stolen from the father's corpse ends up in the possession of a hairdresser (Patricia Arquette) in Pittsburgh, who undergoes a series of attacks on her body—each assault part of the "stigmata" phenomenon that will plague her for the duration of the picture. First, spikes are driven through her wrists, then a crown of thorns is crushed against her forehead, and her feet are impaled with spikes. These gruesome attacks are shown in short blasts that keep the film stylish if sometimes too mysterious. To her rescue comes Byrne, newly assigned by Cardinal Houseman of the Vatican (Jonathan Pryce, as smarmy as they come) to investigate. Celibate Byrne starts to fall in love with Arquette and, while battling with his hormones, realizes he's caught up in a Vatican attempt to suppress the truth she scrawls on her apartment wall. Translated, it says Jesus Christ would prefer you to think of His temple not as a church but as your own body. To the Vatican, this is heresy; hence the conspiracy to keep the discovery hush-hush. Although *Stigmata* is all flashy effects and stylish direction by Rupert Wainwright, and offers too little exposition and many shallow characters, the Tom Lazarus–Rick Ramage screenplay was inspired by a few grains of truth. In 1945 ancient writings dating back to Christ's time, known as the Gospel According to St. Thomas, were uncovered and presented to the Catholic Church. Because the writings espoused the same philosophy as that portrayed in the film, they were rejected as heresy. If only the film had turned out half as thrilling as the background story sounds . . . Nia Long, Thomas Kopache, Rade Sherbedgia, Enrico Colantoni, Ann Cusack, Dick Latessa. (Video/DVD: MGM)

STILL NOT QUITE HUMAN (1992) ★★★ The continuing comedy misadventures of Chip Carson, the humanoid invented by scientist Alan Thicke, finds the likable robot-youth attending the Robotics Convention of America. When Dad is kidnapped and imprisoned in a white dome by an evil scientist, Chip (played with delightful innocence by Jay Underwood) and his pals (a pickpocket and a female cop) go after the dastards. A charming element makes this Disney-produced series appealing. Written-directed by Eric Luke. Christopher Neame, Betsy Palmer, Adam Philipson, Rosa Niven. (Disney)

STILL OF THE NIGHT (1982) ★★★½ Sophisticated, intelligent whodunit in the psychological vein, detailing how psychiatrist Roy Scheider tracks a slasher killer who murdered a patient. It's writer-director Robert Benton's homage to Hitchcock with slasher-flick touches added—a quiet, underplayed approach as Scheider suspects the killer is a beautiful blond (Meryl Streep) having an affair with the murdered patient. The symbolic dream sequence is out of Hitchcock's *Spellbound*; even the Streep character reminds one of Kim Novak in *Vertigo*. Little gore or violence—this could be the only cerebral slasher movie ever made. Idea by Benton and David Newman. Jessica Tandy, Joe Grifasi, Sara Botsford. (CBS/Fox; MGM/UA) (Laser: CBS/Fox)

STIR OF ECHOES (1999) ★★★ Richard Matheson's 1958 novel, *A Stir of Echoes*, is an excellent urban ghost story set in a bustling, overcrowded suburb. Released on the heels of *The Sixth Sense*, the film tells the tale of an adolescent boy (Zachary David Cope) who talks to dead spirits but was largely lost on audiences who thought it was a rip-off. An unfortunate bit of timing, since *Stir of Echoes* is an above-average product. Kevin Bacon, who also served as a producer, portrays a telephone lineman who is filled with angst because his life has gone nowhere and his dreams are unfulfilled. One night, with his wife, Kathryn Erbe, he attends a party where his sister-in-law (Illeana Douglas) playfully hypnotizes him. But there's nothing playful about it when the session accidentally opens Bacon's mind to the supernatural and he begins seeing weird images, some of which prove to be glimpses into the future. Bacon is tapping into a murder involving some neighborhood friends—the rape and killing of a mentally retarded young woman. Unfortunately, screenwriter-director David Koepp didn't shape the story for revelations and surprises but by the numbers, so the viewer is never allowed to participate in the solving of the puzzle—the plot comes to Bacon, rather than Bacon being lured into the plot. Also, Koepp throws away a subplot involving a group of ordinary citizens who share Bacon's extrasensory abilities. It's introduced then quickly forgotten. Still, Fred Murphy's dark, urban photography creates an eerie atmosphere that enhances this good contribution to the genre. In the old days, the studios allowed Matheson to write his own scripts; remember *The Incredible Shrinking Man* and *The Legend of Hell House* and all those Roger Corman movies with Edgar Allan Poe plots? Is this what happens when the young auteurs take over from the old guys? (Video/DVD: Artisan)

STORIES FROM THE EDGE (1996) ★★ This trilogy of half-hour tales has but one relevance to this book: "Take Out the Beast," a morality lesson set aboard a space station where the two-man crew (Gary Kemp and Steven Weber) are assigned to destroy a humanoid robot (Charles Martin Smith). How Smith outsmarts the humans in Oliver Butcher's script will surprise no one. All director Eric Freiser can do is make the ship atmospheric à la *Alien*. And then he falls off the edge.

STORM PLANET. See *Planeta Burg.*

STORYBOOK (1995) ★★ Milton Berle as a chintzy magician, a kangaroo with an Australian accent (voice by Ed Begley, Jr.), and Swoosie Kurtz camping it up as Queen Evilia with her swarmy snake Hiss are about all you'll find of interest in this half-hearted, poverty-stricken attempt to spin a cutie-pie fairy tale. Sean Fitzgerald plays an insufferable kid who steps through his book into a storyland where he is joined by Woody the Woodsman (Richard Moll) and a wise old owl to help King Arthur (William McNamara) recover his sword and regain control of the kingdom. The special effects are nothing and director Lorenzo Doumani brings no magic whatsoever to the script he wrote with Susan Bower. Wasted in uninspired roles are James Doohan as the boy's grandfather and Jack Scalia as the father (in one of the smallest cameos ever). Spell this one Grim, not Grimm. Brenda Epperson-Doumani, Gary Morgan, Robert Costanzo. (Video/Laser: Republic)

STORY OF SUPERMAN, THE (1990) ★★ This 52-minute documentary, made exclusively for the video market, covers the history of the Man of Steel from his inception as a comic-book superhero through the radio show and movie serials of the late '40s, then spends a lot of time on George Reeves in the TV version. Only two things are of interest in this droning, poorly written history: scenes from a World War II propaganda film that Reeves starred in ("The Last Will and Testament of Tom Smith") and amusing TV commercials about a different kind of "cereal"—Kellogg's Corn Flakes. For completists only. (Burbank Video)

STORY OF UGETSU, THE. See *Ugetsu.*

STRAIGHT JACKET (1982) ★½ Unconvincing psycho-killer drama mixing in 2 characters who have the ability to foresee the future: a young wife (Kory Clark) who just moved into a house previously the scene of a decapitation murder, and a cop (Aldo Ray) recently kicked off the force. The acting borders on the amateurish and the Phillip Pine–Larry Hilbran script unfolds in a poor manner, so there is no suspenseful climax. Directed by coproducer Martin Green. Chuck Jamison, Bobby Holt, Andy Gwyn. (Genesis; Neon; Ariel International; from Marquis as *Dark Sanity*)

STRAIGHT ON TILL MORNING. See *Dressed for Death.*

STRAIT-JACKET (1964) ★★★½ While this William Castle horror thriller has none of his gimmicks, and its techniques now seem dated, it features a wonderfully campy performance by Joan Crawford as a murderess who chops off the heads of her adulterous husband and his lover and is sent to an institution for 20 years. She gets to revive her "cheap tramp" characterization of the '40s, and she does it up without director Castle restraining her, when she shows up to live with daughter Diane Baker. Right away she behaves oddly when handyman George Kennedy, in a great sleaze role, chops off the head of a chicken. And what do you know. Pretty soon heads are rolling again as Crawford turns into one batty broad suffering from hallucinations. Robert Bloch's script is one of his favorites—producer-director Castle left most of it intact. Beware red herrings—the script is full of them. Rochelle Hudson, Howard St. John, Leif Erickson. (RCA/Columbia)

STRANDED (1987) ★★★ Entertaining sci-fi actioner, in which a family of aliens accompanied by a robot guard escape their war-ravaged world for asylum in a farmhouse on Earth. What follows is a siege situation with black sheriff Joe Morton facing not only the aliens but prejudice from deputies and townspeople. An assassin-alien in human form is also involved as the tense situation unfolds. This Robert Shaye–Sara Risher production is a respectable piece of work directed by Tex Fuller. Susan Barnes, Ione Skye, Cameron Dye, Michael Greene, Gary Swanson, Barbara Hughes. Maureen O'Sullivan appears as the besieged grandmother. (Video/Laser: RCA/Columbia)

STRANGE ADVENTURE OF DAVID GRAY, THE. See *Vampyr* (1932).

STRANGE ADVENTURE OF JONATHAN HARKER, THE. See *The Heritage of Dracula.*

STRANGE BEHAVIOR (1981) ★★½ Aussie–New Zealand production (also known as *Dead Kids*) in which a crazed doctor murders high school students after conducting weird experiments on their bodies. The acting is overblown and the plotting by producer Michael Condon and director Michael Laughlin out of a horror pulp, but the film has a sense of freshness and features a strong cast: Michael Murphy, Louise Fletcher, Fiona Lewis, Scott Brady. (RCA/Columbia; from Scorpio as *Small Town Massacre*)

STRANGE CASE OF . . . !#*%. See *The Maltese Bippy.*

STRANGE CASE OF DR. JEKYLL AND MR. HYDE, THE (1968) ★★★ U.S.-Canadian TV production produced by Dan Curtis and starring Jack Palance as one of the most effective Jekyll-Hydes in the cinematic history of Robert Louis Stevenson's horror classic. Directed by Charles Jarrott from a telescript by Ian McClellan Hunter. Makeup by Dick Smith. Denholm Elliott, Torin Thatcher, Oscar Homolka, Leo Genn, Billie Whitelaw. (On Thrillervideo with Elvira; MPI)

STRANGE DAYS (1995) ★★★★ You will run the gamut of emotional reaction to this breathtaking, audacious and sometimes infuriating futuristic murder mystery written by James Cameron and Jay Cocks and directed with episodic proportions by Kathryn Bigelow. Set Dec. 30–31, 1999, as a collapsing society prepares to welcome in a new century, *Strange Days* deals uncompromisingly with sleazy lowlife con man Lenny Nero (Ralph Fiennes) as he sells his illegal "tripwires"—human events visually and emotionally recorded on CDs via a special headset unit and providing a virtual reality experience to "wirehead junkies" on playback. Just like ex-cop Lenny, Los Angeles is collapsing into anarchy and social ruin. Lenny suddenly finds himself at the heart of 2 whodunit murders—one of a popular black singer (staged in the fashion of a Rodney King incident), the other of a young woman raped and strangled, her death recorded on a CD. As Lenny wises up to life with the help of his only true friend, limousine driver Mace (Angela Bassett), elements of racism slam this daring movie in new, exciting directions. At times the violence becomes almost unbearable to watch, but the imaginative ideas underlying the script also make the violence mesmerizing. Also mesmerizing is an escape from a submerged car and the breathless New Year's Eve climactic sequence. You may love or hate *Strange Days*, but you still have to say: "What a movie!" Juliette Lewis, Tom Sizemore, Michael Wincott, Glenn Plummer. (Video/Laser: Fox)

STRANGE EXORCISM OF LYNN HART, THE. See *Daddy's Deadly Darling* or *Pigs.*

STRANGE HOTEL OF NAKED PLEASURES, THE (1975) ★ This was produced by Brazilian horror master José Mojica Marins and directed by his right-hand man, Marcello Motta. The plot involves a hotel where guests check in to undergo their most hideous dreams—which then come true. (S/Weird)

STRANGE INVADERS (1983) ★★★ In the style of monster invader movies of the '50s, this is a blend of comedy and thrills, effects and chases in telling its genre tale of space creatures plotting our overthrow in a midwestern town in 1958. Paul Le Mat gets involved when he discovers his ex-wife is one of *them* and now her pals are coming to look for her daughter, who's an alien too. Well, half an alien. Le Mat and Nancy Allen end up on the run. Good direction by Michael Laughlin, who cowrote with William Condon. Michael Lerner, Louise Fletcher, Fiona Lewis, Kenneth Tobey, June Lockhart. (Vestron) (Laser: Image)

STRANGE JOURNEY. Early title for *Fantastic Voyage.*

STRANGELAND (1998) ★ It's hard to think of a more unpleasant way to spend 90 minutes than watching a psychotic madman nicknamed Captain Howdy sew shut his victims' mouths with thick cord, thrust pins and needles into their bodies, and hang them from hooks. This is entertainment? Director John Pieplow (remember *Jurassic Women?*) must think so, the way his camera lingers on all the unpleasantness. Dee Snider, whose previous claim to fame was writing the music for *Pee-Wee's Big Adventure* and *One Crazy Summer*, portrays Howdy, and he also wrote the screenplay and produced this abomination in and around Colorado Springs and Denver. This is a gross glimpse into the underworld of body piercing, in which Snider's religiously crazed killer spouts H. G. Wells prose and says things like, "The dead are so dreadfully dead, when they are dead." He also remarks, "There are thousands hacking at the branches of evil," in reference to how he uses Internet chat rooms to pinpoint his victims and invite them to "parties." There's something else disturbing about this movie, and that's the portrayal of a cop named Mike Gage by actor Kevin Gage. After his daughter (Linda Cardellini) is tortured and nearly killed by Howdy, he brings the sadomasochist to justice. Well, sort of. After Howdy is sentenced to three years in a fruitcake house, he is released by a liberal judge as "rehabilitated." But then Robert Englund and other upstanding citizens drag off the seemingly reformed captain to lynch him, with Gage looking the other way. But Englund, in a role as unpleasant as Snider's is sickening, fails to finish the job. (Would you believe the branch of the hanging tree breaks?) This botched lynch job sends the cap'n into a new cycle of kidnapping and torture, and it's Gage who rips the ring off the cap'n's nose and finishes him off in a church by hanging him from a swaying hook and setting him on fire (but only after his dumb daughter has allowed herself to be kidnapped a second time). Now, here's the most disturbing thing about his movie: The cop sets the church on fire, too, and doesn't even call 911. This is the kind of movie that could finish off the career of Elizabeth Peña, who is cast as the long-suffering wife of Gage. Aka *Dee Snider's Strangeland*. (Video/DVD: Artisan Entertainment)

STRANGENESS, THE (1985) ★★★ Inspired by *The Boogens*, this is "lost mine" stuff as geologists enter the legendary Golden Spike Mine, closed years before when workmen mysteriously vanished. There's a cruel boss, a writer who talks in deathless prose, an experienced old mine hand and other clichéd types. Long stretches of nothing, extended periods of ennui, with an occasional glimpse of a tentacled creature animated by stop motion. No feeling of menace as the film plods to a routine climax. Directed by David Michael Hillman, without any "strangeness." Dan Lunham, Terri Berland. (Trans World; Premiere)

STRANGER IN THE HOUSE. See *Black Christmas*.

STRANGER IS WATCHING, A (1982) ★★★ Unsettling mixture of suspense and violence, directed by Sean Cunningham, the mastermind behind *Friday the 13th*. Even though this is a better-crafted movie and has a superior plot (adapted by Earl MacRauch and Victor Miller from a book by Mary Higgins Clark), it was a flop. What Cunningham fails to realize is that audiences prefer slasher movies in which the killer is a faceless killing machine. That rule is broken as we follow killer Rip Torn when he kidnaps a TV reporter and a young girl and hides them in the New York subway system. Also, the reporter (Kate Mulgrew) is so well drawn that it becomes unbearable to watch when a screwdriver is thrust into her stomach. Cunningham might have done better to stress the kidnapping plot and the capital punishment aspects, going for inherent suspense in the Hitchcock tradition. James Naughton, Barbara Baxley, Roy Poole. (MGM/UA)

STRANGER ON THE CAMPUS. See *Monster on the Campus*.

STRANGERS FROM OUTER SPACE. Early title for *It Came from Outer Space*.

STRANGEST DREAMS. See *Invasion of the Space Preachers*.

STRANGE WORLD OF COFFIN JOE (1968) ★ Brazilian filmmaker José Mojica Marins, famous for his gory horror movies, helmed this trilogy of tales about a doll maker. Necrophilia comes into play in this shocker, which is part of a series starring the character of Coffin Joe (played by director Marins). Others: *At Midnight I'll Take Your Soul, This Night I Will Possess Your Corpse* and *The Bloody Exorcism of Coffin Joe*. (S/Weird; Tapeworm)

STRANGE WORLD OF PLANET X. See *Cosmic Monsters*. (X marks the splotch)

STRANGLEHOLD. See *The Haunted Strangler*.

STRANGLER OF VIENNA, THE. See *The Mad Butcher*.

STRATOSTARS. See *War of the Robots*.

STRAYS (1991) ★★ Would you believe a TV-movie with the "horrifying monster" a feral housecat? That's what producer-writer Shaun Cassidy sells you in this absurd catnip. Lawyer Timothy Busfield and novelist Kathleen Quinlan live in a forest, unaware the mean tabbie has invaded their attic with a band of feline accomplices. The film's tone, dialogue and satire are similar to those in *Arachnophobia* as the humans engage in inane chatter and petty jealousies when it appears Busfield's client (Claudia Christian) is trying to win him away from Quinlan. Director John McPherson has fun when the cats jump out of the woodwork, what with a lightning storm outside, but the clichés are so drearily familiar that this never has more than half a life. William Boyett provides the film's only relief from tedium as a wise-cracking veterinarian. (Video/Laser: MCA/Universal)

STREET ASYLUM (1989) ★★★ Wings Hauser gives a powerful performance as Arliss Ryder, a betrayed L.A. cop who unknowingly becomes a guinea pig in an experiment to turn police into killers who willingly slaughter street criminals. With a cybernetics device implanted in his back that turns his impulses animalistic, Hauser is controlled by his boss Alex Cord (in a role oozing with menace) as the leader of a special unit called Strike S.Q.U.A.D. (Scum-Quelling Urban Assault Division). In one bizarre piece of casting, G. Gordon Liddy plays a police chief running for reelection, a sado-masochistic fruitcake who enjoys having domineering prostitutes whip him. The disturbing script by John Powers captures an aura of madness and paranoia and is loaded with eccentric street people such as Brion James's insane preacher. Director Gregory Brown uses the alleys and backstreets of Hollywood to good advantage to give this urban nightmare tale an edge of realism. Roberta Vasquez, Sy Richardson, Jesse Doran, Jesse Aragon. (Magnum) (Laser)

STREET FIGHTER (1994) ★★★ If there is any

reason to watch this comic-book movie, based on the popular Capcom video game, it's for the final screen performance of Raul Julia as the crazed dictator General Bison, who intends to take over his country of Shadaloo (in the Far East) with zombie soldiers. Julia, dressed in a costume that harkens back to Hitler for its symbols, rants and raves and carries on in often brilliant style, elevating this dumb material far beyond what it deserves. Not so with Jean-Claude Van Damme as the heroic, battle-toughened Colonel Guile, who intends to destroy Bison with his army of Allied Nations troops. He seems incapable of knowing what to do with his unidimensional role, and as a result this is one of his weakest vehicles. As for the high-tech sci-fi gadgets (a stealthy armored speedboat, a virtual-reality machine that turns sane men into monsters, bizarre satellite transmissions), the film is a visual delight, and its various action plots, though messy and intercut to the point of confusion, carry one along. It was written-directed by Steven E. de Souza. Ming-Na Wen, Damian Chapa, Kylie Minogue, Simon Callow. (Video/Laser: MCA)

STRIPPED TO KILL (1987) ★★½ One can almost hear director Katt Shea Ruben insisting her movie be filled with realistic, gritty glimpses of striptease artists—their angst, sleazy bosses, tough working hours and compromised personal lives—and producer Roger Corman insisting on a slasher-killer plot for box office. Neither seems to win although all those ingredients, and then some, are here. What goes awry is the premise that cop Kay Lenz, going undercover as a stripper, falls in love with the profession, while a strangler knocks off shapely dancers one by one. Another problem with the Andy Ruben–Katt Shea Ruben script is its incoherent ending, which defies description with a chase, a fire, an identity revelation and a mess of other stuff. Greg Evigan as Lenz's macho partner and Norman Fell as the club owner add verisimilitude to the anguish and there are some arousing strip dances, but the film is too stripped of humanity. Pia Kamakahi, Tracey Crowder, Debby Nassar. (MGM/UA)

STRIPPED TO KILL 2: LIVE GIRLS (1989) ★★ If ogling bountiful tits and asses is what you seek in movie-watching, jump to it, because that's all this Roger Corman production has: sexually desirable women wearing kinky, provocative outfits and dancing to very exotic, erotic numbers. Writer-director Katt Shea Ruben knows the psychology of the stripper, and imbues her topless dancers with male sex-fantasy traits, ranging from lesbian overtones to sadistic undertones. This is as big a mess as *Stripped to Kill* with its plot contrivances and alleged surprise ending, and vacillating characters. In this mishmash stolen from Cornell Woolrich, dancer

Maria Ford keeps dreaming she has a razor between her teeth and is slashing throats of dancers, waking up to find blood on her mouth. Actually she is having psychic dreams (further details would give away the woeful whodunit plot) and becomes suspect in the murder case when L.A. cop Ed Lottimer investigates. You do have to admit, though, that Karen Mayo Chandler, Birke Tam, Marjean Holden and Debra Lamb are something to watch as they perform red-hot strips. (MGM/UA)

STRONGEST MAN IN THE WORLD (1962). See *Mole Men vs. the Son of Hercules.*

STRYKER (1983) ★★ Low-budget quickie script by Howard R. Cohen (of *Saturday the 14th* and *Space Raiders* infamy) is a swipe of *Road Warrior*, set in a post-Armageddon world where tribes of strangely dressed survivors fight over water. Stryker (Steve Sandor) is an unadorable hero who engenders zero sympathy. This mess was directed without care by Cirio H. Santiago in the Philippines, and it's one corny action scene after the other. Andria Savio, William Ostrander. (Starmaker; Embassy; from Bingo as *Savage Dawn*)

STUCK ON YOU (1982) ★ A hodgepodge of visual gags (juvenile and otherwise) spliced together under the guise of being a comedy by that traumatized Troma team of Lloyd Kaufman and Michael Herz. Divorce court's Judge Gabriel (Prof. Irwin Corey) leads a divorcing couple (Virginia Penta and Mark Mikulski) through time to demonstrate why there's a battle of the sexes (from caveman days to the reign of Napoleon and Josephine). He's an inventor with a device that stimulates chickens to lay more eggs and there's an awful lot of scatology and chicken humor. You'll see nudity, simulated sex, Martin Balsam in a cameo, a man floating around in a phone booth and other examples of total chaos. Occasionally there's a laugh—but then, 9 writers contributed to the script. The nonstop music track features Neil Sedaka, Howard Greenfield and Junk Rock. Directed by Kaufman (as Samuel Weil) and Herz. (Troma)

STUFF, THE (1985) ★★½ Another strange, strange satirical horror tale from the bizarre, bizarre mind of writer-producer-director Larry Cohen. A gooey substance bubbles up from the earth and becomes a delicious yogurtlike dessert called the Stuff. When industrial spy Michael Moriarty tries to learn the formula, he uncovers the real truth: The dreams that the Stuff is made of are nightmares. It's a living substance that takes over mind and body, oozing out of gaping mouths and attacking in a flowing wave of glop. It's kind of the Blob, sort of. Cohen treats this horror premise as a joke. One minute he's reminding us of fluoride in water and poisonous preservatives in food, in the next he's spoofing the military and advertising world. Andrea Marcovicci portrays the marketing expert–love interest and Paul Sorvino is an Army officer. Patrick O'Neal, Garrett Morris, Scott Bloom, Alexander Scourby (in his last role). Jim Danforth and David Allen worked on the effects. (New World)

STUFF STEPHANIE IN THE INCINERATOR (1987) ★★½ A thoroughly unusual and surprising role-playing thriller in the Hitchcockian vein that will have you guessing when three millionaires get together for their annual staging of a horror play. Catherine Dee, William Dame and M. R. Murphy assume new characterizations and engage in double crosses as each tries to outfox the other. What is real and what is staged? You won't know until it's all over. Produced-directed by Don Nardo, who co-wrote with Peter Jones. Dennis Cunningham, Paul Nielsen. (Video/Laser: Media)

SUBSPECIES (1990) ★★★½ Classical vampire tale, reminiscent of the gothic Hammer species, from the Charles Band–Full Moon production house. European locations enhance this morbid yet fascinating account of three women visiting a Transylvanian castle where Radu—an evil count with bony fingers, and resembling Nosferatu—holds sway over miniature gargoyles and the "bloodstone," a device that gives him powers of evil. David Allen's effects are effectively used by director Ted Nicolaou, who emphasizes the gory as well as more sublime elements in the Jackson Barr–David Pabian script. It moves slowly at times but the film is stamped with good production values. Michael Watson, Angus Scrimm (in a cameo), Laura Care, Anders Hove, Michelle McBride, (Video/Laser: Paramount)

SUBSPECIES II. See *Bloodstone: Subspecies II.*

SUBSPECIES III. See *Bloodlust: Subspecies III.*

SUBURBAN COMMANDO (1991) ★★½ A real belly flop for professional wrestler-turned-thespian (a redundancy of terms?) Hulk Hogan, who portrays space ranger Shep Ramsey, a savior of the universe who defeats galaxy tyrant William Ball in a blaze of sci-fi pyrotechnics and then vacations on Earth, living in the home of nerdy engineer Christopher Lloyd and wife Shelley Duvall. If that doesn't make sense, wait. . . . Two bounty hunters from the cosmos (who, strangely enough, resemble wrestlers) drop in on Hulk for a showdown, allowing for Lloyd to be the worm that turns. There's plenty of zappy action when Ball returns from the dead as a lizard monster, but one wonders what drew so much talent to this stranglehold on human brain cells. It was directed (?) by Burt Kennedy and it has Jack Elam as a retired old soldier and Roy Dotrice as Hulk's assignment chief—who deserve to be body slammed for taking such parts. It also has a mean spirit even though it appears to be made for family viewing. Larry

Miller, Jo Ann Dearing, Michael Faustino. (New Line) (Laser: Image)

SUCCUBUS (1971). Video version of *Devil's Nightmare* (Applause).

SUN DEMON, THE. See *The Hideous Sun Demon.*

SUNDOWN: THE VAMPIRE IN RETREAT (1989) ★★★ Offbeat vampire Western, loaded with unusual concepts and bubbling with an infectuous cinematic vitality. Purgatory is a town in the Utah desert (where this was filmed) where Count Mardulak (David Carradine) takes his vampire citizens to start a new life without killing, living off artificial blood made in a factory. But preacherman John Ireland wants vampires to kill humans and leads a revolt against benevolent Mardulak. An undercurrent of satire runs throughout this vigorous action-comedy film with Carradine a standout. Richard Stone's main theme is an amusing pastiche of grandiose Western scores. Accolades to director Anthony Hickox, who cowrote the amusing script with John Burgess. Jim Metzler, Morgan Brittany, Maxwell Caulfield, M. Emmet Walsh, Bruce Campbell. (Vestron)

SUN RA & HIS INTERGALACTIC ARKESTRA: SPACE IS THE PLACE (1974) ★ A muddled fiasco, barely released to theaters (it lasted a week in San Francisco under the simpler title *Space Is the Place*), depicting the life-style of Sun Ra. In what must be the only sci-fi flick starring Mr. Ra, the mystical keyboard musician lands his spaceship outside San Francisco and rounds up blacks to take to a faraway planet in order to escape earthly prejudices and inequities. The surrealistic special effects, along with Ra's terrible acting and vacuous philosophies, are totally impotent. Directed by John Coney from a Joshua Smith (un) script. (Rhapsody)

SUPER FORCE (1990) ★★ A far-out action flick in which astronaut Ken Olandt, recently back from a flight to Mars, dons a jazzed-up armor suit to fight the lousy scumbags who killed his cop brother. G. Gordon Liddy, Larry B. Scott, Marshall Teague. Directed by Richard Compton. (MCA)

SUPERGIRL (1984) ★★★½ Wild and woolly Alexander Salkind production featuring wonderful flying scenes and expensive effects. Kara (daughter of Zoltar, brother of Superman's father) loses a life-giving object, the Omega Hedran, which spells doom for Argo City (on Krypton) unless she can recover it. Jumping aboard the Binar Shoot, a vehicle for passing through the Sixth Dimension, Kara (Helen Slater) comes to Earth, assumes the guise of college girl Linda Lee and engages in adventures with Selena, a wicked witch (beautifully essayed by Faye Dunaway) who uses the Hedran to conjure up evil. What's lacking in David Odell's episodic script are strong relationships and logic.

What saves this are its visual style (thanks to cinematographer Alan Hume) and Dunaway's flamboyant sorceress. She proclaims herself "the ultimate siren of Endor," and becomes Hollywood's greatest villainess. The production is aided by Peter O'Toole (as Kara's father) who reaches Shakespearean heights when he's lost in the Phantom Zone and turns to alcoholism. Slater performs well in her debut role. Effects by Derek Meddings and Roy Fields. Music by Jerry Goldsmith. Directed by Jeannot Szwarc. Mia Farrow appears as Supergirl's mother and Brenda Vaccaro is whimsical as Selena's right-hand gal. Peter Cook, Simon Ward. (USA) (Laser: Image)

SUPER INFRAMAN, THE. See *Infra-Man*.

SUPER KONG. See A*P*E.

SUPERMAN—THE MOVIE (1978) ★★★★★ Super-spectacular $40 million Ilya Salkind production pays homage to the most famous superhero of the comic books, radio, and serials . . . but never in a single style. This beautifully crafted film begins as a space adventure, depicting the origin of Superman, his father Jor-El (Marlon Brando) and the demise of Krypton, all done seriously. It then shifts to our baby hero landing on Earth and tended to by the Kent family, and a sentimental, lyrical quality in the cornfields of Kansas prevails. The more traditional comic book ambience is generated when Kent shows up in Metropolis, writing for the *Daily Planet*, and falling in love with reporter Lois Lane. It's a great affair, with Superman carrying Lois through the skies of the city. And finally, we have Superman's adventures with Lex Luthor, evil mastermind who plans to create an earthquake that will send California into the Pacific. Mixture of styles may have been caused by so many writers: Mario Puzo, David Newman, Leslie Newman, Robert Benton. John Williams's musical score gives the film a true sense of heroic grandeur. Richard Donner directed, and did a wonderful job. Christopher Reeve doubles as Superman and Clark Kent and he's perfect casting. Gene Hackman hams it up as Luthor, Ned Beatty likewise as his bumbling sidekick, and Margot Kidder is perfect as Lois. (RCA/Columbia; Warner Bros.) (Laser: Warner Bros.)

SUPERMAN II (1981) ★★★★½ Entertaining special-effects masterpiece translates the famous comic book to the screen with a joyous sense of wonder. This follow-up to the 1978 box-office smash is a rich mosaic of action, light-hearted romance ("mushy stuff") and a sense of stylistic spoofery, even if director Richard Lester is somewhat dwarfed by the story's enormity. The cast is wonderful, with Christopher Reeve again doubling as the Man of Steel and as Clark Kent, mild-mannered reporter, Margot Kidder again falling in love with Superman, and Gene Hack-

man returning as master villain Lex Luthor. Sarah Douglas, Jack O'Halloran and Terence Stamp appear as Kryptonite heavies who turn the world topsy-turvy with their superpowers. Their destruction of downtown Metropolis is brilliant. The Mario Puzo–David Newman–Leslie Newman script moves moves moves, and you'll love E. G. Marshall as our First Executive with a toupee. Ned Beatty (back as Otis), Jackie Cooper (back as Perry White) and Susannah York (back as Superman's mother) appear briefly. (Video/Laser: Warner Bros.)

SUPERMAN III (1983) ★★★ Alexander and Ilya Salkind, the Brothers Whim of producers, commit an unpardonable cinematic sin: After establishing high standards for effects and scripting in their first 2 Superman epics, they allowed mediocrity to set in. The David and Leslie Newman script is a half-witted affair in which the Man of Steel (Christopher Reeve again) pursues archcriminal Ross Webster (unctuously played by Robert Vaughn). But Superman doesn't seem to have his heart in it—and the same can be said for director Richard Lester, whose *Superman II* was so much more stylized. There's a dull love affair between Clark Kent (also Reeve) and old high school flame Lana Lang (Annette O'Toole) that never builds, and Richard Pryor is plain stupid as computer whiz Gus Gorman, victimized by Vaughn to reprogram the world to create a monopolistic hold on the world's oil. The film comes to life when Superman is weakened by ersatz Kryptonite and turns evil—you'll see Superman drinking whisky and having an affair with sexy Annie Ross. Finally there's a great duel of alter egos when Kent and Superman square off in a junkyard. But the humanity that enhanced the previous films is missing, and no amount of effects magic can make up for it. Jackie Cooper appears as Perry White, and Margot Kidder is in just two scenes as Lois Lane. (Video/Laser: Warner Bros.)

SUPERMAN IV: THE QUEST FOR PEACE (1987) ★★ Superman is no longer so super—Menahem Golan and Yoram Globus took over the series from the Salkinds and proved they were made of putty, not steel. The Harrison Ellenshaw effects are so inferior as to be (1) laughable and (2) disappointing, and the Lawrence Konner–Mark Rosenthal script (based on a Christopher Reeve idea) is a spectacular mess, never leaping a single bound. Christopher Reeve as Clark Kent/Superman is so appealing you want to like this movie, but director Sidney J. Furie gets in the way of a good time. Superman is on a kick to dump all nuclear weapons into a space junkpile, but returning to stop him is Lex Luthor (Gene Hackman), who creates a mighty solar man to combat our stalwart hero. This battle is an insult to the 3 films that preceded it.

Mariel Hemingway as the new owner of the *Daily Planet* provides the film's only charm by exposing her beautiful gams. And that, fans, is the highlight of this distressingly disappointing movie. Sam Wanamaker portrays Mariel's greedy father. Margot Kidder returns as Lois Lane, and except for one flying sequence with Superman is left out of the picture. Jon Cryer, Marc McClure. (Video/Laser: Warner Bros.)

SUPERMAN: THE SERIAL (1948) ★★★ One of the better serials to come out of the Columbia factory from producer Sam Katzman. It's a series of rip-roaring adventures (in 15 chapters) beginning with Superman's origins on Krypton, his coming to Earth in a rocket, his adoption by the Kent family, and his journey to Metropolis to fight crime disguised as Clark Kent. The flying sequences are animated in a cartoonish style—a jarring contrast to the fine live-action footage. Superman's adversary is the sexy Spider Lady, played with a perverse twist by Carol Forman in an appealing black outfit, her main murder device a large electrified web. She's out to possess the "Reducer Ray" and has Kryptonite to keep Superman at bay. Noel Neill is a perky Lois Lane, although her actions are annoyingly dumb. It was directed with style by Spencer G. Bennet and Thomas Carr and stars Kirk Alyn as a square but likable Man of Steel. Pierre Watkin is Perry White and Tommy Bond is Jimmy Olson. In this wonderful cliff-hanger can be seen the antecedents for the TV series with George Reeves. The chapters begin and end with narration read by Knox Manning, who had one of the best voices in radio. (Warner Bros.)

SUPER MARIO BROS. (1993) ★★★ They took the popular Nintendo video game and turned it into a lavish effects extravaganza, jam-packed with action, comedy and computerized graphics. Even so, the result is a mediocre mixture out of control and without the internal logic a good fantasy needs. Bob Hoskins and John Leguizamo are delightful as Brooklyn plumbers who enter another dimension where a kingdom of people descended from dinosaurs is ruled by comical tyrant King Koopa (Dennis Hopper with a crazy hairdo). The plumbers are after a magical pendant and a bevy of kidnapped Brooklyn beauties and the pace is unrelenting as they meet an evil priestess, a pet *T. rex* named Yoshi, henchmen called Goombas (tall dudes with tiny lizardheads) and a zillion funky props, sets and costumes. Nobody can fault the energetic direction by Rocky Morton and Annabel Jankel, the creators of Max Headroom. Fiona Shaw, Samantha Mathis, Fisher Stevens, Richard Edson. (Video/Laser: Hollywood Pictures)

SUPERNATURALS, THE (1986) ★★★½ Well-produced Sandy Howard production that opens in 1865, when Confederate prisoners are forced to walk across a mine field by a Union sadist. A youth surviving that ordeal possesses magical powers that, 100 years later, plague a detachment of Army recruits training in the area where the Civil War massacre took place. Dead rebels are on the march, killing the soldiers one by one, while the boy's mother, in beautiful form, falls for one of the troopers. Macabre, eerie imagery by director Armand Mastroianni richly enhances this offbeat, above-average horror thriller. Nichelle Nichols, Maxwell Caulfield, Talia Balsam, Scott Jacoby, Levar Burton. Excellent music by Robert O. Ragland. (Embassy)

SUPERNOVA (1999) ★★ *Alien* producer Walter Hill walked out on MGM when the studio refused to give him more money to finish this $70 million sci-fi wanna-be epic, and he instantly supernovaed himself out of credit-existence by asking that his name be replaced with the pseudonym "Thomas Lee." It's difficult to say what he saw in this deep-space adventure script by David Campbell Wilson, since Hill had already made the four-picture series that set the standard for this genre. It's like he ripped himself off. The film is set aboard the Nightgale 229, a paramedic rescue spacecraft that receives a distress call from a mining colony and hyperjumps halfway across the universe through time and space to render medical aid. Captain Robert Forester dies quickly, leaving matters in the hands of new captain James Spader, nurse Angela Bassett and crew members Lou Diamond Phillips, Robin Tunney, and Wilson Cruz. Aboard comes only-surviving miner Peter Facinelli with a weird alien artifact that has given him superstrength and a desire to destroy. He starts dumping bodies into space, forgetting to give them spacesuits first. This derivative movie will remind you of *Sphere, Event Horizon, Stargate, Virus* and *Deep Rising*, it borrows that much. It also has some sex-in-freefall but it's soft-R at best. The computer-generated effects are grand (giving the character-weak plot a giant boost) and the film was re-edited by Francis Ford Coppola to hyperjump the story along, though some coherence may have been lost on the cutting room floor. The tagline "It Will Blow You Away" is not true, by the way. It's nothing more than a 90-minute diversion that is quickly forgotten. (Video/DVD: MGM)

SUPERSONIC MAN (1979) ★★ A humanoid alien cruising through space in a capsule is awakened and told he has a mission to carry out on the endangered planet of Earth, where the mad would-be dictator Dr. Goolick (Cameron Mitchell) plans to conquer mankind with a fire-breathing robot. So Supersonic Man, cape billowing in airless space, swoops toward the Green Planet to music that was inspired by *Superman—The Movie*. Once on Earth he confronts Goolick's green-garbed minions, the robot and a comic-relief drunk with basset hound in a series of asinine, uninspired adventures. Mitchell, despite mad-doctor dialogue, is drab and nonthreatening. The effects are mediocre, and the story line too stupid for children or adults. Directed and cowritten by Juan Piquer Simon. Michael Coby, Diana Polakow, Richard Yesteran. (United)

SUPERSTITION (1982) ★★ Haunted house–exorcism package with ample gore effects. Black Lake is haunted by a witch drowned there in 1692, and she also haunts a nearby mansion, allowing for bloody acts of violence that make it appear the house is responsible. What we have here is an exploding head in a microwave oven, a body ripped open by a whirring skill saw ("My, what teeth you have!"), a body gutted and chopped in half by a descending window frame, the toes of a swimmer eaten off, a man hanged in an elevator shaft, a man crushed by a wine press, and a woman nailed to the floor with spikes (including one through her brain). The characters are fodder for the deathmill in Donald G. Thompson's script, including Albert Salmi's inquisitive policeman, Larry Pennell's drunken husband, James Houghton's investigating hero and Lynn Carlin's heroine. James W. Robinson's direction is hampered by flat lighting. Aka *The Witch*. (Lightning)

SURF NAZIS MUST DIE (1986) ★★ Despite its campy title, this Troma production takes itself seriously in depicting war between the Samurai Surfers and the Surf Nazis for control of Power Beach. In "the near future," following an earthquake that's left the L.A. basin devastated, these gangs fight it out and spend enough time riding big waves to slow the plot to a backcrawl. The neo-Nazi band, led by "Adolf" and "Mengele," becomes the target of an irate black mother (Gail Neely) after her son is murdered, and she's a sight as she buys firearms (to "blow away honkies"), rides a motorcycle and pursues Nazi rats in a speedboat. Directed by Peter George. Barry Brenner, Dawn Wildsmith, Bobbie Bresee, Dawne Ellison. (Media)

SURF TERROR. See *Monster from the Surf*.

SURF II (1982) ★★ The big gag: there never was a *Surf I*. Ha ha ha ha! Glub glub. New Wavers in black outfits are aliens who abduct teenagers into an underwater UFO, and Buzz Cola, a new soft drink, turns teens into zombies or women. This foolish sexploitation trash consists of unfunny jokes, such as eating seaweed, crunching on glass, jiggling bare breasts into the mouths of overweight boys and kidding a stupid sheriff, Chief Boyardit. The script by director Randall Badat is impossible to describe as infantile jokes are blended like flotsam on the tide. Joshua Cadman, Linda Kerridge, Cleavon Little, Ruth Buzzi, Lyle Waggoner. (Media; King of Video)

SURGEON, THE (1994) ★★★ Following in the tradition of *Coma, X-Ray*, and other medical thrillers, this Canadian-produced shocker is a satisfying, above-average blend of needle-into-flesh horror visuals, suspenseful cat-and-mouse sequences, taut chases through hospital corridors, slasher-movie clichés, and some unusual science-fiction touches. Director Carl Schenkel brings a vitality and curiosity to all these things in a far better style than most, giving energy to otherwise standard B-movie devices. The screenplay by Patrick Cirillo (from an unfilmed script by Bernard Sloane) provides a few novel twists as Isabel Glasser, a doctor at a major hospital, and promising doctor-to-be James Remar track a killer who is knocking off the patients. Turns out that the lollipop-sucking killer (Sean Haberle) is Glasser's former lover, a onetime doctor who had developed a promising cure for cancer but attempted suicide when some patients died. Now he's back for revenge with a pituitary-gland serum he carries around in hypodermic needles that heal all the wounds that he sustains as he goes on his murderous spree. Cop Peter Boyle thinks he can stop this madman from using Glasser for his ultimate horror experiment, but of course he's wrong. And Haberle, in a good performance for this kind of crazed character, captures her and ties her down for the climactic battle. Malcolm McDowell is around briefly as a doctor experimenting with monkeys, but he dies off pretty fast. Originally made as *Exquisite Tenderness* (a medical term for the point at which pain reaches its most extreme threshold), this horror movie is perversely fascinating—a guilty pleasure, for sure. In supporting roles are Beverly Todd, Mother Love, Charles Dance and Gregory West. (The A-Pix Entertainment video has the added treat of *The Horror Shop*, an introduction with a host who makes ghoulish hospital comments; he continues with voice-over jokes during the closing credits, and then does on-camera plugs for other A-Pix horror videos.)

SURVIVAL. See *Panic in Year Zero*.

SURVIVALIST, THE (1987) ★★ When war with Russia appears imminent, biker gangs in Texas take over the territory, terrorizing Steve Railsback and son. Mindless action in the *Mad Max* vein, without style or interesting characters. This film, written by Robert Dillon and directed by Sig Shore, can't possibly survive. Jason Healey, Marjoe Gortner, Cliff De Young, David Wayne, Susan Blakely. (Vestron) (Laser: Image)

SURVIVAL RUN. See *Damnation Alley*.

SURVIVAL ZONE (1984) ★★ "Welcome to World War IV," proclaims a survivor of nuclear holocaust that has left a handful to rove the nuked landscape. Among them: Bigman and his vicious motorcycle gang, heroic Adam Strong (Morgan Stevens) and Gary Lockwood, who lives with wife Camilla Sparv and children on an isolated farm. The screenplay by producer-director Percival Rubens and Eric Brown has these elements coming together to do battle in what is a predictable (though surprisingly philosophical) portrait of post-Armageddon survival. It finally boils down to routine action and sadistic torture and looks as though it was made in Australia. Zoli Marki, Ian Steadman. (Prism; Starmaker)

SURVIVING THE GAME (1994) ★★★½ Well-written, entertaining variation on "The Most Dangerous Game," in which derelict Ice-T becomes the prey for a small band of hunters led by Rutger Hauer, Gary Busey and Charles S. Dutton. Rugged Canadian terrain enhances the action as Ice-T proves more durable than his stalkers ever imagined. In an odd twist, Eric Bernt's script turns the tables, making Ice-T the stalker, and creating suspense for the baddies. Director Ernest Dickerson spends just enough time on the twisted attitudes of the hunters to elevate this above other "Dangerous Game" remakes. John C. McGinley, William McNamara, Jeff Corey. (New Line)

SURVIVOR (1986) ★ Worthless post-holocaust movie in a quasi–*Road Warrior* vein. Richard Moll is astronaut Kragg, who takes off aboard *Challenger II* to circle Earth 228 times while a nuclear war wipes out mankind. He awakens to find himself shackled to a pipe, and proceeds to enter an adventure with Sue Kiel that makes no sense involving a subterranean city where a madman has Wolf Larsonish dreams of starting mankind over again. There's one good action sequence in which men dangling on chains fight it out, but otherwise this is incoherent, from Bima Stagg's script to Michael Shackleton's direction. Chip Mayer, John Carson. (Vestron) (Laser: Image)

SUSPECT DEVICE (1995) ★★★ Another Roger Corman–produced TV-movie composed of elements from many films. Scripter Alex Simon lifts ideas from *Three Days of the Condor* and *Total Recall* to spin the confusing but fast-moving action thriller about a low-grade government agent (C. Thomas Howell) who is suddenly caught up in a conspiracy and wave of paranoia because he doesn't know who he really is, and the government guys are out to kill him. It's another plot involving cyborgs, a nuclear device that is set to go off soon, and tons of shoot-outs. Director Rick Jacobson just looks the other way and makes it as action-packed as possible as he manipulates the cardboard characters. Stacey Travis, Jed Allan, Jonathan Fuller, John Beck and Marcus Aurelius go along for the ride and make this watchable and diverting—while it lasts, then you're reminded of what a rip-off producer Corman is pulling. (New Horizons)

SUSPENSE. See *Beyond the Door II*.

SUSPIRIA (1976) ★★★½ Short on logic but long on thrills, this is a fan's picture—an Italian import written by director Dario Argento and Daria Nicolodi. Jessica Harper is an American enrolled in a German dance academy, when suddenly a thunderstorm sets the mood for a bat attack, falling maggots, a throat-ripping dog and cackling witches. Commendable "cheap thrills" with Joan Bennett, Udo Keir and Alida Valli. (Magnum) (Laser: Image)

SUTURE (1993) ★★★½ As you start to watch this unusually literate psychological suspense thriller, don't take it literally, and consider that your eyes are about to be challenged by what you see, or think you see. It is an exercise in visual identity, dealing with who we think we are as opposed to who we really are. Case in point: The lookalike brothers who drive the plot of this mystery (written-produced-directed by Scott McGehee and David Siegel) don't look alike at all. In fact, one is black (Dennis Haysbert), the other is white (Mel Harris). And yet for the movie to work, you must assume that they are lookalikes. For that is what all the characters in the movie do. The film was shot in black and white, as if to say this project is also an illusion. This unusual aspect aside, the story plays out like a Hitchcock thriller, with all the plot twists in place. Coproduced by Steven Soderbergh of *sex, lies and videotape* fame. Fran Ryan (as the love interest), Sab Shimono (as the psychiatrist), David Graf (as the cop). Dina Merrill has a guest role. (Evergreen/Hallmark Entertainment)

SWAMP OF THE BLOOD LEECHES. Video version of *The Alien Dead* (USA).

SWAMP THING (1982) ★★ Popular comic-book creature, half-man, half-slime, is the laughingstock of the Okefenokee in the hands of director-writer Wes Craven. The juvenile approach is an ironic shift from his *Last House on the Left* and *The Hills Have Eyes* and will disappoint fans expecting hard-core horror. The monster looks exactly like what it is—a strong-arm actor in a rubber suit. And Craven lingers lovingly on the phony outfit, allowing us to wince for minutes at a stretch. Louis Jourdan has the thankless role of Arcane, Swamp Thing's nemesis, and Adrienne Barbeau streaks through the wilderness, screaming as she is pursued by the creature (for a moment she pauses to bare her lovely breasts). Though trying to play a "ballsy broad" and make Alice Cable a heroine, Barbeau is merely decorative and rescuable. Nicholas Worth, David Hess. The sequel was *Return of the Swamp Thing*, followed by a weekly TV series. (Video/Laser: Embassy/Nelson)

SWITCH (1991) ★★½ Once again writer-director Blake (*Victor/Victoria*) Edwards tackles the fascinating theme of confused sexual roles, but this time it's a fantasy clunker. When womanizer Perry King is murdered by three abused lovers, he winds up in Purgatory, where it's decided (by the male and female voices of God) that he should be given a second chance to find a woman who respects him. But then the Devil (Bruce Martyn Payne) gives him the body of a sexy woman (Ellen Barkin) in his/her quest. What results are unfunny situations in which Barkin (remember this is a male trapped in a female's body) embarks on lesbian and heterosexual relationships. Only toward the climax, when the woman gets pregnant, does the film take on poignancy. Jimmy Smits, JoBeth Williams, Lorraine Bracco, Tony Roberts, Lysette Anthony. (Video/Laser: HBO)

SWITCH IN TIME, A. See *Norman's Awesome Experience.*

SWORD AND THE SORCERER, THE (1982) ★★★½ Producers Brandon Chase and Marianne Chase offer a fantasy reminiscent of Saturday matinee serials as Lee Horsley battles evil in a mythical kingdom, Eh-Dan, ruled by Cromwell (Richard Lynch) and his demon (George Maharis). Prince Talon (Horsley) must also rescue Kathleen Beller. It was well directed by Albert Pyun (from a script by Tom Karnowsky) and has bloody effects as well as good transformations of men into monsters (by Richard Washington). (Video/Laser: MCA)

SWORDKILL. See *Ghost Warrior.*

SWORD OF HEAVEN (1985) ★★ Magical blade, forged from a meteor hundreds of years ago by Zen priests, becomes the object of contention between the evil gang that possesses it and a Japanese policeman, skilled in martial arts (naturally), visiting California. Directed by Byron Meyers. Tadashi Yamashita, Mel Novak, Bill "Superfoot" Wallace, Venus Jones. (LD Video)

SWORD OF THE VALIANT (1984) ★★★½ Entertaining, swashbuckling interpretation of the Legend of Sir Gawain and the Green Knight, awash in colorful dialogue and characters under Stephen Weeks's direction. The Green Knight, a supernatural entity, rides into King Arthur's court and challenges any brave knight to chop off his head. The only catch is, if the swinger misses, the Green Knight (Sean Connery) gets a return swing. A squire (Miles O'Keeffe) accepts the challenge, thus beginning an outré odyssey into adventure, myth and magic as he sets out on a 1-year quest for the answer to a riddle of wisdom. His wanderings take him to the land of Leonette, where he finds love, imprisonment

and new enemy Ronald Lacey. Sets and costumes in this Golan-Globus production are splendid. Trevor Howard is the disillusioned king, Lila Kedrova is the wife of the protector of Leonette, Peter Cushing is a roving fop, Cyrielle Claire is Sir Gawain's love. Photographed by Freddie Young and Peter Hurst. Leigh Lawson, John Rhys-Davies. (MGM/UA)

SWORDSMAN, THE (1992) ★★★ Lorenzo Lamas is adept with epées, sabers and swords in this fantasy adventure mystery cast in the mold of *Highlander.* Lamas portrays an L.A. cop undergoing psychic visions connected with the sword of Alexander the Great, which has fallen into evil hands. Lamas comes under the control of diabolical sorcerer Michael Champion and must break free to duel for possession of the priceless weapon. Writer-director Michael Kennedy has a good sense of ambience and his stunt coordinators stage good swashbuckling sequences, but Lamas is lifeless, although his thrust with a blade is far better than his thrusts with Claire Stansfield in the pallid lovemaking sequences. Still, this is a notch above most fantasy-action fare. Nicholas Pasco, Raoul Trujillo. (Video/Laser: Republic)

SYNAPSE (1994) ★★★ Well-produced futuristic action thriller set in a society where war rages between the dictatorial Life Corporation (ruled by evil Barry Morse) and the Union, a band of rebels fighting to restore freedom. A supplier of guns to rebel chieftain Matt McCoy has his soul essence transferred against his will to the body of a pregnant woman (Karen Duffy) via technology developed by sympathetic scientist Saul Rubinek. So she/he goes on a rampage of violence and destruction, joining McCoy's ranks to get the correct body back. Blazing machine guns, explosions, force fields and other sci-fi hardware enhance this adaptation of Hank Stine's novel *Season of the Witch* by David Gottleib, Dale Hildebrand and director Allan A. Goldstein. Made in Toronto. Chris Makepeace, Nigel Bennett. (Video/Laser: WarnerVision)

SYNGENOR (1990) ★★★ Synthetic genetic organism (hence, *Syngenor*) is a new cyborg designed to fight our wars in the Middle East. Starr Andreeff fights for her life when the cyborg turns rogue. Directed by George Elanjian, Jr. Mitchell Laurance, Charles Lucia, David Gale, Riva Spier. (South Gate; Hemdale)

SYSTEM OF DR. TARR AND PROFESSOR FEATHER, THE. See *Dr. Tarr's Torture Dungeon.*

TAINTED BLOOD (1993) ★★½ Spinning off from the thesis of *The Bad Seed*, this derivative TV-movie is a "whichisit," in which one of two teenagers is the offspring of a family that always passes along homicidal tendencies to offspring. Investigative writer Raquel Welch is trying to determine which one, while telescripter Kathleen Rowell plants dozens of red herrings to throw you off the track. Average for its kind, except for Joan Van Ark's over-the-top performance as a neurotic, hard-drinking mother of one of the teens. Directed by Matthew Patrick. Alley Mills, Kerri Green. (Paramount)

TALE OF A VAMPIRE (1992) ★★½ In foggy, rainy London, a young woman (Suzanna Hamilton) working in a library of the supernatural meets a stranger (Julian Sands) who just happens to be a centuries-old vampire who commits a couple of murders and flashes back to a previous lover who resembles Ms. Hamilton. Along comes a von Helsing–type (Kenneth Cranham) looking for revenge. This British-Japanese production is a gothic tale of romance and neck obsession that is all angst and atmosphere. Directed by Shimako Sato, who cowrote the script with Jane Corbett. Marian Diamond, Michael Kenton. (Video/Laser: Vidmark)

TALE OF TORTURE, A. See *Bloody Pit of Horror.*

TALES FROM A PARALLEL UNIVERSE (1967) ★★ This video version of a Showtime series is strictly for hard-core sci-fi fans who enjoy galactic adventure on a bizarre scale. The computerized special effects are a little rough around the edges but telescripters Paul Donovan, Lex Gigeroff, and Jeffrey Hirschfield make up for it with outrageous plots and characters as a giant spaceship called *Lexx* goes on a search through the galaxy with enough firepower to destroy entire planets. The idea here is that an evil ruler, His Shadow, a floating spirit that takes over various host bodies, is always threatening everyone's existence and it's up to the crew of misfits to save it. And what misfits: the captain, Stanley Tweedle (Brian Downey), is a former janitor who gained access to the key that controls the ship; Zev (Eva Habermann) is a sexy Nordic number who strips to the buff for the sake of skin watching; Kai (Michael McManus) is an almost dead humanoid who occasionally comes out of his incubator to keep the plot moving; and there's a robot head that rolls its eyeballs and makes lascivious comments to Zev because of a program malfunction. Strictly comedy relief, this device. In this episode, *Lexx* and crew search for some way to help Kai get more life force, with Tim Curry as the guest star. This is such an oddball mixture of styles and ideas, under the direction of Ron Oliver, that it may or may not be your hunk of the universe. Best thing is to give it a try. If you dig this one, you might seek out others in this same series: *Giga Shadow* and *I Worship His Shadow.* (Paramount)

TALES FROM BEYOND/TALES FROM BEYOND THE GRAVE. See *From Beyond the Grave* (Graves of Wrath?).

TALES FROM THE CRYPT (1972) ★★★½ Adaptation of 5 E.C. comic stories published in the '50s by Al Feldstein and William Gaines (the latter became long-time editor of *Mad*). The famous panels (drawn by such artists as Johnny Craig, Graham Ingels and Jack Davis) have been recreated faithfully; and thanks to Milton Subotsky's script and Freddie Francis's direction, this comes off as a fun-filled horror film. Four individuals trapped with the Cryptkeeper (Sir Ralph Richardson) are told a narrative foreshadowing his or her destiny. "And All Through the House" deals with Joan Collins fighting off a Santa Claus madman on Christmas Eve; "Reflection of Death" is about a dead man who can't get used to the idea; "Poetic Justice" deals with a St. Valentine's Day gift delivered by Peter Cushing, fresh from his grave; "Wish You Were Here" is a variation on "The Monkey's Paw"; and "Blind Alleys" has Nigel Patrick blundering through a maze of razor blades. *Vault of Horror*, the sequel, adapted 4 more shuddery E.C. yarns. And in 1989 a cable TV series brought the Cryptkeeper back as storyteller. (Prism)

TALES FROM THE CRYPTKEEPER (1993) ★★ Two episodes from the animated TV series for kids: "While the Cat's Away" (by horror director Manny [*Dr. Giggles*] Coto), in which two boys are trapped in a haunted house with a werewolf and other monsters, and "Nature" (by Juan Carlos Coto), in which two picnicking boys are miniaturized and find themselves in the grass with giant ants, spiders and other deadly insects. The Cryptkeeper cracks his macabre jokes in introductions, and for children this is pretty scary stuff, so don't let the young'uns watch alone. (Sony Wonder)

TALES FROM THE CRYPTKEEPER (1994). Two episodes from the animated Saturday morning TV series: "Hyde and Go Shriek" and "The Sleeping Beauty." (Sony Wonder)

TALES FROM THE CRYPTKEEPER (1994). Two

episodes from the animated Saturday morning TV series: "Fare Tonight" and "Caveman." (Sony Wonder)

TALES FROM THE CRYPT PRESENTS BORDELLO OF BLOOD (1996) ★★ This is an insult to the memory of the great E.C. horror comics of the 1950s, and their publisher William Gaines. A low blow delivered in a lowbrow way to the lowest common denominator, *Bordello* makes the previous *Crypt* feature, *Demon Knight*, seem like a classic. Only the most loyal of gore/grue/blood buffs will derive a modicum of satisfaction from all the disgusting imagery and sick, fall-flat jokes that fill director Gilbert Adler's incoherent script (hacked out with the help of Al Katz). It's time for producers Richard Donner, David Giler, Walter Hill, Joel Silver, and Bob Zemeckis—who have allowed the popularity of the TV series to turn them into money-hungry whores—to reread the original magazines to remind themselves what E.C. horror was really about. Those stories were done with a storytelling class and morality—two factors sorely missing from this drecky mishmash of smutty vampire-movie clichés. The worthless plot has to do with the spirit of Lilith (redheaded Angie Everhart) establishing a bordello in a mortuary, where young rocker Corey Feldman is turned into a zombie. Meanwhile, phony evangelist Chris Sarandon makes a farce out of moral issues and Dennis Miller plays a wise-cracking private eye (hired by Feldman's sister, Erika Eleniak) you wish would get killed as soon as possible, he's so dreadful. The Cryptkeeper (voice by John Kassir) makes an all-too-brief appearance. Miss this insult of a movie and do yourself a grand favor. Aubrey Morris, William Sadler. (Video/DVD/Laser: Universal)

TALES FROM THE CRYPT PRESENTS DEMON KNIGHT (1995) ★★★ This full-length horror tale, with opening and closing scenes featuring the Cryptkeeper from the TV series, is more a homage to Romero's *Night of the Living Dead* and Lamberto Bava's *Demons* series than to the E.C. comics published by William C. Gaines, on which the HBO series is predicated. Using an original script by Ethan Reiff, Cyrus Voris and Mark Bishop, *Demon Knight* (under the capable direction of Ernest Dickerson) engages in the eternal struggle of good vs. evil in a literal way by presenting a demon called the Collector (Billy Zane, playing the character zanily) in pursuit of a key-shaped object that contains the blood of Jesus Christ. Presumably if he can get it away from its protector (William Sadler as a guy named Brayker), evil will rule the world. Or something like that. Brayker ends up in an old church turned into an inn-whorehouse run by CCH Pounder, surrounded by an army of demons conjured up by Zane with his green blood. How he and other trapped victims (including

Dick Miller as an unshaven rummy) fight the forces of evil, trying various forms of escape, makes up the plot of this gore-oriented shocker, with touches of black humor swirled in. Anyone expecting the E.C. touch will be sadly disappointed with this film's exploitative use of gratuitous violence and naked women with large breasts. The monsters and effects, however, are well done. Jada Pinkett, Brenda Bakke, Thomas Haden Church, John Schuck, Gary Farmer. (Video/Laser: MCA)

TALES FROM THE DARKSIDE: THE MOVIE (1990) ★★★ A slight variation on the *Creepshow* series—a trilogy of horror stories with a framework linking device. Based on the syndicated TV series from George Romero, this begins in the kitchen of a woman preparing to cook a boy imprisoned in an adjacent cell. To stall for time, the youth reads her stories from a volume entitled *Tales From the Darkside*. The first yarn, "Lot 249," is a mummy narrative inspired by Sir Arthur Conan Doyle and written by Michael McDowell—about how a scheming scholar brings a 3,000-year-old mummy monster to life. This is only moderately frightening, with a twist ending. "Cat from Hell" is a Stephen King idea scripted by Romero in which a hit man is hired to kill a supernatural feline. Grisly ending to this one. "Lover's Vow," the final yarn, has the strongest potential: a starving artist makes a pact with a murderous gargoyle and finds fame, riches and happiness as a result—but the surprise ending falls flat. The makeup (by Dick Smith) and effects are good. Potential is here but director John Harrison never creates a sense of over-the-edge excitement. Christian Slater, Deborah Harry, David Johanson, Rae Dawn Chong, William Hickey, James Remar. (Video/Laser: Paramount)

TALES FROM THE HOOD (1995) ★★★★ A blend of traditional movie horror and social satire, all finely filtered through an acute awareness of the inequalities of the modern world—especially the African-American experience in America—explores our penchant for violence graphically and disturbingly. That the film succeeds as both an entertainment and a comment on black violence in our culture is to the credit of director Rusty Cundieff, who cowrote with Darin Scott. (That Spike Lee is the executive producer only enhances this major contribution to the genre of black filmmaking.) The framework for this anthology film in the *Tales from the Crypt* vein has three street punks (De'Aundre Bonds, Samuel Monroe, Jr., and Joe Torry) visiting a weird mortuary where the equally weird mortician Mr. Simms (Clarence Williams III, in a bravura performance of madness and evil) spins his "cultural legends" of horror: a black activist murdered by rogue cop Wings Hauser returns from the grave for revenge; a boy uses an imaginary monster to avenge the beatings he and his mother receive from her abusive boyfriend; a crooked politician (Corbin Bernsen) gets his through voodoo dolls; a black gang leader is subjected to a bizarre and macabre *Clockwork Orange* type of rehabilitation (this comments on the Ku Klux Klan and features photographs from real lynchings of blacks); and finally the boys come to learn that Mr. Simms is more than he seems in a way-out conclusion. A moral conscience is at work in this entertaining and disturbing film. Anthony Griffith, Michael Massee, Tom Wright, David Alan Grier. (Video/Laser: HBO/Savoy)

TALES OF TERROR (1962) ★★★½ Roger Corman at his producing-directing best, with Richard Matheson superbly adapting a trilogy of Poe stories in "rococo gothic." In "Morella," a maddened Vincent Price faces his wife's ghost in the shapely form of Leona Gage. . . . Slow but eerie, with Price believably sinking into alcoholic insanity. A combination of "The Black Cat" and "The Cask of Amontillado" teams Price and Peter Lorre in a rollicking wine-tasting contest. This tale is played for laughs, and Lorre comes off in excellent form. (Also in excellent form is Lorre's wife, Joyce Jameson.) In "The Case of M. Valdemar," Price is on his deathbed, kept alive by hypnotist Basil Rathbone. Handsomely mounted and entertaining in a preposterous way. Debra Paget, Wally Campo, Maggie Pierce. Aka *Poe's Tales of Terror*. (Warner Bros.; Orion) (Laser: Image)

TALES OF THE PALE MOON AFTER THE RAIN. See *Ugetsu*.

TALES OF THE UNKNOWN (1990) ★★½ Compilation of 4 short tales of horror, produced independently from 1983 to 1989. "Jack Falls Down," directed by John Kim and written by Michael Matlock, deals with a deal with the Devil; "The Big Garage" is writer-director Greg Beeman's parable about a repair garage that traps stranded motorists; "Warped" is writer-director Roger Nygard's tale of revenge and incest; and "Living on Video" is producer-director Todd Marks's comment on how TV invades our privacy. (Action International)

TALES OF TRUMPY. See *The Unearthling*.

TALES THAT WITNESS MADNESS (1972) ★★★ British horror anthology in the style of *Tales from the Crypt*, directed by Freddie Francis and written by Jennifer Jayne (aka Jay Fairbank). Donald Pleasence and Jack Hawkins are strolling through an asylum and meet 4 crazies who spill their yarns: "Mr. Tiger" is about a boy who creates imaginary beasts; "Mel" stars Joan Collins as a bitchy wife who resents her husband bringing a tree into the living room—a tree that is living in a terrifying sense; "Penny Farthing" is a time-travel tale involving a haunted bicycle; and "Luau" is a voodoo-cannibal story with Kim Novak as a rich doll whose daughter is a sacrificial lamb. The final shocker concerns what happens to Pleasence and Hawkins in the asylum. Involving and unusual. Georgia Brown, Donald Houston. Aka *Witness Madness*. (Paramount)

TALL TALE: THE UNBELIEVABLE ADVENTURES OF PECOS BILL (1994) ★★★ An excellent Disney-produced family adventure with fantasy overtones. This is a Western with heart and a grandiose sense of American history as it spins a story of mythical proportions. Young Daniel Hackett (Nick Stahl) is growing up on a farm about to be gobbled up by a railroad syndicate (represented by Scott Glenn as J. P. Stiles) when he encounters a trio of legendary spirits: Pecos Bill (cantankerously played by Patrick Swayze), Paul Bunyan (played like a blustering mountain-man by Oliver Platt) and John Henry (played with steel-driving energy by Roger Aaron Brown). After picturesque misadventures, which include a brief appearance by Calamity Jane (played with hip-shootin' dynamite by Catherine O'Hara), the script by Steven L. Bloom and Robert Rodat gets down to serious business with a showdown between young Stahl and Glenn. *Tall Tale* is funny and larger than life, as it should be, in portraying characters ripped out of the history books. It's all pulled together by director Jeremiah Chechik. Stephen Lang, Jared Harris, Moira Harris, John P. Ryan, Scott Wilson. (Video/Laser: Disney)

TAMMY AND THE T-REX (1993) ★ This video-movie is so bad, it could serve as a primer in how *not* to make a movie. First you have a computerized dinosaur created by crazy scientist Dr. Wachenstein (Terry Kiser). Then you have a teenage boy's brain electronically connected to the T-Rex to animate it and make it "think" through "crystals" and "memory cells." (Are you following this?) Then you have stupid teen girl Denise Richards (Tammy, tell me it's not true) rummaging through a morgue looking for a body in which to put the boy's brain. Then you have her pouring whisky over the brain and dancing a striptease in front of it. Who do you blame for this fiasco, which doesn't end but just sputters to a close? How about director Stewart Raffill, who cowrote with associate producer Gary Brockette. Pity poor John Franklin, Paul Walker, Geroge Pilgrim, Theo Forsett and Buck Flower (as a dumb deputy). (Imperial)

TANK GIRL (1995) ★★★ The stylish, post-Armageddon comic book by Alan Martin and Jamie Hewlett reached the screen as a lavish, no-expenses-spared sci-fi actioner set in the year 2033. It's a bizarre mixture of live action, animation and static comic-book frames as Lori Petty portrays the titular heroine, a captive of the Water and Power Company, which controls the world's resources under the aegis of evil

Malcolm McDowell (playing Kesslee). With machine guns blazing and her tank (an absurdly decorated weapon of war) clanking, Rachel Buck escapes prison, joins the gargoylelike rebels called Rippers (part human, part kangaroo), and with the help of fellow prisoner Naomi Watts takes on W & P with a flaming vengeance. The failure of *Tank Girl* to integrate all of its freakish elements into a whole is the biggest fault of scripter Tedi Sarafian and director Rachel Talalay. But there are wonderful moments, especially when McDowell is oozing his unrestrained wickedness, and there's a charm to Ice-T's portrayal of a Ripper. Don Harvey, Jeff Kober, Scotty Coffey. (Video/Laser: MGM/UA)

TARANTULA (1955) ★★★ Director Jack Arnold tries to recapture the moods of *It Came from Outer Space* and *Creature from the Black Lagoon* but this Universal-International "giant creature" thriller (written by R. M. Fresco and Martin Berkeley) comes off as a lesser effort. Leo G. Carroll, seeking a nutrient to feed the increasing world population, turns a spider into a monster, which, naturally, escapes. John Agar and Mara Corday have a perfunctory, dull romance soon forgotten when Clifford Stine's effects take over. But the effects are only mildly exciting and the film builds unspectacularly to a fiery climax as the ill-tempered arachnid attacks mankind. Clint Eastwood has a bit part as a jet pilot. Nestor Paiva, Ross Elliott, Eddie Parker. (Video/Laser: MCA)

TARGETS (1968) ★★★½ Roger Corman came to Peter Bogdanovich with outtakes from *The Terror* (1963) and asked the writer-producer-director to construct a movie. Bogdanovich needed only a few scenes to concoct a tale about Byron Orlok, an aging horror star who feels he's passé (the real world's horrors are far worse, he believes) and wants to retire. Orlok is played by Boris Karloff in one of his best roles. Meanwhile, Tim O'Kelly, average American, murders his family with a high-powered rifle and snipes at motorists. Later, these divergent elements merge at a drive-in, where Orlok delivers his farewell address. Bogdanovich costars as a Sammy Fuller–type director. In recent years this unusual feature, photographed by Laszlo Kovacs, has taken on cult status. It's damn powerful. Sandy Baron, Mike Farrell, Jack Nicholson, Dick Miller, Randy Quaid, James Brown. Aka *Before I Die.* (Paramount)

TAROT. See *Autopsy.*

TARZAN AND THE GREEN GODDESS. Feature/video version of the 1935 serial *The New Adventures of Tarzan* (Hollywood Home Theater).

TARZAN AND THE LOST GODDESS. See *The New Adventures of Tarzan.*

TARZAN IN GUATEMALA. See *The New Adventures of Tarzan.*

TARZAN'S NEW ADVENTURE. See *The New Adventures of Tarzan.*

TARZAN VS. IBM. See *Alphaville.*

TASTE FOR FLESH AND BLOOD, A (1990) ★★ Outer space creature has a thing for human flesh and arterial fluids—in short, a ravenous appetite for mortals. The thing is stalked by a NASA commander. Directed by Warren F. Disbrow. Rubin Santiago, Lori Karz, Tim Ferrante. (Legacy)

TASTE OF BLOOD, A (1967) ★★ Producer-director Herschell Gordon Lewis's updating of the Dracula legend (aka *The Secret of Dr. Alucard,* as written by Donald Stanford) finds a descendant of the count drinking from a flagon of vampire wine. Whom should he seek out and mark for death? Why, the destroyers of his maligned ancestor. Gore specialist Lewis appears in the cast. Bill Rogers, Elizabeth Wilkinson, Otto Schlesinger. One draggin' flagon, this chalice from no palace. (S/Weird)

TASTE OF FEAR. See *Scream of Fear.*

TASTE OF SIN, A. See *Olivia.*

TASTE THE BLOOD OF DRACULA (1970) ★★★ A tooth-bite above most of Hammer's Dracula films of the period, with Christopher Lee again conveying an aura of menace when three gentlemen in search of lust and thrills engage in a bit of satanism, inadvertently resurrecting the long-dead count. These men and their families meet death in horrible albeit traditional vampiric fashion. Dracula, in a genuinely imaginative climax, faces a new form of death in a recently reconstructed church. Above-average direction by Peter Sasdy, with screenwriter John Elder (an alias for producer Anthony Hinds) atoning for the horrible botch he made of *Evil of Frankenstein.* Linda Hayden, Isla Blair, Geoffrey Keen, Michael Ripper, Ralph Bates. (Warner Bros.)

TC 2000 (1993) ★★★ Although set in a futuristic society where criminals are called "breakers" and cops are "trackers," this is your basic martial-arts actioner. But it's a lively one, with a funky set design and well-choreographed battles as two cops are subjected to brutality and a double cross in their "underworld security force" city. Bobbie Phillips is especially effective in a dual role: as an honest cop and later as a rebuilt sexy android. She's such an attractive woman, she distracts your mind from a lot of this film's ugliness and violence. Written with a lot of plot and directed by T. J. Scott, this Canadian film costars Bolo Yeung, Jalal Merhi and Billy Blanks. (Video/Laser: MCA)

TEDDY. See *The Pit.*

TEENAGE CATGIRLS IN HEAT (1991) ★ You'll feel cold for the duration of this low-budget, regionally produced horror nonthriller depicting how the statue of an Egyptian cat goddess transmutes cats into naked women and causes mortals to commit sacrificial suicide while a nerd with cat-hunting equipment runs around the countryside. One scene has it literally raining cats without dogs. Words are inadequate to describe just how awful this piece of trash is. Directed by Scott Perry, who cowrote with Grace Smith. Gary Graves, Carrie Vanston, Dave Cox.

TEENAGE CAVEMAN (1958) ★★ Despite stone-age production values, an inept performance by Robert Vaughn and horrendous music by Albert Glasser, this is salvaged by the direction of Roger Corman and a strangely shaped script by R. Wright Campbell. Vaughn, from a primitive tribe forbidden to trespass where dwells the Monster That Kills with a Touch, enters the taboo zone anyway, where a surprise ending awaits him (but not you—you can see it coming). There is no truth to the rumor this was originally called *I Was a Teenage Caveboy*, although correct alternate titles are *Out of the Darkness* and *Prehistoric World*. Jonathan Haze, Robert Shayne, Frank De Kova, Leslie Bradley. (RCA/Columbia)

TEENAGE DRACULA. See *Dracula vs. Frankenstein* (1971).

TEENAGE EXORCIST (1991) ★★ Scream queen Brinke Stevens wrote and starred in this spoof of *The Exorcist*, which has a few chuckles but most of it lacks spirit. The sexy Stevens portrays a mousy creature who takes possession of a haunted mansion and is turned into a wanton seductress by a horned demon, but there's no way she'll ever pass for a teenager. Although Michael Berryman, Robert Quarry (as a bumbling "Father Karas") and Jay Richardson strive for laughs, the material just isn't there. There's an occasional special effect but the whole thing is halfhearted. Directed by Grant Austin Waldman. Eddie Deezen, Tom Shell, Elena Sahagun. (Video/Laser: Action International)

TEENAGE FRANKENSTEIN. Video version of *I Was a Teenage Frankenstein* (RCA/Columbia).

TEENAGE MONSTER. See *Meteor Monster*.

TEENAGE MUTANT NINJA TURTLES: THE MOVIE (1990) ★★ The comic book series by Kevin Eastman and Peter Laird tapped into mythology with its 4 turtles turned into crime fighters named Raphael, Michelangelo, Donatello and Leonardo, and a Yoda-like philosopher in the form of an intelligent rat named Splinter. Brought to the screen in a live-action movie, these characters become a collection of costumes designed by Jim Henson's Creature Shop, without the distinctive personalities of the comic books. The direction by Steve Barron is dark when it should be light and airy, and the script by Todd W. Langen and Bobby Herbeck lacks the mythological proportions that might have turned this into a *Star Wars*–like classic, and the villain imitates Darth Vader without possessing his memorable qualities. Although a box-office hit when released, this remains a shabby effort, crude when it needed to be smooth, wisecrackish when it needed to have a touch of class. Read the comic books or play the computer games—this is a disappointing addition to the Ninja Turtle phenomenon. Judith Hoag, Elias Koteas, Joch Pais, Michelan Sisti, Leif Tilden, David Forman, Michael Turney. (Family Home Entertainment) (Laser: Image)

TEENAGE MUTANT NINJA TURTLES II: THE SECRET OF THE OOZE (1991) ★ Even worse than its predecessor, this halfhearted, commercially shaped entertainment is for small fry—adults will find it difficult going as the mutant turtles get involved with the music world so that Vanilla Ice, Ya Kid K and Cathy Dennis can perform. Once again the nemesis Shredder is on hand, and the origin of the shell-backed heroes reveals that a mad doctor (David Warner) was responsible for the ooze from which they sprang. Script by Todd W. Langen, directed by Michael Pressman. (RCA/Columbia; New Line) (Laser: Image)

TEENAGE MUTANT NINJA TURTLES III: THE TURTLES ARE BACK . . . IN TIME (1993) ★★★ Those pizza-loving, sewer-dwelling, fun-loving turtlenecks are off on a new adventure, traveling back to 17th-century Japan where they get into a bloody battle with a nobleman waging war against rebels. Most of the script by director Stuart Gillard focuses on slapstick hand-to-hand combat sequences as Raphael, Leonardo, Donatello and Michelangelo slug it out with Caucasian bad guy Stuart Wilson and warlord Sab Shimono, while that lovely newspaperwoman April O'Neil (Paige Turco) watches from the sidelines. Meanwhile, back in Manhattan, Splinter the intellectual rat puts up with the 17th-century behavior of samurai warriors who travel through time in exchange for the turtle guys. Don't ask—it's too complicated to explain. You either dig the silly humor and slam-bang action or you should go to the opera. Elias Koteas, Vivian Wu, Mark Caso, Matt Hill, Jim Raposa, David Fraser, James Murray. (New Line)

TEENAGE PSYCHO MEETS BLOODY MAMA, THE. See *The Incredibly Strange Creatures Who Stopped Living and Became Mixed-up Zombies*.

TEENAGERS FROM OUTER SPACE (1958) ★★ Evil teenage aliens land on Earth in the company of Gargon, a lobster creature that walks on its hind legs and turns to jelly when the good-kid alien aims his Blaster Zap Gun. Strictly for the teenage set, if teenagers can sit through it. It's doubtful adults will want to. Produced-written-directed-photographed-edited by Tom Graeff, who incidentally also did the music score. Aka *The Gargon Terror* and *Invasion of the Gargon*. David Love, Dawn Anderson, Bryan Grant. (Sinister/C; S/Weird; Filmfax)

TEEN ALIEN (1988) ★★ Peter Senelka directed this horror tale in which a group of partygoers gather in an old mill for a Halloween contest, only to discover a nonhuman amidst their ranks.

Dan Harville, Michael Dunn, Vern Adix. (Prism)

TEEN VAMP (1989) ★★ Bitten in the neck by a prostitute, Beau Bishop turns into a traditional bloodsucker taken for granted by all his friends—what's so special about a vampire? Regional low-budget effort, shot in Shreveport, La., flops miserably. Written-directed by Samuel Bradford. Karen Carlson, Angie Brown, Clu Gulager. (New World)

TEEN WITCH (1989) ★ Pallid comedy with musical-dance numbers in the MTV tradition, complete with an object lesson for Robyn Lively, a witch who discovers her powers at age 16 and uses them to become the best-liked girl in school. Steppin' Lively learns the hard way, however, that you shouldn't always get what you want. Some object lesson. Without special effects, this is so lightweight it blows away on a cloud of nothingness. Director Dorian Walker doesn't even bring the dance numbers to life. Zelda Rubinstein is cute as the fortune teller who guides Lively through her magical stages and Shelley Berman is funny as an English teacher, but they can't salvage this broomstick bomb. Dan Gauthier, Joshua Miller, Caren Kaye, Dick Sargent. (Media)

TEEN WOLF (1985) ★★★ Werewolf tale avoids genre clichés and goes for a shaggy twist: underdog teenager Michael J. Fox learns from Dad about his wolfish genealogy and copes with being hairy on the gym floor during a basketball game. In that respect the Joseph Loeb III–Matthew Weisman screenplay is unique, but nothing is done with the premise, beyond Fox fighting within himself for the human half to succeed without resorting to the talents of the wolf, which include break dancing and other physical feats. James Hampton, Scott Paulin, Jerry Levine, Susan Ursitti. Directed by Rod Daniel. (Paramount; Goodtimes) (Laser: Paramount)

TEEN WOLF TOO (1987) ★★ Without the charming presence of Michael J. Fox, this sequel to the 1985 hit is a bore, duplicating the themes of the original without exploring new territory, and presenting a lethargic cast with little to work with. Jason Bateman, portraying Todd Howard, the cousin of the Fox character, turns up at Hamilton U on a sports scholarship but really wants to study. He's sidetracked into exploiting his werewolf abilities to become the most popular, hairiest guy on campus. Eventually he loses the respect of the good people, and has to regain it in a climactic boxing match that tries to recapture the furor of *Rocky*. Director Christopher Leitch is left high and dry with inadequate material by R. Timothy Kring, from a story by *Teen Wolf* creators Joseph Loeb III and Matthew Weisman. Stuck with hopeless roles are Kim Darby (sympathetic science instructor),

John Astin (insidious Dean Dunn), Paul Sand (absurd boxing coach) and James Hampton (hairy Uncle Howard). Wenches Beth Ann Miller and Rachel Sharp provide the shapeliness the rest of the production direly needs. (Paramount)

TEKWAR—THE [ORIGINAL] MOVIE (1993) ★★★½ A fascinating technological world of the future is created in this TV-movie adaptation of the novel by William Shatner in which former cop Jake Cardigan (Greg Evigan) is brought out of cryogenic suspension. To find out who framed him, Cardigan joins forces with super private eye Walter Bascom (Shatner) to find a missing scientist (Barry Morse). A trip through the Internet (controlled by Matrix Police) is one of the highlights of this above-average "virtual reality" effort, which features pulse guns, androids and cyborgs, and a mind-stimulating drug called Tek that blends fantasy and reality. Directed by Shatner, from a script by creative consultant Alfonse Ruggiero, Jr., and Westbrook Claridge, *Tekwar* is a very satisfying mixture of sci-fi and action, and features interesting romantic subplots. Eugene Clark, Sheena Easton (as Warbride, the rebel leader), Torri Higginson, Sonja Smits. (Video/Laser: MCA)

TELEPATHY 2000. See *Scanners*.

TELL-TALE HEART, THE (1960) ★★ Intensely acted, well-photographed British horror film based loosely on Edgar Allan Poe's story. Laurence Payne portrays Poe, who dreams he's Edgar Marsh, a librarian in a French town where he falls in love with flower shop worker Adrienne Corri, a femme fatale who would rather dally with Edgar's best friend (Dermot Walsh). The librarian, crazed with jealousy, murders his friend and places his body under the floorboards in the library. Soon, the exaggerated beating of a heart drives him to madness. There's a very macabre sequence in which Payne cuts out the heart of his victim, holding the still-pumping organ in his bloody hands. A memorable sleeper directed by Ernest Morris and written by Brian Clemens and Elden Howard. Watch for subtle literary clues hinting at the surprise ending. Aka *The Horror Man, Panic* and *Hidden Room of 1000 Horrors*. (Loonic; Sinister/C; S/Weird; Filmfax)

TEMPTER, THE (1974) ★★ Watch Italian director Alberto de Martino's rip-off of *The Exorcist* (made as *The Antichrist*) and you won't eat for a week after seeing: possessed woman gulping down severed head of toad; possessed woman licking up spilt blood; possessed woman regurgitating wine; possessed woman vomiting scrambled eggs; possessed woman spitting up green slime; possessed woman spewing into the face of a relative. All this gooeyness has to do with reincarnation of a witch burnt at the stake hundreds of years ago. Demonic winds, flying furniture, far-flung objects. What the Devil are

Mel Ferrer, Arthur Kennedy and George Coulouris doing in this Anti-Christ catastrophe? (Embassy)

TEMPTRESS (1994) ★★½ A good cast is wasted in a half-baked, unconvincing tale about a beautiful photographer (Kim Delaney) who becomes possessed by the evil spirit of Kali, the Indian goddess of destruction (remember the Thugee gangs of India?). This Playboy movie-for-video, directed by Lawrence Lanoff, strives for artsy-fartsy craftsmanship but comes up empty and pretentious, with a climax in Melissa Mitchell's script that is strictly from hunger. Among the wasted are Chris Saranson as Kim's disbelieving boyfriend, Ben Cross as Dr. Samudaya (an Indian cult expert), Jessica Walter as the helpful psychiatrist and Dee Wallace Stone as a friend whom Delaney rejects. One major fault in this fiasco is that Delaney fails to convey (or even suggest) she is possessed by anything other than the desire to strip down for some steamy love scenes with Saranson. But not even bare breasts and butts will keep your interest. (Video/Laser: Paramount)

TENANT, THE (1976) ★★★ This adaptation of Roland Topol's novel is either a study in paranoia or an old-fashioned ghost story, and it is to the credit of director Roman Polanski that his script (cowritten with Gerard Brach) works either way. Polanski is effective as a repressed Pole who rents a Paris flat and is haunted by the spirit of a woman who committed suicide by leaping from a window into the courtyard below. He also believes that the building's owner (Melvyn Douglas as a curmudgeon) and other tenants are conspiring to drive him crazy. The takeover of his personality includes Polanski going drag—a grotesque image that enhances the film's ambiguities. The buildup is slow albeit fascinating and Polanski captures nuances of character brilliantly. A mosaic of oddball characters is played by Isabelle Adjani, Jo Van Fleet, Lila Kedrova, Claude Dauphin and Shelley Winters. (Paramount)

TENEBRAE. See *Unsane*.

TENTH VICTIM, THE (1965) ★★★ In the 21st century, war has been outlawed and replaced by the Big Hunt, a means of venting aggression wherein citizens are "licensed to kill"—but alternate as hunters and victims. Anyone surviving 10 hunts is guaranteed financial rewards for life. The game idea sprang from the fertile imagination of Robert Sheckley, and under Elio Petri's direction is savagely satirical and suspenseful, with Ursula Andress as a hunter with a loaded bra (we kid you not) and Marcello Mastroianni as her prey. The adaptation is frequently erratic but the chase and ingenious weapons are engrossing. Not to mention Ursula's bod. Elsa Martinelli is also a shapely huntress, enough to make you go *gggrrrrr*. (Embassy)

TEN TO MIDNIGHT (1983) ★★★ Slasher film with hardened cop Charles Bronson, a Dirty Harry of the '80s, distressed when the legal system thwarts him from taking a sex-crazed killer off the streets. He plants incriminating evidence to put the killer away, but his conscience won't allow him to go through with it. The most interesting characters are Andrew Stevens as Bronson's inexperienced partner and Lisa Eilbacher as Bronson's daughter, chief target of the slasher. The killer is chillingly played by Gene Dare (though his motives are obscure); he murders while totally nude. Polished direction by J. Lee Thompson and a honed script by William Roberts make this a standout: Geoffrey Lewis, Wilford Brimley. (Video/Laser: MGM/UA)

TEOREMA (1969) ★★½ Writer-director Pier Paolo Pasolini spins a dark and sometimes baffling allegory about a saintly visitor to Earth (Terence Stamp) who intervenes with everyone in a certain household, affecting the futures of those individuals as each reacts in a seemingly insane way to the intrusion. Silvana Mangano, Massimo Girotti, Laura Betti. Music by Ennio Morricone. (Tapeworm)

TERMINAL. See *Robin Cook's Terminal*.

TERMINAL CHOICE (1982) ★★★½ Riveting medical psychothriller, holding you spellbound as its diabolical murder plot unfolds. Joe Spano's patients are dying at Dodson Medical Clinic in Toronto because someone is programming life-and-death hospital equipment to kill patients. Investigators Diane Venora and Don Francks move in; suspicious-looking doctors and medical red herrings crop up in Neal Bell's script. Climactic scenes of Spano trapped in a hospital bed are exciting. Strange blending of mystery, computerized sci-fi and whodunit. David McCallum portrays the clinic's owner. Directed by Sheldon Larry. Aka *Death Bed*, *Death List*, *Critical List* and *Trauma*. (Vestron)

TERMINAL JUSTICE (1995) ★★½ Routine action shoot-'em-up stuff with virtual-reality special effects and lightweight sci-fi touches thrown in for The Kitchen Sink Effect. Lorenzo Lamas, his hair wild and unruly, plays a cop of the future with infrared eye implants (he lost his sight in the Russian Cartel Wars of 2008) who loses his partner in a bloody shootout and goes on a vengeful rampage to catch Peter Coyote, a maverick genius scientist who has mastered the art of cloning beautiful women from his own DNA—a "biosex" technique—and selling them as prostitutes. Tod Thawley joins the unkempt Lamas by using Cybertech tracking equipment and other futuristic technology. The Wynne McLaughlin-Frederick Bailey script never stops with its gimmicks and director Rick King uses locations that give this vapid movie at least a touch of gloss, if not class. Chris Sarandon, Kari Salin, Barry Flatman.

TERMINAL VIRUS (1995) ★★★½ Among Roger Corman's post-holocaust actioners shot in the Philippines under Cirio H. Santiago, in which roving gangs of men and women in dusty, funky automobiles shoot it out with superweapons, this TV-movie is perhaps the strangest. First, it stars James Brolin, normally not exposed to this genre. And it actually has a modicum of romance between scientist-of-tomorrow Bryan Genesse and female warrior Kehli O'Bryne. And then it has a terrific shoot-out action sequence in an old rock quarry, in which hundreds of Filipino extras are blasted to bits by women equipped with rocket launchers and submachine guns. Some feminine wiles. Brolin, as an Irishman named McCabe, brings a tongue-in-cheek wise-guy quality to his rather limited role (the script by Joe Sprosty, Jeff Pulice and Daniella Purcell is hardly concerned with character arc). The minimal plot is set in a desert world where sex between man and woman leads to instant death. Only Genesse's snake serum can save mankind from doom. The rest of it is shoot-'em-up with the bad guys led by Richard Lynch, whose only contribution is the use of a mini–rocket launcher strapped to his wrist. Elena Sahagun, Susan Africa, Nikki Fritz. Directed by Dan Golden as a protégé of Santiago. (New Horizons)

TERMINATOR, THE (1984) ★★★★½ One of the best action movies of the '80s, blending fantasy with horror and suspense to create an incredibly satisfying viewing experience. Arnold Schwarzenegger portrays a humanoid robot from A.D. 2029, a time when man has been conquered by robot machines. Schwarzie travels back to present day to assassinate a young woman; one day she will give birth to a child who will overthrow the robot society. The machine-killer begins a cold-blooded reign of terror to find the woman, killing anyone in his way. The pacing is relentless as the intended victim (Linda Hamilton) flees with Michael Biehn's help. James Cameron directs with a real sense for pace, and the script by Cameron and producer Gale Anne Hurd not only has an abundance of action but even works in a relevant love story. Stan Winston's effects are wonderfully graphic; the whole thing is one big success. Schwarzenegger's simple line, "I'll be back," is a classic. Paul Winfield, Lance Henriksen, Rick Rossovich, Dick Miller, Earl Boen. (HBO; Hemdale) (Laser: HBO; Hemdale; Image)

TERMINATOR 2: JUDGMENT DAY (1991) ★★★★½ A blockbuster classic of high-tech bravura, a worthy follow-up to the 1984 classic and a trendsetting epic in terms of its special-effects razzle-dazzle. Arnold Schwarzenegger is back as the cyborg-man from the future, only this time programmed not to kill, but to rescue important individuals from being terminated by his adversary, an advanced form of cyborg-man (Robert Patrick) whose liquid-metal components enable him to change shape and to form parts of his body into lethal weapons. The computerized metamorphosis effects are stunning as T-1000 enters the present timestream to assassinate Linda Hamilton (back as Sarah Connor, the role she created in *Terminator*) and her son John Connor (Edward Furlong). This is one terrific action film, its formula already established by producer-director James Cameron, who cowrote with William Wisher. Medals for the creators of the metal man, Stan Winston and Dennis Muren. Earl Boen, Joe Morton, S. Epatha Merkerson, Castulo Guerra. (Video/Laser: Live)

TERMINATOR 2: JUDGMENT DAY–SPECIAL EDITION (1991). Pioneer/Carolco laserdisc with 15 minutes of new material.

TERRIBLE QUICK SWORD OF SIEGFRIED. See *Long, Swift Sword of Siegfried.*

TERRIBLE SECRET OF DR. HICHCOCK, THE. See *The Horrible Dr. Hichcock.*

TERROR, THE (1963) ★★★ History of this Roger Corman tricky quickie is more fascinating than the film: After finishing *The Raven*, Corman realized Boris Karloff owed him 2 days' work, so he fashioned a script and filmed Karloff's scenes back to back. Later, Francis Ford Coppola, Monte Hellman, Jack Hill and Dennis Jacob added new scenes. No wonder the Jack Hill–Leo Gordon script seems disjointed. Napoleonic officer Jack Nicholson (who directed some scenes) pursues ghostly Sandra Knight into a seacliff mansion owned by Karloff. Supporting players: Jonathan Haze, Dick Miller. Some footage of Karloff was also used in *Targets*. Aka *Castle of Terror* and *Lady of the Shadows*. (World Video; Goodtimes; Genesis; Prism; S/Weird; Filmfax; Sinister/C)

TERROR. Video version of *Shock Chamber* (North American).

TERROR (1973). See *Dr. Frankenstein's Castle of Freaks.*

TERROR AT LONDON BRIDGE. Video of *Bridge Across Time* (Charles Fries).

TERROR AT RED WOLF INN, THE (1972) ★★★ Young woman is lured to a seaside inn for an all-expenses-paid holiday, only to discover the elderly couple running the place is into cannibalism, as is their retarded son. Allen J. Actor's script has tongue-in-cheek subtleties and keeps horror visuals limited to PG. Only the nihilistic ending will leave one feeling let down. Otherwise, a good scare job, a tame *Texas Chainsaw Massacre*. Director Bud Townsend does an okay job, but don't make reservations at the Red Wolf. The food tastes strange there. Originally made as *Folks at the Red Wolf Inn*. Linda Gillin, Arthur Space, Mary Jackson. (Academy; from Cougar as *Terror on the Menu*; from Vogue as *Terror House*; from Electric as *Club Dead*)

TERROR AT THE OPERA (1987) ★★★ Writer-producer-director Dario Argento is back in action as Europe's premiere horror filmmaker, this time setting his macabre machinations in an opera house where a singer becomes the target for a diabolical serial killer. It's a bloody good show Argento offers. Cristina Marsillach, Ian Charleson, Daria Nicolodi. Aka *Opera*. (From South Gate in rated and unrated versions) (Laser: Japanese)

TERROR BEACH. Variant video version of *Night of the Death Cult*, a desert hermit with a mother fixation who kidnaps stranded women.

TERROR CASTLE (1973). See *Dr. Frankenstein's Castle of Freaks*.

TERROR CIRCUS (1973) ★½ The humiliation of women reaches an all-time exploitation low in this first-feature effort from director Alan Rudolph, who went on to direct major Hollywood features, including the cattle-mutilation thriller *Endangered Species*. (He made this under the alias of Gerald Comier.) This has no redeeming values in depicting depraved Andrew Prine, a desert hermit with a mother fixation who kidnaps stranded women and ties them up in his barn. He treats Manuella Thiess, Sherry Alberoni and Sheila Bradley like animals in a circus zoo, making them perform despicable acts. Out in the toolshed, meanwhile, there's a mutated monster (caused by Nevada nuclear tests) that likes to break out and kill. Aka *Nightmare Circus*. (Regal; from Showcase Productions Inc. as *Barn of the Naked Dead*)

TERROR CREATURES FROM THE GRAVE (1965) ★★ Lackluster Italian chiller has the presence of Barbara Steele but not the presence of mind to tell a compelling story, or provide genuine scares. Instead, you're handed nonsense about a terrible plague and how victims are summoned from the dead to avenge an occultist. The photography is okay but, gee, what lousy direction by coproducer Ralph Zucker (aka Massimo Pupillo). Sure cure for insomnia. Walter Brandi, Marilyn Mitchell, Alfredo Rizzi. Aka *The Tombs of Horror, Five Graves for a Medium* and *Coffin of Terror*. (Sinister/C; S/Weird; Filmfax)

TERROR EYES. See *Night School*.

TERROR EYES (1987) ★★½ Supernatural comedy in which the Devil sends a sycophant to help an advertising agent write a horror screenplay. Vivian Schilling stars and wrote the screenplay (with the Devil's help?). Directed by Eric Parkinson. Lance August, Daniel Roebuck, Vivian Schilling, Dan Bell. (Action International)

TERROR FACTOR. See *Scared to Death* (1946).

TERROR FROM THE SUN. See *The Hideous Sun Demon*.

TERRORGRAM (1990) ★★★ Horror trilogy about revenge, with tales ranging from the absurd to the serious, and getting better each time. The mastermind here is producer-director Stephen M. Kienzle. The morality yarns are bridged with narration by the Voice of Retribution (James Earl Jones)—written as a poor man's Rod Serling imitation—and with the appearance in each story of a messenger from Hell wearing a lightning bolt on his cap. "Heroine Overdose," cranked out by Kienzle and Donna M. Matson, is the farcical tale of a movie director (played as a bastard by Jerry Anderson) named Alan Smithee (the alias used by real-life unhappy directors). Smithee, maker of *Cycle Maniacs* and *Driller*, mistreats the women in his life (especially the actresses) and finds himself detoured onto Elm Street. It's played for laughs and has less effect than the next 2 yarns. "Pandora" (written by Kienzle) depicts TV anchorwoman Angela Pandoras (Linda Carol Toner) when she strikes down a boy with her car and flees. She gets hers through a Pandora's Box substitute, and it's rather effective. The best of the tales is "Veteran's Day," focusing on dirty rat Eric Keller (J. T. Wallace) and how a Vietnam casualty he once offended places Keller on the battlefield to learn the true meaning of war. (Monarch)

TERROR HOSPITAL. Video version of *Beyond the Living* (Marathon).

TERROR HOUSE. Video version of *The Terror at Red Wolf Inn* (Vogue).

TERROR IN THE AISLES (1984) ★★★ Compilation of shock scenes from horror, sci-fi and crime movies. Some are from classy or classic movies while others were lifted from schlock. In short, a hodgepodge that has moments of intensity, as when we relive Hitchcock's *Psycho* and *Strangers on a Train*. Other films: Carpenter's *The Thing, Suspiria, When a Stranger Calls, Nighthawks, The Exorcist, Rosemary's Baby* and *Dressed to Kill*. The cassette version has more gore than the TV version. Compiled by Andrew Kuehn and Stephen Netburn. (MCA)

TERROR IN THE CRYPT (1963) ★★½ Christopher Lee heads the cast of this Spanish-Italian supernatural yarn that approaches its subject leisurely, in a sincere effort to build suspense and atmosphere, and to pay homage to J. Sheridan Le Fanu's *Carmilla*. Lee, a nobleman who fears his daughter is possessed by a witch, invites occult experts to his castle to observe her behavior. Several murders occur before the demon is exorcised. Directed by Thomas Miller (real name: Camillo Mastrocinque). José Campos, Vera Valmont. Aka *Cartharsis, Crypt of Horror, The Karnstein Curse, The Crypt of the Vampire, The Vampire's Crypt, Karnstein, The Crypt and the Nightmare, Carmilla* and *The Curse of the Karnsteins*. Stop it, already. (Baker; S/Weird)

TERROR IN THE FOREST. See *The Forest*.

TERROR IN THE SWAMP (1985) ★★ Poachers' Cave, now there's a place to steer clear of, I'm warnin' ya. Seems folks 'round Houma, Louisiana, are turnin' up plumb dead. Course, the reason's mighty clear, them local scientists tamperin' with the nutria water rodent 'n' all, and danged if they didn't go create a giant mootation rat. Reckon 'twern't gonna scare ya too much 'cause it's just one-a-them extras in a hairy suit. Dad rat it. Soon's that picture wrapped, folks ran that Joe Catalanotto and his'n crew 'n' scribblers Terry Hebb 'n' Martin Folse smack outta town and told 'em and them high-falutin' actors, Billy Holliday, Chuck Long and Michael Tedesco, quit givin' us swamp folks a bad name or next time we'll sic them gators 'n' cot'n moccasins on you city slickers, hot damn gotohell. Did y'all know it was to be called *Nutriaman: The Copasaw Creature*? Gertrude, hand me my shotgun! (New World) (Laser: New World; Image)

TERROR IN THE WOODS. See *The Forest*.

TERROR IN TOYLAND (1980) ★★ Is nothing sacred? This, the first of the killer Santa Claus movies that set the stage for the *Silent Night, Deadly Night* series, is the ultimate in crass commercialism and execrable exploitation. The world's first killing Kris Kringle is "an emotional cripple"—a sexually repressed worker at the Jolly Dream Toy Company. He's haunted by 1947 memories of his mother being fondled by Santa at the Christmas tree. Keeping records on which children are naughty or nice, he flips out and takes his bag of goodies into the world. To kiddies he delivers gifts—to adults, death. The only memorable sequence has Santa pursued down an alley by angry citizens carrying torches—homage to *Frankenstein*. But there's no depth to the killer's characterization and writer-director Lewis Jackson never pulls it all together. And the final scene is outrageously out of place in a pseudostudy of a murderer. Brandon Maggart, Jeffrey DeMunn, Dianne Hull, Andy Fenwick. Aka *You Better Watch Out*. (Academy; from Saturn as *Christmas Evil*)

TERROR IS A MAN (1959) ★★★ The first in the Filipino-produced "Blood Island" series, in which impassioned mad doctor Francis Lederer conducts experiments in his lab that turn a man into a leopard (tiger?) creature. To Lederer's island comes shipwreck survivor Richard Derr, an engineer who falls for the doc's attractive wife, curvaceous Greta Thyssen, whose sexuality creates a tension. This film is reminiscent of *The Creature Walks Among Us* in its sympathetic portrayal of the misunderstood beast and the way the shoreline scenes are photographed. Despite a poor monster design, this film is not without interest when human conflict is aroused. Codirected by Gerry (Gerardo) de Leon and Eddie Romero from a Harry Paul Harber script.

Oscar Keesee, Lilia Duban. Aka *The Gory Creatures* and *Creature from Blood Island*. (Filmfax; Sinister/C; S/Weird; on video as *Blood Creature*)

TERROR OF DRACULA. See *Nosferatu* (1922).

TERROR OF DR. CHANEY, THE. See *Mansion of the Doomed*.

TERROR OF DR. HICHCOCK. More complete video version of *The Horrible Dr. Hichcock* (Sinister/C; Duravision; Filmfax).

TERROR OF DR. MABUSE, THE. See *The Testament of Dr. Mabuse*.

TERROR OF GODZILLA, THE. See *Godzilla's Revenge*.

TERROR OF MECHAGODZILLA (1975) ★★ Giant robot monster attacks Earth, realizing the Green Planet isn't going to be a pushover when fire-snorting Godzilla shows up, slamming his tail in anger. Also involved in this Japanese mishmash (along with the kitchen sink) are mechanized cyborgs, Ghidrah, Ebirah, Rodan and a bird monster, Chitanoceras. Godzilla's creator, Inoshiro Honda, directed. This sequel to *Godzilla vs. the Cosmic Monster* was 15th in the series. Aka *The Escape of Megagodzilla*, *Revenge of Mechagodzilla* and *Monsters from the Unknown Planet*. Katsuhiko Sasaki, Tomoke Ai. (Paramount) (Laser: Japanese)

TERROR OF SHEBA. See *The Graveyard*.

TERROR OF THE DEEP. See *Destination Inner Space*.

TERROR OF THE DOLL. Video of the Karen Black episode from *Tales of Terror* (MPI).

TERROR OF THE MAD DOCTOR. Video version of *The Testament of Dr. Mabuse* (S/Weird).

TERROR OF THE MUMMY. See *The Mummy* (1959).

TERROR OF THE SHE WOLF. Video version of *Legend of the Wolf Woman* (Mogul).

TERROR OF THE SNAKE WOMAN, THE. See *The Snake Woman*.

TERROR ON ALCATRAZ (1987) ★½ Aldo Ray is terrible as an ex-convict who burns a cigarette into his girl's chest before he turns killer and razors a retired guard's throat. Then he heads for Alcatraz, where the key to a fortune in stolen money is waiting in Cell #146—but to get it he must cut through a crowd of young people having a party on the island. Ray (playing Frank Morris, a real-life convict who escaped from the island in 1962) meat-cleavers a man in the forehead, drowns a female guard in a vat and generally behaves in an antisocial fashion. This instant video nonclassic has crummy lighting, bad acting and unbelievable behavior. And you see "the Island of Pelicans" in San Francisco Bay in all its touristic decay. Blame the dumb writing on Donald Lewis and the cruddy direction on Marvin G. Lipschultz. Veronica Porsche Ali, Scott Ryder. (Trans World)

TERROR ON BLOOD ISLAND. See *Brides of the Beast*.

TERROR ON TAPE (1983) ★★★ Compilation of grisly scenes from horror and sci-fi exploitation films—we're talking Gross City, folks. Clips are frameworked around video store owner Cameron Mitchell (resembling a ghoul) as he greets customers (a nerd, a macho construction worker, a sexpot in a revealing outfit) and pushes the sickening merchandise. Scenes are from *Vampire Hookers, Return of the Alien's Deadly Spawn, Bloodtide, Cathy's Curse, Frozen Scream, Alien Prey, Color Me Blood Red* and *2000 Maniacs*. You'll see baby alien monsters eat a human head, a hatchet sink into a brain, hairy hands strangle a father in a confessional booth, a needle plunge into an eye, a human arm severed, a boulder dropped on a woman's chest, impaling by pitchfork, a scalping, ad nauseum. For strong stomachs only, and we mean strong! The wraparound was directed by Robert A. Worms III and features Michelle Bauer as the hot tamale let's-romp chick. (Continental)

TERROR ON THE MENU. Video version of *The Terror at Red Wolf Inn* (Cougar; Lettuce Entertain You).

TERROR ON TOUR (1980) ★★ Don Edmonds, noted for his sadistic films about Nazi commandant Ilsa, helmed this minor-league psychoslasher flick in which the stabber runs around murdering prostitutes while dressed as a member of a hard-rock group, the Clowns. It's up to the real Clowns to make fools of themselves while tracking the killer. Mainly an excuse for an abundance of feebly produced rock footage as the amateurish cast misses every beat of Del Lekus's script. Rick Styles, Chip Greeman, Rich Pemberton, Lisa Rodriguez. (Media)

TERROR STRIKES, THE. See *War of the Colossal Beast*.

TERROR TRAIN (1980) ★★ Unsavory college kids, holding a masquerade party on a speeding train, are knocked off one by one by a knife-wielding maniac. Muddled characters make it difficult to swallow the preposterous action. The only exciting moments come when Jamie Lee Curtis, scream queen from *Halloween*, is pursued by the killer through the train. Ben Johnson as the sympathetic conductor and magician David Copperfield are derailed by one lousy script, as is director Roger Spottiswoode. Aka *Train of Terror*. (Key) (Laser: CBS/Fox)

TERRORVISION (1986) ★★ Failed comedy satire from producer Charles Band and writer-director Ted Nicolaou. It's a lowbrow insult when a garbage-collecting alien on Pluton accidentally jettisons a monster into space, which comes to Earth on a lightning bolt and enters a home through its TV screens. The monster, designed by John Buechler, is a gross thing with big teeth and a long tongue and it hogs the camera too long. Folks in the invaded home are a swinging couple (Mary Woronov, Gerrit Graham), a militant grandfather (Bert Remsen) and an obnoxious kid (Chad Allen). An Elvira clone, Medusa, is wasted. Made in Italy. Music by Richard Band. (Lightning)

TERROR WITHIN, THE (1989) ★★½ Another crank-out job from Roger Corman's copycat factory—this time the Chestburster from *Alien* and the suspenseful corridor sequences from *Aliens* are imitated but never surpassed. The setting is a subterranean research station in the Mojave Desert after most of mankind has been wiped out by a virus. Ugly mutations rove the desert, one of them penetrating the security of the laboratory run by George Kennedy, Andrew Stevens (armed with a crossbow, and accompanied by his real-life dog Butch), Terri Treas and Starr Andreeff. The gargoyle monster (designed by Dean Jones) is a disappointing example of a man in a rubber suit. Granted, the climax yields harrowing chase sequences, but the script by Thomas McKelvey Cleaver remains derivative and Thierry Notz's direction is journeyman but hardly inspired. John Lafayette, Tommy Hinchley. (MGM/UA)

TERROR WITHIN II, THE (1990) ★★ Andrew Stevens, star of the first *Terror Within*, reprises his crossbow-packing hero and steps in as writer-director, performing as well as, if not better than, his predecessors. It's pretty much the same old stuff when those "grotesque genetic mutations" penetrate the underground research lab of R. Lee Ermery to carry out the usual killings. This also has the mutations raping women, an ugly birth sequence and the suspenseful battles in the corridors. There isn't anything you haven't seen before in this post-Armageddon world, but undemanding fans will find it an adequate time killer. Stella Stevens (Andrew's mom) portrays a lab assistant. Burton "Bubba" Gilliam, Clare Hoak, Chick Vennera. (Vestron)

TESTAMENT (1983) ★★★★ Powerful antiwar film, depicting in low-key fashion the aftereffects of nuclear holocaust. Hamelin is a small California community beyond the major blast area. However, gamma rays, radiation and fallout take their toll. Focus is on a mother and 4 children (father William Devane is away at the time) as she clutches for hope while despair grows around her. No devastation, no blood and only a few corpses wrapped in sheets—yet this is a gut-wrenching picture. Based on a short-short story by Carol Amen (who says the idea came to her in a vision), scripted by John Sacre Young, and produced by Jonathan Bernstein and Lynne Littman (she also directed) for PBS. Jane Alexander is outstanding as the mother fighting to hold family together. William Devane is strong in the brief father role. Mako, Leon Ames and Lurene Tuttle appear in cameos. Lukas Haas, Clete Roberts. (Video/Laser: Paramount)

TESTAMENT OF DR. MABUSE, THE (1933)
★★★ In this sequel to Fritz Lang's 1922 *Dr. Mabuse, The Gambler*, the evil genius (Rudolf Klein-Rogge) dies broken and alone in an asylum. But the head of the sanitorium becomes infected with Mabuse's megalomania. Shrewd inspector Lohmann (from Lang's *M*, also played by Otto Wernicke) tracks the surrogate criminal. Atmosphere, suspense, social melodrama in the best Lang tradition. Oscar Beregi, Karl Meixner, Theodor Loos. Aka *The Last Will of Dr. Mabuse*. Remade in 1962 as part of a continuing West German series that kicked off with *The Thousand Eyes of Dr. Mabuse*. (International Collection; from Sinister/C and Filmfax as *The Crimes of Dr. Mabuse*)

TESTAMENT OF DR. MABUSE, THE (1962) ★★
Second in a series of West German remakes based on Fritz Lang's early films about a math genius who turns his intellect to crimes against humanity. Confined to an asylum, Dr. Mabuse works his devilish schemes through hypnosis and other acts of terror carried out by henchmen—even after his demise. Hardly up to the quality of Lang's version, yet a sincere attempt by director Werner Klinger and screenwriters Ladislas Fodor and R. A. Stemmle. Wolfgang Preiss is the doctor, Walter Rilla is in charge of the asylum and Gert Frobe is the cop after Mabuse. Senta Berger, Helmut Schmid. Aka *Terror of the Mad Doctor*. (Sinister/C; LSVideo Inc.)

TEST TUBE TEENS FROM THE YEAR 2000 (1993) ★★ Sorry, no sex is allowed by a ruling corporation in the year 2000, a deficient fact of life that causes 3 teenagers to travel back in time to change history. Two of them (Ian Abercrombie and Brian Bremer) pose as girls at the Carmella Swales School for Girls, which is run by a beautiful but cold fish (Morgan Fairchild). After the renegades comes Lex-500 (Don Dowe), an android that tries to be a comedic Terminator (but without much luck). This low-budget hogwash (written by Kenneth J. Hall), first made as *Virgin Hunters*, is an innocuous piece of crap with naked girls taking a shower being the high point of action. It was directed by Ellen Cabot who is really David DeCoteau. Under either name, he's made a very lousy movie that doesn't even halfheartedly try to be funny. Michelle Matheson, Sara Suzanne Brown, Laurel Wiley, Tamara Tohill. (Video/Laser: Paramount/Full Moon)

TETSUO:THE IRON MAN (1988) ★★★ The spirit of the cinema of the grotesque, established by David Lynch and David Cronenberg, lives anew in this Japanese novelty that epitomizes the cyber-punk movement in film and music. Filmmaker Shinya Tsukamoto is either a genius or a madman, and his bizarre movie will either turn you on or sicken you. This is a disturbing yet fascinating treatise on man's phobia of the metals he forges and the out-of-control machines he creates. A taxi driver turns into a misshapen hunk of metal (or is he imagining the transmutation?) made up of tubes, wires, gears, cables, steel tentacles and a whirring drill for a penis. The imagery of the transformation is horrendous, making this unsuitable for the squeamish, especially sequences dealing with Iron Man's sexual interludes. One is reminded of *Godzilla* movies, the torn face of Schwarzenegger in *The Terminator*, and the Japanese obsession with atom-bomb wounds—which some footage seems to duplicate. Way, way out, so brace yourself or you might bolt. (Fox Lorber) (Laser: Image)

TETSUO II: BODY HAMMER (1992) ★½ Another gory body-mutilation marathon from Japan's Shinya Tsukamoto, who wrote-coproduced-directed-photographed this sequel to *Tetsuo: The Iron Man*. Tokyo resident Tomoroh Taguchi is kidnapped by psychopath skinheads and transforms into a cyberman. Gross.

TEXAS CHAINSAW MASSACRE, THE (1974) ★★★★ Strictly an exercise in exploitation, but done with such grotesque style that it now stands as a cult classic in American Grand Guignol. Nowadays it might seem tame but in its day it was controversial, so cruel and sick seemed its macabre touches. Marilyn Burns establishes new screaming records as she is pursued through an orchard by a madman eager to sink his teeth into her neck—the teeth of his chainsaw, that is. Poor Marilyn. She's bound and gagged, beaten, cut with a razor blade, shoved into a canvas sack and forced to sit in an armchair made of real arms. The family of sick characters is played for grotesque comedy. Directed by that mild-mannered sentimentalist Tobe Hooper. Kim Henkel cowrote with Hooper. Gunnar Hanse plays the crazy guy with the buzzing saw. Two sequels followed. Allen Danziger, Paul Partain. (Video Treasures; Wizard; Media) (Laser: Vestron; so-called definitive director's version from Elite Entertainment)

TEXAS CHAINSAW MASSACRE 2, THE (1986) ★★★ Lawman Lefty Enright (Dennis Hopper), brother of one of the victims of the first film, tracks the chainsaw killers using radio disc jockey Stretch (Caroline Williams) as bait. Director Tobe Hooper's new cut-and-tear adventures of the Sawyer family comprise one odd movie—a hip, flip comment on various American mania, personified by the return of Leatherface (chainsaw-whacking specialist), Chop-Top (the idiot with a metal plate in his head) and Grandpa, still trying to hit victims over the head with a sledgehammer, but usually missing. Hooper captures a macabre humor from L. M. Kit Carson's groovy albeit simplistic script, which turns to surreal horror once Stretch is trapped in the underground caverns of an abandoned tourist attraction. Hooper turns Grand Guignol into farce and sociological subtext, and Hopper is a standout with chainsaws strapped to his side like six-shooters. Gory, not for the squeamish, but the satire makes it a must-see. (Media) (Laser: Image)

TEXAS CHAINSAW MASSACRE 3. See *Leatherface: The Texas Chainsaw Massacre III.*

TEXAS CHAINSAW MASSACRE: THE NEXT GENERATION (1994) ★★ Originally entitled *The Return of the Texas Chainsaw Massacre,* this was not released into the home video market until 1998, which tells you something right there. In recapturing the madness and mayhem of the demented, homicidal Sawyer family, writer-director Kim Henkel provides some expected thrills: the crazed Leatherface (Robert Jacks) chasing a damsel-in-distress (Renee Zellweger) through a forest; beautiful women hanging from hooks; the Sawyer house littered with horror props; a dinner table with half the "diners" propped up dead. (From Tonie Perenski he gets the best performance, as she portrays the Sawyer craziness with a touch of tongue-in-cheek class.) However, Henkel stresses certain cruelties to the extreme, making the film frequently difficult to watch. Such as when "W" (Joe Stevens) uses an electric cattle prod to stun Ms. Zellweger repeatedly; or when the absolutely bonkers Vilmer (Matthew McConaughey) crushes Lisa Newmeyer by stomping on her head. Or when Vilmer runs over a body with his truck—and returns for more passes. Two problems prevent this movie from being fulfilling even to die-hard *Chainsaw* freakos: Henkel sets up situations and gimmicks without climactic payoff, and he turns the ending into a baffling metaphysical exercise. Two men in suits, who could be the Devil and a minion, show up. As if they had endowed the Sawyers with their madness as a kind of experiment. Whatever it's all about, it doesn't belong in this politically incorrect series. Does Henkel think he's making an art movie? Pretentious, pal, pretentious. Which may be why your movie sat on a shelf for four years. (Video/DVD: Columbia TriStar)

T-FORCE (1994) ★★★ A terrific, well-edited action picture with stupendous explosions, car chases and other pyrotechnical special effects as futuristic cop Jack Scalia (in a role he makes fun to watch) goes after a gang of cybernauts (known as Terminal Force) who, upon hearing they will be discontinued, rebel against their laboratory creators and go on a killing spree of major proportions. It's swiftly and ably directed by Richard Pepin (who coproduced with Joseph Merhi) and includes a siege on an office building that is a masterful piece of action. Jacobsen Hart's script is lively, with just enough characterizations to pull you into the action-packed story. Scalia, also an associate producer, is a

kick as he runs through rubble and ruin with an oversized automatic. Erin Gray, Evan Lurie, Bobby Johnston, Deron McBee, Vernon Wells, Jennifer MacDonald. (PM Entertainment) (Laser: Image)

THEATER OF BLOOD (1972) ★★★ Macabre black comedy (similar to the Dr. Phibes series with its sick jokes and bloodletting) with Vincent Price as ham Shakespearean actor Edward Lionheart, who so murders scenes from the classics that London's critics murder him in the press. The "murdering" becomes literal when Lionheart has his revenge against the critics and murders them with the help of a band of bums (the true identity of which will surprise you). Death devices are borrowed from Shakespeare, a clever touch to Anthony Greville-Bell's script. Death's labor found, you might say. Diana Rigg, Jack Hawkins, Harry Andrews, Coral Browne, Diana Dors, Robert Morley, Michael Hordern, Dennis Price. Jolly good horror from director Douglas Hickox. Aka *Much Ado About Murder.* (MGM/UA) (Laser: Image)

THEATRE OF DEATH (1967) ★★½ Whodunit-horror story with slasher overtones. Parisian theater presenting Grand Guignol is site of several murders committed by a ghoul or vampire. Could it be that Christoper Lee, head of the troupe, is responsible? Don't count on it, as there are a few surprises. Samuel Gallu directed. Lelia Goldoni, Julian Glover, Jenny Till, Ivor Dean. Aka *The Blood Fiend* and *The Female Fiend.* (VCI; Republic; Sinister/C)

THEM! (1954) ★★★★★ "Giant bug" movies of the '50s tended to be cheapjack affairs, but not this Warner Bros. classic, which holds up as a sci-fi thriller and as a chase-suspense-mystery story, wonderfully concocted by screenwriter Ted Sherdemann and George W. Yates. Director Gordon Douglas captures a maximum of atmosphere in this taut tale of mutant ants (12 feet high) terrorizing the New Mexico desert near the Alamogordo atomic test sites. Superior effects by Ralph Ayers will convince you those giant ants are real and attacking! Intriguing chase to track down the queen and destroy her nest leads to the L.A. sewers—more opportunity for Douglas to build suspense as armies of men move into the slimy tubes. Edmund Gwenn is the aging expert in myrmecology, the science of ants; heroes are James Arness and James Whitmore, with Joan Weldon as Gwenn's daughter, who's also a scientist. William Schallert, Onslow Stevens, Dub Taylor, Leonard Nimoy, Fess Parker. (Video/Laser: Warner Bros.)

THEM (1996) ★★½ This Stephen Cannell TV movie for the UPN network, not to be confused with the 1954 killer-ants classic, is pulp-magazine sci-fi at best, but there's enough weird atmosphere and wisecracking dialogue to make it bearable. A race of ugly extraterrestrials (spearheaded by Tony Todd in a look-alike "Candyman" role) has invaded the mountain-lake town of Whitney and turned many of its citizens into minions (mainly by sticking alien worms down their ears). Others are put into E.T. sacs and hung up in a cave, awaiting further developments. A handful of untainted humans (a scientist, a teenager, a diner operator) finally get wise and band together to wipe out the aliens. The ending suggests this was made for a series that never got past the pilot. (New World)

THEN THE SCREAMING STARTS. See *And Now the Screaming Starts*.

THEODORE REX (1996) ★ A disaster of the highest order, a flop of the lowest degree. Why Whoopi Goldberg would star in a movie in which dinosaurs live in our futuristic society, and one of them is her "grid cop" partner, defies explanation. "Theodore Rex" is a bumbling fool with an idiot's voice, so there's nothing at stake to begin with, and there's nowhere but nowhere for writer-director Jonathan Betuel to go—except into the toilet. This hodgepodge of futuristic sets and hardware, like Whoopi's participation, defies description. Maybe it's so bad it's good, but for most of us it's going to be so bad it's just plain awful. Do they come any worse than this? It's doubtful. Move over, Ed Wood, Betuel is here to keep you company. Armin Mueller-Stahl, Bud Court, Juliet Landau, Stephen McHattie, George Newbern, Carol Kane. (Video/Laser: New Line)

THERE IS A NAME FOR EVIL. See *A Name for Evil*.

THERE'S NOTHING OUT THERE (1991) ★★ An outright spoof on teenager slasher and monster flicks, in which writer-director Rolfe Kanefsky makes fun of all the *Friday the 13th* and *Alien* clichés by depicting a gang of kids in a mountain cabin being subjected to the horrors of a creature from another world—a slimy thing that has the ability to send out a laser beam from its eyeballs that makes humans satisfy its needs. One of the characters is always referring to what these monsters are like in the movies, and uses this lore to outwit the beast. Genre fans should enjoy it the most, since they are more apt to be clued into things than a layviewer. Layviewers should just lay down and forget it. Craig Peck, Wendy Bednarz, Mark Collver, Bonnie Bowers, John Carhart III. (Prism) (Laser: Image)

THERE'S SOMETHING OUT THERE. Video version of *Day of the Animals* (Vidmark).

THEY (1993) ★★★½ A loosely based, updated version of one of the best ghost stories written by Rudyard Kipling, this TV-movie is a heartfelt, emotion-wracked family drama in which father Patrick Bergen, so griefstricken over the car-accident death of his daughter Nikki (Nancy Moore Atchison), begins to fall apart and becomes driven to find out the mys-tery behind the strange children he sees on the grounds of an old Southern plantation where aging matriarch Vanessa Redgrave lives. There's a sublime, ethereal quality to John Korty's direction and a mistiness to Hiro Narita's cinematography that gives this ghost tale a Jamesian twist in modern dressing. The script by Edithe Swensen deals with the conflicts between Bergen and wife Valerie Mahaffey, and is not afraid to cross over into the supernatural realm where the children, "souls, spirits in transit," become frightening spectral images, especially the Owl Girl in white. A subtle, thoughtful ghost story. Rutanya Alda, Ken Strong, Brandlyn Whitaker. Aka *They Watch*. (RCA/Columbia)

THEY CAME FROM ANOTHER WORLD. Original production title of *Invasion of the Body Snatchers* (1956).

THEY CAME FROM WITHIN (1975) ★★★★ One of the best of the disgusting zombie-gore movies in the wake of *Night of the Living Dead*, and one of the best samplings of grue from Canadian writer-director David Cronenberg. Produced by Ivan Reitman, it has the atmosphere of George Romero and a touch of *Alien* before *Alien* was made, and qualifies as a trendsetting film. Residents of the Starliner Towers housing unit in Montreal are subjected to wormlike parasites that turn them into sexually lusting monsters. Its sick humor, ghastly murders and oddball sexual encounters as the high-rise dwellers are taken over and turn on their neighbors with hearty sexual appetites. There are great scenes of the worm creatures popping out of bodies or jumping into mouths, a chilling bathtub sequence, and an unrelenting sense of chaotic horror. Strong stomachs and a sense of humor are prerequisites for this bloody classic. Aka *Shivers, Frissons* and *The Parasite Murders*. Paul Hampton, Barbara Steele, Joe Silver, Lynn Lowry, Allan Migicovsky. (Vestron)

THEY LIVE (1988) ★★★ Ray Faraday Nelson's famous short story "Eight O'Clock in the Morning" served as the inspiration for this John Carpenter–masterminded sci-fi action film, which takes the idea that aliens have infiltrated our society and hypnotized us not to see them. But writer Frank Armitage (is this an alias for Carpenter?) broadens the idea into a statement about how we were conditioned to be automatons by the Reagan Administration in a declining society where the middle class is becoming poorer. Hence, the first half hour of this is compelling, with director Carpenter framing a tent city on the outskirts of L.A. against the high rises of downtown. (He conveyed a similarly stark view of L.A. in *Prince of Darkness*.) And professional wrestler Rowdy Roddy Piper, in his first legit acting role, seems an interesting character, a laconic construction worker caught up in social deprivation. The shooting starts when

George Nada (Piper), by wearing special glasses, discovers half the population is made up of aliens who wear their skeletal makeup outside their bodies. From then on it's downhill as Piper goes through adventures to destroy the aliens. Meg Foster provides a very weak romantic angle in this ultimate statement on our social paranoia. (Video/Laser: MCA)

THEY'RE COMING TO GET YOU (1971). See *Dracula vs. Frankenstein.*

THEY'RE COMING TO GET YOU (1972). Video version of *Demons of the Dead* (Vogue).

THEY SAVED HITLER'S BRAIN (1964) ★ This has been ranked as one of the worst movies ever made, and while at moments it comes close, it never has the ultimate campiness one prefers. The Richard Miles–Steve Bennett story (aka *Amazing Mr. H*, *Return of Mr. H* and *Madmen of Mandoras*) is a muddled affair about a deadly G Gas and its antidote (PAM—Formula D). First a scientist is kidnapped, then a U.S. couple is kidnapped to a South American country (Mandoras) where neo-Nazis (led by Marshall Reed) keep Hitler's head in a special solution. Since a secret agent is wearing a minidress circa 1969, one suspects the film may have sat on a shelf for years before new footage was added to salvage the mess. The poor cinematography in these scenes is another clue to the padding, as most of the film has a professional look thanks to Stanley Cortez. The music track was lifted from Universal-International horror movies. The direction by David Bradley is pedestrian. Walter Stocker, Audrey Caire, Carlos Rivas, Nestor Paiva, Scott Peters. (VCI; United; Video Yesteryear)

THEY WATCH. See *They.*

THIEF OF BAGDAD, THE (1940) ★★★★★ British producer Sir Alexander Korda's fantasy in the Arabian Nights tradition is still the best of its kind—an allegory of good vs. evil, a love story, an adventure of quest, retribution and restitution, a tale of black magic in which a wizard, tormented by love for a woman, is driven to his doom. Above all, this blends metaphor of language with poetic visuals and lush, exotic music. Sabu possesses an ageless quality as the thief who joins deposed king John Justin to fight the wicked vizier, played to perfection by Conrad Veidt, and to romance beautiful June Duprez. Screenwriter Miles Malleson doubles as the dopey but lovable sultan who collects the world's strangest toys. Rex Ingram is the towering, thunderous Djinni, who springs from a tiny bottle uncorked by Sabu. Visual effects and cinematography by William Cameron Menzies, music by Miklos Rozsa. Three directors were needed: Michael Powell, Ludwig Berger and Tim Whelan. Splendid Technicolor adventure; cannot be recommended too highly. (Video/Laser: Nelson/Embassy)

THIEF OF BAGDAD, THE (1960) ★★★ Entertaining Arabian Nights adventure, but 1,001 adventures away from the 1940 version. This Italian production, imported to America by Joseph Levine, stars Steve Reeves as a muscular hero who must pass 7 tests to possess the Blue Rose, the only cure for an ailing princess. But why would anyone face so many dangers for such a flaccid character (played by Georgia Moll)? Made in Tunis and Italy. Directed by Arthur Lubin, Edy Vessel, Arturo Dominici. (Embassy)

THIEF OF BAGDAD, THE (1978) ★★★ TV remake of the 1940 Sabu version, with Roddy McDowall assuming the role of the beggar-thief (and doing a dandy job of it) and the more bland Kabir Bedi playing the prince seeking the hand of beautiful Paula Ustinov (the daughter of Peter Ustinov, who plays the daffy caliph) and looking for the All-Seeing Eye at the Top of the World so he can find the soul of the villain vizier (Terence Stamp, who is splendid). It doesn't have all the magic of the Korda adaptation but it does have its moments, as when Bedi and McDowall ride a Magic Carpet into battle against an army of flying horsemen, and when the genie (Daniel Emilfork, in a delightful cameo) uncorks from his bottle. Directed by Clive Donner from a telescript by A. J. Carothers and Andrew Birkin, this has enough veiled beauties and paradise gardens to make itself worthwhile. Special effects by John (*Star Wars*) Stears. Frank Finlay, Ian Holm, Marina Vlady. (Video Gems)

THING, THE (1982) ★★★★ Outstanding John Carpenter–directed version of John W. Campbell's "Who Goes There?", the classic novella first brought to the screen by Howard Hawks in 1951. While that film is remembered for suspense and characterizations, and not for monster or effects, Carpenter has striven for exactly the opposite values, stressing the shape-changing extraterrestrial beast at the expense of all else. Yet, it is this single facet that makes the film so compelling. Rob Bottin and a team of tricksters create remarkably grisly, gruesome effects—perhaps the most gruesome ever captured on film. According to Bottin, there are 45 different glimpses of the creature as it undergoes change. The stuff of our worst nightmares, this will give children bad dreams and may even upset adults. The cast is topped by Kurt Russell, with strong support from Wilford Brimley, T. K. Carter, Richard Dysart and Richard Masur. The setting is an Antarctic research station where scientists are isolated by a raging storm. Meanwhile the Thing, freed from imprisonment in the ice, where it has been for 100,000 years (next to its crashed saucer), begins taking "shape." The screenplay by William Lancaster (son of Burt) is muddled but as a special effects classic, this is the greatest. (Video/Laser: MCA)

THING ... FROM ANOTHER WORLD, THE
(1951) ★★★★ One-time editor Christian
Nyby is credited with directing this RKO version of John W. Campbell's "Who Goes
There?" but it is generally known that producer
Howard Hawks was on the set as guiding benefactor. Certainly the technique of overlapping,
fast-delivered dialogue is a telltale giveaway.
No matter ... because of its concern for a strong
camaraderie among military men (a standard
Hawks trait), for sprightly dialogue (by Charles
Lederer), for tingling suspense, and because it
captures the frigid atmosphere of an Arctic research station, *The Thing* remains one of the
best sci-fi thrillers of the '50s. Another achievement is composer Dimitri Tiomkin's use of the
theremin to create an unholy chilling theme. A
small band (U.S. Air Force personnel and scientists, including one woman, Margaret Sheridan) at an isolated outpost near the North Pole
retrieves the frozen body of an alien that has
come to Earth aboard a flying saucer. Once the
creature (described as an emotionless vegetable
monster) thaws out, it's on a destructive rampage, needing human blood to survive. The
makeup for the creature (James Arness in a
jumpsuit with putty nose) is a letdown, but
glimpses of the monster are minimized, allowing tension to build unrelentingly. Kenneth
Tobey heads the Air Force personnel, Douglas
Spencer is great as the wisecracking newsman
Scotty, Robert Cornthwaite is memorable as the
misguided scientist. Dewey Martin, Eduard
Franz, Paul Frees, John Dierkes, George Fen-
neman, Tom Steele. (RKO; Nostalgia Merchant;
RCA/Columbia; VidAmerica; Goodtimes)
(Laser: Turner; Image; VidAmerica)
THING IN THE ATTIC, THE. See *The Ghoul*
(1975).
THINGS TO COME (1936) ★★★★ British production from Alexander Korda—directed by
William Cameron Menzies from a screenplay by
H. G. Wells, who adapted his own novel—is a
minor classic in sci-fi set design and effects, although its philosophies now seem muddled and
naively outdated. The epic is broken into 3 prophetic sections. The first depicts war in 1940,
which leads to the Dark Age, when pestilence
(the Wandering Sickness) sweeps the world.
The second section deals with a feudal system
in which neighboring districts wage war. The
third part, set in 2036, depicts man on a higher
plane devoting himself to art and science. A
rocket expedition to the moon is planned, but
reactionaries fear man has advanced far enough
and stage an uprising. Which leads to war. Thus,
history is a cyclical process. Stunning achievement for its time, with a cast that does wonders
with the oft-pedantic dialogue: Sir Cedric Hardwicke, Raymond Massey, Ralph Richardson,
Margaretta Scott, Edward Chapman. Early titles:

*The Shape of Things to Come, The Hundred
Years to Come* and *Whither Mankind*. (Kartes;
Media; Filmfax; Sinister/C)
THING THAT COULDN'T DIE, THE (1958) ★★
Universal-International, once the king of horror,
was foundering when it produced this programmer, for David Duncan's script is wretched and
Will Cowan's direction double wretched, with
studio composer Joseph Gershenson stealing
themes from other films to keep the budget low.
The back-lot studio ranch is the setting for a
feeble story about a girl with divining powers
who finds the head of a 16th-century devil wor-
shipper, which maintains a hypnotic hoodoo
over the cast as the long-dead dastard, once an
enemy of Sir Francis Drake, tries to rejoin his
severed head to its body. But believe us, this
lacks body. William Reynolds, Andra Martin.
Aka *The Man Without a Body*.
THING WITH TWO HEADS, THE (1972) ★½
Imagine the social satire that might have gone
into this horror fantasy about a hulking black
convict (Rosey Grier) who wakes up from an
operation to find the head of a bigoted white
surgeon (Ray Milland) attached to his neck. But
no ... instead we are subjected to gross stupid-
ities as Grier rushes around L.A. to clear himself
of a murder charge and Milland acts like a redneck dolt. Every opportunity for something
amusing or clever is missed by writer-director
Lee Frost. William Smith, Roger Perry, Chelsea
Brown, Don Marshall. Aka *Man with Two
Heads* and *Beast with Two Heads*.
THINNER. See *Stephen King's Thinner*.
THIRST (1979) ★★★ Above-average Australian vampire tale, written by John Pinkney, has
a compelling, perverse nature in its bite when
Chantal Contouri is taken to a country farm to
be "fattened" for the kill by a vampire gang.
Henry Silva has a great death scene and David
Hemmings is outstanding in a surprise-twist
role. Well directed by Rod Hardy. *Thirst* will
quench your need for a good horror movie. (Media; Cult)
THIRST OF BARON BLOOD, THE. See *Baron
Blood*.
THIRSTY DEAD, THE (1974) ★★ Filipino production of minor importance; its feeble story
barely brings it above the level of episodic TV.
Jennifer Billingsley and other beauties are kidnapped from night spots in Manila and taken to
a jungle hideaway where a blood cult hangs out,
dressed in baby-doll nighties, sarongs and bikinis. Seems that John Considine and followers
believe in the god Rahu, whose head is kept in
a red-tinted box. The chicks are needed for
blood transfusions, which are gulped down by
the cult (they give the chicks eternal beauty). A
sensitive love affair develops between Jennifer
and John, but it isn't enough to bring Charles
Dennis's script out of the pulp jungle. Director

Terry Becker offers no style and little adventure when the women break for freedom and a chase ensues. Gore effects are clumsily handled, and the ending unsatisfying. Judith McConnell, Tani Guthrie. Produced as *Blood Cult of Shangri-la*. (Western World; Applause; King of Video; from Simitar as *Blood Hunt*)

THIRTEEN DEMON STREET. TV series from which a compilation was made called *The Devil's Messenger*.

13 GHOSTS (1960) ★★★ Campy but pleasing horror film produced and directed by William Castle, prophet of the great god Gimmick. Filmed in "Illusiono," for which viewers were provided "Ghost Finders": glasses with panels of red (enabling them to see the ghosts) and blue (blocking out the ghosts). Robb White's story: A family inherits a haunted house, unaware a fortune is hidden among the bric-a-brac. Ghosts come and go with the blink of an eye. Thirteen was Castle's lucky number on this ghostly outing. Rosemary De Camp, Donald Woods, Martin Milner, Margaret Hamilton. (RCA/Columbia; Goodtimes)

THIRTEENTH FLOOR, THE (1999) ★★½ "Virtual Reality" strikes again. although this is based on the literate and complex novel *Simulacron 3* by Daniel Galouye, a lot got lost in the translation in the screenplay by Josef Rusnak (who also directed) and Ravel Centeno-Rodriguez. Convoluted movies with O. Henry twist endings need to be carefully worked out, but *The Thirteenth Floor* throws one "Astounding Revelation" after another at the viewer, until finally it all seems more of a mess than it's worth. The labyrinthine narrative concerns an experimental "virtual reality" computer program masterminded by an aging genius played by Armin-Mueller-Stahl and assistants Craig Bierko and Vincent D'Onofrio. They've created a cyberspace reality in the year 1937. When you play the game you spread out on a "control table" that bathes you in eerie green light and you are computer-fed an alter-ego identity of a personality living back then. You wake up in '37 Los Angeles and live through the time and place for two hours, then you have to come back to the present or you might die of complications—call it a bug in the program. Mystery and intrigue abound in this world of swing bands and opulent hotels, but it gets thicker back in present times when Stahl is mysteriously murdered and Dennis Haysbert (playing plainclothesman Larry McBain) investigates. Bierko goes back and forth through time and space to solve the homicide but the mystery only deepens as we realize there may be a layer of "virtual realities" and Stahl's "long-lost" daughter shows up to add to the confusion. If you are willing to accept tricks in storytelling, and suddenly discover that nothing is what it has seemed, you might enjoy this difficult exercise in multilayered tomfoolery and all its mazework of dual identities, duplicity and deception. Don't think this is a special effects extravaganza, however. There is a startling glimpse at how L.A. must have looked back in '37, but otherwise there's a minimum of computerized graphics. *The Thirteenth Floor* is a handsome product, beautifully shot by cinematographer Wedigo von Schultzendorff, and a pleasure to watch. The fact that its exec producer is power-wielding Roland Emmerich might account for how this unusual film got made; otherwise, its non-mainstream elements might have been rejected by Hollywood had the producers less clout at the box office. (Video/DVD: Columbia TriStar)

THIRTEENTH MOON OF JUPITER, THE. See *Fire Maidens from Outer Space*.

THIRTEENTH REUNION. Video version from Thrillervision of an episode of *Hammer House of Horror*. See *Charlie Boy/Thirteenth Reunion*.

30-FOOT BRIDE OF CANDY ROCK, THE (1959) ★★★ Lou Costello's last feature (sans Bud Abbott) stars Lou as a goofy assistant to a crazy inventor who transforms Dorothy Provine into a gigantic representative of the feminist movement and sends her and Lou through a time-travel device. A sad finale to the career of a once-popular film prankster. Directed by Sidney Miller from a silly script by Arthur Ross and Rowland Barber. Robert Burton, Doodles Weaver, Gale Gordon, Jimmy Conlin, Charles Lane. Aka *Lou Costello and His 30-Foot Bride* and *The Secret Bride of Candy Rock*. (RCA/Columbia)

THIS ISLAND EARTH (1955) ★★★★ Sincere adaptation of Raymond F. Jones's novel resulted in a classy Universal-International sci-fi epic with abundant effects by Clifford Stine and Stanley Horsley. The Franklin Coen–Edward G. O'Callighan script is uneven but it's still a pleasure to ogle the space battles and interplanetary travel as Rex Reason and Faith Domergue are transported to the planet Metaluna by E.T. humanoid Jeff Morrow to save the dying world from attack by its rival enemy, Zahgon. It was excitingly directed by Joseph Newman (aided by Jack Arnold and producer William Alland) and crisply edited by Virgil Vogel. The climax is heightened by a 6-foot offspring of a giant bug with exposed brain, eyes as big as saucers and blood vessels outside the skin. Lance Fuller, Russell Johnson, Douglas Spencer, Robert Nichols. Aka *War of the Planets*. (Video/Laser: MCA)

THIS NIGHT I WILL POSSESS YOUR CORPSE (1968) ★ This sequel to *At Midnight I'll Take Your Soul* in the Coffin Joe horror series from Brazilian filmmaker José Mojica Marins, the professional gravedigger performs hideous forms of torture on innocent women. Others in this series: *Strange World of Coffin Joe, Hallucinations of a Deranged Mind, The Bloody Exorcism of Coffin Joe*. (S/Weird)

THIS TIME TOMORROW. See *The Time Travelers*.

THOSE FANTASTIC FLYING FOOLS. See *Blast Off*.

THOUSAND CRIES HAS THE NIGHT. See *Pieces*.

THOUSAND EYES OF DR. MABUSE, THE (1960) ★★★ Fritz Lang returned to West Germany to cowrite (with Heinz Oskar Wuttig) and direct this resurrection of his 1932 classic, *The Testament of Dr. Mabuse*, reactivating the evil genius who turns his intellect to nefarious pursuits. Aka *The Testament of Dr. Mabuse, The Shadow vs. the Thousand Eyes of Dr. Mabuse, Eyes of Evil, The Secret of Dr. Mabuse* and *The Diabolical Dr. Mabuse*, this is not up to the original, but still damn good Lang as Commissioner Kraugs (Gert Frobe) tracks the criminal to the Hotel Luxor. This set off a wave of Mabuse remakes: *The Return of Dr. Mabuse, Dr. Mabuse vs. Scotland Yard* and *The Secret of Dr. Mabuse*. Dawn Addams, Wolfgang Preiss, Peter Van Eyck, Howard Vernon. (Sinister/C; S/Weird; Filmfax; LSVideo)

THOU SHALL NOT KILL. See *The Avenging Conscience*.

THOU SHALT NOT KILL . . . EXCEPT (1985) ★★★ Set in 1969, the year Charles Manson committed several murders, this establishes the premise that a Manson-like crazyman is on a killing spree near Detroit, where Sergeant Stryker (homage to John Wayne in *Sands of Iwo Jima*) is recovering from wounds received in Vietnam. Stryker and 3 Army buddies are all that can stop Manson and his killers from slaughtering hostages. You want to cheer the military guys even though they're as bloody as the Manson-takeoffs and spatter gore all over the place. Makeup man Gary Jones needed buckets of the stuff as the gang is wiped out, each dying a sanguinary death. Brian Schulz, John Manfredi, Robert Rickman and Tim Quill are heroes while filmmaker Sam Raimi portrays the demented cult leader. It's better than a lot of revenge-horror films, with a good score by Joseph Lo Duca. Director Josh Becker wrote the script. (Prism)

THREE FACES OF FEAR/THREE FACES OF TERROR. See *Black Sabbath*.

THREE ON A MEATHOOK (1973) ★ Said to be patterned on the true-life murderer Ed Gein, the madman who wore the skin of his victims and had a mother complex, and who inspired Robert Bloch to write *Psycho*. But that's pure bullroar hype. This movie has not an ounce of psychological depth and is merely an excuse to show beautiful women being axed, hatcheted and chopped to death and then hung up on meathooks to dry. It's a bad gore movie and unworthy of anyone's attention despite the fact it was written-directed by William Girdler as if he were doing a take-off of *Psycho*. Wow, what a turkey. Charles Kissinger, James Pickett, Sherry Steiner, Madelyn Buzzard, John Shaw. (New Pacific; Regal; Video Treasures; Front Row Entertainment)

THREE STOOGES MEET HERCULES, THE (1962) ★★★ Spoof on musclemen epics, with Moe Howard, Larry Fine and Joe De Rita working in Ithaca, N.Y., in a soda shop, befriending the guy next door who just happens to be inventing a time machine. They travel back in time to Greece before Christ to that Ithaca to meet Ulysses, Hercules (portrayed as a dumb grunt master) and Achilles the Heel. The funniest scenes feature the Stooges in drag in a harem, mistaken as hand maidens, and partakers in a Ben-Hur parody as they row a king's vessel on a "holiday cruise." Efficacious and outrageous, with the Stooges trapped in a low-budget continuum. Directed by Edward Bernds from a script by Elwood Ullman. Gene Roth, Samson Burke. (RCA/Columbia; Goodtimes)

THREE WISHES (1995) ★★★½ This is one strange fairy tale. Eschewing the obvious trappings and clichés of the genre, *Three Wishes* is set in 1955 and depicts widowed mother Mary Elizabeth Mastrantonio raising her young sons (Joseph Mazzello and Seth Mumy) in a small California town. Into their lives come wandering, bearded Patrick Swayze and his dog, Betty Jane. There seems to be a simplistic morality lesson that lies at the heart of Elizabeth Anderson's script but it's beefed up with all kinds of object lessons (don't judge people without knowing them; take things at face value, etc.) and subplots designed to tug at the heart regarding the fatherless boys. It's a refreshing piece of work from director Martha Coolidge but it's strange and slow-moving and seems focusless, going all over the place before we find out that the strange Swayze and dog, as if they were genies from magic lamps, are capable of making wishes come true for the family. Phil Tippett provided the nice effects for this unpredictable, sometimes heartfelt and moving story. If you like them different, we grant you *Three Wishes*. David Marshall Grant, Diane Venour, Jay O. Sanders, John Diehl. (HBO)

THREE WORLDS OF GULLIVER, THE (1960) ★★★★ Following *The Seventh Voyage of Sinbad*, producer Charles H. Schneer and special effects artist Ray Harryhausen collaborated to bring Jonathan Swift's satire to the screen, and the results are impressive. Again, Kerwin Mathews portrays the young hero—a traveler who falls overboard and finds himself captive in the land of the Lilliputians, tiny people under the thumb of the Brobdingnags, unfriendly giants from a neighboring island. Mathews befriends the Tiny Tims and battles the towering titans. The wonderful effects capture more of a fairy-tale quality than other Harryhausen efforts.

Romance, action and comedy, with the younger set better served. Directed by Jack Sher. Wonderful music by Bernard Herrmann. Jo Morrow, Peter Bull, June Thorburn, Lee Patterson. Aka *The Worlds of Gulliver*. (Video: Columbia; Laser: Columbia TriStar with Harryhausen interview)

THRILLED TO DEATH. See *Night Warning*.

THRILL KILLERS, THE (1967) ★★★ Ray Dennis Steckler, an eccentric but likable low-budget filmmaker, directs and stars in this high-energy though often laughable psycho-killer smasher-basher in which an escaped maniac, Mad Dog Click, terrorizes assorted passersby when he runs into 3 other escaped nuts, one of whom carries a large ax. A lot of what Steckler does is crude satire and there's an underlying element of naïveté that makes it palatable. The film works best as a chase during its last half hour as Liz Renay runs (and repeatedly screams) for her life. Steckler has built up an odd cult following. Aka *The Maniacs Are Loose* and *The Monsters Are Loose*. (Mascot; Camp)

THROUGH NAKED EYES (1983) ★★★ Hitchcockian TV-movie has a few surprise twists and offbeat characters when high-rise dweller David Soul realizes Pam Dawber—a chick in a nearby building as tall as his—is spying back at him. They strike up a relationship just when a slasher-smasher starts striking folks with his butcher knife. But suspicion is diverted onto Soul, a flutist who behaves oddly and doesn't have easy relationships with people, including his father, William Schallert. Contrived suspense situations by writer Jeffrey Bloom will still have you on the edge of your couch. Directed by John Llewellyn Moxey. (Prism; Media)

THROUGH THE LOOKING GLASS. See *The Velvet Vampire*.

THUNDA. See *King of the Congo*.

THUNDERBALL (1965) ★★★★ Stylish James Bond espionage adventure, set largely underwater and featuring exotic, sophisticated scuba equipment and weapons. Sean Connery, as 007, tracks 1-eyed Largo (Adolf Celi), who has hijacked a NATO aircraft armed with atomic bombs and demands a ransom of £1,000,000. Several punnish quips by 007 flip through Bond's lips—they are part of the charm that continued to cling to these marvelous adventures. Richard Maibaum and John Hopkins adapted the Ian Fleming novel. The undersea photography and full-scale battles make this an outstanding contribution to the series (this story was remade into *Never Say Never Again*.) Claudine Auger plays Domino, and Luciana Paluzzi is a palaluzzi of a woman in her bathing suits. Directed with pizzazz by Terence Young. (Video/Laser: MGM)

THUNDERBIRDS ARE GO (1966) ★★★ Gerry and Sylvia Anderson, who produced some top British TV sci-fi, first became known for *Thunderbirds*, which featured realistic effects and mature story lines around marionette characters shot in the "Supermarionation" process. This full-length treatment demonstrates the excellent puppet-model work and has interesting characters in the Tracy family (each commands a different kind of Thunderbird aircraft) and the love interest, Lady Penelope (called Fab #1). The International Space Rescue Service blasts off for Mars in the Zero-X experimental spacecraft but the project is threatened by saboteurs. A sequence featuring explosions is spectacular for a film of this kind, thanks in part to the effects work of Derek Meddings. Sequels were *Thunderbird Six, Thunderbirds to the Rescue, Thunderbirds: Countdown to Disaster* and *Revenge of the Mysterons from Mars*. Directed by David Lane. Voices by Gerry Anderson, Ray Barrett and Alexander Davion. (Video/Laser: MGM/UA)

THUNDERHEART (1992) ★★★★ While on the surface this is a whodunit, in which FBI agents Val Kilmer and Sam Shepard investigate a murder on the Pine Ridge Reservation in South Dakota, it's also the spiritual study of Kilmer (whose character is part Sioux Indian) and how he rediscovers his roots through strange visions, dreams and other metaphysical experiences brought on by an old medicine man. *Thunderheart* is a taut thriller with an intriguing conspiracy twist to its unusual story, and very well directed by Michael Apted from a script by John Fusco. Graham Greene, Fred Ward, John Trudell. (Video/Laser: Columbia Tristar)

THUNDER MOUNTAIN. See *Shadow of Chikara*.

THUNDER RUN (1985) ★★★ Minor sci-fi actioner set in the deserts of Nevada and Arizona when an aging trucker (Forrest Tucker in his final screen role) helms a Kenmore Supertruck (with indestructible tires, bulletproof windows and trick weapons) through a gauntlet of foreign agents who drive camouflaged Volkswagens (equipped with heat-seeking rockets) and other *Road Warrior*-style vehicles. There's nonsense about a computer code, a tunnel of lasers and a mysterious helicopter. Tuck is carrying a cargo of plutonium for CIA boss John Ireland and wheels the rig with the daring of Mad Max. Crashes are plentiful and well-photographed. Directed by Gary Hudson. John Sheperd, Jill Whitlow. (Media)

THURSDAY THE 12TH. See *Pandemonium*.

THX 1138 (1971) ★★★★½ In an underground society, in the distant future, man lives in a drugged stupor, ruled by a computerized police system that denies citizens the right to feel emotions or sexual desires. George Lucas, in his impressive directorial debut, creates an automated, trance-state world that is a visual exploration of man's dark side. While the future technology and the emotionless behavior of the robots are fascinating, the Walter Murch-Lucas script also probes into man's need to remain individualistic, as captive Robert Duvall breaks loose from the system to escape to the unknown surface world above. Produced by Francis Ford Coppola, who first admired Lucas's short 16mm film that he made at USC entitled *THX 1138-4EB* (aka *Electronic Labyrinth*), this is a major stepping-stone in the path to the *Star Wars* series. Donald Pleasence, Maggie McOmie, Don Pedro Colley, Johnny Weissmuller, Jr. (Video/Laser: Warner Bros.)

TICKS (1993) ★★★½ At first this gross monster movie just seems disgusting. But then because of the energy director Tony Randel brings to the project, and because of cliff-hangers on top of cliff-hangers that screenwriter Brent V. Friedman heaps on the fire, *Ticks* suddenly jumps to life and bites you where it does the most good. The titular entities are mutations of the eenie-weenie-teenie creatures one normally finds on Roger or Spot that have been subjected to a steroid substance in fields of marijuana. First they cocoon in pulsating white hives, then they grow into a shape that resembles an irate crab. The critters take to the fields and byways of America, especially to harass vacationing teenagers Peter Scolari, Ami Dolenz, Rosalind Allen and Alfonso Ribeiro who are out for a good time in the country. But then you've got Clint Howard, playing one of his lowlife creeps who grows the things in his barn, and you've got 2 crazed hunters who take delight in pursuing the most dangerous game of men—man. Mix up these plots with a forest fire and an army of tick monsters that are all gooey and crunchy and icky-looking and you've got a thriller that'll make you scream and laugh in the same breath. Seth Green, Virginya Keehne and Dina Dayrit help out. Rance Howard is in there too as a sheriff who becomes fodder for the beasties. (Video/Laser: Republic)

TIGER CLAWS (1991) ★★★ A serial killer known as the Death Dealer damages the interior organs of his victims without leaving exterior markings except for claw marks across their cheeks. Swinging into action are martial arts cops Jalal Merhi (who also produced) and Cynthia Rothrock, who demonstrate karate and kickboxing skills in what is basically an action picture with minor horror overtones. Rothrock and Merhi are personable players who bring likability to their characters, and director Kelly Makin makes it a workable albeit formulaic picture. Script by coproducer J. Stephen Maunder. Bolo Yeung, Ho Chow. (Video/Laser: MCA)

TIGER MAN (1943). See *The Lady and the Monster*.

TIGHTROPE (1984) ★★★★ Fascinating, perplexing study of a New Orleans cop (Clint Eastwood) investigating brutal sex murders of women in the kinky velvet underworld of perversion. Eastwood is lured into this sordid world and finds he enjoys it—then discovers the killer has a vendetta against him. The subtext finds Eastwood examining his own values, although the main thrust remains the pursuit, craftily built to an exciting climax by writer-director Richard Tuggle, who treats this more like a slasher-horror thriller than a whodunit. Clint's romance with Genevieve Bujold contributes to the theme. One of Eastwood's best. (Video/Laser: Warner Bros.)

TIL DEATH DO US PART. Video version of *The Blood-Spattered Bride* (Vestron).

TILL DAWN DO US PART. See *Straight on Till Morning*.

TILL DEATH (1978) ★½ Tepid, lethargically paced supernatural-ghost tale. Keith Atkinson is locked in a mausoleum with the corpse of his wife (Belinda Balaski), who died in a car crash that he caused. He's snared in a state of limbo, where the spouse rises from her crypt and tries to seduce him into joining her in the Great Beyond. None of this makes sense, and the ending, in which transparent entities menace the helpless couple, sheds no light on Gregory Dana's muddled script. Walter Stocker pointed the camera and coproduced with actor Marshall Reed. Not to have and to hold. . . .

TIM BURTON'S NIGHTMARE BEFORE CHRISTMAS. See *Nightmare Before Christmas*.

TIME AFTER TIME (1979) ★★★½ Ingenious time-travel yarn, written-directed by Nicholas Meyer, in which Jack the Ripper flees Victorian London in a machine built by H. G. Wells, landing in San Francisco in November 1979. Wells, pursuing the slasher, becomes an amusing anachronism as he adjusts to 20th-century customs. David Warner is an intriguing Ripper, remarking to Wells, "We haven't gone ahead, we've gone back; man hasn't advanced beyond barbarism," flipping on the 6 o'clock news to prove it. Malcolm McDowell is the British idealist-writer and Mary Steenburgen the kooky but lovable bank executive who befriends him. This imaginative fantasy is enhanced by a rich Miklos Rozsa score. Charles Cioffi, Shelley Hack, Clete Roberts. (Video/Laser: Warner Bros.)

TIME BANDITS (1981) ★★★½ Thoroughly wacky time-travel comedy zanily directed by Terry Gilliam of Monty Python infamy. Destructive fun as a gang of dwarfs aids a youth (Craig Warnock) lost in a time hole. Gags fly fast and furious, and many stars show up in cameos: Sean Connery is Agamemnon, John Cleese is a hilarious Robin Hood, David Warner is wonderful as the Evil Genius of the Universe. Others in the Gilliam–Michael Palin script: Sir

Ralph Richardson, Ian Holm, Kenny Baker, Shelley Duvall. Absolutely bananas at times, but you'll be too busy laughing to tell yourself none of this mayhem makes sense. Producer George Harrison provided songs. (RCA/Columbia; Paramount) (Laser: Paramount)

TIME BARBARIANS (1991) ★★ A direct rip-off of *Beastmaster 2*, stealing that film's curious blend of sword-and-sorcery fantasy and time-hopping. Set in the magical kingdom of Armana, it depicts a warrior king (Deron Michael McBee) losing his crystal amulet to Mondrok the Cutthroat and being sent through time to modern-day L.A. by wizard queen Ingrid Vold, she in a long stringy blond wig. Muscle guy McBee, also wearing a blond wig and reciting turgid dialogue by writer-director Joseph J. Barmettler, does battle with modern gangs with his sometimes-invisible sword and tracks the bad-guy warrior with the help of a TV reporter in a miniskirt. The effects are minimal, the fighting less than convincing and the plot and dialogue rancid. Jo Ann Ayres, Daniel Martine, Louis Roth, Michael Ferrare.

TIMEBOMB (1990) ★★★½ Rousing action thriller with overtones of *The Manchurian Candidate* in which watchmaker Michael Biehn is the target for superassassins created by a secret government gang run by Richard Jordan and Robert Culp. Writer-director Avi Nesher crams this offbeat adventure with violent action and the pace is unrelenting as Biehn and psychoanalyst Patsy Kensit follow the clues, with cop Raymond St. Jacques tagging along. The sequence in which Biehn undergoes "behavior modification experiments" presents unusual holographs. Tracy Scoggins portrays the sexy assassin Ms. Blue. (Video/Laser: MGM/UA)

TIMEBURST—THE FINAL ALLIANCE (1988) ★★★ Offbeat, satisfying fantasy thriller with shoot-'em-up action, martial-arts mayhem, convoluted plot twists and pseudophilosophy (Zen-style). Scott David King portrays a 350-year-old man, Urbane, who discovered the Japanese secret of immortality in feudal times under the guidance of "the Master" (Gerald Okamura) and now is a CIA agent who suffers amnesia and has brief flashes of his past life. Bad guy Jay Richardson and gang are after the secret with a Japanese band led by Craig Ng. Caught in the middle is the Master (also immortal) and another CIA operative (Michiko) who provides romantic interest and a partner for Urbane during the chases. The script by producer-director Peter Yugal and coproducer Michael Bogert offers an unusual ending. Chet Hood, Jack Vogel. (Action International)

TIME COP (1994) ★★★★ Jean-Claude Van Damme's best action thriller, enhanced by excellent time travel paradoxes and marvelous special effects that include a "time ripple" (in which space suddenly becomes a pool of water flowing in all directions) and a merging of 2 individuals into disintegrating blood molecules. It's the stuff of fascinating fantasy adventure with Van Damme as a member of the Time Enforcement Commission, a police force that tracks those who use time travel for evil gain. His time-hopping adventures (including a jaunt to Wall Street in 1929, on the sets used in *The Hudsucker Proxy*) involve a sadistic senator (Ron Silver, portraying a totally evil opportunist), "rips" in the fabric of time that change events to come and Van Damme's efforts to save his wife who died 10 years earlier. Based on a comic-book series published by Dark Horse, *Time Cop* was written by Mark Verheiden with a breathless quality and directed-photographed by Peter Hyams with high-class production values and a gleaming futuristic technology. For once Van Damme rises to the acting challenge and comes through with a panache that matches his martial-arts prowess. It's about time you saw *Time Cop*. Mia Sara, Gloria Reuben, Scott Bellis, Jason Schombing. (Video/Laser: MCA)

TIME FLYER (1985) ★★★ Satisfying family cable-movie starring Huckleberry Fox as a modern youth who travels through time to 1927 to prevent his grandfather Max Knickerbocker (Peter Coyote) from taking off in a plane to beat Lindbergh to Paris. Writer-director Mark Rosman brings interesting time paradoxes into the story and provides enough pleasant characters to make this minor effort better than average. There's an unusually good ending, with a twist to it you won't suspect. Art Carney, Dennis Lipscombe, Joe Flood, Mittie Smith, Frank Simons, Morgan Upton. Aka *The Blue Yonder*.

TIME GUARDIAN, THE (1987) ★★★ Fanciful and exciting sci-fi special-effects extravaganza in the *Star Wars* mold (with *Terminator* overtones) set in 4039, when Earth has been destroyed by cyborg killer robots called Jen-Diki. A domed city commanded by Dean Stockwell travels through time and space to escape the Jen-Diki, and warriors Tom Burlinson and Carrie Fisher are sent back to 1988 to set up a final apocalyptic confrontation with the half-human metal monsters. They are aided in their desert adventures by wandering Nikki Coghill as they also square off against corrupt Australian policemen. The effects are well done, the pacing by director Brian Hannant (who concocted the script with John Baxter) is intense, and the action is plentiful enough to make this Australian production a welcome treat. Tim Robertson. (RCA/Columbia; Orion) (Laser: Nelson)

TIME KILLER, THE. See *The Night Strangler*.

TIME MACHINE, THE (1960) ★★★★½ Stylish George Pal version of the famous H. G. Wells novel, charming in its depiction of 19th-century milieu and moving at a fast clip as Rod Taylor hops into his ingenious apparatus and travels through several centuries. He arrives at a bleak world in the year 802,701 to find mankind's remnants: the rulers are the cannibalistic Morlocks and the Eloi serve as slave labor and food, working in underground caverns. It's continuously exciting and has a poignant message that avoids being preachy. Taylor is excellent and Yvette Mimieux is cuddly as the soft, warm heroine, Weena. The effects by Gene Warren and Wah Chang deservedly won an Academy Award. Pal produced-directed the David Duncan script. Alan Young, Sebastian Cabot, Whit Bissell. (Video/Laser: MGM/UA)

TIMEMASTER (1995) ★★½ The "kitchen sink" principle is applied to this time-travel/parallel universe adventure in which an outer space culture from Palisades City (on "the edge of the universe"), under the control of entertainment master Michael Dorn, plays virtual reality games that affect events on Earth, just for the vicarious thrill of watching us destroy ourselves. After nuclear holocaust in A.D. 2007 leaves Yellowstone a desert wasteland, time explorer Isaiah (Noriyuki "Pat" Morita) decides to help mankind restore its planet by using a young boy (Jesse Cameron-Glickenhaus) to travel back in time. It's a mess of a plot but several individual moments play well: a Western cow town sequence, a couple of passes through the time continuum where events exist inside floating bubbles; a *Mad Max*–styled action segment, an exciting ski chase in Switzerland, and a graveyard of military aircraft. But the sum of these subtotals don't add up to much. What it was all supposed to mean can only be known to writer-director James Glickenhaus. Morita talks about Einstein like an old martial-arts guru and Duncan Regehr plays Jesse's heroic father. Good effects, though. Joanna Pacula, Michelle Williams, Scott Colomby, Zelda Rubinstein. (Video/Laser: MCA)

TIME OF THE BEAST. See *Mutator*.

TIME OF THE GYPSIES (1989) ★★★½ While this is basically a wonderful and gritty slice of life set in a village of modern Yugoslav gypsies, marked by stretches of comedy and pathos, this film by director Emir Kusturica (who cowrote with Gordan Mihic) delves mildly into the telekinetic powers of a youth (Davor Dukmovic) as he undergoes the rites of passage. (Presumably his father was cursed by a fortune teller, resulting in the boy's unique powers.) Leaving his squalid but happy life behind to take his sick sister to a hospital, and then moving on to Italy to become a thief, that youth must ultimately use his unusual ability to move objects for revenge. This may not exactly be every fantasy fan's cup of tea, but art film lovers will savor its richness of characters and situations. It's a classic of a kind that Hollywood rarely strives for. Bora Todorovic, Ljubica Adzovic. (Columbia)

TIME RAIDERS. See *Warriors of the Apocalypse*.

TIMERIDER: THE ADVENTURES OF LYLE SWANN (1983) ★★½ Time-travel hogwash depicting how a Baja 500 race motorcyclist gets lost in the desert and passes through time portals, which scientists are experimenting with at control center. Just a poor rehash of *Time Tunnel* as Fred Ward lands in the 1880s to be surrounded by outlaw leader Peter Coyote and his ornery gang of mavericks, who'd love to trade their hooves for wheels. Ample stunt riding and horse chases, but production values are those of a TV-movie and the script by producer Michael Nesmith and William Dear (the latter also directed) is predictable, including the time paradox "surprise" ending. Belinda Bauer provides interesting love interest—in fact, she's the only intriguing character. Ed Lauter, Richard Masur, L. Q. Jones. (Video/Laser: Pacific Arts)

TIME RUNNER (1992) ★★½ Traditional literary time paradoxes are at play in this action thriller shot in Vancouver and British Columbia, but ultimately its script (uncredited) is too erratic to be satisfying. The time is 2022 when a civil war on Earth has rebels trying to depose the tyrannical leader Neila (check that spelling backwards, pal). Space jockey Mark Hamill (as Captain Michael Rainier) is caught in a wormhole and sent back to Earth in the year 1992, where he fights the forces of the president-to-be and is present at his own birth. So many elements are undefined and so many sequences devoted to mindless action that this stumbles to an unconvincing conclusion. They try to make Hamill "a new kind of terminator," but it doesn't work, in spite of fluid direction by Michael Mazo and fast-paced editing. Brion James portrays the evil president and Rae Dawn Chong is a scientist of dubious loyalties who helps Hamill. Allen Forget, Gordon Tipple, Marc Bauer, Barry W. Levy. (New Line/Columbia TriStar) (Laser: Image)

TIMESTALKERS, THE (1986) ★★½ Complicated time-travel fantasy explained in bits and pieces, as if it were a jigsaw puzzle in the mind of writer Brian Clemens. This helps to build mystery and curiosity as modern physicist William Devane, following the death of his wife and son in an auto accident, confronts a woman from A.D. 2586 (Lauren Hutton) and begins tracking a strange gunfighter (Klaus Kinski) who keeps bouncing from the past century to the present one via a crystal device. Elements finally come together under Michael Schultz's direction in this diverting entertainment, even if Kinski's performance seems unnecessarily manic. John Ratzenberger, Forrest Tucker, Tracey Walter. (Fries)

TIME TRACKERS (1989) ★★★ Time-travel

fantasy-comedy produced by Roger Corman, who no doubt used props and costumes left over from his remake of *The Masque of the Red Death*. In 2033, an evil scientist working on a "time tunnel" project goes back in time to change history so he can have credit for inventing the device. Eventually the characters end up in 1133 when the Red Duke, a Robin Hood–like hero, is fighting forces of evil in a fairy-tale England. The best feature about this Howard R. Cohen screenplay (he also directed) is the comedy relief provided by Ned Beatty as a modern cop whisked back to days of yore. The cast (Wil Shriner, Kathleen Beller, Bridget Hoffman, Alex Hyde-White, Lee Bergere) romps through this nonsense, but it's timeworn. (MGM/UA)

TIME TRAP. See *The Time Travelers*.

TIME TRAVELERS, THE (1964) ★★ German scientist Preston Foster and companions Merry Anders and Phil Carey are projected into the future to find Earth burned to a cinder by atomic war. Man-eating creatures ravage the surface (the lava beds near Barstow, Calif.) but underground is a colony of survivors using robots to build a spaceship for escape to another planet. Watch for Forrest J. Ackerman in a cameo. Directed by Ib Melchoir, who cowrote with David Hewitt. Later, Hewitt adapted this plot for *Journey to the Center of Time*. John Hoyt, Carol White, Dennis Patrick. Photographed by Vilmos Zsigmond. Aka *Depths of the Unknown, This Time Tomorrow, Time Trap* and *The Return of the Time Traveler*. (HBO)

TIME TROOPERS (1989) ★½ Following nuclear war, society creates a special police force to keep everyone in check. Directed by L. E. Neiman. Albert Fortell, Hannelore Eisner. Aka *Morning Terror*. (Prism)

TIME WALKER (1982) ★★ Sci-fi mummy yarn that gets so wrapped up in unbelievable plot developments, it unravels early in the action—or nonaction, since this is a lethargic, lumbering, 2-bit movie. When archeologist Ben Murphy breaks into King Tut's tomb, he finds a sarcophagus containing an E.T. under wraps. Back at the California Institute of the Sciences, dumb technician Kevin Brophy exposes the long-dead creature to so much gamma force the alien pops up alive, shambling around in search of 5 glowing "jewels" that will enable him to communicate with his home planet. "E.T., Phone Home"—get it? The cast shambles around like so many dummy mummies in need of a director. So where was director Tom Kennedy all this time? Nina Axelrod, Austin Stoker, James Karen. (Charter)

TIMEWARP (1980). See *The Day Time Ended*.

TIME WARP. Video version of *Journey to the Center of Time* (American).

TIME WARP TERROR. See *Bloody New Year*.

TINGLER, THE (1959) ★★★½ Gimmicked-up fright flick from producer-director William Castle, with theaters originally wired to give audiences a "tingle" at "shocking" moments. Disregarding that hokum, though, this is fine Castle Macabre enhanced by a tongue-in-cheek flavor. Scientist Vincent Price discovers each of us has a mysterious element, brought to life by fear, that takes possession of our backbones. Removed from the body, the spine becomes a lobsterlike monster attaching itself to the nearest human and pinches and breaks bones. The best sequence in this campy miniclassic is when the Tingler is loose in a movie theater and everyone runs like hell as the thing crawls through the projector aperture. There is a hand coming out of a tub of blood shot in color, which some TV prints show. Robb White dreamed up the nifty idea. Daryl Hickman, Philip Coolidge, Judith Evelyn, Patricia Cutts. (Laser: Columbia Tristar, with color sequence)

TIN MAN (1983) ★★★ This attempt at a "feel-good" movie has honorable intentions and is shaped in a manner similar to *Charley*. Stone-deaf auto mechanic Timothy Bottoms creates a speaking computer named Osgood (nickname: the Wizard of Osgood), falls in love with Deana Jurgens and has his hearing restored by doctor John Phillip Law. When a major corporation markets his computer, he realizes some things are more important than the material. How Bottoms finds happiness remains the bulwark of Bishop Holiday's script, with the sci-fi taking second position and undermined by a low budget. Produced-directed by John G. Thomas. Law, who normally plays misfits, here plays a sympathetic doctor and he's quite good. Troy Donahue also shines as an ambivalent executive. (Prism; Media)

TIN SOLDIER, THE (1995) ★★½ This is similar to another maturation fantasy, *The Indian in the Cupboard*, in depicting how a youth (Trenton Knight) is helped in growing up by a toy knight (named Yorick) that comes to full-scale life as Jon Voight, who also directed (with the help of Gregory Gieras) this low-key fantasy written by Patrick Clifton from a Hans Christian Andersen story. Unlike *Indian*, this has a hard edge when Knight must join a gang to survive in a new school, and he is ultimately forced to fight a rival, although Yorick in the process teaches him about honor, honesty, human integrity and other morality issues. A lack of action and special effects is made up for by a good cast including Dom DeLuise as a toy-shop owner, Bethany Richards as Knight's depressed mother, Aeryk Egan and Pablo Irlando. A thoughtful movie, but not an exciting one, which makes it of limited interest.

TINTORERA . . . BLOODY WATERS (1977) ★★ This British-Mexican ripoff of *Jaws* is less interesting for its underwater footage of tiger and great white sharks than for its portrayal of the hedonistic life-style of 2 shark hunters (Hugo Stiglitz and Andres Garcia) who enjoy a ménage à trois with beautiful Susan George. Loose morals and plenty of bare breasts will hold your curiosity if scenes of a man's body hanging out of a shark's mouth don't. Director Rene Cardona, Jr., captures an indolent Caribbean flavor and surrounds his handsome, angst-riddled heroes with the sexy, rarely dressed bodies of Priscilla Barnes, Fiona Lewis and Jennifer Ashley. Cardona cowrote the script with underwater photographer Ramon Bravo, on whose novel this anomaly is based. Music by Basil Poledouris. (Media)

TINTORERA . . . TIGER SHARK. See *Tintorera . . . Bloody Waters.*

TITAN FIND, THE. See *Creature.*

TO ALL A GOODNIGHT (1980) ★★★ Another slap at Santa Claus, depicting graphic murders at the Calvin (Klein?) Finishing School for Girls, performed by a homicidal yuletider in a St. Nick costume. Even the blood is slow-moving as the killer fires crossbow arrows into torsos, plants an ax blade in a forehead, hangs a severed head in a shower stall, shoves a knife into a back, and loops a garroting wire around a soft human throat. Directed by David Hess. Jennifer Runyon, Forrest Swanson, William Lauer, Buck West. (Media)

TOBE HOOPER'S NIGHT TERRORS (1993) ★ Robert Englund, portraying the Marquis De Sade with one albino eyeball and the makeup of a degenerate fop, calls everyone "debauched" and "depraved," and he might have added that this Cannon movie produced by Yoram Globus, Chris Pearce and Harry Alan Tower is just as tortured as his soul, since it has been diabolically raped and deflowered of anything even remotely resembling entertainment. What an ugly piece of crap as (mis)conceived by alleged screenwriters Daniel Mator and Rom Globus. Englund also appears as a modern sadist named Paul Chevalier who, in the city of Alexandria, uses his minions (ladies of the night Alona Kimhi, Juliano Merr and Chandra West) to trick a young innocent (Zoe Trilling) to enter his demonic cult where harem women suck on the heads of boa constrictors. Come to think of it, this whole movie sucks. (Cannon)

TOBOR THE GREAT (1954) ★½ Clanking sounds do not emanate from the mechanical man of the title, but from the rusty mind of director Lee Sholem and the unoiled typewriters of screenwriters Phillip MacDonald and Dick Goldstone, who must have intended this "clunker" for 6-year-olds. But even the young will be bored by the spy antics and performances of Charles Drake, Karin Booth, Lyle Talbot, Robert Shayne, Taylor Holmes and William Schallert, who look as though they wanted to

get oiled. Ask yourself: Tobor or not Tobor? Remember, Thor, *Tobor* is a bore. (Video/Laser: Republic)

TO CATCH A YETI (1993) ★½ Inconsequential, kiddie-oriented Canadian TV-movie in which the alleged snowman of the Himalayas turns out to be nothing more than a small furry creature with big, cute eyeballs, a cooing voice and big clumsy feet. In the vein of *Harry and the Hendersons,* "Hank" ends up in the home of little Chantallese Kent, but along comes big game hunter Jake Grizzly (Meat Loaf) and his dumb pal Rick Howland to steal him away for a spoiled millionaire kid. Paul Adam's teleplay displays an appalling attitude of violence toward children and parental indifference that may turn off some viewers. Directed by Bob Keen. Jim Gordon, Leigh Lewis, Jeff Moser. (New World)

TO DIE FOR (1989) ★★★ Two vampires prey on women in L.A. in this trendy video horror film directed by Deran Sarafian and written by Leslie King. One of those bloodsuckers is Vlad Tepish, the original "Dracula" on whom Bram Stoker based his novel. Brendan Hughes, Scott Jacoby, Duane Jones, Steve Bond, Sydney Walsh. Followed by a sequel. (Academy) (Laser: Image)

TO DIE FOR 2: SON OF DARKNESS (1991) ★★★ Dr. Max Schreck (the name of the actor who starred in the German classic *Nosferatu*) turns up at a hospital at Lake Serenity. In actuality he is Vlad Tepish (the madman whom Bram Stoker patterned Dracula after) turned immortal and trying to live a cleaner vampire's existence by tapping into the hospital's blood bank instead of puncturing humans. However, his communal vampire friends prefer to kill their supper, causing a rift in the local bloodsucking community. Caught between these forces are a mother and her adopted baby (the child is secretly Vlad's) and a vampire hunter à la Von Helsing. Rather well done by director David F. Price, who brings zing to the Leslie King script. Good cast, too, with Vince Edwards as the disbelieving cop. Rosalind Allen, Steve Bond, Scott Jacoby, Michael Praed, Jay Underwood, Remy O'Neill. (Vidmark)

TO DIE WITH PLEASURE. See *Blood and Roses.*

TO KILL A STRANGER (1985) ★★ When singer Angelica Maria is forced to murder sex maniac Donald Pleasence, does she report it to the cops? Hell no, the guy was a war hero. So she conceals the body. Meanwhile, there's long-suffering husband Dean Stockwell and a cop (Aldo Ray) and a military officer (*Mad* magazine cartoonist Sergio Aragones). What the hell is a nice guy like Aragones doing in this flick? Directed by Juan Lopez Moctezuma. (Virgin Vision; VCL)

TO LOVE A VAMPIRE. See *Lust for a Vampire.*

TOMB, THE (1985) ★★ Egyptian snake goddess Nefratis, nothing more than a vampire with fangs, is resurrected from her sarcophagus by young dumb adventurers and materializes in L.A. to recover a magical amulet in the possession of archeologist Cameron Mitchell. The acting is really bad, full of modern idiom when it should possess feeling for an ancient culture—blame poor direction on Fred Olen Ray. And the bad dialogue ("I've come to kill you, you mummified bitch!") on Ken Hall. Sybil Danning and John Carradine have pointless cameos. Michelle Bauer is sexy as the vamp but she needs to take acting lessons. Susan Stokey, David Pearson, Richard Alan Hench. (Trans World)

TOMB OF HORROR. See *Terror Creatures From the Grave.*

TOMB OF LIGEIA (1965) ★★★½ Edgar Allan Poe's poem, in which the spirit of a dead woman returns through the corpse of her husband's second wife, becomes a Roger Corman film made in England. Many consider this one of Corman's best—Poe lovers, on the other hand, objected to its overuse of the walking corpse and the fact Vincent Price must kill it over and over again. The literacy of the production is attributable in part to screenwriter Robert Towne and Corman's direction. The 1820s of England is well captured in the set design. Elizabeth Shepherd, John Westbrook, Derek Francis. Aka *House at the End of the World, Ligeia, Tomb of the Cat* and *Last Tomb of Ligeia.* (HBO; Orion) (Laser: Image, with *Conqueror Worm*)

TOMB OF THE CAT. See *Tomb of Ligeia.*

TOMB OF THE LIVING DEAD. See *Mad Doctor of Blood Island.*

TOMBS OF HORROR (1962). See *Castle of Blood.*

TOMBS OF HORROR (1965). See *Terror Creatures from the Grave.*

TOMBS OF THE BLIND DEAD. First in a series of Spanish-Portuguese films from writer-director Amando De Ossorio. See *The Blind Dead.* Others: *Return of the Evil Dead, Horror of the Zombies, Night of the Seagulls* (aka *Night of the Death Cult*). (Paragon; Midnight)

TOMCAT: DANGEROUS DESIRES (1993) ★★½ Eccentric mixture of genetic sci-fi and cat-and-mouse horror (excuse the term) with erotic overtones and bedroom nudity that give this video movie an unusual mood. Scientist Maryam D'Abo has found a way to transfer a genetic solution taken from a cat into the brain of Richard Grieco, who is suffering from a genetic deficiency (whatever that is). Grieco emerges with the characteristics of a cat, and a primitive instinct to kill the sexy women he mates with. This is basically a 4-character scenario (by director Paul Donovan) that moves as languidly as a black cat through a dark alley and has its best erotic scene when blond sex bomb Natalie

Radford masturbates while having a breathless phone conversation with Grieco. There's a good chase sequence through a lumber mill but this is like a cat at the foot of a dead-end alley—it has nowhere to go, and simply ends with a mild meow. Too much mood and erotica and not enough story, but, if you dig mood and erotica, this is catnip. (Video/Laser: Republic)

TOMMYKNOCKERS, THE (1993) ★★★½ Excellent 4-hour adaptation by Lawrence D. Cohen of Stephen King's sprawling, complex novel about an alien force that crash-landed outside Haven Falls (typical of King's New England territory) centuries earlier and now drains the humanity from the people so the aliens can get back into action. It evolves around drunken poet Jimmy Smits and estranged wife Marg Helgenberger and how they come to grips in first unleashing the extraterrestrial menace and then trying to curtail it. Secondary characters include a lovely sheriff (Joanna Cassidy), a town slut (Traci Lords) and the one man who knows about the legend of the "tommyknockers" (E. G. Marshall). A number of weird plot twists are tossed in (the townspeople are inventing crazy new devices, including a novel-writing machine) before the satisfying climax in the haunted woods involving a buried spaceship and some great-looking aliens. Directed by John Power. John Ashton, Allyce Beasley, Robert Carradine, Cliff De Young, Annie Corley, Leon Woods. Also known as *Stephen King's The Tommyknockers.*

TOMORROW NEVER DIES (1997) ★★★½ So you like your James Bond movies filled with plenty of incredibly exciting stunt action, explosive special effects, and as little plot as possible. And as little characterization as you can live without. Then here it is—your all-time Bond action-adventure flick, with Pierce Brosnan essaying the role of the British agent licensed to kill for the second time. He doesn't do much with the historic spy role except shoot by the numbers and behave like a windup action toy, since the Bruce Feirstein screenplay for this, the 18th in the series, is almost pure movement. Lip movement, even for kissing and making other forms of love, is kept to a minimum. After an explosive and exciting prologue in which Bond has to escape in a jet from a terrorist site on the Russian border, about to be blown up by a guided missile, Agent 007 settles into a head-to-head encounter with a crazed communications tycoon (a breathless Jonathan Pryce) and his minions (including blond Gotz Otto, who is reminiscent of Robert Shaw's assassin in *From Russia with Love,* though only in appearance). Seems that Pryce, a hyped-up version of Ted Turner, intends to start war between America and China with the use of a super-stealth (invisible) battleship and then dominate the international media scene. A British warship is lured into Chinese waters and then sunk by a special drilling machine, with the Chinese made to look responsible. Bond's episodic adventures, only loosely knitted together by Feirstein, includes teaming with a Chinese secret agent (Michelle Yeoh) skilled in the martial arts, visiting Hamburg to have a fling with his old girlfriend Teri Hatcher (who now just happens to be married to Pryce's evil Elliot Carver), and dodging a constant spray of machine-gun fire. A chase through the streets of Saigon with Brosnan and Yeoh on a motorcycle with a helicopter in pursuit really does stretch credulity (even in the context of a Bond movie), but far more satisfying is an underwater sequence where Bond explores a sunken British ship. There are also some nice action-sequence escapes from 1) a printing-press plant, 2) the skyscraper headquarters of Carver's media empire, and 3) the "stealth ship" built by Carver to bring about the intended world war. Director Roger Spottiswoode, although he delivers a slick-looking movie, settles for tried-and-true formulas that often make the film look better than it is exciting. Judi Dench is once again a capable M (Bond's assignment chief) in a world dominated by men, Joe Don Baker is back as an American agent, Desmond Llewellyn is the frustrated but ingenious weapons-designer Mr. Q (offering Bond a newly equipped BMW that becomes the centerpiece for an action sequence), and Vincent Schiavelli appears in a brief though funny hitman cameo. (Video/Laser: MGM)

TOMORROW YOU DIE! See *The Crawling Hand.*

TOM THUMB (1958) ★★★★★ Delightful George Pal fantasy musical, which he produced and directed, based on the fairy tale by the Brothers Grimm, about a woodsman, Honest John, who wishes for a child the size of his thumb—and literally gets it in the form of happy-go-lucky Russ Tamblyn, a trampoline star who bounces bubbly in the role. Enchanting, nonsensical mixture of live-action choreography, animation in the old Puppetoon style Pal introduced in the '40s; and music and songs with a touch of sparkling magic. Terry-Thomas and Peter Sellers are wonderfully corny as the villains in the Black Swamp who misuse the minuscule Thumb to rob the King's Treasury. The plot (by Ladislas Fodor) is slight—it's Pal's ability to capture a cinematic lightheartedness that works. Alan Young, Jessie Matthews, June Thorburn. (MGM/UA) (Laser: MGM/UA; Turner)

TOOLBOX MURDERS, THE (1979) ★★★ A favorite film of Stephen King, this perverse murder thriller, designed for gore fans and blood-and-guts connoisseurs, depicts a killer in a ski mask murdering apartment-building beauties with power drill, hammer claws, battery-driven screwdriver and nailgun. Disgusting but

fascinating in its meticulous attention to details (splattering blood, ground-up flesh, woman masturbating in bathtub, like that), *Toolbox* begins falling apart when attention focuses on the aftermath of the grisly, grim murders as a young man searches for his kidnapped sister. Acting is amateurish and the sound is semilousy, but Gary Graver's photography captures the sleazy setting and mundane characters all too well and there's a sense of nihilism that comes through despite the incompetent direction of Dennis Donnelly (son of Tim Donnelly, who plays a cop) and a barely literate script by Neva Friedenn, Robert Easter and Ann Kindberg. Cameron Mitchell is the manager of the apartments, and is it possible he's the killer? A closing credit says this is based on a true story from 1969, but it sure plays like a B movie thriller-driller. Hah! Pamelyn Ferdin, Anita Corsaut, Wesley Eure, Nicholas Beauvy. (United; Video Treasures)

TOO SCARED TO SCREAM (1983) ★★★ *Psycho* lives when a knife-wielding murderer attacks victims in a Manhattan apartment building. Obvious suspect is the doorman (Ian MacShane), a repressed ex-actor who spouts Shakespeare and lives with his invalid mother (played catatonically by Maureen O'Sullivan). Mother? Did we say Mother? Hmmmm. . . . Cops Mike Connors and Anne Archer meet suspects and sex perverts as director Tony Lo Bianco builds suspense with smelly red herrings. Aka *The Doorman.* Leon Isaac Kennedy, Ruth Ford, John Heard, Murray Hamilton. (Vestron)

TOPPER (1937) ★★★★ Classically funny Hal Roach adaptation of the Thorne Smith comedy novel. Constance Bennett and Cary Grant portray a rich couple killed in an accident, but fate decrees they remain on Earth until achieving a good deed. So they straighten out the affairs of henpecked Cosmo Topper (Roland Young) and nagging wife Billie Burke. Delightfully madcap, jammed with visual tricks, utterly refreshing. This led to 2 sequels (*Topper Takes a Trip* and *Topper Returns*) and in the '50s became a long-running TV series with Leo G. Carroll, Anne Jeffreys and Robert Sterling. Directed by Norman Z. McLeod. (Media; Nostalgia Merchant; Video Yesteryear; Video Treasures offers a colorized version)

TOPPER RETURNS (1941) ★★★½ Second Hal Roach sequel to *Topper* is more rollicking high jinks in the Thorne Smith tradition with Roland Young as the sophisticate who solves an "old dark house" murder with the aid of ghost Joan Blondell. The great supporting cast includes Carole Landis, Billie Burke (as Topper's goofy spouse), Dennis O'Keefe, Patsy Kelly and Eddie "Rochester" Anderson. Directed by Roy Del Ruth from a memorable script by Gordon Douglas and Jonathan Latimer. (Video Yesteryear; Kartes; United; Video Classics) (Laser)

TOPPER TAKES A TRIP (1939) ★★★½ The first *Topper* sequel, again with Constance Bennett as the svelte Marion Kerby, a ghost who pops in and out of sight while trying to keep Cosmo (Roland Young) from divorcing pea-brained Mrs. Topper (Billie Burke) during their holiday in Europe. Stuffy characters (such as Alan Mowbray's butler) are an added treat, and Hal Roach's special effects department has objects moving mysteriously as the female ghost performs mischievous deeds. Directed by Norman Z. McLeod. Irving Pichel, Alex D'Arcy, Franklin Pangborn. (Video Treasures; Media)

TORMENTED (1960) ★★ Rock-bottom production values (consisting mainly of Pacific waves crashing on rocks along the California coast) make this Bert I. Gordon–Joe Steinberg production border on the unwatchable. It was the nadir in the career of Richard Carlson, who overportrays a heel who pushes his secret lover off the balcony of a lighthouse when she threatens to blackmail him. Julie Reding, the curvaceous lover, is so busty you want to see more of her tantalizing figure, but she only returns as a superimposed image to haunt Carlson's conscience, insipidly reciting her "revenge" dialogue without conviction. Gordon directed the George Worthing Yates script, a hopeless assignment from anyone's perspective, and he flounders horribly whenever he tries to inject a special effect. The whole thing is contrived, and except for the overwrought performances will bore you into a state of sleep. Susan Gordon, Gene Roth, Joe Turkel, Lillian Adams, Eugene Sanders. (Sinister/C; S/Weird; Filmfax)

TORPEDO OF DOOM (1938). Feature version of the Republic serial *Fighting Devil Dogs*.

TORSO (1973) ★★ Italian gore galore murders with touches of sleazy lightcore pornography dominate this crude, rude, lewd sick hick flick. Suzy Kendall and a bevy of glamor models are on the fringes of a series of hacksaw murders committed by a madman in a hood who strangles his female victims and then fondles their nude bodies with bloody hands. This unsettling "entertainment" climaxes when Kendall (one leg in a cast) is trapped in a villa with the killer as he saws up Suzy's beautiful friends. More-so *Torso*? Less-so messo. Directed by Sergio Martino, who cowrote with Ernesto Gastaldi. John Richardson, Tina Aumont, Luc Meranda. (Prism; MPI)

TORTURE CHAMBER, THE. Video version of *The Fear Chamber* (MPI).

TORTURE CHAMBER OF BARON BLOOD. Video version of *Baron Blood* (Thorn EMI).

TORTURE CHAMBER OF DR. FU MANCHU. See *The Castle of Fu Manchu*.

TORTURE CHAMBER OF DR. SADISM (1969). Alternate video version of *Castle of the Walking Dead* (Magnum; Regal).

TORTURE GARDEN (1967) ★★★½ Above-average horror anthology, skillfully written by Robert Bloch (he adapted 4 of his short stories), and imaginatively directed by Freddie Francis. At a British carnival sideshow, barker Dr. Diablo (Burgess Meredith) offers "special terrors" to his visitors—glimpses into their unpleasant futures. Hence, the Bloch Busters: "Enoch" is the "Weird Tales" classic about a demon cat who eats the heads of its victims; "Terror Over Hollywood" shows why all our favorite movie stars are so beautiful; "Mr. Steinway" is the bizarre look at a haunted piano; and "The Man Who Collected Poe" (the best of the lot) stars Peter Cushing as a sorcerer who brings Poe back from the dead, much to the shock of Poe collector Jack Palance. And then, of course, there's the surprise ending with Dr. Diablo. Beverly Adams, Michael Bryant, Maurice Denham, Robert Hutton. (Video/Laser: RCA/Columbia)

TORTURE ROOM, THE. See *The Torture Chamber of Dr. Sadism*.

TORTURE ZONE. See *The Fear Chamber*.

TO SAVE A CHILD (1991) ★ Failed TV-movie pilot for a series, derivative of the *Rosemary's Baby* genre in which Marita Geraghty, pregnant with child, winds up in a New Mexico community with her doctor-husband. But from the beginning it's apparent the town is evil, and her prenatal paranoia suspicions build quickly. This kind of witchcraft–devil cult tale has been told so many times before, it's totally obvious what's going down, and instead of throwing us surprise zingers, scripter Joyce Eliason simply fulfills our nonexpectations. Director Robert Lieberman is stuck with a bad concept, but he pulls good performances from Geraghty, hubby Peter Kowanko, Joseph Runningfox (as the strange Indian, Toby Coldcreek), Shirley Knight and Spalding Gray. Especially excellent is Anthony Zerbe, who oozes evil. Also shown on TV as *The Craft*.

TO SLEEP WITH A VAMPIRE (1992) ★★½ That old saw about the cheapest way to make a movie—put 2 actors into a single room and let them talk to each other for 90 minutes—is put to practical use by producer Roger Corman in this remake of *Dance of the Damned*, right down to the dialogue. The 2 characters are a nightclub stripper with suicidal tendencies (Charlie Spradling) and a lonely nocturnal wanderer–vampire (Scott Valentine) with the soul of a poet. He locks her up for a night to learn what the daytime is like and they exchange morbid dialogues about the meaning of life and other vital issues for strippers and vampires. The title of this 1-note sleep inducer is all too prophetic, its only lively moments depicting big-breasted women stripping. After that, you need No-Doze tablets. Directed by Adam Friedman from a rewrite by Patricia Harrington. Richard Zobel, Ingrid Vold. (New Horizons)

TOTAL RECALL (1990) ★★★★½ An exciting, breathless sci-fi actioner, capturing the pure essence of what movies are about, with director Paul Verhoeven knocking down the walls of film violence to incorporate his own dark vision of how terrible the human species can be to itself. It's Arnold Schwarzenegger's best acting job as a worker in the year 2084 who discovers his quiet, boring life is cover for a previous identity as a spy—none of which he remembers. His search for an understanding of himself and the treacherous events that suddenly endanger his life lead to a mining colony on Mars and a string of fascinating characters and situations. The pacing of the script (by Ronald Shusett, Dan O'Bannon and Jon Povill, based on a Philip K. Dick short story, "We Can Remember It for You Wholesale") never lets up and exciting twists move the story to a new level of action, and give it an epic quality, as life on Mars is in jeopardy. The story has the bizarre flavor of the *Star Wars* series, though without sympathetic characters. It's a satisfying experience with good-to-excellent effects and makeup (by Rob Bottin). The cast serves the material well: Rachel Ticotin as the mysterious romantic lead; Sharon Stone as the "loving" wife; Michael Ironside as the insidious heavy; Ronny Cox as the conspiracy master. (Live) (Laser: Image)

TO THE CENTER OF THE EARTH. See *Unknown World.*

TO THE DEVIL . . . A DAUGHTER (1976) ★★★ Satanist Christopher Lee is out to transform a young child into a devil goddess in this Hammer film based on a Dennis Wheatley novel (Chris Wicking did the adaptation) and directed with a strong sense of evil by Peter Sykes. Richard Widmark (acting with unusual intensity) portrays an occult writer who tries to stop Lee with the help of a book, *The Grimoire of Astaroth.* The 16-year-old is Nastassia Kinski, daughter of Klaus Kinski. Sykes zooms all over the gloomy landscapes and the final results are pretty good if somewhat muddled. Honor Blackman, Denholm Elliott. (New Star; Continental; CinemaGroup; Republic; from Olympus as *Child of Satan*)

TOURIST TRAP (1979) ★★★½ Low-budget exploitation chiller borrows from *Psycho, Carrie* and *Halloween*, and comes off powerfully with its cat-and-mouse terror, thanks to the imaginative direction of David Schmoeller. Four likable young travelers are lured to a deserted roadside wax museum owned by reclusive Chuck Connors. Stealing the show are numerous mannequins (with gaping, screaming mouths) and masks that litter a madman's torture chamber. The film sinks deeper and deeper into nightmare allegory until reality is nonexistent, and one needn't bother to sort out any logic. Jocelyn Jones, Keith McDermott, Dawn Jeffory, Robin Sherwood, Tanya Roberts. (Media; Paramount) (Laser: Paramount)

TOWER, THE (1992) ★★★ A high-rise office building owned by Intercorp and controlled by a computerized system called Cybernetics Access Structure (CAS), becomes a nightmare for Paul Reiser and Susan Norman, employees trapped overnight when the system has a breakdown and flips into a "terminate intruders" mode. The cliff-hangers are good, and the suspense builds steadily under the direction of Richard Kletter (who cowrote this Gregory Harrison–produced TV-movie with John Riley) but where things go awry is in the dumb love affair that dominates when the couple should be fighting for their lives. (All that's Kletter's is not gold?) Still, it has its scary moments and is a decent time killer. Richard Gant, Annabelle Gurwith, Roger Rees.

TOWER OF EVIL (1974) ★★★½ Snape Island houses a lighthouse and a cache of ancient Phoenician treasures; it is also the romping ground for a murderer who severs hands and heads from corpses and leaves the remains for visitors (including Jill Haworth and Bryant Halliday) to stumble across. Graphic shocker has plenty of bare flesh and sexual activity in addition to its horrors to hold interest—and that's during the film's quieter moments. From British producer Richard Gordon; written-directed by Jim O'Connolly. Dennis Price, George Coulouris, Anna Palk, Jack Watson. Aka *Horror on Snape Island* and *Beyond the Fog.* (Gorgon; VCI; Orion; MPI)

TOWER OF SCREAMING VIRGINS (1971) ★★½ European-made period thriller is more of a swashbuckler in the tradition of Alexandre Dumas than a horror film, although it fulfills the latter category by depicting bloody murders in the Tower of Sin, where the Queen of France and other sexpots hold orgies, concluding them by having brigands slaughter young noblemen the wanton women have lured into their chambers. The action and period production qualities are good and the film satisfies best on an action level. Plenty of nudity and erotic lovemaking sequences. And this deserves a laugh when a lady-in-waiting is named Blanche DuBois. Directed by Francois Legrand. Terry Torday, Jean Piet, Veronique Vendell, Armando Francioli. (Video Yesteryear; Video Dimensions; Sinister/C; Filmfax)

TOWER OF TERROR. See *Assault.*

TOWER OF TERROR (1998) ★★ This Disney TV movie of the supernatural-comedy school, based on an amusement ride at Walt Disney World, has hardly any ghostly special effects and only a modicum of comedy, and therefore is a lightweight, almost negligible film. However, its cast is appealing and there are enough twists and turns in the teleplay by director D. J. McHale to keep it interesting for the kiddies. Down-and-out tabloid journalist Steve Guttenberg hopes to restart his career by exposing what happened on Halloween night in 1939 when five people—including a child star of the Shirley Temple mold and her sour-faced nanny—disappeared while going up in an elevator and a bolt of lightning struck the Hollywood Towers Hotel. Deserted since that night, the gothic, dust-covered, cobwebbed hotel provides for a few eerie settings, but there are no genuine scares or spooky thrills as Guttenberg and niece Kirsten Dunst set out to solve the mystery. A "Book of Souls" used by a witch on that fateful night becomes a key element. Nia Peeples, Michael McShane, Melora Hardin, Alastair Duncan. (Walt Disney Home Video)

TOXIC AVENGER, THE (1984) ★★★ Flaky farce on monster movies, a scattergun of visual gags with some pellets on target and others missing by miles. It's funky and ugly and gory and cruddy and yet takes on a crude charm. Played for parody, *Toxic Avenger* is set in Tromaville, a center for toxic waste, where nerdish 90-pound janitor Melvin falls into a barrel of atomic poison and emerges a mutated crusader who fights crime, his symbol a wet mop shoved into the face of an unconscious foe. Satirical vignettes ensue, depicting brutish fights and a romance between the dippy crime-fighter and a well-developed (her body, that is) blind girl. Amid this hodgepodge are raunchy sex jokes and bouncing bare breasts. Produced-directed by Samuel Weis and Michael Herz. Mitchell Cohen, Andree Maranda, Jennifer Babtist. (Vestron; Live; Lightning) (Laser: Vestron)

TOXIC AVENGER PART II, THE (1989) ★★ If you can set your brain control on Zero, and get into the spirit of slapdash fun, you might have an amusing time watching this sequel to Troma's 1984 hit. That original was fresh and funny, while this is just madcap mayhem. The bad guys from Apocalypse, Inc., are out to take over Tromaville with only the Avenger to stop them—and that's all the plot you'll find. Directors Michael Herz and Lloyd Kaufman (that traumatized Troma team) exercise no control over the barrage of lowbrow sight gags, but at least there's Tokyo location footage (where the Avenger heads to find his missing father). Ron Fazio and John Altamura double as the Avenger, Phoebe Legere reprises her role as Claire, the sexy blind girl, Rick Collins plays the heavy. (Video/Laser: Warner Bros.)

TOXIC AVENGER PART III: THE LAST TEMPTATION OF TOXIE, THE (1989) ★★½ Toxie turns into a Wall Street tycoon in this third entry in the wild and woolly Troma series that goes for the lowest common denominator in screen excitement—in short, it's totally stupid. But there are moments of fun if you can accept the inanities of producer-director Lloyd Kaufman and writers Kaufman and Gay Par-

tington Terry. Ron Fazio, John Altamura, Phoebe Legere, Rick Collins, Lisa Gaye and Jessica Dublin head the whacky cast. (Vestron)

TOXIC SPAWN. Video version of *Alien Contamination* (Lettuce Entertain You).

TOXIC ZOMBIES (1984) ★★ Poor man's imitation of *Night of the Living Dead*, in which hippie marijuana growers are sprayed by a herbicide, Dromax, which gives them hollow eyes and bloodlust. Type-O flows and the gore spurts as the shamblers mindlessly attack picnickers and fishermen. A federal agent enters the area to investigate, discovering a government conspiracy that ordered the spraying. Writer-producer-director Charles McCrann offers little subtext or substance beyond the bloodletting, so this is your basic exercise in exploitation futility. Charles Austin, Beverly Shapiro. (Raedon; Monterey)

TOY FACTORY. TV title for *Necromancy*.

TOY STORY (1995) ★★★★½ The first feature-length film to be completely animated by computer, and a wonderful entertainment for children and adults—a box-office winner for Pixar, the company that designed the system, and Disney. This is set in a world of toys, which come to life whenever their owner is out of the room. *Toy Story* is a joy to behold because screenwriters Joss Whedon, Andrew Stanton, Joel Cohen and Alec Sokolow have given believable human traits to these toys, so that you care about cowboy marionette Woody (voice: Tom Hanks) and spaceman Buzz Lightyear (voice: Tim Allen) as they struggle to maintain a safe place in their owner's world, lest he abandon them for newer playthings. You'll also fall in love with Mr. Potato Head (voice: Don Rickles), Slinky Dog (voice: Jim Varney) and the insecure Rex the Dinosaur (voice: Wallace Shawn), characters who also have distinct human traits. As well as any army of toy soldiers who carry out various missions (commander's voice: R. Lee Ermery). Director John Lassiter is an old hand from Pixar, the Marin County–based company that originally won an Oscar for *Tin Toy*. (Video/Laser: Buena Vista)

TRACES OF RED (1991) ★★★½ An unusually good whodunit with mild slasher overtones, opening in the fashion of *Sunset Boulevard* with a corpse narrating his own story. Jim Belushi stands out as that character, a Palm Beach cop who's involved in a series of murders committed by a fiend who sends him poetry and plays other cat-and-mouse games. The clues have been cleverly planted by screenwriter Jim Piddock and Andy Wolk directs in a clear, no-nonsense style as several plot twists unfold. This is one worth seeing even if its horror content is minimal. Lorraine Bracco, Troy Goldwyn, Faye Grant, Joe Lisi, William Russ. (Video/Laser: HBO)

TRACK OF THE VAMPIRE. Video version of

Blood Bath (1966) (Sinister/C; S/Weird; Genesis).

TRACKS OF A KILLER (1995) ★★★ This "woman in peril" psychothriller has 2 attractions: an intensely crazed performance by Wolf Larson as a homicidal maniac, and an equally intense performance by Kelly LeBrock as a terrified woman trapped in an isolated mountain cabin with madman Larson. Occasionally quipping à la Freddy Krueger (an element of the Michael Cooney script that weakens the suspense a bit), Larson yanks a bullet from Le-Brock's wounded arm with kitchen tongs, stitches up the wound with a hooked needle (without anesthetic), and beats and kicks her with frequent regularity. Larson also sets a forest ranger on fire and a little later pumps 5 bullets into his quivering body. Meanwhile, LeBrock's hubby, James Brolin, struggles through Vancouver snowdrifts to rescue her. Will he arrive in time? Is the Pope a Catholic? Directed by Harvey Frost. Courtney Taylor, George Touliatos. (Live)

TRAIN OF TERROR. See *Terror Train*.

TRANCERS (1984) ★★ Muddled cross between *Blade Runner* and *The Terminator*, set in the 23rd century when half of L.A. is underwater, and a war rages between police and zombielike Trancers. These human killers are trained by Whistler (Michael Stefani), whose adversary is hard-boiled "Angel City Trooper" Jack Deth (Tim Thomerson). Whistler has gone into the past to eliminate the relatives of a special peace council so the council will no longer exist. Deth follows him to modern-day L.A., where he uses a time-stopping wristwatch to save the heroine. A mess of a story line by director-producer Charles Band, who nevertheless made several sequels, some of which are an improvement on this original. Aka *Future Cop*. Helen Hunt, Anne Seymour, Richard Herd, Richard Erdman. (Video/Laser: Vestron)

TRANCERS II: THE RETURN OF JACK DETH (1990) ★★ An unnecessarily convoluted plot showcases the return of future-cop Jack Deth (Tim Thomerson), living in present-day "Old California" with new wife Lena (Helen Hunt) after traveling through time. His old wife Alice (Megan Ward) turns up in his time zone on a mission to nail the evil E. D. Wardo (Richard Lynch), an ancestor of the original film's chief villian, the Whistler. (So where's Whistler's Mother through all this?) Wardo runs Green World Mission, turning out Trancer zombies with Scurb, a drug from 2078 that gives him power over his subjects. Screenwriter Jackson Barr (working from an idea by producer-director Charles Band) tries to make this hodgepodge of time-travel clichés meaningful by giving Deth 2 romances but little here is fresh or interesting if you've already seen *Back to the Future*. Biff

Manard, Martine Beswicke, Jeffrey Combs, Alyson Croft, Barbara Crampton. (Paramount) (Laser: Full Moon)

TRANCERS III: DETH LIVES (1992) ★★ "This is the best thing that's happened to me in two centuries!" exclaims Trancer hunter–private eye Jack Deth in this, the third in this series, in which he is taken from 1992 (where he was trapped in part II) to 2352 and back to 2005 to prevent the origins of the Trancer research. This is by far the least interesting of the *Trancer* movies, showing none of the imagination and wildness that earmarked part II, for example. Produced by Charles and Albert Band, it was written and directed by C. Courtney Joyner and stars Tim Thomerson (his Deth wisecracks are wearisome), Melanie Smith, Andrew Robinson, Tony Pierce, Dawn Ann Billings, Helen Hunt, Megan Ward, Stephen Macht. (Paramount) (Laser: Full Moon)

TRANCERS IV: JACK OF SWORDS (1993) ★★★ In his time-hopping adventures, Jack Deth (Tim Thomerson) is in a parallel universe in the medieval kingdom of Orpheus, where a gang of Trancers called Nobles preys on humans by sucking out their energy. Call it *Jack Deth Meets Robin Hood* when the wisecracking, trenchcoated Deth joins rebels (nicknamed "tunnel rats") to fight the evil ruler (Clabe Hartley) of the Nobles, and the arrows start to fly. Producer Charles Band brings production value to this Full Moon fantasy adventure made in Romania. For the first time in the series, Deth doesn't deal with any of his wives. Lucky break for him. Written by Peter David, directed by David Nutter. Lochlyn Munro, Jeff Moldovan, Ty Miller, Stacie Randall, Terri Ivens, Stephen Macht. (Video/Laser: Paramount)

TRANCERS V: SUDDEN DETH (1994) ★★★ This is a virtual continuation of the adventures in part 4, with Jack Deth (Tim Thomerson) still trapped in the land of Orpheus, where he leads the "tunnel rats" against evil magician Clabe Hartley and the psychic-powered Nobles in the castle of Calaban. It's a competently made Charles Band production, enhanced by Romanian locations and good direction by David Nutter, but the Trancers formula seems wearisome, as if there is nowhere new in Peter David's script to take the idea of a time-hopping, wisecracking private eye. The quest in this allegedly final episode in the series is a magical diamond called a Timond, which will enable Deth to traverse time and space (something about an "open dimensional vortex") and get back to headquarters where boss Harris (Stephen Macht) is waiting. Or it will give that evil magician ultimate power over the folks in Orpheus. The strong supporting cast includes Ty Miller, Terri Ivens, Mark Arnold, Alan Oppenheimer and Jeff Moldovan. (Video/Laser: Paramount)

TRANSFORMATIONS (1989) ★★★ Oddball mixture of supernatural horror and hardware sci-fi when space-cargo pilot Wolf Shadduck (Rex Smith) is taken over by an evil, sexy incubus demon in a dream fantasy. Landing on a mining planet–penal colony complex, Wolf learns from doctor Lisa Langlois that he's carrying a plague—an opinion reinforced by sympathetic priest Patrick Macnee. This bizarre sci-fier takes a twist when its hero begins killing prostitutes—the demom within him taking over. Scriptwriter Mitch Brian's hodgepodge of ideas isn't reinforced by the sparse production and minimal effects in this New World production made at Empire Studio in Rome under the direction of Jay Kamen. Ultimately it doesn't have the budget or the ambience to make its intermixed themes effective. Christopher Neame, Michael Hennessey. (Starmaker) (Laser: Image)

TRANSIT. See *The First Power.*

TRANSMUTATIONS (1985) ★★★ Clive Barker, who cowrote this British low-budgeter with James Caplin, has disavowed the result, but it's a rather offbeat horror film about unsavory Dr. Savary and his drug Thakanicene, a liquid that gives users hallucinogenic euphoria. But the side effects are disfigurement of face and body; the mad doctor (played with wonderful abandonment by Denholm Elliott) is creating an army of zombielike addicts. This physically marred band kidnaps beautiful prostitute Miranda Richardson, bringing in an underworld gang led by Motherskille (Steven Berkoff) and an old boyfriend hired to track down the femme, who has a fatal attraction for all. They are as addicted to her as the poor saps are to the doc's drug—a fascinating parallel in this odd tale, which ends on a metaphysical twist. Director George Pavlou (*Rawhead Rex*) keeps the unpredictable plot moving briskly. Ingrid Pitt appears as Pepperdine, the whorehouse madam. Larry Lamb, Art Malik. Aka *Underworld.* (Vestron) (Laser: Image)

TRANSPLANT, THE. See *Night of the Bloody Transplant.*

TRANSVESTITE. See *Glen or Glenda?*

TRANSYLVANIA 6-5000 (1985) ★★ Nutty newsmen Ed Begley, Jr., and Jeff Goldblum are assigned to find Frankenstein in Transylvania by the editor of a sleazoid tabloid. What they dig up in a back-lot Rumanian village are would-be monsters created by the quite insane Dr. Malavaqua (Joseph Bologna) and assistants Lupi (Carol Kane) and Radu (John Byner), who pose as domestic help. There's a hunchback, a vampire, a Frankenstein hulker, a mummy . . . but you'll be depressed to find out what they really are. Script by director Rudy DeLuca. Jeffrey Jones, Geena Davis, Michael Richards, Norman Fell. (New World) (Laser: Image)

TRANSYLVANIA TWIST (1989) ★★ A witless series of verbal and visual puns, non sequiturs and movie-fan in-jokes as director Jim Wynorski (onetime Roger Corman neophyte) and writer R. J. Robertson spoof vampire and Frankenstein movies. Nerdish Dexter Ward (Steve Altman) and sexy Teri Copley of Arkham, Mass., are searching for the Book of Ulthar, a Lovecraft-inspired volume that could release an "elder god" from captivity. Robert Vaughn guest stars as Byron Orlock, vampire, and he's down for the count. Others in gag roles: Angus Scrimm, parodying his *Phantasm* character; Steve Franken as a Bavarian constable; Ace Mask; Howard Morris and Jay Robinson. The best sequence in this mess produced by Corman is a musical number, "Give Me Some Action," in which Wynorski reruns every explosion ever used in a Corman film. (MGM/UA)

TRAPPED (1989) ★★ Clichéd TV-movie, lacking in originality, depicts the plight of Kathleen Quinlan trapped in a new office building with a slasher killer armed with knife and baseball bat who's seeking revenge against TNX Industries, a company responsible for dumping toxic waste. Every cat-and-mouse trick is pulled out by writers Fred Walton (he also directed) and Steve Feke as the lovely Quinlan, in a short tight skirt and high heels, dangles from ledges, leaps in and out of elevators, and uses her female wits to stay one leap ahead of the murderer. A surprise ending is thrown in for good measure. Bruce Abbott, Katy Boyer. (MCA)

TRAPPED ON TOYWORLD. See *Josh Kirby . . . Time Warrior!*

TRAS EL CRISTAL. See *In a Glass Cage.*

TRAUMA (1982). See *Terminal Choice.* (Melotrauma?)

TRAUMA (1993). See *Dario Argento's Trauma.*

TREASURE OF THE FOUR CROWNS (1983) ★★ Writers-producers Tony Anthony and Gene Quintano, who gave the world *Comin' at Ya!* in 3-D, blend elements of *Mission: Impossible* and *Raiders of the Lost Ark* to depict adventurers stealing valuable crystals from a cult of religious nuts. These crystals have magical and atomic powers "of good or evil," depending on who owns them. The main concern is the 3-D; some effects are good, but logic is discarded for cheap thrills. The caper provides suspense, but otherwise it's condescending. Directed by Ferdinando Baldi in Spain. Anthony and Quintano portray adventurers. Ana Obregon, Francisco Rabal, Kate Levan. (MGM/UA)

TREASURE OF THE MOON GODDESS (1987) ★★★ Mildly entertaining adventure fantasy in the Indiana Jones tradition, but without the pizzazz. Rich guy Don Calfa and bikini-clad "secretary" are at poolside while he recites the adventure, which is shown in flashback: Calfa is the talent agent of small-time sexy blond singer Lu De Belle (Linnea Quigley) who is gig-ging in joints on the fringes of the South American jungle. Turns out her face resembles that of a native idol, so she's worth plenty to the bad guys if they can kidnap her. But Calfa, a sleazy guy, hires adventurer Asher Brauner and his girl (Jo Ann Ayres, a beautiful number) to escort them out. The band winds up in Indian territory with a crooked native chieftain and a cave of magical powers. A lighthearted touch in the Eric Weston–Asher Brauner script makes it bearable; even Joseph Louis Agraz's indifferent direction is forgivable. (Vidmark)

TREMORS (1989) ★★★★½ Rarely does a horror-monster movie satisfy all the needs of the genre . . . but here's one that's funny, scary, suspenseful, packed with action, gruesome, satirical and well-scripted and-acted. It has the flavor of a "mutant monster" film of the '50s as 2 desert-community handymen, Kevin Bacon and Fred Ward, discover there's "something out there" under the ground, tunneling at top speed and popping up to feast on sheep and people. These are giant worms, each with a gaping maw that contains smaller snakelike heads. It's a wild romp for our heroes to keep their feet off the ground when trapped in the isolated town with scientist Finn Carter, gun nuts Michael Gross and Reba McEntire (who blast away at an attacking worm in a hilarious send-up on modern firepower) and assorted survivors. The monsters are the frightening-fun kind and director Ron Underwood keeps it moving as fast as the locomotivelike worms. Script by producers S. S. Wilson and Brent Maddock. Produced by Gale Anne Hurd. (Video/Laser: MCA)

TREMORS 2: AFTERSHOCKS (1995) ★★★ A droll sense of satire underlies this amusing, if not terribly terrifying, sequel to the 1989 box-office hit, in which Fred Ward returns as Earl Bassett and Michael Gross is back as gun-happy Burt Gummer. These roughnecks journey to Mexico with an abundance of ordnance to destroy a new wave of Graboids, gigantic underground worms that prey on earth-walking humans. The script, by producers Brent Maddock and S. S. Wilson (the latter also directed), moves into new worm-eaten territory when the monsters mutate into smaller creatures capable of slithering on land. Christopher Gartin joins the fun as Grady Hoover, a happy-go-lucky adventurer with dreams of capturing the Graboids alive and opening a monster amusement park. A sense of fun rather than horror dominates this direct-to-video feature (Ron Underwood is credited as a producer), although Phil Tippett, Alec Gillis and Tom Woodruff, Jr., contribute some new special effects, making the baby monsters just believable enough to warrant a few limited thrills. (Video/Laser: MCA)

TRIAL, THE (1993) ★★★ Another adaptation of the Kafka allegory about a bank clerk in the city of Prague who is put on trial for no apparent reason. Harold Pinter wrote this adaptation, which was directed by David Jones. It stars David MacLachlan, Anthony Hopkins, Jason Robards, Jr., and Polly Walker. (Orion)

TRIBULATION 99: ALIEN ANOMALIES UNDER AMERICA (1992) ★★★ By pasting together documentary and feature footage, Craig Baldwin creates a sci-fi "documentary" that blends every known conspiratorial and/or crackpot theory into a narrative about aliens, known as Quetzals (from the planet Quetzalcoatl), that have infiltrated our society and are responsible for interplanetary-international events since 1949. Strictly a novelty item, but since it lasts only 48 minutes, its madcap editing and crazy sound track hold one rapt. (Film Threat)

TRICK OR TREAT (1986) ★★ Rip-off of *Phantom of the Paradise*, focusing on a heavy metal rocker (Sammi Curr, played by Tony Fields) who zaps dancers with electric bolts from his guitar. Curr, who uses sadism and death images in his act, has died and gone to rock heaven only to be brought back when a young fan (Marc Price) plays his last record backwards and is ordered to get out there and kick ass. Price finally realizes he's being manipulated by an evil force, and tries to stop Sammi's returned corpse with the help of girlfriend Lisa Orgolini. In a gag appearance, Ozzy Osbourne appears as a TV crusader against rock music. Good effects at the climax can't save this from its adolescent mentality. Directed by actor Charles Martin Smith, written by producers Joel Soisson and Michael S. Murphey. (Lorimar; American; Warner Bros.)

TRICK OR TREATS (1982) ★★ With all the experience Gary Graver has had as cinematographer, producer, director and actor, one would expect he would at least know that a horror film requires a quickened tempo, and not the movements of a lumbago-riddled grandmother. No treat, this *Halloween*-inspired slasher yarn, depicting how baby-sitter Jackelyn Giroux puts up with the Halloween night antics of jokester Christopher Graver while a maniac killer is approaching the house, intent on murdering the woman inside. It takes forever to happen and there's only a minimum of splatter matter. The killer, an escapee from an asylum for the criminally insane, is dressed as a woman, but all of Graver's attempts at drag humor fall as flat as a man who's just had his throat cut by the Boogeyman. David Carradine, Carrie Snodgrass, Steve Railsback and Paul Bartel are wasted in miniroles. Let's all rush over to Graver's L.A. digs and soap up his windows. (Vestron)

TRILOGY OF TERROR (1975) ★★★½ Superior anthology TV-movie produced-directed by Dan Curtis, for which William F. Nolan adapted 2 Richard Matheson stories and Matheson adapted the third. The unusual feature is that Karen

Black appears in all 3 in a total of 4 roles. "Julie" (a Nolan script) is a witchcraft tale involving a sexually unhappy teacher being blackmailed by a student; "Millicent and Therese" (another Nolan script) permits Black to engage in schizophrenia as she portrays diametrically opposing sisters; and "Amelia" (from Matheson's "Prey," which he adapted himself) is a horrifying tale of a doll that terrorizes Black in her apartment. Gregory Harrison, Robert Burton, John Karlen, George Gaynes. (MPI; the "Amelia" episode, a classic of its kind, is on tape from MPI as *Terror of the Doll*)

TRILOGY OF TERROR II (1996) ★★★½ This is a solid sequel to producer-director Dan Curtis's 1975 cult favorite starring Karen Black in three tales of terror. The most remembered, "Amelia," better known as "Prey," depicted her battle with a devil doll possessed by the spirit of a fierce African warrior that kept up an incessant chant during bloody knife-wielding attacks. In this movie made for the USA Network, Curtis revitalizes the formula with three new horror yarns all starring Lysette Anthony, a gifted actress who carries all the mini-chillers successfully. "The Graveyard Rats," scripted by Curtis and William F. Nolan from a Henry Kuttner classic, presents Ms. Anthony as a brunette who schemes with her lover (Geraint Wyn Davies) to get the fortune of her nasty, wheelchair-bound husband Matt Clark. After they push him down the staircase à la Richard Widmark in *Kiss of Death*, they have to break into his coffin in a rat-infested graveyard ill tended by caretaker Geoffrey Lewis. The grisly ending is deliciously over-the-top, but greater things are in store. The second tale, "Bobby," scripted by Richard Matheson with a little help from the classic short story "The Monkey's Paw," has Anthony as a brunette calling on demonic forces to bring her drowned son back to life. The fair-haired boy (Blake Heron) comes back all right, but not quite the way mother intended. The tale has a nice snap ending, the kind Matheson is famous for. But *Trilogy of Terror II* really zings to life with its resumption of the murder spree of that Zuni doll in "He Who Kills," scripted by Curtis and Nolan from Matheson's short story "Prey." Ms. Anthony, a brunette again, is a British-accented ethology expert asked by police to look at the Zuni doll after it's found charred in an oven. The creature, chanting its blood-chilling cries, corners her in her laboratory, and like Karen Black, Anthony undergoes several savage attacks and a few near escapes before . . . ah, but the ending isn't what you might think. Definitely a keeper. (Paramount)

TRIP TO MARS. See *Flash Gordon: Mars Attacks the World.*

TRIP TO THE CENTER OF THE EARTH. See *Journey to the Center of the Earth.*

TROG (1970) ★★ Superridiculous Herman Cohen production is a thorough time waster—it also wasted the talents of Joan Crawford as an anthropologist helping a caveman (a troglodyte, played by Joe Cornelius) find a place in contemporary society, and occasionally taking him to lunch. (This same idea was presented far more maturely in *Iceman.*) Michael Gough overacts as the villain thwarting her research. Director Freddie Francis does what he can with Aben Kandel's stone-age script. *Trog* is a dog. Robert Hutton, Bernard Kay. (Warner Bros.)

TROLL (1986) ★★ Unusually tame, G-rated Charles Band production directed with taste by John Carl Buechler, a special effects man making his directorial debut. The setting is a San Francisco apartment building where little Jenny Beck is possessed by a troll from another dimension. This ugly, undroll troll has a magical ring that turns everyone into mythical creatures or rain forests. The creatures and effects are adequate but the characters are cardboard and the promising themes in Ed Naha's script never developed beyond embryos. Michael Moriarty and Shelley Hack as the parents are wasted, as is Sonny Bono in a cameo (he becomes the rain forest). The standouts are June Lockhart as the guardian over the Tolkien-esque creatures, and her lovely daughter, Anne Lockhart. Nice try, but no *Gremlins*. (Video/Laser: Vestron)

TROLL 2 (1990) ★★ This has the grotesque dwarflike monsters of the original, and gory makeup and bloodletting to satisfy fans, but its juvenile approach and substandard acting (some of the worst in modern memory) make it inaccessible for shocks or suspense. Writer-director Drago Floyd has no idea how to work with actors, and his script, set in the rural burg of Nilbog (check that out backward), jumps all over the place, introducing characters as fodder to kill off. The monsters prey on a family of vacationers, particularly young Michael Stephenson. With the help of his dead grandfather's spirit, the youth not only proves he's the best actor in the cast but thwarts those damn dwarfs. George Hardy, Margo Prey, Connie McFarland. (Columbia TriStar)

TROLLENBERG TERROR, THE. See *The Crawling Eye.* (Trolling for monsters?)

TROLL IN CENTRAL PARK, A (1994) ★★★½ Animators Don Bluth and Gary Goldman helmed this cartoon fantasy in which a fairy-tale creature ends up in New York City. Voices by Dom DeLuise, Cloris Leachman, Jonathan Pryce, Hayley Mills, Charles Nelson Reilly and Phillip Glasser. (Warner Bros.)

TRON (1982) ★★★½ Walt Disney's adventure set in an electronic game world broke cinematic territory with splendid computer-generated images, but story and acting are so ineptly ridiculous that what emerges is a novelty piece with nowhere to go. A major problem is writer-director Steven M. Lisberger's plot. Instead of setting up the characters, he immediately plunges into the computerized Tron world, making one feel lost from the start. A corporate bigwig (David Warner) is stealing the game ideas of designer Jeff Bridges. To find the evidence to prove Warner's conspiracy, Bridges, Cindy Morgan and Bruce Boxleitner are zapped into the other-dimensional world of the computer. Wonderful blending of live action with computerized graphics, but at no time is there a sense of menace—just a playfulness. Nice try, Steven, but no Pac-Man. Barnard Hughes, Dan Shor. (Video/Laser: Disney)

TROUBLE IN MIND (1986) ★★★ Although set in the near future, in a society plagued by a mood of doom and pending war, this film written-directed by Alan Rudolph has few fantasy elements. It is more a surreal situation in which John Hawks, an ex-cop known as "the Hawk" (played by Kris Kristoffersen), returns to Rain City (actually Seattle) where he makes a play for old girlfriend Genevieve Bujold (as a crusty café owner) but falls for Lori Singer, who is married to cheap gangster Keith Carradine. Hawks also is caught up in a war between 2 criminal factions (one of them bossed by Divine playing an ugly vermin named Hilly Blue) and there's one very odd shoot-out. It's a strange film, as only Rudolph can make them, and its character portrayals are superb and real. Joe Morton, George Kirby. (Nelson/Charter) (Laser: Nelson; MCA)

T. R. SLOANE. See *Death Ray 2000.*

TRUCKS (1997) ★★½ It would be easy to dismiss this TV movie (one of those USA Network "originals") as "shiftless" or "a case of stripped gears" or simply write that it "never builds up much speed" and just "races its engine." However, there's a bit more acceleration going for this new adaptation of a Stephen King short story that was first made in 1986 as *Maximum Overdrive* (taken from his collection *Night Shift*). That movie marked the directing debut of King, and he wasn't afraid to run over a kid and do the other stuff that is usually avoided, even in graphic horror films. In redesigning King's concept of large-scale road rigs taking control of themselves and trapping a handful of hapless travelers in a road café, telewriter Brian Taggert has made numerous changes. The setting is now Lunar, NV, a rural spot on the map not far from Area 51. Thousands of years ago a meteorite crashed down here; hence the name. The trapped characters (father alienated from daughter, father and son trying to make a go of it with their roadside café, philosophical fat man, two redneck troublemakers, friendly cook, young married couple) are an unusual lot, and Taggert interestingly offers several explanations for the truck phenomenon. Did that thousand-year-old meteorite have something to do with it? Maybe "alien particles" from a recent comet bombardment are interfering with human-made "energy signals" and somehow the trucks are taking on an "intelligent energy force." Or maybe the nearby secret military base is causing the disturbance. Whatever, this version has its engrossing moments under the direction of Chris Thomson, even if the characters behave rather stupidly at times (necessary, obviously, for all the cliffhanger escapes). The TV version, aired in '97, kept the violence to a minimum, but the new DVD version from Trimark offers up some extra deaths. Another thing that makes Trucks enjoyable is a surprise ending that comes completely out of left field. It takes your breath away and forces you to consider the broader implications of the isolated roadside incident. Timothy Busfield, Brenda Bakke, Aidan Devine, Jay Brazeau, Brendan Fletcher, Amy Stewart, Roman Podhora. (Video/DVD: Trimark)

TRULY, MADLY, DEEPLY (1990) ★★★ Totally offbeat ghost story that deals deeply, passionately with the grief that comes after the death of a loved one. Overcoming that grief and finding a new life is the theme of the script by director Anthony Minghella, who brings a sense of uniqueness to his tale of spirits from the Beyond who impinge on the material world. Juliet Stevenson is the devastated wife recovering from the death of Alan Rickman, who suddenly pops up with other dead souls. There's nothing frightening about them, they just hang around her house watching TV and moving the furniture. It's all in the emotional depth of Minghella's writing and the way that Stevenson captures the despair, and her attempt to find new relationships. Bill Paterson, Michael Maloney. (Touchstone)

TRUMAN SHOW, THE (1998) ★★★½ This thoughtfully whimsical fantasy-parable, written by Andrew Niccol of *Gattaca* fame, is about man and his relationship with two things he frequently takes for granted: 1) the TV set in the living room, and 2) the world in which he lives. Jim Carrey plays Mr. Everyman, Truman Burbank, who lives in an idyllic coastal community called Seahaven with wife Laura Linney, who strangely describes the products she brings into the house as if she were a TV pitchwoman. Unknown to Truman, she is. In fact, everything around Truman is part of a domed soundstage created to resemble the real world, with rising and setting sun and waves that crash along the beaches. And everyone but Truman is an extra or actor pretending to be part of his day-to-day life. Since he was a baby purchased by the government to be the "star" of a lifelong TV sitcom, Truman has been watched 24 hours a day, seven days a week, by the rest of the TV-watching world. Five thousand hidden cameras surround him, and aloft in the dome's control center sits Truman's God, appropriately named Christof. Ed Harris plays the producer-director as if he had become God, so controlling is he not only over Truman but over his entire artificial world. He even calls himself a "televisionary." This character speaks volumes about the broadcasters and network CEOs who control our media, often cloaking their commercialism with high-minded double talk. But as Truman enters his 30th year, Day #10,909, a klieg light drops out of the sky (oops—the technicians on the catwalks goofed) and Truman meets his long-dead father. Other tasty clues suggest that all is not what it seems. And eventually he decides not to accept the reality he thinks he sees and escape to Fiji, where a former love (Natascha McElhone) said she was going. (Actually she really loved Truman and dropped out of the series rather than continue the deception.) This is an unusually laid-back message movie, with Carrey playing his character in a low key that allows him to display a wider range of acting abilities than usual. Director Peter Weir is never bombastic nor does he resort to special effects, preferring to let the themes of the movie speak for themselves. There's a lot to chew on here, and a tasty morsel it is. (Video/DVD: Paramount)

TURBO: A POWER RANGERS ADVENTURE (1997) ★½ This highly inferior, utterly disappointing sequel to *Mighty Morphin Power Rangers: The Movie* (based in turn on the TV series) is an absolute disaster for anyone who isn't five to seven years of age. With a phony-looking dwarf wizard named Lerigot (Joe Simanton in a furry suit and a headpiece with big eyes) and really crummy special effects and miniatures that look exactly like miniatures, *Turbo* is a noisy, confusing story mess (blame scripters Shell Danielson and Shuki Levy) in which the superhero teenagers square off against a lady villain named Divatox, played by Hilary Shepard Turner with her breasts falling out of her armor plating. Hilary, in fact, is the only watchable aspect as she cruises around in a submarine with some ridiculous-looking aliens. The ultimate absurdity is called "Zards," supercharged warrior cars the Rangers drive, which when fitted together turn into an upright, walking robot that battles an ugly demon from hell. The real hell is having to watch this for 99 minutes. Even with two directors at the helm (David Winning and Levy), *Turbo* still has no charge. Jason David Frank, Steve Cardenas, Johnny Yong Bosch, Catherine Sutherland, Amy Jo Johnson, Nakia Burrise, Blake Foster. Paul Schrier, Austin St. John. (Video/Laser: Fox)

TURKEY SHOOT. See *Escape 2000.*

TURN OF THE SCREW, THE (1974) ★★★ TV-movie, originally shown in 2 parts, is an adaptation of Henry James's classic horror novella, written by William F. Nolan and directed by Dan Curtis. The ambiguities of the story are faithfully retained and Lynn Redgrave, as the governess tutoring 2 children seemingly troubled (or possessed) by a dead spirit (or spirits), is superior. Megs Jenkins, Jasper Jacob, Eva Griffith. (Thrillervideo)

TURN OF THE SCREW, THE (1992) ★★★ This modernized adaptation of Henry James's classic novella of the supernatural by British producer Michael White is told in the form of a flashback by Marianne Faithfull during a gathering at her manor. Patsy Kensit portrays the tutor sent by a depraved Englishman (Julian Sands) to Bly House, his isolated estate, to educate his 2 children, only to discover they are possessed by the dead spirits of the evil Quint and his lover, Miss Jessels, a fact housekeeper Stephane Audran would rather ignore. Writer-director Rusty Lemorande strains a bit hard, and turns unnecessarily pretentious in the fright sequences, employing obvious religious and sexual symbols to capture themes of faith and depravity. This is an eccentric, stylish film, zinging to life when the hauntings are in force. To Lemorande's credit, he captures an erotic undertone without resorting to blatant sex, and shows off a commendable experimental spirit. *The Innocents* (1962) is still the best version, with a grand performance by Deborah Kerr, but it remains unavailable on video. (Live)

TURN-ON, THE (1985/1989) ½ Incredibly awful, simply worthless version of a 1985 French movie based on Milo Manara's comic strip "Le Declic," which Roger Corman reedited for the U.S. market, featuring new footage directed by Steve Barnett. It's a horrible mishmash of footage about cynical, unlikable Dr. Fez (Jean-Pierre Kalfon) who invents a black box that arouses sexual desires in women and makes them perform uninhibited sex no matter where they are. This ultimate male fantasy is wretchedly presented, with a plethora of stripteases, voodoo ceremonies and other material shot in and around New Orleans. The original was written-directed by Jean-Louis Richard. To be avoided at all costs. (New Horizons)

12 MONKEYS (1995) ★★★★½ Rarely does movie science fiction come up to the level of this ambitious fantasy thriller directed by Terry Gilliam. The Monte Python alumnus has created a grim albeit literate and fascinating sci-fi masterpiece from a David Peoples–Janet Peoples script based on the 1962 French short subject *La Jetee.* Bruce Willis portrays a hardened convict in a future time (A.D. 2035) who is sent into the past in an effort to prevent 90 percent of mankind from dying from a plague virus. His odyssey through several time zones is a compellingly presented mystery and adventure, with pieces of a grandiose jigsaw puzzle slowly falling into place. Willis appears to be insane and ends up in a mental hospital where he is befriended by psychiatrist Madeleine Stowe and where he meets another oddball patient (Brad Pitt), who will figure prominently in Willis's dilemma in a different time zone. Yes, it is difficult and convoluted, but gradually it all becomes clear that the world is at stake, a plot twist that pushes the film unrelentingly. There are times when Willis's character seems too brutal and callous, and *12 Monkeys* is sadly missing the satiric Gilliam touches that earmarked his *Brazil*. But the political statements the film makes and the final payoff are so great, you will forgive Gilliam his trespasses and be pulled along by this apocalyptic tale that hammers home the evil, dark side of man again and again in a profound way. Christopher Plummer (in a small but pivotal role as a scientist), Jon Seda, Joseph Melito. (Video/Laser: MCA)

12:01 (1993) ★★★½ In 1973 Richard Lupoff wrote the short story "12:01 P.M." for the *Magazine of Fantasy and Science Fiction*, using the idea of a "time loop" that traps a man in a park during his lunch hour and dooms him to live it over and over again. In 1990 Jonathan Heap wrote-directed a 25-minute adaptation (starring Kirkwood Smith) nominated for an Academy Award. This 2-hour TV-movie was produced by Heap, with his old school chum Philip Morton throwing away the minimal plot and using the "time bounce" as a gimmick. Now we have Jonathan Silverman portraying a clerk in an electronics corporation, UTREL, which is running tests of "particle physics," an attempt to accelerate molecules and harness energy. After a bad day at the office, during which lab assistant Helen Slater is murdered, Silverman wakes up the next morning destined to relive the day over again. He stops being an ineffectual nerd and sets out to prevent Slater's murder and the test-firing of a disintegrator ray, which could put all of mankind into a 24-hour time loop. While this may sound like *Groundhog Day*, Lupoff's premise did come first. It's a pretty good thriller and once the time-loop idea is under way, the pacing picks up noticeably under Jack Sholder's direction. Martin Landau plays Dr. Thadius Moxley, the dedicated scientist in charge of the project; Nicolas Surovy is a sinister lab technician; Robin Bartlett is Silverman's bitchy boss and Jeremy Piven is Silverman's prankster pal. (Columbia) (Laser: Image)

12 TO THE MOON (1960) ★★ There are a dozen reasons why this poverty-stricken sci-fi thriller doesn't thrill, and Ken Clark, Anthony Dexter, Francis X. Bushman, Tom Conway and Robert Montgomery, Jr., are five. Tedium galore as Lunar Eagle One lands in the crater Menelaus to encounter lunatic creatures ruled by the Great Coordinator, who threatens to turn Earth into a giant popsicle. This movie sucks, all right. Directed by David Bradley from DeWitt Bodeen's script. Photographed by the great John Alton. John Wengraf, Cory Devlin, Tema Bey and Michi Kobi are 4 more reasons why *12 to the Moon* is less than classic.

20 MILLION MILES TO EARTH (1957) ★★★½ Space probe returning from Venus, damaged by a meteor, crashes into the ocean off Sicily. A tiny dinosaurlike creature (a Venusian specimen) survives the impact but our atmosphere causes it to grow at an accelerated rate—all too quickly it assumes monstrous proportions, crashing through the Roman Forum and the Temple of Saturn while army combat units pursue with flamethrowers. This Columbia low-budgeter (directed by Nathan Juran; written by Bob Williams and Christopher Knopf) has outstanding stop-motion work by Ray Harryhausen, whose Ymir creature is one of his finest; Harryhausen injects personality into the Ymir and evokes sympathy for its plight. Harryhausen's partner, Charles H. Schneer, produced this minor classic. Joan Taylor, William Hopper, Arthur Space. Aka *The Beast from Space* and *The Giant Ymir*. (Laser: Pioneer)

27TH DAY, THE (1957) ★★★ Aliens wish to colonize Earth but cannot conduct warfare—it's against their religion—so they send emissary Arnold Moss to abduct 5 Earthlings from different countries. In his UFO, Moss gives each captive capsules that could, on telepathic command, destroy all human life within 27 days. It's the aliens' way of giving us a chance to commit suicide. Or, if we don't use the capsules, we win and they'll go away. Realizing the power they hold, and how that power could be misused by less scrupulous individuals, the principals disperse to hide and contemplate. Main focus is on Gene Barry and Valerie French as they wrestle with their consciences and fall in love. Message science-fiction with strong anti-Communist overtones in the vein of *Red Planet Mars*, adapted by John Mantley from his own novel. This film's blatant political stance definitely reflects its time and place. William Asher directed. George Voskovec, Stefan Schnabel, Paul Birch, Ralph Clanton. (Video/Laser: Columbia TriStar)

20,000 LEAGUES UNDER THE SEA (1954) ★★★★ Classic Disney adventure (based on the Jules Verne novel) spares no expense to re-create Captain Nemo's atomic sub, the underwater kingdoms, the giant squid and other Verne-esque wonders. Kirk Douglas, Peter Lorre and Paul Lukas are survivors of a whaling ship ramming who find themselves on the *Nautilus*, under the command of the brilliant but demented Nemo (James Mason), who wages war against those who wage war. The effects are remarkably grand for their day, especially the squid attack as men armed with harpoons try to dislodge the multitentacled giant off the sub's hull. This remains the film that best captures the flavor of Verne and his inventions. Directed by Richard Fleischer, written by Earl Fenton. (Video/Laser: Disney)

TWICE DEAD (1988) ★★ The old haunted house tale retold as a juvenile slasher splasher, occasionally diverting but ultimately disappointing with its plethora of clichés. An actor who hung himself in the old Tyler estate in the '30s is back in the '80s to haunt a newly arrived family. The main problem with director Bert Dragin's script (which he cranked out with producer Robert McDonnell) is that the spirit's intentions are never clear—one minute it's trying to strangle young Tom Breznahan, the next it's warning him his sister Jill Whitlow is being raped. The film deteriorates into disappointing practical jokes when the 2 teenagers in the family are forced to ward off threatening punks. The concluding supernatural gore murders are humdrum stuff. Sam Melville, Brooke Bundy, Joleen Lutz, Jonathan Chapin. (Video/Laser: Nelson)

TWICE-TOLD TALES (1963) ★★★ Lushly photographed anthology highlighting three fantasy-horror tales by Nathaniel Hawthorne, Vincent Price in each. Writer-producer Robert E. Kent has selected: "Dr. Heidegger's Experiment," in which Price and Sebastian Cabot experiment with a rejuvenation serum that returns their youth and brings long-dead Mari Blanchard back from the grave; "Rappaccini's Daughter," a strange yarn in which a woman's touch brings instant death, and a plant that destroys any who touch it; and "The House of the Seven Gables," a traditional haunted house–family curse story (and weakest of the three). Director Sidney Salkow's pacing is slow, but rich detail in Kent's script and good ensemble acting make the film a stylish one. Brett Halsey, Beverly Garland, Richard Denning. Aka *The Corpse-Makers, Nathaniel Hawthorne's Twice-Told Tales* and *Nights of Terror*. (MGM/UA)

TWILIGHT OF THE COCKROACHES (1988) ★★★ The Asian roach (a species known as *Blattas orientalis*) is given sympathetic treatment by Japanese producer-director Hiroaki Yoshida in this curious blend of live action with animation. The people are real—it's the roaches that have been cartooned into the world as misunderstood, maligned creatures, so dwarfed by the lumbering humans that they seem vulnerable to danger. This unusual treatment makes this full-length allegorical cartoon offbeat entertainment, with Yoshida drawing parallels to the Holocaust and to the behavior of today's Japanese people and their willingness to shut their eyes to the rest of the world. Definitely worth it, even if you hate cockroaches. (Streamline) (Laser: Japanese)

TWILIGHT OF THE DEAD. See *The Gates of Hell.*

TWILIGHT PEOPLE, THE (1972) ★★½ A spirit of jungle adventure and good location photography are the best things this Roger Corman–David Cohen film (made in the Philippines) has to offer. The Jerome Small–Eddie Romero script is a rehash of *The Island of Dr. Moreau* and *Island of Lost Souls*, featuring a cave prison of half-human, half-animal experimentations gone awry, including a Goat Guy, a Panther Woman, a winged Bat Creature (on wires yet) and a Dog Daughter. John Ashley plays adventurer Matt Farrell, kidnapped and taken to a jungle stronghold. He's the perfect specimen for the mad doctor's next experiment, but first there's time to fall in love with the scientist's assistant. Director Eddie Romero moves it at a fast clip, with enough action to make it bearable. Aka *Island of the Twilight People*. Good cast all around: Pat Woodell, Jan Merlin, Charles Macaulay, Pam Greer (as that panther gal), Mona Morena and Ken Metcalfe. Ashley doubled as one of the producers. (United; from Direct as *Beasts*)

TWILIGHT ZONE—THE MOVIE (1983) ★★★ Entertaining if not classic homage to the great Rod Serling TV series. Produced by Steven Spielberg and John Landis, this is made up of 4 tales (3 based on TV episodes) and a clever prologue. Landis directed and wrote the prologue and first episode, which stars Vic Morrow as a bigot puzzlingly projected into situations where he is vilified (by Nazis, Ku Klux Klansmen, black American soldiers in Vietnam). While it has the moralistic turnaround Serling loved, Landis's script is weak and makes this the least of the quartet. Providing a warm glow is Spielberg's segment about how old folks in a rest home rediscover youth with the help of a traveling goodwill magician, Scatman Crothers. It's a spiritually uplifting fantasy. Third and best of the yarns is an adaptation of a Jerome Bixby story (scripted by Richard Matheson, directed by Joe Dante) about a youth with the ability to affect physical things by "willing" them. A good cast (Kathleen Quinlan, Jeremy Licht, Kevin McCarthy, Patricia Barry, William Schallert, Dick Miller) adds to the nostalgia. And there's '30s-style animation by Sally Cruikshank and a novel interpretation of life-size cartoon monsters by Rob Bottin. Final episode, directed by Australia's George Miller, is based on the famous TV episode "Nightmare at 20,000 Feet," in which a neurotic (John Lithgow, in the role originated by William Shatner) sees a gnomelike monster on the wing of a jetliner and goes bananas to prevent it from making the plane crash. (Video/Laser: Warner Bros.)

TWINKLE, TWINKLE, KILLER KANE. See *The Ninth Configuration.*

TWINS OF DRACULA. See *Twins of Evil.*

TWINS OF EVIL (1971) ★★★ Predictably plotted sequel to Hammer's *Vampire Lovers* and *Lust for a Vampire*, dealing with the Karnstein family and its vampiric curse. Peter Cushing as a witchhunter of the 19th century seeking to help 2 "infected" 19-year-old beauties: Mary and Madeleine Collinson, altogether beauties who are seen in the altogether in several shots. Tudor Gates's script is heavy with heaving bosoms and unsubtle hints of lesbian love-biting. Directed by John Hough. Dennis Price, Isobel Black, Kathleen Byron, Damien Thomas, David Warbeck. Aka *The Gemini Twins, Virgin Vampires* and *Twins of Dracula*. (VidAmerica)

TWISTED JUSTICE (1990) ★★½ In a futuristic L.A., where new antigun laws require policemen to carry stun guns (or "stingers") instead of lethal firearms, maverick cop James Tucker (played by writer-producer-director David Heavener) uses unorthodox procedure (i.e., a long-barreled revolver) to go after the Bull's-eye Murderer, a rapist who uses the drug "Umbra," which turns him into a superintelligent psychotic, with superhuman strength. Helping Tuck is Shannon Tweed and getting in his way are fellow cops Erik Estrada and Jim Brown. Since this is watered-down action trash, wasting Karen Black in an empty cameo, we refer you to a similar film that is much better trash and more stylistic, David Pirie's *Future Force*, which also spotlights an iconoclastic law enforcer named Tucker. (Arena; K-Beech)

TWISTED SOULS. See *Spookies*.

TWISTS OF TERROR (1998) ★★★ This loosely knit trilogy of horror stories, lifting its narrative styles from *Tales from the Crypt* and *Amazing Stories*, captures a surreal quality usually missing from this type of anthology. Scriptwriter John Shirley sets his stories in a dark world where innocence and guilt are turned topsy-turvy, where sex and retribution are the standards of the night. The only connecting link is a storyteller called simply "The Host," but he's an odd duck, having none of the cackling charm of the Cryptkeeper. No, this creepy yarnmeister is in dire need of a shave, haircut, and bath as he wanders through the upper story of a run-down mansion surrounded by old newspapers with screaming headlines that recount the tales he spins. As played by Joseph Ziegler, he's a total paranoid and recluse, warning us of the dangers "out there." The first yarn is the least effective, with twists within twists that don't hold up to any logic. A young couple, after a car crash, is "rescued" by two degenerates with murderous intentions. The second is pure *Tales from the Crypt* as a traveling salesman, when his car runs out of gas in a small town, is attacked by a German shepherd. After a harrying *Cujo*-style attack, he seeks refuge in what appears to be a hospital. The moment a busty blond nurse rushes forth to help him, you know you are in the Weird Zone. There's some grisly and macabre touches that should please fans. But the best "twisted tale" is the third, which stars Jennifer Rubin as a seemingly lonely young woman trying to get a date in a bar. That's when Nick Mancuso shows up. Given the O. Henry convolutions and surprises director Douglas Jackson has to deal with, to describe anything further would be giving away too much. The cast includes Carl Marotte, Andrew Jackson, and Françoise Robertson. Production qualities are consistently high throughout. (Paramount)

TWITCH OF THE DEATH NERVE. Video version of *Bay of Blood* (MPI).

TWO EVIL EYES (1990) ★★★ Inspired by the macabre genius of Edgar Allan Poe, George Romero and Dario Argento teamed up to make this anthology. Romero's contribution, a loose version of Poe's "The Facts in the Case of M. Valdermar," plays more like an episode of "The Twilight Zone" and is the kind of material you see when someone is imitating Romero. Adrienne Barbeau is fleecing her dying husband and supernatural forces from beyond the grave are unleashed when her accomplice-doctor uses hypnotism. It's just okay, with Tom Atkins reprising his cop from *Night of the Creeps* and Ramy Zada, Bingo O'Malley and Jeff Howell assisting. The better half of this duo is Argento's "The Black Cat," an amalgamation of elements from Poe yarns. Harvey Keitel plays Rod Usher, a crazed crime photographer who murders his wife and hides her blood-spattered corpse behind a bedroom wall. The outcome is predictable but Argento brings stylish touches to "The Black Cat" (which he wrote with Franco Ferrini). John Amos, Sally Kirkland, Kim Hunter, Martin Balsam. (Media/Fox) (Laser: Image)

TWO FACES OF DR. JEKYLL, THE (1961) ★★★ Hammer pulls a switch on the overworked Robert Louis Stevenson split-personality plot: Instead of a good-looking doc turning into an ugly brute, a not-so-handsome chap transmutes into a handsome playboy who falls for London's can-can girls. Directed by Terence Fisher from a Wolf Mankowitz script. Paul Massie, Dawn Addams, Christopher Lee, Oliver Reed. Strictly a game of Hyde-and-seek, produced by Michael Carreras and Anthony Nelson Keys. Aka *House of Fright* and *Jekyll's Inferno*. (Columbia TriStar)

2000 MANIACS (1964) ★★ Revolting exploitation material panders with scenes devoted to dismembered arms and legs, chopped-up bodies and heaped intestines. Setting is the modern South where rednecks are still fighting the Civil War by hacking to death any Northerners who wander through. Rednecks making red necks, get it? It turns out the town of Pleasant Valley, once wiped out by General Grant, periodically appears out of a time warp so the citizens can wreak revenge. Considered the "masterpiece" of gore purveyor Herschell Gordon Lewis, who wrote, and directed under producer David Friedman. One watches at one's own risk. (Wizard; Comet; Rhino; S/Weird) (Laser: Japanese)

2001: A SPACE ODYSSEY (1968) ★★★★★ Producer-director Stanley Kubrick's monumental venture into the realm of science fiction, originally entitled *Journey Beyond the Stars*, is a landmark film combining visual fascinations with a plethora of ideas often left to individual interpretation. Special effects by Douglas Trumbull are an achievement for their time, the music by Johann and Richard Strauss and other classical composers lends the film distinction, and the screenplay (by Kubrick and Arthur C. Clarke) is stunning in its implications. The boggling story begins with a "Dawn of Man" sequence in which apelike creatures (the beginnings of man) are given intelligence after touching a monolithic black slab. By 2001, man is on the moon and preparing to journey to other planets when a similar slab is uncovered that transmits a signal to Jupiter. Astronauts Gary Lockwood and Keir Dullea are assigned to investigate, but their odyssey is endangered by a ruthless, malfunctioning computer nicknamed HAL. How the machine is overcome makes for a suspenseful allegory of man vs. machine. Final journey through the Star Gate is a sensory experience of psychedelic colors and psychotic patterns, heightened to a fevery pitch with music to commit suicide by. The "Star Child" ending is enigmatic and complex. Stunning, intelligent film not equalled by the 1984 sequel. Best seen on a big screen or letter-boxed for TV. William Sylvester, Daniel Richter, Leonard Rossiter, Robert Beatty. (Video/Laser: MGM/UA)

2010: THE YEAR WE MAKE CONTACT (1984) ★★★½ If Stanley Kubrick's *2001: A Space Odyssey* is the Bible of movie science fiction then this sequel (written-produced-directed-photographed by Peter Hyams) is blasphemy. Although this picks up 9 years later as the continuing adventures of HAL, the malfunctioning computer; David Bowman, the astronaut who vanished into the Star Gate; and *Intrepid*, the abandoned space vehicle, it has none of the epic sense of Kubrick's masterpiece—in fact, it mundanely starts on Earth and wastes a half hour depicting needless scenes of Roy Scheider's home life, conversations about a Russian-U.S. rescue mission to Jupiter and other trivial junk.

When the film finally gets into space to recount the important parts of Arthur C. Clarke's story, it must be rescued by Richard Edlund's effects. Credit him for one of the most exciting sequences set in space: the walk of 2 men transferring from the Russian spacecraft *Leonov* to the deserted *Intrepid*. That enigmatic black monolith is back, but the Kubrick ambiguities are gone—replaced by a simplified theme that tells, never suggests, that the floating slab belongs to God. Those who remember *Red Planet Mars* will blanch at Clarke's pseudoreligious miracle that finishes the film—and hopefully the thought of any further irrelevant, irreverent sequels. Scheider, John Lithgow and Bob Balaban as the American spacers work with limited roles, but remain second best to Edlund's effects. Keir Dullea appears briefly as Bowman; among the Russian astronauts are Helen Mirren and Dana Elcar. (Video/Laser: MGM/UA)

2019: THE FALL OF NEW YORK. See *After the Fall of New York.*

2020 TEXAS GLADIATORS (1985) ★★½ A nuked-out Dallas, Texas, is the wild and woolly setting for this rambunctious post-holocaust adventure pitting a band of good-guy warriors called the Rangers against the "New Order" that intends to use them as slave labor in a mine. With the trappings of a Western (saloon brawls, shoot-outs and a tribe of noble Indians), this foreign-produced flick gallops along, its endless action sequences holding one in the grip of its momentum as the Rangers go up against the outcast Catchdog and an army of soldiers equipped with thermal shields, off which bullets bounce. It's absurd comic-book stuff, directed without pretensions by Kevin Mancuso (aka Armand Massaccesi). Harrison Muller, Al Cliver, Daniel Stephen, Sabrina Siana. (Media)

TWO WORLDS OF JENNIE LOGAN, THE (1979) ★★★½ Plagued by her husband coming off an affair, unhappy housewife Lindsay Wagner finds an old dress in a Victorian home and slides into a time continuum, traveling back to the turn of the century to fall in love with Marc Singer. She passes back and forth between her 2 worlds, involved with murder, confused identities and the paradox of changing the past to ensure her future happiness. Nicely written by director Frank DeFelitta (he adapted David Williams's novel *Second Sight*) with well-etched performances by Wagner, Singer, Linda Gray, Joan Darling and Henry Wilcoxon. (USA; Fries)

UFO (1956) See *Unidentified Flying Objects: The True Story of Flying Saucers.*
UFO (1980). See *The Spaceman in King Arthur's Court.*
UFO INCIDENT, THE (1975) ★★★½ Fact or fiction? You must judge this intriguing TV-movie based on an alleged incident that occurred to Betty and Barney Hill while they drove through lonely countryside (an incident detailed in the book *Interrupted Journey*). They were hypnotized by aliens and led into a saucer to undergo biological testing. Only later, with a sympathetic psychiatrist's help, did the frightening details emerge. This thoughtful treatment deals with the trauma of UFO abductions but also leaves doubt as to exactly what happened. Provocatively directed by Richard A. Colla, with James Earl Jones and Estelle Parsons convincing as the couple. The doctor is excellently essayed by Barnard Hughes.
UFORIA (1980) ★★★ Eccentric but entertaining portrait of 3 free-spirited souls, with light fantasy touches. Texas drifter-grifter Fred Ward meets a supermarket check-out clerk (Cindy Williams) neurotic as hell and they begin an uneasy romance. Meanwhile, phony evangelist Harry Dean Stanton can genuinely heal although he doesn't know why. Williams's belief in UFOs is twisted by Stanton (against Ward's better wishes) into a new pseudoreligious cult. A compelling character study with surprise ending, although you can probably see it coming. Richard Baskin, Dennis M. Hill. Written-directed by John Binder. (MCA)
UFOS...A NEED TO KNOW (1991) ★★★ Thoughtfully produced, low-key documentary detailing fascinating aspects of the UFO mystery, produced-directed by Bob Brown of Oakland's Video City. Although he and coproducer/codirector Ted Oliphant are believers, they approach cautiously, documenting reports with a sense of balance. This covers the unusual number of UFO reports in and around Fyffe, Ala.; the mutilated cattle mystery; the Roswell crash of 1947 (now well documented). One of the best UFO documentaries of the period. (Video City)
UFO: TARGET EARTH (1974) ★ Producer-director Michael A. deGaetano made this cheap ($70,000) off-target bore that misses Earth by miles. An electronics expert picks up signals of an alien craft submerged in a lake near town and tries to uncover its secrets, but this is an exercise in monumental tedium. Too much talk and not enough action. And no visible monster! Nick Plakias, Cynthia Cline. Aka *Target Earth*. (Simitar; Movies Unlimited)
UGETSU (1954) ★★★★ Academy Award–winning Japanese film, based on stories by 18th-century writer Akinari Ueda, is a weird, evanescent blend of violence and fantasy set in 16th-century Japan. Two parallel stories evolve around a potter and a farmer who abandon their wives to fulfill dreams of glory. The farmer turns samurai warrior and the potter falls for a woman who turns out to be a spirit. Acted in classic Japanese style, often as delicate as brush strokes on a vase, sometimes brutal in its sweaty action, but always beautifully photographed by Kazuo Miyagawa. Translated, the title means "pale, mysterious moon after the rain." Directed by Kenji Mizoguchi. Machiko Kyo, Masayuki Mori. Aka *The Story of Ugetsu* and *Tales of the Pale Moon After the Rain*. (Embassy; Western) (Laser: Voyager)
ULTIMATE WARRIOR, THE (1975) ★★★ A non sequitur among Hollywood's post-Armageddon yarns, predating *Mad Max* and thus a curious anomaly from writer-director Robert Clouse, who mixes intellectual content with standard action. The allegory of intellect vs. brute force is told via 2 groups trapped in a destroyed New York: pacifists led by the Baron (Max von Sydow, in an underplayed role) and sadists and marauders led by Carrot (William Smith). While this has none of the style or combative ingenuity of *Mad Max* and countless clones, it has the strengths of von Sydow and Yul Brynner as a "street fighter" named Carson (after frontier scout Kit, who blazed new trails in a wilderness?) to bolster its sagging story. Rivalry is over a tomato patch—symbol of the old world lost and the beginning of a better one. A chase through an abandoned subway is a highlight. Despite good moments, it ultimately falls flatter than the corpses Brynner so easily chalks up. Joanna Miles, Richard Kelton, Stephen McHattie. (Warner Bros.)
ULTRA WARRIOR (1992) ★★½ Hodgepodge of footage from assorted Roger Corman post-Armageddon movies has been inserted into this derivative *Mad Max* clone lacking distinction. Dack Rambo portrays a warrior of 2058 assigned to track down "zerconium," a substance needed to make bombs to stop invading aliens

from turning Earth into a blazing sun. The Atlantic Seaboard is "Oblivion," a radioactive zone where he confronts a villain (the Bishop) in boring battles. Characters are clichéd and made unappealing by an indifferent cast: Meshach Taylor, Clare Beresford, Mark Bringelson, Charles Dougherty. It was, like a hundred other *Mad Max* rip-offs, directed without an ounce of ingenuity by Augusto Tamayo and Kevin Tent. (New Horizons)

UNBORN, THE (1991) ★★★ Disturbing, cautionary parable about mankind's poisoning of fetuses, told as a paranoid thriller in the vein of *Rosemary's Baby* but with the horrific elements springing from the scientific and not the supernatural. Brooke Adams is artificially inseminated by seemingly benevolent Dr. Meyerling (James Karen), but he's a geneticist conducting experiments to create a superhuman being. Adams's nightmares are compounded by her manic depression and inability to deal with the "monster" growing inside her. Although the final "baby" is not that convincing, and in the evil vein of Larry Cohen's *It's Alive*, the message in Henry Dominic's script comes shrieking through. Producer-director Rodman Flender does a creditable job lending this premise ambience and paranoia. Jeff Hayenga, K. Callan, Jane Cameron, Kathy Griffin. (Video/Laser: RCA/Columbia)

UNBORN II, THE (1993) ★★ Loose sequel to *The Unborn* has another patient of Dr. Meyerling giving birth to a deformed baby with an urge to chew up people after biting them in the neck. Mother Michele Greene faces the challenge of holding off baby killer Robin Curtis. This Roger Corman production, directed by Rick Jacobson, works best as an action thriller, with car chases and intense shoot-outs overpowering the horror sequences, which are unconvincing because the hideous baby-monster is unconvincing. Scott Valentine portrays a neighbor who befriends Greene. Leonard O. Turner, Brittany Powell. (New Horizon) (Laser: Image)

UNCLE WAS A VAMPIRE (1959) ★★★ Christopher Lee is in peak form doing a parody of his Hammer version of Dracula in this silly albeit pleasant Italian horror comedy in which he turns up at a hotel for young romantics, where his nephew-owner (rascally Renato Rascel) has been reduced to working as a bellhop. Once Rascel is bitten by his 400-year-old uncle and grows fangs, he begins biting the necks of all the beautiful women at the resort. Only the kiss of the hotel's sweet gardener (Sylvia Koscina, a fragrant flower herself) can save him from eternal bloodsucking. Rascel's nerdy and hammy performance has its amusing moments, and there are bikini and negligee-covered cuties and scenic coastal photography to hold one's attention in this mild terror-error laughfest directed

with the touch of a feather by Stefano Steno. Kay Fisher, Lia Zoppelli, Susanna Loret. Aka *Hard Times for Vampires, Hard Times for Dracula* and *My Uncle the Vampire*.

UNDEAD, THE (1973). See *From Beyond the Grave*.

UNDERSEA KINGDOM (1936) ★★★ Rousing if frequently corny 12-chapter Republic serial (the studio's second after *Darkest Africa*) stars Ray "Crash" Corrigan as a naval officer with superstrength who finds himself on the Lost Continent of Atlantis battling Monte Blue, who has a disintegrator weapon. Robots, submarines and other fantastic weaponry keep the story moving, as does the lively direction of Joseph Kane and action specialist B. Reeves Eason. It's a gas even if the acting is old-fashioned and creaky. Lois Wilde, C. Montague Shaw, Lon Chaney, Jr., Smiley Burnette. (Nostalgia Merchant; Republic; Filmfax; Sinister/C) (Laser: Republic)

UNDERSEA MONSTER. See *Viking Women and the Sea Serpent*.

UNDERSTUDY: GRAVEYARD SHIFT II, THE (1988) ★★½ The "blood is the life" theme of *Dracula* and *Camilla* and its sense of perversity are the strongest elements of this portrait of a vampire who takes a job as the leading "bloodsucker" in a low-budget flick being shot on an L.A. soundstage. There are times when writer-director Gerard Ciccoritti gets pretentious with dialogue, and the story line is a jagged mess as the film skips around from reality-reality to the reality of the movie. Although Mark Soper etches an unusual monster, it is Wendy Gazelle who is central focus as an actress who is seduced away from her editor-boyfriend and turned into a vampire herself. Ciccoritti is aspiring to something different but stumbles in the process, and the film feels staged and claustrophobic, as stifling as the interior of a vampire's dirt-lined coffin. A very loose sequel to the equally strange *Graveyard Shift*. (Virgin Vision) (Laser: Image)

UNDERWORLD (1985). Variant video title for *Transmutations* (Vestron).

UNDYING BRAIN, THE. Video version of *Brain of Blood* (Premiere).

UNEARTHLING, THE (1984) ★ Really bad *E.T.* imitation, of the "it came from outer space" school. A meteor crash-lands on Earth in a forest that just happens to be full of (1) dumb teenagers, (2) some nightingale egg poachers and (3) a young boy who has seen the crash. Out of the crash hulks a plastic-suited creature with the nose of an anteater. This is the father alien, who goes around killing everyone. Meanwhile, the insufferable kid finds an alien egg and hatches it. Out pops a cute version of the father, who goes "coo" to tug at your heartstrings. The script by J. Piquer Simon (who also directed) and Jack Gray goes nowhere. *The Unearthling* is the un-movie of the decade. Ian Sera, Nina Ferrer, Oscar Martin, Susan Blake.

UNEARTHLY, THE (1957) ★★★ Enjoyable sleaze, grade-Z fashion, with John Carradine as a mad doc who discovers a 17th gland containing the secret of youth, "prolonging life for thousands of years." So naturally he kidnaps innocent people and exposes them to electricity bolts and deformities. His assistant, Lobo, is lumbering Tor Johnson. Myron Healey is a sympathetic criminal seeking refuge in the doc's recuperation center and sexy Allison Hayes is an intended victim. Carradine, always on the verge of hysteria, asks "Did you sterilize my #23 scalpel?" and plays morbid organ music during dinner. Producer-director Brooke L. Peters manages a silly "buried alive" sequence from the script by Jane Mann and Geoffrey Dennis. Roy Gordon, Arthur Batanides. (Rhino; Filmfax; Sinister/C)

UNEARTHLY STRANGER (1963) ★★★ John Neville wakes up to discover his lovely wife (Gabriella Lecudi) sleeps with her eyes open. Her peculiar traits increase—until Neville realizes he has married an alien, sent to Earth to kill scientists in the space project Neville is working on. However, when the E.T. falls for Neville, the plan goes awry. Thoughtful British sci-fi thriller from producer Albert Fennell suggests and implies, rather than shows, the horrors at work. John Krish directed the Rex Carlton script. Jean Marsh, Philip Stone, Warren Mitchell, Patrick Newell. Aka *Beyond the Stars*. (Movies Unlimited; Wade Williams)

UNFORGETTABLE (1996) ★★★½ Director John Dahl sets up an impactful suspenser in the Hitchcock tradition, showing off his mastery as a stylist behind the camera. And although Bill Geddie's thriller plot (tinged with elements of the fantastic) seems frequently contrived, Dahl manages to hold the taut yarn together and charges ahead with more spine-chilling sequences. The use of jarring sound effects and imaginative editing are effective in this dark, twisted tale of a medical examiner (Ray Liotta, who brings a sense of manic obsession to his paranoid role) seeking the murderer of his wife with the help of lab experimenter Linda Fiorentino, who has perfected a serum that allows transference of memory from one brain to another. Liotta undergoes harrowing and incredible ordeals as he relives his wife's murder and the slaughter of seven people in a drugstore. Geddie's script is loaded with surprises and plot twists that pull you ever deeper into Liotta's edge-of-insanity performance, and the swift pacing and editing help to make you forget how contrived it all is. Peter Coyote is super as a hard-bitten cop and he is ably supported by Christopher McDonald, Kim Cattrall, Kim

Coates, Duncan Fraser and David Paymer. (Video/Laser: MGM)

UNHOLY, THE. See *The Demon*.

UNHOLY, THE (1988) ★★★ Well-produced, well-acted but slow-moving and sometimes ponderous religious parable of good vs. evil. A demon from Hell named Daziadarius, which manifests itself on Easter weekend, sucking up priests and/or virgins, is haunting a church to which Ben Cross is assigned after Cross survives a 17-floor fall without injuries. Guiding Cross in his fight are an Archbishop (Hal Holbrook) and a blind priest (Trevor Howard, in one of his last roles) and working to lead him astray is a nightclub owner (William Russ) who presents a devil-cult show and a young beauty (Jill Carroll). The Philip Yordan–Fernando Fonseca script is high-class though the monster looks like something out of a grade-B effort, and its actions are unsavory, in a sexual manner of speaking. Camilo Vila directs with an emphasis on religious symbols, and Ned Beatty brings unrest to his role as a sympathetic cop. Claudia Robinson, Nicole Frontier. (Vestron) (Laser: Image)

UNHOLY HOUR. See *Werewolf of London*.

UNIDENTIFIED FLYING OBJECTS. See *UFO*.

UNIDENTIFIED FLYING OBJECTS: THE TRUE STORY OF FLYING SAUCERS (1956) ★★★ A rereviewing of this film reveals it as a remarkable and important semidocumentary report, reflecting a positive attitude toward the existence of UFOs through what appears to be careful, thoughtful documentation: interviews with observers of UFOs, movie footage of UFOs taken in Montana and Utah (and never disclaimed by the military), and Air Force personnel involved with Project Bluebook in the '50s talking on camera. What makes this Clarence Greene–Russell Rouse production seem so remarkable today, given the current climate of conspiracy, cover-up and lack of military confirmation of UFOs, is the cooperation given by the Air Force and its willingness to admit to "unknowns" right on camera. (Most of the film is a reenactment with occasional touches of film noir, and many of the participants appear as themselves in the film.) Tom Towers, a real-life L.A. news reporter, portrays a public information officer named Albert M. Chop, who is assigned to look into UFOs. He tells the UFO story from 1947–52 in first-person voice-over. At first skeptical, Chop/Towers turns into a firm believer. The high point is a reenactment of the July 1952 incident in which at least 14 UFOs hovered above the White House on two separate occasions, disappearing when fighter planes came on the scene, reappearing when the fighters left. Director Winston Jones brings a chilling sense of reality to this segment of Francis Martin's fact-filled script. This film should be reexamined by serious UFO researchers and studied for its implications. Aka *UFO*.

UNIDENTIFIED FLYING ODDBALL. See *The Spaceman in King Arthur's Court*.

UNINVITED, THE (1944) ★★★★ Those who saw this in the '40s, or discovered it on TV in the '50s, always remember it fondly as one of the few good haunted-house movies. However, now that we have been carried to the heights of atmospheric and shock filmmaking, one might accuse Paramount's adaptation of Dorothy Macardle's novel *Uneasy Threshold* of being slow-moving and talky. But anyone searching for old-fashioned story-telling—with fascinating characters, strong motives, scintillating dialogue, a setting that serves as a metaphor for character—will find this demonstrative of '40s Hollywood at its best. Ray Milland and sister Ruth Hussey buy a mansion, Windward House, on the Cornish coast to be confronted with subtle hints of a haunting: wilted flowers, a weeping voice, a gust of wind on the stairs, a room turning cold, the smell of mimosa. Recommended for the fine script by Frank Partos and Dodie Smith, the gentlemanly direction of Lewis Allen, and the performances of Milland, Hussey, Gail Russell, Donald Crisp, Cornelia Otis Skinner and Alan Napier, the latter as the village doctor. (Video/Laser: MCA)

UNINVITED (1987) ★★ For a monster movie to work, the terrorizing entity must have a modicum of scariness and/or believability. If not, the horror turns into uninvited comedy. The monster in *Uninvited*, resembling a Muppet reject that's always popping out of a cat's mouth, is so obviously faked as to invite uninvited laughter. Writer-producer-director Greydon Clark has assembled a fine cast: Alex Cord as a sleazy underworld character, George Kennedy as his gunsel, Clu Gulager as a drunken sycophant and Toni Hudson as a woman hired to sail Cord's yacht. And there's possibilities for character relationships as we see Cord—a man of power and wealth—fall prey to evil desires and bubble-headed sexpots. But rather than trust in his own abilities, Clark resorts to *Alien* clichés. Clare Carey, Eric Larson, Beau Dremann. (New Star) (Laser: Image)

UNIVERSAL SOLDIER (1992) ★★★ What's that old saying? All brawn and no brain? Apply that adage to the script by Richard Rothstein, Christopher Leitch and Dean Devlin and you've got *Universal Soldier*. As a sci-fi action picture it's nonstop violence when Vietnam War adversaries Jean-Claude Van Damme and Dolph Lundgren kill each other in combat and reappear years later as cyborgs controlled by "mad doctor" Jerry Orbach. The hardware, technology, combat and martial-art sequences are explosive

and exciting but the plot (Van Damme regains part of his humanity and goes on the run with TV news reporter Ally Walker, with Lundgren on their heels) is comic-book fodder. So, settle in for exploding and overturning vehicles and anticipate the mano-to-mano battle royal between the stars during the last 15 minutes. Directed by Roland Emmerich. Ed O'Ross, Leon Rippy, Ralph Moeller. (Columbia TriStar) (Laser: Live)

UNIVERSAL SOLDIER II: BROTHERS IN ARMS (199?) ★★ All brawn and no brain—that describes your average *Universal Soldier*, not to mention this time-killer. A "Unisol" is a dead human (male species) that has been "regenerated" and placed under the mind control of Command Center. Emotionless, cold, a total killing machine. Or so it was portrayed in Jean-Claude Van Damme's 1992 actioner directed by Roland Emmerich. While Jean-Claude went on to make a terrible '99 sequel, this was a TV movie made for the Movie Channel based on the same premise starring Matt Battaglia, a heartthrob hunk-a-guy on TV's *Days of Our Lives*. He portrays GR-44, another reject Unisol, who's on the run with newspaperwoman Chandra West (of TV's *Highlander*). Battaglia walks zombielike through Peter M. Lenkov's script along with his brother Unisol GR-5 (played by action star Jeff Wincott) in order to stop Gary Busey from selling off reprogrammed-for-evil Unisols to a Chinese mercenary. Nobody snarls, chortles, and screams commands like Busey and he does it here in an apparent sympathetic attempt to stave off total disaster for director Jeff Woolnough. Busey is aided in his nefarious activities by a sinister White House official played by Burt Reynolds, who spends most of his time talking on the phone from the West Wing. It's a setup for more sequels, including *Universal Soldier III: Unfinished Business*. (Paramount)

UNIVERSAL SOLDIER III: UNFINISHED BUSINESS (1998) ★★ Another TV movie made for the Movie Channel and repackaged for video starring Matt Battaglia as a reject "Unisol" (a mindless killing machine created by the U.S. government to be the perfect combatant) and Chandra West as a journalist who knows too many secrets and must always stay on the run with GR-44. Since the original project created too many flawed troopers, the Unisol Project is creating test-tube babies to be trained from scratch. Fleeing to Canada, the couple hopes to find a news outlet to report the secret project to the world, but it's a never-ending series of shoot-outs and narrow escapes. Like its predecessor, *Universal Soldier II: Brothers in Arms*, this was written by Peter M. Lenkov and directed by Jeff Woolnough. (Paramount)

UNIVERSAL SOLDIER: THE RETURN (1999) ½

If ever there was a movie indicating an actor's career has plummeted into a bottomless abyss, it is this weak sequel to the 1992 Roland Emmerich–directed vehicle starring Jean-Claude Van Damme. Why Van Damme would surrender whatever standards he may have left to make this cliché-riddled (and bullet-riddled) retread is beyond comprehension. From the outset it's a bad direct-to-video premise, although the film did play briefly in theaters before being relegated to the cardboard-box world of vidflicks. The Unisol 2500 Project is still going at a secret Dallas installation, but the government is threatening cutbacks. Van Damme and daughter (Karis Paige Bryant) are hanging around the computer one day (the program is nicknamed SETH), when it goes paranoid, electrocutes its programmer (Xander Berkeley), and reprograms the Universal Soldiers to kick the asses of the good guys. That's when the script by William Malone and John Fasano deteriorates into nothing more than a series of three kind of scenes: 1) Van Damme and a stupid woman TV reporter (Heidi Schanz, in one of the worst feminine parts written in years) trying to escape death inside the cordoned-off installation, 2) hundreds of government soldiers being blasted by the Unisols with their big-bad automatic weapons and rocket launchers, and 3) Van Damme karate-chopping his way through numerous hand-to-hand encounters with Bill Goldberg (as a brute of a Unisol named Romeo, because he's so lovable), Michael Jai White (whose brain gets cybernated with SETH so SETH can walk around on two legs), and other enemy Unisols. Director Mic Rodgers contributes nothing in the way of substance and just lets it run free and wild as a mindless action epic. Kiana Tom hangs around the edges of the story as a sympathetic partner to Van Damme but has nothing much to do but wince when Romeo pulls down her pants in one scene. And as the good-guy general, Daniel Von Bargen lets his mouth fall open more than once when he sees how much firepower those mean bad old Unisols have to blast his units away into nothingness. Speaking of nothingness, that best describes this utter waste of time. Ironically, the TV movie *Universal Soldier II: Brothers in Arms* is a better piece of work. It may not be saying much, but Van Damme should take heed. (Video/DVD: Columbia TriStar)

UNKNOWN, THE (1927) ★★★ Although not a horror story in the traditional or gothic sense, this silent-screen collaborative effort between director Tod Browning and "Man of a Thousand Faces" Lon Chaney, Sr., is a morbid, creepy tale of revenge that will have your skin crawling. Chaney is at his most anguished as a killer fleeing the police who takes the unlikely disguise of Alonzo the Armless, a circus performer who seemingly has no arms and throws knives with his feet. Alonzo falls prey to his own emotions—mainly his love for Nanon, played by Joan Crawford at her most alluring. To win that love Alonzo has his arms surgically removed, only to discover too late that Nanon loves another. How Chaney seeks revenge against his rival (a happy-go-lucky gypsy) is one of the strangest, and most lurid, plot devices ever. It's a hallmark of dark cinema, suggesting the grim overview of life shared by Browning and Chaney and scriptwriter Waldemar Young. S. Norman Kerry, Nick De Ruiz, John George, Frank Lanning. (Enrique J. Bouchard; Dark Dreams) (Laser: MGM/UA)

UNKNOWN WORLD (1951) ★★★ Effective Robert L. Lippert sleeper, filmed in the Carlsbad Caverns, depicts an expedition corkscrewing into the core of the Earth with a giant duralumin-powered drill mounted on the front of their "mole ship." These human burrowers, searching for a new place for mankind to live so decent people can escape the threat of atomic attack, discover conditions at Earth's center to be harmful to reproduction. The Millard Kaufman script is neat and unpretentious. Directed stylishly by Terrell O. Morse. Bruce Kellogg, Victor Killian, Jim Bannon. Aka *To the Center of the Earth*. (Prism; Sinister/C; Filmfax)

UNMASKED: PART 25 (1990) ★ British spoof of American slasher flicks finds Gregory Cox wearing a mask like Jason's as he knocks off folks. Producer-writer Mark Cutforth and director Anders Palm have fun with black comedy, but it's rather feeble, old chaps. Fiona Evans, Edward Brayshaw. (Academy)

UNNAMABLE, THE (1988) ★★ Another adaptation of an H. P. Lovecraft tale, falsely advertised as being in the league of *Reanimator*. Except for an offbeat female monster named Alyda (well played by Katrin Alexandra and imaginatively designed by effects man R. Christopher Biggs) this has nothing to offer but tedious haunted-house clichés as 4 students from Miskatonic University are pursued from floor to floor by the demonic form, which enjoys ripping out your heart, bashing your head against the floor until it cracks open like an eggshell and slashing your throat so blood gushes out. Another plot has to do with Randolph Carter (named after a Lovecraft character) and his nerdish companion poring through old, musty books and incantations, seeking the answer to the mansion's mystery, which may have something to do with tree monsters—writer-director Jean-Paul Ouellette never makes it that clear. *Unnamable*, unless you're looking for a gore flick with a good monster, is unnecessary. Charles King, Mark Kinsey Stephenson. (Vidmark) (Laser: Image)

UNNAMABLE II, THE (1992) ★★★ Writer-director Jean-Paul Ouellette returns with an adaptation of H. P. Lovecraft's short stories "The Unnamable" and "The Statement of Randolph Carter," picking up on the same night that *The Unnamable* ended, with all the dead bodies being carted away by sheriff Peter Breck. Antiquarian John Rhys-Davies of Miskatonic University (located in Arkham County) joins with Randolph Carter (Mark Kinsey Stephenson) in tracking down the mystery surrounding that winged, big-breasted she-demon named Alyda. It is discovered that within the hideous monster is imprisoned the innocent soul of a young woman (Maria Ford). Girl watchers will appreciate the fact that once she's been separated from the evil spirit through an incantation Ms. Ford spends most of the film stark naked, covered only by a mane of wild flowing hair. The rest of *The Unnamable II* is exploitation gore thrills as the creature destroys, with her superhuman strength, most of the characters as Carter and Ms. Ford run around Arkham County. It's an okay horror picture in that regard, but it's far from the literate cosmic-horror level that makes Lovecraft so great to read. Charles Klausmeyer, Julie Strain, David Werner, Siobhan McCafferty. (Video/Laser: Prism)

UNSANE (1984) ★★★ Nobody makes a psychothriller as well as Italy's Dario Argento, and in this retitled version of *Tenebrae*, writer-director Argento is at his best. Mystery novelist Anthony Franciosa turns up in Rome to find himself involved with a mad killer enflamed by Franciosa's writings. There's bloody ax murder after ax murder, an excellent sequence in which a Doberman pursues a hapless female victim, and constant twists of plot. It's fun trying to guess what Argento will throw at you next. John Saxon has a small role as Franciosa's agent and the victims include Eva Rubins, Carola Stagnaro and John Steiner (the latter as a policeman hooked on mystery fiction). *Unsane* is inspired. (Media; Fox Hills has a heavily edited version; also in video as *Shadow*)

UNSEEN, THE (1980) ★★★ Despite a trite-sounding plot (3 beautiful TV newscasters are secluded in a house with a madman and, one by one, are brutalized and murdered), this is a strange, sometimes enthralling low-budget flick, made in and around Solvang, Calif., a Danish-style village of windmills and smorgasbord restaurants. Written by Michael L. Grace, it takes one of the hoariest clichés of horror movies—the animalistic, "unseen" entity living in the cellar—and gives it a new sense of mystery, even compassion. Not that the film aspires to anything more than it is—it just does what it sets out to do well under Peter Foleg's direction. Barbara Bach, Sydney Lassick, Stephen Furst, Karen Lamm, Lelia Goldoni. (VidAmerica)

UNTIL DEATH DO YOU PART. See *Possession: Until Death Do You Part.*

UNTIL THE END OF THE WORLD (1991) ★★★ Difficult, diffused Wim Wenders oddity that mixes elements of film noir and high-tech sci-fi without it all coming together in a cohesive fashion. The year is 1999 and a nuclear rocket has gone awry over Earth. Exotic, mysterious Solveig Dommartin gets involved with a private eye, a novelist (played by Sam Neill), a satchel of stolen money, hold-up men and other types before the meandering story shifts to Australia where her boyfriend William Hurt meets his scientist-father (Max von Sydow), who has designed a camera that transfers images into brain waves that a blind person can "see." Photographing in 15 countries, the cultish German director intended this as a metaphor for our unending search for ourselves and the meaning of life. It's so dense and pretentious that you might laugh at it, not with it. For diehard Wenders fans only, or those who don't mind being baffled (as well as tortured) by inaccessible characters and unfathomable plot. (Video/Laser: Warner Bros.)

UP FRANKENSTEIN. See *Andy Warhol's Frankenstein.*

UP FROM THE DEPTHS (1979) ★ "Down to the Depths of Despair" better describes this amateurish imitation of *Jaws*, which features ridiculous characters, phony effects and a holiday feeling that betrays any cinematic drama. Charles Griffith, an old Roger Corman alumnus, directed in the Hawaiian Islands, hamstrung with a terrible script by Alfred Sweeny, who is said to have used *The Creature from the Haunted Sea* as his guide. Sam Bottoms wins worst acting award bottoms-up. In this picture, you root for the killer fish and hope the dumb white-eyes get eaten. (Vestron)

URBAN LEGEND (1998) ★★★ You know an urban legend. It's a story you heard from your mailman who heard it from his uncle in Hoboken who got it from a cop in Detroit. It's some terrible cautionary tale. And of course it really happened. Like the one about the baby-sitter who got threatening phone calls—only to realize they were coming from an extension upstairs. Or the one about the wealthy woman who gave her poodle a shampoo and, to dry out the dog quickly, popped the pup into the microwave. Or maybe it's the one about the hitchhiker who . . . well, at Pendleton University, the hottest urban legend going around is about the girl who sped away from a gas station when the attendant got weird, not realizing that an ax murderer was hiding in her backseat. Only trouble is, this really happens; it opens the picture, in fact. Also, there's an urban legend around the campus that 25 years before, in one of the dorms, a killer knocked off everyone by slitting their throats. You have to admit, Silvio Horta's script gives a refreshing spin on the slasher genre by depicting the crimes of a mad killer who is knocking off the students and using infamous urban legends as inspiration. Director Jamie Blanks really has fun with this wild premise, and although the genre is unavoidably riddled with cliches that this movie does nothing to avoid, there is a sense of a good time. The cast is made up mainly of TV personalities (Alicia Witt of *Cybill*, Jared Leto of *My So-Called Life*, Rebecca Gayheart of *Beverly Hills 90210*) and a couple of old pros: John Neville as the dean and Robert Englund as an instructor who specializes in urban legends. The latter even indulges his students by providing "pop rocks" (a kind of candy) and soda—a lethal combination according to one urban legend around campus. The one performer who really has a good time is Loretta Devine as a security guard who emulates Pam Grier when she draws her .45 automatic, and who's always trying to save the screaming heroines from the awful slasher. And for sensuality there's Tara Reid, a sexy blonde with a talk-radio show on campus. Nobody else in the cast quite captures the depth of her fear as she's pursued through her radio facility (her disheveled clothing falling away to reveal her awesome figure) by the ax murderer, who always strikes in a furry parka. Speaking of urban legends, did you hear the one about the killer with a hook hand who stalked occupants of cars on lovers' lane? Yeah, it came from a pal of my uncle in Denver who heard it from this retired fireman in Chicago. One dark night this car pulled up, see, and lurking in the dark was . . . (Video/DVD: Columbia TriStar)

UROTSUKIDOJI. See *Legend of the Overfiend.*

V (1983) ★★★ Four-hour miniseries written-produced-directed by Kenneth Johnson. Fifty giant saucer-shaped motherships from another galaxy appear, crewed by humanoids here to exchange precious commodities to save their dying planet. But these E.T.s are 2-faced conquerors, wresting control of TV networks to take over the world. Guerrilla units led by Marc Singer fight back by zapping the humanoids with their own ray guns and stealing their shuttlecrafts. It is then that V (from the World War II phrase "V for Victory") deteriorates into mock heroics and a plot about bigotry and betrayal patterned on Nazi Germany. The special effects are good, the art design derivative. The best touch is when a high school band greets the first aliens to Earth with the theme from *Star Wars*. (Warner Bros.) (Laser: Japanese, as *V1*)

V: THE FINAL BATTLE (1984) ★★½ Six-hour continuation of *V*, but without creator Kenneth Johnson. Producers Daniel H. Blatt and Robert Singer took the helm, hiring Richard T. Heffron to direct and a mess of hacks to carry on the story. Primarily action and intrigue in the TV vein, designed to introduce a weekly TV series that was short-lived. Jane Badler stands out as an alien bitch in charge of the invasion. Marc Singer is back as the hero, with Faye Grant. (Warner Bros.) (Laser: Japanese, as *V2*)

VAGRANT, THE (1992) ★★½ This Mel Brooks production is an interesting but failed experiment in surreal paranoia, with Bill Paxton as a yuppie accountant who buys a fixer-upper and becomes terrorized by a brute of a man, monstrous in behavior. This unpleasant character is played with relish by Marshall Bell, but motives for the harassment are never clear in Richard Jeffries's script. It's played as a comedy and Paxton is a nerdy klutz, which makes it difficult to root for him since he's his own worst enemy, and not the vagrant. Occasionally the surreal elements serve the premise, and director Chris (*The Fly II*) Walas struggles to bring style and pacing to the material, but the ambiguities underlying the vagrant's motives defeat good intentions. And Michael Ironside's cop adds to the lack of focus. Mitzi Kapture, Colleen Camp (as a goofy, horny real estate lady), Stuart Pankin, Marc McClure. (MGM/UA)

VALLEY OF GWANGI, THE (1969) ★★★½ Excellent Charles H. Schneer production, made in Spain, with brilliant stop-motion effects by Ray Harryhausen and a romantically pleasing story by Willis O'Brien (scripted by William E. Bast). It's an exciting turn-of-the-century Western (directed by James O'Connolly) in which cowboy James Franciscus discovers a forbidden valley of prehistoric creatures. A *Tyrannosaurus rex* is lassoed and hogtied in one helluvan exciting sequence, then displayed in a traveling circus. Up there with the best of Harryhausen's work. Gila Golan, Richard Carlson, Freda Jackson, Laurence Naismith. Aka *Gwangi, The Lost Valley,*

The Valley Where Time Stood Still, The Valley Time Forgot. (Video/Laser: Warner Bros.)

VALLEY OF THE MISTS. See *The Beast of Hollow Mountain*.

VALLEY TIME FORGOT, THE. See *The Valley of Gwangi*.

VALLEY WHERE TIME STOOD STILL. See *The Valley of Gwangi*.

VAMP (1986) ★★★ Above-average teenage comedy blending horror and laughs when members of a frat party step into the After Dark Club—and a comedy Twilight Zone—to meet Grace Jones (as Katrina, an Egyptian mummy goddess). She and her strippers are literal femme fatales who put the bite on the boys. This New World comedy has a few scary-fun moments as well as humor. Directed stylishly by Richard Wenk. Chris Makepeace, Sandy Baron, Robert Rusler, Billy Drago, Brad Logan. (New World) (Laser: Image)

VAMPIRE (1979) ★★★½ Effective vampire tale—one of the better TV productions—features the trappings of the gothic thriller but crypt-oligizes them intelligently and chillingly. Jason Miller and E. G. Marshall are superb as vampire hunters stalking Richard Lynch, an 800-year-old bloodsucker, in San Francisco. Made on location, this is unresolved so the story would segue into a weekly series, but it was never picked up. Well directed by E. W. Swackhamer; written by Steve Bochco and Michael Kozell. Jessica Walter, Barrie Youngfellow.

VAMPIRE AND THE ROBOT, THE. See *My Son, the Vampire*.

VAMPIRE AT MIDNIGHT (1988) ★★½ Bodies drained of blood are dumped out of a limousine as it dashes about the lonely streets of L.A.— the pastime of a nocturnal bloodsucker who's pretending to be a psychologist. The focus of this low-budget horror feature—with more erotic ambience than most—is a beautiful blond pianist (she looks great in white-and-red outfits) and her relationship with a cop working on the case, who's trying to keep her from falling under the doc's hypnotic spell. These characters (especially the sexy blond) put meat on the bones of this lean, mean tale. Directed by Gregory McClatchy. Jason Williams, Gustav Vintas. (Key)

VAMPIRE BAT, THE (1933) ★★★ Mad scientist Lionel Atwill (as that wonderfully dedicated but demented Dr. Otto von Niemann) sneaks around leaving puncture marks in the necks of victims—but is he a vampire? Edward T. Lowe's script and Frank R. Strayer's direction are outdated, but this is worth seeing for the cast: Melvyn Douglas as leading man, Fay Wray as screaming heroine, Dwight Frye as crazy henchman. (Sinister/C; Western; Filmfax; Goodtimes)

VAMPIRE BEAST CRAVES BLOOD. See *Blood Beast Terror.*

VAMPIRE CASTLE. See *Captain Kronos—Vampire Hunter.*

VAMPIRE CIRCUS (1972) ★★★ Three-ring Hammer midway of horror, set in 1810 Serbia in a village wracked by plague. Paying a visit to the community is a Big Top with low entertainers: vampires and other types capable of transmutation into animals and grotesque night creatures. The owner of the circus, a vampire himself, is seeking revenge against those who murdered his cousin. Graphically gory in the Hammer tradition. Directed by Robert Young. Adrienne Cori, Laurence Payne, Thorley Walters, David Prowse (Darth Vader's body), Lynne Frederick, Skip Martin. (Fright)

VAMPIRE COP (1990) ★★ The title character (William Lucas) dons blue to evoke red from victims in this regionally produced (Florida) minor horror item. Written-directed by Donald Farmer, who's also in the cast. Melissa Moore, Mal Arnold. (Panorama; Atlas)

VAMPIRE HUNTER D (1985) ★★★ "This story takes place in the distant future, when mutants and demons slither through a young world of darkness." So begins this superbly animated Japanese adventure in a vein of dark fantasy in A.D. 12,090, when a race of vampires rules like feudal land barons and a subclass of half-vampire, half-human warriors takes on the role of vampire hunters. "D," who resembles a samurai swordsman with a touch of Dr. Strange, is a sinister traveler hired by a young woman to protect her from Count Magnus Lee. She's kidnapped and "D" fights 3 sisters who turn into deadly serpents and other characters endowed with magical powers. It's a rip-roaring adventure directed by Toyoo Ashida. (Streamline)

VAMPIRE IN BROOKLYN (1995) ★★½ There is such a strong on-screen sexuality between Eddie Murphy and Angela Bassett that it's a shame this vampire movie didn't take itself more seriously. Instead, the Charles Murphy–Michael Lucker–Chris Parker script (idea by Eddie Murphy) is a mixture of gore thrills, spoofery and black-ghetto humor that is, at times, awful. And just plain stupid. Too bad—it's a step down for director Wes Craven, who's capable of better. The Murphy-Bassett chemical sizzle provides the only moments when there's something to sink one's teeth into. Murphy portrays the vampire Maximilian (a "connoisseur of death"), who arrives in Brooklyn aboard a rusty freighter in search of Bassett, a homicide cop whose mother once studied the supernatural in Haiti (an element of the story never made very clear, and poor exposition at that). References to Blacula, John Shaft and Mr. Tibbs are a reminder that this film belongs to the genre of black-culture movies, and that when such movies are bad, they are stinky. This is very stinky. Zakes Morae, Kadeem Hardison (as a decomposing "ghoul," perhaps the only really funny thing in the entire film), Allen Payne. (Video/Laser: Paramount)

VAMPIRE KILLERS. See *The Fearless Vampire Killers.*

VAMPIRE LOVERS, THE (1970) ★★★ Initial entry in Hammer's Karnstein series with Ingrid Pitt as the beautiful, busty Mircalla (sequels were *Lust for a Vampire* and *Twins of Evil*). It features a sensuous sex romp between two gorgeous babes (heavily edited by U.S. censors) who engage in streaking and breast-biting. Peter Cushing is General Spielsdorf, the exorcist who must behead Mircalla (an anagram of "Carmilla"). Directed by Roy Ward Baker from a Tudor Gates script. Pippa Steele, Madeline Smith, Kate O'Meara, Douglas Wilmer, Dawn Addams, Ferdy Mayne. (Orion; Embassy) (Laser: Japanese)

VAMPIRE MEN OF THE LOST PLANET (1971) ★★ Muddled horror–sci-fi fiasco (written by Sue McNair) in which vampires from another planet attack Earthlings with such frequency that Dr. Rynning (John Carradine) sends rocket *XB-13* to the faraway planet, where astronauts discover dinosaurs, squabbling cavepeople and Spectrum X, a freaky frequency that makes the color red dangerous to have around, and which accounts for scenes tinted a reddish hue. This Al Adamson–directed olio has everything but the sinking kitsch. Its only distinction is that the cameraman was William Zsigmond. Features footage from *Unknown Island* and *One Million B.C.* and there are persisting rumors that footage was lifted from a Filipino horror flick. Robert Dix, Vicki Volante, Joey Benson, Bruce Powers. Aka *Blood Monster, Creatures of the Prehistoric Planet, Creatures of the Red Planet, Flesh Creatures of the Red Planet, The Flesh Crea-*

tures, Horror Creatures of the Lost Planet, Horror Creatures of the Prehistoric Planet, Horror Creatures of the Red Planet and *Space Mission to the Lost Planet.* (From Republic and Vid-America as *Horror of the Blood Monsters*)

VAMPIRE OF DR. DRACULA. See *Frankenstein's Bloody Terror.*

VAMPIRE OVER LONDON. Video title for *My Son, the Vampire* (Sinister/C; S/Weird; Filmfax).

VAMPIRE PLAYGIRLS. See *Dracula's Great Love.*

VAMPIRES, THE (1961). Video version of *Goliath and the Vampires* (Sinister/C).

VAMPIRES (1988) ★★ At a private Connecticut school, mad doctoress Jackie James uses a machine to extract the energy from her girl students; Duane Jones plays an occultist. Aka *Abadon.* Produced-directed by Len Anthony; written by James Harrigan and Anthony. Orly Benair, Robin Michaels, John Bly.

VAMPIRES (1998) ★★★ A hell of an exciting, violent, gore-filled genre movie that entertains without letup, with director John Carpenter treading into controversial areas when he presents some blatantly anti–Catholic Church material. James Wood (as a lifelong vampire stalker named Jack Crow) seems well suited for the horror genre as he leads his Team Crow, specially trained warriors that track down and destroy nests of vampires. This adaptation of John Steakley's novel *Vampire$* opens dramatically with the destruction of nine vampires in a lonely farmhouse, and introduces imaginative vampire-killing equipment. But the superpowerful, unstoppable Master Valik (Thomas Ian Griffith) escapes. Totally pissed off, the caped entity shows up that night at the Sun-God Motel, where Crow and his team are celebrating with assorted hookers. The massacre that follows is graphically presented as heads are severed, bodies are split apart, and the Master shoves his arm through torsos. Survivors Crow, his best friend (Daniel Baldwin), and a hapless hooker (Sheryl Lee, a beauty from TV's *Twin Peaks*) escape and are themselves pursued by the Master, who rounds up other unkillable Masters to help him complete the foul deed. The Catholic Church gets blamed for creating vampires 700 years ago through an ungodly ceremony and screenwriter Don Jakoby spices up this subplot with a peace-loving priest—Tim Guinee, who quickly becomes a vampire killer out of necessity—and a cardinal of questionable character played by Maximilian Schell. The ending, which involves a giant crucifix called the Berziers Cross, gets a little ridiculous with its parade of melodramatic resolutions, but hey, guys, it's only a vampire movie. Maybe that's why Carpenter and Jakoby decided to dig at the Catholics a bit—in a genre movie it doesn't seem so profane. Among the members of the Team Crow are Cary-Hiroyuki Tagawa, Mark Boone, Jr., and David Rowden. (Video/DVD/Laser: Paramount)

VAMPIRES AND OTHER STEREOTYPES (1992) ★★ This semiprofessional effort is a tale about two demon hunters (Bill White and Ed Hubbard) who descend into Hell with three beautiful women. It brims with monstrous special effects (a wall of talking monster heads, a wall of wriggling arms and hands, a giant rat, a crawling hand, and assorted horned demons) but the end result is no more scary than a visit to a carnival's monster funhouse. The pacing established by writer-editor-director Kevin Lindenmuth is lethargic and clumsy, and despite some mildly good performances (Wendy Bednarz, Anna Dipace, Suzanne Scott) there is no forward thrust, or sense that the story is going anywhere. (Brimstone)

VAMPIRE'S CRYPT. See *Terror in the Crypt.*

VAMPIRE'S EMBRACE (1993) ★½ Amateurish stab at a black-comedy bloodsucker tale set in suburbia fails miserably due to incompetent handling by all concerned, especially writer-director Glenn Andreiev. He doesn't have the cast or the writing skills to spin this crazed yarn about an average stiff (Paul Borgese) who comes to realize his wife (Sarah Watchman) is a vampire, feeding on town folks in the company of another ghoulish creature (Edna Boyle), who sleeps in a coffin in a graveyard mausoleum. The whole thing is wretchedly performed, and George Higham's makeup is lousy beyond words. Shot in and around Jacksonville, FL, this is one you want to avoid at all cost. (EI Independent Cinema)

VAMPIRE'S KISS (1988) ★★★ And now for something completely different in the vein (heh heh!) of vampire movies . . . here's a strange tidbit about a New York literary agent (Nicolas Cage) who gets it in the neck from a Manhattan vampire and goes insane, turning into a bloodsucker—or so he thinks. We can see his reflection in a mirror—but he can't! It is the ambiguities of the Joseph Minion script that no doubt appealed to director Robert Bierman. But in avoiding genre conventions, *Vampire's Kiss* moves off on such an oddball tangent, into a region of hallucinatory dreams, it's tough to peg. It's more a study in madness as Cage makes life hell for his secretary, stands up his girlfriend, fantasizes himself in the office of his shrink (Elizabeth Ashley in a nonresponsive role) and carries a stake, requesting he be put to death before he attacks innocents. It works neither as a comedy nor as a satire, and floats in a void of its own. Catch it if you're a vampire completist. Maria Conchita Alonso, Jennifer Beals. (HBO) (Laser: Image)

VAMPIRE'S LAST VICTIM, THE. See *The Play-girls and the Vampire*.

VAMPIRE'S NIECE. See *Fangs of the Living Dead*.

VAMPIRES OF BIKINI BEACH (1987) ★½ Insufferable teenage monster flick, a rank amateur effort shot in L.A. on a shoestring, and having the appeal of same strung through the eyelets of a raunchy tennis shoe. Two dumb teens find a "Book of the Dead," and then find themselves in the thick of a vampire cult led by a caped cornball named Demos, who intends to raise an army of vampire zombies to take over the world. The vampires are ham personified, and every cliché is paraded before your weary eyes as this wretched waste of man-hours unfolds. The title is cute, but everything else isn't. Todd Kauffman, Jennifer Badham.

VAMPIRES OF HARLEM. See *Blood Couple*.

VAMPIRES OF PRAGUE. See *Mark of the Vampire*.

VAMPIRES OVER LONDON. See *My Son, the Vampire*.

VAMPIRE'S THIRST. Video version of *The Body Beneath*.

VAMPIRE'S TOMB. Original working title for the project that grew into *Plan 9 from Outer Space*.

VAMPIRES VS. HERCULES. See *Hercules in the Haunted World*.

VAMPIRE VIXENS FROM VENUS (1995) ★ Simply put, this is simply awful—dumb and stupid, to boot. Three ugly aliens from Venus land on Earth and transform themselves into sexy bimbos who lure young guys into traps and turn them into pieces of raw meat. It's played as a comedy, and includes a moronic British policeman who isn't a bit funny. Michelle Bauer tries to spice it up, but writer-producer-director Ted A. Bohus is strictly bogus as a filmmaker. Leon Head, Theresa Lynn, J. J. North, Charlie Callas, Leslie Glass.

VAMPIRE WOMEN (1971). See *The Heritage of Dracula*.

VAMPIRE WOMEN (1973). See *Crypt of the Living Dead*.

VAMPYR (1932) ★★★★ German masterpiece photographed by Rudolf Mate (who later became a Hollywood director) and produced-directed by Carl Theodore Dreyer, whose script (written with Christen Jul) is based on J. Sheridan Le Fanu's *Carmilla*. It remains one of the few horror films to so well capture the nightmarish qualities of a dream. A visitor (Julian West) to a peculiar inn in a strange village is given a book on vampirism and plunged into a cryptic world of shadows, coffins and vampires. *Vampyr* has, in recent years, taken on a cult following and been recognized as a minor art classic. Aka *Adventures of David Gray, The Strange Adventure of David Gray, Not Against the Flesh*

and *Castle of Doom*. Henriette Gerard, Sibylle Schmitz, Rena Mandel. (Kino; Video Yester-year; S/Weird; Filmfax) (Laser: Image)

VAMPYR: A SOAP OPERA, THE (1993) ★★ Oddball updated version of Heinrich Marschner's 1827 opera, in which vampirism has assumed a form of big business in modern society. Omar Ebrahim, Fiona O'Neill. (CBS/Fox)

VAMPYRES. Video version of *Vampyres—Daughters of Darkness*. (Magnum)

VAMPYRES—DAUGHTERS OF DARKNESS (1975) ★★ R-rated version of the X-rated *Vampyres*. Lesbian bloodsuckers Fram and Miriam (Marianne Moore and Anulka) prey on campers vacationing on the lawn of their castle—until one of them makes the mistake of falling in love with handsome Murray Brown. The theme is: every lesbian vampire should own a castle. They certainly have a gay time in the crypt with Joseph Larraz directing. Aka *Daughters of Darkness* and *Daughters of Dracula* (Magnum; from Majestic as *Satan's Daughters* and Lettuce Entertain You as *Blood Hunger*)

VANISHING BODY, THE. Rerelease title of *The Black Cat* (1934).

VANISHING SHADOW, THE (1934) ★★½ Twelve-chapter Universal serial with Onslow Stevens as an invisible avenger who goes after the murderers of his father with a robot, a Death Ray and other futuristic inventions. Directed by Lew Landers. Ada Ince, Walter Miller.

VARAN THE UNBELIEVABLE (1958) ★★ Varan was described by a critic as a flying squirrel with jet-propelled nuts, by another as a prehistoric bat . . . what the hell is this thing called Varan? Beats the hell out of us, but kiddies will squeal with delight at this U.S. version of a Japanese monster movie directed by Inoshiro Honda. Pure action as the Godzilla carbon copy beelines toward Tokyo, encountering resistance from a naval officer. Scenes with Myron Healey were added for U.S. appeal by director Jerry Baerwitz. Effects by Honda's partner, Eiji Tsuburaya. Kozo Nomura. Aka *Baran* and *The Monster Varan*. (VCI; United)

VAULT OF HORROR, THE (1973) ★★★ Sequel to *Tales from the Crypt* consists of stories adapted from the E.C. comics of the '50s edited by William Gaines and Al Feldstein. Milton Subotsky's black-macabre script recaptures only some of the E.C. flavor, but horror fans will still enjoy. Five people trapped in an underground tomb with the Vault Keeper listen as he spins 5 yarns that run the gamut: vampirism, limb dismemberment, body snatching, voodoo, Satanism. "Midnight Mess," stars Daniel and Anna Massey; "The Neat Job," Glynis Johns and Terry-Thomas; "This Trick'll Kill You," Curt Jurgens; "Bargain in Death," Edward Judd and Michael Craig; and "Drawn and Quartered,"

Tom Baker. Roy Ward Baker directed. Aka *Tales from the Crypt Part II* and *Further Tales from the Crypt*. (Nostalgia Merchant; Media)

VEGAS IN SPACE (1991) ★★ This homegrown film from San Francisco's drag-queen community is an outrageous, campy spoof of sci-fi space adventures, emphasizing uninhibitedly wild hairdos, glitzy costumes and a self-mocking of the gay scene. As an underground oddity and an anomaly of moviemaking, it's a popular film-festival item and was released theatrically by Troma in 1993. It's the work of impresario Phillip R. Ford, who produced, directed, edited and conceived the no-state-of-the-art effects. It was designed as a showpiece for drag-queen Doris Fish, who helped Ford shape the script with Miss X (another drag queen). Fish plays the captain of a spaceship assigned to investigate the disappearance of jewels on the planet Clitorius. But since no males are allowed on the planet, Fish and other crew members take sex-change pills, turning into women. There's no attempt at serious filmmaking, so what gives the film its unusual edge is its blatant badness and lack of cinematic art. It works better as an audience-participation experience. Except for a few sexual innuendoes and double entendres, there is nothing sexy about the film—it is never lascivious. Only the clothing and hair are in bad taste. Doris Fish died of AIDS in 1991, the month the film opened in San Francisco. Two months later another cast member, Tippi, who plays "Princess Angel," died of AIDS. Among the drag queens: Miss X as Veneer, Queen of Clitorean Police; Ginger Quest as Empress Nueva Gabor; Timmy Spence as Lt. Dick Hunter; Ramona Fischer as Lt. Sheila Shadows; Jennifer Blowdryer as Futura Volare; and Sandelle Kincaid as Babs Velour. (MCA)

VEIL, THE. See *Haunts*.

VELVET VAMPIRE, THE (1971) ★★★ Commendable attempt by director Stephanie Rothman and cowriters Charles S. Swartz and Maurice Jules to create an unusual vampire picture. Aka *The Devil Is a Woman*, *Through the Looking Glass* and *The Waking Hour*, this has strong sexual overtones that heighten the suspense when travelers Michael Blodgett and Sherry Miles stop at the ranchero of Celeste Yarnall, unaware she is a sensual vampire and a descendant of horror writer Sheridan Le Fanu. There's time wasted with desert dune-buggy footage, but once Yarnall focuses on her targets, male and female, the going gets sensuous. How the vampire is laid to rest belongs to the Flower Child Generation. Sherry Miles, Gene Shane. (Embassy; Impulse; Simitar) (Laser: Image)

VENGEANCE. See *The Brain* (1962).

VENGEANCE IS MINE (1976) ★★½ An eccen-tric, disturbing portrait of a farmer (Ernest Borgnine) who tortures 2 escaped convicts (after shooting one in the chest with a shotgun) by hanging them up on chains in his cellar and refusing them food and water. What's weak and fascinating at the same time about this independent feature is that Borgnine's motivations are never explained. All he succeeds in doing is alienating the granddaughter (Hollis McLaren) he loves, so what was the point of all the mayhem (which includes an intense attack by 2 police dogs on one of the criminals). Borgnine gives one of his better performances and Michael J. Pollard does a good job as a crazed psychocase. A most unusual script by Robert Maxwell and director John Trent, who filmed in the South. Cec Linder, Al Waxman, Louis Zorich. Originally made as *Sunday in the Country*. (Paragon; Video Gem; Video Yesteryear; from Lettuce Entertain You as *Blood for Blood*)

VENGEANCE OF FU MANCHU, THE (1968) ★★ Lackluster Harry Alan Towers production (third in the British series) with Christopher Lee as the diabolical Asian mastermind who forces a surgeon to create an exact duplicate of Scotland Yard's Nayland Smith in an insidious plot to substitute the chief law enforcers with killer clones. Strangely lacking in action. Directed by Jeremy Summers from a Towers script. Howard Marion Crawford, Tsai Chin, Horst Frank, Maria Rohm, Tony Ferrer. Preceded by *The Face of Fu Manchu* and *The Brides of Fu Manchu* and followed by *Kiss and Kill* and *The Castle of Fu Manchu*. (Warner Bros.)

VENGEANCE OF SHE (1967) ★★★½ The best thing going in this loose Hammer sequel to the Ursula Andress version of H. Rider Haggard's *She* is the sexy Olinka Berova, who turns up on a millionaire's yacht in a daze, uncertain who she is or why she's mysteriously drawn to a lost city in the nearby desert mountains. Berova, an exotically attractive blonde with a marvelous figure, parades around in various stages of disarray in the company of heroic Edward Judd while high priest John Richardson tries to lure the beauty into the Eternal Flame and thereby find eternal life in the kingdom of Kuma. Peter O'Donnell's script is compelling enough to hold one's interest, the Hammer production values are strong and director Cliff Owen focuses on the shapely form of Ms. Berova frequently enough to take one's mind off any inadequacies of story. Andre Morell, George Sewell, Colin Blakely, Noel Willman, Jill Melford. Aka *Ayesha, the Return of She* and *Ayesha, Daughter of She*.

VENGEANCE OF THE MONSTER. See *Majin, Monster of Terror*.

VENGEANCE OF THE MUMMY. See *The Mummy's Revenge*. (Mummy Deadest!)

VENGEANCE OF THE ZOMBIES (1972) ★★ Spanish fright job directed by Leon Klimovsky (the hombre who gave us *Saga of Dracula* and *Vampyres*) and starring that Holy Toledo monster star Paul Naschy. Indian sage named Krisna (is his first name Harry?) arranges, through a magical chant, to raise a woman from the grave, who is turned into a killing machine for purposes of revenge. Montezuma's revenge could be next. Script by Jacinto Molina. Mirta Miller, Vic Winner, Luis Ciges. Aka *Revolt of the Dead Ones* and *The Rebellion of the Dead Women*. (Home; Sinister/C; All Seasons; S/Weird; Filmfax; from Vogue as *Walk of the Dead*)

VENGEANCE: THE DEMON. Once-proposed theatrical title for *Pumpkinhead*.

VENGEFUL DEAD, THE. Video version of *Kiss Daddy Goodbye* (Premiere).

VENUS RISING (1995) ★★½ A 21st-century sci-fi thriller, with modest virtual reality sequences, depicting the plight of a sensitive woman (Audie English) trying to adjust to life on the mainland after escaping from K314, a prison-colony island on which she grew up a complete innocent. Coupled with her efforts to begin a new life is a romance with a hit man assigned to murder her, some strange virtual reality encounters, and the reappearance of a homicidal young man who escaped with her. This slow-moving film, partly shot in Hawaii, is marred by moments of mediocre filmmaking and some drab dialogue by screenwriter-director Leora Barish. (Edgar Bravo is credited with directing extra scenes.) Joel Gray and Morgan Fairchild are wasted in cameos. Billy Wirth, Costas Mandylor, Meredith Salenger, Ivory Ocean. (IRS/Columbia Tristar)

VIBES (1988) ★★ What might have been a rousing fantasy adventure in the fashion of *Romancing the Stone* turns up a lame duck for producer Ron Howard. Psychics Jeff Goldblum and Cyndi Lauper (he has the power of psychometry, she makes predicitons via an Indian spirit guide) are lured to Ecuador by a strange character named Harry Buscafusco (Peter Falk) to find a room of gold in a lost city high in the mountains. Little of the adventure and comedy promise of this premise—concocted by screenwriters Lowell Ganz and Babaloo Mandel, who gave us *Splash*—pays off as the romantic team finds that almost everyone else they've encountered in the film is in on one scheme or another. Richard Edlund provides mildly interesting special effects surrounding a pyramid-shaped stone that gives off powerful psychic energy, but director Ken Kwapis has little to work with. The Goldblum-Lauper duo is quite appealing, though. Julian Sands, Googy Gress, Michael Lerner, Ramon Bieri. (RCA/Columbia) (Laser: Japanese)

VICE VERSA (1988) ★★★ An amusing, oft clever use of the plot device of switched personalities in 2 bodies—in this case a somewhat neurotic, humorless department store executive (Judge Reinhold) swaps souls with his adolescent son (Fred Savage) through the magical powers of a Thai art object that resembles a devil's mask. Reinhold steals this show with his portrayal of a youngster in a man's body, capturing the nuances of a wide-eyed kid having the advantages of an adult's body. To the credit of screenwriters-producers Dick Clement and Ian LaFrenais, they keep the ridiculous Thailand elements to a minimum, and play down the danger element as art collectors–thieves Swoosie Kurtz and David Proval pursue father and son for the relic. Director Brian Gilbert is far more interested in social satire. Corinne Bohrer, Jane Kaczmerek, Gloria Gifford. (Video/Laser: RCA/Columbia)

VIDEO DEAD, THE (1987) ★ Uninspired video original, another variation on *Night of the Living Dead*, only this time the zombie monsters come out of a TV set. Written-produced-directed by Robert Scott in and around San Francisco, this features gore effects, zombie makeup and a dumb plot. Rocky Duvall, Roxana Augesen, Sam David McClelland. (Embassy)

VIDEODROME (1983) ★★ Bungled David Cronenberg picture, grotesque and repulsive under his writing and direction. James Woods is a sleazy cable TV station owner, looking for porn programming, who stumbles across a sadistic series called "Videodrome." Watch enough sex and violence and a new organ grows in your brain that creates hallucinations. Eventually your mind and body evolve into something more wholesome. It's a plot by the Moral Majority to cleanse the nation. If you're having trouble following this critique, wait until you see this botched mess. Rick Baker's effects are ugly, and the sex and violence were heavily cut by Universal for an R rating. (Note, however, that Cronenberg restored the footage from his X-rated version for video and laser.) Deborah Harry of Blondie is the beautiful female lead, but her character is quite unsavory; she and Woods as sadists are a turn-off. Sonja Smits, Peter Dvorsky, Les Carlson. (MCA; A & E) (Laser: MCA)

VIDEO WARS (1984) ★ Inept Italian spy spoof, in which dumb superspy Scattergood (billed as George Diamond, but don't believe it), the head of SOB (Subversive Operations Bureau), is assigned by a video-happy President to stop a villain named Reichmonger, dictator of the kingdom of Vacabia, which has programmed the video games of the world to brainwash everyone for conquest. Absolutely nothing happens in this Mario Giampaolo produced-directed fiasco except a bevy of beauties show off their breasts and legs, and a dumb Norwegian beauty (Joan Stenn, as Miss Hemisphere) tries to lay the hero. (Best Film & Video)

VIENNA STRANGLER, THE. See *The Mad Butcher*.

VIEW TO A KILL, A (1985) ★★★ Something misfired in Roger Moore's seventh (and last) 007 outing. Despite the massive destruction and opportunities for excitement, director John Glen's pacing is strangely lethargic. Part of the trouble is a minimum of offbeat gadgets and machines; a less-than-rugged Moore, whose quips are as weary as his physique; and a Richard Maibaum–Michael G. Wilson script lacking humor or freshness. Master villain Max Zorin plots to destroy Silicon Valley and the world microchip market by creating earthquakes to shake up the San Andreas Fault. The film's only saving Grace is the lithe Ms. Jones as May Day, a tigress who makes Christopher Walken's Zorin a wimp in comparison. Tanya Roberts as heroine Stacey Sutton is an attractive eyeful but her acting abilities are minimal. Patrick Macnee is pleasant as Bond's undercover companion but he never gets a chance to display the ability of Steed the Avenger. There's a shoot-out on the Eiffel Tower, a high-speed fire engine chase down Market Street in San Francisco, a cliff-hanging climax on the Golden Gate Bridge, and the blowing up of an underground cavern . . . but it just sits there and dies. (Video/Laser: CBS/Fox; MGM/UA)

VIKING SAGAS, THE (1995) ★★½ Minor touches of magic and the supernatural, with a few prophecies thrown in, charactize this action film, which has the advantage of being photographed on location in Iceland. The script by Dale Herd and Paul R. Gurian (the latter doubling as producer) is somber and humorless, without colorful characters, so the film suffers a great deal in terms of story and character, but the action sequences under Michael Chapman's direction are packed with gore and violence, so the real star of this picture is the action coordinator. And Ingibjorg Stefansdottir is some beauty. Ralf Moeller plays the heroic warrior out to avenge the murder of his father at the hands of the usurper Ketil the Black (Hinrik Olafson), and he shoots a mean arrow and wields a wicked "Ghost Sword." (New Line)

VIKING WOMEN. See *Viking Women and the Sea Serpent*.

VIKING WOMEN AND THE SEA SERPENT (1958) ★ Rock-bottom Roger Corman programmer (he produced-directed) depicts a water beast that functions as deus ex machina by intervening at the last minute between bands of warring Vikings. Scenes are so dark, the ocean waves so phony and the man-beast relationship so ambiguous, the only horror to be pondered is: Who designed the crummy monster? Too bad the creature didn't swallow the good guys along with the bad—that would really give him indigestion. The people are that tasteless. Originally made as *Saga of the Viking Women and Their Voyage to the Waters of the Great Sea Serpent*. Abby Dalton, Gary Conway, Susan Cabot, Brad Jackson, Jonathan Haze. Aka *Viking Women* and *Undersea Monster*.

VILLAGE OF THE DAMNED (1960) ★★★½ Faithful version of John Wyndham's *Midwich Cuckoos*, thanks to director Wolf Rilla, who co-wrote the adaptation with Stirling Silliphant and George Barclay. A small community in England is isolated by a strange invisible shield and its inhabitants afflicted by prolonged sleep. Later, the village's pregnant women give birth to hollow-eyed children who possess irresistible hypnotic powers and grow up to dominate adults, especially their fathers. Ultimately, these singular alien children will have a devastating effect on mankind. This British film generated a sequel, *Children of the Damned*, equally well done. George Sanders, Barbara Shelley, Michael Gwynn, Laurence Naismith. Remade by John Carpenter in 1995. (MCA) (Laser: MGM/UA, with *Children of the Damned*)

VILLAGE OF THE DAMNED (1995) ★★★½ This is a sincere effort to remake the successful 1960 adaptation of John Wyndham's famous sci-fi novel, with the script by David Himmelstein remaining faithful to the original material (excepting that the British setting has been changed to a Monterey-like California setting). However, neither director John Carpenter nor Himmelstein has expanded on the theme to give it modern relevance, and all that remains are a few of the original movie's startling images restaged, but without any attempt to inject modern effects or techniques. The memorable image that must have attracted Carpenter to this project—white-haired evil children who zap folks with their blazing eyeballs—is recaptured verbatim. But so what? Where's some new clout to stir up a little excitement? Once again a strange invisible shield is placed by an unseen force around a small town, causing 10 women to become pregnant and give birth to babies that grow into the strange children. Christopher Reeve portrays the doctor whose life is turned topsy-turvy by events, and Kirstie Alley is the sinister doctor-scientist who keeps tabs on the alien experiment for the government. This is a dark, unrelenting portrait of evil and science gone amok, unrelieved by the slightest hint of comedy. It will fill you with a sense of déjà vu but little else other than the desire to see the original again to be reminded of just how good it was. Mark Hamill, Linda Kozlowski, Michael Pare, Meredith Salenger. (Video/Laser: MCA)

VINDICATOR. See *Wheels of Fire.*

VINDICATOR, THE (1984) ★★★½ Above-average, well-produced Canadian blend of horror and sci-fi (originally *Frankenstein '88*) reminiscent of *Man-made Monster* and *The Indestructible Man.* Obsessed (and certainly mad) scientist Richard Cox takes the victim of an accident (David McIlwraith) and turns him into a cyborg, who escapes and commences a rampage of death and destruction because of his evil programming, even though he's a good guy who would rather go after the crooks. Bounty hunter Pam Grier (her name is Hunter) is hired to track the robot killer with a gun that fires "vaporized acid," and she's one ruthless bitch. There's some nice sewer sequences, good battles and destruction scenes, a violent rape and a sense of cinematic style emerging from director Jean-Claude Lord. Stan Winston created the cyborg look, which is more messy than dressy. Teri Austin, Maury Chaykin, Denis Simpson. (Key)

VINEYARD, THE (1989) ★★ Japanese madman with a penchant for blood traps victims on his island. His blood-drinking gives him immortality, but will the theme immortalize this movie? Directed by Bill Rice and James Hong from a script by Hong, Douglas Condo and James Marlowe. James Hong, Karen Witter, Michael Wong, Cheryl Lawson. (New World) (Laser: Image)

VIOLENT BLOOD BATH (1985) ★★½ The presence of Fernando Rey as a magistrate haunted by memories of sending a serial killer to the guillotine enhances and upgrades this foreign-produced psychothriller, which costars Marissa Mell as his long-suffering wife. It appears that the serial murderer has returned from the grave when a new wave of identical crimes begins, forcing Rey back onto the case to work with police. The script by John Tebar and director Jorge Grau (said to be based on a "theme" by Guy de Maupassant) has enough character content to set this above most of its kind. Aka *Penalty of Death* and *Night Fiend.* Esparaco Santoni, Elisa Laguna. Shown on TV as *Night Fiend.* (World's Worst; VidAmerica)

VIOLENT JOURNEY. See *The Fool Killer.*

VIOLENT MIDNIGHT. See *Psychomania* (1963).

VIPER (1993) ★★ Crummy TV-movie about a wheelchair-bound inventor (Dorian Harewood) who creates a new law-enforcement vehicle for a futuristic society, and a criminal suffering from amnesia (James McCaffrey) who drives the prototype auto to prove its worthiness. Director Danny Bilson coscripted with Paul De Meo. Joe Nipote, Sydney Walsh, Jon Polito.

VIRGIN AMONG THE LIVING DEAD, A (1971) ★ Young heiress is haunted by her family's secrets after arriving in the family's stomping grounds in British Honduras—where the stomping is literal. Directed by Jess Franco. Footage was used from *Zombie Lake* to make this more commercial in the U.S. Paul Muller, Christina Von Blanc, Britt Nichols. Aka *Among the Living Dead.* (Lightning; Wizard; from Edde as *Zombie 4*)

VIRGIN HUNTERS. See *Test Tube Teens from the Year 2000.*

VIRGINS FOR THE HANGMAN. See *Bloody Pit of Horror.*

VIRGIN VAMPIRES. See *Twins of Evil.*

VIRTUAL ASSASSIN (1995) ★★★½ Like *Project Shadowchaser* and *Armed and Dangerous*, this is an excellent if derivative spin-off of *Die Hard*, in which a high-tech high-rise lab is taken over. The caper is the master plan of Brion James, a demented, albino gang leader with designs on stealing a computer virus that could throw the world into "total chaos." The only man standing in the way of his global conquest is ex-cop now-janitor Michael Dudikoff, who overcomes his personal demons to crawl through ventilators, ride elevators and rush through corridors, shooting it out with crazed gunmen. There's also a robotic police probe called C.Y.C.L.O.P.S. that roves the corridors in this explosive actioner loaded with sci-fi gimmicks and futuristic hardware. The roller coaster ride is tense, and James gets to etch one of his over-the-top villains with gusto. And Suki Kaiser is good as the computer gal. Good adventure stuff from writer Eric Poppen and director Robert Lee. John Cuthbert, James Thom, Topaz Hashal-Schou (Turner/Prism)

VIRTUAL COMBAT (1995) ★★★ Another genre olio of standard martial-arts hand-to-hand fighting and futuristic gadgets and technology starring kickboxing champ Don "the Dragon" Wilson. This time he's a "grid runner," a Las Vegas–to-L.A. cop in pursuit of a killer clone created from a virtual reality program by mad scientist Turhan Bey. Dante (Michael Bernardo, with the telepathic voice of Michael Dorn) goes around bragging about his invincibility while bashing cop after cop and chasing after a sexy cyborg lady (Athena Massey), but finally meets his match in Wilson. Why a cyborg creation would possess the magical ability to make swords appear out of thin air is never dealt with in William C. Martell's script—hey, it's a movie, right? Andrew Stevens proves he's a capable director of B-movie material, and gives mother Stella Stevens a bit role as a face on a computer screen. You've seen it all before but you'll still enjoy it. Ken McCleod, Dawn Ann Billings, Rip Taylor, Carrie Mitchum. (Video)

VIRTUAL SEDUCTION (1995) ★★★½ A devastating indictment against the potential misuse of virtual reality and how it could turn us all into a mindless culture that wants to experience life without living it. An unusually provocative Roger Corman TV-movie, with a thoughtful, emotion-filled script by Michelle Gamble-Risley, William Widmaier and Paul Ziller, *Virtual Seduction* depicts Jeff Fahey as a "guinea pig" for Cybernetics, a company with a new Virtual Reality Pod. Inside this singular unit, Fahey re-creates the beautiful young woman (Carrie Genzel) who was murdered on the eve of their marriage. The company (represented by anything-for-progress Frank Novak) wants "a virtual reality more real than reality," and to Fahey that's what he's getting. There's a sexy lovemaking sequence in which he and Genzel smear paint all over their bodies. Meanwhile, real-life girlfriend Ami Dolenz tries to save Fahey with the help of sympathetic cyber-technician Meshach Taylor, as Fahey sinks deeper and deeper into the pseudoreality of the Pod. Ziller also directed this comment against uncontrolled progress. (New Horizons)

VIRTUOSITY (1995) ★★★ Brett Leonard (*The Lawnmower Man, Hideaway*) always manages to direct interesting if not entirely perfect tales with unusual twists, and he does it again in this curious blending of virtual reality, computer microchips and modern serial killers. During V.R. experiments to train police officers in tracking violent criminals, video game serial killer Sid 6.7 (Russell Crowe) is brought to life through a microcrystal and goes on a killing spree, having been given the characterizations of 181 real-life serial killers (including, strangely enough, Adolf Hitler.) When former cop Denzel Washington is brought out of prison to track Sid 6.7, it's the beginning of violent action sequences, as Sid 6.7 can rejuvenate himself after taking numerous bullet hits. Eric Brendt's screenplay captures the intensity of the personal vendetta between Washington and Crowe, and drives the picture to the point that you forget the weaknesses and concentrate on the suspenseful conclusion. Kelly Lynch, Stephen Spinella, William Forsythe, Louise Fletcher, Kevin O'Connor. (Video/Laser: Paramount)

VIRUS. See *Invasion of the Flesh Hunters*.

VIRUS (1995) ★★ Although based on Robin Cook's novel *Outbreak*, this should not be confused with the feature film *Outbreak*, which was released almost simultaneously with the airing of this TV-movie. Both deal with the deadly Ebola virus (which first broke out in Zaire in 1976), but this quickly deteriorates into a "woman in peril" thriller with heavy conspiratorial overtones, following a predictable formula that seems to earmark many of Cook's stories. Beautiful Nicollette Sheridan portrays a doctor new to the ranks of the Centers for Disease Control who uncovers an attempt by a secret group to unleash Ebola on the American public. Roger Young's teleplay, directed by Armand Mastroianni, is but a series of manipulative scenes to put Sheridan into trouble as quickly as possible, and stack the deck against her. Nothing special about this screamer. William Devane, Stephen Cafrey, Barry Corbin, Dakin Matthews, William Atherton.

VIRUS (1998) ★★★ A rousing if thoroughly clichéd disaster-at-sea thriller, of the familiar trapped-on-a-ghost-ship genre, but with science-fiction rather than supernatural explanations. This is pure over-the-top action stuff, based on a Dark Horse comic-book series of the same title, that cuts immediately to the chase when a transparent UFO collides with a Soviet space station and electrifies everything on board. Bolts of electricity are carried down to the satellite dishes of the Soviet research ship *Academic Vladislav Volkov*, where scientist Joanna Pacula watches in horror as her crewmates are destroyed. Cut to a salvage tug, the *Sea Star*, captained by a half-crazed Donald Sutherland, heroic engineer William Baldwin, wise navigator Jamie Lee Curtis, and a handful of other "cannon fodder" types. Seeking refuge from a South Pacific typhoon that is slowly sinking the tug, the crew finds the Soviet ship floating empty except for the surviving Pacula. (If this plot by comic-book creator Chuck Pfarrer and Dennis Feldman rings a bell, it's almost identical to that of *Deep Rising*.) With hopes of claiming the ship as salvage, the tug's crew soon realizes it isn't that easy—that a formless alien intelligence has taken control of the central computer and robotic equipment on board, and is creating half-human, half-mechanical killing machines. Director John Bruno, an Oscar-winning special-effects artist (*Ghostbusters, Terminator 2*), realizing he has cardboard cutouts for characters, goes for blazing action, creepy corridors, grisly human-machine combinations, and cliffhanger after cliffhanger as the crew members are eliminated one by one in their attempt to escape. The one interesting element about the alien intelligence, that it looks upon mankind as a "virus" that needs to be exterminated, is never expanded on. Produced by Gale Anne Hurd, *Virus* is visceral stuff saved by sheer chutzpah and energy. Marshall Bell, Sherman Augustus, Cliff Curtis (hey, he was also in *Deep Rising*), Julio Oscar Mechoso. (Video/DVD: Universal)

VISIONS (1990) ★★ Joe Balogh suffers from visions that could hold the answer to who is killing the hoboes in and around Portland, Oreg. Psychic/slasher film that is all too familiar by now. Produced-directed by Steven Miller from a screenplay he wrote with Tom Taylor. Alice Villarreal, A. R. Newman, J. R. Pella. (Monarch)

VISIONS OF EVIL (1973) ★★ So sad about *So Sad About Gloria* (this TV-film's original title), a sad statement of a sadistic shadow play showing slaughter and the same sanguinary sad plot about seducing a sad skirt into a state of sad insanity. Sad for director-producer Harry Thomason and sad for Dean Jagger, Lori Saunders, Lou Hoffman, Bob Ginnaven, and sad for you, the viewer. For sad-ists. (Prism)

VISIONS OF MURDER (1993) ★★★ Above-average TV movie for the Lifetime network in which Barbara Eden portrays a psychiatrist receiving psychic images of a naval officer whom she suspects murdered one of her patients—his wife. How she convinces ex-hubby/cop James Brolin occupies most of the telescript by Julie Moskowitz and Gary Stephens, which deals with the psychology of the characters quite well. Directed by Michael Rhodes, *Visions of Murder* is a good time-killer.

VISITANTS, THE (1987) ★★ E.T. creatures from beyond space land on Earth in the 1950s and, just for laughs, settle down to suburban life. Directed by Rick Sloane. Marcus Vaughter, Johanna Grika, Nicole Rio. (Star Classics; Trans World)

VISITING HOURS (1982) ★★★½ Better-than-average slasher film (first produced as *The Fright*) that often follows killer Michael Ironside, so that we are as much with him as with the victims. A Canadian production, this also focuses on Lee Grant as a TV reporter fighting for women's rights who is stalked by Colt Hawker (Ironside) in a hospital. Tautly directed by Jean-Claude Lord and scripted with an understanding of movie terror by Brian Taggert. Linda Purl, William Shatner, Lenore Zann, Harvey Atkin. (Video/Laser: CBS/Fox)

VISITOR, THE (1980) ★★½ Offbeat imitation of *The Omen*, dealing with an archangel who comes to Earth to ward off a force of evil from Hell. This allegorical mumbo jumbo is told with odd camera angles, unexplainable effects and pseudoreligious symbolism that baffles rather than enlightens. Directed by Giulio Paradisi. An Italian-U.S. production with a top cast: Glenn Ford, Mel Ferrer, Shelley Winters, John Huston, Sam Peckinpah, Lance Henriksen. Aka *Get Well Soon*. (Embassy; Sam Goldwyn) (Laser: Sam Goldwyn)

VISITORS, THE (1988) ★★★ Swedish variation of *The Amityville Horror* is an effective supernatural chiller with several scary sequences, undermined only by mediocre English dubbing. Before the haunting begins, however, writers-producers Joakim and Patrik Ersgard take the time to establish the psychological tensions between a young insurance executive and his wife and their 2 children when they move into a country home. Their conflicts set into motion the forces of demons imprisoned in an attic room—wallpaper falls off the walls, a strange sliding noise can be heard behind the walls and finally a demon's image appears. Director Joakim Ersgard brings a peculiar edge to some of the char-

acters that borders on satire, but the atmospheric sequences work well. Keith Berkeley, John Force, Joanna Berg, John Olson. (Vidmark) (Laser: Image)

VOLCANO MONSTER, THE. See *Gigantis, the Fire Monster*.

VOLERE VOLARE (1993) ★★★ Rollicking, absurd Italian comedy in which a daffy but lovable sound effects man (Maurizio Nichetti) turns into a cartoon version of himself after falling in love with an equally daffy gal (Angela Finocchiaro) who specializes in partaking in kinky (but innocuous) sex games with her goofy clientele. Loaded with zany sound effects, sight gags and a gallery of wonderfully bizarre personalities. Written-directed by Maurizio Nichetti and Guido Manuli. (Video/Laser: New Line)

VOODOO (1995) ★★★ A strange sense of conspiracy hangs over this low-budget, direct-to-video supernatural thriller, enhancing its otherwise routine production qualities and commonplace script (by associate producers Bria Dimuccio and Dino Vindeni). Corey Feldman portrays an unusual college student whose fraternity house turns out to be home for a voodoo practitioner (Joel J. Edwards), who intends to make Feldman his sixth and final sacrifice before assuming full evil powers from the snake goddess Ezili. Director Rene Eram gets good performances from Sarah Douglas (as a medical-school teacher), Diana Nadeau (as the innocent heroine), Ron Melendez, Maury Ginsberg and Jack Nance—enhancements to a tale involving death-like suspended animation, Haitian charms to ward off evil, waxy figures with pins sticking in them and powdery substances. (A-Pix)

VOODOO BLACK EXORCIST (197?) ★ Despite its title, this U.S.-Spanish co-production is your basic mummy movie, and about as poor a mummy movie as you will ever have the displeasure to find. Known as a "loa," or evil spirit, a thousand-year-old Haitan prince and his sarcophagus are cruising on a pleasure boat to Haiti (complete with sexy women for shower and bikini scenes, and a few severed heads) when the avenging spirit rises and injects his enemies with curara poison, turning them into zombie slaves. Rock-bottom editing, acting, writing by S. Monkada and dubbing will curse this mummy monster flick for another thousand years. Undirected by M. Cano. Aldo Sambrel, Tanyeka Stadle, Ferninand Sancho, Alexander Abrahan. (Dura Vision)

VOODOO BLOOD BATH. See *I Eat Your Skin* and *Zombies*.

VOODOO DAWN (1989) ★★ Weak production values, a lack of tension and a loosely structured story line by John Russo, Jeffrey Delman, Thomas Rendon and Evan Dunsky make for one cold *Voodoo Dawn*. Two students go looking for a friend who is researching migrant workers in the South, unaware that their friend has been turned into a flesh-craving zombie by a crude dude with a machete. There's an attempt to repeat plot elements of *Night of the Living Dead* but director Steven Fierberg's pacing is far too lethargic to dry the dew off the grass of this *Dawn*. Only interesting moment is when a demon head rises up from a man's stomach à la *Alien*. Raymond St. Jacques, Theresa Merritt, Gina Gershon. (Academy) (Laser: Image)

VOODOO DOLLS (1990) ★★ School maidens fall victim to the ghoulish ghosts residing in an old institution of learning that teaches them the true meaning of ABC: Apparitions, Blood and Corpses. Directed by Andre Pelletier. Maria Stanton. (Atlas Entertainment)

VOODOO ISLAND (1957) ★★ Boris Karloff's performance as hoax buster Phillip Knight is the saving grace of this Howard W. Koch–Aubrey Schenck low-budget, low-energy production filmed on Kauai Island, Hawaii. Eager to debunk reports of voodooism, Karloff, associate Beverly Tyler and assorted adventurers end up on an island where man-eating plants (and not very convincing ones at that) are on the attack. Richard Landau's script has Karloff realizing the supernatural does exist and includes an affair between angst-ridden explorer Rhodes Reason and the naive, sexually awakening Tyler. Sluggishly directed by Reginald LeBorg. Murvyn Vye, Elisha Cook and Jean Engstrom provide secondary characters. Aka *Silent Death*.

VOODOO MAN, THE (1944) ★★½ Fun in a perverse way, this is so appallingly bad. George Zucco is a voodoo cult leader with a TV "spy" device who works in cahoots with hypnotist Bela Lugosi and John Carradine, a drum-beating Igor-type whose light bulbs are rather weak. Lugosi is kidnapping women with a phony roadblock detour, encasing them in sexy nightgowns and putting them into trances in the hopes he can transfer one of their souls into the corpse of his wife, who has been dead 22 years. This is attempted while Zucco utters nutty mumbo jumbo. Under William Beaudine's direction, Lugosi is the world's biggest hambone, with the Carradine character taking close second. The Monogram production values (with producer Sam Katzman at the helm) are distressingly poor, and the acting is so bad it could put you into a catatonic state. Wanda McKay, Louise Currie, Henry Hall, Michael Ames.

VORTEX. Video of *The Day Time Ended* (Value).

VOYAGE TO THE BOTTOM OF THE SEA (1961) ★★★ Visually exciting, good-humored Irwin Allen production designed for the young set with big names to appeal to parents: Walter Pidgeon, Joan Fontaine, Peter Lorre, Robert Sterling. The biggest star remains the atomic sub *Seaview*, with panels of flashing lights and fluctuating gauges. (This set was used in the TV series of the same title.) The Van Allen Radiation Belt surrounding Earth has caught fire; the mission of *Seaview* is to fire a missile to put out the blaze. But complications erupt aboard the ship when a saboteur goes to work. Barbara Eden, Frankie Avalon, Michael Ansara, Henry Daniell, Regis Toomey. Originally directed by Allen as *Journey to the Bottom of the Sea*. (Video/Laser: Fox)

VOYAGE TO THE PLANET OF PREHISTORIC WOMEN (1968) ★★ Not a sequel to *Voyage to the Prehistoric Planet*, just more footage lifted from a 1962 Soviet film, *Planet of Storms*, which Roger Corman repackaged for U.S. consumption. New footage directed by Peter Bogdanovich (under the name Derek Thomas) features Mamie Van Doren and other statuesque cuties in furry bikinis. These buxom dolls portray psychic humanoids who enjoy close encounters with stranded Earthnauts. And nauts to you, too, earthy ones. It was written (?) by Henry Ney. Aka *Gill Woman* and *Gill Women of Venus*. (Sinister/C; S/Weird; Filmfax)

VOYAGE TO THE PREHISTORIC PLANET (1965) ★★ Highlights from Soviet sci-fi movie *Planet of Storms*, the story of cosmonauts exploring Venus, plus new footage shot by writer-director Curtis Harrington that features Basil Rathbone, Faith Domergue and Marc Shannon. Roger Corman spliced it together with Elmer's glue. Same old plot: Earthmen crash-land on an alien world to face new dangers from E.T.s, robot men, centuries-old lizards, etc. Voyage to prehistoric tedium. (Nostalgia; Sinister/C; Filmfax)

VULTURE, THE (1967) ★★ Akim Tamiroff as a creature with a bird's body, legs and wings, but retaining human head and arms? That's only the beginning, bird lovers. Dig the inept performances of Robert Hutton and Broderick Crawford, groove on the belly-flopping, ersatz suspense. The vultures must be picking the bones of writer-producer-director Lawrence Huntington. (IVE)

VULTURES (1985) ★★ Jim Bailey in 5 roles (you figure out which characters) is the highlight of this gore-murder thriller told in whodunit fashion. Yachtsman Stuart Whitman is accused of the crimes, but we know better as he pursues the clues. Average for its type. Written-produced-directed by Paul Leder. Yvonne De Carlo, Aldo Ray, Greg Mullavey, Maria Perschy. (Prism)

WAKING HOUR, THE. See *The Velvet Vampire*.
WALK LIKE A MAN (1987) ★★ What old-pro director Melvin Frank (who made films with Norman Panama) is doing as producer-director of this ridiculous comedy is a question to ponder. Howie Mandel portrays a young man raised by wolves brought back to civilization to live with his original family. It's played for farce as Howie chases fire engines, walks like a canine and bays at the moon. Christopher Lloyd and Colleen Camp yuk it up as crazed family members out to get the youth's fortune, and they can be funny at times. And despite absurdities and sometimes tasteless slapstick antics, there is a crude charm Mandel brings to Bobo that may evoke a few chuckles. As the sympathetic woman who trains Bobo in the ways of civilization, Amy Steel is a nice counterbalance, but this still plays like an inane sitcom. Scripted by Robert Klane. (MGM/UA)
WALK OF THE DEAD. Video version of *Vengeance of the Zombies* (Vogue).
WARD 13. See *Hospital Massacre*.
WARHOL'S FRANKENSTEIN. See *Andy Warhol's Frankenstein*.
WARLOCK (1983). Video version of *Skullduggery* (Paragon).
WARLOCK (1989) ★★★ Intriguing idea is executed in a mildly interesting way. Warlock Julian Sands of the 17th century is transported to modern times and a witch hunter named Giles Redferne (Richard E. Grant) follows after him. The warlock intends to carry out the Devil's plan of destruction but Lori Singer (as L.A. lady Kassandra) joins Redferne in thwarting the evil. Producer-director Steve Miner injects atmosphere and brooding qualities, but the story line by David Twohy is too weak to sustain for long. (Video/Laser: Vidmark)
WARLOCK 2: THE ARMAGEDDON (1993) ★★½ Only the recurring presence of Julian Sands qualifies this as a sequel when the titular force

of evil (the son of Satan) turns up in modern times in search of powerful runestones in the possession of assorted humans. Only 2 Earthlings (drab characters played by Chris Young and Paula Marshall) have the supernatural power to fight him in a small California town, and it's a rather ordinary dual of wizards, wherein any special effect is permissible, whether it makes sense or not. The film is dark and humorless and has little appeal beyond Sands's personification of evil, so you could end up rooting for him instead of the boring kids, both of whom have to be killed and brought back to life to have the superpowers to battle Sands. Where's the imagination and humor director Anthony Hickox brought to the *Waxwork* series? It's sorely and blatantly missing. (Vidmark)
WARLORDS (1988) ★ If anyone brings to life this umpteenth copy of *Mad Max*, it is Dawn Wildsmith as a wild and woolly adventuress who has survived a nuclear war and is in the country (near Vasquez Rocks) escaping bands of mutants. It's another Fred Olen Ray low-budget potboiler, the producer-director working with a skimpy, almost nonexistent script by Scott Ressler. David Carradine, in the Mad Max role, seeks his missing wife, abducted by warlord Sid Haig. There's comedy, but the premise is so weak, the performers (Robert Quarry, Brinke Stevens, Fox Harris and Ross Hagen) have nothing to work with. Especially bad, in this compendium of supertired clichés, is a talking head named Ammo that Carradine carries in an old box. *Warlords* is a dud with a thud. (Vidmark) (Laser: Image)
WARLORDS OF ATLANTIS (1978) ★★★½ Fourth and last film in a series of picturesque fantasy adventures from producer John Dark and director Kevin Connor, starring Doug McClure. He portrays an intrepid hero transported via diving bell into an undersea kingdom of 7 cities inhabited by treacherous Martians. Characters and situations in Brian Hayles's script are preposterous but Roger Dickens's monsters are visual delights: a giant octopus; a multiarmed mollusk with rolling eyeballs; a snake-fish; a thing with flippers called a Zarg; a flying fish with bad overbite; a scaly millipede. Cyd Charisse, as Atsil the High Priestess, fares well because she gets to display her shapely legs. Still, it's the octopus who has the real class. Shane Rimmer, Peter Gilmore. Originally made as *Seven Cities of Atlantis*. Previous titles in this series: *The Land That Time Forgot, At the Earth's Core* and *The People That Time Forgot*.
WARLORDS OF THE 21ST CENTURY (1981) ★★★ Gas costs $59 a liter after the great Oil Wars and what's left of mankind on New Zealand (farmers and isolated groups) is subjected to roving bloodthirsty pirates, whose only nemesis is the Hunter (Michael Beck), an avenging warrior à la Mad Max. Made as *Battletruck*, for

chief villain Straker (James Wainwright) pillages with an armored oil carrier bristling with firepower, the story (cowritten by director Harley Cokliss) centers on how the Hunter and Straker face off, with Straker's daughter (Annie McEnroe) caught in the middle. (Embassy)

WARLORDS 3000 (1992) ★★ While this has the external trappings of a *Mad Max* imitation, set in a futuristic desert when radiation storms ravage the landscape and drug-crazed psychotics drive dune buggies, it has some semblance of plot and interesting characters who clash on an emotional level instead of participating in the same old physical violence. Jay Roberts portrays Nova, a soldier seeking the drug dealer responsible for having his family slaughtered, who falls in love with his nemesis's daughter (Denice Marie Duff). The story is told in the memory voice-over, giving the script by Ron Herbst and producer-director Faruque Ahmed a literary element. By no means is this a great picture, but it's engaging (after a clumsy start) and has well-staged action. Steve Blanchard, Wayne Duvall, Dawn Martel, Jeff Sable. (Columbia TriStar)

WARNING, THE. See *It Came . . . Without Warning.*

WARNING SIGN (1985) ★★★½ Engrossing action thriller in the style of *The Andromeda Strain*, tautly directed by Hal Barwood, who cowrote and coproduced with Matthew Robbins. At the isolated Utah plant of Biotek, a secret government germ warfare plant, a bacteria is unleashed that infects the "rage" area of the brain and turns victims into homicidal maniacs. Trapped in the plant is security guard Kathleen Quinlan, while outside, her sheriff-husband Sam Waterston tries to solve the mystery being kept hush-hush by government toady Yaphet Kotto. The performances are excellent, the script exciting, the action full of twists as they seek an antitoxin to stop the monsters. (CBS/Fox)

WAR OF THE ALIENS. See *Starship Invasions.*

WAR OF THE COLOSSAL BEAST (1958) ★★½ Producer-director Bert I. Gordon's sequel to *The Amazing Colossal Man* finds the ever-growing 60-feet-tall Colonel Manning (played this time by Dean Parkin) not destroyed at Boulder Dam but down in Mexico, snatching taco trucks off the highway in hopes of finding something that will stick to his king-size ribs. As in most Gordon films, the effects are pedantic, and the same could be said for George Worthing Yates's script. One of the soldier boys remarks, "There's no place in this civilization for a 60-foot man." He said it. Roger Pace, Sally Fraser, Russ Bender. Aka *The Terror Strikes* and *Revenge of the Colossal Man.* Music by Albert Glasser. (Columbia TriStar)

WAR OF THE GARGANTUAS (1967) ★★ Sequel to *Frankenstein Conquers the World* was reedited for the U.S., with a sequence explaining

connection to the first film dropped; hence, links are tenuous at best. With Inoshiro Honda directing and Eiji Tsuburaya at the effects helm, you're in for a monster extravaganza: a giant octopus battles another entity of green-hued evil and the greeny takes on a brown-hued beast. The only thing that happens by "occident" is Russ Tamblyn as a scientist. Aka *Adventure of Gargantuas* and *Duel of the Gargantuas.* Kumi Mizuno. The planned sequel, *The Frankenstein Brothers,* never got produced. (Paramount/Gateway)

WAR OF THE GODS. See *Battlestar Galactica.*

WAR OF THE MONSTERS (1966) ★★ Toho's sequel to *Gammera the Invincible,* with that friendly snapping turtle, Gammera, doing battle with Barugon the Dinosaur, a creature surrounded by a force field. Kids will cheer the chest-pounding, noisy encounters; adults will snooze. Directed by Shigeo Tanaka. Kojiro Hongo. (S/Weird; from Celebrity as *Gamera vs. Barugon*)

WAR OF THE PLANETS. See *This Island Earth.*

WAR OF THE PLANETS (1965) ★ Turgid is the best word to describe this uninspired Italian adventure (aka *The Deadly Diaphanoids* and *Diaphanoids, Bringers of Death*) set on space wheel Gamma I, which is invaded (on New Year's Eve) by invisible, bodiless beings from Mars called Diaphanoids. Coming to Gamma I to investigate is Tony Russell and spacesters armed with rifles that spit flame a few feet, and ray guns called .38s. The aliens, described by screenwriter Ivan Reiner as "bodiless patterns of energy," speak through humans, while the human response is "Good God" or "Incredible." The only exciting moments provided by director Anthony Dawson (real name: Antonio Margheriti) are when astronauts form the words "Happy New Year" while floating through space à la Busby Berkeley, and when they dance to "Auld Lang Syne" while cavorting in the void. This film's sequel was *Wild, Wild Planet.* Lisa Gastoni, Franco Nero, Carlo Giustini.

WAR OF THE ROBOTS (1978) ★½ Ambitious Italian space opera, but condescending and insulting to audiences. A race of robots (in metallic suits, wearing blond wigs) kidnap a beautiful woman; a squad of rocket jocks (including a Texan, yet) slip into warp drive and pursue across the galaxies, meeting weird aliens in papier-mâché caverns and firing laser beams hither and thither. Armies of extras, massive sets and tons of action can't compensate for Alfonso Brescia's inept direction (he's credited as Al Bradly). Special onions to Marcus Griffin for his awful electronics "shuffling" score, the dumbest ever, and to Alan Forsyth for inferior effects. Except for leading man Antonio Sabato, the credits would appear to be Anglicized pseudonyms: Melissa Long, Patricia Gore, James Stuart, Robert Barnes and "a special performance" by Mickey Pilgrim. Pilgrim's Progress? Aka *Robots* and *Stratostars*. (United; VCI; from Mogul as *Reactor*)

WAR OF THE SATELLITES (1958) ★★ Aliens you never see (producer-director Roger Corman's economic ingenuity at work) don't want us fooling around in space, so one takes over the body of scientist Richard Devon aboard a satellite. But he (it) falls for Susan Cabot, a foolish act that makes him vulnerable to Earthlings who suspect something is awry. Something is awry—the tepid script by Lawrence Louis Goldman, who banged it out for Corman after the Russians launched *Sputnik*. According to legend, Corman directed it in 8 days—1 day longer than it took God to create the universe. Dick Miller, Michael Fox, Robert Shayne.

WAR OF THE WORLDS (1953) ★★★★★ George Pal's commendable version of H. G. Wells's novel of a Martian invasion—imaginatively depicted in the Oscar-winning effects of Gordon Jennings. Alien saucers land in isolated areas of California and zap everything in sight with greenish Death Rays. Barre Lyndon's script, focusing on research physicist Gene Barry and scientist Ann Robinson, sometimes sinks into clichés, yet it unfolds with such compelling swiftness and breathless action that the invasion takes on epic proportions. One suspenseful sequence depicts a bug-eyed Martian, another shows Barry searching for Robinson through war-ravaged L.A. The opening prologue is beautifully rendered, with the planets described by the splendid voice of Sir Cedric Hardwicke. One of the few sci-fi classics of the cinema. Directed by Byron Haskin. Carolyn Jones, Robert Cornthwaite, Paul Frees, Jack Kruschen, Les Tremayne, Alvy Moore, Charles Gemora (as the Martian). (Video/Laser: Paramount)

WARRIOR AND THE SORCERESS, THE (1984) ★★★ Interesting and entertaining barbarian-and-sorcery *Conan* copy, with director John Broderick showing an influence of Japanese samurai movies. Here he copies *Yojimbo* when the Dark One, a laconic warrior (and the only survivor of his race), hires out to 2 warring factions in the village of Yabatar, shifting sides as fortunes of war shift. David Carradine is good in this variation on the wandering gunslinger. Oddities include the Protector (a giant octopus-monster), a green lizard that whispers into the ear of its master, a 4-breasted dancing assassin, and the sorceress, who forges the mighty sword of Ura for the Dark One and rushes about through the entire picture with her glistening, beautiful breasts bared. Above average for Roger Corman. Luke Askew, Maria Socas. (Video/Laser: Vestron)

WARRIOR OF THE LOST WORLD (1985) ★ Silly

Mad Max rip-off, with the absurd premise that evil Omegans, led by Prosser (Donald Pleasence), are fighting the good guys, the Outsiders, on an Earth that has been devastated by radiation wars. Robert Ginty comes riding by on a rocket-launching "supersonic speedcycle" equipped with Einstein the Computer, which espouses such comments as "Bad Mothers" (cops) and "Very Bad Mothers" (more cops). Ginty agrees to help Persis Khambatta rescue her father (Harrison Muller) from Prosser's stronghold, so there's plenty of explosive action that allows Fred Williamson (as Henchman) to crash the scene, guns blazing to synthesized music. Director David Worth's script makes little sense, but the action is nonstop. (HBO)

WARRIORS (1994) ★★½ Your basic action movie with 1 odd twist: the U.S. military has created an elite squad of assassins out of soldiers who have been traumatized in combat by incarcerating them in Ft. Monroe. When super-soldier Gary Busey busts out of the fort to secretly meet with his father, aided by prostitute Wendi Fulford, authorities assign Internal Security cop Michael Pare—Busey's one-time buddy—to terminate him with extreme prejudice. Some of the action as staged by director Shimon Dotan is downright ridiculous, taking the edge off an otherwise okay script by Alexander Epstein and Benjamin Gold. (Republic)

WARRIORS FROM THE MAGIC MOUNTAIN See *Zu: Warriors from the Magic Mountain.*

WARRIORS OF THE APOCALYPSE (1987) ★★★ Another post-Holocaust action adventure that starts off in the *Mad Max* mode (civilization wiped out by war; 150 years in the future surviving bands rove a desert landscape wiping each other out) and then shifts to a "Lost City" saga with overtones of *She*. Trapper leads his motley lot into a forest with the promise that somewhere ahead lies the Mountain of Life, a Shangri-la where existence is eternal. On the way they wipe out a tribe of natives led by Giant Bill, discover a pygmy band that can heal wounds and resurrect the dead, and Amazon warriors armed with bows and arrows and huge bosoms. The Lost City is ruled by an exotic wench and a treacherous high priest and they shoot it out with laser bolts from their eye sockets. The lost race, behaving like Aztecs, conducts fertility rites and sacrifices yet has machinery to turn ruined terrain into lush jungle. The monosyllabic script by Ken Metcalfe is a mishmash of clichés and the action under the direction of Bobby A. Suarez is wall-to-wall, stopping only long enough to put on white see-through gowns. Michael James, Debrah Moore, Franco Guerrero, Mike Cohen. Aka *Searchers of the Voodoo Mountain* and *Time Raiders*. (Lightning)

WARRIORS OF THE WASTELAND (1983) ★ Inferior, imbecilic *Mad Max* rip-off by Italians finds 2 unlikable antiheroes (Timothy Brent, Fred Williamson) roving the nuked countryside 2019 A.H. (After Holocaust) in ridiculous automobiles, seeking an evil band (the Templars, Administrators of Revenge) that is slaughtering innocent folks. Absurdly dressed men ride redesigned motorbikes, fire silly zap guns (which give off inane electronic sounds) and no doubt wonder why director Enzo G. Castellari doesn't demand the Method style of acting. Suitable only for insomniacs in the wasteland of TV. George Eastman, Anna Kanakis, Thomas Moore. (Simitar; HBO; from Impulse as *The New Barbarians*)

WAR WIZARDS. See *Wizards*.

WASP WOMAN, THE (1960) ★ Producer-director Roger Corman gives us a "stinker" in need of more production sting. Strictly a bottom-of-the-hive programmer (scripted by Leo Gordon under such titles as *The Bee Girl* and *Insect Woman*) with Susan Cabot as a Wacky Anglo-Saxon Protestant . . . a cosmetics manufacturer seeking an eternal youth formula from wasp enzymes. Once she's an oversized member of the Hymenotpera clan, she turns predacious and goes on a murderous spree, sticking it to all the guys but good. It's the wasp-ish budget that does in *The Wasp Woman*. Anthony Eisley, Michael Mark, Frank Wolff. (Sinister/C; S/Weird; Rhino; Filmfax)

WASP WOMAN, THE (1995) ★★ This modernized remake of Roger Corman's 1960 schlock shocker is only notable for its incredibly hilarious wasp monster, which is what aging cosmetics company owner Jennifer Rubin turns into whenever she gets jealous of her sex with her male partners. It's a huge creature with big breasts that keep getting bigger each time she transmogrifies. Leo Gordon's original script was rewritten by Daniela Purcell and Guy Prevost and now includes a fellatio scene that will have you falling down laughing. This silliness about wasp hormones turning a human into a "bee girl" was directed by Jim Wynorski with his usual lack of subtlety and his continuing penchant for bimboesque big-breasted beauties. Doug Wert has the thankless role as Rubin's cameraman and lover. Maria Ford, Melissa Brasselle, Daniel J. Travanti (as the crazed doctor who invents the serum). (New Horizons)

WATCHER IN THE WOODS, THE (1980) ★★ Disney attempted to escape formulaic kiddie movies with this adaptation of a Florence E. Randall novel, but the results are too silly to make it an adult movie and not silly enough to make it a kiddie treat. Music writer David McCallum, wife Carroll Baker and daughters Lynn-Holly Johnson and Kyle Richards move into a secluded mansion owned by sinister old bat Bette Davis. A strange psychic force emanates from a nearby forest, but is never explained as the teens, overwhelmed by ESP powers, help Davis's long-lost daughter. Apparently an alien probe has taken her and trapped her in another dimension, and there's a shower of fireworks by Harrison Ellenshaw that passes as effects. The film, directed by John Hough and adapted by Brian Clemens, Harry Spalding and Rosemary Anne Sisson, was never released theatrically, even after new footage was added by doctoring director Vincent McEveety. Ian Bannen, Georgina Hale, Richard Pasco. (Disney)

WATCHERS (1988) ★★ Had this modest sci-fi–horror thriller been given decent effects, and had the script by Bill Freed and producer Damian Lee (from Dean Koontz's novel) been developed as a juvenile fantasy instead of a bloody adult affair, *The Watchers* might have been watchable. A government experiment produces 2 creatures: a golden retriever with superintelligence and a monster called an OXCOM (Outside Experimental Combat Mammal). There's a third experiment gone awry but you'll have to figure that one out yourself. The monster is never shown and this never delivers as a bloodletting vehicle. Nor does the supersmart dog integrate strongly into the plot to become a dominating element that would please younger audiences. Directed by Jon Daniel Hess. Corey Haim, Michael Ironside, Duncan Fraser, Blu Mankuma. (IVE) (Laser: Image)

WATCHERS II (1990) ★★ The golden retriever, Einstein, is back in this moderately effective "science-gone-awry" horror action film, communicating telepathically with Marc Singer, who must destroy a monster called the Outsider (or AE-73), an escapee from a top-secret military project. Based on Dean R. Koontz's novel, with adaptation by Henry Dominic. Directed by Thierry Notz. Tracy Scoggins, Jonathan Farwell, Irene Miracle, Mary Woronov. (IVE) (Laser: Image)

WATCHERS III (1994) ★★★ Parts of this Roger Corman production play like a virtual remake of *Predator*, with a team of *Dirty Dozen*–type commandos trekking through a South American jungle in search of the Outsider, that man-made genetic monstrosity designed for combat, programmed to work in conjunction with the benevolent golden retriever named Einstein. Wings Hauser and his team are unwitting victims of a U.S. government–controlled experiment to test the killing power of the Outsider, until Hauser becomes the stalker of the stalker. Enhanced by rugged jungle locations, and well directed by Jeremy Stanford, this is a better-than-usual work for Corman. Michael Palmer's script (borrowing ideas from Dean R. Koontz's novel *Watchers*) is totally derivative of other actioners, but makes for a good adventure entertainment that is marred only by a beast-creature that sometimes looks more ludicrous than hideous. Gregory Scott Cummins, Daryl Roach, John K. Linton, Lolita Ronalds, Ider Cifuentes Martin. (New Horizons)

WATCH ME WHEN I KILL (1981) ★★ Italian psychothriller concocted in the vein of Mario Bava, but lacking the stylistic nuances and cinematic verve of that master of the macabre. Director Anthony Bido turns it into a plodding, almost incomprehensible "killer on the loose" concoction featuring 3 mildly interesting deaths: a pharmacist is knifed in the back, a woman's head is shoved into a bubbling stewpot, and a man is strangled in his bath with a thick cord. The explanations are ludicrous; no writing credits are provided. Coproduced by Herman Cohen. Aka *The Cat with the Jade Eyes*. Richard Stewart, Sylvia Kramer. (HBO)

WATER BABIES, THE (1978) ★★★ An unusual children's film, based on Charles Kingsley's novel, that blends an amusing Dickensian live-action comedy (set in 1850s England) with an underwater animated adventure executed by Miroslaw Kijowicz. A crooked chimneysweep (Mr. Grimes, played grimly and grimly by James Mason) and his young charge (Bernard Cribbins) run afoul of a witch's spell and end up as cartoons, with an evil shark as the representation of Mason. Charming and quaint, and directed with nice touches by actor Lionel Jeffries, the film is suitable for adults, too, with Billie Whitelaw, Joan Greenwood and David Tomlinson contributing character bits. Michael Robson and Jeffries did the adaptation. Aka *Slip Slide Adventures*. (Nelson)

WATERWORLD (1995) ★★★½ Ballyhooed as the most expensive movie ever made (at a rumored $200 million), this sci-fi adventure set in a future time when the ice caps have flooded the entire Earth (except for a mythical place called Dry Land) offers plenty of comic-book heroics and stunts that will please action fans. But its lack of a sympathetic character and its use of caricaturized villains make it a movie without much of a heart. You want to be drawn into the funky, soggy world where a lone adventurer named Mariner (Kevin Costner, playing a muscular hero without moral values) battles gangs of marauders called Smokers and their one-eyed leader (Dennis Hopper, playing a comedic buffoon who projects not an ounce of menace), and there are times when his adventures with heroine Jeanne Tripplehorn and her daughter Tina Majorino (whose backside contains a map providing clues to Dry Land) verge on delivering some of the humanity that the story (by David Twohy and Peter Rader) needs so desperately. But director Kevin Reynolds seems incapable of allowing Costner to open up his heart very much, something that would have enhanced Mariner, a half-man, half-fish mutation capable of swimming for long periods underwater and performing feats of derring-do to rival Douglas Fairbanks and Errol Flynn. And he sails an ingeniously rigged trimaran bristling with fascinating gadgets and weapons. Criticisms aside, this *Mad Max* imitation is one of the best of its kind and sports such wonderful action and destruction scenes that they alone are worth admission price. Definitely an E-ticket ride. Michael Jeter, Gerard Murphy, R. D. Call, Kim Coates. (Video/Laser: MCA)

WATTS MONSTER, THE. See *Dr. Black and Mr. Hyde*.

WAVELENGTH (1983) ★★★ Thoughtful morality tale thanks to writer-director Mike Gray, who fashions a philosophical story that indicts militaristic attitudes toward aliens. Robert Carradine, a burned-out guitarist in Hollywood, meets psychic Cherie Currie who mentally "hears" wails of help from E.T. humanoids (dubbed Beta, Delta and Gamma), captured from a downed UFO and caged in a secret installation near Carradine's home. The couple penetrates the system to help the trio escape. Its one weakness is that youngsters with shaved heads play the aliens, when credibility calls for a more realistic rendering. Keenan Wynn is along to help the escape plan work. Effective sound track by Tangerine Dream. (Video/Laser: Embassy)

WAX MUSEUM. See *Mystery of the Wax Museum*.

WAXWORK (1988) ★★★½ Intriguing premise—spectators who innocently step inside waxwork horror exhibits are teleported into another world—is enhanced by the imaginative, stylish work of writer-director Anthony Hickox (great-grandson of British film distributor J. Arthur Rank and son of late director Douglas Hickox), who loads this weird tale with effects and bloodletting. The setting is a residental "house of waxy horrors" (presided over by sinister David Warner), where teenagers and investigating police become part of the tableaux after undergoing horrible deaths. A plethora of characters and monsters fight it out in a messy melee during the fiery conclusion. In cameos are Patrick Macnee (an antimonster nut in a wheelchair), Miles O'Keefe (as Dracula) and John Rhys-Davies. Zach Galligan (of *Gremlins*) is the male lead, followed by Deborah Foreman and Michelle Johnson. (Vestron) (Laser: Image)

WAXWORK II: LOST IN TIME (1991) ★★★½ Off-the-wall but entertaining sequel to *Waxwork*, starting where the first film ended as Zach Galligan and Monika Schnarre flee the burning wax museum, pursued by a severed hand. Accused of killing her stepfather, Schnarre travels with Galligan through time to gather evidence of her innocence, undergoing an odyssey that is essentially a series of horror-movie parodies.

The stopovers include Dr. Frankenstein's lab; a haunted house (this sequence is in black and white, imitating Robert Wise's *The Haunting*); a spaceship terrorized by an Alien-like creature; and King Arthur's court, where an evil sorcerer tries to take over the throne. These adventures are presented tongue-in-cheek and colorfully by writer-director Anthony Hickox, who goes a bit berserk by having the climactic battle cross a series of time zones and include all the genre's heaviest villains: Dr. Jekyll, Jack the Ripper, Godzilla, Romero's walking dead in a shopping mall, and Nosferatu. A definite crowd pleaser. John Ireland (as the king), Martin Kemp (Frankenstein), Bruce Campbell, Juliet Mills, Patrick Macnee, David Carradine, Jim Metzler, Michael Des Barres, Joe Baker, Marina Sirtis, Sophie Ward. (Live)

WAY AND THE BODY, THE. See *What!*

WEB OF THE SPIDER (1972) ★★ Stylish Italian supernatural thriller holds one's attention as it opens in a country tavern where Edgar Allan Poe (Klaus Kinski at his wildest) is telling a terror tale. Journalist Anthony Franciosa is challenged by Poe to spend a night in Blackwood Villa, a haunted castle. Once ensconced, Franciosa meets 2 beautiful women who fight over him. The redhead is a real knockout. What Franciosa is really seeing are spectral images of long-dead occupants of the castle, and he must relive the horror of their deeds. This remake of *Castle of Blood* was directed by Anthony M. Dawson (Antonio Margheriti) and based on Poe's "Danse Macabre." Aka *In the Grip of the Spider, And Comes the Dawn . . . But Colored Red* and *Dracula in the Castle of Blood*. Michele Mercier, Peter Carsten, Karin Field. (Filmfax; Sinister/C)

WEIRDO (1989) ★½ Freaked-out lowlife (Steve Burington) is on a murderous rampage in this horror thriller written, directed and produced by Andy Milligan. It's dripping with ineffectual gore murders. Jessica Straus, Naomi Sherwood, Lynne Angus. (Raedon)

WEIRD SCIENCE (1985) ★ Absolutely awful teenage sex-fantasy comedy, more excruciating than titillating—a complete misfire from writer-director John Hughes. Two idiotic juvenile nerds (Anthony Michael Hall, Ilan Mitchell-Smith) feed ridiculous material into a computer to create a perfect woman. What comes out, amid a lot of pyrotechnic nonsense, is Kelly LeBrock, a real beauty. Following this, the plot rambles on with no coherence; LeBrock possesses unexplained witch powers that make things come and go at will, including some appalling biker characters. The cast—Bill Paxton, Suzanne Snyder, Robert Downey, Jr.,—must still be trying to live down this fiasco. Final insult is the title, stolen from the E.C. comic that featured some of the best illustrated sci-fi stories

of all time. Editors William Gaines and Al Feldstein would have used Hughes's plot to line garbage cans. (Video/Laser: MCA)

WEIRD TALES. See *Kwaidan*.

W.E.I.R.D. WORLD (1995) ★★★ Oddball TV-movie from the producers of *Tales from the Crypt* and inspired by E.C. sci-fi comic-book stories from "Weird Science" and "Weird Fantasy." It gets off to a slow, talkie start as we are introduced to various scientists working at "the Institute," an abandoned Air Force base on a salt flat where research is being carried out on the Kronos Device (time travel), the FRANS security robot (Free Roving Android Neutralizing System), and a reverse aging process. At times the telescript by A. L. Katz, Gilbert Adler and Scott Nimerfro plays like "Scientific Days of our Lives," but eventually it gets down to some exciting sequences with surprise twists. Good atmosphere is injected by director William Malone. This appears to have been intended as a pilot for a series. Dana Ashbrook, Marshall Bell, Paula Marshall, Audie England, Kathryn Morris, Miguel Nunez.

WELCOME TO BLOOD CITY (1977) ★★ Peculiar Canadian sci-fi mystery (made as *Blood City*) leaves many details clouded in uncertainty and lacks a stylish separation between reality and fantasy sequences. The results are chaotic—and intriguing. Samantha Eggar and Barry Morse are on a research team that is placing potential "kill masters" for an ongoing war into hallucinatory states to determine which are strongest. The fantasy realm becomes a *Westworld*-type place where test subject Keir Dullea is exposed to the sadism of sheriff Jack Palance and bloody gunfights. The Stephen Schneck–Michael Winder script really gets weird when scientist Eggar projects herself into Dullea's alternate reality, and watches tapes of them making love. The main problem is drab camera work, a lack of effects (these would have enhanced the lab sequences), and indifferent direction by Peter Sasdy. The film ends on a metaphysical note and leaves moral ambiguities as cloudy as ever. (Interglobe; Lightning; Pan-Canadian)

WELCOME TO OBLIVION (1990) ★★ Another *Mad Max* rip-off, starring Dack Rambo as the silent hero who, in the wake of nuclear war, goes on a mission in a mining zone called Oblivion. He's assisted by mutant Clare Beresford. Directed by Augusto Tamayo, who filmed in Peru. Meshach Taylor, Mark Bringelson.

WE'RE BACK! A DINOSAUR'S STORY (1993) ★★★ Excellent feature cartoon for children, a Steven Spielberg production in which a scientist (voice by Walter Cronkite) brings a group of dinosaurs to modern day via his time-travel device, and the creatures interrelate with kids. Based on Hudson Talbott's book, this fine animated special was written by John Patrick Shanley and directed by Dick and Ralph Zondag. Other voices by John Goodman, Jay Leno and Martin Short. (MCA)

WEREWOLF OF LONDON (1935) ★★★ One of the earliest of Hollywood's werewolf films, not as exciting as Universal's *The Wolf Man*, which established movie-lycanthropy traditions this failed to generate. Robert Harris's script seems very dated as botanist Henry Hull seeks a plant that blooms only in the Tibetan moonlight. During his expedition he is bitten by a savage beast. Returning to London, Hull turns into a 4-legged monstrosity. Although Jack Pierce created memorable makeup, Hull does little to bring the role to life. Directed by Stuart Walker. Warner Oland, Valerie Hobson, Spring Byington. Aka *Unholy Hour*. (Video/Laser: MCA)

WEREWOLF'S MARK, THE. See *Frankenstein's Bloody Terror*.

WEREWOLF'S SHADOW, THE. See *The Werewolf vs. the Vampire Women*.

WEREWOLF VS. THE VAMPIRE WOMEN, THE (1972) ★★ West German–Spanish fly-by-night werewolf film, the third in a series starring Paul Naschy as the monster with a silver bullet in his heart, resurrected by pathologists who should have seen *The Wolf Man*. In this follow-up to *Frankenstein's Bloody Terror* and *Night of the Werewolf*, Waldemar Daninsky pairs with cuddly cuties to create a vampire baby. Writers Jacinto Molina (Naschy) and Hans Munkell mix up the legends a bit, but variety is the spice of death, and the images by director Leon Klimovsky are quite striking if the story is not. Gaby Fuchs, Patty Shepard, Andres Resino. Aka *Shadow of the Werewolf, The Werewolf's Shadow* and *The Black Harvest of Countess Dracula*. The next film in this series is *Assignment Terror*. (Hollywood Select; Horizon; Filmfax; S/Weird; Sinister/C; from AIR as *Blood Moon*)

WEREWOLF WOMAN. See *Legend of the Wolfwoman*.

WEREWOLVES ON WHEELS (1971) ★ With surfing music blaring on the sound track, a motorcycle gang roars through the countryside, hurls curses, attends impromptu orgies, drinks barrels of beer and roughs up monks who just happen to be staging a Satanic rite. In retaliation, the cyclists are cursed with lycanthropy, and their ranks begin to thin even as their blood is being thinned. What follows is unintentional comedy, sleazy bloodletting and nudity, with the entertainment value being a flat-out zero. We're all for exploitation but, please, do it with class, and give us someone to care about before killing them off. This dumb road release was carelessly directed by Michel Levesque, based on a script he cranked out with David M. Kaufman. Stephen Oliver, Severn Darden, D. J. Johnson,

Billy Gray, Barry McGuire, Owen Orr, Anna Lynn Brown. (Unicorn)

WES CRAVEN PRESENTS MIND RIPPER (1995) ★★★ If you can have *John Carpenter Presents Body Bags*, why not this title? Hardcore horror fans will not be disappointed with this gory, fast-paced TV-movie derivative of *Alien* set in a secret underground test lab where the government is conducting T.H.O.R., a program to produce a supersoldier. In the Jonathan Craven–Phil Mittleman script, a virus injected into a human guinea pig produces a crazed killer who runs wild through the dingy corridors of the lab, a monstrous tongue extending out of his mouth to kill scientists and other hapless victims. Scientist Lance Henriksen turns up with his cowardly son and daughter to help save his fellow scientists from the scourge. Since the killer seems unkillable, the bloodletting and mayhem are never-ending. If you like 'em graphic, satisfaction is guaranteed thanks to Joe Gayton's direction. John Diehl, Giovani Ribisi, Gregory Sporleder, Dan Blom, Claire Stansfield.

WES CRAVEN'S NEW NIGHTMARE (1994) ★★★★ Among the myriad sequels that have been made of popular horror films, this ranks as one of the most original (and the most important to the genre), for it dares to expand the horizon of its predecessors and explore fresh territory— a rarity in the canon of horror movies. Writer-director Craven, who created the *Nightmare on Elm Street* series, brings Freddy Krueger back one more time (number this 7) for a challenging premise in which actors from the series portray themselves in a strange story mixing movie reality with Hollywood reality. Wes Craven (played by himself) is writing a new Krueger script when his star Heather Langenkamp (played by Heather Langenkamp) and her son Dylan (Miko Hughes) are plagued by oddball dreams and other supernormal incidents punctuated by a series of earthquakes. The same can be said for Robert Englund (played by Robert Englund), who begins painting macabre scenes blending death and Freddy. It seems that the spirit of Krueger is a genuine evil that can only be laid to rest if another movie is made, and Dylan is the key to Krueger's reentry into the world of mortal men. Craven daringly concentrates his imaginative script on Langenkamp's and Dylan's psychological traumas, while devoting only small portions to the kind of bloody gore murders that permeated the earlier *Elm Street* movies. With John Saxon and New Line producer Robert Shaye also appearing as themselves, *Wes Craven's New Nightmare* is a clever idea wonderfully executed with an apocalyptic climax in Krueger's underground netherworld (incorporating some graphic but effective computerized special effects) that brings a crowning touch to the Krueger series. After this, Craven has to be considered one of the best directors in the horror genre. David Newsom (as a special-effects man married to Langenkamp), Tracy Middendorf (as Dylan's loyal baby-sitter), Fran Bennett (as a misguided but well-meaning doctor). (Video/Laser: New Line)

WESTWORLD (1973) ★★★½ In premise and visuals, this is superior sci-fi, written-directed by Michael (*The Andromeda Strain*) Crichton. What's missing are meaty characterizations for Richard Benjamin and James Brolin and a reason for the malfunctioning of Westworld, an amusement center of the future, where vacationers enact fantasies. This is a rich man's Disneyland, consisting of Western, medieval and Roman themes. The idea is to live the dangers of the periods without undergoing physical harm. But harm is in everyone's way when the center malfunctions and the robots kill tourists. Yul Brynner portrays an android gunslinger who uses real bullets and sets off a chase through the sets. But since we care little for Benjamin, it's hard to take the horrors seriously. *Futureworld* is a sequel that fares better as a story. Dick Van Patten, Steve Franken. (Video/Laser: MGM/UA)

WHAT! (1965) ★★★ Italian-French-British gothic, heavy with atmosphere and period costumes and set in a mansion on a cliff, where everyone acts sinister or hysterical. Daliah Lavi is haunted by the visions of a murdered count (Christopher Lee as a sadistic chauvinist) and she flits about the castle in negligees, gasping at muddy footprints and a gnarly hand that's interminably reaching for her. For the U.S. market the sexual depravity scenes were heavily cut (What??), so what's left is a lot of skulking around under Mario Bava's direction. If you enjoy corny melodramas, by all means. Tony Kendall, Harriet White, Isli Oberon. Aka *Night Is the Phantom, The Whip and the Body, The Body and the Whip* and *Son of Satan.*

WHAT EVER HAPPENED TO BABY JANE? (1962) ★★★½ Contemporary Grand Guignol yarn directed by Robert Aldrich, who established a subgenre of thrillers in the '60s about batty old dames. It helped to rejuvenate sagging careers. Bette Davis and Joan Crawford are sisters who have left acting to live in a gloomy old house. Bette gradually goes off her nut, torturing her crippled sister and driving herself to the brink of insanity. Nothing more horrible than a dead bird on a food tray is shown—the horrors are psychotic ones implied by screenwriter Lukas Heller, taking off from a novel by Henry Farrell. Victor Buono, Anna Lee, Bert Freed. (Video/Laser: Warner Bros.)

WHAT EVER HAPPENED TO BABY JANE? (1991) ★★ TV-movie remake of the Henry Farrell novel that was first adapted by Robert Aldrich in 1962 with Bette Davis. This time the actress

sisters are played by Vanessa and Lynn Redgrave. Vanessa is the sympathetic, bedridden former movie star hated by her demented sister and kept a prisoner in her own mansion. The update by Brian Taggert focuses on intriguing if lurid material about the freaky folks in Hollywood these days. The grotesqueries of Lynn's performance are what make this notable; there's little else except graphic murders, but even these do not build suspense; instead, they only add to the unsavoriness of it all. Directed by David Greene. John Glover, Bruce A. Young, Amy Steel, Samantha Jordan, John Scott Clough.

WHAT THE PEEPER SAW (1973) ★★★ Offbeat British psychodrama, interesting for its ambiguities and hints of conspiracy. Mark Lester is a perverted little bastard who may have drowned his mother—or so suspects stepmother Britt Ekland, the only one to penetrate to the roots of the boy's "bad seed" tendencies. Father Hardy Kruger refuses to believe it, so psychiatrist Lilli Palmer gets to make it appear Britt is off her rocker and commits her. Screenwriter Trevor Preston is interested in the psychological interplay among his intriguing characters, and how they step in and out of shadows cast by the aberrant mind. Directed with a minimum of flash and dash by James Kelly. Aka *Night Child, Night Hair Child* and *Child of the Night* (VCI; Interglobal)

WHAT WAITS BELOW (1983) ★★★ Intriguing fantasy adventure from producer Sandy Howard, with Robert Powell as a soldier of fortune called upon by a U.S. military unit in South America to help with the installation of a sonar device in an underground cavern. Director Don Sharp captures tension and suspense as the expedition (Timothy Bottoms, Anne Heywood, Richard Johnson, Lisa Blount) works its way into the cavern's depths to discover an Alien-esque rock monster and a race of albino-skinned Lemurians. When the action erupts there's plenty of it. (Lightning)

WHEELS OF FIRE (1984) ★★★ There's never a dull moment in this nonstop display of car chases and gun battles, which amounts to another *Mad Max* retread, directed-written by action master Cirio H. Santiago. The hero is Trace, the heroine is Stinger and the villain is Scourge in a post-Armageddon world of dune buggies, souped-up autos and tons of desert dust. There's a tribe of white-haired, cannibalistic Sandmen in a cave, a dwarf fighter, samurai swords, a flamethrower, batteries of artillery and mortars, a clairvoyant woman warrior and peace lovers called the True Believers. What else could you want? Totally mindless, yet fascinating as it unfolds at a dashing pace without logic. Gary Watkins, Laura Banks, Lynda Wiesmeier, Linda Grovenor. Aka *Vindicator*. (Video/Laser: Vestron)

WHEELS OF TERROR (1990) ★★★ The first half of this TV-movie, designed in the manner of a slasher flick by screenwriter Alan B. McElroy, resembles *The Car* in its setting (small desert community) and the fact that we never see the killer driver. The second half takes on its own flavor as school-bus driver Joanna Cassidy, after seeing her daughter abducted by the killer car, chases after the black sedan in a prolonged car chase. It is during this exciting sequence that director Christopher Cain struts his artsy-fartsy stuff, and *Wheels of Terror* is at its best. Marcie Leeds, Arlene Dean Snyder. (Video/Laser: Paramount)

WHEN A STRANGER CALLS (1979) ★★★½ Chilling premise: baby-sitter Carol Kane receives weird calls . . . then realizes a killer is in the house with her, calling from an extension. After this shocking start, the story deteriorates into standard chase fare as cop Charles Durning, years later, pursues the killer after he escapes from an asylum. Finally, the story returns to the baby-sitter and again becomes a genre scare flick with moments that will make you leap with fright. Recommended to all baby-sitters. Directed by Fred Walton, who coscripted with Steve Feke. Rachel Roberts, Colleen Dewhurst, Ron O'Neal, Tony Beckley. (Video/Laser: RCA/Columbia)

WHEN A STRANGER CALLS BACK (1993) ★★★½ Emphasis in this TV-movie sequel to the 1979 shocker *When a Stranger Calls* is on the psychological terrors endured by baby-sitter Jill Schoelen who, 5 years after an ordeal at the hands of a kidnapper, is terrorized anew by her assailant. Carol Kane, the victimized baby-sitter in the original, and Charles Durning, the cop on the case, are back as investigators helping Schoelen solve the mystery of someone breaking into her apartment and leaving behind clues to frighten her. The cat-and-mouse aspects of the script by director Fred Walton (who cocreated the characters with Steve Feke) dominate, and there are eerie and scary sequences, although explanation of who and how and why is lacking. Gene Lythgow, Karen Austin. (MCA)

WHEN DINOSAURS RULED THE EARTH (1970) ★★★ Spectacularly built blond Victoria Vetri is some eyeful in this Hammer sequel to *One Million B.C.*, which depicts early man squaring off against prehistoric creatures and the elements (including the formation of the moon). Jim Danforth headed a team of effects artists, while Val Guest wrote-directed. Ms. Vetri is a member of the Rock Tribe rescued by Robin Hawdon of the Sea Tribe. Cast out from their respective bands, they rove the barren surface, make love in caves and encounter snakes, crabs and dinosaurs. Effects are not up to the Harry-

hausen standard, but it's solid entertainment. Patrick Allen. (Video/Laser: Warner Bros.)

WHEN THE BOUGH BREAKS (1993) ★★ This starts out as one weird serial-killer movie, and has plenty of weird music by Ed Tomney and atmospheric photography. Credit must go to Ally Walker for her unusual performance as a forensics expert assigned to help the Houston police (headed by Martin Sheen) solve a perplexing case. Pairs of severed hands are being found all over the city—hands that once belonged to children between the age of 5 and 12. Walker, an outsider within the male world of cops, finds a link that takes her to a mental institution, where a mute youngster (Tara Subkoff) takes her on an odd psychological journey into the heart of a child murderer. Although it's clear that the child has a psychic link to the killer, the script by director Michael Cohn never ties together numerous loose ends and leaves more questions unanswered than answered. Hence the climax, while well done, is a letdown. As the "suspect analyst," Walker is a hyper, chain-smoking, fast-talking high-strung investigator, and the one reason to see this oddball slant on the now-clichéd *Silence of the Lambs* theme. Ron Perlman, Robert Knepper, John P. Connolly, Scott Lawrence, Jimmy Medina. (Turner)

WHEN THE DARK MAN CALLS (1995) ★★½ Clichéd "woman in peril" TV-movie, predictable at every alleged plot twist because you've seen it all done before, only better. Joan Van Ark portrays a psychiatrist who doubles as a Toronto talk-show host (WRAP radio) who just happens to not remember what happened many years ago when her mother and father were brutally murdered in their bedroom. Geoffrey Lewis went to prison for 25 years for the crime, and now he's out, seeking revenge against Joan for some dark reason. Who really committed the gory murders? Joan, always wearing miniskirts, thinks maybe she did it—or was it her former husband? Everyone looks like a suspect as she keeps flashing back to the murder scene in black and white. Stuart M. Kaminsky's novel was adapted by coproducer Pablo F. Fenjues and directed by Nathaniel Gutman. James Read, Barry Flatman, Frances Hyland, Chris Sarandon. (Paramount)

WHEN THE DEVIL COMMANDS. See *The Devil Commands.*

WHEN THE GODS FALL ASLEEP (1972) ★★½ This is a sequel to *The End of Man* from Brazilian horror-señor José Mojica Marins, the hombre who gave us the Coffin Joe movies. This is the continuing supernatural adventures of a priest on a mission to save mankind. Pretty weird stuff. (S/Weird)

WHEN THE SCREAMING STOPS (1973) ★★½
A school of nubile young women . . . a scaly monster brought to life by moonlight . . . an underwater cavern where tigerskin-clad cuties dwell . . . the Sword of Siegfried . . . it's the "kitchen sink" theory as applied by writer-director Amando De Ossorio in this naive, silly tale based on an old legend that Lorelei stands guard over the gold of the Rhine River, killing when the moon is full. The amphibious green slime monster with big teeth is more comical than frightening, and an eye-filling parade of curvaceous cuties in bikinis and other skimpy costumes will please males. But these facts don't necessarily make for a good movie. Tony Kendall stars as a thick-skulled hunter brought to the school to kill the monster. Mild lesbian overtones show up. Helga Line, Silvia Tortosa, Josefina Jartin. Aka *Grasp of the Lorelei* or *The Lorelei's Grasp*. (Lightning)

WHEN TIME EXPIRES (1998) ★★ This lethargic, actionless Showtime TV movie is a bungled attempt by writer-director David Bourla to put across a convoluted time-travel yarn. A "timeline analysis" (Richard Grieco portraying Travis Beck), who works for a "League of Planet's Ministry," arrives buck naked in the Texas desert while shapely Cynthia Geary watches with a keen eye. In a nearby lazy town, Grieco waits several days just to carry out his assignment—to put a quarter in a parking meter. While waiting, he learns that Geary is a barmaid (he finally woos her but not for several reels, since sex might interfere with his assignment). Grieco also talks to a used-car dealer (Pat Corley) through a TV-set "interface," converses with a couple of fellow time-traveling agents who may be mercenaries, assassins, or just misunderstood nice guys, gets into a barroom brawl with muscular meanies, and has dinner with the barmaid's father (Chad Everett). There's talk of an apocalytic destruction of Earth and a smattering of time paradoxes are thrown into the swirl, but no amount of dialogue can tie together Bourla's kitchen-sink approach to science fiction. You'll end up with time on your hands, with only seconds to spare, as your own interest in this failure expires. Mark Hamill, Tim Thomerson, Ron Masak. (Hallmark)

WHEN WORLDS COLLIDE (1951) ★★★★½
Producer George Pal's above-average version of the Edwin Balmer–Philip Wylie novel, with an intelligent script by Sydney Boehm that deals convincingly with man's social disintegration when a star dubbed Bellus passes so close to Earth it causes destructive earthquakes, tidal waves and other mayhem. Mankind's only hope is to build a rocket ship to take a handful of humans to a satellite planet, Zyra—and thus begins the race to survive. Among those in the project are millionaire John Hoyt and lovers Richard Derr and Barbara Rush. Chesley Bonestell was technical advisor; Gordon Jennings won an Oscar for his effects. Directed by Rudolf Mate, who turned this into one of the best sci-fi films of the '50s. Mary Murphy, Larry Keating. (Video/Laser: Paramount)

WHERE ARE THE CHILDREN? (1985) ★★★
Mildly horrific adaptation of Mary Higgins Clark's novel, but missing the hard edge such a suspense tale needs. For a story about a madman who kidnaps 2 children and holds them hostage, with the intent to murder them, this has too few graphic shocks—fans would call this Zev Braun production "wimpy." Jill Clayburgh portrays the children's hysterical mother, whose history suggests she could be responsible for the kidnapping. The supporting cast is good, especially Frederic Forrest as the kidnapper (wearing a pillow to give him added weight), and Max Gail and Barnard Hughes. Scripted by Jack Sholder and directed by Bruce Malmuth. (RCA/Columbia)

WHERE TIME BEGAN (1977) ★★ Spanish version of Jules Verne's novel by writer-director Juan Piquer Simon is inferior to the 1959 adaptation, *Journey to the Center of the Earth*. The pace is sluggish, the characterizations dull. The film gains life when the monsters appear. Even though they are laughable dinosaur and King Kong imitations, they beat the monotony of the expedition into the bowels of Earth. Kenneth More stars as the professor in charge. Ivonne Sentis, Frank Brana, Pep Munne, Jack Taylor. Aka *Fabulous Journey to the Center of the Earth*. (Embassy)

WHISKEY AND GHOSTS (1967) ★★ Obscure Italian comedy Western from producer Carlo Ponti captures a Three Stooges flavor with its sagebrush silliness, and it's just dumb enough to evoke mild chuckles. Napoleon B. Higgins, a nerdish snake-oil salesman, is pursued across the desert by Mexican outlaws (stereotypes at their worst) while Davy Crockett's ghost (depicted as a chubby, whiskey-guzzling drunk in a derby with ho-ho-ho humor) helps Higgins out of life-threatening situations. Eventually, the spirits of Johnny Appleseed (!) and Pecos Bill (!!) are added to the craziness. An anomaly made when spaghetti Westerns were big, so overtones of that genre appear within this melee of Western wackiness. The dubbing, though, is bad. Directed by Anthony Dawson. Tom Scott, Fred Harris, Mariel Martin.

WHISPERING SHADOW, THE (1933) ★★½
Some old serials, no matter how bad the acting or scripting, have a nostalgic twist that make them enjoyable. Unfortunately, this 12-chapter Mascot serial, from producer Nat Levine, is not one of them. This hogwash is difficult to sit through without continually wincing, even with the presence of Bela Lugosi as the mysterious

Professor Strang, the owner of a wax museum, whose daughter (Viva Tattersall) becomes involved in a search for jewels from a Baltic nation hidden in a moving and storage warehouse. Lugosi hams it up as one of several suspects in the case who could be "The Whispering Shadow," a nefarious cackler who uses radio Death Rays that kill unfaithful accomplices and a machine that casts his ominous shadow onto walls while he diabolically laughs and issues dire threats. Directed without style by Albert Herman and Colbert Clark, and with poorly choreographed fights and action sequences, this serial is strictly from hunger and one of the poorest of its decade. Henry B. Walthall, Karl Dane, Viva Tattersall. (Captain Bijou; Sinister/ C; Nostalgia; VCI)

WHISPERS (1990) ★★★ Unusually good Canadian adaptation of Dean R. Koontz's novel about a woman (Victoria Tennant) terrorized by a knife-wielding attacker—but nothing is what it seems when assailant Jean LeClerc returns from the dead to terrorize her anew. She and cop Chris Sarandon set out to find out if he's dead or not. The trail leads to devil worship, vampires and an army of deadly cockroaches, all cleverly arranged by writer Anita Doohan and carefully shot by director Douglas Jackson. The film also has an unusual homosexual touch, which we cannot elaborate on without giving away the ending. Peter MacNeill, Linda Sorenson, Eric Christmas, Jackie Burroughs. (Live) (Laser: Image)

WHISPER TO A SCREAM, A (1989) ★★ Stripper Nadia Capone takes a job as a telephone-sex lady, creating sensuous personas that turn on a murderer and make him kill the dancers at Nadia's club. Canadian psycho-killer flick unfolds in predictable fashion. Director Robert Bergman cranked out the script with producer Gerard Ciccoritti. (Virgin Vision) (Laser: Image)

WHITE DWARF (1995) ★★★ A Francis Ford Coppola TV production, intended as a series pilot, in which fledgling doctor Neal McDonough is sent to a distant galaxy to learn medicine under the tutelage of Paul Winfield, a humanoid alien on a planet divided into the Dark Side and the Light Side, where civil war constantly rages between the 2 factions. McDonough is subjected to numerous alien cultural anomalies (a shape changer; a parasitical creature that crawls through one's stomach; a dangerous animal that can be mesmerized by the human voice; a pair of surgical gloves that slide onto one's hands as if they were alive; strange royalty). The teleplay by coproducer Bruce Wagner is thoughtful if a bit ethereal and complicated, and director Peter Markle has the advantage of digital computer effects to help pull off his difficult assignment of making sense out of a hodgepodge of characters and situations. Ele Keats, Joey Andrews,

Tara Graham, Beverly Mitchell, CCH Pounder. (Cabin Fever)

WHITE LIGHT (1990) ★★★ Offbeat Canadian-produced mixture of "cops vs. the underworld" action and a mild supernatural plot in which deep-cover cop Sean Craig (Martin Kove) is shot by an assassin and has a 6-hour near-death experience, meeting beautiful Rachel (Allison Hossack). Returned to the living, Kove tracks down his old nemesis, searches for the mysterious Rachel and meets a lady scientist conducting experiments with "tetradetoxin," a drug that simulates the death experience. Ron Base's script is unusual enough to sustain interest despite familiar ingredients, and director Al Waxman brings moments of sensitivity to the romantic interludes. Filmed in Toronto. Martha Henry, Heide von Palleske, James Purcell. (Academy) (Laser: Image)

WHITE OF THE EYE (1986) ★★★½ Off-the-wall, unusually original portrait of a psycho killer and what happens when he goes off the deep end. This is not a slasher film—it's a study of people in an Arizona town and how they react to a series of wealthy-housewife murders. Sometimes the characters behave in such a bizarre way that credulity is stretched to the breaking point, but director Donald Cammell keeps it balanced with his fine cast by always emphasizing the perversensss of the unpredictable script by China and Donna Cammell. This will not be everyone's cup of tea, but those who appreciate the metaphor (complete with apocalyptic climax) will groove on its cinematic delights. David Keith, Cathy Moriarty, Art Evans, Alan Rosenberg. (Paramount)

WHITE TRASH ON MOONSHINE MOUNTAIN. See *Moonshine Mountain.*

WHITE ZOMBIE (1932) ★★½ Long hailed as a lost classic, this was rediscovered in the '60s, then condemned by some fans who wished it had remained lost. Want the truth? It's creaky and awful, only occasionally enhanced by the symbolic imagery injected by producer Edward Halperin and director Victor Halperin. Yet it's historically important because of Bela Lugosi, whose performance makes this worth viewing. Yes, he's in dire need of restraint as he overplays Legendre, a sweetless sugar plantation owner in the West Indies who holds sway over an army of zombies. Heavy-handed, turgid viewing, yes, but it's a wonderful glimpse into Hollywood's schlocky past. Voodoo lore was borrowed by writer Garnett Weston from William Seabrook's nonfictional *Magic Island.* Madge Bellamy, John Harron. (Prism; United; Kartes; Quintex; Sinister/C's and Filmfax's versions includes a "lost" interview with Lugosi) (Laser: Roan)

WHITHER MANKIND. See *Things to Come.*

WHO? (1974). See *Robo Man.*

WHO? (1975). See *Beyond the Door*.

WHO CAN KILL A CHILD? See *Island of the Damned*.

WHO FELL ASLEEP? See *Deadly Games*.

WHO FRAMED ROGER RABBIT? (1988) ★★★★★ An instant classic, an instant masterpiece, an instant Hollywood innovation—a feature that blends live action with animation in a seamless style, creating a unique universe set in 1947. This is the kingdom of Hollywood where cartoon characters ("toons") live and breathe with humans, working in cartoons but taking "human" jobs during lean times. You really have to credit animation director Richard Williams and Industrial Light & Magic for major contributions to the effect. Almost every cartoon character conceived through 1947 has a featured role or cameo in this entertaining production from Steven Spielberg and Disney. The Jeffrey Price–Peter S. Seaman script (based on Gary K. Wolf's novel *Who Censored Roger Rabbit?*) stars Bob Hoskins as private eye Eddie Valiant trying to help cartoon star Roger Rabbit duck a murder charge. Directed with incredible vitality by Robert Zemeckis, the film really gets weird when Hoskins goes to Toonville, a community where all animated characters live. A subplot involves a scheme to get rid of cable cars to make room for freeways—giving this an odd twist of social relevance. The 1 human-animated character is sexy songstress Jessica (voice by Kathleen Turner). Christopher Lloyd excels as the villain, Judge Doom, Joanna Cassidy portrays Valiant's girlfriend, and Stubby Kaye lends his own cartoonish presence as a comedy writer. Highlights include Daffy Duck and Donald Duck performing a piano duo, cameos by Tweety Bird and Sylvester (voices by Mel Blanc), and a guest spot by Lena Hyena. You'll need to see this more than once to catch all the characters and visual gags. (Video/Laser: Touchstone)

WHO KILLED COCK RUBIN? See *The Maltese Bippy*.

WHO SLEW AUNTIE ROO? (1971) ★★½ Minor horror themes barely qualify this as a fright flick, yet it always evokes a rowdy response from viewers who recognize the Hansel-and-Gretel parallels to this modern tale of 2 children living with auntie Shelley Winters. She wants to toss them into the oven in what passes for a gingerbread house. The script (Gavin Lambert, Jimmy Sangster, Robert Blees) meanders but the cast works hard to make the feeble ideas work: Mark Lester, Ralph Richardson, Hugh Griffith, Lionel Jeffries. Despite its slightness, and only average treatment by director Curtis Harrington, this comes out a winner. Aka *Whoever Slew Auntie Roo* and *Gingerbread House*. (Vestron)

WICKED CITY (1992) ★★★ A fascinating, action-packed, animated Japanese fantasy-adventure feature set in a land where mankind is at war with "the black world," from which monsters come through the time-space continuum to attack humans. An uneasy treaty exists between the worlds, but renegades break it and a "black guard" agent is assigned to protect a diplomat for the new treaty signing. Monsters (including a spider-woman) and effects are exciting and frequently sexual; the film has a heightened sense of eroticism, and the mood captures the bizarre flavor of the comic-book novel by Hideyuki Kikuchi. Directed by Yoshiaki Kawajiri. (Streamline)

WICKED GAMES (1993) ½ This is a scuzzbag movie, a slimeball flick, unworthy of even those strange beings who go out of their way to find and savor the worst films imaginable. A regional video obscenity made in Amateur City (Palm Beach, Fla.), *Wicked Games* is a wretchedly produced hunk of junk about a serial killer in a copper mask who slaughters prostitutes and other unfortunates with knives, barbed wire and anything handy. Unwritten and undirected by Tim Ritter, its costars Joel D. Wynkoop and Kermit Christman are also unproducers. Lori Zippo, Kevin Scott Crawford. (Twisted Illusions)

WICKED STEPMOTHER (1989) ★ Writer-director Larry Cohen makes pretty strange films, touched by Cohen peculiarities—but this time he didn't mend his wicked, wicked ways and came up with what ranks as the rankest of his work. Bette Davis plays a witch who presumably shrinks people (why or how is never explained) and tries to move in on Lionel Stander, who shares living space with daughter Colleen Camp and son-in-law David Rasche. Along comes Barbara Carrera (looking exotic as usual) as a witch who casts meaningless spells—an excuse for some meaningless effects poorly done. The only funny scene is a police lineup of old-lady types, but after that it's a misfire. Another good actor unfortunate enough to get involved is Tom Bosley, who portrays the cop on the case. (MGM/UA)

WICKER MAN, THE (1972) ★★★★½ This oft-admired film sports a top British cast (Britt Ekland, Diane Cilento, Ingrid Pitt, Christopher Lee) but received poor distribution on 2 occasions: when initially released in a butchered form, and again in 1978–79 in reedited form, with director Robin Hardy touring the U.S. to flack for the film. In its complete form, this retains an unusual power in depicting the inhabitants of a Cornish village who act strangely when a constable turns up to investigate a disappearance. One of the highlights of this unusual story is an erotic nude sequence involving the comely Ms. Ekland. And Lee considers it one of his best. The literate script is by Anthony

Shaffer. Ian Campbell, Aubrey Morris, Edward Woodward. (Media; Republic)

WILDER NAPALM (1993) ★★★½ A thoroughly wacky comedy fantasy depicting a set of whacked out, eccentric characters. The brothers Wilder (Arliss Howard) and Wallace (Dennis Quaid) Foudroyant are bitter enemies and have feuded for years. Wilder just wants to be a fireman but Wallace, a cheap carnival clown, wants to exploit a little strange thing they have: the ability to start fires and to whirl fireballs like a pitcher hurls a curveball. As Wallace says, "We're just one big thermal-nuclear family." When the feud extends to Wilder's nymphomaniacal wife (Debra Winger, in one of the strangest roles of her career), the brothers let fly with their pyrotechnic skills, exploding buildings, blasting holes in walls and ceilings and, in general, setting fire to their lives and the lives of those around them. The film's idiosyncratic behavior will delight you and/or annoy you as its bizarre characters cut loose, aided a little bit by Jim Varney's circus roustabout and M. Emmet Walsh's fire chief. Vince Gilligan's script is clever and fresh, and Glenn Gordon Caron's direction of it reminds one of just how good TV's "Moonlighting" once was. Personal taste will ultimately dictate how much you like this oddball piece of filmmaking and performing—frankly, it set me afire. Mimi Lieber, Marvin J. McIntyre. (Video/Laser: Columbia TriStar)

WILDEST DREAMS (1987) ★ Brainless sex comedy with a little bare-breasted nudity and simulated rolling in the hay when nerdish James Davies, hungry for love and sex, uncorks Heidi Paine (as the genie Dancee) from an Egyptian vase and is granted the wish of having beautiful women fall in love with him instantly. However, each woman is so overbearing that Davies keeps asking for another. It's a series of tasteless sight gags, dumb verbal jokes, big hooters and other prurient interests from writer Craig Harrall and producer-director Chuck Vincent. Cork it and forget it. Deborah Blaisdell, Ruth Collins, Jill Johnson. Aka *Bikini Genie*. (Vestron) (Laser: Image)

WILD JUNGLE CAPTIVE. See *Jungle Captive.*

WILD MAN (1989) ★ Magical ring on the finger of secret agent Eric Wilde (Don Scribner) enables him to return to life whenever he gets killed by bad guy James L. Newman. The ring comes from Indian medicine man Fred J. Lincoln, who also directed this video actioner. Michelle Bauer, Kathleen Middleton, Travis Silver, Ginger Lynn Allen. (Celebrity)

WILD PALMS (1993) ★★★ In A.D. 2007, L.A. attorney James Belushi wakes up from a dream about a rhino in his pool, setting into motion events that lead him to realize he is at the core of a conspiracy that involves a quasireligious communications organization secretly planning to control the world through a form of TV virtual reality. This intriguing theme by Bruce Wagner is told in such an offhanded, convoluted and slow-moving fashion in this 6-hour "TV event" that interest drifts unless one is dedicated to keeping track of the many characters, their dual loyalties and a past that is constantly mingled with the present. You will need to appreciate the eccentric and bizarre as this futuristic cautionary tale unfolds. Robert Loggia is strong as the messiah of the cult (the Fathers), David Warner is intense as the leader of the underground fighting the cult, and Angie Dickinson is superb as a torture expert for Loggia. Others who do well with difficult roles are Dana Delany, Kim Cattrall, Ernie Hudson, Bebe Neuwirth, Nick Mancuso, Robert Morse and Brad Dourif. Various episodes were directed by Peter Hewitt, Keith Gordon, Kathryn Bigelow and Phil Joanou. Music by Ryuichi Sakamoto. (ABC)

WILD THING (1986) ★★★ Unusual urban fantasy patterned after the *Tarzan* myth, springing from the imagination of screenwriter John Sayles. In 1969 a child witnesses the murder of his mother and father at the hands of drug dealers. The youth escapes and grows up wild in the city slums to emerge in modern day as a Robin Hood on a rope, who swings from the parapets to rescue the innocent from the evil elements of the Zone, a depressed area of an American city, the "home of the down and out, outlaws and outcasts." Rob Knepper plays Wild Thing as a naive innocent (he calls sex, for example, "body bump") and has his first romance with Kathleen Quinlan, who has just arrived to work in a relief mission. Wild Thing's battle is with drug kingpin Chopper and he stalks baddies with a crossbow. A fascinating, though not-always-successful tale of messed-up Americana, with director Max Reid capturing the coarseness of city life and its decadence and decency. Robert Davi, Maury Chaykin, Betty Buckley. (Paramount; Goodtimes)

WILD, WILD PLANET (1967) ★ Dull, dull Italian sci-fi set in A.D. 2015 spends too much time setting up a premise that never gels—a miniaturized scientist (Massimo Serato) plots to kidnap representatives of the United Democracies with the help of intergalactic robot female pirates. This unofficial sequel to *War of the Planets* was directed by Anthony Dawson (Antonio Margheriti). Tony Russell, Lisa Gastoni, Franco Nero, Charles Justin. Aka *Criminals of the Galaxy* and *The Galaxy Criminals*. (S/Weird)

WILD WILD WEST (1999) ★ Of all the movies based on the popular TV series of 1965–69, which mixed western settings with science fiction and horror, this is undoubtedly the worst, primarily for its utterly ridiculous casting. After the success of *Men in Black*, director Barry Sonnenfeld and actor Will Smith teamed up again, thinking they could parlay big bucks out of this tongue-in-cheek action film. They ended up spending big bucks all right, but without ever earning them back. And oh, what a disaster when you consider the ludicrously misguided script by S. S. Wilson, Brent Maddock, Jeffrey Price, and Peter S. Seaman. For starters, Secret Service agent James T. West, operating out of Washington, D.C., in the post–Civil War years for President Ulysses S. Grant, was white when played by Robert Conrad (at least that was true the last time we looked). To replace him with a black actor (Smith) is to go against the traditions of the show and to dishonor the memory of those who made it one of the few memorable series of the sixties. And then to inject racial humor into the plot, such as West escaping from a Ku Klux Klan–style lynching, just heaps insult upon injury. With Kevin Kline taking over Ross Martin's role as master of disguises Artemus Gordon, the film sinks into a hopeless morass. Martin would have sent Kline back to acting school if he were alive. While the TV show was rather coy about its tongue-in-cheek attitude, Sonnenfeld turns the action into cartoonish slapstick that belongs in a picture like *Inspector Gadget*. Those who fondly remember Michael Dunn's portrayal of archvillain Dr. Miguelo Loveless will be further appalled to see him replaced by a wheelchair-bound Kenneth Branagh, who does nothing with the role that the dwarfish Dunn did. (The arbitrary changing of his first name to Aliss is indicative of the uselessness of this movie.) Loveless has designed a giant spider machine that seems to have stepped out of a Jules Verne adventure and there is Salma Hayek around for love interest. Go back and look at the old TV episodes again—it's a helluva lot more fun than watching this drippy dreck. (Video/DVD: Warner Bros.)

WILLARD (1971) ★★★½ Stephen Gilbert's novel, *Ratman's Notebooks*, is material that proved a difficult mousetrap for director Daniel Mann and scripter Gilbert Ralston to set. You'll never be suckered in by its cheesiness; it's too unbelievable in depicting how a 27-year-old failure (Bruce Davison) trains an army of 500 rats to do his evil bidding, which includes murdering a sadistic boss (Ernest Borgnine). Sondra Locke plays Bruce's girlfriend in a miniskirt, Elsa Lanchester is the demanding, dying mother and Michael Dante is a fellow office worker. The sequel, *Ben*, was also a money-maker but just as mousy. (Prism) (Laser: Image)

WILLIAM SHATNER'S STAR TREK MEMORIES (1995) ★★★★ Excellent 1-hour reedited version of a TV special hosted by Shatner, in which all the show's principals, as well as writer D. C. Fontana, talk about how the "Star Trek" series began and evolved. (Paramount)

WILLIES, THE (1990) ★ Anthology of horror stories suffers from slow pacing and padded material. Three teens (Sean Astin, Jason Horst, Joshua Jon Miller) spend the night trying to gross each other out with bloodcurdlers. Some are sickening vignettes ("Tennessee Frickasee," "Haunted Estate," "Poodle Soufflé") but most of the film is devoted to 2 lengthy tales: "Bad Apples," in which a picked-on kid gets his revenge with a monster in the boys' room at a high school; and "Flyboy," a perverse, pathological study of a fat boy (Michael Bower) with a fetish for collecting dead flies. Naturally, the flies get their revenge for having their wings pulled off, with the help of Spivey's Own Miracle Manure. There's something unappetizing about this film (you actually want to see Bower knocked off, he's so despicable) when it should have had a sense of fun. Blame writer-producer-director Brian Peck. Ralph Drischell, Kathleen Freeman, Ian Fried, James Karen, Jeremy Miller, Clu Gulager. (Prism) (Laser: Image)

WILLIS O'BRIEN: A COMPILATION. Highlights from films featuring the stop-motion animation of the man who invented it, Willis O'Brien. Included: *King Kong, Lost World* and *Mighty Joe Young*. (On Video)

WILLOW (1988) ★★★½ A George Lucas production that tries to regain the magic and excitement of the *Star Wars* series, but which misses by a considerable distance. However, Lucas fans will consider it the best game in town until something better happens along. It is full of lavish (if not wondrous) special effects and the action is plentiful, even though the characters don't have the charm and mythical qualities to make them memorable. *Willow* recounts the episodic adventures of a dwarf (called a nelwyn) returning a lost baby to civilization, unaware that the cooing infant, a princess destined to ascend to the throne in Daikini territory, has been ordered killed by the wicked sorceress Queen Bavmorda. The nelwyn, Willow (Warwick Davis), leads his miniband into a plot involving a Han Solo–like renegade named Madmartigan (Val Kilmer), the evil general Kael (Pat Roach) and 2 pocket-sized adventurers. The film conveys 3 points of view during the action sequences, creating amusing effects. Bob Dolman's screenplay borrows from many sources to spin the far-ranging tale. Since there's never any doubt as to a happy ending, one's attention is held by the parade of little people, warriors, magicians, killer animals and monsters. Directed by Ron Howard with a rough edge. Joanne Whalley, Jean Marsh, Billy Barty, Patricia Hayes, Gavan O'Herlihy, Kevin Pollak, Phil Fondacaro. (Video/Laser: RCA/Columbia)

WILLY MILLY (1986). See *Something Special*.

WIND, THE (1986) ★½ Deserted village on the windswept Greek island of Monemvassia is the setting for this psychoterror flick, which holds the suggestion that the ubiquitous breeze sweeping the desolate place is supernatural. Producer-director Nico Mastorakis (who cowrote with Fred C. Perry) fashions cat-and-mouse slasher games when adventure writer Meg Foster is attacked by next-door neighbor Wings Hauser. Boyfriend David McCallum, back in L.A., is too far away to do anything so his is a thankless role. Every twist is predictable, there's little suspense in Mastorakis's lethargic style, and the setting, with its catacombs and ruinous atmosphere, ultimately has too little story to service. Robert Morley, Steve Railsback, John Michaels, Tracy Young. (MGM/UA)

WIND OF DEATH. See *The Last Man on Earth*.

WING COMMANDER (1999) ★★★ Although this is based on a computer game that's been popular for years, it comes across as a comfortable extension of the first *Star Wars* movie (with its battle between fleets of fighter spacecraft), TV's *Battlestar Galactica*, and scenes from *Star Trek* movies where the crew goes falling all over the place every time a proton torpedo is fired. It has all the clichés one would expect: spectacular spacecraft engaged in maneuvers and battles, lightweight characters who get moved around like chess pieces for the space battles, and an alien race of reptilian creatures bent on conquering our solar system. There are entire sequences that play like scenes from old World War II submarine and aviation epics. So *Wing Commander* is like putting on a pair of well-fitted metallic boots for a space walk. Freddie Prinze, Jr., plays the Luke Skywalker counterpart, a brand-new fighter pilot arriving in a distant quadrant of space where war with the evil Kilrathi race has broken out. An interesting racial prejudice disrupts his arrival because his mother was a "Pilgrim," a member of a group of early space explorers who eventually abandoned their human ways. This is a key element in whether things get done right or not, and is one of the few psychological conflicts in the film. Saffron Burrows is Prinze's "wing commander" and Matthew Lillard and Ginny Holder are among his fellow hotshot pilots. Among the older officers are Jurgen Prochnow, Tcheky Karyo, and David Warner, who all do a commendable job to save Earth from destruction. Chris Roberts, who created the computer games, was given command of the script and the direction, and they are in capable hands. Pure and simple sci-fi space adventure, with hardly a complicated thought to slow it down. (Video/DVD: Fox)

WINGED SERPENT, THE. See *Q: The Winged Serpent*. (Queue up to see it!)

WINGS OF DESIRE (1987) ★★★ West German director Wim Wender creates a mesmerizing, poetic effect in this fable about 2 angels (without wings, halos or harps) hovering above Berlin and listening to the thoughts of inhabitants. (They are beautifully underplayed by Bruno Ganz and Solveig Dommartin.) As they reflect on the human condition, Ganz is overtaken by the desire to be human, and transforms into flesh and blood so he can indulge his love for a circus aerialist. The film is told in stark black-and-white images except when Ganz feels human or turns human. Peter Falk, portraying an actor making a movie, becomes a key figure in this philosophical, brooding and moving tale. Sequel: *Faraway, So Close!* (Orion) (Laser: Image)

WINTERBEAST (1993) ★★ When folks begin disappearing mysteriously from a wintertime resort, a park ranger begins to figure out that the hotel is built on Indian burial grounds. Hmm. Tim R. Morgan, Mike Magri, Dori May Kelly. Directed by Christopher Thies. (Tempe; Movies Unlimited)

WIRED (1989) ★★½ Very strange biographical movie based on Bob Woodward's study of comedian-actor John Belushi's drug overdose death in 1982. That book was a serious attempt to learn the truth of Belushi's death and to explore the devastation drugs has on our culture, but this movie is a supernatural comedy in which Belushi's spirit (Michael Chiklis) comes alive on the coroner's slab and is led through a life recap by taxi driver and guardian angel Ray Sharkey. J. T. Walsh plays Woodward, shown investigating the death. All of this, plus assorted flashbacks into Belushi's career, is never blended in Earl MacRauch's script. Just when you get caught up in the serious drug issues, and the impact of Belushi's self-destruction, the comedic fantasy elements intrude and deaden the effect. Larry Peerce's offbeat direction, in which present and past are often shown in the same scene, is finally defeated by trivialization. Bad taste prevails. Lucinda Jenny, Alex Rocco, Gary Groomes, Patti D'Arbanville. (IVE) (Laser: Image)

WIRED TO KILL (1986) ★★★ The futuristic post-holocaust world in this low-low-budget actioner is different from Mad Max's, so at least it strives for originality. The time is 1998, and while there is a semblance of law and order, the world is pretty screwed up when Emily Longstreth, freshly kicked out of her home, teams with electronics inventor Devin Hoelscher, who's just had his legs broken by a sadist (Merritt Butrick) and his band of perverts. The gimmick is that the incapacitated Hoelscher must use the girl to carry out his dirty work, aided by a robot named Winston. Directed-written by Franky Schaeffer. Frank Collison, Tommy Lister, Jr., Kim Milford. A little better than usual for this genre. (Lightning)

WISHBONE CUTTER. Video version of *Shadow of Chikara* (MNTEX).

WISHMAKER, THE (1979) ★★½ Slow-paced, gentle-mannered German TV-movie based on "The Goosegirl" by the Brothers Grimm, in which the legendary 3 wishes are granted a poor blacksmith's son as he searches for a beautiful princess who is ostracized by her wicked father-king. The lad learns wisdom through his youthful mistakes and the teachings of a sagacious witch. Decent production values and a sincere cast turn what might have been a dreary experience into okay family fare. Directed by Ursula Schmenger. Ingrid John, Günter Nauman, David Schneider. (Video Gems)

WISHMAN (1991) ★★★½ Modern fairy tale set in L.A.: Garbage collector Paul Le Mat loves from afar beautiful Quin Kessler, who is kept a virtual prisoner by her guardian and a mean old housekeeper named Crabb. Enter Geoffrey Lewis as Liggett Hitchcock, a genie who has lost his magic bottle and some of his powers, and Staten Jack Rose, a charming con man played by Brion James. The hapless guys team to help Kessler escape her plight and to reclaim the bottle, which has ended up in a museum. The humor is only mildly funny and the make-a-wish potential is never fully utilized, but writer-director Michael Marvin makes this a pleasing concoction with his personable characters. Paul Gleason, Nancy Parsons, Gailard Sartan, Liz Sheridan. (Monarch)

WISHMASTER (1997) ★★★ Forget Barbara Eden, Ali Baba, and Robin Williams. Genies, or djinns, are evil creatures, tricking you with their three wishes and then destroying you in the most hideous ways so you will never live to enjoy the fruits of the wishes. Bad guys, get it? This blatant exercise in excessive violence and gore at least has the enhanced presence of the talented Andrew Divoff as the master djinn (or "wishmaker" of Persian folklore), who has been freed from imprisonment in a red gemstone ("The Stone of Secret Fire") to walk the earth. While he often appears in heavy makeup as the ugly demon, Divoff also appears as "Nathaniel Demarest," a pseudo-human making his deals with greedy individuals and then tricking them so that while they get their wishes, it is in the least desirable form. Such as when a bodyguard admits to Divoff that he would like to "escape" his job, and ends up in a Harry Houdini–like water torture chamber, thoroughly tied up and struggling to "escape." A security guard tells Divoff "you'll have to go through me" and so Divoff does—literally. Divoff has a menacing voice and presence, but when you add the double entendre dialogue of scriptwriter Peter Atkins, the djinn comes up a win. A prologue (voice by Angus Scrimm) tells us that djinns 3,000 years ago ("in a time before time") were condemned unholy creatures trapped between heaven and hell. Any person who frees a djinn is entitled to three wishes, but upon granting the third wish, the djinn and his pals will be free to unleash their evil fury upon a helpless world. So it is that a certain djinn (Divoff) is freed from imprisonment when a statue being brought to America is accidentally dropped on a pier and the gemstone concealed inside is smashed open. The djinn makes a psychic link to Wendy Benson, the woman he must now trick into making the mandatory three wishes. Benson, meanwhile, is investigating the broken gemstone through museum curator Robert Englund, gem specialist Chris Lemmon, and street bum Buck Flower. Eventually the djinn uses perky, sexy Jenny O'Hara as a hostage to lure Benson into a den of horrors. Atkins's plot is minimal, with many set pieces of bloody action and gory disembowelings and beheadings. Other forms of brutal butchery are enacted along the way. These grisly special effects are the work of a special-effects team known as KNB EFX Inc., one member of which is Robert Kurtzman. That *Wishmaster* marks Kurtzman's directing debut may explain why the film is routine rather than special. Aka *Wes Craven's Wishmaster* and *Wes Craven Presents Wishmaster*. Kane Hooder, Tony Todd, Jenny O'Hara, Tony Crane. (Video/DVD: Artisan Entertainment)

WISHMASTER 2: EVIL NEVER DIES (1998) ★½ This djinn-unleashed-upon-the-earth thriller is watchable only for the unusual performance of Andrew Divoff as the human embodiment of an evil 3,000-year-old genie that intends to destroy mankind and fulfill an ancient Persian prophecy. Divoff has a stone-faced demeanor and a voice that oozes menace. At first he is an "Ahura Masda" diety imprisoned in "The Stone of the Secret Fire," a red gemstone that is part of a statue in a U.S. museum. When small-time robber Holly Fields and her boyfriend bust into the museum, she accidentally frees the "wishmaster." Once embodied in Divoff, the genie grants wishes in a literal kind of way. If a cop says, "Freeze," putting his service weapon on the genie, then the cop turns into a frozen statue. Or if someone wishes for a lawyer "to go fuck himself," then . . . well, you get the picture. That's about all that is clever in the script by director Jack Sholder (who did better work in *The Hidden*). The rest of the film shows Divoff granting wishes, rapping out double entendre black humor, and claiming each wishee's soul in the foulest way. There's also Fields and her love affair with a priest (Paul Johannson) as they marshal the forces of good to fight evil. Hohum stuff. Divoff, who has a field day with this role and makes it fun, is much more interesting to watch as he finally amasses his needed 800 souls by opening his own Las Vegas casino. Just wish to hit a jackpot and see what happens to your spirit. When Divoff turns into the djinn (genie to you moderns), he looks like your standard demon from hell with makeup by Anthony C. Ferrante. And the final showdown in Divoff's casino is more funny than frightening. Incidentally, onetime director Alfred Sole is credited as production designer. Bokeem Woodbine, Carlos Leon, Robert Lasardo, Oleg Vidov, Tommy "Tiny" Lister, Jr. (Video/DVD: Artisan)

WISH ME LUCK (1995) ★½ Incomprehensibly imbecilic rip-off of "I Dream of Jeannie," made with a debilitated teenage mentality, in which a well-stacked blond genie (Avalon Anders) is sent by Ali Baba (he lives off Earth, in a castle in a cloud) to Earth to help his banished son discover his "manhood." She thinks this means he has to get laid within 48 hours, and she gets some sexy bimbo-brained cheerleaders to help her climax the deal. There's no imaginable reason to watch this goofy crap, which is the equivalent of being lashed 1,500 times by an unusually savage cat-o'-nine-tails. The not-so-magical writer-director is Philip J. Jones, who should be put into a bottle and corked for all eternity, to avoid him ever getting his hands on a movie camera again. Zen Gesner, Christine Harte, Raymond Storti, David Sobel, Tom Carroll, David Jean Thomas, Tom Kane.

WITCH, THE (1982) See *Superstition*.

WITCH ACADEMY (1993) ★½ One of producer/director Fred Olen Ray's better excuses for girl watching, thinly veiled as a horror comedy written by Mark Thomas McGee. Such cuties as Ruth Corrine Collins, Suzanne Ager, Michelle Bauer and Priscilla Barnes romp around in Frederick's of Hollywood outfits, their giant breasts threatening to fall out of the inadequate material, while they harass mousy, sexually repressed Veronica Carothers because she wants to join their sorority. Robert Vaughn pops up as the Devil to turn shy Veronica into a redheaded sexpot in a revealing red outfit, so he can unleash stupid-looking monsters on the beauties, not to mention libido-happy professor Jay Richardson. No actual nudity, but plenty of things are half exposed. (American Independent)

WITCHBOARD (1986) ★★★ Sincere effort to tell a terror tale with good characterizations underlies this low-budget supernatural thriller utilizing the Ouija board as a horror device. Unfortunately, the first half could be called *Witchbored*, with writer-director Kevin S. Tenney in need of more panache for his planchette. Finally, the murders begin after Tawny Kitaen dabbles with a 10-year-old spirit, unaware she is communicating with a mass murderer back from the grave and stalking prey with his ax. The gore is light but the impact is there at the chaotic climax, a blending of slasher and *Exorcist*-type thrills. Todd Allen, Stephen Nichols. (Continental; Magnum) (Laser: Image)

WITCHBOARD 2: THE DEVIL'S DOORWAY (1993) ★★ A few spectacular effects—that's about all writer-director Kevin S. Tenney brings to this sequel to his 1986 hit, which again uses the Ouija board as a device linking our world to the spirits. Ami Dolenz moves into a loft apartment, finds the "witchboard" and communicates with the spirit of a dead woman who claims to have been murdered. A series of *Omen*-inspired gore-murders occurs, but Tenney doesn't set up interesting characters or circumstances to build on the mystery of who the dead woman is, or who killed her. Timothy Gibbs, John Gatins, Laraine Newman, Julie Michaels. (Video/Laser: Republic)

WITCHBOARD: THE POSSESSION (1995) ★★½ Good special effects of David Nerman morfing into a horned demon enhance this otherwise predictable, by-the-numbers supernatural thriller, the third in the *Witchboard* series created by Kevin S. Tenney, who this time collaborated on the script with John Ezrine but did not direct. That chore went to Peter Svatek, who does an okay job depicting how unemployed stockbroker Nerman is taken over by the spirit of fertility god Nargor and how girlfriend Lockey Lambert tries to save him using anti-evil charms, etc. Cedric Smith, Donna Sarrasin. (Video/Laser: Republic)

WITCHCRAFT (1989) ★★ Brand-new mother Anat Topol-Barzilai moves into the gothic house of her mother-in-law and has visions that suggest demons are close at hand. This was such a successful video release that it inspired sequels. Directed by Robert Spera. Gary Sloan, Mary Shelley, Deborah Scott. (Video/Laser: Academy)

WITCHCRAFT II: THE TEMPTRESS (1989) ★★ Ridiculous sequel is supposed to be deadly serious but it turns out hysterically funny. The offspring from the original, now a teenager living with adoptive parents, is the spawn of the Devil, and a buxom, blond witch in black lingerie and high heels (played by supersexy Delia Sheppard) hams it up trying to seduce him into her coven. She acts more like a dancer in a cheap burlesque club than an evil spirit, and eventually the best thing going in this movie are her large breasts, which threaten to rip apart her Frederick's of Hollywood costumes. Charles Solomon, as the young man, is inadequate to the occasion, but his facial expressions are a joy to behold. They aren't what director Mark Woods wanted, but the editor left them in anyway. Mia Ruiz, David L. Homb, Kirsten Wagner. (Video/Laser: Academy)

WITCHCRAFT III: THE KISS OF DEATH (1991) ★★★ A marked improvement over *Witchcraft II*, with Charles Solomon back as an L.A. D.A.

who has the power of a warlock but refuses to use it for evil. He meets a warlock who does use his powers for evil, kissing women and turning them into sex slaves. The warlock falls for Solomon's girl and sets Solomon up for the kill. Solomon turns to an African witch doctor for help. Screenwriter Gerry Daly injects interesting characterizations and director R. L. Tillmans handles his assignment adequately, considering the low budget and limited effects. Lisa Toothman, Dominic Luciano, Leana Hall. (Academy)

WITCHCRAFT IV: VIRGIN HEART (1992) ★★★ Charles Solomon is back as lawyer Will Spanner, who is again called on to use his warlock abilities when he defends a man accused of a ritualistic murder. Involved are a British talent agent and his sexy charge, a stripper named Belladonna (played by pinup Julie Strain). Call it a Strain on the eyes. Directed by James Merendino. Clive Pearson, Jason O'Gulihur, Lisa Jay Harrington. (Academy) (Laser: Image)

WITCHCRAFT V: DANCE WITH THE DEVIL (1993) ★ This sleazy Satanic melodrama, a major deterioration in the series with some of the crummiest special effects in many a year, finds Charles Solomon missing from the cast as the warlock who fights evil forces. He has been inadequately replaced by Marklen Kennedy, who now has William's powers (as a character named Will Spanner) but is controlled to murder by an evil entity from Hell named Cain. As portrayed by David Huffman, Cain is the only thing worth watching as he gathers assorted human souls to prepare for Satan's return to Earth. But not even his performance (hammy but enjoyable) can raise this stinker from the lower depths of Hollywood moviemaking. Many of its sequences consist of steamy lovemaking scenes with Kennedy and Carolyn Taye-Loren, a huge-breasted minion for Cain. Bordering on slobbering porn, *Witchcraft V* fizzles but never sizzles. Written by Steve Lymon and James Merendino, directed tastelessly by Talun Hsu. Nicole Sassaman, Kim Bolin. (Academy)

WITCHCRAFT VI: THE DEVIL'S MISTRESS (1994) ★ Does each new entry in this long-running series get a little worse than the last? It seems so as these *Witchcraft* things become more raunchy with explicit sex between big-boobed beauties and male studs. In this supernatural adventure involving divorce attorney Will Spanner (Jerry Spicer)—a warlock who has the powers to fight off Satan's evil minions—he confronts Savanti (Bryan Nutter), another warlock, who intends to use an eclipse as part of his L.A.-based plan to bring the Devil to Earth to rule again. Such huge-breasted babes as Debra Beatty and Shannon Leod wield their exotic wiles, a couple of goofy cops working on a serial-killer case have various psychics examine a victim's bra, Nutter goes nutty (and hammy)

as the Evil One, and director Julie Davis (who wrote the nonscript with Peter Fleming) wastes every opportunity. The effects, as in *Witchcraft V*, are the worst. How do they get these things financed, anyway? Craig Stepp, Kurt Alan, John C. Holiday. (Academy)

WITCHERY (1988) ★★ An island off the coast of New England is haunted by witch Hildegard Knef, the spirit of a sexy movie actress who committed suicide by jumping out a window. With the help of cackling hags, who make the Cryptkeeper and the Vault Keeper seem beautiful by comparison, she performs assorted *Omen*-style murders. Among the unfortunate souls (a boatload of people stranded on the island) are a photographer, a magazine writer, two realtors, Linda Blair with a kid, and an ugly man and his wife. The graphic, unpleasant-to-watch murders include a voodoo-doll puncture job, a human mouth sewn shut by thread (this one will keep you in stitches), a body hung upside-down and burned alive in a fireplace, a crucifixion (nails and all) and another body through a window. This Italian gory story was written by Anonymous and directed by Martin Newlin, better known in Rome as Fabrizio Laurenti. Catherine Hickland, David Hasselhoff, Annie Ross. (Vidmark)

WITCHES, THE (1989) ★★★ Director Nicolas Roeg spins a satisfying witchcraft tale that walks a fine tightrope between being a child's fable and an adult's delight. Outstanding in her first screen role in almost 15 years is Mai Zetterling as the grandmother of bespectacled youth Jasen Fisher. The lad listens with wide-eyed wonder to her tales of witches and their devious ways. Good thing, because when the boy and Granny spend a holiday in a seacoast hotel in England they encounter a coven holding a convention, presided over by the grand High Witch—Anjelica Huston in an excellent performance. Her plot is to poison the children of England with sweets and it's up to Jasen, after he's been turned into a mouse, to outsmart the cackling coven. The characters are delightfully funny and the witches convey the witty treachery that Margaret Hamilton conveyed in *The Wizard of Oz*. Executive producer Jim Henson provided the effects and Allan Scott adapted Roald Dahl's book. Rowan Atkinson, Bill Paterson, Brenda Blethyn. (Video/Laser: Warner Bros.)

WITCHES' BREW (1985) ★★ Originally shot in 1978 as *Which Witch Is Which?*, this failed to stir the cauldron and underwent reshooting before being sold to cable TV. It's a comedy rendering of Fritz Leiber's *Burn Witch Burn* (though uncredited), showing the humorous side to suburban witchcraft. Richard Benjamin is a university professor whose wife (Teri Garr) uses her witch's powers to help him get ahead, but he forces her to throw away her good-luck charms . . . leaving him wide open to the witches-wives of 2 rivals, and their mentor, witch Lana Turner. The old biddy conspires to enter Teri's body, allowing for cheap effects. The jokes are thin, the production qualities cheap. Directed by Richard Shorr with new footage by Herbert L. Strock. A Strock of bad luck? (Embassy)

WITCHES OF EASTWICK, THE (1987) ★★★½ Three divorced women living in a New England village steeped in American tradition discover they have witchy powers and, one by one, are willingly seduced by a newcomer to town, Daryl Van Horne, who is none other than the Devil incarnate, here to engage in a battle of the sexes that is intellectual and visually exciting thanks to the special effects of Rob Bottin. Jack Nicholson is brilliant as the seductive chauvinist male who employs supernatural tricks (such as levitation) to tease his conquests. The talented women are equally up for the occasion: Susan Sarandon is a suppressed music teacher turned into a passionate redhead; Cher is a sculptress, showing her dramatic and comedic acting abilities; and Michelle Pfeiffer is a local newspaper reporter, beautiful and vulnerable. Veronica Cartwright should also be singled out for her performance as the woman who realizes what Van Horne is up to and tries to stop him. There's wonderfully witty dialogue by Michael Cristofer, who adapted John Updike's novel, and director George Miller treats the material on an epic scale, suggesting we are seeing the supreme battles of good over evil, man against woman, and other cosmic themes. It is, however, Nicholson's performance that will endure. One could be critical of the ending, which goes berserk with nauseating effects (the Road Warrior in Miller coming out, perhaps?) but this is still a superior entertainment. Richard Jenkins, Keith Jochim, Carel Struycken. (Video/Laser: Warner Bros.)

WITCHFINDER GENERAL, THE. See *The Conqueror Worm.* (Death wormed over?)

WITCHFIRE (1985) ★½ Since she's also the associate producer, leading lady Shelley Winters can go bonkers in grand style, cackling with a madness that will delight your perverse soul. When her psychiatrist is killed in a car crash, madcap Shelley plots to escape the Institute for Living (better known as the Asylum for the Utterly Crazed). She and 2 other batty dames (Frances De Sapio and Corrine Chateau) take refuge in the rural house where Shelley once set fire to her parents. The babbling old broad thinks she's a witch, but not once does anything supernatural happen, no matter how many incantations she recites from her battered book. One lousy video movie—substandard in every respect. Pay homage to director Vincent J. Privitera. Gary Swanson plays a hunter estranged from his son, but that's a subplot that has nothing to do with anything. Aka *A Sonnet for the Hunter.* Peter Masterson, David and James Mendenhall. (Lightning)

WITCH HUNT (1994) ★★★½ This sequel to *Cast a Deadly Spell* continues HBO's nostalgic fantasy adventures of L.A. private eye Phil Lovecraft (named after Howard Phillip Lovecraft, the beloved horror writer), whose capers are set in the '40s and '50s. The year 1953 finds magic still being commonly practiced by many (some for good, some for evil) and Lovecraft up to his neck in black magic. Fred Ward has stepped aside as the world-weary dick and Dennis Hopper fills his shoes admirably as he gets involved with a congressman (Eric Bogosian) holding hearings to stop the practice of magic and with a beautiful film actress (Penelope Ann Miller). Also around is the cop named Bradbury (Christopher John Fields) and a weird guy named Finn Macha (played oh so weirdly by Julian Sands). Joseph Dougherty's telescript tends to be a bit too talky this time, but director Paul Schrader captures the essence of a parallel-universe L.A. of the '50s and enhances the depth of the characters to make up for the lack of action. Sheryl Lee Ralph, Valerie Mahaffey, Lypsinka, Alan Rosenberg. Produced by Gale Ane Hurd. (HBO)

WITCHING, THE. Video version of *Necromancy* (Paragon).

WITCHING OF BEN WAGNER, THE (1990) ★★★ Are teenager Bettina Rae and her grammy Sylvia Sidney, who live in a little shack on the edge of Mirror Lake in Utah, really witches capable of "bazinko" curses? One never knows for sure in Malcolm Marmorstein's teleplay when realtor Sam Bottoms, wife Harriet Hall and son Justin Gocke move into the community and get involved with the alleged curse makers. This is a pleasant TV-movie ably directed by Paul Annett on location. It's based on a novel by Mary Jane Auch. (Warnervision/Leucadia)

WITCHKILL. See *The Witchmaker.*

WITCHMAKER, THE (1969) ★★★ William O. Brown wrote-produced-directed, for producers L. Q. Jones and Alvy Moore, this poor man's glimpse at witches and warlocks sneaking through the misty Louisiana bayou. Much of this is ludicrous exploitation, especially the scenes in which Luther the Berserk (John Lodge) hangs up women by their heels, slices their throats and lets the blood drip to the ground. The swamp country makes for some chilling, atmospheric sequences in Brown's plot, which has psychic researchers Moore, Anthony Eisley and the beautiful dolls investigating the bogland. Before long the gals are drifting through the foggy landscape in sexy negligees,

which stirs the blood of some creeps in a cave—
and those creeps include horror movie host Seymour. Retitlings include *Legend of Witch Hollow* and *Witchkill*. (Cinema Concepts;
Interglobal)

WITCH OF TIMBUCTOO, THE. See *Devil Doll.*

WITCHTRAP (1989) ★★½ Due to flat, nonat-
mospheric lighting, mediocre actresses and inadequate effects, *Witchtrap* limps along without
much conviction. It's also been mistitled, as it
has a warlock as its chief villain. Writer-director
Kevin S. Tenney did a better job with *Witchboard* than with this haunted house tale
involving a warlock (J. P. Luebsen) who returns
from the dead to reclaim his missing heart when
a team of psychic investigators invade his gothic
domain. Only James W. Quinn as private eye
Tony Vicente and Linnea Quigley as a psychic
video technician seem at home with this material, the rest of the cast being strangely amateurish. Kathleen Bailey, Rob Zapple and Judy
Tatum head the paranormal experts. Tenney appears briefly as the owner of the house who
hires the private cops and psychics. (Magnum)
(Laser: Image)

**WITH HERCULES TO THE CENTER OF THE
EARTH.** See *Hercules in the Haunted World.*

WITHOUT WARNING (1980) ★ Here's a warning: Beware this sci-fi terror tale (a predecessor
to *Predator*) in which an alien stalks Earthlings
for trophies to adorn his spaceship walls. Martin
Landau (playing Fred Dobbs, get it?) and Jack
Palance deserve the Overacting Awards of
1980; they are genuinely terrible as would-be
victims of the creature, who uses ugly disc-
shaped suckers for "bullets." *Slurp sqwk glump*—
those are sounds made by the Incredibly Hungry
Disc Beasties. They are effective, even if Greydon Clark's direction isn't. Cameron Mitchell,
Neville Brand, Sue Ane Langdon, Larry Storch,
Ralph Meeker. From a script by Lyn Freeman
and D. Grodnik. Aka *It Came . . . Without
Warning* and *The Warning*. (HBO)

WITHOUT WARNING (1994) ★★★ "None of
what you are seeing is actually happening" is
the disclaimer that precedes this TV-movie that
tries to recreate a real-life event as a network
might televise it (see *Special Bulletin* for another superior example of this offbeat genre).
Sandor Vanocur is the anchor of "Evening
World News" who interrupts regular programming to cover the sudden, simultaneous landing
of 3 asteroids in different parts of the world:
China, France and the U.S.A. The broadcast,
"Asteroid: Fire from the Sky," is a brilliant pastiche of news coverage as reporters from all
over the world begin to track the story. (Homage
is paid to this idea's inspiration, Orson Welles's
"War of the Worlds" radio broadcast of 1938,
by having one of the flaming rocks land at Grov-
ers Mill, Wyo.) Gradually, this turns into sci-

ence fiction as it becomes apparent that an
intelligent extraterrestrial force is behind the
landings. *Without Warning* is an insightful survey (as written by Peter Lance, and directed by
producer Robert Iscove) of TV news, with Arthur C. Clarke making a surprise appearance as
himself from Sri Lanka. There's a sci-fi climax
that'll knock you out of your seat. Incidentally,
the original broadcast was on Oct. 30, 1994, 56
years after Welles's "War of the Worlds." It was
produced by documentarian David L. Wolper
and features Jane Kaczmarek, Bree Walker
Lampley and Dwier Brown. A great example of
TV imitating itself for dramatic effect—and
working.

WITNESS MADNESS. See *Tales That Witness
Madness.*

WIZARD OF GORE (1970) ★★★ One of the
great camp-gore classics from the king of blood
and guts, producer-director Herschell Gordon
Lewis. The Allan Kahn script has a mad magician named Montag the Magnificent (Ray
Sager) who performs horrifying mutilations on
the stage (all faked), but then does them for real
with members of the audience after the show is
over. See a woman cut in half and watch another
spiked to death. Strong stomachs required. Ray
Sager, Judy Cler, Wayne Ratay. (Rhino; Select;
New Star; Continental)

WIZARD OF MARS, THE (1964) ★½ Low-
budget slop of the "gee whiz" school, its
schlocky story borrowed from *The Wizard of
Oz*. Four astronauts rocket to the Red Planet,
crash-landing in a wilderness. By following a
"golden road" they find a civilization ruled by
wizard John Carradine. Time on the planet is
frozen, and only by unfreezing it can the Earthlings return home. The effects are inadequate to
the ambitions of screenwriter David Hewitt,
whose chores extended to producing-directing.
Forrest J. Ackerman served as technical adviser,
but to what avail is unclear. Turgidly acted by
Roger Gentry, Vic McGee, Eve Bernhardt, Jerry
Rannow. Aka *Journey into the Unknown*. (Republic; Genesis; from Star Classics/Genesis as
Horrors of the Red Planet and from Regal as
Alien Massacre)

WIZARD OF OZ, THE (1939) ★★★★★ Pe-
rennial MGM classic (produced by Mervyn
LeRoy, directed by Victor Fleming) continues
to be enjoyed by new generations enthralled
with the magical story-telling of L. Frank Baum,
whose fairy tale was adapted by Noel Langley.
Judy Garland is the young Kansan, Dorothy,
who is knocked out during a tornado (in black
and white) and wakes up (in color) in a fantasy
kingdom. Taking the Yellow Brick Road to adventure, she meets the Scarecrow (Ray Bolger),
the Tin Man (Jack Haley) and the Cowardly
Lion (Bert Lahr). The fantastic kingdom of Oz
is ruled by Frank Morgan and threatened by the

wicked witch (Margaret Hamilton) and her swarm of deadly flying monkeys. Then, of course, there are the Munchkins. Cedric Gibbons's art design always looks fresh and vibrant, the songs and music are unforgettable and the exaggerated acting perfectly captures the proper note. Enjoy the Munchkin merriment, because you will never discover a film as wonderful as this one. Billie Burke, Charles Grapewin. (Video/Laser: MGM/UA)

WIZARDS (1976) ★★★★½ Tolkienesque masterpiece of animation by Ralph Bakshi, depicting a future when mankind, following atomic holocaust mutation, is divided into two camps: the mechanized armies of Blackwolf the Tyrant, whose followers are a motley collection of frog creatures and demons, and the peace-loving elves who practice wizardry. The artwork is stunning, especially the brutal clash of armies in which Bakshi combines animation with live-action stock footage. The influences of comic-book artists Wally Wood, Frank Frazetta, Berni Wrightson and Al Williamson are pronounced. The narrative by Bakshi is sometimes garbled and the characterizations uneven, but these minor problems do not distract from the film's visual power. Bakshi's best! Originally shot as *War Wizards*. (Video/Laser: CBS/Fox)

WIZARDS OF THE DEMON SWORD (1991) ★ Producer-director Fred Olen Ray, a champion of the B movie, tackles sword-and-sorcery themes with tacky, campy, so-bad-it's-good results. The Knife of Aktar, key to unlimited power, is fought over by hammy conjurer Lyle Waggoner and roving swordsman Blake Bahner, who's trying to help maiden Heidi Paine and her imprisoned father Russ Tamblyn, with advice from the Seer of Roebuck (Hoke Howell). With all of its non sequiturs and silliness, this has to be seen to be believed. Camera work by Gary Graver. Jay Richardson, Dawn Wildsmith.

WIZARDS OF THE LOST KINGDOM (1984) ★ Cliché-riddled, amateurish sword-and-sorcery nonsense, distinguished only by the blasé, tongue-in-cheek performance of Bo Svenson as Kor the Conqueror, a wandering swordsman who befriends a youth who is "Simon, song of the good wizard Wilford, magician of the Kingdom of Axum." Simon and his "fuzzface" companion, a furry thing called Goldpack, are searching for a magical ring, and so is Chirka, the evil sorcerer. They throw rays of light at each other but the conflict is minimal and forced, and even Svenson can't sustain his performance under Hector Olivera's feeble direction. There's a hobgoblin, an insect woman who turns into a monster, 5 walking corpses and assorted *Star Wars*-style aliens. As the kid says, "Pretty neat stuff, huh?" Vidal Peterson, Thom Christopher, Barbara Stock. (Media)

WIZARDS OF THE LOST KINGDOM II (1990) ★★½ David Carradine's presence as legendary swordsman the Dark One helps this Roger Corman production a little, but director Charles B. Griffith's script is slow-paced and generic as Carradine, Bobby Jacoby and wizard Mel Welles unite to fight forces of evil in the sword-and-sorcery tradition. Susan Lee Hoffman, Lana Clarkson, Blake Bahner, Sid Haig, Henry Brandon. (Media)

WIZ KID, THE. See *Zapped!*

WIZ KID, THE (1989) ★★½ Inconsequential German TV-movie has a nerdy kid creating a more aggressive clone of himself and outsmarting some baddies who want to kidnap him. For moppets only. Directed by Gloria Behrens. Narcisa Kukavica, Jake Wood. (Vidmark)

WOLF (1994) ★★★★ Amazing, isn't it, when skilled filmmakers can take an old B-movie plot, update it, give it modern sensibilities—and presto—a tired old idea lives again in exciting, new form. This is nothing more than a remake of *The Wolf Man*, with Jack Nicholson as a fiction editor who is bitten by a wolf one snowy, stormy night and slowly transmogrifies into a hairy creature with all the symptoms and anguish of Lawrence Talbot. However, it's full of excellent dialogue (by Jim Harrison and Wesley Strick) and stylish makeup effects by Rick Baker. And director Mike Nichols proves he knows his genres by giving *Wolf* an odd atmosphere. And Michelle Pfeiffer is superb as Nicholson's lover. A howl of a good film! James Spader, Kate Nelligan, Richard Jenkins, Christopher Plummer, Eileen Atkins. Music by Ennio Morricone. (Video/Laser:Columbia TriStar)

WOLFEN (1981) ★★½ This adaptation of Whitley Strieber's novel might have been a winner, but . . . if you excite an audience's expectations for a monster, you'd better pay off. But when these titular entities (mutant wolves with superintelligence) reveal themselves, the film falls faster than a diarrhetic wolf hound's doodoo. Instead of creatures seemingly capable of ghastly gore murders, we are shown ordinary wolves with slight makeup. The disappointment is ultradevastating. Up to then, *Wolfen* is a graphically suspenseful thriller about a killer pack running in the ruins of the Bronx. Director Michael Wadleigh, who cowrote with David Frye, also made bad changes in Strieber's plot. There's business about Indians (they were once pushed off their land, just like earlier generations of wolves) but that remains secondary to Albert Finney as the cop in pursuit of the 4-legged killers. The Steadicam wolf's-eye-view shots in the Bronx ruins are marvelous; if only the pay-off had paid off. Gregory Hines, Diane Venora, Edward James Olmos, Tom Noonan. (Video/Laser: Warner Bros.)

WOLF MAN, THE (1941) ★★★ Classic Universal thriller establishes the mood and lore for the werewolf genre, and presents sympathetic Lon Chaney, Jr., as Lawrence Talbot, a student attacked by a werewolf (Bela Lugosi) who, under the full moon, turns into a marauding, slavering monster. Jack Pierce's time-lapse makeup is outstanding and Curt Siodmak's script explores the trauma and torment of lycanthropy in sympathetic fashion. Maria Ouspenskaya recites the famous "werewolf curse" poem and Claude Rains portrays the father who gropes to understand his son's malady. Produced-directed by George Waggner. Ralph Bellamy, Evelyn Ankers, Warren William. (Video/Laser: MCA)

WOLF MAN, THE. See *Legend of the Wolfwoman*.

WOLFMAN, THE. See *The Curse of the Werewolf*.

WOLFMAN: A CINEMATIC SCRAPBOOK. See *Wolfman Chronicles*.

WOLFMAN—A LYCANTHROPE (1978) ★★ Although his films rarely play outside the South, Earl Owensby is a producer of money-making genre flicks. In this one, set in Georgia near the turn of the century, Owensby inherits the Curse of the Glasgow Family and turns into a hairy killer under the full moon. Written by Darrell Cathcart and directed by Worth Keeter. But Owensby was howlin' all the way to the bank. Kristina Reynolds, Maggie Lauterer. (Thorn EMI)

WOLFMAN CHRONICLES (1991) ★★★ Nice compilation of movie trailers and clips that traces the cinematic history of the werewolf on screen, described by writer-director Ted Newsom as a tribute to the "wildest beast men and wolf women." It starts with the first attempts by Universal (*Werewolf of London, The Wolf Man, The House of Frankenstein*, etc.). Lon Chaney, Jr., who played the hairy beast frequently, is profiled, and there is rare footage from an episode of TV's "Route 66" in which he played a wolfman opposite Boris Karloff and Peter Lorre. Lugosi is shown as a hirsute being in *The Ape Man* and *Return of the Vampire*. Although the track is occasionally poorly mixed, the previews are wonderful, including *Cry of the Werewolf, She-Wolf of London, The Undying Monster,* and *The Mad Monster*. The film also traces the screen history of Jekyll and Hyde monsters. A collector's item. (Rhino)

WOLFMAN OF COUNT DRACULA, THE. See *Frankenstein's Bloody Terror*.

WOLF MAN'S CURE, THE. See *House of Dracula*.

WOLF WOMAN. Video version of *Legend of the Wolfwoman* (Lobo Lady Lopes Loosely!) (VCI).

WOMAN FROM DEEP RIVER. See *Make Them Die Slowly*.

WOMAN IN BLACK, THE (1989) ★★★½ Chilly British ghost story in the best literary traditions of H. R. Wakefield and M. R. James. Adapted from a Susan Hill novel by Nigel Kneale, creator of the "Professor Quatermass" series, this TV-movie under the direction of Herbert Wise has moments that will freeze your bone marrow as it captures the eeriness and supernatural ambience in and around Eel Marsh House, a manor on a fog-shrouded moor where solicitor Adrian Rawlins is cleaning up the estate of a deceased recluse. A psychological study of Rawlins's mounting fear as he hears ghostly sounds and sees the spectral image of the dead woman, which serves as an omen for dire events. Bernard Hepton, David Daker, Pauline Moran, David Ryall. (BFS)

WOMAN'S OBSESSION, A. See *Bad Blood*.

WOMEN OF THE PREHISTORIC PLANET (1966) ★★½ Old-fashioned low-budget sci-fi movie, extinct as soon as "Star Trek" showed everyone how it should be done. Cheapies from the '60s era such as this were loaded with inexpensive "interior rocket" sets, studio-bound "exteriors" that always looked it, phony props and awful effects—call it the "dark ages" of space movies. Wendell Corey is a wise starship commander; John Agar is his adventurous second in command; Stuart Margolin appears in an early role; Merry Anders is a sexpot in space; Keith Anders is an officer; Irene Tsu is a crewmember who goes native; and nightclub comedian Paul Gilbert performs terrible variations on his act. The plot follows a starship to a distant planet on a rescue mission to save the crew of a hijacked ship. The scenes with the lizard monsters are laughable, and the "surprise ending" to director Arthur C. Pierce's script features one of the hoariest clichés in "speculative fiction" history. They sure don't make 'em like this anymore—thank God! Aka *Prehistoric Planet Women*. (Paragon; King of Video)

WOMEN OF TRANSPLANT ISLAND. See *The Deadly and the Beautiful*.

WONDER WOMEN. See *The Deadly and the Beautiful*.

WONDERFUL ICE CREAM SUIT, THE (1999) ★★★ This magical tale first appeared in Ray Bradbury's 1960 collection, *A Medicine for Melancholy*, and it remains one of his enduring miniclassics. It was presented as a one-act play by the Pandemonium Playhouse in the 1960s, and then in the nineties it was staged as a musical with music by José Feliciano. Bradbury's own screenplay blends elements of all three into a kind of musical fantasy (with one dance sequence that reminds one of MGM in the forties) that Stuart Gordon has brought to the screen with obvious love and affection. Five down-and-out Mexican-Americans are wandering the streets of a border town when they decide to chip in and buy a $100 vanilla-white suit in a shop owned by Sid Caesar and Howard Morris. When each amigo slips into the "threads," it alters his personality—each becomes the individual he dreams of being but cannot become because of social restrictions. The ice-cream suit strips away poverty and hard times. Joe Mantegna (lovable con man and rogue), Esai Morales (he wants to be a ladies' man), Gregory Sierra (a soapbox intellectual), and Clifton Gonzalez (the shy one who dreams of being a rogue, too) stand together against the sloppiest of the five—a bum wallowing in filth played by Edward James Olmos. But even Olmos (whose *Vamenos* hasn't taken a bath in many years) finally slips into the suit to become a "new" man. There's some comedic action in a cantina that is in keeping with Bradbury's tongue-in-cheek attitude toward Mexican culture and finally a poignant and melancholy realization among the five that their friendship can't last forever—the bonding brought about by the suit is but an object lesson. This was an unusual project for Gordon, who usually goes for the jugular in his horror films, and he deserves praise for restraining himself and capturing as much Bradbury on film as is possible. (Video/DVD: Touchstone)

WORKING STIFFS (1989) ★½ Semiprofessional comedy of the macabre, running barely an hour, which comes up with a solution to labor shortages. Carl Worm of the Consolidated Temps Company, an employment agency, kills his clients, resurrects them with a voodoo rite and sends them out to work for cheap wages. This tongue-in-cheek farce has many clever lines but writer-director Michael Legge lacks the experience to pull it off with a cast of amateurs: Beverly Epstein, Bruce Harding, Tony Ferreira, Alan Kennedy. (Sideshow Cinema)

WORLD APARTMENT HORROR (1991) ★★ From director Katsuhiro Otomo, who gave us *Akira*, comes this live-action horror-action flick depicting a gangster (Hiroki Tanaka) and his efforts to evict Asian immigrants from an apartment building haunted by a supernatural monster. Also written by Otomo with Keiko Nobumoto. Yuji Nakamura. (Video Search of Miami)

WORLD GONE WILD (1988) ★★ Undistinguished *Mad Max*–type post-holocaust actioner made palatable by Bruce Dern's portrayal of Ethan, a guru who throws off funny one-liners and acts out of synch with the rest of the cast and story. The time is A.D. 2087, after the Big War, and mankind suffers from a lack of water except for Lost Wells, a hippie-style community, which is besieged by Adam Ant and his army of pseudoreligious followers—men in white robes who keep machine guns tucked underneath. The Jorge Zamacona screenplay relies on standard action clichés and borrows from *The Magnificent Seven* by having Dern and girlfriend Catherine Mary Stewart look for mercenaries to help them stave off a pending attack. These characters are colorful if familiar: Michael Pare as a silent hero type, Anthony James as a cannibal, Rick Podell as a gunslinger, Julius Carry III as a nitro man and Alan Autry as strongman Hank. Directed by Lee H. Katzin, an old hand who deserves better material than this rehash. (Video/Laser: Media)

WORLD IS NOT ENOUGH, THE (1999) ★★★ This marks the 19th entry in the James Bond series, so to keep the franchise alive and going, everyone obviously felt obligated to work harder to top previous efforts under producers Michael G. Wilson and Barbara Broccoli. That extra-hard effort shows in spots, and in other spots the formula reveals a decided weariness. And in the person of Pierce Brosnan, there seems to be only a shadow of the presence that previous actors—Sean Connery, Roger Moore, Timothy Dalton—brought to the role of British secret agent 007. He is given so little to do beyond leap from high places, fight bigger-than-life villains, fire pistols, and bed beautiful women. Hence, *The World Is Not Enough* is a mixed bag of action, spoof, satire, and sex. It certainly opens grandly with a motorboat chase through downtown London on the Thames River, with Bond actually ending up on top of an enormous white dome built for the new millennium in Greenwich. Such set pieces always open the Bond adventures, and this is one of the best, with its incredible aquatic acrobatics. From there, gentleman spy James is off to former Soviet Union republic Azerbaijan to protect a deceased industrialist's daughter Elektra (Sophie Marceau) from Istanbul terrorists. A skiing action sequence at breathtaking heights points to one problem with Michael Apted's direction. Instead of cleverly working out a chase between Bond, Elektra, and Soviet agents flying above in parachute-rigged snowmobiles, Apted allows hundreds of rounds of automatic weapons' fire to miss Bond (stretching the credibility of even this series) while he makes himself an easy target. Why can't spectacular action sequences like this one be worked out to highlight Bond's ingenuity rather than just the terrible marksmanship of the villains? Speaking of villains, the main adversary here, a terrorist named Renard (Robert Carlyle), is one of the less interesting bad guys in the series. Because he has a bullet in his brain that is pressing against certain nerves, he is supposed to have no feeling and possesses superhuman strength. However, neither of these elements is used imaginatively, and Renard plays out like a dime-a-dozen villain. The action includes a ridiculously named and dressed nuclear scientist (Christmas Jones, played by Denise Richards in halter and shorts) who becomes the gal-in-peril who finishes out the film with Bond, even though there is no good reason for her being there. Judy Dench is back as assignment boss "M" (and actually gets embroiled in the action when she is imprisoned by the baddies), Samantha Bond appears too briefly as Miss Moneypenny, Desmond Llewelyn has his usual good time as frustrated weapons designer Q, and John Cleese pops up for some tongue-in-cheek tomfoolery as Q's right-hand man, R. The screenplay by Neal Purvis, Robert Wade, and Bruce Feirstein doesn't waste time moving from place to place, often sacrificing credibility for plot. Perhaps in a Bond film nobody cares. The action concludes with another superb action set piece, aboard a nuclear submarine that crashes to the ocean floor vertically, allowing characters literally to climb the walls. This is a marked improvement over *Tomorrow Never Dies*, the previous entry. One can only hope that Brosnan will be given a little more personality and a few personal touches in the next slam-bam outing. This film definitely cries out for that. Robbie Coltraine, Maria Grazia Cucinotta, Michael Kitchen, Claude-Oliver Rudolph. (Video/DVD: MGM)

WORLD OF HORROR. Video version of *Dario Argento's World of Horror* (Vidmark).

WORLD OF YOR, THE. See *Yor: the Hunter from the Future.*

WORLDS OF GULLIVER, THE. See *The Three Worlds of Gulliver.*

WORM EATERS, THE (1981) ★ Crazy Guy (Herb Robins, who also wrote-directed this sleazy exploitationer) talks to worms and forces people to eat them (remarkably disgusting, wouldn't you say?) and turns them into worm monsters. May have been intended as a horror comedy, although with the eccentric Robins at the helm, and T. V. Mikels producing, anything

is possible. Worm your way out of watching unless you have a taste for wriggling, crawly things. (WesternWorld)

WOULD YOU KILL A CHILD? See *Island of the Damned.*

WRAITH, THE (1986) ★★★ Supernatural spirit is at work in an Arizona town where tough guy Packard Walsh (Nick Cassavetes) holds sway over an odd collection of gang members, including Skank, Gutterboy, Oggie and Rughead. The Wraith (Charlie Sheen) is equipped with an Incredible Killer Rifle and a customized sports car to knock off baddies when he isn't making love to Sherilyn Fenn. Pointless revenge fantasy clumsily written by Mike Marvin but at least interestingly directed by him when it comes to car chases and stunts designed by Buddy Joe Hooker. Giving the film its only touch of comedy is Randy Quaid's Sheriff Loomis. He's cynical and funny and provides ironic counterpoint to the mayhem and death. Too bad the story isn't about him instead of those ridiculous teenagers. Matthew Barry, Griffin O'Neal, Jamie Bozian, Clint Howard, Chris Nash, David Sherrill. (Lightning) (Laser: Image)

WRESTLING WOMEN VS. THE AZTEC MUMMY (1965). Video of *Doctor of Doom* (Budget; Filmfax; S/Weird; from Rhino as *Rock 'n' Roll Wrestling Women vs. the Aztec Mummy*).

WRITER'S BLOCK (1992) ★★★ This TV-movie, perhaps inspired by Stephen King's *The Dark Half*, depicts mystery writer Morgan Fairchild undergoing trauma when someone, the Red Ribbon Killer, begins to duplicate the murders in her book. What's intriguing about this psychological study of the writer is whether the killer is real or an entity created by her imagination and now stalking her. Better than usual for its genre. Michael Praed, Mary Ann Pascal, Cheryl Anderson, Joe Regalbuto. Written by Elisa Bell and directed by Charles Correll.

X. See *X—The Man with the X-ray Eyes*.

XENIA (1990) ★★★ Unusually literate vampire film opens at the Crest Theater in Sacramento, Calif., where film producer Dennis Edwards (producer-director of *Xenia*) meets movie critic Dana M. Reeves (also producer-director of *Xenia*) to see *Xenia, Priestess of Night*, a horror film made by mysterious director Andre W. Wiers, who has the credits *House of Varicose Veins, Cry of the Shanker Sore* and *The Crawling Gallbladder*. This becomes a film-within-a-film as they watch the black-and-white movie unfold, opening this up to a parody of movie criticism and genres. And the "Xenia" within *Xenia* is a turgid piece—purposely designed to spoof techniques of '50s filmmaking. Hmm, some esoteric piece of work. Watch for Bob Wilkins, one-time "Creature Features" host of the San Francisco Bay Area, in a cameo. Herb Lightman, Matias Bombal, Sharie-Marie Jonsin, Timothy Gray, Dale Meader, Roberta Shepps.

X-FILES, THE (1993) ★★★★ This 1-hour pilot for the popular Fox network series depicts the exploits of 2 FBI special agents (played by David Duchovny and Gillian Anderson with great angst and paranoia) who investigate strange phenomena cases. After this episode involving UFOs and abductions, *The X-Files* went on to become a TV hit, covering a variety of fascinating subjects including many that would come under the heading of "urban legends." Writer-producer-creator Chris Carter was inspired by "The Night Stalker" series but wanted to deal with so-called supernormal mysteries and how they could be explained in terms of modern science and technology, instead of traditional supernatural ones. The troubled characters of agents Fox Mulder and Dana Scully (he's a believer, she isn't) and the air of conspiracy surrounding their FBI superiors have given this series a popularity resulting in collec-

tor comic books and other sidebar merchandising. Directed by Robert Mandel.

X FILES, THE (1993-94) ★★★★ Excellent episodes from the incredibly popular Fox network series have been reedited to include previously unshown footage, with two episodes per videotape. Tape 1: "The Pilot Show" and "Deep Throat." Tape 2: "Fallen Angel" and "Eve." Tape 3: "Ice" and "Conduit." There is added commentary by producer Chris Carter. If you're a fan, you gotta have these. (Video/Laser: Fox)

X-FILES, THE (1998) ★★★★ Except for a lot of megabucks for special effects and its use of widescreen Panavision, this plays like a glorified episode from the hit TV series created and produced by Chris Carter. The film looks and feels exactly like a video episode. And for that, this $60 million version should satisfy the ravenous appetite of any of the millions of loyal followers of the Fox Network series, which first came to the small screen in 1992 as a sleeper and built over the next two seasons into a mega-hit. All that conspiracy stuff involving the FBI, a secret cartel (run by John Neville), and aliens from space has been recycled and given some new dimensions by Carter and his cowriter/coproducer Frank Spotnitz. How does it click for nonfans or those generic moviegoers who know nothing about alien abductions and UFOs? My own feeling is that it's too convoluted for its own good and you do need to have some background about the series. However, both kinds of audiences gave it thumbs-up and it was a more-than-adequate summer hit. David Duchovny as the paranoid-driven Fox Mulder and Gillian Anderson as the sometimes disbelieving Dana Scully stay in character as they start out by tracking the mystery behind the bombing of a federal building in Dallas. Once again the sinisterly driven FBI is trying to break up their partnership. Martin Landau turns up as one of those half-crazed, *Deep Throat* scientists who slips Mulder information that could be true or half-baked. Nothing is what it seems as the FBI agents track the human-alien conspiracy to white domes in a cornfield (that means bees will be buzzing very quickly), a North Texas cave where horrible things happened back in "15,000 B.C.," and finally to Antarctica, where a climactic duel is fought between Mulder and saucer-equipped alien entities of evil. Rob Bowman, a veteran of the TV series, directs with a strong sense of atmosphere identical to that of TV episodes. Neville gets a fair amount of screen time as the double-dealing cartel chieftain, but the rest of the regulars turn up too briefly, almost perfunctorily: Mitch Pileggi as agent Walter Skinner, William B. Davis as the lurking Cigarette-Smoking Man, and those three editors of the *Lone Gunmen* tabloid of the paranormal: Dean Haglund, Bruce Harwood, and Tom Braidwood. Well and good, Chris Carter. (Video/DVD: Fox)

X FROM OUTER SPACE (1967) ★★ X for xcruciating . . . yet another Japanese creature bonanza for moppets produced by adults with children's minds. Guilala, a giant stegosaurus that spits steel spears, grows from a single cell into a monster after being brought from space attached to a spacecraft's hull. The monster goes on the same old rampage, destroying the nearest city—destruction-prone Tokyo. Cowritten and directed by Kazui Nihonmatzu. Starring the impulsive Eiji Okada and the erratic Shinichi Yanagisawa. Aka *Gilala* and *Big Space Monster Guilala*. (Orion) (Laser: Image, with *Yongary, Monster from the Deep*)

X-RAY. See *Hospital Massacre.*

X–THE MAN WITH THE X-RAY EYES (1963) ★★★½ One of Roger Corman's strangest films, hampered by inadequate effects and other budget woes yet singularly compelling as it unfolds an allegorical plot about Dr. Xavier (Ray Milland), who discovers a way of seeing through objects—to the heart of the universe! The climax to the Robert Dillon–Ray Russell script was inspired by the Bible and is utterly gross, yet producer-director Corman succeeds in jolting you. John Hoyt, Don Rickles, Dick Miller, Diana Van Der Vlis, John Dierkes. Aka *The Man with X-ray Eyes*. (Video/Laser: Warner Bros.)

X–THE UNKNOWN (1957) ★★★ This Hammer rammer is sometimes confused with the Quatermass series, and although Dean Jagger portrays a sympathetic scientist similar to Quatermass, it is a vehicle unto itself, being Jimmy Sangster's first script. It is sci-fi reeking with eerie atmosphere as a sludge monster rises from a Scottish bogland to seek out radioactive materials on which to feed. Good effects and great gloominess achieved by director Leslie Norman. Leo McKern, Anthony Newley, Edward Judd, Edward Chapman.

XTRO (1982) ★★½ A touch of *Alien*, a little blending of *Poltergeist* and a modicum of *Venom*—in short, your average rip-off movie with nothing original thrown into the bargain. This British sci-fier starts with Philip Sayer being abducted by E.T.s, then returning to Earth 3 years later, reprogrammed to suck on other people's flesh and give his young son psychic powers. There's silly baloney about toy soldiers coming to life that seems at odds with the *Alien* imitations. One doesn't know whether to laugh, scream at the gooey, horrendous effects or just go blind. Is masturbation the answer? A few hideous moments might have your skin crawling, but in general a waste of time. Directed with little imagination by Harry Bromley-Davenport. Bernice Stegers, Simon Nash, Danny Brainin, Maryam D'Abo. Scripted by Robert Smith and Iain Cassie. Produced as *Judas Goat.* (Thorn EMI/HBO) (Laser: Image)

XTRO 2: THE SECOND ENCOUNTER (1991) ★★★ Once in a great while a film derivative of a classic is inspired enough to transcend its own imitative weaknesses to take on a life of its own. This Canadian film is such a "sleeper." Although a rip-off of *Aliens, Xtro 2* eventually builds a momentum of suspense, action and characterization that sends it spiralling above other imitations. This achieves what *Alien³* did not. The setting is a computer-controlled research center for Project Nexus, an attempt to send explorers, after altering their body structure, into a "parallel universe." What's waiting for them returns in the transference machine and . . . you guessed it, it's an Alien-like monster who sets out to kill those sequestered in the project lab. The monster is an effective one, the cast is sharp and the pyrotechnics and effects well produced. But it's the tension captured by director Harry Bromley-Davenport that elevates this to classy status. For once, a rip-off script (this one by producer John A. Curtis, Steven Lister, Robert Smith and Edward Kovach) spurts fresh blood. Jan-Michael Vincent, Paul Koslo, Tara Buckman, Jano Frandsen, Nicholas Lea, W. F. Wadden. (New Line) (Laser: Image)

XTRO 3: WATCH THE SKIES (1995) ★★★ This opens with a clever pastiche of a 1955 newsreel, which leads into a modern science-fiction adventure involving a military conspiracy to cover up a UFO/alien experiment. The government testing dates back to the '50s on an island once used to intern Japanese POWs during World War II. Marine Corps demolitions expert Sal Landi and a ragtag band of leatherneck misfits are assigned to go to the island, where they unleash the imprisoned alien, which moves about inside a force field, displays a long orange tongue, and has a device that drills into human ears and brains. How the Marines are betrayed by their superiors (including Robert Culp back at headquarters) and are wiped out one by one accounts for most of Daryl Haney's script. Haney, incidentally, also plays one of the Marines and was an associate producer. Directed by Harry Bromley-Davenport, *Xtro 3* has occasional moments of inspiration, but one wishes the film had ended on a more upbeat note, given how much you come to sympathize with Landi's character. Jim Hanks, Andrew Divoff, Karen Moncrieff. David Barton has created a neat alien. (Triboro) (Laser: Image)

YANKEE IN KING ARTHUR'S COURT, A. See *A Connecticut Yankee in King Arthur's Court.*

YELLOWHAIR AND THE FORTRESS OF GOLD (1984) ★★★ Under the direction of Matt Cimber, this is a mixture of spaghetti Western violence and Indiana Jones humor when a white woman raised by Indians (Laurene Landon) and Pecos Bill (Ken Robertson) search for the Treasure of Kings while pursued by an outlaw gang and Mexican federales, both led by sadistic brutes. The fantasy element surrounds a legendary tribe of Comanches (Tulpan Warriors) who turn to plastic when they're shot. Includes imitative snake attack scenes and temple sequences, and a magic horn. Its lightheartedness makes it palatable. Aka *Yellowhair and the Pecos Kid.* (Lightning)

YELLOWHAIR AND THE PECOS KID. See *Yellowhair and the Fortress of Gold.*

YELLOW PHANTOM (1936). Feature version of the serial *Shadow of Chinatown.*

YESTERDAY MACHINE, THE (1962) ★★½ Cheaply produced regional sci-fi time-travel adventure, entertaining for its campy qualities in depicting pipe-smoking small-town cop Tim Holt (in his final screen role) and newsman James Britton tracking down a Nazi fanatic who has figured out a way of accelerating the velocity of time to send test subjects in and out of the past, all for the Third Reich. As directed by Russ Marker, Professor Ernst Von Hauser (delightfully played by Jack Herman, as if he were doing an impression of Sid Caesar's Professor Von Knowitall) explains his pseudophysics—or "superspectronic relativity"—to Britton in a hilarious scientific double-talk sequence. Meanwhile, there's fun in watching bleach-blond torch singer Ann Pellegrino sing, scream and fall into Britton's arms every time she's in danger. Be forewarned: You have to get a kick out of semiamateurish efforts to enjoy. Linda Jen-

kins, Jay Ramsey. (Video City; Sinister/C; S/ Weird; Filmfax)

YESTERDAY'S TARGET (1996) ★★½ Offbeat though muddled time-travel adventure (made for cable) with time paradox plot twists and telekinetic trickery. Three psychics with superpowers from 2025 are amnesiacs in modern times but slowly remember their assignment to protect a young boy (the first of a new brainy bunch who spend 11 months in the womb) and protect him from special government man Malcolm McDowell, who sends clairvoyant LeVar Burton and other toughies after the threesome. Too much plot in Dave Bourla's telescript hampers this attempt at unusual sci-fi, though director Barry Samson does all he can to hold it together, and the cast is good: Daniel Baldwin, Stacey Haiduk, T. K. Carter, Richard Herd, Trevor Goddar and Burton, who is especially fine.

YETI: THE GIANT OF THE 20TH CENTURY (1971) ★★ Italian "giant monster" nonepic tells the tale of a 50-foot Yeti, discovered in an icefield in the wilds of northern Canada by a scientific expedition. The Yeti, a tall dude covered with plenty of hair and photographed to look very big against blue-screen backgrounds, shows benevolence toward those who treat him decently. But the bad guys show up to exploit the monster, and the police have no understanding of this poor creature when he decides to take a stroll, so rampaging and mayhem result. The effects are obvious, the acting is of the "gee whiz" school and the attempts to humanize the beast fall flat. Then there's a Lassie-type collie that runs around, creating yuks for the Yeti. Directed by Frank Kramer (real name: Gianfranco Panolini) with no polish; the photography is rough too. Phoenix Grant, Jim Sullivan, Tony Kendall, Eddy Fay. Aka *Big Foot.*

YOG—MONSTER FROM SPACE (1971) ★½ Aka *Space Amoeba*, this Japanese sci-fi sukiyaki depicts an alien amoeba that comes from outer space on the hull of a space probe, infecting various life forms on Earth and turning them into Godzilla-like destructors who bear such names as Ganime, Kamoeba and Gezora. Scientists work day and night to devise a method of stopping the infection, finally settling on bat cries from old *Dracula* sound tracks. . . . No, that's not it. . . . What really gets them in the end is an erupting volcano. Oops, is that giving something away? Directed by Inoshiro Honda. Akira Kubo, Atsuko Takahashi, Noritake Saito. (Sinister/C)

YONGARY, MONSTER FROM THE DEEP (1967) ★★ South Koreans joined with the Japanese to produce this "horror" about a hulking monster (who looks not unlike Godzilla) freed from its centuries-old cave by an atomic blast and on his way to destroy Seoul, capital of South Korea. Yongary does differ from Godzilla in that he drinks gasoline for breakfast, lunch and dinner . . . but Yongary still runs out of petrol before the first reel is over. You really have to like men in monster suits to tune in. Directed by Kiduck Kim. Starring the unflappable Yugil Oh and the undiscouraged Chungim Nam. Aka *Monster Yongkari* and *Great Monster Yongary*. (Orion) (Laser: Image, with *X from Outer Space*)

YOR: THE HUNTER FROM THE FUTURE (1983) ★★½ Lowbrow fantasy escapism, but energetically on the level of a Saturday serial and hence palatable entertainment. Italian director Anthony Dawson, a master at cheap imitations of whatever trend is popular, never aspires to more than he delivers. At least the noisy sound track will keep you alert, even if the acting will deaden your brain cells. *Yor* starts as a caveman pastiche with muscular hunk Reb Brown rescuing beautiful Corinne Clery from a prickly dinosaur and fighting off hairy Neanderthals. Just when you think you're in for another *One Billion B.C.*, the medallion around Yor's neck leads him to a post-holocaust control center ruled by the Overlord, winner of a Darth Vader lookalike contest, who has an army of robots and a nuclear bomb. Ray guns zap, metal explodes, rockets burst in air and there's more pyrotechnics than the Fourth of July and World War II combined. The Cro-Magnon plot is from a popular book by Juan Zanotto and Ray Collins. John Steiner, Carole Andre, Alan Collins. Aka *The World of Yor*. (Video/Laser: RCA/Columbia)

YOU BETTER WATCH OUT (1980). Original theatrical title for what is now on tape from Saturn as *Christmas Evil* and from Academy as *Terror in Toyland*. See *Terror in Toyland*.

YOU'LL FIND OUT (1940) ★★★½ Three reasons to see this RKO send-up of the "old dark house" genre are Boris Karloff, Peter Lorre and Bela Lugosi, who spoof themselves as a terrifying trio involved in a phony séance in a mansion where bandleader Kay Kyser and his group (comedian Ish Kabbible, Harry Babbit, singer Ginny Sims) are stranded. A new recording device called the "sonovox" creates weird voices, and Kyser indulges in his radio "Kollege of Musical Knowledge" nonsense, with nostalgic musical numbers thrown in. It's an entertaining mix reflecting the essence of the '40s through James V. Kern's nonsensical script. Dennis O'Keefe and Helen Parrish provide obligatory love interest. Lorre is amusing with his bulging eyes and long cigarettes, Karloff is charmingly menacing as the mansion host and Lugosi hams it up with a turban as a mystic. Produced-directed by David Butler. Aka *Here Come the Boogie Men*. (Budget; Hollywood Home Theater) (Laser: Image)

YOU NEVER CAN TELL (1951) ★★★ It would be a cheap shot to call this film a dog. Despite its unpromising story line, it is quite funny. King, a German shepherd, becomes heir to a fortune, then is poisoned by a one-time trainer from the K-9 Corps (Charles Drake) who wants to inherit, marry Peggy Dow and settle down very rich. King arrives in Beast-atory, where he is turned into a "humanimal" and allowed to return to Earth to uncover the dastardly trainer. Back on Earth as private eye Rex Shepard (Dick Powell), King is the brunt of jokes about fire hydrants, dog food and handy tree trunks, and indulges in verbal puns of his own. Sounds like a dog, yeah, but it's done with such goodheartedness that the "dog-eared" script by director Lou Breslow and David Chandler wins you over. Also very funny is Joyce Holden, as a onetime race horse reincarnated as a human to help King solve the caper. Albert Sharpe, Sara Taft, Will Vedder. Aka *One Never Knows* and *You Never Know*.

YOU NEVER KNOW See *You Never Can Tell.*

YOUNG AGAIN (1986) ★★★½ The opposite of *Big*—instead of a youth's wish to be in an adult's body being granted, 40-year-old business executive Robert Urich wishes he were in the body of a teenager again, and along comes guardian angel Jack Gilford to grant the wish. Now in the body of K. C. Reeves, Urich returns to his hometown and to the high school, where he strikes up a new relationship with Lindsay Wagner, the girl that got away when he was a teen. This Disney TV-movie deals poignantly with the problems of a teenager trying to date a woman old enough to be his mother, and is a charming morality tale. Directed by Steven Hilliard Stern.

YOUNGER AND YOUNGER (1993) ★★ What is this oddball movie about? The script by coproducer/director Percy Adlon and Felix Adlon seems to be about our search for spiritual love, and how men fall out of love with women when they lose their sexiness. Certainly it is a story about several eccentrics working in a selfstorage office, with the focus on womanizing owner Donald Sutherland, who only realizes how much he loves his dowdy wife after she dies of a heart attack. (He was upstairs at the time making love to a bimbo on his Wurlitzer.) The dead wife (not the bimbo) comes back in his visions as a femme fatale and he yearns after her like a puppy, though to what end is never made very clear. (He seems more taken with her physical look than her inner qualities.) Is he supposed to be happy as he rides away with her ghost on his motorbike? A sublime, ethereal flavor is strived for, but director Adlon doesn't quite pull it off. What should have been bittersweet is just bitter. There's an interesting supporting cast: Brendan Fraser, Sally Kellerman, Lolita Davidovich, Julie Delpy, Linda Hunt.

YOUNG FRANKENSTEIN (1974) ★★★★½ Hysterically funny Mel Brooks takeoff on the Universal horror films of the '30s, in particular *The Bride* and *Son of Frankenstein*, since sequences from those films are parodied. Director Brooks, who cowrote the script with Gene Wilder, is wild and ingeniously creative, though some of the satire works and some falls flat. Peter Boyle is the singularly inane creature created by Dr. Frankenstein (Wilder), while Marty Feldman is the hunchbacked Igor, Cloris Leachman the daffy woman hanging around the Frankenstein castle, and Madeleine Kahn the eventual "bride." Watch for Gene Hackman as the blind hermit in the forest. You'll scream—with delight. Aka *Frankenstein Junior*. (Video/Laser: CBS/Fox)

YOUNG HANNAH, QUEEN OF THE VAMPIRES. See *Crypt of the Living Dead*.

YOUNG HARRY HOUDINI (1987) ★★★½ Excellent 2-hour Disney movie for TV presenting Harry Houdini as an adult, telling a story of his childhood to an admirer. Flash back to 1886 as young Erich Weiss runs away from home to pursue his dream to become a magician. After a nifty train sequence, in which the lad demonstrates a practical use of escaping from handcuffs, he meets a traveling magic show and becomes a disciple of sleight-of-hander José Ferrer, who inspires the boy to keep after his dream. A mute Indian named John Parker teaches young Weiss how supernormal powers (such as the ability to fly astrally) can be brought into play if only you believe in yourself. This is nostalgic and warm, full of colorful period characters and a sense of a boy learning to be a man. Wil Wheaton, Jeffrey Demunn, Kerri Green, Barry Corbin, Roy Dotrice, Ross Harris, J. Reuben Silverbird. Director James Orr cowrote with Jim Cruickshank.

YOUNG MAGICIAN, THE (1987) ★★★ Pleasant Polish-Canadian TV production, fourth in the "Tales for All" series, in which a youth named Peter (Rusty Jedwab) learns the power to move objects, often at a rapid velocity, only to discover he's looked upon as a freak—until police need his help to avert a major disaster. Writer-director Waldemar Dziki never allows the material to ignite as much as one might like, but it's passable entertainment. Edward Garson, Natasza Maraszek. (Family Home Entertainment)

YOUNG POISONER'S HANDBOOK, THE (1994) ★★★½ Although this is based on a true story about a British teenager who poisoned his mother to death, went to prison then was paroled only to poison again, it plays like a psycho-thriller; with its dark humor and insight into abnormal psychology, it will chill you to the marrow of your bones. Director Benjamin Ross (who coscripted with Jeff Rawle) brings a surreal touch to this British production, and evokes from Hugh O'Conor (as the poisonous youth) a compelling performance that really gets into the nitty-gritty of a twisted, sexually perverted brain. This will frighten you more than any monster or slasher movie because it captures the essence of truth behind homicide. Antony Sher, Charlotte Coleman, Roger Lloyd Pack, Ruth Sheen.

YOUNG SHERLOCK HOLMES (1985) ★★★★ This rousing action adventure, perfect in technical aspects and handsomely cast, was produced by Steven Spielberg and directed by Barry Levinson. It's a tribute to the Victorian detective by portraying him and Watson as students at a boys' school, solving a mystery in the Sir Arthur Conan Doyle tradition. The first third, especially, captures the antecedents of the Holmes canon and the restraint of Doyle's storytelling and has Chris Columbus's best writing. The Holmes stories were, after all, studies in ratiocination and deduction and only occasionally lapsed into wild and woolly adventure. But when the "Rover Boys" stumble across an Egyptian death cult in the gaslit heart of London, this slides into an Indiana Jones adventure with mock derring-do and heroics. And because there's nightmarish hallucinations, Spielberg and gang have an excuse to drag out special effects: a dead squab that comes to life on the dinner plate like a killer buzzard; gargoyles that attack an old inventor in a curio shop; French pastries that become cutesy-pie animated imps; graveyard horrors with rotting corpses. Spielberg twice apologizes in the credits for taking liberties but apparently had permission to use the characters (or was it just a blessing?). Many Holmesian props (pipe, Inverness cape, violin, deerstalker's cap) are cleverly introduced. (Video/Laser: Paramount)

YOU ONLY LIVE ONCE. See *Mission Stardust*.

YOU ONLY LIVE TWICE (1967) ★★★★ Lavishly produced James Bond thriller from Albert Broccoli and Harry Saltzman (their fifth), with Sean Connery carrying the load as the urbane, sophisticated, implausible Agent 007. Blofeld (Donald Pleasence), mastermind of SPECTRE, returns with a plan to hijack U.S. and Soviet space capsules and blackmail the world. Gadgetry, superweapons, seductive women, unstoppable action—all enhanced by John Barry's music, as Bond finds himself in Japan. Durably directed by Lewis Gilbert and swiftly paced by scenarist Roald Dahl. Akiko Wakabayashi, Karin Dor, Bernard Lee, Charles Gray, Robert Hutton, Tsai Chin. After this, Connery left the series not to return until *Diamonds Are Forever*. (Video/Laser: MGM/UA; CBS/Fox)

YOUR TEETH ARE IN MY NECK. See *The Fearless Vampire Killers*.

ZAPPED! (1982) ★★ Pathetic comedy that falls on its face as Scott Baio discovers he has telekinetic powers after a high school lab explosion. The intellectual height of this undernourishment is to have Baio cause a girl's blouse to pop open or have her dress fly off. Willy Aames is around as a cardboard character to say "Gee whiz." So belabored that not even teenagers, for whom producer Jeffrey D. Apple intended it, will sit still for long. Director Robert J. Rosenthal was defeated before he started with the script he and Bruce Rubin wrote as *The Wiz Kid*. Scatman Crothers, Roger Bowen and Sue Ane Langdon have dumb cameos. (Video/Laser: Nelson/Embassy)

ZAPPED AGAIN (1989) ★ Lamebrain sequel to a fantasy comedy that was lousy to begin with. Rebellious Todd Eric Andrews, a student at Ralph Waldo Emerson High, discovers a prune juice that gives him telekinetic powers, which he uses to elevate Linda Blair's dress over her head or to get even with sadistic coworkers. In fact, too little use of visual humor prevails—director Doug Campbell is stuck with boring dialogue and inane characters. *Zapped Again* zapped him good, as it did Sue Ane Langdon, Karen Black, Lyle Alzado and Kelli Williams in empty-headed roles. (Video/Laser: Embassy/Nelson)

ZARDOZ (1973) ★★★½ Visually exciting sci-fi fantasy set in 2293, but writer-producer-director John Boorman is heavy-handed and unnecessarily symbolic when Sean Connery (as an Exterminator, a man entitled to impregnate women) infiltrates the Vortex, an intellectual society segregated from the rest of the world's savagery. It evolves into a political-social allegory (with esoteric literary overtones) and is composed of incongruous, unfathomable elements. For hardcore fans who appreciate experiments in the outré—general audiences may find this enigmatic. Charlotte Rampling, Sally Anne Newton, Sara Kestelman, John Alderton. (Key; CBS/Fox) (Laser: CBS/Fox)

ZEBRA FORCE (1977) ★★★ Well-produced cops-and-robbers actioner set in L.A. spotlights Vietnam vets who take on the Mob to rid society of drug dealers. The twist: the white soldiers turn into blacks when they strike against Richard X. Slattery and his guys, then revert back to whites in the blink of an eye. Without explanation! Their leader is a one-armed lieutenant who needs a sound tube against his throat to speak. An implausible twist ending rounds out the action of this unusual film. Odd, and disconcerting, to say the least. Written-directed by Joe Tornatore. Mike Lane, Rockne Tarkington, Glenn Wilder, Anthony Caruso. The sequel, *Code Name: Zebra*, has no fantasy. (Media)

ZEDER—VOICE FROM DARKNESS. See *Revenge of the Dead*.

ZEDER—VOICES FROM THE BEYOND. See *Revenge of the Dead*.

ZELIG (1983) ★★★★½ Brilliant Woody Allen pastiche of biographical-documentary films, comprising staged scenes and historical black-and-white footage into which Allen has been matted. Leonard Zelig is a schmuck of the first order, whose shyness and alienation from society have given him a unique talent: the chameleon ability to take on the characteristics of others. This wonderful parody spotlights Allen with Eugene O'Neill, Herbert Hoover, the crowd at Hearst's Castle, and Hitler during a Munich rally. It's a classic Allen gag carried off ingeniously. Mia Farrow is the mousy psychiatrist who tries to break Zelig of his malady, and you'll see real-life people (such as Susan Sontag) making fun of themselves by participating in this colossal lampoon. Three cheers for the klutzy Mr. Zelig, and 4 cheers for the unprecedented Allen. (Video/Laser: Warner Bros.)

ZERAM (1991) ★★½ Japanese sci-fi actioner in which a lovely alien humanoid battles the monster Zeram (a fugitive E.T. from another galaxy), which has a strange, mushroomlike flattop from which a snake with a human head emerges. As the fights go on and on, the creature mutates into other forms so the heroine (and 2 comedy-relief buffoons) keeps bringing out new weapons to blow it asunder. Good visuals, but inept plotting (by Hajime Matsumoto) and acting by Yuko Moriyama. Directed by Keita Amemiya.

ZERO BOYS, THE (1986) ★ Gang of youths well known for wilderness survival takes shelter in a deserted house in the forest only to become targets for drooling killers equipped with bowie knife and crossbow. It's never explained who the killers are, so it's hard to generate interest in the cat-and-mouse games writer-producer-director Nico Mastorakis plays in this *Friday the 13th* clone. Not even the big-breasted women in the gang have much to show. Daniel Hirsch,

Kelli Maroney, Tom Shell, Crystal Carson. (Lightning)

ZERO POPULATION GROWTH. See *Z.P.G.*

ZETA ONE (1969). See *Alien Women.*

ZIPPERFACE (1992) ★★ A serial killer in a black leather suit and a mask with a zipper across his lips resembles Jason of the *Friday the 13th* series, what with the machetelike knife he keeps plunging into the beautiful bodies of actresses-prostitutes. Or chops their heads off with. Poor Palm City will never be the same as the female mayor cries for an arrest and female cop Donna Adams searches for the fiend and reads her lines badly. The script by Barbara Bishop and Mark Troy (from an idea by producer-director Mansour Pourmand) is more of a whodunit with an occasional gore murder as red herrings are set up—smelly fish that won't fool you in the slightest if you're wise to slasher flicks fashioned as murder mysteries. A substandard, poorly acted production strikes an extra-bad note of incredulity on several occasions. This sleazy movie with mild nudity and unimaginative R-rated love scenes is easy to miss. Jonathan Mandell, David Clover, Trisha Melynkov. (Action International) (Laser: Image)

ZODIAC KILLER, THE (1971) ★★ Chintzy, amateurish rendering of a true murder case that rocked San Francisco in the late '60s, and which remains unsolved to this day. Several citizens were indiscriminately murdered by a man who played a dangerous cat-and-mouse game by taunting police with cyphers and other clues. This version, concocted with the help of one-time *Chronicle* reporter Paul Avery, is wretchedly conceived, with little directorial style from producer Tom Hanson or scenarists Ray Cantrell and Manny Mendoza. A couple of the murders are graphically effective—especially sunbathers being stabbed to death by the hooded killer—but otherwise the staging and editing are poor. Oddly enough, the closing voice-over of the killer is chilling as he describes how the law works to protect him. Hal Reed, Bob Jones, Ray Lynch and Tom Pittman make up the nonprofessional cast, which is aided briefly by the appearance of Doodles Weaver. (Academy)

ZOLTAN, HOUND OF DRACULA. Video version of *Dracula's Dog* (Thorn EMI/HBO; Republic).

ZOMBIE (1979) ★★★ Unauthorized sequel to Romero's *Dawn of the Dead*, set on St. Thomas Island where Tisa Farrow and Ian McCulloch battle zombies, resurrected via voodoo rituals by fiendish doctor Richard Johnson. Heads are blown off in abundance (that's the only way to stop a zombie, remember?) and director Lucio Fulci and scenarist Elisa Briganti allow this Italian exploitationer to reach ridiculous extremes—such as having a zombie attack and bite a killer shark and having a human eyeball punctured. But that's what this "walking dead" genre is all

about, right? Auretta Gay. Aka *The Island of the Living Dead, Zombie 2* and *Zombie Flesh Eaters.* (Magnum; Wizard; Lightning) (Laser: Image)

ZOMBIE 2. See *Zombie.*

ZOMBIE 3. See *Burial Ground.*

ZOMBIE 4. Video version of *A Virgin Among the Living Dead* (Edde).

ZOMBIE ARMY (1993) ★★ Soldiers are turned into out-of-step members of the marching dead. Eileen Saddow, Jody Amato, Steven Roberts, John C. Kalinowski. Directed by Betty Stapleford. (Tempe)

ZOMBIE BRIGADE. See *Night Crawl.*

ZOMBIE CHILD. Canadian video version of *The Child* (CIC).

ZOMBIE CREEPING FLESH. See *Night of the Zombies* (1983).

ZOMBIE FLESH EATERS. See *Zombie* (Yummy!).

ZOMBIE HIGH (1987) ★★ Honorable intentions to make a meaningful horror film, with social overtones, are handicapped by mediocre filmmaking and sound, so at best this is a poor man's *Stepford Wives* with conspiratorial vibrations thrown in. And the title is misleading, as this is not a "walking dead" melodrama in the George Romero tradition. So don't look for brain-hungry corpses brought back to life. At Ettinger Academy, student Virginia Madsen discovers a plot to turn the alumni into automatons, and she is threatened with a lobotomy to give her eternal life via a crystal implanted in her brain. All she and the others need is a daily fix of blood and brain tissue, a concoction created by the campus's Dr. Frankenstein, Dean Eisner (Kay Kuter). Horror fans will find Ron Link's direction too mild and the social relevancy too weak for this to work either way. Richard Cox, James Wilder, Sherilyn Fenn, Paul Feig. Aka *The School That Ate My Brain.* (Cinema Group; Simitar; Continental)

ZOMBIE HOLOCAUST. See *Dr. Butcher M.D.* (*Medical Deviate*)

ZOMBIE HORROR. See *Burial Ground.*

ZOMBIE INFERNO. See *Night of the Zombies* (1983).

ZOMBIE ISLAND MASSACRE (1984) ★★ A Caribbean island is the setting for this tale of vacationers being slaughtered by what appears to be a killer zombie tree. Huh? But all is not what it seems. Screenplay by Logan O'Neill and William Stoddard. Directed by John N. Carter. David Broadnax, Rita Jenrette. (Fox Hills; Media)

ZOMBIE LAKE (1985) ★★ Corpses of Nazi soldiers slaughtered in a World War II battle rise from the depths of a very nonpicturesque lake to attack nude women swimmers, who spread wide their legs while the camera photographs them from below. The rotting troopers fondle bare breasts and asses. Gee, an art horror movie with redeeming values. Directed by Jean Rollin (billed on some prints as J. A. Lazer) and co-written by Jesse Franco. Howard Vernon, Britt Carva, Robert Foster, Fred Sanders. Aka *Lake of the Living Dead*. (Lightning; Wizard; VCI)

ZOMBIE NIGHTMARE (1987) ★★ Mediocre Canadian horror film, shot in Ste. Anne de Velle-vue, and released to video once distributors saw no hope for theatrical. It goes to the trouble of setting up the character of a young boy who, after seeing his father knifed to death by toughs while rescuing a young girl being raped, grows up to be a macho good guy who prevents 2 hoods from robbing a market. He is promptly run over by a carload of delinquents. Mother comes along and turns the corpse over to a local witch, Molly Mokembe, who proceeds to res-urrect him from the dead. Now our hero (Jon-Mikl Thor) becomes a zombie killer with a baseball bat who goes after the gang. The mur-ders (as conceived by scriptwriter David Wel-lington) aren't exciting and the fights poorly staged by director Jack Brauman. Adam West has a small but pivotal role as a cynical police-man—why he took this part is a bigger mystery than any of the voodoo and mysticism under-lying the witch's mumbo jumbo. Music lovers may grove on the rock track that features "Zom-bie Night" by Knighthawk and other renditions by Motorhead, Girlschool, Thor, Deathmask, Fist, Virgin Steel and Battalion. Tia Carrere, Manuska Rigaud, Frank Dietz. (New World)

ZOMBIES, THE (1966). See *Plague of the Zombies*.

ZOMBIES (1961) ★ Crude, dumbly conceived junk piece (originally *Voodoo Blood Bath*) about a Miami Beach writer lured to a Carib-bean island to solve the mystery of some fright-faced natives and a doctor (Robert Stanton) searching for a cure to cancer. This exemplifies sleazy thrills as William Joyce runs around with floozy Heather Hewitt to solve the unmysterious mystery. Credit (or discredit) Del Tenney for writing-producing-directing this mess. Assistant director was William Grefe, who went on to di-rect *Stanley* and other schlock. *Zombies* was re-packaged in 1971 as *I Eat Your Skin* and double billed with *I Drink Your Blood*.

ZOMBIES. See *Dawn of the Dead*.

ZOMBIES OF MORA TAU (1957) ★★ Columbia producer Sam Katzman must have been in a trancelike state when he read Raymond T. Mar-cus's script. Edward L. Cahn must have also been in a deep sleep when he accepted the as-signment to direct. Otherwise, why bother? Gregg Palmer and Allison Hayes (the 50-Foot Woman) sleepwalk through roles as adventurers in search of diamonds in an underwater hiding place guarded by hollow-eyed insomniacs. Ray Corrigan, Morris Ankrum, Gregg Palmer . . . zzzzzzz. Aka *The Dead That Walk*. (RCA/Co-lumbia)

ZOMBIES OF THE STRATOSPHERE (1952) ★★★ This 12-chapter entry in Republic's sci-fi serial cycle of the early '50s is the third and final adventure in a trilogy of "flying man" sa-gas, the others being *King of The Rocket Men* and *Radar Men from the Moon*. In this one the guy with the jet-rocket backpack is Larry Martin (Judd Holdren) of the Inter-Planetary Patrol, a watchdog of the solar system. The "zombies" are actually Martians Marex (Lane Bradford) and Narab (Leonard Nimoy), who land on Earth and persuade an evil scientist (Stanley Waxman) to help construct a hydrogen bomb and explode it, forcing Earth out of its orbit. Fred C. Brannon directed this campy cliff-hanger, the charm of which comes from its now-antiquated but delightful-to-watch space vehicle effects, fre-quent fisticuffs, and underwater photography in which the Martians appear to walk along the bottom of the ocean. An obvious inspiration for the 1991 feature *The Rocketeer*. Aline Towne, Tom Steele, Wilson Wood, Jack Shea. (Repub-lic; Nostalgia Merchant; Video Connection; the TV feature version *Satan's Satellites* is on video from Admit One) (Laser: Republic)

ZOMBIES ON BROADWAY (1945) ★★★½ When the owners of the Zombie Hut, a night-club on the Big Street, announce they'll have real-life dead zombies performing onstage, they're forced to send schmucks Wally Brown and Allen Carney to the West Indies island of San Sebastian to bring back the real dead Mc-Coy. Darby Jones, the wonderful bug-eyed zom-bie corpse in *I Walked with a Zombie*, is back for more shenanigans, this time strictly for laughs, as he stalks Anne Jeffreys and the 2 id-iots through potted jungles, occasionally carry-ing off a body. Bela Lugosi portrays Dr. Renault, the madman perfecting his walking dead, in his usual wide-eyed style. Taken as a period piece, it's quite funny with Sheldon Leonard in a good role as the nightclub owner. Director Gordon Douglas guides the cast through the inanities of the Laurence Kimble–Robert Kent script quite well. Ian Wolfe, Frank Jenks. Aka *Loonies on Broadway* (Turner; IME) (Laser: Image)

ZOMBIETHON (1986) ★★★ Compilation video of the goriest scenes from zombie movies, with new wraparound footage produced-directed by Ken Dixon. Various women pursued by walking dead enter the El Rey Theater to sit in a crowd of zombiers and see clips from *Zombie* (1979), including the infamous eye-gouging and shark-biting sequences; *Zombie Lake*, with emphasis on bare flesh and wide-open legs; *Oasis of the Zombies*, a foreign film with Afrika Corps sol-diers stalking the living; and *Astro-Zombies*. Only with this final camp classic does this video take on a fun quality; otherwise, you really have to love zombies to find enjoyment. Other clips from *The Invisible Dead, A Virgin Among the Living Dead, White Zombie* and *Fear*. (Wizard; Lightning; Force)

ZONE OF THE DEAD. Video version of *Alien Zone* (Monarch).

ZONE TROOPERS (1986) ★★★ Simple-minded, mildly enjoyable World War II fantasy from Empire International, which resembles a segment of TV's "Combat" when GI dogfaces in Italy shoot it out with German troops. Four survivors flee into the forest and encounter Bug, an E.T. creature with an insect's head who evaporates Nazi war machines with his disintegrator ray. Bug is part of a band of alien troopers stranded on Earth and since they understand war, and can tell the good guys from the bad guys, they side up with the dogfaces to blast dirty Nazi rats into another dimension. Unusually gentle for a Charles Band production, with nostalgic '40s tunes on the sound track. Directed by Danny Bilson; okay effects by John Buechler. Tim Thomerson, Timothy Van Patten, Biff Manard, Art LaFleur. (Lightning)

ZONTAR: THE THING FROM VENUS (1968) ★ Described as a new version of Roger Corman's *It Conquered the World* . . . but why resurrect that old turkey? Well, don't laugh because this film is so inept, it's a minor cult favorite among those who love good-bad movies. The story reaches new lows in screen sci-fi as John Agar opposes a space monster capable of dominating the human mind. Too bad a spark of creativity didn't dominate the mind of writer-director Larry Buchanan. See it. You won't believe it. Susan Bjorman, Anthony Houston, Warren Hammack. (Video Dimensions; Sinister/C; S/Weird; Dark Dreams; Filmfax)

ZOO, THE. 3-D video version of *The Bubble* (3-D TV Corp.).

Z.P.G. (1972) ★★ Which stands for Zero Population Growth, in case you haven't been following Earth's current population problems. And which stands for Zero Picture Grabber, if you've already seen it. Geraldine Chaplin plays a wife in the 21st century who defies antibirth laws and has her baby anyway (hubby Oliver Reed helped, of course). The city is surrounded by a deadly smog, forcing the cast to wear gas masks, but masks might be more in order for the audience to prevent them from gagging on this turgid sociological sci-fier. Directed by Michael Campus, scripted by Max Ehrlich and Frank DeFelitta. Aka *Edict; Zero Population Growth* and *The First of January*. (Paramount)

ZREAKS. See *Children Shouldn't Play with Dead Things*.

ZU: WARRIORS FROM THE MAGIC MOUNTAIN (1983) ★★★ Hong Kong–produced fantasy of a wild and woolly nature, with adventurers of the 10th century entering a mountain in China and facing such rivals as Evil Disciples, Blood Crows, Flying Swords, Evil Force, Heaven's Blade and wizards, warlocks, priestesses and other entities endowed with magic. It gets out of hand under Tsui Hark's direction, often becoming ridiculous when the cast is ricocheting off the walls, yet there is a free-spirited feeling to this rambuctious production, and a sense of breathlessness, that enables a Western audience to embrace this pastiche of the West's sword-and-sorcery quest fantasies. And that's it, pal, there ain't no more.